E1 SUNBURST

THE COMPLETE ENCYCLOPAEDIA OF
PHOTOGRAPHY

THE COMPLETE ENCYCLOPAEDIA OF
PHOTOGRAPHY

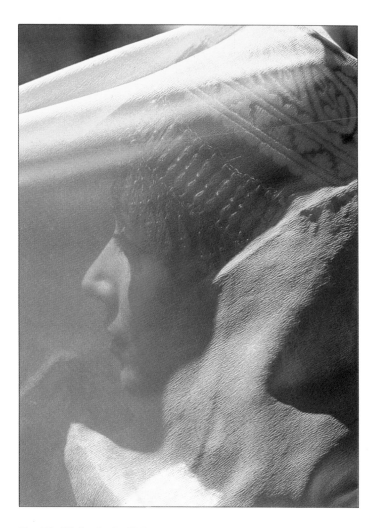

MICHAEL LANGFORD

EBURY PRESS

The Complete Encyclopaedia of Photography
was conceived, edited, and designed by
Dorling Kindersley Limited, 9 Henrietta Street,
London WC2

Project editors   Joanna Godfrey Wood
                         Jonathan Hilton

Art editor   Michelle Stamp

Editor   Phil Wilkinson

Designers   Calvin Evans
                         Nick Harris

Picture researcher   Caroline Lucas

Managing editor   Joss Pearson

Art director   Stuart Jackman

First published in Great Britain in 1982 by Ebury Press,
National Magazine House, 72 Broadwick Street,
London W1V 2BP

Second impression 1983

ISBN 0 85223 229 2

Typesetting and reproduction by Reprocolor Llovet S.A.,
Barcelona
Printed in the Netherlands by Royal Smeets Offset B.V.,
Weert

Contents

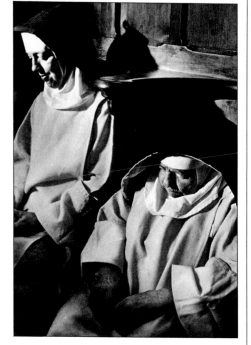

11   **INTRODUCTION**

12   **The art of photography**

14   NATURAL LIGHT

16   **Light direction**
16   Side-lighting
17   Back- and rim-lighting
17   Front-lighting
17   Viewpoint and lighting

18   **Light quality**
18   Hard lighting
19   Semi-diffused light
19   Soft lighting

20   **Light and subject properties**
20   Materials
21   Surfaces
22   Color and surface

22   **Light and color**
23   Time of day
23   Visual response

24   **Lighting contrast**
24   Tonal range
25   Tonal distribution
26   Lighting contrast and color
27   High key
27   Low key

28   **Light as subject**
28   Shadows
29   Rim-lighting
29   Silhouettes
30   Weather
30   Sun and flare
31   Reflections
31   Night photography
32   Light as the main picture ingredient

34   SUBJECT ELEMENTS

36   **Line**
36   Straight lines
37   Curved lines
37   Line combinations

38   **Shape**
38   Change with viewpoint
38   Shadows and reflections

39   Shape counterpoint
39   Shape as subject

40   **Pattern**
40   Change with viewpoint
40   Choice of subject
41   Pattern combinations
41   Interrupted pattern
42   Pattern and color
42   Pattern and scale

43   **Texture**
43   Detail and scale
44   Texture as a design element
45   Lighting and texture

46   **Form**
46   Choice of subject
47   Ephemeral form
48   Light on form
48   Form interpretation
49   Form distortion
49   Form suppression

50   **Color**
50   Association and mood
51   Saturation, hue, and brightness
51   Unexpected color

52   **The inner elements**

54   COMPOSITION

56   **Format proportions**
56   Horizontal image
57   Square format
57   Vertical format

58   **Divisions of the frame**
58   Placing the horizon
59   Using simple divisions
60   Frames within the frame
60   Finding frames
61   Forming related compartments

62   **Viewpoint**
62   Moving in close
63   Change of background
63   Extreme high and low viewpoint
64   Vertical change
64   Influence of distance
65   Horizontal change
65   Moving around the subject
66   Viewpoint and subject meaning
66   Critical viewpoint

67 Emphasis
67 Positioning the subject
68 The Golden Mean
68 Unconventional framing
68 Tone theory
68 Tone interchange
69 Emphasis through tone
70 Emphasis through color
70 Complementary color
71 Color contrast
71 Isolated color
72 Lead-in lines

72 Structure
73 Thematic shapes
74 Related color
74 Opposed color
75 Color themes
76 Balance
76 Symmetry
77 Balancing tones and shapes
77 Dynamic balance
78 Balance of color
79 Weight of color
79 Imbalance and tension

80 Depth and distance
81 Linear perspective
82 Viewpoint and linear perspective
82 Aerial perspective
83 Overlap and false attachment
84 Using false attachment
84 Depth through scale change
85 Depth illusion

86 Timing and movement
86 Framing the action
87 Peak of action
88 The critical moment
88 Picture sequences
90 The camera's portrayal
90 Controlling the setting
91 Blur as a movement device
91 Abstraction by blur
92 Juxtaposition and transient
     relationships

93 The whole image

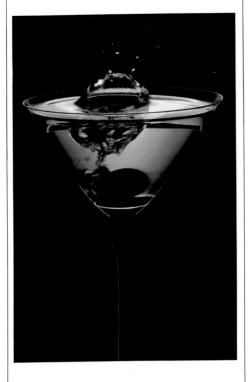

**96 The techniques of
     photography**

98 CAMERAS AND THEIR CONTROLS

100 Camera principles
100 The essential features

102 Camera types
102 35 mm SLR cameras
104 Direct vision compact cameras
106 Rollfilm SLR cameras
107 TLR cameras
108 Sheet film cameras
109 Instant picture cameras
111 SLR systems and functions

112 Lens controls
112 Pinhole images
112 Refracting light
113 Basic converging lens
113 Camera lenses

114 Focusing
114 Focusing and subject distance
114 Fixed focus lenses
115 Focus setting aids
115 Autofocus lenses
116 Using focus control

116 Aperture
117 Changing apertures
117 The f number system
117 Lens "speed"
118 Depth of field
118 Technical considerations
119 Depth of field scale
119 Standards of sharpness
119 Maximum depth of field
119 Choosing depth of field

120 Focal length and camera size
120 Angle of view
120 Lens and camera movements
121 Movements on 35 mm cameras
121 Movements on sheet film cameras
121 Controlling converging lines
122 Controlling reflections
122 Improving depth of field
123 Controlling shapes

124 The shutter
124 How shutters work
125 Shutter settings
125 Shutter and aperture relationships
126 Shutter firing systems

127 Using slow shutter speeds
127 Supporting the camera

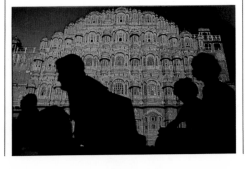

128 Moving camera, static subject
128 Panning moving subjects
128 Exposure considerations

129 Using fast shutter speeds
129 Controlling the freezing of action
129 Exposure considerations
130 Camera shake
130 Choice of interpretation
131 Focal plane distortion
131 Chopping shutter
131 Special-purpose, high-speed shutters

132 Exposure and its measurement
132 Film speed figures
133 Correct exposure
133 Using the exposure meter
133 How camera meters work
134 Cell types
135 TTL systems
136 Using a hand-held meter
137 Advantages of hand meters
137 Exposure values
137 Solving exposure problems
138 How meters can be misled

138 Exposing with flash
139 How flash works
140 Flash guide numbers
141 Self-regulating flash
141 Diffused flash
141 Flash meters

142 FILM

144 How films work
144 Black and white film process
145 Instant picture black and white film process
145 Chromogenic black and white film process
146 Color negative film process
146 Color positive film process
146 Color peel-apart film process
146 Integral film process

148 Choice of film
149 Sizes and packs
150 Choosing color camera film
151 Color temperature
152 Choosing black and white camera film
152 Reciprocity failure
153 Film care
153 Picture economy
153 Film box information

154 Expressing film response
154 Graph information
155 Curves for different films

155 Manipulating film response
155 Black and white film response
156 Uprating black and white film
156 Downrating black and white film
156 Using filters
157 Special black and white films
158 Uprating and downrating color film
158 Using filters
159 Special color films

160 LIGHTING

162 Light sources
162 Light source quality
162 Available lighting
164 Tungsten lighting
164 Color temperature meters
165 Flash lighting units
166 Lighting accessories

167 Lighting in the studio
167 Amateur studio set-ups
168 Professional studio
169 Controlling lighting
169 Contrast
170 Glare
170 Local lighting
171 Copying
171 Lighting enclosed detail
172 Silhouette lighting
172 Low-key lighting
173 High-key lighting
173 Lighting polished surfaces
174 Lighting glass

174 Controlling mixed lighting
175 Balancing light
175 Light sources in the picture
175 Lighting large areas
176 Reducing contrast with flash
176 Simulating sunlight

176 Advanced flash techniques
177 Using single units
177 Using multihead flash
178 The freezing power of flash
178 Red eye

179 Special effects lighting
179 Colored light sources
180 Physiograms
180 Creating light trails
181 Projecting slides on objects
181 Back projection
182 Front projection
182 Coloring shadows
183 Using mirrors
183 Ultraviolet lighting

184 ADDITIONAL EQUIPMENT

186 Wide-angle lenses
186 Technical features
187 Perspective effects
187 Practical considerations

188 Fisheye lenses
188 Technical features
189 Practical considerations

189 Telephoto lenses
189 Technical features
191 Catadioptric lenses
191 Telephotos for rollfilm formats
191 Perspective effects
192 Practical considerations

192 Zoom lenses
193 Technical features
193 Lens performance
194 Practical considerations
194 Zooming effects

195 Close-up equipment
195 Image magnification
195 Equipment for close-up
197 Technical aids
197 Close-up picture making
197 Compensating exposure
197 Useful calculations

198 Filters and lens attachments
198 Polarizing filters
198 Special effects attachments
201 Non-effects filters
201 Neutral density filters
201 Attachment holders

202 System cameras and accessories
202 Motor drives and camera backs
203 Tripods and camera supports
203 Bags and cases
204 Viewfinder accessories
205 The 35 mm SLR system
206 The rollfilm camera system
207 The sheet film monorail system

208 Special cameras and lenses
208 Special cameras
210 Special lenses

211 Future design trends

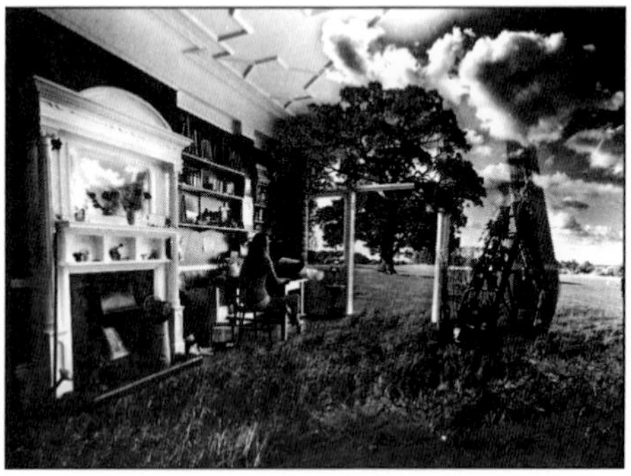

212 Post-camera techniques

214 FILM PROCESSING

216 Film and paper image formation
216 Black and white materials
217 Chromogenic film and paper theory
219 Silver dye-bleach material
219 Photo color transfer process
220 Effects of reciprocity failure

220 Processing controls
220 Film processing equipment
221 Agitation
222 Processing chemicals
223 Negatives and printing conditions
223 Grain and development
224 Time and temperature
224 Compensation processing

225 Preparing to process
225 Loading film tanks
226 The processing sequence
227 Washing and drying
227 Mounting and filing

228 Assessing results
228 Black and white film
229 Pushing and holding back
230 Color negative film
231 Color slide film

232 PRINT MAKING

234 The darkroom
234 Basic requirements
235 The complete home darkroom
236 Printing equipment

240 Printing controls
240 Print processing solutions
241 Time, temperature, and agitation

242 Exposing the paper
242 Color theory
243 Paper grades
244 Preparing to print
244 Making a contact sheet
245 Making a black and white enlargement
246 Making a negative/positive
     enlargement
247 Making a positive/positive
     enlargement
248 Print faults

248 Special printing techniques
249 Local density control
250 Additive printing

251 Local color control

252 Print finishing
252 Retouching and spotting
252 Airbrushing
253 Mounting and storing

254 SPECIAL EFFECTS

256 Alternative printing techniques
256 Image distortion
257 Photograms
258 False color
259 Liquid emulsions
260 Sandwich printing
260 Multiple printing

261 Specialized darkroom materials
261 Registration systems
262 Lith emulsion
262 Tone and color separations
263 Masks and overlays

264 Image manipulation
264 Screens
265 Bas-relief
266 Posterization
266 Shadow and highlight masking
267 Solarization

268 Workroom techniques
268 Toning
269 Montage
269 Hand coloring

271 New technology

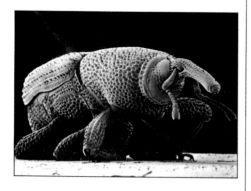

272 The specialized subject

274 Scientific and technical photography
274 Equipment and techniques
275 Contracting time
275 High-speed photography
277 Enlarging small subjects
278 Photomicrography
280 Miniaturizing the subject
280 Revealing the invisible
283 Kirlian photography
284 Holography
284 Periphery photography

285 Medical and forensic photography
285 Equipment and techniques
285 Record photography
286 Radiography
286 Using ultraviolet
287 Thermography
288 Using infrared
288 Surveillance and inspection
290 Isotope scanning and sonography

290 Astronomical photography
291 Equipment and techniques
292 Photographing the solar system
292 Photography and space exploration
295 Analyzing starlight

296 Aerial photography
296 Photographic materials and techniques
296 Basic aerial photography
297 Medium-altitude photography
297 Photogrammetry
298 Remote sensing

300 Natural history photography
300 Equipment and techniques
300 Animals
301 Birds
302 Insects
302 Underwater life
303 Plants and flowers

304 Sports photography
304 Equipment and techniques
304 Individual sports
305 Team sports
306 Water sports
308 Climbing and mountaineering
309 Caving

309 Architectural and landscape photography
310 Equipment and approach
310 Architectural exteriors
311 Cities and industrial landscapes
311 Interiors
312 Landscape photography

314 Editorial and advertising photography
314 Equipment and techniques
314 Still life
316 Fashion photography
318 Advertising approaches

320 The human figure
320 Equipment and techniques
321 Groups
322 Individual portraits
322 Photographing stage performers
323 The nude

324 Reportage photography
324 Equipment and techniques
325 Press photography
326 Photojournalism
327 Manipulation after shooting

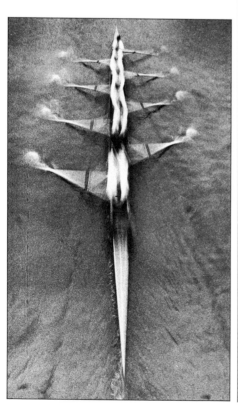

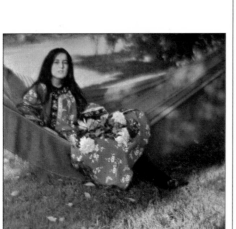

328 Photographic styles

330 High Art photography
330 The themes of High Art
330 The Pre-Raphaelite influence
331 Techniques
332 High Art's leading exponents
333 Pictures and exhibitions of the High Art movement

334 Pictorialism
334 The major influences on Pictorialism
335 Techniques
336 Exhibitions and secessionist movements
338 The impressionistic approach
340 The naturalistic approach

342 Straight photography
342 The influences of art on Straight photography
343 Techniques
343 Individuals and movements of Straight photography
346 The influences of Straight photography

347 The documentary approach
347 Equipment and techniques
348 Early documentary photographers
350 The external influences
350 The illustrated magazines
352 The Farm Security Administration project
353 Magnum Photos
355 The war photographers
355 The individualists

357 Dynamism
357 The influences of modern art on Dynamism
358 The major exponents of Dynamism
360 Techniques

361 Structuralism and Abstraction
362 Mixed media images
362 The influences of art on Structuralism and Abstraction
363 The Bauhaus
364 Leading exponents of Structuralism and Abstraction

368 Metaphor and Symbolism
369 Equivalents
370 The leading exponents of Metaphor and Symbolism

373 Romanticism and the dramatic
374 The pictorial origins of Romanticism
375 The leading exponents of Romanticism and the dramatic

378 Surrealism
378 Art origins and influences
379 Techniques
379 The leading exponents of Surrealism

384 SUBJECT GLOSSARY

393 GLOSSARY

422 INDEX

431 ACKNOWLEDGMENTS

Introduction

Photography is an active and creative medium. At a basic level, using a simple, automatic camera, the photographer must make challenging decisions about the content and composition of a photograph. At an advanced level, photography offers a vast range of creative possibilities. This book explores the world of photography from the practical details of equipment to the widest range of its uses. It shows photography by both artists and scientists, compares yesterday's approach with today's and attempts to predict the methods of tomorrow.

In its early years photography suffered from the fact that it combines elements of both art and science. The confusions and controversies this has caused have only resolved themselves comparatively recently, helped probably by the influence of movies and television — both requiring similar combinations of technology and visual expression. Today most people agree that it can be both. Photography is a medium, and the camera is merely a tool — it is the person using it who determines the balance between its art and its science. After all, a pen can be used to trace both a diagram of a circuit or to create an imaginative composition. Photography is simply drawing with light.

Combinations of seeing and recording skills are required in the use of all visual media. In photography you must have some practical knowledge of equipment and materials as well as a basic grasp of compositional guidelines, if you are to exploit the camera's possibilities. In the early days of photography, the technical aspects were awesome and limiting — it was necessary to place cameras on stands, to make complex exposure calculations, and to master lengthy darkroom processes. In contrast, today's cameras are easy to use, and often automatic. In the case of some models, the problem now lies in finding a way of overriding a built-in automatic process in order to achieve other than uniform and unimaginative results.

Sophisticated modern equipment and films now make picture taking possible under almost any conditions and today there is as strong an interest in photographs themselves as in the equipment used to produce them. The photograph has become an important medium, whether in books, magazines, on television, or in exhibitions, and there is now a sufficient body of work available to see what a vast range of subjects and approaches is possible. The photographs we take do not have to resemble those taken by other photographers any more than our expression of personality through choice of words, dress, or decor must be similar to those of other people — many photographers have recognized the modern camera as an important creative tool.

This book is divided into five main sections: *The art of photography, The techniques of photography, Post-camera techniques, The specialized subject,* and *Photographic styles.* Each section is structured so that it is self-contained, but a cross-referencing system also links it to the rest of the book. It can therefore either be read as a complete unit or referred to for information on individual topics. Each topic starts with an introductory column of text, to give a broad understanding, and then goes into fuller detail, subdivided under specific headings.

The first section, *The art of photography,* is concerned with the skills of seeing and composing pictures. It demonstrates the way light dictates how things appear, and the relationship between lighting, viewpoint, and subject form and surface. Central to this section are suggestions for ways of strengthening pictures through the use of simple practical methods of composition.

Sections two and three, by contrast, are technically orientated and take the reader through the main items of equipment and the methods used in general photography today. *The techniques of photography* is concerned with cameras, lighting, lenses, film, and general accessories. The section tackles every major aspect of photographic equipment, explaining not only its function but also its potential for creative control. *Post-camera techniques* deals with what can be done with the image once the film is removed from the camera. This area covers general principles of darkroom technique and more detailed practical advice. Straightforward processing and printing in color and black and white is followed by a comprehensive range of more advanced manipulative darkroom and workroom techniques.

The fourth section, *The specialized subject,* examines the ways in which photography is put to use in highly professional areas, such as in space exploration, scientific and medical research, and sport and fashion. It shows the wide variety of photographic images produced by professional photographers and explains the special equipment used and problems involved.

Section five, *Photographic styles,* gathers together some of the pictures of the world's leading photographers, past and present, and compares their styles and approaches, tracing links with art movements and technical and stylistic influences of all kinds.

The last pages of the book contain two glossaries. The first is a practical guide to popular subjects, offering basic suggestions and reminders of the main techniques and points to concentrate on. It can be used as a quick-reference source before shooting. The second glossary provides definitions of all the terms you will encounter in the book, as well as those used in general photographic parlance.

Throughout the main text and at the foot of each introductory column you will find cross references directing you to related topics for additional reading. As a whole the book aims to give an overview of photography as it is practiced, used, and discussed in the 1980s, including numerous recent developments that will shape its future.

The art of photography

This section of the book is important for anyone who contemplates using a camera. Rather than dealing with the technical aspects of photography, it concentrates on seeing, and on using a feature common to every camera – the viewfinder. The photographer must use the viewfinder in the same way as a painter uses a sketch book or canvas – as a frame within which to organize a picture in the strongest and most effective way. To use it well calls for the ability to *notice* things – to see clearly the basic elements which make up the appearance of subjects.

The most fundamental qualities required to take a good photograph are an ability to see in a perceptive way, and to have a positive enjoyment of creating and looking at pictures. Other aspects are secondary. The camera may impose limitations on what you want to produce, but without first being aware of the qualities of the subject that you want to capture, there is little point in taking a picture.

Many people underrate their ability to see and make pictures, believing that visual sense is either a gift you are born with or one you will never possess because it cannot be learned. In fact, anyone can develop and intensify the skill of seeing, as long as there is the will, time, and a real interest in the task. This can, in turn, sharpen your sense of sight – enabling you to get more out of your surrounding environment and derive more enjoyment from any visual experience, however mundane.

The pages ahead cover the many different facets of the way we see objects. They discuss the ways that light can change a scene's appearance, the visual qualities of objects themselves, their surface textures, colors, or shapes, and how these can offer a vast range of effects. Most of these are common aspects of the world about us, but usually we are too preoccupied with the directly useful aspects of objects to see them in this way. For example, a road is merely a means of getting from one place to another, rather than an interesting aesthetic shape or a division in a landscape. Evening sunlight falling across a wall means that it is the end of the day, rather than being a changing display of abstracted light and pattern. It is this simple but often unused ability to notice things without being conditioned by their function which is important for photography.

Visual "language" and composition

Composition is the ability to organize what you see in front of you within the boundaries of a flat, two-dimensional photograph. Taken to extremes, composition can become a straightjacket which stifles originality and experimentation, but it can also offer guidelines and suggestions on how to put picture elements together which really do help to improve pictures. In the days of the Bauhaus design school, aspects of composition were referred to as the "grammar of design" or the "language of vision". While these titles may seem pretentious today, they do refer to ways of expressing visual ideas through pictures, just as thoughts can be expressed clearly through certain well-proven word structures. Picture composition should therefore be thought of as a consensus of what works, rather than as an inflexible set of rules. Make an evaluation of the suggestions you find here and decide whether or not they work for you. Do not be afraid to reject anything that seems restricting or with which you do not agree. If you are an experienced photographer, it may be your very reactions against certain rules of composition which give your work its individual flavor. Many photographers in the *Photographic styles* section of the book have very effectively broken away from the accepted norms and rules of picture structure.

Today, there is a fashion for making pictures which intentionally break all the rules in order to avoid being "photographers' pictures", preserving instead the naïve, snapshot-like quality of photography. At the same time, the very acts of aiming the camera and deciding when to release the shutter are factors influencing composition. Taken to extremes, photographs shot totally at random may produce a tiny percentage of interesting results, but quickly become hidebound according to the random technique adopted. Despite these radical "anti-structural" approaches, the fact remains that if your pictures are intended to communicate ideas to others, composition can certainly help to strengthen and simplify what you are trying to express.

Later in the book, in *The techniques of photography* and *Post-camera techniques* a discussion of the machinery and processes of photography will offer numerous imaginative techniques and ways of enhancing the image you have composed in the viewfinder, suggesting many different interpretative possibilities. Photography has its own technical qualities which you can use to intensify or add to the subject, including, for example, freezing or blurring movement, altering the apparent subject perspective, or converting its natural colors into black and white.

The importance of light

Light is fundamental to photography – it is what sound is to music. In this section the principles affecting the color and shadow-forming qualities of light are explained, with the accent on existing lighting conditions such as daylight or domestic interior lighting. (Photographic lighting, which follows the same visual principles, is discussed in *The techniques of photography*.) Light direction, quality, and color are compared under different conditions – as are the various ways of controlling the mood of a scene with color or by overall lightness or darkness. This is where the photographer can make good use of the various forms of weather conditions and times of day rather than opting only to use the bright sunlight usually considered to be the best light for picture taking. Comparisons are also made between the effects of lighting on different materials and surface finishes. Light is an exciting, universally available ingredient that you can experiment with – observing its various effects without actually taking a photograph. A desk lamp, tracing paper, and pieces of cardboard, plus some very simple subjects are ample to explore the basic principles in a straight forward way.

The subject within the frame

The basic, visual qualities of things are covered here under the simple headings of line, shape, form, pattern, texture, and color. In practice, most subjects actually combine some or all of these features, but as a photographer, you have the power to emphasize some and diminish others — usually by your choice of lighting and viewpoint. Viewpoint in particular is a very basic area of picture making. It is all too easy to develop the habit of taking pictures from a standing position, at a fixed distance from the subject. Simple actions such as bending the knees, finding a higher viewpoint, or moving very slightly to the left or right can improve the relationship between picture components, and the way they relate to the frame edges.

This opens up the wider topic of how much to include within the frame. The viewfinder, after all, is selective and can only show a small part of the scene before it. The shape and proportions of the final picture, the placing of the horizon, and the positioning of the main subject, are often very open decisions, which only the photographer can make. The way one element relates to areas of color and tone can produce emphasis or confusion, harmony or discord. Lines formed by the edges of objects or shadows, for example, can be used to create a sense of movement or calm, or to draw attention to the key element, such as a face. They are also invaluable for helping to create a sense of depth and distance through convergence, or they can add a sense of dynamic action through zigzag pattern and sharp angles. Photographing a moving subject and conveying the concept of time carries its own more complex problems. Whether to use blur to create a sense of movement or to freeze the subject and make use of the peak of action are also creative decisions that the photographer must make.

The points made in this section can be applied to subjects of all kinds. Picture composition, like any other vocabulary, helps you to present your subject using a whole range of slants and different emphases. It may help to make strongly subject-orientated photographs, such as portraits, more powerful and direct. Or it may help you to find pictures in things you might otherwise pass by. It will also encourage you to appreciate photographs for their inherent structure alone. This, in turn, may lead you to experiment with abstract images, where the subject is no more than a raw color or line.

Relationship to technique

Another major aim of this section is to put into context the technical sections of the book that follow. Practicing a technique for its own sake has little meaning. Camera and film techniques are primarily ways of transferring your ideas into a photographic image. Unless you have something to express or communicate, photographic equipment might just as well be used as a device for recording rather than interpreting the subject. Pictures need not be particularly important or profound — perhaps they are only a record of everyday events and happenings. But in each case they can be far more than mundane records. Perhaps in one shot, shape and texture can be emphasized, while in another it is the lighting or the juxtaposition of objects or frames which adds an extra personal element. Having decided what you are aiming to achieve and portray in the picture, it is essential to have the relevant technical know-how.

One of the problems with many photographers is that the camera is just not used enough. Like any other technical or aesthetic skill, without constant practice, the ability to *see* and *realize* is no longer an automatic reflex. It is like learning to ride a bicycle or drive an automobile — once learned, the technique is best absorbed and used subconsciously. You can then concentrate on the particular challenge of each individual subject — treating it with a mixture of a proven visual approach and experimental ideas.

Natural light

The form of energy called "light" is fundamental to seeing and to photography. It communicates information about our surroundings to our light-sensitive receptor – the eye. And in the process of creating a photograph, it forms images via lenses and mirrors, and initiates chemical changes in the film which record these images in a permanent way.

For photographers, light has two intimately linked, important features. First, it has physical characteristics, explained by factual, scientific principles. These determine how it illuminates objects and creates images. Second, it engenders an emotional, subjective response in the human observer. We interpret the light effects we see selectively, according to our personal experience.

Light's physical characteristics

When light strikes the surface of an object, much of the energy bounces off, or "reflects". The effect is like a jet of water striking a flat surface. Just as parts facing the jet become wettest, while others remain dry, so the "lit" side of an object reflects more illumination than shielded, or shadow, areas. The result is that variations of light and shade reach the eye or camera in the form of rays of different intensities. Light rays are then bent, or "refracted" by a lens, and concentrated to form a small image on the film, which represents the scene before us.

Our main source of natural lighting is the sun. Radiations from the sun spread outward like ripples, in a mixture of wavelengths. Different wavelengths appear as different colors, every color of the spectrum being contained in the sun's "white" light. Surfaces that reflect only certain wavelengths and absorb the rest look colored. The more selectively an object reflects the light, the richer and deeper in color it appears. Colors also owe their appearance to the scattering of some wavelengths more than others by the contents of the air. For example, the atmosphere at dawn or dusk absorbs some of the wavelengths from sunlight, leaving it orange-colored. Objects therefore literally change in their color appearance according to the time of day, weather conditions, and the intensity and quality of the lighting.

The subjective response

Differences of light and shade and color communicate key information about objects around us. They define shape and outline, and tell us a great deal about texture and three-dimensional form. Experience since childhood influences our interpretation of visual clues, and also conditions our subjective response. We associate differing levels and qualities of light with different moods, and attribute emotional qualities to colors. Reds and yellows seem "warm" and embracing, perhaps through identification with flames and sun. Blues and greens appear "cool" and remote, while muted colors suggest a somber mood, and brilliant, contrasting colors attract attention, giving a sense of exuberance.

Handling light effects

Light can transform the appearance of surroundings, dramatically emphasizing or suppressing detail, and altering color and apparent shape. For the photographer, the intensity of the lighting itself is often the least important factor – it can be measured objectively with an exposure meter, and duly compensated for. But most of light's more subtle influences cannot be allowed for by any technical means. For example, there is no way in which camera settings can convert hard-edged, distinct shadows to softer, gradated shading. Neither can they change light directed from one side into lighting from the front, nor compensate for the effect light has on colors. All these are fundamental visual changes, and are much more obvious in an isolated photograph than in real life.

The qualities of objects themselves are equally important. In identical lighting, a transparent object can differ greatly in appearance from one which is opaque or translucent, and an object with a shiny surface will look quite different from one which is dull or textured. In practice, all these factors interrelate. Photographers must develop a conscious awareness of the many subtle effects of light, and realize how they affect the photographic image, both separately and in combination. Then they must learn to choose and apply these effects creatively to any subject – from portraits and landscapes to still life.

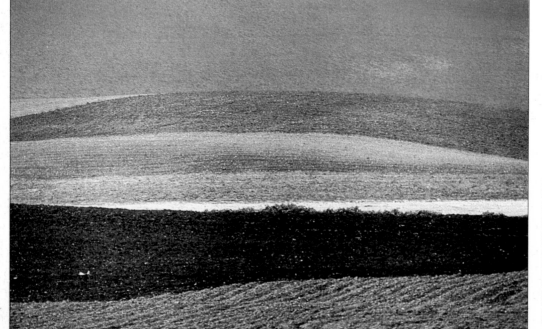

Soft, even front-lighting
This landscape by Franco Fontana (left) comprises simple, abstract strips of tone and color, like a geologist's cross-section. Light has permeated every element in the picture, illuminating but flattening, and revealing minimal modeling and texture. The whole picture seems to occupy one plane. Only the changing granular structure of the soil itself gives clues about scale and distance.

Harsh, low back-lighting
Dennis Brokaw's composition of glistening sand and water (facing page) shows effective exploitation of harsh, low back-lighting. Tiny ripples catch the light and reflect it upward as intense highlights, counteracted by deep shadow. The direction of the light conveys all the information on color, texture, depth, and the relative heights of different surfaces, while contrast helps to give a sense of brilliance and luminosity. The photographer chose a viewpoint which gave the right lighting direction, at a time of day when the sun was low, and warm in color.

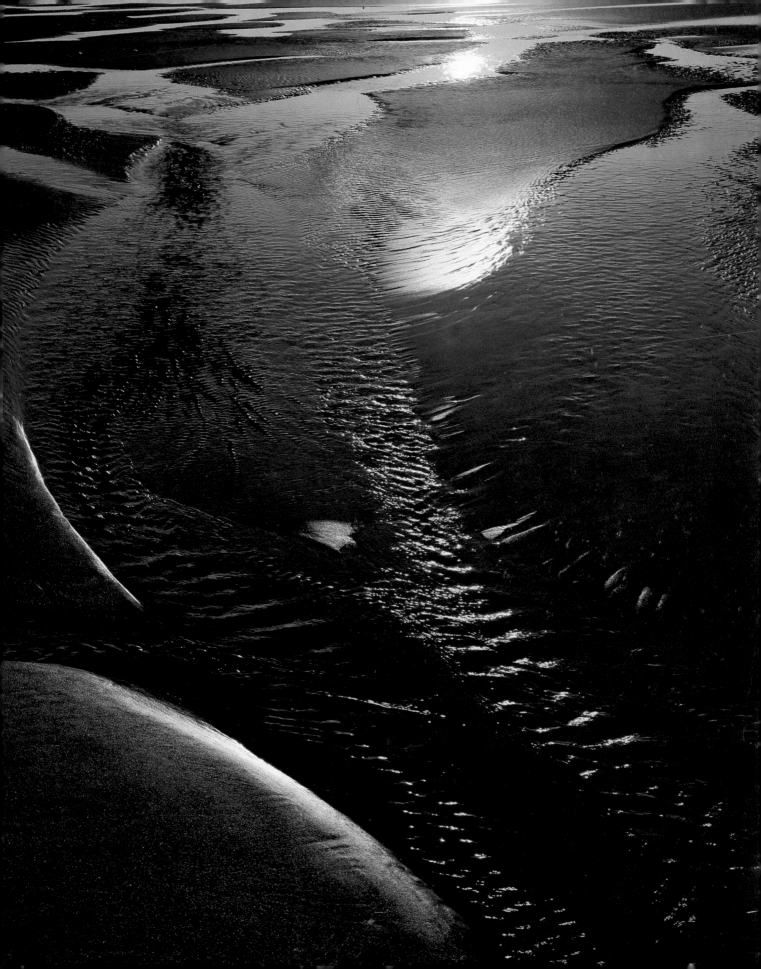

Light direction

The height and direction from which light reaches a scene have a fundamental influence on its appearance. According to the position of the light source, different facets of the subject are either illuminated or cast into shadow. Careful choice of direction makes it possible to emphasize the important parts of the subject, and suppress into shadow any distracting details. In addition, it can make the actual form of objects look three-dimensional or flattened, surface texture appear enhanced or suppressed, and colors look brilliant or muted.

Psychological influences

These changes are mostly objective, physical ones, but lighting direction has strong psychological influences, too. For example, natural scenes are usually lit from above, so objects lit from below our line of sight appear inherently "unnatural". Even directing light horizontally rather than vertically produces associations with dawn or dusk.

Light direction through the day

Throughout daylight hours, as the sun moves gradually across the sky, any object or structure facing east is frontlit in the morning and backlit in the afternoon. The longest shadows are cast at dawn or dusk, and the shortest ones are cast at noon.

The location of the light source in relation to the subject controls the direction and length of the shadows it forms. The principle is simple – sun, shadow edge, and the part of the object that formed it normally all lie in one straight line. If an object is static it is possible to predict when a particular facet will be lit, and the direction shadows must therefore take.

The movable object

Although the sun's position is a fixed factor at any one time, many subjects are movable. Whenever possible, it is best to pick shadow directions that will enhance the important visual qualities of the subject and strengthen the lines of the composition.

Look at the care with which a photographer such as Bill Brandt uses lighting direction to control the visual appearance of human forms. Brandt can make the fingers of a pair of hands seem hewn out of rock, using side-lighting. With flat frontal lighting his nudes become white featureless shapes (see *Leading exponents of Structuralism and Abstraction,* pp. 364-8).

See also
Form *Light on form,* p. 48. Lighting in the studio *Controlling lighting,* p. 169. Medical and forensic photography *Record photography,* p. 285. Aerial photography *Basic aerial photography,* p. 296.

Side-lighting

Light coming from one side shows three-dimensional objects and surfaces in strong relief. Because the light rays are traveling at right-angles to your line of sight, you can see the formation of both lit and shadowed areas very distinctly.

Protruding parts of the subject, and other isolated objects, catch the light, and rounded objects show gradation between their light and dark sides. Across this middle zone texture is greatly exaggerated.

Side-lighting strongly reveals the depth in three-dimensional subjects, but gives much less overall detail and information than front-lighting. This is because of the often harsh contrast between lit and unlit areas, and the long shadows. The more numerous and complicated the shapes present in a scene, the more harsh side-lighting will transfer a confusion of shadows from one object to another, making it more difficult to distinguish individual objects from one another.

It is important to realize, too, that unless an object is completely symmetrical, its appearance will differ greatly according to its position in relation to the side-lighting. To take an extreme example, a profiled face loses all detail from its features if it is lit from behind the back of the head. If the light source is moved only slightly toward the front, the small details and complexities of skin texture will start to become clearly visible once again.

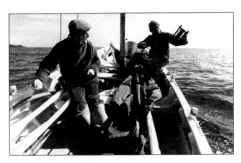

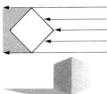

Different surfaces
Side-lighting (above) gives a confusing mixture of shadows and highlights across complicated surfaces. Simpler structures, mostly on one plane, respond better (left).

Shadow contribution
Nick Walster's picture (below) shows how well a simple, mainly two-dimensional subject responds to harsh side-lighting. Objects protruding from the building cast dynamic, angular shadows, which make a geometric contribution to the composition.

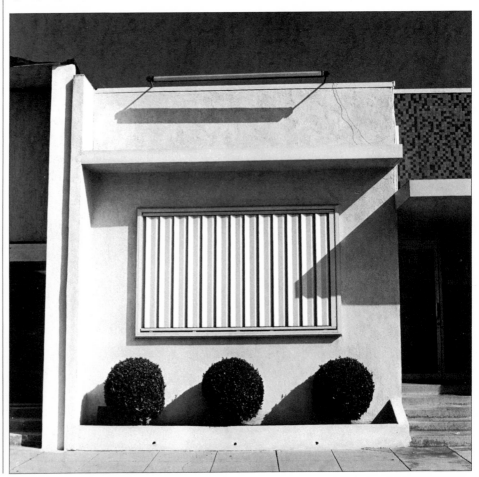

Back- and rim-lighting

When light comes mostly from the rear of the subject, shadows must form toward the photographer. If the whole background is brightly and evenly lit, an opaque object appears in the foreground unlit and so silhouetted. This happens most naturally with objects set against the sky shortly after sunset. Objects reveal their complete outlines, giving a stark, black

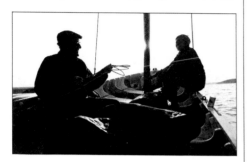

Silhouette shapes
Back-lighting (right and above) from the sun directly ahead silhouettes shapes — most detail merges into flat, simplified, dark tone. Notice how the sun "eats into" the boat's mast.

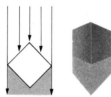

appearance. But moving around the subject in full daylight makes it possible to achieve a backlit effect if you want the subject to appear as a simple shape, or a silhouette. Colors are much reduced and this can be useful to emphasize shape even further or eliminate hues which are not wanted.

When the rim of the subject (the top if the sun is high) reflects some light directly, this can form a brilliant outline, which emphasizes shape. This effect, known as "rim-lighting", is strongest when the background is dark and the light source itself is only just outside the

Rim-lighting
Back-lighting can give a rimlit effect (right), which emphasizes shape against a dark background. In hazy conditions, rim-lighting helps to give an effect like a halo.

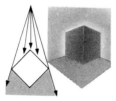

picture area, and shaded from view. When you use rim-lighting on its own, however, you may find that detail within the object is hidden in the contained shadow, which suppresses color and texture, while three-dimensional subject form often appears to be reduced to a flat, black area which looks two-dimensional.

Usually some light reflects back from surroundings into the shadow area, but this is at such a low level that the brilliance of other areas overwhelms it visually. Another kind of rim-lighting takes place when a subject in misty or smoky conditions completely hides a compact light source, such as the sun. Particles then scatter the light, illuminating the air all around the subject, giving a "halo" effect. You can often see this result on tree shapes in a forest which is laden with mist.

Front-lighting

In a frontally lit scene, the light comes from directly behind the photographer. Shadows tend to fall behind the parts of the subject that formed them, and are mostly hidden. Lighting from this direction floods surfaces with illumination, revealing maximum detail in the subject, but minimizing texture. Three-dimensional objects lose most of their appearance

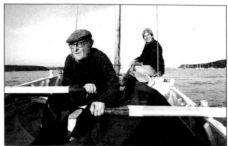

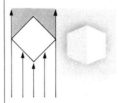

Flat detail
Lighting from the front (above and left) gives plenty of detail, yet has a flattening effect on form. Shadows are mostly hidden directly behind the objects that produced them.

of form and depth. Colors, however, are often rendered brilliantly when they are lit in this way. Front-lighting is also a good way of producing the maximum amount of glitter from a highly reflective surface such as glossy paint or glass.

You can use front-lighting as a safe way of achieving acceptable results in photography. Simple camera guides suggest that beginners should always take pictures with the sun over one shoulder. A more sophisticated application of this tip can help to produce pictures in which all the objects appear to occupy a single plane, or at least give a very limited impression of depth. Figures appear "pinned" to their backgrounds. However, there are pitfalls to avoid when you use front-lighting. Portraits of people looking directly at frontal sun-lighting frequently show eyes screwed up against the glare. A cast shadow of the photographer may also appear in the foregrounds of pictures (although this may be an effect you want to achieve intentionally). Around noon in particular, frontal lighting from the sun can give short, hard, ugly shadows under noses and chins. (The same effect can happen when you mount a flash unit high on top of the camera — see *Advanced flash techniques,* pp. 176-8.)

Viewpoint and lighting

Even though you can alter your own viewpoint in relation to almost any subject, this will not alter the way in which it is lit and shadowed. Altering your viewpoint will, however, affect how much of the lit and shadowed areas you can see, ranging from a view of the totally lit surfaces only, to a view where only the shadowed surfaces appear. Another factor to consider is the degree of glare from reflective surfaces when you view them from particular angles in relation to the light. This glare gives an increase in contrast between the brightest and

darkest areas, which in photographic terms can either help to give dramatic effect, or destroy subject detail that you want to preserve. Equally, from some viewpoints there will be reflective surfaces which redirect some light back into the shadow areas. At other times, nearby grass and trees, for example, may cause problems by tinting shadows green, in which case you must choose a different viewpoint or time of day when these surfaces do not act as reflectors and produce these unwanted effects.

Fixed lighting, changed viewpoint
Although the mill (right) was lit from the same direction throughout, changing viewpoint has given a different lighting direction in each picture. From viewpoint **1** the sun sidelights the mill from the right. Moving around to viewpoint **2** and shooting into the sun, the now totally shadowed surfaces have a flattened, semi-silhouetted appearance. Viewpoint **3** results in a picture side-lit from the left. Compare these results with the series of two people in a boat (above).

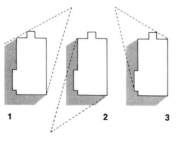

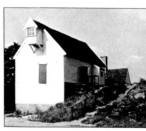

3

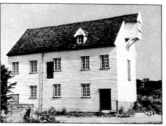

1

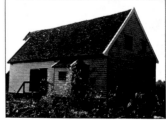

2

Light quality

Light direction is only one of several lighting factors influencing a scene. Shadows are not always hard-edged; often they have soft outlines, and give little contrast between shadowed and lit areas.

The "hardness" or "softness" of shadow areas is an indication of light quality. Hard-quality light tends to give stark, dramatic effects. Shadows contribute strong lines and parts of subjects are often well defined. With soft-quality light we are less conscious of shadows, and the form of the subject itself dominates over shadow lines.

Size of the light source
The relative size of the light source controls light quality. For example, the sun in clear weather is small in relation to the sky as a whole, and gives hard-quality illumination. When a cloud passes in front of the sun, light is diffused and scattered – intensity is reduced, but the whole cloud is now the light source, and its larger area gives a less-abrupt edge to shadows. In overcast conditions, the whole sky becomes one even light source. Illumination is so diffused that shadows virtually disappear. Truly shadow-less lighting occurs when this still down-ward-directed light is matched by diffused lighting from below (reflected from snow or sand). The softness of light at late dusk is particularly noticeable when the sky alone is still strongly illuminated and air particles reflect even, scattered light.

Light quality in practice
Photographers must learn to distinguish between lighting quality and lighting intensity. It is vital to notice the shadow qualities which various-sized light sources produce. Although lighting intensity is often greater when the source is hard and direct, quality and intensity are really two quite independent factors. The full moon, for example, gives hard lighting like direct sunlight, even though its intensity is less.

By careful choice of lighting it is possible to create shadow of a quality that suits the mood, subject, and structure of a picture. Hard lighting might suit a portrait of a man hard at work, but it could destroy a romanticized portrait of a mother and child. It is interesting to see how well known photographers use light quality in all its different forms to add atmosphere to their work. For example, look at Arnold Newman's controversial portrait of the German industrialist Alfried Krupp (see *The illustrated magazines,* pp. 350-1). The hard, low-angled light contributes an almost demonic effect.

See also
Light as subject, pp. 28-32. **Texture** *Lighting and texture,* p. 45. **Light sources** *Light source quality,* p. 162; *Tungsten lighting,* p. 164. **Lighting in the studio** *Lighting polished surfaces,* p. 173. **Advanced flash techniques** *Using single units,* p. 177; *Using multihead flash,* pp. 177-8. **Straight photography** *Individuals and movements of Straight photography,* pp. 343-6.

Hard lighting

Hard lighting gives shadows with sharp, clear outlines. The more compact (point-like) the light source is, and the farther it is from the subject, the sharper shadows will be. Try restricting the light from a window on an overcast day by partly drawing opaque curtains, and notice how shadows in the room become sharper. Light is being made to come from a small source, and since it travels in a straight path, it must form abruptly edged shadows, and give harsh contrast between lit and shadowed areas. This will vary according to whether any of the reflective surfaces near by return a little illumination into the shadowed areas (see *Tonal range,* p. 24).

Hard lighting is excellent for emphasizing the texture of a surface, or strong shapes, and for revealing brilliant color. The clear-cut shadows it gives create extra lines which you can use in order to add a sense of structure to the picture. High contrast between light and dark areas can make a subject stand out well from its surroundings, especially when you use side-lighting.

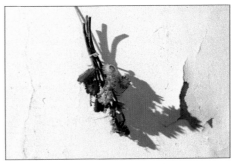

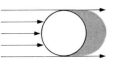

Compact light source
A distant, compact light source (such as the sun in a clear sky) produces a clear division between lit and shadowed areas, as shown in the diagram. The photograph (above) shows how, on a far more intricate subject, shadows are sharply defined, and modeling is crisp. Color and texture are easy to identify.

Hard light abstraction
In this simple composition by Robin Bath, hard noonday sun projects sharp, downward shadows which are exactly the right length and angle to duplicate the design of the tiles. Notice, too, how the harsh light reflected from angled louvers in the window shutters makes the paintwork glisten. This helps to break the picture's otherwise severe symmetry. The clothes line, some distance in front of the wall, has cast its shadow outside the picture frame.

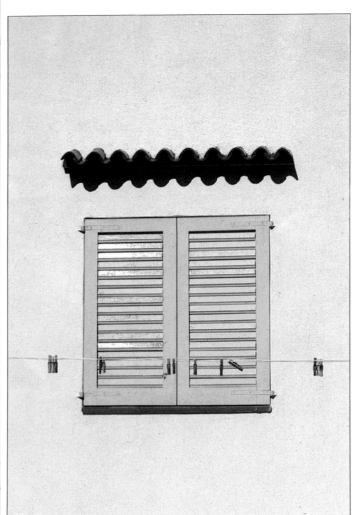

Semi-diffused light

Lighting becomes softer in quality the larger and closer the light source is to the subject. Try holding tracing paper to intercept light from a small domestic lamp and watch the effect on shadows. The reason for this change is that a wide light source projects light toward the subject from a much wider range of directions, and this creates a far more gradual change from light to dark areas on the subject itself. Shadows cast by this kind of light are still clearly defined, but they now have softer edges. Semi-diffused light coming from one side only

Scattered light

When the light source is diffused (for example, if the sun's rays are mostly obscured by intermittent, or thin, cloud cover), the light's rays are scattered and reach the subject from a much wider area, as shown in the diagram. The photograph (below) shows how shadow edges are far less clearly defined, possessing softly gradated edges.

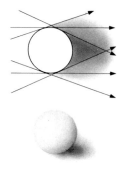

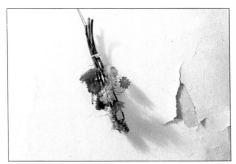

gives enough visible shadow to help show form and texture. But it allows more flexibility than hard lighting, because there is none of the extreme contrast which causes problems if light height and direction are not perfect for the subject. Semi-diffused side-lighting gives roundness and form without empty black shadows. Color appears slightly more muted than with hard light, but detail throughout is good.

Soft lighting

Heavily diffused, "soft", lighting gives an almost shadowless effect. This occurs when you use a large-area light source, such as an overcast sky. Even on a clear, sunlit day you can still find diffused-quality lighting. People sitting in the shadow cast by a building, for example, are only illuminated by light scattered from the

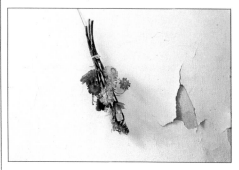

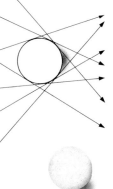

Diffused light

Totally diffused light (such as sun shining through a completely overcast sky) reaches the subject from many different directions, as shown in the diagram. The picture (above) shows how all parts of the subject receive some illumination, revealing full detail, but very soft shadow and less texture than in harder lighting. Separation of the subject from its background is also far less obvious than in other conditions.

blue sky. Here lighting quality equals overcast daylight, although it is bluer in color (see *Time of day*, p. 23). When shooting a small subject you can create soft lighting artificially by placing it in shadow, and then directing light toward it from a large white surface (a large sheet of white cardboard, for example) held angled so that it reflects the direct sunlight.

Indoors you can produce heavily diffused lighting by illuminating the wall and ceiling of a room with several lamps. Large, floor-to-ceiling windows draped with muslin have a similar effect. The closer you place your subject to the light source, the softer the lighting becomes. This is because the light source grows effectively larger in relation to the subject, and encompasses more of it.

Heavily diffused lighting can appear less spectacular than hard lighting. But it can be more rewarding and manageable than other lighting types. The photographic process tends to exaggerate contrast, and soft light gives delicate modeling, muted colors, and shading rather than shadows. It can be excellent for subjects with complex mixtures of forms and surfaces. Soft lighting, therefore, offers by far the greatest freedom when you are choosing lighting for a subject — in terms of lighting direction and viewpoint.

Soft light detail

Henry Wilson's picture of the interior of an Indian temple shows how totally diffused light can reveal minute detail in a complicated structure. Reflections from ceiling and walls outside the picture area have scattered most of the daylight, giving an even luminosity to the carved pillars and polished stone floor. Hard lighting would have produced a complicated grid of cast shadows, which would have confused this already complicated subject even further, and spoiled the picture's atmosphere.

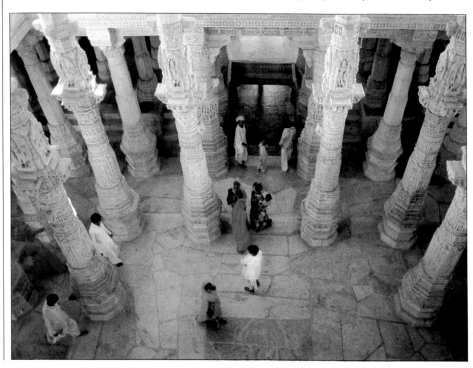

Light and subject properties

The appearance of objects in our surroundings depends on the kind of lighting they receive and on their physical properties. Materials and surfaces can respond differently to lighting direction and quality, giving a rich visual range. Materials are either opaque, transparent, or translucent. A solid, opaque object often looks so because of the light reflected from its surfaces, or because of the way in which it blocks light coming from an illuminated background. Transparent materials, such as clear glass and plastic, are recognizable as much by the light reflected from other objects and transmitted through them, as by the material itself. Transparent objects can also refract light rays, so that we see transmitted areas of light and shade which are not directly behind them. Light is transmitted by translucent materials, too, but this time in a scattered form, as though through tracing paper.

Tones and colors
In any given amount of light, one object can appear relatively bright, because its tone reflects a large percentage of the illumination reaching it, and another look darker, because it absorbs most of the light. A surface with a shiny, glossy finish will show richer tone and color values than one with a matte surface. Rounded forms tend to give gradated changes in tone, and angled, flat surfaces tend to give more abrupt tone-value changes. Color is influenced both by an object's material and by its surface finish, as well as by the color of the light (see *Light and color*, pp. 22-3).

Interpreting subject properties
All these complex visual characteristics communicate vital information. We can tell immediately that one item is smooth while another is polished, one textured, and yet others rounded or flat. It depends how the light is physically modified by the subject. In photography, the challenge is often to bring out the richness of subject qualities. This becomes problematic when different materials occur together. If this is the case, lighting either has to be a compromise to give reasonable results for them all, or it will emphasize and enhance one at the expense of the others.

See also
Texture *Lighting and texture*, p. 45. **Lighting in the studio** *Controlling lighting*, p. 169; *Glare*, p. 170; *Lighting polished surfaces*, p. 173; *Lighting glass*, p. 174. **Editorial and advertising photography** *Still life*, pp. 314-15.

Materials

Light direction is the most important lighting factor to consider when you are revealing the qualities of different materials. Front-lighting generally minimizes the differences between transparency, opacity, or opalescence, while side- or back-lighting emphasizes their separate qualities. This is because all three visual characteristics are based on the material's ability to stop light, or to allow it to pass through.

Opaque materials
An opaque material is one which does not allow light to pass through it. The majority of objects are opaque and therefore rely mostly on surface reflection for their visual description — which generally means using front- or side-lighting. But since opaque objects block light, you can emphasize interesting shapes and suppress other features if you use back-lighting. If you want to create a silhouetted

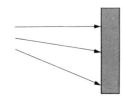

Absorption of light
Opaque materials absorb light, converting it into heat, and dark materials absorb more light than pale ones. Few surfaces absorb all light — some is always reflected back.

shape and suppress other features totally, show the subject against a bright area of background, such as the sky. Lighting used in this way can make even a white-toned object look completely black.

Translucent materials
Objects that are translucent allow light rays to pass through them, but at the same time scatter the light in all directions. They enable you to make free use of side- or back-lighting, which gives them a milky, self-illuminated appearance. Examples of such materials include paper, clouds, leaves, and thin porcelain. When objects made from translucent materials are lit from the front they become virtually indistinguishable from light-toned, opaque objects. Translucent materials make

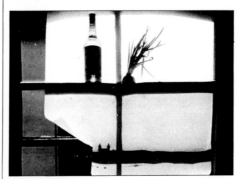

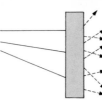

Diffused transmission
Translucent materials transmit light, but scatter it (right) — objects cannot be seen clearly through them. Paper (above) reveals shadows but diffuses subject details.

very good diffusers when you want to convert hard-quality lighting into soft.

Transparent materials
Clear, transparent materials transmit light freely, without changing its quality, although some losses due to absorption always occur. Light rays reaching a flat surface of clear material, such as sheet glass or water, at right-angles, pass through it without any change of direction. But if light strikes the surface at an angle, its direction is bent, owing to refraction. At acute angles, the light mostly reflects off the surface of the material — as though from a highly polished mirror.

It is only possible to see smooth, clear-glass objects by means of subtle visual clues. Background and surroundings are all-important. Against a dark ground you can identify curved or angular, transparent materials mostly by their surface sparkle. Small or distant light sources reflect as small, bright highlights. Large, diffused lamps or reflectors will form larger, "spread" highlights, which tend to follow the form of the object. When you look at transparent objects from some distance in front of a white background, their shapes are delineated by black outlines, due to refraction of the light away from you, along the edges of

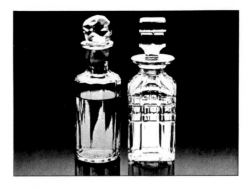

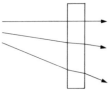

Direct transmission
Transparent materials (above) transmit light, but cause it to bend, or "refract" (right). The degree of refraction alters according to the angle at which the rays of light hit the subject.

the material. The larger the amount of dark-toned surfaces you have both to the left or the right of the object, the stronger and more definite the black outline will become.

Shaped, transparent objects can function as crude lenses. Clear, rounded glass objects placed one behind the other form patterns of distorted shapes. Transparent materials also have the ability to trap light that is applied along one edge. The illumination is reflected from the front and back surfaces and only escapes where there are indentations.

Surfaces

Every material has a top surface which has its own light-reflecting characteristics. Surface qualities range from smooth and highly reflective, through sheenless matte, to rough texture. Look at the varied surfaces of human skin and the fabric of clothing. Wind-ruffled water, the leaves of plants, metals, stones and pebbles, all have surface characteristics which are very different from one another.

Even if the underlying material of two objects is exactly the same, surface finish differences will give them contrasting appearances. The influence of surface finish is obvious when you

compare, say, a newly washed car with one covered by a film of dust. The glossier the surface, the richer tonal detail and colors seem. Matte surfaces dilute colors, and make black materials look more like dark gray. Glossy-surfaced subjects also demand more lighting care — quite insignificant alterations in the position of the light source or in viewpoint can make very noticeable differences in the placing of highlights and glare spots (a point to watch for when composing the photograph).

Glossy surfaces

Any material which has a smooth, glossy surface tends not to scatter the light but reflects it in one direction only. This means that from one vantage point you see a glaring "hot spot" of light, if the light source is hard, or a larger patch of reflective sheen if it is soft and diffused. From all other viewpoints the object is free of surface finish reflections. Its underlying color is brilliant and details are easy to pick out. This

is a spectacular change when you compare it with an object that is made of the same material, but which has a matte surface.

Choose your viewpoint carefully for glossy surfaces — it is important to try to estimate

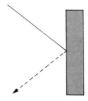

Direct reflection
Light reflects from a surface like a bouncing ball. If a line, or "normal", is drawn at right-angles to the surface, angles of incoming light, and reflected light, are equal.

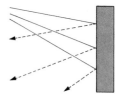

Specular reflection
Rays reflected from a glossy surface (right) retain their direction in relation to each other. Highlights and reflections (below) are characteristic features of very glossy surfaces.

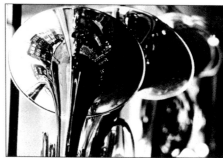

where to stand so that you can either avoid or make use of surface reflections.

Textured and matte surfaces

A textured surface has a raised structure. This may be anything from a range of distant mountains to a close-up of weathered wood (see *Detail and scale*, p. 43). You can emphasize

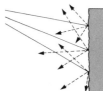

Diffuse reflection
Light rays striking a matte surface reflect according to the many facets of its "micro" texture. Because of this the light is scattered in many different directions at once.

the form and structure of any textured surface by using oblique, glancing light, to shade in dips and highlight raised surfaces.

Matte-surfaced materials have a microscopically textured top surface. This reflects hard lighting and scatters it in different directions, giving an effect similar to diffusion. Diffused light becomes further diffused. The result is that hot spots are absent, but there is a little surface reflection visible from all viewing angles — diluting even the richest blacks to very dark grays.

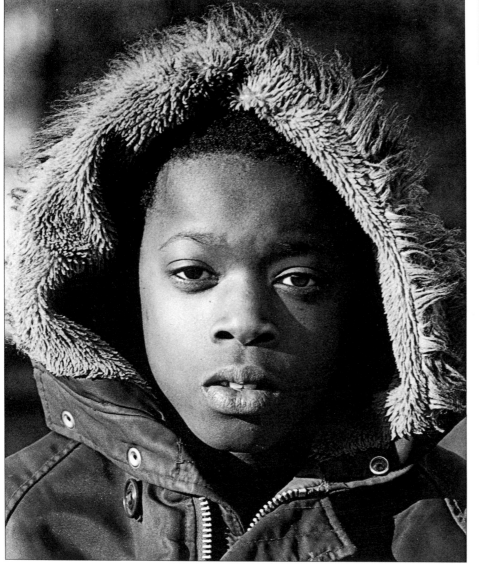

Mixed surfaces

Most everyday subjects in fact contain a wide variety of different surfaces, each of which responds in its own particular way to various kinds of lighting. This close-up portrait of a boy, by Stephen Godfrey, shows glossy, matte, and textured surfaces combined in the same subject. The boy's lips and eyes are glossy, and his skin and jacket matte, while his hair and hood lining are strongly textured.

Color and surface

A colored object with a glossy surface generally has a richer, more "saturated" appearance than an object of the same color with a matte surface. Look at a paint sample book, and compare the different ways the same color appears when it has been treated with a glossy, semi-gloss, and a matte finish. To take another example, compare the different effects created by glossy and matte finishes on photographic prints.

This difference is particularly evident if the lighting is hard and generally frontal. Provided you choose a viewpoint which avoids direct flare, a glossy surface acts as a very color-selective reflector. Objects with matte surfaces, however, always reflect a little white light from the top surface, which mixes with and dilutes the colored wavelengths reflected from pigment underneath. Whatever vantage point you choose, a color with a matte finish will have a slightly more pastel look. Overcast and heavily diffused lighting will reduce these surface differences. Some of the heavily scattered light tends to reflect toward you from glossy surfaces, too, forming a more diluted mixture. Lighting is also generally dimmer when weather conditions are overcast, and so the ways in which we perceive color strength is markedly affected by our inherent inability to

see quite as brightly when the light is poor as when it is completely clear (see *Visual response,* facing page).

You can expect maximum brilliance from a color, therefore, when it has a smooth, high-gloss surface, brilliantly lit by hard-quality lighting from an angle which does not reflect a glaring hot spot toward you. It is helpful to have dark surrounding surfaces which will not reflect and scatter light back at the surface. The identical shade looks most "washed out" (or desaturated — see *Saturation, hue, and brightness,* p. 51) if its surface is matte, and is lit from several different directions by diffused, low-intensity lighting. This is even more likely to happen if the subject is very closely surrounded by other surfaces which are light-reflecting as well.

Light and color

The sun's visible radiations range in wavelength from 400 to 700 nanometers. Most of the time, rays of all these different wavelengths exist in sunlight, forming a mixture which looks uncolored and white. In practice the exact composition of this white-light wavelength mixture varies according to time of day and weather conditions. A reminder of its true color content is visible in the rainbow, or when light passes through a prism. Refraction caused by the rain droplets or by the glass then separates out the various different wavelengths into individual bands of color — an effect which is known as "the visible spectrum".

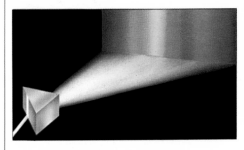

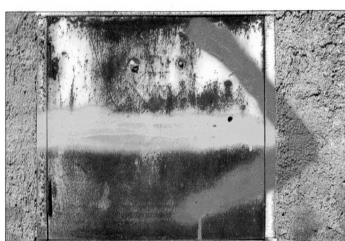

Smooth and textured
A dusty or textured surface (below) acts as a color diffuser, weakening it, while a smooth one reflects it directly, showing color at full saturation. The painted

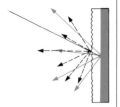

arrow (left) shows saturation variations when paint covers both rough and smooth surfaces.

Glossy
Hard light on a glossy surface (below and left) gives strong, pure color. The light reflects directly from the

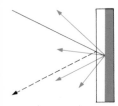

pigment, with only a few rays reflecting from the surface to provide highlights. These small areas contain little or no color.

White light spectrum
When a narrow beam of white light passes through a glass prism obliquely, it is split up into its component colors. The glass alters the direction of the light's short (blue) wavelengths more radically than its red wavelengths. The colors are spread out as individual bands in the spectrum.

Color appearance
The color an object appears to have depends on its physical make-up, pigment and surface finish, and on the color, intensity and quality of the lighting. A rich green material only looks green because it has the ability to reflect or transmit the green wavelengths in white light and absorb the other colors. (In orange light, green looks dark because there are hardly any green wavelengths present.) When daylight is tinted at dusk, colors of matching hue look lighter, and colors from the more remote, blue end of the spectrum sequence appear darker. Articles such as fabrics can look one hue in direct sunlight and another when the light is tinted by green foliage, or reaches the fabric from a clear, blue sky.

With a few materials color appearance is also affected by the ultraviolet content of the sun's radiations (wavelengths somewhat shorter than 400 nanometers). Ultraviolet light is not visible, but it makes certain substances "fluoresce" and produce visible light. Fluorescent papers, poster colors, and washing powder additives all work in this way, giving a slight "extra brightness" in daylight.

See also
Color, pp. 50-1. Structure, pp. 72-9. Depth and distance *Aerial perspective,* pp. 82-3. Choice of film *Color temperature,* p. 151. Controlling mixed lighting *Balancing light,* p. 175. Special effects lighting *Colored light sources,* p. 179.

Time of day

Direct sunlight at noon has an approximately even distribution of color wavelengths. Toward the beginning or end of the day, fewer short (blue) wavelengths are present. When the sun is low in the sky its light passes through the earth's atmosphere obliquely. Air molecules in the atmosphere always scatter a small proportion of light rays traveling through it, the most scattered being the short wavelengths (this is why the sky looks blue, not black). But sunlight reaching the atmosphere obliquely must pass through hundreds more miles of these molecules than at noon. They progressively filter out more short wavelengths, leaving only orange and red-colored radiations. This

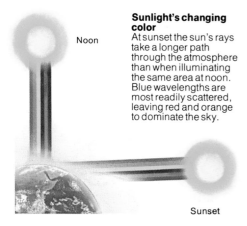

Sunlight's changing color
At sunset the sun's rays take a longer path through the atmosphere than when illuminating the same area at noon. Blue wavelengths are most readily scattered, leaving red and orange to dominate the sky.

corresponds with the color of the sun at dawn and dusk which gives the sky its characteristic warm, rosy tints.

Changes in weather conditions throughout the day influence color, too. When the air contains many water particles — haze, mist or cloud — these tend to absorb light, mostly in the blue region of the spectrum again. The sky looks less blue and more white than at noon on a clear day. For the bluest lighting of all, look at the illumination from a clear sky as it affects shadows at midday. Very few long wavelengths are present and subjects in these shadowed areas have a very strongly blue-biased appearance.

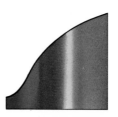

Dawn
Early sunlight (left) contains few blue wavelengths. The whole scene (below) is bathed in orange light. Similar color effects can occur directly before dusk, depending on the weather.

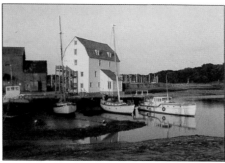

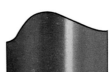

Noon
By late morning (left) daylight contains a more even mixture of wavelengths. The widest variety of subject colors are seen (below), increased dramatically in brilliance by the strong lighting.

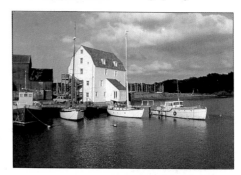

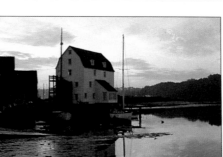

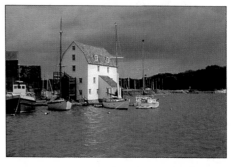

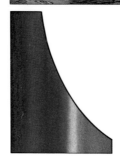

After sunset
After the sun has set (left), blue-rich wavelengths dominate the light. These wavelengths illuminate building and boats (above) from parts of the sky behind the camera. The last direct light from the sun tints high clouds and sky background. The still water reflects the clouds.

Storm light
Sunlight before or after a storm (above), at any time of the day, creates dramatic lighting effects. Lit surfaces set against the dark sky seem to have a greater brilliance of tone and color. White objects stand out starkly. In changeable weather conditions, the whole mood of a scene can be transformed

within minutes. Usually the most brilliant colors are seen in distant landscapes when sunshine follows directly after a heavy shower of rain. This is because of the exceptionally clear atmosphere — the air is literally "washed" clean.

Visual response

The eye sees colors at the two extremes of the spectrum, deep red and deep blue, as "dark" and colors in the middle of the spectrum, such as yellow-green, as "bright". As light dims, our response to color changes. First, our idea of the brightest color shifts from yellow-green toward green-blue. At late dusk, green-blue looks lighter than red. Then, as illumination drops still further, color receptors in the eye no longer function and we see the world in black and white. The response of the eye to color is at its most sensitive when illumination is brightest. In brilliant, glaring sunlight colors have to reflect more light, and because of this they appear more "colorful" to the eye. They are at their brightest and are fully saturated (see *Saturation, hue, and brightness*, p. 51).

The color of our surroundings is therefore ephemeral. It changes according to the time,

weather, and our viewpoint relative to lighting direction, as well as the wavelength-reflective properties of objects themselves. Despite this we tend to remember scenes and situations as they were colored at the time. Color in pictures is very evocative. We tend to associate blue-dominated scenes with coolness. Greens and yellows seem to have more cheerful, spring-like associations. Oranges and reds give a sense of enclosure and warmth. The different combinations of colors in a scene create their own emotive responses, too. Strong, bright, contrasting hues have a brash liveliness, whereas desaturated colors, which match closely, seem to create a much quieter and far more somber mood.

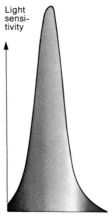

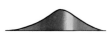

Light sensitivity

Rods

Cones

Eye response
The millions of tiny light receptors in the eye are a mixture of two types. "Cones" give a different response according to wavelength (below), allowing us color vision. The more numerous "rods" are many times more light sensitive (left), but see colors only as tone differences. In twilight we see with the rod receptors only, not the cones.

Lighting contrast

Lighting contrast is the difference between the amount of illumination reaching the brightest and darkest parts of a scene. The greater this difference, the wider the "tonal range" of the scene. Contrast is generally greater in hard-quality lighting than in soft. The nature of the subject is also important. A mixture of dark- and light-toned, reflective and non-reflective surfaces will produce greater overall contrast than a single-toned surface, even though both receive the same lighting.

Atmospheric conditions

The level of lighting contrast in sunlit scenes varies with atmospheric conditions, and the time of day and year. Some parts of the world have their own characteristics, often based on altitude, or their proximity to the equator. Flat terrain or areas surrounded by water, for example, tend to have low-contrast lighting. Common forms of natural, high-contrast lighting occur when atmospheric conditions are clear and the sun is shining directly, but dark clouds and/or dark nearby surroundings absorb most scattered light from the sky and prevent it from reaching shadows.

Lighting direction also affects the appearance of contrast — side- or back-lighting both present larger areas of shadow than front-lighting, so the eye is more conscious of the tonal range.

Eye and film response

The eye is sensitive to the tonal contrast of its surroundings. It is the juxtaposition of lightness and darkness that most clearly separates one object from another. In conditions of extreme contrast (such as back-lighting from low sun), the eye cannot see detail in shadows and highlights located very close together.

While this extreme lighting range is difficult for the eye to accept, it is even more difficult to capture on film. The process of photography tends to increase contrast — wherever subject tones are much lighter or darker than a certain limited range, all tonal differences are lost, merging either into stark white or solid black.

Lighting contrast has its own psychological associations, too. Low-contrast conditions help to produce a gentle, moody atmosphere. If tones are mostly light or "high key", the effect is delicate and open. Predominantly dark, somber tones produce a "closed-in" feeling.

The effect of high-contrast lighting on color is to increase richness of hue in the brightest areas, because the eye is more color-sensitive to high-intensity illumination. In general, the effects of contrast are less obvious in color pictures.

See also
Emphasis *Tone interchange*, pp. 68-9. **Lighting in the studio** *Contrast*, p. 169; *Low-key lighting*, p. 172; *High-key lighting*, p. 173. **Controlling mixed lighting** *Reducing contrast with flash*, p. 176.

Tonal range

In photography, lighting contrast is more important than lighting intensity. You can compensate for dim or bright overall intensity by choice of film or exposure settings. But light contrast, along with reflectance characteristics of objects, affects the tonal range of a scene. A figure sidelit at night in a dark street, for example, has a tonal range too extreme for film to record fully, at any exposure setting. To overcome this, you can move the subject away from the light source and toward a pale-toned surface, such as a white wall. Directly lit areas become less bright, while shadows, now receiving some light back from the reflecting surface, become more brightly lit. This reduction of lighting contrast contracts the entire tonal range.

The same principle applies to lighting a small, fixed object, harshly illuminated from one side in dark surroundings. If you bring a very reflective surface gradually closer to the shadow side, you can see how reflection of spilled light increasingly illuminates detail. To create the opposite effect and expand the tonal range, remove any reflective surfaces that happen to be near by. They may be illuminating shadow areas that you want to keep as dark as possible.

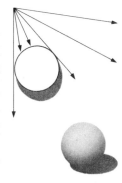

Hard, direct light

The diagram (left) illustrates how hard lighting from one side strikes an object, casting a strong, well-defined shadow. The picture (below) shows this effect in practice. Very little light reaches the shadowed part of the subject, and it is difficult to see and photograph detail in both lit and shadowed areas together. The resulting image contrast is very high.

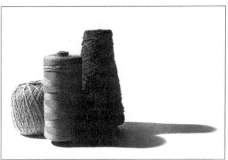

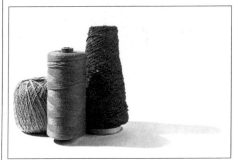

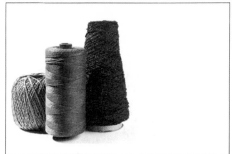

Semi-diffused result

For the result above, a large sheet of paper was placed vertically about 3ft (1m) from the yarns. Its matte surface has reflected some scattered light back into the subject, as shown in the diagram (left). This has added some light to the shadowed areas of the subject. Contrast is considerably lower than in the hardlit version.

Soft result

The photographer brought the sheet of paper much closer to the subject to produce the soft result (above). Being closer makes the reflector effectively larger (left), so that the reflected light "fills in" the shadows at both the side and front of the yarns. Contrast in this picture is very low. Little shadow is visible on the flat surface.

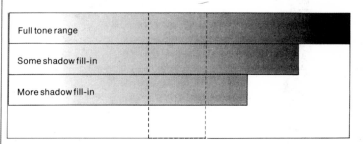

Full tone range			
Some shadow fill-in			
More shadow fill-in			

Exposing for brighter tones   Exposing for darker tones

Tone and exposure

The diagram (left) represents the tonal range of a scene. The top scale shows the full range produced in contrasty lighting. The two lower scales show the ranges given in softer light. In photography, you will be able to record only part of the full range, exposing for either end or the middle of the scale.

Tonal distribution

Lighting contrast, modulated by the way it affects objects which themselves possess relative brightness and darkness, gives the tonal variations we need to distinguish most of our surroundings. But our response to tonal differences is also subjective — the eye is easily deceived. A particular tone can look light when you see it next to a black background, but dark against another, lighter one — an effect that is known as "simultaneous contrast" (see *Tone theory,* p. 68).

The general, overall distribution of tones present in a scene can also help to set the mood. This is largely based on our associations with the natural environment — strongly contrasting tone values, for example, suggest drama and vitality, and a limited tone range suggests tranquillity.

Predominantly pale tones

In picture terms, a scene consisting mainly of pale tones is known as "high key" (see *High key,* p. 27). A person with fair hair, dressed in light-colored clothing, standing against a pale-toned background and lit with soft, frontal lighting would probably only show deep tone in the eyes and other tiny areas of shadow. The effect is delicate, open, and optimistic. Landscapes full of light-toned buildings, snowscapes, or scenes with large areas of pale sky, all lend themselves to high-key treatment.

It is advisable to leave a small area of dark tone to prevent the picture looking flat, and to improve the relative luminosity of the rest. Do this by using soft lighting if possible, plus any nearby reflective surfaces for extra light.

Predominantly dark tones

The opposite effect — scenes in which most of the tones come from the dark end of the scale — is known as "low key". Results are more dramatic than high key, and may give an impression of enclosure and mystery. High-contrast lighting is usually helpful for creating low-key effects. In the art world there are many painters who have worked successfully using this "tenebrism". Rembrandt, for example, used very dark scenes for his portraits, relieved by faces and hands picked out by small areas of light. In photography, look at the work of Bill Brandt (see *The illustrated magazines,* pp. 350-1), or Yousuf Karsh (see *Leading exponents of Romanticism and the dramatic,* pp. 375-7) for very similar effects.

Apart from picking a background and other large-area elements in the scene which are dark in tone, shadows created by direction and restriction of the light source are also important. Look at the ways in which theater and television use high-contrast lighting to pick out key elements in a low-key scene and set an atmospheric, often somber, mood.

Sometimes you can change the appearance of a portrait from high to low key, with consequent change of mood, by moving the subject into a dark, shadowed area, where it is illuminated by a "slot" of light from a doorway or window.

High key
The landscape by Mark Fiennes is dominated by white and pale gray tones. Mist rising from the water scatters the light within the atmosphere, so that even dark objects appear only mid-gray. A few of the nearest elements appear almost black, but these are kept small. The whole mood of the picture is highly delicate and luminous.

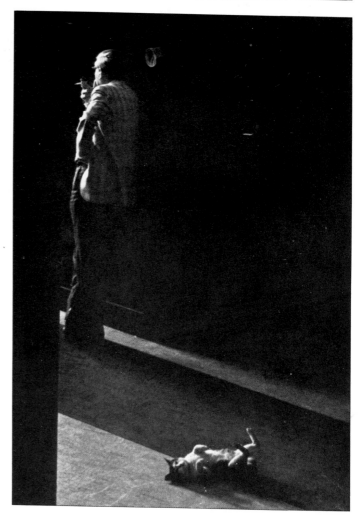

Low key
The man and cat in Bina Fonyat's picture are illuminated by two "slots" of side-lighting coming through a door and window. Solid black, filling most of the picture, adds a note of mystery, and usefully eliminates superfluous detail. Despite the harsh contrast, lights pick out the relevant details of the subject with great economy.

Lighting contrast and color

The presence or absence of color strongly affects our visual response to lighting contrast. First, colors within the subject can themselves give it a contrasty or flat appearance. Second, the colors of areas picked out by the direction and quality of the lighting can dominate the picture. Third, depending on the color of the light (see *Light and color*, pp. 22-3), the colors in a scene can either take on a "flat" appearance, or look more contrasty.

Subject characteristics
Color relationships present in the subject itself give it an inherent visual contrast, of a very similar nature to ordinary tonal contrast (see *Tone interchange*, pp. 68-9) though far more varied. Different colors from widely spaced parts of the spectrum create a much stronger "color contrast" (see *Color*, pp. 50-1) when

they are placed next to each other, than shades of one or two colors that are harmonious, and of similar saturation.

Lighting direction and intensity
You can make color a major element, or suppress it almost entirely, by the direction of the light. If the subject is opaque, harsh back-lighting will all but destroy colors by under-illumination and flare. You can photograph a brilliantly colored flower directly against the sun and produce an image which is practically black and white. But if the flower is translucent, results show a colored shape against white.

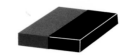

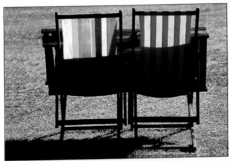

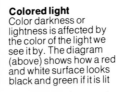

Colored light
Color darkness or lightness is affected by the color of the light we see it by. The diagram (above) shows how a red and white surface looks black and green if it is lit by green light. This is because, unlike white light, green contains no red wavelengths for the pigment to reflect.

Hard side-lighting gives the greatest mixture of shadows and highlights. Because we tend to notice the color in a highlit area far more than in a shadowed one, every surface that has light falling directly on it takes on a special importance. You must therefore be fully aware of how patches of bright color like this are distributed through a photograph, and how they affect its overall composition.

There is also a vital difference between the responses of color film and the eye to color and lighting intensity. "Correct" exposure approximates eye response and shows most color in highlights, least in shadows. But by intentionally overexposing you can "burn out" highlights so that colors here look bleached, and the color in shadows is brightened instead. The softer and more frontally directed the lighting is, the less contrast, and therefore the less opportunity, there is to adjust your colors (or to "tune" them) so that they appear the strongest at any one particular tone value.

Lighting color
The color of the light itself affects the light or dark appearance of colored subjects, and consequently alters contrast, too. In orange light, yellow and red surfaces become difficult to distinguish from white, while blues darken. A blue object, partly lit directly by the setting sun, and partly lit (in shadow areas) by blue sky light, produces a far less contrasty result than an orange object under exactly the same conditions.

Light intensity and color
In this picture by Robin Bath, the Mediterranean boat is painted all over in the same bright colors, but the areas which are exposed to strong sunlight look far more brilliantly colored than those in the shade. This is because the human eye sees brightly lit parts of a colored subject as possessing the strongest color. The eye's color sensitivity is greatest at high illumination levels — fine differences of color and detail are much easier to distinguish. Dimly lit colors look less colorful than they really are, and therefore seem to merge together more readily.

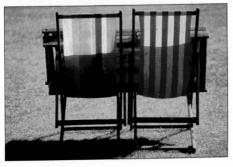

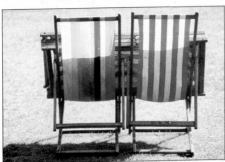

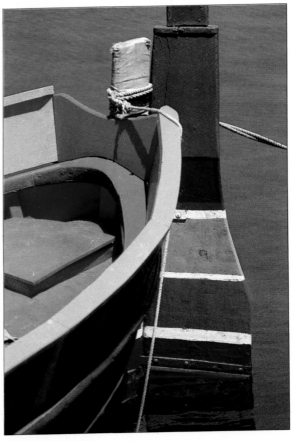

Color emphasis by exposure change
In photography, you can shift strong color from the lightest to the darkest parts of the picture by exposure alteration, like changing the brightness control on a television. The series of pictures (above) shows how, with contrasty light, you can expose to move color brightness from the brilliantly lit top to the shaded bottom, of the striped deckchairs.

High key

Color pictures are called "high key" if the average tone and color values are pale, while dark, rich colors are excluded or kept very small in area. Aim for minimal contrast, and colors diluted with white so that they look pastel. You can achieve this by using very diffused frontal lighting, and by choosing subject and exposure carefully. It is best to organize your composition so that most of the color is in the darker tones of the subject. Then, by exposing (or slightly overexposing) for these areas, you will be able to keep all tones and colors nearer to white than black, and achieve a general air of delicacy rather than heaviness or flatness. Another way of using lighting is to back-light the subject, and then calculate exposure for the shadow areas only.

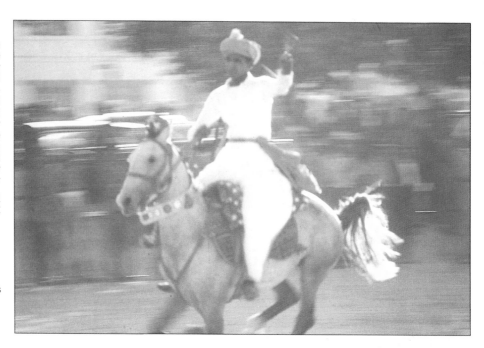

Diluted color
The extreme color delicacy in Roland Michaud's picture of a charging horseman was achieved by shooting into the overcast sun, overexposing the subject, and panning.

Low key

Low-key color pictures contain mostly dark, rich colors, with large areas remaining engulfed in shadow. Strongest, saturated colors exist in mid-tones and highlights, while shadow hues are often suppressed by directional (generally hard) lighting. It is therefore important to see that all surfaces which are to appear colored are lit, and that you expose the photograph for these illuminated parts and not for the shadows. If it is possible to choose your background, use one which is as dark as possible, if not black. In addition, you can use rim-lighting to pick out shape without actually illuminating large areas (see *Back- and rim-lighting,* p. 17).

Try to avoid excessive contrast, for although this can look dramatic, it destroys most colors. The secret is to limit the lighting to the areas where it is absolutely necessary. In terms of color photography, this is usually the areas, or even odd spots where color is most vivid and eye-catching. This may mean that the subject of your picture becomes less important than its colors. Sometimes you can create low key simply by having some dark relevant object in the near foreground to fill large parts of the picture. Another aid is to frame the photograph so that you feature a "patch" of light — outdoors this could be created by a gap in foliage or between buildings, or indoors by an area of soft but localized light from a window. By moving back you can make the light patch relatively small in your picture, the remainder being dark and featureless. Look at the way painters such as Caravaggio handled these "tenebral scenes", and compare this with the high-key color effects used by the Impressionists.

Enriched color
In this low-key indoor portrait, by Roland and Sabrina Michaud, the dominance of dark tones gives colors extra luminance and richness. The directional daylight is carefully limited, but it is not harsh. Picture information is entirely based on the highlit areas, so that the eye is immediately drawn to them. Notice the excellent texture and form that this kind of highlighting gives to the woman's hand.

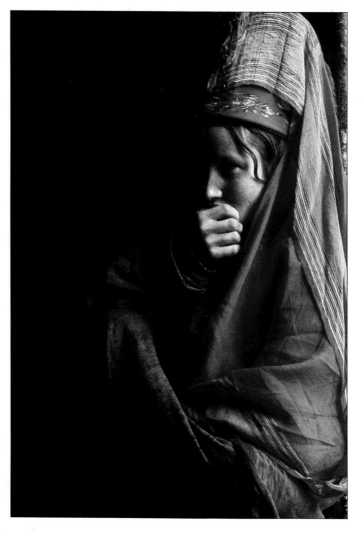

Light as subject

For centuries, light has been a compelling theme for artists, as a subject in its own right. Among painters, Vermeer, Turner, and the French Impressionists are outstanding examples — all in their different ways fascinated by the play of light on an object's surfaces. In photography, the work of Edward Weston, Clarence John Laughlin, and Clarence White in particular continues and develops this preoccupation.

Lighting effects can range from the grand to the minute in scale. An aerial view of a vast city just after sunset is transformed by the evening light into abstract patterns of purple. Sunlight reflected from the inside rim of a cup forms a sparkling pattern of curves on the liquid's surface. The glancing light of dawn or late afternoon will tint the edges of fine seaweed, sand dunes, or huge cliffs alike. A reflection in a puddle, or in the gleam of an eye, can be as telling as a whole cityscape reflected in a lake.

Different light sources

Light as a photographic subject does not have to be "bright". Candles, bonfires, torches, matches, and oil lamps all have atmospheric qualities which can be powerful in photography, despite their weak output. Mixed lighting — the inclusion of differing light sources, such as daylight and domestic lamps, in one scene — shows areas of the scene tinted in different, unexpected colors. Weather conditions sometimes give a similar effect, as do reflections. Subjects reflected in a colored surface appear changed in hue or shape, or are multiplied into repetitive patterns, according to the surface and angle of the reflector.

Light associations

Light has psychological significance, too — strange or unfamiliar forms of lighting suggest a disturbing mood, and command our attention. A face above a candle, for example, or a room in a house surrounded by snow, or an airplane flying above sunlit, white cloud, all receive unnatural, "up-turned" light, with a disquieting effect.

Light symbols

The sheer power of the sun, and other intense light sources, is difficult to communicate in photographs, so symbols must be used. The most common symbol is light spread — either general flare, or the sun's disk extended into a many-armed star. The sun and other compact light sources tend to appear like this anyway if we look at them with eyes screwed up. We therefore accept this kind of representation as signifying brightness, whether drawn, painted, or produced in a photograph by a starburst filter, or similar light-spreading attachment (see *Special effects attachments*, pp. 198-200).

See also
Lighting in the studio *Silhouette lighting*, p. 172; Controlling mixed lighting *Light sources in the picture*, p. 175. Special effects lighting *Physiograms*, p. 180; *Creating light trails*, p. 180; *Ultraviolet lighting*, p. 183.

Shadows

Shadow — basically the absence of light in relation to surroundings — can have as important an influence on picture building as light itself. Shadows appear attached to objects in two main ways; they are either cast or contained. Cast shadows fall on another surface, away from the object itself. Contained shadows remain inside the boundaries of the overall shape of the object. In most lighting situations, though, both cast and contained shadows occur simultaneously.

All shadows give you important clues about subject shape and form. Cast shadows in par-

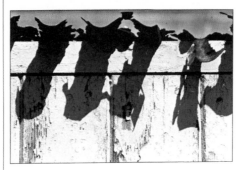

Cast shadow pattern
The picture by Carol Sharp (above) shows the ability of shadows to dominate a scene. Harsh, oblique sunlight casts shadows of corroded roofing across the wall of a shed. It is as though we can see end-on and top views of the complicated metal shapes simultaneously.

ticular offer extra information, often showing how high things are, or how near or far they are from other elements. A view downward from a tall building may reveal little more of people and traffic than tiny circles or rectangles. But the long, hard shadows each casts in evening sunlight show you a side view of each object too, elongated and spread out across the street surface. A cast, two-dimensional shadow of one object often forms a pattern which interrelates with other objects and patterns on the surface on which it lands. For example, the sun casts a well-defined shadow of just part of the shape of one building on another. This has the effect of changing the first building's apparent outline beyond all recognition.

Always give shadow shapes the same attention as the lit areas of a scene. Sometimes you can exclude the object forming a cast shadow altogether. You can show the shadow of a huge tree behind you spread out over a field in front, its branch shapes reaching out in a pattern toward the horizon. If you keep the sun behind you, it is also possible to include your own shadow in every scene you photograph, forming strange associations and giving a kind of continuity. We identify shadow, like darkness generally, with mystery. It is possible to use it to create an atmosphere of tension and surrealism — for example when shadows cast across the ground beyond a doorway prove the presence of a mysterious person or object out of sight, beyond the frame edges (see, for example, Franco Fontana's picture, p. 83).

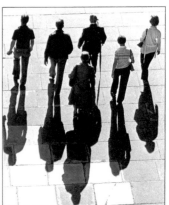

Repeating pattern
High viewpoint, and the long shadows cast by late afternoon sun show this small group of figures as a double pattern. If you view the picture the other way up, you will see how much shadow and subject shapes differ. The picture is by Forrest Smyth.

Shadow and direction change
Shadow lines falling across a pillar in this picture by John Chitty are cast by an unseen grid. Notice how they change direction and bend to follow the pillar's form. Straight lines falling on the pillar resemble fluting.

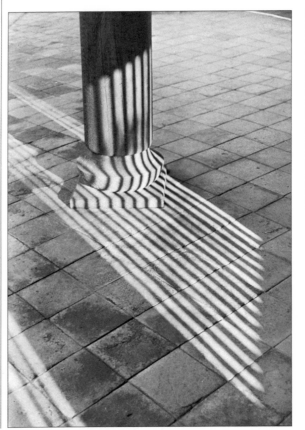

Rim-lighting

Rim-lighting is a means by which you can show a dark subject against a dark background without losing its outline. When the light source is mostly behind the subject (see *Back- and rim-lighting*, p. 17), but also higher or to one side of it, a narrow strip of highlight will pick out the rim of the subject's top or side. A great deal depends upon the nature of the surface — objects made of glossy, dark glass or smooth, black leather will give a clearer and longer highlight than something that has a matte surface. If the background is also dark, you can show up almost the entire outline of a subject by positioning several lights directly behind it, so that its entire near edge is illuminated.

Rim-lighting is therefore an excellent way of simplifying normal surface detail into graphic edge-line pattern, like a white line drawing on black. It is also a method of local emphasis (in a similar way to a halo in painting). Sometimes, in advertising photography, products are emphasized in this way, combined with sufficient frontal lighting to reveal detail as well. In fact, most photographers use rim-lighting as an adjunct to other lighting. For example, when a subject is sidelit against a dark background, its shadowed half will soon become merged and lost in darkness unless you pick it out by rim-lighting.

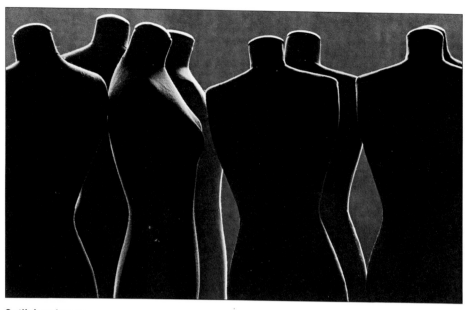

Outlining shapes
This picture of tailor's dummies by Trevor Melton, shows how rim-lighting can simplify a scene. The dummies are in fact light-colored. They were lit by overcast daylight coming through wide windows, from above — each one reflecting a little scattered light on the flanks of its neighbor. Precise framing creates a highly structured picture.

Silhouettes

Silhouettes, with their stark, definite outlines, have an eye-catching simplicity. The subject communicates itself to the viewer by means of its shape alone — continuous shadow, for example, swallows up all form, color, and texture. Notice the visual strength of a tracery of tree branches, or the imposing shape of a building against an evening sky. The sun silhouettes any figures standing against it — a profiled face by a lighted window, or a figure standing on the brow of a hill obscuring the sun itself, becomes a strong, black shape.

The best lighting arrangement for silhouetting small subjects is to place them against an evenly and brightly lit, white surface (such as a sunlit, white wall). You can silhouette larger subjects against a white, overcast sky, or at night you can show figures against a lighted display, such as a store window. Indoors, you may be able to light an unpatterned, even wall. Technically, getting an even background is very important and not always easy. You may, for example, require several lamps to light a large area of wall evenly. The background also must be substantially brighter than your subject, but not glaringly so. The photographic process, from judging exposure to making the final print, increases contrast. This is particularly true of black and white photography.

Take care over choosing viewpoint for silhouettes — especially for portraits. Only the outer edge of the subject communicates information, so you must exploit it to the full. Often a very slight shift of the person's head or hands is enough to transform a featureless outline into a very revealing portrait which is full of interest and conveys personality.

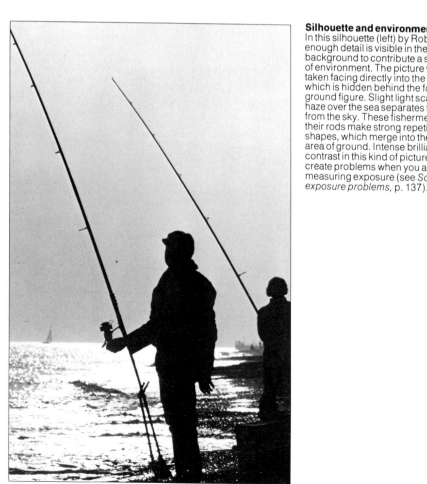

Silhouette and environment
In this silhouette (left) by Robin Bath, enough detail is visible in the background to contribute a sense of environment. The picture was taken facing directly into the sun, which is hidden behind the foreground figure. Slight light scatter by haze over the sea separates the boat from the sky. These fishermen and their rods make strong repetitive shapes, which merge into the dark area of ground. Intense brilliance and contrast in this kind of picture may create problems when you are measuring exposure (see *Solving exposure problems*, p. 137).

Weather

Changing weather conditions have a powerful effect on light, whether in terms of its color, intensity, or quality. Photographers must be aware of this and exploit it in their pictures. Total cloud cover softens and dims the light, and often alters its color, too. Exact effects vary with its thickness and content – sometimes in industrial areas pollution gives a strong, yellow tinge – but the usual color shift is toward blue. Color slides, particularly, have a tendency to show a cold cast, and with all films it is advisable to add a pale-pink haze filter (see *Non-effects filters,* p. 201), which does not affect exposure. Provided you do not underexpose, results are often much brighter and more colorful than the subject appeared.

Lighting shortly before or after a storm is especially rewarding for landscape pictures. Often quite small patches of sky light up in colors which differ radically from the light on the land. Subtle, delicate areas of colored light pass across the scene, changing it completely in mood and character within a matter of minutes. Some subjects may be picked out in brilliant light against an almost black sky.

Snow cover on the ground also has a special effect on lighting direction. Natural scenes, which we normally see lit from above, now have almost as much illumination reflected upward from below. Indoors, ceilings look much brighter than usual, thanks to illumination bounced off white surfaces outside the windows. Interior detail is much more evenly lit. Outdoors, snow in the absence of sun has a leaden appearance, often with a blue cast. Sunlight is essential to convey the sparkle of snow and frost, but a blue sky makes any patches of shadow appear intensely blue, which may spoil the shot.

Do not dismiss poor-light weather conditions as impossible for photography. Often the most interesting lighting conditions occur in mist, frost, and rain, when familiar surroundings look different and strange. You must have the patience to wait and watch – and the technical confidence to work when other people have put their cameras away. New kinds of weather-proof equipment and cameras mean that you can take pictures in storms and many adverse weather conditions without worrying about your equipment's safety.

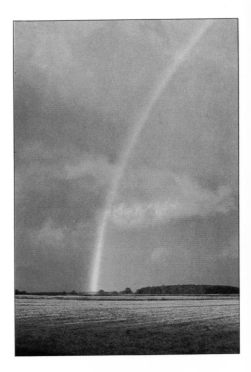

Rainbow
Andrew Watson found the evening sunlight rear-lighting a sudden summer shower. Notice how light color enriches golden stubble, but suppresses the color of green foliage.

Sun and flare

Shooting directly into a bright light source, such as the sun, is often a direct and powerful way to add luminosity and radiant light to a picture. If the sun is just outside the frame, it may be possible to "spill" flare light into the picture to suggest glare. Sometimes you can add "flare spots" – colored, shaped patches of light – to the image itself. The size and shape of the spots depends upon the lens aperture setting you use; and quite small shifts in viewpoint affect them radically, too. Make sure that you notice these aperture flare spots if they occur and either compose them carefully as a constructive ingredient of the picture, or avoid them altogether by shading the lens.

If you include the sun in the picture and you want to flare it into a star shape, make it as small and point-like as possible (partially conceal the sun behind something). If you use the smallest possible lens aperture, it will pull the sun naturally into a modest star shape. For a much more exaggerated result, use a starburst filter (see *Special effects attachments,* pp. 198-200). Looking through greased glass makes the sun's light scatter into shadow parts of the scene, helping to create a luminous, high-key image. Backlit haze or mist gives a similar, spread-light effect.

The actual character of pictures taken directly into the light depends on the amount of exposure you give. It is best to take several versions at different exposure settings (see *Correct exposure,* p. 133). Too little exposure shows the light source as a white disk in a largely black scene, like moonlight. Too much exposure gives a bleached result with detail in the shadow areas only.

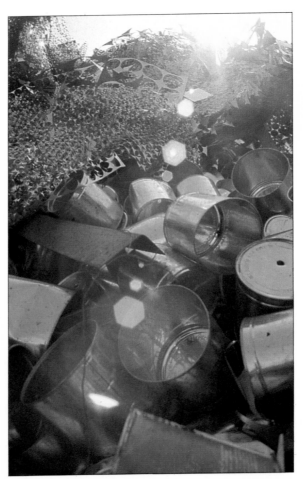

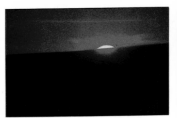

Sunset
This sunset picture (above) by Andrew de Lory was made through a deep-red filter. Intense light and slight scatter by the filter itself has spread the sun locally into the black foreground area.

Flare spots
In Robin Bath's picture (left) direct, bright sunlight has spilled into the camera lens from the top right-hand side of the frame. Each glass element of the lens forms a ghost reflection of the hexagon-shaped aperture (see *Aperture,* pp. 116-19). These patches spread across the image like a string of beads, shape-linked to the tin cans.

Reflections

The ways in which light is reflected from mirror-like surfaces are well worth exploring for the interesting effects they can give. It is important to remember that the angle of incidence always equals the angle of reflectance (see *Surfaces,* p. 21). This is like bouncing a ball – the more square-on you are to the surface, the more light is simply reversed in direction, so you see yourself reflected in the surface. Looking at the mirror from a more oblique viewpoint brings you light from objects that are more obliquely placed in relation to the mirror. This concept makes it easier to gauge where you should position yourself in order to either include or exclude reflections coming from windows, glossy paintwork, or from wet streets after rainfall.

Mirrors on walls are often a good way to present two views in one picture – the reflected scene together with the mirror's surroundings. If you choose an oblique viewpoint you can show a figure and its reflection side by side.

Often at dusk, with the setting sun directly behind you, walls and windows of painted buildings opposite will glare and glitter magically. Oblique reflections seen in a flat surface,

such as glass and still water can form repeated images, turning shapes into patterns. If the surface is transparent, like a store window, you can create superimposed images containing objects you see through the glass and reflections from other objects along the street. Eugène Atget, Ernst Haas, Robert Frank, and Lee Friedlander (see *Forming related compartments,* p. 61, and *Leading exponents of Metaphor and Symbolism,* pp. 370-3) have all produced strange, surrealistic photographs by this imaginative method of composition.

Objects reflected in irregular or curved surfaces – rippled water, bowed or crumpled foil – are distorted and abstracted. Look at the strange images of the human form created with distorting mirrors by André Kertész during the 1930s (see *Form distortion,* p. 49).

Try to show structural or actual relationships when you are exploring the possibilities of reflections. You can do this by using a small mirror, or puddles and other natural sources. If possible, look through a reflex camera, rather than using the eye alone – you will find that results vary according to whether you focus on the reflection, or the mirror itself.

Night photography

Apart from an obvious lack of light, extreme contrast is one of the main characteristics of night photography. You may be able to see the details inside a lit building, along with its dark exterior, but this is usually beyond the range of photographic film. Where possible, shoot at dusk, when some sky light is still present to illuminate shadows. Results often look more realistic than genuine night pictures. Another way of handling contrast problems at night in towns and cities is to work after rain has wet roads and sidewalks, and use the bright reflections of the surrounding lighting (from shopping centers, store windows, and cinema and theater entrances – all of which can provide a bright, even spill of light) to add extra illumination to the picture. With mobile subjects, such as a person, you have maximum flexibility, and can move him or her at will to make use of these light sources. However, avoid top-lighting from nearby streetlights. Although it may be tempting to use their available light, their direction and harshness combined may cast deep and unattractive shadows over the subject's eyes and nose.

For moonlit landscapes, it is best to shoot at late dusk with an early-risen moon in the sky, perhaps also showing some distant, half-hidden artificial light sources. When working by the light of the moon alone, you may have to exclude the moon itself because of its movement during very long exposure. In the absence of any artificial lights, landscapes under a full moon can photograph almost as if they are sunlit, provided that the exposure given is long enough.

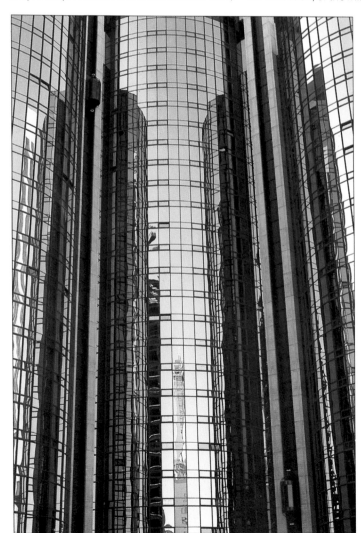

Found reflectors
Heat-reflecting glass used in many modern buildings can form spectacular mirror surfaces. For this photograph Brian Rybolt has used these twin towers to reflect each other and the sunlit block across the street. The formal pattern of windows contrasts well with the mirrored distortions. Quite small changes of viewpoint would have given these reflected structures a totally different distribution.

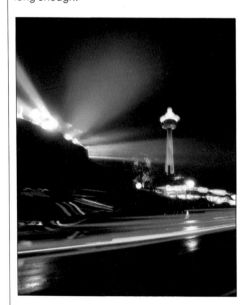

Niagara
In Robert Estall's picture of Niagara (above), he has turned his back on the falls to show the flood-lighting coming through the mist, the rotating observation tower, and the road. An exposure of several minutes has recorded the road patterned by light trails from moving cars (see *Supporting the camera,* p. 127). When you shoot pictures at night rather than at late dusk, make sure that the frame is well distributed with interesting detail.

Light as the main picture ingredient

Light as it exists around you presents unlimited opportunities for creative pictures. Watch the way that patterns formed by sunlight and cast shadow envelop ordinary, everyday objects, and transform their appearance into something new and unusual. Silhouettes formed by back-lighting give stark shapes. It is all too easy to see, even notice, the natural designs created by light but dismiss them without considering them as serious subject material for photographs. Think of the way in which harsh sunlight coming through a window can cast a hard-edged shadow which picks out every minute detail of the window frame and exterior foliage as it falls across a floor. In addition, notice how light sparkles brilliantly from a reflective glass object on a window ledge. Outside, look at the way in which the sun can form shafts of light which slice through a wooded landscape — particularly if the atmosphere is laden with mist or dust particles.

Whenever possible, use existing light for its infinite variations and subtleties. (The reason for this is that flash used on the camera, although a technical convenience, often destroys these natural lighting qualities by giving a harsh burst of frontal illumination.) Ordinary, everyday lighting can be both atmospheric and symbolic, too — often possessing nostalgic qualities. The flickering light from a camp fire, or the solitary lighted window of an isolated house at dusk becomes a symbol of invitation. The glare of a flared sun, or the softness of overcast weather form a reminder of particular seasons, or different parts of the world. Bobbing lines of flame torches at night and strings of colored lights are reminders of special processions and festivals. The soft, moody light of banks of votive candles in a dark cathedral is evocative of a hushed atmosphere of worship.

Photography can record light in ways which reach far beyond the scope of the naked eye. One of these is the recording of moving light sources — traffic, fireworks, fairground carousels — so that they trace out tracks of light over an extended period of time (see *Supporting the camera,* p. 127). You can take this simple technique a stage further and take pictures of stars at night, but using a much longer exposure. If the shutter is left open over a long period of time (several hours), the resulting photograph will show an intricate pattern of the tracks made by stars, or the moon, as the Earth turns on its axis.

For the most part, it is the simple visual incidents created by light which are the most rewarding. We often notice them, but tend to underrate them as photographic subject matter. The way morning light spills around drawn curtains, or forms a brilliant pool of light when it is refracted through a glass bottle can be just as exciting as the most elaborate floodlit building at night.

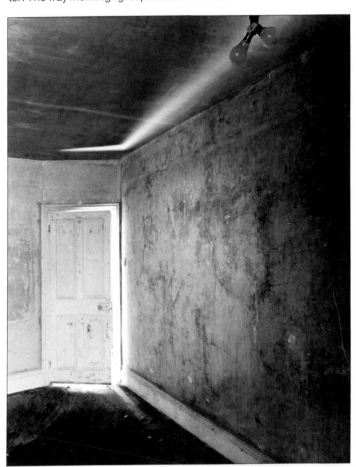

Light spill
Keith Collie's composition (left) creates an arresting subject out of something that we see all the time — light spilling into a room from a barely opened door. It shows that even the simplest light formations are worth observing carefully and using in pictures. The market scene by John Chitty (facing page) shows the same idea, but on a much larger scale. Rays of sunlight, "sliced" by a grid, and traveling through a dusty atmosphere, form a "curtain" across the bazaar. It separates the boys in the center from other figures behind. The projected pattern of bars and the spots of light on the ground add a sense of luminosity and depth.

Light abstractions
Carol Sharp's sequence of photographs (below) exploits the strong linear patterns formed by sunlight and shadow on louvered shutters. Notice the wide range of results you can obtain by working close to a very simple subject.

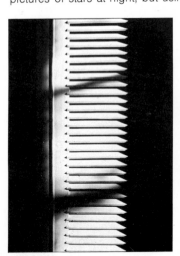 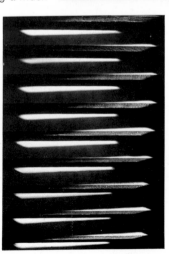 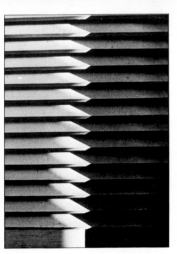 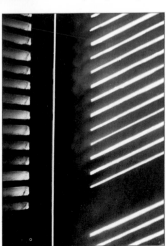

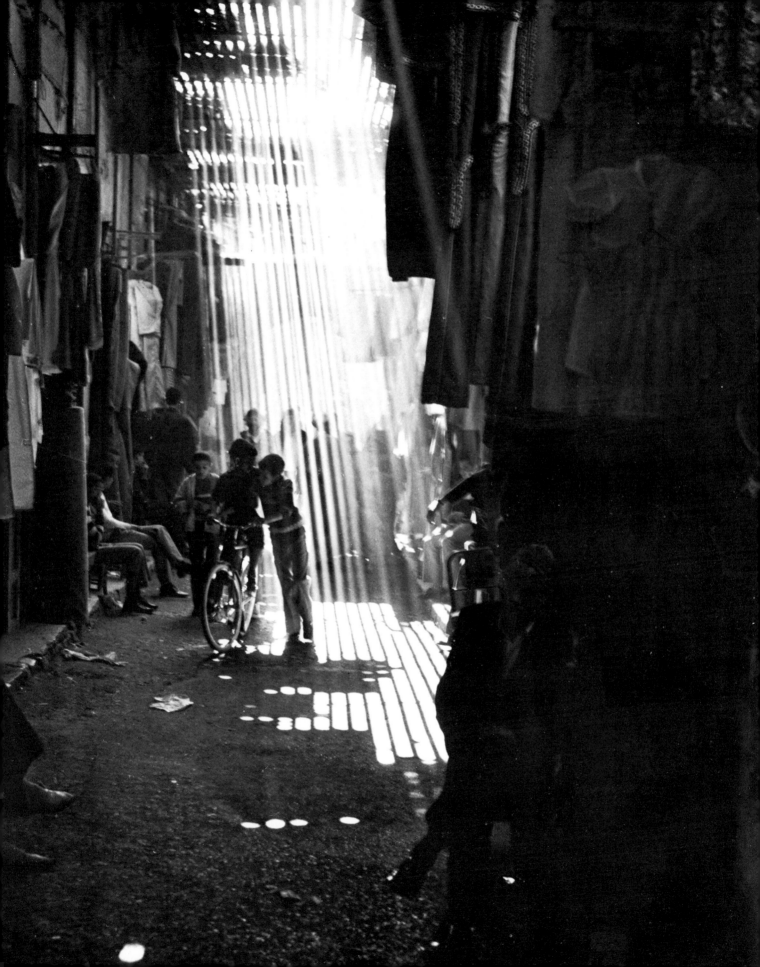

Subject elements

Unlike many forms of drawing or painting, straight photographs have to come directly "from life". A photographer has to recognize the potential of a subject within a real, often complex, situation, and then apply visual controls such as lighting, vantage point, and framing, to stress or eliminate certain features. This selective and interpretive process has to be carried through by using the strongest possible composition in the frame, and in turn, the practice of photo-technical skills.

Photography can serve simply as a visual notebook — a straightforward record of events, people, and places. It can also treat the subject itself as a means to an end — a source of colors, shapes, and forms from which an image can be created. The picture structure then becomes as important as its content, if not more so. But in either case, the ability to recognize the basic visual qualities of a subject, whatever its actual function or significance happens to be, is an essential skill for the photographer to possess.

Objects as subjects

In everyday life, objects are seen simply, categorized, and taken for granted. A length of lumber (with knot holes, grain, and texture) is merely a piece of wood, and a familiar office building (with its intricate pattern of repeated shapes) is no more than a giant block. Seeing things as they really appear at the time is often easiest in a completely unfamiliar environment. Initially, so much is fresh and strange that it arouses our attention and perception strongly. In photography, it is important to keep this visual sensitivity alive. A family group may consist of familiar people, but it is also a collection of shapes and forms, of various textures, set against a background, with its own color and pattern characteristics. A building may be important because it is someone's house, but it is also a structured form with textured surfaces and a dominant color scheme. The contents of a refrigerator, or a supermarket counter, are not merely consumable items, but show a rich variety of forms, colors, patterns, and shapes.

Stressing the elements

With practice, a photographer can develop and strengthen this awareness greatly. Try picking out each visual quality of a subject in turn, taking photographs which will enhance the chosen element and suppress the others. An exercise like this can lead on to exploring the visual potential of a much greater range of subjects, many of which are not obviously photogenic. Whether in a portrait, or a landscape, or a close-up of a natural or manufactured form, there is an extra quality to see and portray — the visual expression of a point of view. The specific features the photographer chooses to portray depend on a personal assessment of what is important to him or her, on individual taste and sense of design. The challenge is to communicate these feelings to others through the medium of photography.

Exploration of the visual qualities of ordinary objects was pioneered by European and American photographers in the late 1920s. Look at the work of Albert Renger-Patzsch, Karl Blossfeldt, and Edward Weston for examples of outstanding straight photography that reveals the inherent qualities of natural and man-made subjects. Today this kind of perception pervades all forms of photography, from the totally objective record, to the picture that is intended to be a highly expressionistic personal statement.

The classic subject elements — line, shape, pattern, form, and color — are found in moving subjects just as in static ones. Vehicles, crowds, water ripples, or blowing clouds can all produce ephemeral visual effects to be selected and isolated by the camera. The gestures, expressions, and body language characteristics of individuals also have powerful visual qualities. Selecting the right moment to show the way a person sits or walks may add perceptive information to a straight portrait. Photographers must be able to see, forecast and, if necessary, organize conditions that reveal strongly the visual elements and qualities of any particular subject.

Small scale
Alfred Lammer's photograph of a seed head shows how an extreme close-up of an ordinary, natural object can reveal unexpected subject qualities. Look at the delicate green and red color relationship, the complex texture, the bold pattern, and the strong sense of form, which are all combined in this intricate, decorative structure. One way to adopt a fresh appreciation of ordinary, everyday things is to examine them in close-up and observe qualities in them which we either fail to notice or else take for granted.

Abstract, natural pattern
This picture of sea-eroded rocks by Dennis Brokaw (facing page) illustrates color and pattern in a natural shoreline. The subject, from this viewpoint directly overhead, loses some of its context and becomes a fascinating design in its own right. Photographing subjects like this, in this way, can be useful when the aim is to make a record. But here the photographer has selected position, framing, and lighting deliberately, in order to create a strong abstract design out of a subject that we might easily discount as a subject for a photograph.

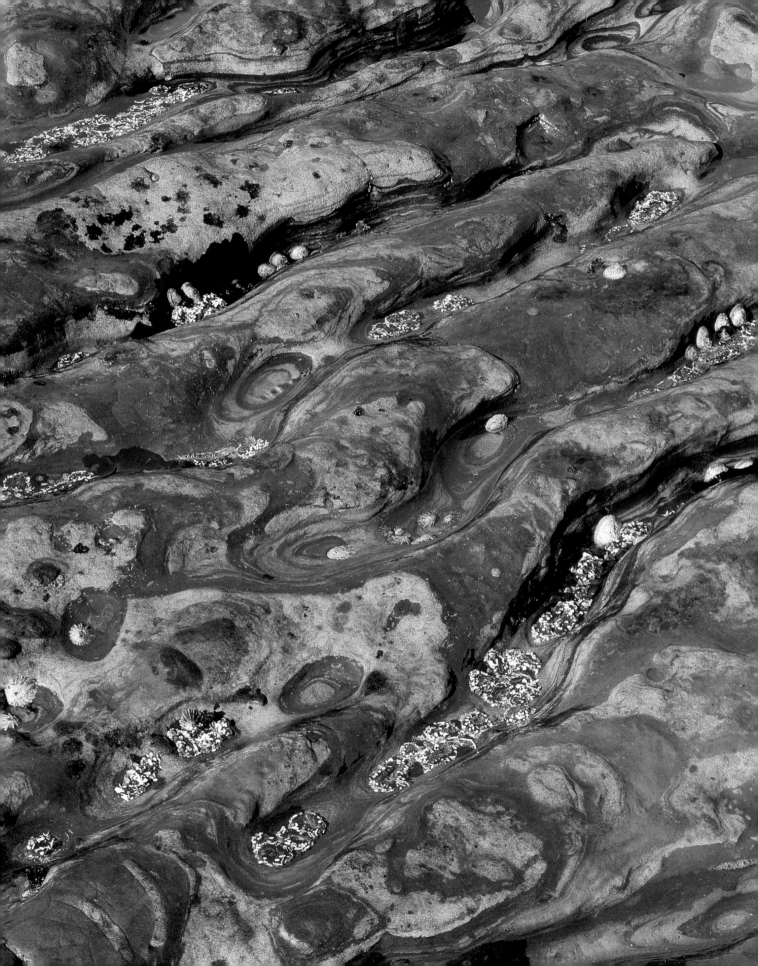

Line

Many different subjects convey a sense of line. Some, like roads or railroad tracks, consist of physical lines. Others contain lines less obviously — the continuous border between one distinct tone and another (such as the horizon), or the lines created by a cast shadow. Often, the eye reads a near-continuous line through the relationships between different elements and juxtapositions at various distances. Plant forms in the foreground, a building in the mid-distance, and hills and clouds behind may, collectively, create strong, flowing lines.

Another source of line is movement. The blur of a moving figure or streams of traffic at night, or even a shift of the camera itself, will draw out highlights into streaky lines, tracing the action.

Mood influences
Lines of different shapes and angles contribute their own influences to a scene. Predominantly horizontal and vertical lines give a more static impression than do lines running at a variety of acute angles to each other. Curved lines as directional forces have associations with encompassment, flow, and repetition. Look at the curves of a

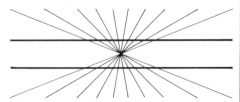

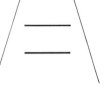

Line illusion
Line appearance is influenced by others near by. Radiating lines (above) make horizontals seem bowed, while converging ones (right) make them seem to be different lengths.

range of hills, or the naked human form. Our identification with particular linear structures is based on associations and experience. Oblique, angular lines, for example, relate to our memory of moving forward, or falling, and so give a sense of action or dynamic balance.

Subject lines not only contribute to mood but also help to give the illusion of depth and distance by means of linear perspective. Lines can also form paths which the eye can travel along, to direct attention to the main subject, or they can contribute organization to a scene by dividing it up into compartments.

See also
Divisions of the frame *Forming related compartments*, p. 61. Emphasis *Lead-in lines*, p. 72. Depth and distance *Linear perspective*, p. 81. Structure *Thematic shapes*, p. 73. Dynamism, pp. 357-61.

Straight lines

The influence straight lines have on a scene depends on the angle they make with each other, and their relationship with the sides of the frame. Like all lines, they are also affected by their degree of dominance (tone and color in relation to surroundings) and repetition. Scenes containing mostly vertical and horizontal lines suggest a formal sense of order and stability. (This particular use of line is evident in many kinds of institutional architecture.) Straight, horizontal lines, which occur particularly in landscapes, help to give an impression of calm, tranquillity, and space. A structure or a scene containing predominantly strong verticals lines tends to have a sense of height and grandeur. Tightly angled, convergent, irregular lines give a dynamic, lively, and active effect.

You will often find that you can alter the direction and effect of dominant subject lines by changing viewpoint. Coming down low and looking upward at vertical lines makes them seem to converge toward the top of the frame (see *Extreme high and low viewpoint*, p. 63). If you look at horizontal, parallel lines from an angle ("sideways-on"), they converge toward a single vanishing point on one side of the frame only (see *Viewpoint and linear perspective*, p. 82).

Where one type, or set, of lines seems to contribute greatly to your subject, try to keep them dominant, and exclude any other contradictory lines as much as possible. You can make the wanted lines look strongest by showing them against plain rather than complicated backgrounds, which contrast with them in tone or color. And sometimes you can find and use a foreground shape which echoes the lines of the main subject, accentuating them and making them a more strident element of the picture.

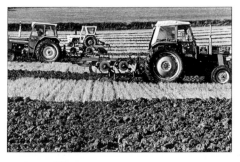

Horizontal lines
The picture (above) by Trevor Melton is dominated by horizontal lines (counterpointed by circles). In spite of the tractors' movement, the overall effect is static and ordered, with a sense of space. Viewpoint was carefully chosen so that lines run parallel to the top and bottom of the picture.

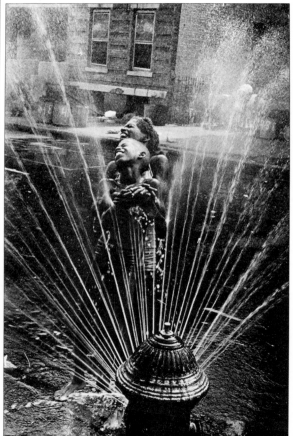

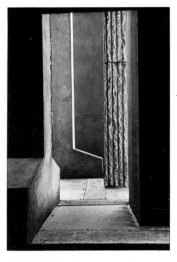

Vertical lines
The lines (above) in Trevor Melton's composition of concrete structures help to give a feeling of stability and calm. Different material surfaces provide visual variety, without destroying the quiet atmosphere.

Angled lines
The exuberant and dynamic mood of children playing in a fire hydrant (left) is enhanced by the strident use of diverging, diagonal lines. The picture is by Leonard Freed.

Curved lines

Curved lines have their own special grace and flow. The eye scans them with a natural ease and enjoyment, in the same way as we might react to the harmony of music. Curves have greater dynamic influence than the more static vertical and horizontal straight-line structures. Their sense of movement and flow seems to add a sweeping and even sensuous atmosphere to a picture.

Curved, linear structures abound in both natural and man-made objects. Rolling landscapes, windblown water, sand- or snow-scapes, or a meandering river scene all offer this type of linear structure, as do many modern buildings, curved staircases, automobiles, and boats. The human form is a particularly rich source of graceful curves. Look at the flowing lines of a bare back or shoulder, or the elegance of a wrist or hand, perhaps emphasized by subtle rim-lighting. Extreme close-ups of plant forms of all kinds can have very similar qualities to this (see *Plants and flowers,* p. 303).

It is usually the case that soft-quality directional lighting, giving gradated shadows, is most in harmony with this type of line structure. You will see that light from a low angle, side or rear, gently picks out and emphasizes raised, curved forms to produce lines that are strongly edged because of lightest areas directly contacting darkest ones.

Choice of viewpoint is important — the higher your position is in relation to the curves of a landscape, the more open the lines tend to appear. Sometimes you will be able to find a viewpoint from which one undulating curve appears to fit exactly within another, or which points directly toward another similar curve — producing a harmonious image, which is full of rhythm and unity.

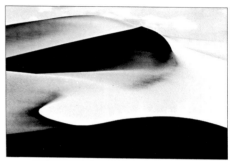

Sense of flow
Low-angled side-lighting (above) gives a mixture of strong lines, forms, and tones, but it is the curved lines which dominate the composition, sweeping the viewer through the landscape. The picture is by Andrew de Lory.

Line combinations

In practice it is rare to find different types of line present in a subject in complete isolation. Most scenes contain a mixture of wanted and unwanted lines and it is difficult to strengthen some and eliminate others. But having a variety of lines in a composition can be a positive asset, provided they work together in some way. A great deal depends upon the visual effect you want to communicate. In a picture of a natural, growing form, you might want to show lines flowing into each other in a harmonious way. There would be differences in line length and degree of curvature, but each could reinforce the other to form a complete, branching structure. In a picture which is intended to convey feelings of discord and confusion, you could make several lines which run in different directions and come into conflict with each other, add to the mood of the subject.

On occasions you will be able to subdue unhelpful subject lines by merging them into shadow areas. The time of day you choose will make a big difference to the appearance of the subject (see *Time of day,* p. 23). You may also be able to pick a viewpoint that makes unwanted lines distant and less noticeable. For example, it is possible to conceal the severe horizontal and vertical lines of the subject behind an acute-angled foreground shape if your picture is mostly concerned with liveliness and activity. You can even crop unsuitable surroundings from the picture completely by choosing a high or low viewpoint, and so feature the main subject against cloud forms or plain ground detail.

Natural line
This detailed photograph of tree roots by Ansel Adams is structured using a rich mixture of natural lines, which interlace and weave like serpents. The composition as a whole seems to symbolize the flow of life.

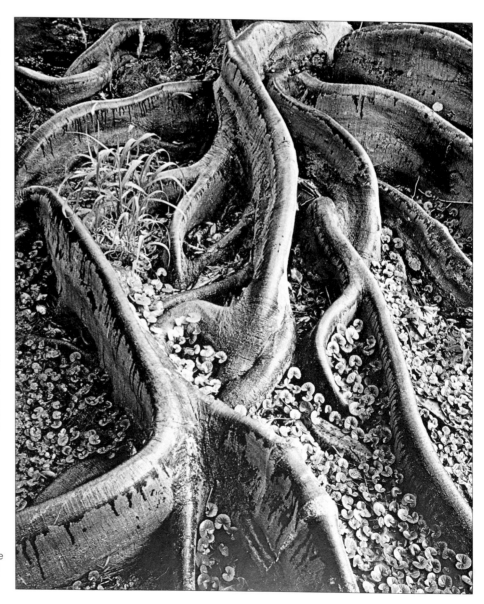

Shape

Shape is a primary means of identifying and distinguishing objects — trees from figures, or one vehicle from another. Even at the periphery of the eye's field of vision, where other detail is indistinct, we can still make out vague shapes — this is a basic necessity for our survival. Shape is the foundation to which color, texture, and other qualities are added in order to provide a total concept of form.

Sources for shapes

Shadows are a particularly rich source of strong shapes. Hard shadows, cast obliquely on flat, textured or undulating surfaces, form distorted shape mixtures. A silhouette can be formed by any lighting situation which creates a fully "contained" shadow (see *Shadows,* p. 28). Features in a landscape set against the sky at dusk, or figures in front of a bright, even-toned background, appear as stark, black shapes with dramatic outlines. Occasionally, it is the white areas on either side of the subject that seem to create the shapes instead. It is also possible

Shape illusion
Shape can either be formed by objects themselves, or by the spaces between them. This sometimes creates strange illusions. In this diagram it is possible to see either a single black vase, or two white faces looking at each other.

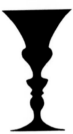

to create new, combined shapes from several overlapping objects.

Viewpoint considerations

Viewpoint is a vital consideration when finding shapes in three-dimensional subjects. A minute shift in position can make large differences to the edge outline, and to the relationship of one shape to another at different distances. For example, the dark silhouette of a head turned profile-on loses all its important features when the subject turns full face. Viewpoint selection also allows emphasis of the chosen subject's shape by setting it against the most contrasting tone or color available.

Shape associations

Some shapes immediately relate to specific objects. Others — particularly distorted shapes — become caricatures, even abstract patterns. Elongated and angled shapes can create a sense of action or instability, and form convergent lead-in lines (see *Lead-in lines,* p. 72). Formal shapes often suggest stability. And playing one shape off against another can communicate interpretive concepts such as menace, humor or love.

See also
Divisions of the frame *Frames within the frame,* p. 60.
Viewpoint, pp. 62-6. Structure *Thematic shapes,* p. 73.
Lighting in the studio *Silhouette lighting,* p. 172. Focal
length and camera size *Controlling shapes,* p. 123.

Change with viewpoint

It is vital to try out as wide a variety of viewpoints as possible when you are showing (or concealing) shape. Most objects are not completely symmetrical, and moving around them gives various shape-change options, as well as different backgrounds. Look, too, at the way selection of viewpoint height is capable of affecting shape (see *Extreme high and low viewpoint,* p. 63).

When a shape is obtrusive but inappropriate to the theme of the picture, or too assertive, you can conceal it by changing viewpoint to show it against a background of similar tone or color. Another solution is to move in close and exclude the shape edges, or move farther away, so that the shape is no longer dominant. In place of this, merge the assertive object with other lines and shapes behind or in front.

Shadows and reflections

Shadows cast from objects lit by low sunlight or a similar harsh light source create enlarged or elongated shapes. Shadow shapes change according to the angle of the surface on which they are cast. Shape is most elongated across surfaces at right-angles to the object — for example, the ground in the case of vertical structures. Across surfaces parallel to the object the shadow retains its true object shape. When your scene contains several planes like this the original shadow can be bent and broken up into interesting variations of shape. You can take this effect even further if one of the planes has a coarse texture or curves which cause additional changes to the shadow. Shadows cast by a regular structure, like a picket fence across undulating ground, often give shape variations of this kind. If choice is possible, it is preferable to use large, relatively plain surfaces to receive cast shadow shapes — otherwise the whole effect can become overcomplicated and confuse the eye. You

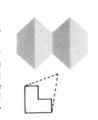 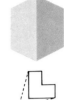

Moving around
The more irregular the subject shape, the more its outline will alter as you move around it. This L-shaped block takes on an entirely different appearance according to the position from which you view it. Cast shadows and the direction and quality of lighting may add further variations.

will often discover situations where a cast shadow attached to the subject which formed it, together form one complete shape. A backlit, triangular shape, for example, projects a triangular shadow on the ground — together, the object and cast shadow form a diamond shape. The same kind of attachment occurs with reflections. Look at the way a mountain skyline appears when you see it across the still water of a lake. The mountains and their reflections merge as a symmetrical shape, forming bands of tone or color.

Reflected shape
In this picture of a horse wading, the photographer has shot right into the sun, so that the subject is totally backlit. This has flattened color and connected the subject to its reflection, producing a strong shape. This choice of light direction has emphasized the horse's outline. The photograph is by Hans Silvester.

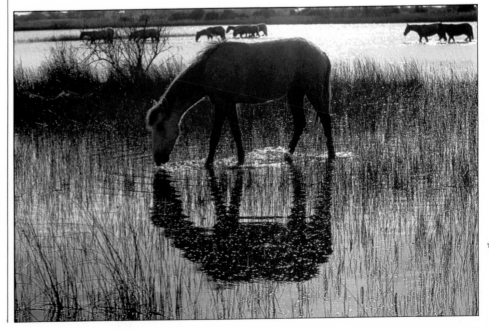

Shape counterpoint

Look out for situations in which one shape completely encloses another. A delicately shaped shadow may fall over other, more strident shapes on a wall, or on the ground. An example might be a bunch of berries enclosed in the shape of a cupped pair of hands. An open structure, such as an arch, silhouetted on a skyline might surround the figure of a person standing directly behind or in front of it. In similar situations, look for two or more different shapes which have some kind of association. You could create this effect by making one form of foliage enclose another that is totally different in scale, or make a circular, man-made shape encompass one that is rectangular or square.

You can also link counterpoint of shape to the function of the two subjects themselves. For example, a foreground full of baseball gear, such as the bold shapes of helmets, could flank the distant view of the team. Objects reflected in water, off glass or glossy-painted surfaces give plenty of opportunities to relate one object to the shape of the reflecting surface itself. Look at the way an irregular puddle of rainwater can contain the severe shapes of modern buildings reflected in it. A more straightforward use of shape counterpoint is to use archways, windows, or doorways as shapes to enclose the shape of a figure (see *Finding frames*, p. 60). This gives the composition added coherence, and helps to draw the eye in to the main subject of the picture (the figure).

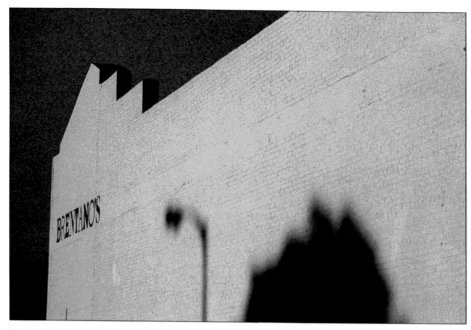

Shadow as counterpoint
Franco Fontana used the similarity in shape between two buildings to create this composition. From his chosen viewpoint, the shadow of one counterpoints the structure of the other. Yet the two predominant shapes do not correspond with each other perfectly, and the eye keeps on traveling from one to the other – comparing their similarities and differences. The additional shadow of a street light and the written sign contribute extra interest and variety to this simply structured composition.

Shape as subject

As shape is such a powerful subject quality, the boldest shape in a scene will tend to dominate the composition, even to become the subject itself. (There is a danger here that a strong but unimportant shape – perhaps the shadow of an object out of the frame – will "steal" the viewer's attention away from the main subject. If so, shift viewpoint slightly to remove it.)

The power of strong shape to dominate a scene is very apparent when an object is seen on the skyline or against an expanse of sea, snow, or some other contrasting, plain area. Shape is also dramatized by a low viewpoint – things look more "monumental" and powerful when you look up at them. Tall buildings take on almost triangular shapes (see *Extreme high and low viewpoint*, p. 63), and figures seem to loom dramatically over you. You can often use this technique to introduce an atmosphere of tension, or even menace, into your pictures.

You can also use shapes as symbols in photographs with the same directness and simplicity of communication as road signs. The shapes of two people embracing can sum up the relationship between them. The shape of a cyclist straining on the brow of a hill can express pain and tension. Look at the way Robert Doisneau uses shape humorously (see *Leading exponents of Surrealism*, pp. 379-83), and Harry Callahan uses it graphically (see *Leading exponents of Metaphor and Symbolism*, pp. 370-3).

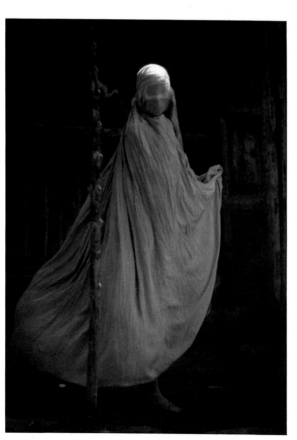

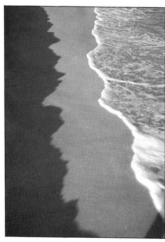

Semi-abstraction
In Neill Menneer's shot of a wave meeting sand meeting shadow, subject matter is less important than the simple, related shapes, and the harmonious color scheme it offers.

Complete shape
This picture of a veiled woman forms a bold shape, complete in itself, which is strengthened by a series of fold lines leading to the lit headdress. The picture is by Roland and Sabrina Michaud.

Pattern

Pattern is created by repetition, whether of lines, shapes, forms, or colors and tone values. The eye is naturally attracted by scenes containing pattern. A repeated visual theme can create harmony and rhythm, and give a sense of liveliness (but, if overdone, produces monotony). If a shape repeats itself many times, it can gain strength, even if the subject is just a close-up of pebbles on a beach.

Choice of pattern
There are two problems to watch for when using pattern in photography. First, single overall pattern, though it is attractive at a glance and might well make a good design for a fabric, can be too uniform to sustain interest for long as a picture. A break in the pattern, or irregularity in the design is usually necessary to give variety, and perhaps provide a center of interest. Second, an assertive pattern can create such a strong overall design that other important objects may lose their individual identity.

Using pattern
Photographers must therefore handle pattern with care, to make it a positive element in a picture. Used well, it can help structure pictures – pattern and lack of pattern forming compartments or dividing up the frame.
Pattern often suggests comparisons. (For example, we tend to study a row of people

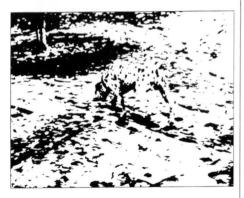

Meaningful pattern
This fragmentary series of blobs is a photograph of a dalmatian dog. Once you have identified it, it is surprising how much other subject detail you can see as well. The picture, by Ronald James, shows how pattern can be strongly destructive of subject form.

dressed in exactly the same way, for variations in expression.) It also allows one scene to form a reminder of another. A great river estuary seen from the air has a pattern resembling other natural forms on a much smaller scale, such as the veins of a leaf.

See also
Viewpoint, pp. 62-6. **Special effects lighting** *Physiograms,* p. 180; *Creating light trails,* p. 180. **Close-up equipment** *Equipment for close-ups,* p. 195. **Filters and lens attachments** *Special effects attachments,* pp. 198-200. **Scientific and technical photography** *High-speed photography,* pp. 275-7. **Straight photography** *Individuals and movements of Straight photography,* pp. 343-6.

Change with viewpoint

Pattern is rarely immediately obvious in our surroundings. It often has to be searched for, and an unusual viewpoint will often reveal it. This can mean looking directly above your head or below your feet, or climbing to a high vantage point, or crouching close to the ground. An oblique viewpoint is one of the most valuable to use when photographing pattern – you will see similar-sized objects with variations in scale and position. Rows of identical plant pots, for example, will gradate in size from the foreground to the background (a wide-angle lens will help to exaggerate the effect – see *Wide-angle lenses,* pp. 186-7). In this kind of controlled situation, where you are able to move objects around at will, you can add variety of pattern by placing more pots in the foreground, much closer to the camera. They would echo the shapes of the other, more distant pots, and perhaps add a frame, too.

An oblique viewpoint of a flat surface can turn a circular pattern or shape into an ellipse, or give a grid or square converging lines. These new shapes may fit more happily within your picture – you either relate them to other shapes, or use them to lead the eye to the main subject of the picture.

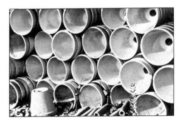
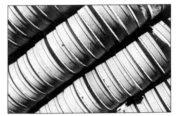

Close viewpoint
Commonplace objects, such as these stacked flower pots offer a number of different pattern variations. With subjects like this, it is important to use a close viewpoint for tight framing, to enhance abstract effect.

Choice of subject

Once you start consciously to search for pattern, you will discover it in all sorts of both natural and man-made objects. A shelf loaded with bottles, a wrinkled face, even an extreme close-up of a column of type in the telephone directory offer possibilities for patterns. Sometimes you will find similar patterns in quite different elements together in the same scene, so that with well-chosen viewpoint and lighting you can relate the two, linking them with a visual thread. At other times patterns that are entirely different in character from each other work well together in the same picture and complement each other. An example of this could be a landscape containing the severe parallel furrows in a plowed field and a sky which is dotted with small, white clouds.

Look at the way harsh light can make coarse textured, plain surfaces appear patterned. Cast shadow is another means of counterpointing one type of pattern with another. This can happen, for example, when shadows of irregular tree shapes fall on the face of a building with a formal pattern of windows. Similar examples occur in macro or even micro forms – notice how harsh, oblique sunlight shining through a comb casts a pattern of lines across your hand. Another unexpected, briefly formed set of patterns occurs in the arrangement of moving subjects, such as a group of walking figures or a flight of birds. A pattern of sailboats for one moment relates to the dark background pattern of buildings across a harbor. At night, rows of streetlights and the illuminated windows of office buildings are two examples of patterns created by light.

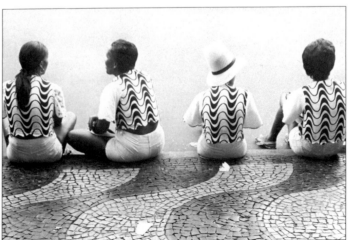

Related pattern
Look out for naturally occuring patterns which relate. Notice, in this picture by Bina Fonyat, how the two main patterns relate in their strong use of line, yet differ in distribution and detail. The plain background and differences in head shapes complement and add interest to the picture. Soft, diffused lighting was a vital ingredient, since cast shadows would have confused an already complex picture.

Pattern combinations

Patterns rarely occur in complete isolation — usually you will find that a pattern is either a part of the subject, or that it "fights" for attention with it. Alternatively, you may find that you can combine two different patterns together to create yet another.

Pattern camouflage

An object patterned in a similar way to its surroundings can be very difficult to "read" and identify — this is exactly the principle of animal and military camouflage. The original shape is there, but the object merges with the immedi-ate environment, because its pattern boundaries conflict with its actual outline. The same loss of identity occurs with "fussy" paintings hung on stridently patterned walls, or details in a scene dappled with the cast shadows of leaves. In real life you may be able to distinguish an object under these conditions by looking at it very carefully (aided by slight head movements and the eye's stereoscopic vision), but in a two-dimensional photograph, this separation often disappears, particularly if the picture is black and white so that color cannot help you identify it. Sometimes pho-tographers use destructive light patterns intentionally in order to create ambiguity, or to give a new look to over-familiar forms.

Pattern juxtaposition

A happy juxtaposition of two or more kinds of shape, which complement each other and create a design of their own, can form strong, effective pattern. An irregular pattern of rounded shapes, for example, can act as a foil to a severe grid of straight lines in another part of a scene; or a shape can enclose a totally different kind of pattern. In other cases, it is possible to interweave two or more types of shape — for example, in a park where tree shapes plus people and fences may collectively give a mixture of related shapes, which offer variety and interest without confusion.

Choosing a setting

Overcast skies or snowy landscapes make ideal backgrounds for isolating a mixture of different pattern elements as prominent black shapes, and eliminating most other details. A low viewpoint will reveal a mixture of shapes against a leaden sky; a high one will make the snow itself the backdrop. The more complex and numerous the shapes, the more necessary it is to choose soft, even lighting and to avoid shadow altogether.

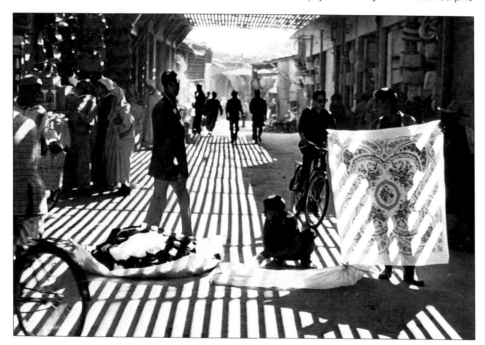

Destructive pattern
This market scene by John Chitty shows how a cast pattern of sunlight and shadow can have a destructive effect on the actual subject matter in the scene, but at the same time add a powerful ingredient to the scene's atmosphere.

The lines link up the various, diverse objects and figures and bring continuity to them. Converging lines at the top and bottom of the photograph lead the eye away into the far distance (see *Lead-in lines*, p. 72).

Interrupted pattern

Unless you break unrelieved, regular pattern, however striking it is, there is a danger of it becoming monotonous. As soon as you interrupt a formal pattern, the point where the break occurs becomes very prominent, so it is important to make sure that whatever is emphasized in this way is worthy of such attention. For example, you can use this area to locate a face or figure, to introduce an entirely different shape, or to emphasize whatever you intend to form the point of interest in the picture (see also *Positioning the subject*, p. 67). Notice how a more irregular pattern seems to allow the eye to continue scanning the scene, finding interest in each small variation of design.

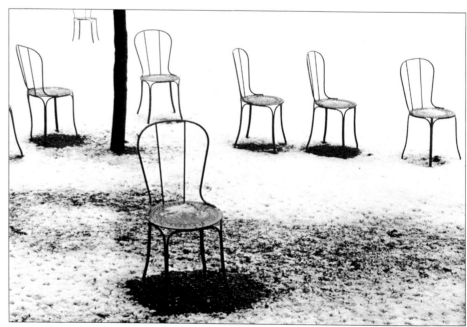

Breaking pattern
Snow-covered ground and a simple arrangement of identical metal chairs all facing in the same direction provide a compelling pattern. The tree trunk, positioned on the intersec-tion of thirds draws the eye, providing a vital pause in the pattern. The photograph is by John Chitty.

Pattern and color

Color adds an extra dimension to pattern in a scene, just as it does to decorative designs of all kinds. Shapes that are otherwise similar create a varied pattern because of their color differences. A subject that barely contains pattern at all in terms of its tones and shapes may be distributed as a very coherent pattern in color. (When shooting in black and white, you must therefore be careful to avoid patterns which rely heavily on subtle variations in color content for their effect. Green and red, for example, often reproduce as remarkably similar tones of gray.)

Even when colors are muted and subtle, they can counterpoint linear and tonal pattern in an interesting way. This is especially true when only a few hues are present, and are grouped and distributed throughout the subject so that they color just a few of its shapes and areas.

Sometimes colors confuse or destroy an otherwise effective pattern because of awkward positioning. You may be able to subdue these areas by choosing lighting conditions which either mask them with shadow or swamp them in an overall tint, such as light from the setting sun or a color filter (see *Special effects attachments,* pp. 198-200).

You can also form color patterns by using mixed lighting (see *Special effects lighting,* pp. 179-83). Artificial lighting from a room can project a pattern of warm-tinted light on the ground and other nearby surfaces outside. If the exterior is lit by dim daylight or streetlighting, color differences can be quite strong.

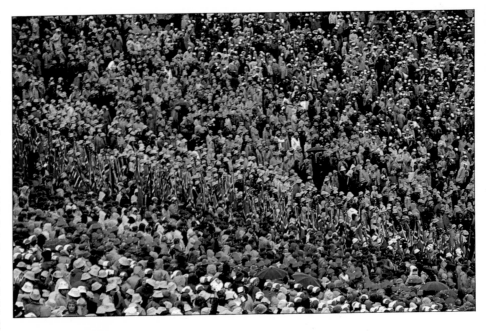

Pattern through color
This distant view of a Norwegian rally by Per Eide (above) is patterned by ribbons and patches of color, many of which would be indistinguishable in a black and white photograph. From a distance they read as if they were spots of pigment in an impressionist painting, forming curved bands of color, reminiscent of a wooded hillside in fall. The more you examine the picture, the more patterns of related shapes and colors you will discover. Each hat is almost identical, for example. This mass of repeated shapes is broken by the line of upright flags running across the center.

Pattern and scale

One of the intriguing qualities of pattern is that you can find surprisingly similar designs in objects which are very different, in both scale and function. The veins of a leaf resemble the bare branches of a tree. The curl of a spiral staircase can look like a shell or an unfolding plant. A careful choice of lighting and viewpoint will help when you are making comparisons like this either through pairs of pictures or by including both in the same frame (Jerry Uelsmann mixes images with this in mind — see *Leading exponents of Surrealism,* pp. 379-83). Or, it may be possible to find subject elements which combine together to form a pattern of their own, either confusing the subject's identity, or concealing it completely. The picture of the flock of birds shows how strong shadows and reflections can do this. It can occur on any scale, whether the main subject is a group of high-rise buildings casting hard downward shadows, and reflected in a harbor, or whether it is a cluster of tiny flowers each throwing a minute shadow.

Sometimes choosing the right viewpoint will allow you to show the structure or surface pattern of one object repeated several times at different distances from the camera, so that scale changes create variety of pattern as well as depth. A view across rooftops may include the detailed pattern of nearby tiles forming the immediate foreground, and behind this distant roofs forming the same pattern on a much smaller scale. You can also add variety to a regular pattern over a flat surface by viewing it

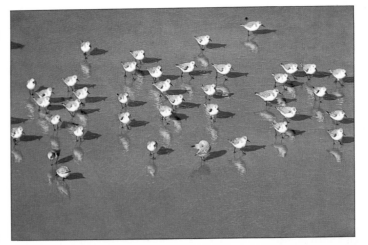

from an oblique angle to give diminishing scale. Or try looking at a reflective surface obliquely, so that both object and its reflection are visible together. This can produce a kaleidoscopic effect. There are many reflection pattern possibilities in store windows, where displays behind the glass combine with reflections of distant objects situated on the other side of the street.

Scale in nature
In this picture of a flock of sanderlings, high viewpoint, and a plain, reflective background create the intriguing treble pattern made up of the birds, their dark shadows, and the light reflections of their bodies. Small items, such as sea anemones (below), shells, or flowers, in close-up, are all excellent sources for natural pattern. The sense of design is heightened, in this picture of sea anemones, by framing tightly and looking directly down on to them. Both pictures are by Dennis Brokaw.

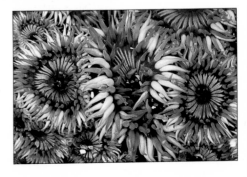

Texture

"Texture" refers to the tactile qualities of things around us, such as smoothness, roughness, and silkiness. A photograph must convey these qualities by the way they appear to the eye, rather than to the touch — and the play of light is a major influence.

Pattern is easily confused with texture. Imagine a totally flat paper surface showing strong pattern formed by color and tone differences, and then compare this with completely plain paper, which has been strongly textured by crumpling and straightening.

Texture acts as a "light modulator", and under suitable lighting conditions will create patterns out of shadow shapes. Pattern on its own, though, does not always contain texture.

Interpreting texture
In practical terms, textural differences distinguish between otherwise similar-looking surfaces — wood and metal, or hair and hide, for example. Visual memories, as well as our tactile experience, allow us to read a wide range of textures by sight alone. More subjectively, texture can also suggest the character of objects — peeling paint and ageing skin, for example, both have textures that are evocative reminders of the passage of time.

Texture uses
Texture, therefore, adds information and pattern to a scene. It contributes to realism, and is a quality to recognize and use in most areas of photography. But if a picture is mostly concerned with shape, color or tone, it is important to suppress texture. In a silhouette, for example, texture would almost certainly detract from the shape.

Many of the "straight" photographers, such as Edward Weston, Walker Evans, and Karl Blossfeldt, exploit subject texture with great skill. (Walker Evans uses hard side-lighting repeatedly, to enhance the textures and three-dimensional qualities of corrugated-iron buildings, weatherboard houses, and people's faces — see *The Farm Security Administration project*, p. 352.)

The picture surface
The surface of the final picture itself can supply texture. A painter may choose canvas, paper, or wood as a base medium, depending on the way the surface relates to the painting. Photographers can use textured printing papers or even light-sensitized fabrics (see *Liquid emulsions,* p. 259). Montages can be built up from prints on different materials, stuck on a common base. All these textural influences help to break down the illusion of truth to reality which is an inherent quality of most photographs. They emphasize instead its two-dimensional surface.

See also
Lighting *Light source quality,* p. 162. Lighting in the studio *Controlling lighting,* p. 169. Straight photography, pp. 342-6.

Detail and scale

Almost every surface has some form of texture that suitable lighting is capable of revealing. Look around at sidelit objects made from such basic materials as stone, wood, or metal. These may be either new or old, corroded or worked. Each surface has its own characteristics. Notice the differing textures of snow, sand, fabrics of all kinds, fruit, and vegetables. The skin texture of people of different ages is capable of immense variations. Notice the hand of a young child in that of an old person. Some textures are ephemeral and constantly changing in detail, such as tiny ripples spreading out on water, or a whole landscape of crops blowing in the wind. Other forms of texture exist only because of the distance from which they are seen — for example, a city from the air.

Texture close-ups impose several technical constraints. The picture must be pin-sharp, for example, and exposure considerations are important (see *Exposure and its measurement,* pp. 132-8). It is advisable to be selective about rendering texture. Detailed surface information can be confusing and distract from the main interest of the subject. Try to use texture to add information, to give emphasis, perhaps to make comparisons, and also to contribute to the design of the photograph.

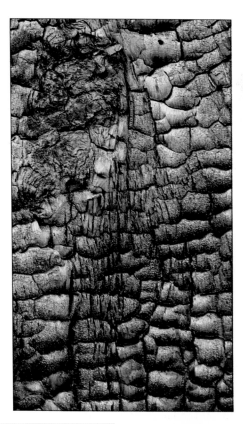

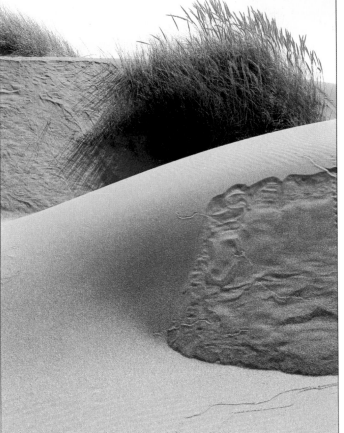

Texture and sheen
This detail of cracked, burned wood, by Dennis Brokaw, shows how close-ups can be a rich source of textures. Photographed in shadow, the soft light adds a glisten to its complex surfaces, forming an abstract pattern resembling the hide of an animal.

Broken texture
Dennis Brokaw's shot of sand dunes is harshly illuminated by direct sun. Although sand is the dominant subject, interplay between smooth and coarse surfaces, and the curving form of the dune itself, give a satisfying variety of texture and scale. The picture is reminiscent of part of a naked human form, or a cast piece of sculpture.

Texture as a design element

The visual appearance of texture depends, quite simply, on the contrast between illuminated elevations and shadow-filled depressions. When this effect shows up strongly, you can really imagine how the surface would feel if you could touch it. In a design sense, texture is a rich source of pattern, too, just as pattern can produce visual texture of a kind. Both add structure as well as information and meaning to objects. Textures which are fine or coarse, linear, or dotted all make slightly different contributions in the same way that different types of marks drawn on paper give different shading. Look at the actual texture created by brushstrokes on the surfaces of paintings. Art students make "tactile charts" from contrasting bits of textured materials as part of their learning experience in dealing with different kinds of surfaces.

Even though the camera does not have the same freedom of expression as a pen or brush, you can make all kinds of visual statements by using texture and pattern. (There are also post-camera printing techniques to give pseudo-textural effects – (see *Screens,* pp. 264-5). You can often set one type of surface detail against another to "sharpen" the appearance of each. Look at the way smooth, rounded eggs seem even smoother and more rounded when they are enclosed in a wire cage or set on rough sacking (or burlap). The complicated, criss-cross texture of a wrinkled face or a pair of hands seems to be emphasized when it is set against a completely plain, unpatterned background.

Notice how textural contrast and interchange are used by architects, industrial designers, potters, and sculptors. One piece of work may require a flawlessly smooth surface to emphasize sensuous curves and imply a sense of continuity. Another contains rough-hewn texture to break up large, plain areas, and form irregular, decorative pattern, which changes according to the direction and quality of the lighting.

Photographers, in a similar way, can be creative in their pictures by recognizing textures in things around them, and stressing whichever one helps to make the point of the picture. For example, jaggedness may be the central impression given by a landscape, and this could be picked out by using a viewpoint which includes rock in the immediate foreground, sidelit with hard illumination. In terms of contributing to the design of a picture, strong, hard-edged shadows in evening light, when the sun is low in the sky, can form definite lines which guide the eye to a more distant main element in the composition (see *Lead-in lines,* p. 72).

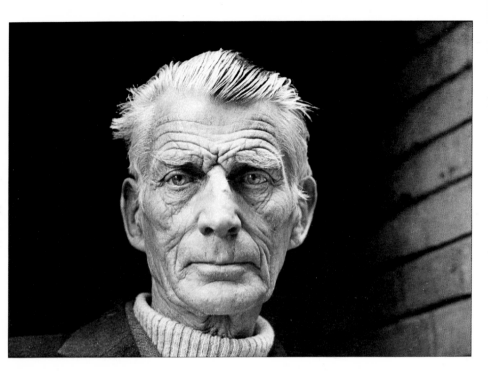

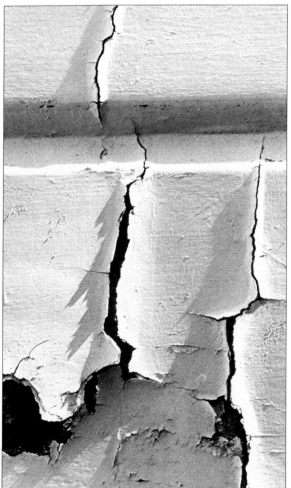

Facial texture
Jane Bown's portrait of playwright Samuel Beckett makes powerful use of the subject's skin texture. The intricate lines of face, hair, and sweater are counterpointed by the expanse of simple background.

Working close up
The texture of peeling paint recorded by Carol Sharp is picked out by hard side-lighting – the thick, curling crust is almost tangible.

Relating textures
The textural relationship between hands and dough forms the main feature of Andrew de Lory's picture. The soft, spongy qualities of the dough, and the pressure exerted by the hands are very strongly communicated.

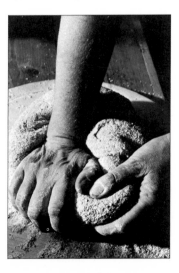

Lighting and texture

The quality and direction of lighting can transform the appearance of texture. Look at the way hard sunlight rakes the wall of a room, or the side of a house across the street, revealing its texture. The more your subject consists of surfaces just on one plane, such as a single wall, the freer your choice of lighting will be. Generally, soft, front-lighting will minimize texture and hard, oblique lighting will exaggerate it. For extreme emphasis of texture, wait until the sun's rays are almost parallel to the surface, picking out all the ridges and protrusions, and producing a strong pattern of light and shade. If overdone, this harsh, "skimming" light gives an excessively dramatic, sculptured appearance — delicate variations vanish into deep shadow or burned-out highlights. (A similar kind of exaggeration occurs when close-up pictures of textured subjects are over-enlarged.) More subtle textures, such as skin, deserve a softer but directional light, especially when the surfaces themselves are either softly rounded or abrupt and angular, as opposed to being predominantly flat.

For showing up texture across horizontal surfaces, such as waves, cobbled roads, or wooden floorboards, oblique sunlight is excellent. Try to pick a glancing light that comes mostly from behind the subject, so that the surface textures produce short, hard-edged

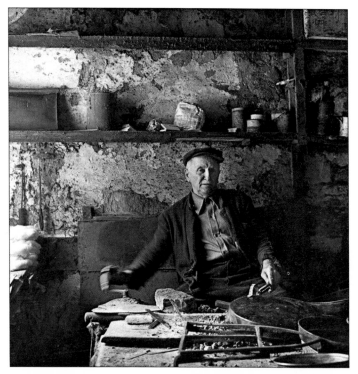

Complex, mixed surfaces
The interior scene (left) by Amanda Currey is full of different, complicated surfaces and forms. Hard lighting might have emphasized the texture of the wall and table, but would have given harsh cast shadows everywhere else to confuse and destroy detail. Soft, directional lighting from one side is the best solution for this subject.

Simple, single surfaces
In the picture (below) by Nick Walster the subject consists mostly of two planes — the roof and wall. By selecting the right time of day, the photographer has caught hard sunlight skimming both surfaces, exaggerating the texture of corrugated sheeting. The whole image has become structured with a strong linear pattern.

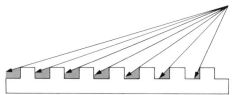

Hard light, single plane
Hard light from an acute angle (above) exaggerates the appearance of corrugations, bumps, or bends in a surface. Each tiny protrusion casts a long, black shadow. The farther away the light source is from the surface, the more equally formed the resulting shadows will be.

shadows which come forward, and each raised part of the subject is outlined by a rim of highlight.

Surfaces and planes

For a less extreme way of revealing texture, use a soft but directional light source. This means using hazy sun, or another form of diffused or reflected illumination (see *Light source quality,* p. 162) to give more gradated shadows. The choice of lighting to show off texture becomes critical when your subject consists of a whole series of different planes — vertical, horizontal, square-on, and various angles. Hard, shadow-forming lighting, which reveals excellent texture along one surface, will flatly illuminate another at right-angles to the first, and may totally shadow a third. Unless you can alter your viewpoint, it is better to pick soft, overall lighting and compromise the conflicting subject requirements. Or, you can choose lighting which best reveals texture across the most important surfaces, and then use this as a method of emphasis.

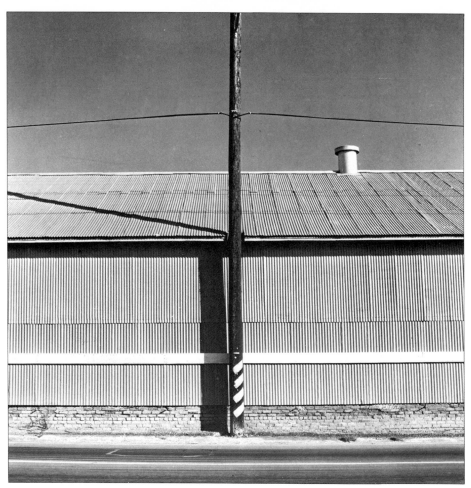

Form

What makes an object like an orange or apple look bulbous and spherical, instead of flat and circular? Viewing an object with two eyes as we move around it and look at it from different angles, can prove that it has a "body" with a three-dimensional structure. Gradations of light and the way they reveal solidity (or three-dimensional form) give equally important clues. Since photographers deal in two-dimensional, static pictures, it is the ways by which they can show form that are most important in making structures appear realistic.

Light, color, and shape
The main factors contributing to the appearance of form are shading (mostly tone values created by lighting), color, and shape. Lighting direction can transform the appearance of objects from apparently flat shapes to their true rounded or angular forms. It can also emphasize or exaggerate form in much the same way that it controls the appearance of texture (miniature form). Color is an important factor, too, because it can act as a substitute for, or strengthen, tone difference. For example, the variegated colors of a flower or fruit may show off its form, even in flat, frontal lighting.

Shape is closely related to form. We recognize many familiar objects initially by their shape, and we then take their form as understood. Once we have perceived a cup and saucer by its shape and it has become a recognized object, we tend to gloss over its other details. In the same way, the recognized object at once takes precedence over any indeterminate background details.

Control of form and shape
The main aim in photography is to make both form and shape work for the purpose of the picture. This can mean emphasizing, subduing, or distorting, to make even familiar things take on a new intensity of appearance. Still lifes, landscapes, and nudes are all subjects that are rich in form, but the photographer can choose, through viewpoint, lighting, and printing, to throw form content away and present instead only flat, two-dimensional shape. (A silhouette or totally frontal lighting on the subject will both achieve this effect.) Landscape photographs by Ansel Adams, for example, are usually full of richly varied forms. He is able to render the natural qualities of weathered wood, stone, and flesh with dramatic intensity, using highest technical standards of straight photography to express his feelings (see *Individuals and movements of Straight photography,* pp. 343-6). Compare this approach with Franco Fontana's interpretation of landscape. He consciously suppresses subject form to translate the scene into shapes of flat color or pattern (see *Leading exponents of Structuralism and Abstraction,* p. 364-8).

See also
Lighting in the studio *Controlling lighting,* p. 169 The human figure *The nude,* p. 323. Straight photography, pp. 342-6.

Choice of subject
Initially, it can be difficult to recognize a subject's form without being influenced by its content—what it actually happens to be. One of the best exercises to try, in order to gain an appreciation of form, is to collect together a number of simple objects, similar in color and generally devoid of pattern. Eggs, smooth stones, wood and paper shapes, can be grouped or viewed separately, under various kinds of lighting. Try hard, soft, and semi-diffused light, changing its direction and height. Observe how each lighting variation alters each object's appearance in terms of its volume. Looking at the subject with the eyes almost closed may help you to visualize it in terms of broad areas of tone only.

You will even find it useful to gather up a collection of household odds and ends, such as a sauce bottle, a soft-drink can, a shoe, and a tennis ball, and spray them all uniformly with matte, white paint. Immediately it is easier to see them as semi-anonymous objects, and compare them with each other as forms alone. (In classic art education students always start by drawing the "white world" of plaster casts. Only when they are able to grasp an appreciation of pure form can they graduate to natural, full-color subjects).

Try identifying form in large-scale things such as landscapes, people—anything from a crumpled paper bag to a sailboat on a lake. Even the way a loosely hanging roll of paper catches the light gives it a spiral form full of surface texture. The human body, as well as being a form with characteristic and personal qualities, is a whole series of structures as well. The graceful sweep of an arched back, the slopes and curves of the shoulder and arm are

Macro form
This fungus is a detail taken from a picture by Dennis Brokaw, showing that even small subjects can be rewarding sources of form. The delicate, symmetrical structure is emphasized by top-lighting and a viewpoint which shows it against a dark background.

Revealing human form
In this fine study of human form, Christian Vogt uses soft, directional lighting from the left to pick out undulations of muscle and flesh. At the same time, subtle use of fill-in and background lighting retains subject outline throughout. Notice how shadow detail is never completely empty and flat.

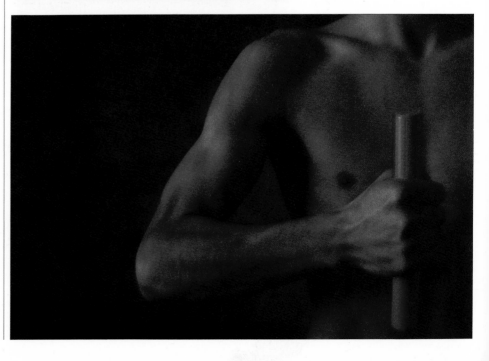

all rounded, three-dimensional forms.

By learning to recognize form in things, you can then make visual decisions. A personal appreciation and understanding of form is vital in order to decide whether a three-dimensional object is interesting enough in itself to become a photographic subject. Often form will be more a part of the attraction of the subject, to be used along with other qualities, such as color. Alternatively, you may think that a particular form is the ideal way to express a symbol or a concept. Having first decided what you want your picture to say, it is then possible to solve more practical problems. Should one form dominate another? In what lighting, and from what viewpoint, will the

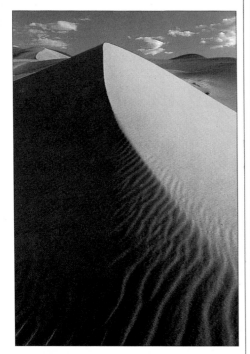

Form in landscape
Very low side-lighting on undulating landscape helps to describe its rounded forms. This photograph of a windblown sand dune by Andrew de Lory shows

how the lighting has both enhanced form and displayed texture. Lighting contrasts are dramatic.

roundness of a sphere or the squareness of a cube be most strongly communicated? Thinking about these problems and the specific skills they demand leads inevitably on to the technical aspects of photography itself (see *The techniques of photography,* pp. 96-211).

Ephemeral form

Forms need not necessarily be solid, tangible things. They can be constantly changing, either gradually or at speed. Cloud formations are probably the most common of the transient structures that we see around us. Look at the way their form alters with changes in the direction of light as they cross the sky. Some of the most dramatic three-dimensional cloud forms can be seen from an airplane, from above. Other examples of ephemeral form include fabrics, such as a flag or sail

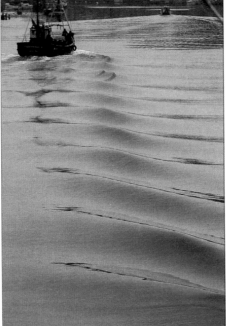

blowing in the wind, and the often complex, delicate structure of flames or moving water. A photograph is quite unlike a drawn or painted image, because it has the capacity to freeze completely these briefly created forms and capture every detail. You must, therefore, look out for them and use them in a similar way to permanent structures, but take special care over timing and reacting quickly to the changing situation. It may be necessary to take a series of photographs in order to obtain a single successful result.

By using very fast shutter speeds or flash it is also possible to record forms which last for too short a time for the eye to appreciate them. This means that even a splash of water or a bursting balloon is capable of revealing structure if it is caught on film (see *Using fast shutter speeds,* pp. 129-31). To take the opposite extreme, a slow shutter speed (see *Using slow shutter speeds,* pp. 127-8) is capable of capturing three-dimensional movements traced out in light. These can range from straightforward subject matter, such as lines of traffic headlights streaming across a busy junction at night, to the stage-lit shapes of ballet dancers in action. Subjects like these can show a gradual build-up of net-like, three-dimensional forms on film which occur too rapidly for the eye to appreciate at the time.

Water ripples
This river scene by Roger Jones shows a passing boat creating temporary three-dimensional form. Each wave crest reflects a dark, elongated shape. A similar effect occurs on a smaller scale if a pebble is thrown into a pond, for example.

Wind-blown fabrics
The clothes on this washing line take on strange, distorted forms, held for a brief moment. Each item seems to possess its own life and character. The effects are created by bleaching and toning the final print (by Giuliana Traverso).

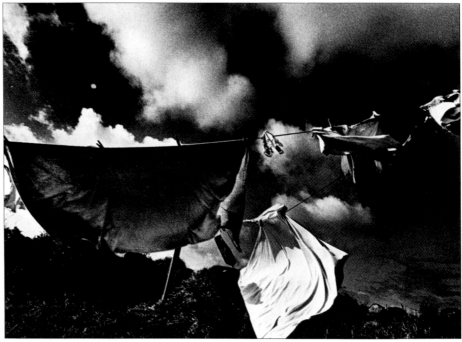

Light on form

The quality and direction of lighting is of critical importance to the appearance of form. Notice how some buildings appear to change in volume and form according to the weather and the time of day. Strongly directional sun, or light at dawn or dusk can make a building look boldly structured. Overcast front-lighting can make the building seem flattened.

Notice the gradated or abrupt tone changes which light creates on each form in your picture. These, plus shape and shadow, will help the final image stand out from the paper, whatever your subject. In general, the best lighting to use is soft, directional illumination from one side, or from above. Wholly frontal

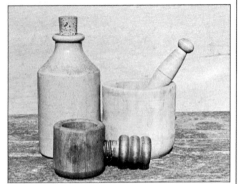

Flattened form
Front-lighting (above), with the light coming from behind the camera, has a flattening effect on the appearance of form. Shadows are hidden behind and below the objects, giving little modeling.

Enhanced form
In this version (below) the objects are lit by the same quality lighting, but it is now coming from the photographer's right. Each item has roundness and volume, suggested by the tonal gradations.

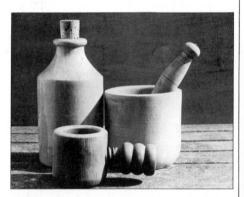

lighting flattens form, giving equal lighting values practically everywhere. Back-lighting often separates a subject well from its background and emphasizes shape, but also gives a forward-facing shadow within which form may be lost. It can be tempting to opt for harsh side-lighting. Although this will show form across a single plane (see *Lighting and texture,* p. 45), for many subjects the result is too contrasty. The parts of the subject which face away from the light become heavily shadowed and their appearance of three-dimensional form is severely flattened.

Form interpretation

Before you can start to use and interpret form, you must learn to recognize it as a quality existing in all three-dimensional objects. Understanding it is like appreciating the richness of a language. The more you expose yourself to it, the wider your vocabulary becomes. You will be able to use form both to structure your pictures' composition, and to help express their content more clearly.

Form as structure

You can savor form purely as structure — whether bulbous, jagged or hollow. You can enjoy some kinds of form, such as a streamlined aircraft, for their austerity and grace. Others, like an overgrown ruin, may possess great variety of form, as well as richness of color, which can enhance the building's evocative, even romantic, appeal.

As a photographer, you must decide what is the strongest aspect of a particular form. Initially, this may emerge from studying your re-

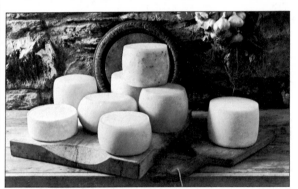

sults, but you must learn to identify salient features when you first see the subject. In turn, the expressive strength of your pictures will help other people rediscover the visual aspects of everyday things to which they had only a conventional, automatic reaction.

Form as symbol

Sometimes concern for form is strictly functional, for example to identify something. Alternatively, you can light and view a subject so that it looks dominating and monumental, or you can reveal simple objects as more interesting than the most highly acclaimed sculpture. Plant forms can become symbols of fertility and life, corroded forms of decay and death. You can even imply movement by the curved sweep of stone steps, or a swirling cloud of leaves. In human situations, forms become symbols of social significance, like the authoritarian figure of a soldier, or the broken shape of a destitute refugee.

Pure form
Form is the central theme of this picture of cheeses by Andrew de Lory. Soft lighting from one side picks out each variation of these rich, rounded forms. Darker surrounding objects add a sense of environment to this highly structured picture.

Found form
Form plays an important part in this photograph of a coat draped over the back of a chair. Its striking visual qualities show how even the most commonplace objects can reveal a dramatic sense of three-dimensional form. The picture is by Keith Collie.

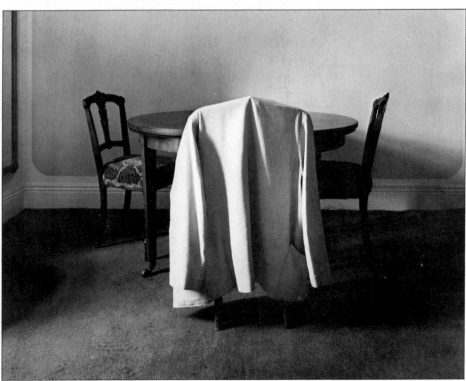

Form distortion

You can change, or distort, familiar objects into startlingly new forms by careful selection of lighting, viewpoint, and simple optical methods. The most accessible of these is reflection. Bill Brandt changes the appearance of the human form in his pictures into flat, white shapes. André Kertész recasts the body into strange structures by showing it reflected in distorting mirrors. In black and white photography, particularly, it is possible to create a distorted image by combining shapes and shadows with forms. If a strongly geometric shadow is attached to a geometric form, it seems to become part of that form. In the same way, you can group together objects so that they become a collective form — a mixture of overlapping shapes and shadows which bears little relationship to the individual elements of the picture, but which has an interesting visual structure of its own.

Changing form
André Kertész's elongated nude was photographed in a curved distorting mirror. Reflection devices and unusual optics allow objects to be interpreted as new, unfamiliar forms (see *Leading exponents of Structuralism and Abstraction*, pp. 364-8).

Form suppression

It is not always necessary or desirable to show the richness and realism of subject form. You may prefer to concentrate on another quality present, such as shape, color, or pattern — either for its own sake, or to make some point about the scene as a whole. It may be that the best way to portray the sinister, clawing look of a gnarled old tree, for example, is by showing it in silhouette, so that its roundness, color, and detail remain concealed. At other times you will want to compare two elements in a scene by suppressing most of their qualities except the ones that they have in common, and where showing form would only confuse the image. For example, in a portrait of an old man standing by a weather-beaten barn door, you may want to emphasize the similarity between skin and wood textures.

The easiest way to minimize form is to look at the subject against the light (see *Back- and rim-lighting,* p. 17). Another method is to use the totally opposite effect and flood the subject with frontal illumination. If the light source is soft and aligned closely with your lens, results can look quite shadowless — something like a pencil drawing without shading.

You can also simplify the visual form and shape of a subject by looking at it through translucent material, such as rippled window glass, to spread and diffuse detail. Other methods of abstraction include recording the scene out of focus (see *Using focus control,* p. 116), or using a slow shutter speed to allow the subject to move and record as blur (see *Using slow shutter speeds,* pp. 127-8).

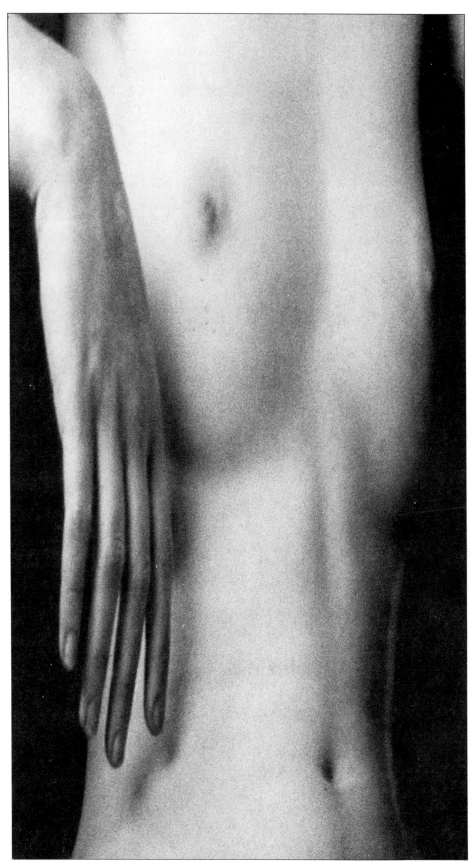

Color

The contribution color makes to a scene is immediately apparent if you adjust the controls of a television set between black and white and color. Color is loaded with extra information about the subject. It can separate out previously similar tones of gray and so pick out fresh shapes and forms. It can also "pull together" dissimilar objects, making them part of color schemes which are harmonious, or discordant, or affect mood through the dominance of one particular color over all the others.

Color choices
Color has such emotional power that it can create or destroy mood. So it is important to recognize how color is affecting a subject. Sometimes the photographer may want to "warm up" or "cool down" a scene by waiting for a change in the lighting (or using a lens filter), or even just by altering viewpoint. The color, intensity, and direction of light, the subject material and its surface qualities all alter the appearance of things from moment to moment, so that subject color is seldom a precise, constant feature.

Objective and subjective color
For objective definitions of color, when a color match is required, it is possible to use comparative color charts. These contain many hundreds of color patches, which vary according to the three indices – hue, saturation, and brightness.

Photography shares some of the jargon of these objective color-classification systems. For certain "critical" subjects, such as commercial products and food-stuffs, the photographer must control color very precisely because it is vital to the sales message. But usually it is unnecessary to aim for perfect color accuracy.

We react subjectively to color, and can use it as a manipulative influence in unexpected ways – from an intense blanketing of false color, as used by Pete Turner, to the more muted color combinations in landscapes by Ernst Haas.

None of these ways of choosing or presenting subject colors is more "correct" or better than any other. They are simply different. The main point is to decide on the purpose and mood of the picture – beware of condemning colors as being inaccurate when in fact "accuracy" would turn a personal interpretation of the subject into dull photographic record.

See also
Light and subject properties *Color and surface,* p. 22. Light and color, pp. 22-3. Emphasis *Emphasis through color,* p. 70. Structure *Related color,* p. 74; *Opposed color,* pp. 74-5; *Color themes,* p. 75; *Balance of color,* p. 78; *Weight of color,* p. 79; *Balance and tension,* p. 79. Depth and distance *Aerial perspective,* pp. 82-3. Choice of film *Color temperature,* p. 151. Light sources *Available lighting,* pp. 162-3. Controlling mixed lighting *Balanced light,* p. 175. Filters and lens attachments, pp. 198-201. Image manipulation *Posterization,* p. 266. Workroom techniques *Hand coloring,* pp. 269-70.

Association and mood

Color relates to the emotions, and it can make sizeable differences to the ways we react to objects and situations – we are far more critical of the color of some things than others (the color of food, for example).

The influence of subject color on mood works in two ways. There is the psychological effect of one particular hue, which dominates the entire scene. And there is the way in which groupings of different colors form either acceptable or discordant color schemes.

The collective use of colors creates fundamental changes of mood. Compare the usually somber color scheme of a waiting-room with the strident colors of a fashion store. For quiet effects, mix elements that have colors adjacent to each other in the spectrum and are fairly desaturated. Rich, saturated colors from well-spaced parts of the spectrum gain contrast from each other. Like the brilliant colors of a flower bed or a fairground carousel, they shout for attention.

Try to make use of color schemes to add coherence to your pictures, and help you interpret scenes expressively. Often this means taking care over viewpoint choice – to exclude unwanted hues and emphasize wanted ones. The less colorful the subject is itself, the more its appearance changes with weather conditions and the color of light. Time of year affects color and mood in pictures according to your geographical location. In temperate climates the changing seasons bring their own

color schemes – spring with its explosion of growth and blossom, high summer with its wider color range, often muted by heat haze, fall with its rich, warm hues, followed by the blue tints of winter. This annual cycle permutates with the changing light throughout each day (see *Time of day,* p. 23), so that the way our surroundings appear, in terms of color, is constantly altering.

Warm and cold hues
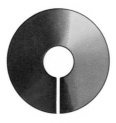
The color wheel is taken from the white light spectrum (see *Light and color,* pp. 22-3). Blue, cyan, and green are all "cold" colors, and yellow, orange, and red are "warm". If warm and cold colors appear in the same picture, the cold ones will often seem to recede, while the warm ones advance.   Cold   Warm

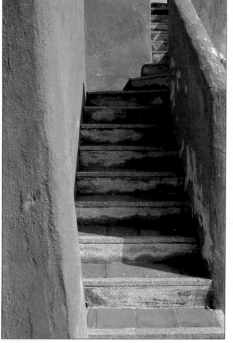

Using warm colors
In his photograph of a Sardinian stairway John Sims makes use of pink and orange hues to give a mood of enclosed sun and warmth. Light reflected from the wall helps to tint the shadowed areas of stone. The stairs lead the eye to a tiny square of blue sky, which is particularly powerful as a focal point because of the unexpected color contrast.

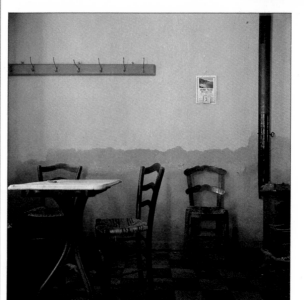

Using cool colors
The predominant blue and green coloring in this interior shot by Amanda Currey, creates an atmosphere of cool and shade. This is helped by soft, directional daylight from the single window, and reflection from the glossy paintwork, which adds an overall greenish hue to the whole scene.

Saturation, hue, and brightness

When describing or comparing colors it is helpful to use some basic technical terms. The first is "hue" – simply the name of the color, the band of wavelengths our eyes recognize as blue, or red, for example. Second, the word used to describe color purity is "saturation". You will find fully saturated colors in the visual spectrum refracted out of white light by a prism (see *Light and color*, pp. 22-3). If you add white, gray, or black the color becomes diluted, or desaturated – just as it would on an artist's palette. (Painters call mixtures of color and white "tints", and mixtures of color and gray or black "shades".) Pastel colors are desaturated, and vivid colors saturated. If a pure red is desaturated it becomes pastel pink, and if a green is at the dark end of the saturation scale it becomes olive.

In practice an object which carries a strong pigment may look pale and desaturated because of the effect of its top surface. A dull, matte surface can reflect sufficient diffuse, white light from the sky to dilute the color beneath, whereas a glossy surface gives a more saturated appearance. Color degradation happens, too, when your subject is illuminated by light reflected off a nearby surface of a different color. Misty or hazy weather conditions will often add a scattered, blue appearance to the light.

It is usually easier to use subjects containing a mixture of many hues if they are all in desaturated form. Strong, saturated colors create assertive, often garish effects. One successful and simple way of changing colors from saturated to desaturated is to alter your lighting from hard frontal to soft diffused or reflected light. Obviously, if you are working in artificial light indoors this is much easier to control.

The third term, "brightness", means the amount of colored light actually reaching the eye. Colors generally look stronger on bright days than on dull days, because the color sensitivity response of the eye improves with the brightness of the light. Films, however, do not share this same change of response – it is surprising how a photograph taken in extremely dim-light conditions can reveal a wealth of subtle colors which the eye fails to notice.

Unexpected color

You can find color in all kinds of unexpected situations. Orange evening sunlight may still color the tops of trees after the rest of the landscape is in semi-darkness. A one-colored door set in a plain wall forms an eye-catching frame for a figure. Contrasting and varied fragments of color distributed throughout the scene attract the eye at first, but by selecting a more limited color scheme, appropiate to the subject and general atmosphere, you can impose a discipline. For a fall scene this might be red or gold, or for a misty landscape, blue or gray. Take advantage of environments with minimal color – perhaps a single hue possessing a full range of gradated tones from dark to light. To add further dramatic emphasis you can juxtapose very small areas of bright, isolated color with surroundings that are mostly neutrally colored or plain (see *Isolated color*, p. 71).

Saturation
This chart shows two hues (red and blue) at different degrees of saturation. The two center squares show the colors at their purest and most saturated, equal to each other in brightness. To the right, the squares are increasingly desaturated by the addition of white. The more white that is added, the more pastel and diluted the colors appear to the eye. Squares to the left of center are also decreased in saturation, this time toward black.

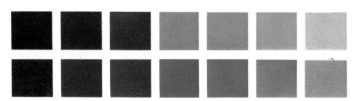

Colors look like this when the light illuminating them contains a strong proportion of a complementary color (see *Complementary color,* p. 70). It also occurs, visually, in dim lighting conditions. The two pictures of many-layered torn advertising posters (below) illustrate the different moods created by red and blue when they are fully saturated, and desaturated. The limited range of bold, saturated red and blue (below left) gives the picture a lively, festive atmosphere. Whereas desaturated, bleached pinks and pale blues (below right), illuminated by warm lighting, create a more harmonious, integrated mood. Both photographs are by Robin Bath.

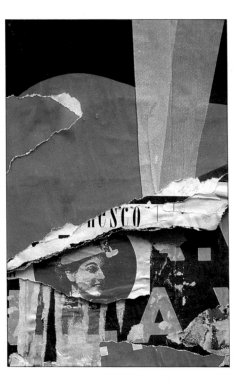

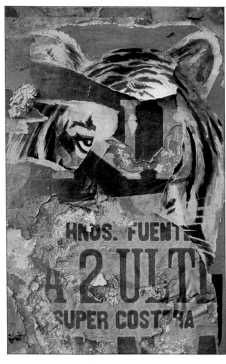

Relating by reflections
Tony Foo's picture of a scene reflected in a puddle shows how you can combine two physically remote areas of color simultaneously. The red roofs give an unexpected splash of color among several other strong hues. It dominates the composition, contrasting with the bright green of the grass, and the sky's strong blue, despite the small area it occupies.

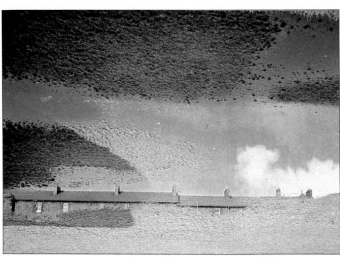

The inner elements

As well as possessing structural qualities like line, form, shape, pattern, and color, every subject presents its own particular content and meaning. At one level, a photograph is made in order to serve as a record — because it reveals important information. At quite another level, it can act as a symbol that has a more universal meaning. A close-up picture of an unknown baby's screaming face can epitomize the pent-up fury and indignation that young children express so well. Another picture — also of a crying baby — becomes a symbol of neglect and the inhumanity of mankind.

Symbols become a kind of personal vocabulary for expressing feelings and opinions. The fact that visual communication is something that has to be learned is very apparent from looking at old movies, which today seem so slow and ponderous. Audiences at the time lacked the experience of reading this kind of image in terms of following subtleties of character and plot, let alone symbol and metaphor. The use of symbols is common practice in advertising and documentary photography. At its very crudest level, the appearance of a product alongside another "desirable" status symbol implies that acquiring one will lead to the other. It is possible to symbolize the power and dominance of one person over another by the use of dynamic shape, relative size, and expression. Less obviously, an unfolding flower can become a symbol for freedom, a candy wrapper or automobile can make a statement about our modern consumer society.

By showing merely a detail, by capturing a brief gesture, or by concentrating on the play of light on a surface, a photograph can express something more than simply the subject content. A brand-new fence directly in front of an old decaying one suggests something about youth and age. Sometimes the subject itself merely provides the raw materials for semi-abstract colors and tones, which are, in turn, used to suggest concepts like calm, strength or delicacy.

Humor, including irony, is a particularly difficult concept to communicate. In photography, this can often be put over by a sense of ambiguity — perhaps an expression, or the juxtaposition of elements briefly frozen in time (see *Juxtaposition and transient relationships,* p. 92).

Another more personal and poetic approach is to produce photographs which are intended to be a metaphor. The subject and its selected qualities are recognizable, but are only the starting point in decoding the picture. Alfred Stieglitz defined such images as "equivalents" — a way of producing the intangible from the tangible. Surfaces and textures are no longer merely factual descriptions of the subject. They can become subjects themselves which possess a deeper significance of their own. For example, the qualities of clouds or sea-washed rocks become metaphors for life or eternity (see *Equivalents,* pp. 369-70).

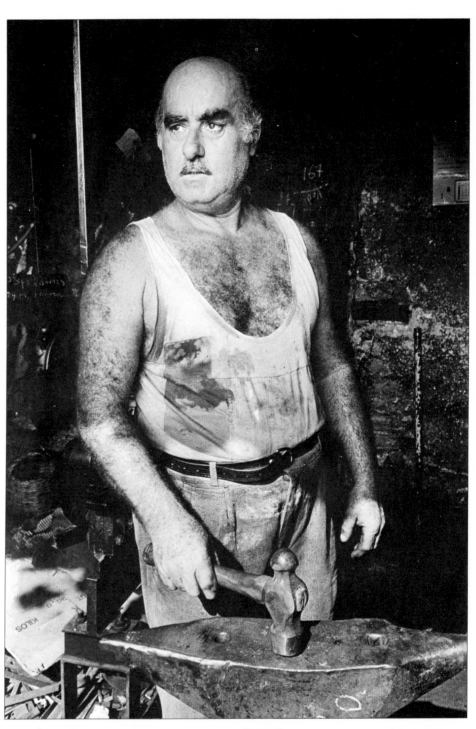

Strength
The photograph of a blacksmith by Jan Ung seems to capture the subject's inner qualities as a strong, blunt working man, as well as his obvious physical strength. The picture has all the qualities of a propaganda poster — perhaps concerning the rights of workers and equality, or some similar theme. The severe yet calm and thoughtful expression on the man's face, as he gazes at something out of frame, contributes a certain sense of tension and anticipation to the picture.

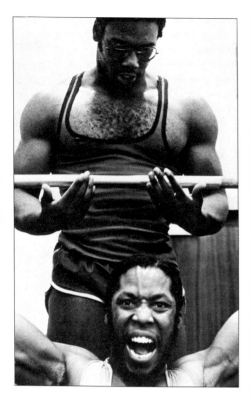

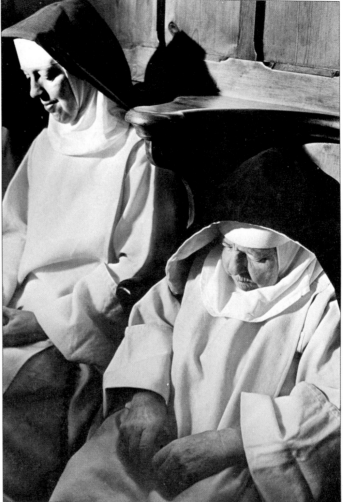

Tranquillity
A sense of peace and calm is communicated by the two nuns in the picture by Jan Ung. There is also an atmosphere of caring between the two figures — the younger woman seems to be protecting the older one. Notice the repeated use of oval shapes in this picture.

Aggression
The weight-lifter's expression (above) suggests aggression, contrasting strangely with the mild background figure. The tension of the weight-lifter's own arms and hands is only hinted at. The photograph is by Milton Colindres.

Grace
Jan Ung's portrait of a dancer at rest (below) has an informal sense of grace. The girl's casual attitude suggests repose and relaxation, but the curves of the arched leg and the precisely placed pointed toe seem to imply hidden reserves of strength.

Humor
The fixed, inflexible pose of statuary can act as a foil to briefly occurring events. In Robert Doisneau's picture the bird obviously sees the stone protrusion as a convenient perch. Yet by including the clenched hand in the picture, the photographer suggests that the stone figure does have human feelings after all.

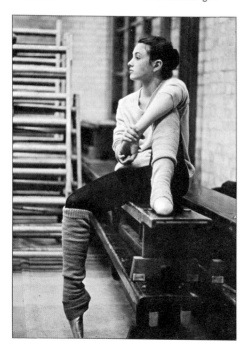

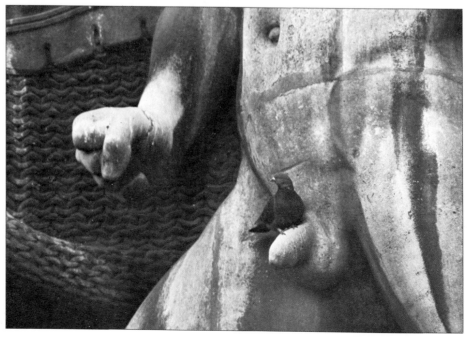

Composition

Composition is concerned with image structure — with methods of visually expressing a subject by arranging it in the strongest way in the frame. The preceding sections show how light alters the appearance of a subject and its surroundings, and how the photographer must develop a personal appreciation of the various qualities of each subject and exploit them. This section discusses the different ways in which photographers can present what they see as effectively as possible within the confined area of a picture with only four sides and two dimensions.

A photographer, like a painter or designer, has to think carefully about each image in terms of its subject content, structure, and the concepts it puts across. There are innumerable ways of presenting the most important element within a photograph or drawing. Its relationship to picture edges and corners, as well as to the other picture contents, can give it emphasis or suppress it. And by exploiting shapes and colors, it is possible to coordinate the whole picture into a powerful visual statement — whether it has passive or active qualities, is either atmospheric or explicit, or possesses a harmonious or discordant mood.

There are important differences between drawn and photographed images. The most fundamental one is the fact that the painter has to build up the image, choosing and steadily adding information, while the photographer has the opposite problem. The mass of information which faces the camera is recorded by it quite without discrimination — so it is the photographer's task to learn to decide what information to include, and what to exclude, so that the picture's meaning is unquestionably clear, and easy to "read" and understand.

Image "grammar"
Visual composition resembles literary composition in several ways. A written statement may either be full of jumbled words which only confuse ideas, or employ phrases that express the idea clearly and simply. In the same way, a photograph, a drawing or painting can either be a mass of confusing and conflicting information, or a well-coordinated visual statement.

Composition has no tightly controlled rules. But symbols and other "visual phrases" can help to communicate visual ideas. Although it can never be quite as clear-cut as a written language, photographers do need to absorb a form of recognized visual grammar. This provides a grounding of structures which they can either use or reject very quickly and almost instinctively, when composing a photograph.

Think of compositional skill as one of the most effective ways of communicating ideas to others. It can also be a main ingredient of an individual style of work. Looking at the work of Arnold Newman (see *The illustrated magazines,* pp. 350-1), Ralph Gibson and André Kertész (see *Leading exponents of Structuralism and Abstraction,* pp. 364-8) — all photographers making a very considered use of composition — reveals their own characteristic choices of picture structure. In practice, the basic elements, or grammar, of composition overlap and intermingle in every picture. Each is just as important as the other, but for the sake of clarity in this section of the book they are isolated and identified as distinct, separate topics.

Seeing and composing
How does the world actually look? When we look at a scene, our eyes give a broadly horizontal, rectangular field of view. It is only possible to see the center of this area in extreme detail at any one moment, although by scanning the scene, we can see a much larger area sharply. The edges of the scene, when observed by the static eye, appear much less distinct. In these peripheral, or outer, zones, we are still able to make out broad shapes and notice any movement immediately, but individual colors and precise details are far more difficult to assess.

What we see in a scene also depends on the amount of attention we are devoting to it — the brain directs the eye immediately to the main object of interest and centers it in the field of view, to the virtual exclusion of all else.

As soon as we try to transfer an image of a scene to a two-dimensional surface (whether a sketchbook, canvas, or a photographic film), major changes take place. Initially, the world is suddenly

bounded by the hard, distinct edges of the recording medium (in the case of photography, it is the edges of the camera viewfinder). Edges and corners cut the lines and shapes within the scene. Much of what the naked eye sees is excluded altogether. Quite small adjustments of viewpoint in relation to the subject make noticeable differences to the picture. This affects not only what is included in the frame but also the relationship between objects that are near by and those that are more distant.

Unlike television or movies, photography is a static medium. It cannot continually scan the scene, giving a general impression of it. The photograph has to be taken from a single viewpoint, and it is important to make firm decisions concerning the position of the

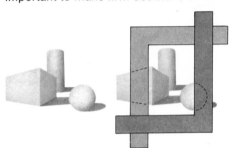

The composing frame
A slide mount, two L-shaped pieces of cardboard, or even two hands cupped into a crude rectangle, can act as a composing frame. Looking through it with one eye closed will isolate part of the scene, making it possible to see how shapes, lines, patterns and forms relate to picture edges.

horizon, the main point of interest, the distribution of colors, or the use of balance.

The photographic image has been termed "seeing for keeps", not because it exactly matches seeing, but because one view (and usually one moment) can encapsulate the scene, make the point, or express the mood. Composition is even more important to a photographer than to other visual artists. The drawn image can, by its very nature, be partly composed from several viewpoints. The artist can always move slightly so that the juxtaposition of two objects does not spoil the picture, and unwanted things can always be excluded entirely. But photographers have to commit themselves to composition much earlier on in the process. Often this means compromise. Whatever technical skills the photographer possesses, certain visual structures are permanently set down with the firing of the shutter — the best possible image must be extracted rapidly from a chaotic environment, and quick, instinctive decisions made on what format to use, the distance of the subject, and the most suitable viewpoint.

Taking photographs is, literally, committing yourself to paper — observing and reacting to surroundings, and translating them to a two-dimensional surface.

Picture structure
This portrait by Roland and Sabrina Michaud contains many compositional devices that can be used to create an effective photograph. The extreme simplicity and isolation of the subject, by excluding extraneous material and details, is due to the choice of close viewpoint. The delicate, harmonious coloring helps to attract the eye, and a strong triangular shape created by man and bird together, makes our attention travel from the man's head, to the bird, to the man's hand, and back again. The main focal point of the picture, the man's face, is classically placed in the frame, on an intersection of thirds. Background tone areas interchange with the two figures, emphasizing their shapes, as well as providing the whole picture with additional balance.

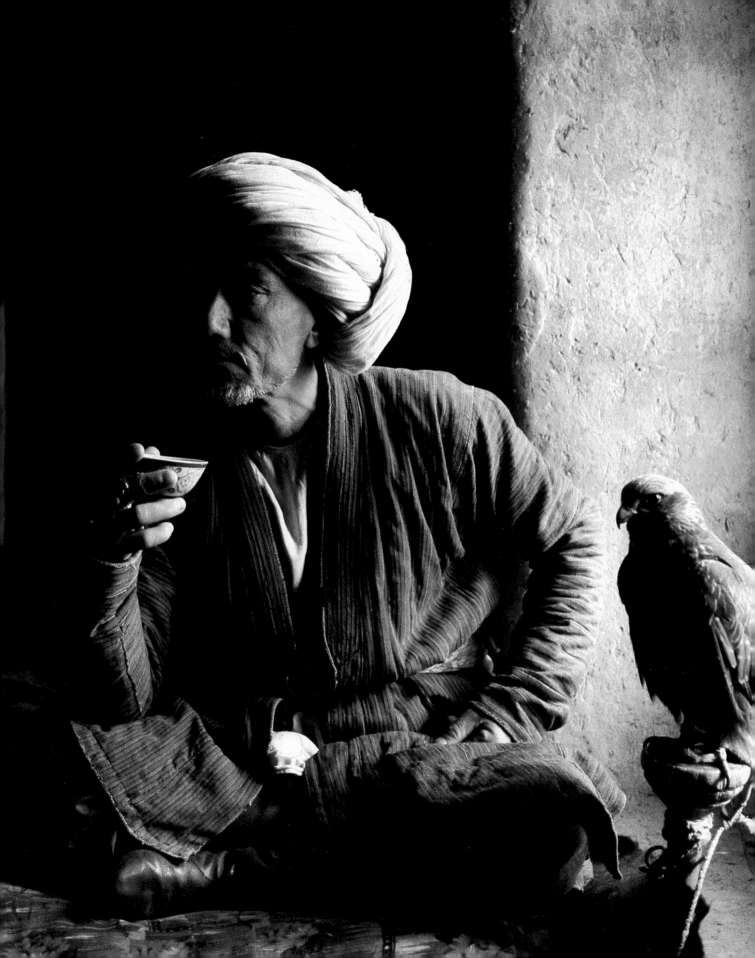

Format proportions

Picture composition begins with the proportions of the picture format itself, whether it is square or rectangular. Most cameras have a rectangular viewfinder, so the first compositional decision is whether to hold the camera horizontally or vertically. This immediately influences the relationships between most of the picture components.

Decision on format can depend on subject shape. Upright formats are called "portrait", and horizontal ones "landscape". These terms have a long history in painting, but in photography, shape and subject conventions barely exist. It is usually more relevant to consider the picture's function. Magazine covers require vertical pictures, whereas photographs for television must be horizontal. If proportions are dictated in this way, but the subject is unsuitable in shape, it is often possible to use a natural "frame within a frame" to fit one within the other (see *Frames within the frame,* p. 60).

By looking through the viewfinder we exclude parts of the scene, and this demands further compositional decisions. The viewfinder also allows us to "home in", isolating relationships between objects which might otherwise be lost.

Format shapes also have some powerful physical associations. A long, low shape seems to have greater stability than a tall, narrow one. The more extreme the proportions are, the stronger these influences and differences become.

See also
Structure *Balance,* p. 76. **Choice of film** *Sizes and packs,* pp. 149-50.

Horizontal image

Of the two options offered by a rectangular picture, horizontal proportions seem to look the most "natural". This is probably because our eyes are set horizontally and we naturally view the world approximately within this shape, rather than a vertical or square shape. We are conditioned, too, by the proportions of movie and television screens, both of which use horizontal formats. The majority of cameras are primarily designed so that they can be comfortably held this way around, and it usually seems unnatural to turn them sideways.

We usually scan pictures from the left to the right, but much depends upon the content of the picture itself, too. A strong center of interest attracts the eye first. Probably because of these eye movements and the dominance of picture base in a horizontal format, horizontal lines and space in the scene itself are emphasized and expanded. Whether the photographer is aware of it or not, the picture seems to have an inherent sense of stability, whereas a vertical picture can seem unsteady.

Horizontal format is a natural choice for portrait pairs or groups, and any subject where horizontal features and actions are to be emphasized. In landscapes it helps to increase the importance of the horizon. It is also much easier to communicate the idea of movement to the left or right in a horizontal frame – particularly if it is important to suggest that the subject is just entering or leaving the scene (see *Framing the action,* pp. 86-7).

Most of these influences are increased if you work within a format with slimmed-down proportions, which you can achieve, for example, by cropping in post-camera work. Horizontal pattern is intensified and landscapes are given a sense of panorama. With groups of objects or people the shape can help to stress separation, owing to its strong sideways pull. Very large prints, or paintings, with these extreme proportions have a "wrapped around" effect, which helps to give the viewer a greater sense of involvement with the contents of the scene.

Horizontal framing
Placing the subject (right) in a horizontal format emphasizes its horizontal lines, and minimizes verticals. The man seems to be working his way along the wall, with still some way to go.

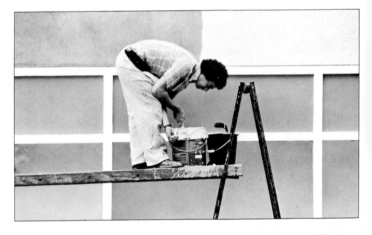

Extreme horizontal cropping
The narrowly cropped picture (below) by Andrew de Lory, exaggerates the horizontal "pull" between the man and his horse – the two main subjects.

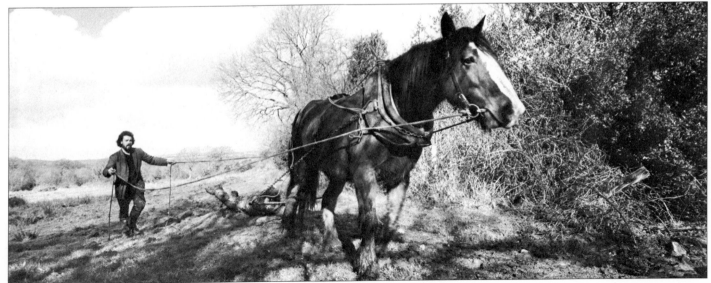

Square format

The symmetry of a square format makes it the most neutral type of picture shape to employ. Neither horizontals nor verticals dominate; each corner tends to pull away from the central area. The format has an equal and balanced feel to it, but the picture can easily become dull and less stimulating than a more "committed" shape, with its potential to intensify the composition. This is one reason why many people find it difficult to compose pictures within a square. Although cameras which take square-shaped pictures do not have to be turned on their sides for different-shaped compositions, it is quite common for results to be cropped to a rectangular format in order to strengthen them. Photographers are not alone in this preference. In any art gallery you will find that square canvases tend to be rarer than other shapes — but this is no reason for avoiding the square format altogether. It is a very suitable shape to use if you want to take photographs which are completely symmetrical (see *Symmetry*, p. 76) and which work because symmetry contributes to their qualities of stability and balance. In addition, this format is a perfect choice for making pictures which rely for their success on the way in which the

Vertical format

The composing space offered by a rectangle with vertical proportions is complementary in several ways to a horizontal rectangle. Its "pull" is mostly vertical. The eye tends to scan from top to bottom (or vice versa), comparing and relating objects it finds in these two areas, rather than in zones to the left and right. A feature of pictures with extreme vertical proportions is that separation between the two ends seems far greater than when the same shape is horizontal — you have to work your way up a tall, thin picture with a more conscious effort. In its less extreme form — the normal 35 mm camera format held vertically — this shape can be used whenever you want to give your main subject a more imposing and dominant appearance. This approach is particularly suitable if you want to position your main subject high up in the frame. It is interesting to note that the same theory applies to architectural design. A building that is structured with a predominant number of strong vertical lines has a far more powerful and monumental appearance than one which is structured with a predominant number of horizontal lines, and which appears to "hug" the ground very closely.

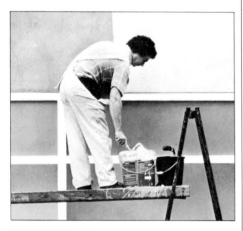

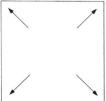

Square framing
A square format (left) influences composition least of all the formats. The shape "pulls" equally into the corners. Square pictures (above) impose symmetry, which can work well with right-angled lines.

corners and edges of the frame relate to subject elements within the picture. This means the ways in which they align with each other, intersect with other objects, and how they contribute to, and interact with, shapes.

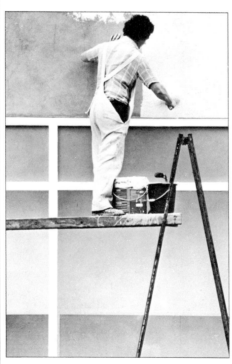

Vertical framing
This picture (above) shows how framing within a vertical format emphasizes height and vertical lines generally. There is now less stability — placing the main subject high creates tension and a sense of precarious balance.

Extreme vertical framing
Very few subjects seem to work well within extreme vertical proportions. This portrait (right) by Jacques-Henri Lartigue is an exception. Moving up or down the picture, the eye encounters one element after another, each of which contributes information about the subject.

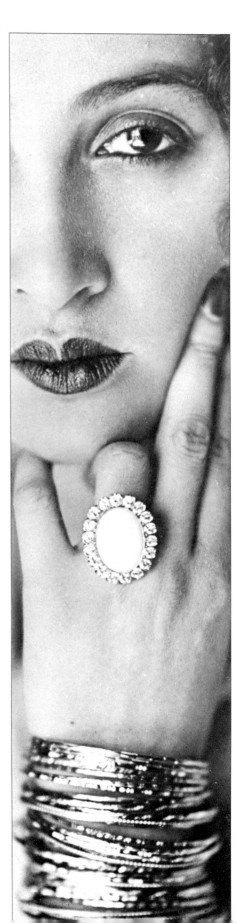

Divisions of the frame

Photographic composition is seeing, selecting, and organizing pleasing pictures. The four sides of the frame act as a cropping device. They truncate parts of figures, buildings, or landscapes, giving them an effective shape or area in the frame. The frame sets the subject position and allows the photographer to place the horizon, and other dominant lines, to form divisions and compartments. The photographer must think of the frame almost as a sheet of paper, assessing the subject not as it appears in reality, but as it looks within the format's four sides.

A few subjects, such as studio still lifes, allow the photographer complete control, but usually composition involves selecting from briefly existing, live situations. This means that different elements must be aligned in the strongest possible way.

Historical background
In the earliest days of photography, composition followed conventions established by painters. Photographers frowned upon the cropping of figures by the picture edges, and shapes created by overlapping forms. They grouped their subjects centrally and showed them complete, from "easel" height. In the late nineteenth century these conventions broke down when photographers began to use hand-held cameras to take "snapshots", often in ignorance of artistic principles. This freedom encouraged more experimental composition in photography, and in art. Degas' compositions, which sometimes showed figures halved by the frame edges, seemed shocking at the time. It is now accepted that structures or figures cropped off at the sides of the frame suggest a continuation of the scene outside the frame; that walls and posts cropped at top or bottom divide the frame into compartments, and that it is possible to alter picture proportions by running the horizon very low or very high.

Divisions and ratios
The main controls in photographic composition are choice of distance, viewpoint, and angle. Tilting the line of sight up or down, for example, alters placement of the whole scene within the picture space. Ratios of one area to another change, and any item of interest can be moved around easily. It is possible to use the frame to discover how a composition would look with more or less sky, or to decide where a natural division should run.

Placing the horizon

Often the horizon is the main division of areas in open landscape. Other strong horizontal divisions occur between sea and sky, or road and sidewalk. The flat top of a wall in the foreground or background of a picture has the same effect, and so has the junction between a floor and wall.

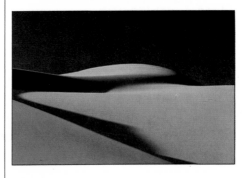

Centered
Framing the horizon halfway down the picture gives approximately equal divisions of sand and sky. Top and bottom halves seem to compete for attention. In relation to higher and lower horizon positioning, the visual effect seems to be very weak.

Centered horizon
Framing the picture so that the horizon is central divides your picture into two equal halves, which have equal "pull", and there is a danger that this will detract from any single point of emphasis. A great deal depends on the variety of tone values and shapes in each half. Sometimes central division can create complete symmetry throughout the entire picture. So unless this is a considered, essential element in your picture, you will achieve greater variety and interest by repositioning the horizon higher or lower.

Low horizon
Tilting the camera upward has the effect of shifting the horizon position down toward the bottom of the picture. Now the sky provides most of the environment, and the picture

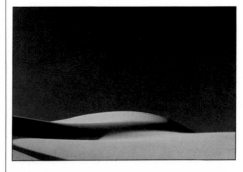

Low
Pointing the camera upward lowers the horizon. Composition is simplified, and there is a sense of endless, open sky. If you try cropping still more from the sand area, you reach a point where the heavy area of sky becomes oppressive, and the picture loses far too much of its subject content. It becomes unbalanced.

seems to have a more "open" feel. With fewer foreground objects, differences in scale within the picture are minimal, giving a more distant, detached impression. This is often a good way to simplify a picture. However, you should leave sufficient tonal weight at the bottom of the frame to give the composition stability and balance (see *Balancing tones and shapes,* p. 77). It is important to judge carefully the ratio of space required to achieve this — ground detail that is dark and shadowy has a stronger tonal "weight" than pale tones and colors, so you can afford to show far less of it.

High horizon
Simply tilting the camera downward makes the horizon move toward the top of the picture format. The uneven division this produces immediately gives variety — your eye tends to compare the contents of the narrow top strip with the larger area below. If the ground area is darkest in tone the whole scene takes on an enclosed feeling, and even becomes somber in mood. Foreground is emphasized and provides most of the environmental clues for the main subject. Since you are now including ad-

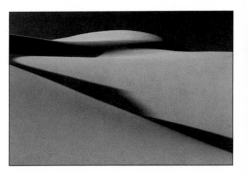

High
The high horizon allows the foreground to become an important feature in the picture. The angled shadow adds a dynamic line, helping to add a sense of movement to the scene. The relationship between lines and picture edges seems to work best with this particular choice of framing.

ditional elements that are relatively close to you, the scale difference between nearest and farthest parts of the picture is more marked, giving a greater impression of depth (see *Depth through scale change,* pp. 84-5). Cropping out the sky can also eliminate pattern which may well compete distractingly with the picture's main subject.

Using simple divisions

Using a line to break up the picture into divisions is a powerful and useful compositional device for many kinds of subject. Horizontal divisions tend to be more natural and familiar than vertical divisions, but there are many ways of creating and using vertical divisions, too. Because they are less familiar, the photographer has to use them with more deliberation and care. Objects to use for this purpose are easy to find. The tightly cropped side of a building, the vertical edge of a window or doorway, or a straight flight of steps when viewed from directly above, can all be used to create effective vertical dividing lines.

One reason for doing this may be to draw attention to the main subject, by placing it so that it breaks the line. But division also allows you to create varied pairs of shapes within the one picture format, and invite comparison between the contents of each area. In this way we can make connections and suggest relationships — particularly when the divisions are vertical rather than horizontal. For example, you can divide a picture vertically with the side of a window frame, so that one area shows the inside of a house, and the other area shows the outside. This technique has the immediate effect of drawing attention to the two separate areas, making us compare and contrast the objects or people encapsulated within them.

Another important function of divisions is to cut off parts of the subject, for example when a figure is partly concealed behind a wall. This is a way of simplifying and creating a more formal design, and also of challenging the viewer's imagination to fill in unseen features. On another level, breaks and divisions can be starting points for experimenting with abstract structure in pictures. For example, you can make a point of looking for subjects which allow you to fill one area with heavily textured wood, and another, say, with brick, to produce juxtaposed pattern designs.

Simple divisions are a useful way of controlling color relationships in a composition, especially still life subjects which allow you more time and care to be spent on selection. It is a worthwhile project to seek out areas of fairly plain color — then by distance and viewpoint vary the size of each area included, to adjust color relationships. For example, by looking up, you can relate part of the top of a white or colored building to blue sky. The blue area could occupy a rectangular quarter of the frame or a narrow strip down one side. The russet color of the building could fill up the remaining area, but be further divided by converging vertical lines into plain areas of light and dark, because of shadows.

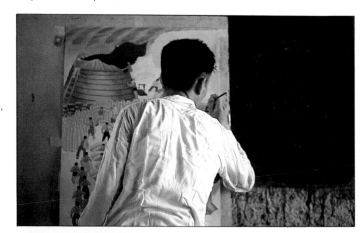

Vertical division
In this picture of a Chinese painter vertical division is made extremely strong by the contrasting tonal areas. Victoria Barclay has chosen viewpoint and framing which makes the figure break this line, so that it becomes the dominant element. Most of the rest of the picture consists of rectangles of different sizes and proportions. Each contains different pattern or color detail.

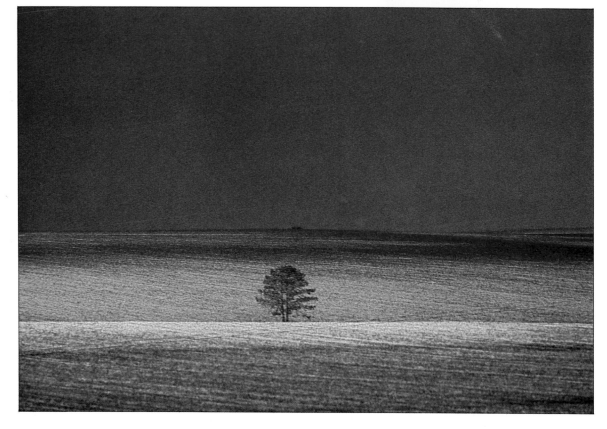

Horizontal division
In this semi-abstract landscape, parallel horizontal lines give colored divisions which enclose the single recognizable element, the tree. Viewpoint and angle are of key importance to the design — shifting the horizon position would change the proportion of blue to yellow, moving toward the subject would widen the central green and gray bands. The picture is by Franco Fontana.

Frames within the frame

The borders forming the edges of the photograph or picture are not the only means of framing a composition. It is often possible to exploit some naturally occurring "frame" within the scene itself, and use this as if it were a separate picture in its own right. Any subject in front of or within these frames draws our attention, without this emphasis seeming too contrived. Even when the main subject does not fall within the frame outline, the frame contents automatically take on an importance of their own. For this reason it is best to make sure that details within the frame are at least relevant to the theme of the picture. It is also possible to choose a frame which contributes to the picture as a whole, telling the viewer something extra about the subject within it. Another idea is to look for a frame which does the exact opposite – adding humor or incongruity.

Photojournalists covering a newsworthy event often look out for a potentially effective frame first of all, and then wait for interesting action to occur within it. Henri Cartier-Bresson and Eve Arnold both often work in this way (see *Controlling the setting,* p. 90).

Framing uses

Usually the most compelling reason for using frames within a picture is to hide otherwise distracting detail, or fill up an uninteresting foreground. The only view possible of a famous building may also show an ugly car lot. Unsightly junk might surround a sparkling new industrial plant, or an empty foreground of bleached grass might well spoil the view of a superb coastline. In any of these instances the photographer may not be able to vary distance of viewpoint, but by working close to ground level or adjusting position slightly to the left or right, may be able to use foreground vegetation to screen and frame at the same time. For fashion photography and landscape work, professional photographers often carry branches of foliage from one location to another so that they can use this device to fill spaces if necessary.

Divisions and comparisons

It is also possible to use internal frames to form divisions within the picture. These can invite comparison between the contents of two areas, and even suggest what is happening outside the confines of the photograph. Including part of a mirror, for example, can encapsulate the scene behind the photographer and add it to details of the environment in the rest of the photograph. Showing just one window of a train packed with commuters can suggest the whole congested scene inside the train. It is possible to take concepts like this even further if, for example, the window forms only one small area in a composition filled with an expanse of empty platform, or an open stretch of countryside.

Finding frames

Often the simplest and most natural framing devices are the most successful. Architectural details, such as windows, or arched doorways, form obvious frames. A silhouetted arch, for example, could form a curved, black frame for a landscape instead of the usual picture rectangle. Make sure that the shape you use adds character to the shot – a store entrance flanked by pots and pans gives a much more interesting silhouetted frame than a bare doorway. It is possible to use upright framing shapes of this kind to allow vertical subjects to work within a horizontal-format picture.

You can find frames almost everywhere, and at any distance. A gap in trees on the horizon can frame a face aligned in front of it quite close to you. A hole in a fence or a space between two people a few inches away will form a blurred but identifiable foreground shape to frame a parade of soldiers in the distance.

Sometimes it is cast shadows which provide internal frames – backlit arches or windows forming clear-cut patches of light on the ground. From a high viewpoint it may be possible to see a pattern of cast shadow shapes, each one encircling a different item.

Frames do not necessarily have to be hard-edged. You can make them diffused and gradated, with the contained picture area fading away on all sides. You can do this by choosing a viewpoint that is so close to a frame that it is rendered completely out of focus, while your main subject remains sharp. Or you can use a post-camera process called "vignetting", which gives the whole picture a soft outline (see *Local density control,* p. 249).

When working in color you can choose frames for their contrasting or harmonious hues as well as for their shape and meaning. A single patch of color in a muted background forms a particularly strong frame for a figure.

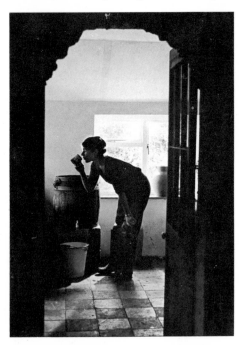

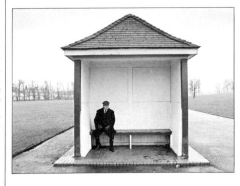

Outdoor frames
The bleak park shelter in Stephen Godfrey's composition shows how a frame's individual character can help to make the point of a picture. It becomes a symbol of loneliness. The off-center figure relieves the picture's symmetry, emphasizing the man's isolation.

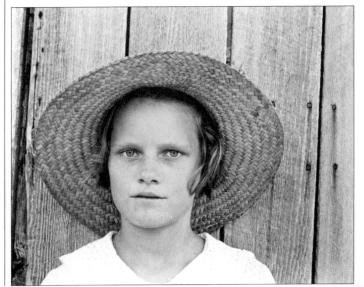

Indoor frames
Sometimes doorways and windows can be used as frames together (above). Andrew de Lory used an internal doorway as a long, silhouetted, foreground frame. The squarer sunlit window behind the figure forms a white background frame. Another window out of sight adds some extra illumination to the figure.

Local frames
This portrait of a share-cropper's daughter by Walker Evans (left) shows how well a hat can act as an eye-catching frame for a face. It also contributes a flowing elliptical line to the picture structure.

Forming related compartments

Another way of dividing up the picture frame is to exploit an actual, physical object, such as part of a wall, door frame, streetlight, or some other foreground object, to cut the frame vertically (or horizontally) in half. This kind of picture division might initially seem destructive to composition — particularly when you compare it with the more traditional methods of framing up, which help to contribute a sense of unity and completeness to the picture. But in fact, the eye is often intrigued by two centers of interest and likes to contrast and compare, making its own discoveries. You can often use this to add a sense of tension and unease to the picture, just because the eye moves restlessly from one compartment to the other.

Two clear-cut compartments in a picture, like a pair of doors or windows, can be used simply to "set apart" two subjects or areas from things going on elsewhere. The general surroundings can effectively form a third compartment. Alternatively, photographers use complex mixtures of compartments as reminders of how objects and structures are cropped by one another in real life, creating confusing clues to form, shape and scale — and producing a symbol of the complications and tensions of daily life.

Compartments can create natural divisions which may help communicate concepts such as separation or conflict. A photograph taken from a high vantage point may show a lonely figure enclosed in a backyard, relative to another isolated figure in a garden across the street. Themes such as rich and poor, young and old can also be expressed in similar ways. Try to ensure that both compartments contain sufficient interest, either in actual content, or strength of mood, to match or contrast with each other. You will often find this happening naturally, for example when you look at a row of telephone booths or windows and see a number of compartmentalized scenes taking place simultaneously. Automatically you begin to compare the social aspects of each compartment, or the expressions on people's faces, or simply their different shapes.

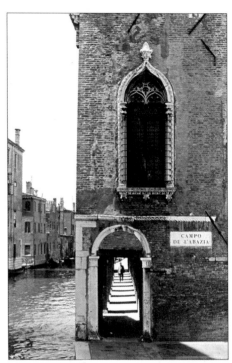

Revolving doors
Complicated vertical lines split the frame in half in Lee Friedlander's picture (below). The two anonymous figures, stepping toward each other, seem mysteriously connected.

Frames and compartments
In this Venetian scene (right) by John Chitty, horizontal and vertical lines as well as arches are used to divide up the frame. Each area holds something of interest to draw the eye.

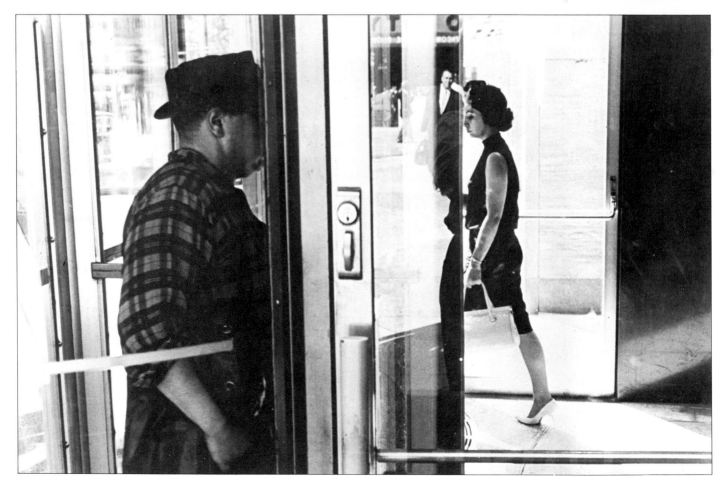

Viewpoint

Viewpoint is the single most important means of selection and control in photographic composition. The exact position the photographer chooses fixes a whole series of relationships. A shift in viewpoint to the left or right, upward or downward, immediately changes the position of near objects in relation to distant ones. Gaining height can change the predictable background of a scene, and emphasize or feature horizontal surfaces. Lowering viewpoint to ground level has the opposite effect – horizontal planes in the foreground become condensed. Moving nearer or farther away changes the apparent size of near objects much more drastically than distant ones, altering relative scale. Moving around the main subject can change the whole atmosphere of a picture. Often very minor shifts make a dramatic difference to the way subject shapes and elements "fall into place", turning an average picture into one full of structure and purpose. Where subject shape is an important element, a considered viewpoint can strengthen it by freeing it from a cluttered background. In the early days of photography, cameras were large and awkward, but today's small models allow as much freedom of viewpoint as the eye itself.

Breaking away from conventions

To explore composition fully it is vital to check all the viewpoint possibilities of each particular subject or situation. Pioneer work in this sort of freedom exists in pictures by László Moholy-Nagy, Imogen Cunningham, and Alvin Langdon Coburn. Their experiments with viewpoint included bird's eye and worm's eye views of familiar objects, as well as extreme close-ups. Viewpoint can transform the way a person relates to an environment or situation. From one angle, two people shake hands against a blank wall. From another, they shake hands in front of a cheering crowd.

Often viewpoint has to be decided primarily in relation to the existing lighting. It may be important to show a shape starkly as silhouette and suppress internal detail by shooting against the light. Front- or side-lighting is best for emphasizing texture, form, or color. When working by available light (rather than with controllable lighting), the photographer must therefore choose viewpoint in relation to lighting direction, and then decide the best possible use of camera distance and height.

See also
Shape *Change with viewpoint,* p. 38. **Depth and distance** *Viewpoint and linear perspective,* p. 82. **Sports photography** *Individual sports,* pp. 304-5; *Water sports,* pp. 306-8. **Architectural and landscape photography** *Architectural exteriors,* pp. 310-11.

Moving in close

One of the most important viewpoint changes you can make is to isolate the most significant subject in the scene by moving in closer to it. This has the effect of enlarging everything and simplifying the composition by cropping out extraneous information. Decide how much you can exclude from the scene without destroying the statement you intend to make. Concentrate on the essentials. One of Walker Evans' pictures, summing up the plight of American farmers during the Depression, shows no more than a row of hands holding tin plates. This simple image made a concise, revealing statement, saying as much about hunger and poverty as a picture taken from a more distant viewpoint, showing the whole scene. Photographer Robert Capa said, "If your pictures aren't good enough, you're not close enough". You may, for example, be able to make a far more telling statement about a sporting event by moving right in close to show upturned seats and discarded beer cans than you can by showing a remote, general view of the pitch itself.

Moving in close gives you the ability to limit the camera's mindless tendency to record too much, irrespective of its importance. By showing less you can, effectively, suggest more, and create pictures with greater impact. Ask yourself whether showing a whole or half figure is necessary when the picture is really carried by the facial expression. Sweeping landscapes are notorious in photography for reproducing in a detached, generalized way – scattered with small, ineffective pieces of information. The essence of the particular locality may be better summed up by showing a carefully selected area of rock or foliage rather than featuring the whole view. It is important to remember, too, that it is not always possible (even with a lot of thought and planning) to attempt to cover a subject in a single photograph. Moving in close to feature a detail from the scene is often an effective way of "changing key" and showing the same subject, but in a completely different light.

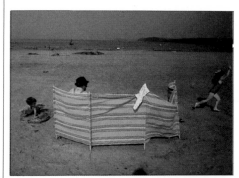

Simplifying the scene

In this beach scene (left), by Neill Menneer, there are several elements present, any of which could make a picture in its own right. But because they are distributed haphazardly across the frame, they conflict, and produce a muddled image. To simplify the material available and make a stronger image, the photographer moved in close to the windbreak (below). Here he could cut out extraneous details and restrict himself to simple shapes and colors. His picture sums up the same situation, a lively seaside, but far more graphically, and leaves it to the viewer to imagine the unseen details.

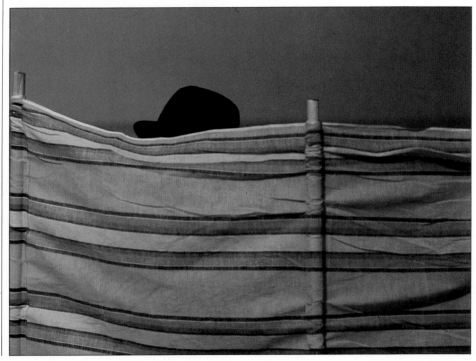

Change of background

Sometimes, when your main item of interest is against an open landscape or plain studio backdrop, the exact relationship between one and the other is not particularly critical. More often backgrounds contain detail and information which contribute a strong sense of environment. They can add rather than detract from the subject of your composition.

In candid photography, backgrounds tend to be especially difficult. Often you are visually concentrating on the main subject, coping with the techniques of photography, and at the same time trying not to overinfluence the situation you are showing. Under these conditions it is easy to spoil results with a confusing, muddled background, or one which is misleading about the true environment. One solution is to anticipate – find the right background and setting first, and then wait for the event to take place (see *Controlling the setting*, p. 90). You can show the opening ceremony of a new building from a meticulously planned viewpoint, so that the cutting of the ribbon will appear against the impressive background of the project itself. You must then wait for the key moment before shooting.

Whatever your subject, try to adopt the habit of visually checking all the other details around the main element which are included in the frame. Often it is possible to make a last-minute viewpoint shift to one side, or stand tall or crouch low, so that background either contributes more relevant information, or forms a simpler, less cluttered setting.

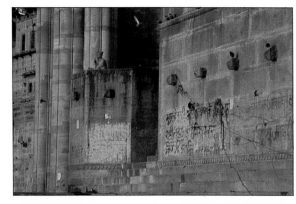

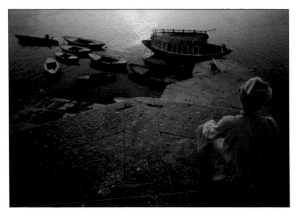

Man at prayer
Both these pictures show the same subject, a man praying, but a change of background affects the overall atmosphere and the color scheme of the pictures radically. In the top version, a low, distant viewpoint shows the bright figure perched high up in the walls of the temple. The background locates the subject in a recognizable and dramatic setting. Warm, frontal lighting pervades the entire scene. For the bottom version, the photographer altered the subject's apparent setting by climbing up behind him and looking down over his shoulder. From this viewpoint the background is now the river below, giving the subject quite a different setting. Shooting toward the sun now mutes most of the color, except for the man's brilliant red robes and headdress. These two very different compositions demonstrate how, for most subjects, there is a wide variety of viewpoints to choose from. A location may offer several quite different viewpoints – any of which can produce good, individual images. The photographs are from a sequence by Henry Wilson.

Extreme high and low viewpoint

A picture drawn or photographed from an unusually high or low viewpoint (well above or below normal eye level) seems to have its own special atmosphere, which is quite different from the effects of changing viewpoint horizontally. This is probably because our movements in everyday life involve mostly a horizontal shift of viewpoint. Horizontal scanning also comes more naturally than vertical scanning. The result is that horizontal variations of viewpoint are all more familiar to us and seem less dramatically different than do vertical changes. For example, if you look at a vertical structure from a very low, worm's eye viewpoint, it seems to taper toward the top. This is because the top is much farther away and therefore smaller in scale than the bottom. The overall effect is very noticeably distorted.

Exactly the same thing happens when you look at a long, low object from the side and it tapers toward a vanishing point in the distance (see, for example, the picture of crushed cars, p. 82). But the distortion is far less apparent than with vertical tapering, because we are more accustomed to observing situations in this way.

Raised or lowered viewpoints not only give strong, unfamiliar shapes but can make vertical objects look more diminished or dominant. Just as a statue of a hero or heroine is mounted on a high plinth to give it a more monumental

appearance, a person photographed from below seems to possess added strength. While looking down on a person tends to produce the opposite effect. It is useful to experiment with high and low viewpoints to help break away from the habit of taking eye-level pictures. Start by taking a set of pictures all from below knee level, or above head height.

Low down, looking up
A low viewpoint of this old man (corresponding with the diagram, far left), gives him a dominant and imposing air. The photograph is by Henry Wilson.

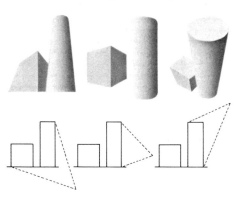

Viewpoint effects
A low viewpoint (far left) makes vertical structures appear to taper toward the top. A high viewpoint (near left) has the opposite effect. A square-on view (center left) preserves the subject's true lines.

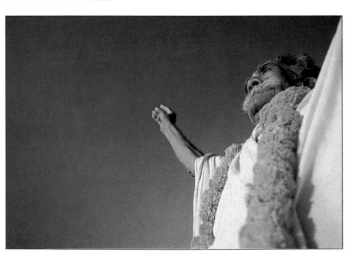

Vertical change

Shifting your position vertically gives not only a higher or lower view of a scene but also the ability to change picture content radically without altering your ground distance. As you raise viewpoint and tilt downward, any objects in the foreground become less different in scale from those in the background, and so less dominant. Horizontal subject surfaces become increasingly square-on and fill more of the frame − vertical surfaces become more oblique and therefore smaller. The ground, or

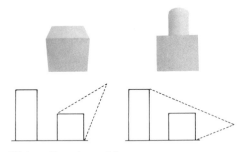

High and low viewpoint
A high viewpoint (above left) makes vertical lines converge downward. Distant subjects can be excluded from the frame, as ground area behind the subject now becomes the background. A low viewpoint (above right) makes foreground vertical surfaces more dominant, background areas become part of the picture.

floor, begins to fill the frame completely, excluding any horizon or sky. A high viewpoint is therefore a good way of excluding these natural divisions and concentrating on shapes and lines within the horizontal plane. This technique works well with small, close-up subjects, but it also applies to distant views. If you take a picture looking down at the ground from a tall building, it will show an almost map-like terrain. Shadows cast across the ground take on a special prominence, although you can hardly see the vertical structures that form them. Marks on the ground, roofs, and open spaces will create divisions and compartments in the frame.

By complete contrast, shifting to a lower viewpoint and tilting your camera upward, gives prominence to all the vertical surfaces in the scene, plus the sky and other background areas. Ground details may now form merely a simple line or contour. Anything in the foreground of the scene is enlarged or exaggerated. It is quite possible to fill most of the frame with a few blades of grass, very close at hand, with the top of the picture showing a distant building. A very low viewpoint also allows you to include parts of the subject that you would not normally notice at all, such as extremely low-level details on buildings, and low forms of vegetation, which are usually on the extreme edges of our field of view at normal eye level.

Influence of distance

The nearer you approach an object, the larger it looks. As viewpoint distance increases, so things look smaller. Such facts may seem all too obvious, but it is harder to accept that, as you move back, the objects that were closest to you diminish at a much faster rate than objects farther away. In a garden containing two identical trees, one some distance in front of the other, relative size differences will seem greater from a close vantage point than at a distance. This means that you can help to make one object dominate another by moving as close to it as possible. This scale change through viewpoint distance allows you to make, for example, the face of a child at a schoolhouse gate as large and important as the school behind or, by moving back, have the building dwarf the child. It depends what you intend the mood of the picture to be, and what you consider to be the relative importance of these elements.

You can experiment with size relationships by holding a pen up and seeing how its height compares with the far side of the room. Moving

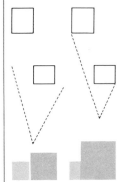

Increasing distance
When a scene contains objects at different distances, the nearest objects look larger (far left). If you move closer (near left), this reduces the distance to the near object proportionally more than to the far one (here it is almost halved). The near object grows larger at a faster rate than the object behind, and dominates it.

your head forward a fraction can make the pen double in size in relation to the wall. Notice that it is impossible to keep your eye focused on the close pen and the far wall simultaneously. This same physical problem is a feature of camera lenses, too, when you are using them for close-up work (see *Depth of field*, pp. 118-19). Another factor that you will have to deal with is that moving back, to reduce size differences, can make the entire scene far too small in the frame, while moving right in close may not necessarily include all the information you wish to show. Artists are able to overcome this problem by choosing their viewpoint to give correct size relationships, but then drawing what they see from a narrow or broad "cone of vision". Photographers are able to achieve this same effect by changing lenses − the steep perspective associated with wide-angle lenses, for example (see *Wide-angle lenses*, pp. 186-7), allows you to move in close to a nearby subject (to make it large in the frame, without obscuring the more distant elements of the scene).

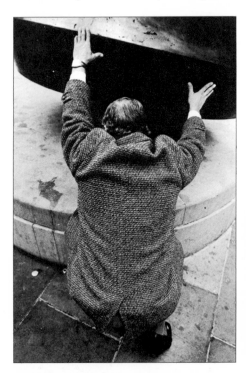

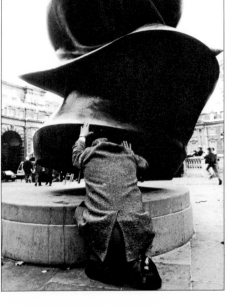

Viewpoint height adjustments
These two pictures show how slight viewpoint height alteration can dramatically affect both the appearance and meaning of a picture. The version above left, using a high viewpoint, shows a man peering under a mysterious structure. The picture is strongly composed, but it is frustratingly lacking in information. The version above right uses a
higher viewpoint, which includes distant information and remainder of the main subject. Meaning is now clear, but the picture is considerably weaker as a composition. (The pictures echo the principles shown in the diagrams above).

Horizontal change

Most scenes and situations consist of a number of objects at different distances from the camera — forming overlapping foreground, mid-distance, and background areas in the picture. Moving your viewpoint more to the right, therefore, makes foreground objects shift to the left in relation to the background, and vice versa. The deeper the scene, the more a limited shift in viewpoint will make dramatic changes to the structure of your picture. Hard lighting contributes, too, by creating

Sideways shift

These pictures (below) show how an area which is enclosed on three sides changes appearance when viewpoint shifts sideways (see diagram, right). From the extreme right-hand position (below left)

all buildings are in shadow. From the central viewpoint (below center) the foreground has moved to the right and the background to the left. The third viewpoint (below right) continues this movement.

greatest possible differences between lit and shadowed areas. Shifting your viewpoint can therefore place objects against dark rather than light backgrounds, and even change the mood of your picture from high to low key (see *High key* and *Low key,* p. 27). For these reasons you should always spend time — if the nature of the subject allows — making small position adjustments to explore the various arrangements of shapes and lines available.

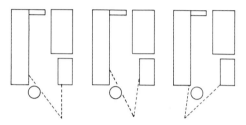

It is much easier to follow these compositional changes if you check through the viewfinder, or a card frame (see *The composing frame,* p. 54), so that you will be able to see how the image will change within the confines of the format you are using. It is important to be aware of the differences between the camera's and the eye's view of a scene.

One problem is that as you shift viewpoint, all objects at the same distance move by equal amounts — the unwanted along with the wanted. Generally, it is best to pick a viewpoint that gives the best alignment of the most important elements, setting them within a design which adds prominence and strength. You may find that, although your chosen viewpoint works for the main subject, the position of the other, secondary, items must be remedied either by moving in closer to the main subject, or, if this is not possible, by cropping the picture during printing.

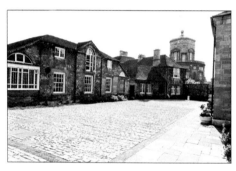
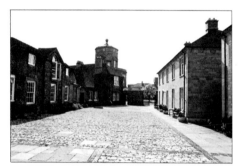
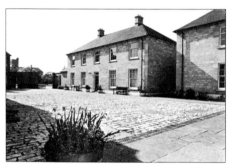

Moving around the subject

Moving in an arc around a free-standing subject makes significant changes to those parts that are visible. It can also transform the background and alter the direction of light within the picture. Greatest compositional change occurs when your subject is surrounded by background or foreground details which differ on all sides. In practice, selection is usually restricted by factors such as other objects blocking the view, or conflicting with assertive background or foreground detail, and the fact that a certain view of a fixed subject is not acceptable. If your subject is movable — a figure, for example, which you can turn as you move position — changes can effectively alter the direction of light on form — in the same way that you would move a spotlight around in the studio (see *Lighting in the studio,* pp. 167-74). Unlike the studio, however, these changes also give different background shapes, tones, and colors. In content, too, both background and foreground can contribute considerable variations to the apparent environment of your subject — changing its appearance radically.

Moving around your subject may also provide a good way of revealing unknown or unexpected aspects. You will find more unusual views by working in this way, and you may even find different subjects to include as you move around. Photographing a complete sequence of pictures in this way is also a thorough method of making an all-round record of a subject from all possible angles.

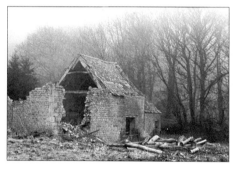

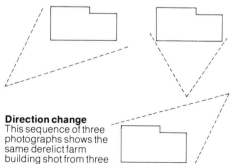

Direction change

This sequence of three photographs shows the same derelict farm building shot from three different viewpoints. The diagrams show where the photographer was standing in each case. The first version (top left) shows the building backed

by trees, while the second (top right) makes it look long and low in an open environment. In the third version (above right), it is sur-

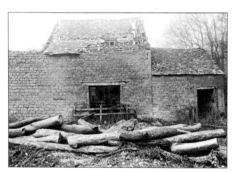

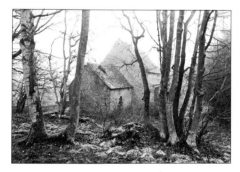

rounded by trees, which dominate the foreground. Soft, overcast lighting conditions give the greatest amount of freedom when you are

selecting viewpoint for a fixed subject.

Viewpoint and subject meaning

Viewpoint is a great aid to intensifying the significance of a picture. A child playing in the street might be shown alone or be framed within the foreground shape of a barbed-wire barrier and armed soldiers. A view looking down a long pedestrian subway makes the lines of walls, floor, and ceiling appear to converge to one point, like the radiating strands of a spider's web. Some distance down the corridor a sinister figure waits, like a spider.

Photographers sometimes choose viewpoints intentionally to make pictures which pose questions. One way is to leave a piece of information out of the picture that is vital to our understanding of it, as in Tony Ray-Jones' photograph (right). Pictures of this kind are planned to be ambiguous, and often have a surreal quality. They allow us to imagine what is happening, and think of all the possible reasons, but never be absolutely certain of what is happening.

By thinking carefully about viewpoint, you can avoid showing the expected and the obvious in your pictures. Henri Cartier-Bresson, for example, has often photographed processions and other public events — but by turning the camera away from the main event to show bystanders' reactions, he has demonstrated how it is possible to reflect one scene in another, in a highly original way. This technique also has the effect of adding a strong human element to the scene, too.

Another idea is to show a child's eye view of the world by the simple method of using a child-height viewpoint. Other children look "normal" height, while adults tower over the scene like giants. Furniture, animals, and automobiles take on a different perspective. Viewpoint can also turn the specific detail into a general statement. Photojournalist Robert Frank, in his photo-essay *The Americans*, often hides the faces of individuals behind juke boxes, flags, signs, and other symbols of American contemporary life, in order to make the mixture of people and objects represent the society as a whole (see *The individualists*, pp 355-7).

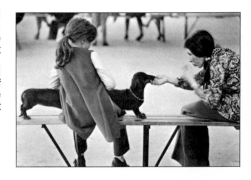

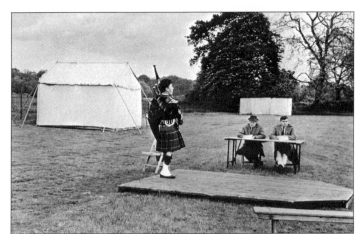

Creating ambiguity
Both these pictures pose questions because of the viewpoint chosen by the photographer. Robin Laurance's (above) exploits shape with a subtle, gentle humor. Tony Ray-Jones' (left) is far more puzzling because of unexplained activity in a field. He has chosen a viewpoint which turns the scene into a complete mystery. The two judges and the piper are separated from the scene's "missing link" — the piper's unseen audience.

Critical viewpoint

With most subjects there is some latitude in viewpoint choice to achieve a particular type of image. Variations of a few feet in any direction will have little effect. With others only one viewpoint will do. Sometimes this is because one object must be framed exactly within another. In another instance the sun must reflect from one particular spot, or flare through a gap in background detail. Often lines between two objects will only appear to attach — or separate — by the correct amount when they are seen from one particular spot.

Often, too, a pattern or relationship cannot be shown really strongly from a normal eye position. You may then have to go to great lengths to choose and find your way to some vantage point from which all the elements sit well in the frame. Most critical of all are those picture structures which rely on something very close to the frame edges, or lead to an object in the far distance. A figure on the horizon, framed in a design of wrought-iron railings in the foreground is one example. A face reflected in the wing mirror of an automobile is another. Errors of only a few inches in framing can destroy the effect here, and it is essential to have camera equipment which will let you see precisely what the lens will record on film (see *35 mm SLR cameras*, pp. 102-4).

Positioning the elements
Although this beach scene by Chris Bell would appear, to the casual eye, to allow successful results from a variety of viewpoints, in fact, the reverse is true. Only this one spot, a viewpoint just above the pebbles, gives the right balance of elements. Small shifts to the left or right would make a great difference to the relationship between the shadow and the tower. Moving forward would enlarge the anchor in relation to the rest of the picture, while lowering viewpoint would raise it closer to the horizon.

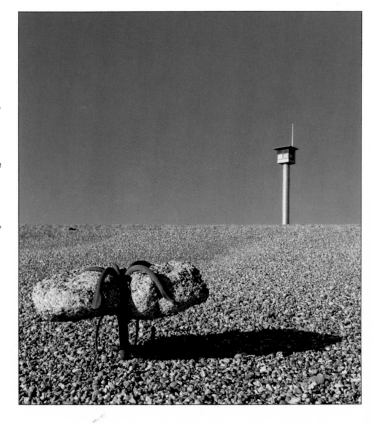

Emphasis

Pictures composed around one main item of interest — such as a building, a natural feature in a landscape, a person's face or eyes, or one figure among many in a candid, documentary photograph — have a certain coherence and unity. A point of emphasis is, therefore, usually something to look for, even though it may consist of no more than a simple break in an abstract pattern. The next step is to decide how best to stress or show off the chosen feature, using the rest of the picture area as a setting — both to direct the eye, and to add extra environmental information.

Emphasis devices
There are several compositional devices for drawing attention to the center of interest. Positioning within the picture format is important, since some positions attract more attention than others. Another technique is to organize the subject lines and shapes, usually by choosing the right viewpoint, so that they form lead-in lines. Lighting can create emphasis too, by directing attention through tonal contrast. Changes in color similarly attract attention — for example, when background and subject are of strongly contrasting hues. These emphasis devices, used singly or together, can give effects ranging from the subtle to the powerful. They often serve to call attention to "central" qualities recognized in the subject itself; but they can also create artificial centers.

Composition based on one main point of interest is evident in the work of most photographers, and many painters. It is interesting to look, for example, at photographs by portraitist Arnold Newman, photojournalist W. Eugene Smith, and much of the work of Margaret Bourke-White, or Alfred Eisenstaedt (see *The illustrated magazines*, pp. 350-1, and *Magnum Photos*, pp. 353-4).

Not every picture needs a single point of interest in order to have a successful structure. Sometimes two features of equal importance can add a sense of vitality to a picture by making the eye scan the scene, comparing the two. Or if the picture contains two separate "compartments" (see *Forming related compartments*, p. 61), it is possible to place a center of interest in each. A few contemporary photographers go out of their way to avoid any visual node at all. Lewis Baltz and Franco Fontana are two examples of photographers who have produced work which relies entirely on rhythms of light and texture running in bands across the frame (see *Abstraction by blur*, p. 91).

See also
Depth and distance *Linear perspective*, p. 81. **Lighting in the studio** *Local lighting*, p. 170; *Low-key lighting*, p. 172; *High-key lighting*, p. 173.

Positioning the subject

Placing the most important element of a composition exactly in the center of the frame gives the picture an obvious formal emphasis. But the resulting image tends to be static and monotonous. Look at a range of photographs and paintings, each of which has a single main point of interest. You will notice that the pictures which have centrally placed subjects appear totally harmonious, but seldom offer any visual surprises. In psychology this effect is described as having a "leveled" state. It is a safe, neat, almost foolproof, compositional solution. However, the pictures that result from this approach can seem unoriginal, and look as though they lack inspiration, spontaneity, and individuality.

There are other subject positions which give a much more active, or "sharpened" emphasis, particularly when the main element of the picture is placed off-center both vertically and horizontally. Perhaps this is because the effect of the composition is slightly unstable and unexpected. In addition, there is a third state, neither leveled nor sharpened, in which the main subject appears to be ambiguously placed, so that the eye has to search the picture for a compositional balance (see *Dynamic balance*, p. 77). There are no fixed rules for

Thirds
Each one of these four points (below) is positioned exactly on an intersection of thirds. Use the diagram as a guide to position the main subject interest.

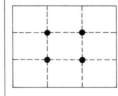

Using thirds
This photograph by Henry Wilson positions the head of a man at prayer exactly on the intersection of thirds. It well suits this image of tranquillity and contemplation. The space left empty by this positioning enhances the overall atmosphere of the picture. (Many photographers opt for the 5:8 Golden Mean ratio, which is a less extreme version.)

photographic composition, but certain subject locations give much stronger pictorial results than others, and are therefore more often used.

The rule of thirds
Divisions of space used in classical painting are just as applicable to photography. One method of organizing the space in either a painting or a photograph is mentally to divide your picture area into "thirds", both vertically and horizontally. This places an imaginary grid of lines over the frame, which can act as a guide for dividing up any composition. It suggests where you might locate any of the subject's major vertical and horizontal divisions (including the horizon in a landscape). In particular, the grid creates four off-center intersections, each of which offers a sharpened position for the main point of interest. The Golden Mean, a similar, more ancient, guide to proportion, sets these divisions at 5:8 (see *The Golden Mean*, p. 68).

The rule of thirds may appear to produce a state of imbalance in a picture — the subject may monopolize one side of the frame, even though it is placed on one of the intersecting guidelines — and weigh the picture down on one side. One solution is to counterbalance a small, vividly colored subject with a large, continuous area of light-colored background on the other side (see *Weight of color*, p. 79).

Test out composition guides on existing photographs and paintings, and decide which works best. They provide a quick aid to positioning figures, or placing strong dividing lines. In practice, they are frequently broken to suit particular subjects, especially when you require a dynamic mood (see *Unconventional framing*, p. 68). But they are well worth using as start points in photographic composition.

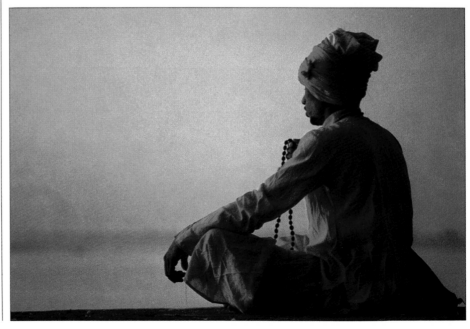

The Golden Mean

The Golden Mean, or Golden Section, is a positioning guide for emphasis, similar to the intersection of thirds (see *Positioning the subject,* p. 67). It has a long history as a canon of proportion in the worlds of painting, sculpture, and architecture, traceable to before the first century BC.

For centuries the Golden Mean was supposed to possess a hidden harmonic, in tune with the universe. You will find it used frequently in paintings of the Renaissance. It also lays down the proportions of an "ideal" rectangle, having a ratio of 5:8. This became an architectural standard for the proportions of rooms, columns, and complete buildings. Most people find that the main subject location determined by the Golden Mean is so close to that set by the intersection of thirds, that the same visual preferences apply to both positions, and the results created by using them are very similar.

Golden Mean principle
The Golden Mean rectangle is constructed from a square. A line drawn from the center of one side of the square to an opposite corner becomes the radius of an arc. This arc defines the rectangle's base line. In the resulting rectangle, the ratio of distances **A** to **B** equals the ratio of **C** to **A**.

Unconventional framing

One of the dangers of composition is that general guidelines may be treated as hard and fast rules. The Golden Mean was still widely used by painters one hundred and fifty years ago — just before the invention of photography. It was therefore adopted by early, art-conscious photographers and extolled as one of several requirements to make "good" pictures. Certainly, one carefully placed point of interest often works well for pictures with a classical, static balance (see *Symmetry,* p. 76). But it is important not to apply any one guideline slavishly, particularly in a medium as versatile as photography. Choosing to place the main subject away from the recommended position, and using two or more areas of prime interest, may well enliven your composition. Breaking these rules intentionally can add strong dynamic interest to a scene. This is because it encourages the eye to scan the image actively — just as it scans a wider scene in real life. If you handle this approach to composition with care and skill, your results will communicate a powerful impression of dynamism.

Avoiding convention
In his picture of the Meiji Shrine, Tokyo, André Kertész ignored commonly used framing guides. The two figures balance each other at the extreme edges of the frame. Ground tone and roof lines link the two, and the empty central area adds a sense of space.

Tone theory

The way a tone appears to the eye is influenced by its surroundings. A small, light-toned area against a mass of dark seems to expand and be emphasized, whereas a small, dark area in a sea of light appears to contract. In the same way, a particular tone of gray seems to alter in value depending on whether it is placed against a light or a dark background. It appears paler when it is against a dark background, and darker when it is against a light background. This illusion is known as "simultaneous contrast".

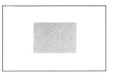

Simultaneous contrast
The single, central rectangles in the three diagrams are all exactly the same tone of gray, but their appearance is affected by the tones surrounding them.

Gray surrounded by black looks lightest. The fourth diagram shows how tone interchange can totally separate one area from another.

Tone interchange

Strong differences in tone between the main subject and its surroundings suit a theme which has impact and drama. The more contrasty this interchange of tones, the more graphic and attention-attracting your chosen point of interest will become. An image of, for example, a somber-toned welder silhouetted against a brilliant spray of sparks, or a backlit, white boat on an inky sea, will stand out from the two-dimensional picture surface. Sometimes you can limit contrast to the main subject area only. For example, you could position a dark figure against a light sky and frame it with a small window, arch, doorway, or other opening of some kind, while the remainder of the scene consists of a whole variety of different mid-tones.

The best way to give subtle emphasis without destroying a gentle mood is through the use of softly gradated tones. This can be particularly effective when it is applied to portraits. A face that is very softly lit from the right side can be made pale gray, gradating to dark gray on the left side. It is then sometimes possible to align the face with background tones which gradate in the opposite direction — so that the face stands out very dramatically from its background.

Gradual tone interchange can give subtly emphasized results that are not over-obvious. By selecting tone differences that are very slight and subtle, you can underplay the effect and still have maximum control over your results.

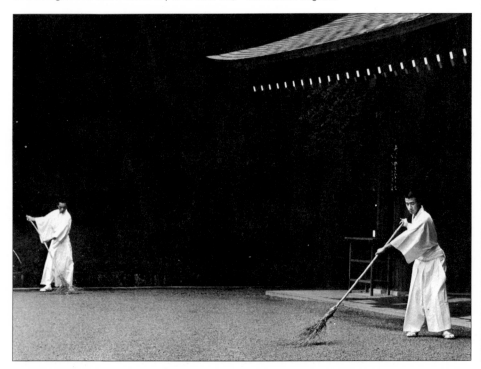

Emphasis through tone

Tones – the range of values in a scene between black and white – are like notes on a piano keyboard. Playing a very deep note immediately after a very high one creates surprise and attracts attention. In the same way, if you set a very dark tone against a very light one (or vice versa) in a picture which mostly consists of mid-tones of gray, the area of abrupt tone contrast will immediately draw the eye and hold our interest.

Often this form of emphasis occurs unintentionally. A bright slice of background between an arm and a body in a portrait, or a backlit halo of light around a dark head of hair, can steal attention from more important features. Provided you notice this problem at the time, it may be possible to adjust your viewpoint slightly, so that you realign the main element and background in a more positive way. For example, a portrait that is noticeably rimlit may create tone contrast in the wrong area – taking attention away from the person's face. By just turning the head slightly, to profile, you can shift the tone contrast emphasis to the face instead.

Tonal emphasis is especially important in black and white photography because of the absence of contrasting colors (see *Color contrast,* p. 71). In color photography, tone values usually mix in with colors, due to lighting direction and reflective qualities of the different subject surfaces. In fact, tone differences are then very useful for creating local emphasis without disturbing the mood created by a scheme which uses only one color.

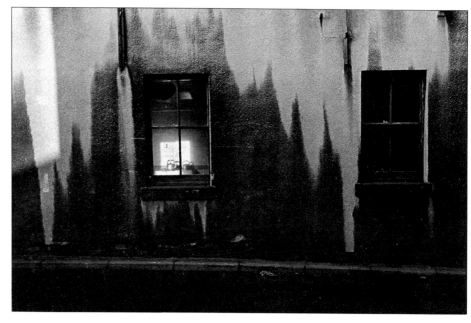

Tonal composition
This picture by Trevor Melton relies on tone interplay for its success. The kettles, picked out in the only white area, a sunlit patch of wall, form a striking point of emphasis. Similar tonal effects often occur in landscapes, when the sun illuminates one small part of a predominantly gray scene, picking it out and drawing attention to it. This particular picture suggests a strong contrast in mood as well as a contrast in dark and light tone. The bright patch of light suggests that this bleak, dreary building contains someone's home.

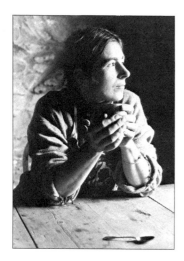

Using contrasting tones
This portrait by Andrew de Lory (above) shows how tonal interchange (placing light tones against dark, and vice versa) can emphasize a face, and make the subject stand out from its background. In Mark Fiennes' riverside scene (right), a strong contrast between dark and light tones produces a strongly silhouetted main subject. Misty detail in the distance and the featureless sky provide a suitable high-key background.

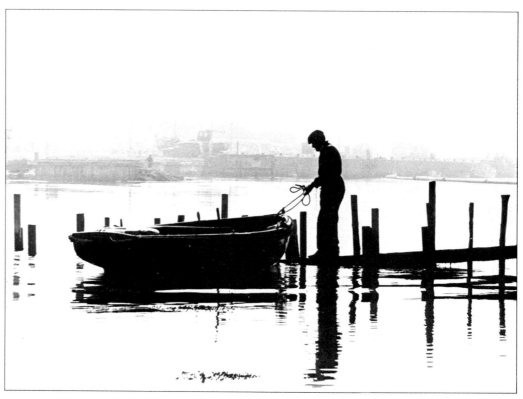

Emphasis through color

Color offers another dimension in which you can control where emphasis falls in a picture. This does not mean that a composition has to be particularly colorful — if most of the hues in a scene are restrained, one element forming a single splash of color takes on great strength. Your main subject may itself be relatively free of color, but if it is backed up with, or is framed within, an isolated patch of color, the same principle of color emphasis can make the picture work.

Some hues seem to seek attention more than others. Red has associations of activity and assertiveness, and objects of this hue tend to come forward or "expand", whereas blues seem to "contract" and hold back. Yellows look brighter and are therefore associated with light. When many colors combine in one subject, the effect does not necessarily have to be a distracting muddle. It depends what other hues are also present in the scene, the context

or mood of the subject matter, the nature of the lighting, and the ways in which we react to colors in general.

To give greatest color contrast between the most important element in the picture and its immediate surroundings, use two colors which complement each other (such as yellow and blue) which come from opposite sides of the color wheel. The conflict in hue will have a dramatic effect, giving the main subject in the scene an emphasis, even when its surroundings have tone values which are the same, or very similar.

Color attraction
Per Eide's landscape uses the dramatic contrast between the rust-red roof and the green field behind to emphasize the main element of the picture —

the barn plus its reflection. In black and white, the red and green areas would merge as a single tone, and the lighter wall and foliage would form similar grays.

Complementary color

The color circle is based on the white light spectrum. Its three main segments are blue, green, and red. These are the primary colors of light (together, they make up "white light"). Directly opposite each primary there is a negative, "complementary", color. In the case of blue, this is yellow, for green it is a purply red called magenta, and for red the complementary is a greenish blue, or cyan. Each complementary color consists of a mixture of the other two primaries — those immediately adjacent to it on the wheel.

You can tell by looking at the wheel which colors form the most striking contrasts with

Color circle
The diagram (right) shows the blue, green, and red primary colors of light. Each one is positioned opposite its complementary color. Yellow is the complementary of blue, magenta of green, and cyan of red.

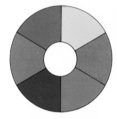

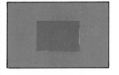

Complementaries
Stare at one of these three rectangles (above and right) — then at a white surface. You will experience "successive contrast".

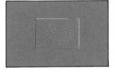

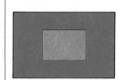

Adjacent colors
The rectangles (left) show how neighboring colors influence our assessment of a particular tone. The center of each rectangle is an identical tone of neutral gray. Most people see the top gray center as pink-tinged and the bottom one as blue-tinged — colors which are complementary to the red and green surrounds.

each other. But when you are judging a color or tone in a scene, it is easy for the effect of adjacent colors to fool the eye. Near-neutral color seems to take on a tint complementary to any strong surrounding color — an effect known as "simultaneous color contrast". By staring fixedly at a colored shape, and then transferring your gaze immediately to a clean, white surface, you can experience an illusion which proves the existence of "negative" colors. Briefly, you will see the same shape in its complementary color on the blank surface — an effect that is called "successive contrast".

Color contrast

Color contrast is especially useful to help you solve the problem of how to emphasize the main subject when the lighting is flat and both subject and background consist of very similar tones. A red figure will look strident against green grass. Similarly, a yellow tree will show up strongly against blue sky. But contrasting colors need not necessarily be fully saturated, bright colors in order to act as a point of emphasis in a picture. Desaturated, soft hues can equally attract attention and emphasize, or even become, the main point of interest. You can also use a mixture of contrasting saturated and desaturated colors together.

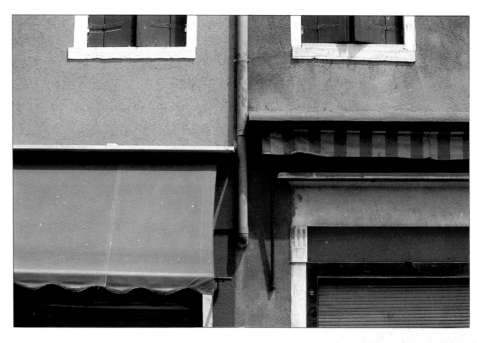

Using color contrast
In this abstract of walls, blinds, and windows, John Sims uses a mixture of saturated and desaturated, contrasting colors to create a structure. The colors are so important that they have become the picture's main subject.

Isolated color

When a small, highly colored object appears in a predominantly gray scene, it can have an influence out of all proportion to its size. This influence is much greater than that of the corresponding tone in a black and white picture. A quite small area of red, for example, may require balancing with a much larger area of gray to produce equilibrium. This effect, known as "isolated color" can therefore be a powerful way of emphasizing your chosen main subject in a scene. It is especially effective in dull, overcast weather, or in drab locations which are mainly gray or muted in color. The eye is automatically attracted by the variety and sparkle that a distinct, bright hue can give to such conditions, so it is important to frame it carefully.

When learning to use isolated color in this way it is useful to seek out small patches of individual color and try framing them so that they dominate the picture. For example, in a garden a backlit urn full of bright flowers appears strong and colorful when shown against a background of dark, shadowy hedge. Compare this with the scene when it is seen from the sunlit side, where the flowers are just one of many competing areas of color. Sometimes a large block of color can be isolated by masking down with dark foreground objects. A child against a brightly colored garage door can be photographed from indoors, so that she is isolated — framed by a dark window surround. In the same way, at night a patch of light reveals just part of a large, colored billboard. On a gray winter's evening in the city the scene is enlivened by a neon sign high up on a building. Small reflective surfaces are another good way of localizing color. A mirror hanging on a wall can introduce a reflected patch of sunlit color into a scene which is otherwise muted by shadow. Or a pool of water can show a brightly colored detail reflected off the paintwork of an automobile.

A break in color
This striking picture of a window in a leaf-covered wall is by Hans Silvester. It uses a small break in a frame filled with regular pattern and strong color to emphasize its main feature. The isolated purply blue sky reflected in the window seems to be made stronger by the red and yellow leaves dominating the rest of the photograph.

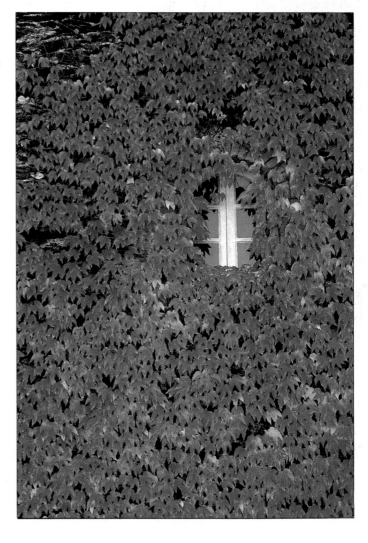

Lead-in lines

One of the best ways to emphasize a particular part of a picture is to direct the eye to it with lines. You can place the main subject so that it breaks the horizon, or some other structurally important line (see *Placing the horizon*, p. 58). On the other hand, you can frame lines in a scene so that they converge at a particular point, where the main subject is placed (or you can position it across one of the lines *en route*). For example, a road diminishing into the distance can lead you to a tiny figure which dominates the picture.

Lead-in lines are perhaps the most easy-to-find, yet effective, devices for giving emphasis. They guide the eye to a stopping point, and at the same time, help to connect foreground with background. Lines have special influences, too. If they start very close to you, the change in scale between the foreground and background will be very noticeable. Lines that converge strongly like this usually run diagonally across the frame, giving a dynamic lead-in to the center of interest. A curved line creates a far more gentle, flowing effect (see *Curved lines*, p. 37).

You will find potential lead-in lines in all sorts of situations. Making them work for your particular subject depends largely on your viewpoint. Straight lines of city sidewalks, fences casting long shadows, or telegraph poles, all converge into the distance when you look at

them end-on (see *Linear perspective*, p. 81). Ropes securing boats, or wind-blown streaks of cloud in a clear sky make good lead-ins, and strong bands of tone or color can also work in this way.

Another important factor is lighting direction. Sometimes side- or back-lighting can be too strong, so that shadow lines overwhelm your main subject. There is also a danger that they will accidentally draw all the attention to an unimportant area. When you are setting up a portrait, for example, choose a viewpoint that relates lines and the main interest constructively. For candid work, photographers sometimes choose lead-in lines first, and then wait for the action they are aiming to capture to occur at the picture's point of emphasis (see *Controlling the setting*, p. 90).

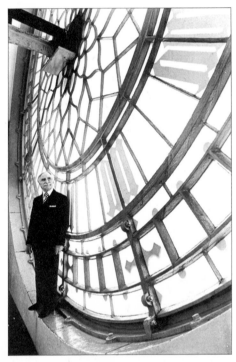

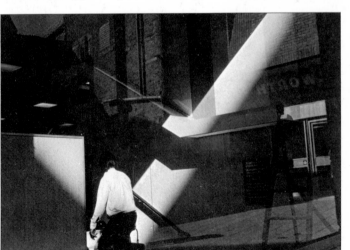

Linear flow
A series of objects diminishing in size against a plain background, as in the diagram (above), can act in the same way as physical lines, to lead the eye through a scene. When composing pictures, try to make a path from foreground to background (or the reverse) visually interesting. One way to do this is to plan subject "stopping points" on the way.

Curved lead-in lines
The sweeping lines (above) of the clock face at London's Houses of Parliament provide dynamic lead-in lines. They also form an appropriate setting for a portrait of the building's custodian. The picture is by Nic Barlow.

Sunlight and shadow
Peter Lester waited until the white-shirted figure (left) coincided with the ends of two shafts of sunlight. They draw attention to the figure by "pointing" like an arrow.

Structure

Photographers, like many artists, often consciously structure their work – using deliberate, formal arrangements to create a sense of order, completeness, and unity. Our visual perception is responsive to physical order and balance.

One way of structuring an image is to arrange the various components to give a clear overall shape – this "completes" the composition, rounding it off like a completed musical phrase or a well-written sentence. The classical, unified structure is the triangle or circle. But other simple, formal shapes are also used. Look at examples of shape structures in portraiture by Arnold Newman (see *The illustrated magazines*, pp. 350-1), or at the constructed images of Jerry Uelsmann (see *The leading exponents of Surrealism*, pp. 379-83).

Color structure
Color is another important means of structuring pictures. A photographer can create a unified, harmonious color scheme throughout a picture, perhaps by selection of subject matter, or by using tinted light (see *Time of day*, p. 23). It is also possible to build a structure with opposed colors, by placing merged "blocks" of similar-colored elements in opposition to complementary-colored areas, so that shapes are formed.

Formal or informal structures
There are times when imbalance and lack of order are appropriate to the spirit of the picture. Try analyzing very formally structured paintings and photographs to determine whether, or how, they show a sense of completeness, and if this helps the content and concept of the picture.

Structures offer a firm base to build a picture on, just as frames and compartments do (see *Finding frames*, p. 60, and *Forming related compartments*, p. 61). This is especially applicable to portraits, still lifes, and groups. They also demonstrate that the photographer must be able to see and exploit subject matter in terms of its graphic, abstract, visual qualities, as well as seeing and showing its significance and worth in terms of content.

See also
Divisions of the frame, pp. 58-61. Timing and movement *The critical moment*, p. 88. The human figure *Groups*, p. 321. Editorial and advertising photography *Still life*, pp. 314-5. Structuralism and Abstraction, pp. 361-4.

Thematic shapes

All the pictures on this page contain compositional structures based on simple shapes – the circle, the triangle, the L-shape, or the S-shaped curve. These shapes can be formed by line, or by weight of tone, pattern, or the placing of shapes. Ideally, a structural shape – like shapes of objects themselves (see *Shape*, pp. 38-9) – should relate and contribute to the mood of the picture. L-shaped structures are generally the most tranquil and static. A side view of a woman sitting with her hands in her lap is one example, an architectural view with a tall building on one side and long, low blocks in the distance, near the base of the picture, is another. A shape which counters the vertical/horizontal picture shape, such as a triangle, will provide more sense of flow and movement. An S-shape or circle encourages the viewer to explore picture content quite actively. The eye tends to zig-zag restlessly across the frame and back again. There are many other variations of the basic shapes which are very effective, too. For example, the oval shape works just as well as a regular

circle, and a semi-circle just as well as an ordinary triangle.

In practice, you can often form shapes through lines of motion or force as effectively as with found shapes. Blur, position in the frame, even expression or the direction in which someone is looking may be enough to encourage the eye to complete a particular path. You can sometimes rearrange individual items to form shapes that are more pleasing overall. This is particularly true of groups of still-life objects – the smaller being grouped around the larger to give a triangular structure. The same applies to the grouping of figures. Foreground or background "frames" also help to create or complete shapes. To take the idea a stage further, you can sometimes find structures which fit within one another. Or, you may find two structural shapes which contrast or compete for attention, but which can be positioned so that they overlap sympathetically within the same picture.

There is a danger that if compositional shapes become too assertive they may domi-

nate the subject itself – so that structure overpowers content. It is usually best to adopt shapes that occur naturally, rather than force your subject into an artificial structure. When taking a portrait of a person sitting behind a desk, for example, the hands stretching out across the desk top often naturally form a triangular shape with the face (look at the work of Arnold Newman to see how he makes frequent use of this construction in his formal portraits). Another example might be two people haggling over a bargain in a market, shown in profile, forming an oval shape that adds structure to a subject which already holds the viewer's interest.

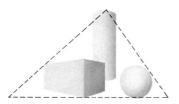

Grouping
Simple groups of objects (above) often form shapes which have a natural rhythm for the eye. The commonest shape, the triangle, is particularly effective if it is off-center. It avoids predictable symmetry and is more satisfying.

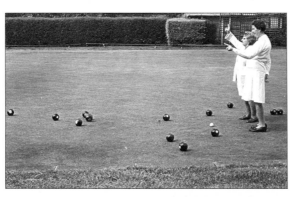

Structural shapes
This picture of bowls players (left), by David Agar, is structured around an elongated L-shape. Its static atmosphere, plus a slight sense of movement suits the nature of the subject well. In Jan Ung's picture of a machine operator (below left), an off-center, triangular shape is produced by the man's head, his elbow, and the machine. The viewer's eye tends to travel around the picture, from one point to the next. In the picture of the horse and stable hand (below), Milton Colindres chose a moment to shoot when the horse turned around, arching its neck. This gives the picture an oval structure which frames the more distant man. None of the three shape structures shown on this page is overassertive, but each gives its subject matter strength.

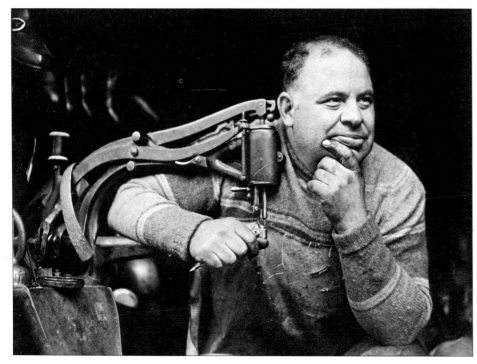

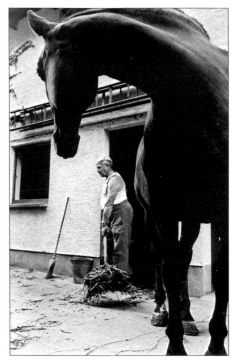

Related color

It is possible to "pull together" a picture containing a number of diverse shapes and forms, and give it continuity by using color skillfully. In the same way that you might exploit any other kind of visual structure, it is often worth taking pictures for the color itself, making color combinations and themes the main point of the photograph which can be appreciated for their own sakes.

One approach is to explore harmonious, restricted colors, perhaps choosing subjects which have only two or three muted hues, similar in saturation. As an alternative, you can structure the picture around the interplay of only two colors, or, by careful selection and framing, show one color in various degrees of saturation, with the rest of the picture consisting of blacks, whites, and neutral grays. In landscape photography, the presence of water is very helpful for this technique. The surface of a lake or river reflects and takes on the color of the sky and surrounding landscapes, increasing the area of variations on a single color scheme. Look at the work of artists such as Whistler in his *Thames Nocturnes,* and at Monet's treatment of the same subject. On a smaller scale, puddles and pools can do the same job, and often separate the different areas of color more far efficiently than larger expanses of water can.

Interchanged harmony
Neighbors in the spectrum, red and yellow are harmonizing colors (below). Interchange is an effective device for separating an object from its background.

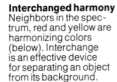

Color interplay
In this street scene (below) by Robin Bath shadow cast by the low sun suppresses the neutral tones of sidewalk and street. All the lit areas contain harmonious colors. Reflections from pools of water bring this same color scheme down to the bottom of the picture, but in a contrasting shape. This relates the different areas of the scene with each other.

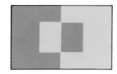

Opposed color

Different parts of a picture will structurally separate or merge because of the way they fall naturally into color groupings. The simplest example of this occurs with the clear division in a landscape between blue-dominated sky areas and the green or brown of the land. (In the same scene in a black and white photograph, both areas might combine as similar gray tones, making clouds and the pale stone walls of houses into the areas which separate most strongly, instead.) Opposed colors occur in mixed lighting conditions, too. A scene inside a room, lit by domestic lamps, makes the daylit garden outside seem to have a bluish cast. A photograph taken to show the interior in correct color, makes the outside detail through the window merge into one compositional block, because of its lack of warm colors. Opposed color "compartments" also occur when one side of a street or one part of a landscape is bathed in evening sunlight, while the rest is lit by the blue sky. Even a colored wall on one side of courtyard can merge with nearby white objects by tinting them with reflected light, turning this part of the picture into a single compositional element which opposes the colors in the rest of the scene. You can create similar effects artificially with colored flash or studio lamps, or by using a split filter over the lens to tint different parts of your picture in opposing colors (see *Special effects attachments,* pp. 198-200). You can also give whole areas a common color cast by local filtering during printing (see *Local color control,* p. 251).

Opposed, strong color
Color strength or brilliance is relative. Much depends on the influence of lighting direction and intensity, subject surface qualities, and the colors and tones of adjacent objects.

Divisive colors
Opposed colors (below) do not necessarily have to be exactly complementary to one another, but as a general rule they should be well separated in the color spectrum and fairly well saturated.

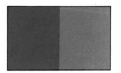

Muted, opposed colors
This deceptively simple picture by Amanda Currey (below) shows how well a composition can work when it is restricted to two opposing colors. In reality, the bench, ground, and trees all differ in their muted hues. But the early evening sunlight has swamped all these foreground objects in pinky-orange illumination, merging them into one common color. Beyond these forms, the pastel and saturated values of blue give a strongly separated backdrop. Limitation of color seems to suit the simplicity of subject shapes here.

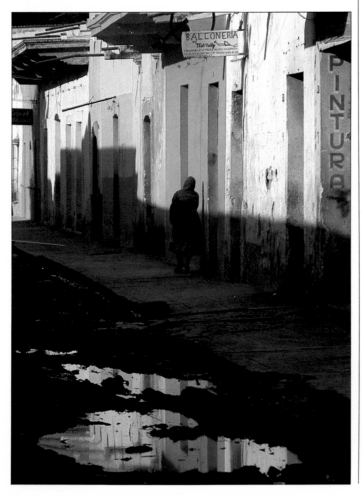

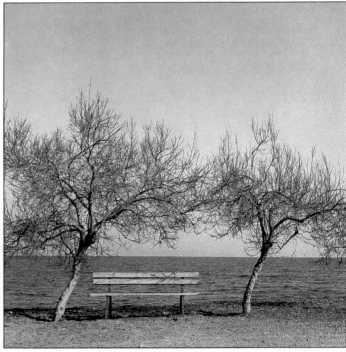

Strong colors generally seem to have more positive, "advancing" qualities than less saturated colors. Strong yellows always appear brighter than yellow in the spectrum. They tend to come forward, particularly when they are directly next to darkish, complementary colors. Bright reds, too, advance and expand stridently, as well as having the most emotional, active overtones of all the colors. Strong blues tend to be more passive, seeming to

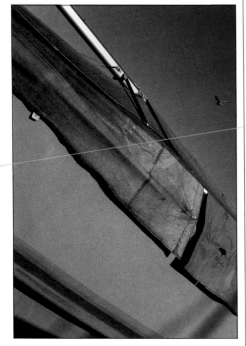

Strong, opposed color
John Sims' photograph of the hull of a boat (above) shows the possibilities of moving in close to a subject for the sake of its colors alone. The richness of the rust-red hull is played off against the deep blue sky and canvas cover, relative areas of each being balanced by very careful framing.

retract visually, possibly due to our associations with the bluish haze of distant views (see *Aerial perspective,* pp. 82-3). In addition, strong colors can seem "heavier" than weaker ones (see *Balance of color,* p. 78), so they have to be used with care, while small areas of strong color in a neutral, or "weaker" background can give a simple subject emphasis in the frame (see *Isolated color,* p. 71).

Equal patches of many colors can give a lively, though confusing, result. Rather than making areas of opposed, strong colors the same size in a picture, it is often effective to structure a composition which contains areas of strong color that are quite unequal in size. To exclude unwanted hues when you are framing a picture, either move in closer, or re-frame totally. You can always reduce the size of a large, dominant area of color by cropping all but a part of it from the frame.

Color themes

Color composition requires more careful handling than black and white picture building. This is because you are forced to consider both tone and color values, and colors have strong links with the emotions. Colors also need to be more accurate than tones in pictures, if you want results to reproduce the original subject objectively.

Try assessing scenes for their color values rather than for their subject content. Decide how these colors could be distributed within the frame, and whether some should be reduced or intensified. Try limiting your picture to a single predominant hue (plus black, white, or neutral gray). Or try finding pairs of colors, preferably using one that is more saturated than the other.

To intensify colored areas, move in closer and pick an angle from which the color is least diluted by glare and other surface reflections. A polarizing filter can help you to do this (see *Polarizing filters,* p. 198). Try to work in strong light, which tends to emphasize the richness of colors, or make them seem stronger by isolating them in a scene containing mostly black or dark-gray tones.

You can remove or reduce an unwanted color by cropping it from the frame, or choosing a viewpoint that hides it. Or you can soften colors by diffusing the image by movement blur, or by using a soft-focus lens attachment. A color filter suppresses color complementary to its own hue.

Muted and restricted color
Bright colors attract attention, but for many people pictures composed of a muted or limited range seem more evocative and atmospheric than poster-like, bright hues.

For muted effects, your subject should have subdued contrast and an absence of saturated colors. These effects tend to occur with adverse weather conditions — particularly in mist, fog, or light rain.

Another approach to the restrained use of color is to pick a subject with widely ranging color saturation, but limited to a single hue. This could, for example, be a close-up of rock forms. It is then possible to reserve the normal tone range for revealing subject form, but use the limited color scheme to determine mood and atmosphere.

Harmonious variations
Two different colors can sometimes be so similar (see the diagram below) that they can provide subtle hue combinations when

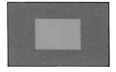

they are used together in a composition. This means that you can choose subjects which contain intermingling colors, for their sake alone, rather than for the sake of their content. The same effect occurs in black and white photography when delicate shades of gray mingle.

Monochromatic color
Look around for subjects based on one or two closely related colors. This picture by John Sims (below) uses only rust-red and

yellow, both in desaturated forms, and mixed with areas of white. The drainpipe seems to divide one tinted area of wall from the other.

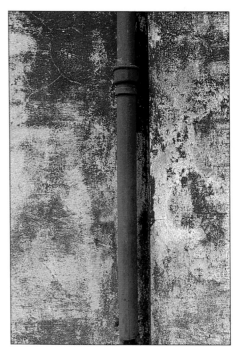

Muted colors
Fred Dustin's picture (left) consists solely of undefined shapes and colors showing through a shaded window streaming with condensation. This technique is a good way of muting and mixing colors to give non-realistic images. Other ways to create such soft, color-blending effects are to move the camera during exposure (see *Moving camera, static subject,* p. 128), or to shoot intentionally out of focus (see *Using focus control,* p. 116).

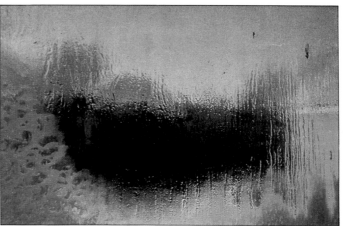

Balance

The need for balance is one of the most important influences on human visual perception. We have an inbuilt sense of equilibrium that gives a natural reference base when we make visual decisions. Eye and brain react rapidly and accurately when judging balance or imbalance in visual patterns — just as they have to in establishing and maintaining the stability of the body.

Balance in composition means distributing the various masses of tone and color, shapes and lines within the frame, so that they collectively give a sense of equilibrium. The most obvious way of doing this is by creating symmetry. You can position the main element right in the center of the picture and place repeating structures to the left and right of it, or to the top and bottom, and so be sure of achieving a completely balanced effect. The end result tends to look ordered but static and lifeless.

Variety and balance

Pictures must offer variety as well as balance. It is possible to avoid rigid symmetry, yet create a sense of balance and completeness. Photographers tend to do this intuitively — shifting vantage point or distance to change the placing and spacing of objects until they look "right". When we analyze the resulting composition the various blocks of tone exert their own individual "weight" — the whole scene pivots at its center, with everything equally balanced. For example, in a landscape at dusk, a large, dark mass such as a cottage or tree may break the horizon just left of center. In the distance another much smaller object also breaks the horizon, but this time very close to the right-hand edge of the picture. It forms a compact block of dark tone. The resulting picture contains both balance and variety.

Balance and atmosphere

Balance in the formal, painterly sense ideally suits those pictures which convey a feeling of repose and order. The use of vertical and horizontal lines, with the main subject centralized or at the intersection of thirds (see *Positioning the subject,* p. 67), all contribute to this static effect. Angled lines, changes in scale and greater variety of shapes give a more forceful, dynamic image structure. They force the viewer actively to scan the scene, the actual movement of the eye adding a sense of energy and action, without destroying the sense of balance and stability.

An understanding of balance also means that a composition can be made to look imbalanced intentionally, to create tension. The result can be awkward, or stressful, and contribute substantially to a situation where the photographer wants to use compositional stress to match picture content.

Symmetry

You can find symmetry of structure in many natural forms, and in man-made objects of all kinds. A leaf, an architectural structure, or a decorative pattern all possess this most balanced of designs. Even an asymmetrical subject, when it is joined to its own shadow or reflection, creates a symmetrical pattern or shape. Visually symmetry has associations with a high degree of formality and order. It can therefore be the right compositional choice for formal groups of people, and certain interiors, such as churches. It can also imply consistency and uniformity, and so work for pictures of items coming off a production line, for example. This could also work for a formal group of people wearing uniforms, arranged in rows, where it is necessary to show a regular, undisturbed pattern and convey a sense of order in the photograph.

We are initially attracted by the regularity of symmetry, but a totally symmetrical picture desperately lacks variety. We seek out even the slightest break in symmetry and it consequently takes on an importance of its own. It is possible to use this exaggerated importance to contribute a sense of variety. For example, in a picture of a room centered squarely on the fireplace and flanked by two people in equally spaced chairs, you immediately compare their expressions and the different ways they are sitting. Looking around the room you begin to find other things breaking the symmetry — objects on the left half of the mantelshelf are different from those on the right. Two similar-looking, rectangular objects hang on either side, but on closer inspection you see that one is in fact a mirror, while the other is a calendar.

Symmetry is therefore counterpointed by variety in detail, in the same way that pattern needs to be broken (see *Interrupted pattern,* p. 41). You have the advantage of a firm, balanced, structural design, but you can also make the viewer examine detail which might be overlooked in a less formal approach. Make sure that these details, however small, add relevant information to the environment or person, and to the mood of the picture. Personal oddments are usually far more interesting and tell us a great deal more about the subject, of say, a portrait, than do impersonal, nondescript objects.

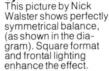

Symmetrical balance
This picture by Nick Walster shows perfectly symmetrical balance, (as shown in the diagram). Square format and frontal lighting enhance the effect.

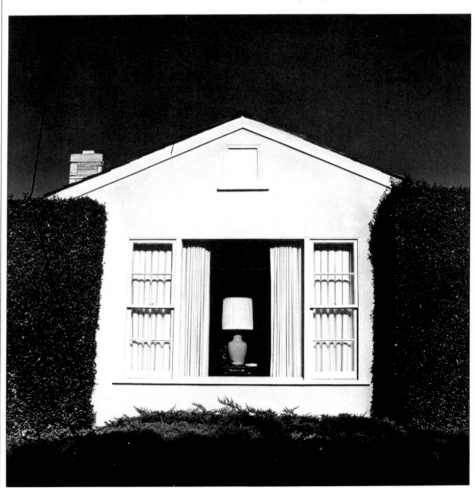

Balancing tones and shapes

Think of the various elements in the picture, with their different areas and tonal values, as each possessing perceptual "weight" which can attract our attention in varying degrees, depending on the subject content as well as the picture structure. A particular figure, or a humorous or aggressive situation, receives our sharpened attention even when it appears very small in the frame. Local contrast — the difference between an object and its immediate surroundings in terms of tone, color,

shape, and scale — boosts its importance. Lines which lead the eye into the picture (see *Lead-in lines*, p. 72) can also give an emphasis to a particular element or area of the scene.

"Weight", then, depends upon many factors, all of which have to be judged in the context of the picture as a whole. The challenge is to balance these factors within the proportions of the frame, so that they give a reasonable sense of order without a loss of variety and liveliness. This is mostly done by using an in-

built sense of what "looks right". Just as the human body caught off-balance automatically stretches out an arm or a leg to counterbalance instability, so the positioning of large quantities of subject matter just to the right of the center may need balancing with a small object well to the left. The best way to learn this is by photographing groups of small, still-life objects, which you can move around as you wish. Keeping one fixed viewpoint, you can make a whole series of pictures altering the relative positioning of individual items, and the structure of the group as a whole.

Lighting plays a fundamental role in altering tone values and the massing of shapes. It affects the relationships between the object and its background as well as between one object and another.

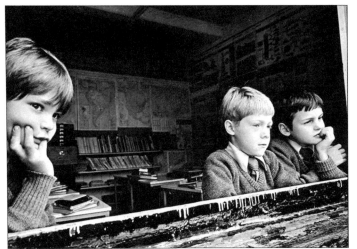

Shapes
The boys (left) in Jan Ung's picture are placed to provide balance. The largest, on the extreme left, balances the two smaller figures on the right.

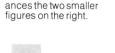

Tone and shape
In Andrew de Lory's landscape (right) the smaller, darker, tree has equal weight to the larger, lighter group. The diagram (above) shows how this relationship works in theory.

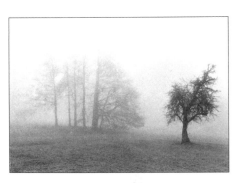

Dynamic balance

Composition that makes use of order and balance, the frequent use of vertical and horizontal lines, and the simplicity of one center of interest is usually considered to be "classical". This approach ranges from the paintings of Ancient Greece and Rome, to the work of individual modern artists, but it is of limited value to photographers. The camera allows for greater variation of viewpoint than is normally available to painters, and photographers can consequently follow photography's own dynamic compositional rules (although many modern artists also use a dynamic approach which is directly influenced by the camera's individual way of seeing).

Dynamic balance in a picture means that the eye is actively encouraged to move from one object to another, yet without a sense of destructive division of interest. It is often possible to achieve this by using two elements — one clearly the center of interest, but the other counterbalancing and complementing it. Try to make use of differences in distance, and therefore, scale. This kind of approach works much more successfully when the two objects relate to each other in some way — by content, structure, or symbolic relationship. You can present a meaning which goes far beyond the actual content of the scene.

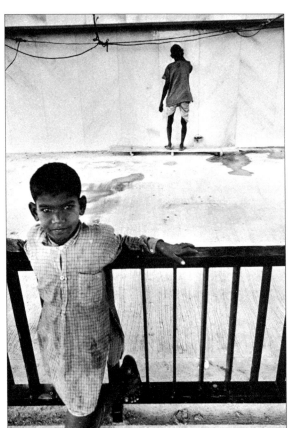

Dynamic composition
The two figures in Bina Fonyat's picture are positioned asymmetrically in the frame. One boy fills a large area of the lower, left-hand corner of the frame, while another takes up a much smaller area in the top, right-hand corner, though slightly more centrally. This makes them seem to pull away from each other, an effect which is enhanced by the fact that they face in opposite directions. Our

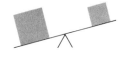

eyes move from one figure to the other, giving the composition both dynamism and balance. By concentrating most of the scene's tonal weight in the bottom and left of the frame, the photographer has given his picture an additional sense of tension (as demonstrated by the diagram).

Balance of color

When working in color, you can apply much the same principles of balance in composition as when dealing only in tone values. "Dark" and "light" colors, however, cannot literally be translated into equivalent tones because their visual power, and therefore compositional weight, varies according to surrounding hues. In addition to this, problems of color balance worsen when a scene contains several different, fully saturated colors — whereas a mixture of strong and muted shades (see *Opposed color,* and *Color themes,* pp. 74-5) of the same color is much easier to handle.

One approach to color balance is to make the color of the main subject itself dominate the picture, so that other, weaker colors play a supporting role. Another approach, in a scene which has relatively large, colorless areas, is to balance the picture in tonal terms, and to use an overall color simply to provide mood. A third alternative is to create a symmetrical color balance, using approximately equal areas of complementary hues. (This effect can be predictable — so if possible, try to add interest by breaking the areas of color up into different shapes.)

The most important factor to consider in balancing a color composition is the attention-attracting power of quite small areas of color when they are contrasted with their surroundings. To experiment with this, put together compositions which contain mostly black, gray, or white, balanced against a patch of strong color (see *Isolated color,* p. 71). It is easy to control the size of this area of color by altering your distance from the subject, or

by moving your viewpoint so that it is either partially obscured by another object, or is cropped by the frame.

In a controlled subject situation, such as a portrait, you can determine color balance by choice of lighting, clothing, and surroundings. A hat, for example, may be the boldest but smallest area in a photograph, balanced against a larger but more centralized shadow area. In found situations, however, the variety of color often makes it hard to believe that you can really control color balance. Photographers lack the total control enjoyed by painters. But in practice you can often remove or introduce color quite easily. When photographing a group of yellow-clad musicians

in a courtyard, for example, you can transform the dark stone ground to yellow, too, by choosing a low viewpoint behind flowers of a similar color. By moving your viewpoint very slightly, it may be possible to alter the picture totally and produce a different version by including a shadowed bush so that the yellow foreground is replaced by dark green.

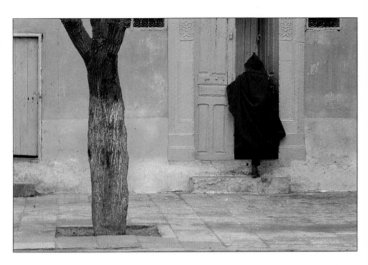

Color in a supporting role
The tree and the hooded figure are the main sources of balance in this picture by Victoria Barclay. They balance each other out. But the background colors are important because they provide balance for the black and gray tones in the picture. The effect would be quite lost in a black and white picture. The colors also form a muted background wash which helps to link the elements with each other.

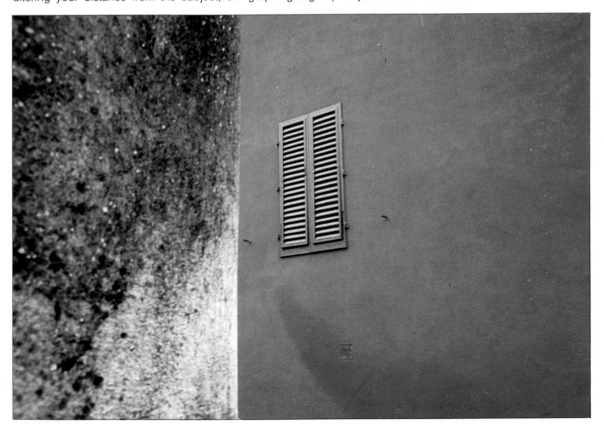

Balancing tone and color
Franco Fontana structured this composition through precise adjustment of the relative areas of red and gray. As demonstrated by the diagram, the large area of red is perfectly

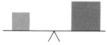

balanced by the smaller areas of gray tone. Framing was critical in the picture — slight adjustment to the left or right would alter the relationship of the window shutters to the gray wall. The tendency of red to "come forward" makes it difficult to decide which surface is, in fact, nearer to the camera.

Weight of color

When they are fully saturated, certain colors are much darker than others and seem "heavier". For example, a fully saturated blue seems much "heavier" than a fully saturated yellow. This phenomenon is known as "color weight", and it plays a crucial role in photography. When taking pictures in color, it is possible to balance a large area consisting of "light" color with a much smaller area of a "dark", or "heavy", color.

The visual weight of a particular color does not necessarily appear the same to the eye as it does on film. In color photography, it is usually possible to follow your own judgment. But when photographing in black and white, it is essential to learn how colors translate into tone values. This is the reason why many photographers feel that black and white film is far more demanding to work with than color. This

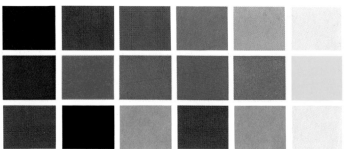

color chart (above) shows how ordinary black and white panchromatic film (which responds to all wavelengths in the color spectrum) alters the apparent weights of fully saturated colors. You will see that the weights of colors on this film are not always what you would expect. Cyan and green are noticeably darker than

their gray equivalents, while blue seems considerably lighter.

The color of the viewing light, its brightness, and simultaneous contrast (see *Complementary color,* p. 70) from adjacent hues, are also factors which affect the weight of color dramatically.

Tonal equivalents
The center row in this diagram contains fully saturated spectrum colors in order of apparent weight. The top row shows an equivalent scale of grays. The bottom row shows how the colors appear on panchromatic film. This records colors so that they have visual weights that are noticeably different.

Imbalance and tension

Stability and balance will not provide ideal compositional solutions for every photographic subject. If you want to introduce a sense of tension into a picture, for example, you may have to reverse suggestions for creating balance. You could, for instance, place a figure stepping off a sidewalk at the extreme edge of a picture which contains very little else. Viewing this, we look for something to provide a balancing weight on the opposite side of the picture, find nothing, and so question what is happening. Is the figure arriving or leaving? Has something just happened, or is it about to take place? The unorthodox composition makes us uneasy. But it is vital to recognize that this is as important a means of communication as producing a classical, balanced composition. It creates a visual sense of discord that can transform a commonplace situation or event into an arresting

image. The more ordinary the subject is, the easier it is to introduce a sense of imbalance. A subject that is intrinsically interesting might well detract from the meaning and purpose you intend the picture to have.

This method of composition has many purposes, and can be a powerful and striking means of self-expression. It can suggest many different emotions (aggression, isolation, discord, ambiguity, or awkwardness), and several notable photographers make it a feature of their personal style. For example, you can discover it in the work of Garry Winogrand, Lee Friedlander, and Harry Callahan.

Pictures like this can be surprisingly difficult to make, for like atonal music, they seem to conflict with our natural inclinations. Rules and principles of balance and order in composition are frequently rationalizations of deeply ingrained standards of human perception.

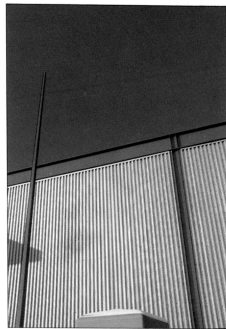

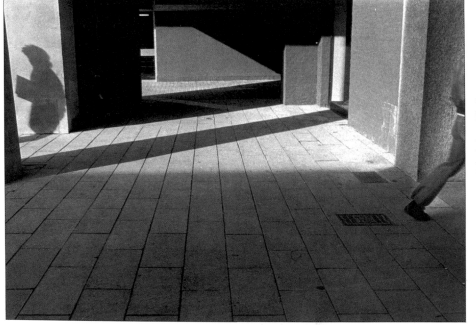

Tension in moving subjects
The picture (left) by Peter Lester shows how fast reactions can freeze rapidly moving subjects and produce strangely disquieting results. Two anonymous figures are moving quickly out of both sides of the frame — one has almost disappeared, only the shadow of the other remains. The eye glances from one to the other, and the overall impression is one of unresolved tension.

Imbalance in color subjects
In the abstract composition (above) by John Sims, the visual strengths of fully saturated red and yellow are used to create a sense of imbalance. Although they appear in minute quantities compared with the blue and white areas, they attract attention, drawing the eye to one side of the picture only.

Depth and distance

The portrayal of three-dimensional scenes containing a complex but familiar mixture of height, breadth, and depth is one of the most demanding aspects of composition. In life, we perceive depth largely because we have binocular vision — the offset viewpoints of our two eyes providing comparative information from which we judge the distances of near and far objects. The actual movement of our eyes and head, as we scan the scene, helps this process, making near and far elements apparently shift in position. Experience also allows us to interpret clues such as size, tone and color, and shape correctly in terms of the nature of the object, and its distance. We know, for instance, that a vehicle does not physically shrink or change shape as it is driven away, and that distant hills are not necessarily actually bluer and paler than close-up fields.

Two-dimensional, still photographs and paintings must convey depth by illusion, and deliberately use familiar visual clues to help us imagine we are seeing objects at different distances. The classic clues to depth are: scale changes; the foreshortening of shape and convergence of lines due to linear perspective; and the shift of colors and tones and lessening of contrast due to aerial, or atmospheric, perspective. The overlap of near and far subjects, and the placing of more distant elements higher in the frame are additional indicators of the relative distances of objects.

Maximum or minimum depth?

By recognizing all the factors which contribute to the illusion of depth in pictures, photographers can then choose whether to employ a dramatic form of extended depth, which uses the picture plane merely as a window by which the viewer is swept into the scene, or whether to combine factors which have a flattening effect.

The success of the maximum depth approach depends on subject choice and the requirements of the picture. Detail is rendered sharp from the nearest to the farthest elements (see *Maximum depth of field,* p. 119). It is generally used when results must be objective and realistic — in architectural photography, for example. (It is also a technique used frequently by Ansel Adams and Bill Brandt.)

Images with minimal depth appear to keep their information all on, or near, the surface of the picture plane. It is possible to show such a compression of space that the image resembles a flat, two-dimensional pattern. Photographs of this kind have become something of a hallmark of such photographers as Lewis Baltz and Franco Fontana.

Historical background

At what point do a few marks, different tones, and colors on a flat sheet of paper take on a realistic representation of a scene? It is remarkable how readily we can read a surface that is basically only a patchwork of pigment, dye, or photographic silver as recognizable subjects at different distances. The problems of creating the illusion of space on a flat surface have always challenged artists. Early Egyptian drawing is conspicuous for its lack of depth. An oblique view of a row of warriors shows the nearest ones as exactly the same height as others farther away. This is entirely logical, since people are approximately the same size in real life. But when depicted in this way, scenes look very unreal, because the artist has not provided the visual clues we use to perceive depth. We know objects at different distances have constant properties. For many painters, the greatest single aid to portraying depth and distance was developed in the fifteenth century when the principles of perspective drawing were first demonstrated. Accurate perspective, in a painting or drawing from one fixed observation point, arose from showing oblique lines converging to one or more vanishing points on the distant horizon.

Photographic techniques and depth

The rules of linear perspective have to be learned by freehand artists, but are largely

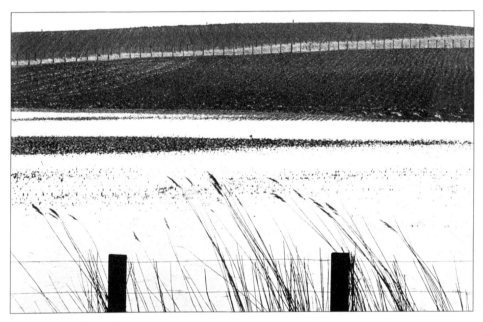

Suppressed space
In this landscape, Carol Sharp uses several devices to suppress the impression of depth and distance, and present the subject as flat pattern. There are no lines running into the picture which would show linear perspective, overlap of forms is minimal, and flat lighting helps to minimize tone change with distance.

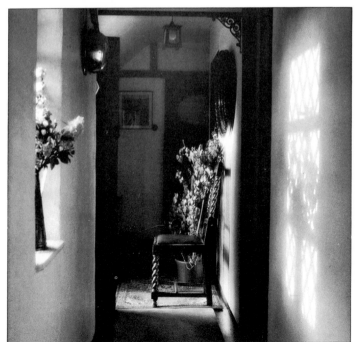

Extended depth
This cottage corridor, by Amanda Currey, gains most of its sense of depth from linear perspective. Oblique surfaces converge to a central vanishing point. Strong side-lighting picks out objects and creates shadows at different distances, so that scale change is made very clear.

handled for the photographer by the camera itself. Similarities between the eye lens and the camera lens (see *Camera principles,* pp. 100-1) mean that most camera lenses "draw" perspective in a highly realistic way. (A shorter focal length lens and closer viewpoint will give an exaggerated idea of perspective — see *Wide-angle lenses,* pp. 186-7.) You can help the illusion further by choosing scenes that contain plenty of linear forms positioned both near and far, and by picking a viewpoint which will show vertical and horizontal surfaces obliquely, so that they converge into the distance. If these surfaces carry a regular pattern (such as brickwork or a checkered floor) the effects of linear perspective appear all the more strongly. The use of light and shade, particularly side- or back-lighting help to separate out objects at different distances by making them vary in tone. Also you can use a mixture of subject colors which "come forward", together with more recessive hues.

Additional space-enhancing factors are the actual picture width and overall size. Wide-screen movies have proved the added depth and realism of a "wrap-around" image. Panoramic stills cameras (see *Special cameras,* pp. 208-9) give a similar effect, plus curved linear perspective in the horizontal dimension. A big enlargement of any photograph, even though viewed from farther away than for normal-sized prints, somehow makes us more conscious of being "surrounded" by visual information, with a corresponding sense of realism and depth.

Other useful depth devices are concerned with limiting detail. This includes the blurring of detail of one object in relation to another by means of movement, or by restricting sharp focus to one narrow zone (see *Depth of field,* pp. 118-19).

An alternative means of enhancing the impression of depth is to use three-dimensional photography. Equipment varies, but the principle is to record two or more viewpoints simultaneously each time the shutter is pressed. The final prints or slides then combine these images in such a way that each eye sees a slightly different viewpoint, just as they would if viewing an actual scene. As a result the photograph literally seems to stand off the page.

See also
Aperture *Depth of field,* p. 118. Focal length and camera size, pp. 120-3. Wide-angle lenses, pp. 186-7. Fisheye lenses, pp. 188-9. Telephoto lenses, pp. 189-92. Zoom lenses, pp. 192-4.

Linear perspective

The simplest, most basic, way to explore the nature of linear perspective is to look through a viewing frame (see *Composition,* p. 54) at a draft board or a sheet of graph paper placed on a flat surface. Using an oblique viewpoint (and looking with one eye only) compare the shape of the squares with the edges of the frame. If your viewpoint is from the center of one side, the set of lines running across your view on the paper will look parallel with the top and bottom frame lines. The lines at right-angles, however, running away from you, appear to converge, as the gaps between them decrease with distance. This is an example of one-point perspective.

Next, change to a subject which has volume — something box-like, such as a building. Choose a viewpoint opposite the edge of one corner, looking horizontally. You can see two faces of the building at right-angles to each other, but each tapering into the distance in opposite directions. This is known as angular, or "two-point", perspective. In imagination you could extend the two tapering faces of the structure until they converge to two vanishing points. Both points are on an imaginary horizontal line running across your "picture", one well to the left, and the other to the right.

Move closer to the subject and the convergence of each of the two sides appears steeper. This is because the nearest corner grows larger more rapidly than the farthest corners. The building looks much deeper and more massive. The same principle applies whether you are looking at a block of buildings, a small box, or a lump of sugar. Cubic or rectangular shapes are easiest to conceive in perspective terms, but the same visual

changes happen with circular and irregular shapes, too. If a pattern of circles was painted on the sides of the building, you would see them become increasingly elliptical as perspective increases.

"Three-point", or oblique, perspective involves three vanishing points. Imagine looking down at a cubic block, like a packing case, from one corner. All the horizontal lines in the object converge toward vanishing points to left and right (this time high in the "frame"). The vertical lines now converge, too, because you are looking down at the object. They lead to a third vanishing point that is situated some distance below the bottom edge of the picture.

All these forms of linear perspective — in one, two, or three, planes — grow steeper the closer you are to the subject, and become less when distance is increased. In photography it is unnecessary to actually know how to draw perspective accurately, but you still need to be able to make conscious use of its effects for structuring pictures and creating a sense of depth. Basic understanding of linear perspective is also important in learning to use different lenses (see *Additional equipment,* pp. 184-94). It is interesting to note that the invention of photography in the nineteenth century meant that the camera increasingly took over the role of precise perspective drawing. But at the same time artists turned away from strict geometrical perspective accuracy.

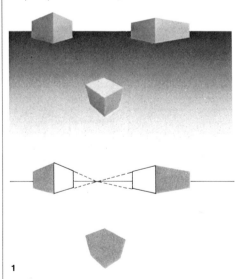

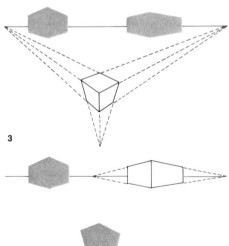

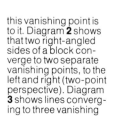

3

1

2

Vanishing points
The diagram (above left) shows a "scene" containing three blocks. Their shapes as shown here, on paper, are far from square, but because they have been drawn using linear perspective, we read them as realistic, three-dimensional forms. Diagram **1** shows single-point perspective. Oblique surfaces facing each other taper toward one common vanishing point. The more oblique the surface is to you (left-hand block), the closer this vanishing point is to it. Diagram **2** shows that two right-angled sides of a block converge to two separate vanishing points, to the left and right (two-point perspective). Diagram **3** shows lines converging to three vanishing points (three-point perspective), because you are now looking down on the foreground block. Notice how perspective is steeper because the object is nearer.

Viewpoint and linear perspective

Linear perspective is a powerful means of implying depth, especially when your subject has clear-cut outlines and contains strong pattern or texture. (It is completely lost over areas of plain sky or ground detail.)

The exteriors and interiors of buildings, patterned floors, roads, and fences all reveal convergence strongly when you look at their dominant lines from an oblique angle. Hard lighting will help to emphasize linear forms, and also cast shadows which create additional lines and patterns. Viewpoint is the key to perspective, so decide carefully whether a slight shift to the left or right, up or down, will give a more interesting visual structure. As convergence becomes shallower in one plane, you usually find that another steepens. Move farther back to flatten perspective on all planes at once. (You can overcome the problem of the consequent small subject size by using a telephoto lens – see *Telephoto lenses,* pp. 189-92 – or by enlarging a part of the picture only, in post-camera processes.)

Using two-point perspective creates two sets of lines converging toward two separate vanishing points. Along with a sense of depth and distance, you now have two potential centers of interest, created left and right by these lead-in lines. You can often make use of a device, such as a feature on the distant horizon, in one or both areas, or crop the lines short. The eye travels through the picture along these lines (see *Lead-in lines,* p. 72) relating center and edges in a dynamic way. So, as well as using this device for adding a feeling of depth and distance to a picture, you can use it for connecting foreground with background.

Often your subject will contain pairs of parallel planes – walls in room interiors, passages, or buildings on either side of a street. From an oblique viewpoint, perspective then

gives linear convergence to one centralized vanishing point, sometimes called "central projection". Moving your viewpoint sideways, upward, or downward shifts this point of emphasis around the frame, but as long as you include both facing planes, it remains within the picture area. If possible, arrange that this vanishing point contains a subject that has a particular significance, since it is so efficiently emphasized by the lines that lead to it.

Objects breaking any of these powerful diagonal lines also naturally attract attention, as they break a pattern. A good way of exploiting central projection is to have some nearby foreground object – such as a man's head and shoulders – placed so that the linear perspective of the street behind surrounds him with radiating lines. Altering camera lens aperture (see *Choosing depth of field,* p. 119), will allow you to control precisely the sharpness of the lines in relation to the figure.

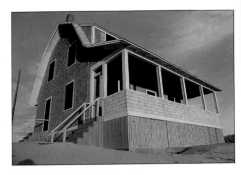

Three-point perspective
In this picture of a house, by Andrew de Lory, a close viewpoint, with the camera tilted upward, makes the lines of the building converge toward three separate vanishing points. Convergence is always more pronounced in an actual picture, because shapes can be closely compared with the straight lines and corners of the frame.

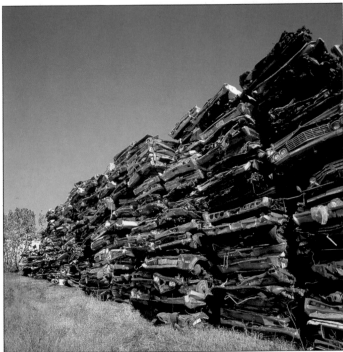

Convergent lines
For this stack of old vehicles, Robert Estall has chosen an oblique viewpoint and used perspective to create a tight, wedge-shaped image. To the left, the eye is rapidly directed to the end of the stack, where it is "stopped" by a tree.

Aerial perspective

Aerial, or atmospheric, perspective is the use of subtle tonal or color variations to suggest planes at many different distances. The phrase comes from landscape work and means the depiction of atmospheric effects. Distant objects in landscapes tend to look progressively paler in tone and colder in color, depending on the content of the atmosphere. The classic example is a view across a range of hills. Each ridge separates out as a different color shade and tone value.

The reason for this change with distance is that we are looking through miles of air laden with water and dust particles. These impurities impede the passage of light and gradually eliminate the detail of features, leaving only silhouette shapes where objects at substantially different distances overlap. Hills, buildings, and trees appear in delicate but clearly separate tones because air impurities between one group of objects and another scatter light, making the air seem slightly luminous. Areas that would normally be either full of detail or a black silhouette "fill in" with flat, bluish-gray tone. The scene resembles a series of cardboard cut-out shapes overlapping one another. The farther away the viewer is from the scene, the more this fill-in occurs, and consequently the contrast between the objects that are most distant and the sky steadily decreases.

The tendency in aerial perspective toward cold, blue colors is due to factors similar to those that cause sunlight to grow more orange at dusk (see *Time of day,* p. 23). Air molecules scatter light most readily from the short-wave, blue end of the spectrum, and the more air we look through, the greater its blue haze effect, although water vapor and dust or smog particles tend to absorb some of this blue from the air, leaving a more grayish cast. This is why, when we look across a range of hills, each "cardboard cut-out" tends to gradate to a paler color and tone in its lower parts, due to greater moisture content in the valleys. The tone contrast makes the upper area of each individual ridge stand out even more strongly. This adds to the theatrical effect.

Although all the features of aerial perspective are obvious to the naked eye, we respond to them largely unconsciously when judging depth and distance. This is why they are such an important aid to suggesting distance and scale in composition. Photographic film adds its own particular influence, too. Unlike the eye, all films are responsive to some ultraviolet light. Since the atmosphere scatters UV even more readily than blue wavelengths, photographs show marked tone and color recession.

For fine examples of the moody, depth-creating use of aerial perspective, look at landscape painting by Claude, Turner, Pissarro, and Monet. Many landscape photographers exploit this device very effectively, too. Photographers such as Ernst Haas (see *Major exponents of Dynamism,* pp. 358-61), Ansel Adams, and Albert Renger-Patzsch (see *Individuals and movements of Straight photography,* pp. 343-6) all make a point of using it.

Exploiting aerial perspective

In landscape work, exploiting aerial perspective means waiting for the most appropriate

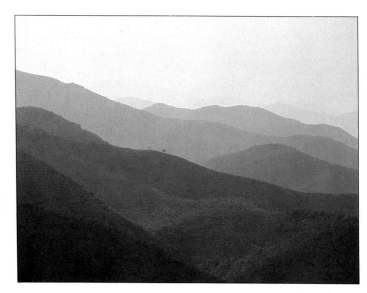

Distance in landscape
This mountain landscape by Robert Estall gives a strong impression of depth and distance, because of aerial perspective. Notice the changes in color as well as tone, from foreground to background. Values become increasingly weak toward the horizon, as moisture in the atmosphere dilutes color and detail.

Overlap and false attachment

Most photographers have, at some time, taken a portrait in which a tree, or a pole, seems to be "growing" out of the subject's head in a destructive or comical way. This overlap, which makes one object look as though it is joined to another is called "false attachment". It can be treated as a fault, or used positively.

Overlap, on a large scale, can either create a claustrophobic compression of space, or can help to make a picture look deeper. Lighting and viewpoint are the most important factors in determining this. Soft, frontal lighting minimizes tonal separation, whereas hard side- or rim-lighting helps to pick out and separate objects. A distant, high viewpoint helps to minimize patterns which recede rapidly, and plays down sharp changes in scale, while a close viewpoint shows maximum amount of difference between near and distant objects.

Overlap and false attachment allow you to join up lines which are actually at different distances from each other. If one corner of a roof coincides with the ridge of a hill behind, and another joins up with a foreground structure, the overall effect is of flattened depth. If all these features are similar in tone or color, the eye runs their shapes together, so that they form a single backdrop. To create a dramatic sense of depth, adjust your viewpoint so that all the various features appear at different levels. You can show their variety of form by using side-lighting to enhance tone differences.

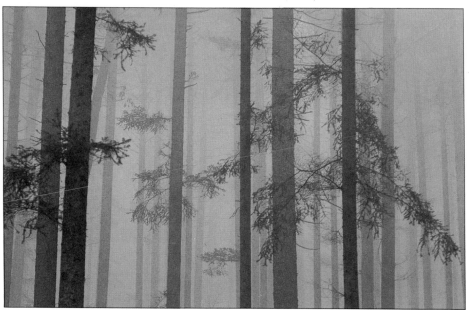

Mist for aerial perspective
Thick mist in dense woodland gives an exaggerated form of aerial perspective, on a smaller scale.

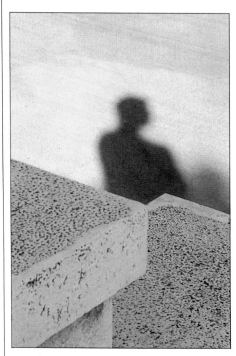

Structure through false attachment
Franco Fontana, in his shadow composition, makes careful use of false attachment as a structural device. Precise viewpoint choice joins together the lines and angles of the foreground stone slabs, and places the cast shadow of an unseen figure as though resting against them. It is difficult for the viewer to understand where the figure is actually standing.

natural conditions, and then carefully selecting viewpoint. A summer heat haze, smoke, or fall mist will give maximum depth and atmosphere. City pictures at dusk, when some haze is present have a much stronger feeling of depth than when the air is clear. Back- or side-lighting is preferable to front-lighting. It is also best to choose a viewpoint which shows several widely distanced objects overlapped — try to include some objects in the foreground and mid-distance.

To minimize depth and maximize distant detail, choose a time when heavy rain has literally "washed" the air clean, and the sun is behind you. A UV filter or pale-pink haze filter (see *Special effects attachments,* pp. 198-200) will further reduce color shift toward blue with distance. Viewpoint should be as square-on to the scene as possible, and preferably high enough to avoid all foreground. Alternatively, you can create a false impression of aerial perspective by using strong colors in the foreground together with weaker background colors. It is possible to apply most of these aspects of aerial perspective to subjects indoors, too. Any scene with dark or shadowed objects in the foreground and increasingly lighter objects toward the background seem to possess more depth than when these tone values are reversed. This is one reason why flash mounted on the camera reduces the sense of perspective unnaturally by reversing the dark to light progression.

Using false attachment

It is often possible to create carefully structured images using false attachment by intentionally lining up objects at different distances within the frame, so that they form a relationship with each other. You must be able to align the objects with absolute accuracy. Not all cameras allow you to do this with sufficient precision. (Direct vision cameras will not give you a precise preview – see *Direct vision compact cameras*, pp. 104-5.)

Choose the moment or the viewpoint which shows forms overlapping to create patterns. For example, a small flower may center on a larger, more distant, flower of similar form. False attachment can be a rich source of surrealistic images. A traffic sign hiding part of a figure, or a fist held out so that it conceals the owner's face both create visual ambiguities. They can express things about people and situations – becoming symbols of the relationship between man and machine, or of a faceless society. Look at the work of Christian Vogt for examples of this (see below, and *Leading exponents of Structuralism and Abstraction*, pp. 364-8).

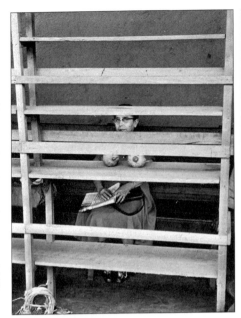

Humorous attachment
Elliott Erwitt used false attachment to create this visual pun (above). Often in candid pictures the people featured have no idea of their relationship to objects in front or behind them. People standing in front of billboards can be particularly rich sources of humorous pictures.

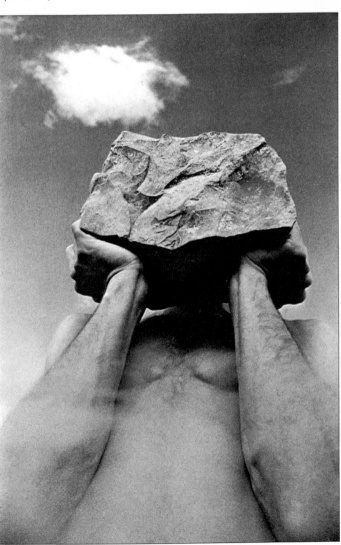

Attachment as symbol
In his picture of a man with a rock held in front of his face, Christian Vogt has made simple but powerful use of false attachment. Low viewpoint makes the rock's vertical lines converge, so that its shape corresponds with that of a head. Shape is further reflected in the white cloud above. The picture takes on symbolic connotations.

Depth through scale change

One of the visual clues to depth in a scene is the variation in size between things that are near, and those that are far away. A large figure in the same picture as a small figure will appear closer to you, provided that the figures both relate appropriately to other depth clues in the image (such as linear perspective). You can see this result clearly if you cut two figures from such a print, and reverse their original

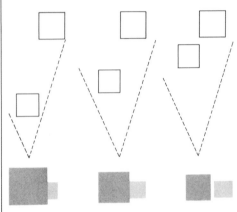

Distance and size
In these three comparative situations, the rear object is the same distance from the viewer throughout. It therefore remains the same size. If the other, identically sized, block is located progressively farther away from the viewer, it looks noticeably smaller each time.

positions. This explains why, on a plain, light background such as snow or sand, it can be very difficult to determine whether two objects are identical in size but situated at different distances, or different in size but situated at the same distance.

The apparent size of physically identical objects depends upon their relative distances from you. A post will look twice the height of another if it is only one-half as far away. If the ratio of distances between you and the near and far objects is 1:4, the near one will look four times the size of the far one, and so on. The higher this ratio is, the greater the sense of distance will be.

It is therefore always possible to increase depth by organizing the composition so that the nearest object in the scene is much closer than the farthest object. In a landscape, include a tree or figure very close to you in the foreground. Sometimes, when photographing buildings, for example, a slight shift of viewpoint to one side will be sufficient to bring an additional foreground element into the frame. This will give an indication of the building's scale, as well as providing an increase in the depth of the picture. Unless you want to use foreground objects to give an impression of environment, it can be effective to show them as shadows only, so that they appear just as shapes. This means that you can avoid showing extraneous details which conflict with, or distract attention from, the main subject of the picture.

To flatten depth, lower the ratio of distances by moving back from any near objects. A tele-

Abrupt scale change
This portrait by Willem Diepraam corresponds with the close-up block (facing page, far left) in the diagram. The man's head, dominating the frame, makes the back ground recede rapidly. The effect of depth is further enhanced by the oblique view down the street.

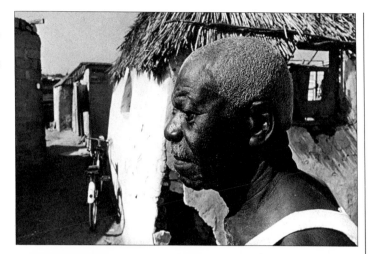

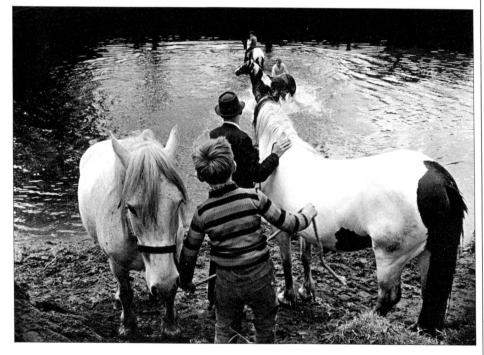

Depth illusion

The eye's sense of depth and distance can be deceived by structures that are carefully designed to have false perspective. This kind of illusion is used regularly in the theater, where flat surfaces are painted with scenes, using artificially steep perspective to give the audience an impression of greater depth than really exists. In photography, the single "eye" of the camera is used from one close, fixed viewpoint, and the same idea can be taken much further.

One design, the Ames room, is constructed so that, from the correct viewpoint, it appears to be a normal, six-sided, cubic room. In fact, the structure itself is quite different. Typically,

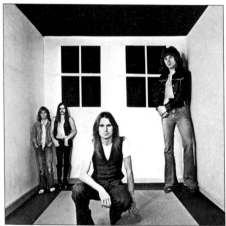

Distorting room
A room with distorted proportions was used to give an illusion of very different figure sizes. The figures on the left are standing twice as far from the photographer as the others. The man on the right is only a few inches behind the one in the center. The diagram shows the room from the back, illustrating its irregular shape, which converges to a vanishing point at one side. The Ames room is designed to be looked into from one

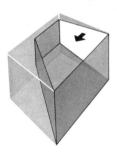

particular viewpoint only – marked with an arrow. From any other viewpoint, the effect is completely lost.

photo lens (see *Telephoto lenses,* pp. 189-92) will still allow you to fill the frame from this new viewpoint. (This type of lens also has the effect of suppressing perspective.) Notice, too, how any viewpoint that positions you about the same distance from all the objects in a scene has a space-reducing effect. A row of automobiles that gave a vivid impression of depth from a viewpoint close to one end becomes a flat pattern from a completely square-on viewpoint. They all look exactly the same size, and no one vehicle looks larger or more important than any of the others.

Although viewpoint is the most important practical factor in controlling relative scale, lighting makes a significant contribution, too. Strong tonal contrast created by harsh back- or side-lighting draws attention to shapes. Cast shadow can form secondary shape comparisons. Detail of texture and form of nearby objects sometimes emphasizes their nearness. In photography certain distorting

Gradual scale change
Careful viewpoint choice, making the figures and horses decrease steadily in size with distance, gives a vivid impression of depth even though the nearest and farthest

elements are actually quite close. The eye is drawn quickly to the top of the picture by the curving, inverted funnel-shape of the group. The picture is by Stephen Oliver.

lenses, too, such as extreme wide-angle, fisheye types (see *Wide-angle lenses,* pp. 186-9) add to the effect of scale change. Unlike the human eye's capability, they allow you to move right in close to a foreground subject. This results in a marked size increase in the subject, but still includes the whole scene, and gives maximum depth of field.

the rear wall doubles in height from right to left, but is angled away steeply. This allows diminution of size with distance to exactly counteract change in height, making the wall look square-on. The other walls and the floor are sloped to link up imperceptibly. When you see several people situated in different parts of an Ames room, they appear dramatically different in height, because of their widely varied distances. However, you are so convinced by the room, and preconditioned to believe that rooms are always regular in dimension, that it is the people who look false instead.

Timing and movement

Still photography is not capable of "replaying" changes in time and space. Yet much of our understanding and appreciation of what we see depends on recognizing characteristic forms of motion, and observing changes over time. The problem of encapsulating timing and movement in a still image is similar to the challenge of representing depth and distance. It is necessary to use visual symbols.

Compositional methods

There are several compositional methods which will help to communicate movement. Most are used in drawing and painting, as well as photography. The position of a moving subject in the frame is important – it can appear either to be just entering the scene, or just about to leave it, depending on where it is placed. Creating blur of various kinds, to separate moving and static objects, or to give the viewer an impression of movement, is another useful technique. Dynamic picture structure – the use of diagonal lines and tight angles – contributes symbols of activity. The massing of color and tone, the use of scale and perspective can also all contribute to the impression of being in motion. Another way of working is to create a short sequence of images – our experience of reading strip cartoons makes it easy for us to understand sequences of separate images as being expressions of continuous events.

Sense of moment

Perhaps more than any other factor, it is the photographer's choice of the exact moment in time to fire the shutter which determines how an action will look. This sense of moment is vital for all kinds of animated subject. Moving subjects, as well as transient expressions, shapes, and forms changing because of altered angles, call for rapid reactions from the photographer. At the moment of firing the shutter, all these relationships become fixed, and invite closer scrutiny. The untypical expression is now permanent, the false attachment cannot be separated. Faced with this challenge, and having to make instantaneous decisions, photographers must snatch compositional guides, such as the use of lines, tone, and balance, as and where they can. It is a measure of the talents of photographers such as Elliot Erwitt and Robert Frank that their pictures are strongly structured, and at the same time capture the essence of rapidly changing events.

See also
The shutter *Shutter firing systems*, p. 126. Using slow shutter speeds, pp. 127-8. Using fast shutter speeds, pp. 129-31. Special effects lighting *Physiograms*, p. 180; *Creating light trails*, p. 180. Zoom lenses *Zooming effects*, pp. 192-4. Filter and lens attachments *Special effects attachments*, pp. 198-200. Scientific and technical photography *Contracting time*, p. 275; *High-speed photography*, pp. 275-7. Natural history photography, pp. 300-3. Sports photography, pp. 304-9. Reportage photography, pp. 324-7. Dynamism, pp. 357-60.

Framing the action

You can imply action and movement by the actual location of an object within the confines of the frame. The amount of space remaining around an object, in relation to the four sides of the picture, can be interpreted in several different ways. It is as if we were looking at the action on a stage in a theater. A large space facing a figure which is positioned at the extreme end of the frame will suggest that the figure is about to move forward. To use another example, it is quite possible to take a picture of a train from the side either so that it is centrally placed in the frame, with equal lengths of track ahead and behind. Or you can frame it so that it is off-center, so that it seems to be either

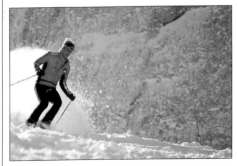

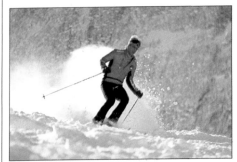

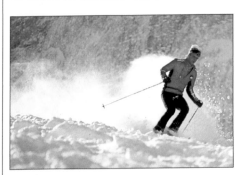

Deciding position
The three shots of the skier show how you can frame the same subject in different ways. In the top version the figure is entering the frame, and the picture conveys a sense of potential movement by showing the distance he still has to travel. The middle version, with the figure centered in the frame, is indecisive, and shows the least sense of movement. In the third shot, with the skier leaving the frame, the cloud of snow behind him and the space to the left of the frame, emphasize the distance he has traveled.

arriving at the scene or leaving it.

A figure lying spreadeagled at the bottom of a tall, narrow picture which is mostly filled with wall and is just revealing a patch of sky at the top of the frame, for example, could suggest that the figure has just fallen off the wall. The same situation, framed so that he appears at the top of the frame instead, and showing sand and sea in the foreground, could suggest that the figure has just dragged himself out of the sea. Some fine sports pictures, originally shot with the action in the center of the frame, have been cropped and printed at an angle in order to add a sense of imbalance – transforming an average action picture into a dynamic sports photograph.

Dynamic structure

You can suggest movement and action through the dynamic structuring of the subject itself (see *Dynamic balance, p. 77*). For example, choosing a viewpoint which tilts and converges the tightly composed lines of a bicycle will suggest movement even when it is in fact completely stationary. Whenever an object is positioned in contradiction to the normal horizontal/vertical axis, movement seems to be implied. There are many naturally occurring examples of this effect. Portraits containing numerous angles, buildings made up of strongly converging lines, or a swirling circular staircase, all harness our own inbuilt visual sense of movement.

Notice that the eye readily follows linear forms, and that we can almost "feel" the en-

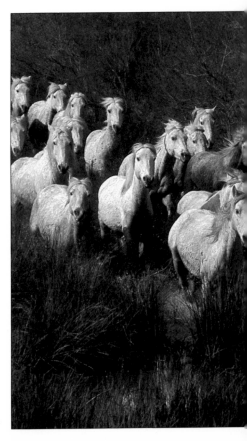

ergy in dynamic structures. This is a compositional aid which is easy to combine with other movement symbols, such as blur, for additional effect. To show a skier or a surfer, for example, try to choose a viewpoint which shows the lines of the water or snow spray shooting out at an angle, preferably backlit as well, so that they add strong diagonal lines to the picture structure.

To help achieve these effects on a more practical level, try using an extremely high or low viewpoint which will accentuate lines which converge and tilt. A wide-angled lens with a short focal length, will exaggerate these effects further (see *Wide-angle lenses,* pp. 186-7).

Peak of action

In many activities, particularly sporting events, there is a crucial moment when the action reaches its "peak" — for example, the split second when a high-jumper's leap changes from ascending to descending, as he slides over the crossbar. Choosing this very moment to fire the shutter can encapsulate and express the drama of the whole event very effectively. Peak of action is not necessarily confined to strenuous activity — it can apply to far more subtle, less obvious, movements, too. A person's expression on seeing something thrilling or horrifying can be just as much a peak as a boxer delivering his knock-out blow. Even waves crashing, or wind-gusted trees, can reach maximum movement at one particular instant. Sometimes there may be more than just one chance to capture the peak of action. Several horses passing over the same jump, repeated bursts of sparks in a fireworks display, or the same movements happening again and again in a dance performance, are all events that show similar actions happening repeatedly, which you can predict and plan for very precisely.

In some sporting events — any kind of jumping, for example — the action does in fact slow down just as it reaches its peak. So, with a certain amount of knowledge of the subject, plus a considered choice of viewpoint, and shutter speed to freeze or blur (see *Using fast shutter speeds,* pp. 129-31, and *Using slow shutter speeds,* pp. 127-8), capturing such key moments can be easier than it might seem. But for

most fast actions, the "trigger" route from eye to brain to finger absorbs too much time. You must have the patience to study the action and anticipate the moment. Anticipation is much easier if you have first-hand knowledge of the subject — this is why so many top sports photographers are themselves ex-participants. Often they can judge the moment so exactly that they can literally press the shutter the instant *before* the peak of action, so that reaction time is eliminated.

Ultra-fast events in science or nature subjects — and many activities which can take place under controlled conditions — can be made to activate the shutter themselves. You must know the physical position or time when peak of action will occur, then use automatic triggering, perhaps with a beam-breaking device, to fire the shutter and flash (see *Shutter firing systems,* p. 126). Camera motor drives offer a fast "burst" of images, but do not necessarily guarantee that any one exposure will coincide with the peak of action. Even at the fastest rates, far more time is spent transporting film than recording the action (see *Motor drives and camera backs,* p. 202). If one frame *does* capture the peak, a short sequence that includes "before" and "after" shots can be a good way of making a sequence of photographs which shows the activity as a chain of connected actions.

Diagonal framing
In this photograph of galloping wild horses in the Camargue region of the South of France, the impression of movement has been greatly emphasized by careful framing choice. The long, diagonal line the horses are tracing across the horizontal frame gives the picture an atmosphere of dynamism. The composition is made even more dramatic by the way the white animals are emerging from their dark background, and a high viewpoint has enabled us to see the animal's features distinctly. The photograph is by Hans Silvester.

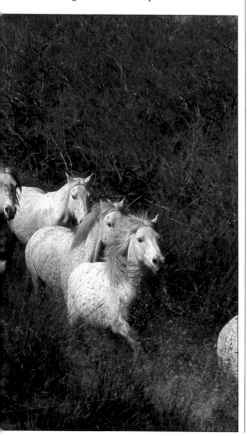

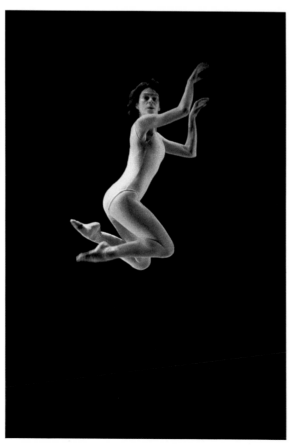

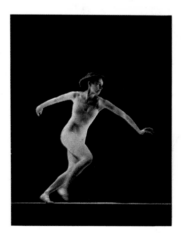

Run-up
This picture (above) shows a dancer just about to jump. The blurred foot emphasizes her movement, but the picture also conveys her reserves of energy. There is a sense of anticipation of the leap to come.

Peak
At the highest point of the leap (left), the dancer is in slowest motion. It may be difficult to decide when this moment has arrived, and when to fire the shutter, since body shape may be changing constantly. The same problems apply to many kinds of sports photography. Both pictures are by David Buckland.

The critical moment

In a situation which is changing continuously, there is often one moment when all the elements come together perfectly to form an effective image. You can sometimes capture such a critical moment by chance, but more often it is a matter of anticipation, fast reaction, and even your own organization of the event itself. Whichever way you work, it will be helpful to use a small, unobtrusive camera with a quiet shutter. A motor drive attachment or a power winder may also be useful, but they tend to be noisy and attract attention. Carrying a large amount of conspicuous equipment will also tend to draw attention when it is least convenient.

The critical moment can influence a picture's structure as well as its content. You may have to wait until a vehicle moving along a distant, winding road is in exactly the right position within a landscape to balance the picture. A figure at one end of a sidewalk may complete the structure of a picture when reaching the convergence of several perspective lines. It may even be necessary to wait for a matter of hours before a gap in storm clouds allows a solitary beam of sunlight to illuminate the metal roof of a building.

In human situations, critical moments produce strong pictures where content is important. Quick reactions will enable you to capture transient expressions which sum up relationships. You may even be able to make these expressions occur in formal photographic sessions. A well-known instance of this happening was when the portraitist Yousuf Karsh produced a characteristic likeness of Sir Winston Churchill by snatching the cigar from his subject's mouth just before firing the shutter. The resulting picture is considered remarkable for its portrayal of personality.

Most press and sports photographers are adept at finding critical moments whenever events are happening quickly. Others, such as Lee Friedlander, Jacques-Henri Lartigue, and Henri Cartier-Bresson combine rapid reactions with an uncanny ability to be in the right place at the right time. This allows them to record events which are less spectacular, because the subject matter tends to be ordinary, even mundane, but create unique images from everyday human events, which take on a deeper significance.

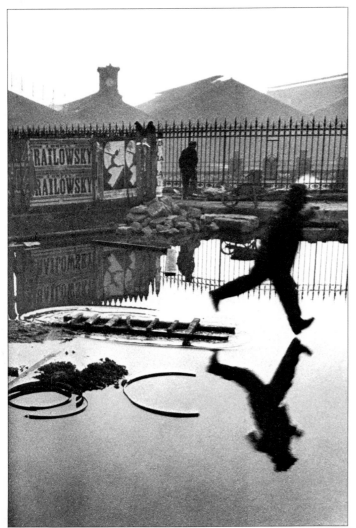

The decisive moment
Henri Cartier-Bresson's famous picture of a man leaping over a puddle was taken at precisely the right instant. A second sooner or later, and the impact of the picture would have been completely different. Although the subject is commonplace and not especially dramatic in itself, the picture is full of suspense and tension, coupled with humor. The man's heel is just about to come into contact with the water, so that we are left wondering how deep it actually is. The picture's framing intensifies the suspense, because we cannot see how far it is to the other side of the water. The reflection contributes to the picture's structure because it emphasizes the man's feet and his position, suspended in mid-air.

Picture sequences

Any set of shots from a film you have taken forms a picture sequence — a record showing the order in which you worked. It can illustrate the progress of a journey, how an event took place, or, in the case of a group of portraits, how your subject's expression altered.

Short picture sequences which you plan and edit provide a more interesting and varied way of communicating ideas. It is possible to plan sequences depicting changes in time (for example, by recording changing events from a static viewpoint) or representing changes in space (by changing viewpoint while photographing a static situation). Sequences can provide penetrating explorations of social behaviour in which picture content is vitally important, or analyze variations of picture structure, when the subject is less crucial.

Narrative themes
If a sequence has enough consistency from one picture to the next, the viewer will be able to read it as a picture story. As soon as you show two or three pictures of an identical setting, the eye notices any differences between them. It is usually best to keep a static viewpoint, so that the picture in the viewfinder becomes like a stage on which events can unfold. In this way you can narrate stories. You will need to define the beginning and the end of the sequence clearly, or give the sequence a cyclic form, so that you can start to read it at any point. You can create a false conclusion, overturning the viewer's expectations by providing a surprise or shock in the final frame.

An alternative way of working is to change viewpoint from picture to picture. You can continuously pull back the camera from the main subject, each time revealing something new about the surroundings. Each picture will show a surprisingly different background, but the images will remain linked by featuring the main element in the same position. Changing viewpoint can also be useful when you are recording an argument or conversation. Modifications in framing can show when one speaker is becoming dominant.

If you change viewpoint in a regular way you can scan a large area of a static subject. It is possible to record a whole room, gradually rotating the camera through 360°, using rows of pictures to record whole areas of wall and ceiling.

Long-term changes
Sequences can also record events over a period of time, allowing comparison later. The construction or demolition of a building, children growing up, the stages in converting a room or completing a painting, can all be covered informatively in this way. It is important to take the pictures for such a sequence from the same viewpoint and distance, with similar lighting and background conditions, whenever this is possible. Scientific and nature photographers use sequences of pictures taken at regular intervals (see *Contracting time,* p. 275) to record and analyze movement and change. High-speed sequences can show the path of a bullet or the flight of a bird through the air. Slower series can illustrate the growth of plants, or a chicken hatching from an egg.

Death comes to the old lady

Duane Michals specializes in making picture sequences that tell a story. As this example shows, his images often involve strange or mystical events. The pictures are carefully staged, and make extensive use of the special image qualities of photography, such as blur, manipulation of tonal values, and change of scale, to create disturbing results. The first and last pictures are the most important. In this sequence, the first sets the scene, and the last provides an unexpected climax. In all sequences economy is essential. Each picture takes the narrative a step further, preserving continuity without using unnecessary images. Each frame contains an image which is strong in its own right, and they combine to make a tightly structured whole.

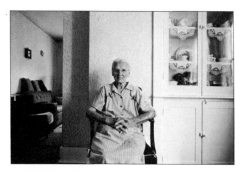

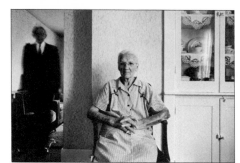

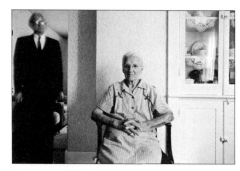

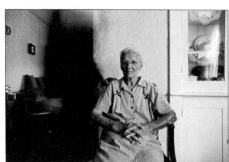

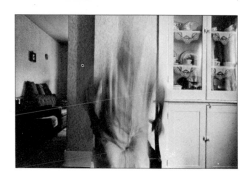

The demolition of an hotel

These pictures by David Agar show five stages in the destruction of an old hotel. The photographer has used the sequence to make an objective record of the event, and also to illustrate the passage of time. Framing, viewpoint, and lighting have been kept as consistent as possible, allowing the viewer to measure the changes in relation to constant surroundings. It should be possible to read a good sequence at a glance, so look for clear indications that the subject has changed significantly in each frame.

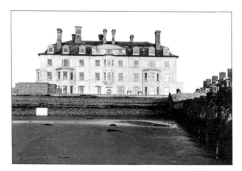

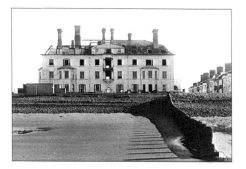

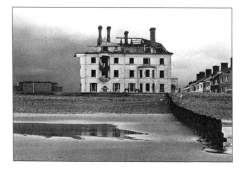

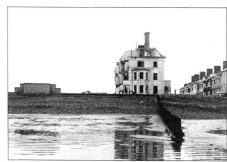

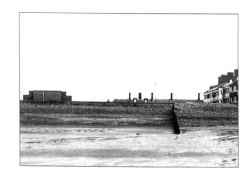

The camera's portrayal

The development of the camera itself has influenced the way in which movement has been portrayed in pictures of all kinds. Early cameras and photographic equipment required exposures of many seconds, even minutes, during which time wind-blown trees blurred, and moving pedestrians and carriages recorded as indistinct streaks. What were actually considered by photographers to be errors, deeply interested the artists of the day – particularly Corot and the Impressionists. They took the lead from these so-called mistakes, and used them to symbolize movement in their paintings.

As equipment improved and briefer exposures became possible, the camera showed that it could reveal actions that were actually far too rapid for the eye to follow. Eadweard Muybridge in America, and Etienne Marey in France both devised systems which would produce frozen sequences, so that they could analyze the rapid movements of both humans and animals. The art world was shaken to discover that many famous paintings showed actions, such as horses galloping, totally inaccurately. Muybridge went on to make hundreds of sequences, covering the many movements of birds, animals, and athletes. When these were published, they were quickly adopted by artists and used as standard visual references for drawn illustration. Objective painters followed the accuracy of the camera, and from the 1880s onward, it is possible to observe marked changes in the ways moving objects were shown in paintings. Artists were able to correct the mistakes they had been perpetuating (this included many of

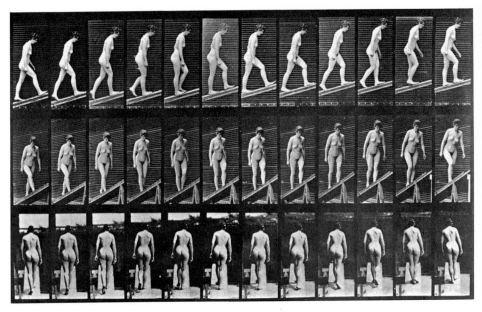

the most notable artists of the day).

Other influences, particularly the much greater freedom of composition within the format, and the use of the actual picture edges (see *Unconventional framing*, p. 68), originate from the results of hand-held snapshot cameras, which were introduced around the beginning of the present century. Although derided by many people, these naïve pictures were eventually to help set photography free from the pretensions and restrictions of aping more formal art.

Analyzing movement
To produce this sequence of pictures, showing a woman walking up a sloping surface, Eadweard Muybridge used fast-shutter cameras working simultaneously from three viewpoints. Muybridge was one of the first photographers to analyze body movement accurately. Some of his pictures freeze actions occurring too fast for the human eye to follow. By presenting these pictures rapidly in sequence, the subject appears to move, a fact which influenced the inventors of the movie process.

Controlling the setting

With advanced planning, you can strengthen action by controlling the setting and positioning the moving subject, in a considered way. You may have to shoot candid pictures as and when they occur, and a sense of confusion may well be an intrinsic part of the scene. But for most action pictures, you should plan your viewpoint so that the setting is exactly right, and then wait for the event to take place. Results will be less cluttered and there is often time to choose a vantage point which will give the most effective lighting and composition. You can make sure the subject is strongly emphasized by devices such as line, juxtaposition of color and tone, and actual positioning within the confines of the frame. Ideally, the surroundings should contribute a dynamic flow to the action, as well as giving it a context and meaning. Photographing a road cycle race from a rooftop viewpoint, for example, can make the gray buildings on either side of the street converge toward the ribbon of color and action in the center. In a sprint, all the excitement and effort is concentrated around the finishing line, so you can compose the picture around the line itself, in advance. An object like a diving board or a gymnast's beam can also offer a fixed point of reference to compose a picture around.

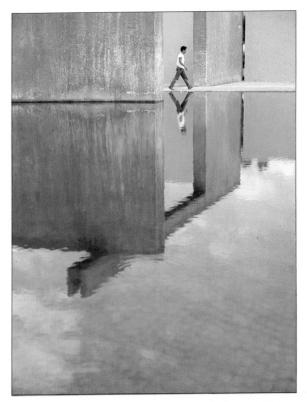

Adding life to a scene
The setting of wall and reflection was carefully selected by the photographer, who then waited for the moving figure to appear and move to the right position before pressing the shutter. In a situation like this, reaction time in shooting is critical. The figure's shape and placing in relation to the background can change in a fraction of a second. The photograph is by Robin Bath.

Blur as a movement device

We are very used to experiencing blur, even if we are not actually conscious of it. Simply rotating the head rapidly turns nearby static objects into blur. Looking at the ground while walking or running shows detail dissolved into lines. Looking out of the side window of a moving vehicle allows a more leisurely study of blur — especially of the way in which the effect decreases with distance. Static objects just beyond the window glass look blurred when you are barely moving, yet from an airplane, the landscape miles below seems blur-free, even at supersonic speeds. Seen from a vehicle, the pattern of blur is mostly dominated by streaks of light, rather than by dark tones — minute highlights are drawn out into lines.

One of the great strengths of photography is that it can capture blur pattern just as you experience it in reality, whereas drawing and painting cannot. It can also control the degree and type of blur, and even create it deliberately, or remove it altogether. By choosing whether to use blur, where to allow it, and how much, you can control the amount of apparent movement you show quite precisely. You can effectively speed it up, slow it down, or even halt it completely.

You have several options with most moving subjects. By keeping a static viewpoint, you can show the moving subject blurred, but static surroundings blur-free. Alternatively, if you are moving with the same speed and in the same direction as a moving subject (for example, one car driven alongside another) you can show it sharp and clear, against blurred surroundings. A picture like this gives a much stronger sense of participating in the action. You can produce it by swinging the camera ("panning") to keep the subject static in the frame (see *Panning moving subjects*, p. 128). A practical example of how this works is the way in which you can decipher the name of a

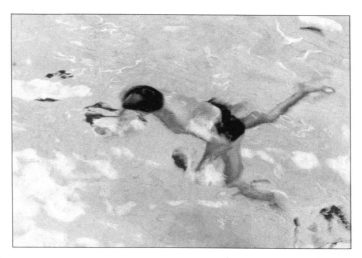

Softening detail
In the photograph of a swimmer, Tony Foo has exaggerated the water's distorting effect by using a slow shutter speed and panning.

Zoom and blur
Robert Estall used a zoom lens for his picture of Christmas illuminations. A long exposure and adjustment of the zoom control produced blur which gives an impression of movement.

train station from a moving train, by rapidly scanning the sign in the opposite direction to the train's movement. This briefly makes the sign static enough to read the letters.

Viewpoint, in relation to direction of movement, changes the pattern of blur. A side-on view gives mostly vertical or horizontal lines. When you are looking obliquely, lines converge toward an out-of-frame vanishing point. Driving a car down a street, particularly at night, makes you aware of blur lines diverging from a central vanishing point. Pictures with these dynamic structures seem to be rushing toward or away from you. The shape of the lines, too, suggests the smoothness or roughness of movement. Slight or open-curved lines may be the result of smooth travel and so you can use them to symbolize calm and tranquillity, while rough, wiggly lines are a symbol of jerky movement. Equally, lines which conflict and tangle with each other can suggest conflict and confusion.

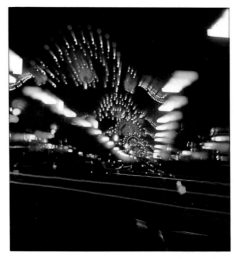

Abstraction by blur

Blur mixes the colors of the image together in the same way that an artist smears paints into each other on a canvas. Since light rather than pigment is involved, blurring has a shadow-filling, lightening effect. Results can often be abstract. Long exposure and fast, sideways-on subject movement create streaks of tone and color. A figure wearing a jacket decorated with bands of color, running against a dark background, forms a pattern of colored horizontal bars at a close viewpoint. At night, the slow movement of pinpoints of light traces out abstract lines. This means that you can think of a scene which contains moving, colored components as a potential palette, rather than as being interesting for the sake of its subject matter alone.

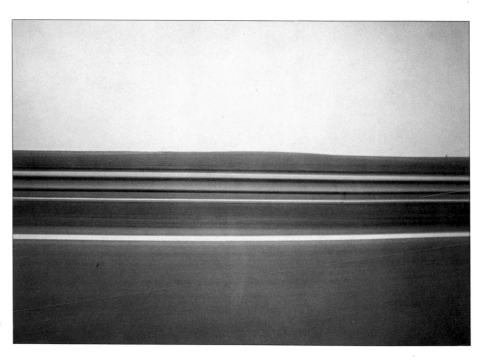

Pattern and blur
Franco Fontana's picture shows a highway taken from a moving vehicle. The fast horizontal movement makes vertical detail in the picture disappear — exaggerating the eye's impression of the scene. Each separate area of color in the image — the road surface, the crash barrier, and the grass — becomes a single abstract, horizontal band.

Juxtaposition and transient relationships

Photography's time-freezing facility is capable of revealing even the slightest actions. It can also capture briefly grouped people and present them as though they relate to each other in some permanent and significant way. The opportunities for these transient relationships in pictures are endless. A small boy momentarily walks in front of a policeman, but a photograph taken at this instant seems to show the man escorting the boy. A woman in a crowd blows on her cold knuckles while a totally unrelated man stands behind her with a bandaged jaw.

Like the false attachment of structures (see *Overlap and false attachment*, p. 83), transient relationships often occur by accident. The mere fact that two people are included in the same frame is often convincing in itself — they appear to be connected in some way. Sometimes such a coincidence takes on symbolic significance. An elderly man and a child passing in the street, for example, can epitomize youth and age.

Juxtaposition

You may be able to anticipate the juxtaposition of two or more elements in a picture, or plan it in advance. Photo-humorist Robert Doisneau, for example, has based many pictures on relating formal statues to people and things. Featuring a group of stone figures heavily coated with bird droppings, he planned his photograph to coincide with a flight of helicopters passing overhead.

You can also show the strange ways people become "cut-into" by parts of objects nearer to the camera. At any one moment in a street scene, the front of one person will be obscured, another person may be emerging from behind something, and a third may appear cut in half by a pole. False attachments can sometimes briefly form entirely new subject structures.

Two soldiers on guard cross each other's path at regular intervals. Shown from one side at the very moment of passing, their marching forms combine into a semi-symmetrical design. An interesting shape or setting often requires a second element added to make the complete statement. The cast shadow of two people embracing (the subjects being outside the picture format) can gain tension and mystery if by slight change of viewpoint you can include a third figure as a black foreground silhouette. Apart from using straight photography, it is also possible to create juxtaposition by double exposure, either in the camera or during printing processes (see *Multiple printing*, pp. 260-1).

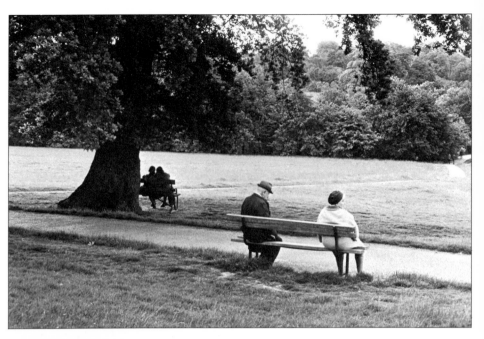

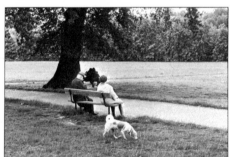

Implied relationships
John Chitty's two pictures show how the combination of perfect viewpoint and timing can affect dramatically the juxtaposition of elements in a picture and make all the difference to its meaning. The first, smaller, version bunches all the elements together, and confuses them. The extra element, the dog, only adds to this confusion. In the second, larger, version, the photographer moved a few yards, allowing him to emphasize the distance between the two old people, and clearly show the younger couple in the distance. The picture suggests how relationships can drift apart (even though we do not know if the two older people are even acquainted).

Humor and juxtaposition
Robert Doisneau's street scene suggests a fleeting relationship between two people. Although the woman seems cut off from the world in her telephone booth, she is momentarily associated with the man as the dogs touch.

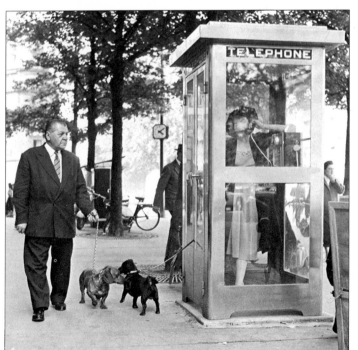

The whole image

Photographic composition, whether it is used as a means of artistic self-expression, or as a way of showing an object or an event more strongly, has inherited its own particular scope from many sources. Some of the guidelines of composition are traditional and come directly from well established principles (see *Positioning the subject,* p. 67, and *Golden mean,* p. 68). Other compositional aids, such as the selective use of blur and local sharpness, as used for example by Ernst Haas, come from the technical capabilities of the camera itself. These, in turn, influenced painters, and were adopted by them (for example, Giacomo Balla, Marcel Duchamp, and Francis Bacon). Composition in the fine arts in recent years has become more flexible, and the classical rules, which were thought essential, have lost their authority. Today, a more innovative and experimental climate exists, which leaves artists of all kinds free to express themselves without either being shackled by a set of rules, or using them as a substitute for ideas (for example Robert Frank and Ralph Gibson).

In this first section, the different areas of composition have been isolated and discussed as separate items. In practice, they rarely occur separately, and the photographer is usually confronted with several compositional problems simultaneously. For example, placing the subject in the strongest position in the frame, choice of format, proportion, and the use of lead-in lines all have to be considered. For emphasizing the key elements in a more complex scene, viewpoint, color or tone contrast, and the placing of frames within the frame, are all important. And when stressing depth, linear and aerial perspective, as well as viewpoint choice, are crucial devices to consider.

Composition and the subject

When photographing a static subject, there is time to make a considered judgment and adopt compositional guidelines which will best enhance the final result. If the subject is moving, the photographer may be able to capitalize on aspects which will turn it into a dynamic picture ingredient. Strong colors, angled lines, tight framing, and blurred movement will all add force and energy. But horizontal and vertical lines, muted hues, and viewpoints which make the subject look static, should all be rejected.

In photography, moving subjects have an extra quality. Unlike other media, photography can freeze movement in unexpected, unpredictable ways. The rapid, fleeting expression or the chance juxtaposition of two moving elements may make a picture which has a significance far beyond the subject's mundane nature.

With both static and moving subjects, composition can contribute substantially to mood and atmosphere. The color scheme, the proportion of light to dark, the amount of contrast and detail, are all important factors, too. While viewpoint in relation to the lighting direction and quality may completely transform the character interpret-

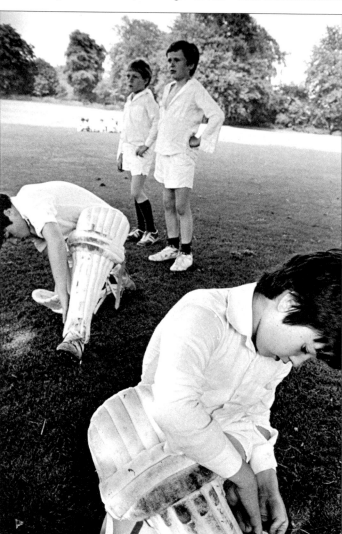

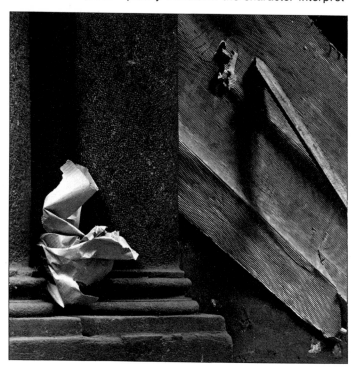

Documentary
Jan Ung's picture (left) is one of a series documenting life in an English public school. In this shot of boys preparing to play cricket, the photographer has chosen a viewpoint to frame the background figures between those in the foreground, emphasizing change of scale. This arrangement also leads the eye across the frame, giving the composition a dynamism which conveys the subject's sense of impending action. Because of this subject's transitory nature, it was essential for the photographer to react rapidly , in order to be sure of capturing the decisive moment.

Still life
This still life by John Goto (above) relies on the quality and direction of the light, and the careful placing of the picture's elements. The surface qualities of the wood, cardboard, and stone give richness of detail, while the different shapes provide visual variety. Low-key tonal values add atmosphere, while the light-toned paper acts as a point of emphasis.

ation and personality in a face, or the appearance of a building or landscape.

The art of photography

Composition is just one "tool" that photographers can make use of. But it must be used in conjunction with a sound knowledge of the basic ways in which light behaves, and how it interreacts with the physical properties of the subject itself. The direction, quality, and timing of light, and the ways it affects the surface textures, lines, shapes, patterns, forms, and colors offer infinite possibilities.

There is always a danger of using composition without thinking about its relevance to the subject. It should be used positively, as a way of strengthening pictures, not as a set of rules to restrict them. Like verbal grammar and phraseology, composition is a living, changing language.

An individual style

Photography has a vast range of possibilities and a broad appeal. Many photographers have chosen just one area and have explored it exclusively. Alexander Keighley became expert in his romantic use of natural light, while Edward Weston chose to explore the richness of structure and form, often irrespective of the nature of the subjects themselves. A few photographers move through many compositional approaches as their style changes. André Kertész has changed from the atmospheric interpretation of pictorial subjects through experimental distortions of form, to periods of surrealism, and a concern for structure.

As shown in the final section of this book (*Photographic styles,* pp. 328-83), photographers no longer form societies or "schools" as they did in the nineteenth century. Instead, their work is published and exhibited, so that what perhaps began as a personal eccentricity can widely influence other photographers.

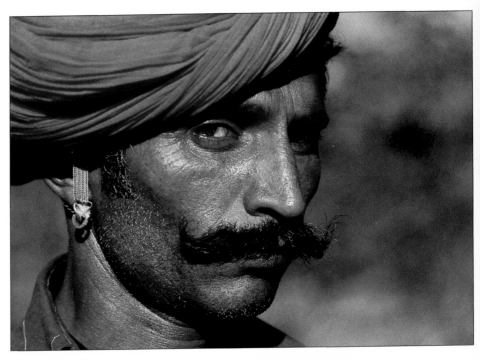

Portrait
The portrait (above) by Henry Wilson makes good use of photography's ability to record fine detail. The hard light emphasizes the reflective quality of the subject's skin, while tight framing and brilliant colors contribute strongly to the composition. The photographer has captured a momentary expression, conveying character.

Street figure
In the shot of a street sweeper (below) by Henry Wilson, the most important element is the atmosphere created by lighting. Backlighting exaggerates the dust in the air, suppressing surface colors and narrowing down the color range of the entire composition. Striking tonal emphasis and a powerful sense of shape are also important features of the picture.

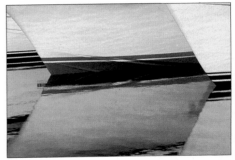

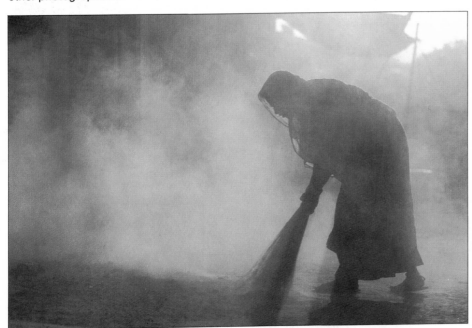

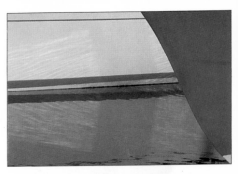

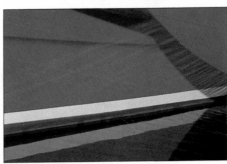

Subject qualities and picture structure
Milton Colindres, in his picture of a crouching man, combines qualities in the subject (form, shape, and pattern in particular) with a strong picture structure. The resulting image is complete and satisfying. The perfect reflection produces a powerful sense of symmetry and balance, and warm evening sun tints the whole picture, giving it continuity, and revealing three-dimensional form.

Abstracts
In the group of three abstracts (facing page), parts of boat hulls and their reflections are used as graphic picture ingredients. With precise framing, the photographer, Carol Sharp, has used areas of tone and color as movable elements in her compositions with the same freedom and control as if the images had been painted on canvas.

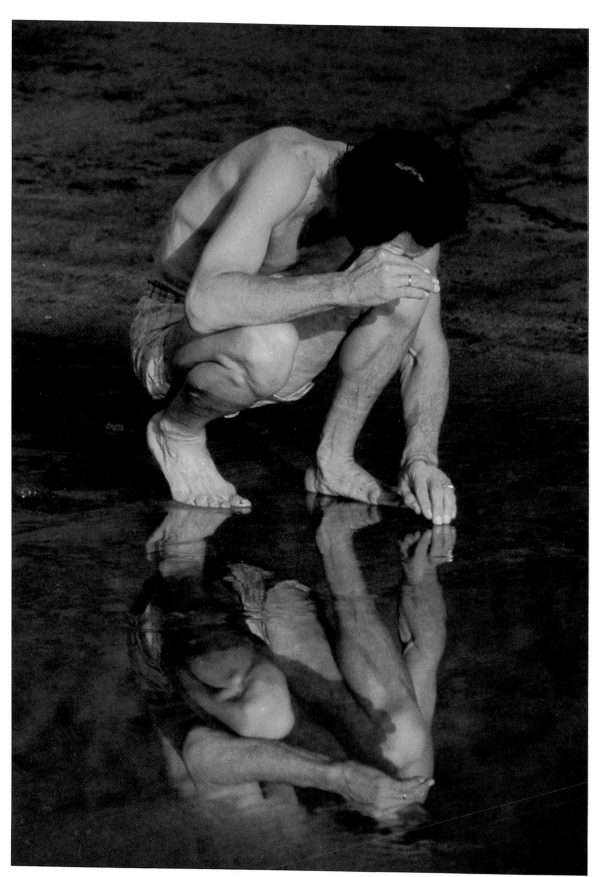

The techniques of photography

This section is concerned with the "machinery" of photography — equipment and processes by which you control what you see in the viewfinder and translate it into a negative or positive film image. Techniques have passed through enormous changes since the first photographs were taken in the early nineteenth century. Cameras, which were once large, primitive wooden boxes, have become diminutive devices packed with electronics. Optical, electronic, and engineering advances have been perfected to the level where cameras are so ingenious they are enjoyed and collected for their own sake. In fact, like expensive cars or sound equipment, ownership of the equipment can eclipse the purpose for which it was made.

In this section the function of cameras, films, lenses, lighting, and general photographic accessories are explained in detail, but regarded throughout as tools to make pictures. Relative features are compared from the point of view of the accuracy and control of visual results they make possible.

Because the technology of photography is changing and improving at an ever-increasing rate, a flexible attitude is essential. The cameras most amateur photographers will be using by the end of this century will almost certainly record images magnetically instead of photochemically, and today's wet processing of films (and papers) will probably be a thing of the past. None of these advances will occur overnight, however, and new technology can only be introduced at a rate acceptable to the average user. Anything that speeds up and simplifies the transition between the eye and final print (without loss of manipulative control when desired) is to be welcomed.

Since the 1890s film, in rolls, has gradually taken over from the old glass plates. Cameras themselves have reduced in operating complexity as well as in size, and have become infinitely more versatile. Lenses and films have increased in their ability to resolve fine detail so that today's 35 mm cameras offer a potential picture quality that was only available with a sheet film camera a generation ago. Automatically monitored exposure, which was initially frowned on by both amateur and professional, has now been accepted as a highly useful feature (provided it can be overridden by the user for difficult situations, such as back-lighting, or for particular effects).

The growth of the SLR camera
The greatest trend in camera development has been the growth of the 35 mm single lens reflex (SLR) camera design. Because of its popularity, prices for this product have dropped in real terms, and this has enabled more people than ever before to use a precision camera. In many ways, the SLR camera is easier to use than a separate viewfinder type camera (especially if the SLR is of the auto-programmed exposure type). The non-reflex camera is never quite accurate in showing within the viewfinder exactly what is being recorded by the film, especially at close subject distances. Also, as you focus a non-reflex there is no sharp/unsharp distinction in the appearance of subjects at various distances, as seen in the viewfinder of an SLR.

This is not to say that you cannot take excellent photographs on a direct viewfinder camera. Many photographers prefer the bright viewfinder display and quieter operation offered, but eventually most photographers do progress to an SLR camera. The ability to preview precisely the framing and sharpness of the picture as it will be recorded allows a much more direct link between the original scene and the final print or slide. For similar reasons, photography in color is visually more direct than photography in black and white. You see and compose in color, and so it takes additional experience to forecast how a picture will look in tones of gray. Before the 1940s, acceptable color materials hardly existed, and therefore photographers, at all levels, used black and white. Since that time, color film has been dramatically improved, and now dominates not only the popular market but also most fields of commercial magazine, fashion, and advertising photography. With few exceptions, the SLR and color film have become accepted as the norm.

The scope of cameras and their controls
The techniques of photography, as described in this section, begin with the major types of cameras in use today, and the function of each of their controls. Then, the main controls common to most cameras — focusing, aperture, and shutter settings — are discussed in terms of their individual and collective effect on the photographic image.

Each of the controls found on the camera allows you to alter the appearance of the resulting picture in a particular way. Simple cameras have few controls and are therefore easier to use, but they do tend to produce uniform results. A lens with focusing adjustments, for example, is more demanding to use than a fixed focus lens, but it does enable you to emphasize objects at chosen distances from the camera and make objects at other distances unsharp. This effect is known as selective focus. In principle, much the same applies to having a wide range of shutter speeds — you can select settings to freeze or blur movement, as well as helping to control the total amount of light received by the film.

Variable lens apertures offer yet another option. They allow you to choose between having just the picture element you have focused on rendered sharp, or extending this sharpness through many nearer and farther objects, too.

Like composition through the viewfinder, as discussed in *The art of photography,* all these controls are important for creative picture making. They introduce factors that are essentially photographic. At the same time, and for a fuller understanding, this section shows the optical and mechanical changes each control makes inside the camera.

Photographic lighting
Another major area of photographic control concentrates on lighting and how you can use and manipulate it in conjunction with exposure. This includes most forms of artificial light — from camera flash to large studio single and multihead systems, as well as the complete range of continuous-

light tungsten units and accessories. It also discusses general studio practice when lighting a variety of subjects and how to circumvent particular problems that can be associated with them.

In the process of seeing and constructing photographs, lighting has so far been discussed as something found, something that already exists. Now in this section we look at lighting equipment and the techniques of actually setting up lighting schemes for different subjects. Considerations such as controlling the quality, direction, and distribution of light are similar in purpose to those in *The art of photography,* but not in practice.

The use of lighting under controlled conditions to reveal objects and surfaces in a variety of ways is one of the greatest challenges and attractions of photography. Like stage or display lighting, it is a way of expressing mood and atmosphere, as well as showing descriptive detail. Flash, in particular, is often very badly used in this connection.

Lighting schemes and their effects are very subjective. In fact, some photographers can be clearly identified by their use of particular lighting effects — in the same way that movies and still pictures can often be dated by the way lighting has been employed.

Lighting, whether available or photographic, can only be successfully rendered on the film if it is correctly interpreted and measured, and this information transferred to the camera controls already mentioned. The measurement of exposure, from totally automatic systems to the personalized use of a separate hand-held meter is therefore carefully explained. Another important factor that governs exposure is your choice and speed of film. All the main types are compared, and diagrams show in detail how each film type is designed to work.

Camera systems and accessories
One of the greatest attractions of the modern single lens reflex camera (35 mm or rollfilm) is the fact that you can remove and change your camera lens. Changing from a normal to a wide-angle, or to a telephoto lens, creates major differences in the appearance of the subject. Each lens type affects the way you must regard potential subjects. These effects are taken to extremes with fisheyes and ultra-long focal lengths, and other special lens types. Zoom lenses, which allow you to vary the focal length, are another alternative. Zooms, despite their versatility, cannot yet act as a substitute for a full range of fixed focal length lenses.

Other forms of optics that dramatically alter our perception and observation of our surroundings include the many different kinds of close-up attachments and accessories. These, like interchangeable lenses, are most easily used in conjunction with a single lens reflex camera. As each accessory is attached, its precise effect on image size, sharpness, and perspective can be seen on the focusing screen.

Lens attachments now extend well beyond close-ups. You can either buy or make a device for almost any visual effect — from a diffuser that will transform highlights into large star shapes, to filters that will tint different areas of the picture in five or more colors. It is easy to become reliant on these special effects attachments as a substitute for ideas and imagination. Used occasionally and well, however, they can help intensify visual effects and add elements of fantasy.

One of the main points to emerge is the ability to build up a personal camera kit as your interest in photography develops. Starting with a single camera body and lens, you can select from a vast range of extra lenses, in addition to flash, motor drives, remote shutter releases, and close-up equipment. Camera systems illustrated toward the end of this section feature attachments that will even allow you to connect your camera to a microscope or telescope. These applications, and others such as special optics for scientific and medical photography are dealt with in more detail in *The specialized subject* section. Eventually you can develop a well-tailored "tool kit", which exactly suits your particular interest in photography.

With this possible long-term commitment in mind, it is important to think carefully about selecting the best size and type of camera in the first place. The camera formats that offer you this flexibility are the 35 mm single lens reflex, 6 × 6 cm single lens reflex, and, to a more limited degree, sheet film cameras.

Cameras and their controls

The devices we call cameras have a history almost a thousand years older than photography itself. As far back as the tenth century, people are known to have observed solar eclipses using a darkened room with one small hole in the window shutters. This simple arrangement caused a clear image of the sun to fall as a disk of light on the white wall opposite the hole.

Historical evolution

Throughout the sixteenth century many descriptions were published of these "camera obscuras" (darkened rooms), and they were used as novelties to project scenes of sunlit exteriors. The simpler types used a hole to allow light to enter the room, but others used a telescope lens fitted over a larger hole to give a brighter and sharper image. In all cases, the scene projected on the wall appeared upside down.

By the seventeenth century, movable camera obscuras were in use. These were usually black tents or adapted sedan chairs fitted with a lens. Inside, there was a drawing board, which allowed the occupier to trace over the projected image on paper. Smaller, portable box-like camera obscuras were standard artists' aids by the eighteenth century. They were especially helpful when accurately sketching linear perspective and the relative scale of objects at different distances. Most devices by this time used a 45° mirror between the lens and a ground-glass screen situated on the top of the box. This screen provided a convenient horizontal surface for tracing, and turned the detailed image the right way up (although at the same time it reversed it left to right).

With so little known about light-sensitive chemicals, it was not until the 1830s that "gentlemen scientists", such as William Fox Talbot in England, and Nicéphore Niépce and Louis Daguerre in France, managed to produce permanent images in the camera obscura by the direct action of light. The first photographic cameras (the word "obscura" was soon dropped) consisted of two large wooden boxes, sliding inside one another for focusing. The lens was at one end and a glass focusing screen (replaceable by a plate coated with light-sensitive chemicals) at the other. Cameras were always used on stands until improvements in lenses and materials (1870s) made it practicable to use hand-held types, fitted with shutters to give "instantaneous" exposures. During the past hundred years, designers have solved many other technical limitations, and four interrelated camera types have evolved. Large sheet film cameras (now mainly used by professionals) have features most similar to the earliest designs. Rollfilm cameras developed as a way of introducing photography to the general public (from 1888). Miniature (by comparison) 35 mm cameras gradually ousted the larger rollfilms (1950s). Reflex cameras, based on the old camera obscura reflex system, have been made for all these sizes. In the last twenty years the 35 mm single lens reflex has become the world's most popular camera.

Plate cameras

When the first practical photography process was introduced (in 1839), the camera that went on sale was a wooden box with a brass-mounted lens at the front and a ground-glass focusing screen at the back. This type of camera mostly formed a picture 7 × 5 ins (18 × 13 cm). The photographer set up the camera, peered at the upside-down image, and focused by sliding the back away from the front. This slide control was soon replaced by more flexible, accordion-

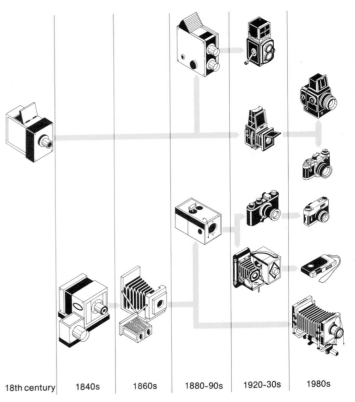

18th century | 1840s | 1860s | 1880-90s | 1920-30s | 1980s

Development of camera technology

The reflex camera obscura of the eighteenth century inspired the design of twin lens and single lens reflex cameras. The basic wooden boxes of the Fox Talbot and Daguerre era evolved into the folding camera and its stereo counterpart. The sheet film camera is a sophisticated modern descendant. The box camera is a further side development. Its basic simplicity has been retained in today's compact and direct vision cameras aimed at the snapshot market. With these, the size of both camera and film format has been progressively reduced. These reductions in camera size have been accompanied by steady improvement in film resolution.

type leather bellows connecting the front of the camera to the back. Large plate cameras were ideally suited to static landscape photography. Initially, exposures of about ten minutes were necessary for most scenes. Smaller models, giving pictures about 2½-3 ins (6-8 cm) high, were used for portraits because the small images were brighter and exposures were only about one minute. As better light-sensitive materials appeared, and lenses were designed that produced brighter images, photographers could no longer conveniently make exposures by removing and replacing a cap in front of the lens. Mechanical shutters giving exposures measured in fractions of seconds were needed.

Today, glass plates have been replaced by sheets of film (generally 5 × 4 ins / 12.5 × 10 cm), but this type of large-format camera is still used in some fields of professional photography. It gives images of excellent quality because of the minimal degree of enlargement necessary and, more importantly, each exposure can be processed individually. Sheet film cameras also allow optical manipulations, known as "camera movements", not possible on other camera types (see *Movements on view cameras,* p. 121).

Rollfilm cameras

Large cameras could not conveniently be hand held, and were too slow and awkward for most people to use. As a further deterrent, until the 1870s plates had to be chemically prepared by the user. Once the first manufactured camera materials became available, it was evident that an enormous demand existed for simple "point-and-shoot" amateur cameras. George Eastman revolutionized

Daguerre camera

This camera, constructed by Alphonse Giroux of Paris in 1839, gave a 5 × 7 ins (13 × 18 cm) daguerreotype image on a silvered metal plate. Long exposures were necessary, which made portraiture an uncomfortable experience for the sitter. The preparation and processing of the plates was equally laborious, so such cameras became almost the exclusive preserve of professional photographers. Only the most dedicated of amateur photographers could cope with this.

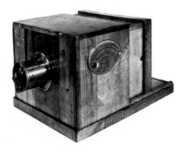

camera design and popular photography by introducing the first Kodak camera in 1888. His innovation was a hand-held box with a lens set for all distances beyond about 6 ft (3 m). It had a spring-powered shutter, and contained a roll of light-sensitive paper (soon replaced by film), which allowed 100 exposures before reloading. The user just pointed the camera, pulled a string to set the shutter, and pressed a button to fire it — a simple key arrangement wound on the film. Eastman's slogan for his camera was "You press the

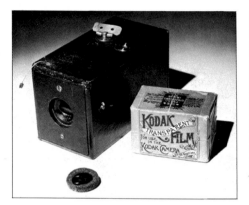

Box camera
Eastman's Kodak camera of 1888, measuring only $6\frac{1}{2} \times 3\frac{3}{4}$ ins (16 × 9 cm), was very simple to use, and ideally suited to casual photographers. A cord tensioned the shutter, and a button released it at 1/25 sec. It had no viewfinder or manual controls, apart from a wind-on crank. Processing and reloading of the 100-exposure rollfilm was performed by the manufacturer. It was the first mass-market camera design.

button, we do the rest", and the statement was literally true. After the last picture was taken, the photographer sent the whole camera back to the Eastman Kodak factory for processing and reloading. Eastman's brilliant invention allowed ordinary, non-technical people to take up photography, provided they kept to distant subjects in bright light. As a result of this popularizing, the term "snapshot" was coined, and millions of snapshot cameras with daylight-loading rollfilms sold world wide.

Throughout the first 30 years of this century, both box type and folding leather and metal rollfilm cameras dominated the amateur market. Their success was largely due to the fact that they produced cheap, album-sized prints by contact printing directly from the negative. The trouble was that even the folding type cameras were bulky to carry. With the improvement in 35 mm format cameras (see below) following the Second World War, rollfilm cameras gradually became less popular.

At the height of the rollfilm camera's popularity, hundreds of models and over twenty sizes of film were available. Today, most rollfilm cameras are high-quality types used mainly by photographers who value the excellent image quality possible with large rollfilm negatives. The modern equivalent of the snapshot camera is the simple 110 pocket camera, with its tiny, drop-in film cartridge (see *Direct vision compact cameras,* pp. 104-5). Large-format, separate viewfinder cameras are still designed for instant picture materials. This is because instant picture cameras have to produce prints of a useful size without enlargement (see *Instant picture cameras,* pp. 109-10).

Miniature cameras
Perforated lengths of 35 mm film, as we know them today, came about when Thomas Edison was designing his first movie equipment in 1889. Rollfilms for the first Kodak cameras were $2\frac{3}{4}$ ins (7 cm) wide. Slit down the middle, these became 35 mm wide. Edison's assistant cut perforations down each edge so that the film could be cranked through the camera.

When Oscar Barnack, a designer working for E. Leitz in Germany designed a little still camera for use on microscopes, he built it to accept short lengths of 35 mm film. Leitz marketed it in 1924 as the LEItz CAmera (Leica), the first 35 mm "miniature" camera. It had a metal body with screw-out lens focusing, and a top-mounted viewfinder. As the camera had a blind-type shutter just in front of the film, it was possible to fit alternative lenses. Distances for focusing, though, had to be guessed.

For professionals, this quality, miniature camera revolutionized candid documentary work. But enlargement was necessary to give

useful sized prints, and this deterred many amateurs. In addition, early 35 mm film had poor ability to resolve fine detail. Small-format cameras (the term replacing "miniature") have become popular in the last twenty years, mainly due to the development of the "single lens reflex". Improved film, lenses, and processing facilities have followed. Today's popular descendant of the Leica viewfinder camera is the 35 mm compact.

Reflex cameras
Another type of camera design was based on the old reflex camera obscura, which allowed visual focusing and composing of a right-way-up image on a ground-glass screen. One approach, toward the end of the nineteenth century, was to mount a reflex obscura on top of a box-structured photographic camera. The photographer then had two lenses — one to view the scene, and one to photograph it — mounted above each other. For focusing, they were both linked so that they moved either backward or forward together. The bottom lens was used to expose the plate through a mechanical shutter like any other camera. The complete device was called a "twin lens reflex", and was very bulky. By 1928 this twin lens reflex camera had shrunk to rollfilm size. The first example was the Rolleiflex, which used the pioneering Zeiss Tessar lens.

An alternative "reflex" design was based solely on the reflex camera obscura — by having a light-sensitive plate at the back of the box and making the mirror hinge upward, out of the light path, just before exposure. A blind opening or closing in front of the plate acted as a shutter. To use this "single lens reflex" the photographer looked down into a tall hood shading the focusing screen on the top of the camera, then pressed a lever to shift the mirror and fire the shutter. The image on the focusing screen was reversed left to right, and was very dark with a small lens aperture — but the single lens

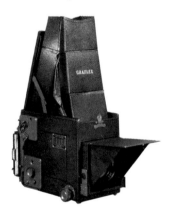

Early single lens reflex design
The Graflex is a quarter-plate single lens reflex camera, which was used by professional photographers in the 1920s and 1930s. A new feature for its time, which was particularly useful in portraiture, was a hinged mirror behind the lens. This allowed the user to see the image the right way up on a viewing screen. The screen was shaded by a hood to give a bright image. This mirror swung out of the way when the shutter was pressed, allowing light to reach the sensitized plate, and so form an image. The camera had a variety of shutter speed settings and control over aperture and focus, but could still be folded down into a compact box when not in use.

reflex allowed great accuracy in both composing and focusing.

During the late 1930s German manufacturers brought out two or three rollfilm and 35 mm single lens reflexes, but they were awkward to use, mechanically complex, and unreliable. It was during the post-war years of the 1950s that SLR design really gathered momentum. This was mostly due to Japanese entry into the field of precision camera manufacture, and their decision to concentrate on improved 35 mm SLR designs. (A Swedish rollfilm SLR, the Hasselblad, was developed during the Second World War and began to have an impact on professionals prepared to work as small as $2\frac{1}{4} \times 2\frac{1}{4}$ ins/6 × 6 cm. For the most part, however, European manufacturers failed to exploit the potential of the SLR camera at the time.)

The drawback of viewing a left-to-right reversed image on a tiny ground-glass screen was overcome by the addition of a penta-prism-shaped block of glass above the screen. This directed the light to a magnifying eyepiece at the back of the camera and gave a right-reading image. The lens aperture mechanism was engineered to stay at its widest setting (to give the brightest possible image for focusing) until the moment of exposure. The 35 mm SLR format became increasingly popular as the camera mechanisms became more reliable and increased production lowered the cost. Today, most professionals as well as amateurs use the format extensively.

Camera principles

Today's cameras are far more ingenious than the apparatus used for early photography, yet they still have certain basic features in common. Essentially, every camera is a light-tight box, holding light-sensitive film at the back, and fitted at the front with a hole covered by a lens. The lens elements may be fixed in one position, which greatly limits the lens's ability to focus selectively on different parts of an image (see *Using focus control,* p. 116). In some cases the lens may shift forward or backward to focus on objects at varying distances. A hole, or

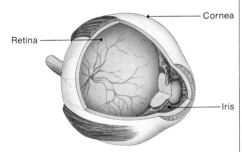

Retina ── / ── Cornea

Iris

The camera's eye
Cameras and the human eye function in similar ways. Light enters via a lens (cornea and lens in the eye) and passes through a diaphragm (iris), which expands or contracts to regulate it. Now focused, light reaches the film (retina); in the case of the camera, by means of a shutter. Cameras also have a viewfinder as a sighting device.

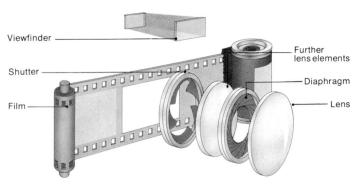

Viewfinder

Shutter

Film

Further lens elements

Diaphragm

Lens

diaphragm, just behind the lens helps to control the brightness of the image. This is usually variable in size, so that it is possible to select a small hole in bright lighting conditions, or a larger one in dim light.

Controlling light
Somewhere in any camera there must be a shutter. This prevents light from the image reaching the film until the photographer is ready to shoot. The shutter also controls the length of time light is allowed to act on the film. With all but the simplest cameras, there is a choice of several shutter speeds. This permits the photographer to choose a shorter exposure time when conditions are bright, or a longer time when lighting is poor. Between them, the size of the diaphragm opening and the shutter speed control the total exposure given to the film.

Aiming the camera
The next essential feature is some means of aiming the camera and composing the picture. Each of the main camera types has a different form of viewfinding arrangement. The cheapest and simplest is a tube-like optical sight, usually built into the camera body close to the lens. Since the photographer looks through it, directly at the subject, this is known as a "direct vision viewfinder". A better system, though, is achieved with "reflex" viewing, which uses a mirror to reflect light taken in through the lens itself to a viewing and focusing screen.

Camera and eye comparisons
In several respects the photographic camera and the human eye are quite similar. The eyeball has a clear gristle lens at the front, just behind a transparent outer layer, known as the cornea. It is able to focus an

(upside-down) image on the concave back of the eye – a light-sensitive network of millions of cells called the retina. Lens and retina are kept at a constant separation by clear fluid filling the eyeball. A pigmented iris situated near the lens slowly enlarges or reduces its effective diameter in response to changes in lighting conditions.

Unlike the camera, the eye lens focuses not by moving backward or forward, but by changing its curvature. Muscles compress the lens and make it bulge slightly for close subjects. This focusing action is much faster than the focusing of any camera lens. In terms of image quality, however, the eye has a much poorer lens than most cameras. It only resolves fine detail in the center of the retina, where the greatest concentration of nerve cells is located. Outside this area, only a general impression of object shapes and tones is registered. The nerve cells (called rods and cones) translate the image light pattern into electrical signals, which pass through optic tracts to the brain (where the image is "read" as being the right way up).

Despite these basic similarities, modern cameras offer many extra features. These range from automatic light measurement and exposure setting to interchangeable lenses, powered film wind-on, and autofocusing. A number of cameras are completely automatic in their technical settings but, in practice, this tends to limit creative picture-making options.

The essential features

Looking at the range of cameras available, it is easy to be confused by the diversity of models and formats, all offering different features. But to understand how light is directed to the film surface, most of the refinements must be stripped away, leaving the features essential to all cameras – lens, exposure controls, viewfinder, and film transport system.

Viewfinding
The first truly "popular" camera, George Eastman's brilliantly original No. 1 camera, did not have a viewfinder at all. Instead, sighting lines were impressed on the top of its box-like form to help the user aim it in the right direction. Modern cameras use one of four main viewfinder devices (see below), varying according to camera type. The direct vision viewfinder is both cheap and compact. But because it shows the subject from a viewpoint slightly to one side of the lens, it is not very accurate. This can be deceptive for tightly framed scenes, and the degree of viewpoint error increases as

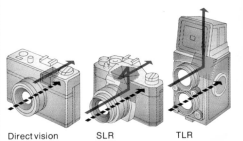

Direct vision   SLR   TLR

Sheet film camera

Viewfinders
Only in the single lens reflex and sheet film cameras does light reach the viewfinder (red line) along the same path through the lens as light reaching the light-sensitive emulsion (broken line).

the subject nears the camera (see *Direct vision compact cameras,* pp. 104-5). If the camera accepts a variety of lenses, then the viewfinder must somehow adjust to indicate the different amounts of scene transmitted by each lens that you can use on the camera.

Twin lens reflex cameras allow you to see the image to be photographed through a separate top lens (see *TLR cameras,* p. 107), which is identical to the picture-taking lens. This system is excellent for focusing (both lenses moving backward or forward together), but it suffers from similar inaccuracies of framing as the direct vision camera above.

Sheet film cameras combine absolute accuracy of framing and focus, provided that they are set up properly (see *Sheet film cameras,* pp. 108-9). Light enters the lens and travels directly to a focusing screen, which you must replace with a film holder containing a piece of sheet film for every exposure.

Of all the viewfinder systems, only the single lens reflex type offers complete accuracy of framing and focusing yet remains a camera that is easy to hand-hold (see *35 mm SLR cameras,* pp. 102-4).

Focusing

There are two basic advantages of a lens that allows focusing movements. First, you can focus on objects that are closer than would be possible with a fixed lens. Second, you can take pictures in which only certain image planes are in focus (useful when a scene contains cluttered or distracting detail). A focusing lens, used at wide aperture – for shallow depth of field – allows you to emphasize a chosen object, and suppress others nearer or farther away by rendering them out of focus.

The focus control ring that moves the lens to different positions may simply be scaled in symbols denoting far distance, mid-distance,

Controlling focus

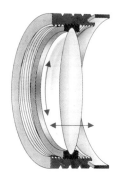

Focusing the lens involves moving it toward or away from the subject so that light waves can be made to converge in sharp focus on the film plane. This is usually done by rotating a control on the lens barrel, as here, or by turning a ratcheted focusing knob to move the lens panel back and forth, and thus vary the distance.

and close subjects. Focus controls on more advanced cameras, however, are marked with a scale of actual distances in feet and/or meters. To help focus a direct vision viewfinder camera, the viewfinder itself may also contain a rangefinding device (see *Direct vision compact cameras*, p. 104-5). In a reflex camera you can check image sharpness by looking at the focusing screen.

An increasing number of cameras now offer some form of automatic focusing. There are three main systems to choose from (see *Auto-focus lenses*, p. 115), available for some instant picture cameras and 35 mm format models. With most systems, the lens sets itself for the correct distance of whatever subject is in the center of the frame.

Exposure controls

Camera controls allow you to regulate the amount of light the film receives from the subject in two ways. First, the shutter speed controls the duration of the exposure (see *How shutters work*, pp. 124-5). Second, the lens aperture controls the brightness of the image (see *The f number system*, p. 117). For maximum exposure (in very dim light), use a slow shutter speed and a wide aperture. In bright lighting conditions, though, use a fast shutter speed combined with a small aperture. The wider this range of exposure combinations, the greater the range of lighting situations under which you can take pictures.

Low-cost cameras generally offer least flexibility. They may, for example, merely have a two-speed shutter (marked with symbols indicating sunny and cloudy) and a fixed-size aperture. With advanced models, you must balance the increased flexibility with the fact that they are more complicated to set and use.

Most 35 mm cameras contain a light-sensitive cell facing the subject. This cell measures

Aperture control

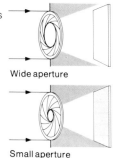

Wide aperture

Small aperture

As the aperture increases in size, more light is admitted and the image becomes brighter on the viewing screen. Each f stop on a rising scale (usually between around f 2 and f 16) halves the amount of light entering the camera. On a descending scale, the amount of light is doubled. The higher the f number, the smaller the aperture.

the level of illumination, and may control one or both of the exposure settings. Single lens reflex cameras usually contain an internal cell, and fully automatic models have their shutter speed and aperture settings programmed directly by its response. But for fuller control over the final appearance of your results, it is better to have a camera offering manual control – or at least one which you can switch between automatic and manual.

For manual cameras with no light-measuring cell, hand-held exposure meters are available that recommend the appropriate shutter speed and aperture settings for the conditions (see *Using a hand-held meter*, p. 136). Such a device is essential when you are using a sheet film or rollfilm camera.

The lens

The lens forms a sharp image of the subject on the film. Basically, it is a piece of glass, thicker at the center than at the edges. In reality, several lenses together (known as elements) are used to produce even sharpness over all of the picture.

Simple camera lenses are often fixed in a position that will bring into sharp focus most of a scene in front of the camera. The smaller the aperture (the hole which allows light to pass through the lens), the greater this zone of sharply recorded detail (see *Depth of field*, p. 118). Advanced cameras are likely to be used in a wide range of conditions and, there-

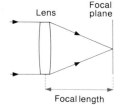

Focal length

Focal length and focal plane

The lens converges subject light to a point of sharp focus on the focal plane. With a simple lens and a distant subject this lens-to-focal-plane distance is called the focal length.

fore, also require wide apertures to cope with dim light. As apertures become wider, so the zone of sharp focus becomes narrower, making it increasingly important for you to be able to focus selectively on different parts of the scene (see *Choosing depth of field*, p. 119).

Film transport systems

Camera designs differ both in their viewfinding arrangements (direct vision and reflex) and in the size of film they take. In general, the larger the film size the better the quality of the final result. This is because the film image requires less enlargement. Conversely, large

films mean larger, more awkward cameras and, usually, more expensive running costs.

The three most popular film sizes are 110 (16 mm wide), 35 mm, and 120 rollfilm (65 mm wide). There is also a range of sheet film sizes for view cameras (see *Sheet film cameras*, pp. 108-9).

Each 110 film comes in a long, rectangular plastic cartridge, ready to drop straight into the camera. After the last exposure, you open the camera back and remove the whole cartridge for processing.

With 35 mm film, the picture size is four times bigger than with 110, but the cost per frame is about the same. 35 mm film is generally slower and more awkward to load because you must position the film cassette on one side of the camera and attach the end of the film to a fixed "take-up spool" at the other side. After the last exposure you wind the film back into the cassette before opening the camera back.

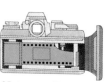

35 mm cassette   110 cartridge

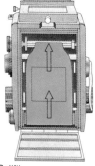
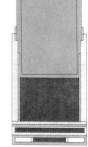

Rollfilm   Sheet film

Film loading

35 mm film comes in a cassette, into which it is rewound after exposure. 110 cartridges simply drop into the camera and do not need rewinding. You load rollfilm into one side of the camera, wind it across, and remove it from the other side. A piece of sheet film is loaded in darkness into a holder and covered by a sliding sheath. The holder slips into the back of the camera.

Rollfilm is attached to and wound up inside a long length of opaque backing paper. You fit the roll of film and paper in one side of the camera, and attach the start of the paper to a removable spool on the other side. The paper draws the film across the camera as the film advance control is used. After the last exposure, all the film and backing paper will be wound round the take-up spool, which you can remove for processing.

Camera types

All cameras have certain basic common features, despite differences in size, structure, brand, and price. But it is possible to sort practically every camera into one of five main types, according to its design.

The first type, recognizable by the characteristic bulge of the pentaprism housing, and the lack of a front viewfinder window, is the 35 mm single lens reflex. This is the most versatile camera design, and for this reason is most suited to serious photography. The 35 mm SLR viewing system allows for accuracy in composition, and a wide range of interchangeable lenses and accessories allows the photographer to tackle almost any subject. The variety of models provides cameras in a very broad price range.

The second type is the compact direct vision camera. It has a separate viewfinder above or to one side of the lens, and is available in two common sizes, taking pictures on 35 mm and 110 film. 110 compacts are very small and slip easily into the pocket, while even the 35 mm version is much smaller than many of its SLR counterparts, having a shallower body, shorter lens, and no pentaprism. Compact cameras include the simplest, low-cost models, but the 35 mm cameras at the top of the range can produce images of the same quality as the best SLRs. (Many photographers start with a simple compact, before moving on to the more flexible SLR.)

Cameras using medium-format film make up the third category. These include rollfilm SLRs and the few remaining twin lens reflex cameras. Both types are box-like in appearance, and heavier than 35 mm SLRs and compacts.

Sheet film cameras form the fourth type. These use still larger picture formats (5 × 4 ins / 12.5 × 10 cm, or larger). Most require a tripod or stand, making them less mobile, less versatile, and more specialized than other camera types, but capable of producing enlargements of superb quality.

The various instant picture cameras are related to medium-format direct vision and SLR types. But instant picture film requires special features built into the camera, such as spring rollers and reversing mirrors. These put the design of instant picture cameras into a special category.

See also
Additional equipment, pp. 184-5. System cameras and accessories, pp. 202-7. Future design trends, p. 211.

35 mm SLR cameras

The single lens reflex is the most versatile camera design. The majority of SLRs are made for the 35 mm format, but there are also several medium-format models (see *Rollfilm SLR cameras*, p. 106), and some smaller types for the 110 format (see *Direct vision compact cameras*, pp. 104-5). The main advantage of all SLRs is their facility for allowing exact composing and focusing.

All SLRs show you the image exactly as it is formed by the lens. The camera achieves this with a 45° mirror positioned between lens and film, angled to reflect the light up to a viewing screen near the top of the camera. To expose the film, this mirror swings up just before the

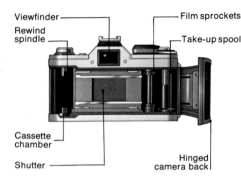

Camera functions
The view of a shutter-priority, automatic 35 mm SLR (right) shows the location of the major camera features. The camera back (above right) is open to show the layout of the film transport mechanism. The color-coded diagram (below) shows the relationship of the systems involved in the operation of the camera.

Key
- Viewfinding
- Metering
- Shutter
- Aperture
- Focusing

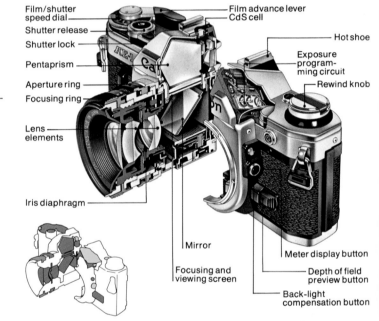

shutter opens, allowing light to pass through to the film at the back of the camera. This means that you cannot see the subject at the moment of exposure, but the exposure sequence is usually so rapid that this is hardly distracting at "normal" shutter speeds.

The SLR's mirror reverses the upside-down image produced by the lens, so that you view the subject the right way up. But the mirror also reverses the image left-to-right. This is corrected by the camera's pentaprism – a block of glass with silvered surfaces that is situated at the top of the camera. The pentaprism's sloping top surfaces reverse the image without turning it upside down, so that you view the image oriented correctly.

It is fundamental to SLR design that the distance light has to travel from lens to focusing screen (via the mirror) is equal to the lens-to-film distance. When you focus the image sharply on the viewing screen, it will also be sharp when it reaches the film. The precise viewing and focusing offered by the SLR makes it possible to check the whole image visually at any aperture setting, to see the change of view provided by different lenses, and the effect of filters and other attachments. Another advantage of the SLR is the wide

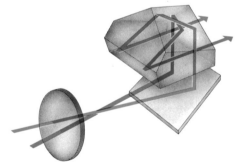

Pentaprism
The lens inverts light from the subject, which is then reversed by the mirror. Reflected by the several facets of the pentaprism (a solid block of optical-quality glass), the image is seen in the viewfinder as the right way up and laterally corrected once more.

choice of films available. These range from color transparency (for slides) to both black and white and color negative film (for prints), all available in a selection of brands and in differing sensitivities to light (indicated by an ASA or DIN number on the film container). Because of the SLR's popularity there is a wide, and growing, range of models to choose from. The sophisticated types offer a variety of features, supplemented by a system of accessories capable of coping with the demands of the most exacting photographer.

Viewfinding

The SLR viewing system enables you to see clearly the parts of the image that are in sharp focus. As you rotate the focusing ring on the lens, you can observe the changes in the appearance of the image on the focusing screen. Most screens have focusing aids built-in to make these changes more apparent. With one type of screen, for example, the image detail in the central circular area appears split in two

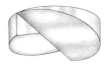

Split field
A double wedge (above) in the focusing screen has two intersecting surfaces. When light is focused sharply on the plane where the surfaces meet (far right), the image in the viewfinder is seen as

continuous. Unfocused (above left), the image appear discontinuous, or split.

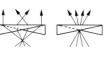

Microprism
In a ring surrounding the split image (above) is a group of microprisms. Accurately focused light is sharply defined as single points (far right). Unfocused light disperses in a shimmer-

ing effect (above left), appearing as a cluster of points.

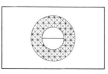

Fresnel screen
Embossed concentric circles below the focusing screen redirect edge light to give more even illumination.

A grid is sometimes engraved on the screen as an aid to aligning horizontal and vertical lines.

when the image is out of focus. As you correct focus, the two halves come together. Many screens also have a microprism ring around the central area. This breaks up the image into a shimmering pattern until focus is perfect. Plain screens, and screens engraved with a grid are also available (the latter is particularly useful when you need perfectly straight horizontal and vertical lines – see *Viewfinder accessories,* p. 204). Most SLRs allow you to

focus and compose with the lens at maximum aperture, providing the brightest possible image. A preview button situated near the lens controls closes down the aperture temporarily to the one selected for exposure, enabling you to see any changes in "depth of field" associated with different apertures (see *Depth of field,* p. 118).

Exposure settings

Most modern SLRs have a built-in exposure meter consisting of a light-sensitive cell made of either cadmium sulfide (CdS) or silicon. To take full advantage of SLR design, the meter cell is housed inside the camera body where it can measure the intensity of the light entering the camera through the lens. This system is known as through-the-lens (TTL) metering.

Depending on the manufacturers' design, these cells may read the light from different parts of the image (see *TTL metering,* p. 134). But the basic procedure for "reading" the light and operating the camera's exposure controls varies, depending on whether the camera works in a "manual" or "automatic" exposure mode. On all models you must first set the ASA or DIN number of the film to give the meter a

Metering
In cameras fitted with through-the-lens (TTL) metering, cells inside the camera body monitor light passing through the lens. These are usually of either the cadmium sulfide or silicon type.

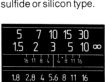

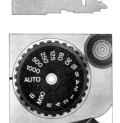

Exposure settings
Working manually, you set the shutter speed by turning a dial, usually mounted on top of the camera (above right). This model also has an automatic setting. You adjust the aperture by

rotating a ring on the lens barrel, marked with distance settings in feet and meters (above left).

Electronic exposure
On some automatic cameras an exposure mode dial replaces the conventional shutter speed control. This aperture-priority model can be set to either automatic or manual modes. Set on manual, pressing the forward button causes LEDs in the viewfinder to climb sequentially, indicating progressively faster shutter speeds. Press the rear button and slower shutter speeds will be shown on a descending scale in the viewfinder display.

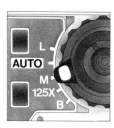

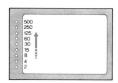

reference point. On a manual camera you can then compose and focus, and adjust either the shutter speed or the aperture setting until an indicator in the viewfinder signals that exposure is "correct".

On a semi-automatic camera you select either the aperture or the shutter speed (depending on whether the camera is an aperture or shutter priority type – see *TTL systems,* p. 135), and the meter itself sets the other control. The viewfinder display shows the setting chosen by the camera. Many of these cameras have a control which allows some form of compensation in difficult lighting situations, such as back-lighting (see *How meters can be misled,* p. 138).

On fully automatic models, the camera will set both shutter speed and aperture, allowing

Exposure sequence with automatic diaphragms
1 The shutter covers the film. Light passing through the lens at full aperture is reflected by the mirror to the focusing screen and eyepiece. **2** On releasing the shutter, the mirror swings up and the lens stops down automatically to the taking aperture, ready for exposure. **3** Finally the shutter opens and admits light to the film. When the shutter closes after the exposure, the diaphragm opens up once more to full aperture, and the mirror returns. This restores the image to the focusing screen.

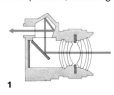
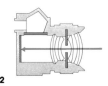
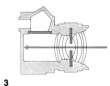

the photographer to forget about exposure altogether, and concentrate on composition. SLRs with this facility are known as "multimodes". They also offer operation in aperture and shutter priority modes.

Many automatic cameras have a manual override, which means you can make your own exposure settings in preference to those selected by the camera. This is essential if you want to keep creative control over results, and is particularly useful for special effects, which do not rely on technically correct exposure. In most cases, the viewfinder display also tells you what exposure the camera would set in its automatic mode.

Flash facilities
SLRs accept a wide range of electronic flash units – and some also work with flash bulbs. You can connect both types to the camera's "hot shoe" (an electric terminal on top of the camera), or by means of a synchronization cord, which you plug into a socket on the camera body. When using the hot shoe, the flash is mounted on top of, and supported by, the camera itself. With the synchronization cord, however, you must either hold the flash in one hand or mount it on a bracket or stand.

The SLR has a focal plane shutter consisting of two blinds that pass across the focal plane

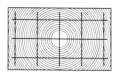
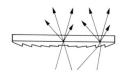

(just in front of the film). The space between the blinds and their speed of travel determine exposure time. As the duration of the flash is usually briefer than the shutter speed set, it is the flash and not the shutter that determines the actual exposure. But to expose the film evenly, the flash must fire when the shutter blinds are fully open. At speeds of 1/60 sec or longer (1/125 sec on some cameras), the second blind is retarded sufficiently in relation to the first, for the whole frame to record. It is essential, therefore, to set the correct shutter speed when using electronic flash.

Lenses and accessories
Most modern lenses have a twist-on, twist-off bayonet mount, which is easy and quick to use. This mount system allows you to connect a wide range of lenses to the basic camera body. You can, for example, change from the standard lens to a wide-angle, or telephoto.

Bayonet mounts made by different manufacturers are, generally, not compatible – so it is essential to use lenses with the correct mount. Lens mount adaptors are available, which allow you to use one manufacturer's lens on a different manufacturer's camera body, but these may interfere with the automatic operation of the lens aperture.

Lens hoods eliminate the "flare" caused by light entering the lens from outside its angle of view. Made in plastic, rubber, or metal, most are designed for a narrow focal length range, although adjustable versions are available for use with wide-ranging zoom lenses.

Bayonet mount
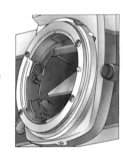
You attach the lens to the camera body by aligning a mark on the rear of the lens barrel with a similar mark on the lens mount. Turn the lens until it locks firmly in place. To remove the lens, depress the release button and turn the lens in the opposite direction.

Practical handling considerations
The SLR's main advantage is that its through-the-lens viewing system enables you to make accurate visual decisions concerning composition, focusing, and exposure. It is the only camera type to offer a really wide range of accessories, from extreme telephoto lenses for natural history work, to ultra-wide "fisheye" lenses for special effects, and from underwater housings to accessories for remote control photography, and copying. Extension rings or bellows are easy to fit and enable you to focus the lens on objects only a few inches away (see *Equipment for close-up*, pp. 195-6). It is also possible to attach the camera body to a microscope (see *The 35 mm SLR system*, p. 205). If you do not have access to such advanced equipment, the SLR is still versatile. You can use attachments such as filters and mirrors in front of the lens to create special effects, and it is always possible to preview the results on the focusing screen, and measure precisely the exposure you require for an accurately rendered photograph.

Direct vision compact cameras
Internally, the direct vision camera is similar to any basic camera (see *The essential features*, pp. 100-1). The lens is usually fixed to the body, there is an aperture just behind the lens, and most types have a bladed lens shutter. The film transport mechanism has a safety device that stops you taking a picture unless you have wound on the previous exposed frame of film.

Compacts are available in both 35 mm and 110 formats, and the two types have certain common features. These include their focusing, viewfinding, and use of built-in flash. The main differences between the two types of camera are the method of loading film, picture

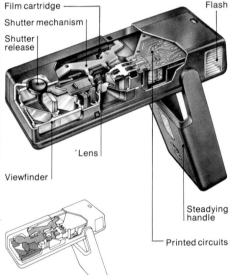

Film cartridge — Flash
Shutter mechanism —
Shutter release —
Lens
Viewfinder
Steadying handle
Printed circuits

size, the range of films available, and the degree of control over exposure.

In order to produce the same size print, the 110 negative must be enlarged four times as much as the 35 mm negative. This means that camera shake, the structure of the film itself, and any marks the film may have accumulated in the camera and during processing, are more noticeable. Film suitable for the 110 format is available only in a limited range of roll lengths and sensitivities, whereas the whole range of film for 35 mm SLR cameras is also suitable for 35 mm compacts (see *Choice of film*, pp. 148-50).

110 cameras use drop-in film cartridges, which are easy to load and do not require rewinding. This is a more convenient arrangement than the 35 mm cassette, but the extra packaging makes the much smaller 110 film cost as much per frame as 35 mm film.

Some 110 cameras offer slide-over lens change (for close-up or telephoto effects). Built-in, automatic metering, motor drive, and flash are also available on some models. Many 35 mm compacts offer these types of features, and some provide an autofocus facility (see *Autofocus lenses*, p. 115). A small number of more sophisticated 35 mm compacts takes a limited range of interchangeable lenses. One model has silicon-cell TTL metering that measures light falling on the film plane.

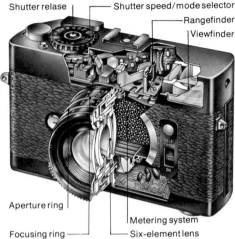

Shutter relase — Shutter speed/mode selector
Rangefinder
Viewfinder
Aperture ring —
Focusing ring —
Metering system
Six-element lens

110 and 35 mm compacts
Like the early box cameras, today's snapshot cameras, such as the 110 compact (left), are designed for ease of use rather than creative picture-taking. The advanced 35 mm compact (above) has greater flexibility. Focusing, aperture, and shutter speed are adjustable, and the 35 mm format allows a wider range of film to be used. This model will accept interchangeable lenses.

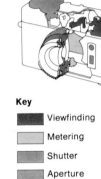

Key
- Viewfinding
- Metering
- Shutter
- Aperture
- Focusing

Viewfinding
All compacts use a direct optical sighting device, which shows the subject plus a suspended white line to indicate the area that will be included in the picture. Because there is no reflex mirror to move out of the light path, the viewfinder shows the subject throughout the exposure. Although the viewfinder window is fitted as close as possible to the lens, discrepancies of viewpoint between the lens and finder always occur. This is particularly obvious at close distances. To help compensate

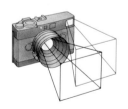

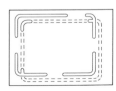

Parallax error
Because the lens and viewfinder in a direct vision camera see the subject from slightly offset viewpoints, parallax error may result, especially with close subjects. Frame the subject slightly off-center toward the lens. Allow for the viewfinder being above the lens axis. Correction lines are marked in some viewfinders to allow for this (below left). Solid line is for distant subjects, broken line is for close-ups.

for this "parallax error" the white line may have additional marks to denote picture limits with the subject at the closest position the lens will render sharp. This aid ensures that your picture is centered, but it will not safeguard against a misalignment of near and far objects.

Some models have symbols at one side of the viewfinder frame to indicate correct exposure or focus. There may also be an indicator to warn of insufficient light.

Focus settings
When you look through a direct vision viewfinder the image is always sharp, even though the subject may be at the wrong distance for the lens focus setting. If your camera has a lens with adjustable focus, you must set it to the correct distance for your subject. Some models use a feet and/or meters scale, but others have only symbols to indicate distances (a mountain for distant subjects, a portrait for near subjects). With a fixed focus lens you must be careful not to come too close to the subject.

As a focusing aid, some models use a rangefinder viewing system (left). This produces a

Distance scales
Direct vision cameras may use either a conventional feet/meters scale, or a system of symbols representing typical subject distances.

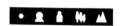
Distance symbols

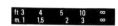
Distance settings

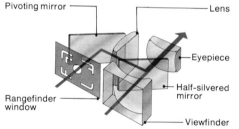

Pivoting mirror — Lens — Eyepiece — Half-silvered mirror — Viewfinder — Rangefinder window

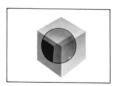
Unfocused

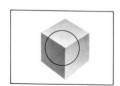
Focused

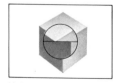
Unfocused

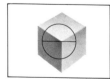
Focused

Rangefinder focusing
The eye sees the subject directly through the viewfinder. Light also enters a rangefinder window. From here it is reflected by a mirror, which pivots as the lens is focused, into the viewfinder (top). You see a double or split image (above) until focus is correct, and the two images are superimposed.

double or split image in the viewfinder until you adjust the lens focus control to the correct setting. Many 35 mm compacts now have some form of autofocus. On most models, slight pressure on the shutter release button causes the lens to shift forward until it has focused on the object in a specified area of the frame — usually the central zone.

Exposure settings
The simplest cameras provide two or three weather symbols to help you set the correct exposure. These may change the shutter speed or lens aperture. Most compacts, though, have automatic exposure setting. You set the ASA or DIN rating of the film in a small window, and a light-sensitive cell measures incoming light, and adjusts aperture or shutter speed settings, or both. Most models give a read-out in the viewfinder to tell you what exposure the camera has chosen. As with single lens reflex cameras, both aperture and shutter

Exposure symbols
Simplification of exposure settings into "sunny" or "cloudy" symbols offers rudimentary control over lighting. An aperture scale allows more precise adjustment.

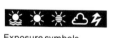
Exposure symbols

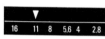
Aperture settings

priority models are available (see *TTL systems*, p. 135), as well as fully automatic cameras. A light in the viewfinder warns you when there is insufficient illumination for correct exposure, and when you should, therefore, use flash. A substantial number of 35 mm compact models have a delayed-action shutter setting, which enables you to include yourself in the picture. A tripod or a stable surface is necessary with this technique.

Flash facilities
Simple compact cameras accept flashcubes or flash bars (see *Flash lighting units,* pp. 165-6). Others have a small electronic flash built into the camera body. You either switch it on manually or, on automatic models, it comes into use when lighting conditions would otherwise result in underexposure. This arrangement is convenient, but for creative work the flat, frontal lighting given by camera-mounted flash destroys subject form and texture. It is better to use a camera that accepts a separate electronic flashgun on a long cord, which you plug into the camera (see *Flash lighting units,* pp. 165-6). In all cases, the shutter fires the flash when the blades are fully open.

Lenses
Some 110 compacts have a pair of additional lenses that slide over the main lens and viewfinder to give a telephoto effect. This increases the focal length of the lens to make your subject appear bigger in the frame. Other models have a close-up lens which slides over in the same way. Supplementary lenses, which clip over the camera's prime lens, are also available for some models. One 110 camera with SLR viewing incorporates a 25-50 mm zoom lens. This gives a choice of angles of view between "normal" and short telephoto effect.

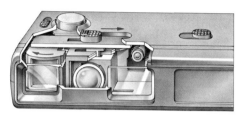

Supplementary lens
The fixed lenses of most compact cameras are designed for subjects 6 ft (1.8 m) or more away. With some models, you can slide a supplementary lens over the prime lens to enable you to photograph close-up subjects sharply. A telephoto attachment increases the magnifying power of the lens thus making distant subjects seem closer to the camera.

A few expensive 35 mm compact cameras accept interchangeable lenses. A mechanical system inside the body alters the viewfinder to correspond with the field of view of the lens in use. This mechanism is controlled by coded notches on each lens fitting. The camera body must have a focal plane shutter to allow lens changing without fogging the film. Recent designs also incorporate through-the-lens metering to allow for the change in field of view with different lenses.

Frame-line finder
Some sophisticated direct vision cameras will accept interchangeable lenses. Though the viewing area remains the same, lines corresponding to the field of view of the lens in use automatically appear in the viewfinder. You can preview the results of using various focal lengths by adjusting the frame-line finder

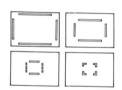

manually, by means of a switch on the camera body. Only a very limited number of lenses is available for this type of camera.

Practical handling considerations
Compact direct vision cameras are more convenient to carry and often quicker to use than other camera types. 35 mm compacts, particularly, offer a high degree of automation, and can provide technically successful results under wide-ranging conditions. Most compacts are relatively inexpensive and designed for ease of operation.

Picture composition controls, however, are more limited than with other types. Precision framing and focusing of close-up subjects is seldom possible. You cannot actually see the effects of depth of field (see *Depth of field,* p. 118), or of filters you may want to attach to the lens. Except with the most expensive models, you also lack a range of lens focal lengths comparable to that available for SLR cameras. It is impossible to use a zoom lens. The standard lens fitted to a compact camera usually has a short focal length. This can distort close-up subjects (an effect that becomes particularly noticeable in portraits). Compacts are useful when you require a small, light, unobtrusive camera. But 110s are so small and lightweight, they can be difficult to hold still during exposure.

Rollfilm SLR cameras

Rollfilm single lens reflex cameras work on the same principle as the 35 mm version (see *35 mm SLR cameras,* pp. 102-3), where a hinged 45° mirror reflects the image up to a horizontal viewing screen. A major design difference, however, is that on most models the familiar pentaprism is replaced by a focusing hood. This is mainly because the glass required to direct the light to an eye-level viewfinder is expensive, and can make the camera heavy and awkward to use.

The three most common formats of rollfilm SLR are the 6 × 6 cm (also known as the 2 $\frac{1}{4}$ × 2 $\frac{1}{4}$ ins), the 6 × 7 cm (the only type featuring a camera with a pentaprism as standard), and the 6 × 4.5 cm. The same 120 or 220 film (the only difference is roll length) is used for all the cameras.

As well as accepting interchangeable lenses, nearly all models take alternative film "backs". Each back is a light-tight magazine containing a rollfilm and take-up spool. A slide-in darkslide stops the film fogging when you remove the back from the camera (even partway through a film). Having preloaded backs is an obvious advantage when you need to change films quickly, or change from color to black and white in mid-roll.

Of particular interest to the professional is the instant picture film back. This allows the photographer to preview the results of a scene or complicated lighting set-up before snapping the ordinary film back on the camera.

Viewfinding and focusing

With most rollfilm SLRs you hold the camera at waist level and look down into the hood to see the image on the focusing screen. The absence of the pentaprism means that the image appears reversed left to right. Because of this, you may, initially, find the camera difficult to use (especially if held on its side). On some rectangular format models the camera back rotates to change from portrait to landscape picture shape. On the most popular, rollfilm SLR format, 6 × 6 cm, this problem does not exist because the camera produces only a square image.

For easier focusing, the standard focusing hood contains a fold-up magnifier, but other focusing hoods are made for eye-level use. A direct vision finder is also available, which clips on top of the camera, and is ideal for sports work or panning a moving subject, where the laterally reversed image on the viewfinder screen may be confusing.

Exposure settings

Few cameras of this format offer built-in exposure metering, but you can buy instead an

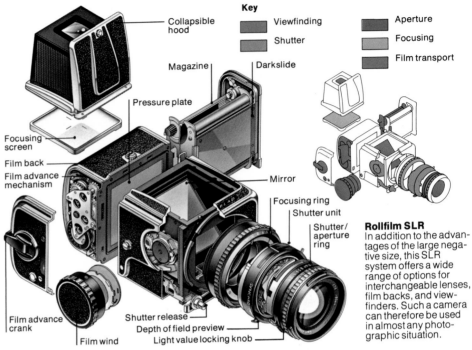

Key
Viewfinding
Shutter
Aperture
Focusing
Film transport

Collapsible hood
Magazine
Darkslide
Pressure plate
Focusing screen
Film back
Film advance mechanism
Mirror
Focusing ring
Shutter unit
Shutter/ aperture ring
Film advance crank
Shutter release
Depth of field preview
Film wind
Light value locking knob

Rollfilm SLR
In addition to the advantages of the large negative size, this SLR system offers a wide range of options for interchangeable lenses, film backs, and viewfinders. Such a camera can therefore be used in almost any photographic situation.

accessory metering hood that fits over the focusing screen without interfering with viewfinding. For the most part, though, these cameras are still intended for use with a separate, hand-held meter (see *Using a hand-held meter,* p. 136). Both the lens aperture and the shutter speed are controlled manually. As a precaution, some models have a device that stops you taking a picture while the darkslide covers the film (or prevents you removing the film back while it does not).

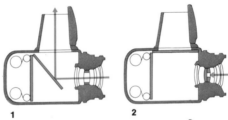
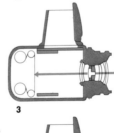
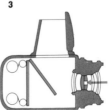

Exposure sequence
1 With diaphragm and leaf shutter fully open and capping shutter in front of the film closed, the mirror reflects light through the focusing screen. **2** On firing the shutter, the lens stops down and the mirror swings up. Leaf shutter closes and **3** capping shutter opens. As the leaf shutter fires, light reaches the film. **4** Capping shutter closes. Winding on opens the leaf shutter and diaphragm, and the mirror returns to 45°, returning the image to the focusing screen.

With rollfilm SLRs you have a choice of either focal plane or leaf shutter built into each lens. Usually, with this type of camera, the mirror does not return instantly after exposure. Winding on the film lowers the reflex mirror and restores the picture to the focusing screen (see below left).

Flash facilities

You can connect this format camera, via a synchronization cord, to any electronic flash-gun or studio flash equipment. Those models with leaf shutters will synchronize with flash at any shutter speed, but models with focal plane shutters are restricted to quite slow speeds because of the size of their shutter blinds (see *How shutters work,* p. 124-5).

Lenses and accessories

Rollfilm SLRs use a bayonet system for lens changing similar to that of the 35 mm SLR. The range of lenses is more limited, though, and each lens is more expensive. Each rollfilm SLR has its own system of accessories, which may include motor drives, extension rings, optical effects boxes, and clip-on meters (see *The rollfilm camera system,* p. 206).

Practical handling considerations

The main advantage of using a rollfilm SLR is the large film image size (approximately four times bigger than 35 mm). This means less enlargement and a resulting improvement in image detail and quality. There is also the convenience of film changing using the magazine system. Against this, every item of equipment is much more expensive, bulky, and heavy to carry. Film is also more expensive and there is less choice than with 35 mm. Improvements in the image-resolving power of modern 35 mm films and lenses are eroding the basic advantage of this larger-format camera.

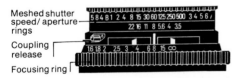

Meshed shutter speed/aperture rings
Coupling release
Focusing ring

Coupled aperture and shutter speed settings
With some lenses for rollfilm SLRs, the shutter and aperture rings are cross-coupled. As you change speed, the aperture control moves automatically and compensates for any change in exposure.

TLR cameras

Although only a limited range of twin lens reflex (TLR) cameras are presently made, thousands are still in use. They are mechanically much simpler than single lens reflexes. Two identical lenses — mounted together on a single panel, one above the other — focus forward or backward in unison. The top lens forms a viewfinding/focusing image on a screen at the top of the camera. When a leaf shutter behind the lower lens is fired, light passes through to expose the film. TLRs use the same film as rollfilm SLRs, but magazines and film backs are not available.

Viewfinding and focusing

TLR cameras are designed for waist-level use, although there is a magnifier in the hood, which allows you to use it at chest level, too. The picture shown on the screen is reversed left to right but it does not disappear at the moment of exposure (as a reflex mirror does not obstruct the light path to the film). For panning action pictures, where you need a correctly

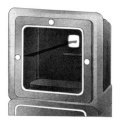

Eye-level finder
At times when the waist level finder is inconvenient to use, such as when panning a fast-moving subject, the front of the hood can be hinged down to give direct vision through a simple eye-level "sports finder".

oriented image, a simple, eye-level, direct vision finder folds out of the hood. On some models you can fit an accessory pentaprism.

As the viewing lens is separate from the actual taking lens, you may have to raise the camera slightly after composing and focusing to compensate for parallax error. Some models have a correction bar beneath the focusing screen to show the true top of the picture when framing a close subject. The viewing lens may have a larger aperture than the taking lens. To aid focusing it is set at maximum aperture. It is therefore not possible to preview the effects of

Parallax error

To correct parallax error, caused by the viewing lens being above the taking lens, the camera should be raised by the distance between the lenses. The distance can easily be measured if the camera is mounted on a tripod. A mechanical device called a paramender can also be used to raise the taking lens quickly to the correct level.

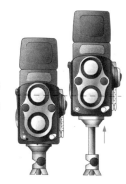

using a small lens aperture, although there is normally a depth of field scale.

Exposure settings

No TLRs have built-in light meters linked to the exposure controls. Like rollfilm SLRs, they are mostly used in conjunction with a hand meter (see *Using a hand-held meter*, p. 136). Some

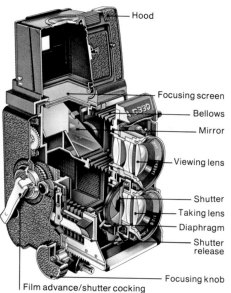

Hood
Focusing screen
Bellows
Mirror
Viewing lens
Shutter
Taking lens
Diaphragm
Shutter release
Focusing knob
Film advance/shutter cocking

Key
Viewfinding
Shutter
Aperture
Focusing

models have meters attached to the outside of the camera body — the cell points toward the subject, and a meter protruding from one side reads out the exposure settings. Most TLRs have separate wheels for aperture and shutter.

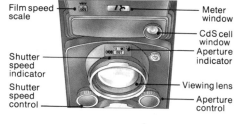

Film speed scale
Shutter speed indicator
Shutter speed control
Meter window
CdS cell window
Aperture indicator
Viewing lens
Aperture control

Exposure sequence
Light enters the upper (viewing) lens and is reflected on to a viewing and focusing screen by a fixed mirror **1**. The lower (taking) lens moves in parallel with the viewing lens during focusing. The taking lens has an aperture diaphragm with a leaf shutter behind. This opens **2** to admit light to the film. The subject is visible on the screen at all times during the exposure, which can be convenient for panning.

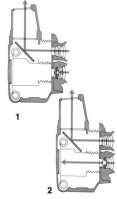

The settings you select may appear in a small window above the top lens, depending on the particular model.

Flash facilities
A connection (often near the lower lens) allows you to attach the synchronization cord from any flash unit. As TLRs have bladed shutters, they can be used with flash at any speed setting. For on-camera use, you must mount the flash unit on a L-shaped bracket, which screws into a socket on the camera base plate.

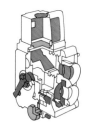

Rollfilm TLR
The twin-lens design makes the TLR bulky. Because of the separate viewing and taking lenses, interchangeable lenses (for a model which will accept them) must be bought in pairs. Some makes have interchangeable focusing screens. All have additional direct vision finders formed by apertures in the hood to enable you to shoot from eye level. Motor drives, coupled or TTL metering, and film magazines are not available for such cameras.

Lenses and accessories
Interchangeable lenses for TLR cameras are supplied in coupled pairs. Because changing lenses involves the expense of replacing both the viewing and taking lenses, there is only one model made at present with this facility. To stop the film fogging, a light-tight flap covers the film while the lens panel is off the camera body. Choice of lenses is very limited.

In comparison to other camera types, there are few accessories — the TLR is not designed as part of an elaborate camera system. You can buy push-on close-up filters in pairs, and it is possible to use such accessories as filters, diffusers, and prism attachments. You hold each one in front of the top lens to preview the

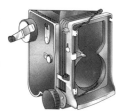

Changing lenses
A few TLR models allow the use of interchangeable lenses, which clip over this fitting and are secured by a wire catch. Choice of focal length is, however, very limited because of the high cost involved in changing both lenses.

results, and then move it down in front of the bottom lens for shooting.

Practical handling considerations
Apart from offering a convenient format at a reasonable price, the TLR allows you to view the subject throughout the picture-taking sequence — even during exposure itself. It is quieter to use than the SLR, having fewer moving parts. Also, the rollfilm image requires less enlargement than 35 mm results.

The main disadvantages of this camera type are parallax error (between viewing and taking lenses) and that the viewing image is reversed left to right. The lack of TTL metering can also prove a problem to those used to 35 mm SLR cameras. Also the cost of a pair of lenses (one with a shutter) is high if you want to change to telephoto or wide-angle.

Sheet film cameras

Most of today's sheet film cameras (also known as view cameras) have either a mono-rail or baseboard design. Monorail types are built up in units on a metal rail, clamped to a tripod or stand. These units hold the lens panel and ground-glass focusing screen, fitted between bellows. You move either lens or screen along the rail, altering the distance between them, in order to focus the image. Baseboard types work in the same way, except that the fo-

Baseboard camera

This will accept inter-changeable lenses. The baseboard carries a distance scale to aid focusing. This model also has a coupled rangefinder and an optical direct vision finder, making it suitable for hand-held photography as well as studio work.

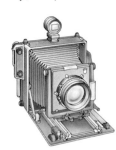

cusing screen back is hinged to a folding metal or wooden baseboard, and this board has tracks for the lens panel unit.

The majority of cameras take 5 × 4 ins (12.5 × 10 cm) photographs. Some types are in the 5 × 7 ins (12.5 × 18 cm) or 10 × 8 ins (25 × 20 cm) formats, although all are adaptable to take smaller sized images. Sheet film cameras are slow to set up and operate, but they are still invaluable for architectural, still-life, and some portrait photography. They are also the choice of a few photographers who demand a considered approach to subjects such as landscapes and architecture.

Viewing and focusing

Sheet film cameras normally have no separate viewfinder. You must first set up the camera on a tripod, open the shutter, and set the lens aperture to its widest diameter. Then, by looking at the upside-down image on the full-sized focusing screen, some of which are marked with a grid for precise viewing, you compose the picture and focus it sharply. For very close

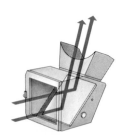

Reflex focusing hood

An alternative to a darkcloth, this focusing hood masks off stray light which would make the image on the focusing screen hard to see. It also contains a mirror to correct the inverted image produce by the camera lens and seen on the screen.

subjects it is essential that the lens is well forward of the screen. If necessary, add extra lengths of bellows. The view camera image is difficult to see unless you block off any ambient light surrounding the focusing screen. You must use the photographer's traditional "darkcloth" to cover your head and the back half of the camera, or else a hood with eyepiece. Some hoods contain an angled mirror to show the image the right way up. Monorail cameras allow independent swinging or tilting of the front and back of the camera. These "camera

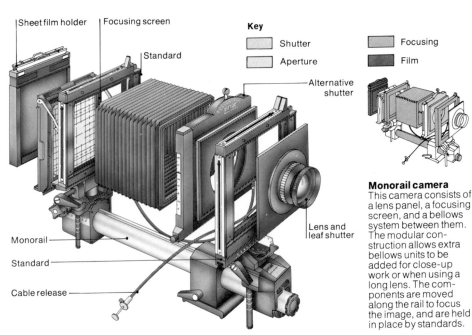

movements" give additional control of image shape and sharpness (see *Movements on sheet film cameras,* p. 121).

Exposure sequence

Most photographers use a hand meter to read exposure with a view camera. (A few monorail cameras have a meter with a probe to measure light from any part of the focusing screen image.) Once you have set lens aperture and shutter speed controls (usually on dials sur-

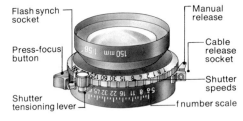

Bladed-shutter lens

In addition to the shutter speed and aperture setting control, this lens has a press-focus button. When you

depress this button the shutter blades open instantly, allowing the image light through to the focusing screen.

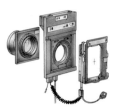

Shutter

This universal shutter can be used with less expensive lenses without built-in shutters. It links up with the film holder.

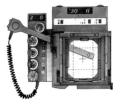

Metering

A very accurate light-sensitive probe permits selective metering at the film plane on some sheet film TTL-equipped models.

Key
- Shutter
- Aperture
- Focusing
- Film

Monorail camera

This camera consists of a lens panel, a focusing screen, and a bellows system between them. The modular construction allows extra bellows units to be added for close-up work or when using a long lens. The components are moved along the rail to focus the image, and are held in place by standards.

rounding the lens), the shutter blades close and then tension, ready to fire.

You load sheet film into a light-proof holder in the darkroom. When the holder is inserted in the camera, the film takes up the position previously occupied by the ground-glass focusing screen. Next, you must pull out the light-proof cover in front of the holder, and fire the shutter to expose the film. Reverse this process to remove the exposed film, and to return the image to the focusing screen. Some view cameras have mechanical or electrical links between the front and back of the camera. And with some types, the shutter automatically closes and tensions when you insert the film holder, reducing the lens diaphragm to your selected aperture. You remove the film holder to restore the image to the focusing screen and reopen the aperture.

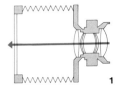
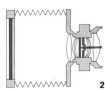
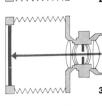

Exposure sequence

1 The image is focused and composed with the shutter open. **2** The lens is stopped down and the shutter closed. A film holder is inserted into the camera and its front cover removed, leaving **3** the film ready for exposure by firing the shutter. **4** With the shutter now closed the cover is reinserted so the entire holder can be removed for processing.

Flash facilities
The shutter on a view camera has a connection that accepts the synchronizing cord of a flashgun or studio flash, and synchronizes with flash at all shutter speeds. You may have to disconnect flash when focusing, to prevent the open shutter from triggering the circuit.

Lenses and accessories
Each size of view camera will accept a modest range of lenses. You remove the front lens panel and change it for another one, ready mounted with a different focal length lens. (Usually each lens has its own bladed shutter.) As wide-angle lenses have to be quite close to the focusing screen, you must replace the normal bellows with bag bellows, which occupy less space. A number of models have an electronic remote control accessory that you attach close to the focusing screen. Push buttons allow you to set lens aperture and shutter speed from this position – a wire passes sig-

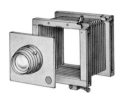

Interchangeable lenses
Lenses of different focal length are mounted on standard panels for easy interchange. Each has a diaphragm and usually a shutter as well.

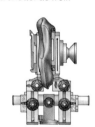

Bag bellows
You can use short, bag bellows with wide-angle lenses, which need to be positioned closer to the screen than other, longer focal length lenses. They are more flexible than a standard bellows, thus allowing freer shifts and swings.

nals to an electronic aperture and shutter unit located at the lens. Special camera backs are available that modify the basic view camera so that it accepts film of a smaller format, or instant picture film packs.

Practical handling considerations
The large size of the view camera negative produces excellent image quality and detail, and makes retouching work easy. As every exposure is on a separate piece of film, you can process each to suit the particular subject. (Unlike other films, where processing is a compromise between the varying needs of dozens of images.) Composing on the focusing screen avoids parallax error and because the aperture stops down you can preview exact depth of field.

Large-format monorail cameras are not suitable for hand-held work, or any subject you have to compose and shoot quickly. Equipment and materials are expensive, and awkward to set up, dismantle, and carry around. But the degree of camera movements is unmatched by any other camera type. Provided you know how to use them (see *Movements on sheet film cameras,* p. 121), the movements of a view camera are an important technical aid to the creative control of image shape, sharpness, and depth of field.

Instant picture cameras

Instant picture materials give you a finished print a few seconds after exposing the film. The special cameras designed to take instant pictures follow broadly the same principles as direct vision viewfinder or single lens reflex types (see *Direct vision compact cameras,* pp. 104-5 and *35 mm SLR cameras,* pp. 102-4). They differ a great deal in design, however, because of the larger format of the picture materials. An instant picture camera must form an internal image big enough to give an album-sized print (because there is no enlargement process); and the image must be transmitted to the light-sensitive material in such a way that

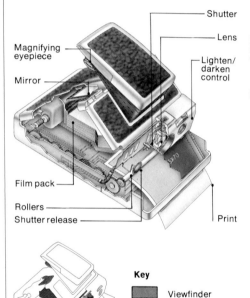

Magnifying eyepiece

Mirror

Film pack

Rollers

Shutter release

Shutter

Lens

Lighten/ darken control

Print

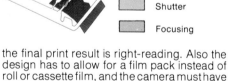

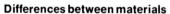

Key

▨ Viewfinder	▪ Film
▨ Shutter	▫ Metering
▨ Focusing	

the final print result is right-reading. Also the design has to allow for a film pack instead of roll or cassette film, and the camera must have spring-loaded rollers to eject each print.

Differences between materials
Cameras made for Polaroid and Kodak integral (single sheet) print materials have the film pack arranged in different ways in relation to the lens. Polaroid material forms the image on the surface that faces the lens during the exposure. This means that the camera must always reflect the image off an internal mirror between lens and surface if the final print is to be right-reading. Kodak material produces the images on the back of each exposed sheet; so cameras for this type of material do not need a mirror.

Loading arrangements
Each manufacturer's camera takes its own, specially designed, drop-in pack of 10 sheets of color material. Polaroid prints give a picture size of 3×3 ins (7.5×7.5 cm), and Kodak $2\frac{3}{4} \times 3\frac{1}{2}$ ins (7×9 cm). After insertion of the pack, and the camera is closed, the protective sheet that covers the unexposed pack ejects.

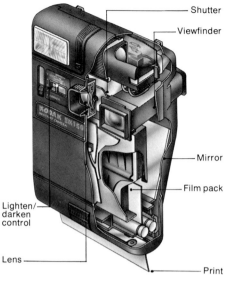

Shutter

Viewfinder

Mirror

Film pack

Lighten/ darken control

Lens

Print

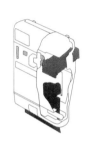

Camera types
Some instant picture cameras (above) have a direct vision view-finder. The focusing distance of the lens is fixed, and will only give sharp results with subjects 6 ft (1.8 m) or more away, even though the image always looks sharp in the viewfinder. With more advanced models (left), you can vary focus and see the results through the SLR viewing system. In both cases, exposure is automatic. The small diagrams show the position of the main camera features.

Thereafter, each exposed sheet is ejected through rollers (the pressure these rollers exert starts the material's internal processing). At first, the plastic sheet looks white, but the picture quickly appears and the colors soon gain full strength.

Viewfinding and focusing
Direct viewfinder types of instant picture camera have the finder very close to one side of the lens, and so you must compose your image to compensate for slight parallax error, especially when working at close subject distances (see *Direct vision compact cameras,* pp. 104-5). You focus the lens by estimating the distance to the subject and setting this on the lens mount. Some models have fixed focus, and others have an autofocus device, which uses ultrasonic waves to set the lens automatically, focusing on whatever is closest in the scene (see *Autofocus lenses,* p. 115).

The single lens reflex instant picture camera allows you to see and focus the image formed by the lens through a unique optical system. The image is reflected off a mirror covering the unexposed film, and then picked up by an eyepiece at the top of the camera. When you take the picture the shutter closes, and the mirror rises to 45° (obscuring the eyepiece). Next, the shutter fires, and the image is reflected off the underside of the mirror on to the now unobscured film surface.

Some SLR models have a sonar autofocus-

Autofocus SLR
The SLR system allows you to see in the viewfinder whether or not you have focused the lens correctly. With some models, focusing is done automatically by transmitting ultrasonic signals toward the subject from a disk above the lens.

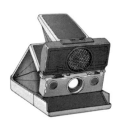

ing system that allows you to use the reflex system for viewfinding, while the autofocus mechanism keeps the image sharply focused. This enables you to change position without having to reset the lens focus.

Exposure settings
Instant picture cameras are designed for simplicity of use. Shutter speeds and apertures are not shown, and, therefore, cannot be manually controlled. A light sensor facing the subject controls the settings (usually variations in shutter speed) to give a correct exposure. Since you can check results almost immediately, a "lighten/darken" overriding

Exposure controls
Set the control to "lighten" if the main subject is much darker than the rest of the picture. Use "darken" for light subjects with dark backgrounds.

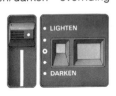

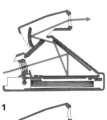

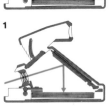

Exposure sequence
1 In the Polaroid SLR (above), light reaches the eye through the lens and a series of mirrors.
2 When the shutter fires, the mirror covering the film rises and its underside reflects light on to the film. The mirror then returns to cover the film.

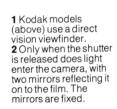

1 Kodak models (above) use a direct vision viewfinder.
2 Only when the shutter is released does light enter the camera, with two mirrors reflecting it on to the film. The mirrors are fixed.

control is fitted so that you can take a second, corrective picture. A warning signal in the viewfinder shows that the camera will set a long exposure – this enables you to use a firm camera support or change to flash.

Flash and accessories
Instant picture cameras accept flash bulbs, bars, or electronic flash, designed to suit particular models. Some flashguns designed for conventional cameras are not compatible. Several models have built-in electronic flash. In each case there is a simple recommended subject-to-flash distance, according to the light output of the unit. Other accessories include a flash diffuser, delayed action release, and telephoto and close-up clip-over lenses for the SLR variety.

Backs for other formats
Special instant picture backs are made to fit sheet film cameras, rollfilm SLR cameras, and some 35 mm reflex models. These replace the normal film holder, magazine, or camera back (see *The rollfilm camera system*, p. 206). Since there is no special mirror system in conventional cameras, a different type of Polaroid material is used to give a right-reading print. The lens image forms on one sheet of material, which is ejected through rollers from the back in face contact with receiving paper. After a set time, you peel the sandwich apart to reveal an image the right way round. In the past, am-

Instant picture backs
Many rollfilm and sheet film cameras will accept an interchangeable back holding instant picture film. You can use these to make a final check on exposure, lighting, and composition before shooting the same scene on conventional film stock. Some photographers also use instant picture material for their final composition.

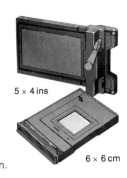

5 × 4 ins

6 × 6 cm

ateur cameras were made for this film type.
Backs take 10-sheet packs of material mostly $3\frac{1}{4} \times 3\frac{1}{4}$ ins (8.2 × 8.2 cm) but only the center of the film is used on rollfilm cameras. Since you can interchange these backs with regular film backs, photographers use them for quick lighting or exposure checks. Some peel-apart material is made for 10 × 8 ins (25 × 20 cm) cameras, housed in a single-exposure holder. After taking the picture, you pass the sandwich through motor-driven rollers in a table-top unit to give an 10 × 8 ins (25 × 20 cm) print.

Lenses
A professional rangefinder instant picture camera is available that takes Polaroid peel-apart material and has interchangeable lenses. Lenses are bayonet mounted (see *35 mm SLR cameras*, pp. 102-4), and produced in wide-angle, standard, and medium telephoto focal lengths. Each lens has manual aperture settings, and its own built-in shutter. In addition, a close-up kit, consisting of a focusing

Interchangeable lenses
Instant picture cameras used by professionals have, in addition to a 127 mm standard lens, a choice of 150 mm portrait and 75 mm wide-angle lenses, with viewfinders to match. Close-up kits give focusing down to $5\frac{1}{2}$ ins (14 cm).

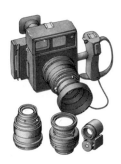

Telephoto lens
This lens from the Polaroid system simply attaches to the front of the normal camera lens. It gives an image magnification of × 1.5 that of the prime lens fitted to the camera.

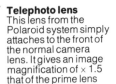

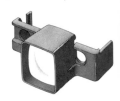

screen and several screw-in lenses, allows you to focus down to $5\frac{1}{2}$ ins (14 cm).

Practical handling considerations
The unique feature of immediate results means that instant picture cameras have two special, quite different roles in photography. First, the cameras, with their automatic controls, are ideal for the amateur without any technical knowledge, who does not want processing delays. However, the cameras are bulky to carry around, despite a print size which is small in relation to enlargements from conventional film. The light-sensitive material is more expensive to buy than other types, and extra color prints can only be made by copying the original. The limited range of technical controls, lenses, and other accessories prevents the work of the photographer without a conventional camera from progressing and developing.

The other important role for instant picture equipment is in professional and applied photography. An instant picture back quickly slips on to a large-format professional camera to give an on-the-spot check of lighting, composition, and exposure. Cost here is much less important than the assurance that the models, sets, and technical equipment all work together as planned. This enables the professional to take the final photograph on regular film with much less risk of an expensive reshoot. SLR, interchangeable lens rangefinder, and special-purpose instant picture cameras give high-quality, immediate results in professional, scientific, and technical areas.

SLR systems and functions

The diagram on this page summarizes the manual operations of a typical 35 mm SLR camera, and their mechanical and electrical effects. The camera offers manual selection of lens aperture and shutter speed, and the through-the-lens meter makes open-aperture exposure readings.

The diagram traces the connections between the external setting controls (left-hand column), the functioning of the camera's mechanical parts, and the electrical links to metering, flash, and motor drive circuits (center and right). The operational sequence reads from top to bottom, and it assumes that the photographer has already loaded the camera, but has not yet wound on the last exposed frame of film.

Setting the film speed alters a variable resistor that forms one of four influences on the exposure meter read-out. The others are lens aperture (sensed from the setting on the lens), shutter speed setting, and light from the image (sensed by the meter cell). Switching on the meter energizes the whole circuit.

Operating the wind-on lever positions unexposed film, changes the frame counter, and tensions the shutter blind spring for firing. (On this particular camera, it is possible to bypass film transport by pressing a multiple exposure button, allowing the superimposition of several images on one frame.)

After focusing, you select lens aperture and shutter speed. When selecting aperture it is good practice to check depth of field visually, holding down the preview button that temporarily closes the lens aperture to the f stop you have chosen.

Selecting shutter speed programs the delay that will occur between the two shutter blinds when they pass across the front of the film. At this stage it is possible to set the self timer for delayed release of the shutter, or to lock up the mirror in order to reduce vibration.

Releasing the shutter activates the lens aperture mechanism in a way similar to that of preview button. It also raises the mirror. The first shutter blind begins to travel, starting to uncover the film. The delay set by the shutter speed control determines how much later the second blind begins to follow on, covering the film again. The chart shows what happens when you use a fast shutter speed (upper path), so that only a slit created by the two blinds passes across the film. This is not suitable for flash, because the second blind has already partly covered the film before the first completes its travel. With a shutter speed of 1/60 sec or less (lower path), the first blind has completed its travel, leaving the film fully uncovered, before the second moves. This allows a full flash image to record on the film.

As soon as the shutter has fired, the motor drive, if used, is electrically activated. The lens reopens mechanically to its widest aperture for viewing and focusing, and the mirror returns to its 45° position to reflect the image to the focusing screen. The camera is ready to take the next picture.

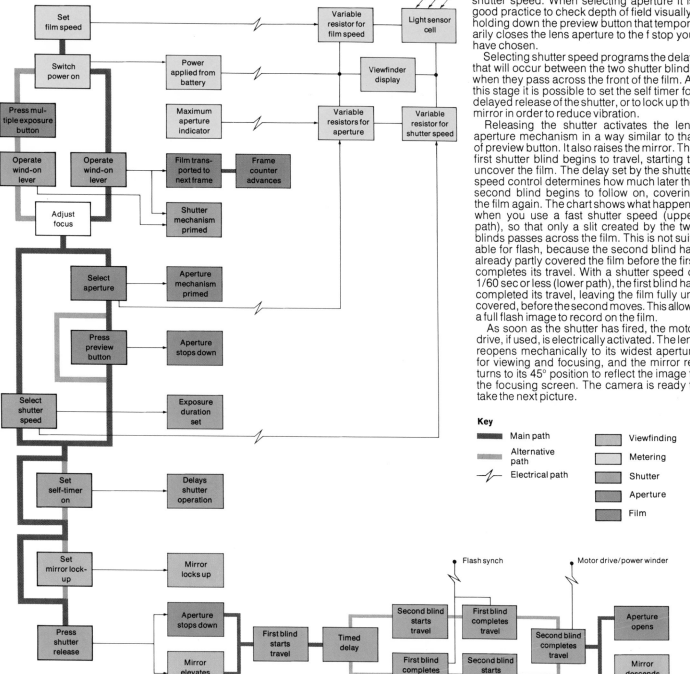

Manual functions   **Mechanical/electrical functions**

Key

Main path
Alternative path
Electrical path

Viewfinding
Metering
Shutter
Aperture
Film

Lens controls

The first part of the camera to be discussed in detail is the lens, and its two controls — focusing and aperture. It is perfectly possible to form an image in the camera without having a lens at all — simply using a small hole, in the same way as the earliest camera obscuras. The image, however, would be too dim and unsharp for serious consideration. Basically, a glass lens is essential to bend light rays reflected from the subject, so that they come into coherent focus on the film surface as a bright, clear (and, incidentally, upside-down) image.

Focusing

Since the distance required between lens and film to produce a clearly focused image changes, according to the distance of the subject being photographed, some form of focusing movement is usually necessary. On most lenses this is achieved by moving the focus control ring, which physically racks the lens forward or backward. The photographer can check the results of this movement by either referring to a distance scale on the lens barrel itself or by viewing the image changes (on rangefinder, reflex, and view cameras). Some recent camera types have automatic focusing, which uses sensors in the camera body to determine subject distance and adjust the position of the lens to allow for this.

Aperture

Focusing allows any chosen part of the scene, up to the nearest limits, to be sharply rendered. Elements within a scene that are nearer or farther from the point on which focus is set may also appear sharp. This factor is mostly controlled by the diameter of the lens aperture, which the photographer can alter within the design constraints of the particular lens, by moving the aperture ring.

If the lens has an adjustable aperture, it allows the photographer to decide whether to limit narrowly the area of sharp focus (and so concentrate attention), or to make nearly everything in the picture equally sharp (and of equal "weight"). Lenses also vary in their light-bending power (or "focal length"). Each camera format has its own standard size of film. In order to include the same amount of a scene on these different size films, different focal length lenses are necessary. For example, a 50 mm lens on a 35 mm camera ("standard" for that format) would have to be changed to an 80 mm lens on a 6 × 6 cm camera (again, "standard" for that format) to include the same scene on the larger film.

See also
Additional equipment, pp. 184-5.

Pinhole images

You can make a camera using any light-tight box with a small pinhole in one face to allow light to enter. Because light travels in straight lines, rays passing through the hole that have been reflected from the top of an object reach the bottom part of the film only. Rays from the bottom of the object reach the top of the film only. The image formed, therefore, is upside down, very dim (because the hole is small), and not very clear.

The loss of image clarity is due to the fact that each cluster of rays that passes through the pinhole forms a beam of light which gradually

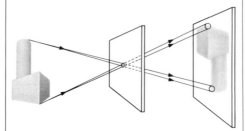

Pinhole camera
A pinhole limits light from each part of the subject to a particular part of the film. The image consists of tiny patches of light, as the rays still diverge. Try this for yourself by mounting an SLR camera on a tripod and removing the lens. Tape aluminum foil tightly over the lens mount and pierce it in the center with a needle. The viewfinder image will be dark, but in bright light an exposure of around 4 sec with ASA 100 film will yield a recognizable image of the subject (below). Because this method of image formation is so imprecise, it is best to bracket exposures.

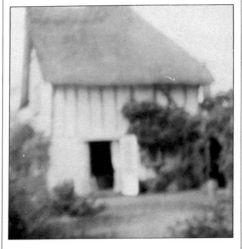

grows wider the farther it travels from the object. So, a speck of light from the object can only become wider and form a much larger patch of light on the film surface (see above). The smaller the pinhole the smaller the patch of light becomes, but there is no way it can ever form a sharply defined picture. Something, therefore, has to be used to bend the light rays together after they reach the hole, so that they form a coherent image.

Refracting light

When light passes from one substance (such as air) to another, denser medium (such as glass or water) it slows down slightly. If the light direction is oblique, this slowing effect creates "drag" on one side of the beam, causing the light to swivel and change direction. The bending of light in this way is called "refraction". Optical illusions created by the refraction of light are all around us — for example, a stick

Refraction
When light passing obliquely through one transparent medium, such as air, reaches a denser medium, such as water or glass, it will bend toward a right-angle drawn at the point of entry. If it then re-emerges into a less dense medium it bends in the opposite direction. Refraction makes a stick appear bent where it enters a pool of water, or water appear less deep than it really is.

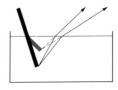

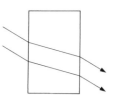

appears to bend at the point where it enters water, and a swimming pool to look shallower than it really is.

As light enters glass from air obliquely, it bends more perpendicularly to the surface of the glass. Returning from the glass to the air, it bends in the opposite direction, and so be-

Prism
When an oblique light ray passes through a prism which has angled faces, refraction at each surface gives it an overall change of direction.

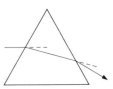

comes less perpendicular.

If you have a piece of glass with the front non-parallel to the back (a prism, for example), a beam or ray of light can be changed in its overall direction. Instead of angling upward, it can be redirected downward. If you place two prism blocks of glass one on top of the other (in a crude lens shape), you can make a diverging beam of light converge.

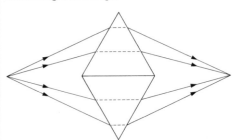

Converging lens principle
When two prisms are placed base-to-base, light rays from a point source are refracted so that they converge to a point again after passing through the prisms.

This is the principle of the converging lens and it is capable of forming an image that can be focused on a screen.

Basic converging lens

A lens which has at least one convex surface and so is thicker in the center than it is at the edges will cause rays of light to converge (just what the pinhole fails to do). When used in place of a pinhole in the camera, this type of lens gives a much brighter image because of its wider diameter. It is also capable of resolving much sharper detail – provided it is placed at the right distance from the film plane. If this distance is incorrectly set, all detail will dissolve into patches of light again. Results may be even worse than those formed by a simple pinhole. Once this distance is correctly set to give a sharply focused image of a distant object, the distance between the lens and image on the focusing screen is known as the

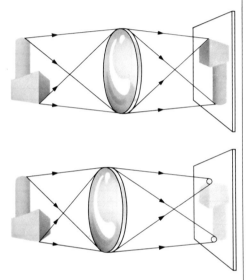

Converging lens
Light from a subject passing through a converging lens is changed from a diverging beam. It can focus a clear, inverted image on a screen (top). Unlike a pinhole image, you can only focus the image sharply at one particular distance from the lens for each subject distance. At other lens-screen distances (above), the image becomes unsharp.

focal length of the lens. A converging lens has what is described as a positive focal length, and so is sometimes called a positive lens.

You can think of the simple converging lens as a magnifying glass. If you look at an image formed by a magnifying glass, though, you will see that it has several defects. When the center is sharp the image around the edges is blurred and distorted, and there is a general mistiness about the whole scene. Photographs taken with a lens having these defects are too unclear for general use.

Camera lenses

A modern camera lens is very much more complicated than a simple magnifying glass, although it operates on the same principle. Lenses for cameras may consist of many elements (each one an individual lens) arranged in groups – often six or more pieces of glass differing in their shape, type of glass, and spacing, one to another. This complexity is necessary to correct the optical errors (or "aberrations") always associated with a single, simple lens. The requirements of lenses for different format cameras vary greatly. Much has to do with the area to be filled, the maximum aperture which is acceptable, the weight and size of the lens itself, and the degree of enlargement of the resulting film image.

Every lens transmits a circular field of light (although only the area actually encompassing the film is used), and the level of illumination toward the edges of this field falls off

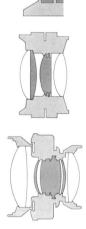

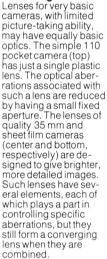

Lens design
Lenses for very basic cameras, with limited picture-taking ability, may have equally basic optics. The simple 110 pocket camera (top) has just a single plastic lens. The optical aberrations associated with such a lens are reduced by having a small fixed aperture. The lenses of quality 35 mm and sheet film cameras (center and bottom, respectively) are designed to give brighter, more detailed images. Such lenses have several elements, each of which plays a part in controlling specific aberrations, but they still form a converging lens when they are combined.

rapidly. The area of the field of light usable for sharp image formation increases as the lens is stopped down. On relatively simple cameras, the lens may be fixed at quite a small aperture (such as f 8). This greatly reduces the complexity of the lens, as many aberrations disappear at this size of aperture setting. On the other hand, many different groups of elements are necessary to correct any aberrations on a standard 35 mm SLR lens, which may have a variable 8-10 stop aperture control. This complexity increases again when lenses are designed for view cameras (see *Sheet film cameras,* pp. 108-9), where the lens must be able to cope with lens movements as well (see *Movements on sheet film cameras,* p.121).

To achieve a balanced result, the lens designer has to calculate how best to combine converging elements with weaker (concave shaped) diverging elements, so that they will counteract each other's distortions. The final image must be equally sharp overall. Straight lines, for example, must record without bowing. There must be no color fringes (the focusing of light of different wavelengths, and hence color, at different positions), and the light must not scatter from bright to shadowed parts of

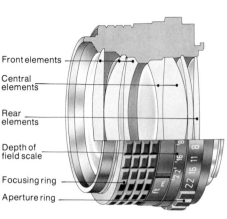

Front elements
Central elements
Rear elements
Depth of field scale
Focusing ring
Aperture ring

Standard lens for 35 mm cameras
This typical design makes use of both converging and weaker diverging elements. Their relation to one another, and how they affect the light path, is shown below. Precise optical engineering must be allied to a sufficiently rugged construction to withstand a normal amount of wear and tear.

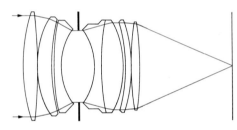

the image. At the same time, the lens has to be of the required focal length, have the widest possible aperture, and not be too expensive or delicate to manufacture and assemble.

The most complex, highly corrected lenses, such as zooms (see *Zoom lenses,* pp. 192-4), may have 14-16 elements. Without special care this volume of glass and the numerous air/glass surfaces alone would produce a degraded image – like looking through a similar number of windows. To avoid this type of distortion, only exceptionally clear and colorless optical glasses are used. Each surface is coated (bloomed) with several microscopic layers of antiflare substances. These layers absorb the proportion of light that would otherwise reflect and scatter between the lens elements and generally flatten image contrast and brilliance. The front and back external glass surfaces of the camera lens have a tougher coating than the inside surfaces because they are exposed to the atmosphere and impurities present in the air.

Focusing

The camera lens must be set in the right position in relation to the film in order for it to form a clear, sharp image. This exact distance depends on the focal length of the lens and the distance of the main point of focus from the lens. The closer the subject is, the greater the distance between lens and film has to be.

Fixed focus lenses have their position set for the best possible compromise between distant and moderately close subjects. Most lenses, however, are focusable, using the focus control ring. It is possible, with detachable lenses, to fit an extension ring or collar between lens and body to further increase this focusing movement, and so allow the focusing of closer subjects. The limiting factor is determined by the fact that corrections for image faults are no longer as effective when the subject is very close to the lens. Special lenses, called macro lenses, are specifically designed for this type of work. Some regular lenses have an adjustment ring, which repositions some of the internal elements for optimum correction when it is set to "macro mode". Another way of focusing on close objects (suitable for fixed lenses too) is to add a weak converging lens to the front of the lens.

Focusing aids
The most obvious focusing aid is the focusing screen that is found on reflex and view cameras. Another aid is the rangefinder system used on some direct vision cameras. Autofocus systems take this a stage further and automatically set lens distance to suit subject distance.

Having the option of focusing on one particular distance means that the photographer can emphasize parts of the scene within this zone. This effect is particularly noticeable if the main subject is close to the lens. But just how extensive the area of sharp focus will be also depends on the focal length of the lens and the lens aperture.

Being able to render different parts of a picture selectively out of focus helps overcome one of the main problems in photography – the recording of unimportant and distracting information. Sometimes a photograph will benefit from there being no point of sharp focus. Outlines will tend to soften, and a more abstract impression of spreading light and color will result. The important thing is to have full control over the results through the knowledgeable application of lens focusing.

See also
Emphasis, pp. 67-72. **Close-up equipment** *Close-up picture making*, p. 197.

Focusing and subject distance

Most camera lenses cannot focus very close and very distant objects at the same lens-to-film setting. Rays of light from a close object reach the lens in a more steeply diverging beam than light rays from an object farther away. As each lens has a set light-bending power (determined by the elements' shape and glass type, and their grouping within the lens), rays passing through it from close objects require a greater distance in which to come together again (to form a sharply focused image on the film plane). To increase this distance, you must focus the lens pro-

Distant subject

Near subject unfocused
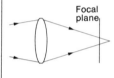

Near subject focused
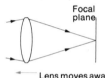

← Lens moves away from focal plane

Focus and subject distance
Light from a distant subject (top) travels in near-parallel lines, and is brought to focus at the film plane. With the lens in the same position (center), diverging light from a source nearer the camera would, however, be brought to focus at a point behind the film plane. Therefore the lens has to be moved nearer the subject (bottom), so that light can be focused on the film plane itself.
A lens with an adjustable focus control allows you to compensate for different subject distances, but only within the design constraints of that particular lens.

gressively more forward the closer the subject is to the camera.

In practice, the physical distance you have to shift the lens between focusing on something on the horizon, the infinity mark (∞) on the lens barrel, and something at, say, 20 ft (6 m) from the camera is quite small. To change the focusing setting from 20 ft to 5 ft (1.5 m), though, requires a bigger lens shift. But to change focus from 5 ft to 2 ft (60 cm) requires a greater lens movement than both previous changes together. You can check this by looking at the focusing scale of any lens – close subject settings are farther apart than distant subject settings. A lens for very close focusing work, therefore, has to come well forward of its "normal" position. This may (depending on subject) be further than the normal rotating thread on the lens barrel will allow.

One solution to this type of problem is to fit an extension tube or bellows unit between the lens and camera body. These greatly increase the lens-to-film distance, and therefore allow much closer focusing (see *Equipment for close-up*, pp. 195-6).

Fixed focus lenses

Lenses that are set in one focus position are designed to render sharply subjects that are both far away and "reasonably close" to the camera. Usually the lens is set for a subject distance somewhere between these two limits, and relies on the smallness of the lens aperture (which must also be fixed or very limited in its adjustment) to extend the zone of sharp focus over the required range of subject distances (see *Depth of field*, p. 118).

A fixed-focus lens will never produce a photograph with an unsharp background, and there are distinct limitations to the nearest subject distance it can render sharply. The zone of sharp focus is greater with a small-format 110 camera than with a fixed-lens 35 mm type, as the 110 has a shorter focal length lens fitted

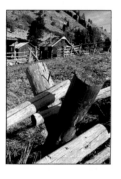
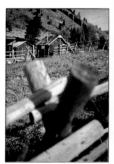

Fixed and variable focus lenses
With a small-aperture, fixed focus lens (above left), sharp focus extends from infinity to a point a few feet from the camera. You cannot choose which areas of the picture you wish to be sharp or unsharp, as you can with a variable focus lens (above right). Having the ability to focus selectively gives you the option of creating different subject emphases within the frame.

as standard. Large-format cameras, with lenses of longer focal length, can only sharply record subjects 6 ft (2 m) or farther away (see *Camera lenses*, p. 113).

You can use a fixed-lens camera for close-ups by attaching a weak converging lens to the prime lens. This will collect the steeply diverg-

Distant subject
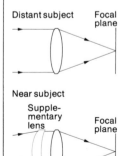

Near subject
Supplementary lens

Close-up attachments
Fixed focus lenses are designed to bring light from a distant subject, traveling in almost parallel lines, to a point at the plane of focus. When the diverging rays of light from a near subject pass through a supplementary (converging) lens they are refracted and thus reach the main lens and focal plane along the same path as rays from more distant subjects.

ing light from a close subject and present it to the camera lens as if coming from further away. Each close-up lens attachment works for one particular subject distance, so you will need several to cover a range of close-up subject distances.

Focus setting aids

Unless your camera is fitted with an actual focusing screen, you must have some means of knowing what settings to make on the focusing control of the lens. Symbols engraved on some focusing rings aim to simplify this by indicating typical distances for portraits (head and shoulders), groups, and distant views. More often you will find a scale of distances, ranging from the nearest objects the lens is capable of focusing on, to objects at infinity, which effectively means the distant horizon.

With practice, you can guess distances beyond about 8 ft (2.5 m) fairly accurately. Sometimes you can calculate closer distances by knowing, for example, that a person's head at a certain distance from the camera exactly fills the frame. If the camera has a direct vision finder, it may also incorporate an optical rangefinder. It works on the principle of showing two views of the same subject (one through the viewfinder itself, and one reflected by a mirror or prism from a window farther along the camera body). When the two views coincide on the focusing screen, the subject is in focus. The closer the subject is to the camera, the more the mirror or prism behind the far rangefinder window has to be angled to show the same part of the scene as the direct view (see *Direct vision compact cameras,* pp. 104-5). By having a mechanism that makes the mirror or prism swivel according to the focusing position of the camera lens, the rangefinder gives positive focusing preferred by some to that of the reflex system.

Autofocus lenses

Some cameras have fully automatic lens focusing systems. There are three main ways in which a lens can "sense" a particular subject distance — either by comparing contrast, scanning with invisible infrared radiation, or by measuring with sound waves.

Contrast-comparing autofocus works in a way similar to an optical rangefinder. The autofocus unit gives one fixed view of the subject, and another via a pivoting mirror linked to the camera's lens focusing control. Both views are projected on to light-sensitive electronic panels. These compare the patterns of light and dark, and halt the lens movement when the image contrasts are identical. In practice, you must make sure that your main subject elements appear in the marked area of the viewfinder — the measurement area of the autofocus unit. The lens starts off in the infinity position (close to the camera body), but then moves forward as you begin to press the shutter release until it is halted by the "in focus" signal. A unit of this type can be fooled by repetitive patterns and low-contrast subjects. It also needs bright subject illumination.

sary, and cannot be confused by subject contrast and patterns. However, shooting through glass may cause inaccurate focusing, as the system will "read" it as a subject position.

The ultrasonic system uses inaudible 1/1000 sec "bleeps". A large transmitting disk sends out the signal and a timing circuit measures how long it takes for the sound to reflect back from the nearest object in the scene. The unit controls a rapid-drive motor which shifts and so focuses the lens. This system works in darkness, measuring for the center of the frame but always focusing on the nearest object. Windows, railings, or vegetation may, therefore, fool the system.

The danger with all autofocus systems is that the unit may read the wrong part of the scene. Even with the most popular system — the contrast-comparing method — it is possible to photograph two people, for example, and unwittingly allow the sensor to measure the background area between them. Or you may often want your main subject off-center in the picture. The better autofocus cameras allow you to make the focus settings with the subject center frame, then lock the lens position while changing to a more off-center composition before shooting. These systems are, however, becoming more sensitive and accurate all the time.

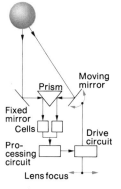

Contrast-comparing autofocus
The subject is imaged through a fixed mirror on to one set of light-sensitive cells. A second, moving, mirror, linked to the lens focusing mechanism, seeks an electronically measured contrast match for a second set of cells. When both images present the same contrast, the lens will stop automatically in the correct position.

Infrared autofocus systems send out a narrow beam of invisible IR light from one window and use a pivoting mirror to scan the scene. Another window, backed by an IR detector cell, acts as a receiver for the beam reflected by any subject within the system's "target area" as outlined, again, in the camera viewfinder. Depressing the shutter starts the scan and then the mirror and the lens movements stop when the strongest signal is received by the detector. This system works well in daylight and in dark conditions where a flash is neces-

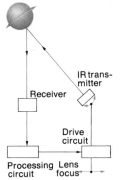

Infrared autofocus
As the lens begins to rack out toward the subject, infrared light from the transmitting diode on the right scans the subject. It is beamed back into the receiving sensor, and when the strength of the IR signal reaches its maximum, showing that the lens has moved sufficiently forward for the subject to be correctly focused, the sensor triggers the autofocus mechanism to stop.

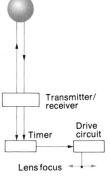

Ultrasonic autofocus
Pulses from the timer activate an amplifier and power circuit. An ultrasonic signal is beamed at the subject from the transducer. The timer sends regular counting signals to an accumulator until the echo returns to the transducer. It then stops counting. The signal's travel time is computed from the accumulator data and a motor drive focuses the lens.

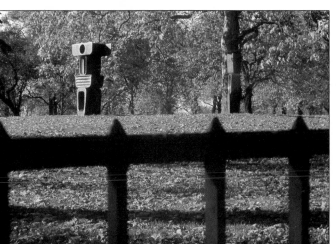

Problems with autofocus systems
The picture (left) illustrates the drawbacks and limitations of some autofocus mechanisms. The pronounced areas of light and shade would confuse contrast-comparing autofocus. Though the sculpture is the main subject, an ultrasonic or infrared model would probably focus on the fence, as this is the nearest solid object to the camera. The off-center position of the sculpture would also cause problems with these types of autofocus, as most systems are set for centrally placed subjects.

Using focus control

A major advantage of having a focusable lens, apart from the fact that it allows you to record the main subject sharply, is that you can determine emphasis. By separating items that you want to be detailed and clear from unimportant items at other distances, you emphasize the former creatively. This "differential focus" effect applies particularly to close-ups, because the lens must be so far forward that distant detail becomes very unsharp.

When you are taking candid shots and do not want to attract the attention of your subject, it is often possible to find something at approximately the same distance from the camera but in another direction. By prefocusing on this surrogate subject, there is less chance of your real subject being aware of you. Another useful technique is to prefocus on a spot on the ground you expect your subject to pass over. This is of particular value in sports photography, where subjects move very fast. It is also advisable to familiarize yourself with which way to move the lens control to focus on a subject moving toward or away from you. This is of particular value if you must continuously adjust focus on a fast-moving object. Interesting results are also possible if there is no point of focus in the picture. Study the appearance of lights and reflections on the focusing screen with the lens defocused.

Focusing problems can result if reflections are a prominent part of a composition. If your picture contains reflections in mirrors or water, for example, bear in mind that the contents of the reflection are further away from you than the surface itself. If a mirror 6 ft (2 m) away is reflecting something beside you, you must set the focus control to 12 ft (4 m) to show the reflected detail in sharp focus.

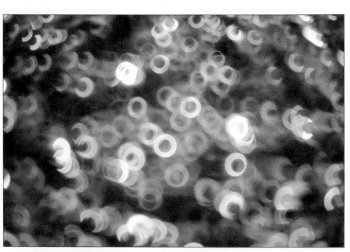

De-focused imagery
With no point of sharp focus in the picture (by John Sims), bright highlights spread into abstract disks, which match the frontal appearance of the lens.

Differential focus
By focusing sharply on the figure of the tribesman, and using a wide aperture setting, Jurgen Schadeberg was able to isolate him from the background. The shallow depth of field makes the other figures record less distinctly.

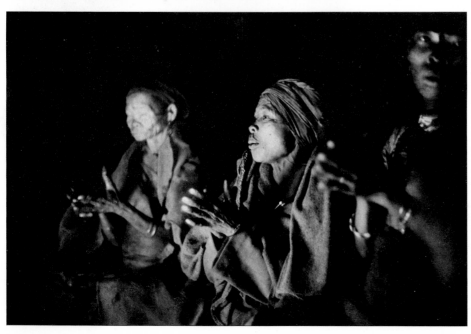

Aperture

Apart from lens focusing, the other major control found on the lens varies the size of the lens aperture. On simple cameras, the aperture control may simply shift a piece of metal containing holes of different sizes across the back of the lens. However, more elaborate cameras have a series of blades which reduce (stop down) the size of the aperture continuously – similar in effect to the iris of the eye.

The aperture has two important influences on picture results. First, it controls image brightness, allowing more or less light through to the film, depending on subject lighting. A lens with a wide range of aperture settings is, therefore, usable in widely varying lighting conditions.

Second, the lens aperture controls the amount of a scene that is recorded sharply at any one focus setting. This means that a picture taken with a very wide aperture will show sharp detail only in that part of the subject where the lens is focused. The same scene taken at a smaller aperture will produce a picture with a wider zone of sharp subject detail. This zone of sharpness is referred to as "depth of field".

The choice of aperture is often determined by the requirements of producing the "correct" exposure – to compensate for shutter speed, for example. At other times, though, the photographer will want to manipulate depth of field consciously. A shallow zone of sharp focus will, for example, concentrate attention on a very specific area of a composition.

Determining depth of field

Since depth of field exerts such a powerful influence on a picture's appearance, most cameras offering variable apertures also have some way of indicating what sort of results to expect when different apertures are used. This may be a depth of field scale of distances near the focus scale of the lens. SLRs usually have a depth of field preview button on the body or lens. The button manually closes the aperture down to the preselected value chosen by the photographer for that exposure (something that normally only happens an instant before the shutter fires). With the lens stopped down the photographer can see precisely the area that will be in sharp focus by examining the focusing screen image. This facility is not available on either TLRs or direct vision cameras, because the screen image is not formed by the picture-taking lens. With a view camera, the aperture stops down or opens up each time the aperture ring is moved, and the varying effects of depth of field are evident on the focusing screen.

See also
Emphasis, pp. 67-72. Depth and distance, pp. 80-5. Exposure and its measurement, pp. 132-8. Additional equipment, pp. 184-5.

Changing apertures

In the early days of photography apertures were literally flat pieces of tin, each with a hole of different diameter stamped out of it. They could be slipped, one at a time, through a slot in the lens, and were known as "stops". Photographers carried little leather packets of stops, and selected them according to the lighting conditions. Changing from a large to a smaller hole became known as "stopping down", a term still used today. Later, the system was made more convenient – the holes were punched in a disk or strip of brass, which could be rotated or moved sideways through the lens barrel to bring different-size apertures into the center of the light beam.

Today's simple cameras may use a similar arrangement. A sliding control, often marked in weather symbols depicting bright sun, hazy sun, and cloudy conditions moves a strip of metal behind the lens so that a hole of one size replaces one of another. There are no half-way positions. The majority of modern cameras, however, use an iris diaphragm. This is an arrangement of overlapping metal leaves constructed so that rotation of a ring on the lens barrel varies the diameter of the hole continuously – from wide to narrow. A diaphragm allows you to change from one aperture to another quickly and simply, and you can also use it at intermediate settings.

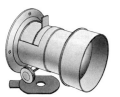
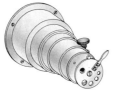

Early aperture settings
Small pieces of tin known as "stops", each of which had a hole of different diameter, were inserted into a slot in some early lenses to regulate the amount of light entering the camera and reaching the light-sensitive emulsion. Later models had a single brass disk stamped with a range of holes, which was revolved to select the appropriate aperture.

Automatic diaphragm
The f number required is set by turning the aperture ring on an SLR camera's lens. This primes the iris diaphragm so it is ready to stop down to the pre-selected aperture when the shutter is released. Until then, it remains wide open for easy focusing. Depth of field can be monitored with the preview control which stops the lens down to the chosen aperture and then goes back to full aperture.

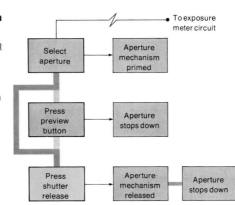
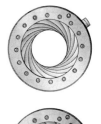

The f number system

Over the years an internationally agreed scale of f numbers has been devised, and appears on virtually all iris diaphragm controls. They usually run f 22, 16, 11, 8, 5.6, 4, 2.8, 2. The higher the f number, though, the smaller the aperture. F 16 has a diameter one-sixteenth the lens focal length, whereas f 4 is one-quarter the lens focal length.

Another important feature of the system is that a change from one f number to the next either halves or doubles the amount of light that passes through the lens. A picture taken at f 5.6 is twice as bright as one taken at f 8, but only half as bright as one taken af f 4. This doubling or halving relationship is very convenient when related to shutter speeds (see *Shutter and aperture relationships*, p. 125), which are marked in a series of halving or doubling fractions of a second. If, for example, you enlarge the aperture by two stops, you can increase the shutter speed by two settings, allowing film exposure to remain constant while varying picture effects. For example, a wide aperture gives shallow depth of field, and the faster shutter speeds stops subject movement, preventing blur.

f stop	22	16	11	8	5.6	4	2.8	2	1.4
Light admitted	1	×2	×4	×8	×16	×32	×64	×128	×256

F numbers
This table shows how each f stop on a descending numerical scale doubles the amount of light let in by the previous stop. This is because, as the diameter of a circle is doubled (change of two f numbers), its area increases fourfold. Thus a setting of f 8 lets in four times as much light as f 16.

Lens "speed"

It is clearly an advantage to have a lens with a wide range of f numbers. Wide apertures – f numbers less than f 2, for example – are especially useful if you expect to work in dim lighting conditions and do not wish to use a slow shutter speed. Unfortunately, wide-aperture lenses are difficult to design with the same image excellence as small-aperture types (most optical errors greatly increase at low f numbers). This fact explains why wide-aperture lenses are more expensive than lenses with small apertures.

The maximum aperture – sometimes referred to as the "speed" of the lens – is engraved, together with focal length, around the front glass element of the lens. Sometimes this aperture departs from the regular series. For example, a lens may provide a maximum aperture of f 1.8 (half a stop wider than f 2).

At the opposite end of the f number scale, apertures seldom exceed f 16 or 22. The aperture could be designed to close to smaller numbers still, but this arrangement also begins to introduce new optical errors (such as diffraction), so that again image quality in the final result deteriorates.

Lenses for larger format cameras tend to have less lens speed – and so are called "slower" – than those designed for the 35 mm format. For example, standard lenses for the 35 mm format commonly have a maximum aperture of about f 1.4, whereas on rollfilm cameras a lens with a widest aperture of f 2.8 is regarded as "fast". F 3.5 or even wider is the typical maximum aperture for a lens designed for use on a view camera.

Lens definition
Most lenses give their best performance at mid-range aperture settings, such as f 5.6 and f 8. Beyond this, there may be a noticeable fall-off in image quality. Generally, this will be more apparent at the edges rather than at the center of enlargements from the same negative.

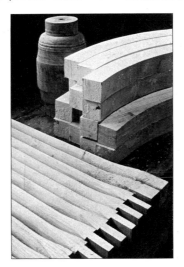
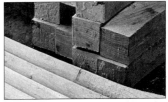
Center

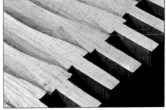
Edge

Depth of field

Stopping down the lens reduces its effective diameter and narrows every beam of light passing through the glass. This has an interesting effect on parts of the image that were previously out of focus because they were either nearer or farther away than the part of the image actually being focused on. What were previously patches of light creating unsharp detail become narrower until they are indistinguishable from points of light and, therefore, record as areas of sharp detail. The result seen on the film is that the zone of sharp detail recorded at one focus setting becomes deeper. When this happens, depth of field is said to have increased.

Depth of field increases both in front of and behind the point focused on as the lens aperture is stopped down. This effect is shown, too,

on a depth of field scale found on the barrel of most lenses that are not fixed in one focus position. For any particular focus setting the scale indicates the distances of the nearest and farthest objects that will also appear "acceptably" sharp in the picture.

A single lens reflex camera normally displays the image on the focusing screen at the widest aperture setting available on that particular lens, whatever the f number you have actually chosen to make the exposure. This is a double convenience. First, the image is bright and easy to see. Second, focusing is much more critical with the lens at its widest aperture because depth of field is at its shallowest. To preview the results of using different apertures, press the depth of field button found on most SLRs. This closes the aperture

down to the one you have preselected for your exposure. The image will dim (unless you have preselected the widest available aperture), but you will be able to see the limits of sharp focus.

Reading depth of field
Most lenses have a fixed depth of field scale next to the distance markings on the focusing ring. This has two numerical scales, one either side of a central mark, corresponding to the aperture settings of the lens. The mark aligns with the distance at which you have fo-

cused the lens. Reading off the aperture you are using against the focusing ring markings shows you the nearest and farthest distances between which objects will be in focus. At small apertures or more distant subject focus settings, this zone of sharp focus could be quite extensive.

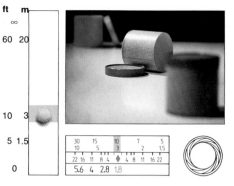
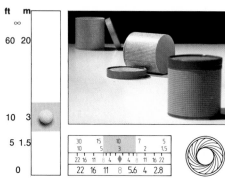
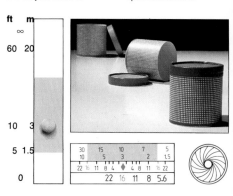

Technical considerations

The use of depth of field is important because it affects image appearance and picture composition. If your camera has features such as variable aperture, focusing control, and interchangeable lenses, each of these will affect the zone of sharp detail in different ways. And by understanding how the technical factors

work, it will often be possible to use them as creative image-making devices.

Depth of field is dependent upon lens aperture, subject distance, and focal length. The smaller the aperture the greater the depth of field becomes at any one focus setting. Subject distance is also important — if you focus on

a close subject, depth of field will be less than when you focus on a distant subject. The reason for this is that the lens must shift position far more when focusing on near subjects than on far subjects, and depth of field is affected by the cone of light made between the lens and film. In practice, this means that you have to take more care to set lens focus accurately for close subjects, knowing that there will be less depth of field to cover any errors.

The third factor having an effect on depth of field is the focal length of the lens itself — the longer the focal length the less the depth of field at any particular focus and aperture setting. This is because a long focal length lens has to move position more than a lens of short focal length in order to focus on the same range of subject distances. This means that a 35 mm format camera, which has a 50 mm lens as standard, will produce greater depth of field (at any particular aperture or focus setting) than a rollfilm camera, for which 80 mm is the normal focal length.

Factors affecting depth of field
Aperture, subject distance, and the focal length of the lens all have an effect on depth of field. As shown at near right, depth of field increases as aperture size decreases. At very close distances (center right), depth of field is drastically reduced, and tends to extend more equally in front of and behind the subject in focus. The longer the focal length of the lens, the shallower the depth of field, as can be seen (far right) by comparing the standard lenses for various film formats. Similarly, wide-angle (short focal length) lenses always give greater depth of field than telephotos. This makes depth of field an important consideration in lens choice.

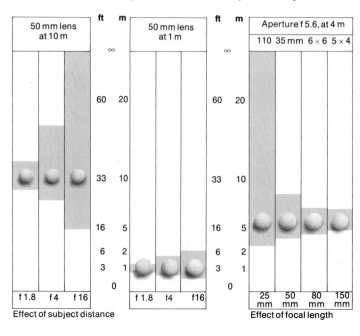

Effect of subject distance

Effect of focal length

Depth of field scale

You can learn a lot by studying the depth of field scale engraved on the camera lens. First, the pairs of f numbers give a constant reminder that greater depth of field results from using a higher f number. Second, you will see from the spacing of the distance figures that there is much greater depth of field at the more distant subject settings. From looking at the depth of field scale you will notice that if you focus the lens at infinity and use a small aperture, part of

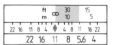

Hyperfocal distance
With the camera lens set at infinity, the nearest sharp point to the camera is at the hyperfocal distance. By focusing the lens for this distance, the view is still sharp at infinity, but depth of field now extends back toward the camera to half the hyperfocal distance.

the potential depth of field is wasted. In focusing a landscape, for example, in which you wanted everything from the distant horizon to very near the camera to appear sharp, you would do better to focus for about 33 ft (10 m) and stop the lens down to about f 11 (or to an even smaller aperture). At f 11 depth of field will extend from infinity back to about 16 ft (5 m) from the camera (assuming a 35 mm camera fitted with a 50 mm lens) – much closer than if you focused just for infinity.

For each aperture marked on your lens you will find that there is a different lens focusing distance that you can use to produce depth of field from infinity back to half this focus setting. These are known as "hyperfocal distances". Cameras that have fixed lenses are generally set to their hyperfocal distance for their maximum aperture in order to give the widest possible zone of sharp focus.

Standards of sharpness

The zone of sharp detail given by depth of field does not suddenly become unsharp at its nearest and farthest limits – the effect is gradual and continuous. A point of light coming from the subject is only reproduced as a true point on the film when critically focused on by the lens. The effect known as depth of field is only possible because the eye accepts the disks of light representing object points at other distances (other than the one being focused on) as being "acceptably sharp", too. These disks gradually grow larger the farther the objects are from the part of the scene on which you are focusing.

Most manufacturers of 35 mm cameras assume that a patch of light 1/30 mm in diameter or smaller will be acceptable on the film as a sharp reproduction of a point of light. (This is known as the "least circle of confusion", and assumes an average degree of enlargement, and also how the picture detail on the print will look to an observer with average vision viewing it from a normal reading distance.) Different circle of confusion standards apply to other camera formats – the smaller the negative the greater the enlargement required.

Maximum depth of field

Maximizing depth of field allows you to make objects at widely ranging distances from the camera all appear acceptably sharp. This is achieved most easily if you use a small aperture and pick a viewpoint as far as possible from the nearest of the objects in view. A camera with a short rather than long focal length lens is also an advantage.

When focusing, try to visualize which part of the scene should form the critical "core" of sharpness, taking into account that depth of field will extend both beyond and in front of this point. If your subject is a close-up portrait, for example, focus the lens for the person's eyes – the key part of the face. If you are photographing a feature in a landscape, make this the point of critical focus.

Some scenes may contain two elements at greatly varying distances, both of which you want sharp. The best way to focus the lens in this case is to set it for a distance about one-third within the required depth of field. If, for example, the near element is 9 ft (3 m) from the camera, and the far element 24 ft (8 m), you will have a depth of field requirement of 15 ft (5 m), and should focus for 14 ft (4.5 m) – one-third within the required sharpness zone.

Stopping down the lens tends to extend depth of field about twice as far beyond the point of sharp focus as it does in front of it. This holds true except for close subject distances. When working closer than about 3 ft (1 m), this pattern changes and depth extends equally either side of the point of focus. With a sheet film camera, you can use the independent front and back movements (see *Movements on sheet film cameras,* p. 121) to extend depth of field substantially.

Choosing depth of field

Whether to make all elements within the scene sharp, or to go for more localized detail, depends on your particular subject and interpretative approach. Maximum depth of field gives maximum information, bringing out detail everywhere. This is valuable in scenes, such as landscapes or interiors, where a wealth of interesting detail may contribute to the mood and atmosphere.

Using a small aperture to maximize depth of field can create problems – in dim lighting, for example, a small aperture may be prohibitive because it also reduces the amount of light passing through the lens. To compensate you will have to use a slow shutter speed (see *Shutter and aperture relationships,* p. 125), or a more light-sensitive film.

Shallow depth of field dictates to the viewer. It emphasizes objects at one distance and veils everything else, to a greater or lesser extent, in unfocused blur. This "differential focus" is a useful device for implying depth and softening distracting detail that may clutter the background or foreground. It is possible to make unwanted areas unrecognizable, or remain as soft shapes, which still suggest the surroundings. You could use shallow depth of field, for example, to draw attention to the eyes in a portrait, or to pick out a few people in a crowd, or to picture someone within a naturally occurring foreground frame, which is gently softened in outline.

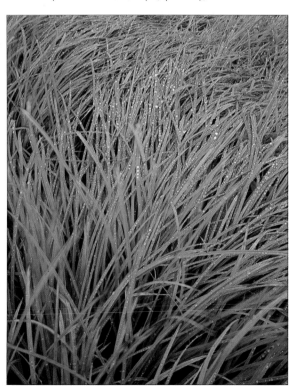

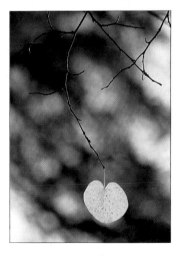

Shallow depth of field
Robin Bath used a wide aperture to create a limited depth of field which isolated the sharply focused leaf (above) against an out-of-focus background.

Extensive depth of field
Dennis Brokaw stopped his lens well down so that depth of field extended through almost the whole picture.

Focal length and camera size

The amount of a scene a camera includes from any one viewpoint depends on the focal length of its lens and the size of its picture format. Designers of fixed-lens cameras aim for a compromise between too wide a view (which might make everything look too small and far away), and too narrow a view (which may not include enough of the subject). It is general practice for normal, or "standard", lenses to have a focal length approximately equal to the diagonal measurement across the camera's picture format. This means that although each size of camera has a different focal length standard lens, it takes in approximately the same angle of view.

Cameras such as single lens reflexes and sheet film types allow the standard lens to be removed and another (of either shorter or longer focal length) to be fitted instead. Changing focal length will give a wider or narrower angle of view. The lens must fill the whole picture area with an image of even quality. It would be futile to take a standard lens from a 35 mm camera and try using it as a short focus lens on a 6 × 6 cm rollfilm camera. Although the lens has the correct focal length, it is only designed to fill an area 24 × 36 mm. On the larger format camera, the picture corners would appear darkened and unsharp.

Camera movements
Lenses for sheet film cameras can usually fill a larger area than the camera's picture format, which is, typically, 5 × 4 ins (12.5 × 10 cm). Cameras of this type allow the lens to be used off center – either above, below, or to one side of the picture center. Using the lens like this produces some very useful effects. You are able, for example, to include the top of a tall building without pointing the camera upward and so forming converging vertical perspective lines. In addition, offsetting or tilting the front and back parts of the camera independently provide control over image shape and sharpness. It is possible to take apparently square-on views of reflective surfaces such as mirrors, without showing the camera. If your subject includes a plane at an oblique angle to the camera, you can double or treble depth of field over this plane by using camera movements. Some of these camera movements are also available in a limited form with rollfilm and 35 mm cameras.

See also
Depth and distance, pp. 80-5. Additional equipment, pp. 184-5.

Angle of view

The angle of view of a lens depends on its focal length and the size (measured across the diagonal) of the picture format. For example, a 50 mm focal length lens used on the usual 35 mm

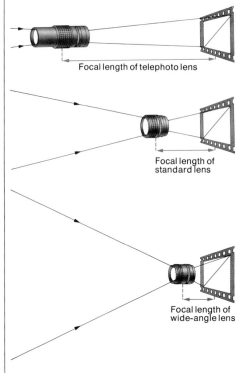

Focal length and angle of view
The focal length of a standard lens is similar to the format diagonal. Lenses with longer or shorter focal lengths must be placed farther from or nearer to the film to focus the image, and give a narrower or wider angle of view.

film frame (24 × 36 mm) produces a 43° angle of view. In practice, when any lens is focused on close subjects it moves out farther from the film, and gives a slightly narrower angle of view. A shorter focal length lens, or larger format, gives a wider angle of view. Longer focal length, or smaller format, produces a narrower angle of view.

Standard lenses have an angle of view of about 40°-45°. To some extent, this parallels human eyesight. (Look through the viewfinder of an SLR held vertically, keeping both eyes open. The subject through the finder is about the same size as the subject seen directly.) To achieve a similar angle of view, a 6 × 6 cm rollfilm camera requires an 80 mm lens, while a 5 × 4 ins (12.5 × 10 cm) camera must have a 150 mm lens. All three cameras are designed to include the same amount of a scene, even though their picture sizes vary greatly. A difference between them, though, is the amount of depth of field each individual one offers (see *Depth of field*, p. 118).

Covering power
If you hold a camera lens so that it forms an image on a sheet of paper, you will see a patch of light containing miniature details of the sub-

Film area
Covering power (circle), though adequate for the format (square), must be greater if shift is used.

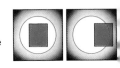

ject. This image patch must be larger than the camera's picture dimensions, or the corners of every frame will be darkened and blurred. Each lens, therefore, has sufficient covering power to fill its own format. Even then, this assumes that the lens will be directly opposite the film center. If it is to be shifted off center, it will require much greater covering power.

Lens and camera movements

The most common lens movement – focusing backward and forward – is practically universal A few lens and camera designs offer additional movements. One of these is a sliding movement of the lens, either up, down, or sideways from its normal location in the center of the frame. This shifts the image in the same direction, but because the lens is much closer to the film plane than to the subject, a small lens shift equals a much larger change to the image. Lens shift movements allow you to set up the camera off center to the subject and then "slide" the wanted parts of the image on to the film. Without this facility you would have to

angle the camera obliquely, causing perspective lines to distort (see below).

Tilting and swinging movements (pivoting about the horizontal and vertical axes) are useful if your subject is mostly on one long oblique plane, such as a floor or wall. Pivoting the lens so that it becomes slightly more parallel to the subject increases depth of field.

On sheet film cameras you can also tilt and swing the camera back. This helps increase depth of field when photographing oblique surfaces. It can also distort linear perspective, by enlarging the image at one end of the picture and diminishing it at the other.

Avoiding reflections
The photographer needed a square-on viewpoint, but using a conventional lens he included his own reflection. Moving the camera to one side, and recentering the image with a shift lens, has preserved the viewpoint but cut out reflections.

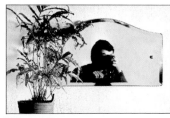

Without shift

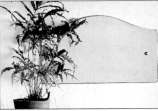

With shift

Movements on 35 mm cameras

Several lenses for 35 mm SLR cameras offer a special shift device. Turning a control knob on the lens moves it a few millimeters sideways so that it is off center on its mount. You can convert this to an upward or downward movement by rotating the whole lens through 90°. Shift lenses are much more expensive than normal types, not only because of the mechanical extras, but also due to the greater covering power any lens must have to be used in this way.

A few shift lenses also have the facility to

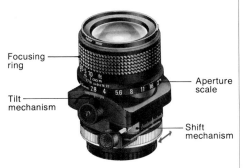

Shift lens for 35 mm cameras
This perspective control (PC) design has a swing movement in addition to upward-downward shifts. These become sideways shifts by rotating the mount through 90°. There are very few shift lenses made for 35 mm format.

pivot slightly, so that the lens is no longer parallel to the film. This is a useful device for improving depth of field (see *Depth of field,* p. 118). Angling the lens means that, again, it is no longer aimed at the frame center, and must, therefore, have exceptional covering power to be effective. This is why pivoting is only found on lenses designed for shifting too. You can see the effects of shift and pivoting movements on the SLR focusing screen and decide on the exact effect before shooting.

Movements on sheet film cameras

For really comprehensive camera and lens movements, a sheet film camera is unbeatable. The monorail design in particular (see *Sheet film cameras,* pp. 108-9) offers maximum swings, tilts, and shifts of both the front and back of the camera. For shift movements, the lens support unit at the front moves sideways by about 1 in (2.5 cm) to the left of right. Since the focusing screen unit itself has similar facilities, you can move it in the opposite direction to double this amount of shift. The same applies to vertical upward or downward shifts (respectively, rising or drop front).

Both the lens panel and camera back will pivot horizontally and vertically. In fact you can even set the back and front at right-angles to each other. The limiting factor here is not the flexibility of the connecting bellows, but the covering power of the lens. Be careful to look for good image quality and evenness of illumination on the focusing screen.

Controlling converging lines

When you aim a camera squarely at a subject such as a building, which has strong vertical lines, these lines will appear parallel to each other and to the sides of the frame. As soon as you tilt the camera, though, the lines appear to converge on a distant vanishing point, creating a distorted result.

Sometimes, convergence (especially if it is slight) gives an irritating result. Vertically designed buildings seem to taper, and the two sides of a street lean toward each other. To avoid this, you must keep the back of the camera absolutely vertical. If this excludes the top of the building from the picture, you can shift the lens upward. As it moves, it will bring in top parts, but lose some of the bottom of the scene. Using a camera without lens shift, you would have to move backward until the whole building was included, and then greatly enlarge the resulting small image.

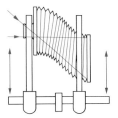

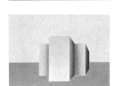

Shift movement and converging verticals
Raising or lowering the lens panel or camera back (above) keeps the film plane parallel to a vertical subject. The lens can be raised above the center of the film to include the top of the subject. Angling the camera brings the bottom of the film closer to the subject than the top, making parallel lines appear to converge (top right). Using shift movements gives the results above and below.

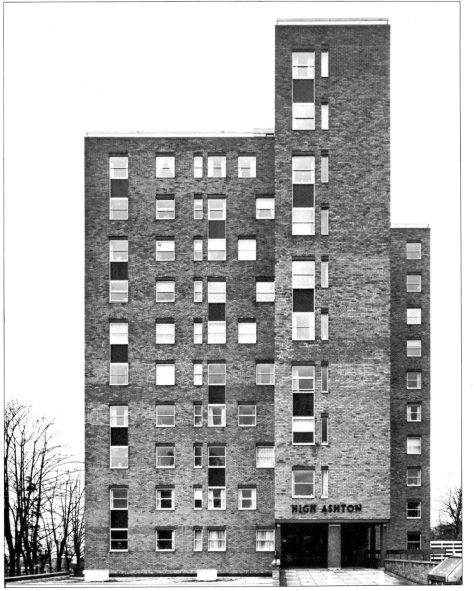

Controlling reflections

There are times when you want to photograph a reflective surface without also revealing yourself or the camera. The subject may be a shop window, a mirror on the wall, or even a close-up of glossy paintwork. Using an ordinary camera without the benefit of movements, you would have to choose an angled viewpoint, or somehow disguise the camera equipment, perhaps by shooting through a hole in a large sheet of paper or cardboard (see *Underwater life*, pp. 302-3).

With shift lens facilities (see *Movements on 35 mm cameras*, p. 121), you take up a viewpoint just sufficiently to one side of the surface to avoid reflections, making sure, though, to keep the camera back parallel to the surface.

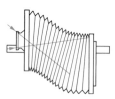

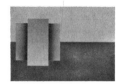

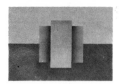

Sideways shift
Without movements, the subject may have to be shown obliquely, with converging horizontals, or framed off-center (top right). By moving the camera back to one side, but still parallel to the lens panel (above left), the lens shifts the image to the center of the film

(above right). Use this to avoid perspective distortion caused by altering the viewing angle that you would otherwise have to use.

Part of the subject will then be out of the frame — but if you side-shift the lens, the wanted parts will "slide" on to the focusing screen. The reflective window or mirror appears in the picture as if it were taken square-on, but there is no reflection of you or the camera equipment.

Shifting the vanishing point
Because the lens is normally positioned opposite the center of the film, perspective lines on inward-facing subject planes converge toward the center of the picture. A normal, square-on view of a room, for example, shows the floorboards as a symmetrical pattern with a single straight line in the middle and increasingly converging lines to the left and right. Squares on a ceiling also form converging lines pointing toward a distant vanishing point.

Lines created in this way in photographs can prove to be important compositional devices — they can lead the eye to one key element in the background, for example (see *Lead-in lines*, p. 72). Having a lens shift control allows you to change this structure. If you give the lens a full sideways shift you will transfer the center of the converging lines to one side of the picture instead of having them in the middle of the frame.

De-centering perspective
Without movements, the parallel lines of the floorboards would have converged on the center of the picture. By using sideways shift (below), Trevor Melton moved the apparent vanishing point to one side, so that the lines draw the eye toward the vase placed off-center in the frame. This produced a more dynamic composition than would be possible with symmetrical, converging lines.

Improving depth of field

You will sometimes find that a scene almost entirely exists on one oblique plane. Examples of this include a reclining figure, the façades of a row of houses, or a landscape of flat terrain — all subjects where the main interest may lie on one continuous surface stretching from the near foreground into the far distance. In cases like this, even the smallest aperture coupled with the longest possible shutter speed may

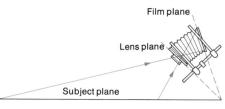

Scheimpflug correction
For maximum depth of field over an inclined subject plane (above), tilt the lens and film planes until all three intersect at an imaginary point. Trevor Melton used this technique to create extreme depth of field in the picture below. Added control was given by using the very small minimum lens aperture that is available on most sheet film cameras.

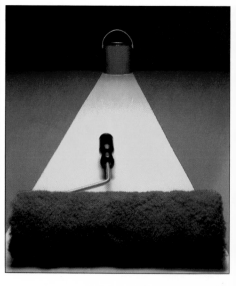

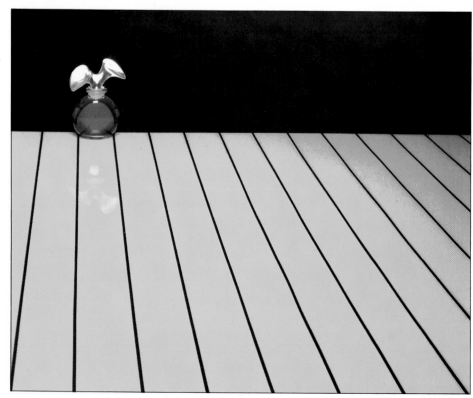

not produce sufficient depth of field for your picture. This is especially true if the nearest elements you want to render sharply are particularly close to the camera. You may also find that if exposure becomes too long, a distortion known as "reciprocity failure" will occur (see *Reciprocity failure*, p. 152).

The way to create massive depth of field using a view camera is to tilt the lens so that the subject plane, lens surface, and camera back all converge toward one point. Even at the widest aperture there is an immediate gain in depth of field. With the lens stopped down as well, sharp detail can easily extend from a few inches in front of the camera to infinity. This arrangement of lens and camera back is an old professional device, discovered by T. Scheimpflug in 1894, and known as the "Scheimpflug correction".

Effect with 35 mm cameras

If you are using a small-format, 35 mm camera, tilting of the lens alone is generally sufficient to produce an enormous extension of depth. With a large-format camera, greater lens tilting and some tilting of the back as well may be necessary to have an equivalent effect. When you have both front and back tilts available, front tilting will angle the lens off center and place the greatest strain on lens coverage. Tilting the back requires only normal lens coverage but gives some image distortion which you can use to alter perspective (see *Controlling shapes,* right).

Improving depth of field is the most useful result of using these types of camera movements. It is especially helpful in close-up work, when depth of field is always restricted. Bear in mind, however, that the extension only works over one plane at a time. If your improved depth of field surface is one of many in the picture, all at different angles to each other, the others may become less sharp as you improve the sharpness of the chosen plane.

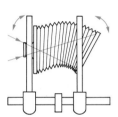
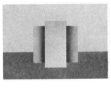
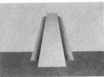

Back-tilt
Tilting the camera back makes the film plane less vertical (above). You can use this to dramatize height, as in the picture (below) by Trevor Melton. When you view the subject square-on (top right), the verticals appear parallel, and the subject squat in shape. Tilting the back produces dramatically converging verticals and makes the subject appear taller (above).

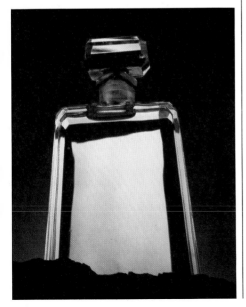

Controlling shapes

It is possible to control the apparent shape of objects by angling the view camera back. A normal, square-on view of the front of a building, for example, taken with the camera back parallel to the subject, will show it as a distortion-free, rectangular form. If, however, you turn the camera slightly so that the back is no longer parallel to the subject, and then swing the lens so that it is pointing directly at it, one end of the building will look bigger than the other end. At the same time, the picture will no longer be in focus at both ends at once — unless you stop the lens well down. Falsely steepening perspective in this way is, finally, limited by depth of field, which becomes progressively shallower the more you angle the camera back in order to change the shape of your subject.

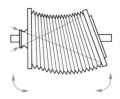
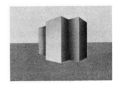
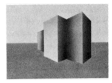

Swing
The back of the camera can be swung to one side (above left) to distort the shape of the subject (above right). One side will then appear smaller, and the other larger, than they would without movements (top right). The cassette box (below) was actually square-on to the camera, but stopping down and using swing has exaggerated perspective.

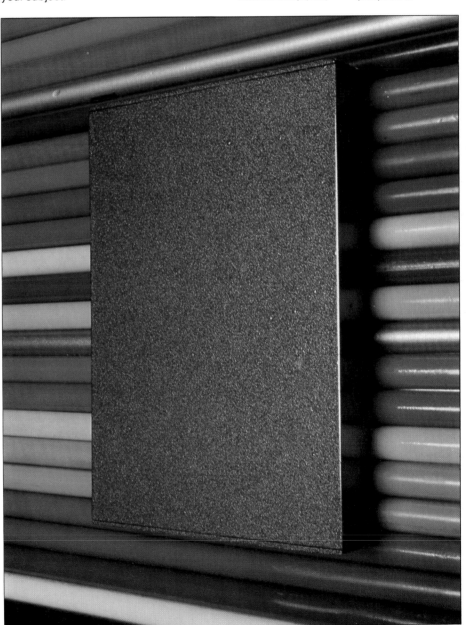

The shutter

The third main camera control is the shutter. For about the first twenty years of photography, shutters were unnecessary. Exposures were so long that photographers simply uncapped the lens, timed the exposure with a watch, and covered the lens again. Gradually, as lenses were made with wider apertures, and the light sensitivity of photographic plates improved, exposures were reduced to fractions of a second. These advances necessitated some form of mechanical timing device. At first, there was a variety of push-on types – wooden drop shutters acting like a guillotine, and others working as hinged flaps.

The most popular shutter was a small roller blind in a box that fitted over the lens. It was tensioned by pulling a cord. To fire the shutter, the photographer pressed an air bulb on the end of a tube. Most roller blind shutters offered two settings, "instantaneous", with a speed of about 1/30 sec, and "time" or "B", which allowed the photographer to hold the bulb squeezed in for a manually timed exposure. By the 1880s, shutters using mechanical blades began to be built into lenses and camera bodies.

Modern shutters

Today's cameras use sophisticated descendants of these two early designs – either a bladed shutter in or near the lens, or a fast-moving blind in front of the film, known as a focal plane shutter. A shutter in the lens exposes the entire picture at one time, even at its fastest speeds. This makes it possible to use flash at any shutter speed, through a synchronizing circuit which is completed the moment the blades are fully open. A focal plane shutter offers still faster speed because it sweeps the film with a narrow slit. This makes fast-speed synchronization with flash more difficult because only part of the film plane is uncovered at one time. At slower speeds (usually 1/60 sec) the whole of the film plane is unobstructed. However, focal plane shutters are necessary in most single lens reflex cameras to leave the lens clear of shutter blades and show an image (via a mirror) on the focusing screen. They are also essential to allow lens changing in mid-film.

A camera shutter has two main functions. It controls the time light from the image is allowed to act on the film and, therefore, directly affects exposure. In addition, it allows the photographer to choose the exact time at which to expose the film and to freeze of blur moving subjects.

Movement blur gives a different pictorial result to an out-of-focus image. Focus separates objects by distance. The shutter speed separates objects by the amount they move while light is acting on the film. It is therefore possible to show static things in detail and abstract moving elements.

See also
Timing and movement *Peak of action,* p. 87; *The critical moment,* p. 88.

How shutters work

A shutter must let light pass to the film and act evenly on it for a precisely measured time, according to the interval set on the shutter control. This is easiest to achieve with a shutter situated close to the lens. Here the light beam is at its narrowest and so least physical movement is required to cover and uncover the film. Lens shutters on the simplest cameras have a single, spring-loaded blade, or they may use a rotating disk with a cut-out section. As you press the shutter release the spring is tensioned until it flips the shutter briefly out of the way of the light beam. Often there is only one shutter speed – about 1/60 sec.

Multibladed lens shutters have cutlass-shaped, thin metal leaves, which swing open or shut when a ring is rotated. A spring controls the opening and shutting stages, but there is an adjustable pause between the two, timed by an electronic delaying circuit or a clock-

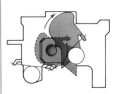

Sector shutter
A mechanically triggered, spring-loaded blade blocks the light path in this simple direct vision camera.

When the shutter is released, the blade flips out of the light path briefly, allowing light to reach the film.

work-type escapement of gears. You use one lever to tension these shutters, and fire them with another. These shutters are most often used on 35 mm compact cameras and rollfilm twin lens reflexes (see *Direct vision compact cameras,* pp. 104-5 and *TLR cameras,* p. 107), where tensioning is coupled to the film wind-on.

Sheet film cameras also have bladed shutters, but here setting and firing are two separate actions. Some monorail models have a large, panel-type bladed shutter, which fits behind the lens panel. This means that you do not have to use lenses that each have an expensive internal shutter.

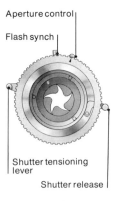

Aperture control
Flash synch
Shutter tensioning lever
Shutter release

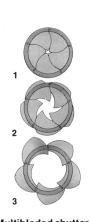

1
2
3

Multibladed shutter
These shutters are built into the lens itself. The rotation of the outer ring moves the overlapping blades out of the way. Counter rotation closes the blades after exposure.

Focal plane shutters

Focal plane shutters operate as close as possible to the film surface. Most of them consist of a pair of opaque fabric blinds. The blinds follow each other across the film surface, forming a gap between them that allows light to expose the film. The blinds are spring-loaded and must be rewound after each exposure. The camera's film advance lever is linked to the blind rewind/reset mechanism, which repositions the blinds for the next exposure. To prevent the film being exposed again, the blinds automatically overlap at this stage.

Focal plane shutters have a constant blind speed, and you vary exposure by altering the width of the slit between the blinds. Narrowest slits give the fastest speeds. At about 1/60 sec the slit becomes as wide as the picture format itself, so allowing flash synchronization. For slower speeds still, the second blind is delayed – either electronically, or mechanically by a system of gears.

In 35 mm cameras fabric focal plane shutters move across the longest dimension of the

Typical focal plane shutter operation
With the shutter set and tensioned, the first blind starts to travel as soon as you release the shutter. At slow speeds (1/60 sec or longer) the second blind does not move until the first blind

completes its travel. With faster speeds, it will start to move when the first is still part way across the film surface, exposing the film, in fact, via a traveling slit.

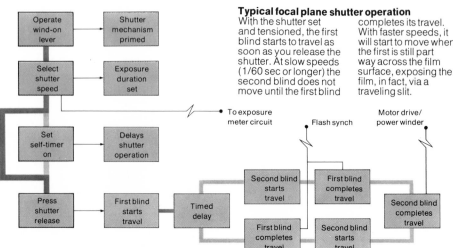

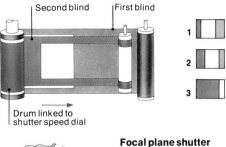

Second blind | First blind

1
2
3

Drum linked to shutter speed dial

Focal plane shutter
Two blinds, located immediately in front of the film plane, follow each other in sequence according to the speed setting. Some blinds travel vertically.

format. (The rolled-up blinds would be difficult to house horizontally.) A growing number of these cameras now use focal plane shutters with two or three metal blinds, traveling vertically. Since the blinds cover a shorter distance, the shutter can be more compact and rapid, with a slit that synchronizes with flash at faster speeds.

Timing the shutter
The traditional way of timing slow shutter speeds (1/15 sec or longer) is to bring into action a train of clockwork-type gears. These spin, dissipating power from a spring, and delaying the closing of the blades or blind. Lack of space limits the size of the gear train, and restricts the longest timed speed to 1 second.

Electronic shutters, on the other hand, have two tiny electromagnets. One opens the shutter, and the other releases the blade-closing movement or second blind. The gap between energizing these devices is timed by charging a capacitor through one of a series of transistors. The rate of charging depends on the transistor you switch into the circuit. Low charging takes the longest time — for the shutter will not close until triggered from a full capacitor.

In controlling the shutter in this way, you change from one speed setting to another by switching electronically, instead of shifting mechanical cams. The shutter becomes an extension of the camera's exposure measuring circuit, controlled by it automatically if required. First pressure on the shutter release button often switches on the light-measuring meter, and may also begin charging the flash.

Electronic shutters also greatly extend the range of speeds, and slow, accurately measured exposures of up to 8 or 10 seconds are possible. Electronics are much more compact than mechanical gears and can be housed in any convenient space in the camera. But there must be some form of battery to power the system. (This is no problem for modern small-format cameras, which already carry a battery for the light-measuring circuit.) In the event of battery failure, sophisticated cameras have a fail-safe system, allowing you to use one mechanically timed speed.

Shutter settings
Like the aperture scale of f numbers, there is a universally adopted series of shutter speed settings. Each change of setting either halves or doubles the time the shutter remains open. Most focal plane shutters, which offer a comprehensive speed range, have a fastest setting of 1/1000 sec and a slowest speed of 1 sec. For longer times you select the setting marked "B" and keep the release depressed for as long as required. Some cameras with electronic shutters and automatic exposure metering offer timed speeds from 1/2000 sec to 8 sec. The fastest speed safe to use synchronized with flash is marked clearly on the dial, often in a different color.

All cameras that offer slow speeds (1/15 sec or longer) should have a socket to accept a cable release, and a threaded hole on the baseplate to allow you to attach a tripod (see *Tripods and camera supports*, p. 203). Bladed shutters tend to have a maximum speed of 1/250 sec or 1/500 sec. The simplest cameras with sector shutters may have only two speeds, marked in weather symbols, or linked to "film type" settings.

The larger bladed shutters built into sheet film cameras seldom work faster than 1/250 sec. One lever tensions the shutter, another fires it (see below). Often a third lever or catch allows you to open the blades and hold them open for focusing and composition, whatever the shutter speed set. Most pre-1955 cameras have non-standard marked speeds featuring 1/5, 1/10, 1/25, 1/50, and 1/100 sec. This system was abandoned because the time increments are not regular.

Shutter and aperture relationships
Long exposure to a dim image is as effective on the film as short exposure to a bright one. (This reciprocal relationship breaks down at extremes, however — see *Reciprocity failure*, p. 152). Often the light level in a scene alone will determine what settings you must make. For example, a brilliantly illuminated light-toned subject may need your fastest shutter setting combined with the smallest lens aperture. Dark subjects in very dim lighting might require the slowest shutter setting and widest aperture. But more often light intensity allows you to make a choice of settings, like those shown below, which give the same exposure effect on the film with different combinations of time and intensity.

Slow shutter, small aperture
If you choose a slow shutter speed and stop the lens well down, the picture will have an extensive depth of field. On the other hand, any movement of the subject or camera during the relatively long exposure may produce a blurred image. Provided that the picture is of a still object, and the camera is firmly supported, blur will not be a problem. If you are hand-holding the camera, however, you may not want to pick a shutter speed slower than 1/60 sec (depending on focal length — see *Camera shake*, p. 130) because of the possibility of slight camera movement.

Again, if the subject is a moving figure or vehicle, or you are shooting from something moving, you can choose a shutter speed to give a controlled degree of blur. It is impossible to preview this effect as you can in the case of depth of field (although an instant picture camera will give you a rapid check). Nor is the degree of image movement easy to measure, depending as it does on subject distance, angle of movement in relation to the camera, as well as the subject's speed.

The use of slow shutter speeds is an important device to symbolize movement in a still photograph. Do not always regard blur as a fault to be avoided — it is well worth exploring as a creative photographic device and can add an extra dimension to your work.

Fast shutter, wide aperture
A fast shutter speed setting, combined with a wide lens aperture, reverses all the influences discussed above. Depth of field is minimized, but this may not matter if the subject itself is largely a two-dimensional surface. A shallow depth of field is also useful if you want to localize sharply focused detail as a means of emphasis, while the brief shutter speed will probably eliminate camera shake, and also give a detailed, more "frozen" image of any moving elements within the scene.

Simple cameras with fixed focus lenses seldom have shutter speeds faster than about 1/125 sec. This is because the aperture is small (to maximize depth of field), and if the camera had fast shutter speeds too, the film would not receive sufficient exposure in dim lighting situations.

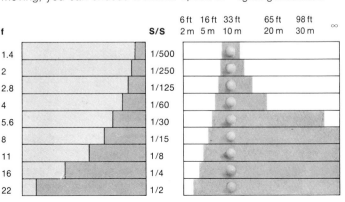

f	S/S
1.4	1/500
2	1/250
2.8	1/125
4	1/60
5.6	1/30
8	1/15
11	1/8
16	1/4
22	1/2

6 ft 16 ft 33 ft 65 ft 98 ft ∞
2 m 5 m 10 m 20 m 30 m

Shutter, aperture, and depth of field
You can use different combinations of shutter speed and aperture to let the same amount of light on to the film (see far left). However, the image will not be the same in each case. Each aperture has a different effect on depth of field (left). With the lens focused on 33 ft (10 m), the shaded areas show the amount in sharp focus at each f stop.

Shutter firing systems

You need not fire the shutter using direct finger pressure on the release button. Most SLR cameras are equipped with a delayed action release, or you can trigger the shutter through a direct mechanical or electrical link. It is also possible to use a radio, light, or sound system, so that no direct, physical connection to the camera is necessary. With devices like these, you can take pictures at a considerable distance from the subject — provided that the camera is firmly supported and set for a particular viewpoint and focus.

Sometimes the distance between photographer and camera is only a few inches — just enough to avoid blocking the light, or perhaps to allow you to hold a flashgun at full reach. Longer distance firing, though, allows you time to include yourself in the frame. This can be useful to fill an empty area in a landscape, for example, or simply to make up a family group. Working at a distance also means you can leave the camera set up to photograph timid or dangerous animals.

To photograph inaccessible locations, you can set up the camera in a tree, on a moving vehicle, at the end of a ski jump, or even hanging from a balloon. In most of these cases it is best to use a motor drive (see *Motor drives and camera backs,* p. 202), so that you can take a series of pictures without having to retrieve the camera to wind on the film.

Cable releases

The traditional cable release works on the same principle as the bicycle brake cable. It screws into the threaded shutter release socket found on all but the simplest cameras. As you press the plunger at one end, a piece of stiff wire protrudes from the other, and fires the shutter. Most releases have a lock on the plunger so that you can keep the shutter open with the camera set to "B". Cable releases of this type are usually not longer than 3 ft (1 m). Twin and triple cable releases are also available for more than one camera.

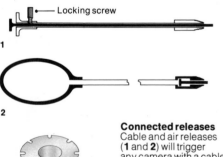

— Locking screw

1

2

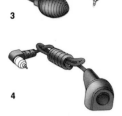

3

4

Connected releases
Cable and air releases (**1** and **2**) will trigger any camera with a cable release socket, over distances between 3 and 23 ft (1 and 7 m) respectively. Wind an air release around a core (**3**) to avoid kinks and bends, which will block the air flow. You can use an electric cord release (**4**) with electrically triggered shutters, but if it is too long electrical resistance may build up and prevent the shutter firing.

When you require a longer shutter release you will have to use an air-operated type (up to about 23 ft/7 m) or an electric release (which can be practically any length). The air release is a thin, flexible air tube with a plastic squeeze bulb at one end and a piston at the other, which screws into the camera shutter release socket. Air releases work well as long as you avoid pinching the tube.

Electrical releases have a push switch on an electric cord. They plug directly into most cameras that have electronic shutters, and provide the most reliable method of triggering the shutter over long distances. These releases are also available with a cable release adaptor for use with mechanical shutters — the current energizes a small battery-powered electric plunger at the camera end, and this presses home a cable release screwed into the camera accessory shoe.

Delayed action timers

Most modern cameras have a built-in delayed action shutter release. You operate the mechanical types by pushing down a lever, and waiting for it to return slowly and trigger the shutter. A series of gears creates the delay, which is characterized by a buzzing noise.

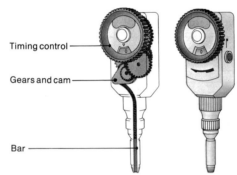

Timing control —

Gears and cam —

Bar —

Accessory delayed action timer
If your camera has no built-in timer, you can screw an accessory delayed action timer into the cable release socket. The gears push down a bar, depressing the shutter release. With the built-in kind, gears or electronic circuits pull down the release.

Electronic delayed action timers are only found on cameras with electronic shutters. When you press the start button the device operates silently, showing a flashing light, which increases in frequency as the moment of shutter release approaches. Both types of timer provide a variable delay lasting between about 3 and 12 seconds, and must be reset for each picture.

Intervalometers

Intervalometers are timing units that allow you to program a series of exposures at intervals of seconds, minutes or even hours. They are designed to work in conjunction with a camera and motor drive. You simply set the required intervals between pictures, release the shutter for the first exposure, and leave the camera to do the rest. Most intervalometers have a frame counter that halts the series when the camera has taken a preset number of pictures.

Remote releases

Remote releases do not have any physical connection to the camera, and are ideal in rough terrain, or wherever the photographer is mobile. To operate them you press a button on a small transmitter pack. This sends out a pulse (either ultrasonic, infrared, or radio) to a receiver mounted on the camera, and trips the shutter electrically. You can also use remote releases with the cable release adaptor described above.

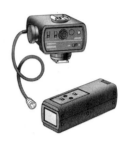

Unconnected releases
Totally remote shutter releases use a transmitter to send a triggering signal to a receiver supported in the camera hot shoe. The ultrasonic variety shown here is effective over a distance of about 33 ft (10 m).

Ultrasonic types have an effective working range of about 33 ft (10 m), and the transmitter must be pointed at the receiver. With infrared types you must have clear line-of-sight between transmitter and receiver, but working distance is about 200 ft (60 m). Radio-pulse remote releases are the most expensive but offer the widest working range (up to several miles). You can also use them underwater. These releases operate on citizens' band or hobby frequencies, which in some countries can only be used with an appropriate licence.

Triggers

With both types of release (connected and remote) you can set the camera up so that the subject itself triggers the shutter. This is of immense value with natural history subjects. To release the shutter, you need a tiny, but inexpensive, light-sensitive silicon cell, and a light source (preferably filtered to give red or invis-

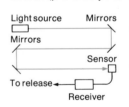

Light source   Mirrors

Mirrors

Sensor

To release ◄—

Receiver

Self-triggering systems
You can widen the "net" by reflecting the path of the triggering light with mirrors. Another system uses microphones to pick up the sound of the approaching subject.

ible infrared radiation only). The cell is wired through a solid state amplifier and battery to whatever shutter firing electronic release you are using.

You must arrange the light beam so that it crosses the likely path of the subject, and shines on the light-sensitive cell. As soon as the subject interrupts the light, the amplifier acts as a switch, and fires the set-up and prefocused camera and/or flash. The whole trigger sequence takes about 1/25,000 sec.

Using slow shutter speeds

Slow shutter speeds (1/30 sec or longer) may be necessary for taking pictures in dimly lit interiors, for night shots, and in similar situations, where this is the only method of accumulating enough light to expose the film adequately. More creatively, though, these slow speeds allow photographers to add an extra dimension to their pictures — that of movement and action through blur. Subject movement while the shutter is open can record the flow of an event rather than its frozen detail. It is effective with a range of subjects, such as dancing, sports and athletics, or quite simple actions like people walking, traffic flow, and bird and animal movement. The blending of colors by blur seems to enliven the most prosaic subjects by adding elements of abstraction. Sometimes results of this kind happen accidentally, but to use them as a means of breaking away from record photography and achieve a more interpretative approach, it is essential to explore and develop the different effects of blur.

Types of blur
There are four main types of blur result possible using slow shutter speeds and time exposures. In the first type, all picture detail appears blurred, either because the camera moved while exposing a static subject, or the camera was still, but a moving subject completely filled the frame. Another, very different, result is possible when stationary parts of a scene record clearly, but moving objects are blurred. This occurs when the camera is held static. In the third type, moving elements record clearly, but stationary ones blur. For this type of result the camera must move in the same direction and at the same speed as the moving elements. The fourth main type of result is a superimposed mixture of sharp detail and blur, generally unlike normal vision, and created by combining a long shutter setting with flash.

Practical considerations
It is possible to regulate the amount of blur by choice of exposure time. An exposure of 1/15 sec, for example, doubles the length of streak recorded at 1/30 sec, and so on. (It also doubles the amount of light reaching the film.) For blur results it is therefore usual to use a small lens aperture and slow (low ASA) film. Some forms of blur result are possible with simple cameras having fixed speed shutters of about 1/60 sec. But the greatest possibilities occur with slow speeds and, in particular, a "B" setting — which means that there is no lower limit to exposure time.

See also
Line, pp. 36-7. Special effects lighting *Physiograms,* p. 180. Zoom lenses, pp. 192-4. Sports photography, pp. 304-9. Dynamism, pp. 357-61. Metaphor and symbolism, pp. 368-73.

Supporting the camera
Often with slow shutter speeds you will want to show static objects sharp by keeping the camera absolutely still — especially when poor light dictates a long exposure. Or you may want a sharp background as a foil to an element that moves, and so blurs, during exposure.

With care, it is possible to hold a camera and lens steady at 1/60 sec. You must squeeze the shutter release gently when doing this. For settings longer than 1/60 sec, some support is usually necessary. Resting your elbows on a chair, table, or floor should give a "safe" 1/15 sec exposure. Pressing the camera against a door frame, wall, or pillar may increase "safe" exposure to 1 sec. Often, you can wedge your camera firmly and fire the shutter with a cable release to minimize vibration. If no cable release is available, you can use the camera's delayed action release.

The best support, though, is a tripod (see *Tripods and camera supports,* p. 203). A good tripod is strongly constructed and offers a wide range of adjustments. A camera clamp is a more portable alternative to a tripod.

As well as recording static objects sharply, holding the camera perfectly still also allows you to reveal subject movement and change, which is too slow for the eye to notice. A time exposure of the night sky can reveal the curved tracks of stars as the earth rotates on its axis (see *Equipment and techniques,* pp. 291-2).

Controlling blur
Blur at slow exposures depends on the subject's distance from and angle to the camera, as well as its speed of movement in relation to the exposure time given. Focal length is also a factor. Telephoto lenses exaggerate a subject's apparent movement. Subject tone also influences blur. A pale object against a dark background appears to spread out, whereas dark objects moving against a light background seem to shrink.

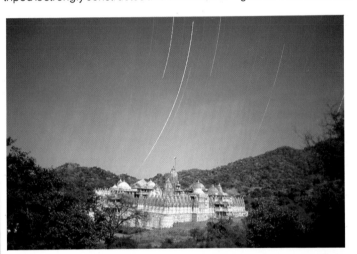

Static camera, static subject
Henry Wilson used a time exposure of several hours to make this picture at night in India. The earth's rotation has caused the stars to record as trails of light.

Moving camera, moving subject
A mixture of camera and subject movement caused the partial blurring evident in David Buckland's photograph of a group of dancers.

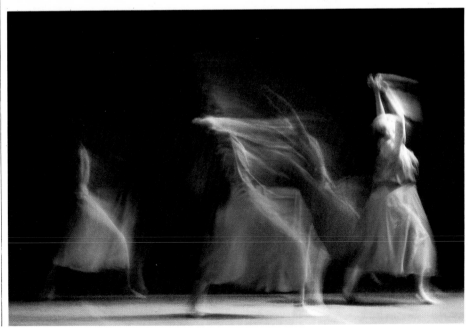

Moving camera, static subject

Camera movement with static subjects can produce a variety of effects. By moving the camera slightly during exposure you can create a streaking of the whole image. This is sometimes so minimal that the softened detail looks like the result of poor lens quality. You can use this effect as an abstraction device. Shifting, rotating, or moving forward with the camera, during exposures of 1/8 sec or longer, will make highlights record as parallel, curved, or radiating lines.

The more contrasty the scene, the more dramatic the results will be. Subjects such as streets at night, illuminated decorations, and backlit tree foliage all possess bright, point-like highlights, which are pulled into clearly defined, abstract shapes by camera movement. Results are usually linear — each line matching the camera's movements — but varying in size according to object distance and focal length. Flatter overall lighting gives more confused tones and colors, and a more abstract effect.

Camera movement can also impart a false sense of movement to an image. Swaying toward a static vehicle during a 1/2 sec exposure, for example, can make it seem to be rushing toward you. You can give a blur trail to a white statue against dark foliage by shooting at 1 sec, holding the camera static at first, and then swinging it sideways.

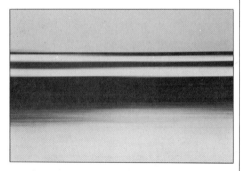

Panning static subjects
By panning across the scene and using a slow shutter speed, David Buckland recorded this seascape as horizontal bands of tone. This technique is particularly useful for abstracting otherwise prosaic scenes and subjects.

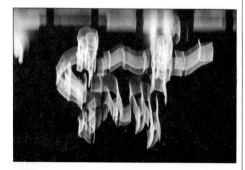

Vertical panning
Andrew de Lory produced this abstract image by focusing his camera on a neon sign and then panning vertically during exposure. Bright areas of the sign have recorded as streaks against a dark background.

Panning moving subjects

Panning is the technique of moving the camera in the same direction as a moving subject, so that the subject remains stationary in relation to the film. The eyes perform the same action when watching a game like tennis, keeping the ball in view. With a camera you should frame the subject in the viewfinder while it is some way away. Have the lens focused for the distance the subject will be when it is nearest to you. Looking through the viewfinder, follow the subject in a smooth, continuous action, keeping it in center frame. When it passes the chosen point, press the shutter re-

Panning technique
Pre-focus the lens on a ground point you expect the subject to pass over. As the subject approaches, swing the camera in a flat arc, following the direction and movement of the subject. Continue the pan after releasing the shutter gently.

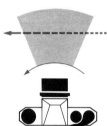
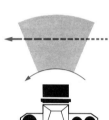

lease while continuing panning in order to avoid abrupt cessation of movement.

SLR cameras are not ideal for panning since they do not show you the image during exposure. You may have to observe the movement by looking over the camera top. The best camera to use is a direct vision type. Reflex cameras without a pentaprism show the image reversed left to right (see *35 mm SLR cameras*, pp. 102-4).

Panning abstracts stationary background and foreground detail into streaks, which vary in length according to the panning rate and shutter speed used. The subject stands out relatively sharply, showing greatest detail where its direction and speed match the camera's "sweep". For most subjects moving at right-angles to the camera, 1/60 or 1/30 sec are effective shutter speeds for panning.

You can extend the effect of panning by moving the camera fractionally too fast or too slow, so that the subject blurs slightly. A related technique is to blur the background by photographing your subject while traveling alongside it in a vehicle.

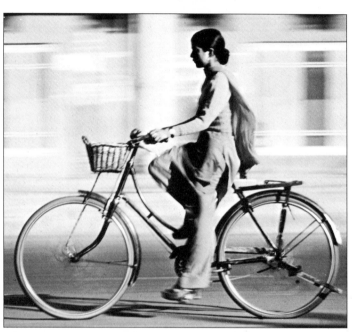

Panning moving subjects
Henry Wilson followed the movement of the approaching cyclist, releasing the shutter when she was sideways-on to the camera. The cyclist stands out sharply against a background, which the action of panning has reduced to blurred streaks, thus suggesting the illusion of much faster motion than in fact existed. For this technique to work properly, it is important to keep the camera moving steadily in the direction of the subject, even after you release the shutter.

Exposure considerations

It is difficult to forecast precisely the effects of blur, and, wherever possible, you should try to take several exposures at different shutter settings. In bright lighting conditions there is a possibility of overexposure. To cut out enough light to allow an exposure time as long as 1/4 or 1/2 sec, even at the smallest aperture, you may have to use a gray (neutral density) filter. These are available in various densities — the strongest type cuts the light down to one-hundredth of its actual value (see *Neutral density filters*, p. 201).

Neutral density ("ND") filters are ideal for eliminating moving vehicles and pedestrians from busy street scenes. An ND filter may, for example, allow an exposure time of 30 sec. Most moving objects then occupy any one position for such a short part of this exposure time that they do not appear on the film at all. (Exposures longer than 1 sec, though, may have less than the expected exposure effect on film, and an even greater time may be required — see *Reciprocity failure*, p. 152).

Using fast shutter speeds

The faster shutter speeds, 1/125 sec up to 1/1000 sec or briefer, are useful when subject conditions are very bright, or when the photographer has chosen a wide lens aperture for reasons of depth of field. (These brief speeds help prevent overexposure.) They also have an increasing "freezing" effect on subject movement. The shutter begins to capture action too rapid for the eye to see clearly, and presents the subject in full, explicit detail. Camera movement itself is no longer important. It is possible to pick out strong, briefly formed action shapes of athletes, dancers, children, or animals, literally in mid-air. Taken to extremes, special equipment can freeze fast moving machinery or even missiles in flight, and then make measurements of velocity and distance directly from the image.

Suitable shutter speeds
From this it would be easy to assume that using the fastest possible shutter speed is the correct way of interpreting all moving subjects. The faster the shutter speed, though, the more the photograph departs from our visual memory of the scene – the spray of a fountain becomes pellets of ice, for example. So although the factual content of the subject is recorded distinctly, it is all too easy to destroy the atmosphere of the event. It will often be more evocative, for example, to pan a moving subject in order to blur surroundings and show one element moving against another, reproducing the scene as the viewer sees it.

Practical considerations
Other factors to consider when using fast shutter speeds are mostly practical. As light has less time to act on the film, strong illumination, fast film, and a wide lens aperture will probably be essential. This can create problems if the subject demands extensive depth of field. The precise moment chosen to fire the shutter is also decisive. It is essential to choose the instant when the action is at its peak. Most normal shutters only offer an upper limit of 1/1000 sec (sometimes 1/2000 sec). High-speed flash or a specialist shutter system may be necessary for greater action-stopping power.

See also
Filters and lens attachments *Polarizing filters,* p. 198. Scientific and technical photography *High-speed photography,* pp. 275-7. Natural history photography *Insects,* p. 302.

Controlling the freezing of action

Like the effects of camera shake, the degree of blur depends on how much the image moves while the shutter is open. The shutter speed required to freeze movement depends on four main factors. First, the size of the image of the subject in relation to the picture as a whole is important. A close viewpoint or a long-focus lens will both produce a large image. This has a magnifying effect on subject movement. For example, a swaying flower in close-up will seem to move more violently than a speeding motorcycle in the distance, and so will require a briefer exposure.

The second influence on apparent subject movement is its direction and speed in relation to the camera. If something is moving quickly toward you, for example, its image grows larger although it is not shifting appreciably within the frame. The same subject photographed from the side presents you with very much faster apparent subject movement. Action and movement at 45° falls between these two effects. The third influence is the standard of sharpness you require in a "frozen" image. It is vital to consider this in the light of how much enlargement the film will receive when printed.

Minimal blurring, which might be acceptable in small prints, becomes unacceptable when enlargement is substantial.

The fourth factor is the actual time that the shutter is fully open. Freezing action means having a shutter with the mechanical capability of opening and closing very quickly. It can also mean using a light source, such as flash, which gives out a pulse of light much briefer than the actual exposure time set. In other words, provided there is little ambient lighting, you can use 1/60 sec shutter speed (the usual speed for flash synchronization) but know that the effective exposure is only 1/1000 sec or briefer (depending on the duration of the flash).

For the maximum stopping effect on image movement, avoid large, close images, select a viewpoint head-on to the action, and try to choose the moment when the subject has least movement (see *Peak of action,* p. 87). Where practicable, use flash at the recommended synchronized shutter speed. Alternatively, set the fastest speed your shutter will offer and use existing light instead of a flashgun (see *The freezing power of flash,* p. 178).

Freezing movement
These photographs of a trotting race were both taken at the same shutter speed. The side view shows much more blur as a result of subject movement than does the head-on shot. A shot taken at 45° would fall somewhere between the two.

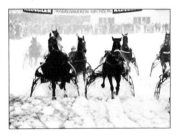 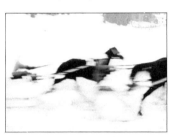

Shutter speed to stop movement
(using normal focal length lens)

Speed of subject	Distance to subject	Movement toward lens	Movement at 45° to lens	Movement at 90° to lens
Under 5 m/h (8 km/h)	16 ft/5 m	1/60	1/125	1/250
	33 ft/10 m	1/30	1/60	1/125
	66 ft/20 m	1/15	1/30	1/60
Over 5 m/h (8 km/h)	33 ft/10 m	1/250	1/500	1/1000
	66 ft/20 m	1/125	1/250	1/500
	98 ft/30 m	1/60	1/125	1/250

Choice of shutter speed
This table suggests the longest shutter speeds you should use with a static camera to freeze image movement. Factors to take into account are the direction and speed of the subject, and also its proximity to the camera. At very close subject distances it is extremely difficult to freeze all traces of movement whatever speed you use.

Exposure considerations

If you are likely to be using the fastest possible shutter speeds, line up the best equipment and materials for the job. For pictures taken on a jostling dance floor, for example, electronic flash may be ideal. Most subjects here are likely to be within flash range, and the flash unit itself will probably give 1/1000 to 1/10,000 sec exposure time, according to subject distance. When the action is outdoors or in large auditoriums, your subjects are likely to be too distant for a camera flash to give sufficient illumination. It would be better to use fast film (push processed to give extra speed if necessary – see *Compensation processing,* p. 224), and the widest aperture lens available. Working at full aperture, though, usually results in a very shallow depth of field. You can minimize this potential problem by choosing a viewpoint from which all the important elements are at about the same distance from the camera. 35 mm cameras, with their good depth of field and wide aperture lenses have a distinct advantage over larger-format models for this type of photography.

Camera shake

You may decide to use a fast shutter speed mainly in order to avoid camera shake. The "safest" slow speed at which you can hand hold a camera depends on the steadiness of your own hands, vibration of surroundings, the mechanics of the camera itself, and the focal length of the lens. Usually it is safe to take pictures at 1/125 sec or faster without camera shake. 1/60 or 1/30 sec is often safe too, provided you brace yourself. For slower speeds you should use a tripod or clamp, or at least support the camera against a firm surface, such as a wall. Cameras, too, vary in the way operating the shutter release imparts vibration to the camera body as a whole. Single lens reflex cameras, for example, produce more vibration than direct vision types, because of the movement of the reflex mirror. Electronic shutter releases are much smoother in operation than the more usual mechanical tripping button. Whichever camera you use, a short cable release may help give a smoother action, even with the camera hand held.

Focal length is important because it affects image size. The longer the focal length (and hence the larger the image) the briefer the first "safe" shutter speed will be (because any movement will be more obvious). If you can hold a 35 mm camera with a 50 mm lens still at 1/60 sec, you should modify this to 1/125 sec with a 100 mm lens, and 1/250 sec with a 200 mm lens, and so on. Changing to a 28 mm lens should make 1/30 sec safe to use. Finally, camera shake assumes an "average" degree of enlargement of the camera image. Large

prints, or slides for projection, must exhibit very high standards of image sharpness. Even the slightest camera shake would be obvious — so it is best to use a still faster shutter speed when conditions allow or support the camera with a sturdy tripod.

Safe shutter speed and focal length

Focal length (mm)	24	28	35	50	100	135	200	400	600	1000
Longest safe shutter speed (sec)	1/30	1/30	1/30	1/60	1/125	1/125	1/250	1/500	1/1000	use a tripod

Note: Use these figures as a guide only. Individual lens designs vary in weight and length — factors which affect their handling stability. With zoom lenses, the slowest safe shutter speed will be that for its maximum focal length no matter what zoom setting you use.

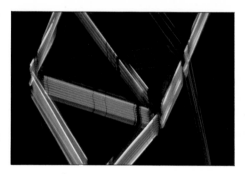
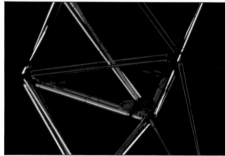

Camera movement during exposure
To photograph this neon sculpture at night, Andrew de Lory had to use a telephoto lens and a slow shutter speed. Camera shake produced a blurred image (above left). Using a tripod (above) the result is much sharper.

Choice of interpretation

The degree of blur or sharpness you decide to record is largely subjective. Sometimes, extremely short exposures reveal a brief structure or pattern, which blur would otherwise destroy. A close-up of a droplet falling into liquid, for example, can show a dramatic symmetrical design; a skier or hurdler will form graceful shapes for a frozen instant. On the other hand, many subjects, such as a bustling crowd, waves breaking on the shore, buses, and automobiles, are all remembered for their movement as much as any other quality. It is as

important to catch the essence of such scenes as to show their every graphic detail.

Just what shutter speed to use either to blur or freeze action is difficult to predict accurately. You have to guess subject speeds and distances, and different parts of the same subject will tend to move at different rates. The best technique is to bracket — make several exposures at different settings (see *Correct exposure,* p. 133). When varying your shutter speed settings, you can compensate each for exposure by changing the aperture setting.

Instant pictures provide the best on-the-spot check of results. Instant picture backs for conventional cameras are invaluable for the photographer who wants to preview the subject and so achieve exact effects.

Blurring or freezing movement
Per Eide used different shutter speeds to take these two photographs of a waterfall. With a time exposure of several seconds, the water records as a flowing, misty blur. With a much faster speed, its movement is arrested in a fixed pattern. Vary aperture to compensate.

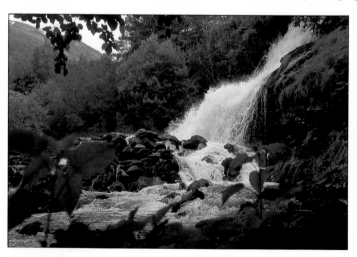
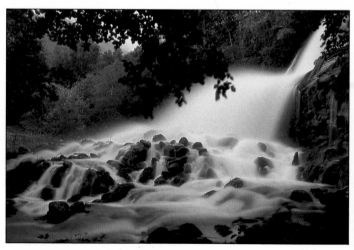

Focal plane distortion

Early focal plane shutters of the 1920s were mainly fitted on professional plate cameras, which took pictures with an image size of about 5 × 4 ins (12.5 × 10 cm). Here, the blind slit had to travel a full four inches across the emulsion surface in order to expose the whole image. In fact, one end of the plate was exposed about 1/100 sec before the other, and if the image moved during this time, its shape became distorted. The greatest distortion occurred when the blind slit and image moved at right-angles

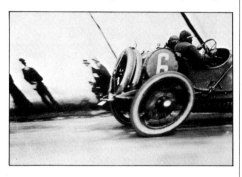

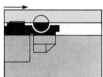
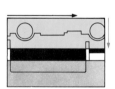
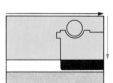
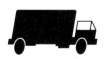

Image distortion
The distortion visible in Jacques-Henri Lartigue's 1912 picture of a speeding car was caused by the slow speed and length of travel of the plate camera's shutter blinds. The diagrams show how this happens with a large focal plane shutter during exposure. The degree of subject movement has been exaggerated to make the effect more obvious.

to each other (see above), because this produced a 45° slanted appearance. This often added to the impression of speed. Effects like this rarely, if ever, occur with today's cameras, owing to the much shorter travel path of the 35 mm format focal plane shutter. For scientific work, however, when subjects may be extremely fast moving (see *High-speed photography,* pp. 275-7), focal plane shutters are still avoided.

Chopping shutter

A chopping shutter is basically a disk with cut-out apertures, which you spin just in front of the camera lens to give a series of very brief shutter speed images on one frame of film. You can easily improvise this device by securely clamping a large black cardboard disk on to a power drill. As an effective alternative you can stand a bicycle upside down, filling in the spaces between the spokes of the back wheel with black paper or cardboard to form the disk. The apertures should be two 10° segments cut from opposite sides of the disk to give aerodynamic stability. If the disk spins at 40 revolutions per second you will get 80 exposures every second, each 1/1500 sec. By firing the camera shutter at 1/15 sec, the film will receive six of these 1/1500 sec exposures. A faster spin speed or smaller segments will produce

Special-purpose, high-speed shutters

There are special shutters and complete cameras for scientific use, which can provide one or several pictures at extremely brief exposures. Generally, this type of equipment uses electronics as a substitute for mechanical parts. These shutters and cameras are often used for analysis of explosions or ultra-fast chemical reactions.

The Kerr cell
This cell consists of a small glass tank of liquid with polarizing filters at both ends (see *Polarizing filters,* p. 198). It fits in front of a standard camera. Since the filters are crossed, no light can pass through the tank. When a high-voltage pulse is passed through the liquid, it temporarily twists the plane of polarization, so that

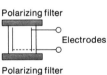

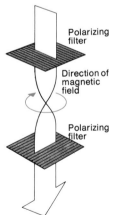

High-speed shutter
Light polarized by the first of the Kerr cell's crossed polarizing filters turns through 90° when a high voltage pulse is applied to electrodes in the nitrobenzine-filled tank. It is then able to pass through a second filter and reach the film. Effective shutter speed is as brief as the electric pulse.

light passes through the second filter. The shorter the pulse the briefer the exposure. Because there are no blades or blinds to open and close, exposures as short as one-two-hundred-millionth of a second are possible. The camera's own shutter is used to reveal the film before the Kerr cell has fired, and then to cover it afterward.

Image tube units
These units are used for purposes similar to Kerr cells, but really they are a form of television camera. A lens on the front of the unit

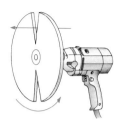

Calculating exposure
With a chopping shutter arrangement (left), you calculate the length of each exposure by the size of the segments in relation to the speed of rotation. Use the shutter speed to control the number of images in the frame.

briefer exposures, and by selecting a faster shutter speed you will cut down the number of exposures per frame. For best results, your subject should be mostly white or light colored, strongly lit, and positioned against a dark or black background. If using flash to illuminate the subject, do not use a shutter speed faster than the correct synchronization speed for your camera.

forms an image on a television tube. A very brief electronic pulse then activates a trigger, and, as this happens, a frozen image taken at this duration is formed on the back of the unit. A camera back forms part of the unit.

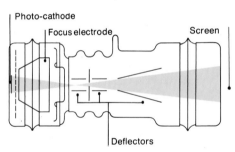

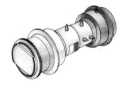

Electronic transmission
An image tube unit (right) is about the size of a 200 mm lens. A cathode (left in the diagram above) receives an image from a normal camera lens (not shown) and converts it into electronic signals. These are channeled by a series of deflectors and when triggered flash a brief image on a phosphor screen at the rear of the image tube. The image is copied using a camera with a macro lens. Such a unit is capable of giving exposures of extremely brief duration (below). An image tube unit is usually part of a much larger, high-speed camera system for specialized scientific work.

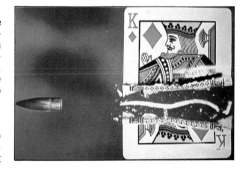

Exposure and its measurement

Exposure is affected by both the intensity of the light and the time for which it acts on the film. Like filling a jug with water, it is possible to let in a large volume for a short time, or a small amount over a longer period. So it is with exposure. A large amount of light for a short period will, within limits, give the same result as a small amount of light over a longer period of time.

For a film to be correctly exposed, it must receive enough light for it to record faithfully all the tones and colors of the original scene. If it receives too little light, the final result will have dark and featureless shadows, possibly merging with mid-tone areas. If, on the other hand, it receives too much illumination, the lighter, highlight parts will appear bleached and lacking in detail.

In practice, four factors influence the amount of exposure given to a film. The first is the subject – the brilliance of its illumination, and the amount of light it reflects. The second factor is the light sensitivity of the film. "Fast" films are more sensitive, and therefore require less exposure than "slow" types. The other factors are shutter speed and lens aperture. Sometimes, especially with moving subjects, shutter speed will be the most important setting, and it will be necessary for the photographer to adjust the aperture to give the right amount of light when the shutter is open. In some cases, for mainly static situations, depth of field may be the deciding factor. This makes the aperture setting critical, and shutter speed must be set to the right period to compensate for the chosen light intensity.

Films today use an international series of sensitivity ratings or speed numbers, which accurately relates one film to another. The one remaining variable, therefore, is subject brightness, and this must be measured by the photographer or the camera itself.

The history of camera design is paralleled by the development of exposure aids to help measure subject brightness. Notebooks and tables provided the first aids to correct exposure. Early photographers took great pride in their ability to judge sub-

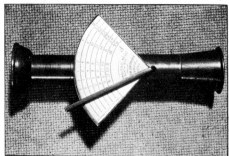
Extinction meter, 1870s

ject and lighting conditions (although they often had to make desperate attempts at exposure compensation when developing plates later). The photographer would rely mainly on a close examination of the image on the focusing screen. He would first stop

the lens down to its smallest aperture, then slowly reopen it, until the point where it was just possible to see detail in important shadow areas. Having established this aperture setting, he then gave the picture a standard exposure time.

The first exposure meters ("extinction meters") worked on the same principle. They consisted of a small tube with an eyepiece at one end and a series of increasingly dark translucent numbers at the other. The photographer pointed the meter toward the subject, and noted the number that was barely visible. Scales on the outside of the

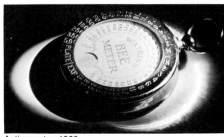
Actinometer, 1903

tube related this reading to plate speed, showing the correct shutter and aperture settings. The accuracy of this type of meter was dubious because the eye's iris gradually opens wider in dim conditions, so that the longer the eye looks at a number or screen image, the more it sees.

Between the 1880s and 1930s, the most popular exposure aid was the "actinometer", shaped somewhat like a pocket watch. This had a small, cut-out section in the face, and contained a piece of sensitive paper that

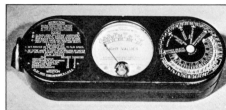
First Weston meter, 1932

darkened on exposure to light. The photographer timed how long the paper took to reach a neutral gray tone, then set this time on a calculator dial to find aperture and shutter settings. Some designs had a small pendulum on a chain to help time the seconds. The main drawbacks of this type of meter were that the paper was insufficiently sensitive to colored light, and reacted too slowly to be used indoors. Photoelectric meters, which started to appear in the early 1930s, were much easier to use.

See also
Emphasis *Emphasis through tone,* p. 69. **Assessing results** *Pushing and holding back,* p. 229.

Film speed figures

The earliest photographic plates were made by the photographers themselves, who learned to judge the sensitivity of their product largely by experience. But when plates, and later film, became a manufactured commodity (see *Film,* pp. 142-3) unrealistic claims were often made for their "speed", or sensitivity to light. Scientists, therefore, had to devise a universal numerical system to relate one product to another. The first to do this were two British chemists, F. Hurter and V. C. Driffield, who published a list of H & D speed numbers in 1890. Most materials had H & D numbers of 100 or less.

Over the years many similar systems of classifying film speed have been used, as the testing of materials altered to match changing practice in the use of films and developers. Some systems were unique to one exposure meter, or a single film manufacturer. Others were nationally based.

Today we are in a transitional period, with two official international systems in common use. ASA (American Standards Association) figures are most widely used outside Europe.

Equivalent film speed ratings			
ISO	ASA	DIN	GOST
25/15°	25	15	22
32/16°	32	16	28
50/18°	50	18	45
64/19°	64	19	56
80/20°	80	20	70
100/21°	100	21	90
125/22°	125	22	110
160/23°	160	23	140
200/24°	200	24	180
400/27°	400	27	360
1250/32°	1250	32	1125

Film speed equivalents
The system of speed-rating the sensitivity of films is gradually being standardized, using the ISO figure as the norm. This combines the ASA and DIN figures pre- viously used. Soviet bloc countries, however, use their own GOST system. This table shows how the different speeds compare.

A simple doubling of the ASA number indicates a doubling of film sensitivity. In most of Europe, however, DIN (German industrial standard) numbers are preferred. An increase of three in the DIN number means a doubling of film speed. In an effort to combine both schemes, the International Organization for Standardization (commonly referred to as ISO) at present quotes the two figures together, distinguishing the DIN number by a degree sign.

Changes of this kind take place very slowly, because millions of cameras and exposure meters marked in ASA or DIN numbers alone are still in use. Many film packages therefore show ASA, DIN, and ISO figures.

In the USSR and Eastern bloc countries, a GOST (Russian standardizing authority) number appears on film products. Today's medium-speed films are rated at ISO 125/22°, which is equivalent to approximately 4000 H & D.

Correct exposure

For most subjects, "correct" exposure means recording full detail across the whole image. Over- or underexposure destroys detail at one end of the tone scale, as well as making the picture generally too light or too dark.

With low-contrast scenes you have greatest latitude for exposure error. But with a contrasty, harshly lit subject, even slight errors will give marked differences in results. You must be accurate in reading exposure, since both extremes of tone may only be just within the range the film can handle (see *Manipulating film response*, pp. 155-9).

Many photographers "bracket" — take one picture at the meter's suggested settings, and others with slightly less and slightly more exposure. A bracketed series for a low-contrast subject might have three pictures with a one-stop difference between each. For a contrasty subject, or for color slides, take four or five at half-stop intervals.

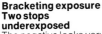

Bracketing exposure
Two stops underexposed
The negative looks very pale and thin. Dark areas in the original are empty and transparent, and will print as solid black without detail.

One stop underexposed
Though empty shadow areas are still evident, highlight areas reveal quite good detail. Dark areas will fill in on the finished print.

Correct exposure
This negative received twice as much exposure as the frame directly above it. Shadow areas are much improved in detail, while highlights are not too dense. There is a good balance of tones throughout.

One stop overexposed
In comparison with the first frame, this negative has a very dense appearance. Detail in highlight areas has begun to merge into one dark tone.

Two stops overexposed
The image now exhibits an overall grayness in all but deep shadow areas. When printed, it will produce a washed-out print with a limited tonal range.

Using the exposure meter

Modern meters greatly reduce the failure rate in pictures caused by exposure errors. They are accurate in the majority of photographic situations. But no meter is infallible. The more varied the conditions under which you work, the more likely it is that faulty readings will occur. Knowledge of how meters view and read scenes helps in recognizing situations where the system may break down. There are also times when you will want to override the meter — for example, to help create lighter or darker effects and so enhance the picture's mood (see *Emphasis through tone*, p. 69).

Each image consists of a range of brightnesses. Film is also capable of recording a range of brightnesses, within certain limits, each time you take a picture. The challenge of a good metering system is always to indicate a level of exposure that sets the subject within the recording limits of the film in use. If the meter mis-matches the two, either the detail in the subject's highlights will be destroyed (overexposure), or the shadow detail will be dark and unreadable (underexposure). There is least room for error with contrasty lighting, because the image then has a much wider brightness range, which may even exceed the contrast range of the film.

In addition, the meter must "see" the subject correctly. The obvious arrangement is for it to view the whole scene that the camera will record. This often gives good results. At other times one part of the picture (such as a face) is much more important than anything else, and the reading must be made for this, even though it occupies a small area. Basic, low-cost cameras overcome the problem of exposure by eliminating as many variables as possible. Users should limit their picture taking to specified "good" conditions, and the camera may only have a cloudy/sunny control to change the aperture by a difference of perhaps two stops. Only one speed of film is recommended. One solution provided by film manufacturers is to include an exposure table with each film. This provides a guide for a few set outdoor lighting conditions, but is not comprehensive enough to include detail such as the reflective qualities of the subject.

Fortunately the cost of light-sensing electronics has now fallen to the point where quite low-cost cameras can have sensitive metering systems built-in.

All but the cheapest (and larger format) cameras now have a built-in meter. In most direct vision models, the light-sensing part of the circuit faces the subject directly. It takes a general view of the whole scene included by the camera's fixed lens. The only way it will measure small parts of the subject is if you take the whole camera close to the subject.

The majority of 35 mm SLR cameras have the light-sensing cell inside, measuring the light coming through the lens (TTL). It may read from the whole picture area or from one small chosen section — and does this no matter which lens you attach to the camera body.

A third form of exposure meter is the hand-held type. This gives you the flexibility of either taking a reading from the camera position, or moving closer to the subject and reading the most important areas individually for a very precise result.

How camera meters work

A typical in-camera meter consists of a battery powering a light-sensitive cell, which points at the subject. A film speed setting control, scaled in ASA or DIN numbers, sets up a resistance in the circuit. On some cameras, changing the film speed control progressively covers or uncovers the cell itself, making it

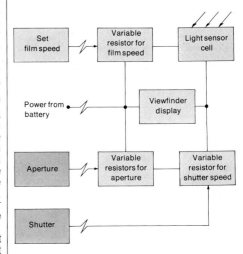

either more or less sensitive to light. (A notch in the film cartridge automatically engages with the meter to make the correct ASA setting on 110 cameras.) An additional variable resistance is created by whatever shutter and/or aperture settings the camera offers. Finally, the circuit is linked to a display board, which causes exposure indication signals to appear in the viewfinder.

Non-TTL metering

Most direct vision, fixed-lens cameras have an external cell placed as close to the lens as possible (often mounted in a ring surrounding the front element of the lens itself). This helps overcome one of the main problems associated with non-TTL metering cameras — that of using lens attachments, such as filters (see *Filters and lens attachments*, pp. 198-201),

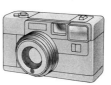
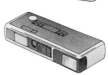
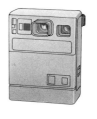

Simple built-in meters
The 35 mm compact (top) has a meter window by the lens, which automatically adjusts shutter speed according to the light falling on it. The 110 compact (center) has a fixed shutter and a sliding sunny/cloudy exposure control. A photoelectric cell linked to a viewfinder display indicates when lighting is sufficiently low for flash to be necessary. The instant picture camera (bottom) links exposure measurement with two-step automatic aperture and shutter adjustments. None of these systems offers much flexibility.

which reduce the amount of light entering the lens and, therefore, exposure. With an external cell in this position, anything slipped over the lens also covers the surface of the cell, which automatically compensates for the reduced level of illumination. On some non-TTL metering cameras you must hold the filter over the cell, to ensure correct exposure, before attaching it to the lens. The cell should have the same angle of view as the lens, so that it "reads" the same area of the subject. In a 35 mm SLR the cell can be in one of a number of positions inside the body.

TTL metering
According to the position of the cell, a TTL exposure meter will measure slightly different parts of the picture area. The most common

Meter cell positions
The cells behind the pentaprism give an integrated reading of light falling on the focusing screen. Other cells monitor image brightness on the film surface or shutter blind. These cells can be selective in their reading.

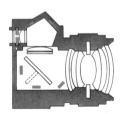

arrangement, usually based on a pair of cells in the pentaprism, measures nearly all of the the picture as seen on the focusing screen, but gives preference to the central area. This is known as "center-weighted" measurement. It provides a high degree of accuracy for most subjects, assuming that the most important elements in your composition are positioned near the center of the frame.

Some cameras provide an "overall averag-

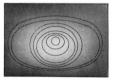

Center weighted

Shutter blind

Metering areas
The center-weighted meter reads from the whole of the picture area, but with emphasis on the central portion. It is biased toward the lower half of the frame, to avoid excessive influence from the sky. With some models, light is measured from a random pattern on the shutter blind itself. Again, this is center

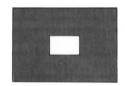

Spot reading

weighted. Spot meters read from a small center portion only, which is shown on the focusing screen.

ing" of the entire format. Measurement is accurate provided that your composition has a fairly even mixture of light and dark areas.

A few cameras measure light only from a small central area, which is marked as a circle on the focusing screen. This "spot reading" can be very accurate provided that you position the spot carefully to coincide with the key element in the composition, such as the face in

a portrait. (An exposure measurement lock enables you to take the reading, and then readjust the composition off center.) Some expensive SLR cameras provide both spot and center-weighted metering. You can change from one to the other to suit subject conditions and personal preference.

Viewfinder signaling
A built-in meter tells you whether the camera's shutter and aperture settings are correct for its reading of the subject, by signaling in the viewfinder, alongside the focusing screen. On some cameras, the viewfinder simply shows whether exposure is over, correct, or under. On automatic models, the meter often tells you what shutter and/or aperture the camera is automatically setting. You must decide whether the shutter speed selected by the

Viewfinder displays
Some cameras show if the aperture/shutter speed combination you have selected is correct by the movements of a needle against plus or minus marks, which represent over- or underexpose. Modern cameras show this by means of light emitting diodes opposite the appropriate mark. These cameras also indicate the aperture and shutter speed you are using as part of the viewfinder display.

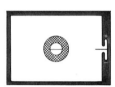

Match needle

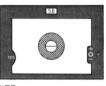

LED

camera is suitable for your subject, or whether the depth of field associated with the aperture is sufficient, and modify or override the camera controls accordingly.

Older type cameras present this information as a needle moving over a scale. This needle can be difficult to read against dim images, and the delicate mechanism is easily damaged if you drop or jar the camera. A further disadvantage of this mechanical system is that it is not quick enough to respond to changing light conditions when compared to the ultrafast reading given by recently developed (silicon blue) light sensors.

In more recent cameras, tiny light-emitting diode (LED) signals show the meter's reading, taking their power from the camera's battery system. Adjacent diodes can give information on other camera settings, including flash, so that you can make all necessary exposure adjustments without removing the camera from your eye. Some recent models use liquid crystal diode (LCD) signals in the viewfinder, to provide a digital read-out display of exposure information.

Cell types
Selenium metering cells are the only ones in use that generate their own electric current. They therefore require no battery. The current they create varies in direct proportion to the intensity of the light received. A problem with power-generating cells is that they must be large to be reasonably sensitive. This is acceptable for a hand-held meter, and on some low-cost direct vision cameras, where there is sufficient space. From the late 1930s, scaled-

Selenium cell
Light falling on the cell generates current in proportion to its intensity, thus producing a meter reading.

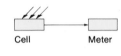

Cell   Meter

down selenium meters were sometimes built into the top of cameras, though they were not linked to the camera controls. They enabled the photographer to set both shutter speed and aperture manually by referring to the meter read-out.

In the late 1950s cadmium sulfide (CdS) cells were first developed. These are much smaller than selenium cells, so it was possible to house them inside the camera body, making feasible SLR through-the-lens metering systems. CdS cells are photoresistant. They

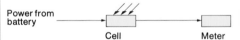

Power from battery   Cell   Meter

CdS cell
Cadmium sulfide cells are powered by battery. They react to light falling on them by increasing in resistance. The meter

is highly sensitive to low light levels, but reacts slowly if the light changes, producing a "memory" effect.

do require battery power, but with modern miniature batteries this does not create a space problem. CdS cells respond very well in dim light, but they are over-sensitive to red, and are also slow to react to the light, suffering from a "memory" of previous light levels.

In addition to selenium and CdS, two other cell types are used in modern meters. Silicon blue cells (SBCs) are extremely small, have a response about 1000 times faster than CdS cells and do not suffer from memory. But they

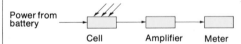

Power from battery   Cell   Amplifier   Meter

Silicon blue cell
These are smaller and more responsive to changes in light levels than CdS cells, but generate signals so

small that an amplifier has to be used before they can be indicated on the meter in the viewfinder display.

become unreliable in extremes of temperature. Gallium arsenide phosphide cells have a similar performance to SBCs, but they are much less sensitive to temperature extremes. Like SBCs, they are linked to a viewfinder signal light rather than a moving needle display, and this system makes full use of their rapid response to light.

TTL systems

It is now possible to build an exposure meter compact enough for its components (light-sensitive cell, battery, a variable resistor marked in film speed numbers, viewfinder read-out, and linkages to the exposure controls) to be housed in various convenient spaces in the camera body. A built-in meter reduces the amount of equipment you have to carry, and can give a direct exposure read-out in the viewfinder. TTL meters give accurate readings no matter what lens or attachment you use (though with some filters, exposure compensation may be necessary – see *Filters and lens attachments,* pp. 198-201).

A TTL meter can be coupled to the camera in one of four modes of operation: manual, aperture priority, shutter priority, and fully automatic. Some models offer one automatic mode, plus the option to use the camera manually. A few cameras are multimodes, offering operation in a number of different modes.

Manual

A manual metering system has a viewfinder signal indicating whether exposure is under, over, or correct. You are free to alter shutter speed, and/or aperture until the viewfinder display shows that exposure is correct. On the other hand, the system is flexible enough to allow you to ignore "correct" exposure whenever conditions, or your own interpretation of the subject, requires this. Apart from sophisticated multimodes, manual cameras are the most versatile, provided that you understand fully the effects of shutter and aperture controls on the image's sharpness and depth of field (see *Shutter and aperture relationships,* p. 125 and *Depth of field,* p. 118).

Aperture priority

The majority of semi-automatic cameras offer aperture priority operation. With this system, the photographer selects the preferred aperture to give the depth of field required, and the meter itself sets the correct corresponding shutter speed. With an electronically timed shutter, the circuitry for this type of operation is

simple and inexpensive. Aperture priority exposure works well with static scenes. The mode's major limitation is that it can give inadequate control over moving subjects. You can, however, operate many models manually, so that it is easy to choose the shutter speed.

Shutter priority

On certain cameras, the semi-automatic system works the other way round: you select the shutter speed, and the meter sets the aperture. The circuitry for shutter priority is slightly more cumbersome than that for aperture priority, because each lens must have electrical

contacts that allow the meter to control the aperture. Shutter priority is a useful mode when you require control over subject movement and camera shake. This is ideal in sports and other action photography, but it can be restrictive in other work where manipulating depth of field is of major importance. Many models feature a manual override which helps overcome this problem.

Many semi-automatic cameras – both aperture and shutter priority models – show in the viewfinder the setting that the camera has selected. This means that it is possible to control depth of field on a shutter priority camera by altering the shutter speed, and watching the effect this has on the lens aperture. Similar manipulation of the shutter speed is possible on aperture priority cameras offering this type of viewfinder display.

Fully automatic

Cameras with a fully automatic mode use their own program of shutter and aperture settings according to lighting conditions, leaving you free to concentrate on composition. The view-

finder may show the camera's settings, but on some simple models there is no indication of the exposure set. If you want to make full use of the visual potential of the shutter and aperture controls, a fully automatic camera is restrictive unless it also offers a manual mode.

Multimode

Some advanced cameras offer a selection of exposure modes. This range of options adds to the complexity of the controls, and to the price of the camera. On the other hand, a multimode model provides a unique flexibility, giving you the features of several types of SLR cameras in one.

Program mode

Some 35 mm SLRs have a program mode, in addition to shutter and/or aperture priority automatic functions. On the program setting, the camera itself combines appropriate speed and aperture settings, in accordance with the lighting conditions. You simply set the aperture ring to A (for automatic) and the mode selector to P (for program). The viewfinder may display the settings the camera has selected, as a reminder of blur and depth of field implications.

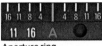
Aperture ring

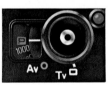
Mode selector

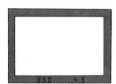
Viewfinder display

Manual functions   **Mechanical/electrical functions**

[Flow diagram – aperture priority:
Set film speed → Exposure meter circuit
Set shutter speed to auto → Exposure meter circuit
Select aperture → Aperture set → Shutter speed computed
Press back-light control → Exposure increase/decrease
Press shutter release → Aperture stops down → Shutter fires at computed speed]

[Flow diagram – shutter priority:
Set film speed → Exposure meter circuit
Set aperture to auto → Exposure meter circuit
Select shutter speed → Shutter speed set → Aperture computed
Press back-light control → Exposure increase/decrease
Press shutter release → Iris closes to computed aperture → Shutter sequence continues]

Key
- ▬ Main path
- ▬ Alternative path
- ⤙ Electrical path
- ☐ Metering
- ☐ Shutter
- ☐ Aperture

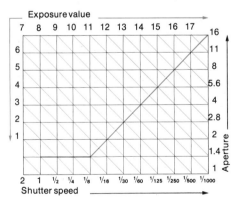

Programed shutter/aperture combinations
The selection of speed and aperture is made according to lighting conditions, shown in the diagram above as exposure values. The combination selected takes into account the ASA rating of the film being used. Shutter speed and aperture change alternately, down to speeds where a tripod is essential to avoid blur.

Using a hand-held meter

A hand-held exposure meter uses a light-sensitive cell to register the level of illumination in exactly the same way as a meter built into the camera. Some inexpensive meters still use a selenium cell, which does not require a battery. Other models, however, use CdS cells — these are more responsive to low light levels, but you must wait several seconds for the meter to register the full reading. The majority of modern meters incorporate a fast-reacting silicon cell of the type used in flash meters (see *Flash meters,* p. 141) and in measuring exposures under the enlarger (see *Printing equipment,* pp. 236-9).

In normal use you set the meter for the ASA speed of the film in the camera, and point the meter at the subject. On most selenium and CdS types, a needle swings across a scale to a figure, which you then must set against a mark on a large calculator dial. On another part of the dial the various combinations of shutter and lens aperture settings that will produce a correct exposure appear aligned. It is left to the user to decide which combination to use — taking into account the desired depth of field and degree of subject blur. Some silicon cell meters have LCD digital read-outs to take full advantage of the cell's immediate response. The read-out is again often transferred to an exposure calculator dial to give a full range of exposure options.

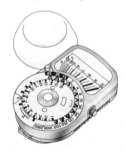

Selenium cell meter
The selenium meter is simple and reliable, and does not require a battery. Use a diffusion cone to make incident light readings. The cone effectively widens the acceptance angle of the light meter's cell. This is especially useful when highlight details are important.

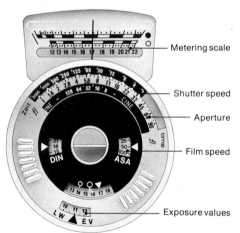

Hand-held meters
First, set the film speed in the circular calculator dial. The number indicated by the meter needle is keyed in to the dial, which then shows the range of shutter speed and aperture combinations you can use to obtain correct exposure, or an EV (exposure value) setting.

Metering scale
Shutter speed
Aperture
Film speed
Exposure values

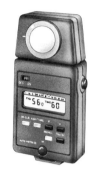

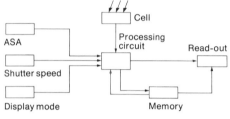

Silicon cell meter
This battery-powered meter has an LCD read-out for shutter speed, aperture, exposure value, and film speed. It also has an analog memory function. The hemispheric diffuser giving incident light readings is built-in. Its clear, simple read-out makes this meter almost as quick to use as an on-camera type.

Cell
ASA
Processing circuit
Read-out
Shutter speed
Display mode
Memory

Spot meters
Spot meters allow you to take a subject range reading (an average of highlight and shadow readings) without getting in too close. This is possible because of their very narrow viewing angle (as little as 1°). Some ordinary CdS meters have narrow-angle adaptors, fitted with an aiming viewfinder so that you can accurately "sight" the meter.

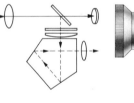

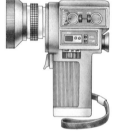

Digital spot meter
This silicon cell meter uses a single lens reflex system. Subject angle of view is 9°, but readings are taken from a center spot with a 1° angle of acceptance. A digital LCD in the viewfinder shows the exposure value, while f stops are shown digitally on the meter body. Use such meters to measure unapproachable subjects.

Reflected reading
By pointing a hand meter toward the subject from the camera position you will obtain an accurate reading, provided that the subject is fairly evenly lit and has an equal distribution of light and dark tones. For this to hold true, the meter should have a cell with a similar acceptance angle to that of the camera lens (most meters match standard lenses). If the subject is a landscape, you should point the meter downward slightly so that it registers a little more land than sky, which, in most pictures, assumes less importance.

Incident reading
A hand meter also makes it possible for you to measure light striking the subject instead of reflecting from it. You must fit a white plastic diffusing cone over the cell to reduce the light in-

tensity and gather it from a 180° angle of view and then hold it near the subject pointing back toward the camera. With this arrangement a single light reading will ensure that highlights are not overexposed (important because we are most conscious of color and detail in light parts of a scene). On most meters you convert the readings to camera settings through the calculator dial in the usual way.

Duplex reading
A duplex light reading is useful for subjects such as backlit scenes with strong lighting and bright highlights. To take this type of reading, fix the diffusing cone over the cell as above and point the meter toward the subject. Take another reading pointing toward the camera, and then take an average of the two.

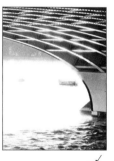
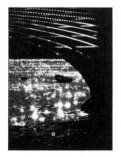

Incident reading Reflected reading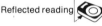

Averaging meter readings
The reflected light reading gives an under-exposed result, due to intense highlight areas affecting the reading. The incident light read-ing overexposes the highlights. An average of these two different results (below) gives the best compromise exposure.

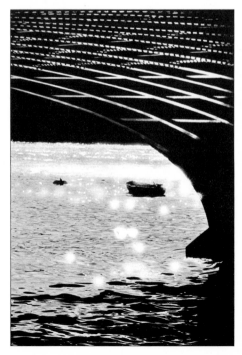

Advantages of hand meters

You can use one hand meter with any number of cameras of any size or type. Hand meters are standard equipment for most photographers who use larger format cameras without TTL metering. Hand meters are also invaluable for checking the performance of TTL meters. For reading subject brightness range hand meters are often easier to use than the camera meter — for example, you can leave the camera set up in position while you move in close to take a light reading from a very specific part of the subject. Hand meters also allow you the option of taking incident light and duplex readings. Against these advantages a hand meter is slower to use than built-in types, and cannot follow fluctuating lighting conditions as closely as a modern TTL meter.

Exposure values

You will find that part of the calculator dial on most hand meters also gives read-outs in single figure "exposure values" (EVs). This is because some cameras (certain Hasselblad and Rolleiflex models, for example) have shutter and aperture settings that can interlock. Changing aperture then conveniently alters the shutter too, and vice versa, so that the exposure level remains constant. This feature is useful if you suddenly change from a subject requiring extensive depth of field to one requiring fast shutter speed. The point at which you intermesh the two scales can be given a value, as shown in the table below. If your camera offers this facility, EV numbers will be marked somewhere near the f number and shutter speed setting rings.

Exposure values

EV	f-stops				
	4	5.6	8	11	16
6	1/4	1/2	1 sec	2 sec	4 sec
7	1/8	1/4	1/2	1 sec	2 sec
8	1/15	1/8	1/4	1/2	1 sec
9	1/30	1/15	1/8	1/4	1/2
10	1/60	1/30	1/15	1/8	1/4
11	1/125	1/60	1/30	1/15	1/8
12	1/250	1/125	1/60	1/30	1/15
13	1/500	1/250	1/125	1/60	1/30

Exposure value scale
For the same exposure value, each combination of aperture and shutter speed admits the same amount of light to the film. If EV 13 is indicated, your exposure will still be correct whether you choose to use 1/500 at f 4 for a fast-moving subject, or 1/30 at f 16 for a subject requiring great depth of field.

Solving exposure problems

Meter manufacturers try to design systems that will give acceptable results for all conditions. Sometimes, however, the type of subject, or simply the type of result you are aiming for, means that problems occur.

Very dim light

In very dim lighting conditions such as a dark interior the TTL meter may not seem to respond at all, even with the lens aperture wide open and a shutter as slow as 1/2 sec. One way to obtain a reading is to turn the film ASA dial slowly to a higher setting until a correct ex-

Exposure adjustment in stops

Reading obtained at (ASA)	Actual film speed (ASA)				
	25	50	100	200	400
50	+1				
100	+2	+1			
200	+3	+2	+1		
400	+4	+3	+2	+1	
800	+5	+4	+3	+2	+1
1600	+6	+5	+4	+3	+2
3200	+7	+6	+5	+4	+3
6400	+8	+7	+6	+5	+4
12800	+9	+8	+7	+6	+5

Low-light readings
If you cannot get a meter reading with the ASA dial showing the actual speed of the film in the camera adjust the ASA setting until you reach a speed at which you can obtain a reading. Then read down the table to find the number of extra stops you will need to give for correct exposure for your film. Unless the lighting level remains the same, you must remember to return the ASA dial to its original setting before the next exposure.

posure is indicated. Then multiply exposure time by the number of times true film speed divides into the number set on the film speed dial.

For example, with controls set to 1/2 sec at f 1.8, you may have to change the ASA dial to 1250 in order to obtain a "go-ahead" reading. If the film is in fact only ASA 125 you must multiply the exposure set by ten times — giving 5 sec at f 1.8 (see *Reciprocity failure*, p. 152). Return the setting on the ASA dial to normal before the next exposure. Given the same problem with a hand meter, take a reading from a piece of white cardboard, then give six to eight times the exposure.

Unapproachable subjects

It is important to be able to recognize the types of conditions that are likely to cause problems for an exposure meter. Sometimes a subject has a very dark or light background that will mislead a meter in a general reading, yet you cannot move near to it for a close-up reading. The particular shot may be a candid one of people or animals you do not want to disturb. In a situation like this you can usually make a substitute reading instead, from something nearby. For a picture of a distant person (where flesh tones are important), you can

take a reading from your own hand — hold it in either shadow or light, depending on the type of lighting falling on the face of the subject. For a picture of a distant field, for example, you can take a light reading from the grass beneath your feet (if the lighting is similar). With practice you will find that you can match most types of objects. Often you will be able to hold the substitute up in line with the subject in order to pre-check by eye whether the two match (approximately) in brightness.

Backlighting

When the lighting is mostly directed from behind the subject, you have to decide whether you want a black silhouette result, or a picture with good detail in the shadow areas and everything else "burnt-out" through overexposure. If the subject is a building set against the sky, you can make the building a silhouette by reading exposure only from the sky. For the opposite effect, take the reading off the building itself. An exposure meter always tries to reproduce a single tone or color as midway between maximum light and dark. Measuring the sky gives a picture with the sky mid-toned and the building black. Measuring the building makes this mid-toned and the sky bleached white. Some modern 35 mm SLRs have a backlighting exposure correction. This assumes shadow detail is most important and opens up the aperture by about $1\frac{1}{2}$ stops.

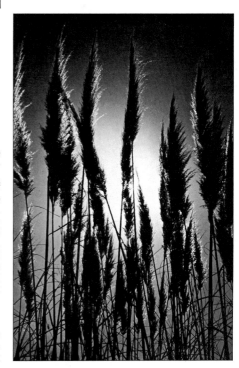

Shooting into the light
Robin Bath gave $1\frac{1}{2}$ stops extra exposure above the meter's indicated reading so that the would be able to record shadow detail and tone in this image of pampas grass. Taking the reading from the sky alone would have recorded the pampas in silhouette alone, standing out in stark relief against the sun's powerful white light in the background.

How meters can be misled

No meter, either built-in or hand held, is completely foolproof. The main problem occurs when a picture contains an unimportant area (such as a featureless background) larger and much lighter or darker than the main subject. You can see this for yourself by setting up an object in a room with a bright window area somewhere in the background, but to one side. Take a TTL light reading from a viewpoint that includes the background but excludes the window area, and set the correct exposure. Next, slightly shift the framing (while watching the meter read-out) until more and more direct window light is included in the picture area. You will see that although the light (and therefore the exposure required) on the main subject remains constant, the meter changes from "correct" to "overexposure" as the proportion of window light included in the frame increases. The same will occur when you use a hand-held meter from the camera position to take a reflected light reading (see *Using a hand-held meter*, p. 136). All meters tend to average what they see, being unable to distinguish between important and unimportant items. Therefore, the largest part of any scene within its measurement area will have the greatest influence on the meter reading.

Before taking a meter reading, try to assess the picture in terms of area. For example, if important light and dark areas are present in roughly equal amounts (or the subject and its surroundings are of similar brightness), one general reading will probably produce a correct exposure. If, however, most of the picture is dark in tone, with only one or two small but equally important light-toned areas, a general light reading will lead to an underexposed result. If the circumstances are reversed, the result will be overexposure. The best way to overcome these problems is to take close-up readings of both light and dark areas, and then set exposure for midway between them. If you are using a meter that reads the overall scene

or the type that weights the reading in favor of whatever is in center frame (see *How camera meters work,* pp. 133-4), simply move the camera (without refocusing) until light, then dark areas completely fill the picture area.

With some types of TTL meters you may obtain misleading readings when the light comes mostly from behind the camera position. This is particularly relevant if the user wears glasses while focusing. Light can enter the camera through the viewfinder eyepiece, and meter cells around the pentaprism will react to this extraneous light as if the image is brighter than it, in fact, is. You can fit a rubber eyecup to most cameras, which ensures that no light can enter the camera from this direction and cause underexposure.

Old or inefficient batteries can also be the cause of erratic and misleading meter readings. Most advanced cameras, which offer TTL metering facilities, incorporate a battery test button and LED signal. To be sure of consistently accurate metering, it is advisable to renew your camera batteries at least once a year and to carry spares at all times.

Overriding the meter

Had Henry Wilson accepted the direct reading for this Kashmir scene (below), the meter would have allowed extra exposure for the figures, due to its center-weighted bias, and thus overexposed the background. Instead, he moved forward and took a reading from the building alone. Having set the camera accordingly, he then stepped back into the crowd. By this means, he was able to give correct exposure for the building, but record the figures in deliberate silhouette.

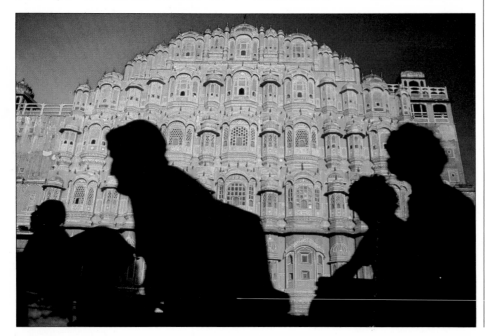

Exposing with flash

As early as 1851 William Fox Talbot had demonstrated that photographs could be taken by the light produced by a spark. During the nineteenth century photographers often took pictures by the light of a burning magnesium ribbon or (more often) by the brief flash given by igniting ground up magnesium powder. By the 1930s magnesium/aluminum foil had been enclosed in a large "flashbulb" filled with oxygen,

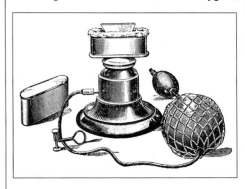

Flash powder device, 1888
Magnesium powder was inserted below a spirit lamp, and the netted ball pumped up with air. When the tube clip was released, the powder was blown into the flame. This type of flash arrangement was impossible to synchronize with the camera shutter.

ignited by a battery connected through the shutter mechanism.

It was not until the 1940s that portable electronic flash of reasonable output became practicable. The first unit weighed about 30-40 lb (14-18 kg) and gave out less light than today's smallest flashbulbs. Unlike flashbulbs, which only last for one exposure, electronic flash units produce light by briefly discharging electricity through a gas-filled tube. Each tube lasts for thou-

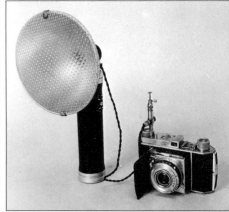

Electronic flash, 1947
This flash unit could be synchronized with all cameras, including those with focal plane shutters. A heavy, self-contained power pack was carried in a separate case. Such units were expensive, and (despite their size) less powerful than modern flash bulbs.

sands of flashes. Improvements over the last 20 years in miniaturizing electronic components has dramatically reduced the size of this form of flash. Today, units with a very useful output are built into even the simplest and cheapest cameras, while larger, independent units can illuminate large studio sets. Apart from a few large types, flashbulbs have also been miniaturized, and they are now mostly used in cubes or multibar units.

The main characteristic of flash is its short duration. This means, however, that most of the ways of measuring exposure of subjects when under continuous illumination are impracticable. Flash also makes the shutter speed set on the camera much less important in exposure terms. As long as the shutter is fully open when the flash discharges, it is the flash duration itself that determines exposure time (about 1/100 sec for bulbs and 1/1000 sec or less for electronic flash). With both types of flash, correct exposure depends on the distance of the subject from the flash and the lens aperture, taking into account the speed of the film in use. With electronic flash it is possible to vary the duration of the flash via the light sensor found on nearly all modern units. On some advanced cameras the photographer can program an electronic flash unit into the circuitry of the camera, so that some of the normal TTL metering can be used.

Flashbulbs represent quite a low initial cost to the photographer, but each bulb must be discarded after one firing – so the cost is continuous. On the other hand, an electronic flash unit will cost much more to begin with, but one set of flash batteries may last for hundreds of individual firings. The actual number of flashes per set of batteries is difficult to calculate – more distant subjects require greater flash output to illuminate successfully.

See also
Light quality, pp. 18-19. The documentary approach, pp. 347-57. Dynamism, pp. 357-61.

How flash works

The simplest types of flash units are the flash cube, flipflash, and flash bar. Each one contains enough bulbs to allow you to take several pictures before changing the complete unit. Each bulb is so small that almost no current is necessary to fire it. Some cameras that accept these flash units have lens shutters containing a small peizo-electric crystal instead of a battery to generate sufficient power to ignite the bulb as the blades begin to open. In this way, the shutter is fully open when the zirconium wire contents of the bulb have burned to maximum brilliance. Bulbs are tinted blue to overcome their natural orangey light and match daylight and electronic flash. Bars, cubes, or flipflashes plug directly into the camera body. You fire larger bulbs, though, with a small battery, wired through synchronizing contacts in the camera shutter.

Electronic flash
Camera-mounted electronic flash units are powered by batteries. Large studio units use the domestic electricity supply. With both types, the current charges a capacitor, which you can think of as a storage tank. When a trigger circuit is completed through the camera shutter, this capacitor discharges through a flash tube to produce an instantaneous flash of high-intensity light. The capacitor then takes up to a few seconds to recharge ready for the next exposure – an indicator light glows to show you when it is fully recharged. Units vary greatly in their recharging time, depending on the design of the circuitry and the condition of the batteries. Some flash units can be used with a motor drive attachment (see *Motor drives and camera backs,* p. 202), and therefore they must recharge completely in a fraction of a second.

You mostly attach electronic flash units to the camera through a "hot shoe" – an accessory holder equipped with electronic contacts connected to the shutter. On some compact cameras small flash units are either built into the camera body or you can clamp them to it. Large flash units, including studio types (see *Flash lighting units,* pp. 165-6) connect to the camera through a long synchronizing cord, which you either plug into the hot shoe or a socket in the camera body near the lens. The flash cord allows you more flexibility in directing the flash light, in order to avoid the very hard, flat lighting that often characterizes flash used mounted on the camera hot shoe.

All electronic flash units incorporate a test button to fire the flash. You can use this to fire the flash manually if you want multiple flashes

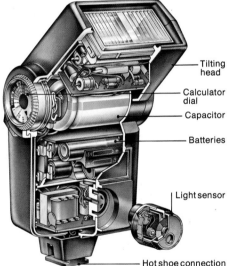

- Tilting head
- Calculator dial
- Capacitor
- Batteries
- Light sensor
- Hot shoe connection

Automatic electronic flash
Flashguns such as this are compact, portable, and economical. They can be programed to adjust the duration or power of the flash to match the subject distance at your working aperture. A sensor calculates when sufficient illumination has been given. You synchronize the flash unit with the camera either by mounting it directly on the camera's hot shoe (above right), or by means of a synchronizing cord if you are using the flash off camera. With some models, you can retain the automatic facility with off-camera flash

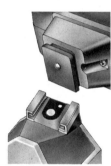

by removing the sensor and attaching it to the hot shoe. The flash can also be fired manually. With many models you can alter the direction of the flash by tilting the head to bounce light off any convenient reflective surface.

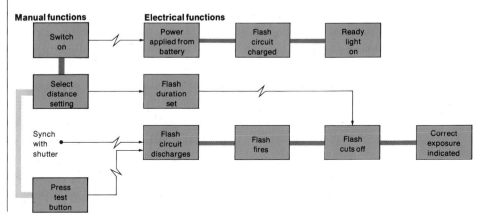

Manual functions   **Electrical functions**

Switch on → Power applied from battery → Flash circuit charged → Ready light on

Select distance setting → Flash duration set →

Synch with shutter → Flash circuit discharges → Flash fires → Flash cuts off → Correct exposure indicated

Press test button

during a long exposure or if you want to combine the frozen quality of flash with the blur of subject movement recorded by ambient lighting. Use the test button to discharge the flash before switching it off.

Flash synchronization
As electronic flash fires without delay when triggered, a lens shutter must complete the firing circuit when the blades are fully open. All larger format cameras have an external socket for flash with a switch marked "X" for electronic, and "M" for bulb flash. Focal plane shutters trigger electronic flash when the first shutter blind has cleared the picture format. Provided that the second blind has not started to cover the frame (usually 1/60 sec, or longer), the flash will record a complete picture.

M setting

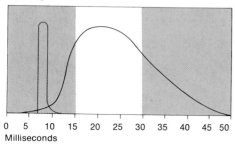

X setting

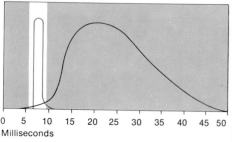

X and M synchronization
With the M setting (top), the shutter is fully open (clear area) when a flash bulb (black line) reaches peak intensity. If you use the M setting with electronic flash (red line), the peak will have passed before the shutter opens. The X setting (above) is timed so that electronic flash fires when the shutter is open. With bulb flash on X, however, the shutter will have closed before the flash reaches full intensity.

Flash guide numbers

The farther the subject is from the flash the less light it receives, and the wider you must set the lens aperture in order to expose the film adequately. The small size of most flash sources means that they conform to the "inverse square law". This law states that doubling the distance between subject and light source quarters the light, and so you have to open the aperture two full stops (setting the aperture to half its original number). Changing distance from 3 ft (1.5 m) to 6 ft (2 m), for example,

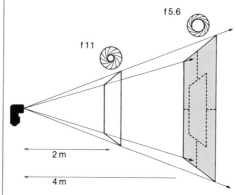

Flash distance and exposure
The flashgun above has a guide number (meters) of 22. If flash-to-subject distance is doubled, illumination is spread over four times the area, and becomes one-quarter as bright. Two stops more exposure is required. Self-regulating flashguns, however, will automatically compensate for this.

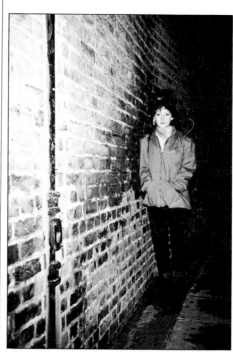

Flash fall-off
The picture (above) shows how light from a flashgun diminishes in intensity the farther away the subject is from the light source. This is particularly noticeable outside at night.

means changing from lens aperture f 8 to f 4.

The power of flash bulbs and electronic units is rated in "guide numbers" (GNs). To calculate a guide number you multiply the f number by the distance of the subject to the flash (either in feet or meters). Unless otherwise stated, guide numbers relate to ASA 100 film. If a guide number is 185 (feet)/56 (meters) you must use f 11 when the flash is 16 ft (5 m) from the subject. Always divide the

Exposure table
Simple flashguns have a data panel such as this to help you calculate correct exposure. Read down the column under the speed of your film and across from the estimated subject distance to find the right aperture setting to use. With ASA 80 film, for instance, and a subject 10 ft (3 m) away, the table suggests you use an aperture of f 5.6.

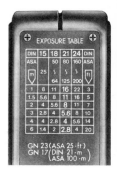

guide number by the distance (in feet or meters) to find the f number.

To determine the flash factor with film slower than ASA 100, you divide the guide number by 1.41 for each halving of the film speed. Therefore with ASA 50 film and a guide number of 185 (feet)/56 (meters) the result is 131 (feet)/40 (meters). With ASA 25 film the result is 185/56 divided by 1.41, divided by 1.41, or 93 (feet)/28 (meters). When using film faster than ASA 100 you multiply the guide number by 1.41 for each doubling of the film speed. With ASA 200 film, therefore, the flash factor is 261 (feet)/79 (meters), while with ASA 400 film it is 185/56 multiplied by 1.41, multiplied by 1.41, or 368 (feet)/111 (meters), and so on. With multihead flash you also multiply the guide-number (see *Using multihead flash*, pp. 177-8).

If you have a simple camera without adjustable aperture, and equipped with a built-in flash, you will normally find instructions telling you the optimum range to use for correctly exposed flash pictures. Simple flashguns often have a calculator for various film speeds and flash-to-subject distances.

Typically, the smallest electronic flashguns have a guide number when used with ASA 100 film of about 50 (feet)/15 (meters). Used with a simple camera having a fixed f 8 lens, correct exposure is given when the subject is about 6 ft (2 m) from the flash. Subjects closer than this will appear overexposed, and anything farther away will be underexposed. Larger units usually have guide numbers between 100-132 (feet)/30-40 (meters), while powerful, and expensive, studio types may offer 330-500 feet)/100-150 (meters).

Certain assumptions about the reflective qualities of the subject and its surroundings have to be made in the assigning of guide numbers. Often they refer to pale flesh tones in a domestic room with "fairly reflective" walls. If your subject is darker than this, and especially if you are shooting outdoors where there are no close surfaces to help reflect light back, you may have to halve the guide number to achieve correct exposure.

Self-regulating flash

All but the simplest electronic flashguns include a small diode light sensor that points directly at the subject. The sensor gives such an instantaneous response that it is able to measure the amount of light reflecting back from the subject and so cut off (quench) the flash when enough light is received. Illumination is therefore regulated according to subject distance. Working close up, flash duration may be as short as 1/10,000 sec, whereas at 10 ft (3 m) the same unit may give a flash duration of 1/1000 sec. Another advantage of this system is that the sensor takes account of any method you use to soften the lighting — perhaps by diffusing the flash with tracing paper, or tilting the flash head to reflect the light off the ceiling or walls — provided the sensor still views the subject directly.

For a correct exposure you must set the film speed and aperture on a tiny computing circuit

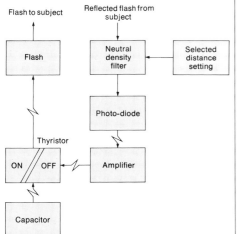

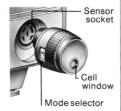

Remote flash sensor
A light cell in the sensor measures the amount of light reflected back from the subject when the flash is fired. This is automatically computed against the setting previously made on the mode selector, which corresponds to the f stop and flash-to-subject distance used. When the correct amount of reflected light has been received, the

flash cuts off. Assuming there are no misleading reflective surfaces, the sensor will work well.

Sensor socket
Cell window
Mode selector

in the flash head. It often shows on a scale the maximum distance (full duration flash) and minimum distance (briefest clipped flash) over which you can work.

"Dedicated" flashguns plug into the camera and integrate with its electronic system. In some advanced 35 mm SLRs this means that the unit automatically changes the camera shutter to a speed suitable for flash. It also picks up ASA information of the film loaded and signals in the camera viewfinder when it is fully charged and ready to fire. On cameras with internal meters, which can read light reflected from the film itself, the camera meter acts as a flash sensor for controlling exposure.

Diffused flash

To create a softer quality light you can diffuse the flash by placing translucent material such as tracing paper a few inches in front of the tube, or pointing the flash head at the ceiling or walls and bouncing the light on to the subject. If your flash does not have a sensor, you will have to make allowances for the inevitable loss of light due to scatter and absorption. To measure the degree of absorbency of any translucent material, first take a normal light reading of a large, bright area, such as the sky. Next take a reading through the material. If the difference in readings is one f number, the dif-

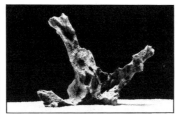

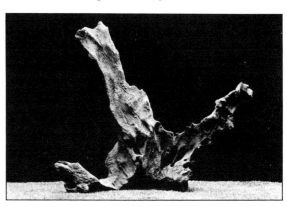

Light quality
The harsh light of directional, frontal flash (above) can be softened (right) by using a diffuser or bouncing light off a reflective surface. This will remove hard shadows and give softer modeling of subject features.

fuser halves the light and you must open up one stop whenever you use it over the flash. For bouncing, open up one to two stops (depending on the reflective qualities of the surfaces). If you are using a manual flashgun for bouncing, measure distance as being from gun to surface to subject. Bouncing light from a colored surface (or diffusing with colored material) will introduce a color cast if you use it in conjunction with color film. Flash sensors that always point at the subject automatically take into consideration the light lost through diffusing or bouncing.

Flash meters

Flash lighting affects film exposure in terms of intensity and duration. A conventional exposure meter only measures the intensity of light, as the duration of normal lighting is continuous. Flash meters, therefore, are designed to measure duration as well.

Multiple-function flash meter
This digital meter has both reflected and incident light measuring modes. A liquid crystal display gives either f number or exposure value indications, as required. The meter can be used with a connecting cord for synchronized flash, or without the cord for continuous light readings from studio lamps, single-burst electronic flash, and multiple or repeated flash. Camera shutter speeds can be dialed in to give a read-

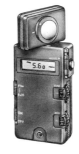

ing for fill-in flash. The head can be turned to take readings from any angle, while the controls and readout remain visible to the user.

Flash meters are similar in size to normal hand-held exposure meters, and you use them to take incident light readings by standing near the subject and pointing them back toward the camera position. Some have a synchronizing cord that fires the flash when you press a button on the meter. Others are cordless, and you must fire the flash using the test button to record a reading. As soon as the test flash fires, the meter displays the f number you require for the ASA value of the film in the

Built-in meter
Some flashguns incorporate a simple form of metering. After setting the estimated flash-to-subject distance, fire the gun at the subject using the open flash button. If the correct exposure indicator lights up, the subject is

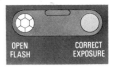

within the range of the flash at that particular setting.

camera. Most flash meters have a 12-stop aperture range, which goes far beyond the range of apertures offered on most popular camera lenses.

Most units are accurate to within one-third of a stop, though more sophisticated models are accurate to within one-tenth of a stop. This degree of accuracy is especially important when you are exposing expensive, large-format color transparency material, which has little exposure latitude. Some flash meters do double duty as continuous light exposure meters. You use a switch to change from a flash mode to a continuous-light metering mode for normal light readings.

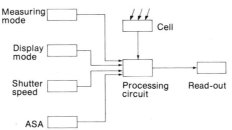

Measuring mode
Display mode
Shutter speed
ASA
Cell
Processing circuit
Read-out

Film

The invention of photography dates from the discovery of light sensitive chemicals suitable for recording an image in a camera obscura. For nearly four hundred years, scientists had known that silver compounds darkened on exposure to the sun's rays. In the early eighteenth century, research in Germany by Johann Schulze showed that light caused such changes, and not heat as previous observers had thought. By 1800, Thomas Wedgwood, son of the English potter Josiah Wedgwood, was producing printed images using this principle. He placed white leather covered with silver nitrate solution under ink drawings on glass. Light forms a negative image in darkened silver. But Wedgwood could find no way to stop the reaction, and halt the darkening of the image.

It was probably the Frenchman Joseph Nicéphore Niépce who made the first chemically formed picture taken with a camera obscura, in 1826. Niépce used lithographic materials instead of silver — a coating of white bitumen on pewter metal, which hardened after exposure to light. After exposure for about eight hours, Niépce removed the unhardened areas of bitumen by washing it in lavender oil. The result was a permanent picture, in recognizable tones, but with fragmented detail (see below).

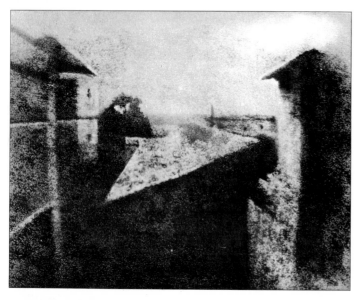

The world's oldest surviving photograph
This historic image was produced by Nicéphore Niépce about 1826. It was taken from the workroom window at his home near Châlon-sur-Sâone.

A pigeon loft (left), the sloping roof of a barn (center), and part of the house (right) can be identified, though shadows have filled in most details.

The daguerreotype
The first practical photographic process was invented by another Frenchman, Louis Daguerre. In 1839 he published details of his daguerreotype process. This used a polished silver plate, which the photographer left exposed to iodine vapor in a box until a coating of light-sensitive silver iodide formed. Exposure for four to five hours produced only a faint visual change, but Daguerre then treated the plate with warmed mercury vapor, to give an intensified, positive image. He halted the chemical reaction by bathing the picture in salt solution, to "fix" the image. Daguerreotypes proved immensely popular. In a few years, improvements in the process, and in lenses, reduced exposure times to about 20 seconds — making portraiture possible.

Negative/positive photography
Each daguerreotype was unique, and it was impossible to print copies. In addition, the image was reversed left to right unless the photographer used a special mirror camera. The Englishman William Henry Fox Talbot overcame these problems with his rival process, the Calotype. Fox Talbot's method was to treat paper with silver nitrate solution, and expose it in a camera for about one minute to a subject lit by strong sunlight. He then treated it again in the same solution to strengthen the image, and fixed it in hyposulfate of soda ("hypo"). Fox Talbot's results were negatives (reversed tonally as well as left to right), so to finish the process he pressed the negative against a similarly sensitized sheet, and exposed it to sunlight. In this way he could make any number of positive prints.

Fox Talbot's system was less popular than Daguerre's because the negative's rough paper fibers destroyed fine image detail. But

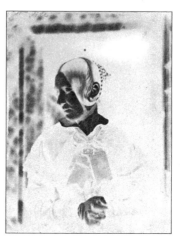 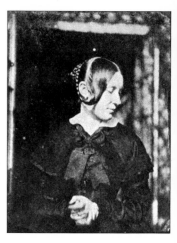

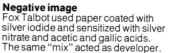

Negative image
Fox Talbot used paper coated with silver iodide and sensitized with silver nitrate and acetic and gallic acids. The same "mix" acted as developer.

Positive image
The fixed negative was waxed to make it translucent and then contact printed (by sunlight) on to paper sensitized by the same method as before.

when, in 1851, Scott Archer discovered that it was possible to use collodion (soluble guncotton dissolved in a mixture of ether and alcohol) to attach silver compounds to glass, the negative/positive process became dominant. But it was not an easy process to use. The photographer had to prepare the collodion glass plates and expose them while they were still wet. Processing in developer, to blacken the exposed parts, and fixing, to dissolve the remaining parts, had to take place immediately. Location photography therefore required a darkroom tent. Time exposures were still necessary, with the camera firmly secured to a tripod.

Films
Most of these problems were solved in the mid-1870s by the use of emulsion: a mixture of silver halide compounds in gelatin. It was possible to use plates with the new gelatin emulsion when they were dry. This meant that plates could become a marketable commodity, and greatly popularized photography, even though most plate cameras were still bulky and awkward to carry.

In America, George Eastman introduced rollfilm in 1889. This had its emulsion ready-coated on a flexible base. Soon adventurous photographers adapted gas-powered magic lanterns to make enlarged prints on emulsion-coated paper. For the first time, exhibition-size prints could be made from relatively small, hand-held cameras. By the beginning of this century, the fastest films had improved to a speed equivalent of approximately ASA 20. It was soon common for chemists to process these films for the amateur.

The search for color
All the hues of the visible spectrum can be produced by combining light of three colors — blue, green, and red. These are called the primary colors of light. Because it is possible to make any hue by *adding* light of these colors, they are also known as the additive primaries. The complementary colors are yellow, magenta, and cyan. Each is made by adding the two adjacent primaries in the

color wheel (see below), and each is the complementary of the opposite primary color. Thus magenta, for example, is made up of red and blue, and is complementary to green.

The principles of color photography were well understood by the 1860s. It would be necessary to have three records of the camera image – on three emulsions, each sensitive to one of the primary colors. By making prints in the complementary colors, and superimposing them on paper, a full color record could be formed. At this time emulsions were sensitive to blue light only. In 1906 sensitizing dyes were discovered, which when added to black and white emulsions made them "panchromatic" (responsive to all colors).

The way was now open for the development of color photography. The early color photographers took three separate negatives of each individual subject through deep blue, green, and red glass

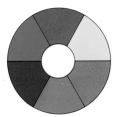

Three-layer color
This view (below) was taken in 1877 by Louis Ducos du Hauron. Three exposures were made on early gelatin emulsion plates through blue/violet, green, and orange/red filters. He produced complementary positives (see left) in light yellow, red, and blue by the carbon process, on gels which were then superimposed. The plates used were sensitive to blue, green, and only some yellow wavelengths of light.

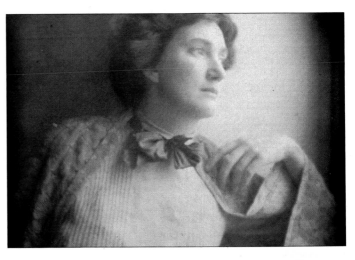

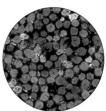

Autochrome process
This Autochrome plate by Alvin Langdon Coburn was made in about 1908. One side of a glass plate was coated with a screen of microscopic grains of transparent potato starch, dyed red, green and blue/violet (right). Gaps were filled with carbon black. The plate was coated with a panchromatic emulsion, and exposed through the back so that the grains acted as color filters. Reversal processing of the plate gave a positive color slide.

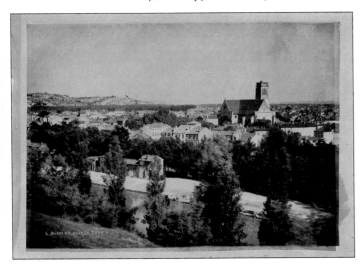

filters. Then they made lantern slides, and combined these with mirrors and similar filters to the ones used to take the photographs in a viewer to see a full colored result. The first commercial color plates were the Autochrome types of 1907. They used a mosaic of colored dots to produce a colored transparent image, in a similar way to the method in which a modern television screen builds up its full-color picture.

Modern color materials date from 1936, when Kodak introduced Kodachrome. This was the first film that used a stack of three emulsion layers on a single base. It was processing alone that turned the three recorded images into separate colors. The resulting images were in the form of color slides. The first negative/positive color prints used triple emulsions in both film and paper, and appeared during the mid-1940s. These were expensive, the colors were inaccurate, and they were impossible for the user to process at home.

Quality slowly improved, and eventually new materials appeared that were much quicker and simpler for user processing. Silver dye-bleach materials (Cibachrome) appeared in the mid-1960s. This positive/positive process allowed direct printing from slides. The speed and resolution of both color and black and white materials has also improved. But the number of black and white products available decreases each year. From the early 1970s, the majority of photographers have used color for most of their work.

Black and white material has changed its role, and is now used only by a minority of photographers.

Instant picture materials
Instant pictures date from 1948, when Dr Edwin Land developed and improved a document copying process to make it suitable for general photography. The first instant picture process used a roll-film-type camera, and gave positive sepia prints in one minute. Each picture was exposed on part of a roll of paper. The camera user then pulled the paper through internal rollers, which spread processing chemicals over the paper and brought it into contact with a second, receiving paper. The camera ejected the two sheets of paper, which the photographer peeled apart after one minute. On one sheet there was a throw-away negative, and on the other there was a permanent positive print.

In 1963, Polaroid produced instant color print material in a peel-apart form. In 1972 they improved this process by the invention of single-sheet material, which the camera ejected as a white card. This then chemically formed a color image in normal light. Kodak followed this in 1976 with their own instant picture color material, based on similar principles.

Instant color print
Dr Edwin Land's early experiments with instant picture processes gave sepia or black and white results, but by 1951 he was producing color dye images such as this. Over a decade was to elapse before a subtractive color dye transfer process yielding an instant color print could be marketed.

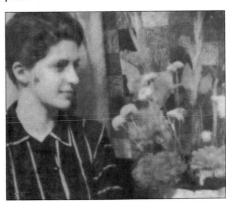

How films work

Both black and white and color films make use of light-sensitive salts of silver and are processed in chemicals that can distinguish between light and dark parts of the exposed image. It is easiest to understand the action of black and white materials first, as they still form the underlying basis of all color film materials.

Black and white films
A typical black and white film consists of a silver halide emulsion coated on a plastic, non-stretch base. In practice, several layers of emulsion are coated in order to give the film the best possible characteristics. Halides themselves are very small—an area one millimeter square may contain one million crystals or "grains" — and they are thinly coated to allow the utmost image resolution. A top coat of gelatin helps protect the halides from abrasion. The back of the film also carries a gelatin coat to prevent curling as the film is successively wetted and dried during processing. A dye is added to this anticurl layer or to the base to stop the spread of light during exposure.

Color films
All color films have several layers of black and white silver halide emulsions. Effectively, three emulsions are used — one responding to blue light, one to green, and one to red. The varied colors present in the camera image form different latent images in each layer. After development each latent image forms a visible image in a different color. In films (not instant picture material) this is done chemically. Films start without any colors at all, but are processed to give images in yellow, magenta, and cyan — the colors complementary to blue, green, and red light. With color negative film, processing forms an image with reversed colors and tones. When it is enlarged on color paper, which also has multilayer emulsions, the result is a positive color print. Color slide film has basically the same structure, but is designed to undergo extra processing stages to form a direct positive image.

Instant picture material already contains three layers of fully formed dyes, as well as three layers of halides. A built-in processing chemical releases colored dye from the dark parts of the image in each emulsion layer. In "peel-apart" material the colors diffuse out on white receiving paper rolled in face contact with the exposed surface. "Integral" material functions similarly within a single-sheet, multilayer sandwich.

Black and white film process

The yellowish or gray-looking surface of unused film is in fact the light-sensitive layer of silver halide emulsion. Silver halides consist of colorless compounds of silver mixed with halides (potassium iodide, potassium bromide, or potassium chloride) in gelatin. The gelatin is a vital component of the film structure. It not only anchors the chemicals to the plastic film base, but also swells enough during processing to allow the easy access of other liquid chemicals without disturbing the position of halides forming the image.

Light causes the silver halides to break down into dark metallic silver. Modern emulsions, however, are not designed to go this far.

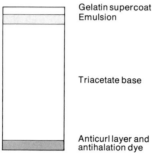

Film structure
The light-sensitive emulsion is protected from handling damage by an extra gelatin layer. Roll and 35 mm films have a 0.1 mm thick

cellulose triacetate base, sheet film uses stiffer polyethylene. A balancing gelatin coating on the back of the film inhibits curl.

Even a minute exposure to light is sufficient to create changes on an atomic level within the halide crystals themselves, according to the light and shade areas contained in the camera image. The emulsion now carries a latent or invisible image, which you must keep away from

Negative formation
These diagrams represent a greatly magnified area of conventional black and white halide film.
Latent image After exposure in the camera there is no visible difference between the crystals which received light, and the dark parts of the image.

Latent image

Developer Developer chemicals in water soak into the gelatin, reaching the halides and causing the light-struck crystals to form black metallic silver.

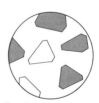

Developer

Fixing and washing
The next main solution, fixer, causes all remaining undeveloped silver halides to become soluble. They are then removed by washing, leaving only the black silver. Dark parts of the film now represent the lightest parts of the original subject, forming a negative image.

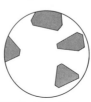

Fixing and washing

light until after development. Development magnifies millions of times the atomic changes in the halide crystal structure, producing a visible result.

If the film is a conventional black and white type, developer chemicals first turn the most exposed areas (representing the lightest parts of the image) black or gray. The remaining parts are still creamy and would eventually darken in normal light. The next "fixer" chemi-

Direct positive formation
Some fine-grained black and white films can be specially processed to give a direct positive image on film. This results in a black and white slide.
Latent image
Exposure in the camera forms invisible changes in crystals which received light.

Latent image

First developer This solution darkens light-struck halides to black silver. At this stage, the image is basically negative.

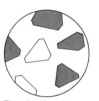

First developer

Bleach and fog
Instead of fixing, the film is treated with a special bleacher. It dissolves away black silver without affecting any undeveloped halides. The halides which remain are then fogged to light (or treated chemically) so they can be developed in the next solution.

Bleach and fog

Second developer
This solution is similar to the first developer. It darkens the remaining halides to black silver. Dark parts of the original image therefore reproduce dark on the film. Finally, by-products are removed by fixing and washing.

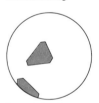

Second developer

cal, therefore, helps dissolve away undarkened halides so that these parts are left clear (representing the darkest parts of the image). Finally, you must wash the film to remove all chemicals and by-products of processing. The result is a photographic negative. (Some modern black and white films are designed to be given a different processing routine — see *Chromogenic black and white film process,* facing page.) You can then enlarge each negative on light-sensitive black and white printing paper to produce a negative of a negative — a positive print.

Film is usually panchromatic, meaning that it gives tonal reproduction of all image colors. Printing paper is normally insensitive to colors other than blue, as it is only intended for use with black and white negatives. This also allows you to handle it safely under convenient orange darkroom lighting. You can process some black and white negative film to produce direct positive images (see above).

Instant picture black and white film process

Instant picture black and white films use the same silver halides as traditional black and white films, but work on a unique "silver transfer" system. The emulsion is coated on a sheet of paper or film (the negative layer). Included in the silver halide layer are the developer chemicals necessary to produce a positive print.

After exposure to the camera image the paper or film is brought in contact with gelatin-coated receiving paper (the positive layer), and jellied activator chemicals spread between them. The positive layer is not light

Positive
Base
Sink layer
Receiving layer

Negative
Reagent
Halides + developing agents
Base

Film structure

Negative material which is exposed to the image in the camera has a paper or film base. Its light-sensitive emulsion contains silver halides plus inert developing agents. An attached pod contains jellied

alkali reagent to activate developer, plus weaker halide solvent. Positive material has a gelatin image-receiving layer with invisible trace elements, and an underlying gelatin sink layer.

sensitive, but it does contain a substance that renders unexposed silver halide particles developable. The pod also contains a silver halide solvent such as sodium thiosulfate (a chemical most commonly used in fixation to convert unused silver halides into a soluble form).

During development the negative (exposed) layer and the positive (receiving) layer are in close contact. The activated developer chemicals develop the exposed silver halides in the normal way. Any unexposed silver halides in the negative layer are made soluble, and these diffuse across to the positive receiving layer where they, too, are darkened into metallic, black silver, forming a positive image. All you have to do is time this process, then pull the two sheets apart to get a permanent, positive image on the receiving paper.

The peel-apart negative is usually not reusable, and so you simply throw it away. Some Polaroid instant picture films (Type 665 and Type 55) use a film base instead of paper and give negatives that you can enlarge in the same way as normal film images. As soon as you peel the negative away from the positive, you must soak the negative briefly in a solution of sodium sulfite to clear the image. Before reuse, it must be washed and dried. This process removes all chemical residue, which would eventually stain the negative. The resulting image is very fine grained, and produces enlargements of excellent quality. All instant picture film made for black and white is of the peel-apart variety.

  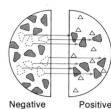

Latent   Negative   Positive

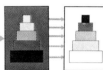

Image   Latent   Negative   Positive

Image formation

Exposure forms a latent image in the silver halides. When activated and sandwiched with positive material, developer chemicals turn light-struck halides to black silver. Remaining halides, released by the solvent chemical, migrate to the receiving layer. They combine with the trace materials and become converted to black silver. Most transfer occurs from image shadow areas,

Negative

giving a positive. By-products are absorbed into the sink layer. If exposed material has a film base it can be cleaned in a special clearing solution to give a negative for enlarging.

Chromogenic black and white film process

Chromogenic film development usually only applies to color negative film, and it is a process in which oxidation products of color developer combine with color couplers (present in the film emulsion) to form dyes of precise and known characteristics.

Some recent black and white films also make use of chromogenic processing. These films are designed with more than one layer of silver halide emulsion. Unlike color negative films (see *Color negative film process*, p. 146),

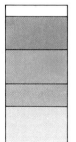

Gelatin supercoat

High-speed emulsion with color couplers

Low-speed emulsion with color couplers

Antihalation layer

Emulsion support

Film structure

A typical black and white chromogenic film has several emulsion layers of different speeds, to extend its general response to various light levels. Each emulsion contains colorless dye

couplers linked to the silver halides present. A gelatin topcoat protects against abrasions. Antihalation dye prevents light scatter, and the back of the film has an anticurl layer.

each layer has identical color sensitivity, so that the dyes produced as a result of development are the same except for hue.

Processing not only causes the dye image to form, but also bleaches away all the film's silver. The result is a monochrome dye negative rather than a multicolor negative suitable for color printing.

The chromogenic negative has a dark sepia or reddish image appearance, according to brand. This color maximizes density when you print on black and white bromide paper (see *Print making*, pp. 232-3), which is sensitive to blue light only.

The reasons for producing a negative in dye instead of silver are threefold. First, a negative consisting of dye molecules has a finer structure than black silver grains, and so gives enlargements with finer resolution (particularly important with 35 mm film, which is generally enlarged further than rollfilm or view camera format film). Second, with a dye film of this type you can still produce negatives that will give successful black and white prints when the film is far more overexposed or underexposed than is acceptable with a silver negative film (see *Chromogenic film and paper theory*, pp. 217-19). Chromogenic film is, therefore, ideal for documentary and candid subjects, where you very often have no time to alter settings to match changing light. Third, you can process most black and white dye films using the same process and chemicals employed for color negative film (see *The processing sequence*, pp. 226-7).

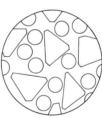

Latent image

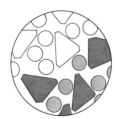

Color developer

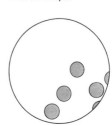

Bleach/fix

Image formation

Latent image After exposure, no visible change occurs to the silver halides in the single layer of chromogenic film emulsion shown here. Circles represent dye coupler molecules. Each one is linked to a crystal, and remains colorless at this stage.
Color developer The first processing solution forms black silver in exposed areas. The by-products of this development then convert couplers adjacent to the crystals into colored dye. Usually this has a reddish or brown tint, depending on brand.
Bleach/fix The second processing solution dissolves away all the black silver and remaining silver halides. Only the colored dye molecules are left unaffected, and remain to form the final negative image. Most chromogenic black and white films use the same processing chemicals and routine as color negatives.

Color negative film process

As color negatives are intended as inter-mediates for making color prints, their characteristics are designed to suit color paper. During processing, a single color developer solution forms black silver along with a different color dye in each emulsion layer. Then the silver is removed along with the remaining unexposed silver halides, leaving only the dye images.

If you could peel apart the layers of a negative after processing, the top one (originally

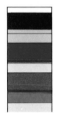

Protective overcoat
Blue-sensitive emulsion + yellow coupler

Yellow interlayer
Green-sensitive emulsion + magenta coupler
Interlayer
Red-sensitive emulsion + cyan coupler

Antihalation layer
Base

Film structure
Each emulsion layer has a different dye coupler that remains colorless until processed. The yellow interlayer acts as a

filter during exposure, preventing blue light from reaching the green- and red-sensitive layers. It is removed in processing.

sensitive to blue) would show yellow wherever blue light existed in the original image. The middle layer (green-sensitive) would record magenta wherever green existed, and the bottom layer (red-sensitive) would have cyan wherever red was present.

Color negatives are designed to be enlarged on paper capable of giving a positive image. You can use either chromogenic negative/positive paper (see *Chromogenic film and paper theory,* pp. 217-19) or photo color transfer paper (see *Photo color transfer process,* p. 219).

Image formation
Latent image This diagram shows part of the green-sensitive emulsion layer. Large shapes represent silver halides, circular shapes are couplers capable of forming magenta dye. After exposure there is no visible change to the film.

Latent image

Color developer
Halides corresponding to parts of the image that contained green light have developed to black silver. By-products of this cause adjacent couplers only to change into magenta dye.

Color developer

Bleach and fix These stages stabilize all the silver salts. Both the black developed silver and the remaining halides (with their unused couplers) are made soluble and removed by washing.

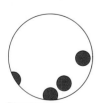
Bleach and fix

Color positive film process

Color positive films are generally designed for projection or direct viewing as slides. There is no overall color mask as with negatives, and all tones and colors are positive, matching those of the original subject. To create a direct positive image the camera film is first developed in black and white developer to give black silver negatives in each layer. However, it is the remaining silver halides that are important, because instead of fixing, the film receives an additional color development. This developer only forms dye in the areas unaffected by the first developer — and this gives a positive color image in each layer.

You have to expose color slides much more

Image formation
Latent image Color slide film has a sequence of layers similar to color negative film (left). This diagram represents part of the middle, green-sensitive emulsion. After exposure, it carries an invisible, latent image.

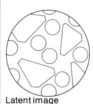
Latent image

First developer
The first solution, a black and white developer, changes halides exposed to green light to black metallic silver. Neither developer nor by-products affect the color couplers at this stage of the process.

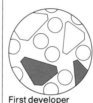
First developer

Color developer
All remaining undeveloped halides are fogged chemically and acted upon by color developer. This forms black silver and creates by-products that cause the couplers attached to these halides only to turn into magenta dye.

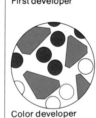
Color developer

Bleach and fix A bleach solution and fixer cause all silver present to become soluble. It is then washed from the film. Where green light was absent, the film now carries an image in magenta dye.

Bleach and fix

carefully than negatives, because the "one-step" result gives you little opportunity to correct any errors (in printing, for example). Also you must be careful to use film that is compatible with the type of light source predominating, because different films are made for daylight and tungsten (see *Available lighting,* pp. 162-3). You can correct color negative film to a large extent using color conversion filters during printing.

It is possible to make a print from a color slide, but you must use paper capable of producing a positive from a positive. There are three types of paper available — silver dye-bleach paper (See *Silver dye-bleach material,* p. 219) chromogenic reversal paper, and photo color transfer.

Color peel-apart film process

Each of the three different color-sensitive emulsions in instant picture material has a ready-formed layer of complementary dye directly below it. Developing chemicals are mixed with this dye, and these only function when an activator is present. You begin by exposing the light-sensitive material (usually

Positive material
Base
Acid layer
Spacer
Mordant layer
Alkaline pod

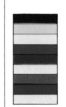

Negative material
Blue-sensitive emulsion
Yellow dye + developer
Spacer
Green-sensitive emulsion
Magenta dye + developer
Spacer
Red-sensitive emulsion
Cyan dye + developer
Base

Material structure
The top part of the cross-section shows the positive material ready to receive the image diffused upward from the multilayered

negative material. Jellied activator spreads between the two, and they remain in contact while picture formation takes place.

Integral film process

There are two types of single-sheet, integral color print instant picture materials — Polaroid and Kodak. Each is ejected from its appropriate camera as a multilayered card on which the image appears, without any peeling apart.

The Polaroid material contains a pod of activator mixed with thick, white pigment. The pod contents are spread within the internal layers as the card passes through rollers on its way out of the camera. The pigment shuts off the layers from light while they are processing, and also forms a white base through which released colors diffuse and form the final image. Internally, the anchoring or releasing of dye proceed as in peel-apart material.

Kodak materials are different in several respects. The activator contains carbon black instead of white, and the released dyes mi-

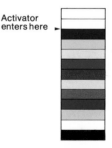
Activator enters here →

Clear plastic layer
Image-receiving layer
Blue-sensitive emulsion
Yellow dye + developer
Spacer
Green-sensitive emulsion
Magenta dye + developer
Spacer
Red-sensitive emulsion
Cyan dye + developer
Timer
Neutralizing layer
Black plastic base

SX-70 material structure
This integral, color instant picture material has lower layers containing light-sensitive halides and dyes. The top layers are clear,

receiving the dye image when released by the negative. Jellied activator enters just before the image-receiving layer.

paper) to the camera image. When you pull the film tab, the exposed layer is placed in face contact with a sheet of receiving paper, and rollers in the camera break a pod of jellied activator as the two papers leave the camera.

Development begins at once. Where halides have been affected by light they anchor the dye directly below them (see diagram right). Where the halides are unaffected by light, the underlying dye is free to rise to the top of the exposed sheet and transfer to the receiving layer. For example, in the blue-sensitive layer, parts of the original image that were not blue allow yellow dye to transfer. The green-sensitive layer causes magenta dye to rise where green was not present. In the white parts of the camera image all layers are exposed and all dyes immobilized. In black parts all three dye layers transfer.

When you pull the two sheets apart, the receiving layer carries a full-color, positive image. Like color slides, the one-step nature of the process means that your exposure must be accurate and the type of lighting must suit the color balance of the material. Peel-apart instant picture material is intended for use with daylight or flash. It produces distorted colors when used with other light sources (see *Color temperature,* p. 151). Color balancing filters are available to correct this effect (see *Using filters,* pp. 158-9).

Exposed material　　　**Activated material**

Subject

Image

Emulsion　Dye　　　Receiver　Emulsion　Dye

Positive　Negative　　　　　Positive　Negative

Image formation
Positive and two negative layers of material are shown (left). Magenta dye, linked to developer molecules, lies behind the green-sensitive halides. Triangles represent acid

molecules. In processing, alkali reagent activates developer to turn exposed halides to silver. Here, dye is locked in. Remaining dye transfers as a magenta positive.

---

grate in the opposite direction to a white surface at the back of the card. Because of this difference you must use the manufacturers own cameras to obtain a right-reading image (see *Instant picture cameras,* pp. 109-10).

Like peel-apart instant picture materials, integral materials produce dark results when underexposed, and pale, bleached pictures when overexposed. A further common factor is that integral instant picture material gives correct color in daylight or flash.

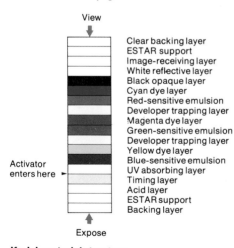

View

Clear backing layer
ESTAR support
Image-receiving layer
White reflective layer
Black opaque layer
Cyan dye layer
Red-sensitive emulsion
Developer trapping layer
Magenta dye layer
Green-sensitive emulsion
Developer trapping layer
Yellow dye layer
Blue-sensitive emulsion
UV absorbing layer
Timing layer
Acid layer
ESTAR support
Backing layer

Activator enters here ▶

Expose

Kodak material structure
This material is exposed through its clear base. Activator enters between layers four and five. Dyes are

released upward, passing through an opaque white layer, to form a color print on the card's opposite face.

Exposed material　　　**Activated material**

Subject

Image

Emulsion　Dye　Receiver　　　Emulsion　Dye　Receiver

Latent image　　　Developed image

Image formation
Shown (right) is a simplified representation of the green-sensitive emulsion, with overlaid magenta dye, and gelatin receiving layer. Special halides form silver in unexposed areas when acted upon by developer. As shown (far right), spreading alkaline activator within the material first causes the latent image in each emulsion to develop as

a black and white positive. Oxidation by-products formed by development release the adjacent chemi-

cally bound dye. This gradually diffuses into the receiving layer, and appears as a magenta image (magenta appears where green was absent in the original). Other layers release yellow dye where blue light was absent, and cyan where there was no red. Where parts of the subject were black, all three emulsion layers are unexposed, form

black silver, and release all three dye colors, re-forming the original subject color (see diagram above).

Choice of film

The first decision to make when choosing film is whether results are to be in black and white or color – this basic decision strongly influences the way photographers compose their pictures. Decide also how much color will contribute to the mood and information content of the picture. If in doubt, shooting on color negative film will allow both color and black and white results.

Film for camera types
In practice, choice of film will also be determined by the type of camera. 110 size cameras, for example, only accept a very small range of films – the choice for black and white negatives and color slides is particularly limited. There are no black and white materials for cameras taking integral instant pictures. Another factor that should make the decision easier is the physical form the final result should take – either color print or slide, or black and white print or slide. Perhaps other types of result will be required too – for example, slides as well as prints, or black and white as well as color.

Film speed and response
Another important factor in choosing the right type of film for a particular subject is film speed. A very slow (low ASA) film will probably be ideal for brightly lit subjects, or any subject where a degree of movement blur is required for an interpretative effect. A very fast film (high ASA) will be better for dim lighting conditions or any moving subject that has to be frozen in action. A fast film may, however, be too fast to allow the photographer much choice of camera controls in brilliant lighting, and the coarse, grainy pattern of the film structure may be another deciding factor.

It is important to bear in mind the differences between eye and film response. Inside a room lit with domestic tungsten bulbs, for example, the eye accepts the illumination as "white", just as outdoors it accepts daylight as white. In fact, the artificial lighting is much more orange in content. Color film cannot adapt in this way – its three layers are designed to reproduce one particular light mixture as truly white. Most films are balanced for daylight (including flash). Some films, though, are designed specifically for tungsten studio lamps.

Non-standard results
Sometimes accurate reproduction of the image seen through the viewfinder is not required. Results may be more powerful with a strong "warm" or "cold" cast, and these can be chosen to suit the mood of a picture. Other effects are possible using unusual film types with infrared-sensitive or high-contrast emulsions, or by giving the film incorrect processing.

See also
Light and color *Time of day*, p. 23. Color *Association and mood*, p. 50. Format proportions, pp. 56-7. Filters and lens attachments *Non-effects filters*, p. 201.

Black and white films

Brand name	ASA	35 mm	Roll	Sheet	Other	Notes
Kodak Ortho Type 3	12*	●**		●		High contrast
Agfaortho 25	25	●**	120	●	Mx	Orthochromatic
Agfapan 25	25	●**	120	●	Mx	Slide processing available
Kodak Panatomic X	32	●**	120			
Agfa Dia-Direct	32	●				Slide film
Ilford Pan F	50	●**	120/220			Slide processing available
Kodak High Speed IR	50*	●				Infrared film
Agfapan 100	100	●**	120		Mx	
Kodak Plus X	125	●**	120		Ma	
Ilford FP4	125	●**	120/220	●		
Kodak Verichrome Pan	125		120/620/127		110/126	
Agfapan 200	200			●		
Kodak Tri-X	400	●**	120/220	●		
Agfapan 400	400	●**	120/220	●		
Ilford HP5	400	●**	120/220	●		
Kodak Royal X	1250		120			
Kodak Recording 2475	1250	●				
Ilford XP1	400-1600	●	120			XP process kit
Agfa Vario XL	125-1600	●	120			C41 processing

Color reversal films

Brand name	ASA	35 mm	Roll	Sheet	Other	Process	Notes
Kodachrome 25	25	●				K14	
Agfachrome 50S	50	●**	120	●		Agfa 41	50 L for tungsten
Agfacolor CT18	50	●	120/127			Agfa 41	
Ektachrome EPY 50	50	●	120		Ma	E6	Tungsten film
Kodachrome 64	64	●				K14	
Ektachrome ER64	64	●	120/127	●	110	E6	
Agfacolor CT110/126	64				110/126	Agfa 41	
Ektachrome Infrared	100*	●				E4	Infrared film
Agfacolor CT21	100	●	120/127			Agfa 41	
Agfachrome R100S	100	●	120	●		E6/Agfa 44	
Fujichrome 100RD	100	●	120			E6	
Ektachrome EPT 160	160	●	120			E6	Tungsten film
Ektachrome ED 200	200	●	120			E6	
Ektachrome EL 400	400	●	120			E6	
Fujichrome 400	400	●	120			E6	

Color negative films

Brand name	ASA	35 mm	Roll	Sheet	Other	Process	Notes
Agfa CNS	80	●	120/620/127		110/126	Agfa N	
Agfacolor 80S	80	●**	120	●	110	Agfa N	
Agfacolor N100S	100		120	●		C41	N80L for tungsten
Kodacolor II	100	●	120/620/127		110/126	C41	
Vericolor IIS	100	●**	120/220	●		C41	Tungsten available
Fujicolor F-II	100	●**	120		110/126	C41	
Agfacolor 400 CNS	400	●	120		110	C41	
Kodacolor 400	400	●	120		110	C41	
Fujicolor F-II 400	400	●	120		110	C41	

*ASA estimate
**Cassettes and bulk film available
Mx Film for Minox miniature cameras
Ma Film for Minolta miniature cameras

Instant picture films

Brand name	ASA	Image	Image size (cm)	Notes
Polaroid Type 665	75	B&W print	7.3 × 9.5	Reclaimable negative
Polacolor 2, Types 88/108	80	Color print	7 × 7.3/7.3 × 9.5	Daylight/flashcubes
Polacolor 2, Type 668	80	Color print	7.3 × 9.5*	Daylight/electronic flash
Polacolor 2, Type 558	80	Color print	9 × 11.7*	Daylight/electronic flash
Polaroid SX70	150	Color print	8 × 8	Daylight/electronic flash
Kodak PR10	150	Color print	6.7 × 9	Daylight/electronic flash
Polapan Type 552	400	B&W print	9 × 11.7*	Fine-grain film
Polaroid Types 87/667	3000	B&W print	7 × 7.3/7.3 × 9.5**	General-purpose film
Polaroid Type 55***	50	B&W print	9 × 11.5	Reclaimable negative
Polapan Type 51***	320	B&W print	9 × 11.5	High-contrast film
Polapan Type 42****	200	B&W print	7.3 × 9.5	Fine-grain film
Polaroid Type 46L****	800	B&W slide	6.2 × 8.3	Continuous tone film

*Sheet formats also available   **Sheet and roll formats also available   ***Sheet only   ****Roll only

Sizes and packs

The most widely used films are made in the form of drop-in plastic cartridges, metal cassettes, rollfilm (film rolled within backing paper), and sheet film of various sizes. With the exception of sheet film, all are designed to be loaded and unloaded from the camera in normal lighting. Most instant picture materials take the form of film packs, or large individually packed sheets of film.

Cartridges

Plastic film cartridges contain both feed and take-up compartments within the unit, with a length of film threaded between the two. The film is backed by light-proof paper. Because this film is designed for basic cameras, the backing paper has pre-printed frame numbers that can be read through a window cut into the camera back and cartridge. This reduces camera complexity and cost. Most cartridges are

made for 110 size cameras and contain film 16 mm wide. Some are made for older 126 cameras – these use 35 mm wide film. In both cases, the cartridge tends to hold the film in the

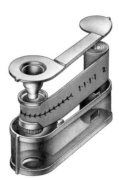

110 cartridge
The sealed plastic cartridge drops straight into the camera. Film is attached to the backing paper a few inches from its leading end. During use, both are drawn from a feed chamber until completely wound on to an internal spool. The cassette's location determines both the position and flatness of the film plane within the camera.

image plane with less precision and flatness than other forms of camera systems. There is a single perforation per frame, which prevents the camera's film advance mechanism from winding on more than one frame at a time.

Cassettes

Metal cassettes are made for film that is 35 mm wide. This type of film still carries the double row of perforations inherited from the time when it was cut-down movie stock. The end of the film is shaped, and protrudes from the cassette through a light-tight, velvet-lined slot. The inner end of the film is attached to a spool within the cassette. The first few inches of film are

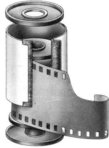

35 mm cassette
As shown here in exploded form, 35 mm cassette film is wound on a single spool in a light-proof metal or plastic container. In the camera the film is drawn out through a slot (light-trapped by black velvet) as exposures are made. It is finally rewound into the cassette. Some types can be used again.

designed to be wasted as it is attached to the take-up spool in the camera and wound on in normal lighting. 35 mm film has no backing paper – the camera itself has mechanical linkages connected to the film transport system, and tallies the number of photographs taken. During operation the film winds on to an open take-up spool permanently fitted within a chamber in the camera body. You must rewind it into the cassette after all the frames are exposed before opening the camera.

Rollfilm

Rollfilm has no perforations and is attached by its leading edge to a length of opaque backing paper. This paper is long enough to be threaded through the camera and on to an identical take-up spool without exposing the beginning of the film to light. Frame numbers are printed on the backing paper, although most advanced rollfilm cameras measure the

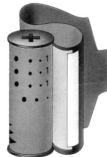

Rollfilm
In a rollfilm, the light-sensitive film is rolled in wider, light-proof backing paper. The film is taped to the paper about 10 ins (25 cm) inside its leading end, which is taken up on another, identical spool situated in the far side of the camera. The tail end of the opaque backing paper is also longer than the film.

number of frames mechanically. After the last frame is exposed the film is completely wound on to the removable take-up spool – the last part of the backing paper is longer than the film and protects it from light when you open the camera back and remove the exposed film.

Formats

The most common picture sizes and film formats are shown below. 6×7, 6×6, and 6×4.5 cm nominal formats all use 6.2 cm wide rollfilm, and vary according to camera design.

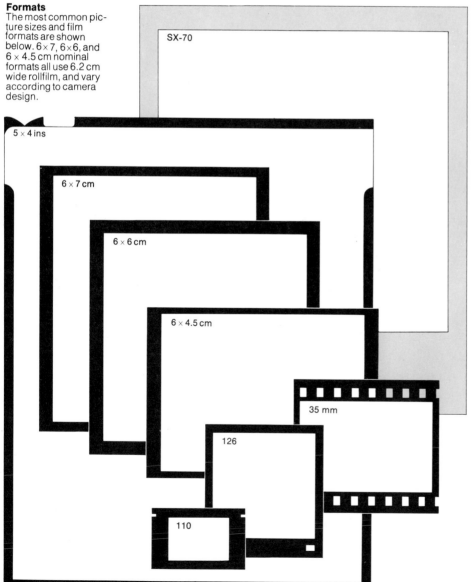

SX-70

5 × 4 ins

6 × 7 cm

6 × 6 cm

6 × 4.5 cm

35 mm

126

110

Today's rollfilms are limited to 120 and 620 (both 6.2 cm wide but with different spool flanges) and 127 size (4.6 cm wide).

Sheet film
Sheet film for use in general photography is made in about four different sizes — the most popular is 5 × 4 ins (12.5 × 10 cm). Sheets are packed 10, 25, or 50 to a box, and are intended to be unpacked and loaded into camera film holders in the dark. A notch is cut into one side of each sheet, and when you hold the sheet so that the notch is in the top edge at the right-hand corner, the emulsion will be facing you.

Boxed sheet film
Sheet film is packed in boxes, often interleaved with black paper. In the dark, use the notch to determine the position of the emulsion side of the film. With some makes, its shape also denotes the emulsion type.

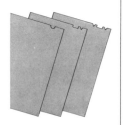

Some manufacturers code notches in such a way that you can identify the types of film from the cut-out shapes.

Instant picture material
Integral materials are sold in packs containing 10 sheets. The cardboard cover sheet automatically ejects when you insert the pack in the camera. Peel-apart materials are also sold in film packs. These contain eight stacked pairs of negative and positive sheets, which are brought together after exposure when you pull a film tab. Both are then withdrawn as a sandwich from the back of the camera through rollers. Large-format peel-apart material is drawn into a special daylight-loading film holder. After exposure, the holder feeds the

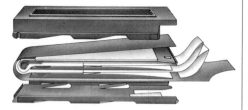

Instant picture packs
Peel-apart material is stacked so that pulling a tab after exposure (right) brings exposed and receiving sheets into face contact. They are then withdrawn through rollers.

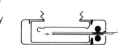

sheet into a small bench processor where the exposed material is withdrawn, placed in contact with receiving paper, and pressed with motorized rollers to spread developing agent between the two. Several types of black and white instant picture material are made in rollfilm form, mostly for use with instrument-recording equipment.

Choosing color camera film

There are many factors involved in choosing a color film because there is a wide range available. You must first decide on what form your final result is to take — either slide or print. Color slides are best shot on film designed to produce a final film positive image (although you can make them from color negatives). If you are likely to want several slides of the same subject, it is best to take several identical exposures — this gives better image quality than duplicating a single slide. You can make good-quality color prints from a slide original provided that subject contrast is soft rather than harsh, and the exposure and color rendering are accurate. If you are in any doubt, or might later want to make black and white prints as well as color prints, you should choose color negative film instead.

Color balance
Another factor governing film choice is the color of your lighting. If you are shooting with daylight, electronic flash, or blue flash bulbs (or mixtures of any of these), a daylight-balanced film is the obvious choice. Other light sources have a different color content. If you want results with a normal color rendition when using studio or domestic lighting as the main illumination, then use film designed for tungsten sources. Weak domestic bulbs still give a warm cast and you may have to correct this with filters (see *Non-effects filters*, p. 201).

If light sources in a scene are mixed, decide which part you want to show with accurate colors and choose a film type to suit that particular area. For example, if a room is partly lit by daylight and partly by domestic tungsten bulbs, shooting on daylight film will make areas near the windows correct in color, but other parts will appear orange. The same picture shot on tungsten film will make the window areas appear blue, while the tungsten-lit areas will appear correct.

Sometimes you are likely to find that the camera is loaded with daylight slide film and you want to take pictures under artificial light. If the film is already partly exposed with day-

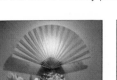
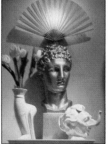
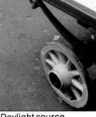

Tungsten source   Daylight source

Daylight-balanced film response
The sensitivity to blue, relative to red, of color films designed for daylight-lit subjects is matched to the color contents of average daylight. Subject colors then reproduce accurately (above right).

When daylight film is used to record scenes under tungsten lighting, the reduced blue and increased red wavelengths present result in a warm cast (above left). Both pictures were taken on slide film.

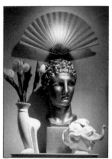
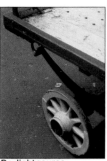

Tungsten source   Daylight source

Tungsten light film response
Color films balanced for subjects under tungsten lighting are more sensitive to blue, and less sensitive to red, than are daylight films. This compensates for the reduced blue and richer red content of the

light. Subject colors record accurately in tungsten lighting (above left), but if the film is used in daylight (above right) the results are excessively blue. You can use filters to compensate for this.

light images, you can shoot with a blue color balancing filter over the lens. Matching the color balance of film and lighting is vital for slide material and instant pictures. For color negatives, though, it is much less important because you can use color filters over all or part of the image during printing. This is why few color negative films (other than types intended for critical professional work) are made balanced for tungsten illumination.

Differences between brands
Each brand of film uses slightly different dyes, and these produce subtle variations in coloring. Once again, this is most noticeable with slide films. Ektachrome, for example, tends to produce "colder" colors than Kodachrome, and Agfachrome gives stronger greens. There are also variations in color response between different brands of color negative film, although differences here are affected by controls during printing, including the use of other manufacturers' printing papers. Choice between brands in terms of color response is largely a matter of personal preference. It is not advisable, though, to mix materials in any one set of prints or slides.

Emulsion speed is an important consideration. The fastest color films do not match the maximum speed of black and white. But color films, like their black and white counterparts, all show an increase in grain size as emulsion speed increases (see *Choosing black and white camera film*, p. 152). Grain in color slides and negatives consists of "blobs" of colored dye rather than clumps of black silver grains. You can sometimes use these dye blobs to give a delicate "pointillist" effect (see *The impressionistic approach*, p. 338-40).

When you are choosing between color slide films, bear in mind that some types are not intended for processing by the user. You must send these "non-substantive" films back to the manufacturer, as the chemical, color-forming "couplers" are not present in the emulsion layers (see *Chromogenic film and paper theory*, pp. 217-19).

Color rendition

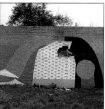

Kodachrome 25

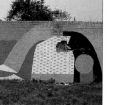

Agfachrome CT18

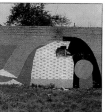

Fujichrome 100RD

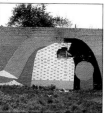

Ektachrome EL400

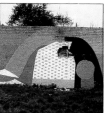

Ektachrome EL400 (uprated 1 stop)

Grain enlargement

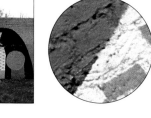

Brand variation
Even with the correct film for the light source, each brand gives slightly different colors and contrast. The pictures above were taken under identical lighting conditions, on five types of daylight slide film. Part of each image is also shown greatly enlarged. Fuji and

Agfa films clearly have a warmer balance of color than Ekta-chrome. Notice how variations appear strongest in pastel or neutral areas. Uprating and pushed development coarsen contrast and grain. Each result would probably be acceptable in isolation.

Color temperature

"White" light is a mixture of wavelengths, which vary according to the light source itself and conditions between source and subject. For example, the blue content in sunlight decreases between noon and dusk because of atmospheric conditions (see *Time of day*, p. 23). Tungsten bulbs give out proportionally more red wavelengths and less blue than the sun. Light from a blue sky contains hardly any yellow and red wavelengths at all, and this accounts for the cold blue cast noticeable in shadow areas illuminated largely by skylight.

Scientists classify these mixtures of wavelengths by heating metal under controlled conditions, until it gives off light matching the color appearance of the source under test. The temperature of the metal at this point (measured on the Absolute scale and quoted in kelvins) is called the color temperature of light. Color temperature gives a useful and internationally agreed scale of figures to describe wavelength mixtures in white light.

As you heat metal it first glows deep red, then orange, and through the spectrum increasingly toward bluish light. Light sources that have a relatively low color temperature are therefore richest in wavelengths at the red end of the spectrum. Higher color temperature light sources are rich in blue light. Candle light,

for example, gives an orange light and has a temperature of 1800 K. Most electric light bulbs give color temperatures in the range of 2000-3500 K, according to their wattage. Direct noon sunlight averages 5000 K. Selective absorption by cloud, or light scattered from blue sky instead of coming direct from the sun, produces a much higher lighting color temperature.

Most color films are balanced for daylight — their emulsion layers are designed to give color-free reproduction of white and neutral gray when a subject is lit by 5500 K illumination (a mixture of direct sun and skylight). Film balanced for tungsten light is corrected to give the same effect for 3200 K light sources. To give color-free reproduction of neutral-toned subjects under lighting other than 5500 K or 3200 K, try to use the nearest suitable type of film and adapt it to the light source with color filters. This correction process is unnecessary if the very color of the lighting on a scene is an important picture feature. Toward dusk, sunlight may only be 2000-3000 K. A sunset shot on unfiltered daylight film records all the warmth you can see by eye. But if you were to record the same scene on film balanced for tungsten light, the sun's light could be made to look almost white.

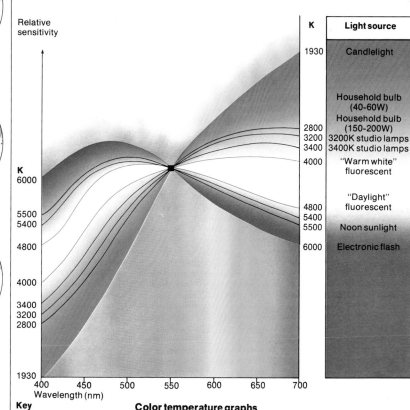

Relative sensitivity

K	Light source	Filter
1930	Candlelight	82C + 82C
	Household bulb (40-60W)	82C + 82B
2800	Household bulb (150-200W)	82C
3200	3200K studio lamps	
3400	3400K studio lamps	81A or 82A
4000	"Warm white" fluorescent	30M + 10Y
4800	"Daylight" fluorescent	30M + 20Y
5400		
5500	Noon sunlight	85B
6000	Electronic flash	85B

Wavelength (nm)

Key

Daylight film parameters

Tungsten film parameters

Color temperature graphs
Each graph represents the mixture of wavelengths present in various white light sources. A candle here has the lowest color temperature, emitting far more red than blue wavelengths. Very overcast conditions give reduced red/increased blue content. Blue and red lines suggest the limits within which daylight and tungsten light films might be used, centered on 5500 K and 3200 K respectively. The filters modify light to give acceptably accurate color on tungsten light film within its parameters.

Choosing black and white camera film

With black and white film you must still decide whether you want the final image to be either slide or print. The vast majority of all black and white film is designed for prints, but it is possible to purchase film specially for reversal processing to slides. Most black and white films are panchromatic and reproduce all the colors as shades of gray. This tonal representation varies in strength according to the "color weight" present in the original scene (see *Weight of color,* p. 79). A few films, infrared types, for example, have a different color/tonal response, and are more suitable for special effects photography.

Speed and grain

For the most part, choice of black and white film means choice of ASA speed. Bear in mind that grain is coarser the faster the film. There is also a change in contrast — in general, slow films are slightly more contrasty than fast films. Most photographers keep to one brand of medium-speed (ASA 125 or 400) film for most work. This is an advantage because you can learn how a particular film responds to different degrees of lighting contrast and the effects of over- and underexposure. But some subjects demand different films. In a delicate high-key portrait, for example, or for recording fine detail in a close-up of weathered wood, you might do better to use a fine-grain film of about ASA 32. The same choice might apply to pictures of dancers, traffic, or any subject where you want to create a sense of movement through blur, by using a slow shutter speed.

Fast film such as ASA 1000 or more is a good choice for hand-held candid photography indoors without flash. Often, you can freeze action in indoor sport such as boxing or badminton. Another reason for choosing a fast film is that it allows you to use a long lens at a shutter speed brief enough for hand-holding.

Sometimes, grain rather than any other factor dictates choice of film. You may want to break away from the objective recording of subjects. Grain appears most strongly in the mid-tone grays of the image and will be very noticeable in softly lit forms, especially if you boost contrast during printing.

Versatility

There will be times when you cannot predict accurately the type of lighting conditions you are likely to meet. One of the disadvantages of lengths of film over individual sheets is that you might have to finish the roll under very different lighting conditions than when you started it. The most tolerant black and white films in terms of exposure are the chromogenic dye types. Pictures can be overexposed or underexposed (by rating the film anywhere between ASA 125-1600 to suit the subject) within the same roll of film. You then process the film for the highest rating used (see *Compensation processing,* p. 224). The negatives will vary in density, but they print with considerably less loss of detail than if you used regular silver image film in this way.

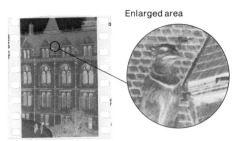
Enlarged area

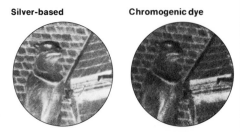
Silver-based   **Chromogenic dye**

Slow ASA 32

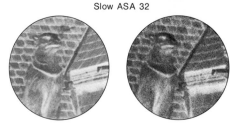
Medium ASA 125

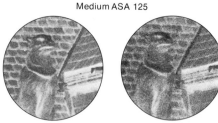
Fast ASA 400

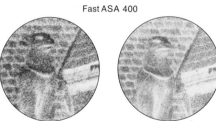
Ultra-fast ASA 1200

Comparative film types
The left-hand column shows enlargements from four silver image films, each exposed correctly following recommended ASA ratings and processing times. Fast film shows more grain, less image detail. The right-hand column shows enlargements made from one chromogenic film, given C-41 processing. Each frame was exposed at a different ASA rating. Between ASA 125 and 1200 negatives remain printable, but the ASA 32 result is too overexposed. At ASA 1200 dye images give better detail than silver images. The "broken" appearance of the enlarged chromogenic negatives is due to dye globules rather than silver grains.

Reciprocity failure

A photographic emulsion is most sensitive to light of a particular intensity. This is contrary to the Reciprocity Law of photochemistry, which states that as long as the exposure (light intensity multiplied by time) stays constant, then the film response will be the same. For example, if you double the time the shutter stays open and close the aperture by one stop, the result on the photographic material should be identical. The Reciprocity Law, however,

Exposure compensation for reciprocity failure (in f stops)					
Typical general-purpose films	**Exposure time** (sec)				
	1/1000	1/125	1/8	1	10	100
Black and white	—	—	—	+1	+2	+3
Color slide (daylight)	$+\frac{1}{2}$	—	—	+1*	+2*	+3*
Color slide (tungsten)	—*	—*	—	—	+1	+1$\frac{1}{2}$
Color negative	—·	—	—	—	+1$\frac{1}{2}$*	+2$\frac{1}{2}$*
Instant picture (integral)	—	—	—	—	+1*	+1*

* Shifts in color balance may occur

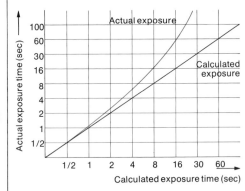

Compensating for reciprocity failure
The table and graph show reciprocity failure exposure compensation for typical films. The table shows how to compensate using lens aperture. The graph shows how to extend exposure time. Differences between metered time (black line) and time required (red line) increase rapidly.

starts to break down when illumination is either very weak or extremely bright.

The film speed marked on the box assumes that the most commonly used camera shutter settings — approximately 1/8 to 1/500 sec — are chosen. Longer exposures to a very dim image, or extremely short exposures to a bright one, make films behave as if they were less fast. This failure is slight to begin with, but at about 10 sec and slower it becomes substantial. Types and brands vary in their reciprocal failure. Generally, tungsten light slide films are adjusted to give less speed loss at long exposures than at short ones. Some professional color films come in two versions — "S" type, corrected for 1/8 sec or shorter, and "L" type intended for 1/8 sec or longer.

Film care

All photographic emulsions are sensitive to chemical fumes, X rays, and physical abrasion. They also contain gelatin, which is an organic substance liable to grow mold if left for long periods in humid conditions. Processed films contain dye or silver images that gradually change or fade, even if protected from light. Color materials are always more susceptible to change than black and white emulsions, because their layers may alter in sensitivity at different rates, upsetting color balance.

Storing unexposed film

Before buying film, make sure it is not close to its expiry date (marked on the outside of each packet). If film has been stored at the right temperature and humidity, its usable life will be greatly extended – perhaps even past its expiry date. In the short term, you can store films at a room temperature of 65° F (18° C) or less.

For longer term storage, film should be kept in a refrigerator at a temperature of 56° F (13° C) or lower. For extremely accurate results you can buy a stock of film all from the same batch, and then test it for precise speed and any adjustment of color balance by filters. Refrigerate the film until it is required.

To protect the film against high humidity it is sold in snap-over plastic containers or in sealed foil wrappers. If you keep the film in cold storage, it is essential to give it time to reach approximate room temperature before unsealing the container. If this is not done, there is a strong posibility that moisture may condense on the cold emulsion surface.

Handling care

Temperature also affects film when it is loaded in the camera. In a closed, sealed vehicle, for example, the temperature can reach a level high enough to alter the speed or color balance of the emulsion. Always keep film away from motor exhausts, boiler fumes, wet paints, or solvents. You should load film faster than ASA 400, and all infrared films, indoors. As a general rule, it is always best to load even slow film in the shade. At airports be careful not to allow unprocessed film to go through X ray baggage inspection. Film always accumulates X ray dosage, so even if each inspection gives a very mild exposure, several exposures will probably result in damage. Often, the processed negatives have an uneven veiling of tone and slides appear bleached. "Radiation protective" envelopes are of little value. Try to have film processed within a few days of exposure in the camera, because exposed material deteriorates far more rapidly than unexposed material when subjected to the effects of damp and humidity.

Caring for exposed film

Do not store any processed material in conditions of high humidity as this will promote the growth of fungus. Light tends to fade images over a period of time. Slides will survive projection about 250 times at 15 seconds each before any color change becomes noticeable. Even when stored in a dry, dark environment, color negatives start to deteriorate after six years, color slides after 10-25 years, and black and white silver negatives after 50-100 years.

Warm-up times of color film packs		
Type of film	For 11°C rise	For 42°C rise
Rollfilm	$\frac{1}{2}$ hr	1 hr
35mm cassettes	1 hr	$1\frac{1}{2}$ hr
Sheet film (10-sheet boxes)	1 hr	$1\frac{1}{2}$ hr
35 mm bulk tins	3 hr	5 hr

Processed film storage	
Temperature (at 15-40% RH)	Dye life extended by
24°C (75°F)	×1
19°C (66°F)	×2
12°C (54°F)	×5
7°C (45°F)	×10
−10°C (14°F)	×100
−25°C (−15°F)	×1000

Picture economy

Cartridge films for the 110 format are sold in 12 and 24 exposure lengths. Cassettes for the 35 mm format contain film for either 20 or 36 full-frame exposures. Some types are also sold in 12 and 72 exposure lengths as well. The number of frames per rollfilm depends on the particular format of the camera – 120 rollfilm, for example, gives 12 exposures for 6 × 6 cm cameras or 10 exposures for 6 × 7 cm cameras. Rollfilms with a special thin base allow 24 6 × 6 cm exposures on a similar film spool (these are known as 220 size).

The longer the length of film you buy, the cheaper each exposure becomes. 110 film, however, is not available in bulk lengths. For the 35 mm format, bulk lengths of film are available in tins of 16 ft (5 m), 56 ft (17 m), or 98 ft (30 m). These are usually used in conjunction with 250 frame SLR camera backs and motor drives. But for the more modest user of film, economies can be made. Film loaders are available that you can use to cut these lengths of film down to reload normal length 35 mm cassettes. A 16 ft tin holds enough film for about 115 exposures, and reduces the cost per frame by about 50 per cent. Bulk film is also sold for rollfilm cameras. This is really aerial photography stock, double perforated, 70 mm wide, and designed for special cassettes that fit into camera backs for rollfilm SLR magazine cameras.

Film box information

The box your film is packed in shows all the information you require to set your camera ready for use. This includes type of film, size, number of exposures, speed rating, batch number, and date stamp. Often the ASA number is incorporated with the name of the film. Generally, brand names ending in "color" are color negative material, and those ending in "chrome" are color slide films. Both black and white and color film should be processed by the expiry date shown. In many cases you can extend this time by careful storage. However it is risky to buy film that is close to or beyond its expiry date – color film in particular may prove slower than expected and it may also produce a color cast.

1 Film type
2 Film format
3 Number of exposures
4 Speed rating
5 Expiry date
6 Batch number

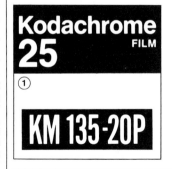

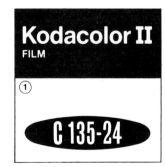

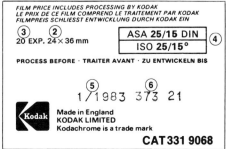

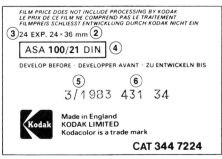

Expressing film response

In technical literature, beyond the simple data packed with the film, the response of emulsion to light is often expressed as a graph. The graph represents the characteristic performance of a film ("characteristic curve" for short). One advantage of describing and comparing films in this way is that a lot of information can be expressed concisely and accurately. Provided the photographer knows how to read them, graphs allow quick comparisons between details such as relative film contrast and exposure latitude, and the effects of development – including combined exposure and development manipulations.

Brightness range

The mixtures of tones and colors in a camera image can be thought of as a scale of brightnesses. This forms the "input" to the film. The visible image on film after processing is the resulting "output". Plotting the brightnesses of input against the differing tones of output gives a shaped line. Film curves prove how underexposure gives inadequate contrast and therefore detail in shadow parts of the picture. They also show the improved performance of chromogenic black and white negative materials over conventional silver image films.

The technical aim when exposing a photograph is to produce the best possible negative or slide on the film, giving the least amount of exposure. The wider the range of brightnesses in an image (for example, the more contrasty the lighting conditions) the more critical it is to give exactly the correct amount of exposure. Scenes with only very limited tones can be more over - or underexposed and yet fit within the useful part of the curve.

Film response curves

Characteristic curves can be drawn for all types of films – black and white negatives, color slides, and color negatives. Since color materials have three dye images, three curves are usually shown. This gives extra information, such as the fact that the layers may become unbalanced at extreme underexposure, and the way over-manipulated processing of color negatives may produce opposing casts in both shadows and highlights.

Two effects, however, are not shown on film response curves. One is the coarseness of grain structure, which is built into the film and exaggerated by development. The other is that in silver image films overexposure tends to scatter light within the thickness of the emulsion and, as a result, gives still poorer image resolution and contrast. Grossly overexposed images always tend to be less sharp. (This effect is greatly reduced in dye image film.)

Graph information

Characteristic curves for films are prepared under strict laboratory control. First, an extremely wide range of known brightnesses is exposed on to the film (using a transparent scale of gray tones ranging from clear to almost opaque). Normal camera subjects also form a scale of brightnesses (see below), although these are generally much more limited than the laboratory scale and so fit within the test range. After processing the film image, each resulting tone area is assigned a density value by means of a light source and a light-measuring instrument. The latter plots out the densities that have been formed for each brightness. If the result was an exact replica of the test brightnesses, the plot would be a straight line at 45°. In practice, with a normal black and white film, it is less steep and flattened out at the top and bottom.

Interpreting the graph

If you are interested in understanding the process control of your film, it is essential to be able to interpret film characteristic curves. These curves show the relationship between the camera exposure and the resulting densities formed in the emulsion. Each measured density is plotted against the logarithm of the exposure (or brightness) that it represents. The logarithm is taken so that a very wide range of brightnesses can be shown in compact form along the graph's horizontal axis (an increase of 0.3 in the logarithm of exposure means the doubling of exposure). There is always some density in the film regardless of exposure – this is called the "fog level". The graph proper starts just above this, at a point known as "threshold exposure". The "toe" is where the graph flattens out below the straight line portion. The top of the graph is called the "shoulder". When exposing a negative film you should aim to use the film response mostly over the straight line portion of the curve.

Indicating exposure effects

Taking the curve as a total performance graph, a so-called "correct" exposure should make your camera image coincide with the lower part of the curve, excluding the flattened-off toe. Such an image would result in a negative with densities more compressed than those in the original scene, and with its shadows slightly more compressed than other tones. To compensate, printing materials are designed to expand the shadow end of the scale.

Underexposure of the film shifts image tones too far to the left, so that half the shadows

use the flattened out toe of the curve, and so details merge into transparent film on the negative. Overexposure shifts image tones too far along the scale to the right, so that highlights correspond to the flattened shoulder of the curve, where they begin to merge into dense silver on the negative. The more contrasty the camera image is the more of the full curve it occupies, and so the less latitude you have for any exposure error.

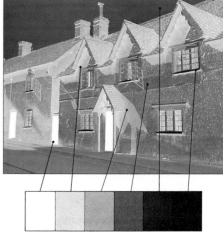

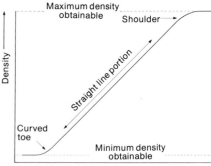
Gray scale

Characteristic curve
The negative image (top) is basically a range of density values. They can be plotted on the vertical axis of the graph (above) against the image brightness that caused them (as plotted on the horizontal axis). The curve shows the transition from one to the other.

Levels of exposure

The three scales of tone (near right) show in simplified form negatives that have been given under-, normal, and overexposure. The excessively dense negative results from giving all the subject brightnesses too much exposure, so they fall on the upper parts of the curve (far right). Underexposure has the opposite effect.

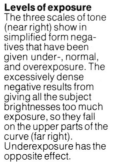
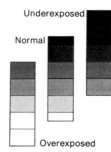
Underexposed

Normal

Overexposed

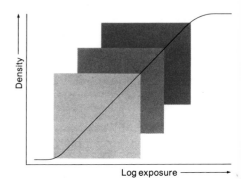

Curves for different films

Every film has its own characteristic curve. A chromogenic black and white film, for example, has a final image in dye instead of silver, and this produces a longer straight line curve. A line or lith film produces extremely contrasty results, and the characteristic curve for this type of film is steeply angled. Color slide film forms a back-to-front curve because it is processed to give a direct positive image. The three dyes forming a color image must be plotted separately (through complementary colored filters) to show how accurately color balance is maintained at all densities. Color slide film must also be plotted for each separate dye layer. The one below has been purposely overdeveloped to show the "cross-curved" effect that often results.

Chromogenic black and white negative film
The long straight-line portion of the characteristic curve shows that the film (here push-processed by one stop) can tolerate a wide exposure range without flattening of tones.

Black and white line film
The curve for this negative film is farther to the right, denoting slower speed. Steep angle and high maximum density show it reproduces few, if any, grays between clear film and dense black – ideal for line subjects.

Color slide film
Three curves are shown, one for each emulsion layer. Curves should ideally coincide, as here, especially toward the toe, for casts are always more noticeable in the palest subject tones.

Color negative film
Curve plots here are often offset, due to the effect of the warm-colored mask, but should be substantially parallel. This film has been push-processed for extra speed, but shows deteriorating color balance.

Color slide film
"Crossed curves" show this film gives a magenta cast in shadows, cyan cast in highlights. The cause is over-extended development. Chemical errors can have similar effects.

Manipulating film response

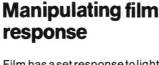

Film has a set response to light in ASA speed and color balance, provided it is treated as the manufacturers recommend. With most products, suggestions are based on conditions that will produce utmost accuracy of subject color and detail. Sometimes, however, lighting conditions are so dim that underexposure cannot be avoided, and so it is better to manipulate the film to gain every bit of speed response even though color or tone values suffer.

Changing film speed
All films can be exposed at speed ratings different to the ones recommended. Rating a film at a higher ASA is known as "uprating". It means that the whole film is underexposed by a fixed amount by setting the exposure meter to a higher ASA number. To compensate for this, the film must receive extra development ("pushing") to bring out maximum detail in the film.

Sometimes the opposite manipulation is required – film has to be "downrated", perhaps to avoid overexposure or to reduce contrast in a harshly lit scene. To compensate for this, film must be given reduced development time ("held back").

All professional film laboratories offer a developing service for film that has been pushed or held back. It is usual for a photographer to have part of a roll of a film from a larger batch test-processed under normal procedures first.

Using non-standard films
Another form of manipulating results is possible by using film that has an unusual response. Special black and white films, for example, are sensitive to infrared wavelengths. False-color slide films contain an infrared-sensitive emulsion along with the red- and green-sensitive layers. Both these types of film "see" and record images in a form very different to the picture seen in the viewfinder. Films with extreme contrast give strong graphic results but have very low speed and are more easily used in the darkroom, making images from pictures shot on regular film. It is also possible to give slide or negative film unorthodox processing to alter its color response.

Using filters
Colored filters offer the photographer an easy way of causing dramatic changes to the image recorded by regular films. A black and white film, which may normally record green and red as similar gray tones, can be made to record one very dark and the other very light by the use of a colored filter over the camera lens. Colored filters can also be used in conjunction with colored films to tint the image – either to make the films' color balance compatible with the light source illuminating the subject, or to give intentionally incorrect color.

See also
Filters and lens attachments *Non-effects filters*, p. 201.

Black and white film response

Most general-application black and white films have panchromatic sensitivity, meaning that they respond (in shades of gray) to all the colors of the spectrum. Some films, though, are orthochromatic, and others blue-only sensitive instead. Blue-only sensitive films are unaffected by wavelengths longer than about 500 nanometers (nm). The earliest photographic materials had this type of response. Emulsions in this category are still used for copying black and white prints and negatives, and you can safely handle and process them under orange or yellow darkroom lighting.

Orthochromatic films have their "natural" blue sensitivity extended to include green wavelengths as well. Again, these films are mostly used for copying whenever red sensitivity is not essential. The extra sensitivity helps

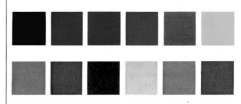

Blue-only sensitive
This film makes greens and warm colors appear dark on the final print. The graph shows how response is lost beyond 500 nm.

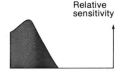

Orthochromatic
This type of emulsion is highly sensitive to green but not to red. On the print, reds appear dark, and greens and blues are light in tone.

Panchromatic
A print from this film shows colors as tone values similar to visual brightness. The emulsion is sensitive to virtually the whole spectrum.

to add some speed to its white light response, without resorting to larger silver grains. You must use deep red safelighting at all times.

You can use panchromatic films for all subjects irrespective of whether they are full of color or just monochrome. Most of these films have sensitivity limits of about 650 nm. Longer wavelengths (650-700 nm) would otherwise appear unnaturally pale and overexposed on the print. You must handle panchromatic films in complete darkness.

All types of black and white and color film are sensitive to ultraviolet and X ray radiation (see *Equipment and techniques*, p. 274).

Uprating black and white film

Uprating film speed and subsequently pushing processing is especially useful when you want to shoot in dim existing light conditions without using flash, or in any conditions when the film you are carrying is not sufficiently fast. In practice, you can uprate most black and white silver negative films one or two stops (this means setting the ASA dial to twice or four times the film's recommended speed). Some of these films can be pushed still further. For each amount you uprate the film you must remember to give additional development time

later (see *Compensation processing*, p. 224).

Bear in mind that certain image qualities have to suffer — otherwise there would be no reason for using the normal rating. Pushing always increases contrast as well as grain. It can result in poor detail in shadow areas, so avoid using it where these areas form an important part of your picture. Also, try not to shoot contrasty subjects — your final results may just consist of white, burnt-out highlights and dense or featureless gray shadows. Uprating film works best with softly lit subjects.

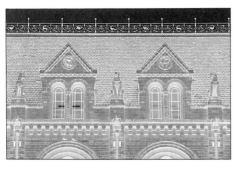

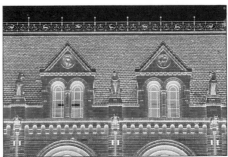

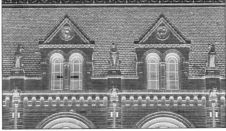

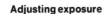

Adjusting exposure
The exposure compensation dial on some SLR automatics allows you to make subtle adjustments (in ⅓ stop increments) to the given film speed. This gives you more control than turning the ASA dial.

Uprating film speed
The negative (above left) was taken on ASA 400 film, exposed and developed normally. The more grainy, contrasty negative (above right) was shot on the same type of film, uprated to ASA 1600 and given extended development. Deep shadow areas record as clear film, and will reproduce as gray or black areas without detail in the finished print. In flat lighting, uprating and pushing development helps to improve contrast.

Downrating black and white film

Downrating film works in the opposite way to uprating. You must overexpose the film by setting the ASA dial to a setting lower than the recommended film speed. To compensate for the effects of overexposure you must curtail development time. There are two reasons for using this technique — one is to reduce the grain response of the film, and the other is to reduce contrast in the film image. Downrating is a useful technique when you are photographing a high-contrast subject, such as interiors where you want to maintain detail in shadowy corners as well as the view as seen through the windows. As a starting point, try downrating your film speed to about one-half the recommended setting (this is the equiv-

alent of overexposing by one stop). Some cameras have an exposure compensation dial (see above) marked in stops alongside the ASA dial. This also displays a signal to stop you using the override setting after the particular film is finished.

Downrating film speed
In comparison with the ASA 400 negative given normal exposure and development (below left), a negative downrated to ASA 200 and given less development time (below right) loses contrast. Taken to extremes, this gives a negative with excessive flatness. The technique is very useful if lighting conditions are too contrasty. It also helps to reduce grain.

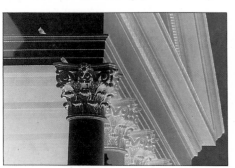

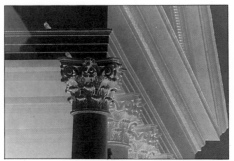

Using filters

You can manipulate the way black and white film reproduces subject colors by using colored filters over the camera lens. Filters consist of dyed glass, plastic, or thin, colored sheets of gelatin. These are most often used to create contrast between colors that would otherwise reproduce as similar tones of gray, or to improve tonal separation between pale colors and white. If you want to darken a particular color you should photograph through a filter complementary to that color. If, however, you want to lighten a particular color, then shoot through a filter that matches it in hue as closely possible. The deeper the color of the filter you use, the stronger the effect.

You can see this for yourself by looking at bright colors through different filters and noticing the changes. Looking through a red filter you cannot distinguish red from white, while rich greens and blues appear very dark. In the same way, a deep red filter will darken blue sky and so make the contrast between sky and clouds much stronger. It will also absorb ultraviolet wavelengths scattered by the atmosphere in distant views. These invisible radiations have an effect on all photographic films, making distant parts of scenes paler than they appear to the eye. The absorption of ultraviolet

Effect required	Filter						
	Yellow (8)	Yellow-green (11)	Orange (16)	Red (25)	Deep red (29)	Blue (47)	Green (58)
Natural sky	•						
Increased cloud/sky contrast			•				
Strong cloud/sky contrast				•			
Dramatic cloud/sky contrast					•		
Simulated moonlight				(underexposed)	•		
Natural sunset	•						
Dramatic sunset			•				
Natural haze effect	•						
Enhanced haze effect							•
Reduced haze/increased contrast in distant subjects			•				
Stronger haze reduction/increased contrast in distant subjects				•			
Natural foliage/flowers	•	•					
Lighter foliage							•
Increased texture in sunlit materials			•				
Natural skin tones (tungsten light)							•
Natural skin tones (daylight)			•				

light corrects the film's overresponse, but you can achieve the same correction without affecting other wavelengths by using a colorless ultraviolet absorbing filter on the lens.

Other useful filters include various shades of green (to lighten green foliage) and yellow (to darken blue skies slightly). Typical panchromatic film (see *Black and white film color response,* p. 155) differs from the eye's response to color brightnesses, especially in the blue and yellow-green bands (see *Weight of color,* p. 79). Film is more sensitive to blue, so blue appears pale on the final print. Using a pale yellow "correcting" filter both darkens blues and lightens tonal reproduction of colors in the middle of the spectrum.

Each filter is marked to denote the factor by which you must multiply unfiltered exposure time (or make equivalent aperture adjustments) to compensate for the light the filter absorbs. Do not rely on a TTL meter when you are using a deep colored filter, because the response of the light-sensitive cell may be uneven. Also, different types of cell have "blind" spots for different colored filters. When particularly accurate results are necessary, it is best to bracket your exposures. Ultraviolet absorbing filters require no exposure increase.

Effect required	Filter						
	Yellow (8)	Yellow-green (11)	Orange (16)	Red (25)	Deep red (29)	Blue (47)	Green (58)
Lighter red/orange tones	●		●	●			
Darker red/orange tones					●		
Dark red/orange tones							●
Lighter blue/purple tones					●		
Darker blue/purple tones	●						●
Dark blue/purple tones			●	●	●		
Lighter green tones	●	●					●
Darker green tones			●				
Dark green tones				●			
Very light yellow tones	●						
Lighter yellow tones			●	●			
Darker yellow tones					●		
Typical filter factor	×2	×4	×2.5	×8	×14	×8	×4

Filters for black and white film
The main use of filters in black and white photography is to alter the way colors record as tones on panchromatic film. The tables show the principal applications. You can use polarizing, soft focus, and starburst filters with black and white film but some special effects filters are suitable only for color film. Most filters require some adjustment to be made to exposure, though the precise filter factor varies from make to make. Most filters have an exposure compensation indication.

Special black and white films
Some black and white films — mostly 35 mm and sheet film types — have emulsions with unusual responses. They are usually designed for special applications, but you can use them for general photographic subjects, too.

Infrared film
Unlike normal panchromatic film, infrared black and white film is sensitive to wavelengths into the near-infrared end of the spectrum. Wavelengths between about 700 and 900 nm

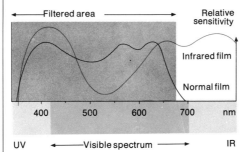

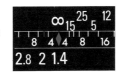

Using infrared film
Unlike panchromatic film, shown by the black line in the graph above, infrared film responds to UV, blue, red, and IR wavelengths. A deep red filter over the camera lens is essential to absorb wavelengths up to about 700 nm, so that only the film's IR sensitivity is used. Lenses focus infrared light at a different distance to white light. So, when using infrared film, focus visually and then transfer the setting to the red IR mark on the lens focusing scale (above right). The picture by Trevor Crone (below) demonstrates the unusual recording qualities of infrared film.

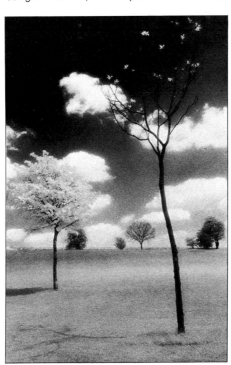

are invisible to the eye but are present in sunlight, flash, and tungsten lighting. Many subject surfaces reflect infrared in quite different amounts to their visual light appearance. The green chlorophyll in living foliage reflects infrared very strongly. So does human skin. If you shoot on film responding to infrared these types of subjects appear snowy white – almost glowing – against darker less IR reflective surfaces. Blue sky appears almost black and atmospheric perspective is destroyed (see *Aerial perspective,* pp. 82-3).

Infrared material is designed mostly for medical, forensic, and aerial survey work. As this material is also sensitive to red and blue light, for the strongest effects you can restrict it to record infrared wavelengths only by using an IR transmitting filter over the lens. This filter absorbs all visible light and looks like a piece of black glass. You cannot see the image through an SLR camera with this filter in place. You must either use a direct vision viewfinder camera instead or fit the filter just before exposure with the camera on a tripod. Many photographers prefer to use a deep red filter for general subjects. This gives almost the same results but allows you to use reflex viewing.

High-contrast film
High-contrast lith film is made in 35 mm and sheet film sizes. When you develop this type of film in special lith developer (see *Processing chemicals,* p. 222), it gives negatives with solid black and clear white only (all half tones eliminated). This material is very slow (about ASA 12) and is insensitive to red light, which therefore reproduces as black on prints. When using high-contrast film to photograph subjects directly (it is normally used in the darkroom or as document copying film) it is advisable to bracket your exposures. The film has very little exposure error latitude – one stop out either way will result in black or clear film. There is one type of Polaroid instant picture black and white print material for 5 × 4 ins (12.5 × 10 cm) cameras that also gives a high-contrast result (type 51). This material has a higher speed – ASA 125).

Ultra-fast material
Black and white material faster than about ASA 1000 has a very coarse grain pattern and, in extreme cases, lacks the subtleties of tone values present in "normal-speed" films. Most of these very fast materials were developed for surveillance and instrument-recording purposes in dim lighting conditions. Kodak make ultra-fast film in 35 mm and rollfilm formats (about ASA 1250). Polaroid make type 410 for $4\frac{1}{4} \times 3\frac{1}{4}$ ins (10.8 × 8.3 cm) instant picture cameras (ASA 10,000).

Uprating and downrating color film

You can uprate the ASA speed of color film and then push development time, or downrate it and hold back development in the same way as black and white film (see *Uprating black and white film* and *Downrating black and white film,* p. 156). The difference with color film is that this type of manipulation often upsets color balance as well as affecting emulsion speed, contrast, and grain.

Negative films

Color negatives are much less tolerant of manipulation than slides. This is because negatives have to be pushed or held back by altering the first processing stage — color development. (For slides on the other hand, the first stage is black and white development — see *Chromogenic film and paper theory,* p. 217-19). Any alteration to color development has generally unpleasant effects on colors. Final prints may exhibit one tint in shadows and another complementary tint in the highlights. For example, shadows look slightly green while highlights have a magenta tint. You cannot correct errors such as these using any form of filtering during printing (see *The effects of reciprocity failure,* p. 220). Another limitation to pushing or holding back negative films is that they are closely matched to color paper characteristics. And, in comparison with when you are using black and white printing paper, you have little, if any, choice of paper contrast grades to give correction. A negative distorted in tone or color qualities therefore gives an even more distorted print.

You can uprate color negatives by about one and a half stops, depending on how critical subject rendition must be. Prints tend to show desaturated colors, opposed tints in highlights and shadows, and have a generally flat, low-contrast appearance, particularly in the shadow areas. The lowering of contrast is generally due to heavy fog level. Downrating is limited to about half a stop. The most restrictive effect of this manipulation is excessively low contrast, producing flat and lifeless prints. Holding back can also lead to such short development times that you will find it impossible to process the whole film evenly, leading to further problems with the results.

Slide films

Color slide film responds to speed manipulation better than color negatives. You can uprate most types by two stops (four times the recommended ASA value), or downrate it by one and a half stops (one-third its stated ASA value), although this varies with the type of film. With Kodachrome, for example, home processing is not possible, and only very limited compensation processing is offered by the few specialist laboratories handling it.

The more you uprate the film the warmer the colors become, and the more contrast is emphasized. If pushed too far, slides often have gray and featureless shadows and bleached highlights. Downrating tends to make the colors colder. This shift toward the blue end of the spectrum is accompanied by reduced contrast and somewhat less brilliant colors.

It is best not to use either pushing or holding back as a method of color control — your results will be far more accurate and predictable if you use color filters. Uprating is primarily a means of boosting film speed if you have no other means of achieving sufficient exposure. Sometimes uprating one stop can also help with extremely flat lighting — landscapes in overcast conditions, for example. Both pushing and holding back developing times can save results (despite some loss of quality) when a test indicates that you have accidentally under - or overexposed a batch of films that cannot otherwise be saved.

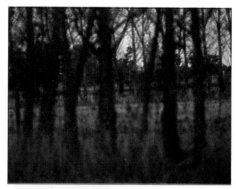

Uprating color slide film
David Buckland took these photographs on ASA 200 film. For the shot (left), he uprated the film to ASA 800 (i. e. by two stops) and push-processed it. Though the grain is enhanced, colors remains fairly faithful to those of the original. However, at ASA 1600 (above) the color balance has been noticeably altered, while graininess has increased to a level that would be unacceptable in most photographic situations. Both pictures exhibit increased contrast.

Using filters

Color filters used for color films are broadly divided into color balancing filters (also known as light balancing filters), and paler color compensating filters. A color balancing filter such as Kodak 80A (blue) allows you to take pictures in tungsten lighting with daylight type film. Conversely, if you must shoot a few frames of tungsten light in daylight, you can use an 85B (strong orange) filter. Other balancing filters help you to match film to most types of fluorescent tubes (see *Available lighting,* p. 162). In all cases, try and use the correct film because balancing filters absorb some light. They all have exposure factors, which means that the film becomes effectively less fast. Kodak filters with even numbers shift colors toward blue, while filters with odd numbers have a red effect on the image.

Some balancing filters are also available in large sheets of acetate, which you can place over lamps or even windows. Use these whenever there are two incompatible types of lighting present — for example, when you have to take a portrait indoors partly lit by daylight and partly by light bulbs. You should work with film correctly balanced for the dominant light source. In this case it may be best to shoot on daylight film and match the artificial light source by covering the bulbs with sheets of 80A acetate for the correct color balance.

Compensating filters are much paler than balancing filters, and they are made to "warm up" or "cool down" slightly the colors present in the image, particularly when you are using slides or instant picture material. Often the reason for using these filters is subjective,

Filters for use with color film

Filter	Filter factor*	Effect	Film type
Color balancing filters			
80A	×3	Cooler	Daylight
80B	×2	Cooler	Daylight
80C	×1.7	Cooler	Daylight
85B	×1.7	Warmer	Tungsten
85C	×1.3	Warmer	Tungsten
Filters for fluorescent light			
40M+30Y or FL-D	×2 ×2	Natural	Daylight
30M+10Y +85B	×2.5	Natural	Tungsten
40C+40M or FL-W	×2.3 ×2	Natural	Daylight
30M+20Y	×2	Natural	Tungsten
Color compensating filters			
1A/B		Warmer	Daylight
81 series	×1.2-1.7	Warmer	Daylight
82 series	×1.1-1.5	Cooler	Daylight
86B	×1.8	Warmer	Daylight

*These factors are approximate, varying slightly with different makes of filter. Check the manufacturer's recommendations before using.

such as gently enhancing the mood of a scene. Sometimes, though, you may have to use a compensating filter to help correct the color distortion produced by overlong exposure of the film (see *Reciprocity failure*, p. 152). Color compensating filters are made in the three primary and three secondary colors, and in various strengths.

Color compensating filters are very helpful if you want your slides or instant pictures to be strictly objective records. This is important with subjects such as food, silverware, glassware, or when copying paintings. If test shots indicate a color cast in any direction, view through a color compensating filter of the complementary color. Decide which strength filter makes mid-tone areas of the slide or print appear correct in terms of color, then use a filter half this strength over the lens when reshooting the picture. A result with a greenish cast, for example, may look correct through a CC10M filter, so you should shoot using a CC05M filter on the camera lens.

Color negative films do not require this degree of "fine tuning". The type of error that requires a compensating filter on slide film can be dealt with by filtering a negative during the printing stage. You can also usually correct the cast caused by using the wrong light source (such as tungsten lighting with daylight film) during printing (provided two or more sources are not mixed). This does, however, demand the use of strong filters and makes the task of judging filtration more difficult. Whenever practicable, use a color balancing filter to bring film and light into line at the camera stage.

Conditions in which film and filter are used

In tungsten lighting (3200K).
With 3400K photolamps, or in tungsten light.
With clear flash bulbs (3800K).
Daylight, or daylight-balanced flash.
As above. Paler than 85B, cooler effect.

With "daylight" fluorescent light.

With "daylight" fluorescent light.

With "warm white" fluorescent light.

With "warm white" fluorescent light.

To reduce bluish cast in strong sunlight.
To reduce bluish cast caused by shade, overcast lighting or strong sunlight. Each gives increasing warmth to color tones.
To cool down marked reddish tones in daylight, according to degree. Cancels out effect of 81 series.
To correct heavy blue light or strong shade.

Special color films

A few color slide films designed for use in the camera have special characteristics. The most spectacular of these is infrared color film. Others feature reduced or increased contrast, tailored to suit particular applications. Most are made in 35 mm only.

Infrared film
Infrared color slide film is designed to produce a false color record of the image formed in the camera. Unlike black and white infrared film, it contains a mixture of infrared-sensitive and visible-light-sensitive emulsions. The top layer consists of a green-sensitive emulsion that produces a yellowish positive image, the next layer is red sensitive and gives a magenta image, and the final layer is infrared sensitive and produces a cyan image.

The result of this unusual combination is that familiar objects record in strange, new colors. Living vegetation, which strongly reflects infrared, appears magenta or red on the final slide image. Grass and leaves may reproduce a brilliant red color, especially when sunlit and during their maximum growth period in spring. Human skin appears wax-like — lips record as yellow and the colored iris of the eyes as black. Most red objects, including red flowers, and red painted or dyed materials, photograph as bright yellow. Non-infrared-reflecting surfaces such as dead vegetation or green paint appear as bluish-purple. Blue skies retain their natural color.

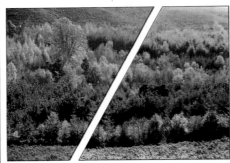

Daylight film   Infrared film

False color
Compared with regular color film, unfiltered infrared film renders

foliage with a strong magenta cast (varying with the time of year).

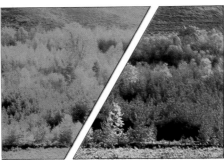

Red filter   Yellow filter

Infrared with filters
You can further distort image colors by using colored filters. Green,

red, or yellow will produce dramatic, unpredictable changes.

Infrared color film is intended for special applications such as aerial or forestry survey to detect dead vegetation, and military use to identify camouflage from natural surroundings. It also has some applications for fashion photography or with any subject where you want startling effects using totally false colors.

The only type of infrared color film available is Infrared Ektachrome. You must expose this film through a deep yellow filter to curb the otherwise excessive response of the three emulsion layers to ultraviolet and blue. If left unfiltered the film produces pictures with a strong blue cast. If you use a red filter over the lens, results will have an overall yellow cast.

For strongest false color results it is best to photograph in direct sunlight, but avoid strong lighting contrast. The film itself gives more contrast than normal color slide materials, so your exposure must be particularly accurate. It is best to bracket exposures for each picture. Do not focus the lens using the infrared mark on the camera's distance scale as for black and white photography — this may render the image out of focus in some color layers. Simply focus the lens visually, but do not use the lens at its widest aperture.

Photomicrographic film
Photomicrographic color slide film is a slow (ASA 16), fine-grain 35 mm material with higher than normal contrast. This is a helpful quality whenever you are recording low-contrast specimens through a microscope, or copying line drawings and other artwork where extra contrast would give a brighter, cleaner result. You can also use it to exaggerate contrast effects by copying regular prints or slides. For accurate color rendering you should use daylight or flash illumination. As with infrared slide film, there is only limited exposure latitude and you should give a series of bracketed exposures.

Slide duplicating film
If you copy slides to make duplicate color slides on normal camera materials, you will probably find that the results are too contrasty. Another side effect is that color gradation becomes coarser. 35 mm slide duplicating film is specifically designed to give lower than normal contrast. It is balanced to give correct color reproduction under tungsten (3200 K) studio type lighting. Low-contrast slide duplicating film is also available in sheet film sizes.

Lighting

After the development of the camera, and the invention of light-sensitive materials for recording a permanent image, the pioneer photographers turned their attention to the problems of lighting the subject. At first this was simply a matter of finding enough light for the invention to work at all. Brightest possible intensity was paramount – even in strong, direct sunlight photographers barely had enough illumination to allow exposure times short enough for portraiture. Understandably, faces appeared with closed eyes and agonized expressions.

The introduction of a fast (f 3.6) portrait lens by Josef Petzval in 1840, and Wolcott's mirror lens, also in 1840, helped to reduce exposure times to about one minute, and so allowed portraits indoors to be taken in direct sunlight. Alexander Wolcott opened the world's first daguerreotype portrait studio in America in 1840. To gather enough light, he used large mirrors hinged on the outside walls to direct sunlight through the windows. To provide the sitter with some measure of protection from the heat and glare, he placed a narrow-sided tank of copper sulfate solution in the light beam to act as a blue filter. Blue absorbs most heat, and the filtered-out red rays had little effect on exposure as early photographic emulsions were only sensitive to blue light. Portrait studios of this time were invariably glasshouses – they offered protection from the weather without wasting light. They were often set up on the roofs of houses – clients were received at street level and then had to climb endless stairs to reach "the camera room".

From the late 1840s the introduction of slightly faster photographic emulsions made it possible to have studios facing away from the direct sun, and so make use of the less variable and softer quality of skylight. These daylight studios were carefully designed with glazing across the roof, continued on down one side wall to ground level. Light could reach the sitter in a great arc, from directly overhead, down to the horizon, and stretching in depth from the background (curtains or painted backdrop) almost to the camera. The photographer could operate blinds running just inside the glass to diffuse or block out different areas and so produce a variety of lighting schemes. Opening blinds nearest the camera gave reasonably diffused frontal lighting, while opening those nearest the sitter produced side-lighting.

For the most part, the aim of the professional portrait photographer was to make a recognizable likeness which would sell. This attitude discouraged experimentation, and frontal, detail-enhancing lighting was most commonly used. The more adventurous use of daylight was left to amateur photographers, especially from the 1860s. Julia Margaret Cameron, for example, deliberately limited the level of illumination to produce an interpretative, creative effect (see *Early documentary photographers*, pp. 347-9), even though this resulted in uncomfortably long exposure times for the sitter.

Artificial light

For these early portrait studios to be commercially viable photographers had to extend their working day. This meant breaking away from their total dependence on natural lighting. London photographer Antoine Claudet probably took the first experimental portrait using artificial light in 1841. As a light source, he used a jet of oxygen gas projected through a flame of hydrogen directed on a disk or cylinder of lime ("limelight"). Used as a direct lighting source, this device produced very harsh results, but it tended to suit the then popular daguerreotype process, which gave very flat, low-contrast pictures. Exposure time was about 15 seconds. Lamps using ordinary domestic gas were also tried – one such device had 68 gas flames and developed 1200 candlepower, but produced so much heat that it almost roasted the sitter.

By the 1860s studios were working after dark using either limelight or the newer electrically powered arc lighting. The first all-electric studio opened in Regent Street, London in 1877. It had a 6000 candlepower dynamo and a huge carbon arc lighting unit slung from the studio ceiling, which the photographer could move to different positions. Exposure using collodion plates was about 3-10 seconds. Arcs were used to give intense point source lighting, but they could also be diffused or pointed toward large white reflectors to reduce contrast. The front of the reflector was filtered blue to minimize the glare from this powerful light source.

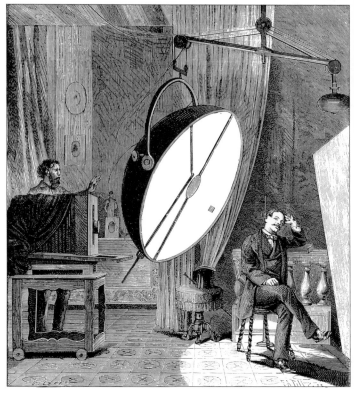

The world's first all-electric studio
Early studios were dependent on daylight, which placed limitations on the length of the working day, especially during the winter months. However, in 1877 H. Van de Weyde opened a studio in London's Regent Street which used electric light as the sole source of illumination. The 6000 candlepower carbon arc lamp was mounted in a 4 ft (1.25 m) reflector.

A 4 ins (10 cm) diameter mirror directly in front of the carbon points screened the sitter from direct rays. Despite his nonchalant pose, conditions would still have been far from ideal for the sitter.

Even as late as the 1930s studios were still using three kinds of electric light source. Arcs gave the strongest light output but they were troublesome to operate – the carbon rods required frequent adjustment and fumes were given off. Mercury vapor lighting (similar to today's bluish street lighting) were used in banks of strip tubes. These were powerful units but were totally lacking red wavelengths. The coming of panchromatic emulsions sensitive to red meant that veins, freckles, and other facial blemishes were apparent. The third lighting source was the light bulb, which created illumination by passing electricity through tungsten wire. This was initially known as "half watt" lighting because early units consumed half a watt of electricity per candlepower of light produced. These new tungsten lights were at first not entirely suitable as they were blue deficient, but the advantage they had over other sources was the fact they could be run off domestic electricity supplies. Improvements to the light quality of tungsten units and the introduction of photographic emulsions balanced to compensate for the lack of blue content in the light output have led to the diverse range of tungsten-powered floods and spots available today.

Flash lighting

Henry Fox Talbot first used light from a spark to take experimental photographs of close objects in 1851. And while the "better" professional studios struggled with limelight in the 1880s, the less expensive studios, and most amateur photographers, were using "magnesium lighting" – the forerunner of photographic flash.

Magnesium burns with an intense bluish white light. At first a magnesium ribbon was held in tongs and burnt slowly for a few seconds or minutes. The advantages of this light source were its low cost and portability.

Magnesium gives a brighter, much briefer duration light if ground up into powder. Various forms of flash powder were made — most ignition systems used an air ball to blow the powder into a gas flame. Flash duration varied between 1/10 and 10 seconds depending on the amount of powder used. As magnesium burns it gives off a dense white smoke. Some studios used a ceiling hood lined with wet canvas to absorb the smoke and ash.

From the 1880s "flashpowder" (a mixture of ground magnesium and an oxygen-producing chemical) became available. Large quantities could be burnt in about 1/30 of a second after the application of a spark, and flashguns were made incorporating a flint-type gas lighter. By spreading flashpowder in a long shallow tray and igniting it at the center, photographers could produce a lighting quality similar to today's soft floodlighting.

Flashbulbs date from 1929. They were originally the size of an electric light bulb, and contained crumpled magnesium foil in an atmosphere of oxygen. Low voltage from a battery was used to ignite an internal fuse and the bulb burnt for about 1/25 of a second. For the first time photographers could synchronize flash to fire with the opening of the shutter. This was of special use to newspaper photographers such as Weegee (see *The individualists,* pp. 355-6), who often had to "snatch" a picture even in the poorest lighting conditions. Smaller and more efficient bulbs (using zirconium wire) are used for cubes and bar flashes today.

Practicable electronic flash dates from the 1940s. Since that time, better electronic components have allowed improvements in two directions. Compact hand units have become even smaller and well able to compete in power with flashbulbs. Larger units are powerful enough to provide complete studio requirements. The lack of heat and continuous glare makes photography more comfortable for the sitter or model, and the photographer has the freedom of movement that comes with using the camera without a tripod. The flexibility of different lighting heads and the abundance of power has in recent years encouraged photographers to return to simpler, daylight-quality style, using flash illumination bounced off white studio walls or large reflectors.

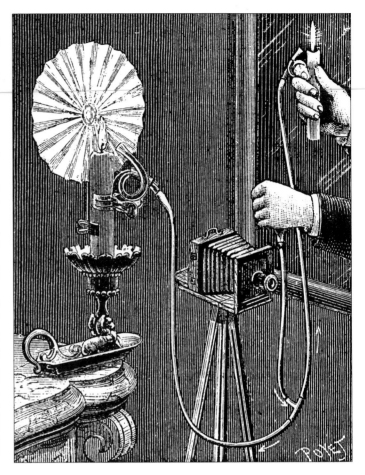

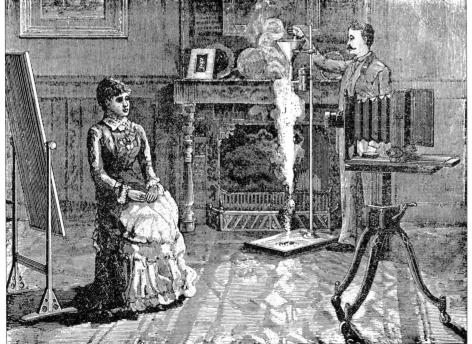

Magnesium flash powder

Magnesium could be ignited in several ways: by blowing it into a candle flame (above), pouring it through a funnel and applying a flame to it as it fell (left), or placing it on a tray and using a flint and wheel, triggered by a lever on the handle (below), to make a spark. Flash duration was from 1/10-10 sec.

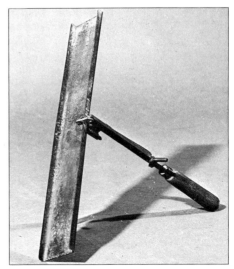

Light sources

Whatever lighting equipment the photographer uses, certain principles remain the same. The first is that the quality of light depends on the size of the light source in relation to its distance from the subject. The more compact and distant the source, the harder and more distinct the shadows.

With compact sources a second principle applies: lighting intensity reduces at a regular rate as subject distance increases. If the distance between light source and subject is doubled, subject brightness drops to one-quarter. Each time a subject moves in relation to a light bulb or flashgun, the photographer must alter exposure. The principle also applies to sunlight, but here it can be ignored, since any changes in distance on earth are minutely small when compared to the sun's remote position. But the situation changes indoors. When sunlight enters through a small window, the window is effectively the light source.

These principles of distance and intensity also apply with obliquely lit surfaces. The more distant the light source, the less the relative difference between illumination levels of the nearest and farthest parts of the subject, and so the more evenly the subject appears to be lit.

The third general feature of lighting is its color content. This depends on the way the light is generated, as well as on certain factors such as filtering, or reflection from colored surfaces between source and subject. The color content of a light source is usually expressed as its color temperature.

Types of light source
There are four main types of light source used for photography. Two are forms of "available light": first, natural sources such as the sun, and second, man-made sources such as domestic bulbs, tubes, and street lamps. A third form of lighting is produced by studio spotlights and floodlights designed specifically for photography. Finally, there are the various forms of amateur and professional flash lighting.

Lighting is infinitely variable, and forms an absorbing and creative area of photography. Sometimes the factual information a photograph must convey determines the best type of lighting. But often lighting choice is a matter of personal style and interpretation.

See also
Light quality, pp. 18-19. Light and color, pp. 22-3. Color, pp. 50-1. Choice of film *Color temperature,* p. 151.

Light source quality

Light travels in straight lines, and this fact influences the shadow quality produced by all types of lighting. A minute, point source makes three-dimensional objects cast harsh, sharp-edged shadows, especially if the light is at some distance from them. A large source, placed close so that it effectively "wraps" the subject with light, illuminates every part of the subject's surface, and so casts no shadow at all. Every light source has an effect somewhere between these two extremes.

You cannot normally change lighting quality with the camera controls, but you can alter it by interposing something between the source and the subject it is illuminating. Translucent material scatters hard light so that it becomes non-directional and soft. The same applies when you turn a hard light source away from the subject and point it toward a white, matte surface, which diffuses and reflects soft light

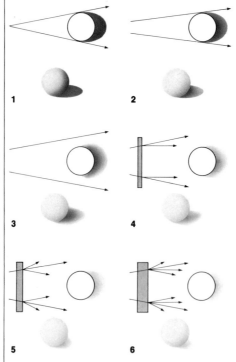

Light sources
Point sources **1** give the harshest shadows. Spotlights **2** also give harsh, directional light and strong shadows. A floodlamp **3** gives much softer light. Diffusing the light **4** enlarges the source and

therefore further reduces shadows. The more opaque the material **5** and **6** the softer the shadows become. Virtually shadowless results are possible.

back toward the subject. The opposite change — from soft light to hard — is also possible. Partly closing curtains at a distant window when shooting indoors, or masking a floodlamp using cardboard with a hole in the middle, hardens (but also dims) the light.

Multiple hard-light sources produce multiple shadows. You can make them give softer light by grouping them behind diffusing material (see *Lighting accessories,* p. 166).

Available lighting

The term "available" or "existing" light generally covers natural and man-made light sources not specifically designed for photography. The earliest photography was by available light, and it remains the mainstay of photographers today. With modern fast lenses and sensitive films, you can capture the natural atmosphere of available light without relying too much on the frequently artificial appearance of flash and studio lighting.

Color
Natural light and artificial light sources vary in color temperature (see table opposite). You must decide whether or not to filter an image so that it matches the color balance of your film. In landscapes, for example, the lighting color is an integral part of the scene. For close-ups, portraits, and copying work, where the sun itself is not visible, the blueness of overcast conditions, or orange light late in the day, often become unacceptable. Filters can be useful to correct this, especially with slide film.

A subject containing a mixture of tungsten and daylight poses problems. But you can use this combination to produce an effective result — particularly if the picture features a contrast between a warmly lit interior and a "cold" exterior. In general, the eye accepts the warm cast of tungsten light more readily than a cold, blue cast, especially if flesh tones are included. So daylight film is the best to use unless the area lit by daylight is small.

Sometimes an entire area, such as the interior of a large store, is lit by fluorescent tubes. Most tubes give a greenish result in color photographs. The table opposite suggests filters for color-balancing different types of tubes to Kodak films. Often you will not be able to identify tubes, so you should bracket with different filters.

Certain floodlamps used on buildings do not give a full spectrum (red and green, for example, often look black). Filtering cannot correct these sources, and it is best to avoid them as the main source of illumination, unless you want false color effects (see *Coloring shadows,* p. 182). A few sources (moonlight, light from a television set, and the pale blue tungsten bulbs sometimes used in stores) have approximately the same color temperature as daylight.

Contrast range
Contrast poses one of the main problems when using existing light. With many subjects you can often reduce contrast by moving the subject away from a nearby light source toward a reflective surface. The illumination will be weaker, but the contrast lower. (Early daylight portrait studios made great use of matte white reflector boards to help illuminate the shadow areas of a figure with diffused light.) Most interiors at night are lit by lamps at or near the ceiling, and this produces "top light", casting shadows over people's eyes, especially near the center of a room. A light-toned table surface, horizontally positioned papers, or an open book will all help reflect diffused light back up to reduce contrast. Avoid colored surfaces — particularly if they are not shown in the picture, and so cannot give context to a local tint that they are likely to produce.

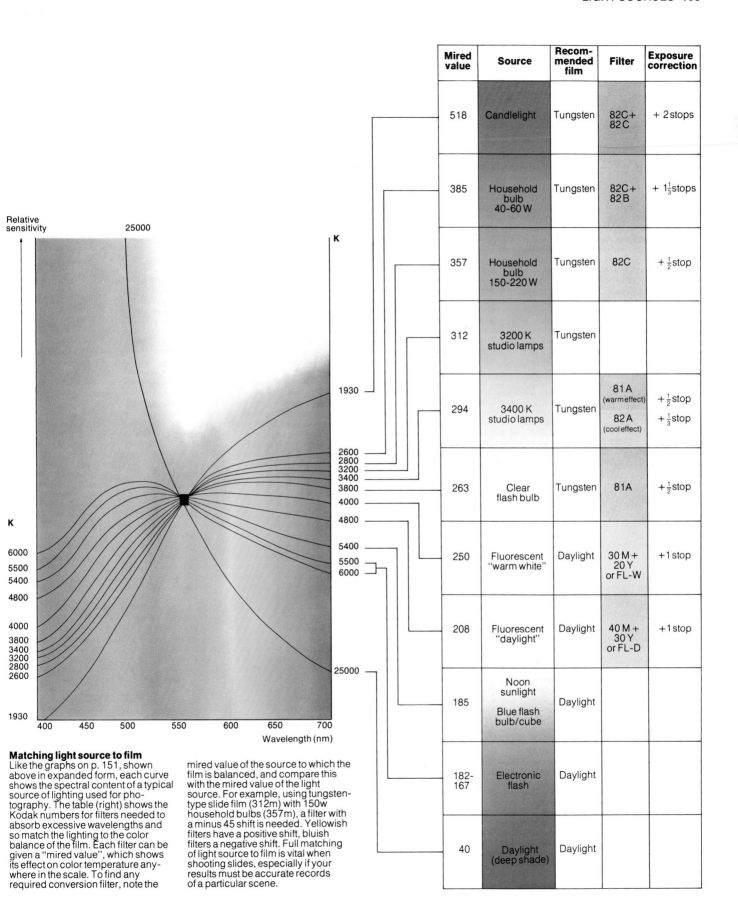

Mired value	Source	Recommended film	Filter	Exposure correction
518	Candlelight	Tungsten	82C+ 82C	+ 2 stops
385	Household bulb 40-60 W	Tungsten	82C+ 82B	+ 1⅓ stops
357	Household bulb 150-220 W	Tungsten	82C	+ ½ stop
312	3200 K studio lamps	Tungsten		
294	3400 K studio lamps	Tungsten	81A (warm effect) / 82A (cool effect)	+ ½ stop / + ⅓ stop
263	Clear flash bulb	Tungsten	81A	+ ½ stop
250	Fluorescent "warm white"	Daylight	30 M + 20 Y or FL-W	+1 stop
208	Fluorescent "daylight"	Daylight	40 M + 30 Y or FL-D	+1 stop
185	Noon sunlight / Blue flash bulb/cube	Daylight		
182-167	Electronic flash	Daylight		
40	Daylight (deep shade)	Daylight		

Matching light source to film

Like the graphs on p. 151, shown above in expanded form, each curve shows the spectral content of a typical source of lighting used for photography. The table (right) shows the Kodak numbers for filters needed to absorb excessive wavelengths and so match the lighting to the color balance of the film. Each filter can be given a "mired value", which shows its effect on color temperature anywhere in the scale. To find any required conversion filter, note the mired value of the source to which the film is balanced, and compare this with the mired value of the light source. For example, using tungsten-type slide film (312m) with 150w household bulbs (357m), a filter with a minus 45 shift is needed. Yellowish filters have a positive shift, bluish filters a negative shift. Full matching of light source to film is vital when shooting slides, especially if your results must be accurate records of a particular scene.

Tungsten lighting

Photographic tungsten lighting equipment is of two main types – units that give hard-quality lighting because they have compact lamps, and units with larger lamps giving soft, diffused light. Lamps of each type also differ in intensity of illumination (generally according to wattage), and in their distribution of light (wide or narrow angle). Some sources use a simple tungsten filament, while more sophisticated units use tungsten halogen. Both types must be handled with care.

Hard-lighting units

An arc lamp provides the hardest lighting, because it is essentially a point light source. However, arcs are no longer used in still photography because of their inconvenience. The nearest equivalent is a compact filament, clear glass, spotlight bulb (see below). Spotlights

Spotlights

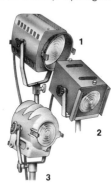

These units incorporate a compact, clear glass lamp and a fresnel lens, giving a bright beam with strong shadows. With most units, the fresnel lens can be moved to adjust beam width. A 650W spot **1** and two or three 150W spots **2** will cope with the majority of studio situations. A miniature spot **3** will highlight small areas of the subject.

give their hardest lighting when focused to produce a broad beam. The rays then most closely resemble lighting radiating from a single point. This type of unit can also be adjusted to give a narrow beam. Another important form of hard lighting is the compact broadlight. This has a short tubular lamp, and a small, open reflector. These units give a much broader distribution of light than spotlights, but form similarly hard shadows. Both kinds of light source use tungsten halogen lamps, which are more compact, and have a longer life without discoloration than regular tungsten types. They also produce a light that is about 25 per cent brighter than that of tungsten filament sources. They do, though, become very hot during use.

You can also buy a low-cost integral reflector lamp that has a silvered reflector built into the glass bulb. The bulb therefore forms the complete lighting unit. It has a regular tungsten filament, and you cannot focus it. The lighting quality given by an integral reflector lamp is slightly softer than a spotlight; it is also often less even.

Soft-lighting units

There are many different units designed to give soft, diffused lighting. They all have a wide distribution of illumination and are generally described as "floodlights". Some types (see below) use a large, frosted glass bulb in a bowl-shaped, matte white reflector. Others have clear glass bulbs or long tubular tungsten halogen lamps, arranged so that they can only illuminate the subject indirectly. They face inward and "bounce" off a shallow reflector. In

Floodlights

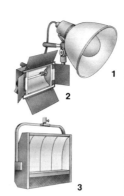

Most floods use a large, opalescent lamp to spread and diffuse the light. The wider the reflector, the less intense the light, and the softer the shadows formed. As well as the standard 500W flood **1**, there are smaller but harder broadlights **2**. A large softlight **3** uses integral bounce lighting for softest shadows.

all cases the larger the reflector, the softer the light. You can convert hard-light sources to soft lighting by turning them to bounce illumination off a reflector board. For a similar effect, you can place a diffusing attachment over the front of the lamp.

Color and intensity

For color photography, it is important for all your lights to work at the same color temperature (see *Available lighting*, pp. 162-3). You should therefore buy bulbs designed to give a color temperature of 3200 K, which suits film balanced for tungsten light. If you are using instant picture daylight material under tungsten lighting, fit a blue compensating filter over the camera lens. Sometimes, if you mix tungsten lamps with daylight or flash (which is balanced to match daylight), you must use blue acetates over the front of each tungsten lamp in order to match their color output with daylight-balanced film.

Light intensity depends on the wattage of each lamp, and the effect of the reflector or focusing arrangement used for each unit. Most still photography studios use spotlights of 500 W, with 1000 W floods, and sometimes small 250 W spots for still-life work. All should have a color temperature of 3200 K.

For tungsten lighting on location, tungsten halogen broadlights on lightweight stands are available. You can pack and carry three or four of these in one case. Another useful location light (although primarily designed for television and movie work) is a battery-powered tungsten halogen lamp. You must wear a shoulder-slung power pack, or battery belt. Typically this can run a single 250 W lamp for 30 min. The batteries take between one and seven hours to recharge. Battery lamps are ideal for the "painting with light" technique (see *Lighting large areas*, p. 175) used to illuminate still lifes and architectural interiors, especially in locations where there is no regular electricity supply.

Color temperature meters

Special hand meters are available for reading the color temperature of daylight and tungsten type light sources. Most models work by comparing the red and blue content of white light, since the relative proportions of these colors change with every fluctuation in color temperature (see *Color temperature*, p. 151). The meter has two separate light-sensitive cells, covered by deep blue and red filters. Each cell feeds the needle read-out movement, "pulling" it in opposite directions. The needle may shift right of center for red-rich lighting, or toward the left for lighting in which blue predominates.

You simply set the meter's center line position according to the color balance of your film, then point the meter toward the light source (not the subject). You press a button to take the reading. If the needle is in the central position, the light source matches your film. Displacement to the left or right indicates the color and strength of the correction filter you should place on the camera lens in order to avoid a color cast.

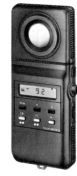

Color meter

Three filtered photocells (for blue, green, and red light) give an accurate measurement of white light. The meter reads chromaticity co-ordinates (for color temperature) or illuminance (for exposure), which are calculated by the microprocessor and diplayed digitally. The meter can measure color temperature ranging between 1600 and 40,000 K.

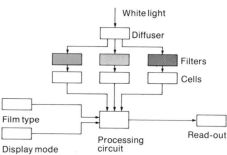

Color temperature meters are expensive but useful if you are making transparencies of subjects demanding critical color accuracy. They are also invaluable if you have to use tungsten lighting of uncertain color temperature, or when a fluctuating voltage supply makes the color of your lamps unreliable. But these meters do not give accurate color content readings for all light sources. Units such as sodium lamps and some fluorescent tubes produce a "non-continuous" spectrum, with some wavelengths totally absent.

Flash lighting units

Simple cameras use flashcubes or bars that you mount directly on the camera. These are fixed units and so you cannot alter the lighting duration. With flipflash (see *Flash lighting units*, pp. 165-6) you can fire up to four bulbs simultaneously (to vary lighting intensity), but this system is still not flexible enough for most photographic situations. A camera-mounted

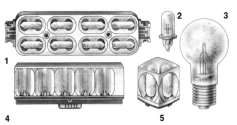

Types of bulb
Flipflash units **1** and flash bars **4** house 8 or 10 flash bulbs. Reverse the unit after you have fired half the bulbs. Single expendable bulbs are designed for amateur **2** or professional **3** battery

guns. A flashcube **5** has four bulbs. The cube rotates with the film wind to bring a fresh bulb into position. Flashcubes are, however, being superceded by more flexible forms of portable flash.

electronic flashgun provides a light source with more creative potential.

You mount most flash units on the camera, close to the lens, and they deliver hard, direct light. The spread of the beam across the subject should be related to the angle of view of the camera lens. For cameras with interchangeable lenses, plastic attachments fit over the flash head to make the beam wider or narrower. More powerful and sophisticated units have a pivoting head, so that you can bounce light off a wall or ceiling to create softer, less directional illumination. Avoid colored or dark surfaces. Some flashguns accept a "bounce board" for outdoor use, but this adds con-

Twin flash unit
In this self-regulating flash, the reflector rather than the head rotates for bounced flash. A small, supplementary tube built into the body then gives direct fill-in flash. This direct light is about one-seventh as bright as the main flash. At all times, the light-sensing cell stays pointing at the subject.

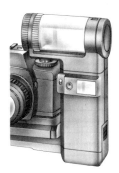

siderably to the bulk of the unit. Some guns form part of a flash system, which also includes filters, a sensor, and a bracket so that you can mount the flashgun to one side of the camera. Certain pivoting flash units contain a small additional flash tube, which remains pointing directly at the subject while the main tube bounces general lighting.

Hand-size flash units can be useful in the studio, but larger flash units designed specifically for studio work are much more powerful. They work off the domestic main supply.

Studio flash
In this mains-powered model the flash tube and power pack are combined in one unit. The flash tube is behind a sheet of diffusing plastic, with a 150W modeling lamp centrally placed.

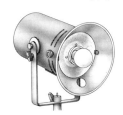

Studio units stand quite separately from the camera and have a power pack to store the charge, which is either built into the head or forms a steady base for the whole unit. Each head contains a tungsten modeling lamp close to the flash tube, so that you can see the direction and quality of the lighting that will be

produced when the flash fires. The flash tube is usually compact, and you can fit it with a range of reflectors. For the softest light, you can turn and direct it into a large white reflective umbrella. Small, narrow reflectors give hard lighting, and cowlings are also available to convert the head into a flash spotlight.

It is usual to use two or three studio flash

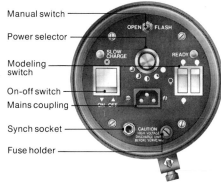

Manual switch
Power selector
Modeling switch
On-off switch
Mains coupling
Synch socket
Fuse holder

Studio flash controls
Five different power levels allow you to vary the intensity of the flash. The modeling light adjusts to the setting selected and allows you to preview shadow effects. A synchroniz-

ing cord connects the unit to the camera or a flash meter, though it can also be fired manually for special effects such as double exposure.

units at a time, positioned in a similar way to tungsten studio lamps (see *Lighting accessories,* p. 166). You can link one flash unit to the camera with a long synchronization cord. For each of the others you can use "slave" triggering units, which have light-detecting cells. Each slave reacts to the camera-triggered flash and fires its flash unit in unison. An alternative system uses a small infrared-emitting device on the camera with detectors on every unit. This arrangement has the advantage of leaving the camera totally free of cords.

The power of a studio electronic flash is

Slave unit
To fire several flash units simultaneously, synchronize one with the camera and attach cordless slave units to the others. These will react to light from the prime flash instantaneously.

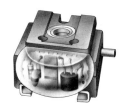

often expressed in joules (j). One joule is equivalent to one watt burning for one second. Single-head units often have a power of about 1000-1500 j. If you use one power pack for two heads, the power of each head is halved. The type of reflector also greatly influences the amount of light on the subject. A flash meter (see *Flash meters,* p. 141) is the best way to measure exposure with studio flash. You can also use a flash sensor mounted on the camera, or rely on the camera's own TTL meter if this is suitable for flash.

Other more specialized flash heads include ring flash. This has a circular tube behind a dif-

Flash system
You can increase the versatility of some flash units by adding accessories. Reflector and diffuser attachments soften the light, while you can use filters to change the color temperature or create special effects. Regu-

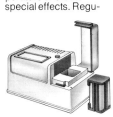

Battery charger

late the flash angle to suit the angle of view of a moderately wide-angle or telephoto lens by using adaptors. Use extension cords for off-camera operation.

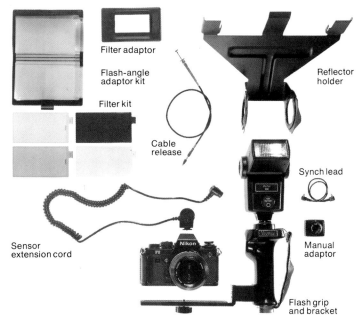

Filter adaptor
Flash-angle adaptor kit
Filter kit
Reflector holder
Cable release
Synch lead
Sensor extension cord
Manual adaptor
Flash grip and bracket

fuser which fits around the camera lens. It produces shadowless, frontal lighting ideal for close-up work (see *Flash lighting units,* pp. 165-6). Flash heads are also available for use with front projection units (see *Front projection,* p. 182).

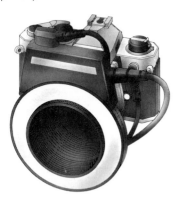

Ring flash
One problem with shooting close-ups is getting sufficient light between camera and subject. Oblique lighting may be unsatisfactory, and light- ing from behind the camera causes shadows. The ring flash unit gives shadowless frontal lighting from a circular flash tube that fits around the lens.

You can use powerful studio lamps of 5000j or more with "window light" heads. These are large area floods (up to 6 ft/2 m square) containing several long flash tubes behind diffusing material. They produce a light similar to a large, north-facing window, and deliver consistent light in flashes of 1/1000 sec or even faster. Special stroboscopic flash units are de-

Window light
Powerful flash tubes behind a large diffusing screen give bright illumination the quality of overcast daylight. They are used on stands or on a boom for overhead lighting (right).

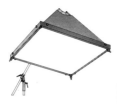

signed to produce a long series of very brief flashes at regular, pre-set intervals. You use them for multi-image pictures of moving objects (see *High-speed photography,* pp. 275-7). The light output from each pulse of a stroboscopic flash is weak when compared to studio electronic flash, because the electronics are designed to give fast repetition rather than a single, accumulated flash. Set to maximum frequency, the light flickers at a speed so fast that the illumination they give seems to be continuous.

Lighting accessories

To use artificial lighting effectively, you must be able to position a lamp or flash head at practically any height or angle. Telescopic stands will support a lamp up to 7-8 ft (2-2.5 m) from the floor. Each stand must be strong and stable, so that it is not top heavy when at full height. Spotlights and large floods therefore require heavy-duty stands with a firm, solid base. These often have wheels for easy maneuverability. With a studio boom you can pos-

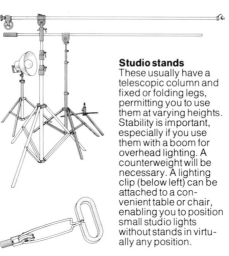

Studio stands
These usually have a telescopic column and fixed or folding legs, permitting you to use them at varying heights. Stability is important, especially if you use them with a boom for overhead lighting. A counterweight will be necessary. A lighting clip (below left) can be attached to a convenient table or chair, enabling you to position small studio lights without stands in virtually any position.

ition a lighting unit above the subject. (If you tried to do this with a regular lighting set-up, the stand would appear in the picture.) But most booms safely support only lightweight heads, and in a small studio they take up a great deal of space. Booms which take a counterweight allow you to use heavier lighting heads. You can also attach small heads to chair backs, or the tops of doors, using lighting clips. This arrangement is especially useful when you are working in a domestic interior, although clips

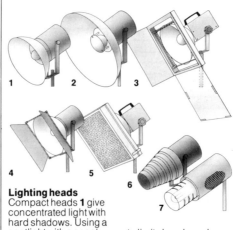

Lighting heads
Compact heads **1** give concentrated light with hard shadows. Using a spotlight with a snoot **6** or a spot projector **7** gives a narrow beam of hard light. A floodlight with a wide reflector, **2** or a spot with a large diffuser, **5** gives softer light with less distinct shadows. Barn doors **4** enable you to limit sharply and shape a hard light beam, and control light spillage. They may also have a holder **3**, into which you can insert filters for color conversion or special effects, or diffusers to soften the light.

are not as easy to move as stands with wheels.

Spotlights, broadlights, and most small floods have brackets at the front to hold accessories which alter the quality or direction of their light. You can use these attachments on both tungsten and studio flash heads, with similar effects. For example, by attaching a "scrim" of wire gauze you can soften and dim the light without color change. "Barn doors" consist of four adjustable flaps that you mount on the front of the lighting unit to control the beam width. They also prevent light spilling into the camera lens when lamps are directed from the side or rear of your subject. Filter holders enable you to insert colored acetates for special effects or color correction. Blue

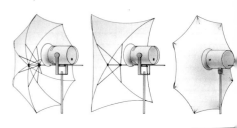

Soft light attachments
If, instead of pointing the light source directly at the subject, you bounce it off a large reflective surface, the light will be softer and more diffused. You can use a folding umbrella reflector (top row) or direct the light through a translucent screen (right). With a large umbrella diffuser (top right) light bounced off the inside surface is further diffused through material surrounding the light. This type of lighting effect is often used in conjunction with a harder, more directional lighting unit like a spotlight.

color balancing filters, or polarizing materials for copying (see *Copying,* p. 171) are particularly useful. The holder should be situated well forward of the front of the unit, so that the lamp's heat does not damage the filters. With "snoots", you can limit the beam's spread, to produce harder, more concentrated illumination. An adjustable spot projector will produce the same effect from a greater distance.

To spread and soften the light, several attachments are available. You can use either a honeycomb diffuser, or one of a range of umbrella-type attachments. With some types you can achieve almost shadowless illumination. This is particularly useful in lighting conditions where shadow conceals form and reduces detail.

Lighting in the studio

The value of studio lighting is that it is completely under the photographer's control. The direction and nature of the light from each lamp can be altered one step at a time, and the photographer can monitor these changes and observe their effect on the set as a whole. In addition, experience with studio lighting helps greatly when using and adapting available light.

Improvising
A specially designed studio is not essential. It is possible to work with small, still-life subjects using nothing more than a table, a single, improvised light, and some white cardboard reflectors. More space, and two or three photographic lights, greatly add to versatility. It is also important to be able to drape the windows, to exclude all uncontrollable existing light.

Most photographers use studio lighting to create a natural appearance, using one dominant light source above camera level (simulating the sun) and adding diffused illumination to lighten the shadow areas (to imitate general skylight). It is essential to avoid "over-lighting" — using lighting units too close to the subject, and from too many directions at once.

It is best to explore thoroughly the possibilities of a single light source at a time, using it from different heights and positions, and discovering how to use it in conjunction with reflectors. By adding lights one by one, it will be possible to build up the lighting while being aware of the precise function that each unit fulfils. One lamp might illuminate only the background, while another could highlight a particular edge or surface of the subject.

Lighting effect
Lighting balance and contrast pose particular problems. Even with effectively placed lights, some dimming, or limiting of the area that each illuminates, is often necessary. The amount of adjustment will depend on whether the image is color or black and white. On color film, color contrast may separate the different elements and planes of the subject, without it being necessary to improve lighting contrast.

Every subject, and each camera viewpoint creates a fresh lighting challenge. Portraits in general call for a more flexible approach to lighting than still lifes. But in all areas of photography it is vital to solve each lighting problem according to the demands of the subject.

Amateur studio set-ups

For simple studio work, a desk lamp, table, some sheets of uncreased blotting paper, and a number of pegs and clips can be sufficient for most lighting situations. For color work, a 3200 K photographic lamp for tungsten-balanced film, or flash for daylight-balanced film, will provide the correct color content. Avoid rooms decorated in vibrant color schemes, as casts may result.

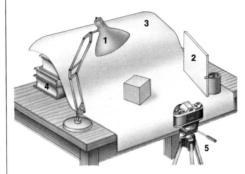

Single light source
1 Desk lamp. 2 White reflector board. 3 Background paper. 4 Books used as support. 5 Camera mounted on tripod.

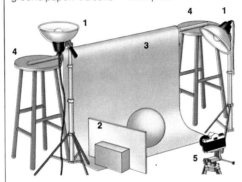

Two light sources
1 Photofloods mounted on stands. 2 White reflector board. 3 Roll of paper. 4 Stools used as support. 5 Camera mounted on tripod.

Basic home studio
1 Blind. 2 Floodlamp. 3 Barn doors. 4 Umbrella reflector. 5 Studio flash unit. 6 Reflector boards. 7 Power pack for flash. 8 Background paper on moveable frame. 9 Telescopic stand. 10 Twin-shank studio tripod. 11 Mirror. 12 Glass-sheet.

If you require more space, use a wide roll of background paper supported by poles. Colored papers provide a variety of backgrounds, although black or white papers and colored gels over the lights give similar versatility. You can attach lamps to stands or clips, leaving enough room to accommodate a wide choice of lighting positions. Sheets of stiff white cardboard, plastic, or plywood can act as reflectors. One hard and one soft lighting unit provide a working minimum for most subjects.

With 6 ft (2 m) wide background paper, and this type of set-up, you should be able to tackle still lifes, child and animal studies, and adult half-length and head-and-shoulders portraits.

Home studios
If you can devote an entire room to studio work, try to use one with generous dimensions. Ceiling height is particularly important, since you will require space for high, low, and upward-angled viewpoints. To calculate floor space, you must first work out the typical lens-subject distance you will require, and then allow additional space for working behind the camera and for separating the subject from its background. An extra 3-6 ft (1-2 m) is an absolute minimum for this. To accommodate lights, a room width of 12 ft (4 m) is best.

Lightproof curtains or blinds are essential for full lighting control. Paint the walls and ceiling matte white to avoid color casts. You should use lights that are mobile and flexible. Braced poles between floor and ceiling make useful lighting supports. With tungsten lights you can preview lighting effects, but operating heat can be uncomfortable. Two tungsten halogen compact lamps fitted with barn doors and scrims provide a flexible lighting system. They give light as hard as that from more expensive spots, and you can bounce them off walls and ceiling for a floodlit effect. Multihead flash is excellent for portraiture and frozen action shots taken in the studio.

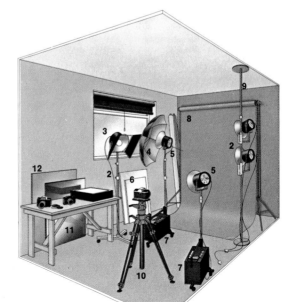

Professional studio

Modern professional studios usually have very high ceilings, and a large floor area. A typical commercial studio has about 650-750 sq ft (60-70 sq m) of usable floor space. This is in addition to the space required for storing equipment. The largest items are folding reflector boards, and "flats" (sheets of wood on frames that you clamp together to create small enclosed areas, or to construct room sets).

The whole studio must be as flexible as possible. Some walls hold racks of wide background papers in various colors. You can suspend these rolls from wall brackets. Concave movable floor coving helps to shape vertical and horizontal surfaces into one continuous sweep of paper. The most useful colors are whites and grays. You can use filtered lights to tint them different colors.

If you are to take full advantage of the studio's height, you must be able to get the camera up high. Some studios have a balcony, but step ladders are more flexible, allowing a greater variety of camera positions. For both tungsten and flash lighting, you will require adjustable stands, including some with booms. In addition, there are low-level supports for cameras and lighting heads. These are useful for photographing small objects, as well as for pictures taken from a low viewpoint. In order to vary the quality of studio lighting, you can use umbrellas or other reflecting and diffusing attachments. One wall of the studio may carry a large reflective screen for front projection (see *Front projection,* p. 182). This screen may also be useful for bounced lighting effects.

To support the large cameras often used in studio work, a strong, single-column stand is ideal. This allows instant height changes down to floor level and also provides a tray for accessories. For photographing small objects, you will require a bench, small background rolls of paper, and a light box.

Studio layout

Most professional studios are a minimum of 20 ft (6 m) square. High ceilings are a great asset. Matte white walls and ceilings can act as bounce surfaces for diffusing light. While all equipment should be readily accessible, maximum use should be made of available floor space. This allows the photographer to move around the subject, and light it from any direction. Be generous with power points, and mask windows and skylights if total control over lighting is required.

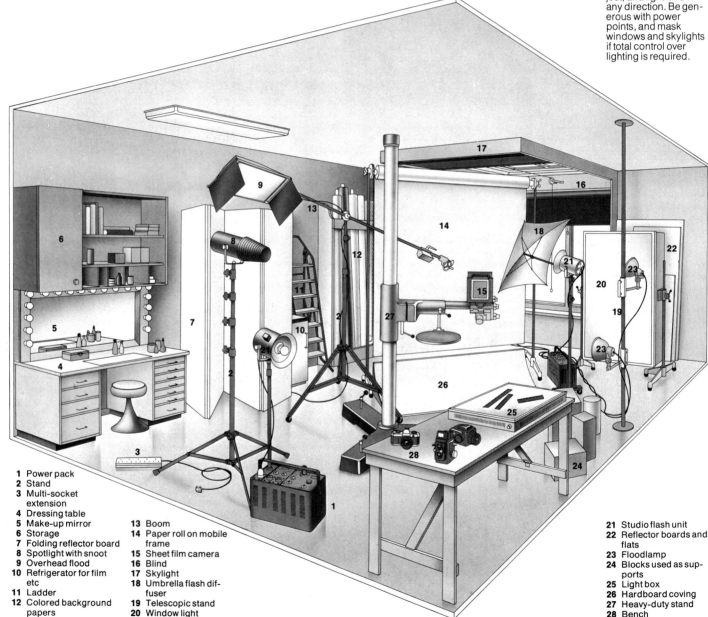

1 Power pack
2 Stand
3 Multi-socket extension
4 Dressing table
5 Make-up mirror
6 Storage
7 Folding reflector board
8 Spotlight with snoot
9 Overhead flood
10 Refrigerator for film etc
11 Ladder
12 Colored background papers
13 Boom
14 Paper roll on mobile frame
15 Sheet film camera
16 Blind
17 Skylight
18 Umbrella flash diffuser
19 Telescopic stand
20 Window light
21 Studio flash unit
22 Reflector boards and flats
23 Floodlamp
24 Blocks used as supports
25 Light box
26 Hardboard coving
27 Heavy-duty stand
28 Bench

Controlling lighting

When first exploring lighting techniques it is best to photograph still-life subjects, though you may eventually use a studio mainly for portraits. Working with inanimate objects gives you plenty of time to watch and consider the effect of each light, and to take a number of pictures with small lighting variations. Viewing and photographing as you proceed also help to make clear the differences between the way your eye sees things, and the way the camera records them on film.

Choose your subject carefully. Often very simple shapes and materials offer the greatest scope. Natural forms in materials such as stone or wood, eggs, onions, a ball of string, or a roll of corrugated cardboard can all form interesting lighting subjects. You can either use a sheet of paper to give a continuous neutral background, or pick a material with a textured surface on which to position your subject. This material should be chosen to form an effective contrast with the subject's texture.

Set up your subject on a table with free space all around it, so that you can place lights in any position. It is important to leave sufficient space between the subject and background, as you may want to illuminate the background without too much light spilling on the subject. Then adjust the camera on its tripod to give the most promising framing and composition. This is the point from which your eye must judge each lighting effect. There are two methods you can adopt. One is to use a "build-up" approach, adding lights one by one. The other is to try variations on an overall scheme.

Whichever method is adopted, you can produce the same results with either tungsten lighting or studio flash units, provided that the heads give illumination of equivalent quality.

The "build-up" approach

Start in the studio with only one key light to create the predominant highlights and shadows in the final picture. This will probably be a hard light source. Ideally, you should have an assistant to hold this lighting unit and move it slowly in an arc over the set from side to side, and then from back to front. While this is happening, you can observe the changes in lighting effect. Look at the surfaces that are emphasized and the shadow shapes cast. Try to decide the best height for the lamp, then move it in a complete circle around the set at this height. When you have found the key light's best position, fix it at that point on a stand or with a clamp.

Next you should decide whether softening the light will improve the appearance. Hold a 2 ft (60 cm) square of tracing paper in the light beam — at first near the lamp, then gradually closer to the subject. When it is nearest to the subject, the largest area of tracing paper is illuminated, and the shadows cast have the softest edges. The glowing paper will also illuminate the whole room, scattering light into subject shadows and reducing contrast.

You should then look at the background. If it is too dark, or too similar to the subject, you can use another light source to illuminate the background paper alone. It is often best to mask this light with barn doors.

Finally, view the scene in terms of contrast. If possible, use an instant picture back on the studio camera to preview precise results. As a consequence, you may want to lighten the shadows. If the room is small, try lighting the whole set by directing a flood toward the ceiling and walls above and around the camera. You may not even require an extra lamp to do this. It may be possible to achieve a similar effect with a sheet of white cardboard tilted toward the subject from near the camera, to reflect some illumination from the key light. You can use other reflectors, clamped nearer the subject to lighten small, heavy shadows.

Using a generalized scheme

The build-up method is flexible, and enables you to produce a variety of effects. But it has some disadvantages. For portraits, it can mean that you force your sitter into a fixed pose or expression for fear of disturbing the lighting. With complicated still lifes, the shapes and surfaces can have so many different lighting requirements that a simpler overall scheme is often a better compromise. In addition, you need an assistant to operate the build-up method really effectively.

One alternative system uses a large diffused floodlight. This is usually positioned fairly high

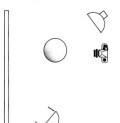

Separating subject and background
This simple set-up uses two floodlights. One, the key light, is angled directly at the subject. The other illuminates the background, so that you can separate it tonally from the subject, as in the photograph below.

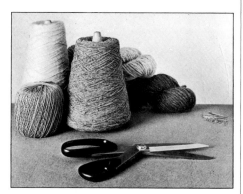

and to one side of the subject. You enclose the set on one side with large reflector boards, which either return the light or are separately illuminated. With this type of arrangement, small changes in the subject's position make little difference to its lighting, which often resembles diffused sunlight or overcast daylight from a large window.

Contrast

One problem with studio lighting is excessive contrast. A single spotlight in a darkened room, for example, can produce brightness differences of several hundreds to one between the lit and unlit parts of a subject. Its effect is like that of a searchlight at night rather than sunlight, which is always accompanied by some light scattered from the sky. No film will successfully record detail in both lit and unlit areas in one exposure.

Your choice of subject and background also affects picture contrast. A white subject sidelit on a dark ground will always show more contrast than a gray subject on a white ground. This is because the gray subject gives less brilliant reflectance from its lit side, while the white background tends to scatter some illumination back to lighten subject shadows.

You can minimize contrast in three ways — by increasing the general level of light, using reflector boards, or changing to a softer main light source. Use a meter to read separately the lightest and darkest areas you want to record in detail. (If the ratio of the two readings is about 4:1 the picture is likely to have fairly naturalistic contrast.) Most films can record higher contrast — you should regard 10:1 as a maximum, but expect some loss of tone and color values. How much loss you can accept depends on

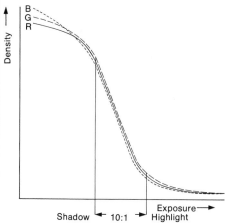

Image brightness range
This characteristic curve of a typical film shows that, for objective results, highlights should not exceed shadows in brightness by more than about 10:1. Outside of range, tones begin to flatten and colors to distort.

how interpretative or objective you want your photograph to be. Sometimes heavy shadows are an essential part of a picture's atmosphere, and slight color distortions in such dark areas pass unnoticed.

When adjusting contrast you may want to lessen the effect of the main light source, without altering its light quality or its position relative to the fill-in light source. If you are using a time exposure, one simple technique is to switch off the lamp (or block its beam with a piece of opaque cardboard) for part of the exposing period. If you switch off the light for 2 sec during a 4 sec exposure, the effect is equivalent to that obtained with a lamp only half as bright.

Glare

There are two types of glare, both caused by light reflected from surfaces. Point light sources produce small, intense highlights, while the reflection of larger area light sources causes varying degrees of opalescent sheen. The sheen effect is produced when diffused light reflects from a material's topmost surface. If the subject is colored, this directly reflected light mixes with, and so dilutes, the colored light reflected from the pigment below (see *Contrast and color,* p. 26). Some glossy surfaces always show glare.

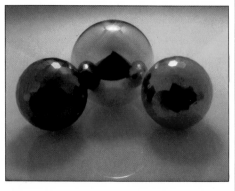

Direct lighting
Frontal lighting from a harsh spot or flash produces intense highlights or glare. Colors appear bright (above). Color photographs appear very bright and shadows harsh.

Dulling spray
Special sprays are available for dulling the surface of polished or highly reflective objects, thus eliminating glare and making colors in the image appear softer (below).

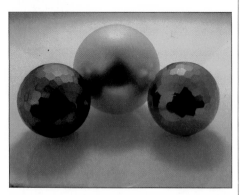

You can even enlarge highlight spots to give a glowing diffused effect by using a starburst filter or soft-focus attachment (see *Special effects attachments,* p. 198-201). You can avoid unwanted glare spots either by using a larger, more diffused light source, or by treating the subject surface itself with a dulling spray containing matte lacquer. It is possible to remove unwanted sheens by picking out exactly the part of the surroundings that is reflecting into the surface, and covering it with black cardboard, or masking it with a cast shadow. You may also find that using a polarizing filter on the camera lens will help to absorb the reflection (see *Copying,* facing page).

Local lighting

Sometimes the lighting of a studio set works well in a general sense, but you also want to give special emphasis to a particular part of the subject. For example, in an advertising photograph, an individual label or product may require picking out. Again, you may need to stress the color of a single bloom in a silhouetted flower arrangement, or draw attention to something held in the palm of the hand. If you can increase the illumination level in the selected area, and expose for this part, the rest of the picture will record slightly darker and subdued. Similarly, in a set-up that is designed to give very soft, shadowless lighting, you can pick out a particular area with harder illumination from behind, to give an emphasizing rim of highlight.

A mirror can often be useful for introducing light into a small area. Another method is to use direct light from a lamp masked with a long conical snoot of black paper. The hole at the end of the snoot should be about 1 in (2.5 cm) in diameter and you should position the lamp as closely as possible to the subject, without including it in the camera's frame of view. A

Picking out details
Use a mirror to reflect part of a spotlight beam on to a particular area of the subject (below). If necessary, you can shape the patch of light by masking parts of the mirror with black tape. Trevor Melton used this technique to pick out the label on a glass bottle (right). He placed

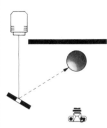

further light sources behind a translucent screen, in the center of which he mounted a sheet of black cardboard to act as the background. Light passed around the edges of this cardboard to pick out the rim of the bottle. No frontal lighting was used, and to prevent any unwanted reflections appearing in the glass, he shot through a hole in a black screen in front of the camera.

slide projector can perform the same function. The slide holder will accept a shaped mask (see *Attachment holders,* p. 201).

Advertising photographers often have to emphasize liquids, such as beer or perfume, and make them look luminous by inserting a light from behind. You can do this by cutting a hole through the background and placing a lamp immediately behind the set, or by using a light positioned out of sight but within the set itself. Small "pencil light" flash heads are available for this type of work. An alternative technique is to pipe light along a fiber optic tube.

Occasionally the part of the subject you want to pick out is self-illuminated. Examples include a candle flame, the face of a digital clock, and the light built into a model building. Many of these subjects will barely show up against strong studio illumination. You can adjust this balance by giving two exposures. You make the first for your studio lighting (slightly underexposing), then switch out all the lights except the self-illuminating object, and give a second, longer exposure to "burn in" the detail of the main point of interest.

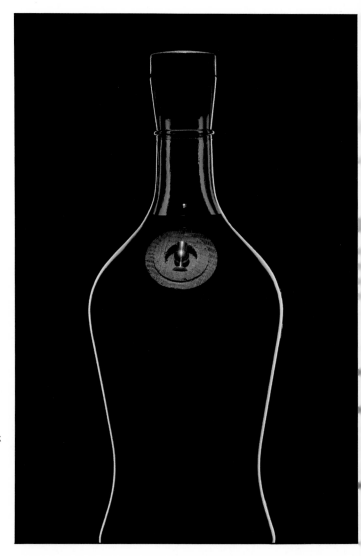

Copying

The type of lighting required to photograph flat drawings, paintings, plans, and photographic prints must be completely even, and have the correct color temperature for your film type. It should not produce reflections or glare spots. The best method is to use two soft light sources such as floodlights, and set these up at 45° to the surface of the original. Do not place the lamps too close, especially with a large original, because this may give more light at the

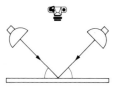
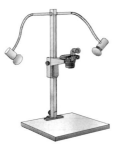

Flat copies
Light a flat original, such as a document or a piece of artwork, equally from both sides. This gives even illumination without glare or reflections. Use floods at 45° (above left) or a special copying stand (above right). If you want to bring out

surface texture, such as the brush strokes on an oil painting (below), light from one side only, with the lamp some distance away for even lighting.

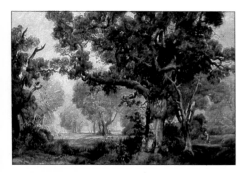

sides than the center. Arranging lamps at an angle should ensure that any glare reflection from the lamps themselves is directed away from the lens. You can place a pencil in the center of the original at right-angles to the surface to ensure that illumination is even. The two shadows cast must be about the same length, and should match in density.

With glass-fronted originals you may find that both you and the camera are sufficiently illuminated to appear reflected in the glass

when you stop down the lens. One way to avoid this is to use a large sheet of black cardboard with a hole in the middle, large enough for the camera lens to protrude through. You position this in front of the camera.

Sometimes an original painting for copying has a strong surface texture that you want to show. In this case, you should light it with a single flood at an oblique angle to the surface. Place the light at the farthest possible distance, so that the nearest side of the original is not brighter than the farther.

Polarized light

Regular light rays from any source (both natural and artificial) vibrate in all the planes at right-angles to their direction of travel. When they are reflected from a smooth, non-metallic surface, such as plastic, glass, or water, they vibrate in only a single plane. This reflected

Polarization
Light waves normally vibrate in many planes. When reflected from a smooth, non-metallic surface, only a single plane remains.

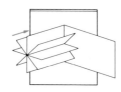

light is known as polarized light. The naked human eye cannot detect the difference between polarized and unpolarized light, although many insects have the ability to do this.

An alternative way to produce polarized light is to use a polarizing filter on the front of the lens (see *Polarizing filters*, p. 198). This allows light to pass in only one plane, but you can also make the filter remove the single-plane vibrations of polarized light. You do this by rotating the filter while observing the effect this has on the image. This is especially useful for photographing subjects behind glass. You simply turn the filter until the reflection disappears. You can use polarizing filters with both black and white and color film.

A polarizing filter will work well if all the reflections are coming from the correct angle, but reflecions of light sources are polarized to varying degrees according to the angle the light makes to the surface. With glass, for example, the greatest polarization usually occurs when the light is traveling at between 30° and 40° to the reflective surface. At other angles, the light will be only partly polarized, so that the filter will not fully absorb the reflection. To suppress specular reflections at all angles it is necessary to place a piece of polarizing ace-

tate over each light source, and fit a polarizing filter over the camera lens. You will still be able to see the subject through the filter because where polarized light reflects from matte surfaces it becomes scattered and de-polarized.

Photographing an oil painting presents a problem that can be solved by the use of polarized light. Using two lamps with polarizing filters to illuminate the subject you may still see a pair of "hot spots" of unavoidable glare from the surface of the varnish. But you can make these disappear by fitting a polarizing filter on the lens and rotating it to produce its maximum effect. All the other highlights from raised parts of the paint will also disappear, so that colors become clearer and more saturated, and the result will be a more faithful reproduction of the original painting.

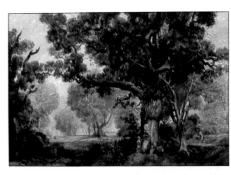

Filter on camera
A polarizing filter on the lens removes some glare caused by polarized light, but some detail is still lost, and colors diluted (above) but quite true to the original.

Filter on camera and lamps
If you polarize the lamps as well, the filter on the lens can totally absorb reflected highlights, restoring the natural warm color to these areas (below).

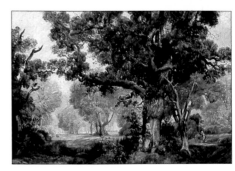

Lighting enclosed detail

Some subjects require flat, frontal lighting. This is especially useful when you want to reveal full detail, rather than show the subject's form. It is often a problem when the objects you want to photograph are tightly enclosed, or very near the camera, so that it is difficult to place front-facing lights without obstructing the lens. Technical subjects, such as the insides of instruments and watches, dental photographs, and record pictures of coins all pose this problem. A solution is to use ring flash (see *Flash lighting units,* pp. 165-6).

A simple, cheap alternative for close-up work is to shoot through a piece of thin glass set at 45° between the lens and the subject. You can place a small lamp or distant spotlight to one side. This will reflect light downward, sharing the same path as that viewed by the lens. Provided that you align the lens and lamp carefully, all the shadows will disappear from the subject. This lighting arrangement is ideal for record photography of small objects. On a larger scale, it provides the basis for front projection (see *Front projection,* p. 182).

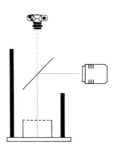

Axial lighting
For totally shadowless lighting use a thin glass sheet at 45° to reflect a light beam down along the same axis as the lens toward the subject. The camera looks through the glass. Black cardboard blocks reflections from the upper surface of the glass toward the lens.

Silhouette lighting

In a silhouette your main aim is to concentrate attention on subject outline and suppress all surface detail into a flat, black shape. The main lighting problem is to create a sufficiently large and evenly lit white background. It is important not to spill so much light that detail within the shape begins to reveal itself. A large studio with a matte white backdrop and dark side walls is ideal. But any room which allows you to position the subject well forward of the background will do.

To create an even spread of background light, you may need up to four floodlights. It is helpful if you can slightly raise your subject (perhaps on a plinth), so that the white background extends down evenly to the bottom of the frame. No other lighting is necessary. For a true silhouette effect, always measure exposure from the background alone (see *Exposure and its measurement,* p. 132-8).

If you want to add slight roundness of modeling on, say, a profiled face, use a small, closely positioned reflector board, angled to return light from the background on to the camera side of the subject. For a silhouette on a colored background, use a colored backdrop or place colored acetates over the lights. You can also use a colored filter over the camera lens. If you want a colored silhouette against a white background, expose the film as you would for a black and white effect, then repeat the exposure on the same frame of film through a colored filter, this time with the subject removed.

You can make silhouettes of small, still-life subjects seem to float in space by supporting them on a sheet of white translucent plastic and then lighting them from below. For a semi-silhouette result, where a little detail is required, you can reflect or add light from the top as well. One problem, though, with using highly reflective plastic or glass is that lit parts of objects may cause specular highlights and even complete double images to be seen as reflections from the surface. A polarizing filter (see *Polarizing filters,* p. 198) added to the front of the camera lens may prevent this.

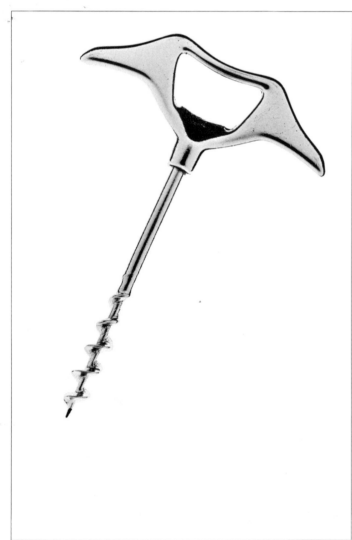

White background
The simplest way to create a silhouette is to light a white background evenly using two floods (below). Place the subject some distance in front of the background well to the rear of the lamps. To prevent stray light

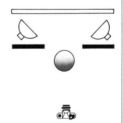

spilling on to the subject, screen off each lamp. Take the meter reading from the background alone. If you want a white, shadowless back-

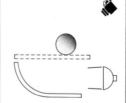

ground, place the object on a sheet of translucent material (above). Reflect light from white cardboard beneath this. To give surface detail (left), return light with a white reflector.

Low-key lighting

In television and stage work, the type of lighting arrangement that makes use of light and shade to create an illusion of solidity and depth is known as "chiaroscuro". In photography, this effect is known as "low-key lighting", because it makes use of predominantly dark tones (see *Tonal range,* p. 24).

Make sure your subject is suitable for this type of treatment. In portraiture, for example, dark hair and clothes as well as a dark background are essential. Because lit areas of the composition are to be very limited, you must direct most lighting from one side and this unrelentingly picks out facial lines and texture. Low-key lighting always gives lit parts great emphasis, so make sure no extraneous information is included by accident. Often, the best position for the main light is high and to one side, with the face turned in profile toward it. This arrangement keeps the lit area to a mini-

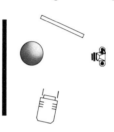

Low-key lighting
Direct a spot with barn doors on to a reflector board (left), and use a matte black background. In the picture below, direct spill from the spot sidelights the front of the locomotive without affecting the background.

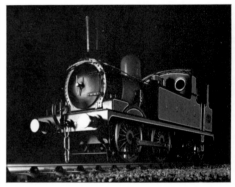

mum, especially if you use a small flood or slightly diffused spotlight. In nearly every case, contrast within the scene will be too great for the film to record unless you return some soft light into the shadow areas using a reflector placed close to the shadow side of the subject. You may prefer to direct another, hard light source from high up and to the rear of the subject to rimlight the top and back of the head. This will also separate the subject from the background.

Exposure must be finely balanced with low-key lighting in order to retain detail in the shadow areas without burning out the highlights. Take your exposure reading from close in on the lit side of the subject, or take the reading with an incident light exposure meter (see *Using a hand-held meter,* p. 136).

High-key lighting

"High-key" means creating a lighting scheme that is essentially light in tone, and is used in conjunction with a pale-toned subject and a light background. If your subject is a portrait, it is important that the sitter have pale skin tones and light-colored clothing and hair. Skin texture (as well as most blemishes) is suppressed by this type of lighting – but the detail and shape of the eyes and mouth are strongly revealed, as in a pencil drawing.

Illumination should be soft and frontal, so that everything is bathed in light – like hazy sunlight from directly behind the camera position. You can combine bounced light from reflector boards close in around the subject with

High-key lighting
Light a pale background evenly with two floods. Illuminate the subject by floods bounced from reflector boards to give soft, frontal lighting. The subject is thus surrounded by reflected light. Use a lens hood to stop stray side-light entering the camera lens and diffusing the image.

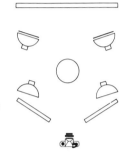

some diffused top light. It is best to light the background separately using evenly spaced floodlighting. Adjust the background tone so that it is just perceptively lighter than that of the subject. A ring flash can also be useful for even, frontal lighting.

When photographing still-life subjects in black and white, you can create soft, overall lighting with minimal equipment using a single floodlight to "paint with light". For this result, hold a diffused flood about 3 ft (1 m) above the subject when measuring exposure. Load the camera with slow film and select a small aperture (or use a neutral density filter – see *Neutral density filters,* p. 201), aiming for an exposure of about 10 sec or longer. In the dark, lock the shutter open, switch on the flood, and move it in a steady arc over the camera while exposing the film. Throughout the entire exposure, keep the light source the same distance from the subject. All the shadow will move and blur during the exposure, and so disappear – the total effect is similar to using a diffused light source as wide as the total movement of the flood. This technique, however, is not suitable for color (if accurate rendition is required) because of the reciprocity effects on color balance (see *Reciprocity failure,* p. 152 and *The effects of reciprocity failure,* p. 220).

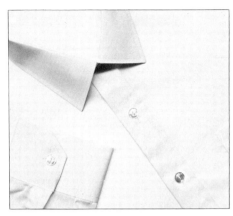

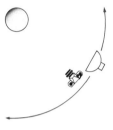

Even lighting with a moving source
Point the flood down on to the subject from above the camera position (left). With the shutter open, move the lamp in an arc. For the picture above, the light was moving left and right.

Lighting polished surfaces

Polished silver, chrome, and other reflective surfaces impose special lighting difficulties. Their surfaces simply mirror all the immediate surroundings, often in a distorted form, which confuses the subjects' own shapes. As soon as you direct a light source on to such a subject, it is returned as one glaring highlight in an otherwise black environment.

One way to overcome this problem is to create a setting that is totally free of highlights or deep shadows – a photographic "tent" of seamless, light-diffusing material, for example, such as tracing paper, muslin, or a translucent plastic dome. Make this as large as possible, so that if any creases or joins do occur, they will be far enough away from the subject that your likely depth of field will not be sufficient to record them sharply. Illuminate the tent evenly over its outside surface, and leave a hole just large enough to accommodate the camera lens.

The subject inside should now be free of all highlights and confusing reflections, but it will probably appear to have an unnatural matte "satin" finish. To restore some of the character of the shiny material, you need to introduce controlled reflections. Do this by adding strips of black cardboard to the inside or outside of the tent. Use the camera's focusing screen (if SLR) to see the precise effect each piece of

cardboard has on the subject (they should create simple shaded reflections that help to define form and not produce shapes that are hard or confusing).

Another approach is to use a large, very diffused flood close above the subject. Wherever dark parts of the surroundings appear reflected in a distracting way, you can soften them by locally applying a coating of a clear, matte lacquer to dull the surface.

Highly reflective surfaces
Sometimes you may want to emphasize the reflective qualities of the subject, rather than suppress them. You can avoid unwanted reflections by shooting through a gap between two white reflectors. Use strips of black cardboard to induce reflections which will bring out the subject's form (below). Shooting in color, use extra reflectors of the same hue as the subject to restore color lost in the highlights.

Light tent
Surround the subject with translucent material on a frame. Use floods outside the screen for diffused illumination, and shoot through a hole in the material. Reflectors give controlled shadows.

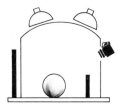

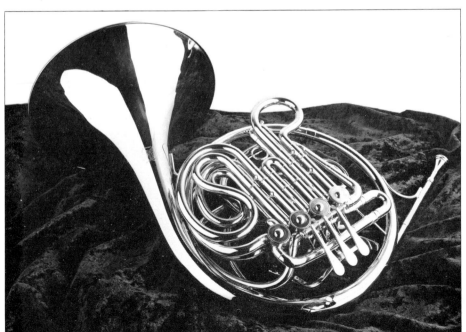

Lighting glass

Photographing transparent glass objects poses its own characteristic lighting problems. There are two main approaches to this type of subject that will help you produce the most effective lighting. The first method is to arrange the object against a dark background, and then light the glass directly from the sides so that the surfaces glisten, and their outlines appear as bright, white highlights. The second method involves positioning the object in front of a lit white background, so that its shape is outlined as a black silhouette.

Both of these methods rely on the fact that glass refracts and reflects light, so that the surroundings — especially to the left and right of the set — have a great influence on final results.

If you use a dark background, it is essential to distance this well behind the glass. Place sheets of white cardboard on either side of the set. These will strengthen the white edge line of the glass, and increase its surface sheen. It is best to direct the lighting partially from the rear, so that it passes through the glass toward the reflector boards. This will produce numerous sparkling highlights, which you can exaggerate if required with a starburst attachment (see *Special effects attachments,* pp. 198-200). You can reduce these highlights — at least in part — with a polarizing filter (see *Polarizing filters,* p. 198). Designs etched or cut into the glass will show as white outlines against a dark background. If you want to avoid a flat background, and produce a result with gradated tones, light the background separately.

If you require a silhouette effect, you should support the glass on a shelf and use your light sources only to illuminate a well-distanced, white background. Sheets of black cardboard on either side of the set and background will help strengthen the subject's dark outlines, but they can make the glass appear unnaturally thick and heavy. Designs cut or etched into the glass will show as dark lines against a white background. If you produce a pure silhouette, the surface texture of the glass will disappear. It is therefore advisable to use a little soft lighting from one side of the subject. This will add a sheen to the surfaces facing the camera. When you require a more dramatic effect, use variegated lighting on the background. This technique will allow you to produce a gradated effect, in which the background is light in tone at the bottom and gradually darkens toward the top.

Both these lighting techniques will show the characteristic reflective surface of glass, while at the same time making clear the shape and form of the object you are photographing.

White background
Trevor Melton backlit these glasses (below) by reflecting light off a white background. Black cardboard behind and to the sides of the subject (right) darkened edges. A reflector gave soft, frontal illumination to the glasses.

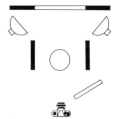

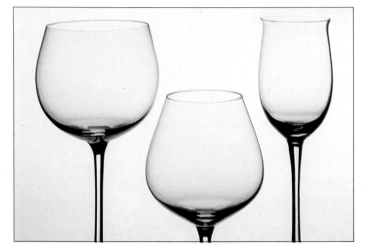

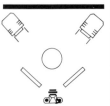

Black background
For the photograph (above), Trevor Melton used a black background. He placed two lamps with barn doors behind the subject, directing their beams partly through the glass and partly on to white reflectors, which created the edge lines.

Controlling mixed lighting

Taking pictures in a studio gives the photographer complete control over lighting and subject arrangement. But studio illumination can provide a highly artificial environment, or produce an excessively austere effect. For a portrait sitter, too, the mass of photographic equipment can often be intimidating and encourages self-consciousness.

Stills photographers, like many film makers, increasingly turn to existing rather than constructed settings. A genuine environment not only seems less contrived, but can also add important extra information about the subject. However, it is often necessary to adapt natural settings. Indoors, a scene can often be improved by simplifying furniture arrangements. Above all, lighting for living and lighting for photography are seldom in accord, and the photographer has to make modifications without destroying the atmosphere.

The main lighting problems indoors are contrast, unevenness, and low intensity. It is often possible to position a still-life subject, or a figure, with a large window to one side and a white reflective surface outside the picture area to lighten the shadowed side. Larger sets, such as those including a whole room, usually require additional photographic lighting. It is essential to add light unobtrusively. Bouncing soft illumination off walls, the ceiling, or reflector boards behind the camera, will add light to the shadows without creating additional areas of shade. Sometimes the existing light is too flat and frontal. Additional lighting, directed as if from a window, is needed to help emphasize form, and show tonally separate objects at different distances from the camera.

The most interesting part of a room may also be the most difficult to work in, if all the existing light is directed toward the lens. It may then be necessary to draw the curtains and illuminate the whole area with photographic tungsten lamps or flash, again aiming for a simple, natural effect. Working in this way also helps to solve technical problems which arise with light sources of different color temperatures.

Another problem, which often occurs with large interiors, is that of directing enough artificial light to fill the darkest, most distant corners of the subject. The answer here is often to use a light source which you move around the subject during exposure.

See also
Light and color, pp. 22-3. Choice of film *Color temperature,* p. 151.

Balancing light

It is often difficult to decide whether available light (indoors or out) will require boosting. In such situations you must be aware that the eye sees contrast at a different level to the camera (see *Camera principles*, pp. 100-1).

Where the problem is lighting of low intensity, it is generally preferable to use a faster film or longer exposure time, supporting the camera with a tripod if necessary. This avoids upsetting a natural lighting scheme and helps preserve a scene's atmosphere.

You may still have the problem of uneven lighting. Indoors, for example, it may be necessary to add light to a dark corner of a room between two windows. To do this, you can

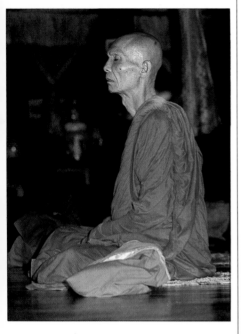

Flash and existing light
Henry Wilson used a mixture of available light from high windows and diffused flash from the camera position to photograph the gold-robed monk (above). Flash adds a little extra detail and subject modeling, without destroying the subdued, peaceful mood of the picture.

conceal a light source within the picture area — use a diffused flash unit or a tungsten lamp. (If you are shooting on daylight color film, you must cover the tungsten lamp with blue acetate to match the color of daylight.)

If you have to fill in shadows across a whole room, you can reflect tungsten or flash light off a large white surface, such as an umbrella reflector, above the camera.

You can often achieve a naturalistic appearance by working entirely in artificial light. For half-length portraits, a large diffused flood, about 2 ft (60 cm) above the subject, and placed to one side, will illuminate the whole picture area. Reflecting the light off walls or ceiling will further soften the effect. If you use tungsten lamps these will approximately match the color temperature of any tungsten room illumination shown switched on.

Light sources in the picture

Sometimes you will want to include actual light sources in the picture. These may be wall lamps, the flames in a fireplace, or the image on a television screen. Outdoors at night, you may want to photograph a subject with a background of illuminated buildings or streets. For most of these situations flash provides ideal illumination for the main subject. Support the camera on a tripod, and arrange the flash heads so that the shadows they cast do not conflict with those caused by the available light. Set your lens aperture to suit the flash illumination, measure the background light source with a meter, and extend the exposure time accordingly. For example, you may require an aperture of f 11, but if you used the regular 1/60 sec flash shutter speed, the background lighting would appear dim. By setting 1/2 sec instead, the light source in the picture will burn in more strongly, but the flash unit will still provide the main illumination. It is important that neither the main subject nor the

Photographing the light source
The candles provided the sole source of light in this picture by Clive Frost (right). Because the high degree of contrast between shadows and flames made exact exposure measurement difficult, he gave several bracketed exposures in order to achieve the desired result. Fast film was essential and a wide aperture has severely limited depth of field. An orange tint, caused by the low color temperature of the light, combined with daylight-balanced film, has suffused the picture, adding to its atmosphere.

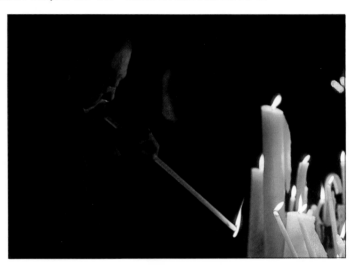

camera move during exposure, unless you want the subject's form to be diffused through movement, or "eaten away".

The background light will often appear orange in color when you use this method, but this is usually acceptable, as it does not provide the main lighting. If your background light source is a television screen, turn down the contrast and take your meter reading from the television image, as if measuring a flat original for copying. Your exposure time must be at least 1/15 sec, or the picture will show uneven bars across the television screen. Longer exposure times also give a full picture, but any action on the screen will blur.

You can combine time exposure and flash outdoors at night. For example, to photograph people in front of a firework display, hold the flash off-camera, so that its light appears to come from the sky. Using the correct aperture for flash, keep the shutter open for several seconds to record the fireworks.

Lighting large areas

You can use "painting with light" for areas which are too big to illuminate evenly with a single source fixed in one position. If you want to photograph a row of houses at night, for example, take up a viewpoint at one end of the street. Leave the camera at this point on a tripod, with its shutter open, and walk along the street, firing a flashgun once opposite each house. Keep the distance between flash and houses constant, in accordance with the flash guide number and lens aperture.

It is possible to treat a shadowy interior in a similar way. Use an aperture one stop smaller than that required for your flash. Measure the ambient light, which will probably require a time exposure. While the shutter is open, fire the flash, either from the camera position, or from a hidden location within the frame, toward the darkest area. If necessary, fire the flash several times. You can alternatively use a blue-filtered tungsten lamp, keeping it moving over the dark parts of the subject during exposure. This method has the advantage over flash of not recording any additional shadows.

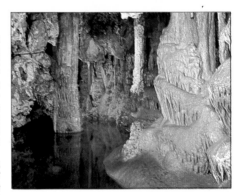

Painting with light
Clive Frost mounted his camera on a tripod, and locked the shutter open for a time exposure. He then moved around the cave, firing a hand-held flash at different areas. He was careful to keep out of direct sight of the camera. This technique revealed detail that with a single flash in such a large area would be obscured by dense shadows. In this situation, bulky studio lights would have been too unwieldy.

Reducing contrast with flash

If you use flash to fill in the shadows caused by contrasty existing light, you can work anywhere, independently of electricity supplies, provided that your subject is not too large or too far away for your particular flash. Flash also matches the color of daylight. It is best to use the flashgun on or very near the camera in order to illuminate all the shadows seen from this position.

With subjects that are harshly sidelit or backlit by the sun, flash should bring shadow illumination up to about one-quarter of the intensity of sunlit areas. You should start by measuring exposure for the strongly lit part of the subject. Then set the camera to a shutter speed suitable for flash, and adjust the lens aperture to one stop smaller than the correct setting at this shutter speed.

When you use an automatic flashgun, set it for an ASA speed twice that of your film. This will produce a shadow-to-highlight ratio of about 1:4. For the same result with a manual flashgun, calculate its correct distance from the subject for the aperture you have set. Then increase the flash-to-subject distance by 30 per cent, or diffuse the flash with one sheet of tracing paper.

All types of fill-in illumination from near the camera have one major disadvantage. Elements in the picture closer to the camera than your main subject will appear excessively filled-in, whereas elements farther away will look under-filled and contrasty. The best way to avoid this problem is to choose a viewpoint from which the main subject is the nearest element in the frame.

Simulating sunlight

On a dull day outdoors you can create a sunlit appearance using artificial lighting, provided that you do not try to light areas that are too large. Flash is the best source to use, because it is portable and its color matches that of daylight. Hold the flashgun away from the camera, high, and to one side, as if its light were coming from the sun, or use a blue-filtered tungsten halogen lamp from the same position.

If you are using this method to shoot a head-and-shoulders portrait, aim to make the "sunlit" parts of the face about twice as bright as those lit by daylight alone. To calculate the exposure required, you should set the shutter to its flash speed, and use an exposure meter to determine the aperture required for the natural daylight. Then set a lens aperture one stop smaller than the one indicated. By dividing your flash unit's guide number (see *Flash*

guide numbers, p. 140) by the aperture you have selected, you can calculate the correct distance between flash and subject.

Unlike real sunlight, this artificial illumination falls off rapidly with distance. Try to avoid viewpoints that emphasize this. A high viewpoint, which shows the ground, may reveal how local the illumination is. A low viewpoint, showing the subject against a plain background of sky, is usually more effective.

Creating the effect of sunlight

In this picture Trevor Melton used flash to simulate the shadow effects of direct sunlight. By choosing a small subject, and placing it quite close to the background wall, fall off of illumination was avoided. The photographer used a small flashgun off-camera, positioning it well back and left of the subject.

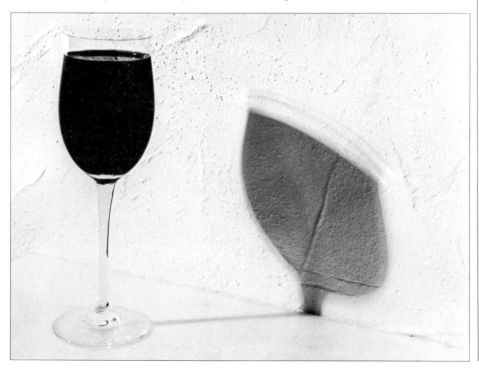

Advanced flash techniques

Many of the principles and practical problems of using flash are the same as for continuous light sources. It is important to pay the same attention to the quality, direction, and evenness of the light, for example, even though the photographer may not actually see the results with flash illumination until the picture is processed.

Several features are unique to flash. One of these is the tradition of mounting a flashgun on the camera, pointing directly at the subject. This is a great limitation to creative lighting. It is convenient to carry a flash unit around in this way, but a photographer would not always choose to have a tungsten lamp mounted next to the lens, or always use the sun directly behind the camera. The result when flash is used in this way is frequently monotonous and regular, with flat, form-destroying frontal light, near objects lighter than distant objects, and backgrounds dark.

Experienced photographers know that, when used imaginatively, even a single flash unit can produce excellent, naturalistic lighting, while several flash heads allow a very flexible approach. Additional advantages include freedom from camera shake (so that the photographer can use a hand-held camera, for flexibility of viewpoint), low operating heat, and a color temperature which matches that of daylight. Most flash equipment is also independent of electricity supplies.

Because of the brief duration of flash light the photographer has to forecast how the final result will appear (unless using studio flash units, which incorporate tungsten modeling lights). It is important to consider contrast, glare spots, the fall of distracting shadows, and unwanted effects such as "red eye". Experience gained setting up tungsten lighting units is invaluable when using flash. Another useful aid is an instant picture camera or back. These are useful for checking the precise visual effect of lighting as well as exposure.

Modern portable flash units are able to approach the flexibility of studio flash lighting, but at considerably less expense. These developments allow the majority of photographers great scope for using imaginative artificial lighting.

See also
Light direction, pp. 16-17. Natural history photography, pp. 300-3. Sports photography *Caving*, p. 309.

Using single units

If you have a single, clip-on flashgun, you can increase its versatility by using an extension cord. You then detach the light source from the camera and position it with the same freedom as you would with a tungsten lamp. To make best use of off-camera flash, practice with a still-life or portrait subject indoors. Set the flashgun on a tripod, so that you can place it at any position, and hand hold the camera. To avoid excessive contrast, place a white reflector board close to the subject's shadow side, in order to reflect a little light back. This will also help produce subject modeling.

Do not place the flash too close to the subject when using it at one side, since lighting will be noticeably uneven. You can base exposure on the flash guide number, always measuring the distance from head to subject. The unit will probably give hard light, like that from a spotlight (see *Tungsten lighting*, p. 164). For soft-edged shadows, place a diffuser in front of the head, or turn the unit to bounce the light off a reflector of white cardboard. Avoid colored surfaces if you are shooting with colored film.

You can use the same technique outdoors, but you will need someone to hold the flash for you. Otherwise, since exposure duration is normally short, you may be able to steady and

fire the camera with one hand only, leaving your other hand free to hold the flashgun some distance from the lens.

Bounce and twin-tube units

Working indoors, you can make use of techniques that involve "bouncing" flash illumination. Use a camera-mounted flash that tilts upward, reflecting light off the ceiling between camera and subject. Do not use too steep an angle, as the subject may be excessively top-lit. (One way to check this is to use a tungsten lamp in the same way.)

Some units overcome this problem by incorporating two flash tubes, a large one for bouncing, and a smaller tube pointing directly at the subject. These flashguns can give more naturalistic light, and being mounted on the camera they form very convenient and flexible units. But problems occur when you move in close toward your subject, or the ceiling is very high or not sufficiently reflective. Unless you can adjust the balance of the two tubes, the fill-in light will become relatively more powerful, and illumination will resemble that from a single flash unit pointed straight at the subject.

Using multihead flash

Mobile, battery-operated multihead flash units can be as flexible as compact tungsten halogen lamps. You can arrange them to light subjects in the same way, although you will have to estimate their exact effect since, unlike tungsten lighting, their illumination is not continuous. An instant picture camera, or back, is a useful aid to judging flash effect.

As with all artificial lighting, it is best to use as few sources as possible, making sure that each one you use is playing a useful role. You might use one head from a high position as the keylight, or sun equivalent. Another head can light the background, while you direct a third into a reflector near the camera, to fill the shadows. You should always place flash heads giving direct light with great care, looking over the top of each unit to check exactly which surfaces it will light, and where the shadows will fall. If you are shooting portraits or action pictures, use a flexible lighting arrangement. Otherwise you will lose much of the freedom of camera and subject positioning that flash provides.

If you bounce flash light it will lose about one-half to two-thirds of its intensity. To avoid excessive contrast you should position the subject nearer to the bounce board than the main light, or use two units to illuminate the

Flash techniques
By changing the method with which you use a flashgun, it is possible to alter the way lighting affects the subject. All these pictures were taken with the camera directly in front of the subject. When the photographer mounted the flash on the hot shoe on top of the camera (right) most of the shadows fell behind the subject, giving a flat image. Using the flash off-camera (far right) produced an image with the shadow clearly visible, behind and to the right of the driftwood. Bounced flash (below) gave stronger modeling. A flash unit with two tubes allowed the photographer to create a fill-in effect (below right), with still better detail in the subject.

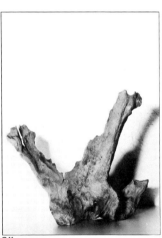

On camera

Off camera

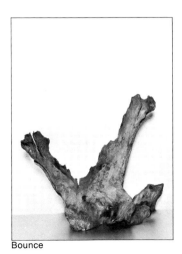

Bounce

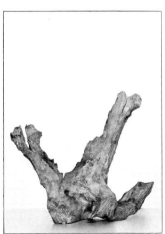

Bounce and fill-in

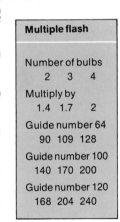

Multiple flash		
Number of bulbs		
2	3	4
Multiply by		
1.4	1.7	2
Guide number 64		
90	109	128
Guide number 100		
140	170	200
Guide number 120		
168	204	240

Using bulb flash
Because flash light falls off with distance, you may have to use more bulbs for increased subject distances (left). A single bulb can give correct exposure over a range of 3¼ ft to 10 ft (1 m to 3 m). Increasing the number of bulbs allows the correct exposure of more distant subjects — four bulbs double flash range. Using more bulbs also alters the guide number (above). The chart shows the factors by which you should multiply flash guide numbers of bulbs grouped together as one light source. Changes for three common guide numbers are shown.

board. Many other variations are possible, including working in conjunction with daylight or with existing interior tungsten illumination. If you use them for interiors where there are domestic lights you can clip orange conversion filters over each flash, and work using film balanced for tungsten light.

Sometimes it is useful to group flash heads together and use them as a single, powerful light source — for example, if filling shadows in a large room when bright daylight is entering through the windows. Using two flash heads in this way, you multiply the guide number for one unit by 1.4. When you group three heads together, multiply the guide number by 2. You can use the same system for flipflash bulb units. You press buttons at the back of the unit to make up to four bulbs fire at once. To provide still more light, attach the camera to a tripod and fire an electronic flashgun repeatedly, completely covering the lens during each flash recharging period.

When calculating exposure only on the basis of flash guide numbers, use the guide number of the main flash alone divided by its distance from the subject. (Units in other positions are either lightening shadows or illuminating subsidiary elements of the subject.) If the main light is bounced, halve its guide number, and measure its distance over the total light path, via the reflective surface. The most accurate way to measure exposure is by using a flash meter (see *Flash meters*, p. 141). Dedicated flash systems, which work through the camera's own through-the-lens (TTL) meter, or via a sensor mounted on the camera top, will also take the complete lighting scheme into consideration, and give correct exposure.

Multihead studio flash units
The great advantage of studio electronic flash units is that they take their power from the regular electricity supply. They can therefore incorporate tungsten modeling lamps, which are only bright enough to show the position of the shadows and the contrast level of the whole scene. They give illumination that is equivalent to flash in everything except intensity and temperature. (With most units, the modeling lamp gives only half its normal output when you switch the power pack to half flash power, so you can judge the effect accurately.) You can fire the flash tubes with or without the modeling lamps switched on — the latter are not bright enough to record on film at normal flash sinchronization speeds. Photographers who require the intensity of studio flash, together with the convenience of a modeling lamp when working on location, power these units with a portable generator.

An additional advantage of studio flash equipment is that often the flash recharges in only half the time required with hand units, so that you can shoot at a faster rate. You can also use studio units in conjunction with battery-operated flash units, provided that the studio units are triggered by light-sensing slave units (see *Flash lighting units*, pp. 165-6). One hand flash linked to the camera can then fire all the studio units simultaneously. This technique is ideal when you are taking pictures in a garden, for example, with a building behind that is also internally lit by flash.

The freezing power of flash
The action-freezing effect of flash varies according to the type of flash source. Flash bulbs offer the slowest duration (approximately 1/80 sec for a typical flash bar bulb). Jumping or running figures will often show some signs of blur, especially if you photograph them close up (see *Controlling the freezing of action*, p. 129). Most studio electronic flash units deliver flashes of a consistent speed of between 1/1000 and 1/5000 sec, according to design. With some units, this time is reduced still further when you switch the power pack to half light output. Flash exposures of this duration will freeze all human movement, together with all normal forms of camera shake. They may not prevent blurred detail in a fast-moving spray of water, for example, if you photograph it close up, exaggerating its movement.

Still greater action-freezing capacity is possible if you use a battery-operated electronic flashgun incorporating a light sensor. Since these units are designed to reduce flash duration as a means of regulating exposure, the closer the subject, the briefer the flash. Using such a unit singly, or in conjunction with other heads, flashes may last 1/5000 sec with distant or dark-toned subjects, or 1/20,000 sec if used close up. The briefest flash time will freeze breaking glass, and fast moving machinery such as an electric fan or parts of an engine. For ultra-high-speed subjects, such as a bullet in flight, special scientific micro flash units are necessary.

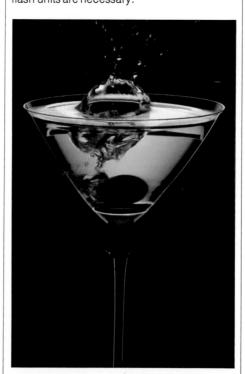

Freezing movement with flash
Trevor Melton took this picture of an olive falling into a glass. He set up the flash lighting using modeling lamps, and tested the result with instant picture film. An assistant then dropped the olive as the photographer pressed the shutter. The flash lighting froze the subject as it was entering the liquid.

Red eye
"Red eye" is a problem unique to flash. It causes a subject's eyes to appear with glowing red pupils instead of the usual black. The fault occurs when a small, hard, direct light source is positioned very close to the camera lens. If the camera is then aimed directly at the subject's face, the light passes through the pupil and illuminates a patch of the pink retina at the back of the eye. This is what the film records. There is a similar effect when an automobile's headlights illuminate the eyes of an animal. You can prevent the problem of red eye by

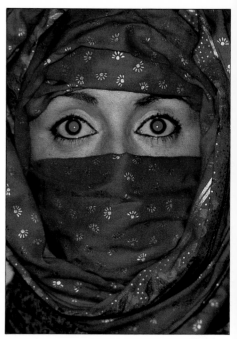

Using red eye for effect
Red eye is normally considered a technical fault, but Trevor Melton has used it here as a special effect. He chose a very small flash gun, of the type normally used on compact cameras. He mounted this on the end of the lens barrel, near the lens hood. This ensured that the lens and flashgun had approximately the same axis, producing the arrangement most likely to illuminate the back of the eyes. Lens and flash were positioned at the same level as the model's eyes. In addition, the photographer chose the red scarf with its gold pattern to pick out the red eyes with their gold highlights, making a unified composition.

using any accessory which places the flashgun a little farther away from the lens. Many compact cameras with built-in flash avoid the problem by having the flash designed to be pulled up before use. The flash units on many 110s are located at the extreme end of the camera for the same reason. For some simple cameras you can buy a flash extender — a plastic tube that raises the flash cube or bar slightly above the camera body. If your combination of camera and flash unit produces red eye, you can offset the effect by diffusing the flash with tissue paper. Bouncing the light off a wall or ceiling, or separating the flashgun from the camera with a bracket and synchronization cord, removes the problem.

Special effects lighting

Photographers usually use artificial light sources either to produce the appearance of natural lighting, or to improve available illumination. But there are sometimes occasions when a theatrical, openly contrived lighting effect is preferable. Light can create spectacular changes in the appearance of a subject, or can itself form the main point of interest in a picture. Used with imagination and control, it can become a highly versatile element, able to turn a commonplace scene into an exciting, expressive image. Shadows, colored light, flare, and light from unexpected directions are all ways of adding to the effect produced by an ordinary subject.

Fashion and advertising photographers often use lighting effects to help create a particular "look", to produce a sense of excitement, or to attract attention. These effects can also save time and money. Front projection, for example, allows the studio photographer to create a variety of abstract or realistic backgrounds.

Scientific lighting applications provide a particularly rich source of techniques. The fluorescent colors induced by ultraviolet lamps give strange, glowing effects. The pendulum movement of a suspended light bulb can trace out formal geometric patterns. Light trails made by hand can produce an effect similar to that of a colored chalk on black cardboard.

Surreal lighting effects are also possible by means of unusual superimpositions. For example, a slide projector can overlay a photographic image on a real, three-dimensional object, or can be used to inject pattern into convenient areas of a subject. Taken in conjunction with high- and low-key lighting schemes, silhouette lighting, and the use of special filters, there is immense scope for experiment.

Working with special lighting effects is also a way of improving photographic technique. Some effects are very simple, while others challenge the photographer to improvise and adapt in order to produce a particular type of result.

See also
Medical and forensic photography *Using ultraviolet,* pp. 286-7; *Using infrared,* p. 288. Editorial and advertising photography *Still life,* pp. 314-15. Dynamism pp. 357-61.

Colored light sources

It is possible to change the colors of particular parts of an object by using a number of light sources filtered in different hues. This effect destroys most of the subject's natural coloring, and if the lighting is directly frontal, most of its form will be suppressed and replaced with flat, colored shape. The change made to the photographic image is often greater and the result more dramatic than the impression gained by the naked eye.

Strongly colored acetate or plastic are effective when placed over spotlights, floodlights, or flash units, especially if you are working with color film balanced for the unfiltered light source. Make sure that your exposure meter will read strong colors accurately, especially red (see *Exposure and its measurement,* pp. 132-8). It is generally best to leave one part of the subject illuminated with unfiltered white light. This will act as a foil to the stronger color effects.

You can light parts of the subject at different distances in contrasting colors, or make one hue gradually merge into another. You can also use filtered light to change the color of a white background area. It is worth experimenting with two differently filtered light sources that overlap on the same surface. Place a patterned shape in one or both of the light paths, so that colored shadows form. For example, green and red lamps overlapped will produce yellow light, but any shape placed in the red beam will turn red and cast a green shadow, while anything in the green beam will have a red shadow.

Instead of using a filter over the light source, you can color your illumination by reflecting white light off a colored surface. The disadvantage of this method over the use of colored filters is that the light direction is less easy to control. But a colored reflector can be very useful to tint part of the subject very slightly. If you illuminate a neutral-toned subject with white light, the result may be cold and stark. You can warm up the lighting by using an orange reflector close to one side.

Coloring the subject
The photographer used a blue-filtered light source to produce this picture of a nude torso. By keeping the lighting directional, the photographer preserved the white background, with only a slight spill of light to produce the colored shadows around the figure. The picture is by Andrew Douglas.

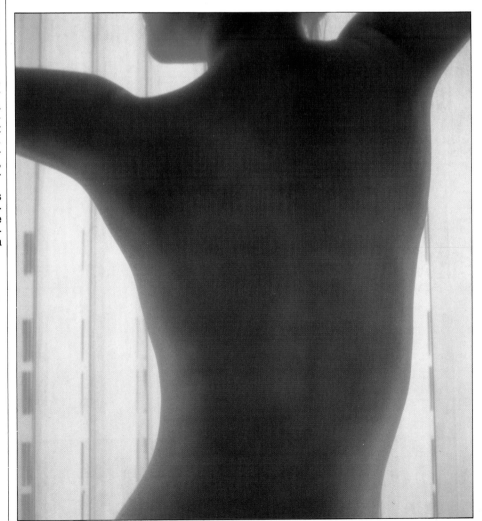

Physiograms

If you include a compact light source in a picture, and move it during exposure it will record as a drawn-out light trail. This effect occurs at night when you use a time exposure to record the lights of moving traffic or fireworks. You can produce similar results by pointing the camera at bright highlights and moving it while the shutter is open (see *Moving camera, static subject,* p. 128).

You can extend this technique by making physiograms — formal geometric patterns consisting of light trails either in a single color or multicolored. A darkened room is necessary, together with a convenient point light source attached to a swinging pendulum. An ordinary domestic flashlight is adequate. Fix it on a long, black cord suspended from the ceiling. It is also possible to work outdoors with the pendulum attached to a balcony or tree. Set the camera on the ground pointing upward. The point of light should appear quite small in the frame, so keep it at the maximum distance from the camera, or use a wide-angle lens. If space is limited, place a mirror (or a flat sheet of reflective foil) on the ground and photograph the light source reflected in this.

It is essential to focus on the stationary light, then stop the lens well down, or use a neutral density filter, so that a time exposure of 10-30 sec is possible. Exposure measurement is largely a matter of trial and error, but if you are using ASA 64 film, 10 sec at f 11 should give good results if you keep the light moving.

Before opening the shutter, start the light swinging in a circle or ellipse. Attaching a second string near the top of the pendulum will allow you to create different patterns by re-directing the light. For colored effects use a series of strong gelatin filters over the lens while the shutter is open. These will also prolong exposure.

Physiograms photographed in this way appear as abstract patterns against a flat, black background. They often work best when shown in some sort of environment, and you can do this by shooting a second, underexposed picture on the same frame of film. An alternative method involves combining the two images by means of sandwiching (see *Sandwiching,* p. 260).

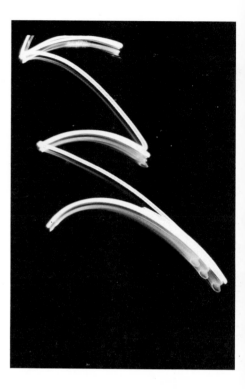

Abstract pattern
Trevor Melton's picture (right) shows how the photographer can create interesting abstract patterns using a moving light source. For this physiogram image he attached a lamp to a cord and set up the camera on a tripod in a darkened studio. He then swung and lowered the lamp during a time exposure, recording the light's path as it moved downward and from side to side. Illumination fall-off, together with dark background paper ensured that the light trail stands out clearly.

Creating light trails

Sometimes you may want to create light trails as blurs and streaks to accompany frozen detail. A studio shot of a dancer, for example, can show a graceful, curved movement blur surrounding a fully detailed figure. You can achieve this type of result by combining flash and a time exposure with tungsten illumination, against a black background.

Position the figure in front of black background paper, and use two tungsten lamps and two flash units, fully shielded from the background and directed from either side to form a band of light. The technique will work best if the figure wears light-colored clothing.

Calculate the aperture required for flash, then measure the exposure time needed with tungsten lamps alone at this aperture. Adjust lamp distances if necessary to arrive at an exposure time of 1-5 sec. Set the camera on a tripod connected to the flashguns. As the dancer starts to perform, you open the shutter, which instantly fires the flash for the frozen image. Hold the shutter open for the time exposure, which records the blur trails. If you want the blur trails to record first, you must fire the flash manually toward the end of the exposure.

Many variants of this technique are possible. For example, you can produce a silhouette

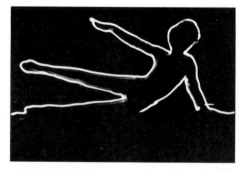

Outlining shapes
Trevor Melton created the outline (above) by moving a small light source around the edge of the subject during a time exposure, keeping it pointed at the camera. With subjects that have simple, interesting, and easily recognizable outlines, this technique is particularly effective. The lamp must move at a constant speed.

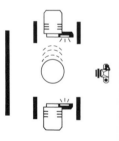

Mixed lighting
A "band" of illumination (above) produced the image (right). Using both flash and tungsten lamps, Trevor Melton made a time exposure to blur subject movement, firing the flash to freeze subject detail.

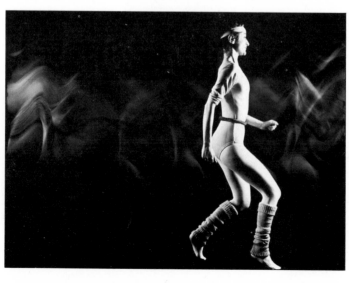

against a background of colored lines. To do this, pose the figure perfectly still and, with the shutter open, move between background and subject with a colored flashlight. You must wear dark clothing so that you do not show up in the final image. Cover a large area with wide sweeping arc movements and cross lines for the best effect.

Other variations with this type of subject include running the flashlight around the outline of the figure, so that a complete tracing in light records on the film. You can also paint the face of the figure with a moving light source, so that you give some detail to an otherwise featureless, dark shape.

Projecting slides on objects

It is possible to project slide images on any static, three-dimensional objects and photograph the results. Nudes, faces, and any objects that offer pale, matte surfaces are all suitable, provided they are not themselves strongly patterned. Undulating surfaces in front of a black background probably offer the best results.

Work in a darkened room with a slide projector supported firmly on a table. Most projection lamps operate at 3200 K, so if you are using color film, choose a type suitable for tungsten light. Instant picture color material will require a bluish balancing filter (see *Using filters,* pp. 158-9). Your camera and subject must be static, since a slow shutter speed will probably be necessary. It is important to avoid confusion between the projected detail and features on the receiving surface — it is easy for one to limit the effect of the other, so that a confused image results. It is worth building up a collection of slides showing simple textures, broad patterns, and bands of color. Sunsets, brickwork, leaves, close-ups of lettering, cracked mud, or jewelry can all work well.

Experiments with form

Positioning the projector close to the camera will suppress the subject's visual form, so that it appears as a flat shape, filled in with the projected detail. If you direct the projector obliquely from one side, the form of the subject will show up in a mixture of slide detail and shadow. It is often helpful to use a heavily snooted light source placed well to the rear on the subject's shadowed side. This will rim-light the edge sufficiently to complete its shape. It is also possible to use two projectors — one from either side — so that the two images merge at the frame center.

You may want your subject to appear filled with projected detail against a white background. If so, place an unlit white object against a pale-toned, well-lit background. You can then project a transparency into the dark shape from the front. Using this method, you can cut an apple in half and fill it with the image of a seated figure; a slide of an office building at night, for example, projected on a white coffee pot, produces a satisfying shape that is full of illuminated windows.

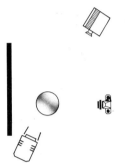

Projection from the side
You can produce interesting effects by placing the projector at the side of the subject (left). A light source positioned toward the back of the subject can illuminate the side that the projected slide does not cover. It is best to use barn doors on the light source. This will help to direct the light more accurately.

Large-scale projection techniques

Projection techniques can be very effective on a larger scale. Shooting at dusk, against the prevailing light, you can project a slide against the white external wall of a house. Even when working with small objects, projection allows you to create spectacular changes in scale. You can cover a basket of eggs with the tiny faces of a crowd, or project the image of a flower on something much larger, such as a white umbrella.

Using a projector
Paul Rozelaar took the picture (right) by projecting a previously photographed slide on the model. This created the bold lines, giving the subject pattern. Strong light from the front helps

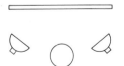

maintain form. The diagram (above) shows how you can light the background while projecting the transparency against an unlit, white object. Make sure the lighting units do not produce hot spots.

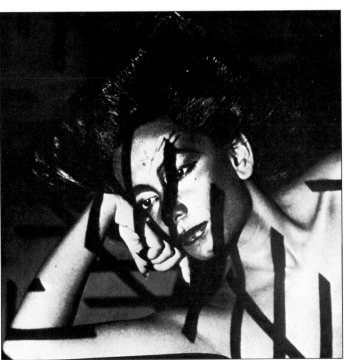

Back projection

Back projection is a convenient method of creating false backgrounds in the studio. Because of limitations of space and screen size it is most effective with still-life subjects and portraits up to half-length. You require a tightly stretched screen of thin, textureless, translucent material, such as tracing paper. (Special plastic versions are also available from the manufacturers of movie screens.) A slide projector located behind this screen forms an image, which you view from the front. Arrange and light the main subject in front of this image.

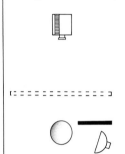

Back projection layout
You must align camera and projector lenses with the center of the translucent screen. The projector must be as far back behind the screen as possible, to give an even picture. (If the image is too dim, give additional exposure with only the projector lit.) Front lighting on the subject must be masked from the screen surface. Reverse the slide for a right-reading image.

If the material of the screen is too dense, the picture will be dim, and may appear unsharp. If the screen is too transparent, it may reveal a glare spot caused by the projector lamp. In either case try moving the projector — farther from the screen to cut glare, nearer to brighten the image — always aligning it with the screen center. Sufficient space is also required between the screen's front surface and the subject, so that you can light the subject without also illuminating the screen.

Matching the images

For naturalistic effects the direction and quality of the lighting in the slide for projection must match the illumination of the studio subject. You can match clouds and landscapes lit by direct sunlight by lighting the items in the studio with a spotlight. Place this high up so it appears to be shining from the same direction as the sun in the background. Keep any reflector boards or fill-in lights you require close to the studio subject, to minimize their effects on the screen. It is also important to establish the correct balance of light intensity between foreground and projected background. You can usually judge this by eye, comparing the midtones and highlights of real and projected detail. You must also examine the perspective of the two elements to make sure they match. If the slide was taken with a long-focus lens, use a similar lens for your studio picture, taking up a camera position well back from the set.

This separate control of background and foreground permits many additional effects. During a time exposure, you can move the projector sideways, or zoom its lens. This will make the studio objects appear to be moving in the final result. It is also easy to create "impossible" scale relationships with this technique, and to project abstract backgrounds.

Front projection

Front projection provides an alternative method of using a transparency to form the background of a composition created in the studio (see *Back projection,* p. 181). It is a more flexible technique than back projection, and requires less space. But it is also more expensive, because you require a special highly reflective screen and a semi-silvered mirror. Instead, you can use a special front projection unit. You still require a flat plastic screen coated with microscopic glass beads, similar to those used on road signs. Such a screen is highly directional – any light that strikes it reflects directly back to its source. If you view the screen from other angles, therefore, it is difficult to see the light at all.

Set up the camera facing the screen, with the lens pointing directly at the screen center. Place the projector next to the camera, so that

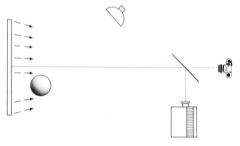

Front projection technique
It is essential to align camera and projector on the same axis (above). The screen must reflect the image along a narrow path back to the camera. Ray Massey used front projection for the surreal image (below). He projected the dramatic red and golden sky on a screen behind the set that forms the foreground. The technique has allowed the photographer to combine effects that would not have existed together in real life.

it forms a right-angle with the camera lens. You must then position the semi-silvered mirror at 45° to the projector, so that it reflects the background image on the screen. It is essential that the camera lens aligns exactly with the image reflected from the mirror. When seen from the camera, the projected transparency will appear evenly and brilliantly illuminated on the beaded screen.

Provided that you align camera and mirror correctly, and that the camera and projector lenses are of the same focal length and equidistant from the mirror, the shadow cast by each studio object on the screen will be exactly covered by the object itself.

Figures or objects that you place between camera and screen will have some of the background image projected over them. But even if they are white, they will only reflect about one-hundredth of the brilliance of the image coming from the screen.

Shooting at the exposure required for the screen image reduces any object in the projector's light path to a dark silhouette. It is therefore necessary to increase the illumination of these dark shapes by lighting them from either side with studio lamps. As with back projection, it is important to make sure that lighting in the studio and on the transparency relate in direction and intensity when you look through the camera. An advantage of the front projection system is that any illumination spilling from the studio lights on to the screen is mostly reflected back toward the lighting units, rather than to the camera.

Most front projection systems are designed for use with studio flash. The projector contains a flash tube and modeling light, and you can use regular studio flash units for the other illumination. A further advantage of special front projection units is that they incorporate a mounting for the camera. This is useful because it guarantees correct alignment.

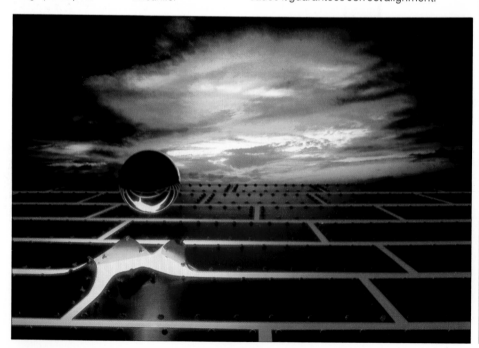

Coloring shadows

You can create unusual effects in otherwise normal images by turning all the shadows into areas of flat color. You do this in the camera by "fogging" an exposed but unprocessed piece of film to light from a colored surface. You must make two exposures. In the first, photograph the subject in quite contrasty lighting. You

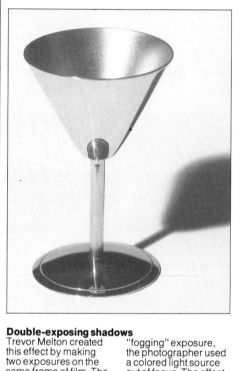

Double-exposing shadows
Trevor Melton created this effect by making two exposures on the same frame of film. The first was lit for a high-contrast effect, giving strong blacks and whites, with few mid-tones. For the second, "fogging" exposure, the photographer used a colored light source out of focus. The effect of this exposure was to tint the shadows, without affecting the white subject areas, which were already burnt out.

should read exposure for the highlights only. It is important to notice where the shadows fall, bearing in mind that it is in these areas that false color will conceal all detail.

Then reset the shutter without winding on the film, and make a second exposure to an even-colored surface. Paintwork, cardboard, blue sky, or any other convenient surface of a suitable hue will be effective. It is best to make the second exposure completely out of focus, in order to diffuse all detail. You should underexpose by half a stop. If you overexpose, the color will begin to affect subject highlights, whereas excessive underexposure will hardly affect even the shadows.

As an extension of this technique, you can make the second exposure to a side-lit textured surface, sharply focused. It is also possible to make the first exposure to an existing image using a copy lighting set up (see *Copying,* p. 171). This also makes it easier to take several versions forming a series of bracketed exposures, and to bracket the fogging exposure.

Using mirrors

If you keep close, careful control over your lighting, a semi-silvered mirror offers a simple way of superimposing images. Place the mirror at 45° to the camera lens. From this position the camera will be able to see one object directly through the mirror and at the same time see a second object reflected in the glass from one side. Both objects must have dark backgrounds. If, for example, you want to combine two faces, use a spotlight to illuminate the left-hand half of one face, and a second spot to light the right-hand half of the other, as seen from the camera. Looking through the camera viewfinder, adjust the positions of the two figures so that the vertical shadow edges running down each face merge into each other, and a new composite "face" is formed. You can adjust the size of each figure by moving it nearer or farther away. Use a small aperture to keep both elements sharp.

Using this technique you can produce a wide range of interesting and even surreal juxtapositions. You can photograph a fish with a tail at each end, or place a flower of one species on a plant of another. You can also fit images inside one another. Working with two sitters, it is possible to experiment by lighting one head frontally, but casting a shadow over the face, so that only the surrounding hair is visible. You can then combine this with the other head lit frontally, but use a snooted spotlight to illuminate the features and not the hair.

Juxtaposition with mirrors
Nic Tompkin's picture shows how it is possible to juxtapose objects using a semi-silvered mirror. Keeping the elements separate has

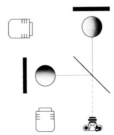

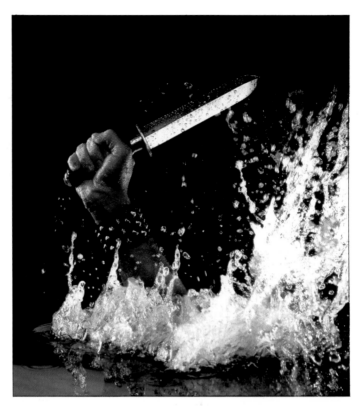

several advantages. First, the hand remained dry, allowing numerous exposures with minimal inconvenience to the model. Second, the technique enabled Tompkin to produce the water effect by dropping an object into the water, thus producing a bigger splash than the hand and dagger would have made moving upward.

Ultraviolet lighting

Ultraviolet lamps, as used for stage and store display lighting, give out little apparent illumination. They radiate weak purple light, but also produce UV wavelengths, which the human eye cannot detect. The main visual effect of UV radiations in darkened surroundings is to make certain materials "fluoresce", or produce visible light. Some objects glow bluish-white, others appear a luminous green or red. Shirts and towels of certain man-made fibers, fluorescent papers, toothpaste, and solutions of powdered chalk all glow strongly.

This effect can turn white garments into magical, self-illuminated forms, leaving the wearer as a dark, almost imperceptible shape. Equally it can make apparently similar natural objects (such as leaves) distinctly different. UV fluorescence is also used in forensic photography (see *Using ultraviolet*, pp. 286-7).

If you want to reproduce these visual effects as seen by the eye, it is essential to place a UV absorbing filter over the lens, and shoot on daylight type film. All films are sensitive to UV radiation, and without this colorless filter your photographs will record a strong overall bluish cast as well as the visible fluorescence. For most subjects it is worth duplicating shots with and without the filter. Generally it is best to work with a filter, adding a little visible light from a regular photographic lamp when you want to relieve the harsh contrast of the fluorescence alone. In this way you will see exactly what the film is going to record. Measure the fluorescent areas normally with an exposure meter, and give additional, bracketed exposures half and one stop more, in case your meter over responds to the ultraviolet.

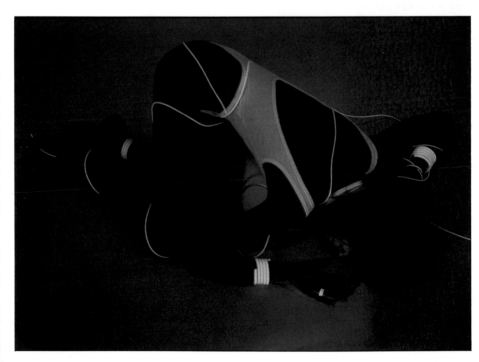

Ultraviolet effect
For the striking result (above), Nic Barlow used an ultraviolet light source to give the unnatural coloring. Regular color film responds to ultraviolet radiation, giving a bluish-white result, but ultraviolet does cause certain substances to fluoresce in bizarre false colors.

Additional equipment

The large range of accessories available is an important reason for the popularity of single lens reflex cameras. There is a particularly wide selection of lenses for SLRs, although rollfilm, large format, and some direct vision models also have interchangeable lenses. The SLR has popularized lens interchangeability for three main reasons. First, the viewing system shows the photographer the subject exactly as rendered by the lens. It is therefore easy to see the changes that occur in angle of view, focus, and depth of field whenever lenses are changed. Second, the lenses are quick to remove and attach to the camera body at any time, even in mid-film. Third, a vast range of focal lengths is available, at wider maximum apertures and cheaper prices than lenses for larger formats.

A choice of lenses gives the photographer the versatility to tackle a wider variety of subjects than would have been possible with a single standard lens. It provides a much greater selection of creative options – in particular, perspective. Lenses of short focal lengths (wide-angle lenses) give a wider angle of view than standard lenses, enabling the photographer to include larger subjects. A wide-angle is a useful choice for confined spaces, such as interiors and narrow streets, and for landscapes where the immediate foreground is also important. A wide-angle lens will include the same amount of a subject as a standard lens from a shorter distance away, with the result that a steeper perspective effect is created.

Long focal length (telephoto) lenses produce the opposite effect. Like telescopes, telephotos are invaluable for filling the frame when it is necessary to be some distance away from the subject. They are therefore often useful in sports and candid photography. Telephotos can also be chosen to include the same amount of the subject as with a standard lens, but seen from farther away, resulting in flattened perspective.

In addition to these lens types, variable focal length ("zoom") lenses are available. These are often more bulky than lenses of fixed focal length, but their prime advantage is that they make it necessary to change lenses much less often. Few zooms yet cover a range of focal lengths from wide-angle to telephoto, but it is possible to cover a good range using two zooms, or even a single zoom and a fixed focal length lens.

The development of glass and lens design

Many of today's lens designs were inconceivable 10 or 15 years ago. Computer technology, information theory, chemistry, and industrial engineering are now important aspects of a task which once involved laborious mathematical calculations and lengthy physical processes. With the aid of a computer, designing the shape and structure of a complex new lens can now take only hours, instead of several years of effort.

Nicéphore Niépce probably used a single, crescent-shaped lens to take the first pictures in the 1820s. This was a converging lens, with a cross-section formed by two arcs of different radii, like simple eyeglasses used for reading. It was necessary to use this lens at a small aperture – typically f 11 – in order to help reduce the major aberrations (image errors) produced by a single lens element. The effect of these aberrations was to produce distortion of shape, imperfections of focus, and color fringing.

Lens designers aim to reduce each image error to a minimum, without making the others worse. Chromatic aberration was one of the most important problems lens designers had to face. When a lens refracts white light, each wavelength is bent by a slightly different amount. In a single lens element the differences in refracton mean that blue light comes to a different position of focus to red, blue being refracted most and red least of the components of light. The amount by which colors are "dispersed" in this way varies according to the type of glass, and is independent of the refractive

Simple meniscus lens

This was probably the type of lens used by Nicéphore Niépce in making the world's first photograph in 1826. They are still used in snapshot cameras today. The convex and concave surfaces reduce spherical aberration and astigmatism.

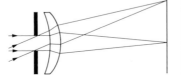

properties of the glass. If the designer balances two lens elements, one in a strongly converging shape in glass of weak dispersing power, the other of weak diverging power but strong dispersing power, most of the dispersing effects are cancelled out. Many other lens aberrations can be corrected by balancing elements in this and similar ways.

By the 1920s, designers had pioneered today's main lens types. Some, like the Zeiss Sonnar f 1.5, had impressive speed. Others, such as the Cooke triplet, overcame the major aberrations using only three elements. But there were other problems of lens manufacture. Lens makers had to use glass with the required characteristics.

Low dispersion and high refractive index (light-bending power) were the main requirements. During the 1930s, with developments in glass manufacture, the approach to lens design changed. Rather than using traditional crown and flint glass types, designers conceived lenses requiring glass with particular characteristics, and then commissioned glass makers to research and produce these materials. Consequently, a range of new materials was introduced into glass manufacture, the most important being rare-earth substances such as lanthanum. Early rare-earth glasses had many im-

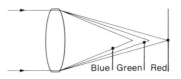

Axial chromatic aberration
This causes light of different wavelengths (and therefore different colors) in the spectrum to be brought to focus at different points. If uncorrected, chromatic aberration will cause "color fringing" in photographs.

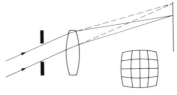

Barrel distortion
The effect of barrel distortion is that light passing through the lens bends away from its true path (broken line), so that the edges of the field form barrel-like curves in the photographic image.

Pincushion distortion
In this form of curvilinear distortion, the position of the f stop causes light to bend away from its true path in the opposite direction. The photographic image then curves inward like a pincushion.

Principal lens aberrations		
Aberration	**Cause**	**Effect**
Astigmatism	Non-symmetrical refraction	Vertical and horizontal subject planes focus at different distances
Spherical	Inability of lens to bring light rays passing through its edge and center into focus	Overall soft focus
Chromatic	Inability of lens to bring all wavelengths of white light to the same point of focus	Multicolored fringe to white objects, particularly in frame corners
Pincushion or barrel distortion	Variation of magnification between center and edges of image	Lines at image edge curve outward (barrel) or inward (pincushion)
Curvature of field	Inability of lens to form a sharp image on one flat plane	Image is sharp at center or at edges, but not both at same focus setting

Such lens aberrations often occur collectively, giving poor image detail, especially toward the edges of the picture.

purities and proved too colored or dark for photographic use. But advances in manufacturing methods solved most of these problems, and today virtually every high-performance lens contains at least one element made of rare-earth glass.

New glass types brought their own problems. In particular, with glass of high refractive index, internal reflections from the surface of each lens element were high. Until this major difficulty was overcome with modern lens coatings, designers had to use a limited

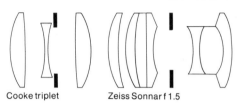

Cooke triplet   Zeiss Sonnar f 1.5

Multielement lenses
Two revolutionary lens systems that greatly influenced subsequent lens design were the three-element Cooke triplet of 1893, and the very fast Zeiss Sonnar f 1.5 of the 1920s.

number of elements, attaching several together with transparent cement to minimize the number of air-to-glass surfaces. Such lenses were expensive to manufacture and assemble.

Another important and recent development has been the production of aspherical lens elements. Traditionally, glass was always ground and polished using a rotary mechanical movement that leaves a surface contour forming part of a sphere. But a lens designer must be able to specify whatever shape is required. It was necessary to devise special manufacturing techniques before aspherical shapes could become practicable. Since the 1960s these have contributed greatly to the design of many lenses with extreme maximum and minimum apertures.

The next step is likely to be "gradient index" glass, in which the refractive power of an element will be weaker at the edges than at the center. Like aspherical surfaces, this will lead to optics of higher quality, with fewer elements, and therefore lighter and more compact camera lenses.

Lens design and user requirements
As well as these general requirements of quality and compactness, the lens designer has to know the limits of subject distance over which each particular lens must give uniformly high standards of image quality. The farther limit is set at infinity, while the nearer limit can be fixed by limiting the forward movement of the lens. Attaching extension rings or bellows between lens and camera body for extreme close-ups is one way of decreasing this limitation. But often standard lenses with large maximum apertures (f 1.4 or less) give disappointing results when used in this way, since corrections already are stretched to their limits to provide the fastest possible speed. On the other hand, macro lenses are designed to give even performance from infinity to a few inches, although to achieve this performance, the lens may have to operate at one to two stops smaller maximum aperture than a standard lens.

The popularity of the SLR camera has made it important to devise a range of focal lengths that will work with the hinged mirror viewing system. This has meant producing short focal length lenses of retrofocus design to accommodate the mirror's movement, and long lenses that are not too large and front-heavy for the camera body. These features do not have the same importance for sheet film cameras because of its different viewing system.

Camera systems
Today's cameras are complemented by a vast range of lenses, but in order to take full advantage of the flexibility of modern camera and lens designs, a number of other items are necessary. Most manufacturers therefore make their cameras part of an extensive system of photographic equipment, comprising a comprehensive array of items. Such systems offer facilities for specialized work, as well as accessories that make general photography much easier. In the former category there are bellows, extension tubes, and lens reversing rings for close-up work, copying equipment, motor drives, and special effects filters. Viewing aids (interchangeable hoods and focusing screens), and certain filters are useful in a wider range of applications. In addition, independent manufac-

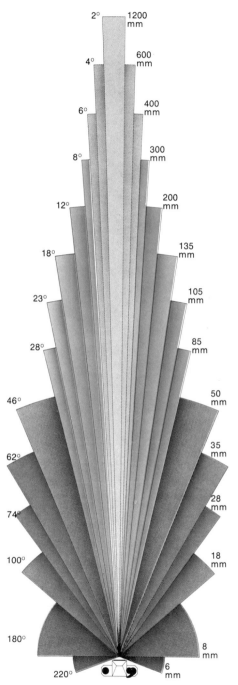

400-1200 mm
Useful when the inaccessibility of a subject precludes the use of a lens with lower magnifying powers. Size and weight, risk of camera shake, a small maximum aperture, and limited depth of field are restricting factors to their use.

85-300 mm
These lenses are portable, relatively light, and have sufficiently wide maximum apertures to permit handholding with fast shutter speeds in favorable light. The longer the focal length, the shallower the depth of field, and the more pronounced the compression of perspective becomes. Such properties can be used creatively.

50 mm
Regarded as the "normal" or "standard" lens for the 35 mm format. The image size in the viewfinder is roughly equal to the eye's view of the scene. These lenses offer the widest maximum apertures.

18-35 mm
Wide-angle lenses have a large depth of field. They are ideal for use in confined spaces or when close contact with the subject is needed. The shorter the focal length, the more distortion toward the edge of the field is marked.

6-8 mm
"Fisheye" lenses have a far wider angle of view than the human eye. Horizontal and vertical lines, except in the center of the view, are dramatically distorted. Their creative use is, however, very limited.

Focal length and angle of view
From ultra-telephoto lenses capable of bringing distant subjects into close-up, to the 180° (or greater) panorama of a fisheye lens, the diagram above shows how angle of view narrows as focal length increases. Depth of field also reduces with an increase in focal length, and apparent perspective is altered. All of the focal lengths and angles of view above relate to the 35 mm format.

turers supply essential items such as tripods. Although no one is likely to use all the lenses or accessories in a particular camera system, the vast majority of photographers, particularly those in the professional sphere, find the range of options and the adaptability of a modern system invaluable.

Wide-angle lenses

A wide-angle lens has a relatively short focal length for the size of the picture format it fills. Wide-angles for 35 mm cameras range in focal length from 45 mm to 13 mm. (Fisheye types are shorter still.) While an extensive range of wide-angles is available for this format, there are far fewer for 6 × 6 cm cameras (where wide-angles have focal lengths from 65 mm to 38 mm) and for the 5 × 4 ins (12.5 × 10 cm) format (with 90 mm to 65 mm focal lengths).

Lens features
All these lenses have a broad angle of view, bringing in peripheral rays from the subject that are not included in the field of view of a standard lens. The immediate effect of changing to a wide-angle lens, therefore, is that more of the subject appears on the focusing screen, with everything made slightly smaller. Foreground detail is increased, and this part of the image becomes much more important and dominant. Wide-angle lenses are useful for architectural subjects, especially in enclosed areas, or for any subject where dramatic angles and a steeper-than-normal perspective are necessary.

Another feature of this type of lens is its generous depth of field. Sometimes this makes the lens difficult to focus, due to the problems of seeing which part of the subject is most sharp. Using a wide-angle also means that quite small changes in viewpoint make appreciable differences in picture structure and content. The shorter the focal length, the greater the angle of view, and the more extreme these characteristics.

Design considerations
Angles of view wider than about 85° (given by a 24 mm lens on a 35 mm camera) produce an image radically different from that experienced by the human eye. Shapes near the corners and edges of the frame seem unnaturally stretched and distorted. This is very noticeable with sheet film cameras, where the lens is placed closer to the film center, and projects the image very obliquely into the corners, so that shapes become further elongated.

Even at angles of view of 110° (with a 15 mm lens on a 35 mm camera) modern lens designs can preserve vertical and horizontal lines in the subject as normal and straight in the image. This "rectilinear projection" may require up to 14 lens elements to maintain. Some manufacturers therefore prefer to discard regular optics at such short focal lengths, and produce a fisheye lens, which gives curvilinear perspective.

The most useful, general-purpose wide-angles for 35 mm cameras have focal lengths between 35 mm and 24 mm. These are the most popular choices, and are priced competitively, though cost rises steeply for f 2 and wider maximum apertures. Lenses shorter than 24 mm produce distortions that make them useful for special effects.

See also
Architectural and landscape photography, pp. 309-13.
The documentary approach, pp. 347-57.

Technical features
The range of wide-angle lenses for 35 mm SLR cameras (excluding fisheye types) extends from 45 mm to 13 mm. Lenses of between 45 mm and 35 mm are barely wide-angle — in fact many compact cameras and some SLRs use a 40 mm lens as standard. If you find that a 50 mm lens often has too narrow an angle of view for your compositions, a 40 mm or 35 mm lens could be a good alternative. But you must not come too close to portrait subjects, or distortion will become a problem. Such a lens also allows greater magnification with extension tubes (see *Equipment for close-up*, pp. 195-6), without appreciable loss of image quality. It is even possible to attach a × 2 tele-converter to make a useful 85 mm portrait lens (see *Technical features*, pp. 189-90). However, these

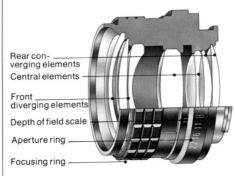

Rear converging elements
Central elements
Front diverging elements
Depth of field scale
Aperture ring
Focusing ring

28 mm lens
In this typical wide-angle lens (above), the retrofocus or inverted telephoto arrangement of elements makes the focal length shorter than the actual distance needed between film plane and rear element. This type of design makes for a compact, easy-to-handle lens.

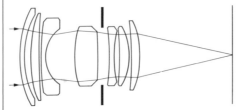

Wide-angle effects
Each of the pictures of the sports car was taken from the same camera position with a wide-angle lens of different focal length. As focal length decreases, the image perspective departs from normal. At 24 mm the nearest parts of the car look unnaturally large, while the farthest details seem too small. The 15 mm lens gives a much greater distortion effect. Although it is not a fisheye lens, the strong "pull" it exerts on oblique surfaces such as the floor means that it must be used with care.

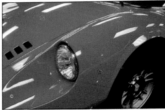

35 mm

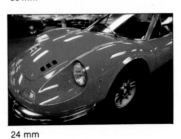

24 mm

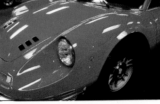

28 mm

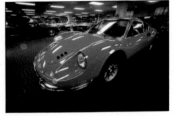

15 mm

shorter focal lengths are more expensive than standard lenses, and for the same cost as a 35 mm f 2.8 lens you could buy instead a faster 50 mm f 1.8.

General-purpose wide-angles
A lens between 30 mm and 21 mm is the best choice if you require only one wide-angle. Due to high demand and competitive prices, a focal length of 28 mm can give good value. Maximum apertures of f 2.8 are common throughout the range, but f 2 lenses are available at a higher price. (Typically an f 2, 24 mm lens is four times the price of a 50 mm lens of the same aperture.) A reasonable degree of differential focus is possible with a 30 mm or 28 mm lens even when used at f 5.6 or f 8, and it is still essential to focus carefully.

If you already have a moderately wide-angle lens, such as a 40 mm or a 35 mm, a 21 mm focal length could form a good addition to your system. But all focal lengths shorter than 24 mm betray their wide-angle characteristics quite strongly. You must be prepared to adapt your technique, avoiding recognizable round or oval objects near the frame edges, and generally using foreground material far more. Typical maximum apertures are f 2.8 for lenses down to 24 mm, and f 3.5 for shorter focal lengths. Recently developed optical glasses have allowed spectacular shrinkage in the design of these lenses, making their compactness another advantage.

Wide-angles for special effects
It is best to regard lenses between 21 mm and 13 mm as useful only for special effects work, although, unlike fisheye types, they are designed to give rectilinear projection. (Many manufacturers only offer fisheyes at 18 mm or 16 mm, since regular wide-angles at these focal lengths have only limited appeal.) Depth of field is enormous with these lenses. With a 15 mm lens, for example, sharpness extends from infinity to about 14 ins (35 cm) when you focus for the hyperfocal distance. Typical maximum apertures are f 3.5 for 21 mm lenses, but often only f 5.6 for 15 mm or 13 mm types. Many of these lenses use "floating" groups of

elements (lens components that mechanically change their position in relation to other, fixed components) to maintain constant image quality at different subject distances. This feature adds to cost, so that a 16 mm lens may be up to twice the price of a 21 mm with the same maximum aperture.

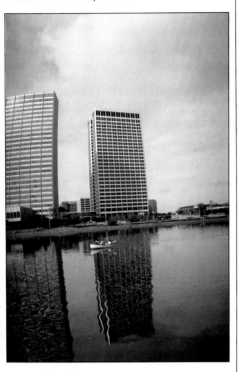

Barrel distortion
John Starr used a low-cost wide-angle lens for the picture of buildings reflected in water. The distortion on the left-hand side is typical of a lens without rectilinear correction. This is a lens aberration known as barrel distortion.

Wide-angle attachments

As an alternative to buying a complete, separate wide-angle lens, you can use an attachment or converter that fits on the front of your standard lens. These attachments contain one or more light-diverging elements. It will convert any model of standard lens to a retrofocus wide-angle type, and it alters neither its aperture or lens-to-film focusing distance. The focusing scale on the standard lens will still be accurate at infinity, but becomes progressively less accurate at other subject distances.

A standard lens plus a wide-angle attachment designed for general use cannot match the quality of a separate, fully corrected wide-angle lens. Even at small apertures you will detect some loss of sharp detail near the picture edges. It is not advisable to use apertures wider than f 5.6.

A typical wide-angle converter will change a 50 mm lens to 30 mm. You can also use it to convert the focal length of a 35 mm lens to 21 mm. The shorter the focal length of the prime lens, the more apparent image distortion will be. Converters that create a fisheye lens effect (see *Technical features*, p. 188) are also available.

Perspective effects

The nearer your viewpoint, the steeper the appearance of linear perspective, and the more dramatic are differences in scale between close and distant objects (see *Viewpoint and linear perspective*, p. 82). A wide-angle lens allows you to work nearer a subject than you can with a standard lens, yet still include the whole scene. Distant objects appear smaller than they do through a standard lens, but close, foreground elements loom large in the frame. Parallel lines photographed obliquely converge steeply into the distance, forming strong lead-in lines, and often adding a dynamic element to the picture.

The wider the angle of view, the more the picture appears unnaturally distorted. This effect would not be obtrusive if you looked at the result close-up, but in practice you usually view prints from an average reading distance of 12-15 ins (30-38 cm). Distortion is quite evident from this distance, and is even more apparent if you hang prints on a wall and view them from still farther away.

Natural perspective is not always a prime requirement in pictures. The wider its angle of view, the more you can use your lens as a device for creating interpretative effects. Shapes can be exaggerated as in the work of Bill Brandt (see *Leading exponents of Structuralism and Abstraction*, pp. 364-8). Important detail in the foreground becomes larger than life, sometimes to the extent of giving deformed or macabre results. The form of a familiar object can be altered, sometimes beyond immediate recognition, and you can make commonplace objects appear new and exciting.

Practical considerations

A wide-angle lens changes your way of looking for subjects. You must become more aware of a scene's nearest elements. Look out for unusual angles, and oblique views of vertical and horizontal lines. Compare lines in your pictures with the unchanging rectangular shape of the focusing screen. The converging verticals formed when you tilt the camera up at tall buildings or similar subjects can create exciting shapes, but very slight convergence often looks irritatingly wrong. For an objective record it is better to avoid tilting the camera. Either move farther away, use a shift lens, or, if you have a sheet film camera, use its camera movements (see *Movements on sheet film cameras*, p. 121).

With a wide-angle lens, all angles in the subject take on an exaggerated appearance. From low viewpoints, people and objects seem to tower above you in a monumental way. Curved roads and pathways sweep dramatically into the distance. Avoid unwanted distortions, especially in portraits. Scenes containing open sky and little foreground detail show least obvious distortion. They can still produce a powerful impression of open space surrounding distant, central elements.

If you use a wide-angle for candid photography, people often think you are much too close to be including them in the picture. Its generous depth of field also helps when you are guessing distances for quick shots, and there is a low risk of camera shake. But be

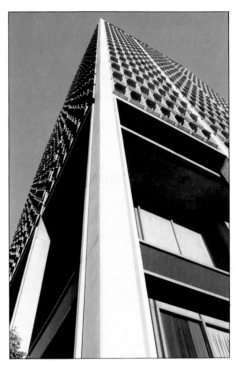

Coverging verticals
Using a close viewpoint with a wide-angle lens, John Starr produced this image of a modern building (above). With a simple architectural subject, converging verticals can provide a good way of creating a more monumental effect, emphasizing the subject's height.

careful when shooting almost into the light – a wide-angle often picks up unwanted flare spots, which may only be clearly visible at the actual working aperture.

Lens hoods and screw-on filters sometimes cause problems. They must suit the lens's wide angle of view. Types intended for standard lenses will cause dark vignettes at the corners of the picture. This will show up mostly when you focus the lens for distant subjects and use a small aperture, so you may not notice the effect when you compose and focus at full aperture. Many extreme wide-angle lenses

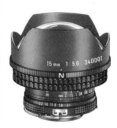

15 mm lens
This extreme wide-angle lens has such a great depth of field that you only need focus at very wide apertures or for close-ups. Because of the shape of the front element, it has to have built-in filters and lens hood.

overcome this difficulty by incorporating built-in hoods and filters.

An additional problem occurs when using flash. A regular flashgun will probably illuminate only the center of the area seen by the lens. You can solve this problem by diffusing the light, or fitting the flash head with an adaptor to give a wider beam of light.

Fisheye lenses

A regular lens produces a circular field of light. A camera normally uses only part of this field – a rectangle of light in the center of the circle that forms the image on the film. To produce the widest possible angle of view it is necessary to use the whole of this circular field, but on a regular wide-angle this poses certain problems. Lens aberrations cause image distortions at the edge of the field, and the image vignettes rapidly into black. In addition, the tube-like shape of the lens limits its angle of view.

One way around the vignetting effect is to incorporate a very large front lens element, which collects light over 180° or more. This also increases the angle of view dramatically. The designer then has to decide how best to present such a vast amount of subject information as an image on the flat plane of film. If maintaining the rectilinear projection of a regular lens is paramount, it becomes necessary to squeeze edge detail wildly out of shape. An alternative solution is to make detail progressively smaller toward the edges of the circle producing an effect like a convex mirror. This automatically makes straight lines appear curved (unless they pass through the precise center of the image).

The result is an unnatural, but very dramatic image, featuring a form of curvilinear image geometry known to lens designers as "equidistant" projection. This means that image magnification varies across the picture according to its distance from the center. Objects which are in reality flat and square-on to the camera bulge out of the frame. Scenes which in actuality "wrap around" the camera on all sides seem almost flat. Close objects near the picture edge are warped into curved shapes.

Circular-image and full-frame fisheyes

With some fisheyes, the camera does not use the whole of the circular field of light produced. A 16 mm fisheye for a 35 mm camera, for example, can deliver an image which fills the rectangular 24 mm × 36 mm format and gives a 170° angle of view. An 8 mm fisheye, on the other hand, gives a circular image, 24 mm in diameter, in the frame center. This covers an angle of view of 180°. 6 mm fisheyes also give a circular image, but have a dramatic 220° angle of view. For 6 × 6 cm format cameras, one 30 mm fisheye gives a 180° angle of view. No fisheyes are made for sheet film cameras.

Fisheye lenses were originally designed for special industrial applications such as photographing the interiors of pipes and other constricted environments. Their use has spread to record photography, and also into fashion and advertising work. They are useful in areas where an eyecatching interpretative approach is required.

Technical features

The 35 mm format fisheyes of 16 mm or 17 mm focal length give a full-frame image, and have a maximum aperture of f 2.8 or f 3.5. They are smaller or similar in size to regular wide-angle lenses of the same focal length, but because they have fewer image corrections, they are less costly. The cheapest types often give rather poor image quality.

Circular-image fisheyes are available in focal lengths from 6 mm to 8 mm, with maximum apertures between f 2.8 and f 5.6. The smaller aperture types are fixed focus, due to their enormous depth of field. Some 6 mm types, in spite of their retrofocus construction, protrude well into the camera body. You must therefore lock up the SLR mirror and use a separate fisheye direct vision viewfinder supplied with the lens.

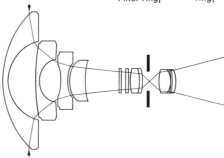

Central elements
Rear elements
Front elements
Focusing ring
Filter ring
Aperture ring

It is possible to focus other wide-aperture fisheyes visually down to about 1 ft (30 cm) using the camera's regular reflex mirror system. These lenses are very expensive and often difficult to obtain. Photographers usually rent rather than purchase them. They are very heavy and bulky and require a sturdy tripod, on to which they are screwed directly.

A camera's regular TTL exposure meter will work with a full-frame fisheye, but a circular image can confuse your meter unless it is strongly center weighted (see *How camera meters work*, pp. 133-4). A separate hand meter may be more accurate. An alternative method is to use the TTL meter with your standard lens before changing to the fisheye. Like other extreme wide-angle lenses, fisheyes will not accept a lens hood or external filters. A set of dial-in color filters is usually contained within the main body of the lens.

Fisheye attachments

As a low-cost alternative to renting or buying a fisheye lens, you can use a fisheye adaptor attached to a regular camera lens. An adaptor that contains several diverging elements will give acceptable image quality when mounted on the front of a standard or moderately wide-angle lens.

This combination can produce results almost as good as a separate fisheye lens, at about one-tenth of the cost. But you must use the smallest lens aperture – f 22 if possible, and f 11 as an absolute maximum. A fisheye attachment fitted to a 50 mm standard lens will give the equivalent angle of view to a 16 mm full-frame fisheye. The same unit used in conjunction with a 28 mm lens forms a circular image, like that produced by an 8 mm fisheye.

An alternative accessory is a "bird's eye" attachment. This contains a convex mirror inside a transparent tube and, when fitted over the camera's prime lens, gives an angle of view of about 200° and a circular image. Its limitations are that the photographer always appears at the center of the image, and image quality is poor compared with that of a separate fisheye lens or even with a conventional supplementary fisheye attachment.

8 mm lens

This fisheye lens (top) has an angle of view of 180°. Fisheyes of even shorter focal length have a yet wider angle of view, such as 220° with a 6 mm lens. The diagram (above) shows the path of light rays through the divergent front element. Convergent rear elements produce the circular image typical of lenses of less than 14 mm focal length. The back focus is greater than the focal length of the lens to allow clearance for the reflex mirror. Dial-in color filters for black and white work as well as ultraviolet or clear filters are common features.

Comparative wide-angles

Wide-angle lenses of this short a focal length are primarily used for special effects. The 16 mm fisheye has an angle of view of 170° but as it fills all of the 35 mm frame, it also has more generalized applications. The 8 mm lens, with its 180° angle of view, is about the shortest focal length you can hand hold. The 6 mm fisheye's angle of view (220°) actually sees slightly behind itself.

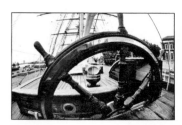

16 mm

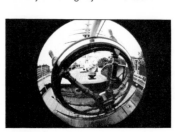

8 mm

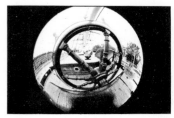

6 mm

Practical considerations

When you look through a fisheye lens, your surroundings seem to shift back in space, and objects within arm's reach appear very distant. Shapes also change. Square rooms seem spherical or flat, and tall buildings curve toward the sky. As you move the lens around, objects seem to change their shapes and proportions according to their position in the picture. Outdoors, the sky fills vast areas of the picture unless you tilt the camera down. This produces a "humpbacked" horizon. Lowering the horizon below the frame center gives it a dished shape. Full-frame fisheyes produce these effects in a less exaggerated form.

The fisheye's extreme depth of field makes it necessary to create emphasis through size and shape, rather than selective focus. One constant problem is excluding irrelevant im-

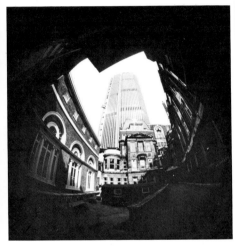

Fisheye for framing

Andrew de Lory used an 8 mm fisheye lens for the picture (above). He took advantage of | the lens' circular image field to frame the modern skyscraper with the older buildings near by.

age content from the wide field of view. You may have to move very close to the main subject, or shoot it through some form of frame. Be sure that you do not accidentally include part of yourself in the picture.

Fisheyes often work well when the main subject is located close to the lens in an otherwise distant, plain scene, such as sky, sea, or sand. For sports pictures it will give impressive "larger than life" effects, provided you can work close enough to the action.

You can use the circular image patch of an extreme fisheye as an integral part of the composition. Pointing the camera vertically upward toward clear sky will reveal a complete circle of horizon detail. Shooting a building from a more conventional, horizontal viewpoint, you can create a symmetrical "bull's eye" effect by framing it carefully within the structure of a wrought iron gate that is situated very close to the camera.

One special hazard of using an extreme fisheye is that it is easy to scratch its large, steeply curved front glass surface. Always protect it with its special concave lens cap when reloading or carrying the camera.

Telephoto lenses

Telephoto lenses have relatively long focal lengths for the size of the picture format they fill. They use an optical system that reduces overall length, and has an effect like a telescope — making the contents of a picture larger than with a standard lens.

With a telephoto lens the photographer can fill the frame even with a distant subject. This is very useful in portraiture, natural history, sports, and candid photography, and for situations where working close-up could disturb or obscure the subject.

Lens features and choice

Telephotos also have more subtle effects on photographic composition. They effectively compress a picture's perspective, just as wide-angle lenses help to expand depth and space.

There is a very wide choice of telephoto lenses. They have been made and improved since the beginning of the century, and modern types have benefited from new glasses, coating, and the use of floating elements. Today some camera manufacturers offer as many as 20 different telephoto lenses for 35 mm SLRs, ranging in focal length from a modest 85 mm to a catadioptric lens of 2000 mm. Some designs at the longer end of the focal length range use mirrors to "fold up" the light path. This allows a shorter, less unwieldy lens barrel.

The widest range of telephotos is available for 35 mm SLR cameras. There is also a reasonable range (from 100 mm to 500 mm) for rollfilm formats. A few are made for sheet film cameras, particularly for baseboard types with bellows too short for use with non-telephoto, long-focus lenses. These seldom have focal lengths longer than 300 mm.

The characteristics of telephotos are the same as for all long focal length lenses. They magnify the image (a 200 mm lens, for example, makes the image of a distant subject four times as large as that given by a 50 mm lens), have very shallow depth of field, and tend to flatten perspective. They also have smaller maximum aperture and slightly lower image contrast than standard lenses, as well as extra bulk and the inability to focus on close subjects. All these features increase with focal length.

Probably the most popular telephoto for 35 mm cameras is the 135 mm. This is a compact lens that is easy to handle and yet provides significant image magnification. High demand for this focal length means that many lenses are made, and cost is relatively low. However there are also some popular telephoto zoom lenses, which compete strongly. Extreme long-focus lenses rise dramatically in price.

See also
Depth and distance *Aerial perspective*, pp. 82-3.
Sports photography *Equipment and techniques*, p. 304

Technical features

Compared with lenses of shorter focal lengths, telephotos are easy to focus accurately. Their shallow depth of field makes it obvious when and where the subject is sharp. (This characteristic also means that you have much less latitude for error when focusing by means of the distance scale on the lens barrel.) It is also important to focus carefully when using infrared film, obeying the special focusing mark on the lens (see *Special black and white films*, p. 157). In sports and candid photography you must practice focusing, to maintain the sharpness of moving subjects while keeping the camera steady enough to avoid image blur.

The focusing movement on most long lenses will not render close objects sharply. The closest marked focusing distance on 135 mm lenses is usually approximately 4 ft (1.2 m). This becomes about 18 ft (5.5 m) on a 600 mm lens, which limits studio use. It is possible to improve these distances by adding extension tubes with most designs (see *Equipment for close-up*, pp. 195-6), but image quality generally suffers as a result.

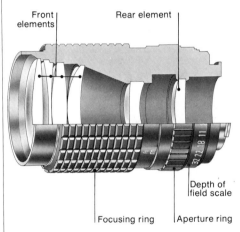

135 mm lens

This is probably the most popular of all telephoto lenses. A typical optical system (below) causes light rays passing through the front (converging) group of elements to be influenced by slightly | divergent rear lens elements. This telephoto arrangement gives the optical effect of a lens positioned much farther from the film, but allows the design to be more compact.

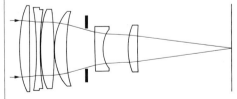

The long focal length of telephotos greatly increases the risk of camera shake, (see *Camera shake*, p. 130), and this, together with the weight and length of lenses over 500 mm, makes them very difficult to handle. A tripod is essential. Lighter, shorter mirror lenses help overcome this difficulty.

Telephotos tend to pick up scattered ultraviolet and blue light wavelengths which lower the contrast and give excessively "cold" images. For landscape work it is therefore best to use a UV or haze filter. Always avoid using poor-quality filters, since they will easily spoil image quality. Many special effects filters (see *Special effects attachments,* pp. 198-200) fail to function as intended when used on telephotos of extreme focal length.

Choice of focal length
Most photographers regard the 85 mm as the shortest useful telephoto. It enables you to work at a comfortable distance for portraiture in most rooms and studios. Lenses are available with maximum apertures of f 1.4 and f 2, giving adequate speed for a wide range of situations. 85 mm lenses are also suitable for use with extension tubes, bringing closest focussing distance down to about 12 ins (30 cm).

The most popular choice for photographers who want to work with a single long focus lens is a 135 mm telephoto, working at f 2.8 or f 3.5. Like the 28 mm wide-angle, its focal length is not so extreme that its influence on image structure is obvious and overwhelming. If you

eventually aim to have two telephotos, a 100 mm or 105 mm lens may be a better first choice, in order to form a useful step between a 50 mm standard lens and a 200 mm telephoto. 100 mm lenses cost about as much as 135 mm types, and are more compact.

A 200 mm lens has a much more dramatic magnifying effect on the image. You will require about 15 ft (4.5 m) to take even a head-and-shoulders portrait. Minimum focusing distance is about 6 ft (2 m) and maximum aperture about f 4, or (at twice the price) f 2.8. Many photographers regard this lens as the most useful for covering spectator sports, especially if lighting is unpredictable.

If you already have a 135 mm lens, a 300 mm could be a good choice for an additional telephoto, although the restrictions of very long lenses start to become evident at this focal length. The lens will have a maximum aperture of f 4.5 or f 5.6, and minimum focusing distance of about 13 ft (4 m). The weight and bulk of a lens of this length make a tripod vital for shutter speeds slower than 1/500 or 1/250 sec. You should use the tripod thread on the

lens barrel. A 300 mm telephoto shows the subject six times larger than with a 50 mm lens, making it a good choice for sport and natural history work, and as an effects lens for landscapes. But perspective compression is obvious in every shot, and it is difficult to track fast-moving sports such as tennis and baseball.

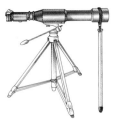

Additional support
With very long, heavy lenses you may need, in addition to a sturdy tripod, the extra support of a monopod, as here, or a second tripod under the front of the lens. This will stop the lens placing undue strain on the lens mount.

The cost of a 300 mm lens is between two and four times that of a 135 mm lens.

Telephoto lenses of around 500 mm are the longest in general use. Wildlife and some sports photographers find them most useful. Differential focus is severe at even small apertures, though this can be an asset when photographing through wire netting or foliage, which disappear in blur. But these lenses are heavy, and maximum apertures small. With still longer lenses, these characteristics are further exaggerated and they are so expensive, and so limited in their application, that it is best to rent them. Handling problems have led to the adoption of lightweight mirror optics (see *Catadioptric lenses,* facing page).

Tele-converters
A tele-converter consists of a tube containing a divergent lens system. You fit it between the camera body and a standard or telephoto lens, and it produces an increase in focal length. A good tele-converter doubles your range of

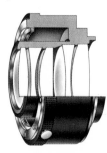

Tele-converter
Attaching a tele-converter behind the normal camera lens will increase its focal length, usually by a factor of × 2. You must open the aperture and/or reduce shutter speed to compensate for light loss. With automatic tele-converters, the camera's meter will allow for this.

long focal length lenses, at relatively low cost. Tele-converters do not only affect focal length. By fitting a × 2 converter, for example, you double the focal length of the lens, increase the f number by a factor of two, and reduce depth of field to one-half. At the same time, however, focusing distances, including the nearest distance, remain unchanged.

The best tele-converters are designed for particular lenses. Others usually give some loss of sharpness, particularly at the picture corners. To achieve the best results, you must match a good converter with a lens of equal quality, since the converter will magnify aberrations the lens may have. It is often preferable to buy a good telephoto and a converter, than two telephotos of average quality.

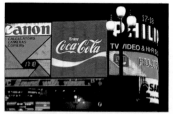

85 mm

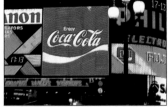

105 mm

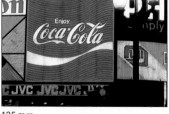

135 mm

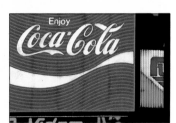

200 mm

Telephoto effects
The group of images of neon signs shows the effects possible with the range of telephoto lenses available in a comprehensive camera system. At the shorter focal lengths, between 85 mm and 135 mm, there is a slight narrowing of the angle of view. The subject begins to look distinctly bigger and apparently closer. The medium telephotos, from 200 mm to 400 mm, continue this process. (With photographs that include objects at different distances, these lenses also compress perspective dramatically.) The longest telephoto lenses (from 600 mm to 1200 mm) exaggerate these effects so much that only a minute area of the subject is visible — in this case only an abstract pattern of colored lines. Few photographers use every lens in the range. Most make a selection of short and medium telephotos, renting the longest lenses.

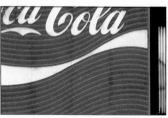

300 mm

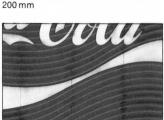

400 mm

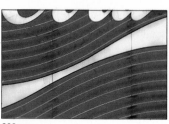

600 mm

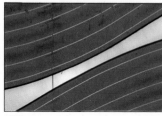

1200 mm

Catadioptric lenses

One way to reduce the bulk and weight of extreme telephotos is to "fold up" the optics, by means of a design that uses curved mirrors as well as lens elements. Light is converged by a mixture of reflection ("catoptric") and refraction ("dioptric") effects, so these lenses are generally known as catadioptric lenses. You can always identify a mirror lens by its drumlike shape, and the opaque central area of the front element, marking the position of one of two mirrors.

Advantages

The mirror system of a catadioptric lens enables the lens designer to accommodate an extreme telephoto focal length within a comparatively short barrel. The distance from the back of the lens to the film can be only about

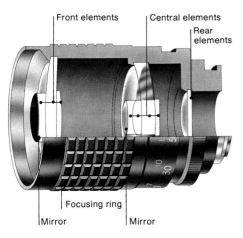

Front elements   Central elements

Rear elements

Focusing ring

Mirror   Mirror

one-tenth of the focal length. A typical 500 mm mirror lens is about 5.5 ins (14 cm) in length, and weighs about one-half of an equivalent focal length lens using regular optics. Their lightness and compactness help create better camera balance, and you can comfortably hand hold lenses up to 500 mm. Mirror lenses are also cheaper since image forming by reflection completely eliminates aberrations that occur due to dispersion, making fewer correcting elements necessary. Additional advantages of mirror optics are that closest focusing distances are much shorter, and that infrared focusing coincides with normal light settings.

Disadvantages

The main disadvantage of mirror lenses is that the aperture is unchangeable. It is impossible

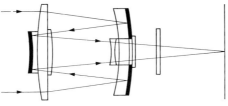

500 mm catadioptric lens
The catadioptric system allows you to have a powerful telephoto lens without it being so long and bulky that it becomes unwieldy. In such lenses, light passing through a weak glass lens (above) is reflected by a mirror behind the central elements on to a second mirror, built into the front element. From this, light is reflected back so that it finally converges on the film plane.

to fit a variable diaphragm to this type of lens, because it causes vignetting. Most mirror lenses therefore have a fixed aperture of f 8 or f 11, and you have no control over depth of field. You can regulate light intensity by selecting from a series of neutral density filters built into the back of the lens. (You can also insert color filters in this position.) Otherwise you

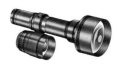

Size comparison
Compared with a normal telephoto, an equivalent mirror lens is compact and far lighter.

must control exposure entirely by means of shutter settings.

Another characteristic of this lens type that may cause problems is that out-of-focus highlights take on a ring-like appearance. This is due to the construction of the front of the lens, and is especially noticeable in pictures featuring glittering water or direct sunlight. The more out of focus detail is, the larger and more overlapping these rings become. Sharply focused highlights are unaffected. This effect can be obtrusive, and you can only avoid it by choosing a plain background or foreground to make the main subject stand out.

Since mirror lenses cannot adequately cover a field of view greater than about 12°, mirror designs are only useful for lenses of 200 mm or over for 35 mm cameras. They are available in focal lengths up to 2000 mm. The longest focal lengths are extremely costly, and useful mainly to the specialist, but some cheaper versions are available that give good image quality.

Telephotos for rollfilm formats

A more modest range of telephotos is available for rollfilm cameras. Because of the difficulty in manufacturing a lens to cover the larger format, and the much more limited demand, these lenses are more costly than their 35 mm counterparts. Lenses for cameras without focal plane shutters usually have small maximum apertures, owing to the space required in each lens to accommodate a bladed shutter. Maximum apertures are usually 1-1½ stops smaller than those of 35 mm lenses.

The most popular telephoto for general long-focus work and portraiture is the 150 mm. A few are available with a maximum aperture of f 2.8. If you choose a longer focal length, you have to make a sacrifice of speed. 200 mm lenses work at f 4 or f 5.6. Lenses of 250 mm and above are large and very heavy, and the range is small. The longest available is a 500 mm f 8 lens, which you can turn into a 1000 mm type with a tele-converter. A 500 mm lens serves a similar sports and wildlife function to a 300 mm lens on a 35 mm camera. Minimum focusing distance is about 28 ft (8.5 m). No mirror lenses are manufactured for use with rollfilm cameras.

You cannot use 35 mm format lenses on medium-format cameras, but you can use a step-down adaptor to fit an 80 mm standard lens for a 6 × 6 cm camera on a 35 mm camera, to give a short telephoto, ideal for portrait work.

Perspective effects

A telephoto lens fills your picture with what would be only part of the image produced by the camera's standard lens. The resulting perspective appears unnatural. Depth is compressed, and objects at various distances seem to be "stacked-up" closely behind each other, although in reality they may be much farther away. The longer the focal length, the greater this compression becomes, just as it does when you look through a telescope.

The reason for this effect is that all the objects in the frame are some distance away, but the lens presents them to the eye as if they were very close. If they were truly close they would differ in scale. The nearest items would appear larger than similar-sized objects behind them, and this is a familiar situation for which the brain has learned to make adjustment. When all the objects you are viewing are distant, however, scale differences are barely noticeable (see *Depth and distance,* pp. 80-5) and our brain senses something structurally unusual. As with wide-angle pictures, a great deal depends on the distance from which you view the final result. Seen from across a room, a telephoto picture appears to have a more realistic perspective than if you held a print at a normal reading distance.

The compression of perspective created by long focal length combined with a distant camera position is often used creatively by

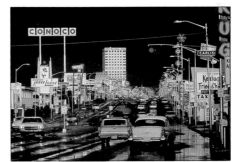

Using the telephoto
To produce the cluttered, vibrant effect of a large city street (above) Ernst Haas used a telephoto lens.

The compression of perspective makes the street seem even more crowded with signs, lights, and vehicles.

photographers. Franco Fontana and André Kertész, for example, often use long lenses to suppress the form of a scene and present it as simple, flat pattern. This can give landscapes an almost abstract appearance, and transforms the scene as viewed by the eye. The foreground will be lost, and the lens pulls the far distance close behind mid-distance objects, greatly compressing normal perspective. Oblique views of surfaces and parallel lines show minimal convergence, and this can give results a static, detached appearance.

Practical considerations

When you change from a standard to a telephoto lens, you have to look at your distant surroundings in order to start selecting potential pictures, while generally ignoring the immediate environment. A moderate telephoto enables you to fill the frame with a face without noticeable distortion. As you will have to adopt a camera position several feet away, the nose and ears of your subject will be relatively similar distances from you, and so will appear undistorted by scale difference (see *Depth through scale change,* pp. 84-5). Results are more flattering to the subject than those taken from a closer viewpoint with a standard lens or a wide-angle.

If you want to photograph a tall building with parallel sides from ground level, use a telephoto to minimize the unattractive effect of converging verticals. You can do this by moving farther away, and so keeping a more horizontal line of sight.

A telephoto is invaluable for picking out details in all types of subject, and is also useful for candid shots, since people will be too far away to notice that you are photographing them. In all cases, the principle applies that when you move farther back to fill the frame with a long telephoto, you reduce the sense of depth in the picture. You can preview this by viewing the scene through an empty slide mount held at the appropriate distance from your eye. For example, holding it at arm's length will give a field of view approximately equivalent to that of a 600 mm lens.

Depth and local emphasis

The telephoto's shallow depth of field is a useful aid to pictorial emphasis. With a standard lens, even at maximum aperture, it is impossible to emphasize distant objects by means of differential focus, because the whole of the background area will appear sharp. But a telephoto enables you to pick out even distant objects from their surroundings. You can

separate a single leaf from a tree full of foliage, or one figure from a crowd. It is also possible to imply depth from the color and tone changes visible in objects at different distances (see *Aerial perspective,* pp. 82-3). This is especially effective in telephoto landscapes, where the lens can make elements that are widely distant (such as hills and valleys) appear closely juxtaposed. Landscapes are also a rich source of tones and colors. Contrast is generally reduced under such conditions, because of the amount of atmospheric haze between the lens and subject.

Variety of functions

In clearer atmospheric conditions, a telephoto lens will help you form patterns from oblique rows of buildings, groups of people, or traffic. Telephoto shots looking down along crowded streets can also suggest a sense of claustrophobia. Sunsets are also rewarding subjects when you are using this type of lens. The sun can be shown as a large red disk of light, positioned close to horizon detail which will seem small and insignificant by comparison. The same foreshortening effect can make a large, distant factory overwhelm a small building some way in front of it.

Whenever using a telephoto, you should expect to do far more walking in order to find the best camera position than you would with a standard or wide-angle lens. Quite considerable changes in camera position are necessary in order to give small differences in the alignment of distant objects.

Mirror lens result

Andrew de Lory took this silhouette with a 500 mm catadioptric lens. In the background, out of focus highlights form rings of light. When using a mirror lens it is best to avoid subjects with brilliant unsharp highlights, except for special effects. Smaller, repetitive foreground shapes can also produce confusing results with this lens type.

Zoom lenses

Zooms (variable focal length lenses) are undoubtedly the camera optics of the future, but at present they are still undergoing development. It is only during the past five years that zoom lenses have begun to compete seriously with fixed focal length lenses in terms of range, image quality, cost, and size.

Zoom lens design dates from the 1930s when they were introduced to meet the demands of the motion picture industry and, later, television. Zooming a lens is a quicker, more convenient alternative to moving camera position (although not giving the same realism of perspective change). It allows the camera user to change rapidly from half-length to close-up without wasting any time or losing the spontaneity of a particular situation.

Although zooms quickly became common for 8 mm movie cameras, there is a massive difference between covering a tiny format to the low optical standard acceptable for moving pictures and filling a much larger still picture format, which will be judged against the quality produced by fixed focal length lenses.

Design challenge

The requirements faced by the lens designer are formidable. A zoom should offer the widest possible variation in focal length (zoom range) but must not alter in the subject focusing or the f number set. At the same time, any alteration to focal length really requires a different optical line-up in order to correct any resulting aberrations. This calls for several groups of "floating" elements – lens components that mechanically shift their positions in relation to other, fixed components as focal length adjustments are made.

Lens construction

Today's 35 mm SLR zoom lenses use between 10 and 20 glass elements, shifting apart or closing together at different rates and directions along tracks worked out by computers. The construction of some zoom lenses offers the benefit of both telephoto and inverted telephoto principles. Zoom range and image quality have improved greatly, while the cost and size of these lenses have decreased. A modern 35-70 mm (1:2 zoom range) lens can be little larger than a standard 50 mm lens, although heavier because of the extra glass.

Zooms were originally limited to long focal lengths, but they are now made to cover a mid range either side of standard for the 35 mm format, and some manufacturers provide a wide-angle range. A few zoom designs are made for other format SLRs such as 110 and 6 x 6 cm.

See also
Sports photography *Equipment and techniques,* p. 304.
Dynamism, pp. 357-61.

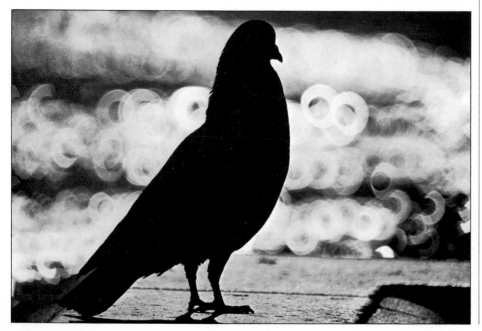

Technical features

The main advantages of a zoom lens are its convenience and flexibility. With a zoom, you also have available a continuous range of focal lengths between the longest and shortest extremes of the particular lens, rather than the stepped and abrupt changes associated with changing fixed focal length lenses. The difference in price between zooms and conventional lenses is becoming less as the production of zooms increases.

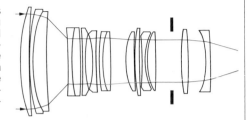

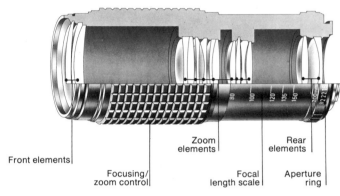

Front elements

Focusing/ zoom control

Zoom elements

Focal length scale

Rear elements

Aperture ring

80-200 mm zoom lens
This short-to-medium telephoto zoom has far more complicated optics than a lens of fixed focal length. It has elements arranged so that their position in relation to one another can be changed from retrofocus to telephoto layout, thus altering focal length. These movements are co-ordinated so the image, once focused, remains sharp at all focal lengths.

Features that still argue against zooms are their image quality and maximum aperture. Image quality does not match that of a good fixed focal length lens when you use the zoom at its widest aperture and shortest focal length setting. Also, zooms tend to have a maximum aperture at least one stop slower than conventional lenses within their range.

Choice of zoom range

You must consider the convenience of a zoom in relation to other lenses you may own. For example, a 35-70 mm zoom can provide a "one-lens outfit", but against this you may pay twice the price of a 50 mm lens, for something that is half the speed and twice the weight. A better solution might be to use a longer focus tele-zoom, plus a conventional 50 mm lens (for its speed and quality), and to complete your lens range eventually add a wide-angle zoom. Bear in mind that the greater the zoom range the longer the barrel — for example, a lens with a zoom range of 1:6 may be twice the length and three times the weight of a more modest 1:3 zoom.

Zoom lens applications

A 24-35 mm or 28-50 mm zoom is very versatile for interiors and applications such as newspaper work (see *Press photography,* p. 325), where you must work close in to the subject and there is usually little time to change lenses. Zooms that span either side of standard focal length include short-range types such as the 35-70 mm, which is physically the shortest length zoom.

Of the large range of tele-zooms, there is greatest choice among focal lengths around 80-200 mm. These offer the best image quality of all zoom lenses — mainly because they remain within the short telephoto range, and they have none of the design problems associated with a lens that spans both telephoto and inverted telephoto. With a zoom of this type, the shortest end of the range makes a good

portrait lens, while the other end of the range can be used by the non-specialist photographer for natural history and sport. Typical closest focusing distance is about 5 ft (1.5 m). Most of these lenses, and others of longer focal length, have a "one-touch" sliding zoom control instead of a separate ring.

Mid- and long-range zooms

Further up the scale there are several quite slow f 5.6 zooms of 100-200 mm, and others working from 100 mm up to 300 mm or 500

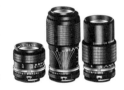

The zoom's flexibility
This 80-200 mm zoom (center) does the work of the 85 and 200 mm lenses on either side of it, as well as giving you continuous intermediate settings.

mm. Those in the range 200-600 mm or 360-1200 mm represent the present extremes of long focal length. Like other extreme telephotos, these are specialist lenses intended for use with tripods. They operate at apertures no wider than f 8 or f 11 and with a closest focusing distance of about 13 ft (4 m).

Macro mode

A number of tele-zooms offer very limited close focusing, but also have a so-called "macro" setting. To use this mode you have to push the focusing ring through a click stop setting — this shifts the position of some internal components into a more favorable configuration to correct aberrations at close subject distances. You can then rotate the focus ring farther, often to subject distances as close as 1.5 ft (46 cm). Potential problems are minimized by the presence of a mechanical connection between the zoom control and the macro mode switch, so that you can only use the macro facility when the lens is set at its shortest focal length.

Lens performance

The performance of zoom lenses varies dramatically. Most do not approach the quality of a fixed focal length telephoto or wide-angle lens. Few, if any, match the performance of a first class standard lens.

You should always examine the image produced by a zoom at its longest, shortest, and mid settings, at widest aperture. You can do this by observing the image on the camera's focusing screen or, better still, by taking a series of test exposures. Compare the results against those obtained from a standard lens in terms of corner sharpness, contrast, and flare. Distortion is shown by straight lines near the frame edges appearing curved. They are usually concave when the lens is set for one end of its focal length range, and convex at the other, and they appear straight at about the mid-range setting.

Slight corner vignetting and lack of sharpness is a sign of insufficient covering power, mostly at the widest angle of view. Contrast is always lower than with a conventional lens.

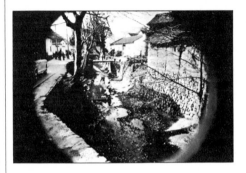

Lens hood vignette
For the picture above the photographer used a zoom lens with a lens hood that was too narrow. At longer focal length settings, the hood was satisfactory, but at shorter settings it appears in the frame as a black vignette. The effect is most noticeable, as here, at small apertures. The correct hood must suit the lens at its shortest focal length setting.

Because of the number of glass surfaces in a complex 15-17 element zoom lens, flare patches can prove to be a problem, especially if you are shooting into the sun. In extreme cases, flare will cause a string of patches across the frame. An efficient lens hood should minimize this effect. To be completely effective, the lens hood should automatically extend as you increase focal length. In practice, however, you can only use a hood suitable for the widest angle offered by the zoom, which leaves the lens relatively unshaded at other settings. A hood suitable for the longest end of the zoom range would cause black vignettes as you zoomed back.

A few older style zooms are really only "varifocal" types. With these you must refocus each time you change focal length. Some of the poorest modern zooms still tend not to hold precise focus throughout the whole range.

Practical considerations

The zoom's great advantage is the tight, precise framing it allows when you cannot move much closer or farther away from the subject. For example, at a sports event, you may find that one fixed focal length lens is too long and does not allow you to include all of the activity, while your next shortest lens renders figures too small and insignificant. The same principle applies to architectural detail picked out from street level, or natural history subjects photographed from a hide. If you mainly shoot on slide material, this framing flexibility is particularly useful as the film is difficult to crop and mask for projection.

For critically structured pictures you must first pick your viewpoint distance to make the best possible visual use of perspective and juxtaposition. Then adjust the zoom so that the required lines and shapes constructively relate to the edges of the frame (see *Moving in close,* p. 62).

With some zooms, however, you may notice some slight degree of line curvature at the shorter focal lengths. Take care when placing critical lines such as the horizon or the straight sides of buildings near the top or sides of the frame, as it is here that distortion is most obvious. Zooms, though, are ideally suited to fast-changing situations such as candids and action pictures. Instead of constantly changing camera position (often influencing the subject by your presence) you can hold your ground and zoom in if the action is far away, or zoom out if it moves closer. To do this quickly you must be able to alter focus and zoom at the

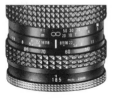 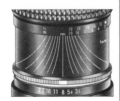

Zoom controls
"One-touch" zooms (right) have a broad ring which you rotate to focus the lens and pull in or out to change focal length. Some designs

have two rings (left). You use one ring to focus the lens and one to control the zoom. This type is not as convenient to use.

same time. Here, the design of the lens itself can be helpful. A lens with a trombone-type sliding control for zooming focal length, which, at the same time, you can rotate to focus the lens, is the easiest sort to use. This double-function, one-touch control is found on most modern zooms.

Whenever possible, focus a zoom lens at the longest focal length setting where depth of field is shallowest, then zoom back to your required image size. If you work the other way round, a slight focusing inaccuracy (covered by depth of field at shorter focal lengths) may produce a very obviously unsharp image at longer focal lengths. Reading exposure with a TTL meter is also more accurate with the lens set to its maximum focal length, because it is then possible to cut out large, unimportant areas, such as featureless skies, for example, and take more selective readings from the most important parts of the subject.

Zooming effects

When zooming, everything moves outward or inward from the center – the detail near the picture's edges shifting sideways more than any other part. If you zoom when the shutter is open, therefore, you record a streaky effect radiating from the center. Results vary depending on shutter speed, direction of zoom, the type of subject, and the background. It is best to use a slow film, small aperture, and, if necessary, a neutral density filter (see *Neutral density filters*, p. 201), aiming for an exposure of at least 1/8 sec. You must operate the zoom control smoothly. Start zooming and fire the shutter during the movement. Try to match your rate of zoom to the shutter speed, making a slower change the longer the exposure. The subject itself can be either stationary or moving. Bear in mind that all lines radiate from the center, giving a strong lead-in effect to whatever is positioned there. Later you can crop the image – enlarge the required portion – to produce an off-center point of emphasis.

Further possibilities
For a mixture of hard detail and movement,

you can open the shutter with the lens focal length static and then zoom for the last part of the exposure only. Other possibilities include zooming and panning a moving subject at the same time. At night, try tilting and zooming illuminated signs and point light sources. All these pictures have a strong "hit-or-miss" element, particularly since you cannot see through the viewfinder while the shutter is open. It is always best to take several versions, varying your technique slightly each time.

Focal length series
Another effect possible with a zoom lens is a sequence of separate exposures "stepped" at different focal length settings, all on one frame of film. This is strongest with a well-defined subject shape against a dark background, and a tripod is essential. Use a camera that allows you to retension the shutter without automatically winding on the film. As a rough exposure guide, take a normal meter reading, divide the recommended exposure time by the number of exposures you propose to make, and set the shutter to this speed.

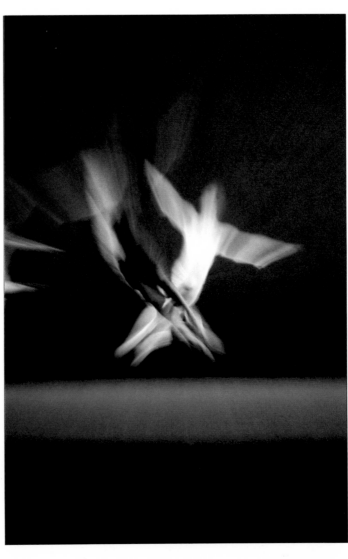

Zooming and movement
In this picture of dancers, John Starr has turned daunting technical problems to good effect. Light levels on stage were very low, so subject blur was almost inevitable. Instead of waiting for a momentary lull for his shot, Starr deliberately chose a slow shutter speed of 1/2 sec and then zoomed the lens during the exposure, catching the performers in full flight. Zooming combined with subject movement has emphasized the agility and grace of the performers, giving their bodies an almost abstract, bird-like appearance. The color distortion evident is the result of uprated film and stage lighting. The localized nature of the light has thrown the background into total shadow, providing a perfect frame for the main point of interest. Effects of this kind are always unpredictable.

Close-up equipment

Most standard lenses have a minimum focusing distance of about 18 ins (45 cm). This is adequate for most situations, but to produce true close-up pictures, with life-size (or larger) images of the subject, the camera must move in much nearer. Working very close can reveal with great clarity the patterns, textures, and colors of ordinary objects. It is also possible to photograph things that are too small for the naked eye to see clearly, either for aesthetic reasons, or to provide a technical record. Some of the most rewarding work involves producing images slightly larger than life size. This branch of photography is generally known as macrophotography.

The single lens reflex is the ideal camera for close-up and macrophotography because of its accuracy in framing and focusing. Most methods of focusing on close subjects use some device to move the lens forward, farther away from the film. The photographer can either select a macro lens, which has its own extensive focusing thread, and is specially designed for working close-up, or use a standard lens with some form of attachment. In all cases, exposure measurement with the camera's TTL meter remains possible.

Close-up attachments
There are four main types of attachment for close-up and macrophotography. The simplest of these is a reversing ring that allows the photographer to turn the standard lens back-to-front, spacing it farther from the film. This gives better image quality, but does not provide any facility for varying the lens-to-film distance. Extension tubes are more flexible. They are available as sets of tubes, of varying lengths, which the photographer fits between camera body and standard lens. An extending bellows unit, placed in the same position, is more versatile still. It provides greater spacing between lens and film, as well as continuous adjustment of this distance. It is possible to use a bellows unit with a standard lens, but combining it with a macro lens will give even greater image magnification. Whichever lens is employed, a bellows unit is the most useful accessory for close-up work.

An alternative method of achieving close-up results is to use a supplementary element placed over the standard lens like a filter. This effectively alters the lens's focal length, producing close-up pictures without spacing the lens farther from the film. This method is therefore suitable for cameras that do not have interchangeable lenses. Sheet film cameras do not normally require special attachments for close focusing, since it is possible to extend their bellows sufficiently, or even to add extra lengths of bellows to monorail types.

See also
Scientific and technical photography *Enlarging small subjects,* p. 277. Natural history photography, pp. 300-3.

Image magnification

There are two ways of expressing image magnification in macrophotography. The reproduction ratio shows the relationship between the subject's dimensions and its size when recorded on film. For example, if you photograph a leaf 70 mm long so that it is 10 mm long in the frame, the reproduction ratio will be 1:7. Magnification (image size divided by object size) is × 0.14. In fact, this rate of magnification is typical of a 50 mm lens, when set for its closest focusing distance.

A life-size image has a reproduction ratio of 1:1 (or a magnification of × 1). A piece of the. leaf 24 mm × 36 mm will then fill up the entire 35 mm format. Working even closer will give an image larger than life size. At a magnification of × 3 (reproduction ratio 3:1) a mark on the leaf 5 mm long would be magnified to 15 mm in length in the image.

The simplest method of testing the limits of your close-up equipment is to take a picture of a ruler and then measure the result on the film. If you use a large format camera, you will be able to measure the image directly on the camera's focusing screen.

Magnification greater than about × 20 will require specialist microscope equipment. Work at this scale, and larger still, is generally referred to as photomicrography (see *Photomicrography,* pp. 278-9).

Equipment for close-up

Although you can use your standard lens for close-up work, the best quality and largest magnifications are only possible with a specially designed macro lens. There are two types, the more commonly used focusing lenses, and the high-quality, more specialized "true" macros used with bellows.

Macro lenses
Among focusing macro lenses, the most common focal lengths are 50 mm and 55 mm, but, unlike standard lenses of the same length, the aberrations have optimum corrections for a subject distance of about 18 ins (45 cm). Maximum aperture is usually about f 4, so that the lens gives good definition when focused for much closer subject distances. Even when focused at infinity, image quality is almost as good as with a normal standard lens.

In order to function efficiently over short subject distances, the focusing mechanism of a macro lens must provide for smooth adjustment of the lens-to-film distance between 50 mm and 75 mm or 100 mm. (At 75 mm, the lens will give half life-size, and at 100 mm life-size, images.) The mechanism that is responsible for this extension normally housed in the deeply recessed hood that is a characteristic feature of macro lenses.

A macro lens is about twice the price of a much faster standard lens of the same focal length. The small maximum aperture is rarely a disadvantage since, when working at such close distances, depth of field is very small. You are much more likely to want to stop down to small apertures, and macros often feature f 32 to maximize depth of field.

This type of macro lens is ideal for extreme close-ups of insects and plants, record photography of small objects such as jewelry, copies of documents, and details of fabrics. Their fully corrected flat field makes them useful for making high-quality copies of postage stamps and color transparencies. A tripod is usually essential, owing to the shallow depth of field and the fact that it is often necessary to use slow shutter speeds.

True macro lenses
"True" macro lenses are mechanically simple, but offer even better image resolution ideal for the highest quality close-up work. Each lens is corrected for a particular subject distance and contains no focusing mechanism – you must use a bellows attachment. These lenses do not have automatic diaphragms, so you must stop them down manually after focusing. The longest focal lengths produce magnifications as great as × 20.

Scientific photographers and natural history specialists use sets of true macros in the same way that they would use groups of microscope objectives. Although true macros produce results of exceptionally high quality, most photographers prefer the convenience of a regular, focusable macro lens.

Supplementary close-up lenses
Using a weak converging element that fits over the standard lens is a simple way to produce close-up results. This presents light from relatively close objects as if coming from infinity. You can still use the focusing ring on the prime lens, though the distance scale is no longer accurate. Quite close focusing is possible: a +4 diopter lens can be used for focusing sub-

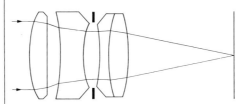

Front element
Central element
Rear elements
Aperture ring
Focusing ring

55 mm macro lens
The optics of a macro lens are designed to give you optimum performance at close focusing distances. The elements are corrected to give equally good definition at both the center and edges of the field under these circumstances. Many models have a minimum aperture of f 32, and you can take advantage of this to gain the maximum depth of field – often crucial in extreme close-ups.

jects as close as about 6 ins (15 cm). Supplementary lenses come in a range of focal lengths. Most manufacturers calibrate them in diopters, a rating calculated by dividing 1 meter by the lens's focal length. A lens rated +1 has a focal length of 1 m, while a 25 cm lens is rated +4. This system is helpful when combining supplementaries, since using two +1 diopter lenses together gives the same focal length as one +2 lens.

The main advantages of supplementaries are their low cost and the fact that they have no effect on exposure. On an SLR camera they do not interfere with the automatic diaphragm. The longer the focal length of the prime lens, the greater the supplementary's magnification. It is best to work with the main lens stopped down, to improve the shallow depth of field.

Reversing ring

For magnifications greater than × 1, your standard lens must be closer to the subject than it is to the film. You can obtain better image quality by reversing the lens, since the elements of

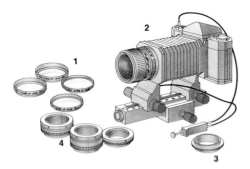

Close-up attachments
Close-up lenses **1**, auto bellows **2**, reversing rings **3**, and extension tubes **4** give different degrees of magnification and image quality. Bellows come out best on both counts, but cannot be easily hand held.

most lenses are recessed farther into the barrel at the front than at the back. To reverse the lens, you screw a thin adaptor ring into the filter thread at the front of the lens and attach this to the camera body. For closer work still, you can fit a supplementary lens or extension tube between lens and reversing ring.

It is possible to reverse all lenses in this way. The effect on magnification depends on the design of the lens barrel. A typical reversed 50 mm standard lens will focus a subject 5 ins (12.5 cm) away, giving × 0.7 magnification.

Reversing rings are cheap, but have several disadvantages. In most cases neither the lens focusing movement nor the aperture-meter coupling will operate. In addition, the rear lens elements facing outward are vulnerable to damage, and the aperture scale can be difficult to read upside down.

Extension tubes

Extension tubes, which you attach between the camera body and the lens, increase the lens-to-film distance, so that you can focus on closer subjects. Even a single tube offers a range of subject distances, because you can still use the focusing mechanism on the lens itself. Tubes usually come in sets of three, each of a different length. By using them individually or in various combinations, up to seven different extensions are possible. In addition, some extension tubes are variable in length. When you use the lens focusing movement as well, subject distances of 4-16 ins (10-40 cm) are possible.

Manual extension tubes do not couple the lens diaphragm to the camera body. More costly automatic types contain a contact, enabling you to use the lens wide open for viewing and metering in the usual way.

Extension tubes make the total image dimmer than normal because of the increased lens-to-film distance, (see *Compensating exposure* p. 197) but a TTL meter will take this fully into account. Because the tubes do not

contain lens elements, overall definition is not affected. But resolution at the edges may suffer slightly, and it is best to stop well down, or reverse the lens, to improve results.

Bellows

Expanding bellows are much more versatile than extension tubes, since they make possible continuous adjustment of the lens-to-film distance. A typical bellows unit, attached to an SLR camera body, gives magnifications of up to × 4 with a 50 mm lens. Minimum extension is seldom less than $1\frac{1}{4}$ ins (30 mm), so the unit will prevent you photographing moderately close subjects if you only have a standard 50 mm lens. A macro lens used alone will help bridge this gap. You can buy bellows units up to about 18 ins (450 mm) in length. Such a unit, when used in conjunction with a short-focus "true" macro lens, will provide impressive magnifications up to × 20.

Regular manual bellows units do not allow linkage of the lens diaphragm to the camera body. Automatic bellows units overcome this problem by means of a linked pair of cable releases. One release connects to the lens panel and stops down the lens to its preset aperture immediately before the other fires the shutter. But you must still make meter readings at the working aperture. Automatic bellows units are expensive: they cost three to four times as much as manual types.

Bellows units are designed for use on a tripod or stand. The shallow depth of field and light loss caused at extreme extensions, in addition to their bulk, make them very difficult to use hand held. Often the design of the tripod attachment clamp makes it possible to shift the whole unit back or forward, as an aid to fine focusing. Some types also provide camera movements, allowing the front panel to swing or tilt (see *Movements on sheet film cameras*, p. 121). This gives your camera some of the facilities of a large-format type for adjusting image perspective and depth of field.

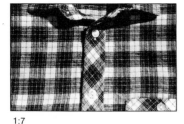

1:7

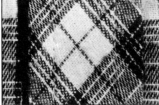

1:1

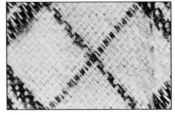

2:1

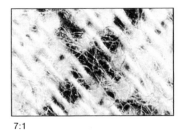

7:1

Close-up range
This chart compares the differing degrees of magnification and lens-to-subject distances at which you can obtain sharp images with the attachments in a typical 35 mm system: 50 mm standard lens, 55 mm macro lens, 2.5 and 4 diopter close-up lenses, extension tubes in various lengths and combinations, and a 208 mm bellows unit.

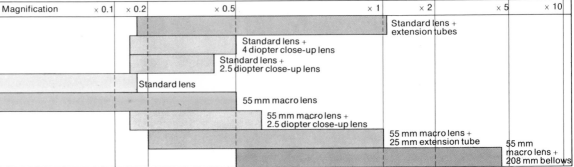

Magnification	× 0.1	× 0.2	× 0.5	× 1	× 2	× 5	× 10

Standard lens + extension tubes

Standard lens + 4 diopter close-up lens

Standard lens + 2.5 diopter close-up lens

Standard lens

55 mm macro lens

55 mm macro lens + 2.5 diopter close-up lens

55 mm macro lens + 25 mm extension tube

55 mm macro lens + 208 mm bellows

Technical aids

Certain specialized items of equipment make macrophotography quicker and simpler. The major difficulty when you are using a direct vision camera is ensuring accuracy of focusing and framing. Fitting the camera with a spacing bracket enables you to determine the correct distance between camera and subject when using a particular close-up lens. The bracket terminates in an L-shaped frame that shows how much of the subject will be recorded without itself appearing in the picture area. With this type of aid you need not even look through the camera viewfinder. You simply bring the frame up to the subject, and compose it by eye within the L-shape.

A four-legged stand holds the camera pointing downward over a flat copy original. The stand's telescopic legs are calibrated with

Vertical copy stand
The camera, with a lens suitable for close-ups, looks downward through the central boss of the copy stand. By lighting equally from opposite sides you can produce evenly lit, distortion-free copies of flat originals. If your subject has a reflective surface, use a polarizing filter or shoot through a hole in black card to cut out glare or reflections.

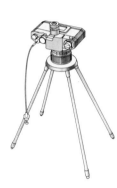

the correct extension for a range of close-up lenses. A device that fulfils a similar function for small subjects is a close-up lens attached to a conical clear plastic base. Placed on a table, it supports the camera at the right height, centers it on the subject, and allows the freedom to use lighting from any direction.

Copying attachments
If you copy color slides and similar objects at life size, you can buy a tube that attaches to an SLR body. It holds the slide, in front of a light-diffusing plastic screen, at one end. The tube also contains a lens (or a supplementary element for the camera's own lens) accurately distanced to produce a life-size image. In ad-

Copying slides
Use a slide copier in conjunction with a bellows and close-up attachment or macro lens. The whole unit is pointed toward any convenient source of daylight, flash or tungsten lighting.

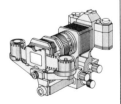

dition, slide copying attachments are available for most bellows units. The majority enable you to vary slide-to-lens distance, to enlarge a particular section of the image.

If you do a lot of slide copying, a special slide copying unit with its own built-in electronic flash is ideal. This is particularly useful for special effects copying work, as well as for making straight duplications. The adjustable light source allows you to use color correction and exposure compensation.

Close-up picture making

In close-up photography it is important to use a camera that allows you to watch the precise image the lens is forming. Depth of field is dramatically shallow and focusing may be difficult. You should start by racking the lens forward or backward to give the approximate image size, then move the whole camera toward or away from the subject until the image is sharp. To simplify depth of field, pick a viewpoint fairly "flat-on" to the surfaces you want to record. Examine the image carefully at the aperture you want to use – strong lighting helps here. Shade or remove distracting unsharp objects. Sometimes shallow depth of field is helpful – you can show detail over a small area, but suggest overall shape with a softer, more generalized shape.

Lighting to reveal form
Pay particular attention to the lighting's quality and direction in revealing form. You can use reflectors to soften shadows or a mirror to redirect sunlight. Indoors, quite small close light sources will be adequate.

With macro work, avoid movement of camera or subject. Tiny movements are magnified by the same factor as the image itself. A clamp or tripod is essential, unless you are using electronic flash.

It is also important to control the color and tone of your background. Use sheets of cardboard in different tones and hues to place under or behind your subject.

Natural structures often prove more rewarding subjects than man-made items. Rocks and stones, vegetables and small flowers, tree bark and thorns are all good subjects.

Equipment choice
When selecting the best equipment to use, it is helpful to know the size of your subject, so that you can calculate the magnification required to fill the frame. For example, an object about 7×4 cm will require $\times 0.5$ magnification to fill the 24 mm $\times 36$ mm film frame. You can then use any close-up attachment that will produce this magnification.

A macro lens is without doubt best in terms of image quality, and it will produce its best results

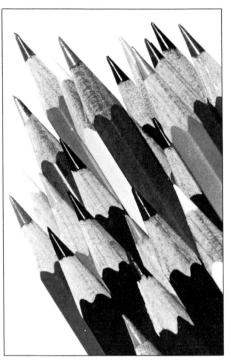

Macro effect
For this picture of pencils, Ian McKinnell used a 55 mm macro lens on a 35 mm camera. This brought out the detail of the wooden sharpened ends, revealing texture and detail where it is not normally noticeable.

at magnifications greater than $\times 1$ if reversed. A short focal length lens will give greater magnification than one with a longer focal length, given the same length of extension tube or bellows. But a long lens will allow greater space between lens and subject. This can be very useful if you want to avoid shadows cast on the subject by your equipment.

It is best to avoid using zooms, or fixed focal length lenses over 200 mm, unless they have a macro mode. Similarly, image quality deteriorates if you use lenses shorter than 28 mm on bellows or extension tubes.

Compensating exposure

When using a camera without TTL metering, some extra exposure calculation may be necessary. This does not apply when you use a supplementary lens, since this will not alter the position of the prime lens in relation to the film. But with sheet film cameras or SLRs with bellows attachments, you can rack the lens to twice or more its normal distance from the film for close subject focusing. This has an effect similar to moving a projector away from a screen in a darkened room – the image becomes progressively dimmer. A similar problem is posed by hand meters, flash meters, and electronic flashguns (unless controlled by the camera meter). All these items work as if the camera lens is at or near its focal length from the film. To determine the factor by which you must increase exposure, divide the square of the lens-to-image distance by the square of the lens's focal length.

Useful calculations

Photographers using sheet film cameras often employ a number of simple optical formulae to calculate exposure compensation and image size. Reproduction ratio relates directly to the ratio of distances between subject and lens, and from lens to image.

Alternative calculations for exposure increase are based on the size of the image on the focusing screen. If the picture on the screen is half the height of the subject (magnification $\times 0.5$), you add one, making 1.5, and square the result, giving 2.25. This is the factor by which you multiply exposure time.

These calculations are accurate with large-format cameras, but are not to be relied on when using the lenses designed for modern 35 mm types. But if you are using a camera without TTL metering, they will be accurate enough for use as the basis of a bracketed series (see *Correct exposure*, p. 133).

Filters and lens attachments

The variety of attachments that will fit on any camera lens includes devices for special effects work and others that help produce more realistic images. Filters are available for both purposes. They absorb light – either reducing certain wavelengths, or lowering the general level of light entering the camera. There is also a number of lens attachments (often incorrectly called "filters") including image-splitting, faceted glass and masking attachments. Most of these are relatively low in cost, and do not require any special technical skills to use.

These lens attachments are primarily intended for SLR and sheet film cameras, which allow the photographer to preview their effect accurately. This is essential for full control of results. Many of the visual effects change according to the rotational or sideways adjustment of the filter, or with the working aperture of the lens, and its focal length. Not all attachments are available in a size large enough for the wide diameter lenses used with sheet film cameras.

Filters for effect

With special effects filters, results vary from a very subtle tinting or darkening of part of the picture, to an extravaganza of colors, streaks, and blurs that swamp the original scene. But these can, if used carefully, turn a commonplace subject into an abstract, expressive image. Many devices stem from attachments home made by photographers to create unusual effects for fashion and editorial illustration. They often produce eye-catching results, but, like false color film and extreme focal length lenses, their effects become tedious if overused. On the other hand, some photographers, such as Francisco Hidalgo, have made extensive and creative use of lens attachments.

It is possible to make attachments out of everyday materials, but a wide range of filters and similar devices in glass, optical resin, or plastic, is widely available.

Filter types

Types such as neutral density filters, polarizers, and single-color filters are generally circular, and screw directly on the front of the lens. Filters that have a local effect on the image, such as dual color and gradated types, are generally supplied in squares, which slip into a special, grooved holder attached to the lens. This holder allows the photographer to shift filters sideways and to rotate them in order to align the effect with any part of the image. It can also simplify the use of the same filter on lenses of different diameters. It is always essential to follow manufacturers' advice regarding the most suitable attachments for particular lenses. Most special effects attachments work best on standard or moderately long lenses.

See also
Architectural and landscape photography *Landscape photography*, pp. 312-13. Romanticism and the dramatic, pp. 373-7.

Polarizing filters

Polarizing filters are generally circular and gray in appearance. They are made of specially stressed plastic, and absorb all light except that vibrating in a single plane (see *Copying*, p. 171). With a polarizing filter you can usually subdue reflections from non-metallic surfaces, such as glass or water, and similarly strengthen the hues of colored objects with shiny surfaces.

Polarizing filters are the only attachments that enable you to darken blue skies in color photographs without altering colors in other parts of the picture. The effect is greatest with clear, deep blue skies with the camera held at

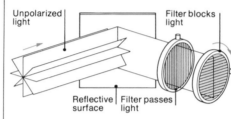

Unpolarized light

Filter blocks light

Reflective surface   Filter passes light

Filter effect
The diagram (above) shows how the polarizing filter blocks polarized light from a reflective surface when you turn it. By doing this, polarizing planes of light and filter are at right-angles. In the example (below left) all the glass planes reflect light. By turning the filter against the planes of polarization of the upper and lower panels, the photographer has suppressed their reflections (below right).

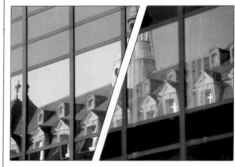

right-angles to the direction of the sunlight. You rotate the filter until the sky darkens to the required tone. The sky will never become completely black, because the filter only removes part of the light. But results can be very dark on clear days and at high altitudes. Most polarizers have a filter factor of approximately ×3, which is equivalent to $1\frac{1}{2}$ stops. You can usually take an accurate TTL meter reading through the filter after rotating it to the most favorable position.

Polarizers are the most expensive filters but they are extremely versatile. You can also use them in conjunction with some special effects attachments. Certain plastics, when positioned between two polarizing filters, appear to have a varying range of colors when you turn one of the polarizers. You can use this combination as a variable color filter. Two polarizers alone, rotated against each other, will operate as a variable neutral density filter without affecting color balance.

Special effects attachments

Lens attachments for special effects range from basic single color filters to elaborate multifaceted attachments for creating multiple images. Both types are available in screw-in form, or as part of a more versatile filter system.

Single and multicolor filters

You can produce striking effects with single color filters. These are available in strong colors, which work best with contrasty scenes, and in a variety of subtler pale colors.

Some filters comprise two or three colors. The colors usually contrast (typically red/blue, orange/green, or yellow/purple), with each half matching the other's density, so that the whole filter has the same factor.

The two-tone color effects are obvious and often garish, but you can create fantasy landscapes with red sky and blue fields, for example, or double-tint lights at night. Even more elaborate effects are possible with a multi-

Single-color filter
The strong red filter (left) stops blue and green light, passing only red. Pale filters are also available, to give a more subtle effect.

faceted attachment, which has a different color on each facet.

The resulting division between colors will vary from an almost sharp line to a gradual mingling of one color into the next. This will largely depend on depth of field – wider apertures give a more gradated effect.

Multicolored filters are difficult to use effectively. But they can heighten the theatrical mood of some scenes, and be effective when combined with a cross-screen attachment.

Gradated filters

Gradated color (and gradated neutral density) filters have a long history. Pieces of glass or sheet gelatin half dipped in pale yellow dye were originally made as "sky filters". They helped counteract the over-sensitivity of early photographic materials to blue, which gave bleached skies. The filter's clear lower half ensured that ground detail did not also darken.

Today, gradated filters are mostly used in color photography to help reduce extreme contrasts of lighting, such as those that occur

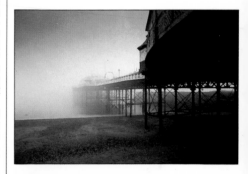

Using gradated filters
Gradated filters can produce subtle effects. To create the picture above John Sims used two filters to form the pink areas at the top and bottom.

between backlit sky and shadowed land detail, or in pictures divided between dark interior and bright exterior detail. They allow you to expose for the dark parts without making the light half "burn out".

With a gray gradated filter you can darken an even, pale sky. Alternatively, you can choose a blue gradated filter that will both darken the sky and restore realistic color. With on-camera flash, you can use a gray filter to shade the foreground parts nearest the camera. It is these areas that tend to overexpose.

Gradated density also means that you can control the transition from filtered to non-filtered areas with the lens itself. Small aperture and a wide-angle lens for example will create the most abrupt transition between filtered and non-filtered areas. This suits pictures with clear, uncluttered horizons. A longer focal length and wider aperture give a more gradual change. With a range of gradated color filters you can easily give a slight tint to a particular part of a picture.

Most gradated filters are square, because you must be able to shift them around the filter holder, as well as rotating them, in order to ensure that they affect the correct part of the image. Using two gradated filters together (one inverted) produces tints that "melt" into each other. In this case, increased exposure is necessary, according to the filter factor shown on the filter mounts.

Center spot attachments
There are two main types of center spot attachment. Regular center spots, or "color circles", consist of a single color filter with a hole in the middle. "Center focus" types comprise a close-up lens with a central hole.

The result with a color circle is a dark or tinted surround, with a central area in which the subject has its normal tones and colors. There is no effect on image sharpness with these types. The longer the focal length of the lens you use, the larger the central patch becomes in relation to the whole frame. Stopping down accentuates the circular shape. You

Clear-spot attachment
The transparent central area in the attachment (left) allows you to tint picture corners and edges. A range of colors is available.

should take TTL readings without the filter in place to expose the center correctly.

With a center focus attachment, the central area remains sharp and the rest strongly out of focus when you focus on the middle of the frame. This device works best with portrait heads surrounded by distracting background detail that you cannot otherwise throw sufficiently out of focus. Similarly, it is possible to isolate a single item from a group, such as a particular flower from a large bunch of blooms.

You must position the main subject precisely in the center, unless you are using a square attachment that will shift sideways. Set a wide aperture to remove any suggestion of the hole edge. Sometimes, light-colored subjects create a slight double image in the circular edge zone. Interesting effects occur when you set the lens to close focus when shooting dis-

tant pin-point lights at night. The out-of-focus highlights created will each contain a small black ring, formed by the structure of the center-focus attachment.

Both types of center spot attachment will betray their structure in any isolated, out-of-focus highlights. In close-up work, for example, background points of light can appear as circles with colored segments or rings.

Prism attachments
Only a few genuine prism attachments are available, but it is possible to produce similar results with a 60° laboratory glass prism. Attach the prism to a holder so that the largest flat surface faces the subject. Then rotate the prism, and shift it slightly up or down, examining the results on the focusing screen. The best lenses to use on a 35 mm camera are between 85 mm and 250 mm. You should choose subjects that have plenty of contrast and strong, simple linear patterns.

Images show the effects of both refraction and dispersion: objects often appear elongated, with multiple images of details

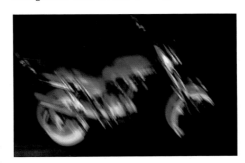

Prismatic image
Andrew de Lory used a glass prism to create this picture of a motor cycle. The prism works best with strong shapes and contrasty subjects against a plain background. The bright highlights appear multicolored.

off-set. There is a great deal of color fringing, specially around well-defined, white objects. The resulting pictures have a blurred, rather impressionistic appearance, similar to an oblique reflection in a thick glass mirror, or to pictures taken using a cheap magnifying glass as a lens. The prism also deflects the lights, so you should expect to have to aim the camera at the sky, or turn it steeply to the right or left when you are photographing a subject that is straight ahead.

Diffraction attachments
Diffraction disks, or "gratings" consists of a sheet of plastic covered with thousands of tiny grooves. White light is "diffracted" into a miniature spectrum of colors by the edge of each groove. The effect is similar to the reflection from a plastic record, or shot silk. As with cross-screen attachments, intense point light sources are necessary to produce strong results. Effects vary according to the design of the disk — from a single string of colors to a circular array of short, multicolored lines or spots around each light source. For the strongest effects shoot silhouettes, so that the diffraction

colors are the only strong hues in the picture. Alternatively, add a muted color filter to subdue and underexpose the scene's true colors. This will not greatly influence the diffraction colors that will still be strongly visible. Interesting effects are possible by giving an exposure of 1 sec or more (with the camera on a tripod),

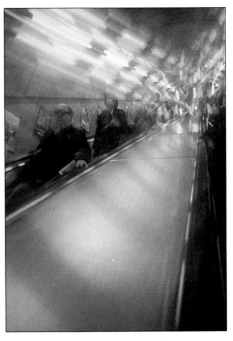

Using the diffraction attachment
Andrew de Lory's composition (above) turns fluorescent lighting into multicolored stripes. He used a plastic diffraction disk over the camera lens. The multiplying and spreading of highlights into crude spectra, and the low contrast are characteristic of this type of attachment. It therefore works best on a subject with strong color or tone.

while continuously rotating the diffraction disk. The array of colored lines radiating from each light source then blurs into concentric colored circles. Diffraction attachments do not require you to make any exposure increase.

Cross-screen attachments
If you photograph a bright point light source through a clear material that has fine lines scratched into it, the light will flare out along the grooves. If the lines are crossed, each bright highlight expands into a number of elongated rays, like a star. This is the principle of cross-screen, or "starburst", attachments. Each one consists of a glass or plastic disk with one surface covered in a finely etched grid of lines. These lines are arranged either at 90° to each other (giving four rays for each highlight) or 60° (giving six rays). Extra sets of lines create additional rays. The deeper the etched lines on the attachment, the stronger the rays, and closely ruled, heavily etched attachments also add colors to the light bursts, and increasingly diffuse image contrast and detail. You will only

see the effect of cross-screen attachments when there are small and intense light sources in the picture. Flatly lit scenes remain unaffected. Wide-angle landscapes that include the sun, strings of light bulbs at night, or sparkling spotlight reflections off glass or jewelry in the studio are good subjects. The attachment

Cross-screen effect
Andrew de Lory used a cross-screen, and stopped well down to emphasize light in the church. The pattern enhances the interior's symmetry.

helps to imply glitter, and can add a romantic or glamorous touch to a whole range of otherwise prosaic scenes.

As you turn a cross-screen attachment, the rays from each star rotate like spokes on a wheel, so that you can set them to the best position in relation to the other elements in the picture. The smaller the lens aperture the thinner the rays. Some cross-screens have two disks, each with parallel etched lines. It is possible to rotate one disk, to vary the angle and number of rays formed. No exposure increase is required for cross-screens but it is best to underexpose the darker parts of the picture slightly if you want to produce the most dramatic results. Another way to make results more striking is to use the attachment in combination with a deep single color filter positioned over the camera lens.

Multifaceted attachments
These devices are also sometimes known as "multivision lenses" and, incorrectly, as "prisms". They consist of thick disks or squares of glass cut to leave multiple facets on one side. When you place them over the lens, several overlapping images of the subject form. With a three-faceted disk, the object in the frame center appears three times in triangular formation. Four- and five-faceted types give one central image encircled by a correspond-

ing number of repeats. It is possible to shift this grouping off-center if you are using a square attachment in a holder.

Some designs have parallel facets, and these space out the multiple images in a straight line. You can make the row of images vertical, horizontal, or angled by rotating the attachment. A type with a circular arrangement of facets produces a ring of images around the center. Some attachments are available that are half plain glass, with four or five narrow parallel facets in the other half. This gives a row of images tailing away to one side — an effect that can give the illusion of movement.

When using a multifaceted attachment, pick subjects with strong, bold shapes against

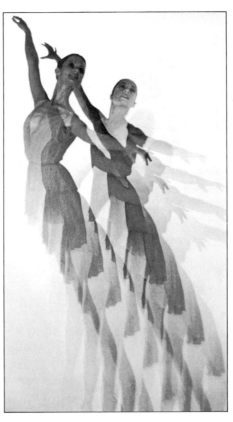

Multiple image
To produce this dynamic multiple image of dancers, John Starr used a multifaceted attachment with vertical divisions. This gives the photograph a strong, upward thrust, appropriate to the subject, and creates an interesting pattern of tones. A different form of multifaceted attachment (left) gives a circular array of images. Simple, clear subjects work best.

plain, preferably dark, backgrounds. Otherwise pictures become confusing, or appear washed out. Try shooting portraits or structures against a deep blue sky, or buildings lit up at night. Flowers can also provide good subjects if set against a black background.

The multiple images appear more spaced apart the longer your lens. Lenses between

85 mm and 200 mm are generally best. With most faceted attachments, the offset repeated images are never quite as sharp or contrasty as the image formed directly through the flat part of the glass.

Split-field attachments
A split-field attachment consists of a close-up lens (usually of about 3 diopters) cut in half and mounted in a frame. The other half of the frame is completely empty. When using this attachment, you can make a very close object in one half of the frame appear sharp, while focusing

Increasing depth of field
The split-field attachment's half lens (left) allows you to increase depth of field by bringing part of the foreground into focus. A blurred central area may result.

the prime lens on a distant subject through the empty section of the frame. The attachment is also useful when the whole scene is distant, and you want half the picture, such as sky or ground detail, to be out of focus.

If you use the attachment with the lens at wide aperture, there is a gradation of focus between close and distant sections of the image. Stopping down creates a more abrupt division. This can suit subjects that divide clearly into foreground and background halves.

You can turn the attachment to rotate the close-up lens around the frame. For realistic effects try to disguise the division by making it coincide with a straight line in the image, such as the horizon, or the edge of a building. Alternatively, position a plain surface or a shadow mid-frame to hide the transition. It is always this mid-distance zone that shows the shift of focus, disclosing the use of the attachment. Split-field attachments do not require any increase in exposure.

Diffusion attachments
There are two types of diffusion attachment. The first type is made of clear glass or plastic, engraved with concentric rings. They soften detail slightly and spread highlights. Use them to destroy harsh detail and enhance mood. You can buy attachments with different grades of diffusion. Some have a clear center, so that the effect is greatest toward the edges. With this type, the more you stop down the lens, the less diffused the image becomes. The second type are fog filters. These have a slight milky appearance. They produce a fairly sharp image, but scattered light dilutes the darkest

Diffuser
Light rays passing through the diffuser split up, softening the image and making colors much paler.

shadows to gray and spreads bright highlights. Colors become muted, and results look realistically misty or foggy. But the light scatter does not increase with distance, as with true atmospheric perspective (see *Aerial perspective,* pp. 82-3). A gradated fog filter helps you overcome this problem. Position it accurately in the holder, so that it affects the top — usually the most distant part — of the image.

Non-effects filters

For general purpose work, most photographers use a number of filters which make the color and tone content of their pictures more accurate. An ultraviolet, or haze, filter is useful with all films, especially color types. It will reduce excessive blue in distant scenes and when the weather is overcast. You can leave the filter permanently attached to the lens to protect it from dust and abrasion.

Yellow-green and deep red color filters are both ideal for adjusting tone values with black

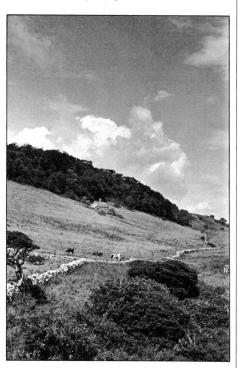

Filters for black and white
To create the landscape picture (above) the photographer used an orange filter to darken the sky, making cloud formations contrast clearly.

and white film. The yellow-green filter darkens blue sky tones, and the red exaggerates this effect. You can also use the red filter with infrared film (see *Special black and white films,* p. 157). Both of these attachments can also produce dramatic effects in color photography, especially when you are shooting directly into the light.

Color balancing filters are invaluable if you often switch from indoor to outdoor locations while using the same film type. A blue balancing filter will balance daylight color film to tungsten lighting, while an orange one will have the reverse effect. A suitable balancing filter for using daylight film in fluorescent light is also valuable. These filters are essential for color transparency film when your lighting type changes, and desirable for color negative film. You can also use a range of pale, color compensating filters to add warmth to or to cool down the color content of images shot on slide film (see *Association and mood,* p. 50), where printing corrections are impressive.

Neutral density filters

Gray neutral density (ND) filters have no effect on image color. They simply reduce the intensity of the light entering the lens. ND filters enable you to shoot at a wide aperture in brilliant lighting or when the camera contains fast film. This facility is specially useful if you want to produce differential focus effects in these situations where, even when selecting the fastest shutter speeds, you would have to stop down to avoid overexposure.

Another use is to allow prolonged exposure to increase the blur of moving subjects. Even at the smallest aperture, you may not be able to use a shutter speed as slow as 1/30 sec for panning a moving object, or 1/8 sec for zooming unless you use an ND filter. For architectural photography in a busy street you can make time exposures with a deep ND filter in place, so that figures and traffic become so blurred that they disappear. At night you can record longer light trails from moving vehicles. ND filters are also essential for exposure control with a mirror lens, which has a fixed aperture (see *Catadioptric lenses,* p. 191). This type of filter comes in a range of strengths, for flexibility of exposure control.

Attachment holders

The simplest method of using a lens attachment is to hold it over the front of the lens with one hand while operating the camera with the other. This soon becomes awkward and irritating. The traditional solution is to buy the attachment as a round disk mounted in a metal rim that screws into the thread on the front of the lens. The disadvantage of this system is that

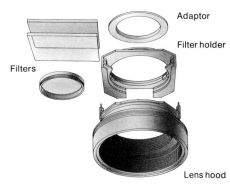

Adaptor

Filter holder

Filters

Lens hood

Filter system
The system (above) features a holder that enables you to change filters quickly. You attach the holder to the lens with an adaptor ring. The system

comprises a wide range of square and some circular types. These are the attachments, such as polarizers, that must be rotated to use them effectively.

lens diameters vary, so you may have to buy filters for your largest lens, and use step-down adaptor rings to mount them on lenses that are smaller in diameter.

Several modern systems use square attachments instead. You must buy a holder with adaptor rings for different lenses, but thereafter one set of square filters and attachments will serve all lenses. The plastic attachments push into grooves in the holder, which will

accommodate two or three attachments at once. Holders also accept low-cost gelatin color correction filters sandwiched in a plastic frame. The main advantage of this system is that it provides an easy opportunity for you to move filters around in front of the lens. This is vital for attachments such as starbursts and polarizers, and useful with split-field, multiple-image, and dual-color attachments. A holder is particularly worthwhile if you use a large number of attachments in special effects work, especially if you want to use them in combination. The system is easy to use and allows rapid changing of attachments. For single attachments, such as color balancing and UV filters, threaded types are generally more convenient. The disadvantage of a square holder is its large bulk compared with individual screw-on disks.

The outer surface of a lens attachment is the front of your optical system. To prevent unwanted flare, which degrades picture content, you should shade the front surface from direct light as much as possible. With all attachments it is essential to use the correct lens hood. Hoods are particularly important with square types, as these rarely have an anti-flare coating. Holders accept a specially designed slip-on hood, while circular filters are threaded to take a screw-on hood, or push-on types.

In all cases, it is vital to ensure that attachments and hoods do not cut into the field of view of the lens in use. Look through the camera with the lens focused on infinity and pointed at a bright, even area of sky. Stop the lens down to its smallest aperture and press the preview button to give maximum depth of field. You should then examine each corner of the frame for signs of vignetting.

Neutral density filter factors

Type and density	Effect on exposure	
	Multiply exposure by	Increase aperture by
ND 0.1	$1\frac{1}{4}$	$\frac{1}{3}$
ND 0.2	$1\frac{1}{2}$	$\frac{2}{3}$
ND 0.3	2	1
ND 0.4	$2\frac{1}{2}$	$1\frac{1}{3}$
ND 0.5	3	$1\frac{2}{3}$
ND 0.6	4	2
ND 0.7	5	$2\frac{1}{3}$
ND 0.8	6	$2\frac{2}{3}$
ND 0.9	8	3
ND 1.0	10	$3\frac{1}{3}$
ND 2.0	100	$6\frac{2}{3}$

Using ND filters
ND filters reduce the amount of light entering the lens. They allow you to use wide apertures (to limit depth of field) or long

exposure times when these effects are not normally possible, such as when using fast film in very strong illumination.

System cameras and accessories

Every photographer's gadget bag contains a personally selected collection of individual items. Some people require only a single piece of camera equipment, with as much as possible built-in. But for most photographers the advantages of a system camera are obvious. Manufacturers offer dozens of items, such as lenses, motor drives, viewing aids, and film backs, that can be added to the basic camera body.

Planning equipment requirements

No one will want or can afford all the items in a particular camera system, but the vast majority of serious photographers find the range of compatible equipment invaluable. By looking ahead and planning, photographers can build the system suited to their own needs, using the choice of film format and type and make of camera as a starting point. A good manufacturer will offer a wide variety of equipment for general work, as well as items useful in a range of specializations. Someone interested mainly in sports and action photography, for example, would be able to build up a system very different from that of a photographer whose major interests were subjects such as architecture and landscapes.

A badly planned camera kit will waste money, and can lead to missed photographic opportunities. An excessive amount of equipment will also pose problems. The photographer can be so weighed down with apparatus, or have to spend so much time changing from one item to another, that picture opportunities are lost, and photography becomes a burden. A well-balanced, versatile outfit improves efficiency. With two camera bodies, for example, it is possible to change from black and white to color film at any time. They can also prevent missed shots when one body fails suddenly or requires reloading. A zoom lens may be a quicker, more convenient lens than two or three of different focal lengths (but it may be too bulky, or not fast enough for typical lighting conditions).

Cost is a vital consideration. The image quality advantages of a larger format camera system must be weighed against the extra price of each item, as well as the possibly more limited range of accessories. Individual methods of working will also influence choice. Some photographers prefer the very considered approach to still-life subjects, landscape, and even portrait photography made possible with a sheet film camera. Others require equipment that is compact, quiet, and unobtrusive.

Motor drives and camera backs

Battery-powered motor drives are available for both 35 mm and rollfilm cameras. They link with the camera's internal film wind-on mechanism through contacts on the base of the body. There are three main types. The most sophisticated models give a continuous sequence of exposure and wind-on at a firing rate of up to six frames per second. They also allow automatic wind-on of individual frames. Their fastest firing rates are restricted by the shutter speed you are using — the most rapid sequences are only possible at speeds of 1/125 sec and faster.

Slightly less elaborate motor drives, often known as power winders, offer similar features but a slower firing rate — typically about two frames per second. Still simpler types do no more than wind on the film, leaving the photographer to press the shutter release in the normal way. These types are generally called autowinders. A number of 35 mm cameras now have built-in autowinders.

Aid to concentration

The great advantage of all types of motor-driven film wind, is that they give you the freedom to watch the subject continuously through the camera viewfinder. You do not have to take the camera away from your eye to wind on the film by hand. This helps you concentrate on the subject, and is especially useful in portraiture and with moving subjects.

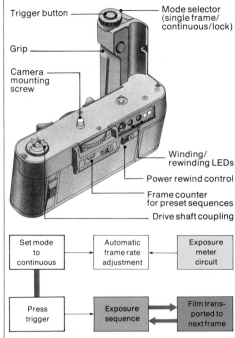

Trigger button — Mode selector (single frame/continuous/lock)

Grip

Camera mounting screw

Winding/rewinding LEDs

Power rewind control

Frame counter for preset sequences

Drive shaft coupling

Set mode to continuous → Automatic frame rate adjustment ← Exposure meter circuit

Press trigger → Exposure sequence → Film transported to next frame

Motor drive
This battery-powered unit automatically adjusts its framing speed to the shutter speed and power source in use, up to a maximum of 6 frames per second. At this speed, you should use the mirror lock-up.

This will minimize strain on mechanical linkages. You can preset the number of exposures you want to make in a particular sequence. Power rewinding in a matter of seconds is possible with this unit.

The more sophisticated types of motor drive also enable you to shoot pictures very quickly. This gives you a better chance of capturing a good picture in rapidly changing situations such as sporting events and brief appearances by celebrities. A motor drive is also an aid if you want to take groups of connected pictures (see *Picture sequences*, pp. 88-9).

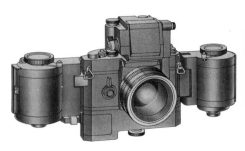

Bulk film back
These are used in situations where it would be inconvenient to change film after every 36 exposures. They can be used for fast sequences, or set up and left to take single pictures over long periods using an intervalometer.

But even at the highest firing rates, film transport takes up most of the time, so there is no guarantee that you will record a particular decisive moment. You can more often capture these images by selective use of the shutter release for single pictures. An additional disadvantage of motor drives is that they attract attention because of their noise.

Remote control

A useful consequence of motor-driven operation is that it makes the camera easy to use by remote control. You can trigger the shutter with any electrical lead, without having to keep returning to the camera to wind on the film. You can also use an intervalometer to fire the shut-

Data back

Most 35 mm SLRs accept a data back containing a small light source which prints preset details such as date, time, or exposure within each frame. Such information is often invaluable in scientific and technical photography.

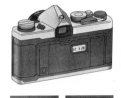

ter at regular time intervals (see *Shutter firing systems*, p. 126). This facility is invaluable in natural history work. To make full use of a motor drive, you can replace the camera's normal back with a bulk film back. This accepts large film cassettes that you must load from a supply of bulk film. Backs for 35 mm SLRs usually give 250 or 750 exposures, while those for rollfilm cameras give 500 exposures.

Some camera systems also offer camera backs that enable you to expose certain data on the film edge during exposure. With most models, you can record the time or date of the picture or, alternatively, details of the exposure settings that you used.

Tripods and camera supports

Camera supports come in all sizes — from simple hand grips to giant, heavy-duty studio stands. Choice depends on the size and weight of your camera equipment, the height at which you wish to work, and the value you place on portability. The smallest tripods are table-top models. These have folding legs and are very compact. You can set them up on a table, stairs, or on top of a wall, to support a small camera, and they are useful for close-up studio work.

The lightest full-size tripods seldom have a center column, and the legs may only extend to about 4 ft 6 ins (1.3 m). At maximum height, the top may become slightly shaky. But these tripods are light to carry and their folded legs

Twin-shank tripod

Braced tripod

Compact tripod

Tripods
Compact tripods are easily carried but are unsteady in high winds or when used with heavy cameras or lenses. Braced models are more stable. Twin-shank tripods are sturdiest, but being heavy are awkward to transport.

are very short and fit into most gadget bags.

Medium-weight tripods often have braced legs and an adjustable center column that is useful when you are making small final height adjustments. Sometimes the center column will reverse, so that you can attach the camera upside down, very close to the ground. This feature is useful in natural history work. Me-

Tripod heads
The simplest tripod is the ball-and-socket head. Pan-and-tilt heads are useful for normal work. Use a balance head for maximum precision.

Ball-and-socket

Two-way pan-and-tilt   **Three-way pan-and-tilt**   **Balance head**

dium-weight tripods are the lightest suitable for 6 × 6 cm format cameras.

Some larger tripods, made of heavy-duty metal, will extend to about 7 ft (2.1 m). These are the standard tripods for sheet film cameras on location, and may weigh 20 lb (9 kg). The largest camera supports are stands and columns designed for use in the studio (see *Professional studio,* p. 168).

It is essential to use a tripod head that gives you adequate control over camera position. The simplest tilting top is a ball-and-socket head that you can lock at any angle. (A large one is suitable for a small camera direct on a

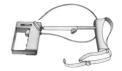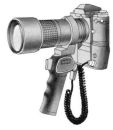

Hand grips
You hold the rifle grip (above left) as you would a shotgun — braced against your shoulder. Steadying the rifle grip requires both hands, so the rear grip incorporates a cable release. A pistol grip (above right) is held in one hand.

table-top.) The most usual head is a "pan-and-tilt" type. It has a panning arm protruding from the back. You turn this to unlock the head and tilt the camera. Undoing another lock allows you to pan moving subjects by using the arm. A scaled-up version of the pan-and-tilt head is available for sheet film cameras on heavy-duty tripods.

When a tripod is too bulky or heavy to carry, you can use one of a number of smaller camera supports. Hand grips are light and compact. Some types brace the camera between your hand and shoulder, like a rifle. Others resemble the handle of a pistol. Both types incorporate a cable release to fire the shutter. Exposures as long as 1/30 sec or 1/15 sec are generally safe. Hand grips also often incorporate a swiveling mount for a flashgun.

For longer exposures, a camera support clamp, which you can lock on the back of a chair, provides a compact support. A monopod is also useful. Constructed like a single tripod leg, it makes exposures of up to 1/8 sec possible if you give steadying downward pressure to the camera. Monopods are much easier to use quickly than most other camera supports.

Bags and cases

Like all precision instruments, cameras and other photographic equipment require careful protection during storage and whenever they are carried about. Never move around with your camera hanging unprotected from your neck or shoulder. Use a cap to cover the lens, or, better, an ever-ready folding case. This provides immediate access to the camera — you simply unbutton the top flap to reveal the

Ever-ready case
This protects your camera from abrasions, dust and the elements, and is usually included with the basic camera. Hard cases are more robust than soft ones.

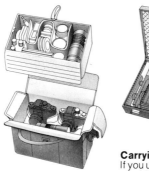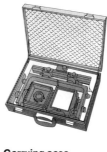

lens, viewfinder, and controls. It is best to buy one that will accommodate the camera even when fitted with a moderate telephoto lens.

As soon as you begin building your own camera system, a carrying bag will become essential. There is a wide range of padded gadget bags with shoulder straps. For SLR outfits a shoulder bag with compartments is generally best. The internal divisions prevent

items bumping against each other, and the bag is compact and usually comfortable to carry — especially if the strap is wide. Make sure that any bag you buy is water repellent. It should be large enough to allow for your system to expand, and it should accommodate a

Gadget bag
This shoulder bag has built-in compartments to stop your equipment moving about in transit.

Carrying case
If you use different combinations of equipment for particular jobs, shape a separate foam insert for each. Carry only what you are likely to use.

supply of film. It is important to be able to open the bag easily and remove the camera without other items falling out.

For comprehensive outfits, and to transport a large-format camera system, a suitcase-type unit in aluminum is strongest and gives most space. These cases are sold with a solid foam interior that you cut out with a sharp knife to form spaces contoured to fit each item of equipment. Such a case undoubtedly gives the greatest physical protection, but is often heavy and uncomfortable to carry. In addition, it will easily be recognizable as containing photographic equipment, and this may lead to theft. A further drawback is that you have to lay the case down whenever you want to open it, so it is inconvenient to use when walking about. One alternative is to use a deep, metal-framed document case.

Camera bags are like tool boxes. You need to store your equipment safely but you seldom have to carry all of it around at one time. Therefore it is often worthwhile buying two bags — one heavy-duty container for storing your entire outfit, the other a light and comfortable type that takes only the items you will require on a particular occasion.

Viewfinder accessories

Some sophisticated 35 mm and most medium-format SLRs offer interchangeable viewing heads. You slide off the pentaprism and eyepiece as a single unit, and replace it with another type. On cameras with this facility, the light-measuring cells, normally housed near the pentaprism, must be redesigned to fit elsewhere — usually under the mirror box.

There are two main types of interchangeable viewing heads — for eye-level and waist-level viewing. Apart from the standard 35 mm eye-level pentaprism head, you can buy a larger "action finder". This is a box-shaped hood with a large rear opening and internal mirrors. It gives you an eye-level view of the whole focusing screen image, even when your eye is several inches behind the camera, or slightly to one side.

Eye-level pentaprism heads that boost the capacity of the camera's TTL meter are also available, allowing you to work in poor lighting conditions. Some eye-level focusing hoods for rollfilm SLRs contain a complete built-in metering system, where this is not provided within the camera itself.

The simplest waist-level finder is a folding hood that you open to shade the camera's focusing screen as you look down at it. It is particularly helpful when working at floor level. Another type has a × 6 magnifying eyepiece to enlarge the screen center. This is an asset when using the camera vertically as a copying device. Both types of waist-level finder show the image upright but reversed left to right.

Many 35 mm SLRs have interchangeable focusing screens. You remove and replace them either through the mirror box with the lens removed, or from above, clipping them into place, if the camera has a removable viewing head. Most systems offer a dozen or more screens. They range from a simple matte screen (suitable for all focal lengths of lens, and imposing least interference on composition) to complex screens with grided patterns (ideal for situations where converging verticals are likely to be a problem). Types with a large area of fresnel (see *35 mm SLR cameras*, pp. 102-4) are easiest to use in dim lighting conditions, while others have varied arrangements of split-image or microprism focusing aids for general use. Choice of screen is mainly a matter of personal convenience and particular interests.

You can attach a number of additional accessories over the eyepiece of most SLRs, whether or not the camera has interchangeable viewing heads. A right-angle attachment is useful for copying, and also when you want to use the camera at ground level. It presents the image as right-reading, and is adjustable to the photographer's eyesight. Another unit magnifies the center of the image. You can also buy correction lenses for your normal eyepiece so that the image is adjusted to your own eyesight. Spectacle wearers often find this useful because glasses can make it difficult to use the viewfinder accurately or comfortably. A rubber eyecup is another valuable accessory, whether you wear spectacles or not. Many TTL systems are affected by strong light entering through the eyepiece, and an eyecup helps create a light-tight seal between the face and the camera.

Interchangeable viewfinders

Use an eye-level pentaprism finder for general work with both 35 mm (above left) and medium format (below left) SLRs. A magnifying finder gives a × 6 image magnification for precision work. A simple folding hood lets you shoot at waist or floor level, or with the camera held above you. An action finder has an extra-large eyepiece so you can hold the camera away from your eye when wearing glasses or goggles, or if you are following a moving subject with both eyes. A right-angle viewer enables you to see the screen from above or one side, if you are copying vertically or shooting from a low angle or in a tight corner. You attach it to the eyepiece of a normal viewfinder. The rotary finder used with medium format SLRs is similar but has its own pentaprism housing.

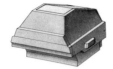
Eye-level finder

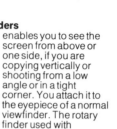

Magnifying finder

Waist-level finder

Action finder

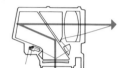

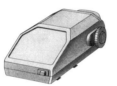
Eye-level finder

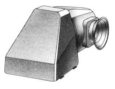
Rotary finder

Right-angle viewer

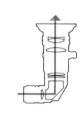

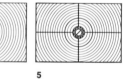

1

2

3

4

5

6

7

8

9

10

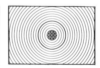

11

12

13

14

Interchangeable screens

1 Fresnel field with split screen surrounded by microprisms. **2** as **1**, without microprisms. **3** as **2** with grid. **4** as **2**, with diagonal split screen to focus horizontal lines. **5** as **4**, with microprism collar and intersecting lines to aid composition.
6 Fresnel screen with clear center spot, for lenses with very long or very short focal lengths, or with small maximum aperture. **7** as **6**, with engraved grid. **8** Fresnel field with circular microprism cluster.
9 as **8**, with larger microprism spot for dim light. **10** Microprism over whole screen area, for very low light. **11** Clear matte field. **12** as **11**, with cross-hairs, used in photomicrography. **13** Double cross-hair reticle and scales for high-magnification work. **14** as **3**, with cross lines and TV outline, used in shooting stills for TV screening.

The 35 mm SLR system

About ten leading 35 mm SLR manufacturers offer their own modular camera systems, each of which may comprise 100 or more separate items. The vast majority of these are compatible with each of the systems' camera bodies. Their compatibility extends to new models, so that you do not have to discard cameras to take advantage of the latest innovations.

In some cases maintaining this principle creates conflicts of design for camera manufacturers. Camera bodies designed 10-15 years ago lack the electronic features of recent designs, and have lens coupling arrangements that would not be ideal if the system were introduced today. But most companies keep their systems up to date by creating additional, newer bodies — models that are more compact, more automatic, or simplified — but accepting both past and current lenses.

It is best to start building a camera outfit with a few items from a good quality system, adding equipment gradually, rather than immediately assembling a wider-ranging collection of low-cost items. Acquiring equipment gradually means that you will become familiar with one item at a time. This experience can be important when deciding future purchases. A quality system is also most likely to produce images of a consistent technical standard, and to remain reliable over a long period of time. The items should also work well together: the layout of controls on lenses and accessories will be similar. Modern system cameras use a bayonet-type lens mounting system, but designs vary and lens mounts produced by one manufacturer are not generally compatible with lenses from another. It is therefore essential to buy lenses either from your camera's system, or from one of the specialist lens makers who produce high quality (but often cheaper) optics intended specifically for other makers' cameras. Filters, flashguns, and tripods are also best obtained from specialist companies.

In practice it is often smaller features that sway personal choice between one camera brand and another. The arrangement of the controls, the legibility of the settings, and the ease of focusing are all important, and you should also take into account the camera's size, weight, and "feel" when handled. A typical basic camera kit might consist of a body with standard, telephoto, and wide-angle lenses (fixed focal length or zoom), plus a tripod and cable release. Filters, a set of extension tubes, a flashgun, and a bag are also important.

The system's components

The 35 mm SLR system illustrated here offers a wide range of equipment, with a particular stress on technical photography. The items divide into certain broad groups. A selection of camera bodies forms the heart of the system. They vary in their degree of automation, size, weight, and the range of facilities they offer. This group also includes devices which provide motorized film advance, together with interchangeable backs for bulk film loading and data recording.

There is a wide range of lenses (though some systems offer an even greater number), ranging from fisheye to telephoto and extreme long-focus types. The system also includes zoom and macro lenses.

For close-up and copying work there are bellows units and a complete vertical copying stand. The system also provides a set of extension tubes, as well as adaptor rings and supplementary lenses.

Flash equipment forms another group. Flashguns are usually "dedicated" to the manufacturer's camera bodies (see *Self-regulating flash,* p. 141). A wider range of flash equipment is available from independent manufacturers,. It is either designed for general use or can be fitted with an adaptor to dedicate it to a particular system.

Specialist attachments for photomicrography are an important part of this system, making its cameras fully adaptable for work at very high magnifications. Remote recording, astrophotography, and underwater photography are all provided for.

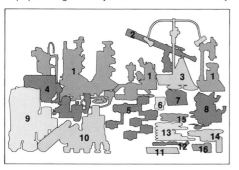

35 mm SLR system
1 Macrophotography, photomicrography and medical equipment.
2 Astronomical photography equipment.
3 Copy stands.
4 Flash and strobe systems, with power pack. **5** Camera bodies, motor drive, power winder, and bulk film magazine. **6** Intervalometer. **7** Bulk film loader. **8** Bellows and slide copying attachments. **9** Carrying cases. **10** Interchangeable lens system. **11** Focusing screens. **12** Data back and viewfinder attachments. **13** Filters.
14 Lens hoods and adaptor rings. **15** Extension tubes and adaptors. **16** Compact flashguns.

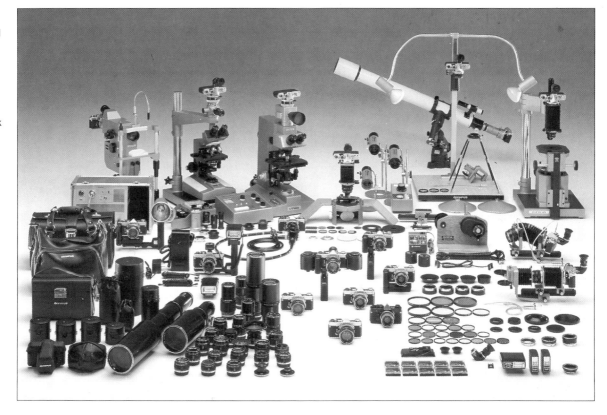

The rollfilm camera system

There are some six rollfilm modular camera systems. Those based on single lens reflex cameras have 6 × 7 cm, 6 × 4.5 cm, and 6 × 6 cm formats, while there is also a 6 × 6 cm twin lens reflex system. 6 × 6 cm is the most popular rollfilm picture format. A square image shape is versatile because it allows you to produce both vertical and horizontal versions of the same picture, by cropping. Professionals normally find this a useful feature when they are asked to adapt their work to clients' specific requirements.

The TLR system is the least costly rollfilm type, but it is much more limited in scope than the SLR systems. There is only a small range of lenses, and since you have to buy them in pairs they are relatively expensive. But the TLR does provide an adequate range of equipment for general photography, and some photographers find its facility for continuous viewing during exposure invaluable.

The system's components

SLR systems provide much more equipment, allowing you to pursue many specializations. The Hasselblad 6 × 6 cm SLR system, shown on this page, is based on a camera body that consists of a simple, but high-quality mirror box. Bodies include completely manual types, and models with electric film wind-on. You choose which of some twenty lenses to attach to the front, the type of film magazine for the back, the hood or pentaprism for the top, and the wind-on device for the side. There is also a specially designed body without mirror or focusing screen. This is designed to act as a wide-angle direct vision viewfinder camera when you use it with a short focal length lens. The body draws its other accessories from the main system. You can also choose between bodies with and without focal plane blinds (the latter type accepting only lenses with built-in bladed shutters). Like 35 mm SLRs, the bodies accept adaptors that enable you to attach them to specialist items such as microscopes. The versatility of the system is extended by equipment for close-up, time-lapse, remote control, and aerial photography, as well as a housing for underwater work.

One advantage of a rollfilm SLR over a conventional 35 mm camera is its facility for changing film magazines, even in mid-roll. This saves valuable time, since you can load a number of magazines in advance and then shoot a whole picture session without breaks. The system also makes it possible for you to change briefly to an instant picture back, so that you can carry out tests on exposure and composition. It is easy to take the same shot on different types of film, trying the same subject in both color and black and white, for example. Magazines are available that accept standard (120) rollfilm, double length (220) film, and bulk film in 250 and 500 exposure rolls. The disadvantage of film magazines is their cost. Each one costs roughly the same as a 35 mm SLR body, so you can achieve similar flexibility with several 35 mm bodies.

There is a good range of high-quality lenses, in focal lengths from 30 mm to 500 mm. But this is not as comprehensive a selection as with most systems in the 35 mm format. Lenses for rollfilm are also appreciably slower than their

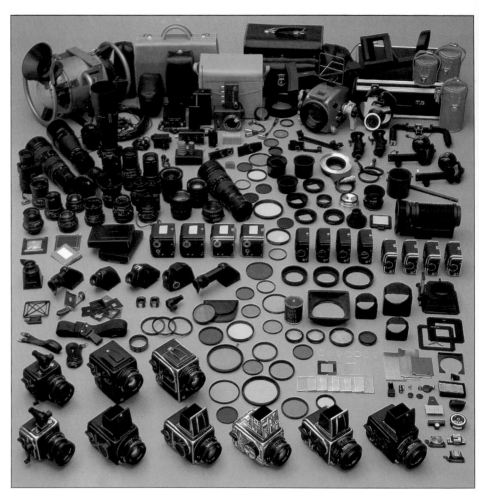

35 mm counterparts. You are also restricted to lenses supplied by the camera manufacturer, and both zoom and fisheye types are expensive and rare.

Viewing aids are available for most applications. Magnifying hoods and pentaprisms for eye-level viewing are among the most useful for general work. There are also clip-on direct vision viewfinders, and wire-frame finders for sports and action photography. TTL metering is not standard on rollfilm cameras, but most systems provide an additional focusing hood with a TTL meter incorporated.

A typical 6 × 6 cm SLR kit might contain either an 80 mm or 105 mm lens as standard (choice of focal length will depend on personal preference), plus a 50 mm wide-angle and a 200 mm telephoto. You require at least two magazines to make full use of the fast film changing facility. A magnifying eyepiece, instead of the standard hood, removes extraneous light when you are focusing and composing. Other essential items are an exposure meter (either a hand-held type, or built into a focusing hood), a tripod, cable release, and a carrying case. A selection of filters and a flashgun will also be useful. You should expect the cost of this outfit to be several times the cost of a 35 mm kit offering similar features. But image quality will be outstanding, and this will be especially noticeable when you make really big enlargements.

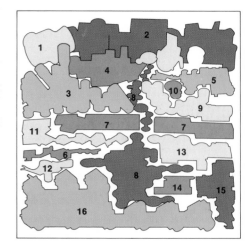

Rollfilm SLR system
1 Underwater housing
2 Carrying cases.
3 Lens system. 4 Timers and remote sensors.
5 Brackets and supports.
6 Viewfinder attachments. 7 Film backs.
8 Filters. 9 Close-up accessories. 10 Ringflash. 11 Focusing and viewing aids. 12 Straps.
13 Lens hoods.
14 Focusing screens and eyepiece correction lenses. 15 Tripod and accessory mounts.
16 Cameras.

The sheet film monorail system

The sheet film monorail camera is the most modular of all types. Each of the basic components — front, back, bellows, and rail — is a separate, interchangeable item. According to particular brand, the monorail itself may be square or round. You either extend the rail telescopically, or add extra lengths. Each system has its own method of pivoting and moving the front and back sections of the camera based on the type of structural support used. Most types tilt and swing the lens about its central axis. This means you can use the range of camera movements without changing the point of focus.

The normal bellows connecting the front and rear supports have a square cross-section, but for wide-angle work you have to change to a more compact bag bellows unit. This allows a much shorter lens-to-film distance. If you want to use the camera for larger format pictures than normal, use the same front support with an enlarger rear support, and conical bellows to connect the two.

On the back of the camera you attach the appropriate focusing screen and one of a choice of light-shading hoods. One drawback of the sheet film camera is that the image appears upside down on the focusing screen. In the studio when you are composing the picture slowly and carefully, this is rarely a problem — but if you prefer an upright image, some systems offer a reflex viewer with a correcting mirror. This has the additional advantage of shading the focusing screen completely from light, freeing you from the traditional photographer's "darkcloth".

The camera back must also hold the film. A sprung back accepts a range of holders for sheet film, pack film, instant picture materials, and rollfilm. These film holders are international in design and, unlike the other components of the system, you can use them with all sheet film cameras, irrespective of brand.

At the front of the camera you mount a lens on a metal panel that clips to the front support. Camera manufacturers do not make their own lenses. You usually buy the camera with blank lens panels, and then have these drilled to suit the diameter of the lenses you have selected. For the 5 × 4 ins (12.5 × 10 cm) format, the focal length choice extends from 65 mm to about 300 mm. Each lens has its own bladed shutter. Alternatively, you can buy a behind-the-lens shutter as part of some camera systems. This enables you to purchase less costly, shutterless lenses. But only a few lenses of this type are available for the sheet film camera format.

The main value of the sheet film monorail camera, apart from the excellent image quality provided by its large negative size, is its range of camera movements. You should make sure these are comprehensive, but also easy to operate and lock. A good 5 × 4 ins (12.5 × 10 cm) outfit would include both square and bag bellows, a sufficient length of rail and bellows for macrophotography, a number of sheet film holders, and an instant picture back. It is best to start with a 90 mm wide-angle lens and a 150 mm or 180 mm standard lens, perhaps convertible to long-focus (see *Special lenses,* p. 210). An exposure meter, a cable release, and a heavy duty tripod or

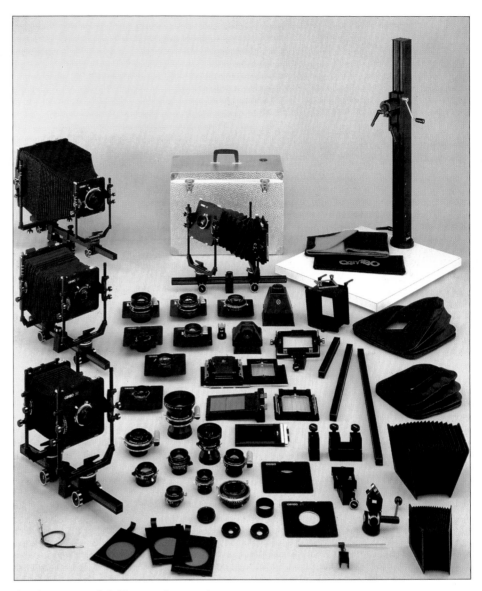

stand are essential. The most accurate exposure meter is a built-in type with a spot probe. This allows measurement of light from particular areas of the image — ideal when you want to make minute adjustments to a studio lighting set-up (see *Sheet film cameras,* p. 108). The latest models give a simple, digital read-out display.

A sheet film camera outfit is heavy and bulky. You may not want to carry the equipment around outside the studio. But a roomy suitcase-type container with subdivisions is still a good investment, as it will give excellent protection to your equipment when it is not in use.

Sheet film system
1 Complete cameras.
2 Carrying case.
3 Darkcloth and camera cover. 4 Copy stand.
5 Lenses on panels.
6 Focusing aids.
7 Lens hood and bellows support. 8 Bellows.
9 Rollfilm backs, film holders and focusing screen. 10 Monorail.
11 Lenses. 12 Monorail supports. 13 Cable release. 14 Filter holders. 15 Soft-focus lens and attachments.
16 Lens panels.

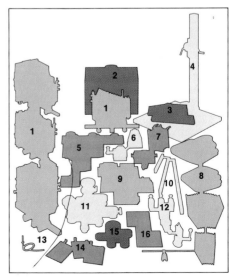

Special cameras and lenses

For general photography a 35 mm or roll-film SLR camera, together with the appropriate lenses and accessories, will produce excellent results, while a sheet film mono-rail camera is ideal for high-quality architectural and studio work. But even the broadest camera system does not accommodate certain branches of photography.

Cameras

Sometimes − with aerial and underwater photography, for example − physical conditions make a more rugged camera essential. In such situations, enlarged camera controls make photography easier, while further modifications, such as different viewfinders for aerial work, and specialized lenses for underwater use, are also useful. Specially designed cameras, with their own accessoires, are therefore best for these branches of photography.

There are also certain image effects that are difficult to achieve with a regular system camera and accessories. To produce a panoramic image in a single shot, for example, a camera that rotates, or that has a rotating lens, is ideal. Three-dimensional photography is another field that requires special equipment. To produce stereo prints, the photographer must not only use a four-lens camera intended only for this type of work, but must send the film to a special printing laboratory.

Lenses

Similar limitations exist with most lenses. The aim of regular wide-angle, standard, and telephoto optical designs is to create a lens that is as versatile as possible within the limits of focal length and covering power. But for specialist requirements a few lenses are available with more limited specifications. These either suit particular shooting conditions, or produce an unusual image quality. Special lenses for standard cameras range from inexpensive anamorphic attachments, for producing a wide-screen image, to sophisticated medical lenses, with built-in light sources, for high-quality close-up work.

The disadvantage of most kinds of specialized equipment is that, because demand is low, costs are relatively high. In addition, the equipment is seldom adaptable for use under more normal conditions. Specialist lenses, for example, often work at small maximum apertures, since their aberration control is generally designed to give excellent performance rather than high speed.

See also
Scientific and technical photography *Equipment and techniques, p. 274; High-speed photography, pp. 275-7.* Medical and forensic photography *Equipment and techniques, p. 285.* Aerial photography, pp. 296-9.

Special cameras

Although these cameras are all designed for specific applications or for producing a particular type of image, they vary greatly in sophistication and price. All except the sub-miniature and stereo types are tools for the specialist. Most other photographers rent these types of equipment, together with whatever specialized lenses and accessories are required for the job.

Multiple-image camera

This type of camera takes four passport-sized portraits on a single sheet of film. You usually use it with 5 × 4 ins (12.5 × 10 cm) peel-apart instant picture material. The body is box-like and contains a set of divisions that split it into four compartments. There are four matched lenses with simple shutters mounted on the

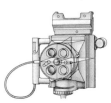

Multiple image camera
Four matched lenses each produce an identical image of the subject in the four quarters of a sheet of instant picture material 5 × 4 ins (12.5 × 10 cm) in size.

front panel. You focus the camera on a ground-glass screen at the back. When you press the cable release the camera records four separated (but identical) pictures, ready for mounting on identity cards or passports. An alternative lens panel contains only a pair of lenses. You use this with a different divider to produce two pictures per exposure. Some models also allow you to expose typed information about the subject with one of the lenses. The print itself can then form an identity card.

Aerial cameras

Special cameras are often necessary for taking hand-held pictures from aircraft − for surveillance, town planning, and military purposes. Cameras for airplane and helicopter use must be simplified, rugged, and easy to operate with gloved hands in a confined space. To make loading simple, they usually take magazines holding enough film for several hundred exposures. Models are available that accept rollfilm 70 mm wide, and there are also 5 × 4 ins (12.5 × 10 cm) aerial cameras with backs taking 50 ft (15 m) rolls of this type of film. The lens (which is interchangeable) has an enlarged focusing scale and there is a wire eye-level sighting frame on top of the camera. Older models have shutter speeds ranging from 1/15 to 1/500 sec, but more recent types provide shutter speeds up to 1/2000 sec. Shutter and film wind-on are

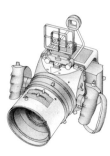

Aerial camera
Cameras such as this are used hand held for air-to-air and general aerial photography. Large handles help you hold the camera steady in the often difficult conditions in which it is used, and controls are usually overlarge and simple. The camera also has a large, direct-vision sight.

generally electrically operated. Cameras of this type can normally record data alongside each image. This enables you to document information about each exposure, and the location of the subject.

Underwater cameras and lenses

Waterproof 35 mm and 110 direct vision cameras are available for use at shallow depths. These also work well in the rain. They have rubber pressure seals on the camera back, and on all external controls. You must maintain these seals carefully with grease. The external controls are large, and the setting dials easy to read under water. Underwater housings for many 35 mm and 6 × 6 cm SLRs are also available. These provide a full range of external controls, and a grip to make the

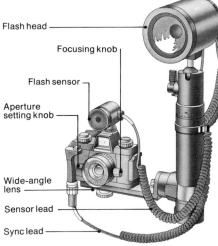

Flash head
Focusing knob
Flash sensor
Aperture setting knob
Wide-angle lens
Sensor lead
Sync lead

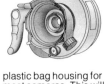

Underwater equipment
The Nikonos (above) is an underwater camera system which can be submerged without the special deep-water housing (right) that you must use on normal cameras. You can use a Nikonos at depths of around 165 ft (50 m). A housing is safe at twice this depth. You can buy an inexpensive plastic bag housing for most cameras. This will let you take underwater pictures just below the surface.

bulky unit easier to handle. Some housings are specifically designed for the tremendous pressures of deep water use (see *Underwater life*, p. 302-3).

Lenses produce particular problems when you use them underwater. Water has a different refracting effect on light from glass or air. When you look through water, objects seem nearer then they really are. This produces increased magnifications when you use lenses underwater. You must use a slightly shorter focal length (for example, 35 mm instead of 50 mm) to give an equivalent view of the scene on land. Better still, a lens of even shorter focal length will help minimize your distance from the subject, cutting down the diffusion caused by particles in the water (see *Underwater life*, pp. 302-3).

For best results you can use a lens specially designed for underwater photography. These lenses are capable of producing very high quality images. On the other hand, the more closely the designer tailors a lens to under-

Using 35 mm format lenses underwater				
Out of water				
Focal length	21 mm	28 mm	35 mm	50 mm
Angle of view	92°	75°	63°	47°
Underwater				
Focal length	28 mm	37 mm	47 mm	67 mm
Angle of view	75°	60°	50°	36°

water use, the poorer is its image quality on land. In general, it is possible to use underwater lenses with focal lengths of 35 mm or longer successfully on land. But you must use lenses that have a shorter focal length underwater only.

Panoramic cameras
Cameras for panoramic photography will take pictures that encompass a view of at least 180° of the horizontal plane. Some types do this by rotating the lens, or the whole camera, on a vertical axis, and exposing through a slit that sweeps past the film, in front of the light-sensitive surface. The image size on 35 mm film is usually 24 × 65 mm.

Panoramic pictures of this kind have unusual perspective characteristics. Lines at the top and bottom tend to curve toward vanishing points to the left and right of the frame. Flat walls photographed face-on, for example,

360° cameras
To photograph the landscape (below), David Buckland used a special camera which rotates through 360° while the shutter is open. These cameras are mounted on a tripod so the horizontal arc remains flat. You should fire the shutter from under the tripod, or use an air release from a distance, to avoid blocking the picture.

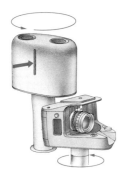

curve away into the distance at either end, while a curved subject — such as a concave row of chairs — appears as a straight line.

Most panoramic cameras have a direct vision viewfinder that gives a "wide screen" view of the scene. When you press the shutter release the lens or camera pivots to scan the subject from one end to the other. Shutter speeds range from 1/125 to 1/15 sec. Some types give a full panorama by turning through 360° during exposure. To use the camera you must mount it on a tripod. It takes 35 mm film and produces an image about 8 ins (20 cm) long. You have to print the image in sections, since there is no suitable enlarger.

Subminiature cameras
Cameras that use film smaller than the 110 format are generally known as "subminiatures". There are very few models on the market. One model, made by Minox, gives pictures 8 × 11 mm on film supplied in specially-made cartridges. It is a direct vision camera with a

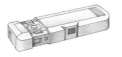

Subminiature camera
Though using an 8 × 11 mm picture size, so-called "spy" cameras have lenses of such quality that moderate enlargements are possible. Use either the maker's own film or a proprietary brand.

Film format

light cell that automatically controls the shutter speed. The body is designed to keep protruding external controls to a minimum. You wind on the film by pushing and pulling out the body casing. Subminiatures — the original "spy" cameras that will slip into a sleeve or pocket — have mostly been superceded by 110 cameras, which are almost as small. But the high quality of the available subminiatures makes them worth considering.

Stereo cameras
Until recently, the only way of producing a three-dimensional (or "stereo") image was to take a pair of transparencies of the same subject from two viewpoints. The viewpoints had to be separated horizontally by about $2\frac{1}{4}$ ins (6 cm) — the approximate distance between your eyes, and you had to view the transparencies through a special holder.

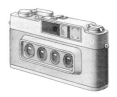

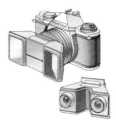

Stereoscopic cameras
The Nimslo (left) gives four images which are combined in processing into one 3D print. You can fit a standard lens with a stereo adaptor (below left).

Light from two distinct viewpoints (above) reaches the film to produce a stereo image which you look at using a viewer (bottom left).

The newly developed Nimslo stereo camera produces a three-dimensional print that you look at without a viewer. It uses four lenses to make four half-frame 35 mm pictures of each scene. You send the exposed film to a special processing laboratory, where an elaborate electronic printer merges the four images into a single print. To do this, the printer uses a lenticular screen. This consists of a finely ridged clear plastic sheet that refracts light. When you look at the same part of the screen, each eye sees a slightly different part of the image, and this discrepancy is responsible for the three-dimensional effect.

The camera accepts ASA 100 and ASA 400 color print film, and a switch on the camera top allows you to set the meter for the film you choose. The camera then sets the required exposure automatically. The four lenses are fixed-focus, which means that you must avoid close subjects, according to the manufacturer's recommendations.

High-speed cameras
A general-purpose camera with motor drive can expose pictures at up to 6 frames per second. But in scientific and industrial photography, where subjects may be very fast moving, a far quicker rate of high-quality "still" pictures is often necessary. Special cameras are used that transport the film continuously behind a rotating shutter. This gives exposure rates of over 1000 frames per second. Exposure duration is short (often only 1/10,000 sec) and a high subject illumination level is required to expose the film properly. Focusing is by a reflex system, and the camera accepts bulk lengths of 35 mm film.

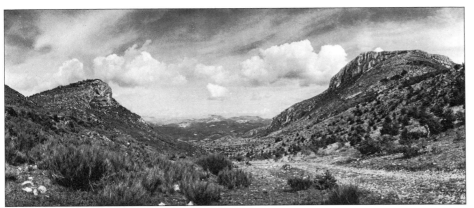

Special lenses

It is possible to carry out certain specialized photographic tasks with a conventional camera body if you use a purpose-built lens. Some of these lenses are designed for 35 mm cameras, others for larger format types. This means that you can take advantage of features available on regular cameras (such as the precise viewing and handling convenience of the SLR), as well as benefitting from top quality specialized equipment.

Anamorphic lenses

Anamorphic lenses where originally developed for the movie industry, where they allowed a wide screen to be filled from a squarer image on the film itself. But a few are available for still photography, either as attachments or complete lenses. The lens has front elements that are cylindrical in cross-section, rather than spherical. Consequently the image formed is stretched in one direction in relation to the other. Depending on which way you use the lens, the viewfinder image will appear stretched horizontally, and squeezed vertically, or vice versa. The image records like this on film, but you can print or project it through a similar lens to correct the image. The result is an undistorted picture with proportions of about 2.5:1 instead of the usual 1.5:1 of a 35 mm frame.

Anamorphic images are used for special distortion effects, wide-screen audio-visual slide shows, wall murals, or for any subjects that would not otherwise fit the conventional 35

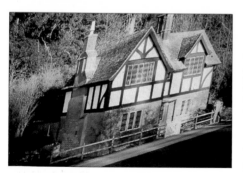

Anamorphic lens
This cylindrical concave lens has a vertical axis of curvature. Because of this, it "squeezes" the horizontal plane only, and compresses a wide horizontal angle of view into a standard frame. Andrew de Lory used an anamorphic lens to create this unusually distorted view of a cottage (above).

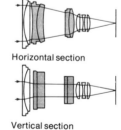

Horizontal section

Vertical section

mm or 6 × 6 cm frame. Anamorphic lenses are also invaluable for copying graphs, charts, or printed text that you want to enlarge or reduce proportionally in one dimension only. In these cases you enlarge the film with regular optics. A few large-format anamorphic lenses manufactured for the printing industry allow a continuously variable range of picture proportions.

A good anamorphic lens gives excellent image quality, but is expensive and quite bulky. Some of the attachments that fit over normally structured lenses give relatively poor image resolution, unless you set the prime lens to its smallest aperture.

Medical lenses

Several lenses specifically designed for medical and dental photography are available. Some are also extensively used by industrial photographers. The model shown below is widely used in general close-up work, because of its convenience of operation. It is a 200 mm, f 5.6 lens with a built-in electronic ring flash and a small focusing light, powered from a plug-in battery pack. A 120 mm version is

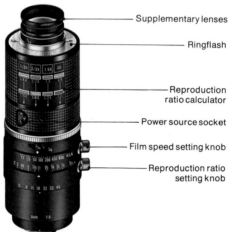

Supplementary lenses

Ringflash

Reproduction ratio calculator

Power source socket

Film speed setting knob

Reproduction ratio setting knob

200 mm medical lens
With its range of six supplementary lenses, built-in ringflash, and focusing light, this lens is an all-in-one close-up system. Magnifi-cation can be preset. The short flash duration allows hand-holding.

also available. A number of supplementary lens elements forms part of the kit. You use these singly or in various combinations to give an image-to-subject magnification between × 0.6 and × 3.

Because the lens has such a long focal length, you can use it well back from the subject. Distancing also helps to ensure that the ring flash produces very flat, even lighting. A fixed, constant-output light source like this greatly simplifies exposure calculation. The unusual lens barrel carries scales on which you set film speed and magnification ratio. Once these are set the lens automatically adjusts to the correct aperture. To focus, you simply move the complete camera backward and forward until the image on the focusing screen is sharp.

Soft-focus lenses

Certain lenses for sheet film cameras give a "soft-focus" effect. This is not quite the same as an out-of-focus image, because the soft-focus lens gives a mixture of focused and unfocused detail. The effect is a slight spreading of highlights and softening of fine detail. It was much admired by early pictorial photographers (see *Pictorialism*, pp. 334-41). Some

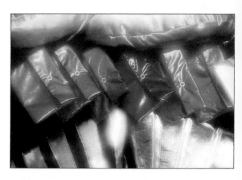

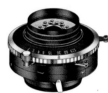

Controlled diffusion
This soft focus lens has interchangeable perforated disks which allow you to vary the degree of diffusion shown in the picture (above) photographed by Andrew de Lory.

portrait photographers use these lenses today – both for aesthetic reasons, and to avoid retouching blemishes, particularly when shooting color transparencies.

Most soft-focus lenses have a pair of elements only partly corrected for aberrations, and a perforated disk. A larger, center hole in the disk forms a sharp image, while smaller holes determine how many of the marginal, aberration-prone light rays are included. Some lenses have a conventional iris diaphragm, enabling you to cut out the peripheral holes, so that the smaller the aperture set, the less soft the result. Other types have no diaphragm, and use interchangeable disks with varying perforations. Each disk has an equivalent f number for exposure purposes. For cameras smaller than 5 × 4 ins (12.5 × 10 cm) format, a range of lens attachments gives similar effects (see *Special effects attachments*, pp. 198-200).

Convertible lenses

Some lenses for sheet film cameras offer a choice between two focal lengths. You can either use them complete or, by removing one section, use the remaining elements as a longer focal length lens. A typical convertible lens has a 150 mm focal length in complete form, but becomes a 430 mm telephoto when you remove the back half.

The altered focal length means that the f

Convertible lens
Some standard lenses (right) can be used as a long-focus lens by removing the rear lens elements. This means that the f number scale will not apply.

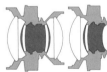

Standard   Telephoto

number scale is no longer correct. A second set of higher numbers is provided in a different color, for use in the telephoto mode. Convertible lenses give best image quality when you use the whole lens. But they can be useful if you have a sheet film camera, but require the longer focal length only occasionally. Try to use it well stopped down.

Future design trends

Compared with the first clumsy daguerreotype cameras and early hand-held types, modern cameras are enormously sophisticated instruments. Pioneer photographers would barely recognize today's SLR as a camera at all. In the same way we may have difficulty identifying the cameras of the near future. Although recent progress itself seems dramatic, there are even more revolutionary developments still to come.

Microelectronic circuitry is ideally suited to a compact, complex piece of equipment such as a camera. Microelectronics have already contributed extensively to changes in camera design and promise to do so even more in the future. In many ways cameras are still too mechanical. Their moving parts are subject to wear and vulnerable to damage. Simple cameras should be more foolproof and at the same time less restrictive in their range of applications. These are challenges to the camera designer that will probably be met with the more extensive use of microelectronic components.

Changes will also take place that will make the technical aspects of photography less complicated and archaic. For example, the use of an expensive metal such as silver as a consumable material is wasteful. Its processing in liquids is primitive and time-consuming. Future cameras will probably allow the photographer to examine results immediately and (unlike present instant pictures) erase images without cost if they are not satisfactory, or store them for enlarging later if they are successful.

Immediate developments
The electrocircuitry at present employed in the majority of cameras (see *35 mm SLR cameras,* pp. 102-4) will spread further. For example, the information link between the lens aperture and the internal meter on an SLR is mechanical, but electronic circuits will perform this task on future cameras. Emulsion speeds will be recorded magnetically on film cassettes, and camera meters will be able to sense this information electronically, so that the user does not have to set a film speed dial.

Built-in motor drives are likely to become much more common, and cameras will feature a self-threading mechanism, which will automatically draw the film on the take-up spool once the photographer has put a film cassette in place. This will save time and lost shots when changing films.

Viewfinder information will become more comprehensive. Frame numbers will be shown as well as the usual exposure settings. But there will be less use of the LED signals that are common today. Instead, information will appear digitally – as words and figures – rather than as lights that the user has to translate. Manual changes of shutter speeds and lens aperture settings will be by pressing small buttons (like those on a pocket calculator) rather than by turning rings. Several of these changes have already appeared on certain cameras.

Automatic focusing will become a common feature, especially if the user can

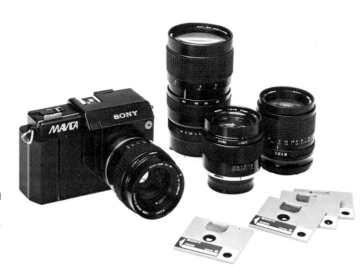

Video still camera
This automatic SLR does not use conventional film. Instead, a solid state imager known as a CCD (charge coupled device) translates image light into electronic signals which record on a small magnetic disk. Each disk records 50 color pictures, which can be individually erased and re-used. A playback unit enables you to see the results immediately on a domestic TV screen.

"lock" the mechanism on a particular subject, and override it when necessary. For SLR cameras with interchangeable lenses, an autofocus mechanism within the camera body is needed to allow autofocus with any lens. Recently introduced autofocus lenses for particular brands of SLR provide a limited range of focal lengths, although an autofocus zoom is available.

Cameras will also have electronic servicing outlets. This will enable any service engineer to link the camera to an analyzing computer, to give a readout of all the camera's functions. This principle is already commonly employed with other types of precision electronic equipment.

Automation in camera manufacturing, together with the enormous and ever-increasing interest in photography, will lower prices still further. The range of features available for a particular price will multiply, and this should affect both automatic cameras designed for simplicity of operation, and elaborate models intended to be as versatile as possible.

Long-term developments
Developments that will take place further into the future depend on components yet to be perfected. These are the liquid crystal display (LCD) and the charge-coupled device (CCD). LCDs are most commonly used in digital watches. They make it possible to render a flat plate either black or transparent, by applying an electric current. This facility may be used to produce non-moving mirrors for SLR cameras. When you press the shutter release you will electronically wipe the reflective surface from the mirror, with the result that light will pass to the back of the camera. A similar LCD inside the lens could act as a non-moving shutter. This could also take the place of an iris diaphragm – the f stop setting will program the size of the transparent aperture in the LCD panel. The resulting exposure system would be completely silent, and not subject to mechanical wear. The camera's only mechanical function would be the film wind-on.

Other likely developments are zoom lenses with much wider ranges than at pre-

sent. The use of plastic elements will make lenses much lighter, and substitutes for metal will lead to lighter camera bodies. But camera size is much less likely to decrease. Experience with some 110 designs has shown that cameras must be sufficiently large to fit comfortably in the hand.

Another development that promises to make photography more convenient is a new type of film pack containing film in the form of a disk. With no need to unwind the film from a spool, processing and printing will be quicker, and it will be possible to process a number of disks at once by threading them on a rod. Special cameras will be necessary to take the new film, and these are expected to be aimed at the 110 market.

The all-electronic camera
A much more radical development is the adaption of video technology to still photography. One still video camera records images on a rotating magnetic disk. Results can then be viewed via a special replayer unit, through a conventional television set. Alternatively, it will be possible to connect a printer, to produce color prints. The electronic signals representing color images can be transmitted by telephone.

The camera uses a flat panel charge-coupled device (CCD) to convert the light into a stream of electronic signals that the disk can record. The main drawback is that image quality, when results are played back through a television set or print-maker, is less detailed than that offered by a conventional photograph. But further research will improve results, as well as opening up further possibilities. For example, contrast control, exposure compensation, and special effects image manipulations normally carried out in the darkroom, should be possible electronically.

The magnetic disk itself also offers a number of advantages. It is relatively inexpensive, simple to load, and re-usable like magnetic recording tape. As the image quality of the still video system improves it is likely to revolutionize the field of photography in future decades.

Post-camera techniques

This section details the routes film originals can travel to produce a wide variety of different photographic results. Practical explanations of the processing of all black and white and color film types is followed by darkroom layout, the equipment needed, and the methods of making enlargements. After the basic and more advanced techniques in black and white and color printing, the final part of the section concentrates on special darkroom and workroom effects. These can be used to create imagery that treats the original camera image as only the starting point for a more personal visual statement. None of the special effects requires extensive additional equipment.

The processing and printing aspects of photography have their own, traditional, mystique. They do, after all, take place in the dark and involve the use of potentially dangerous chemicals and unfamiliar equipment. This attitude is largely based on imagery coming to us from the turn of the century, when darkroom work called for a knowledge of chemistry and carried an element of risk. Today, it is a far more streamlined routine involving relatively little time in the dark, and no more knowledge of chemistry than is required for, say, cooking.

The black and white process

The minute exposure the light-sensitive material receives inside the camera creates a "latent" image. The ability to amplify this invisible image into a permanent, stable picture was the keystone of the first practical photographic process. To "bring out" the image in the daguerreotype process, the exposed light-sensitive silvered plate was held face down over warmed mercury. Mercury vapor clung to light-struck parts of the plate, giving these areas a matte, grayish white appearance. Next, it was bathed in a "fixing" solution to remove any remaining light-sensitive salts, washed, and dried. The result was a direct positive image in shiny metal.

William Henry Fox Talbot's rival calotype process used light-sensitive writing paper. After exposure, the paper was soaked in a silver nitrate solution to turn light-struck areas into black metallic silver, then fixed and washed. Talbot's pictures were therefore negatives, capable of giving any number of positive prints when exposed on similarly treated paper. Subsequent processes such as collodion (1851) and eventually gelatin-coated, light-sensitive glass plates (1876) confirmed the value of negative/positive methods of photographic reproduction.

Photographic plates were processed in open trays in a blacked-out room lit by a red "safelight" lantern containing a candle, gas, or an oil lamp. (Emulsions were blue-only sensitive.) First, the plate was slid face up into an alkaline developing solution, containing a mixture of developing agents with some restraining chemicals to prevent overactivity on unexposed areas. The tray was rocked and the plate watched carefully until the slowly blackening image seemed dark enough. Development was therefore "by inspection".

The plate was then transferred to a tray of fixer — a solution of what in the nineteenth century was known as hyposulfite of soda (since renamed sodium thiosulfate, although the abbreviation "hypo" still remains). The fixer made remaining undeveloped silver halides soluble so that they could be removed by washing. Finally the plate was left to dry. Early rollfilms were treated in the same way, held in a U-shape and passed back and forth through the processing trays. Special trays were made for the purpose with a bridge or roller across the top to keep the long length of film immersed in solution throughout the sequence.

The coming of orthochromatic and panchromatic materials made development by inspection impracticable. Over- or underdevelopment was avoided by the use of a system of "time and temperature" — the lower the temperature the longer the time. A clock and thermometer became essential aids to processing. Trays were no longer much used (especially for rollfilm) and by the turn of the century, crude tanks had been introduced for processing film in a loose roll. Tanks had light-tight lids and allowed the photographer to work in normal light once the tank had been loaded and sealed.

Developers and fixers were mostly made up from raw chemicals by the photographers themselves. There were hundreds of developer formulae, and everyone had their own favorite kinds. As more convenient, prepacked chemicals became cheaper this practice died away, and black and white developers today are limited to about a dozen different kinds, varying in their effect on film contrast, emulsion speed, and grain.

Negatives, whether on film, paper, or glass, have to be printed on light-sensitive paper to produce a "negative of a negative" — an image with correct tonal values and right-reading details. The most popular nineteenth century printing paper was prepared using albumen (egg white) and silver chloride. Albumen paper worked by "printing out", visibly darkening after several minutes exposure to daylight. The paper was placed behind the plate negative in a frame and left in direct sunlight until it was seen to have darkened sufficiently. It was then fixed, washed, and dried. All prints were made by contact, and to produce a large photograph a correspondingly large camera had to be used.

By the 1870s faster "bromide" paper, coated with an emulsion of silver bromide and gelatin, had become available. This paper only required enough exposure to form a latent image, and was then developed and fixed in trays in a similar way to negatives. It was sensitive enough to print on by artificial light, and magic lanterns were converted to act as horizontally mounted projectors (or enlargers). Usual light sources were oil, gas, and daylight directed to enter the enlarger through a hole in the darkroom wall. The introduction of electricity made it possible to use more convenient vertical enlargers. Enlargers made the concept of small cameras attractive, because their small film image could now be enlarged.

Many special printing materials and processes — platinum, gum bichromate, and bromoil, for example — were invented and used by enthusiasts for the particular image quality they produced. All were eventually discontinued, either because of cost or complexity, leaving bromide emulsions, which are still used today.

The color process

For the first thirty years of this century satisfactory color prints could only be made by professionals and advanced amateurs taking three black and white negatives through different-colored filters. Negatives were printed by methods such as the carbon process, which gave an image in any chosen dye. The blue filtered negative was printed in yellow dye, the green in magenta, and the red in cyan dye. Then each print was transferred, in register, to a single sheet of paper to form a full-color picture. Printing was extremely laborious and uncertain.

An easier process invented in 1907 by the Lumière brothers in France made it possible to make a plate-size color transparency. The Autochrome plate (and later, various makes of film) was coated with a mosaic of minute blue, green, and red dyed specks, which acted as filters. Behind this was coated a panchromatic black and white emulsion. The picture in the camera was exposed to light from the subject through the mosaic, so light from blue parts of the subject only passed through and affected emulsion parts behind the blue specks. Red parts registered behind red specks, and green behind green specks. White parts of the subject were recorded behind all three.

Mosaic materials were processed in black and white developer to form a negative, but instead of fixing, the black silver was bleached away and remaining halides fogged and blackened instead. This produced a positive image and is called reversal processing. When the plate or film was held up to the light, only blue and red specks of the mosaic allowed light to pass in blue and red parts of the image. Other mosaic colors in these areas were blocked by blackened silver. In areas where all three filters passed light, the colors mixed to form white.

Mosaic color materials were relatively easy to process, but results were always dim and there was no satisfactory way of making paper prints. Throughout the 1920s and 1930s manufacturers researched ways of improving color materials. It was found that a "stack" of blue, green, and red sensitive emulsions could be coated on one film support, but the difficulty was to make each layer develop into a different colored dye.

Kodachrome, the first of a new generation of tricolor films to achieve this, is processed in a very complicated way. First, a developer forms black and white negatives in all layers, then each emulsion layer is reversal processed, one at a time, by fogging it to the appropriately colored light. After each layer has been fogged, it is treated with its own color developer to form the required color dye image. Processing then – as now – involved many steps and was not suitable for home use. Agfa and then Kodak solved this problem during the late 1930s by incorporating the different colorless "coupler" chemicals in each emulsion layer. A single color developer could then trigger different color images. This "chromogenic" processing was therefore much simpler.

In practice, color slide films are given ordinary negative development, and then the remaining halides are fogged to white light and treated in a color developer to form dyes in these areas. Finally, by bleaching away all silver, leaving just the dye, a positive color slide results. This used to take about eight to ten processing stages. Color negative processing is less complicated as only color developer and its following stages are needed. The same routine is used for color paper processing, which also has triple emulsion layers.

Color negative films and papers first became available after the Second World War, but the chemicals for home processing were not released until a few years later. Chemicals for processing color have always been sold in kits of ready weighed powders or liquids. Each film or paper is designed to be given a particular process, and these are periodically updated. For example, the original Ektachrome (1946) needed E-1 processing, which took one and a half hours. Today's Ektachrome is processed in E-6 and takes only 37 minutes.

Recent developments

Developments in processing, printing, and finishing have progressed in three main directions. The quality of dyes used has been improved, processes have been speeded up, and new materials and equipment have made color processing and printing more convenient to do at home.

During the 1960s a new form of color print material (Cibachrome) was introduced. This silver dye-bleach material contains pure, fully formed dyes within the emulsions. Special processing bleaches the dyes where they are not required for the image – a system opposite to chemical dye formation. In the early 1970s resin-coated paper was introduced to replace the regular fiber-based papers. Having a water-proof base means that chemicals cannot sink into the support, so speeding up rinsing, washing, fixing, and drying times. New color materials such as photo color transfer (Ektaflex), introduced in 1981, also greatly reduce print production times. PCT materials use a form of peel-apart instant picture film to give color prints, and only require one processing solution.

Film processing

The main skills in film processing are loading the film tank and maintaining the precise temperature of the processing solutions. The length of time the film remains in contact with these solutions is another important factor for consideration. Processing is not a long operation – color negatives, for example, take about 30 minutes (excluding drying time), while the longest process takes between 40 and 60 minutes (for color slides). To make best use of your time, and most efficient use of the processing chemicals, film tanks are available that accept several reels of film. For 35 mm black and white and color processing a simple daylight film tank is sufficient. But for color print processing, there are drums available that also accept special inserts for holding film. A multipurpose tank of this type may be very convenient.

Working under a colored safelight is unnecessary and generally unwise with most camera films. The safelight must be extremely dim to be usable with most color-sensitive emulsions. For the short period you have to be in total darkness (from unloading the film container to loading the film tank), it is better to consider using a changing bag – a black opaque cloth bag with light-tight armholes, and large enough for loading small film tanks in a normally lit room. The other basic requirements for film processing are a thermometer, timer, and graduates for the solutions. Films are not dried inside the tank, but hung up clipped to a line to dry naturally, or enclosed in a cubicle equipped with a heated blower unit.

Choice of chemicals

There is a fairly wide choice of developers for black and white negative film processing. To start with it is best to use one of the types recommended on the packing slip accompanying the film. Later you can experiment with other types of developers designed to maximize speed with fast films, or types giving highest resolution with slow films, or extreme contrast with specialized lith materials. Information packed with these developers will state the times and temperatures required for processing.

Stop baths and fixers are common to all developer and film types. It is also possible to reversal process some black and white negative films to give direct black and white slides for projection. You must have a special black and white processing kit to do this, and there are more processing steps.

Color film chemicals are bought in kit form, containing all the necessary solutions. Some are designed for reversal processing slides, others for processing color negatives. At one time, each brand of color film required its own unique type of kit. Today for home processing, this has been rationalized into four different types. Most Kodak films, and products made by Fuji, Barfen, and some 3M and Agfa materials use E-6 chemicals, if they are slide film, or C-41 chemicals if negatives. Films of this kind are sometimes quoted as using "A type chemistry". A few films such as the older Agfa films still use "B type chemistry", which means using Agfa process 41 for slides and Agfa N for negatives. These processes work at a lower temperature but take a longer time. Finally, there are some films – notably Kodachrome – that require much more complicated processing, and this can only be carried out by the manufacturer or at specially equipped laboratories. Your color film container will be clearly marked with the process required if home processing is possible.

Types of result

As shown in the table on the right, the film you expose in the camera need not totally commit you to one type of result. Black and white prints, for example, can be made from color negatives, or color prints from color slides. Black and white films can be processed as black and white slides, or color slides processed as color negatives for special effects. It is even possible to make color prints (of a kind) from black and white negatives. There are also intermediate (low-contrast) materials that allow you to make either color negatives or black and white negatives from color slides, which can then be printed on the appropriate negative/positive paper. In general, however, the most direct route between camera film and the final print material will give you the best quality results.

Black and white films

Film type	Film sensitivity	Film process
Negative – standard silver halide emulsion forming a black silver negative image.	Panchromatic, ASA 25-1600. Infrared.	General fine-grain, high-acutance, or speed-compensating developers.
Negative – silver-dye emulsion forming a dye negative image.	Panchromatic, ASA 25-1600 (no change on camera setting or film).	Chromogenic color developer, as for color negatives.
Positive – silver negative films suitably processed.	Panchromatic, ASA 25-125.	Reversal black and white kit – gives direct positive slides.

Color negative films

Film type	Film sensitivity	Film process
Silver-dye emulsions forming triple dye image. Incorporates dye mask.	ASA 125-600. Most balanced for daylight, but some tungsten.	Kit containing chromogenic color developer compatible with film.
Internegative – similar to above, but lower contrast.	Tungsten light.	Chromogenic color developer kit, as above.

Color slide film

Film type	Film sensitivity	Film process
Substantive – silver-dye emulsion forming triple dye image.	ASA 50-640. Most balanced for daylight, but some tungsten. Also infrared type.	Reversal chromogenic color kit compatible with film.
Non-substantive – silver emulsion without couplers.	ASA 25-64. Daylight balanced. One only tungsten type.	Elaborate machine processing. Not suitable for home processing.
Slide print film.	Tungsten light.	Same as for negative/positive color paper.

Special materials

Type
Black and white bromide emulsions on a variety of surfaces such as linen, opal plastic, metal, and colored base paper. Blue-only sensitive or orthochromatic. Only available in one contrast grade.
Line or lith films. Blue-only sensitive, orthochromatic and some panchromatic types.
Photo-stabilization black and white papers. Blue-only sensitive. The developing agent is contained within the emulsion.

Black and white papers

Paper type	Paper sensitivity	Paper process	Comments
Resin or fiber black and white bromide — variable contrast grade. All finishes —for prints from negatives.	Mostly blue-sensitive. A few orthochromatic types.	General black and white print developer. Some warm-tone developers.	The normal way of working is to print silver or dye image black and white negatives on resin-coated bromide paper. Panchromatic paper is not essential for printing from color negatives, but the usual blue-sensitive papers will produce some tonal distortion. Use direct reversal paper for contact prints and rough proofs only — it has high contrast, and renders red and orange subjects black. For the best results from slides, copy or contact print on regular panchromatic film, and then print this negative on bromide paper.
Panchromatic — for prints from color negatives.	Panchromatic.	General print developers.	
Direct reversal or prints from slides.	Orthochromatic	General print developers.	

Color papers — negative/positive

Paper type	Paper process	Comments
Resin-coated chromogenic paper. Various surfaces.	Chromogenic color developer kit compatible with the paper.	Color negatives are usually printed on regular chromogenic or photo color transfer materials. Filtering and exposing techniques are similar, but processing is completely different. To make color slides or enlarged transparencies, print on special slide or print film. Internegative film gives optimum results when color prints must be made from color slides on negative/positive color paper. Color slides can be printed directly on negative/positive paper to give contrasty, reversed color and tone images for special effects.
Photo color transfer process— exposing on intermediate film, then transfering image to paper.	Single-solution alkali activator. Peel-apart process.	

Color papers — positive/positive

Paper type	Paper process	Comments
Resin-coated chromogenic reversal paper. Available in various surfaces.	Chromogenic reversal color kit compatible with paper type.	Both substantive and the older (Kodachrome) non-substantive films print well on all three printing materials, provided that the image is not too contrasty or overexposed. Chromogenic reversal material has the least stable dyes, and is the most critical to process. Photo color transfer has the quickest processing, using a special print-making unit. Slide print film is a clear-based darkroom material designed for printing color slides from color negatives. All positive/positive papers can be used for direct image formation— in a large-format camera — for color photography. But emulsion speed is extremely slow and the image will appear laterally reversed on the paper (except for PCT).
Silver dye-bleach. Contains silver emulsions plus fully formed dye layers. Available in various surfaces.	Silver dye-bleach color kit designed specifically for SDB paper.	
Photo color transfer process— same as negative/positive prints (above), but different transfer film chemistry. Two surfaces.	Same single-solution activator used for negative/positive photo color transfer materials (above).	

Process/result	Comments
Normal or high-contrast print developer. Forms a black image, which may later be toned.	Available in sheets or rolls (except for metal). Used mostly for display work.
High-contrast developer. Lith film requires special lith developer for best results. Gives black and white result with no mid-tones.	Used for copying line drawings, lettering, and special effects applications such as masks and separations.
Special motor roller transport processing unit. Applies alkali activator, then stabilization solution. No washing stage required.	Used when fast print production is essential. Processed results are complete to damp-dry in only 15 seconds. Results, however, are not permanent.

Film and paper image formation

The present trend is for photographic materials and processes to become standardized as manufacturers discover the best, most efficient, and cheapest ways of making and processing films and papers. Although silver — the basis of most photography — is expensive, no efficient substitute has yet been found. There are other ways of making a permanent photographic image — electronically or electrostatically, for example. The major disadvantages with all these methods are, however, that they cannot match the combination of light sensitivity and image detail resolving power offered by salts of silver.

The newer type of chromogenic black and white film is based on similar principles to those of color negative film and requires the same processing. Silver and dye images are both formed in a color developer. During processing the silver is completely removed, leaving only the dye. On a commercial scale this silver can be recovered and reused.

Starting with a black and white negative it is usual to make a positive print on light-sensitive bromide paper, which may have a resin-coated (plastic) or fiber base. On exposure to the film image in the enlarger, the paper reacts to make a tonally reversed image of the already tonally reversed negative.

Materials for color prints

Color negative materials produce a negative with colors complementary to subject colors and tones reversed. The negative film has a magenta or orange mask that forms during development. It is designed to correct any inaccurate dye response during printing. This film can be enlarged, in a way similar to that used in black and white printing, but using negative/positive color paper. By using negative/positive film instead of paper it is also possible to make a color slide directly from a color negative.

Color slide films are similar in structure to color negative films, but are designed to be reversal processed so that the subject reproduces directly in its correct colors and tones. Starting with a color slide there are several ways of making a color print. In all cases the paper must be capable of forming a positive image from a positive film image.

The new color transfer method of printing can be used to make positive prints from either color negatives or color slides (different exposing material is used in each case). It uses the same principle as peel-apart instant picture film, and only requires a simple alkaline solution to activate the process.

Black and white materials

Modern black and white film is a sandwich consisting of a top coating of gelatin (which protects the emulsion), the emulsion itself (which may consist of several layers of light-sensitive silver halides suspended in gelatin), and the film base or support. The base has to be dimensionally stable, flexible, and tough, and is generally made of a cellulose triacetate. The film has an antihalation layer designed to stop light bouncing back from the film base and diffusing the image. This is particularly noticeable around point sources of light.

Paper structure

Most black and white (and color) paper is coated on a base consisting of paper fiber sealed front and back in clear plastic. Chemicals can-

	Supercoat
	Emulsion
	Baryta
	Paper base

Fiber base
Traditional, fiber-base papers have a barium sulfate (baryta) undercoat to improve whiteness. A thin gelatin supercoat protects the emulsion surface.

	Supercoat
	Emulsion
	Resin coat
	Paper base
	Resin coat
	Antistatic backing

Resin coated
Most modern papers have a fiber base coated with white plastic. Chemicals are then only absorbed by the emulsion, not the base itself.

not sink into the base, so that processing, washing and drying times are shortened. The plastic-coated paper has a layer of silver halide emulsion and a gelatin supercoat at the top to protect the emulsion surface from nor-

mal handling damage. Plastic paper may also have an antistatic backing.

Some black and white papers are still fiber-based only. In this case, the paper carries a layer of baryta to improve its whiteness. Because of the absence of the plastic, the paper base tends to absorb a large amount of processing chemicals. This, in turn, means that you must greatly extend washing time at the end of the processing sequence in order to ensure that all traces of chemical residue are removed. Any chemical remaining in the paper will, in time, cause staining of the image. The paper is also dried differently, and has to be glazed if a glossy finish is required. The availability of many types of fiber-based paper is rapidly declining as resin-coated paper becomes popular.

How the image is formed

Once the film or paper is exposed correctly to light, tiny atoms of silver are formed in some of the silver halides in the emulsion. At this point the changes are too small to detect and the exposed material carries only a latent image. During the processing sequence, the action of the developing agent amplifies the atoms of silver millions of times. In effect, each silver halide grain originally affected by light is completely converted to black metallic silver.

The fixing solution turns the remaining, unexposed silver halides into soluble complex silver salts, which you can remove by washing. The gelatin support performs two functions. First, it swells when in solution and so allows developer and fixation chemicals to penetrate and reach the silver halides. Second, it anchors the silver salts (or silver image) in position on the film or paper base. As most photographic materials are still based on silver image formation, these principles apply to many color films and paper as well.

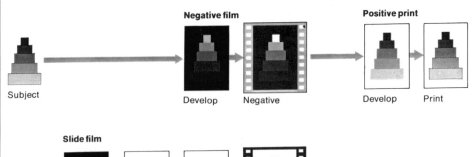

Negative film   Positive print

Subject   Develop   Negative   Develop   Print

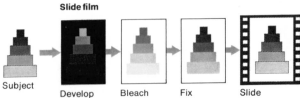

Slide film

Subject   Develop   Bleach   Fix   Slide

Black and white neg/pos
As shown above (top) the image of the subject, after exposure on film in the camera, is made visible by developer chemicals, which convert light-struck halides to black silver. Fixing and washing clears remaining areas of halides, leaving a negative film image. When this, in turn, is exposed on printing paper (via the enlarger) and given similar processing, a positive image results.

Black and white slide
Some black and white negative/positive films can also be processed to produce a direct positive transparency on film (black and white slide). After development, the black silver negative is bleached without affecting remaining halides. These are then fogged to white light and developed, forming a positive slide image.

Chromogenic film and paper theory

Most types of color material, and some black and white, you are likely to use will be based on the principles of chromogenic development. This is a process in which the exhausted (oxidation) products of a color developer combine with colorless color coupler chemicals present in the emulsion to form dyes. Only two commonly available color printing materials do not use chromogenic principles of development. One is silver dye-bleach (SDB) printing paper (Cibachrome), and the other is color transfer paper (Ektaflex). These each use their own system of fully formed dyes incorporated in the emulsion layers.

How chromogenic processes work

For either negative/positive or positive/positive results the principles and general structure of chromogenic materials are the same. The film or paper support has a minimum of three layers of light-sensitive emulsions. This arrangement is referred to as an "integral tripack", and in color materials the three emulsion layers are sensitive to approximately one-third of the visual spectrum each. One of the layers is sensitive to blue light, one to green light, and one to red light.

When exposed color negative film or negative/positive color paper is placed in its chromogenic color developer changes occur in

Supercoat
Red-sensitive emulsion +
cyan coupler
Green-sensitive emulsion +
magenta coupler
Blue-sensitive emulsion +
yellow coupler
Paper base

Chromogenic neg/pos color paper

The three emulsion layers of chromogenic negative/positive paper differ in their color sensitivity and the type of (largely colorless) dye couplers they contain. During color development oxidation by-products turn couplers into cyan, magenta, and yellow dyes wherever exposed halides are developed into black silver. Bleaching, fixing, and washing removes all the remaining black silver and unused silver halides, leaving only pure dye.

two stages. First, the exposed silver halides in each layer are turned into black metallic silver. Second, the by-products of this change (mostly oxidized developer) react with couplers linked with each grain, so that dye is formed along with the silver wherever exposure occurred. In the blue layer an image in yellow dye is formed, while in the green- and red-sensitive layers other couplers form magenta and cyan images respectively.

After the three image dyes have been formed in the emulsions by development, you must dissolve the remaining black silver image in bleach and the unexposed silver halides in a fix solution. This will leave you with an image in pure dye on a paper base for negative/positive prints or on a film base for negatives.

The processing of reversal (slide) chromogenic materials follows a similar routine, but is preceded by an extra black and white devel-
opment stage. This creates black and white negative images in each layer, and it is the remaining halides which are then fogged and chromogenically developed. As a result, parts of the original scene that were not blue record in yellow dye, non-green parts record in the green-sensitive layer as magenta, and non-red parts record as cyan. The final result is a direct positive slide or positive/positive print.

Chromogenic black and white film

Dyes formed chromogenically, by the combination of oxidized developer and color couplers in the film, are the basis of several modern types of black and white negative film. You can process the film with the same kit you use for color negative film. The main difference between these films and color films is that all the

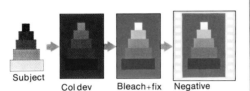

Subject   Col dev   Bleach+fix   Negative

Chromogenic negative process

When chromogenic black and white film is processed, color development first forms black silver negatives plus similar dye images in the various emulsion layers. Next, silver bleaching and fixing leaves dyes, collectively forming a monochrome negative. When color negative film is given this chromogenic processing, the different color sensitivity of each emulsion layer results in a multicolored instead monochrome negative.

emulsion layers have the same panchromatic sensitivity, instead of responding to one-third of the spectrum each. Consequently, the images formed in each layer are identical, except for their dye color — when the processed film is examined, the combined dyes are seen to form a warm black or brown monochrome set of negatives. The dyes used in chromogenic black and white film are designed to produce virtually grainless results. As long as you expose the film anywhere within the limits recommended by the manufacturer (and you can vary exposure from frame to frame) you can use a standard development time to produce negatives of consistent density.

Chromogenic color toning

Chromogenic development principles can also be applied to color toning a finished black and white print — replacing the silver image with a dye color of your choice.

To tone an image chromogenically you must start with a fully processed, washed, and dried black and white print, and then bleach it to "halogenize" the image. This means returning the image areas of the printing paper to the state they were in when you had exposed the paper under the enlarger but not developed it. In the next stage you must redevelop the image in a suitable color developer. Instead of having a color coupler incorporated in the emulsion, you must add a color former to the developer solution. The developer oxidizes as it rebleaches the silver image and combines

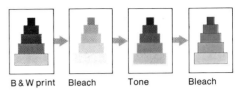

B & W print   Bleach   Tone   Bleach

Chromogenic toning

The silver image in a black and white print, slide, or negative can be converted to a dye by chromogenic toning. First the silver is bleached back to a silver halide (rehalogenized). Then it is redarkened in a color developer containing a color former — creating dye along with the silver. Finally, the silver can be bleached away, leaving only the dye image.

Color toning formulae		
Working-strength developer		
Activol No. 7	2.5	g
Sodium sulfite (anh)	16.7	g
Sodium carbonate (anh)	25.0	g
Potassium bromide	0.58	g
Add water to make 1 liter		
Color formers		
Magenta p-nitrophenylacetonitrile $\frac{1}{4}$ % solution in methyl ethyl ketone		
Cyan Dichlor α — naphthol $\frac{1}{2}$ % solution in methyl ethyl ketone		
Yellow Dichlor acetoacetanilide 1 % solution in methyl ethyl ketone		
Add 60 ml color former to 1 liter working-strength developer		
Bleach A		
Potassium ferricyanide		30 g
Potassium bromide		10 g
Sodium carbonate (anh)		16 g
Add water to make 1 liter		
Bleach B		
Farmer's reducer		
Stages		
Bleach A, wash, working-strength developer (including color former), wash, bleach B (to remove silver image only).		

with the color former incorporated within the developer to form a dye. The final result will consist of a combination of silver image overlayed with a colored dye image. For an alternative result you can use a silver bleach to remove the black silver image, leaving only the dye. Yellow color formers tend to produce the most dramatic results, but you must bleach away the silver afterward.

Negative/positive material

With chromogenic color negative film, the light-sensitive layers are arranged so that the top layer responds to blue light, the second layer to green light, and the third layer to red light. All three layers are sensitive to blue light, so there is a yellow filter underneath the top layer to stop blue light affecting the other two. This filter is bleached away completely during the processing sequence.

An important additional feature of color negative film — one which immediately distinguishes it from all other types — is the presence of a built-in color mask. This gives processed negatives an overall pale pink or orange appearance that varies according to brand. (This is also seen in the creamy, unprocessed emul-

sion, which has a warmer tint.) The mask helps compensate for slight deficiencies in the chromogenic dyes formed in both negative and paper. Magenta, for example, tends to absorb some blue along with green light. By making the normally clear parts of the processed magenta image an equally blue-absorbing pale yellow, the whole layer takes on an even gray-to-blue appearance. (It then simply requires slightly more exposure at the printing stage.) The final color print reproduces green objects as purer green, with less blue tint.

This masking technique cannot be applied to slides, however. They are usually projected or viewed as complete in themselves, and the eye would not accept an overall mask tint. Negatives, on the other hand, are purely intermediary, which is one reason why color prints made from color negatives normally give greater color fidelity than prints made from color slides. As chromogenically formed dyes improve, the necessity for masking grows less. Modern negatives have a much paler mask than that used in materials ten years ago.

Negative/positive chromogenic paper has the red-sensitive layer at the top, the green-sensitive layer in the middle, and the blue-sen-

sitive layer next to the paper base. (This gives a final image with the cyan layer at the top, which, in a print, improves sharpness and depth.) Processing is simple and, as with color negative film, you require only one developing stage. In the color developer silver and dye negatives are formed. The bleach/fix bath (usually combined in one solution) removes the silver image and any unexposed silver halides. After washing you give the print a final stabilization bath with some processes, but with others, stabilization occurs earlier in the processing sequence.

Positive/positive material

Chromogenic slide film is more complicated than negative material, and there are two basic types — "substantive" and "non-substantive". Structurally the two types are similar, but processing differs quite radically. The essential difference between the two is that with substantive films (such as Ektachrome) the couplers are in the emulsion.

With substantive chromogenic film you must first give the exposed material a standard black and white development to form the negative silver images in each layer. This stage is

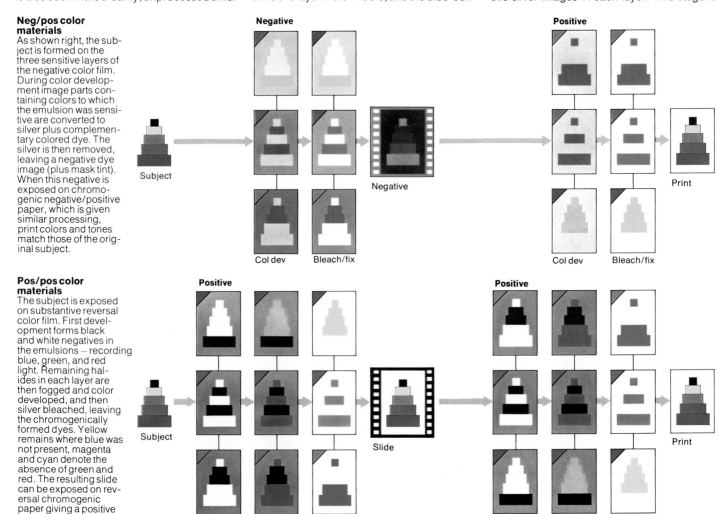

Neg/pos color materials
As shown right, the subject is formed on the three sensitive layers of the negative color film. During color development image parts containing colors to which the emulsion was sensitive are converted to silver plus complementary colored dye. The silver is then removed, leaving a negative dye image (plus mask tint). When this negative is exposed on chromogenic negative/positive paper, which is given similar processing, print colors and tones match those of the original subject.

Subject

Negative

Col dev   Bleach/fix

Negative

Positive

Print

Col dev   Bleach/fix

Pos/pos color materials
The subject is exposed on substantive reversal color film. First development forms black and white negatives in the emulsions — recording blue, green, and red light. Remaining halides in each layer are then fogged and color developed, and then silver bleached, leaving the chromogenically formed dyes. Yellow remains where blue was not present, magenta and cyan denote the absence of green and red. The resulting slide can be exposed on reversal chromogenic paper giving a positive color print.

Subject

Positive

B & W dev   Col dev   Bleach/fix

Slide

Positive

B & W dev   Col dev   Bleach/fix

Print

critical. The next step is a reversal bath or a reversal fogging exposure. This makes all the silver halides that were not affected by the initial camera exposure developable. The second developer is a color developer, which forms a positive silver image as well as oxidation by-products that react with the color couplers present in the emulsion.

If, for example, you had photographed a blue object, then on exposure in the camera, only the blue-sensitive layer of the film would react and develop a record of the object in black silver. After the reversal bath, the unused green- and red-layer halides become developable in the same area, and when these are color developed they form positive images in silver plus magenta and cyan dyes. You must next remove all the silver in the film by bleaching. This bleach in fact converts the silver to silver bromide, which you can remove in a fix bath. (Often the bleach and fix stages are combined in one "blix" solution.) When you view the processed film image by transmitted light the remaining magenta and cyan dyes combine to blue — the color of the original object. What was formerly a film base supporting a complex series of dye images overlaid with silver is now a much simpler series of three images in pure dye.

Older non-substantive chromogenic color slide films do not have color couplers incorporated in their emulsion layers, and this makes them too complicated for home processing. As with substantive color film, the first stage is to process the film in black and white developer to form a negative silver image in the red-sensitive, blue-sensitive, and green-sensitive, layers. But with non-substantive film the next step involves re-exposing the film to red light (to fog the remaining unexposed silver halides in the red-sensitive layer) and redeveloping it in a special cyan-coupled developer. (The color couplers are only present in the color developer, as with color toning.) After cyan dyes form in the red-sensitive layer, a blue-light exposure allows yellow dyes to be developed in a special yellow-coupled developer, and then a white-light exposure allows magenta dye to form in the middle, green-sensitive layer in the presence of magenta-coupled developer. The whole process of color formation in non-substantive film is similar to chromogenic dye toning of black and white prints. But with non-substantive film the processing sequence is so complicated it can only be carried out in an elaborate, highly automated machine. Non-substantive films are also relatively slow. On the other hand they have a fine-grain response, excellent image contrast, and strong, saturated colors.

Silver dye-bleach material

Unlike chromogenic materials in which color dyes are formed as a result of the reaction between the developer and color couplers, silver dye-bleach (SDB) material is manufactured with fully formed dyes present in the emulsion layers. Working on the principle of dye destruction, SDB material gives richer colors than are possible with chemically formed dyes, but is only suitable for making a positive print from a positive film image. The paper has a white plastic base supporting the three layers of light-sensitive emulsion, which is very similar to other integral tripacks. Each emulsion is mixed with a dye color complementary to its light sensitivity. After exposure to the slide in the enlarger, a latent negative image forms in each layer. You must then process the paper in three solutions. The first step is a black and white developer, which forms silver negative

SDB paper
Instead of printing on reversal chromogenic or PCT material, you can use silver dye-bleach paper. This paper has blue, green, and red sensitive halides and complementary colored dyes already present. Processing is simpler — first, development forms black and white negatives. Then special bleacher removes all black silver, plus dyes only from where silver was present. After fixing and washing, the remaining dyes form a direct positive color image.

images. The next step is a bleach solution. This removes the black silver and with it the dye, but only from areas where the negative image was formed by development. The final fix stage dissolves the remaining unexposed halides, leaving a fully formed positive image in pure dye only.

To understand the way SDB paper works, imagine that you are printing from a slide of a predominantly blue object. After black and white development the paper carries a silver image in the blue-sensitive layer only, which is the yellow dye layer. When you bleach the print, the silver image and its complementary dye (yellow) are dissolved in the object area. What you are left with (after fixing) are cyan and magenta dyes in the other layers, which, when combined, reproduce a blue object — the color of the original.

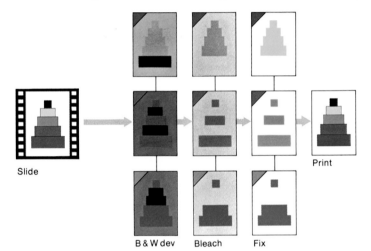

Slide

B & W dev Bleach Fix

Print

Photo color transfer process

Photo color transfer (Ektaflex) is another process that uses fully formed dyes in light-sensitive emulsions. But it works differently from SDB materials, being based on instant picture chemistry. There are three components — a print-size sheet of light-sensitive film, a sheet of non-sensitive receiving paper, and a printmaker. Instead of a chemical kit there is a single alkaline activator, used at 65°-80°F (18°-26.5°C).

To make a color print, first invert the negative or slide to reverse the image left to right. You then enlarge it in the dark on to a sheet of negative/positive PCT film (with negatives) or reversal PCT film (with slides). Filtration and exposure are as with conventional chromogenic materials. Next the exposed film is slid into the activator-filled printmaker and left to soak, face up, for 20 seconds. The receiving paper and film form a sandwich which is rolled out and then, after 6-8 minutes in normal light, peeled apart to give a finished paper print. Identical activator and receiving paper are used for negative and reversal PCT film.

The film component contains three silver halide layers sensitized to red, green, and blue light respectively. Each has a complementary dye layer as well as developing agents. As

soon as alkali penetrates the emulsion layers it activates the developer. If a negative has been exposed on the negative/positive PCT film a positive silver image then develops. Developer oxidation products then release dye from exposed parts of each emulsion layer, and these migrate as a positive color image to the receiving paper.

If you print the image of a red object, which has recorded as cyan on the camera film, and then enlarge it on the PCT film and activate it, a silver positive image forms in the green- and blue-sensitive layers only. All the silver remains in the film support, while the released magenta and yellow dyes transfer from exposed areas and create a red image on the paper receiving layer.

With reversal PCT film, silver emulsions form a direct positive image, and so dye is released from unexposed parts of the film instead. Consequently a color slide of a red object first records in the red-sensitive layer. Exposure inhibits development in this area, and development and the release of dyes occur in the other two layers, magenta and yellow dyes forming red.

Effects of reciprocity failure

When an emulsion (either film or paper) is exposed to light, the fact that it is given a short exposure to bright light or a longer exposure to dim light should not, theoretically, make any difference to the result. In other words, the reciprocal relationship between time and intensity should hold true. However, in practice there is an optimum combination of these two factors. Manufacturers design their materials to perform with a particular ASA or DIN speed and correct color balance when exposed under "typical" time and light intensity conditions (see *Reciprocity failure*, p. 152). Outside of these conditions, materials behave as if slower and, worse still, each emulsion (in color material) may be affected differently, resulting in color distortions. Camera materials (especially color negatives) are carefully matched to suit the characteristics of color printing papers. If the film image has been severely af-

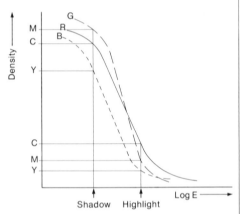

"Crossed curves"
This illustration shows a slide film characteristic curve indicating reciprocity failure. Shadows reproduce with a magenta/blue bias, while highlights are cyan. No filter correction can compensate, for both highlights, and shadows.

fected by reciprocity failure — exposed for several minutes to a dim night scene, for example — it may be impossible to print even though density may seem satisfactory. In extreme cases, the color filters required to give correct color in the highlights could be complementary to the filters required to correct the color cast in the shadows.

Printing materials are generally more tolerant of reciprocity failure, and you can adjust exposure by changing either the duration of the enlarger exposure or the aperture of the enlarger lens. Silver dye-bleach materials are, however, an exception. When making test exposures on SDB paper it is best to maintain a constant time (approximately 20 sec) and adjust exposure by changing the lens aperture setting only. In printing, reciprocity failure may also come into effect when you change magnification. For example, if you calculate that a × 3 enlargement of the film image requires a 10 sec exposure at f 8, then it could be assumed that a × 9 enlargement should require an 80 sec exposure. In fact, this would probably lead to underexposure.

Processing controls

There are three important requirements for film processing. First, a container is needed where light-sensitive materials can be treated without being affected by light. Second, there must be some method of controlling the chemical action by means of accurate timing and ·constant temperature. Third, solutions must be agitated to produce an even result, and this agitation must be consistent to avoid over- or underdevelopment.

As equipment becomes more standardized, film processing becomes simpler. In some cases, the equipment required for processing films is the same as that used for prints. Simplified versions of the type of equipment once only found in commercial processing laboratories are now available for the home darkroom. One type of processing unit can handle black and white and color 35 mm, 110 and rollfilms. With the addition of special adaptors it will also process sheet film.

Equipment

For average, low-volume processing of all film other than sheet film, the simplest processing unit is a light-tight plastic or stainless-steel tank. The tank contains a removable reel with a spiral groove suitable for all usual formats. Once the film is wound on the reel and placed inside the tank with the lid in place, processing can take place in normal light. Chemicals are poured in and out through a light-tight cap.

It is possible to process sheet film in open trays, but it is difficult to maintain the correct temperature critical for color films. Also, open trays have to be used in a blacked-out room. In complete darkness it is easy to contaminate the solutions or scratch the delicate film surfaces. The only exception to this is black and white sheet film processing, where safelighting can be used. These films are conveniently handled in open trays and processing is similar to that used for black and white papers.

Chemicals

Chemicals required for processing color films are now mostly available only in kit form. Chemical manufacturers are standardizing the chemistry of their kits and film manufacturers increasingly bring out new materials that conform to existing processes. In the same way, processing steps are becoming shorter and less complicated. Some stages of the processing sequence, which previously required an extra solution, have now been combined in simple baths as chemical by-products.

Chemicals for conventional black and white films are still sold as separate components. There are, for example, four or five different developers suitable for black and white silver negative films.

Film processing equipment

When you are processing black and white or color films you cannot avoid dealing with chemical concentrates or solutions. You must therefore ensure that the equipment you select is non-corrosive and designed specifically for the job. Some materials that may seem usable can upset the carefully balanced reactions of the chemicals and film emulsions.

Film tanks

The most common processing tank for 35 mm and rollfilms is made of either plastic or stainless steel. Plastic tanks consist of a light-tight body with a screw lid. A plastic spiral (which holds the film) fits inside the tank. When in place, the lid makes a light-tight seal. A light-trapped hole in the top of the lid allows you to

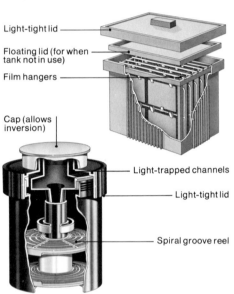

Light-tight lid
Floating lid (for when tank not in use)
Film hangers
Cap (allows inversion)
Light-trapped channels
Light-tight lid
Spiral groove reel

Film tanks
A large-capacity film tank (above right) holds sheet film in hangers. Separate tanks are used for each solution.
The smaller capacity, cylindrical tank will accept all formats of rollfilm and 35 mm using different film spirals.

pour chemicals in and out. Stainless-steel tanks are simpler in construction. They have a metal spiral and they are often closed with a funnel-type metal lid and plastic cap. Larger tanks of both types are made to contain multi-reels so that you can process several films at the same time.

Sheet film tanks

Most sheet films are still processed in a series of deep tanks, each containing a different solution. You must attach every sheet to a stainless-steel hanger before inserting the film into the tank. You then move the film from one container to the next in the dark. Deep tanks are now being superseded by the introduction of film inserts for motor-driven drums.

Tempering boxes and processors

For accurate results, precise maintenance of temperature is vital — especially for color films. The most suitable type of temperature control unit depends on the size and quantity of films

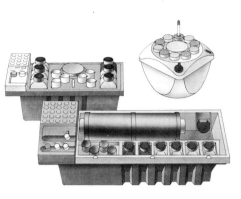

Tempering units
All these units contain temperature-controlled warmed air or water, surrounding the film tank and graduates of processing solutions.

The large unit has a motorized print drum with a film-holding adaptor inside.

you will be handling. For processing 35 mm and rollfilms, a simple tempering (temperature control) box is ideal. These hold the film tank and containers of necessary solutions at the correct temperature either in a bath of heated water or by circulating hot air. For sheet film you can use drum processors, which are primarily designed for prints. All types of drum processors provide some degree of control over agitation in addition to thermostatic control of solution temperature.

Storing and measuring
Chemicals for film processing are mostly supplied in concentrated liquid form. Graduated measuring cylinders ("graduates") in plastic or glass are therefore necessary to allow you to

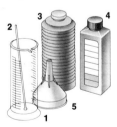

Solution containers
A graduate **1** is used to dilute and prepare solutions, and a stirring rod **2** to dissolve the chemicals. Use an accordion container **3** for developer, and a cheaper, rigid one **4** for fixer. A funnel **5** is useful for pouring.

mix the required solution strength. You will also require non-corrosive storage containers for both concentrated and working-strength solutions. The best types are accordion shaped. You can compress these to exclude any air from the container that may cause the chemical to oxidize.

Time and temperature
Two important factors governing film response to processing are time and temperature. Tim-

Timer and thermometer
Use a clock or digital timer **1** for each processing stage. A dial thermometer **2** or battery-operated digital type **3** fits into the top of the film tank.

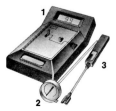

ing units that you can program to carry out the appropriate number of steps are best. For monitoring the temperature of solutions you will need a thermometer. Mercury types can be extremely accurate but difficult to read. Digital types offer the same degree of accuray and are much easier to read.

Washing
For permanent results with both slide and negative film an efficient washer is essential for removing all chemical by-products. Some washers accept the loaded film spiral. For

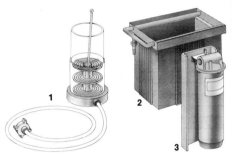

Washing equipment
You can attach film washing units, suitable for several reels of film **1**, to the faucet. Sheet films are washed hanging in a deep tank fitted with sprays **2**.

A cartridge water filter **3** helps remove grit present in some water supplies. Smaller filters are available that fit in a faucet hose.

sheet film it is possible to adapt a deep tank processing unit by adding spray tubes with a hose connected to a faucet. With most water supplies it is a good idea to use a filter to remove any impurities from the water.

Drying
After processing and washing camera film, you can remove excess water using squeegee tongs. Make sure these are scrupulously

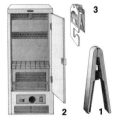

Drying accessories
Rubber-lined squeegee tongs **1** remove excess water from lengths of film. Heated drying units **2** are available for sheet film, and taller versions accommodate long lengths with clips **3** top and bottom to prevent curling.

clean. To dry film, leave it suspended by a film clip in a warm, dust-free area of the darkroom. Use a weighted clip at the end of the length of film to stop it curling. To speed up the process use a thermostatically controlled warm-air drying cabinet.

Agitation
Agitation is necessary for all film processing. The importance of an efficient agitation technique cannot be overemphasized, as it is this that brings fresh chemicals to the emulsion surface. If you overagitate it could produce an excessively dense negative or slide. One-shot chemical processes (which use minimal volumes of solution that are then discarded) linked to overagitation can produce underdevelopment due to insufficient contact between the solution and the emulsion. Too little agitation can have the opposite effect — lack of image density and also the possibility of uneven drying marks. Heavy or pale areas of tone emanating from the sprocket holes of 35 mm film is an indication of either insufficient agitation or exhausted solution.

Chemical application
You should start to agitate the film as soon as you place it in the solution. Whichever system you use — hand tank or machine — make sure that you cover the whole film immediately with an evenly applied solution of chemicals. A large percentage of processing marks are caused by the irregular application of (normally) the first developer.

Hand tanks
The processing instructions that accompany your film will tell you which of the two methods of agitation — intermittent or continuous — you should use with hand tanks. Always agitate using the same technique for every step, unless the instructions say otherwise. If you are using a hand tank you should invert the whole unit the set number of times at intervals recommended by the film manufacturer. During the first few seconds, tap the tank gently against a hard surface to dislodge any air bubbles clinging to the film. If you do not do this clear spots on the film emulsion are likely to result. Normally, with water rinses or wash steps, the flow of water through the tank is sufficient to cause its own agitation.

Deep tanks
Deep tank processing is used with sheet film too large to fit inside a regular film tank. Deep tanks are filled with static solution — one for each step — and they depend entirely for agitation on your movement of the film hangers. Once you have loaded the film, immerse the hanger evenly and swiftly into the first solution. If you fail to do this evenly, a clear line will be visible on the processed film. To agitate, lift the hanger up to the top of the tank and down again, then lift the hanger clear of the solution, drain excess solution back into the tank by holding the hanger at 45°, and return the film to the solution. Between periods of agitation, you can enclose the tank with a light-tight lid and switch the room lights on.

Tray processing
Consistent and adequate agitation is difficult when you are using open trays. The best method is to tip the tray slightly, first from the short side and then from the long side. To avoid any developing marks, make sure that when you immerse the film, the solution runs swiftly and evenly over its entire surface.

Processing chemicals

Most chemicals for film processing come in ready-mixed, premeasured containers of liquid concentrates or in packs of dry powders or crystals. Mixing instructions always accompany these, and they are very specific. You may have to combine certain of these chemicals in the correct order or under the correct conditions. Otherwise they may not mix properly or they may precipitate out of solution. Unusual chemicals for some color toners or special developers, and organic types used in color forming and color developing may be expensive and difficult to locate.

For black and white film processing there are two main chemical solutions – developer and fixer. As the developing solution is basically alkaline, you can use an optional bath of a mild solution of acetic acid to act as a "stop bath". This will immediately halt the action of the developer and minimize the amount of "carry-over" of developer into the fixing solution, prolonging its working life. Chemicals for color film processing are supplied in complete kit form. You must use the correct kit chemistry for your particular film. For example, the majority of slide films, including Ektachrome and Fujichrome, are designed for processing in E-6 chemistry. (The process you require is usually indicated on the film cassette or packing slip.)

There are two other chemicals you can use during the processing sequence. If you add a clearing agent or "hypo eliminator" after you have fixed the film you can reduce washing time by about 75 per cent. Also, if you add a "wetting agent" to the final wash water you will help to eliminate drying marks (see *Assessing results,* pp. 228-31).

Once you have made up a set of processing solutions you should use them as soon as possible. You can, however, store stock solutions. In the case of developers, use an accordion-type bottle. This will exclude all possible air from the container.

Keeping properties for stock solutions

Black and white chemicals (film and paper)

Standard fine-grain developer	6 months
Universal developer	12 months
Standard paper developer	24 months
High-contrast developer (sep. A & B)	6 months
Rapid fixer	2 months

Color chemical kits (film and paper)

Negative	Most first developers	6-8 weeks
positive/	Color developers	2-3 weeks
process	Bleachers	2-6 months
Reversal	Most first developers	2-3 weeks
paper	Color developers	4 weeks
	Bleachers	6 weeks
SDB paper	Developer	12 months
	Bleacher	12 months
	Fixer	6 months

Chemicals for black and white films

Developers*

Standard fine grain
These moderately fine-grained, normal-contrast developers are suitable for most film types. You can use a "universal" developer for processing both films and prints.

High energy (or speed enhancing)
These are powerful, strongly alkaline developers, increasing the speed of the emulsion by as much as 100 per cent. As a result, film grain is often exaggerated.

Maximum acutance
Diffusion of light through the film emulsion can cause loss of detail. These developers form the silver image very near the film surface. This results in a very "sharp" image.

High contrast
Use this type of developer for processing line or lith films. Images will have deep blacks and clear highlights, without intermediate tones.

*There are many proprietary developers for black and white films. Choose the one that offers the characteristics that suit your film or the type of image you are aiming to produce.

Stop baths

Water rinse
A rinse in water for 10-15 sec is adequate to stop development and reduce carry-over into the fixer solution.

Acid
A stop bath containing acetic acid is best to neutralize highly alkaline developer, preserve the fixer, and prevent stains. Always use with lith film.

Indicator
This type of stop bath is yellow when fresh and turns purple to indicate exhaustion.

Fixers

Acid
Acidified "hypo" (sodium thiosulfate) is the cheapest form of fixer

Acid hardener
For most work it is best to use a fixer incorporating an acid hardener. This gives some extra protection to the emulsion gelatin.

Rapid
These contain acidified ammonium thiosulfate plus hardener. They approximately halve fixing time.

Solution storage

Keeping properties of photographic solutions vary according to their chemical contents. Developers in particular react to oxygen in the air, especially if left in open trays or half-empty bottles in a diluted state. Some developers are stored with developing agents and alkali in separate A and B solutions. Powdered chemicals in airtight containers have the longest shelf life. The table above covers typical concentrated stock solutions stored in full, stoppered bottles at about 65° F (18° C). Never refrigerate liquid chemicals – some constituents crystalize out at below 55° F (12.5° C). Shelf life can be extended using accordion type bottles.

Chemical kits for color films

Reversal (slides)

Slide films can be divided into two categories – type A and type B. In principle, both types are the same, but they do have a different molecular structure, and so you must use the appropriate processing chemistry. Chemicals for color films come as complete kits. Most slide films of A-type chemistry, Ektachrome, Fujichrome, and Barfen CR, for example, require E-6 processing. B-type films such as Agfachrome require Agfa Process 41. Several chemical manufacturers sell kits to suit each type chemistry. Most amateur kits contain enough chemicals to process either 6 or 10 films of 36 exposures each. You must return non-substantive slide films to the manufacturer for processing.

Negative

Color negative film processing is simpler than color slide processing. There are fewer stages and therefore fewer chemical solutions required. C-41 (made by Kodak) is the most commonly used negative process – Fuji, Sakura, and Agfa all make negative films that use it. Most photographic chemical manufacturers make color negative processing kits (in general C-41 type). Some of these color negative kits reduce the processing time by combining several solutions in one, so that even fewer stages are required. Often independent kits are cheaper than kits sold by the film manufacturer, and they give equally good results.

Kits for films and papers

Universal kits

Color negative films and color negative/positive color printing papers require similar processing stages. This allows you to use a "universal" kit of chemicals to process both negatives and prints. Most kits are designed for films that require C-41 chemistry processing and negative/positive paper requiring Ektaprint processing. Kits contain all necessary chemicals – color developer, bleach/fix (usually combined in one solution), and stabilizer. When using a universal kit to process prints, you normally have to mix an additive with the color developer.

Negatives and printing conditions

The contrast to which you develop a film depends in part on the lighting conditions of the original scenes you photographed, and also on the equipment you will use to make the prints. With a general-purpose film, the manufacturer's recommended development time assumes a maximum subject brightness range of about 100:1. The development time suggested gives a slope to the film's characteristic curve (see *Graph information,* p. 154), which allows all these light intensities to reproduce as a usable negative. The darkest shadows should be found just above the contrast-flattening toe part of the curve and the brightest highlights below the shoulder part.

This kind of negative prints well on a diffuser enlarger (see *Printing equipment,* pp. 236-9) using normal-contrast paper. However, if you are using a condenser enlarger, which gives a more contrasty result, or prefer using a harder paper, it will be worth reducing the negative developing time or using a less active solution. With experience you can learn to modify processing times to suit your own printing conditions and preferences.

Grain and development

The "grain" of a film negative is the pattern of black silver clumps that have been formed due to the structure of the original silver halides, the amount of exposure, and the degree of development. The basic grain structure is determined during manufacture of the film. The way the emulsion reacts, however, is influenced by the way you expose the film and the form of development you adopt.

Without enlargement the grain structure of a film is too small to see, but the general appearance (or graininess) is of a reasonably even distribution of silver. In fact, this is not the case. Under a microscope the grain appears as irregularly shaped clumps of black metallic silver. Areas of the negative that received a large amount of light have a greater concentration of black silver clumps than areas that received less light. This means that overexposure increases the appearance of grain.

Effect of increased development

Grain structure also tends to become more pronounced as development time increases (for example, to compensate for low-contrast lighting conditions or for uprating film — see *Compensation processing,* p. 224). Often, too, the more energetic the developer the more pronounced the image grain.

Because of all these factors, an enlargement from a fast or "pushed" film shows the grain structure more clearly than a similar-sized enlargement from a slow or "held back" film. The grain structure of printing paper is always finer than the grain structure of film, so that the apparent graininess of a print is usually the result of the film image. Other factors that will affect the appearance of grain are the type of enlarger light source, the size of the enlargement, and the paper surface. Heavily textured paper surfaces, for example, tend to disguise film grain structure.

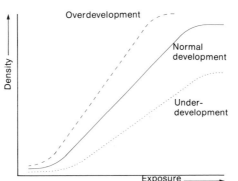

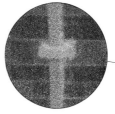

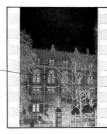

Degree of magnification
The image detail above, like those below, is enlarged 30 times from a 35 mm negative. This is the equivalent of enlarging a whole image to a size of 28 × 42 ins (71 × 107 cm).

Degree of development
The images (right) on ASA 400 film, show how development increases contrast and grain. Characteristic curves (above) show how highlight density builds up more rapidly than shadows.

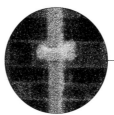

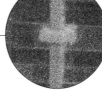

Underexposed/
overdeveloped

Normal exposure/
normal development

Overexposed/
underdeveloped

Slow film
Details on the right are from ASA 32 film negatives. This emulsion is clearly less grainy than faster types, with extra-fine-grain developer producing least grain pattern. High-energy developer gives excessive contrast.

Medium-speed film
These three details, from ASA 400 film, were exposed at the normal rating. The two fine-grain developers reduce grain clumping together to about the level of the high-energy developer used with slower ASA film.

Ultra-fast film
The details here are from ASA 1250 film. The inherent emulsion grain breaks up fine detail, even when it is processed in the finest grain developer.

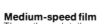

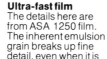

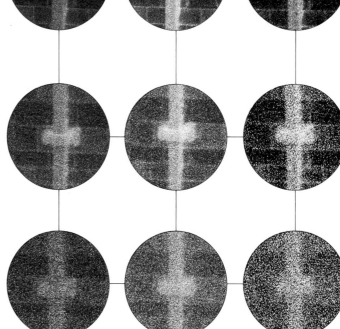

Fine-grain developer
This is effectively the standard developer for 35 mm film — typically D76 or DK50. It gives full film speed with minimum grain.

Extra-fine-grain developer
A developer of this type produces less negative grain, but film emulsion does exhibit some loss of speed.

High-energy developer
This developer will boost ASA film speed at the expense of increased grain. Contrast is also increased.

Time and temperature

The degree of development that you give a film (with standard agitation — see *Agitation,* p. 221) depends on the temperature of the developer and the length of time you allow it to act on the film. If you take care to ensure that your processing controls are always standard, then you can be certain that any deviation in the quality of your film images is due to variations in camera

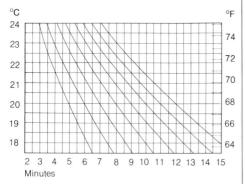

Time/temperature graph
The graph shows time changes to maintain similar results at different developer (Acutol) temperatures. Outside 64°-75°F (18°-24°C) the chemical balance may be altered.

technique. Development times recommended by manufacturers are the basic guide — modified by personal preference and such factors as enlarger type (see *Printing equipment,* pp. 236-9), which determine what makes an ideal black and white negative. Personal preference is not such an important factor in color processing (especially positive/positive), and you must use standard time and temperature for optimum results.

The length of time for which you develop the film determines the degree of image contrast. You normally process black and white silver negative film at temperatures between 60°-70°F (15.5°-21°C). Chromogenic black and white negative film requires the same temperature and processing as color negative film — approximately 100°F (37.8°C).

Controlling temperature

The easiest and most accurate way of maintaining a set temperature throughout the whole of the film processing sequence is by using a tempering box (see *Film processing equipment,* pp. 220-1). These units are worth having even for the most simple film processing.

Basically a tempering box is a large tank filled with water, a heating element, and a thermostat control device. The top of the tempering box has molded insets, into which you place the film tank and graduates of diluted, ready-to-use processing chemicals. If you buy a tempering box make sure it has enough spaces to accommodate the number of graduates required for the most complicated processing you are likely to undertake.

Compensation processing

Whenever you uprate or downrate film in the camera — either to compensate for very dim or very bright lighting conditions, or to increase or decrease the contrast and grain response — you must make a corresponding adjustment to the processing. With all films the processing step that you alter is the first developer. With silver-image black and white film there is only one development stage, and so this is the only point at which you can influence image density. Even with color film, though, it is the initial formation of the silver image in the first developer stage that determines the color response of the film in the second, color developer (see *Black and white materials,* p. 216 and *Chromogenic film and paper theory,* pp. 217-19).

Color shift

Uprating or downrating color negatives or slides can also cause an erratic color shift in the dye layers within the film. Special processing will not necessarily correct this problem. With color negatives it is possible to make further adjustments at the printing stage using printing filters, assuming the color shift is not too great (see *The effects of reciprocity failure,* p. 220). But with slides for projection, you do not have this additional correction stage.

Variable ASA film

Compensation processing may also be unnecessary with black and white dye-image film. Because of its unique characteristics of wide exposure latitude, as long as you rate the film between ASA 125 (ASA 400, depending on brand) and ASA 1600, you can use color negative film processing to produce monochrome negatives of printable density. (This holds true even if you alter each individual

Development time changes
This table gives typical changes in development time that are necessary to help compensate for uprating or downrating the ASA speed of camera film. In practice, this will vary according to film and developer type, especially for black and white work. Side effects, not shown here, include changes in contrast, grain, and color accuracy. Some brands of color film will tolerate development compensation with less noticeable color distortion than others.

frame on the same roll of film.) The rule is, when you process, develop the whole film for the time recommended for the fastest ASA setting you used during exposure.

Developer strength

With black and white film you can adjust its speed, and hence its development time, to compensate for subjects of "abnormal" contrast by using modified developers. Abnormal contrast means that the difference in light intensity between the deepest shadows and the brightest highlights in the subject exceeds the recording ability of the film. This difference (measured in f stops) is known as a subject's "luminance range". (Being able to recognize situations that are likely to exceed the film's contrast-recording range is largely a matter of experience and familiarity with one particular brand of film.) The first step is to downrate the film's ASA speed. Then by diluting a fine-grain black and white developer (see *Processing chemicals,* p. 222), and modifying development time, you can produce negatives of normal contrast with no increase in grain, and minimal compression of tones. If the developer normally requires diluting 1 + 10 for film that has been exposed in standard conditions, change this to 1 + 20 for compensation development, and increase development time in proportion to the change. For example, you should develop the film twice as long if you halve developer strength. This technique effectively holds back development in a similar way to decreasing time in normal-strength solution, but with less risk of uneven development due to very short times.

Compensation processing

Black and white film

Camera exposure	Change in ASA	Development time adjustment
−1 stop	× 2 normal	Increase by 30 %
−2 stops	× 4 normal	Increase by 75 %
−3 stops	× 8 normal	Increase by 160 %
+1 stop	× ½ normal	Decrease by 30 %
+2 stops	× ½ normal	Standard time, but dilute developer

Color negative film (C-41)

Camera exposure	Change in ASA	Development time adjustment
−1 stop	× 2 normal	Increase by 30 %
−2 stops	× 4 normal*	Increase by 80 %
+1 stop	× ½ normal	Decrease by 30 %

* Emergency use only

Color slide film

Camera exposure	Change in ASA	Development time* adjustment *First developer only
−1 stop	× 2 normal	Increase by 30 %
−2 stops	× 4 normal	Increase by 80 %
+1 stop	× ½ normal	Decrease by 30 %
+2 stops	× ½ normal	Decrease by 50 %

Preparing to process

Film should be processed as soon as possible after exposure in the camera. The latent image can be adversely affected by humidity, heat, fumes, or even light leaking into the film container. When home processing film the aim should be to achieve absolute consistency and standardization of technique. Except where film has been purposely uprated in the camera, it is not recommended that you deviate from the manufacturers' processing specifications. This is particularly true of color films.

Present trends
Standardization of equipment, film types, and chemicals means that processing film, both black and white and color, is simple and efficient. Some recently introduced black and white films (Ilford XP1 and Agfapan Vario-XL) can be processed in the same chemicals used for color negative film. Print drums with special inserts can also be used for film processing – these may have the added advantage of mechanical agitation and a tempered water jacket.

Basic equipment
For processing all camera films, except sheet film a simple cylindrical daylight film tank is adequate. These tanks are available in sizes suitable for 110, 35 mm, and rollfilm formats. Daylight film tanks are made either of plastic or stainless steel. The steel ones are preferable for processing color films – they are less likely to harbor chemicals from the previous solution and create contamination. For film sizes larger than rollfilm, deep tank processing is necessary. Although you require a tank of chemical solution for each stage of the processing sequence, the system is economical and simple to operate. Sheet film larger than 10 × 8 ins (25 × 20 cm) has to be processed in open trays (as used for print processing).

Film care
Care of film breaks down into two categories – processing (including washing and drying) and post processing (including filing, mounting and cataloguing). Washing and drying is often considered the most delicate part of the operation. But once the negative or slide is dry it must be protected and filed immediately. Dust, hairs, scratches, and finger marks are all signs of film that has been carelessly treated. As most photographers use more film than they ever print or project, an efficient filing system is essential.

Loading film tanks

Whichever type of tank you use – plastic, stainless steel, or deep tank – practice loading a piece of waste film in daylight first. Only when you are adept at this, even with your eyes closed, should you attempt to start processing in darkroom conditions. With daylight tanks, after you have loaded the film into the tank and placed the lid on top, all further steps can be carried out in normal room lighting. With deep tank processing, however, you must transfer the film from tank to tank and total darkness is necessary while this is taking place.

A few black and white films have a much thinner base than traditional film stock, and because of this 72-exposure lengths can be contained in the normal size 35 mm cassette. To accommodate this extra length, daylight tanks have a special steel spiral and an optional loading mechanism to feed it in. For bulk lengths of 35 mm film (as used with motor drives) still larger spirals are available, together with correspondingly larger stainless-steel tanks.

Using a light-tight bag
If you do not have a darkroom, you can load films using a light-tight bag. Make sure that you place film, scissors, spiral, and all the tank fittings inside the bag before you open the film container. This system is not suitable for deep tank processing.

However simple it may seem to test load a length or sheet of waste film in normal light, it is still easy to make mistakes in the dark. Always treat the film with the greatest care and, when loading, avoid kinking the film as this will leave crescent-shaped marks. It is a good idea to keep a black plastic bag in the darkroom. If things do go wrong you can place the film safely inside before turning on the room lights.

Plastic tank loading
Spirals for plastic daylight tanks are adjustable to accommodate different format films. Before you start to load the spiral, switch off the light, remove the top of a 35 mm cassette using a bottle opener, and trim the shaped film leader square. With rollfilm you must first remove the backing paper from the film. If you are processing 110 or 127 format film, you must break open the plastic cartridge before stripping off the film backing paper.

Film is wound up emulsion side in – the same way you must load it into the spiral. Always hold the film by its edges only and line up the two sides of the spiral so that the entry slots on the outside rim coincide. Gently feed the first

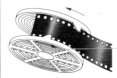

Rim-loading reel
You push the film's cut end into the spiral groove of the reel, and turn the reel halves in opposite directions to wind in the film.

few inches into the spiral groove. Then rotate the two sides of the spiral alternately until you have drawn all the film into the grooves.

If the loading sequence goes wrong, it may be because you have pushed the film into the grooves out of square, or trimmed the leading edge unevenly. Sometimes, after a few revolutions, the film may jam. This could be caused

by using a damp spiral or by buckled film. In either case, do not apply force to free the film. Unwind the film and start again, if necessary beginning from the other end of the roll.

Metal tank loading
With stainless-steel tanks you must first attach the film leader to the core of the spiral. This is the opposite to plastic tank loading, where you feed the film into the grooves from the outer edge inward. Depending on the type of metal tank you choose, it may be easier to leave the

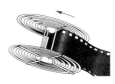

Center-loading reel
When you have clipped the film to the spool core, keep it bowed and rotate the whole spiral to wind the film on to the grooves.

shaped film leader of 35 mm film untrimmed. Metal film spirals are not adjustable, and so you must have a different one for each format of film you wish to process.

When loading a metal film spiral make sure you hold the film's leading edge square to the central core before attaching it to the film clip – bow the film slightly. Once attached, rotate the spiral in the opposite direction to the film feed, keeping the film bowed between your fingers. Continue until all the film is taken up into the grooves. If you feel the film beginning to jam, unwind and start again.

Deep tank processing
With deep tank processing of sheet film you need a minimum of three tanks for black and white chemicals and more for color. Each tank requires a floating lid to prevent chemicals oxidizing. It also has a light-tight top lid so that you can use normal lighting once the film is inside. Tanks are normally wide enough to take individual 10 × 8 ins (25 × 20 cm) film hangers, or several smaller ones together. Each film

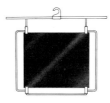

Sheet film hanger
After removing each sheet from its film holder in the darkroom, you clip it at four corners into a stainless-steel hanger. You place this in a special, large-capacity, sheet film tank.

must be suspended on its own hanger, which has a clip at each corner. Make sure you position the film squarely within the frame.

If you are processing more than one piece of film at the same time, take care that the films do not come into contact with each other. This will prevent the free movement of solution over the emulsion, and will retard or prevent development in that area. This also applies to film developed in daylight tanks. If the film is not securely within its spiral groove, it may come into contact with the adjacent loops.

The processing sequence

Before unloading your film from its container, mix up all the solutions you will require for the complete processing sequence and bring them to the correct temperature. If you have a thermostatically controlled tempering box (see *Film processing equipment,* pp. 220-1) this will not present a problem.

Apart from correct solution strength, two important factors governing processed image quality are the temperature of the developer and the length of time you leave the film in the developer. With black and white film you can, within limits, compensate for a change in temperature by altering the time, and vice versa (see *Time and temperature,* p. 224). But with color films (and chromogenic black and white films) some of the chemicals behave differently at various temperatures, so you do not have this option. Instead you must carefully read the instructions with the chemical kit and adhere to the times and temperatures stated.

Importance of agitation

Another influence on image quality is agitation. This is important because it brings fresh solution into contact with the emulsion surface (see *Agitation,* p. 221). With daylight film tanks the most common method of agitation is by inverting the tank. The usual period is an initial 15 second agitation and then 10 seconds at the end of each minute. If you have a plastic tank you can also use an agitator rod to twist the film spiral. For consistent results always use the same technique.

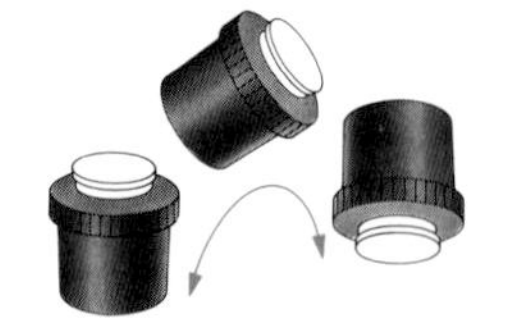

Film tank agitation
To agitate the tank manually, first ensure that the cap is in place. Then gently invert and return the tank, keeping your finger over the cap to avoid spillage.

Temperature control

If you use deep tank processing, maintaining

Film development – typical time and process

Black and white negative film	Developer: D-76 or ID 11 (undiluted)	Developer: Agfa Rodinal (diluted 1+25)	Developer: Paterson Acutol	Wash	Stop bath	Fixer: Kodafix	Fixer: Amfix (diluted 1+3)	Fixer: Paterson Acufix	Wash
Agfapan 25	4/8 min*	4/8 min	6½/9 min	1 min	½ min	4 min	3 min	1–1½ min	30 min
Agfapan 400	5½/8½ min	7/10 min	10/12½ min	1 min	½ min	4 min	3 min	1–1½ min	30 min
Ilford FP4	6/8½ min	6/8 min	7/9 min	1 min	½ min	4 min	3 min	1–1½ min	30 min
Ilford HP5	8/10 min	10/12 min	10/13 min	1 min	½ min	4 min	3 min	1–1½ min	30 min
Kodak Tri-X Pan	8/11 min	10/12 min	11/13½ min	1 min	½ min	4 min	3 min	1–1½ min	30 min
Kodak Verichrome Pan	7/9 min	12/14 min	9/12 min	1 min	½ min	4 min	3 min	1–1½ min	30 min
Temperature	68°F/20°C	68°F/20°C	68°F/20°C	68°F/20°C (±3°C)	68°F/20°C (±3°C)	68°F/20°C (±3°C)	68°F/20°C (±3°C)	68°F/20°C (±3°C)	Room temp or less

* First time is for negatives to be printed on condenser enlarger. Second time is for negatives to be printed on diffused light enlarger.

Black and white slide film	First developer	Wash	Bleach	Wash	Clearing bath	Rinse	Expose to white light	Second developer	Rinse	Fix	Wash
Time Temperature *±3°C	6 min 68°F/ 20°C	5 min 68°F/ 20°C*	5 min 68°F/ 20°C*	5 min 68°F/ 20°C*	2 min 68°F/ 20 C*	½min 68°F/ 20°C*	2½min	4 min 68°F/ 20°C	½min 68°F/ 20°C*	5 min 68°F/ 20°C	30 min 68°F/ 20°C*

C-41 color neg/chromogenic black and white	Color developer	Bleach	Wash	Fix	Wash	Stabilizer
Time Temperature	3¼min 100°F/37.8°C (±0.2°C)	6½min 75°-104°F/ 24°-40°C	3¼min 75°-104°F/ 24°-40°C	6½min 75°-104°F/ 24°-40°C	3¼min 75°-104°F/ 24°-40°C	1½min 75°-104F/ 24°-40°C

E-6 color slide	First developer	Wash	Reversal bath	Color developer	Conditioner	Bleach	Fix	Wash	Stabilizer
Time Temperature ** Times vary if print drum used for processing	6 min** 100.4°F/ 38°C (±0.2°C)	2 min 91°-102°F/ 33°-39°C	2 min 91°-102°F/ 33°-39°C	6 min** 100.4°F/ 38°C (±0.6°C)	2 min 91°-102°F/ 33°-39°C	6 min 91°-102°F/ 33°-39°C	4 min 91°-102°F/ 33°-39°C	4 min 91°-102°F/ 33°-39°C	½min Room temperature

Agfa 41 color slide	First developer	Wash	Stop bath	Wash	Reversal bath	Color developer	Wash	Bleach	Wash	Fix	Wash
Time Temperature *±0.2°C	13½min 75°F/ 24°C	¼min 68°-75°F/ 20°-24°C	3 min 72°-75°F/ 22°-24°C	7 min 68°-75°F/ 20°-24°C	2 min 68°-75°F/ 20°-24°C	11 min 75°F/ 24°C*	14 min 68°-75°F/ 20°-24°C	4 min 68°-75°F/ 20°-24°C	4 min 68°-75°F/ 20°-24°C	4 min 68°-75°F/ 20°-24°C	7 min 68°-75°F/ 20°-24°C

Film processes for black and white and color are constantly being updated and improved. The above stages, times, and temperatures applied when this book went to print, but always read the instructions supplied by the film and chemical manufacturers.

the correct temperature is more difficult as tempering boxes are not made for such large film containers. One method of temperature maintenance is to stand all the tanks in a large container of water, heated to the correct level

Sheet-film agitation

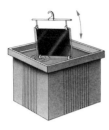

To agitate sheet film during processing in a deep tank, you must first remove the floating lid in total darkness. Then raise the film hanger (or rack of hangers), tilt, and return the hanger to the tank smoothly and evenly.

by a thermostatically controlled water heater. Agitation is equally important for sheet film, although the technique is very different (see *Agitation,* p. 221). The normal agitation period for sheet film is the same used for daylight tanks described above.

As soon as possible after you have switched off the light and loaded the film into the daylight tank spiral or attached it to the deep tank film hanger, you should start to process. With most daylight tanks you place the loaded film in the tank, lock the lid and switch on the lights again. Then you can begin pouring in the first temperature-controlled solution through the entry aperture in the tank top. Bear in mind that processing starts as soon as the solution enters the tank and only ends when the last of the solution has been drained. Always start to pour the solution out about 15 seconds before the end of the allowed time. The exact time will vary according to tank design.

Solution exhaustion

There are two methods of using solutions. You can make up a quantity of working-strength solution and return it to the storage container after each use, noting on the label the number of films processed. You must then increase processing times to compensate for the gradual loss of strength until the active ingredients become exhausted. It is false economy to use

---

Development time increases
(using a one-reel tank of D-76)

1-2 processings	Normal time
3-4 processings	Normal time + 6%
5-6 processings	Normal time + 12%

Then discard the developer solution

---

developer or fixer past its film-processing capacity — this information is normally supplied with the chemical concentrate. A better method of using developer is to make up only enough working-strength solution for each film, and then throw it away after one use. This is more expensive, but your results will be predictable and consistent. All developing solutions have a maximum safe shelf-storage life (see *Processing chemicals,* p. 222), and for consistent results you should not attempt to use them after the expiry of this time.

Washing and drying

Whatever the sequence of processing solutions you will have to wash all films at various stages. This may mean a wash in either still or running water. It is always best to use a filtered water supply, as all water contains small particles of grit that, under pressure, can pit the soft emulsion surface. In some areas a water softener will help prevent scum and drying marks. Read the information leaflet that comes with your film and make sure that each wash stage is carried out adequately. Because washing does not bring about an obvious change to the emulsion, it is incorrect to assume that it is not important.

Black and white film

The final wash for black and white film removes all traces of chemicals and by-products from the emulsion. If you do not wash thoroughly the emulsion will eventually stain. If you have processed in a daylight developing tank you can simply remove the light-tight lid and insert a special wash hose down into the center of the film spiral (see *Film processing equipment,* pp. 220-1). For film processed in deep tanks you can use a spare deep tank fitted with a water inlet.

After washing, add some drops of wetting agent to the final wash water. Wetting agent is rather like mild detergent — it reduces the film's surface tension and promotes even, rapid drying (see *Processing chemicals,* p. 222). You may decide to use a film squeegee to remove excess water before the film drying stage (see *Film processing equipment,* pp. 220-1). If so, the squeegee must be scrupulously clean, free of grit, and rinsed in wetting agent, otherwise you could create scratches down the whole length of the film.

Color film

All the general points mentioned above apply to color film as well, but you must usually give color film and chromogenic black and white film a final soak in stabilizer before drying. This solution gives the dyes greater stability, hardens the emulsion, and acts as a wetting agent. But you must take care as it can be harmful to the skin. You will notice that most films with chromogenically formed images have a milky appearance when wet. This is due to resin globules used to anchor color couplers in the emulsion. It will disappear as the film dries.

Drying

Always try to dry film in a warm, dust-free area. The most efficient method of film drying is in a specially-built cabinet. Sophisticated models have air filters and thermostatic control units. If necessary you can also use these units for drying both silver dye-bleach and resin-coated paper prints. Most color materials have to be dried at a particular temperature, otherwise the dye balance of the three layers may be adversely affected.

Mounting and filing

It is important to establish a good mounting and film system for slides and negatives. The more films you take and process the more difficult it is to identify and locate a particular film image either for projection or printing.

In general, your film storage area should be dust free, out of direct sunlight, have a low humidity, and a temperature not exceeding 70° F (21° C). It is not a good idea to store film in the darkroom — the build-up of chemical fumes or moisture from drying materials may damage the emulsion surfaces.

Filing film

After processing, cut your film into strips of five or six images. You can store each strip in special acid-free paper or plastic sleeves. A better system for easy reference is a binder containing pages of paper sleeves large enough to hold an entire film. If you use this system for negatives you can also mount a

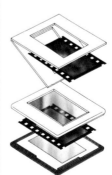

Negative file
You can store negatives in loose-leaf sheets in a binder, together with their contact prints.

contact sheet alongside. Give each page a reference number and mark the corresponding contact sheet with the same number. For large numbers of films you can use a filing cabinet. You should mark the back of any enlargement you make with the same reference number assigned to the contact sheet and film. You can identify individual images on a contact sheet by using the frame numbers on the film rebate.

Slide film

Cut successful images into individual frames and place them in slide mounts ready for projection. There are two types of slide mount. Inexpensive glassless types can be made of cardboard or plastic. The cardboard ones are usually self-adhesive, but are too flimsy to use with larger, rollfilm images. There is a risk that they will buckle in the projector magazine.

Slide mounts
The cheapest mounts are made of self-adhesive cardboard. These are quite strong in transit, but they allow the slide to bow when warmed during projection, causing it to go out of focus. Glass mounts protect the surface during handling, hold the film flat, and allow you to remove the slide at any time for printing. Do not send these by mail.

Plastic, glass-fronted mounts are suitable for all formats and, although more expensive, they offer complete protection from dust, scratches, and clumsy handling. Glass-fronted mounts also prevent slides bowing out of focus due to excess heat when projected. You can keep large numbers of slides in suspension files, which hold between 20 and 25 slides each, inside a metal cabinet.

Assessing results

In general terms, there is little to be gained by departing from the manufacturers' instructions when processing films. Commercial laboratories depend heavily on machine processing not only for speed and efficiency, but also to eliminate the greatest cause of inconsistent results – human error, especially in the area of agitation. When home processing film in small tanks, it is possible to use high-acutance and other specialist developers, but this applies only to black and white work. With color film the correct color kit must be used, and the conditions for use are even more critical. The advantage of complete consistency and control is that it is then possible to use the processed film as a check on the accuracy of exposure and camera work.

Black and white film
For most results in black and white the aim is to achieve a negative with a trace of detail in the darkest important subject shadows, without also allowing delicate subject highlight tones to merge together in dense black silver. This should occur if correct exposure is given – so that all the subject brightnesses correspond to the lower part of the straight portion of the characteristic curve. Should the result be underexposed, negatives will be thin, with deepest shadow detail just clear film. Overexposed negatives will be dense with all values near the top of the curve, giving solid highlights. Underdevelopment results in low contrast and thin shadows – the slope of the characteristic curve being less steep. Overdevelopment has the opposite effects.

Color film
These problems are exaggerated in color negative and slide film. All these films are based on layers of black and white silver emulsions, which must all line up in terms of characteristic curve response. Under- or overdevelopment (beyond acceptable limits for pushing or holding back) results in some layers being affected more than others. The result may be a cast of one color in the highlights and another in the shadows – faults that no color printing filtration will correct. In color film processing, contamination is probably the most common single cause of ruined film. A few drops of bleach, for example, in the color developer will produce a bluish cast and generally degraded image colors.

See also
Light-sensitive materials, pp. 142-3. Manipulating film response, pp. 155-9.

Black and white film

A common temptation in film processing is to extend development time simply to ensure ample density. Overdone, however, this can lead to a negative that has dense highlights, exaggerated grain, and too much contrast to make a successful print.

When assessing your negatives you must first decide whether any faults are the result of camera or processing errors. Although examples on this and the facing page are 35 mm, most of the faults depicted apply equally to other film formats. Common failures due to camera error include film that is completely blank except for rebate numbers (film incorrectly loaded or not exposed); superimposed images (caused by faulty film advance, or loading the same film twice); and some bands of uneven image density (light leaking into the camera body or cassette, or flash used at the wrong shutter speed). Underexposure is also often confused with underdevelopment. The former gives results lacking shadow detail but having normal contrast in mid-tones and highlights. The latter gives weak contrast with highlights gray and thin.

Processing faults often result in patches of uneven density, stains, mottle, clear spots, creased film, or images that are part negative and part positive. Black or white scratch marks, or bands of uneven density parallel to the edges and running the entire length of the film are also likely to be processing faults.

As a general guide, a good black and white negative image should appear rather flatter than a normal black and white print. Many of these black and white processing faults apply to color film as well.

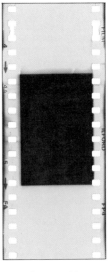
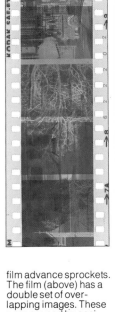

Superimposed images
The strip of film (above) shows no negative images. It has a single, almost totally black frame near the beginning followed by a clear strip of film, showing only the edge numbers. This was caused when the film became jammed inside the camera so that all the exposures were superimposed on this one frame. The film perforations were torn by the camera's film advance sprockets. The film (above) has a double set of overlapping images. These were caused by accidentally reloading a cassette of film that was already exposed. It is advisable to mark exposed films, or rewind them fully into their cassettes. This will ensure that you cannot accidentally double expose.

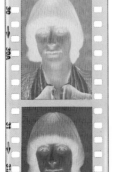

Underexposure
This negative was underexposed by $1\frac{1}{2}$ stops. This results in pale (or "thin") shadow areas as with the girl's hair. These zones will print as flat, continuous black. Highlight areas still show acceptable detail and will probably print well.

Correct exposure
Subject highlights contain more information, but shadow areas are not excessively dense. The whole image shows subject detail clearly, and the negative should yield a print of good quality.

Overexposure
When overexposed by $1\frac{1}{2}$ stops, the resulting negative looks generally dense. Highlight tones, such as the subject's cheeks, tend to merge, becoming flat and lacking in detail. Shadows retain good detail, as in the hair.

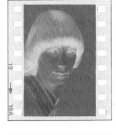

Underdevelopment
Like underexposure, underdevelopment gives a thin negative, but highlights look weaker, and shadows have slightly more detail. The resulting image is low in contrast. This negative had development time cut by 25 per cent.

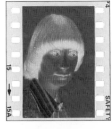

Correct development
With the correct development time, highlights are less dense and shadow areas are improved. The image has correct contrast and density, and, like the correctly exposed image (far left), should print well on normal-grade paper.

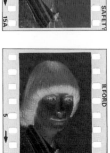

Overdevelopment
A contrasty, bright-looking negative is the result of overdevelopment. Highlights are dense, but the image lacks the excessive shadow detail given by overexposure. This negative had development time prolonged by 50 per cent.

Completely clear
This processed silver image negative film is completely clear — without edge lettering or frame numbers. Placing the film in fixer or stop bath before developer can produce this result. Chromogenic processing can also cause this.

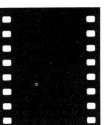

Black
If the processed film is completely black, with the manufacturer's edge lettering obscured, it has probably been fogged severely — either to light, chemicals, or even fumes. This can happen in the camera, or before or during processing.

Clear, with edge numbers
If the film is clear except for the manufacturer's edge lettering, it is probably unexposed. The edge data is printed on the film with light and its presence on the edge of this negative shows that processing was correct.

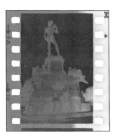

Fogged before exposure
Fogging the film outside the camera causes a gray veil of fog along most of the film's length. It may be due to loading the processing spiral in a room that is insufficiently blacked out. If this effect is even, you may be able to print.

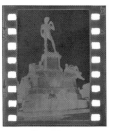

Fogged during development
This film has an overall gray veil, together with pale lines around the frame edge, lettering, and other contrasty detail. It was caused by accidental fogging part way through development. This is a solarization effect.

Exhausted developer
Processing film in exhausted or contaminated developer gives an underdeveloped result that also has a veil of fog. The lines of uneven density extending from the sprocket holes are also typical, and there may be a slight yellow stain.

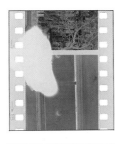

Clear patch
A clear or milky-looking patch on the negative is caused by careless loading of the processing spiral. One loop of the film bowed out and pressed against another, preventing chemicals from reaching the emulsion surface.

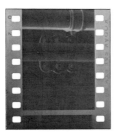

Uneven density
Bands of uneven density (but not fog) along the entire film are due to an insufficient quantity of developer in a roll-film tank. The right-hand half of this image was covered only intermittently by developer during the processing sequence.

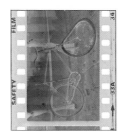

Camera fog
A dark bar across the film is a typical result of fogging caused by briefly opening the camera back. The black scratches also shown here were probably due to grit in the camera body, or on the film squeegee tongs.

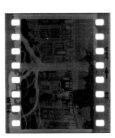

Surge marks
The bands of paler density extending from the perforations across the film are due to excessive agitation. Developer flowed continuously through the holes, creating extra development in adjacent areas of the film image.

Insufficient fixing
If the film appears fogged or opalescent by transmitted light, or milky gray by reflected light, it has not been fixed properly. You can often clear the film by refixing in fresh solution. You must then wash the film thoroughly again, and dry.

Drying marks
The circular marks (some with dark rims) on this negative were caused by drying the film while water droplets were still attached. You can rub these marks off the film base, but not off the emulsion. They can also be caused by splashing dry film.

Pushing and holding back

There is a direct relationship between film speed and film development time. The suggested development times that accompany your chemicals assume that you have exposed the film at the suggested ASA setting. There is also an assumption that you have "correctly" exposed a subject of "average" lighting contrast.

There may be times when you need to uprate the film in the camera (see *Uprating black and white film,* p. 156), and then compensate by pushing (extending) development time. This is a useful technique when illumination or lighting conditions are flat and gray. When light levels are too bright, or lighting contrast is bright, you may have to use the opposite technique (see *Downrating black and white film,* p. 156) for satisfactory results.

Pushing
Uprating film speed alone gives a thin negative (right). With extended development time (below right) the negative of this flatly lit subject is greatly improved. Excessive uprating and pushing (below) gives harsh contrast and a grainy image, which may be suitable for some subjects.

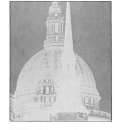

ASA × 2/normal development

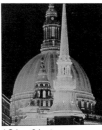

ASA × 8/extreme development

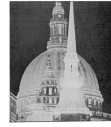

ASA × 2/pushed development

Holding back
Downrating film with normal development produces a dense negative (right). Reducing development time creates a low-contrast result (below right), useful in harsh lighting conditions. Overdone, downrating and holding back give very flat negatives (below), which cannot be corrected by printing.

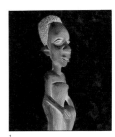

$\frac{1}{2}$ ASA/normal development

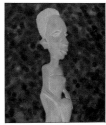

$\frac{1}{4}$ ASA/development held back (minimal)

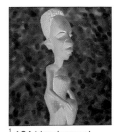

$\frac{1}{2}$ ASA/development reduced (held back)

Color negative film

Color negative films (and chromogenic black and white films) tend to appear slightly opalescent when wet. Wait until the film is completely dry before you try to assess results. Color negatives often seem more fully exposed than they really are due to the presence of a pale orange mask. This makes the task of judging slight color inaccuracies impossible. In addition, all of the subject colors appear as their complementaries on color negatives, but the yellow and magenta dyes tend to merge with the orange mask, leaving only cyan dye clearly visible.

A good way to assess new negatives is to compare them to negatives you know print well and, to reduce the visual effects of the mask, examine them through a filter of the same color. One of the most difficult faults to correct with color negatives is a camera error — underexposure. This is a problem because it produces empty shadow areas, and these usually print with an uncorrectable color cast. Also, the print is likely to look flat and gray.

Pushing and holding back
Unlike black and white film, altering the development time of color negatives affects color as well as image density. If you have uprated or downrated the film in the camera it is possible to partly compensate by altering development (see *Compensation processing*, p. 224). Using C-41 chemistry you can increase development time by 30 per cent to compensate for a 1-stop uprating, or push the film to its absolute limits with an 80 per cent increase for a 2-stop uprating. Downrating 1 stop requires a 30 per cent decrease in development time. These techniques tend to give negatives that are more difficult to print successfully because they no longer fully match the contrast and color characteristics of the paper.

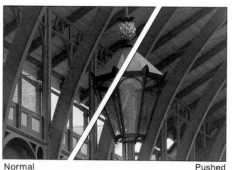

Normal   Pushed

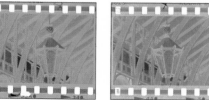
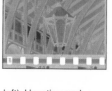

Pushed processing
A color negative exposed at its rated ASA and processed normally is shown with its resulting print (above

left). Uprating and pushing gives coarser colors and contrast (above). Grain is also more noticeable.

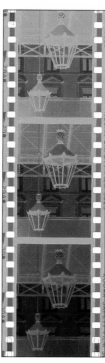

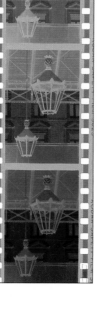

Underexposure
Shadow areas look empty — lacking contrast, detail, and color. Mid-tones and highlights record well and show good detail. These areas may print well, but shadows will look flat and lifeless.

Correct exposure
This negative is darker, with stronger tone and color information in the shadows. Details in the highlights are still distinct and colors can be picked out easily.

Overexposure
Subject highlights are now beginning to look clogged and solid, and the colors too dark to separate clearly. They will print bleached and featureless. Color and tone values in the shadows are, however, excellent.

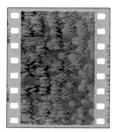

Wrong film
Color slide film processed by mistake in color negative chemicals results in bright, contrasty negatives. Prints will be harsh, with some poor colors due to the absence of the color mask found on all negative films.

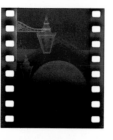

Fogged in tank
This color negative was fogged to a small amount only of white light in the processing tank. This was perhaps due to an insecure lid. Notice how the perforations holes have printed from the adjacent loop of the film in the spiral.

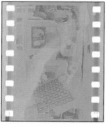

Contaminated tank
It is important to clean and dry thoroughly the processing tank before use. Traces of fixer have produced this pale, patchy cyan staining. The negative has an overall color cast and is probably too thin to produce a successful print.

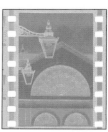

Underdevelopment
This negative was correctly exposed but underdeveloped. Highlight areas are weak and will probably print yellowish. Shadow areas are slightly better detailed than the underexposed version (left). Overall contrast, though, is too flat.

Correct development
Correct exposure and development have improved overall contrast. Highlight areas are darker and details look more contrasty and distinct. The negative is well balanced and should produce a good print if it is filtered correctly.

Overdevelopment
Overdevelopment has formed a brighter, more contrasty negative. Highlights are dense, but shadows are less detailed than in the overexposed version (left). Grain is more pronounced and the resulting print will probably be harsh.

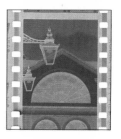

Fogged to safelight
This negative was slightly fogged to an amber safelight during tank loading. The (underexposed) negative has a cyan cast. Fogging to colored light always gives a complementary tint, which you cannot correct during printing.

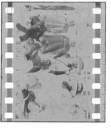

Solution contamination
Contamination of one chemical by another produces a whole range of faults, depending on the process. Here, some bleach/fix has contaminated the developer during C-41 processing, giving fog and local color stain.

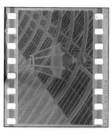
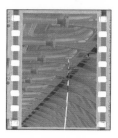

Scratched emulsion
The swollen, wet gelatin emulsion is easily damaged. In this example, grit from the fresh water scratched the emulsion when the film was wiped with squeegee tongs. Abrasions, made before processing, give black scratches.

Color slide film

With color slide film all the image color and tone values should appear as you saw them in the original subject. This makes your task of assessing exposure and processing errors much easier. With slide film you must get everything right at the moment of exposure. Compensating development for incorrect exposure will solve density problems but also alters contrast, and tends to introduce or exaggerate color casts. Subject lighting must also be exact (see *Color temperature,* p. 151), and within the film's exposure latitude.

Use a good, even light source to view and assess your results. Ideally, it should have the same color temperature as the light you use to project them. There are more stages involved in processing slides than other film types, which increases the chances of error. The appearance of faults varies depending on the film brand and process.

Pushing and holding back

It is possible to compensate when developing slide film for a greater variation in exposure than with color negative film. The exact degree, however, depends on film type, and whether you can process it yourself or have to send it back to the manufacturer. To compensate (see *Compensation processing,* p. 224) for uprated or downrated film you only adjust the time of the first developer (not the temperature). Pushing development to an extreme will mean loss of tone, harsh highlights, and overall color casts. Holding back development will reduce contrast and, if taken to extremes, will result in flat colors and probably lead to color cast.

Holding back

Compared with normal ASA rating and processing, slides that are downrated and then held back in processing show reduced image contrast. This can improve a contrast subject. Holding back also helps compensate for overexposure. Results have less rich blacks and highlights may show warmer tones. If this processing technique is over done, however (far right), the resulting image is likely to be muddy in appearance and have a strong color cast.

Pushed

The slide (right) was normally rated and processed. Uprating the ASA speed and then pushing first development time gives better contrast. This technique will often help flatly lit subjects. Pushing also helps compensate for unavoidable underexposure. Most slide films allow for a greater degree of pushing than holding back. Overdone, however, shadows become featureless and unnaturally gray.

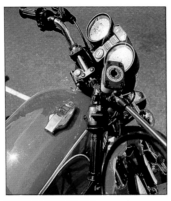
Correct exposure and processing

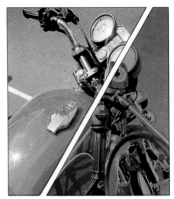
Overexposed ×2, held back   Overexposed ×4, held back

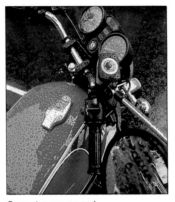
Correct exposure and processing

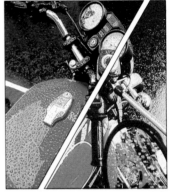
Underexposed ×4, pushed   Underexposed ×8, pushed

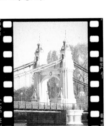

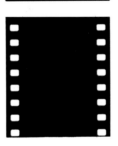

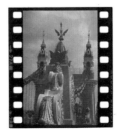

Underexposure
In the shadow areas of this image colors have become clogged and heavy and details are difficult to see. Highlight colors and details are good. Underexposed slides require extra development to compensate.

Correct exposure
This correctly exposed image is not as dark and has more shadow detail. Highlights are lighter, but still show good color and detail. The more harsh the lighting the more accurate your exposure must be.

Overexposure
Overexposed slides have bleached highlights. Only shadow areas have accurate color. This will result in slides appearing weak when projected, and prints will have flat white or gray areas instead of highlight detail.

Overdevelopment
More than normal development (pushing) makes a correctly exposed image pale. Highlights will appear bleached, especially if the subject was contrasty. The slide will be difficult to print on positive/positive material.

Bleach omitted
If the bleach is omitted (or it becomes exhausted) silver remains in the film along with the dye image. The slide is almost black, or shows patchy gray central areas. You can correct this fault by treating with fresh bleacher.

Fogged to light
Slightly fogging film to white light before, or possibly just after, first development, will produce a weak looking image, with flat gray shadows. The film rebates are also less than fully black.

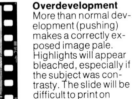

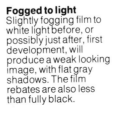

Underdevelopment
Less than normal development (holding back) makes a correctly exposed slide image look dark. Highlights are veiled and shadows may be featureless, producing a flat result. This example only had half the usual first development time.

Bleacher in developer
Like negative processing, contamination of one color slide solution with another gives various degraded image effects. Here, some E-6 bleacher reached the color developer, producing a blue cast in mid-tones and shadows.

Fixer in developer
The magenta cast affecting most dark tones in this slide was due to contamination. A few drops of fixer were allowed to spill into the color developer when the solutions were in adjacent graduates. An overall fog may also result.

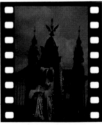

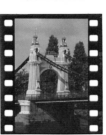

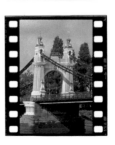

Print making

Print making is a key stage in the photographic process. Second only to camera work, it offers a further set of creative options ranging from the adjustment of cropping, density, and color to complete changes in mood and atmosphere, including special effects. The most important single piece of darkroom equipment is the enlarger. Even if you decide to start printing in black and white, it is sensible to by an enlarger that has filtration facilities (either a drawer or accessory color head) for color printing, too.

There is no one, fixed route for starting to make your own prints. Some people begin with color and progress to black and white, while others do the reverse. It is also possible to start printing from color slides instead of negatives. Each of these starting points has certain advantages and disadvantages.

The advantage of starting in black and white is that materials and chemicals are cheaper, and you can become familiar with basic skills such as assessment of correct exposure and tone values, and local density control, without also having to make judgments about color. Black and white printing, though, still involves the use of open tray processing in a darkroom with the appropriate orange lighting. Although it is not necessarily expensive to set up, black and white printing does demand a lot of space, and tends to be more messy than a color print drum system.

Starting off in color does away with the necessity of having a darkroom. A light-tight closet, large enough to house the enlarger while exposing the paper and loading it into the drum, is sufficient. All other steps are carried out in normal light. A further refinement to this form of working is to use the latest photo color transfer material, which has brought some of the applied chemistry of instant pictures into enlarging. Only one solution is required for processing, used in a processing/laminating unit instead of a drum. The final results are very similar to those obtained by other forms of color printing, but you must carefully compare material and chemical costs before deciding.

The same drum, or photo color transfer unit, can be used with negative/positive materials (for working from negatives) and positive/positive materials (for working from slides). When printing from color negatives there is slightly wider control of tones and colors than when working from slides. Against this, slide images are much easier to judge at the film stage, and they offer the extra bonus of allowing you to project them without extra processing.

Choice of materials

As the tables opposite show, color materials tend to be divided mostly by method of working, so if you have decided to use one system rather than another, there is only a narrow choice of papers — limited perhaps to two surface finishes. Black and white materials, however, are available in a much wider range of surfaces, thicknesses, contrast grades, and emulsion types. You also have a choice of chemicals, most of them usable (like stop baths and fixers) with all black and white paper types. This range is, though, becoming narrower as more color and fewer black and white materials are used. Some of the color and black and white films designed to be used under the enlarger, although not used for ordinary printing, are shown in use later in the section dealing with special effects.

The following pages detail the making of black and white and color prints. At each stage – discussion of equipment, materials, exposing, processing, and print finishing – black and white and color are considered together, so that you can compare the differences in techniques and handling procedures. You will also see what influences on the final image appearance each form of printing will allow. Later, in the special effects section, you will be able to see how black and white and color materials are often combined to create more advanced manipulations.

Black and white papers

Emulsion type	Safelight
Bromide Papers with a mainly silver bromide emulsion give a neutral black image. Regular bromide papers are blue-only sensitive, and are used for most black and white printing. A wide range of surfaces, weights, and contrasts are available.	Orange
Panchromatic bromide This emulsion type is sensitive to all the colors of light. It gives accurate black and white prints from color originals, where blue-only sensitive papers would distort. Available in a range of surfaces, weights, and contrasts.	Preferably none (or dark green)
Chlorobromide Emulsions with both silver bromide and silver chloride give a warm brown-black image. This is more pronounced with additional exposure and less development. Available in a range of surfaces. One contrast grade only.	Orange (some require red)
Document This neutral black, high-contrast matte bromide paper is designed for copying documents by contact printing. It is used for printing lettering where black and white (no half-tones) only is wanted. Limited range only.	Orange
Direct positive This bromide emulsion gives a positive print from a positive image. One type only.	Orange

Color papers

Paper type

Negative/positive (chromogenic)
This is the cheapest, most popular color print material. It works chromogenically, forming a color negative of a color negative. The dyes formed by the paper, and its general contrast, are designed to suit the manufacturer's own brand of film. It is possible, though, to print one manufacturer's film with another's paper. These types of cross-printings can add a richness to some colors, while muting others.

Positive/positive (chromogenic)
This is one of the three types of paper you can use to make color prints from color slides. To form a positive original, you have to use processing similar in principle to color slide film processing. Reversal paper is much lower in contrast than negative/positive paper because color slides, which are designed for projection, are brighter and more contrasty. You can make a print from any brand of color slide film, but avoid images that are overexposed or excessively contrasty.

Positive/positive (silver dye-bleach)
You can also use silver dye-bleach paper to make prints from slides. It works on an entirely different principle to reversal paper, and requires simpler processing. The dyes that make up the final image are already present in the paper's emulsion layers. As a result, image colors are richer and more permanent than dyes that are formed chemically during processing.

Photo color transfer (negative or positive working)
In this process you expose the image on an intermediate sheet of film under the enlarger. If you are working from color negatives, then you use negative type film. When working from color slides use reversal film. Filtration and exposure are similar to those used with chromogenic papers. Exposed film is soaked in a single solution to activate the developer in the emulsions, and then rolled in contact with receiving paper. Dyes transfer from the film to the paper. After 6-8 minutes, you pull the film and paper apart for the finished print.

Base material	Weight	Contrast	Surface
Fiber Fiber-base papers are cheaper than resin-coated types, but they take longer to process. For high-gloss, prints have to be glazed. **Resin coated** Most modern printing papers have a plastic resin layer coated on each side of the fiber base. As the paper fibers are sealed in, they cannot absorb chemicals, and this reduces processing time by two-thirds. Resin-coated prints dry without curling, and glossy types do not require glazing. Image quality matches that of fiber papers. Resin-coated prints are more difficult to mount. **Base tint** Apart from normal white, some papers have off-white or ivory base tints, which may suit your subject.	**Double** Doubleweight is the thickest base. It is available for all sizes. It particularly suits larger prints, which need extra support. **Single** Singleweight is cheaper than doubleweight, and suits prints up to 10 × 8 ins (25 × 20 cm). **Lightweight** A few papers such as document types have extra thin bases. These suit special applications, such as paper negatives for later printing. **Medium** Resin-coated papers are only available in mediumweight. However, the added plastic layers in resin-coated paper makes this thickness very similar to double weight fiber-based paper.	**Graded papers** Bromide papers for general use are made in a range of contrast grades. Low-contrast types give a finer variation of gray tones. Normal contrast is grade 2. Grade 1 (soft) will give normal-contrast prints from harsh negatives. Grade 3 (hard) suits flat, low-contrast negatives. Popular papers are made in grades 0 to 5. **Variable contrast** Instead of buying bromide paper in several grades, you can work with one packet of variable-contrast paper. This paper has two emulsions: one high and one low contrast. By altering the color of the enlarger light you can vary the paper's contrast. You can use a set of lens filters or a color head enlarger.	**Matte** Matte papers are totally lacking surface sheen. Some are smooth surfaced and others are textured. Matte papers are ideal for retouching and artwork, but they do not produce a rich black. **Glossy** Glossy papers give a mirror-like finish. Prints have a deep, rich black and make the most of negative shadow detail. Any retouching will reduce the reflective surface of the paper. Fiber glossy paper must be glazed for the final sheen. **Others** Other paper surfaces include rough and fine luster, velvet stipple, and "silk". The more pronounced textures help to disguise graininess, but they do tend to break up fine detail.

Black and white darkroom films

Normal contrast	High contrast
Normal-contrast "continuous-tone" films produce a full range of tones between black and white. These films are excellent for printing black and white slides from negatives, and for effects such as bas-relief. Some continuous-tone film types are blue-only sensitive and can be handled under normal safelighting. You can think of them as normal-grade bromide paper when exposing and processing. If panchromatic film is necessary (when working from color originals, for example), you should use a slow camera film such as FP4 or Plus X. You must then work in total darkness as no safelight is completely safe.	These types of darkroom films, if properly exposed, will produce images of extreme contrast, with no intermediate shades of gray. You can use them for simplifying a normal photograph, or for making screens, masks, and separations. Most of these films are orthochromatic (blue/green sensitive). There are two main types—line or lith. Line film is processed in concentrated print developer. Lith materials produce a more intense black and slightly finer detail. Lith must be processed in special developer, which is more expensive than print developer. For results from color you will have to use panchromatic lith.

Surface	Chemistry	Advantages	Disadvantages
Most negative/positive papers are available in glossy, luster, or silk finishes. They are all resin coated. Glossy types dry with a high-gloss sheen.	Type A processing suits Kodak and similar products, and type B suits some Agfa products. Kits are available from paper manufacturers and others.	Reproduces the widest range of subject and lighting conditions. Cheapest paper. Simple processing. Wide range of kits.	Working from negatives makes assessment of originals difficult. Prints on type A material show a bluish cast when wet.
Your choice of reversal papers is quite limited. They are usually only available in glossy or smooth luster surfaces. All of these papers are resin coated.	Use chromogenic reversal processing. Most of the independent kits only suit type A. With some kits you must expose the paper to light part way through processing.	You choose an image for enlargement from a positive original. You have the option of projecting the image as a slide. You can mount and display prints.	Reversal paper is expensive. Paper exposure critical. Reversal materials give poorer prints from contrasty original than does negative/positive.
SDB materials are resin coated with a pearl or high-gloss plastic surface, similar to other resin-coated glossy papers.	Special kits are supplied by the manufacturers and are not suitable for other use. SDB paper is tolerant of timing temperature variations.	SDB paper produces a rich, sharp print. It is tolerant of processing variations. Dyes are very stable, so refrigerated storage is not necessary.	SDB is a relatively expensive material. It has a very slow emulsion speed. Glossy prints are very delicate and will scratch easily.
PCT materials are available in glossy, smooth, or matte finishes, and can be used with both types of film.	Same activator used for both films. Negative film is soaked for 17-23 seconds in printmaker tray. Dyes transfer safely in daylight.	PCT material is quick to process. Precise temperature control not necessary. Low-cost chemicals. No washing stage required.	Camera film must be inverted in carrier—makes printing composition difficult. Materials more expensive per print. Minutely poorer resolution.

Color darkroom films

Negatives to slides	Slides to negatives
Using color darkroom film you can print a color negative to make either a large color slide for displaying on a light box or a normal-size color slide for projection. Ektacolor print film is matte surfaced front and back. These surfaces are easy to retouch, and they also reduce reflections—helpful if you want to display a large slide. To produce a 35 mm slide, contact print your negative on Ektacolor 35 mm slide film. The film stock is contrasty and has a clear film base suited to projection. No matter which method you use, you must make exposure and filtration tests, in the same way you would for negative/positive paper.	An alternative to printing slides on reversal or SDB paper involves making an intermediate color negative. With the negative you can print color enlargements on negative/positive paper, which is the cheapest paper. The additional cost of making the negative can be quickly made up for if you intend to produce several prints from the same negative. Quality, too, is often superior using a negative to print from, especially if the slide is contrasty. To make the negative you must contact print from the slide on low-contrast internegative color film. Process the internegative film in regular color film chemicals.

The darkroom

As film and paper processing becomes more streamlined – in terms of equipment, time, and chemical procedures – it is becoming less difficult to set up a home darkroom. Being self-sufficient may not save money compared to prices charged by commercial processors, but it gives, especially in printing, full creative control.

Setting up a darkroom usually means taking over an ordinary room for a short period and then returning it to normal use afterward. The obvious choice for a temporary darkroom is either the bathroom or kitchen, because of the ready supply of running water. If a spare room is available it is possible to build up a fully equipped darkroom where even the most complicated work can be tackled.

Space requirements
Different processes require different amounts of space. For film processing, in daylight tanks, any small area that can be blacked out for the length of time required to unload the film container and transfer the film to the tank spiral is sufficient. A water supply is not necessary, and all the actual processing can be carried out in normal room lighting.

Of all the darkroom processes, black and white printing is the most space consuming. This is because the three processing solutions – developer, stop, and fix – are used in open trays. Color printing uses small amounts of a greater number of chemical solutions poured into a reasonably compact daylight processing drum.

Safety
Whether the darkroom is a professional set-up, converted spare room, or temporary arrangement, it is important to be aware of the safety aspects of working with liquid chemicals and an electricity supply in a blacked-out area. Working in the dark means no windows, so the first consideration is ventilation. Some chemicals, particularly for color processing, can produce noxious fumes, so if you are using them in a darkroom an extractor fan and light-tight louvers should be installed to ensure a supply of fresh air. Whenever handling new chemicals there is always a possibility of an allergic reaction. As a precaution, it is best to wear rubber gloves. When planning the darkroom area, separate dry from wet areas and keep all electrical cables away from liquids. Use cord-operated switches for lights. Most aspects of darkroom safety are common sense – all chemicals should be kept in well-stoppered bottles away from children. Also, because most aspects of darkroom work involve complete darkness at some point, keep the floor area clear of obstructions at all times.

Basic requirements

The basic requirements for any darkroom are an area where you can keep out all external light, an electricity supply, a water supply, and a ventilation system. If necessary you can make use of an area that does not have running water. Instead, use a bucket of water to store processed film or prints until the end of the processing session and then transfer them to a convenient water supply for washing. However limited your space may be, always group similar aspects of the processing sequence together. For example, keep everything to do with film loading into processing tanks, sorting out negatives for enlarging, and exposing the printing paper under the enlarger on the "dry" side of the darkroom. Reserve the "wet" side for all aspects of processing to do with chemicals or wet prints and print and film washing. Unexposed paper, negatives, or prints can be damaged if splashed by water or chemicals.

Temporary darkroom
A bathroom is an ideal location for a temporary darkroom because of its ready supply of running water. Also, most bathrooms only have one small window and so are relatively easy to make light tight. Many bathrooms in apartment blocks do not have windows at all. If this is the case then they will have extractor fans, and this also solves ventilation problems. To make a work surface, use a fitted board to convert the bath tub to a bench. If the tub is too low for comfortable use, place spacers under the board. Leave room underneath for a print washing tray or tank. Arrange the processing trays on absorbent material, such as newspaper, to soak up any spills, and build up the height of the enlarger section of the board so it is above the trays. If there is space in the room for the enlarger to be separate from the "wet"

side, all the better. Should you have to run power cables across the room, make sure they are not near any source of water, and remove them as soon as you switch off the power.

Closet darkroom
A permanent darkroom in a basement or closet is more convenient – you can leave this type of area blacked out with everything in position between sessions. An attic is not a good choice because it tends to be too hot in summer and too cold in winter. In an under-stairs closet darkroom you must position the enlarger at the farthest point from the stairs to avoid the low ceiling. To minimize vibrations, build the enlarger support to a wall and not to be underside of the stairs. In a permanent area you can pay more attention to detail. For example, paint the area around your enlarger matte black but the rest of the room in a light neutral color to reflect the maximum amount of safe-lighting, and finish the work tops with white laminate for easy cleaning.

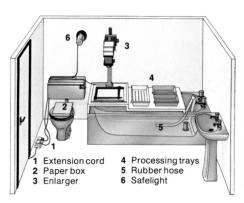

1 Extension cord   4 Processing trays
2 Paper box   5 Rubber hose
3 Enlarger   6 Safelight

Basic darkrooms
You can convert a bathroom (above) into a temporary darkroom. It is essential to keep the enlarger cord away from water, and to remove it as soon as you have finished printing. A bench over the bath can accommodate enlarger and processing trays. It is best to keep the enlarger raised above the liquid level. A window black-out and a foam rubber light seal around the door will be essential. An understairs closet (left) can also be converted for darkroom work. Build the enlarger bench higher than the wet bench. A light-tight ventilator is vital. Because there will be no running water, you will also require a plastic bucket for rinsing hands, and another, empty, bucket to remove batches of prints for washing in the kitchen or bathroom.

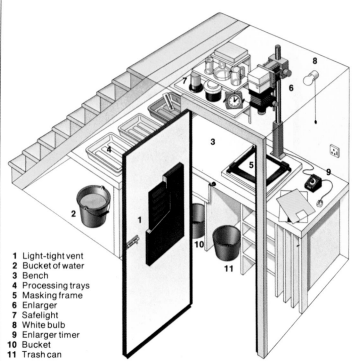

1 Light-tight vent
2 Bucket of water
3 Bench
4 Processing trays
5 Masking frame
6 Enlarger
7 Safelight
8 White bulb
9 Enlarger timer
10 Bucket
11 Trash can

The complete home darkroom

With a large room permanently at your disposal you can build up a darkroom where you can tackle every aspect of processing and printing. The basic principle of organizing all your equipment into a wet side (for processing) and a dry side (for exposing and print finishing) still applies. Make the wet bench large enough to accommodate all the processing trays for black and white work – developer, stop, fix, and wash tray. The bench should also be large enough for a tempering box for chemical solutions and a motorized unit for a color print processing drum. The dry side should be able to accommodate not only an enlarger, but also a timer, color analyzer, mounting press, and trimmer. There should also be room for sorting out negatives or slides for printing, preferably with a light box. Your will also need a stool suited to the bench height. A specially built darkroom should also have adequate storage space. The best floor covering is a practical, hard-wearing material such as seamless PVC,

and all work surfaces should be completely covered with sheets of laminate. (Bare wood will absorb any chemical spills and may be a source of contamination.) For ease of use, work benches should be about 3 ft (1 m) high.

If the room has windows you should make sure that they are completely blacked out. There is a variety of ways of doing this – the cheapest being with heavy-duty black plastic. The best method is to make opaque fabric blinds encased in wood channeling painted matte black. If the room is large, make sure you have sufficient safelighting to cover the entire area. This may mean using two or three separate lights. Run a cord horizontally above head height between the walls so that you can switch on the white light anywhere in the room with wet or dry hands. Another convenient item is a large, flat-bottomed PVC photographic sink. This can replace the top of the wet bench, and should be capable of holding all the trays and wash tanks.

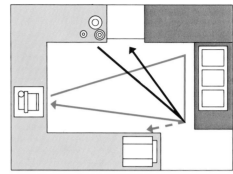

Planned darkroom layout
Darkroom layout should minimize walking movements, while keeping wet and dry areas clearly separated. The diagram (above) shows the room (below) in plan form. It illustrates typical movements while processing (black arrows) and printing and drying (red arrows).

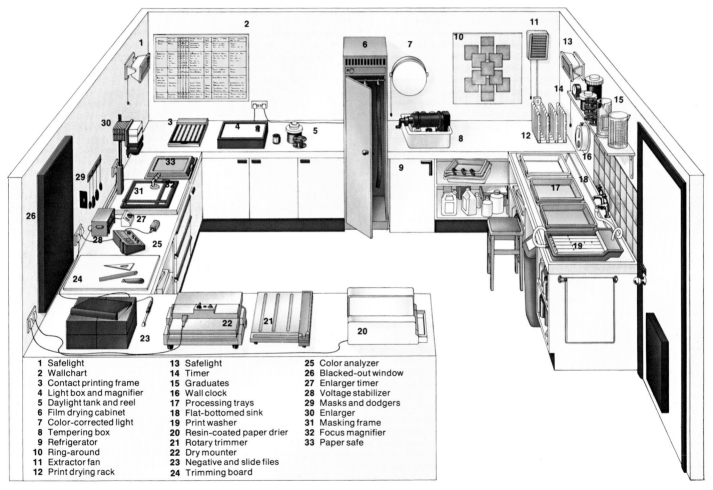

1 Safelight	13 Safelight	25 Color analyzer
2 Wallchart	14 Timer	26 Blacked-out window
3 Contact printing frame	15 Graduates	27 Enlarger timer
4 Light box and magnifier	16 Wall clock	28 Voltage stabilizer
5 Daylight tank and reel	17 Processing trays	29 Masks and dodgers
6 Film drying cabinet	18 Flat-bottomed sink	30 Enlarger
7 Color-corrected light	19 Print washer	31 Masking frame
8 Tempering box	20 Resin-coated paper drier	32 Focus magnifier
9 Refrigerator	21 Rotary trimmer	33 Paper safe
10 Ring-around	22 Dry mounter	
11 Extractor fan	23 Negative and slide files	
12 Print drying rack	24 Trimming board	

Dry side
This half of the room is reserved for activities that do not involve chemicals or liquids. This helps to avoid damage to films, negatives, and paper.

Wet side
You should keep chemicals, tanks, trays, and print washers on this side. Avoid leaving negatives or slides here, as they will be susceptible to damage.

Printing equipment

A modern enlarger and its auxiliary equipment are designed for both color and black and white printing. Equipment for processing the prints, however, differs — black and white materials are processed in simple open trays under orange safelighting, while color prints require a light-tight drum in ordinary room lighting. Black and white work therefore takes up more room. Equipment for color print processing tends to be more compact and sophisticated, and you must maintain high temperatures to minimize the time for each processing cycle. A fully equipped darkroom is expensive, but you can build it up gradually, perhaps beginning with black and white but planning your purchases to cover color requirements too.

Enlarger types

The enlarger is the single most important item in the darkroom. Its quality, together with that of the enlarger lens, largely determines the standard of your prints. The function of the enlarger is to project an evenly illuminated image of the film original. To do this, the enlarger lamphouse contains a light source that shines down through a large condenser lens or is scattered by a diffusing device, before reaching the negative carrier. Below this an enlarging lens, similar to a camera lens, forms an image on the baseboard. The higher you

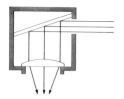

Reflex lamphouse
Positioning the enlarger lamp at right-angles to the downward light path reduces heat and column height. A 45° mirror reflects the light through a large condensing lens.

raise the enlarger on its vertical column the greater the degree of magnification. For each adjustment of height you must move the lens toward or away from the negative carrier in order to bring the image into sharp focus. The condenser system produces the most brilliant image, accentuating both sharpness and

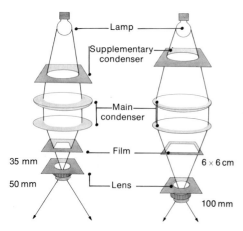

Condenser adjustment
A condenser enlarger directs light through the negative to the lens. If you change negative size (and focal length) you must also alter the position of the supplementary condenser.

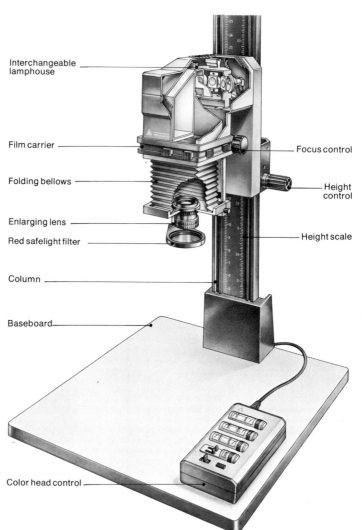

Interchangeable lamphouse

Film carrier

Folding bellows

Enlarging lens

Red safelight filter

Column

Baseboard

Color head control

Focus control

Height control

Height scale

The most important enlarger controls are height adjustment (to alter image size), lens focusing (to control sharpness), and lens aperture (to adjust brightness). The column must be tall enough to give prints of the required size, but rigid enough not to transmit vibrations. Lamphouses are interchangeable — condenser types for black and white, and diffuser heads that mix filtered light for color printing are both available. The red filter under the lens is for black and white

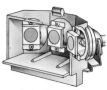

work. It allows you to compose and focus without exposing the paper. Some enlargers, such as the one shown (left), are designed to work additively and use a color head with three separate lamps filtered deep blue, green, and red (above). You change the overall color of the light by electrically dimming or brightening lamps on a control unit. The head itself has no moving filters of the type found on a subtractive color enlarger.

grain. But you must reposition the condensers each time you change lenses for different formats. Any incorrectly positioned condenser may cause off-center darkening of the projected image.

Filter systems

For printing in black and white you only require a red safelight filter. With this in place over the lens you can compose the image and position the paper safely without exposing it. For color printing, however, filters have an entirely different function. You interpose a range of different colored and different strength filters between the light source and the negative to change and control the color balance of your print. Even the most basic enlargers

Diffuser lamphouse
Filtered light enters the scatter box, which uses diffusing plastic and matte reflective surfaces to scatter the illumination. Many color head enlargers use this system.

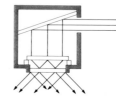

incorporate one or more lamphouse filter drawers, which hold a variety of colored acetate filters. These filters do not have to be of high optical quality, because you introduce them before the light reaches the lens. This system is, however, slow and awkward to handle. With most types of color filtration you move filters partially into the light beam produced by the lamp. Light rays then mix thoroughly inside the matte white interior of a scatter box built into the lamphouse, before passing through a diffuser (or condenser) on to the negative as even-colored light.

Nearly all modern enlargers have an integral "color head" containing two or three filters, which you can "dial" into the light path. Some enlargers have a color head as an accessory that you can change for the simpler black and white lamphouse. Color head enlargers allow you to make a continuous variation in filtration as the filter moves progressively into the light path. With the filter drawer system, filtration tends to be in abrupt steps as you change the composition of the filter pack. Even when there is a color head in place, you can still use the enlarger for printing on black and white paper by simply setting the filter dials to zero.

To obtain the correct response from color printing paper, most color enlargers use complementary-colored filters to remove blue, green, or red wavelengths selectively from the light emitted by the enlarger bulb (subtractive filtration). A few color enlargers use the addi-

Movable filters
The cheapest method of filtration is to use acetates in a drawer. Most enlarger heads use three filters (deep yellow, magenta, and cyan), moved into the light path by dials. Cheaper ones omit cyan.

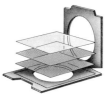

Filter drawer

Two-filter head

Dial-in filters

tive system. These enlargers have three individual light sources, each filtered in a different primary color. You control the relative strength of color by varying the output of the bulbs. The combined, additive effects of these three colors are mixed before illuminating the film. Both the drawer system and the simpler color heads use dyed filters. These eventually fade and must be replaced. More sophisticated heads use dichroic filters — semireflective glass that tints the light by interference rather than absorption — and these remain fade free.

Variable contrast enlarger
When printing in black and white, you select the paper contrast grade most suited to the tonal range of your negative. As an alternative to this, variable-contrast paper is available which alters its tonal response in relation to the color of the light falling on it. You can then use your color enlarger to adjust the contrast of your black and white prints by introducing filters into the light beam. Another option is a variable-contrast black and white enlarger head. This is like a simplified additive color head with blue and yellow lamps only. It enables you (via a control unit) to select the contrast of your paper by pressing a button to alter the color of the enlarger light.

Enclosed enlargers
Some enlargers are made as totally enclosed console units, which you can operate in a room

Daylight enlarger
The enclosed enlarger allows you to print in normal light. You insert the film in a carrier, choose final image size and composition on a print-size focusing screen, then raise the mirror to expose the image on paper housed in a spool at the rear.

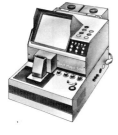

with normal lighting. Generally they produce one or two fixed-size enlargements, and they expose on to a roll of paper that is then machine processed. These units are also known as multiprinters because of their ability and convenience for producing long runs of prints, made "straight" (without selective printing-in). One model has a reflex screen for viewing the image and a zoom lens to vary the magnification. When you press a button to expose, the mirror swings out of the way, allowing the light to reach part of a roll of paper. Enclosed enlargers are much more expensive than conventional types, and they are normally found only in professional darkrooms or commercial laboratories.

Enlarger accessories
In addition to the basic enlarger, there is a range of accessories you will require. You will find these especially useful if you intend to print from more than one film format.

Negative carriers hold the frame of film to be printed flat and square in the light beam produced by the enlarger's bulb. For small-format (35 mm and smaller) a simple glassless carrier will be sufficient. But for film larger than 35 mm, a carrier with glass inserts will ensure that the film does not bow, causing parts of the image to be rendered out of focus. The problem with glass inserts is that as well as the two film sur-

Carrier adaptors
Most enlarger film carriers have interchangeable masks to allow the printing of images on different film formats. Some also have sliding plastic strips (moved by finger tabs) to mask any unwanted areas, and reduce light scatter.

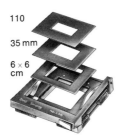

110

35 mm

6 × 6 cm

faces to be kept clean and dust free, you will also have four glass surfaces. As an alternative to having a different negative carrier for each film format, you can purchase a standard carrier (to suit the largest format film you use) and a set of masks so that you can adapt it for use with smaller formats.

The most useful enlarger lens has a focal length approximately equal to the diagonal measurement of the film format with which it

Enlarging lenses
Enlarging lenses are designed to work best close-up. Apertures have click settings that you can feel in the dark. Use 50 mm lenses for 35 mm format, 100 mm or 135 mm lenses for 6 × 6 cm.

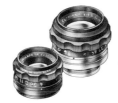

is used. For 35 mm film, for example, you should use a 50 mm lens. You can use your lens with a smaller format film but the enlarger will not produce very large prints. If you use a 50 mm lens for larger than 35 mm negatives vignetting of print edges will probably occur.

Masking frames hold the printing paper flat under the enlarger and cover the edges to form

Masking frames
These keep the paper in position and hold it flat. The simplest **1** is non-adjustable. The adjustable frame **2** is the most common. It gives any proportions or border widths. Borderless types **3** allow you to print the whole sheet and the multiple frame **4** gives up to four borderless prints.

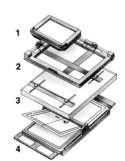

white borders. Some are non-adjustable and are only suitable for one size of paper. Others have movable masking strips, enabling you to make prints in a variety of sizes, and some produce borderless prints. A few types can also be used to print multiple images on the same

Focus magnifier
To aid focusing, you stand this magnifier on the masking frame. An internal mirror reflects light up to a ground glass screen, and you view the image through an adjustable eyepiece. Screen and base are the same distance from the mirror.

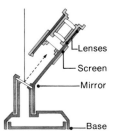

Lenses

Screen

Mirror

Base

piece of printing paper for special effects (see *Multiple printing*, p. 260).

No matter how good the original film image and the enlarger lens system are, your final print will only be sharp if the lens is precisely focused. A focus magnifier is an essential aid whenever the image is dim or eyesight is poor. Basically it brightens and enlarges part of the projected image. You place it on the masking frame, then adjust the enlarger focusing control until the film grain appears sharp on a screen inside the magnifier.

Exposure timers and meters
Print density relies on a precisely timed exposure. For black and white work (under red or orange safelighting) a sweep second hand on a wrist watch will be adequate for basic printing. But for most work, when you will be selectively exposing different parts of the printing paper (see *Local density control,* p. 249), a timing device has the advantage of leaving both your hands free. Timers that you wire directly into the enlarger circuitry are best; they

Meter/timer
This combined unit makes spot readings of highlights and shadows from the projected image. It measures exposure and contrast grade, and also acts as an enlarger timer.

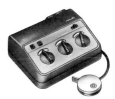

automatically turn the enlarger off at the end of the programmed time.

Many different timers are available. Make sure that the one you select has an extensive range of timed intervals — you can set some for as little as 0.1 sec or for as long as 1000 sec. In very dim lighting, or when color printing in total darkness, a timer that shows a countdown on an illuminated display is ideal. (The display should not be bright enough to fog the paper.) Audible timers that emit a signal every second are also available. Some sound a warning at the end of the timed period.

Advanced timers can also incorporate an exposure meter. Although expensive, these units can pay for themselves by reducing the number of wasted prints. Before use you must program the meter for the speed of the paper (you can determine this by making test prints). Most exposure meters have a diffuser that slips over the lens and mixes the light coming through the film. This gives an integrated or overall reading of highlights and shadows. An optional arrangement is a probe that you can use to measure exposure from small key areas of the projected image.

Color analyzers
Normally when making color enlargements you will have to assess visually several test prints before deciding on the correct balance of filtration and exposure. By using a color analyzer you can greatly reduce the number of test prints, and so make a substantial saving on wasted paper. These units measure the color content of the light projected from the film image. Once set up, an analyzer will assess the intensity of the blue, green, and red light and indicate the necessary filtration for a balanced print on the particular type of paper in use. It does this by comparing the information from the new negative or slide with information programmed into the analyzer from a film image known to give a good result.

For accurate results you must program the analyzer with information regarding the enlarger, film type, and paper batch, and to do this you must first make a perfect print by trial and error. Then, with the enlarger controls undisturbed, take a reading with the analyzer's probe and turn the programming controls to

Electronic analyzers
These analyzers measure key areas of the projected image through a probe that you place on the enlarger baseboard. They compare readings through internal blue, green, and red filters with previous data, and show the filter and exposure settings you will require.

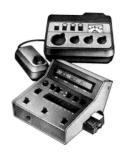

the exposure time and filtration that produced the print. There are two alternative types of reading you can take with a color analyzer. An "integrated reading" produces an average, overall assessment. For this you must use a diffuser over the enlarger lens to scramble all the light from the film image. For a "spot reading" you remove the diffuser attachment, leaving a small measuring aperture on the probe, which you then position on the projected image to read a very selective area of the scene.

Color analyzers range greatly in sophistication. Very simple models may only be suitable for one type of film and paper combination.

More advanced models can be used for both negative/positive and positive/positive enlargement and for additive and subtractive filtration (see *Color theory*, pp. 242-3). Most analyzers also incorporate an exposure meter and can be linked to an exposure timer.

Safelights
When printing and processing paper you must use the type of lighting that will not in any way affect the light-sensitive emulsion. Regular bromide paper for black and white prints is only sensitive to blue light, so an orange safelight can be used. Orthochromatic materials like lith film (high contrast) and continuous-tone process flat film require a red safelight because they are sensitive to a wider area of the spectrum, including green light. Black and white panchromatic emulsions are sensitive to the entire spectrum. You can only view these materials intermittently during processing by a deep green safelight.

In principle, color papers are designed to be sensitive to the full spectrum. In fact, most materials have gaps in their spectral sensitivity

Safelights
Simple plastic safelights are designed for 15 W or 25 W bulbs. The upright type stands on a bench, while the pivoted model is designed for wall mounting. Most safelights accept interchangeable filter screens in red, orange, or deep green for a range of paper types. Some filtered narrow-band fluorescent tubes also act as safelights.

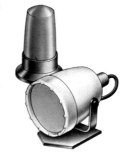

because they are keyed to dyes in the film. You can, if you wish, use a very dark brown safelight with negative/positive paper, and a very deep green (580 nm) light with Cibachrome. A number of safelights use light-emitting diodes (LEDs). These have a very narrow band

Choice of safelighting
The table shows typical recommendations for safelighting with a range of black and white and color photographic materials. Your safelight must have the correct bulb, and should not be closer than about 4 ft (1.2 m). Safelights may also fog materials if they illuminate them for too long. To test your safelight, first correctly expose the film or paper to an image. Then cover part of it with a coin, and leave it near the enlarger or developing tray for at least as long as your usual handling time. Process the image fully and examine it carefully for any trace of a coin shape.

of spectral emission and are safe to use with most color papers.

Safelights come in a variety of designs to be used either free standing on the bench, wall mounted, or ceiling mounted. Nearly all types accept normal, low-wattage domestic light bulbs and allow you to filter the light for a range of different materials.

Contact printing frames
Contact printing frames produce a series of positive images, the same size as the negatives, on one sheet of printing paper. Basically, a contact printing frame consists of a sheet of glass, with plastic guide channels on the underside, hinged to a rigid base. After you have loaded the negatives into the channels

Contact frame
This frame for contact printing has glass with thin channels for strips of film, and a base covered in plastic foam. You can use an enlarger to provide the light source for exposing the paper and negatives.

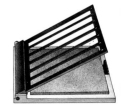

(emulsion-side down), place a piece of printing paper on the base (emulsion-side up). Then lower the glass to bring the negatives and paper into contact, and expose the frame to an even light source. The resulting contact sheet of positives is a vital aid to selection of images for later enlarging (see *Preparing to print*, p. 244). To obtain a sharp set of images you must ensure that the film and paper are in tight contact throughout the exposure. Otherwise there will be slight softening of detail.

General accessories
There are a number of low-cost items you will require for print making and processing. For black and white printing you process the exposed paper in open trays of diluted chemical solutions. There are three different solutions and you must have a tray for each. To avoid the possibility of chemical contamination, buy

Safelight filters (Kodak)		
Filter no.	**Filter color**	**Suitable for**
OA	Greenish yellow	Contact material (blue sensitivity)
OC	Light amber	Black and white bromide including some variable-contrast and Velox contact paper
1	Red	Slow orthochromatic and fast blue-sensitive materials
		Some variable-contrast papers
		Kodagraph Transtar Paper TP5
1A	Light red	Kodalith Orthochromatic materials
		Kodagraph Transtar TC5 and TPP5
2	Dark red	Fast orthochromatic materials
3	Dark green*	Slow panchromatic films
6B	Brown	X ray materials
10	Dark amber*	Kodak Ektacolor papers
		Vericolor slide film 5072 and print film 4111
		Panchromatic printing paper
13	Amber*	Kodak Ektacolor paper 1
*Indirect lighting only		

trays in different colors and always place the same type of solution in the same colored tray.

Print tongs allow you to transfer prints from one tray to another without the risk of contamination. These are also available in different colors — you will require one each for the developer, stop bath, and fixer.

You can make use of certain types of items used in film processing (see *Film processing equipment,* pp. 220-1) for print making. These

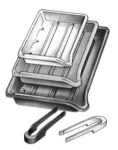

Trays and tongs
Processing trays should ideally be one size bigger than your largest paper sheets. You will require one for each of the three black and white processing solutions. Tongs must have smooth rounded tips to avoid the risk of damage to the emulsion surfaces of prints.

include graduates for mixing solutions, storage containers, certain types of timers, and thermometers. Print thermometers, though, tend to be mounted on back plates and have large, easy-to-read figures.

Print processing units
Print drums and automatic print processors are mostly used for color print processing, although they are also suitable for black and white work. Models range in sophistication from simple drums, which you manually roll along a flat surface (to bring fresh chemicals into contact with the paper), to motorized units, which automatically and evenly agitate the print drum contents.

Automatic print processing units incorporate a motorized print drum and a tempering box. The motor unit ensures thorough agitation at a constant speed, while the tempering box maintains the correct temperature of all processing solutions. With these models, once you have loaded the exposed paper into the drum and closed the lid, the unit is light tight, so that safelighting is not necessary.

The most advanced amateur units incorporate all the features of automatic agitation and

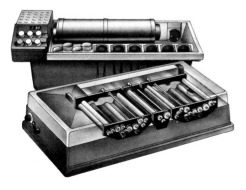

Motorized processors
The drum unit (top) processes prints up to 24 × 20 ins (60 × 50 cm). The automatic roller processor (above) produces twenty 10 × 8 ins (25 × 20 cm) color prints per hour.

temperature control, but with the added facility of roller transport of the exposed paper from solution to solution. You can use the roller processor for both black and white and color print processing, and it is adjustable for all paper types. After you have fed the paper in at the top of the machine it travels along rollers through three baths containing developer, bleach, and stop. The actual development process takes about seven minutes, after which the print is delivered ready for stabilisation and drying. The processing unit is completely sealed, so that once the paper is inside you can switch on normal lighting.

Print washers
It is vital to remove all traces of processing chemicals and unused silver salts from paper prints, other than PCT materials, which do not require washing. Otherwise staining and eventual fading of the image will result. There are many different washers to choose from, and all are suitable for both black and white and color prints. If you are using resin-coated paper (which category includes all color papers and an increasing proportion of black and white) you can drastically reduce washing

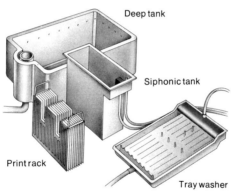

Washing units
A rapid tray unit washes resin-coated paper in approximately 4 minutes. The deep tank unit rapid-washes resin-coated prints in special racks. The large siphonic tank accepts fiber-based prints, too.

time while still removing completely all the by-products of processing.

If you only have a small number of resin-coated prints to process, the best method is to use the high-speed tray washer. This type of unit has adjustable dividers to hold either one large print or up to four smaller ones. A hose from the faucet directs water into one end of the tray, where it flows over both sides of the prints before escaping from an outlet into the sink. Siphonic type washers have a much larger capacity and are more suited to fiber-based papers. Water enters the tank through perforated pipes and this action helps keep the prints separate, so allowing a more effective washing action.

Driers and glazers
You only need the most basic equipment for drying resin-coated papers. Because of the plastic coating, the underlying paper base remains dry. All you have to do is remove

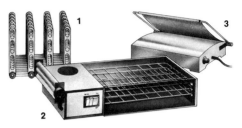

Drying equipment
Let resin-coated papers dry in the rack **1** at ordinary room temperature, or dry them manually with a roll-squeegee and place them in the warm-air drier **2**. The drier/glazer **3** takes fiber-based prints.

excess water from the print surface using a squeegee, place the prints on a blotting sheet or in a vertical rack, and leave them at room temperature. Warm-air driers are available, though, and these dry resin-coated paper in a few minutes. With fiber-based paper there is always the risk of shrinkage and curling as the print dries. To overcome this problem you can by special drier/glazers. These are thermostatically controlled and have cloth lids with adjustable tension to keep prints flat and free of creases while drying. If you want to give fiber-based prints a high-gloss finish, squeegee them face down on a ferrotype plate. With resin-coated paper, the "glossy" variety dries with a naturally glazed finish.

Dry mounters
If you want to display your processed and dried print, before framing it is a good idea to mount it on a piece of rigid, acid-free cardboard. Most professional processing laboratories offer this service, but small mounting machines are available for the home user. Before mounting, make sure that your print is free of any surface grit or finger marks and that it is positioned squarely on the mounting board. Trim off the print borders if necessary.

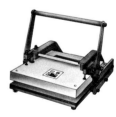

Soft-bed press
The top plate of this press is electrically heated. The press is open on three sides. Its base has a soft lining. To exert pressure on the print, you pull the top bar part of the soft-bed press.

Dry mounting presses all require an electricity supply, and use heat to melt a thin tissue of adhesive material placed between the back of the print and the mounting board. Hard-bed presses allow you to adjust the pressure and are more usually found in commercial use. Soft-bed presses are simpler and lighter in construction, and are more suited to low-volume work. Take special note of the recommended temperature to use with resin-coated papers, because at high temperatures the plastic surface may melt.

Printing controls

The photographic print depends for its quality and effect on a number of factors. The first of these – which is highly subjective – is the camera position. Technical skills apart, there are a set of visual conventions that most photographers react to either consciously or unconsciously. There are also secondary considerations of fashion and style, and in some cases the market for the image is of importance.

Image quality
The quality of the negative or slide used to make the print is of vital importance. Exposure in the camera and the subsequent processing are interrelated, and there are few techniques the printer can use to "rescue" an unsuitable film image. Exposing and printing standards together determine printed image quality. The photographer must also decide which route should be taken from film stage to print stage for the best possible result. For example, each time an intermediate film stage is introduced into the process, quality can be lost in a variety of ways – contrast changes, color balance alters, and each time the image passes through a lens, definition will suffer.

Once the print process is decided, the choice of paper directly affects quality. The two choices here are the surface texture of the paper and the contrast grade (black and white materials). The first choice is largely dependent on the intended use for the print – glossy for the richest tone range, textured or matte to minimize the appearance of grain or to facilitate later retouching. Not all papers are available in a wide range of contrast grades, so it is best to apply a standard exposure/development combination to all camera film originals.

Print density depends mainly on enlarger exposure and, to a certain extent, on development. The apparent density of the print changes with viewing conditions and looks brighter when wet. For assessment of print density view in white light. For color prints, view by daylight or under a daylight-balanced unit. These are essential for color aftertreatments, too, such as retouching, airbrushing or spotting.

Consistent technique
The type of processing unit, processing solutions, time, temperature, and agitation are all critical factors in printing control. Black and white prints are usually processed in trays, and this may itself create problems of inconsistency. Most other types of processing occurs in drums, tanks, or roller transport machines, and results are extremely reliable – the main variables are then limited to control of exposure, filtration (mostly for color), and paper contrast grade (for black and white).

See also
Light-sensitive materials, pp. 142-3. Manipulating film response, pp. 155-9.

Print processing solutions

In the same way as color film processing solutions are becoming more standard and compatible, you can now increasingly use one manufacturer's chemicals with another manufacturer's paper. For example, it is possible to process 3M negative/positive color paper in Kodak Ektaprint II processing solutions. Numerous manufacturers make kits usable with Kodak and 3M negative/positive papers and some chemical kits can be used for processing color negative films, too. Photo color transfer (PCT) materials require the same single activator solution for both negative/positive and positive/positive printing. Black and white papers can be processed in a wide range of print developers, although variable-contrast types produce the best results when you use the developer made by the manufacturer who supplied the printing paper.

Solutions for paper bleaches, stop baths (not essential for black and white printing), and fixers are quite complicated chemical compositions, and you must follow all mixing instructions as carefully as when you mix developing solutions. You must neutralize some color chemicals before disposing of them.

The basic ingredients of stop baths (acetic acid) and fix solutions (sodium thiosulfate) are generally available, and you can buy these chemicals and mix them up yourself at a considerable saving in cost. The chemicals for color developers are difficult to obtain and you will find it easier and cheaper to use kits supplied by the manufacturer.

Chemicals for black and white papers

Developers	Stop baths	Fixers
Universal (fine grain) These developers give neutral blacks on all bromide papers. **Warm tone** Special slow-acting. These give extra-warm images on chlorobromide papers. Or overexpose and use diluted normal developer. **High contrast** There are no contrast-enhancing developers for papers. Use concentrated universal developers. **Rapid processing** These work best with resin-coated papers. They are fast acting and work well at high temperatures.	**Rinse** You can use water rinse only, but fixer deteriorates quickly. **Acid** Acid stop is preferable to water. **Indicator** These start off yellow when fresh and turn purple to indicate exhaustion.	**Acid** Same as film, but diluted. Do not exceed 25 prints (10 × 8 ins / 25 × 20 cm) per liter. **Acid hardener** Special hardener added to prevent damage during washing – essential before glazing glossy prints. **Rapid** Use at half film strength. Excessive fixing may bleach the image.

Chemical kits for color papers

Negative/positive	Positive/positive	
Every color paper manufacturer, and practically all makers of processing chemicals, offer kits consisting of 2 or 3 solutions for negative/positive color paper. Some kits have a wide choice of working temperatures, others are especially low cost. There are two types of negative/positive processing kits. Most are designed to suit type A chemistry papers, such as Kodak products. The other type of kit is designed for Agfa type B chemistry paper. Photo color transfer activator suits both negative/positive and positive/positive PCT materials.	**Reversal** These kits process chromogenic papers for printing from color slides. All modern papers work with the same type of kit, usually containing 6 chemical steps. You can use kits by Kodak, Agfa, and Unicolor, for example. Reversal chemicals are about twice as expensive as kits for negative/positive papers. New reversal kits are reducing the time and number of stages used.	**Silver dye-bleach** These materials require reversal processing, but use entirely different chemical steps to other reversal kits (see left). You need only 3 solutions – developer, silver bleach, and fixer. Most photographers use kits made by silver dye-bleach paper manufacturers (such as Ilford), but there are a few independent kits. These kits cost about the same as chromogenic reversal kits.

Time, temperature, and agitation

You have slightly more latitude in terms of time and temperature when processing black and white paper than when processing color paper. With black and white, adjusting these two variables mainly affects print density. But with color, any marked variation from standard controls may lead to totally unacceptable color casts. However, whatever the print processing system — trays, drum, or roller transport — adopt a consistent approach. Always start your timer at the same point, for example, make sure you monitor the temperature of the solutions at regular intervals, and agitate using the same technique each time.

Black and white prints

Processing black and white prints in open trays easily leads to inconsistency in the temperature and agitation of solutions. The simplest way to control temperature is to maintain the temperature of the darkroom close to that required for the processing solutions (usually about 68°F/20°C).

It is important to immerse the paper evenly and smoothly in the developing solution. Otherwise, a clear line of different density may appear on the print. If you tilt the developer tray forward slightly, lay the paper face down in the bottom of the tray, and then lay the tray down again, the developer will wash back and cover the paper immediately. Turn the print so that the emulsion side is uppermost and agitate by gently rocking the tray.

Color prints

Open tray processing is not really recommended for color prints. The wide color sensitivity of the paper means working either in total darkness or in very dim safelighting. Also, color developer tends to oxidize too quickly in open trays. Print drums are much more convenient to use, because once the paper is inside you can pour chemicals in and out and agitate by rolling the drum on any flat

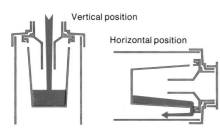

Vertical position

Horizontal position

Drum processing

Chemical poured into the vertically positioned drum is retained in the lid area. It only passes over the paper when you tilt and roll the drum horizontally along the bench.

surface with normal room lights on. Motorized tempering boxes automatically agitate the drum in a thermostatically controlled water bath (see *Printing equipment,* pp. 236-9). When processing color prints you must follow the recommended time and temperature and agitate for the correct periods of time.

Photo color transfer (Ektaflex) prints are processed by soaking the exposed sheet of film in a tray-shaped tank of activator, at room temperature. It is then roller-laminated to receiving paper and left in normal light to transfer.

Development and processing times

Black and white papers

Paper	Process All chemicals at 68°F/20°C	Time
Normal black and white papers Agfa Brovira, Agfa Portriga, Ilfobrom, Ilfospeed**, Ilfobrom Galerie***, Ilfospeed Multigrade****, Kodabrom II RC*****	Developer* Stop bath/rinse Fix Wash: fiber (ambient temp.) resin (ambient temp.)	2 min 10-15 sec 5-10 min 30 min 2-4 min

    ** 2 min in Ilfospeed Developer 2
    *** 2 min in Dr Beers variable-contrast developer
    **** 2½-3 min standard: 1 min in Ilfospeed Multigrade Developer
    ***** 1-2 min standard: suitable for use in Kodak Veribrom developer

    * Standard development in Suprol 1+2 or D163/Dektol 1+3 or Bromophen 1+7

Paper	Process	Time
Special black and white papers Kodak Panalure (color negative to black and white), Kodagraph Transtar TPP5 (color slide to black and white), Kodaprove** (color slide to black and white)	Developer* Stop bath/rinse Fix Wash: fiber (ambient temp.) resin (ambient temp.)	2 min 10-15 sec 5-10 min 30 min 2-4 min

    ** 2-2½ min development

    * Standard development in Suprol 1+2 or D163/Dektol 1+3 or Bromophen 1+7

Color papers (positive/positive)

Paper	Process	Temperature	Time
R14 process Kodak Ektachrome R14 Agfacolor MCN 310	Pre-soak First developer Wash* Reversal exposure** Color developer Wash*** Bleach-fix Wash****	86°F/30°C (±1°C) 86°F/30°C (±1°C) 82°-90°F/28°-32°C 84°-88°F/29°-31°C 82°-90°F/28°-32°C 82°-90°F/28°-32°C 82°-90°F/28°-32°C	4 min 3 min 4 min 20 sec 3½ min 2 min 3 min 4 min

    * Minimum of 4 changes of water
    ** Expose to 100 watt light 16 ins (40.5 cm) away
    *** Minimum of 2 changes of water
    **** Minimum of 6 changes of water

Paper	Process	Temperature	Time
Cibachrome process Cibachrome A II – Process P30	Developer Wash Bleach Fix Wash	75°F/24°C (±1°C) 75°-79°F/24°-26°C 73°-77°F/23-25°C 73°-77°F/23°-25°C 75°-79°F/22°-26°C	3 min 30 sec 3 min 3 min 3 min

Color papers (negative/positive)

Paper	Process	Temperature	Time
Kodak Ektacolor 78 RC, 3M High Speed Professional, Sakuracolor, Fujicolor, Photocolor RC, 3M Easy Strip	Developer Bleach-fix Wash	91.4°F/33°C (±0.3°C) 86°-93°F/30°-34°C 86°-93°F/30°-34°C	3½ min 1½ min 3½ min

Other color papers

Paper	Process
Agfacolor Type 4 MCN + MCS Agfacolor 5 PE	Agfacolor Process 85 Agfacolor Process 90 or Process P Kit

Exposing the paper

For every newly developed film it is advisable to make a contact sheet. A color contact sheet gives an initial guide to the color filtration necessary to make individual enlargements. A black and white contact sheet allows the photographer to make a quick assessment concerning exposure time and print density, and to note any areas on individual frames that may require special printing when enlarged. For both color and black and white work, a contact sheet gives the photographer the opportunity to plan the composition and cropping of enlargements before making a full-size print.

Test strip
After selecting an image for enlargement, the next step is to make a test strip by positioning a narrow strip of printing paper over a representative section of the projected image, and making a series of different exposures by doubling the time of each. When color printing a second test strip is needed to test the effects of filtration. Exposure and filtration values taken from the contact sheet are starting points for the test strips.

Print assessment and terminology
A photographer's assessment regarding print quality is largely based on subjective decisions. There are, however, certain terms that accurately describe the visual appearance of a print. Print density, for example, is the amount of silver (or dye) formed by exposure and development. The difference in density between the brightest highlights and the deepest shadows is known as the density range. The brightness of part of an image is the amount of light reflecting from it at that point. The brightness range, or contrast, describes the difference in brightness between the extreme highlights and shadows. The contrast of a print may be radically different from the contrast of the subject. Sometimes a print needs to be more contrasty to enhance a graphic effect such as subject texture or pattern, or, on the other hand, it may look better with softer contrast because of mood or atmosphere.

In color, the term hue is used to describe one pure color as distinct from another. A hue to which white is added is known as a tint, while a hue to which black is added is known as a shade. Both these forms of dilution give desaturated colors. Some prints will require pure, vibrant colors, while the subjects of others will respond to more muted pastel hues.

See also
Light and color, pp. 22-3. Filters and lens attachments
Special effects attachments, pp. 198-200; *Non-effects filters,* p. 201.

Color theory

Photographic color printing papers are all either based on the principles of chromogenic color formation (see *Chromogenic film and paper theory,* pp. 217-19), dye destruction (see *Silver dye-bleach material,* p. 219), or peel-apart color transfer (see *Photo color transfer process,* p. 219). Whichever system you use will depend on your original film image and preferred manner of working, but in all cases the dyes in the negatives or slides have to balance with the color print material in order to produce acceptable results.

Films and papers
In an ideal situation, a color negative or slide projected on a suitable color material with white light will result in a perfectly balanced print. In practice this is not the case. Imperfections in both film and paper dyes inevitably lead to unbalanced images and color casts. Differences in the quality and intensity of enlarger bulbs, and variations in the types and batch differences of film and paper make this balance impossible. A print made from a color negative without filtration almost always results in a strong overall color cast. This is partly because color negatives include an orange masking layer needed to compensate (to a degree) for deficiencies in the films' chromogenic dyes. For all these reasons, as well as for the control of subject coloration, you must always expect to filter the light source.

Supplementary filters
You can use a basic black and white condenser enlarger for printing in color by placing the appropriate combination of supplementary filters in the filter drawer. This system works on the same principles as dichroic filtration, but the filters eventually fade and need replacing because they do not allow you to make continuous color modifications.

You can also use supplementary filters for correcting small areas of local color cast by holding a filter of the correct compensating color under the lens at the enlarging stage. You must keep the filter moving continuously otherwise a distinct area of different color will result. This technique is similar in principle to selective printing in black and white, where you either hold light away from, or add extra light to, an area of the paper in order to correct print density. To remove a color cast in negative/positive printing use additional filtration the same color as the cast. In positive/positive printing, however, to remove a cast you must use additional filtration that is complementary in color to that of the cast.

Dial-in filters
Most modern enlargers incorporate some form of built-in color head filtering system. The better types use special fade-free dichroic filters instead of dyed gelatin types. Both allow a wide range of color changes, with continuous variation. External dials on the color head are calibrated in values of yellow, magenta, and cyan.

Basic filtration principles
The principle of color printing is the use of colored filters to control the color content of the light illuminating the film image, and of exposure time to control the density of the print.

There are two methods of filtering. The most common method is "subtractive filtration", where you give one exposure and use combinations of the complementary colored filters — yellow, magenta, and cyan — in different strengths to control the color of light. Some modern enlargers now use the much older

10Y   20Y   40Y

Filter strength
Whatever its color, filter density determines whether changes in color balance are large or small. A 40Y filter, for example, subtracts four times as much blue light as does a 10Y filter.

"additive" method of coloring. Additive enlarger heads use three separate light sources, each strongly filtered in one of the primary colors — blue, green, or red. Instead of moving filters, illumination color is controlled by brightening or dimming individual lamps. With both types of filtering systems, you should use infrared and ultraviolet absorbing filters. These block the sensitivity of some of the paper's emulsion layers to near IR and UV wavelengths, and in this way lessen the possibility of color casts occurring.

All the filter diagrams on this and the facing

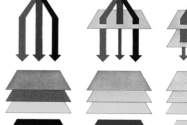

Subtractive filters
Unfiltered light affects negative/positive paper layers equally. A magenta filter subtracts some green, so the green-sensitive layer forms less magenta, giving a greener print. Adding cyan filtration to subtract red forms less cyan, making yellow stronger.

Additive filters
Basic additive printing means giving separate exposure through deep red, green, and blue filters. Each exposure affects one paper emulsion at a time. Relative exposures control the proportions of cyan, magenta, and yellow formed. Triple lamp enlarger heads individually dim or brighten three separately filtered lamps and so only require one exposure.

page refer to negative/positive paper, which records blue, green, and red light in yellow, magenta, and cyan dyes.

Filter effects

To alter the color of your print you either change the acetate filters in the filter drawer, or dial in different filter values on a color head enlarger. If you are using complementary colored filters for negative/positive printing, several aids help you work out the correct filtration and exposure. Once you have made a test strip (see *Making a negative/positive enlargement*, p. 246) you can use special viewing

Filter adjustments
In subtractive negative/positive printing if your print is too yellow when filtered, say, 40Y, then add 05Y to make it slightly more blue. A 20Y filter gives a larger color shift. Reduce cyan to remove a red cast, or add yellow and magenta filtration. Avoid using a final filtration that utilizes all three filters — this has a neutral density effect. If you always subtract the smallest filtration value from the other two, the color of the light will be the same, but illumination is brighter, and therefore exposures shorter (right).

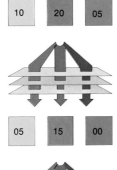

filters to assist in estimating filter changes. As color filters of any type stop (to some degree) the passage of light, any change to filtration may also have an effect on exposure time. Simple calculator disks are available that indi-

Filtration corrections – Negative/positive

Print color	Take out	Or add
Too blue	Yellow	Magenta + cyan
Too green	Magenta	Yellow + cyan
Too red	Cyan	Yellow + magenta
Too yellow	Magenta + cyan	Yellow
Too Magenta	Yellow + cyan	Magenta
Too cyan	Yellow + magenta	Cyan

Filtering options

The chart (above) relates to negative/positive color printing by subtractive filtration. Choosing between "take out" and "add" options (and always eliminating neutral density) means a two-filter head is adequate for most photograpic situations.

cate any necessary corrections.

In negative/positive printing, to correct a color cast you add filtration of the same color as the cast, or subtract its complementary if it is a primary color. In positive/positive printing, to correct a color cast you must subtract filtration the same color as the cast, or add the complementary color if the cast is a primary color.

Paper grades

Black and white paper is made in contrast grades ranging from low contrast, or "soft", to contrasty, or "hard". The grade of paper you use directly determines how the range of tones in your negative will appear in the final print. If, for example, you are printing from a low-contrast negative, a hard (grade 4 or 5) paper will brighten the tonal range by eliminating some of the gray tones. Starting with a contrasty negative, you could use a soft (grade 0 or 1) paper to reduce the contrast on the final

print by reproducing the maximum possible number of intermediate grays.

With traditional paper, you must buy a different package for each contrast grade. As an alternative, you can use variable-contrast paper. Changing filters (supplied as a separate accessory) alters the paper's contrast response in half grades from the equivalent of grade 0 to grade 4 in regular papers. If you have a color head enlarger, you can use its printing filters instead.

Graded papers
These print details were made from a normal-contrast negative on six grades of paper (see inset grade numbers). Soft grades (lower numbers) give most gray tones. Harder grades (higher numbers) form fewer grays, giving harsher results.

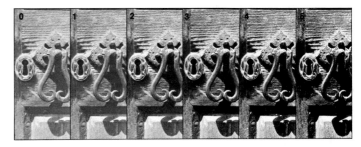

Variable-contrast paper
These results were all made on the same Ilford variable-contrast paper, using numbered filters (inset top) supplied for the product. You can also use color head filter settings (shown at the bottom of the prints).

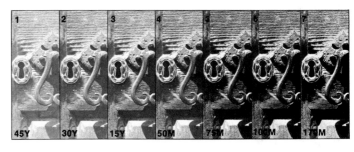

Deciding on grade
First assess your negative enlarged on the white base of your masking frame. The thin negative (near right) has mid-tones to shadows in low contrast. As shown below, it tends to print best on hard-grade paper, which exaggerates tone differences. The correctly exposed and processed negative has a normal tone range and prints well on grade 2 paper — the version on grade 3 is too harsh. The overdeveloped, contrasty negative (top right) prints best on grade 1. This paper's generous range of grays counteracts the coarse tonal range of the negative. In practice, you may not always wish to re-create the original subject tonal range. For example, printing a normal negative on hard paper may give particular emphasis to a strong subject shape. A soft paper, on the other hand, can help a misty, atmospheric image.

Low-contrast negative

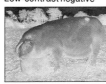

Normal-contrast negative

Contrasty negative

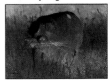

Soft grade (1)

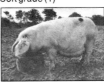

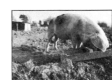

Normal grade (2)

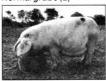

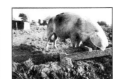

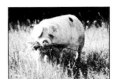

Hard contrast (3)

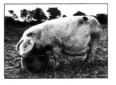

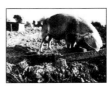

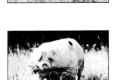

Preparing to print

The first step when preparing a printing session is to make up the required chemical solutions for the complete processing sequence, and bring them to the correct temperature (see *Time, temperature, and agitation,* p. 241). Next you must select either a single negative (for enlargement) or a set of negatives (for contact printing), and make sure that both film surfaces on each image are free of dust, hairs, or finger marks. Also ensure that both the front and rear elements of the enlarger lens are perfectly clean.

If you are making an enlargement, place a single negative in the carrier, turn the enlarger light on, and the white room light off. Then adjust the position of the enlarger head until you obtain an image of the correct size for your paper. For the brightest possible image and most critical focusing, open the lens aperture fully. Next, focus the lens until the image is

Adjusting the enlarger
For large prints you must raise the enlarger head and reduce the lens-to-film-carrier distance. For small prints, lower the enlarger head and extend the lens-to-film distance. The table (below) shows distances for different enlargement ratios. To work out others, subtract (**B**) from (**A**) and divide by (**B**).

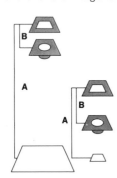

Magnification ratios				
Film height above baseboard (A)	in	19.8	14.4	8
	cm	50.4	36	20
Distance of 50 mm lens from film (B)	in	2.2	2.4	4
	cm	5.6	6	10
Ratio of enlargement to film		8:1	5:1	1:1

sharp on the white surface of the masking frame (use a focus magnifier if necessary – see *Printing equipment,* pp. 236-9). Sometimes, focusing changes the degree of image magnification significantly, so you may have to readjust head height and refocus the lens. Focusing the image carefully for both the center and edges helps you check enlarger alignment. The film plane, lens panel plane, and the plane of the masking frame should all be exactly parallel for sharp images. When enlarging from a negative you have to imagine the print in positive form in order to compose an effective image. Exclude unwanted areas by resetting one or more borders on your masking frame, or shifting the whole frame.

Making a contact sheet

A contact sheet is a useful guide as it reproduces on one sheet of paper all the images from one roll of film. When you are printing negatives it is much easier to decide which images to enlarge and where to crop if you have a sheet of small positives.

Setting up the darkroom is the same in principle for black and white and color, and to make the contact sheet you can use either a special purpose-built contact printing frame (see *Printing equipment,* pp. 236-9), or a sheet of clean glass at least 3 mm thick.

Loading the contact frame
After you cut the film into strips of five or six negatives, open the contact printing frame and place each strip in the grooved slots on the underside of the glass. (Be careful not to leave finger marks on the glass surfaces.) Position the negatives so that when you close the glass they will be emulsion (dull) side down. Then, using the appropriate safelighting, lay a piece of printing paper or PCT film emulsion (shiny) side up on the base of the frame. Bring the glass down so that the negatives and sensitive material are in contact. If you are using a plain piece of glass, lay the material emulsion side up on the bench (or enlarger baseboard) and place the negatives on top emulsion side down. Then carefully cover the negatives with glass, pressing them into contact.

Exposing the sensitive material
When making a contact sheet (in black and white or color) it is impossible to take into account the individual requirements of each frame of film. It is a good idea, though, to make at least two exposures by shading half the sheet of paper (using opaque cardboard) halfway through the exposure time.

Place the loaded contact printing frame on the enlarger baseboard squarely under the lens. For a black and white contact sheet set the lens at about two stops from maximum aperture, and set the timer for 10 seconds. After 5 seconds, shade half the sheet. For color you can use the same aperture, having set filtration at 65Y 35M, or as recommended on the paper packet. Because filtration is an additional variable with color, you may find it a help to uncover progressively the frame to produce three exposures of 5, 10, and 20 seconds duration on the same piece of color printing material.

As a general rule, for black and white you should use a soft or normal grade paper as it will probably produce the best results from a wide variety of different density negatives.

Processing
For black and white processing, immerse the print in a tray of developer for the specified time (usually about 2 minutes), and then transfer it to the stop bath and fix before washing and drying. With color, load the paper into a print drum (with the emulsion inward), switch on white light and pour chemicals at the correct temperature into the drum in the sequence required. PCT film is loaded in darkness into the printmaker for activation.

As for all processing work, ensure consistency of technique. Prepare the volumes of solution before they are required and monitor the

temperature closely. When using a print drum start to drain the solution 10 seconds before the end of each process. Dry the print before trying to assess the results.

Assessing results
Look at the black and white contact sheet in terms of exposure and contrast. If contrast is generally excessive or too flat, you will have to use a different paper grade (see *Paper grades,* p. 243). The processed contact sheet will show two very different bands of exposure. The lighter half received the shorter 5 second exposure. It is likely that the sheet as a whole may require a compromise exposure for the best overall result. If this is the case, estimate the new exposure time and make a fresh set of contact prints.

Assess a color contact sheet for exposure first (although it will also give an overall guide to color casts). As far as contrast is concerned, there is only one grade of color printing paper. You have to assume that once you correct the color cast, and select the correct exposure,

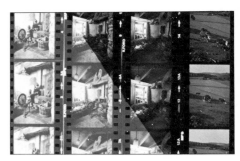

Assessing the contact sheet
The left half of this black and white contact sheet received 5 sec exposure, and the right half 10 sec. Contrast seems about right, and correct exposure will probably be about 8 sec. Differences between dark and light exposure results are most obvious when using a hard grade of printing paper.

the print will show a satisfactory range of tones and colors. Often you can make a second contact sheet testing for color alone. Choose the best exposure from the three shown on the first contact and use this as the basis for making three equal-time exposures, each with a different filtration. After processing and drying, decide which band produces the best overall color and density and make a final contact sheet.

If you use the same paper batch, set the filtration controls to the values used to make the final contact sheet as a starting point for making an enlargement of a single frame. With all darkroom work, keep a notebook of enlarging details such as type of camera film, enlarger magnification, aperture, exposure, and filtration.

Making a black and white enlargement

Study your black and white contact sheet and select a suitable negative for printing. Use the contact sheet image to make some preliminary decisions concerning cropping for best composition (assuming that you do not want to print the whole frame). The final appearance of the print will depend on the type of negative, enlarger illumination, the degree of enlargement, paper type, and the exposure you give it. Image quality will also be affected by the way you process and the condition of the chemicals. Old developer is slow and sometimes produces a high fog level on the paper. All chemical solutions should be within their acceptable temperature range and agitation must be carried out consistently (see *Time, temperature, and agitation,* p. 241).

Test strip

Before starting a printing session make sure that all you need is prepared and conveniently laid out (see *Preparing to print,* p. 244). The first step toward producing a full enlargement is making a detailed test strip. This involves exactly the same technique used in making a test exposure for your black and white contact sheet, but with more steps.

With the negative in place in the carrier (emulsion side down) and the safelights on, set the enlarger head for the correct degree of enlargement and the masking strips of the masking frame for the correct cropping of the image. Focus accurately using a focus magnifier. Then set the enlarger lens to the same aperture used to make the contact sheet. With the red filter in place or the enlarger light off, place a half sheet of printing paper in the frame so that it will include a range of image highlights, shadows, and mid-tones.

Turn the enlarger on, and, using a piece of opaque cardboard, progressively uncover the paper to create exposure bands of 5, 10, and 20 seconds. If the enlarger head is set to the same height used to make the contact sheet, you can modify these times in relation to its print density. If, for example, the contact image is too light you can make the exposure bands

10, 20, and 40 seconds. If the contact is too dark, try 5, 10, and 15 seconds.

Assessment

After processing, the test strip should show a good range of densities. If, overall, the test is too dark, either halve the time or close the aperture down one stop, and vice versa. If the test is too hard with too few mid-tones between good highlights and shadows, you should try a softer grade of paper (see *Paper grades,* p. 243). An overall flatness with good mid-tones but highlights not bright and deep shadows only dark gray is the result of using too soft a paper. If you carry on testing and find that your print is too contrasty whatever the paper grade, then either subject lighting was too hard or you overdeveloped the negative.

Final print

For the majority of negatives, one test strip will give enough information to enable you to make a full-size enlargement. When the test strip is correct, realign the masking frame, refocus the lens, and set the aperture and timer before placing a full sheet of paper in the masking frame.

Black and white from color negatives

For reasons of economy or perhaps to avoid changing camera film stock while shooting, you may wish to print color negatives as black and white. Ordinary black and white paper is not really suitable for this purpose because it is only sensitive to blue light or blue-green light. If used, this type of paper will give you incorrect tonal reproduction of original subject colors, with weak blues and black reds. Because the color negative will incorporate a pink or orange mask, a print made on ordinary bromide paper requires a long exposure and may be low in contrast.

To overcome this problem, special panchromatic black and white paper is made specifically for printing from color negatives (Kodak Panalure, for example). You make test exposures and enlargements in exactly the same way as for ordinary bromide, but you must work in total darkness because of the paper's extended spectral sensitivity.

The final print
Test strips are vital for every enlargement. The one below was exposed for 5, 10, and 20 sec. Always include both light and dark parts of the image when testing for exposure. In this case, the middle (10 sec) strip shows best overall detail. For the full print (right) the whole print was exposed for 10 sec, and then the window area and nearest wall were given an extra 4 sec exposure to bring out additional detail, which would have otherwise been lost as a featureless highlight.

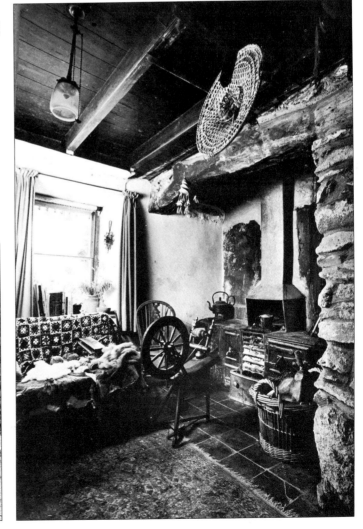

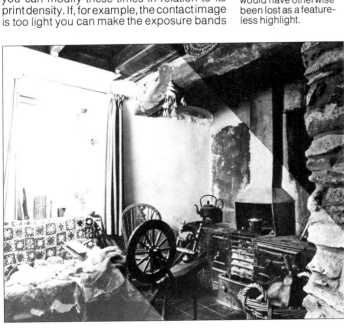

Making a negative/positive enlargement

Making a color print from a color negative is simple with a color analyzer and a processing drum or PCT printmaker (see *Printing equipment,* pp. 236-9). First, select an image from your color contact sheet (see *Making a contact sheet,* p. 244), and then prepare your chemicals, enlarger, and all processing equipment (see *Preparing to print,* p. 244). Make sure that the negative is clean and then place it, emulsion side down, in the negative carrier. Open the enlarger lens to its widest aperture, set the color head for while light, and adjust the enlarger head for the desired degree of magnification. Then compose the image on the masking frame and focus

At this point you should either set the filtration to that chosen for the contact sheet or previous enlargements (if you are still using the same paper batch) or use an analyzer to "read" the color content of the negative. The analyzer will recommend the filtration and exposure. These instruments are programmed for midtones, and will produce a correct assessment as long as the negative has an average distribution of tones. Analyzers, however, do vary, so make sure you read the instructions.

Test print

Once you have set the enlarger filtration, stop the lens down to the aperture used for the contact sheet. Set the enlarger timer and, in complete darkness or suitable safelighting, use a piece of opaque cardboard to make a series of three exposures on a piece of printing paper. Use intervals of 10, 15, and 20 seconds, or adjust these by referring to the best exposure time used for the contact sheet. Next, process the test (see *Making a contact sheet,* p. 244). With drum processing 10 seconds before the end of development pour out the solution, and pour in the bleach-fix. Restart the timer and agitate. Discard this solution also at the end of the step. Carefully remove the print and wash and dry it before assessing filtration.

If the print has no unwanted color cast, then select the exposure that produced the best

density and make a full enlargement. It is more likely, though, that the test will show a cast. In this case, select the best density from the three and prepare to make a filtration test. Using the best exposure time, make three separate exposures changing the filtration by about 10 units each. Mask the paper so that only one strip is showing at any one time. Process the test as before. With the results of these two tests, you should have enough information to make an enlargement. If, however, the second test does not show a neutral zone, pick the best option and make another test varying filtration around that filtration value.

20Y

10Y

20R

20G

10R

10G

Correct filtration

10M

10C

20M

20C

10B

20B

Neg/pos ring-around

To prepare a ring-around first make the best possible print from your chosen negative. Then make further prints changing filtration by 10 units, and another by 20 units in one color direction at a time. Adjust aperture or exposure time to keep all prints at the same density. Finally, mount them on a sheet of cardboard near to where you can judge your test strips (preferably by daylight or color-corrected white light). Th filter references shown against each print in the ring-around (left) indicate the amount of filtration necessary to subtract from your settings to correct that amount of color error. To subtract a primary color cast remove two complementary colored filters. A 10Y plus a 10M, for example, are equivalent to 10R. If you cannot subtract a particular color any further, then add a complementary filter of equivalent strength.

Negative/positive ring-around

Assessing filtration is highly subjective. When looking at a test print from a new negative, it is very useful to have a series of test prints (each differing in filtration in different directions and in increasing amounts). A series of images like this is called a ringaround, and the negative you choose to make one from should be accurately exposed, not excessively contrasty, and include neutral tones as well as an important mid-tone such as a skin tone.

Exposure test

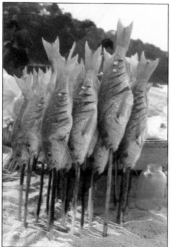

20 sec   15 sec   10 sec

Filtration test

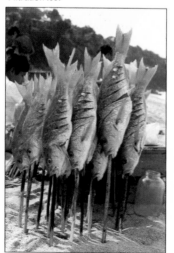

50Y 30M   55Y 30M   65Y 40M

Final print

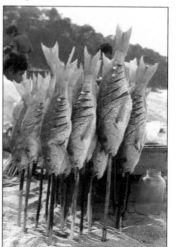

Assessing tests

The first (exposure) test (far left) was exposed for 20, 15, and 10 sec intervals, with filtration set at 50Y 25M. Density was judged to be best at 15 sec, but the print has a slight warm cast. To produce a less orange result, yellow and magenta filtration must be increased by the correct amount. The next (filtration) test (center) was therefore masked off so that only one part of the paper was exposed at a time. The print's top left-hand corner was exposed for 15 sec filtered 50Y 30M. For the middle strip filters were changed to 55Y 30M, and for the final strip 65Y 40M, both also at 15 sec. From this result, 55Y 30M appears most correct, but density now requires a slight increase. The final print (left) was made at the same filtration, but exposure was increased to 20 sec.

Making a positive/positive enlargement

There are three different types of material you can use to make a print from a slide — silver dye-bleach paper (such as Cibachrome), reversal paper (such as Kodak R14), or PCT Ektaflex reversal film. You must set up the enlarger, masking frame, and all processing solutions and equipment as described on the facing page. It is easier to compose the image as the enlarger projects an unmasked positive on the masking frame. But you must make sure that the slide is perfectly clean, as any tiny hairs or particles of dust will print as black marks, which are extremely difficult to remove (see *Retouching and spotting,* p. 252).

Processing variation

For silver dye-bleach, reversal papers, and PCT material, the sequence of testing for exposure and filtration is essentially the same, but processing is different (see *Time, temperature, and agitation,* p. 241). A problem that affects all types of positive/positive material is that of contrast. It is best to print from a slide original which is evenly lit and not particularly contrasty. A slightly overexposed slide will produce a print with washed-out colors and weak highlights. A slightly underexposed slide will give a print with strong, saturated colors. Cibachrome material has lessened the problem of excessive contrast by including a self-masking layer between the blue- and green-sensitive layers of the paper.

Positive/positive contact sheet

You can make a positive/positive contact sheet by placing mounted slides on a sheet of printing paper or PCT film (emulsion side up), and exposing them to light under the enlarger. Set the filtration recommended on the paper packet, and make three separate exposures across the sheet. With some positive/positive paper, short or very long exposures may cause color distortion, so only expose one strip of paper at a time, and vary the lens aperture to change exposures. As a guide, you can use f 5.6, f 8, and f 11. Process

the contact sheet. The red cast on SDB paper will disappear as the print dries.

Enlarging

After selecting a single image, remove it from its mount, and clean and place it in the enlarger film carrier. Switch off the room lights and focus and compose the image on the masking frame. Then, either set the filtration used for your contact sheet (if you are using the same paper batch) or use a color analyzer. Place a sheet of paper or PCT film in the frame and make a series of exposures. Again, vary aperture and not exposure time. From this processed test, pick the strip that produced the best density and prepare to make a fresh print, testing for filtration. The type of filtration adjustment required will depend on the cast shown by the first test. To correct a color cast you simply subtract filters the same color as the cast.

Positive/positive ring-around

As with negative/positive printing, it is useful to make a ring-around for judging color cast with a positive/positive print. Use an original with some neutral and pale colors.

20Y

10Y

20R

20G

10R

10G

Correct filtration

10M

10C

20M

20C

10B

20B

Pos/pos ring-around

To make a positive/positive ring-around, choose a correctly exposed slide containing some near neutral areas (pale colors show up the slightest cast strongly). Silver dye-bleach paper was used for the ring-around on the left. First, a print closely matching the slide was made, followed by others offset in color. SDB material has more filtration latitude, so you may have to choose larger unit differences in filtration than with negative/positive paper. Filter references against each print show what must be removed from your filtration to correct that degree of color cast. Unlike negative/positive printing, this filtration is the same color as the cast. If you are positive/positive printing and have an enlarger with a color head allowing only yellow and magenta filtration, you may have to buy some 10 and 20 unit cyan filters to use in the filter drawer.

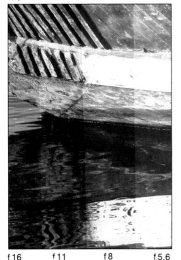

Exposure test

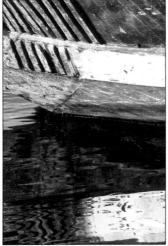

Filtration test

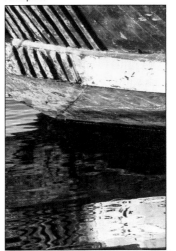

Final print

f 16   f 11   f 8   f 5.6

70Y 15C 60Y 15C 50Y 15C 40Y 15C

Assessing tests

The first (exposure) test (far left) was filtered 40Y 15C. The paper was exposed in strips, with the lens set at f 16, f 11, f 8, and f 5.6. Each strip received 15 sec exposure. Using a constant exposure time minimizes reciprocity failure effects. Density appears to be best in the f 11 strip, but the colors are slightly bluish. The second (filtration) test (center) had all its strips exposed for 15 sec at f 11, but with differing increases in yellow filtration. The first was 70Y 15C, the second 60Y 15C, the third 50Y 15C, and the right-hand strip received 40Y 15C again. The best result is from the 70Y 15C strip, but colors could still be warmer and results are a little dark. For the final print (left) filtration was changed to 80Y 05C, and filtration was 15 sec with the aperture set at the half stop between f 8 and f 11.

Print faults

Modern color print processing chemistry and papers have been refined and standardized to the point where practically all faults can be traced back to user error. In general, those processes that require the higher solution temperatures are more likely to create problems. Incorrect temperature of the developer, in particular, will cause color and contrast errors on both negative/positive and positive/positive color prints. With PCT color material activator and all black and white print processing this is not so critical. Within limits you can adjust for differences in solution temperature by either increasing or decreasing development time. Another very common error

leading to print faults is chemical contamination. Color processing chemicals, especially developers, are very complex and carefully balanced to produce a specific and defined response in the emulsion layers of the printing paper. A drop or two of bleach in the developer solution results in prints which are fogged or show extreme color casts. A major source of chemical contamination is inadequately cleaned graduates and processing drums. Furthermore, if you use a thermometer to test the temperature of one solution and then do not clean it thoroughly before testing another, you will experience the type of problem described below.

Identifying print faults

Typical error	Negative/positive Ektaprint 2	Positive/positive Cibachrome	Kodak R14
Paper placed in masking frame the wrong way round (emulsion side down).	Print will have blue cast and be lighter than expected.	Print will have an unexpected color cast and be too dark.	Print will have an unexpected color cast and be too dark.
Printing filters omitted during exposure of the paper.	Print will exhibit a bright orange color cast.	Strong overall color cast.	Strong overall color cast.
Temperature of developer outside the latitude recommended by the manufacturer.	Print will be too flat or shadows too heavy. There will also be a color cast.	Print will have incorrect color balance and density. (Process a control strip to show it is a process fault, not filtration.)	Incorrect color balance and density.
Developer solution contaminated with bleach-fix solution.	Print will show a magenta or purple color cast, and appear slightly solarized. Depends on the degree of contamination.	Print will appear dull and have a muddy pink color cast.	
Paper loaded into print drum the wrong way round.	Print will have light blotches due to uneven and insufficient development.	Print will have dark blotches.	Dark blotchy densities and colors (after reversal exposure).
Paper fogged to light before processing.	Print will show brownish streaks.	Top layer (yellow) of print will be destroyed, resulting in a purple cast.	Print will be too light, too flat, and have an overall color cast.
Exhausted bleach.	Print will appear too dark and contrast too flat.	Print will have a silvery surface appearance, too dark and muddy.	Silvery appearance and too dark and muddy.

Color printing — comparative exposure and filtration corrections

Print appearance	Positive/positive paper (including PCT reversal film)	Negative/positive paper (including PCT negative film)
Too light	Reduce exposure	Increase exposure
Too dark	Increase exposure	Reduce exposure
Small area dark	Burn in	Shade
Small area light	Shade	Burn in
Too yellow	Reduce yellow filters	Add yellow filters
Too magenta	Reduce magenta filters	Add magenta filters
Too cyan	Reduce cyan filters	Add cyan filters
Too blue	Reduce magenta and cyan filters	Reduce yellow filters
Too green	Reduce yellow and cyan filters	Reduce magenta filters
Too red	Reduce yellow and magenta filters	Reduce cyan filters.

Special printing techniques

Ideally, the image recorded by the camera on film should be an exact representation of all the nuances of color, shade, and tone of the original subject or scene. Taking this a stage further, the printing paper should be able to reproduce all these subtleties, and so render a print that is in all major respects an exact copy of the original. In reality this is not the case. Film emulsions have an uneven response to component colors present in a scene. Above all the three dye layers used in films and papers can, at best, only come close to matching the potentially vast range of colors you can see in the viewfinder.

The quality of processing and printing also plays an important part in image appearance. Many films are now machine printed in commercial laboratories. Although the standard of these is high, they are designed to produce a "standard" print, usually balanced for a mid-gray or skin tone. Where more than 50 per cent of the image is highlight or deep shadow, or where the photographer has exposed for large areas of bright color, a machine print will probably be unsatisfactory.

Selective printing
Photographers can improve most prints by lightening or darkening selected areas during enlargement. The principle is the same in black and white and color negative/positive printing. To lighten a particular area it must be shaded from light during part of the exposure. This technique is called shading or dodging. For the opposite effect a selective area of the paper must receive additional exposure, and the technique is known as printing-in or burning-in. These techniques also work with positive/positive paper, but in the opposite way. Shading light from an area will darken it and vice versa. Color can be boosted in a similar way by additional filtration in selective areas.

Additive printing
With additive printing (exposing the image several times, through different filters) it is possible to exercise finer control over the appearance of a color print. The additional exposures can be made with different overlays in contact with the paper to build up either a straight print of exceptional quality or a whole range of color special effects.

See also
Emphasis *Emphasis through tone*, p. 69.

Local density control

However careful you are with the lighting of your original subject, with the processing of the resulting film image, and your printing, there will be occasions when the final print is unsatisfactory because of areas of incorrect local density. You may also make a subjective decision to alter the visual appearance of a print that is correctly exposed by lightening or darkening selected parts. Practice your dodging technique by turning on the enlarger and moving your hands or pieces of opaque cardboard in the light path until the shadows they create on the masking frame are satisfactory. Use a similar technique to practice burning-in. Make a test strip that includes areas of the print to be selectively printed. From the test, discover the overall exposure required and the necessary increase or decrease to be made by burning-in or dodging. With dodging, subtract the amount of time necessary to lighten the area from the standard time. Then use your hands or a dodger to shade over this area while you expose the remainder of the print. For burning-in, expose the whole print and then use your hands or a piece of cardboard to make an appropriate shape which will allow light through for the additional period of exposure. You can also use a sheet of glass as a dodging tool.

Spray an area of it (corresponding to the area to be dodged) with photo-opaque or black poster paint. Hold this glass about 3 ins (7 cm) above the paper. (When hand-shading it is easiest to position your hands just a few inches below the lens.) With all these techniques, keep the burning-in or dodging im-

plement gently on the move while in use, to avoid sharp outlines of different density. An extension of the burning-in and dodging techniques is vignetting, where you shade off the edges of your print into a light or dark frame.

Vignetting
For a white vignette on a black and white or color negative/positive print you need a piece of opaque cardboard larger than the paper. Cut an aperture in the cardboard and hold it above the paper while exposing through the hole. For a black vignette use the same technique, but after exposing the paper switch the enlarger off and carefully remove the negative. Then shade with the cut-out section of the cardboard (on glass) using it as a shield for the exposed area while you fog the paper edges to the light from the enlarger. For a color positive/

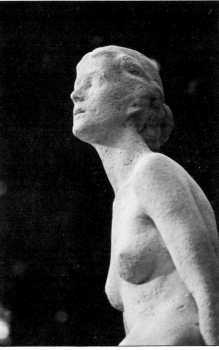

positive print, hold light away from the paper edges for a black vignette, and fog the edges for a white vignette. By modifying these techniques — keeping the cardboard in contact with the paper — you can print sharp black or white, shaped, or regular print borders. Make sure the cut card edges are perfectly smooth.

Burning-in
After discovering the extra exposure required by making a test print, decide which shape aperture (or apertures) will best suit the particular job. One of the most versatile implements to use for burning-in is your own hands. Cup them together so that they shade most of the paper area, leaving just a small gap between them at the bottom. After burning-in, raise one hand to obscure the enlarger light before switching off the enlarger with the other. Hold your hands or the cardboard above the paper and move continuously. The higher up the beam you interrupt the light, the larger and more diffused will be the area shaded. Sometimes it is impossible to remove or tone down an intrusive highlight or excessively contrasty area using this method. In such cases, you can use a small flashlight, suitably masked down with a cone of black paper, to fog a very specific area with non-image-forming light.

Dodging
Before deciding on dodging times, make a test print to determine the area (or areas) affected. Tools for dodging are very simple — appropriately shaped pieces of opaque cardboard attached to thin but stiff non-reflective wire. For certain shapes and areas next to picture edges it is easiest to use the side of your hand or fingers. The basic rules for burning-in also apply to dodging. For a soft, diffused area, hold the dodger high up in the light beam produced by the enlarger. And keep the dodger moving continuously. If you find the wire handle is scattering light on the paper, paint it matte black.

Variable-contrast paper
It is possible to alter the contrast of a very localized area of the print by using variable-contrast black and white printing paper (see *Paper grades*, p. 243). You can use this technique when a photograph prints well at one particular grade except, say, for a small area of underexposed shadow or overexposed highlight which requires extra contrast. First, make a print with the variable-contrast paper filtered for the best overall response. During this exposure, dodge the area requiring special attention. Then switch off the enlarger and change filters (or dial in the appropriate color filters if you are using a color head enlarger). Choose filtration that will create a hard response. Next, print in the area previously dodged using a large piece of opaque cardboard with an aperture cut out of it. You may have to adjust the duration of the exposure to restore correct density.

Fogging-in
Usually, unwanted light areas in the background (near right) can be toned down by locally burning-in. Sometimes, however, these parts can remain noticeable even when given two or three times the main exposure. For the large print (far right) small patches of sky were fogged using a small flashlight cowled with black paper.

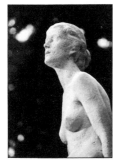
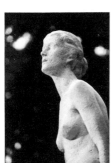

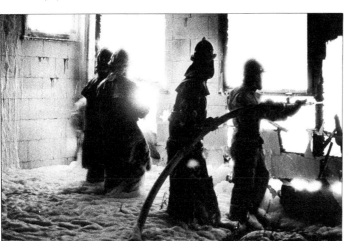

Density control
This backlit image required extensive dodging and burning-in to print all the information on the negative. Hard-grade paper was essential to stop the figures looking flat, but tests showed that the firemen needed 10 sec exposure, and the walls and windows up to 35 sec. The final print was exposed for 15 sec — shading the figures for 4 sec each with a cardboard dodger on wire. The top and sides of the picture were burned-in for an additional 20 sec.

Additive printing

For the basic additive system of color printing you give the paper three separate exposures, each through a different deep-colored primary filter. The first exposure through a blue filter affects only the blue-sensitive layer of the paper, which eventually results in the yellow dye image. The second exposure through a green filter produces a magenta dye response, and the final exposure through a red filter produces cyan dye. With positive/positive paper, the dye response of the paper is the same color as the filter used.

Unless you use a single-exposure additive enlarger (see *Printing equipment,* pp. 236-9), there are two important disadvantages in using the additive printing system. First, you have to make three exposures on a single sheet of paper without shifting the enlarger or masking frame while you are changing filters. Second, you have to make at least two filtration tests, instead of the usual one required in subtractive color printing (see *Making a negative/ positive enlargement,* p. 246 and *Making a*

positive/positive enlargement, p. 247).However, some photographers feel that the flexibility of additive printing more than compensates.

The additional equipment you require for additive printing consists of a filter holder, which you attach under the lens, and the correct color separation filters made of gelatin or high-quality glass. Set up the enlarger and darkroom in the same way as for subtractive printing (see *Preparing to print,* p. 244).

Making a patch chart

The best way to determine exposure when working additively is to first make a test print with only the blue filter in use. Using opaque cardboard, make a series of three exposures at 5, 10 and 20 second intervals (with the lens set at about f 8). After processing (see *Time, temperature, and agitation,* p. 241) you will have a yellow image on negative/positive paper (or a blue image on positive/positive paper), which you can assess for image density. If you find the yellow image too dim to view

properly, look at it through the blue filter. Assuming density is best at 10 seconds, place more paper in the frame and expose it all at this setting through the blue filter. Then change to a green filter and expose the same sheet from top to bottom in three steps – 5, 10, and 20 seconds. Next change to the red filter, and expose from left to right at 5, 10 and 20 second intervals. Process the print.

Assessing the test print

Make careful notes concerning the filters and exposure times for each "square" of your test patch chart. Ideally, your test will have the best color and density in the center patch (10B 10G 10R). When printing additively you make the print lighter or darker by changing all three exposures by the same proportion. If, for example, the center patch had the correct color but was too dark on negative/positive paper you could change exposure to 7B 7G 7R. If it was too light, exposure could be 15B 15G 15R. To change image color you have to change filter exposure individually. A longer blue exposure on negative/positive paper will produce an image with more yellow. More green exposure will increase magenta, and additional red exposure will increase cyan. For the primary colors, to increase red give a longer exposure through the blue and green filters, to increase green give more exposure through blue and red, and for additional blue, give more exposure through red and green.

Testing for exposure
The patch chart test (below) was made on negative/positive paper. An initial test strip through the blue filter showed 10 sec to be correct. Next, a whole sheet was given 10 sec through blue, plus strips of 10, 20, and 40 sec red exposure from right to left. Finally,

10B 40G 40R	10B 40G 20R	10B 40G 10R
10B 20G 40R	10B 20G 20R	10B 20G 10R
10B 10G 40R	10B 10G 20R	10B 10G 10R

green exposures of 10, 20, and 40 sec were made from the bottom to the top. The chart records the total exposure for each "patch"

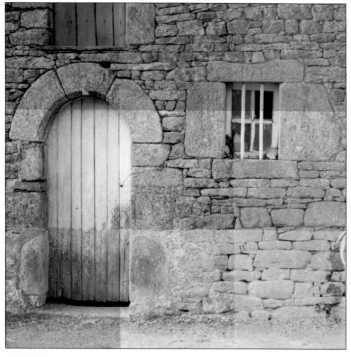

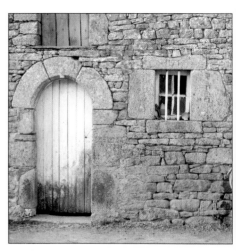

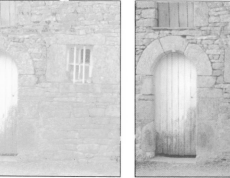

Yellow

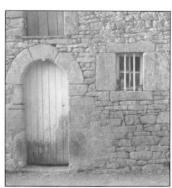

Magenta

Cyan

Deciding the final exposure
Judging the processed patch chart (above left), the center square (10B 20G 20R) shows the most accurate color rendition. You can next make another patch chart with slight adjustments around these figures, or try a complete print (above). Each separate additive exposure affects only one paper emulsion. The blue filter exposure controls the yellow dye image, the green exposure controls the magenta, and the red exposure controls the cyan dye image (left).

Local color control

You can intensify chosen areas of color, or correct local color casts by burning-in and dodging (see *Local density control*, p. 249) through a supplementary filter of suitable value. It is simplest to introduce these filters after the light has passed through the lens, so they must be optically pure gelatin filter types. The acetate filters used in enlargers with color filter drawers (see *Printing equipment*, pp. 236-9) will upset the definition of the image.

Boosting local color

A common problem when photographing landscapes that include areas of sky is that if you expose for the land area the sky takes on a bleached out and featureless appearance. If you are working with negative/positive paper, expose a standard print that is correctly balanced for land detail, density, and color. To intensify color and tone in the sky you may decide to at least double the exposure of the sky area. Hold a 40Y filter just below the lens (as if

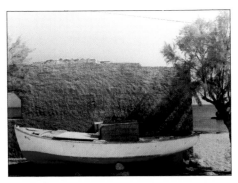

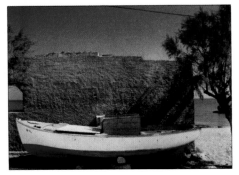

Controlling color
The top print was correctly filtered and exposed for main detail. It was printed on negative/positive paper at 50Y 25M for a 12 sec exposure. The sky area is too weak and colorless. For the second print (above), an additional 15 sec exposure was given to the sky area, holding a 40Y gelatin

filter under the lens. Another method of achieving this effect is to dial in an extra 40Y on a color head enlarger for the extra period of exposure. Take care not to move the enlarger in any way between the two exposures as this will make registering the extra color difficult.

you were trying to remove a yellow color cast), then burn-in the top, sky part of the image, giving the same exposure time again. Use your hand or a cardboard dodger to shade the land. If you are printing from a slide using positive/

positive material, you will have to give the sky less exposure through a blue filter in order to intensify the sky coloring. Using a filter like this will not only alter the color but also cut down the light reaching the paper and so darken it. Only one exposure is therefore necessary, as you use the filter in the same way you would an opaque dodger.

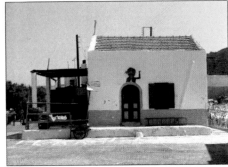

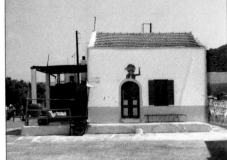

Local corrections
Sometimes density in a color print is correct, but there is a color cast over part of the picture. The top print here received a 10 sec exposure overall on negative/positive paper, with filtration set at 40Y 15M. The general color balance is correct, but the face of the building has a cold

blue cast. For the corrected version (above) the building was shaded throughout the exposure with a 30B filter, used like a dodger. Finally, the building alone was given 3 sec extra exposure through a hole in a piece of cardboard. The filter was still in place over the lens.

Controlling local color casts

Local color casts usually appear in subject shadows or highlights. These could be the result of incorrect film exposure (see *Effects of reciprocity failure*, p. 220) in the camera or mixed color temperature lighting. To minimize or eliminate a color cast using negative/positive paper, hold a gelatin filter the same color as the cast (as you would a print dodger) under the lens and shade the area to be corrected during the normal exposure. This may create an area of lighter density. If so, then hold the rest of the print back and give that particular area additional exposure (still through the same filter).

Working from a slide on positive/positive paper, you must use a filter complementary in color to that of the cast. Again, the filter will cut down the light to that area of the paper,

probably making it too dark. To correct this you will have to give additional filtered exposure while shading the rest of the paper.

Contrast masking

Excessive print contrast can be a problem when printing direct from color slides. To make a less contrasty print you can prepare a very weak contact print made on normal contrast panchromatic film. Sandwich this in exact register with the original slide and enlarge them as one image. When making this "mask" use slow black and white sheet film. Underexpose the film and reduce development by 50 per cent. Following processing, cut the weak negative image out of the sheet and arrange it with the original so that the slide base separ-

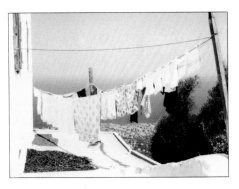

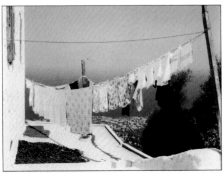

Reducing contrast
The top print was made on positive/positive paper from a contrasty slide. Contrast is too high to give good color rendering and detail throughout. The

second version (above) is the result of combining a very weak black and white negative with the slide before making a print.

ates the two emulsion surfaces. Tape the two together along the film rebates before placing them in the film carrier of the enlarger, preferably between glass. Another method of reducing contrast on positive/positive paper is by "flashing" the paper, to white light after it has been exposed. On the initial exposure, aim for good highlight and mid-tone detail, not shadows. Then carefully remove the slide and replace it with a neutral density (ND 2) filter, and re-expose the paper for the same length of time.

Print finishing

Processed films attract dust and other small air-borne particles easily, and because film often carries a slight electrostatic charge, these can be quite persistent. The photographer must aim to remove any debris before printing, since when enlarged this can seriously mar the look of the finished work.

With negative/positive printing, dust or hair on the film surfaces will appear as clear white areas when printed. With positive/positive printing these same particles will appear as black marks on the print, which are far more difficult to retouch out.

Print retouching
There are two stages to print retouching. First, there is the correction of small light and dark specks using water color, dye or process white, applied with the tip of an almost dry fine brush. This method is suitable for both black and white and color prints. Second, for large areas of print retouching, tones of unsuitable density, or large areas of unbalanced color, it is best to use an airbrush. More accurately, this should be called an air spray as it uses a source of compressed air to spray water-based dye or pigment. With practice, it is also possible to use an airbrush for very fine line work and the addition or enhancement of detail.

Print preservation
After processing and retouching, the photographer may need to decide on the best method of preserving the printed image. For archival permanence, the print must be stored in the correct environment, away from light. But for the prints that are to be displayed, special care must be taken to protect them from fading. Most display prints are first mounted on special acid-free cardboard. They can be sandwiched between two sheets of clear plastic, which not only protects their surfaces but also stops them stretching or shrinking. Other protective devices include UV absorbing sprays, plastic heat-sealing sleeves, or laminates.

Display
Apart from the obvious advantages of mounting and protecting prints, the way they are displayed can affect their visual impact considerably. Glossy prints or prints covered with a gloss laminate offer the richest tone range and tend to have the most dramatic impact. The quality of the print mount, its spacing, and color will all contribute to the general impression. Normally a print looks best on a white or neutral mount, but black can also sometimes be effective. For black and white prints, it is worth experimenting with different pale-colored mounts.

See also
Workroom techniques, pp. 268-70.

Retouching and spotting

It is generally more difficult to remove dark specks or hair marks on resin-coated paper than on fiber-based paper. On the older base you can use a scalpel to scrape away a little dye or silver and the offending mark, but with resin-coated paper this leaves a frilly edge. Also, any tone or color applied to resin-coated paper sits on top of the print surface. To overcome this, after treatment spray the whole print with a gloss or matte finish. To remove white marks you require a fine sable brush, black (neutral) retouching dye or watercolor, and a palette for mixing. Load the brush with the least possible amount of color and stipple the area using just the tip of the brush. You will find that a few closely grouped spots of tone will create the illusion of gray tone. If you have a white hair mark, treat in the same way you would a series of white spots. For black marks use a scalpel or apply process white spotting, then build up the required tone.

To correct faults on a color print, it is best to use a proprietary set of retouching dyes. You will also need a set of fine brushes, a multiple mixing palette, and several pots of clean water for mixing the dyes. If you study your print you will see that the color image is an illusion of a particular color, created by the combination of many colors. This realization can help you when retouching color prints. Instead of applying an area of flat color, which never looks natural, you can use small quantities of different colors until you achieve the correct effect. Pay close attention to the type of brush stroke you use and try to match the texture of the surrounding print. You can often correct light spots by first toning down the area with gray retouching dye. To correct dark or black marks, cover the area with white pigment, and then rebuild the color.

No method of retouching will be completely successful unless the print surface is absolutely clean and grease free. If necessary, clean the print with degreasing agent and cotton balls. For cleaning fiber-based prints you can apply a mild solution of ammonia.

Bleaching
You can remove black spots on black and white prints by dampening the print slightly and spotting with a solution of iodine in potassium iodide (use 0.4 g iodine added to 1.5 g potassium iodide in 100 cc water). When the spot is bleached remove the brown iodine stain by refixing and washing the print. When the print is dry retouch the now white spot. Or you can tone down a black spot so that it more closely balances surrounding density, using Farmer's reducer. First, resoak the print and squeegee off any excess water, which could make the reducer run into unwanted areas. Using a brush, apply the reducer to the spot. When the spot is light enough, refix and wash the print. Any reducer left overlong on the print may stain yellow. You can also bleach color prints, but you must use special color dye reducer kits. With Cibachrome paper, prints are very delicate even when they are dry and therefore you must use the retouching kit supplied by the paper manufacturer.

Airbrushing

To retouch large areas of a print it is easier to use an airbrush. This is a miniature spraygun about the same size as a large fountain pen. You attach it via a tube to an air compressor, which has a filter to stop dust and grit blocking the flow of dye. You can, instead, use a can of compressed air to propel the dye. There is a fine needle running down the center of the airgun from a reservoir on top to an adjustable nozzle at the tip. Any suitable liquid in the reservoir runs down the outside of the needle to the nozzle.

Using an airbrush you can spray a uniform tone or color over an area of print that suffers from patchy density or hue, or from which distracting detail simply needs to be obliterated. It is also possible to transform a print, by adding highlights and shadows, removing or re-creating backgrounds, and adding or changing color. Impressive surrealistic effects are possible if you use an airbrush in conjunction with masks (see *Techniques*, p. 379) to create strange juxtapositions of different elements. In skilled hands, an airbrush can even be used

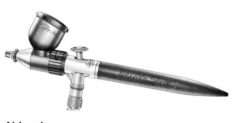

Airbrush
The cup-shaped reservoir holds liquid color. Pressing the top button allows air to flow. Pushing it back gradually allows the paint or dye to be sucked out by the passing air and also controls spray width.

to build up a photographic-looking image from white paper.

Using an airbrush
For spraying black and white prints mix up the required strength of tone using black and white process colors, thinned with water. For color work mix up the dyes on a palette, diluting with water as necessary, and testing by spraying on paper or a scrap print. Make sure that the colors you use are grit free, otherwise you will probably block the fine nozzle outlet. When the color and consistency are correct, load the airbrush reservoir with a hog hair brush (even the fine hairs of a sable brush may block the nozzle). To draw air through the airbrush depress the button on top of the body and, with the button still depressed, pull it gently backward. This will draw the needle away from the nozzle and allow color to be sucked out by the passing air flow. Too little air pressure will create a flat area of tone finer than that of the surrounding photographic image. For realistic effects, the pattern of the tone should match the grain structure of the original print.

Initially, practice various spraying techniques on a waste print. Always prevent the print moving by taping it down securely to the work surface. It requires a lot of practice before you can spray an even tone over a large area, or spray fine lines directly on the print surface. If you make a mistake using pigment colors, you can remove all the color using damp cotton balls, and then start again. Dyes, however, sink into the emulsion, and you will require several spare prints if you make any mistakes.

As with all forms of retouching, the print surface must be perfectly clean and free of grease. Fingerprints in particular will show up as areas of uneven pattern under the airbrushing. The airbrushing accessories you will also require include a sharp scalpel, masking tape, thin cardboard for masking, palette and brushes, in addition to process black and white and a good range of water colors, inks, or dyes. For complicated work, you will also need special adhesive masking film.

Using masks

For precise areas of spraying, where a sharp, clean outline is essential, you will have to use a mask. Make the mask out of thin cardboard and hold it flat on the print surface while you overspray the area. If you hold the mask just a little above the print surface, some color or tone will work its way under for a softer outline. Cover up all areas of the print, except those requiring work.

A better method of masking is to use adhesive masking film. Cover the whole print with the film and, using a sharp scalpel, carefully cut through the film and peel it away to reveal the areas to be sprayed. Take care not to damage the print surface. After you have sprayed that area either remove more of the mask and so build up densities in steps, or replace the first cut-out and remove another. Using this technique, you can spray adjacent hard-edged areas in different colors or tones without the risk of overlap.

Creating effects

On black and white prints, mix white with the black to make an opaque gray with which to obliterate detail completely, or use black to accentuate shadow areas. To create brighter, more pronounced highlights, use a white or off-white mix. If you are working in color, you can remove unwanted color by spraying with process white, and then building up the image again with colors of your choice. An alternative method is to overspray an image color with a dye of another color. You can, for example, spray yellow dye over blue image detail in order to create green.

Before changing colors in the airbrush, fill the reservoir with clean water and spray out several times. And when you have finished working, clean the airbrush out again and keep the button depressed until the airbrush is dry inside. Airbrushed prints are extremely delicate and it is easy to lift off the color or scratch the surface. As a protective finish you can use an acetate overlay, or spray with matte or glossy lacquer. Most airbrushed prints are used for reproduction or as "one-off" artworks. Where duplicates are required, it is best to copy the original carefully on appropriate film, from which prints can then be made.

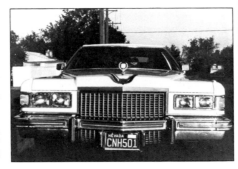

Original print
Make the original print for airbrushing fairly large. (Eventually you may want to copy the finished result and reduce it in size.) As with hand coloring, it is best to sepia tone a black and white image first. The subject here has a distracting background. Reflections darken the hood and hide interior details.

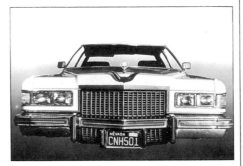

Background treatment
The whole surface is covered with a masking film. This is cut by knife around the body and window outlines, and peeled away from the background. With other parts protected, all the background is sprayed white, gradated downward to dark gray. The car at this stage has an unnatural cut-out appearance – even the wheels are missing.

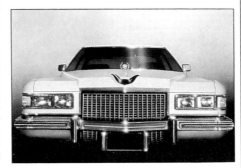

Finishing touches
The mask is further cut away to spray areas requiring slightly less treatment, such as the hood. Similarly, the windshield has also been tinted, and wheels added using handmade masks. Localized use of the airbrush has cleaned up the chrome and been used to add the catch lights. The final detail was added with a fine sable brush, including the removal of rough edges left by the mask surrounds.

Mounting and storing

With resin-coated paper (which is used for most black and white and all color papers) the paper base itself does not become wet and so curling after drying does not present a problem. Fiber-based prints, on the other hand, often fail to lie flat after drying. It is advisable to mount both types of print, especially if they are to be displayed or are likely to be subjected to extensive handling.

Dry mounting

A dry mounting press is rather like a print drier (see *Printing equipment*, pp. 236-9), except that the heating element is above the print. To mount a print you must sandwich a sheet of shellac-coated tissue between the back of the print and a piece of mounting cardboard. When you heat the tissue the shellac melts, gluing the print to its mount. First, place the print face down on a piece of clean cartridge paper and cover it with a sheet of dry mounting tissue. Use a heated tacking iron to stick the tissue to the back of the print at the corners only. Then trim off any excess tissue together with unwanted edges and lay the print and tissue on a piece of mounting cardboard. Using the tacking iron again, carefully lift each corner of the print, and tack the tissue to the cardboard. Next, place the sandwich of print, tissue, and mounting cardboard in the press with the print surface protected with a sheet of silicon release paper. This will prevent damage or unwanted texturing of the emulsion. Then close the press until the print is firmly pressed down on the cardboard.

The heat of the press is controllable, and you must read the accompanying instructions regarding the temperature settings for different types of paper.

Cold mounting

Certain types of papers are too delicate for dry mounting, and the application of heat would destroy the image. Cibachrome should only be cold-mounted using, for example, a double-sided adhesive sheet or tape. This is a simple and effective method of securing prints and is suitable for use with ordinary papers and instant picture material, too. When you are using tape, first cut a length that is sufficient to cover the edges of the print before removing the backing paper. Then lay the tape in position on a piece of trimmed mounting board, and carefully remove the backing. Finally, lay the print gently on the tape and apply pressure from the center outward.

Storing

Like negatives and slides, prints of all types have gelatin emulsions and must, therefore, be kept in conditions of low humidity and reasonably low heat. If you have space in your film storage area (see *Mounting and filing*, p. 227), this will be ideal for your prints.

Whenever you make a print from a negative, in either black and white or color, always mark the back of the print with the identity number you have given the film and, if possible, the frame number as well. This will make the task of finding a negative for reprinting much easier. Take care not to press too heavily on the print as it may show on the print surface. Instead, it is best to use a system of self-adhesive tags.

Special effects

One advantage of having your own processing and printing facilities is the range of special effects manipulations these make possible. Materials and processes can be used and "abused" in all manner of ways to create unusual or non-photographic looking results. These are the type of effects you cannot expect from a laboratory because they concern a particular image idea, which may evolve as the process continues. It is important, however, to become familiar with the straight methods of working first, because during this process you will learn about your equipment and the disciplines that go with it to control results. Having reached this stage, it is well worthwhile experimenting to see what extra forms of image your enlarger can produce.

Most of your time in the darkroom will be spent in producing photographs that are "true" to the original as seen in the viewfinder of the camera, but no routine is inflexible and no photographic material or process has to be used in a particular way. It is also true that when you expose a frame of film in the camera, you often have to compose and shoot in a short space of time — people move, shapes may be distorted by angle, and lighting changes and fluctuates. Later, when you are working in the darkroom there is far more time to consider major or minor changes and to see if these will enhance the total effect of the image. Some photographers regard negatives and positives produced with the camera as only the raw material. Their pictures are actually composed and constructed in the darkroom, sometimes combining many elements from different originals or changing the color scheme completely.

Another method of creating pictures under the enlarger is to place actual objects between the light source and the paper to form shapes and shadows known as photograms. Photograms are as old as photography itself, but came into vogue again through the work of Man Ray and others during the 1920s and 1930s (see *Structuralism and Abstraction,* pp. 361-8). With today's materials, the possibilities for different photogram effects have been extended by the introduction of negative/positive and positive/positive color papers. If the enlarger filtration settings are altered or objects moved part way through the exposure, color and tonal shapes for abstract imagery can be created.

Photograms require the minimum of equipment, but you do need to understand basic black and white or color printing first. Unless you work methodically, you can easily waste a great deal of time and material. As an extension of this method of generating color by filtration alone, you can print black and white negatives on color paper. The color of each area is governed by your filter settings — exposing only one part of the paper at a time to light from the enlarger and shading the remainder.

Combining images

One of the most interesting printing special effects manipulations involves merging one camera image realistically with another on the same sheet of printing paper. Sometimes this can be used to compensate for the deficiencies of straight photography — lack of sky detail in a landscape, for example. Mostly, though, it is used to create incongruous or surreal imagery. Impossible situations can be presented, dreamlike combinations of negative and positive colors, mixtures of scale, or photogrammed and photographed images. This type of work can take hours of skilled shading and printing-in of different elements, with no guarantee of success until the print emerges from the processing sequence. Or, it can be as simple as combining two color slides in the same mount or in the film carrier and projecting or enlarging the result.

A few extra items of equipment will be necessary if you are going to explore the possibilities of composite printing, or techniques such as posterization, which turn normal photographic tone and color values into a stencil painted type image. Register pins on the enlarger baseboard and a punch to make precision holes in paper or film that will receive the image are an example. A good registration system will ensure that prints can be part exposed, then removed (perhaps while you change originals), and exposed again in precisely the same position.

Unusual materials such as extreme-contrast lith or line film are widely used in some areas of darkroom special effects. Printing on film of this type allows you to simplify pictures to pure black and white only by eliminating the continuous progression of tones associated with straight photography. Lith film can also be used to make masks photographically, which you can then use to cover part of a sheet of color paper while you expose other parts to the image at a different filtration. Black and white material can be used in conjunction with color images in many different ways. Simply sandwiching a color slide with a contrasty black and white negative (contact printed from it) will blacken white clouds and all other image highlights. Manipulations of this kind are ways of subtlely manipulating or destroying the reality and familiar photographic qualities of a picture.

In a similar way, the bas-relief process turns subjects depicted in a photograph into strange, flattened-looking forms resembling sidelit low-relief sculptures. This is a surprisingly quick and simple routine, involving the making of one contact print on black and white film to form an offset mask. It is one of the best techniques to start off with as all you will require is a box of continuous-tone darkroom film such as Kodak Gravure positive. Another easy introductory special effects manipulation is solarization. For this, all you will need is line or lith sheet film, and results have a part-positive, part-negative, unearthly appearance.

Daylight techniques

Not all special effects have to take place in the darkroom during printing. Toning, hand coloring, and montage, for example, are all image manipulating techniques you can use on fully processed prints, and in a normally lit room. This is the stage when a montage can be constructed from any number of prints, or virtually any other source such as photographs in a magazine or newspaper, and combined with even greater freedom than multiple printing.

Hand coloring (with water color or oil-based paints), unlike color printing, allows you to decide the color of each individual element in a picture, irrespective of the actual hues. Modern chemical toning kits allow almost as much flexibility. These techniques are useful for the extra, and often highly personal qualities they can add to your photographs. Initially, practice them as techniques to extend your use of the materials involved, then use them selectively and only where the image itself demands such treatment. In general, all special effects should be used with restraint. Any technique applied too often, or without sufficient regard to the actual content of the basic photograph, will tend to lose its impact.

The special effects featured on the following pages begin with techniques that require very little additional equipment. These range from simple shape manipulation to multiple printing. Working methods for lith materials and ways of using film materials under the enlarger for separations and masks develop into typical applications, such as screen images and posterization. Finally, there are several examples of workroom techniques. All of the procedures and processes require practice before you can really understand and control what is possible. The examples presented are often only an example of the type of result that you can obtain — often your own combined use of camera, darkroom, and workroom techniques will lead to highly individual and distinctive images.

**Matching subject
and technique**
In this picture, Francisco
Hidalgo combined a
highlight mask with a
color slide to add an
unreal element to this
large-city street scene.
This darkroom tech-
nique has helped to
intensify colors and lines
— making the final ima-
ge more graphic in
content than completely
descriptive. These sorts
of darkroom technique
are more appropriate, ·
as here, to reinforce the
photographer's ideas
at the time of shooting,
rather than as a substi-
tute for them.

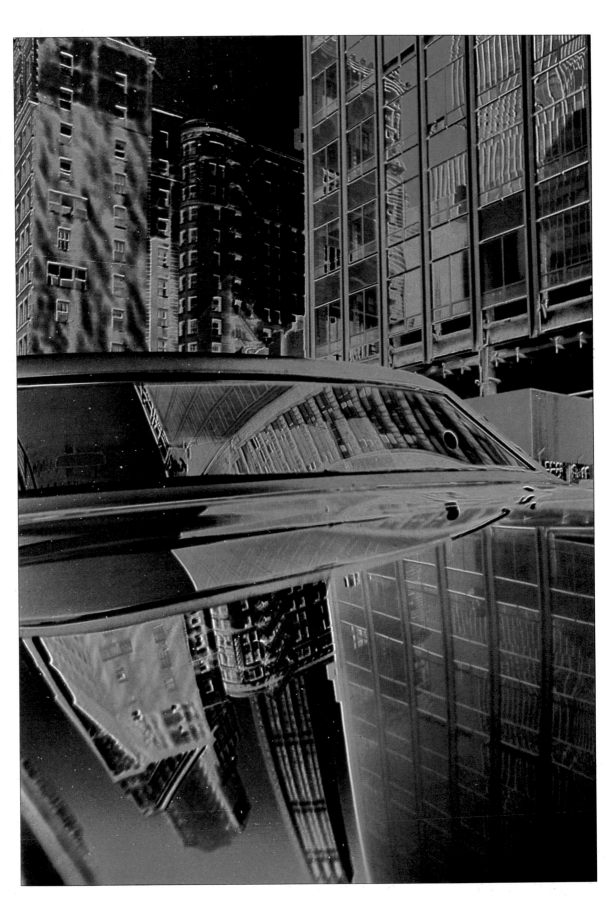

Alternative printing techniques

The first group of special print-making techniques mostly uses standard materials and processing solutions. They do not require any special equipment. Methods are very flexible, results being limited only by imagination, time, and material costs.

The photographic print does not even have to be based on a camera film image. Photograms, for example, are derived from the most fundamental "drawing with light" concept of photography. Two- or three-dimensional objects are placed in direct or close contact with the sensitive emulsion, and exposed to light. Shadows cast by the objects create shapes, and these appear as permanent images after processing.

Image shape changes are possible by simply angling or crumpling the paper on the baseboard of the enlarger. These effects may be useful as caricature, or for correcting camera distortions, or as a means of breaking away from the normal illusion of reality given by straight photography.

Color from black and white
With a black and white negative, the usual route is to make a black and white print. But this is not the only option. Using the appropriate filters and color paper, it is possible to create a range of subtle colors, which closely resemble color toned images, but with a wider choice of hue and saturation. The "false" color images can be of one overall color, progress from black and white to color, or combine colors.

Unusual printing surfaces
For over a hundred years photographers have been coating light-sensitive emulsions on suitable surfaces and exposing them to camera images. The surface texture of the material that carries the photographic image can exert a strong influence on the total effect. With old processes such as gum bichromate, any good-quality drawing paper can be used as a support material. The modern (and more convenient) alternative to this is liquid black and white emulsion, which can be used to sensitize a wide range of flat and three-dimensional surfaces, such as wood, ceramics or linen, as well as paper.

Using multiple images
For some, a straight photographic image is only the starting point for a more complicated visual statement. Sandwich printing, for example, allows the photographer to use combinations of negatives and slides, in color or black and white, by printing them simultaneously. Multiple printing is another method of combining images, but this time by exposing them individually.

See also
Editorial and advertising photography *Advertising approaches*, pp. 318-19. Pictorialism *Techniques*, pp. 335-6. Structuralism and Abstraction *The Bauhaus*, pp. 363-4.

Image distortion

Starting with a straighforward original image, there is a variety of ways in which you can subtly or dramatically distort its shape in the darkroom. Many of these are based on having part or all of the printing paper held at an angle to the image. Parts of the picture nearest to the enlarger lens will then print smaller than parts of the image projected on more distant areas of the paper. Most distortion effects take only a minimal amount of extra time, and provided that you start with a suitable image it is normally well worth the effort to carry through an idea.

Paper effects
One of the major rules when setting up the enlarger is that the planes of the film carrier, lens panel, and masking frame must be parallel to each other for sharp, undistorted prints. This assumes that objective rendering of the film image is required.

If you, for example, crumple and then slightly flatten a piece of printing paper, and expose it on top of the masking frame, the resulting print will look as if the object itself has crumpled up or collapsed. You should use single-weight paper, preferably fiber based, with a matte surface finish. After you have exposed the paper soak it in clean, still water to further flatten it, and then process as normal. Inevitably, parts of the image will be unsharp, and it is likely that the paper may uncrumple slightly

Curving the paper
For this print of a distorted skyline the paper was taped to the baseboard by the top left-hand corner. The paper was then curved upward steeply and attached by its top right-hand corner to a support about 8 ins (20 cm) high. Exposure (at smallest aperture) was 90 sec overall, but the top right area was shaded for 30 sec. In general, this technique works best with a large print. Use a matte surface to minimize light reflections.

during exposure — but these can enhance the weird quality of the imagery. Similar effects are possible by overlaying flat paper with irregularly rippled glass.

Another form of distortion is only suitable for black and white printing, as you must monitor the effect on the paper using the red safelight filter without fogging the paper. Tape the printing paper to the masking frame at two corners, and then curve the paper up, attaching it to a block of wood (or other support). When you like the effect you can see, stop the lens fully down, remove the safelight filter, and expose. Image elements will be either squashed or enlarged, elongated or rendered out of focus. Shade parts of the paper nearest the lens to avoid uneven exposure.

Correcting perspective distortion
It is useful to be able to correct image distortion of the type found occasionally on film originals. The most obvious form of camera distortion you are likely to encounter is converging verticals. This unsightly effect is caused by tilting the whole camera up to include the top of a tall structure. In a similar manner to the way camera movements overcome this problem (see *Controlling converging lines*, p. 121), you can also use enlarger movements to counteract slightly converging lines on a print. Begin by lifting up the masking frame at the side where the verticals are widest. Although the image will go out of focus slightly, prop up the frame in the position where the convergence seems to disappear (or at least appears minimal). Then release the locking screw holding the enlarger head to the column and tilt it so that the film carrier tilts in the opposite direction to that of the masking frame. Make slight adjustments to the angle of the enlarger head (and hence film carrier) until the image appears sharp all over.

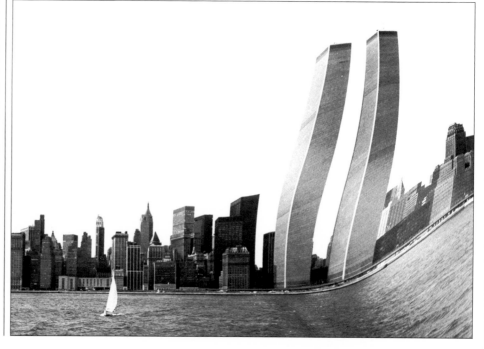

Photograms

Making photograms can be creative and challenging, as well as a useful aid to developing printing skills (particularly in black and white). In negative/positive printing (color and black and white), an opaque object placed on a piece of printing paper and exposed to light will leave a clear white impression of itself after processing. You can achieve the opposite effect in positive/positive printing. The photogram will contain tone or color values if the object is translucent, transparent, or is shifted or moved part way through the exposure. Another influence is whether it is in tight contact with the paper or not, and the direction of the light used to expose the paper. Obliquely cast shadows, for example, will become part of the composition. If you are using color paper (either negative/positive or positive/positive) you can introduce any color you like by manipulating the filter controls.

Using opaque shapes

With opaque shapes on the printing paper you can either produce a degree of realism by using recognizable objects, such as a key or scissors, or create total abstracts by using odd, unrecognizable shapes. Set up the enlarger so that the light will illuminate the paper area evenly. Any light source is sufficient to make a black and white photogram, but the enlarger is probably most convenient. Initially, make a successive set of exposures on normal or hard-grade bromide paper to demonstrate its range from black, through gray, to white. You can then use the test to determine the exposure you want for your photogram.

Arrange a few objects on the paper, using the red safelight filter to check shadow positions. Then set the timer so that the background will print as the tone chosen from your test. You can also give the background an exposure for black and remove the objects one by one so that their shapes print as chosen grays rather than white. Photograms will also act as paper negatives. Make a contact print from one on a sheet of soft-grade paper (pressed emulsion to emulsion under glass) to create a positive silhouette on a white background. If you raise objects on a sheet of glass above the paper they take on a soft appearance, forming a contrast with the hard lines of objects in contact with the paper.

Color effects

Two very different effects are possible when working in color. If you use negative/positive paper you can produce photograms that are complementary in color to that of the object. Or, if you use positive/positive paper, you will be able to create direct positive color photograms. The basic principle of moving objects part way through the exposure to alter density (discussed above) also applies to color. Translucent objects and shapes in contact with the paper may need extra filtration to produce strong coloration. For predictable color effects, first start by testing the filtration and exposure settings that produce a neutral gray on the paper when processed. Having established this, you can introduce the particular color you want by shifting settings away from this neutral filtration. To obtain the strongest colors when using negative/positive paper avoid underexposing.

Variations

Instead of placing objects on top of the printing paper, you can also place small objects in the film carrier of the enlarger. For this you will need a glass insert to act as a support. Any object positioned here will appear greatly magnified on the paper surface. If you line the enlarger bellows with white paper, object colors can be recorded, too. Light from the enlarger will reflect off shiny objects, adding to the final effect. You can also hang small objects inside the bellows, and they will appear framed by the film carrier when printed.

Utilizing simple shapes
The photogram (above) was made by placing two rows of pencils with tips facing on a flat sheet of hard-grade bromide paper. The paper was then exposed to light from the enlarger (with no film in the carrier). Always place objects with great care and observe the shadows they cast on the paper with the red safelight filter in place. Test print, and then give just sufficient exposure to produce a good, rich black.

Gradated effects
For this photogram John Goto placed simple cardboard shapes in contact with the black and white emulsion. He formed the gray tones by removing some objects part way through the exposure. Another method of creating gray tones on a photogram is by using a small flashlight to "spray" light along the outlines of objects. Results can be similar to those that can be achieved with an airbrush and masking.

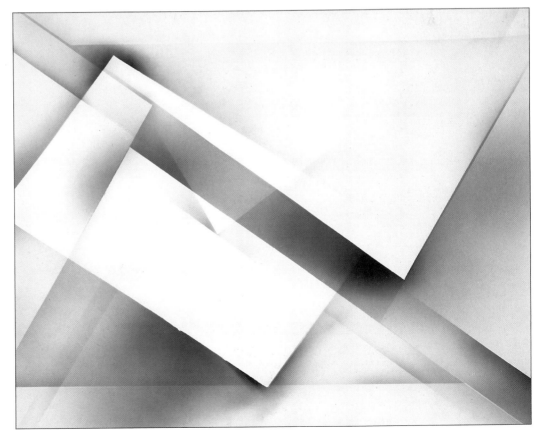

False color

It is possible to create a wide range of colors on negative/positive or positive/positive printing paper without having a negative or slide in the film carrier of the enlarger. Taking this further, you can also enlarge a black and white negative directly on color materials. The technique is the same as for normal color enlarging (see *Making a negative/positive enlargement,* p. 246), except that the negative will not have an orange mask. Results have the appearance of a color toned image (see *Toning,* p. 268).

When you are using a black and white negative for color, sandwich a piece of unexposed but processed color negative film with it. The warm color mask will allow you to achieve a neutral result using less filtration. This means that you have a greater range of filter options to generate the colors of your choice.

Filtration and exposure

Working with negative/positive paper, you must first discover the filtration and exposure necessary to achieve a completely neutral black and white print. This occurs when the color layers (cyan at the top, magenta in the middle, and yellow at the bottom) are formed in the correct proportions. Filtration for such a result from a black and white silver negative might be about 85Y 45M, but this will vary according to your enlarger and paper batch. Try to adjust the lens aperture so that each negative needs the same exposure time — color shifts with exposure due to reciprocity failure (see *Effects of reciprocity failure,* p. 220). In the same way, you must retest for a neutral result when you change color paper batches.

From the neutral position, make a yellow shift test by varying the yellow filter values only by 25 or 50 units in opposite directions (with negative/positive paper increase exposure as the filtration increases, and vice versa). Then make a magenta shift test for colors ranging from magenta to green, and finally a cyan shift test for colors ranging from cyan to red. After processing, results will show a wide range of hues and saturations, and you can simply pick out the color you require and reset the enlarger filtration accordingly. If you remove the black and white negative, you will have a color controlled light source to use for techniques such as photograms (see *Photograms,* p. 257).

Additive printing method

Another method of creating false color is to use the additive printing system (see *Color theory,* pp. 242-3, and *Additive printing,* p. 250). With this system you have to make three separate exposures (unless you have an additive enlarger with three filtered light sources). Each single exposure affects one layer of the color paper emulsion, and is made using the enlarger (set at white light) through one of the primary colored filters. On negative/positive paper, each exposure forms a dye complementary to the color of the light exposure. On positive/positive paper, a dye, or dyes, the same color as the light is formed with each exposure. When using additive filtration to print from black and white negatives you will find that the maximum color intensities that can be generated tend to be stronger than when a subtractive system of filtering is used.

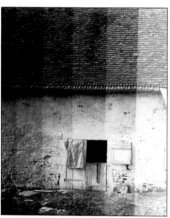

Neutral result

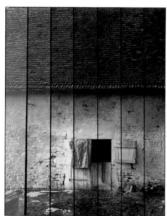

Yellow shift

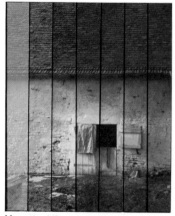

Magenta shift

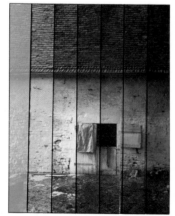

Cyan shift

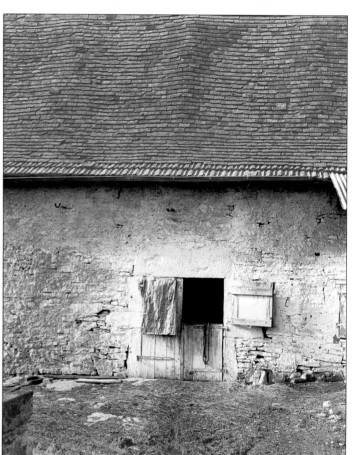

Final result

Color from black and white

These tests were made on negative/positive color paper from a black and white negative. You must first discover the settings that give a neutral color and correct exposure (top left), then shift yellow filtration, magenta filtration, and cyan filtration to discover your "palette" of false colors. For best results, sandwich your negative with a piece of unexposed but processed color negative film.

Final result
For this final version, two of the three image areas were shaded with cardboard each time the third one was exposed. Settings were 40 sec at 125Y 60M for the roof, 46 sec at 98Y 72M (neutral filtration) for the wall, and 40 sec at 90Y 100M for the ground area. You will need to have a reliable method of resetting your filtration in the dark, or you must cover the printing paper with opaque cardboard before turning on the room lights.

Liquid emulsions

You can coat any suitable surface with a light-sensitive emulsion and, when dry, expose it to a negative, then develop it to form a black and white positive image. It is still possible to make up your own sensitizing solution for an old process such as gum bichromate, which also allows a great deal of image manipulation. This is a slow and difficult process, however, and for most work of this type, paint-on liquid silver bromide emulsion products are used instead. With both methods you can create additional image texture by using brush strokes as part of the design. Sometimes it is best to select an image that has associations with the article you intend to print on — a tree, for example, on a piece of wood.

Gum bichromate

Using the gum bichromate printing process you can print an image (by contact only) on a wide variety of paper surfaces, ranging from high-quality cartridge paper to newsprint or even plastic. First, coat the base material with gum arabic dissolved in hot water, plus pigment of any color you wish, made weakly light sensitive by the addition of potassium bichromate (or dichromate). When dry, you expose the paper in contact with any suitable continuous-tone negative to ultraviolet-rich light, which hardens the gum. The paper is "processed" in still water until the gum and pigment from the unhardened highlight areas of the negative completely dissolve away.

The only additional equipment you will need is a drawing board, a camel hair brush (for coating the paper), an ultraviolet light source (sunlight will do), a range of water color pigments, a sheet of glass (for contact printing), and a photographic tray (for processing).

Lightly soak the paper in water and tape it to the board until it is dry and flat. Mix together the gum and sensitizing solution under orange safelighting, and coat the paper using the camel hair brush. To achieve a textured result, use a stiffer brush. Coat enough sheets for your projected number of prints (including tests). If you use very porous paper, it may need "sizing" with gelatin beforehand.

Making large prints

To make a large print from a small negative, first contact print it on film (such as Kodak gravure positive 4135). Then enlarge this positive on a larger sheet of the same film to produce a negative of the size required for the gum print. Place this negative (emulsion side down) on the coated gum paper and weight it down with a piece of clean glass. Make a series of test exposures to ultraviolet light in 30 second steps. Then remove the paper from the board and soak it in a tray of water until all the unhardened gum and pigment has diffused from the image highlights. From this test decide on the exposure required. During processing, you can remove any unwanted image areas using a stiff brush. After processing, tape the paper to the board again so that it dries flat.

Hand coloring

Later, you can hand color areas of the paper (see *Hand coloring*, pp. 269-70) or, with experience, resensitize the paper with another color and expose it once more. Using this technique you can expose the paper to three color separations (see *Tone and color separations*, pp. 262-3) to build up a full color image. Make sure you register the paper each time (see *Registration systems*, p. 261). Initially use magenta pigment in the gum and expose it to a green separation negative. After processing, coat the paper with yellow gum solution and expose it to a blue separation negative, and finally coat the paper with cyan pigment gum and expose it to a red separation negative. Make sure each time that you allow the highlights to wash out completely to avoid a muddy result.

Liquid Light

You can treat surfaces such as cardboard, paper, canvas, or even plastic with a commercially available product known as Liquid Light. This silver bromide product is also suitable for use with three-dimensional objects ranging from wood to ceramics. If the printing surface is very porous first use a thin layer of varnish. Most surfaces at least require a coating of subbing solution, which comes in a two-part kit. This helps the liquid emulsion to adhere evenly. Allow the subbing layer at least 12 hours to dry. The shelf life of the solution is about six months, after which time the fog level starts to increase (an antifog agent is supplied). Warm the surface to be coated slightly before coating, and liquify the emulsion by immersing the whole bottle in a tempering box (at between 95° and 104° F/35° and 40° C). You must use orange safelighting when coating.

Pour a suitable amount of warmed emulsion on the printing surface and drain off any excess. Too thick a coating will lead to a loss of image definition. Brush out any air bubbles. When dry, you can expose flat printing surfaces under the enlarger as you would an

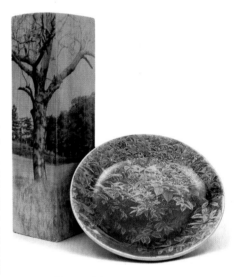

Silver halide emulsion
A length of wood and a white ceramic plate have been used here to carry photographic images. Both were sensitized with silver bromide liquid emulsion.

The wood was exposed under the enlarger at the angle seen in the photograph. The plate was exposed flat-on — after processing the image was blue toned.

ordinary sheet of printing paper. Three-dimensional objects tend to be more of a problem, though, because of the problem of focus. One solution is to make an enlarged film negative (by contact printing from an enlarged film positive), and then wrap the negative round the object. Shade the object if necessary as you expose so that each part receives an equal amount of light. Develop the image by gently sponging it with black and white developer and fixer solutions.

Paint-on emulsions tend to frill or lift at the corners, especially on three-dimensional objects. A thin coating of clear varnish will eliminate this problem and reduce the possibility of the surface being scratched. Before varnishing you can hand color the image (see *Hand coloring*, pp. 269-70).

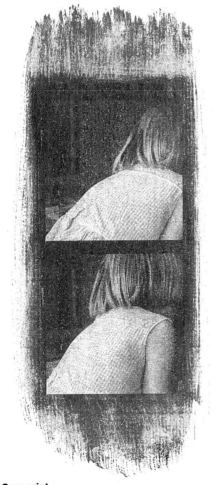

Gum print
Mari Mahr contact printed 6 × 6 cm negatives on paper as the first step in making this gum bichromate print. She used a coarse brush to emphasize the textural effect. The pink dress was then hand colored after the gum print was completely dry.

Sandwich printing

Sandwich printing involves combining two negatives or two slides in the film carrier of the enlarger and printing them simultaneously on one sheet of printing paper. This technique is most often used to create an unusual juxtaposition of image elements that could not occur in reality. You can also combine a negative with a slide to produce a print with a mixture of negative and positive elements. Sandwich printing works equally well in color or black and white.

When using negatives for sandwich printing, information from one negative will show through in the shadow areas of the other. This is because the shadow areas of negatives are less dense than highlight areas. The more contrasty and underexposed the shadows, the clearer the film and, therefore, the more information from the second negative will record on the paper. The opposite is true when using slides — one image appears in the highlight and pale areas of the other.

Matching contrast

For black and white printing, try to choose negatives with similar contrast, otherwise a well-balanced print will be difficult to achieve. In color, the problem is slightly more complicated because you must consider color balance as well as density — not an easy task with color negatives because of the presence of an orange mask. It is usually best to make sample prints from each negative first. When choosing or shooting color slides for sand-

wiching, use images that are overexposed by at least one stop. Otherwise, the combination will be excessively dense for printing.

Sandwich printing is based on trial and error, particularly if you are working from existing images. Overlay images on a light box until you see a combination that is suitable. Slides are much easier to work with in this respect. If you are shooting new material for a particular effect, it is best if the combination is designed so that one of the images is reversed left to right. You can then tape the film images together (carefully along the film rebates) so that they are emulsion to emulsion. This will minimize any focusing problem caused by images being in slightly different planes. With slides, remove them from their mounts first. Film carriers with glass inserts ensure better overall sharpness, as they will prevent the film images bowing out of contact as they warm up slightly in the enlarger. But make sure that all glass surfaces as well as film surfaces are completely clean. Because of the light-stopping power of the film densities, you may find that sandwich prints give a flatter result than you would expect with a straight print.

Sandwiched negatives
This print, by Amanda Currey, is the result of combining two negatives in the enlarger film carrier and printing them simultaneously. When you work with negatives, the details of one image will only show through in the shadow (clear) areas of the other. The small figure was photographed against a large, plain background, which recorded as transparent on the negative. It was therefore easy to register this figure within the equally clear, leotard area of the second, larger figure. Working from slide originals, subject details from one image will show through only in the highlight and light areas of the other.

Multiple printing

Multiple printing is a broad term covering the overprinting of one image on top of another. The techniques range from simply exposing one negative after the other on one sheet of black and white paper, to complicated compositions consisting of numerous separate film images all carefully printed into planned spaces on color paper. It is usually easier to work from similar types of originals — two or more black and white negatives, for example, or two or more color negatives, or slides of the same brand. Make sure, as far as possible, that the film image densities and contrasts balance. This will help for color multiple prints, as filtrations should be similar.

Gather together all the film images you need to make the final multiple print. Place the image from which you intend to print the overall background in the film carrier, and trace its image on a piece of opaque white paper or cardboard. Then make a test on printing paper for exposure (and color, if relevant). Set the aperture for at least a 20 second exposure in the final print to allow you the necessary time for dodging and burning-in (see *Local density control*, p. 249). Place the other film images in the enlarger in turn, and raise or lower the enlarger head until each fits with the sketch made from the previous image. Make test prints from each image with the enlarger head set at the position it will be in for the final print. At the end of this process, you will have test prints for every element, as well as a master sketch showing all the elements in their correct position, which you can use as a printing guide for the final print. For simple multiple prints you

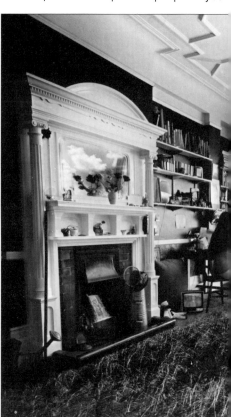

will either be printing in areas of detail into otherwise blank spaces, or exposing one element on top of another. For more subtle effects, you will have to hold back areas as you print the first image, and then print parts of other film images back into these spaces.

After you have printed the first negative (using dodgers where necessary), place the opaque master sketch over the printing paper and change to the second image. Size up and focus, remove the sketch and, with another dodger in place to shield the area printed by the first image, expose the second on to the paper. While printing the second image, you may have to use yet another dodger to shield areas you need left blank in order to accommodate elements from the third image.

Using masks
For the most advanced work you may need masks (opaque shapes that are used in contact with the paper for very definite areas of shading). To ensure alignment of masks, printing paper, and master sketch, use a registration punch system with a fixed pin bar attached to the baseboard of your enlarger. For a complicated multiple print, where you may be using four or five masks, you can use more than one pin bar.

Multiple print
This image by Hag is an example of a very complex multiple print. He used a series of lith film masks to shade different parts of the paper while exposing others. For this particular print Hag used a combination of 35 mm and 6 × 6 cm black and white negative images.

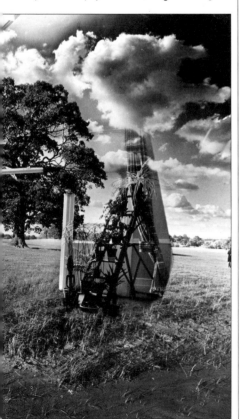

Specialized darkroom materials

Moving on from simple effects, which mostly use standard darkroom materials and equipment, it is well worthwhile experimenting with some of the range of specialized darkroom materials. One of the most versatile products currently available is a high-contrast film, known as "lith" from its original use for photolithography.

Lith film
Lith film emulsions can be used to create three very different types of images. First, because lith films (processed in lith developer) do not normally reproduce subtle half-tones, they can be used to make high-contrast, sharply defined, pure black and white images on film. These can be used for masks in multiple printing and similar techniques. Second, using controlled exposure and development times it is possible to produce a yellow-brown and black image. Third, using sequences of masks in register, and printing by contact on photographic paper, it is possible to manipulate the tonal response in image shadow areas and produce evenly tinted areas of flat mid-tone. This type of technique is used for posterization and other effects.

In order to make film images coincide exactly when printed at different stages on the same piece of printing paper, some form of registration system is essential. To break up full-tone or full-color images into their constituent parts the usual practice is to make tone or color separations on registered sheets of lith film.

Mask making for negatives and slides is an important area of control for darkroom special effects. A negative contact printed on lith film, for example, and then sandwiched with the result, will appear as an image with white shadows. If you make an enlargement on print-size sheets of lith film, and then attach the processed result over a sheet of printing paper, you will create a contact mask, which can in turn be used as a dodger.

Other masks are simply used to help correct excessively high- or low-contrast film images, which would otherwise print badly. They are much less dense and of lower contrast than effects masks. You can still make them on lith film provided it is underexposed and processed in low-contrast developer.

Most lith and other process films (those used for copy and separation work) are manufactured with the emulsion coated on a dimensionally stable ESTAR film base. Using these types of products with a pin bar registration system, the darkroom printer can guarantee perfect alignment of separations for printing special effects.

Registration systems

Special effects techniques, such as highlight masking, posterization, tone and color separations, and masks for multiple printing, demand precise registration. This means the exact matching of masks and overlays in sequence (in any combination), for a variety of exposure steps, working under safelighting conditions, or even in total darkness. The dimensional stability of these materials is of paramount importance, so it is preferable to work with ESTAR base sheet film rather than camera type acetate film.

The simplest method of registration is to punch two or more holes near the edge of the material (whether film or printing paper) and then place it on pins set into a stainless-steel strip (pin bar) or fitted in a special enlarger film carrier, or in a contact printing frame.

Register punch system
The cheapest arrangement is to use an office punch, and make your own pins from wooden doweling. The Kodak register punch system is an expensive but much better device to use for regular darkroom work. It makes one hole longer than the others so that you can locate the emulsion side of punched material easily in the dark.

When making masks or separations from a single negative or slide in the enlarger, attach the pin bar temporarily to the baseboard or masking frame using double-sided adhesive tape. For each exposure (mask making for multiple printing, for example), punch a fresh sheet of film and place it on the pins. When you have made these masks and are ready to make a variety of exposures through them (in sequence), punch a sheet of printing paper first and locate it on the pins – then place the first lith mask on top of it.

For most processes you can use weights to hold the assembly down flat, but for sophisticated work (particularly when you include retouched masks), a vacuum masking frame is ideal. This will hold large sheets of material flat while you set focus and expose. A foot switch allows you to operate the frame and keep both hands free for local dodging and burning-in (see *Local density control,* p. 249). Or you can use a special glass-covered contact frame that has built-in register pins.

Miniature punch
If you print directly from the enlarger with registered film material in the carrier, you will require a special miniature punch that is compatible with the placing of registration pins in the film carrier. Although all the films you use will align exactly, registration is less precise than with the pin bar system. This is due to the fact that you must remove the whole film carrier each time you want to exchange masks or separations. Enlargers are usually not engineered precisely enough to guarantee that the film carrier will always occupy exactly the same position. In general, though, carrier-registered masks are satisfactory if you are only using one mask throughout the whole exposure period (the mask and film image can then be pre-registered and taped together). But if you are engaged in more elaborate work, you should use enlarged, print-sized masks in contact with the paper.

Lith emulsion

Many advanced darkroom special effects, such as color and tone separations, posterization, solarization, and screen and masking effects, require additional film stages. The choice of film for these effects is mostly governed by its contrast and spectral sensitivity, and also by its dimensional stability, speed, and graininess. For most effects requiring high-contrast results, lith film is ideal.

Lith film is made in two different types – 35 mm and sheet film orthochromatic, convenient when working from black and white originals and processed under red safelighting, and sheet film panchromatic, used when working from color originals and processed in total darkness. Both film types are very slow – about ASA 6 and ASA 32, respectively.

Processing

Lith film must be processed in specially formulated lith developer to produce the highest degree of contrast with excellent line detail. The development process is unusual because as by-products of exhausted developer are formed in the emulsion, development becomes more active. The image appears quite slowly initially (in normal-contrast tones), but then image formation suddenly accelerates with a sharp increase in black image density into the mid-tone areas. The process is known as "infectious development". Because of this characteristic, it is vital that you time development precisely. In open trays, the mixed, working-strength developer becomes quickly exhausted – so for critical results it is advisable to use fresh developer for each sheet of film. Immerse the film smoothly in the developer, otherwise it will show a definite surge mark. Because of the development characteristics of lith, some printers agitate vigorously for the first $1\frac{3}{4}$ minutes, and then leave the film in the

tray of still developer for 1 minute to increase detail sharpness. Lith films processed in regular fine-grain developer give a normal-contrast result. If lith film, or its developer, is not available, you can obtain high-contrast results almost as good with line or process sheet films, processed in print developer.

Exposure

You can determine exposure for lith materials using a light meter set for the appropriate ASA speed of the film. Use an incident light reading (see *Using a hand-held meter,* p. 136) when enlarging directly on lith film or when using it in the camera for copying. You may still have to bracket, though, to obtain accurate results (see *Correct exposure,* p. 133), due to the very limited exposure latitude, which is a characteristic of extreme-high-contrast materials.

When any normal-contrast, continuous-tone image is exposed on lith material, and correctly processed, the usual range of tones simplifies into either dense black or transparent film. (Mid-tones may merge with either highlights or shadows, depending on how much exposure the film actually receives.) Underexposure produces completely transparent film, or may just record the brightest highlights as gray or black. Overexposure gives a totally black frame, or only the deepest shadows record as clear film. Overexposure also causes the image to "spread", which results in loss of fine detail. If what should be black parts of the image are brown or gray, you have probably underdeveloped, perhaps because the developer is exhausted.

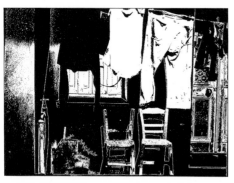

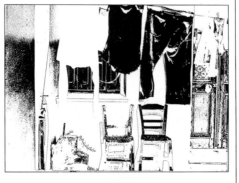

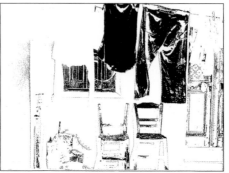

Lith film images

Lith film can create a variety of different effects when used to copy a photographic print or slide. The negative (above) shows the stark image produced by this high-contrast material. When printing from a continuous-tone negative on lith sheet film you can choose to preserve some grays by overexposing and then processing in dilute lith

developer (above right), or by processing in a normal-contrast developer. Given full lith development, all the tones in the original negative are simplified into either black or white (right). Lith film is available in panchromatic form for use with color originals.

Tone and color separations

Different exposures produce different densities in prints, and it is possible to expose specifically for highlight, mid-tone, or shadow detail, allowing other print areas to go either very dark or very light. This is particularly pronounced when working on hard-contrast materials. In separation printing you exploit this effect to form an image in which the familiar, gradated photographic tone values are replaced by areas of flat, sharply divided tone or color (see facing page).

You first print the original camera image (normally a negative) as a series of positive images on high-contrast film. Each positive will be identical in size but differ in the image information it carries – either because of differences in exposure (tone separation) or because it was exposed through a different primary-colored filter (color separation). Color separations are only possible when working from a color original. Finally, you must print the three separations in turn and in exact register.

Making tone separations

Use sheet film (panchromatic type if you are working from a color original) of the same size required for the final print. Set up your original film image in the enlarger and focus, leaving space for registration holes along the edge of the sheet of lith film (see *Registration systems,* p. 261). Fix the pin bar firmly to the enlarger baseboard, then punch a sheet of lith film, and place it on the register pins. Test expose the film in exposure bands, then process in lith developer, fix, wash, and dry the test. If you are working from a negative, your first stage of separations will be positives.

Exposure selection

Select one exposure from the test that only just prints the densest shadows as black. Select a mid-tone exposure where everything from mid-tone to shadows records as black. And finally, select a still longer exposure, which makes the whole image black except for the brightest highlights.

To print the separations into one tone-separated image you must first contact print a negative from each positive (again using lith film, register punching each sheet first). Then, printing by contact on bromide paper, test to find the time each separation negative needs to print a pale gray image. The final stage is printing each separation negative in turn at this exposure on a single sheet of punched bromide paper. If you wish to vary the possible effects, you can print using different combinations of positive and negative separations.

Color effects

For color results you can print from tone separations (described above) on color paper, changing filtration between each part-exposure. An alternative method is to make three separations through red, green, and blue primary filters – either on panchromatic lith (for posterization effects) or continuous-tone panchromatic separation sheet film (for more objective results). Follow the same steps you would if printing color posterizations from tone separations, printing finally on a registered sheet of negative/positive or positive/positive paper (see *Posterization,* p. 266).

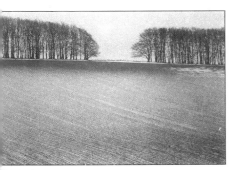

Original

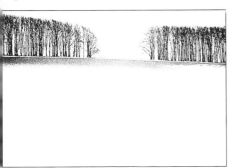

Positive 1

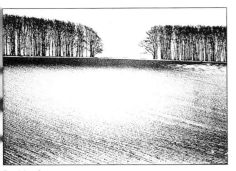

Positive 2

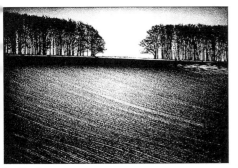

Positive 3

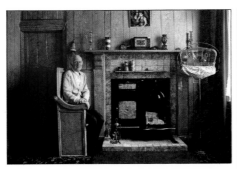

Original

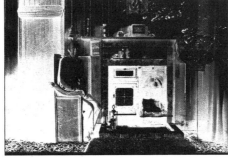

Blue negative

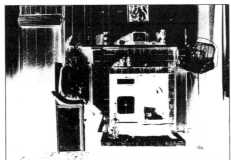

Red negative

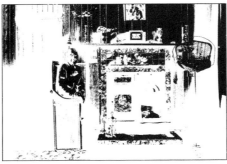

Green negative

Tone-separated images
The set of landscape prints (above) was made from the same continuous-tone negative. The top version, on normal-contrast bromide paper, shows the full tone range of the picture. The other three positives were made on lith film. They were given 3, 6, and 12 sec exposures respectively (top to bottom), and then fully processed in lith developer. Each of the positives has separated a different range of grays into either white or black.

Color-separated images
All three lith negatives of this interior scene were made from the same color slide (top). It was enlarged on panchromatic lith film through deep blue, green, and red filters. Each sheet of film was given the correct exposure. The different separations into black and white are therefore determined by color content. The blue vase and carpet, for example, appear black on the blue-filtered negative only.

Masks and overlays
Masks and overlays on film are used in more advanced darkroom work, sometimes to correct fim and paper response (to create a result that is more in line with reality), or more often to distort tone, or color, or to create other special effects. Masks can be either positive or negative images, usually black and white. They are used in conjunction with other, original, negatives or positives, either color or black and white. You can use them to boost or reduce contrast, or distort shadows or highlights only. Masks can also be used in order to "drop out" (print as white) picture areas without laborious retouching, before printing in elements from a different film original (see *Multiple printing,* pp. 260-1). Masks are either of the same size as camera film and used in conjunction with the film original in the film carrier of the enlarger, or final print size and used in contact, overlaying the printing paper in the masking frame.

Correction masks
Sometimes the contrast range present in a negative or slide is too wide to be printed successfully. In such cases you need to make a mask that reduces contrast by adding a little density to the most transparent parts of the film, without also adding to the dark parts. To do this, contact print a positive image on film from your negative (or a negative image from a slide) on continuous-tone film. This must be underexposed and underdeveloped, giving a weak image. Next, sandwich your mask in register with the original image in the film carrier, and enlarge normally.

If your negative is excessively low in contrast, you may be able to use a film mask to intensify and improve contrast. First, contact print from your negative on continuous-tone film, and slightly overdevelop it. Process and dry this positive and then carefully contact print it on another piece of continuous-tone film to form a negative. This should be slightly underexposed and normally developed. Finally, combine the original and the mask negative in register and enlarge them, giving a long exposure on a hard-grade paper.

Drop-out masks
Drop-out masks are most often used in multiple printing to cover one part of the paper while another is being exposed. Provided your registration is accurate, this can be much more precise than hand shading. If, for example, you had a negative of a tree set in a flat landscape and you wanted to print in a new background, first enlarge the negative on orthochromatic (for black and white) lith material, punched and registered on a pin bar attached to your enlarger baseboard. This will produce a high-contrast positive. Next, use Farmer's reducer to remove all image detail except for the tree. Contact print this (placing emulsion to emulsion) on another registered sheet of orthochromatic lith to produce a negative drop-out mask. You then register punch a piece of printing paper, sandwich it on the pins with the negative drop-out mask and, keeping the original negative in the carrier, expose the paper. Use the first positive mask over the paper instead if you want to print in a new background from another negative.

Image manipulation

The special effects dealt with in this final selection of darkroom manipulations combine and elaborate some materials and techniques dealt with previously. Not all the effects, however, are complex. Bas-relief, for example, relies for its very striking appearance on the simple combination of a film positive and negative of the same subject – printed together slightly out of register. Others, such as screen effects, break the original picture down into image-forming dot and line patterns of density or color (similar, in fact, to the technique used to print the photographs in this book). It is also possible to combine patterned film with the original in the film carrier of the enlarger for a slightly different effect. Screen effects in this context should not be confused with texturizing screens sometimes used in dry mounting. These are canvas-type materials pressed on a finished print to remold its surface texture and give a basically non-photographic appearance.

Screen types and effects are very varied. Half-tone screens consist of transparent sheets ruled with fine lines at 90° to each other. Other commonly used screens include mezzotint, wavy line, and brick patterns. These, used in conjunction with high-contrast film, will convert the continuous tones of an original into a pattern of dots. The dots will all be of the same density (black), but of varying size depending on the darkness of the original. At the correct viewing distance, the eye sees them as a range of tones.

Using separations and masks

In this section, the use of tone or color separations to create posterized images is discussed. Here, more advanced controls possible in color posterization are dealt with. Masks and overlays are also taken a stage further, and are used for highlight and shadow special effects masking. Striking results are possible, and yet only very simple masks have to be made. Basically, masks are used to displace either highlight or shadow detail with strong color or tone to emphasize selected parts of the image. They can also give a surreal mixture of realistic and false subject representation.

One of the most popular darkroom effects is solarization (although, strictly, this should be called the "Sabattier effect"). Solarization techniques can be as simple as fogging exposed printing paper to white light part way through development. More predictable and dramatic effects, though, are possible by fogging darkroom film or using a combination of solarized masks printed along with an unaffected film original.

See also
Structuralism and Abstraction *The influences of art on Structuralism and Abstraction, pp. 362-3.* Surrealism *Techniques, p. 379.*

Screens

You can use screens for effects in two forms. First, you can simply buy or make a low-density film image of a textured pattern, and combine this with any negative or slide when enlarging. The effect is an overlaid combination of pattern and image. Second, and more interestingly, you can use a technique that makes the pattern itself carry the image as a grid of solid dots or lines, which, by their variation of size or thickness alone, re-creates the appearance of shadows and tones. For this second technique you will require the use of a half-tone screen.

Half-tone screens

A half-tone screen usually takes the form of a large gray-looking sheet of film covered with a fine, slightly unsharp pattern of lines. If you enlarge or print your film original on lith film covered by one of these screens, the result will be a half-tone image. During exposure, brightest parts of the image form bright pools of light between each dot or line, while denser image areas form dimmer pools. Because lith film is extremely contrasty, the bright pools record as large dots (or wide lines), and dimmer pools record as small dots or lines.

Half-tone images are used to reproduce photographs mechanically by systems such as lithography or silk screen, which can only reproduce solid black (or color) or clear white. Screening gives the illusion of a range of grays, and the pattern remains unnoticed, provided the screen is sufficiently fine. For special ef-

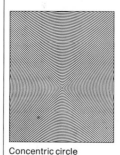
Concentric circle

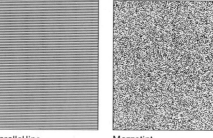
Brick

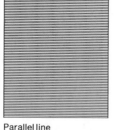
Parallel line

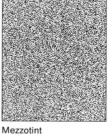
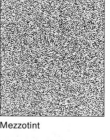
Mezzotint

Screen patterns
The high-contrast prints (left) are from different forms of half-tone contact screens. The original screens are slightly unsharp so line thickness varies with the exposure given. When an image is printed through them, patterns reproduce thickened or thinned where the image is bright or dark.

Half-tone negative
The image of a tree was made by enlarging a color slide on lith film covered by a mezzotint screen. The result seems to contain gray tones, but pure black ink or white paper only is present. Varying thicknesses of the pattern lines give an illusion of intermediate tones of different density.

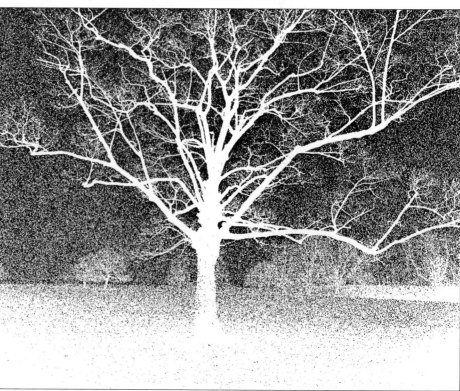

fects work, however, you may want a coarse screen so that the pattern itself becomes a feature. You can achieve this either with a coarse-ruled screen, or a fine one that you enlarge at a later stage.

Further screening effects
The range of ready-made screens available includes parallel line, wavy line, concentric circle, and cross-line grids, in various rulings. You can convert your original continuous-tone (color or black and white) image by enlarging it on a combination consisting of the screen pressed down by glass on top of lith film. For the coarsest effect, contact print the original image by placing it between the glass and

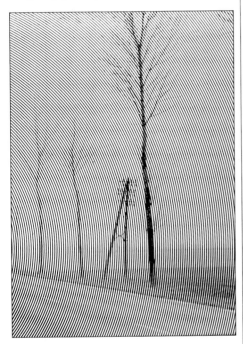

Enlarged screen
You can enlarge part of a half-toned screened negative until the screen pattern becomes so assertive
that it turns the picture into a semi-abstract image.

screen. After you have lith processed your half-tone film image, contact print or enlarge it on bromide paper. If your original was a negative, the resulting half-tone positive must be contact printed on lith film, and this used for making the paper print.

Prescreened film
There is one film available — Kodak Autoscreen — that produces screened half-tones directly from continuous-tone originals. It is only available in sheet form, has a speed of ASA 2.5, and can be handled in red safelighting. As Autoscreen is not fully color sensitive, it is best used with black and white originals. The film carries 133 lines per inch and you process it in exactly the same way as all lith materials. You can also cut Autoscreen down to fit inside your camera for copying. Results, when enlarged, show very coarse screening.

Bas-relief
Traditionally, bas-relief is a type of wall sculpture or engraving in low relief. It has to be lit strongly from the side for the best effect. You can produce an image photographically that is similar in appearance using one of the most simple image manipulations. First, contact print a black and white or color negative on a piece of continuous-tone film (panchromatic if the original is color), and underdevelop to produce a flat, gray positive with no black in the shadows at all. When dry, superimpose the two films on a light box (emulsion to emulsion), and then carefully shift them sideways, out of register. You will notice that a dark "shadow" appears down one side of the subject detail, and a clear "highlight" down the other side. Move the films out of register in the other direction and the shadow and highlight effects will be reversed. Examine these changes with a magnifying glass. When you achieve the de-

gree of offset that gives the best effect, tape the two films together along one edge, place them between glass, and enlarge them on black and white or color paper.

For different effects, you can use lith film instead of continuous-tone film, or print a black and white bas-relief on negative/positive color paper, introducing any color scheme you choose (see *False color,* p. 258). It is also possible to work from a color slide original, making a black and white film negative, which you then superimpose, offset.

Bas-relief effect
For this bas-relief image the original negative was contact printed on lith film. This was then contact printed to form a lith negative. Both lith films
were combined out of register, as a projection slide. Continuous-tone films produce white and black edge lines on a gray background.

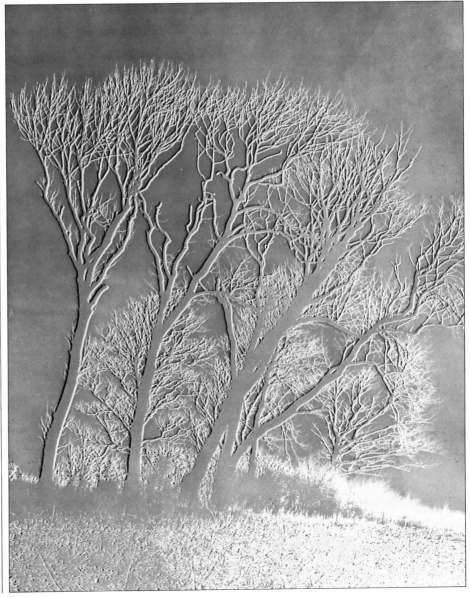

Posterization

Posterization is characterized by distinct areas of flat tone or color. Results tend to be strikingly similar to the simplified image quality produced by silk screen stencil printing, or paintings with even tones of poster color, which rely for their maximum effect on simplicity of design. A posterized photograph has all shading and gradation replaced by abrupt changes from one area of tone or color to another. For best results, choose a photograph that has some of the elements of poster design — bold shapes and uncluttered composition and, usually, a simplified color scheme.

Black and white results

The principle of black and white posterization involves making a series of tone separations to produce three different density negatives and positives on high-contrast lith film (see *Tone and color separations,* pp. 262-3 and *Lith emulsion,* p. 262). Enlarge the original black and white negative on several sheets of register punched lith film (see *Registration systems,* p. 261) to produce positives. Following the procedure on page 262, working with sets of three separations gives a result with areas of black, two distinct tones of gray, and white only. If four separations are made, however, the final print will have three different tones of gray and white only.

Color results

If you start with a color original you can make either tone or color separations using panchromatic lith film instead of orthochromatic. One convenient method of working is to make the color separations through the primary colored filters used in additive printing. Test for exposure so that you produce a set of separations matching in density in neutral-toned areas, but differing in density in colored areas of the image.

To print the color separations, set up your enlarger so that the light source covers the area of the film separations evenly, and set the enlarger to white light. Then, if you are using negative/positive paper, punch a sheet of paper and place it in register under the negative separation that was made through the red filter. Make a test using the red filter again to achieve a suitable cyan dye response, and then repeat for the other separations and filters (see *Additive printing,* p. 250), except that instead of making three successive exposures through a single, color, negative, you expose through a different film separation each time. If you are printing on positive/positive paper you must print from positive separations. Use the deepest cyan filtration your enlarger will produce to print from the red separation, magenta for the green, and yellow for the blue.

The above procedure will give an approximation of the original subject colors, but you can print in the "wrong" filter colors (including printing some separations twice) for more subjective results. If you color print from tone separations, the print will show each different tone area as a separate color (see *Photography and space exploration,* p. 292-5).

Shadow and highlight masking

Shadow and highlight special effects masking produces the best results if you start with a slide and expose on silver dye-bleach paper. With shadow masking you can control part of the shadow end of the density range, replacing the shadows with pure, flat colors. Enlarge your slide to the desired size, leaving room for a pin bar down one side, and then make a test strip on panchromatic lith film. This test is the critical part of the process, because the exposure you select determines the amount of shadow detail you will replace with color. As a guide, highlights and mid-tones should print as solid black.

Making a positive

Remove the slide from the carrier and contact print the mask on to a sheet of orthochromatic lith film to make a positive. Make sure that opaque areas of the mask are dense black and retouch any dust spots. With the slide back in exactly the same place, and the positive mask on the pin bar, expose a punched sheet of color paper. This will produce a print with all shadow areas unexposed. For the next stage, change to the negative mask, remove the slide, and choose filtration that will produce the color you want for the shadows, then expose the paper again before processing.

Highlight masking

For highlight masking, select a suitable slide original and make a same-size copy by contact printing on panchromatic lith film. Underexpose the lith so that when the mask and slide are combined, highlights only become solid blacks. You can then tone this mask a suitable color (see *Toning,* p. 268), and when it is dry combine it with the slide in exact register. Use the chromogenic toning system — the basic color formers are yellow, magenta, and cyan, but you can mix these to form the primaries or any other color. If the highlight mask is ex-

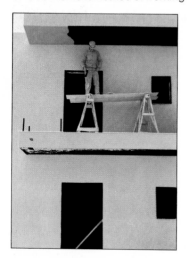
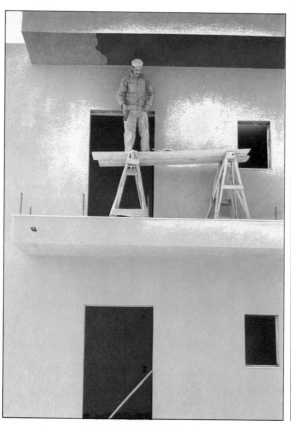

Partial posterization
Two of the many variations, possible when posterization and straight printing techniques are combined, are shown here. Print-sized tone separations were first made on lith film in both negative and positive forms. These were register punched and used in sequence to cover the paper while first the original negative and then colored light was printed through the clear areas of the film.

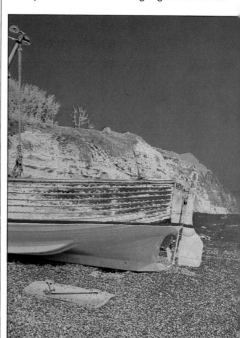

posed accurately, all the whites or highlights in the original slide will be replaced by a single pure color. Make a range of masks and tone them different colors before deciding which gives the best effect. The general appearance of the finished print will be ruined if there are any pinholes or stains in the mask.

Highlight masking has the strange effect of giving your slide an almost fluorescent quality. You can manipulate highlight masked results further by filtering the enlarger to bring masked highlights back to their original color. This will give all other tones in the picture distorted hues.

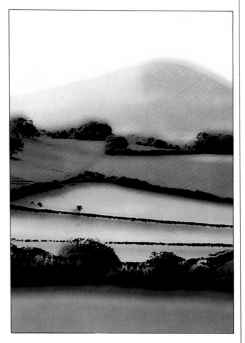

Manipulated shadows
For the result above a print-sized positive lith mask was first made from a slide original. This was pressed in contact with silver dye-bleach paper while it was exposed to the original slide, positioned just out of focus.

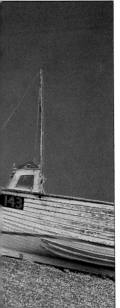

Manipulated highlights
The print (left) was made on positive/positive paper from a color slide original, using two tone-separated lith positive masks. The darker mask was toned pink and the lighter one cyan. Both were printed on the paper in register with the slide image.

Solarization

Your first experience with solarized images is likely to be accidental — fogging film or paper to white light in the darkroom, for example. It is often seen on prints discarded during development, before fixing. The silver image (either on film or paper) that is beginning to form acts as a "negative", through which the fogging light prints as a "positive" image on unexposed emulsion areas. The reaction is well known, but difficult to control. The strength of the part positive/part negative result varies a great deal from print to print, or film to film.

The Mackie line effect
There is a further effect associated with solarized images, known as the Mackie line effect, which causes a fine line of minimum density between positive and negative parts of the solarization. Depending on the stage at which you solarize, the line prints as either clear white or dense black. The factors influencing the appearance of the solarized image are the initial exposure (normally under the enlarger), the first period of development, the intensity of the reversal exposure, and the final development. You will find, however, that solarizing the final print (by fogging it briefly to white light part way through development) is too unpredictable,

Solarizing slides
Another method of solarizing, used by John Starr for his picture of a dancer, is to fog slides during processing. This means interrupting first development to shine a colored light evenly over the wet film. Since results are unpredictable, it is usually safest to work from an existing slide. Copy this, same-size, on slide film, bracketing your exposures. Then experiment with different levels of fogging and with different colored light. The additional contrast produced by copying helps to counteract the flattening effect of direct solarization.

and gives a gray, low-contrast result. It is usually more successful to solarize an intermediate film stage, by first contact printing on sheet film.

Black and white results
Select several negatives that you think might make good solarized images, and contact print these on one sheet of line or lith film. Use a high-contrast material for this because fogging tends to flatten contrast. Tray process the film (as you would paper), but half way through the correct development time transfer the developer tray to the enlarger baseboard. (Place blotting paper down to absorb any spills.) Remove the negative and fog the film to the light from the enlarger. Then finish the full development time and complete processing. Cut out each small image from the film and enlarge directly on bromide paper.

The length of the fogging exposure in relation to the image exposure directly affects the degree of solarization. For example, a 4 sec image exposure and a 16 sec fogging exposure may produce a film with a negative appearance, which will, therefore, print with a positive bias. An 8 sec image and a 10 sec fogging exposure may give roughly equal nega-

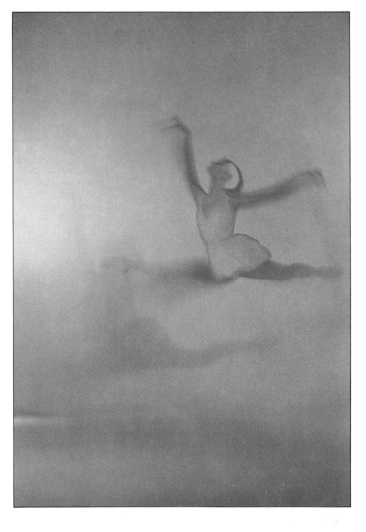

tive and positive elements. Still more image exposure and less fogging gives a result that forms a negative-biased print.

Color results

Color materials are inherently low in contrast and difficult to solarize. Because of this, it is best to make a black and white film image from the color original and solarize this instead. First decide if you want to solarize one color more

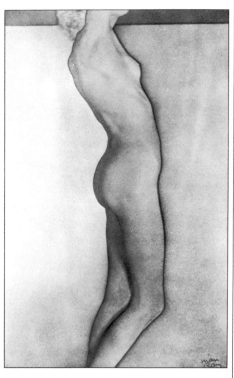

Nude

This solarized image was made by Man Ray in the 1920s. Using sheet film, Ray solarized his negatives during development, producing a result with

mixed qualities of drawing and photography. (Photograph courtesy of Sotheby's, Belgravia.)

than the others. If so, then filter in this color as you contact print from the color original. Use the same technique as described above for black and white results, except that you must use panchromatic film and work in darkness. After processing and drying, set up the solarized image in the enlarger and make test strip exposures on a full sheet of color paper. Process and decide on the most appropriate exposure. Then expose another sheet at this setting. Place the paper in a light-tight box and set your original slide or negative up in the film carrier of the enlarger. Use the test print to align the new image exactly before returning the part-exposed paper to the masking frame, and making a second exposure on to it.

Workroom techniques

Workroom techniques differ from the previous techniques described because they do not rely heavily on the controlled conditions of a darkroom. As long as the work area has a water supply, work tops, and print finishing facilities, it will be sufficient for processes such as toning, montage, and hand coloring black and white images.

Combining images

Montage (the mounting of one or more cut-out photographs on a common photographic background) has been practiced in photography since the nineteenth century. It was one of several techniques used by photographers to create realistic scenes that would have been impossible with a single exposure in the camera. The poor resolving power of early lenses, the slowness of film, and inadequate artificial lighting meant that it was sometimes difficult to photograph a large group of people, for example, other than in small sections. In the early twentieth century montage was expanded to include non-photographic elements such as paintings, typography, and three-dimensional objects.

There are two main approaches to modern montage. The first is the juxtaposition of two or more elements using invisible joins to create incongruity, as in surrealist paintings. The second is the actual emphasis of torn or cut-out photographs.

Adding color

There are two different workroom techniques for adding color to black and white images. The first is toning, where the black metallic silver in the print is converted to a colored chemical dye. There is a variety of methods of toning, some involving the color changing of the whole image area, and some using a more restrained approach. Some of the processes, such as sepia toning, make the image more permanent, whereas metal toners (such as iron) are far less stable.

Hand coloring is the second common method of adding color. Like montage, hand coloring is as old as photography itself. The technique developed initially because black and white photography was considered to limit the realistic appearance of the subject, and so it became common practice to "color up" prints. Today, with color photography's high quality and universal usage, hand coloring is mostly used for false color results. It remains one of the most popular workroom processes, and is often used in magazine and advertising illustration, especially when the aim is to evoke a strong sense of nostalgia.

See also
Editorial and advertising photography *Advertising approaches*, pp. 318-19. Reportage photography *Manipulation after shooting*, p. 327. High Art photography *Techniques*, pp. 331-2. Surrealism *Techniques*, p. 379.

Toning

Black and white prints can be toned as soon as they are fully processed and washed. There are several different toning methods you can use. The first is to displace the black metallic image with another metal, forming a color salt image. The second is to bleach the silver image to "rehalogenize" it, then redarken it in a solution (such as sepia toner) to form a toned image. The third, and most controllable, method involves rehalogenizing and then redarkening it in a form of color developer to which you add the color coupler of your choice. You can then leave the image as a mixture of silver and colored dyes, or bleach the silver away, leaving the pure dye image. All these chemicals are supplied in kit form.

Iron toning

Iron toning gives a strong blue image and intensifies the print — so you should select an image that consists of light tones. The solution is in two parts — the first (1 g of potassium ferricyanide, plus 2 ml of concentrated sulfuric acid in solution, made up to 500 ml with water) and the second (1 g of ferric ammonium citrate, plus 2 ml of concentrated sulfuric acid in solution, made up to 500 ml with water) must be mixed together just before commencing the toning process.

The toner converts the silver to an iron salt, which is blue. Thoroughly soak the print in water first, then place it in the solution and agitate. The blue image will be brighter if you leave some silver as black (untoned). When the print reaches the color you desire, remove it from the solution and wash it thoroughly. If highlights have a blue cast you can clear them in a 10 per cent salt solution.

Sepia toning

Like hand coloring, sepia toning conjures up a sense of the past. To sepia tone a print, which should be one that is fully developed and possesses a rich range of tones, first bleach the print (using a solution of 50 g potassium ferricyanide, plus 50 g of potassium bromide, dissolved in 500 ml of water), diluting further by adding one part of the bleaching solution to nine parts of water. Leave the print in this solution until the image is pale yellow. Remove the print and rinse it for a few minutes. Next, place the print in the sepia toning solution (25 g of sodium sulfide, plus 500 ml of water), and tone until the image shadow areas are a full dark brown. Wash the print thoroughly and dry it. You can partially bleach, then tone, the print, giving a "duotone" of black shadows and sepia highlights for a different effect.

Chromogenic toning

By adding mixtures of basic color couplers (see *Chromogenic film and paper theory*, pp. 217-19) to a suitable color developer, you can tone a rehalogenized print any color you wish. You can also retain the new silver image formed in order to boost the shadow areas of the print, or bleach away areas selectively and then apply a combination of different colored dyes to the same print. The coupler liquids are available in kit form, but are made for basic tints only. By a process of experimentation you can mix these together to produce a wide range of other colors.

Montage

As a method of combining two or more prints on one background, montage has wide scope for creative effects. Image ingredients can be all photographic, or you can combine photographic images with newspaper images, paint, or typographic cuttings. Many different results are possible. You can create surreal effects by using incongruous backgrounds and invisible joining techniques. Or you can emphasize joins between the elements by tearing the edges or cutting them roughly. A montage need not be permanent — you can make a temporary composition under glass and later rearrange the elements.

Planning

It is usually best to design a montage as a preliminary sketch and then photograph the elements individually — specifically to comply with it. Or you can use images from stock.

Set up the enlarger and plan each print by lining up the sketch on the masking frame. Each element should be balanced perfectly for color and contrast if you want to make a montage with invisible joins. But for a rough-cut effect, unbalanced tone and color effects may be what you are looking for.

Print suitability

It is possible to montage any kind of photographic print, but some photographers prefer resin-coated papers because they are more durable — although a disadvantage is that the plastic coating can leave a frilly edge when cut. Thin paper is easiest to mount, and a matte surface makes retouching much simpler.

Invisible joining

Mount your background print on a thick sheet of cardboard first, and remove any surface grease or dust. Cut out each element, paring down all edges to a minimal thickness. Use a scalpel with a new blade and lightly score the surface along the image outline. Hold the print to the light and bend it slightly, to ensure that the blade has cut through the emulsion only.

For complex, intricate shapes, cut out about 1 in (2.5 cm) from the scored line to make a series of "flaps". As you tear away excess paper pull off each flap in turn to avoid tearing off delicately scored image detail. Place the print face down on a clean surface and pull excess print areas away from the back of the print. Finally, remove excess frills of resin or paper fibers by sanding the print back with a fine grade of sandpaper.

Composing the elements

Arrange the elements on the background image, and weight them down with glass. The perspective of the various elements should, ideally, match up. Clean all print surfaces, and then coat the back of each image evenly with glue (avoid rubbery adhesives). Place the prints in position and apply pressure from the center outward. Remove any excess glue, then cover the montage with weighted glass or put it under paper in a cold dry mounting press.

Hand coloring

You can use hand coloring techniques simply to create a full-color image from a black and white print, or you can use it in a more interpretative way to produce impossible color combinations and special effects. Colors used in this way can add a sense of fantasy. When you apply color to the entire print area, it tends to be degraded by the black photographic tones underneath — so try toning the print sepia first. If you still require some areas of hard, black density, then apply the sepia toner selectively, masking off, if necessary, areas of the print that you want left untoned.

Problems with resin-coated prints

Resin-coated prints are not really suitable for hand coloring. The plastic finish means that oil color in particular sits on the surface and always looks like an addition. You can use water colors, oil paints, felt pens, or colored pencils for print coloring. With water colors it is best to work on a slightly damp print. Oil paints should be applied to a dry surface. Water colors, though, require more skill because they sink into the print surface and are difficult to remove if you want to make alterations. But with oils, you can wipe everything off with turpentine and start again if necessary.

Equipment

The basic set of equipment you will require consists of a set of water color retouching dyes or an artist's basic oil color kit. Other essential items are a range of brushes (from fine through to coarse), a sponge, palette, jars for clean water, and turpentine for oil paints. You may also require bleacher and toner solutions, a photographic tray, and a non-absorbent work surface that is larger than your size of print. For your first attempts at hand coloring, choose a small print size.

Water coloring

After you have bleached, toned, and washed your print (if necessary), squeegee it, still wet, flat on your work surface. Make up the tints you will require on your palette, diluted with plenty of water. Add small amounts of concentrated color to this until you have exactly the color you want. For large areas, such as sky, use your widest brush or a swab, moving rapidly to avoid building up noticeable brush marks. It is usually more successful to build up color coat by coat, rather than trying to apply it all in one wash. Sponge off any excess color. You can next work on the more detailed areas, using a finer brush and stronger color. Have a piece of blotting paper nearby to stop color running into unwanted areas. Let the print dry out throughly before you apply the final, smallest, areas of painted color, which may be brighter still. At this stage of working it is best to apply concentrated color with the finest brush you have available. After coloring, your print may wrinkle, so mount it carefully.

Oil coloring

Oil colors make brighter colored prints — you can blend them together quite easily, and results tend to look more professional than water colored prints.

Sepia tone your print first, then let it dry before mounting it. Use only a small amount

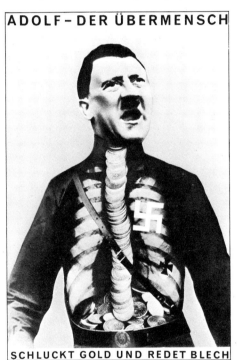

ADOLF – DER ÜBERMENSCH

SCHLUCKT GOLD UND REDET BLECH

Political montage
Many of the well-known anti-Nazi and left-wing magazine covers were created by the photomontagist John Heartfield during the early 1930s. This one was entitled "Adolf the superman swallows gold and spouts trash".

Surrealistic image
Bob Carlos Clarke's image (right) is a combination of double printing, montage, and extensive retouching by airbrushing.

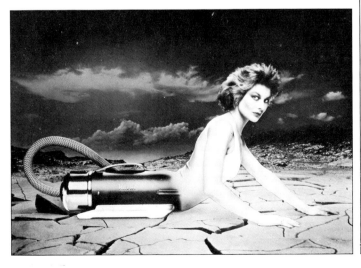

of color from each tube, and mix it on the palette with a few drops of turpentine to make it more viscous. Oils take a long time to dry, so take care to avoid smudging. You can blend colors on the print surface, and rework colors easily, even after many hours. Remove any mistakes with a clean cloth dipped in turpentine, and pick out areas of brightest color at the last stage. Flesh tones worked in this way can be highly realistic.

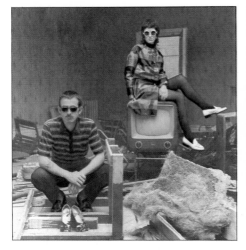

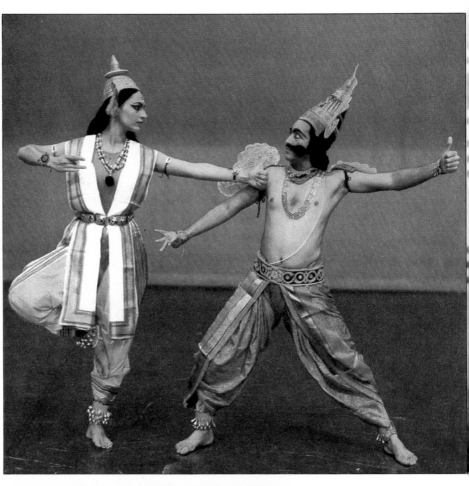

Hand coloring
As a creative technique, hand coloring provides almost unlimited scope for adding emphasis to a picture. For the image above, Amanda Currey first sepia toned a black and white print, and then hand colored only the figures. This has the effect of producing a cohesive double portrait, without removing the sense of chaos of the couple's surroundings.

Hand coloring with oils
To create the highly realistic and totally controlled coloring above, Amanda Currey worked in artists' oils. Beginning on a dry, sepia-toned print, she first colored in the larger areas. After leaving these to dry for 24 hours, smaller details were added. Notice the striking use of white paint.

Using black silver
Paul de Nooijer's approach to hand coloring is highly stylized (left). He frequently uses high-contrast black and white paper, tinting selected highlight and pale-toned areas with water-based dyes. In this way, the rich black silver parts of the image are used to add strength to the busy patterns found in many of his images.

New technology

New technology for the post-camera stages of photography increasingly embraces the use of electronics and computerization. One reason for this is the need to break away from the traditional dependence on silver in photography. Specialized processing laboratories and other large users can reclaim some silver from bleach and fix solutions. But despite this (and despite every manufacturing streamlining), photographic materials remain expensive, and are likely to become more so as the world's supply of silver diminishes.

Another factor prompting change is the inherent slowness and inefficiency of chemical processing. Liquid chemicals take time to penetrate the emulsion evenly; chemical changes are relatively slow; by-products have to be removed; and finally the material must be dried. Ingenious short cuts within the present technology have been devised – instant picture and photo color transfer materials, for example, which have the developers and dyes already built in and only require activating. For other materials, roller transport processing machines accept the exposed paper or film and take it through the required sequence of solutions, and, where necessary, washing and drying automatically. All of these, however, can be likened to steam engines when compared to the speed and flexibility possible with electronically generated images.

Electrochemical interface
Electronic images are already used by laboratories to predict how negatives will look when they are printed. The operator inserts a color negative in a video unit, and the image is displayed on a color television screen in positive form. Turning controls on the console alters density and color balance, and these settings are used to program the exposure and filtration controls on the enlarger that prints the negative by traditional photographic means. Although this enlarger does not look in any way similar to home darkroom models, it employs exactly the same principles.

This electronic previewing of negatives is still some way from complete electronic control – with the ability to create instant effects found, for example, in television broadcasting. One approach is seen in the laser scanning process, originated in the United States. Starting with a fully processed color slide, the image is scanned by three minutely focused laser beams. The light is received by light sensors, which generate signals in relation to the proportion of blue, green, and red present, translating the image into a stream of electronic signals.

Computer "processing"
Once the image is in this electronic form, a computer can "process" the information in various ways, according to how it is programmed. The possible changes include overall or selective contrast reduction, color correction or color distortion, and highlight masking effects. The computer can also generate a negative image and off-

set it with the original positive image to produce a bas-relief effect. Similarly, tone or color separations can be scanned, given any color, and then recombined as a posterized image. It is also possible to reverse out a band of tones in the middle of the tonal range, and exchange single colors.

Visual display
In all these cases, the results are displayed on a video unit, allowing controls to be further adjusted until the image looks exactly the way it should before printing. Finally, this processed signal is used to program three other blue, green, and red point-focused lasers, which scan print on negative color film to expose the modified photographic image. This negative can then be enlarged conventionally on ordinary photographic paper.

As yet there is no suitable way of using laser scanning for original camera exposures. The wavelengths of the lasers do not have a suitably broad scope to "build up" the visible spectrum as do the three silver halide layers in color film.

Applications
Once the image has been encoded as electronic signals (preferably in digital form), most of the special effects in this section, plus many others, can be created. Computer graphic programs can correct or alter shape and perspective, with an action similar to camera movements. Two images can be sandwiched – each element in any required form, negative or positive, color or black and white, and in various relative strengths. A black and white image can be electronically colored, for example, to distinguish clearly one area from another. This feature has applications in medical and astronomical photography (see *Photography and space exploration*, pp. 292-5).

Electronic toning
With the newest systems it is also possible to "hand tone" by marking out an area on a monitor with an electronic pen or cursor. A particular hue is then selected from an "electronic palette", viewable on the screen. When the cursor then touches the marked out image area, it automatically changes to the selected color. Even cut and stick montage effects are possible. For example, a figure of a girl can be scanned from a black and white negative, colored, reduced in size, and repeated across the screen like a chorus line. Next, the operator can recall the full-size figure and superimpose it over the line to appear in the foreground. Any number of images can be scanned and superimposed in this way.

Another application of electronic artwork is electronic retouching. Special equipment can display a scanned slide image, for example, on a color video unit and, by using a cursor to control a crosshair mark on the screen, the operator can make all the types of corrections normally done by hand. To remove marks or blemishes, the faulty picture section is enlarged on the screen, an

adjacent color or tone is selected using the cursor, and this fed into the program for translation into the adjacent blemish. Similarly, any chosen local area of the image can be subtly varied in color and hue – perhaps to correct mixed lighting and resulting color casts. Every correction is lodged in the computer memory, which is eventually used to expose the retouched image back on color film.

Conversion of photographs into half-tone images, essential for reproduction on the printed page, is an ideal application for electronics. An original photograph can be scanned and automatically turned into dot pattern color separations ready for printing in yellow, magenta, and cyan, and black ink. At this point, "feed-back" circuits can adjust the contrast and density of each separation to suit the requirements of the particular printing press being used.

Spread design
It is even possible to compose a full double-page spread of pictures and text for magazines or books entirely electronically. After the spread has been designed on a television monitor, a computer translates the information into a set of images exposed on suitable film. These are then contact printed on an ink printing plate for processing or etching prior to printing.

All of these electronic possibilities already exist. Many are spin-offs from other fields of research such as space technology. Most, however, do require elaborate computer systems having sufficient memory capacity to carry information on the millions of values that make up each color image. The average photographer requires equipment that offers equally fine control of results, but at a price practicable for the home user. This will come in time as new advances and developments increase the memory capacity of microelectronics and dramatically reduce the cost.

Video still cameras
It is probable that some of this new technology will coincide with the availability of high-resolution video still cameras. Such cameras will help to "complete the chain" – converting not just existing slides but actual real-life scenes into electronic signal form. Camera users will be able to take the magnetic recording from the camera then use a preview/editing unit to crop, correct, or manipulate the images, all in normal room light and without the use of chemicals and solutions. The last link in the chain is a low-cost print-out device, which will convert the finalized manipulated image into a result on paper – preferably printed in ink or dye, not using silver anywhere in the process.

The specialized subject

In many fields of photography it is necessary to expand techniques to meet the particular requirements of specialized subjects. The subjects covered in the following pages are wide-ranging, but in each case the most important thing is the way in which photography can convey information about the subject – whether this is done with the objective approach demanded by scientific research and medical diagnosis, or in the more interpretative way favored in areas such as landscape and fashion photography. Each assignment is therefore an exercise in problem solving, in which photography is used as a tool to record the essential information. Because the equipment and techniques are put to practical use in this way, this type of photography is often known as "applied" photography. The degree of specialization is high. Most photographers are professional, and few work in more than one particular field.

The photographer must first know exactly the type of information that is required, then select the appropriate equipment and materials that will achieve the necessary result. The requirement may be a picture of a particular animal in the wild, an advertising shot designed to fill a billboard of specific proportions, or a diagnostic image of a medical condition. It may involve using only the most basic photographic equipment and techniques, yet, like the news picture that sums up an event, it can still demand perfect timing on the part of the photographer. In some circumstances it may be necessary to use the latest, most complex, and most specialized technology to produce the required result.

This section begins with the most objective and technically biased applications of photography – scientific and technical research. This work often requires special cameras, materials, and lighting. The photographer must know which of this wide range of specialized equipment to use. Other scientifically based areas – medical, forensic, astronomical, and aerial photography – present similar problems. They are also dealt with at the beginning of the section.

The more subjective areas follow. These range from the photography of natural history subjects, where a degree of scientific accuracy is still often vital, to subjects such as architecture, landscape, news, and photojournalism, where the photographer is much more free to develop and explore individual interests and opinions.

Each topic features a preliminary summary of the equipment and techniques most generally used, followed by a detailed survey of the subject, and the ways certain photographers approach it. It is therefore possible to grasp the general problems posed by each topic before reading in greater depth about the more specialized techniques that are involved.

Objective approaches

The most objective fields are geared to providing accurate factual information. There is rarely scope for self-expression on the part of the photographer, and details such as magnification ratio, time and date of exposure, and particulars of the equipment used are frequently vital information, without which the picture is practically worthless.

Scientifically based photography often demands the use of the most advanced technology. This is often the case in astronomical photography, which is concerned with the problems of transmitting pictures of distant planets and stars back to earth from remotely operated cameras in space probes. In astronomical research images may be the only tangible results of vast expenditure.

Many of the developments pioneered for space and military purposes — such as electronic image enhancement, high-resolution television, and side-looking radar — are already benefiting other areas of photography. For example, it is possible to use techniques designed to increase the sharpness of pictures from space to improve details in medical and forensic images. Similarly, infrared transparency film, originally developed for detecting camouflage, is now widely used for vegetation surveys, and for special effects, particularly in advertising.

Another influential development is the growth of electronic methods of forming images. According to the demands of the user, it is now possible to form pictures on a cathode ray tube, by means of a charge coupled device, or with an X ray or thermal sensor, as well as on the surface of a regular silver halide emulsion. Each of these methods of recording has its own advantages and limitations, and photographers often use two or more techniques in sequence, for example using one to respond to an image from a lens, and another to intensify, transmit, or otherwise modify this result to make it more useful to the scientist.

Photography also often involves working with invisible forms of radiation. These range from the relatively familiar infrared and ultraviolet wavelengths to gamma rays and ultrasonic waves. Even when photographing through a microscope, scientists now frequently use short-wave electrons instead of light. The modern scanning electron microscope produces images that combine quality, detail, depth of field, and magnification in a way that is impossible with other methods of photomicrography.

Some of the most interesting results come from the simultaneous use of several methods of image production. Airplanes, satellites, and space probes often record the same subject with at least three devices, sensitive to different wavelengths. It is possible to superimpose the results, to emphasize different information. In addition, electronics enable the scientist to code tonal images in a range of contrasting colors, so that important areas stand out more clearly. The visual effect of this is similar to color solarization, and scientists are already using techniques that will become more widely familiar with the introduction of completely electronic cameras in the future.

Conventional photography still has many advantages over electronic imaging methods. For example, many techniques rely on a television tube to produce an electronic image which scientists must then record photographically to produce a permanent result. But even the best high-resolution cathode ray tubes do not resolve fine detail as well as regular silver halide film processed with liquid chemicals. Regular film also has a superior tonal response. Each grain is smaller than the tiniest of the picture elements that make up the image on a television screen. On the other hand, an electronically produced image can provide an immediate result that the user can view without processing. This facility is very useful in scientific applications, where the procedure in one experiment often depends on the outcome of another. When a picture is required quickly, but a high-resolution image is also vital, instant picture materials often provide the best answer. But as electronic image-forming devices are developed further, image quality is likely to improve to a point where results are comparable with conventional silver halide images.

To produce images that are valuable to scientists, the photographer still requires the strong sense of composition necessary to produce effective pictures. It is vital to aim for a result that will convey information clearly, free of distracting surroundings and confusing shadows. When choice is possible, concern for subject qualities such as color, form, and texture is also important. Pictures that are well composed and interesting to look at will make their point more effectively. In addition, the strange and often colorful images produced for technical purposes can have an influence irrespective of their original function. The abstract patterns that appear in photographs of crystals have influenced fabric designs, while infrared and thermal images have formed the basis of illustrations for items such as record sleeves and stage scenery.

The scope for interpretation

Some specialized subjects allow the photographer much more interpretative freedom. These range from natural history and sports to landscape, architecture, portraiture, and reportage. All these subjects call for a combination of technical skills, detailed understanding of the subject and the purpose of the picture, and flair for composition.

These subjects vary in the extent to which they rely on specialized equipment. Many sports and natural history photographers use remote-controlled cameras or automatic triggering devices to overcome problems of difficult locations and subjects that are disturbed by the presence of the photographer. Yet it is still essential to rely on a sound knowledge of the subject itself to produce the best results — many sports photographers are themselves ex-competitors, and successful natural history photographers are often qualified biologists.

Subjects such as architecture, landscapes, portraiture, and reportage rely less on special equipment and more on the particular skills of the photographer. With architecture and landscape, the photographer has time to ensure that the composition is exactly right and to wait for the best lighting. It is also possible to explore these static subjects fully, seeking out revealing details and unusual viewpoints. With reportage and portraiture the reverse is often true. To capture fleeting expressions, and decisive moments that epitomize

a situation, it is vital to be continuously alert. Yet there is still a great deal of scope for the individual to develop a personal style, to stress one feature and play down another, in order to express a point of view.

The demands of specialization

Although the specialized subjects of photography are diverse, the demands on the photographer of accuracy, of working to a tight brief, and of producing consistent results, are similar. This means that photographers must adopt a completely professional approach. The cost of specialized photography is often high. Scientific work calls for expensive equipment, while advertising and press photography frequently involve the cost of traveling to distant locations. In addition, the quality of the pictures produced often has a particular importance. A good news story, an accurate medical diagnosis, or an effective survey of a developing country may all be impossible without photographs showing the required details clearly and accurately. Because of the high cost and the exacting demands, photographers who undertake this work are usually specialists. It is seldom possible to be an all-rounder and still achieve results of a sufficiently high professional standard.

Some specializations impose extreme restrictions on the photographer. In advertising, for example, format proportions, space for lettering, and features to be stressed, will all be specified by the client. Each prop, background feature, and expression has to be planned with meticulous care. Often the photographer works to a drawn layout.

Subjects such as architecture and portraits can also be restrictive. A property developer may want a building to appear in a certain way, and people commissioning a portrait may make similar demands. Even reportage photographers have to work within the constraints of the printed page, although the photojournalist usually has a great deal of scope to develop original ideas and opinions about a particular topic. It is demands such as these that make many of the subjects discussed in this section the preserve of the professional photographer. But the type of results produced, and the techniques used remain interesting and revealing to photographers at all levels.

Scientific and technical photography

Scientific and technological research is involved with the accumulation of facts, often the result of minute and painstaking observations, which eventually lead to new theories and ideas. Scientists therefore require measuring devices of great accuracy, and observation aids that supplement the power of the naked eye. Photography can often supply these needs.

The unaided human eye has distinct limitations as a device for direct observation. It can respond only to a limited range of light wavelengths, and requires illumination within a narrow brightness range – objects are invisible to the eye if light is too bright or too dim. Objects must also move at the right speed. Complicated movements more rapid than about one-tenth of a second are too quick for the eye to see clearly, while changes taking hours or days require impossible levels of concentration. Objects must also be larger than about one-five-hundredth of an inch. In all these cases, the photographic process is a far better tool for analysis than the naked eye.

Historical background
Fox Talbot was the first to show how photography could record subjects that are not clearly visible to the eye. He produced a sharp photograph of a printed newspaper page on a fast-revolving turntable by illuminating the subject with a very brief electric spark. Eadweard Muybridge was another important pioneer. With his sequences of pictures showing running figures he was the first to use photography to analyze movement in a systematic way.

This century, developments have come about more rapidly. In the 1930s, improved stroboscopic and flash illumination allowed briefer exposures and more intense lighting. More recently, tools such as the Kerr cell, the electron microscope, and the bubble chamber have all been coupled with the photographic process.

Industrial applications
In industry, microphotography can provide miniature versions of documents and printed circuits. For the research engineer, photography is a means of revealing invisible air currents that pass over a moving vehicle, or the stresses that are likely to occur in a proposed building. The physicist can use photographic techniques to reveal the structure of crystals. Macrophotography and photomicrography have wider applications. They are employed in all fields that involve the magnification of small and microscopic objects. Devices providing ultra-fast exposures and time-lapse techniques are also used in many areas.

See also
Timing and movement *The camera's portrayal,* p. 90. Aperture, pp. 116-19. Focal length and camera size *Movements on sheet film cameras,* p. 121. The shutter *Shutter firing systems,* p. 126.

Equipment and techniques

Scientific photography varies as widely as science itself. On the most specialized level, the equipment used can do one job only, and would be totally unrecognizable to photographers in other fields. But every area of research also requires certain general-purpose items. These include cameras (from 5×4 ins/12.5×10 cm to 35 mm types), with close-up and macro equipment, multihead and ring-flash, fiber optics, and compact tungsten light sources. A full set of correction, polarizing, and neutral density filters is also essential.

At the same time, a degree of improvization is usually required. Every research and development laboratory uses "one-off" set-ups, and frequently adapts regular camera equipment to solve unusual technical problems.

If photographic records are to be precise, the definition of camera and enlarger lenses must be pin-sharp. It is also vital to use film stock that will give consistent results, and to standardize the color temperature of the light source, and the processing and printing techniques. In this way, if there are variations in pictures taken of the same subject they will reflect changes in the subject itself, not variations in the photographic process.

Using the electronmagnetic spectrum
Scientific photographers (together with those working in medical, forensic, and astronomical fields) use radiant energy in wavebands beyond those that form visible light. The shorter wavelengths of the vast electronmagnetic spectrum include ultraviolet. This causes certain materials such as crystals and bacteria to take on a self-luminous appearance. Even shorter wavelengths, such as X rays and Gamma rays, are used for their penetrative powers. It is possible to record them directly on X ray film, which is coated on both front and back with a special thick emulsion. Electrons in the Gamma wavebands make possible electron microscopes. These wavelengths are much shorter than light, and offer much better image resolution than that possible with regular optical microscopes.

Wavelengths longer than visible light include infrared and heat bands. Scientists use this radiation to make pictures with infrared-sensitive film and thermal scanning cameras (see *Using infrared,* p. 288 and *Thermography,* p. 287). Ultrasonic frequencies, when converted into light images by sonographic devices (see *Isotope scanning and sonography,* p. 290), are also used increasingly widely, particularly in medical photography.

These bands of the electromagnetic spectrum have their own characteristics and limitations. Some, such as X rays, must be generated on earth, because the atmosphere blocks out natural X rays from space. Others, like sound waves, rely on a carrier substance such as air or water for their transmission. They cannot pass through a vacuum.

Scientists have not developed detection devices for frequencies beyond cosmic rays, although it is probable that the electromagnetic spectrum extends to even higher frequencies, which scientists have yet to discover and use. The spectrum extends below the audio bands to electrical alternating current, and probably to even lower, undetected frequencies.

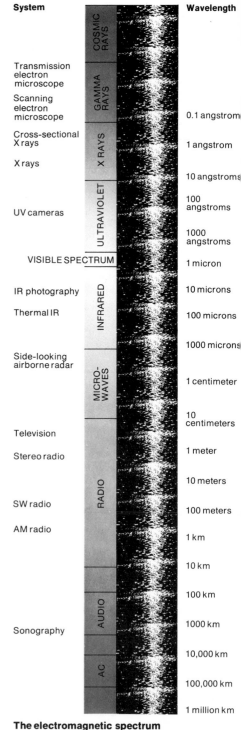

System		Wavelength
	COSMIC RAYS	
Transmission electron microscope	GAMMA RAYS	
Scanning electron microscope		0.1 angstrom
Cross-sectional X rays	X RAYS	1 angstrom
X rays		10 angstroms
	ULTRAVIOLET	100 angstroms
UV cameras		1000 angstroms
VISIBLE SPECTRUM		1 micron
IR photography	INFRARED	10 microns
Thermal IR		100 microns
		1000 microns
Side-looking airborne radar	MICRO-WAVES	1 centimeter
		10 centimeters
Television		1 meter
Stereo radio		10 meters
	RADIO	100 meters
SW radio		1 km
AM radio		10 km
		100 km
	AUDIO	1000 km
Sonography		10,000 km
	AC	100,000 km
		1 million km

The electromagnetic spectrum
Specialized areas of photography use forms of radiation ranging from short-wavelength gamma rays (bands that make possible electron microscopes) to very long sound waves (used for ultrasound body scans). Visible light forms a very small section of the whole spectrum. Wavelengths longer than infrared and shorter than X rays require electronic equipment to convert them into light before photography can take place. To detect radiation from space, scientists send equipment beyond the atmosphere.

Contracting time

To analyze actions and changes that take place over a long period of time, researchers often employ time-lapse photography. Sequences of comparative pictures are invaluable to clarify slow chemical and physical changes, such as the growth of plants or crystals and the corrosion of metals. They also aid the study of traffic flow, enabling transportation planners to improve the layout of complex road intersections. In addition, the physical movements necessary for people to undertake particular jobs can be studied, in order to produce more conveniently designed machinery and working areas.

Time-lapse photography

The essence of time-lapse work is to eliminate all the variables between successive pictures other than the changes that occur in the subject itself. This can be quite difficult when the periods between each exposure run into minutes, hours, or even days. Lighting may change in its quality, direction, and intensity. Subsidiary elements in the foreground and background can move around, and even occasional air currents can cause misleading changes on film.

As far as possible, this type of photography requires laboratory conditions, in fixed artificial lighting. Sometimes, when natural conditions are essential to allow subject growth, or weathering, to continue, the photographer must devise a set-up that creates a controlled environment for each exposure. To record plant growth, for example, a greenhouse environment may be essential. If pictures must be taken at regular intervals a timing device provides the best solution. It is possible to use this technique to make time-lapse movies, as well as still sequences.

Chronocyclographs

To analyze a subject's motion, scientists often prefer to represent movements in the form of light trails. Such pictures, known as chronocyclographs, are invaluable for illustrating work patterns in time and motion study. A subject, for example a person operating a machine, is placed in lighting of fairly low intensity, with the camera positioned to give an overall view from above. The researcher attaches miniaturized lamps to the hands and arms of the machine operator, and by keeping the shutter open throughout the cycle of operation records a series of light trails.

To avoid confusion between the many crossing and overlapping trails, it is advisable to use lamps of different colors. It is also possible to use lamps that pulse at regular intervals, recording on the film as broken lines. Counting the number of breaks in the line tracing any movement from one position to another allows the photographer to calculate the amount of time taken. A more sophisticated method uses lamps that brighten faster than they fade out at each pulsation. These lamps record pointed traces of light on the film, each pointed end denoting the direction of travel.

High-speed photography

Scientific researchers in many fields use ultrafast exposures to record phenomena that move too fast for the unaided eye to perceive. The analysis of projectiles in flight, the recording of explosions, and the investigation of fast chemical reactions all require exposures faster than those permitted by regular cameras. With a series of these pictures, taken either on a single frame or on individual pieces of film, the scientist can study detailed changes that occurred over a minute period.

High-speed cameras

The fastest shutter speed on a regular camera is usually either 1/1000 or 1/2000 sec. These speeds are too slow for many scientific applications. There are two main ways of achieving faster exposures – either using a specialized electronic flash unit, or an ultra-fast non-mechanical shutter such as a Kerr cell or a sophisticate image tube unit (see *Special-purpose, high-speed shutters,* p. 131).

Electronic flash units are capable of giving flashes as short as one-millionth of a second. For small subjects a concentrated laser light source may be used. But neither source will be adequate to freeze movement if the subject is strongly self-luminous. For subjects such as a detonator firing, or a fuse exploding, one of the special shutters or a special high-speed

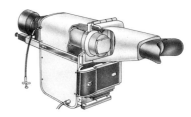

Image tube camera
This high-speed camera incorporates an image tube that will form pictures at rates of up to 20 million frames per second. It uses a specially modified instant picture rollfilm back suitable for use with the ultra-fast ASA 10,000 film that records the image.

framing camera will be essential. The fastest shutter type, the image tube, lays out a matrix of consecutive images on a display screen (see *Special-purpose, high-speed shutters,* p. 131). Image tube cameras can offer rates of up to twenty million pictures per second.

For exceptionally bright subjects, such as plasmas and atomic tests, a series of several shutters may be necessary. First, a bladed shutter opens about $\frac{1}{2}$ sec before the event is photographed. Then a Kerr or Farraday cell fires simultaneously with the action. Finally (because these shutters allow through about 0.002 per cent of the light when closed), a capping shutter, consisting of glass crossed with fine lead wires, is energized electrically. This causes a coating of lead to cover the glass, giving a completely light-tight seal, within about 1/20,000 sec.

Short sequences

Often short sequences of pictures are necessary, with a known time gap between each exposure. Researchers can then plot the subject's distance from the frame edges, and

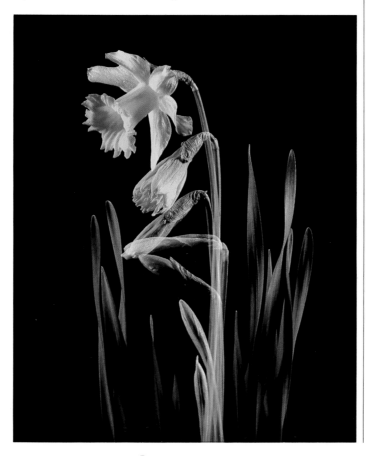

Time-lapse photograph
Jane Burton used the time-lapse technique to record the growth of a daffodil over a seven-day period. In order to preserve natrual growing conditions while giving consistent light for photography, botanists often use a four-fold trigger system. First, a timer activates a mechanism that covers the greenhouse windows, to exclude natural lighting. Second, fixed lamps, or electronic flash units, are switched on. The third stage is to make one exposure, and wind on the film. Finally, the timer switches off the photographic lighting to restore normal growth conditions in natural illumination. See also the sun eclipse time-lapse picture on p. 292.

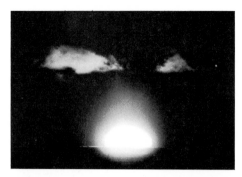

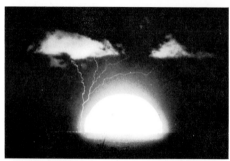

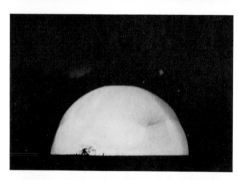

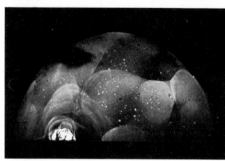

A record of a nuclear explosion
This sequence of images shows the world's first thermonuclear explosion, which took place at Eniwetok Atoll in 1952. The pictures show the brilliant cloud of hot air immediately in front of the explosion's shock wave. On the first two frames, induced lightning is also visible. The bright area to the left of the fireball in the final frame is a vaporized instrumentation tunnel. Scientists in the US Department of the Environment used a high-speed camera to record over 500 frames before the light became too dim for photography at this rate. This stage, known as "light-minimum time", was reached after only 0.07 sec.

calculate its velocity and acceleration directly off the film. This application of photography is useful in showing effects as diverse as a tennis racket redirecting a ball, and a bullet penetrating armored plates. For dark or large-area subjects continuous illumination may be necessary. A special high-speed framing camera together with several powerful lights provides the best combination of camera and lighting equipment.

The slowest high-speed cameras use 35 mm or 16 mm film and operate like motor drives, holding the film still briefly as each frame is exposed. These allow exposures at rates up to about 400 frames per second (fps). At faster rates the film is not strong enough to withstand the strain caused by this action. Cameras with an even faster frame rate keep the film running continuously, and have a rotating prism that acts as a shutter. Such a camera will expose pictures at up to 10,000 fps. This rate is suitable for photographing rapidly moving mechanical parts and liquid sprays. But the prism system does cause a slight loss of fine detail.

For the fastest subjects, such as rifle bullets in flight, a huge rotating mirror camera may be necessary. This holds a length of about twenty frames of film still behind a curved array of lenses. A fast rotating mirror reflects the image through each lens in turn, giving exposures as brief as one-two-millionth of a second and an adjustable framing rate of between 50,000 and eight million pictures per second. The speed of the mirror's travel, and the number of lenses in the camera determine the framing speed. But even at the highest framing speeds there is an interval between pictures during

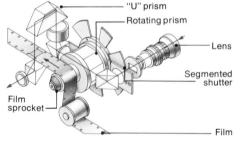

"U" prism
Rotating prism
Lens
Segmented shutter
Film sprocket
Film

1

2

3

Rotating prism
The camera's design (above) links segmented shutter, rotating prism, and film, so that they all move at the same speed, but the shutter and prism travel in the opposite direction to the moving film. In most types the prism itself blocks light from the film **1** until it turns **2**, so that the lower area of the image reaches the uppermost part of the frame. As the prism continues to turn **3**, the center of the image registers. This is followed by the top. This process can take place up to 10,000 times per second.

which no image of the subject records. It is therefore possible to convert most rotating mirror cameras to record one long image of a high-speed subject as a single streak. This provides a semi-abstract, but continuous record of the subject.

The two most common technical problems with these ultra-high-speed cameras are lighting, and synchronizing the camera with the action. Unless the subject is intensely self-illuminated, an immense volume of light is

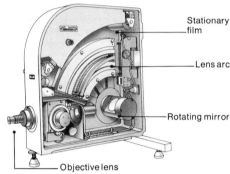

Stationary film
Lens arc
Rotating mirror
Objective lens

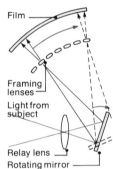

Film
Framing lenses
Light from subject
Relay lens
Rotating mirror

Rotating mirror camera
The camera (above) produces an array of circular images on a strip of film. Light from the subject (right) passes through a relay lens to the rotating mirror, which reflects the image through the lenses to the film. Precise synchronization of camera and subject is essential. Mirror speed determines framing rate.

required at exposures of one-millionth of a second. Sometimes a powerful xenon arc spotlight a short distance from the subject can give sufficient light. This is only brought to full power a moment before exposure. A heat-absorbing filter over the light is usually essential, and even then the heat may be excessive for living subjects. Occasionally the only way to achieve sufficient illumination is to shoot directly toward the light source, so that the subject appears as a silhouette.

To synchronize camera and action a set-up is usually designed so that the subject itself triggers exposure. This technique is invaluable for the rapidly moving subjects of ballistic photography, and is also used in natural history work (see *Insects*, p. 302). A common method involves setting up narrow light beams projecting on photo-sensitive cells in the path of the subject. As the subject enters the frame, it breaks the beam, bringing the lighting to its full strength, and triggering the camera.

Stroboscopic flash
Photographers requiring a simple working method can illuminate the subject with a stroboscopic flash, and use a regular camera. A dozen flashes will give the same number of images on a single frame of film, and a black background will show up the subject clearly,

making direct measurements easy. The image of a golf ball, for example, may have moved 1 mm on film between two flashes fired 1/100 sec apart. If the camera has magnified the subject × 0.001 (see *Image magnification,* p. 195) the ball will have moved 1000 mm in 1/100 sec (a velocity of 100 meters per second). Stroboscopic flash units are cheaper, easier to use, and much more widely available

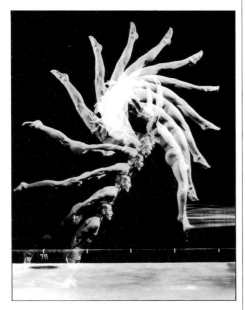

Strobe image
This picture of a diver performing a back dive was taken by Harold Edgerton, the pioneer of high-speed photography. Edgerton used a stroboscopic flash unit to produce the multiple image. The dark background, resulting from fall-off in illumination, makes the image of the figure stand out clearly and ensures that the back-

ground does not record through the figure. This type of image is often useful to sports teachers who want to demonstrate a competitor's movements, to sports participants themselves, and to orthopedic specialists who use this technique to analyze human motion.

than high-speed cameras. Their disadvantage is that they have a relatively low light output, which imposes a limit on the subject speeds they can record. Stroboscopic flash is therefore best suited to analyzing relatively slow-moving subjects, such as human and animal movement.

Enlarging small subjects

When examining small, complete specimens scientists use macrophotography to produce low-magnification enlargements. These are useful to biologists recording subjects such as plants and insects. Researchers in many other fields use macrophotography for routine work, including comparing specimens before and after experiments, and analyzing faults and weaknesses in man-made structures. Macrophotography is also useful for examining miniature electronic components.

In scientific work, the provision of a scale in every picture to establish magnification is usually vital. If you use camera movements (see *Lens and camera movements,* p. 120) to increase depth of field, it is important that subject shape should not be distorted. The same applies when using a short focal length lens from a close viewpoint. "True macro" lenses

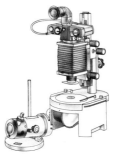

Macro illumination
The arrangement (left) provides even, shadowless illumination for macro work. Light passes up through the stage via a mirror to the subject. A reflector around the front of the lens stops glare by making transmitted light bounce back toward the subject. A right-angled viewer aids composition.

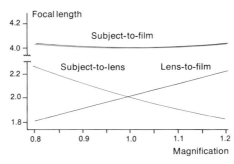

Macro focusing ratios
When the subject is about four times the focal length from the film, and the lens set midway between subject and film, the image is life size. As you increase the lens-to-

subject distance, the lens-to-film distance decreases by an amount that keeps the image sharp. Between magnifications of × 0.8 and × 1.2, focus is maintained.

are often used for high-quality work (see *Equipment for close-up,* pp. 195-6), and a ring-flash unit (see *Flash lighting units,* pp. 165-6) provides the most even illumination. Light reflected from a 45° mirror is best for objects with deep cavities.

With a sheet film monorail camera it is often possible to attach an additional supporting bracket right at the front of the rail. This can accommodate a stage for small objects, and glass or opal plastic for back-lighting if required. Balanced illumination from the rear is particularly useful for giving a shadowless background. With the stage placed at a distance four times the lens focal length from the film, it is only necessary to alter lens position to

give a useful range of magnifications between × 0.8 and × 1.2.

Depth of field is always a problem when working close to three-dimensional subjects. With spherical and conical objects, it is possible to light only the topmost plane that is in

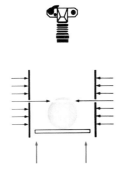

Lighting convex subjects
With a spherical or conical subject, a special method of illumination is sometimes required to extend depth of field. The lens is focused on the nearest portion of the subject, which is illuminated by a "slot" of light from either side. Moving the subject steadily during exposure brings each area into focus.

focus, using a horizontal slot of light from a masked-down source. During exposure, you can then raise the subject slowly, bringing the other parts into focus and light. The whole item will then record sharply, although it will not have regular perspective.

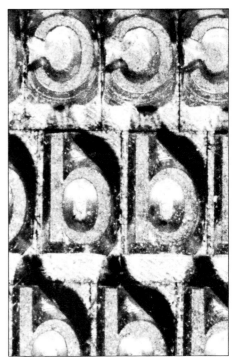

The close-up image
This macro picture of metal type for printing shows one of the many industrial applications of this branch of photography. A 35 mm SLR, with extension bellows and a 20 mm "true" macro lens gave a magnification of × 10. The type shows slight wear that would have

been barely visible to the naked eye. Macrophotography is invaluable in assessing and recording the quality of small metal castings.

Photomicrography

Most branches of science use microscopes in combination with photographic equipment to record subjects too small for regular photography. These fall into two broad categories — optical types, using lenses and giving magnifications up to about × 2000, and electron microscopes, that use a fine beam of electrons to scan the subject, producing magnifications of × 100,000 and greater.

Optical photomicrography
The equipment required comprises a light source, the microscope itself, and a camera body attached to the eyepiece. You can fit any size camera body from 5 × 4 in (12.5 × 10 cm) to 35 mm, but the SLR is the most convenient type for viewing and focusing. The TTL meter is usually accurate, although many microscopes designed with photography in mind have their own built-in light-measuring device. This is essential when working with larger-format sheet- and rollfilm cameras.

Both the preparation of the specimen and its lighting are of key importance. Transparent and translucent specimens, such as organic materials, oils, dyes, or any subject to be shown in silhouette, require illumination by transmitted light from below. Opaque specimens, such as metals or rocks, should be lit

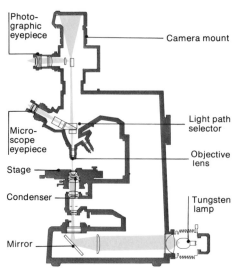

Microscope and camera adaptor
When the adaptor is attached (above) you view the image through a seperate focusing eyepiece. A selector allows the light to pass to eye piece, film plane, exposure meter, or color temperature meter.

Brightfield illumination
Light from the lamp passes through the condenser (right) which concentrates the rays and sends them straight through the subject on the stage to the microscope objective. This produces a characteristic light background (below).

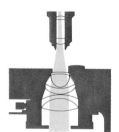

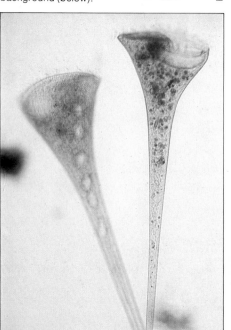

Darkfield illumination
An opaque stop in the condenser (right) directs the light around the edges of the specimen. Light spills obliquely toward the subject from all sides. Only rays deflected from the subject itself reach the microscope objective, giving a dark background (below).

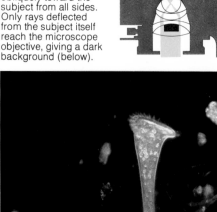

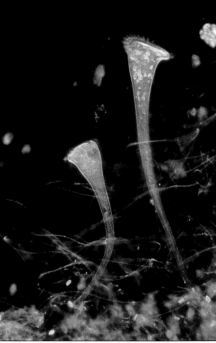

from the viewing direction. You can do this by directing light down the microscope, so that it shares the same axis as the objective lens. Both of these are known as "brightfield" illumination techniques.

A different arrangement, known as "darkfield" illumination, lights the specimen obliquely from all sides. The light may come from below the specimen, but is blocked off in a circular area immediately behind it. This gives the specimen a dark background, but light from outside this zone spills in, to pick out small raised details in the subject.

You can also use darkfield illumination for opaque subjects. Light conveyed down the microscope's optical system emerges around the lens (or "objective") like illumination from a ring lamp. Because the subject is so close to the objective, the light comes from the edge of the subject, picking out the variations in its surface very clearly. Optical microscopes give

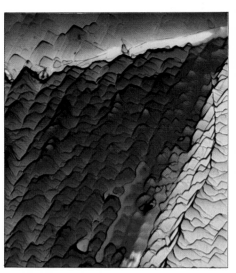

Polarized photomicrograph
The photograph of the vitamin histidine (above) was taken with a camera attached to an optical microscope. The photographer achieved a magnification of × 63. Polarized illumination made the different constituents of the substance show up in color.

very shallow depth of field. Translucent specimens therefore must be prepared as thin, flat sections sandwiched between thin layers of glass. It is impossible to render subjects such as rocks, metals, or crystals sharply overall, unless they are flat and smooth. The higher the magnification, the more acute this problem becomes and the more scientists turn to electron microscopes.

Electron photomicrography
The characteristics of light itself — especially diffraction will determine the magnification limits of an optical microscope. Light rays spread slightly when passing the edge of an aperture or an opaque, sharp-edged object. Long wavelengths show greatest diffraction, but even with the shortest visible wavelengths, it is impossible to resolve subject details smaller than about one micron (0.001 mm). A

microscope that uses invisible electrons instead of light overcomes this problem. When energized by a charge of several thousand volts, electrons behave like light of extremely short wavelengths. It is also possible to control them, using electromagnets in place of the optical microscope's glass lenses.

The first electron microscope, built in 1932, worked by transmission. Its electromagnetic "lenses" focused the electron beam in a way similar to that in which an optical lens focuses light. In the 1950s an improved type, the scan-

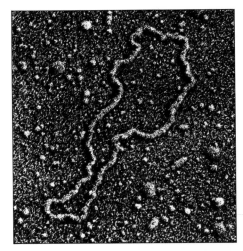

ning electron microscope (SEM), was introduced. It works by bombarding and detecting electrons from one tiny point on the specimen at a time. Scan coils program the beam so that it follows a set pattern, crossing the subject like the spot of light on a television tube. Focus is continuously adjusted as the beam moves over the subject's surface, so that depth of field

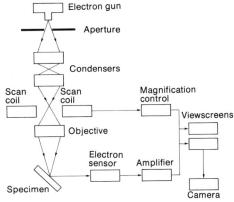

The scanning electron microscope
A condenser forms an electron spot that scans the surface of the specimen. A sensor collects the electrons reflected from the subject, and converts them into an electrical signal. This is then amplified and presented to a cathode ray tube.

is much greater than with an optical microscope. Subject brightness is also rendered faithfully, since each scanning point is shown as a similar point on a television-type viewing screen, where the image appears in black and white. At the end of a complete scan, a full image appears on the screen.

It is possible to record the image by attaching a camera and macro lens over a parallel display tube and exposing long enough to capture a single scan. This tube is a flat-faced, high-resolution type, often using 2000 or more overlapping lines to make up the image. It gives a slow read-out, which the operator cannot read in its entirety, but when fully recorded on film its image is totally free of scan lines. The exposure time required is usually about 70 sec. Scientists often use instant picture material to record results. This is ideal when the outcome of one experiment determines the conditions for the next.

The SEM produces the greatest magnifications at present available (some models offer enlargements of up to six million times, although with loss of image quality), and provides extensive depth of field. This results in a very realistic image, and allows the use of complete specimens instead of slides.

To prevent electrons colliding with air molecules, the microscope interior must be kept in a state of vacuum. This, together with the instrument's complex controls, means that it is very expensive. An additonal drawback is that specimens must be "fixed" chemically.

DNA molecule
The loop-shaped subject (above) is DNA — the substance that transmits genetic information from one living cell to another. Stanley N. Cohen and his team of researchers at Stanford University used a scanning electron microscope to enlarge the subject about 250,000 times. Cohen produced the image during his important series of genetic experiments in 1973, in which he combined DNA molecules from two unrelated bacteria, to give one of these substances new characteristics.

Weevil
This image of a corn weevil was taken with a scanning electron microscope, to give a magnification of × 75. The picture shows clearly the electron microscope's impressive depth of field, producing the three-dimensional image quality quite different to that of the optical microscope.

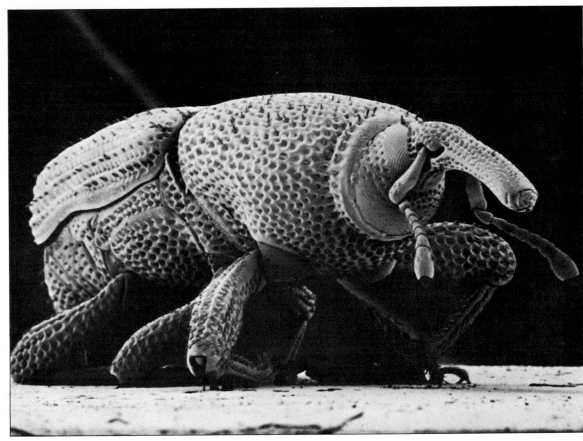

Miniaturizing the subject

Microphotography is the exact opposite of photomicrography: the photographer produces an extremely small image of a much larger object. The technique is useful for miniaturizing documents to save storage space. It is also invaluable in the manufacture of scientific equipment — making hair-line graticules for optical sighting and viewfinding, and producing scales for instruments. Another use of microphotography is for miniaturizing text and illustrations, so that a large amount of information can be stored in a very small space. The text is reproduced on microfilm and read in a magnifying display unit. Microphotography's widest application is in making electronic circuits with up to half a million components per square inch.

The originals for all these applications are two-dimensional. Microphotography is essentially a copying process, dealing with black and white originals, either printed or drawn. A high-resolution macro lens is essential and the

Producing microcircuitry
Complex microcircuitry (shown here magnified × 70) is reduced photographically from original drawings. It is then printed on a high-resolution negative. Light-sensitive silicon is exposed to this image, and further processes turn the result into a network of electrically conductive channels.

main technical challenge is to focus the tiny image accurately.

For the production of graticules, and similar purposes, the photographer forms an image on a high-resolution plate. The plate is extremely slow and insensitive to red, so it is possible to clamp it, emulsion side down, to the stage of a horizontally positioned microscope in the darkroom. The camera lens can then form its image on the emulsion surface from behind the stage. You check its sharpness by viewing the back of the plate through the microscope using it in a similar way to an enlarger focus magnifier.

To produce micro-circuits, the designer begins with a master drawing about 20 ins (50 cm) square, reducing this to 1/500 of its size on a microcopying camera. A composite image is then produced on a high-resolution negative, repeating this original several hundreds of times. This image is then projected on light-sensitive silicon. Chemical processes later alter the silicon's electrical characteristics, and build up deposits that form the components of each circuit.

Revealing the invisible

Research and development work often involves examining properties of a subject that are not normally apparent to the human eye. These range from air flows around objects moving at high speed, to internal strains in certain structures. It is often useful to show these properties in contrasting colors, since the eye distinguishes color differences more readily and clearly than tone differences.

Radiography

The use of X rays, gamma rays, and charged particles to form shadow images on photographic materials is known as radiography. Industrial scientists use radiography to detect cavities in metal castings, fatigue cracks inside engines, and other hidden weaknesses in metal structures. Radiography is also widely used in medical diagnosis (see *Radiography,* p. 286). Unlike light, it is impossible to refract or reflect these types of radiation using a mirror or a lens. They also have the well-known ability to pass through visually opaque objects, penetrating some substances more than others. The higher a substance's atomic weight, the more X rays it will block. Lead's high atomic weight therefore makes it an ideal X ray shield.

With the source of radiation placed on one side of the subject, the scientist tapes X ray film in a thin metal holder to the other side. Highly penetrating rays are generally used — the health hazard present in medical radiography with strong radiation need not be a problem. Most industrial researchers use either "hard" (short-wave) X rays, generated within a tube by bombarding metal with an electron gun, or the even more penetrating gamma rays given off by radioactive isotopes.

In more specialized work, it is possible to use a beam of neutrons from a nuclear reactor to form shadow images. The radiation produced has largely opposite penetration properties to X rays, passing through dense materials such as lead, but not through lightweight hydrogen and carbon molecules. It is therefore possible to use neutrography and radiography as complementary test techniques for analyzing objects made of a mixture of diverse materials.

To improve the response of the double-coated photographic emulsions used for radiography, scientists often use an intensifying screen. This consists of a thin sheet of lead foil placed in direct contact with the emulsion. Radiation causes the screen to emit light or secondary electrons. The screen itself therefore creates the latent image in the sensitive emulsion.

All radiographic work requires specially trained personnel, because of the potential

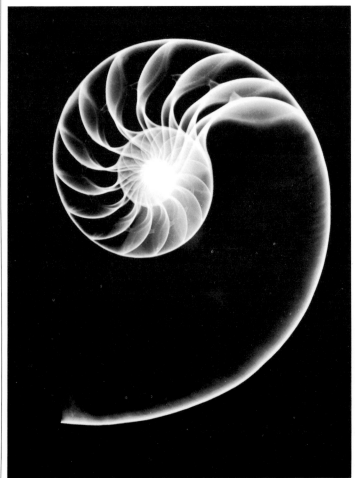

The structure of a shell
The X ray photograph (left) illustrates the internal divisions of a shell. Radiography is invaluable to scientists who want to study objects, such as cast and welded structures, that it is difficult or impossible to examine internally.

Using a wind tunnel
Engineers used a wind tunnel to test the aerodynamic performance of the automobile (right). Designers aim for high aerodynamic efficiency, to reduce drag and give lower fuel consumption. Air passes from the front of the vehicle toward the back. The engineer introduces a jet of visible gas at the front of the vehicle. (The gas tube is visible on the right-hand side of the picture.) The gas passes over the vehicle, and any disruptions in the flow show places where the body is interrupting the air, causing drag. This production model shows the low wind tunnel turbulence characteristic of a modern aerodynamic automobile design.

danger to human life from these sources. Interpretation of the results also calls for great skill and experience.

X ray diffraction

X rays are useful to researchers identifying the atomic structures of crystals. In addition, they are especially valuable in the development of new alloys, and the study of metal fatigue in items such as engines.

A very narrow beam of X rays is allowed to strike a crystal placed on the surface of photographic film. The crystal's internal network of individual atoms diffracts the X rays, scattering their path. The effect is similar to a beam of light striking a hanging crystal ball, and forming a larger pattern of brilliant highlights on the ceiling and walls around it.

The processed film records a complex pattern of black dots. Each arrangement of atoms forms a different characteristic pattern, so that although the atoms themselves remain unseen, the scientist can compare and analyze their arrangement in the crystal.

Aerodynamics and hydrology

Most big engineering projects, from new automobile or aircraft designs to proposed harbors, bridges, and tall buildings, are tested extensively in model form. Wind tunnels or water tanks are the tools used for testing the effects of anticipated air or water flow. The method of showing the flow can be very simple. If tufts of cotton are attached to the test surface in a wind tunnel at regular intervals, these act like miniature flags, blowing in different directions to reveal the air currents. To give a continuous record of the air flow over an object, it is also possible to use jets of colored gas. Eddies and interruptions in the path of the gas indicate points on the subject where air flow is interrupted.

In a water tank it is possible to reveal surface currents by using floating candles. To monitor

ripples or small wave patterns, a method known as the "starry sky" technique is sometimes employed. A grid carrying a large number of small lamps is clamped high above the water. The photographer makes a time exposure of the changing reflections to record the wave patterns.

In all these cases it is essential to choose carefully the duration and also the frequency

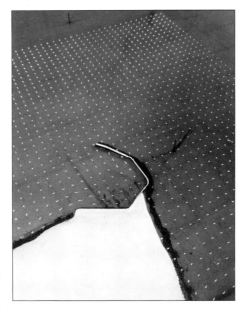

The "starry sky" technique
The pattern of light trails (above) is the reflection of a grid of lights suspended from the ceiling above the model of a proposed coastal development.

The varying shapes recorded during a time exposure demonstrate clearly how wave patterns change as a result of the extended sand bar and coastline.

of the exposures, particularly in relation to subject movement. A series of regular, brief exposures shows up changes in subject position, while a longer, single exposure shows each movement as an elongated track.

Polarized light

In additon to its uses in general photography (see *Copying*, p. 171, and *Polarizing filters*. p. 198) polarized light can form a simple but revealing scientific tool. Its two main applications are in analyzing the stresses in structures, and in polarized photomicrography. Both techniques use the property of "birefringence".

A birefringent material has the ability to divide a beam of polarized light into two parallel beams, polarized at right angles, with one traveling faster than the other. If the two beams are recombined, for example, by passing them through a polarizing filter, interference between the two merging beams creates colors. For example, a crinkled sheet of clear plastic, placed between two polarizing filters, shows yellow and cyan coloring. The lines and colors that appear in this way denote the presence of stresses in the plastic.

To make a photo-elastic analysis of an engineering structure or building support beam, the scientist constructs a model in clear, unstressed birefringent plastic. This is then set up between two polarizing filters and placed under stress with sets of weights and clamps.

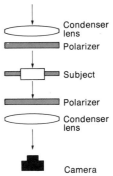

Using polarized light
A parallel light beam passes through the subject. When the two polarizers are crossed, no light can pass through the system. As the light penetrates the birefringent specimen, the single plane polarized light divides into two planes of polarization, aligned with the subjects' main stress areas. The second polarizer passes one plane, so stress patterns appear.

Condenser lens
Polarizer
Subject
Polarizer
Condenser lens
Camera

Photographs taken with the model unstressed show no change in image color. But as the strain on the model increases, bands of color appear, gradually increasing in their number and brightness. It is possible to identify the parts of the structure most vulnerable to stress by their greater concentration of these interference patterns.

A similar arrangement can be used in photomicrography to reveal colors in crystals, and so greatly increase the information about their structure and identity. The method is suitable for both transmitted and reflected light setups. In a transmitted light microscope, the polarizing filters must be placed below the stage and near the eyepiece. They are crossed in relation to each other, so that only light affected by the birefringent specimen is visible. Turning either one of the filters or the subject changes the colors.

With both stress analysis and polarized photomicrography it is possible to add a

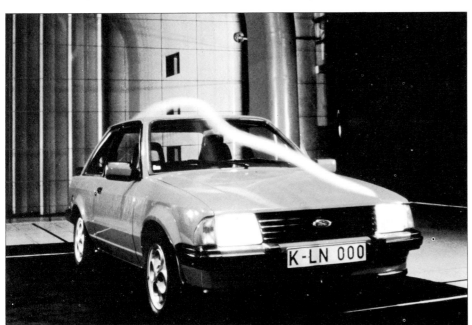

further component — a retardation plate — between the subject and the viewing polarizing filter. This helps to slow down the two birefringent light beams, to give stronger, more brilliant colors in the final image.

Bubble chamber photography
A bubble chamber consists of a tank containing liquid helium. Research physicists use this device in the study of sub-atomic particles. A particle accelerator — a tubular ring encircled by electromagnets — builds up a flow of fast-moving, minute particles in the tank. These are directed at a "target", which may be metal, or

Recording cosmic rays
The particle tracks (right and below) were produced by scientists using a large bubble chamber at the CERN laboratories in Switzerland. They illustrate the effects of cosmic rays — high-speed particles and energy that bombard the earth from outer space. To produce these results, a particularly powerful ray collided with a molecule outside the frame, making over one hundred particles of atomic debris pass through the chamber. The resulting vapor trails appear on the image as lines.

a number of other particles moving in the opposite direction.

The collision occurs in a large, glass-walled tank containing liquid helium at an extremely low temperature. As the minute, invisible nuclear particles stream into the tank, they lower the liquid pressure so that expansion takes place and minute visible gas bubbles form, like vapor trails behind an aircraft. Wherever one particle strikes and splits another these tracks show the creation of still smaller, sub-atomic particles, some of which only last for a tiny fraction of a second.

The photographer's task is to record these

interactions accurately, usually in three dimensions. Two or three cameras are used simultaneously from separate positions and the bubble chamber is edge-lit by extremely brief electronic flash, often with a darkfield arrangement — a scaled-up version of this type of microscope illumination (see *Photomicrography,* pp. 278-9). The camera's different viewpoints allow stereo viewing of the results and exact plotting of each collision in three-dimensional space.

Precise camera positioning and total film flatness (best achieved with a vacuum film holder) are vital to permit precise measurements. For this reason, too, it is necessary to filter the light source, so that it produces a narrow band of wavelengths giving minimal chromatic spread and dispersion. Results are usually in black and white.

Certain apparatus for detecting the collision of particles uses a glass chamber filled with neon and helium gas in an electric field. Colliding particles form tiny luminous streamers in the gas. These are barely visible to the naked eye, but recorded on film through an image intensifier (see *Surveillance and inspection,* pp. 288-9) their brightness increases by a factor of about two thousand.

Schlieren photography
Schlieren photography provides a method of making visible air or gas currents, or vapors of different temperatures, because of differences in the way they refract light. It was originally devised to detect irregularities in clear optical glass. Modern uses range from recording air flow in wind tunnels and gas jets from nozzles,

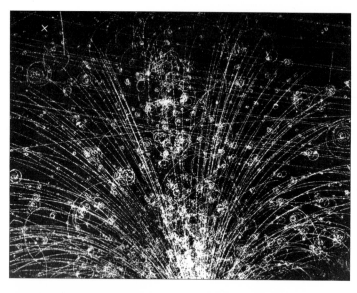

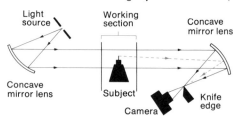

The principle of Schlieren photography
As light rays pass through a subject of varying density they are refracted and deflected past, or into, the knife edge stop.

Image brightness therefore corresponds to variations in refractive index, and to subject density.

to the analysis of shock waves in ballistics. The effect produced shows the vapor darker than its surroundings. It is also possible to make different gases appear colored, so that the variations have strongly contrasting hues. A primitive form of schlieren occurs when hard sunlight passes through air rising above a domestic radiator, casting smoke-like shadows on a far wall.

In schlieren photography, hard light illuminates the subject from the rear. (In wind tunnel work, the light passes through a pair of optical windows across the airflow). A mirror or large lens focuses the light beam to a point, and the photographer also focuses a camera on this point to record the effect.

If the air around the subject shows any variations of refractive index (see *Additional*

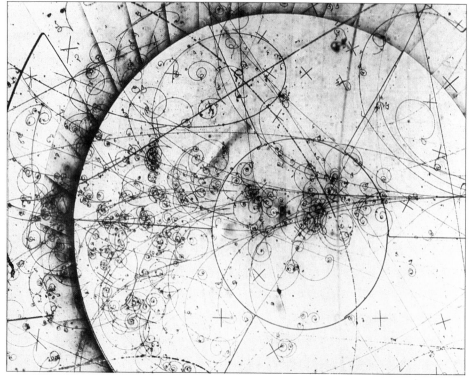

equipment, pp. 184-5), some of the light rays will be slightly displaced. (With an atmosphere that has a uniform refractive index, the camera will show a clean silhouette image.) A knife edge or color filter placed close to the light beam will cause the displaced rays either to appear black to the camera, or to pass through the filter and become colored.

The challenge for the photographer is to adjust the filter or knife edge effectively, giving the system its greatest sensitivity, without creating unevenness. Very fast shutter speeds are often necessary, and for moving subjects

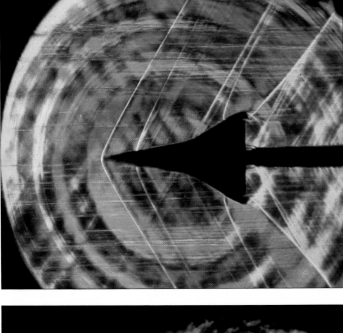

such as liquid sprays, flash may be essential.

When a color filter is used for the schlieren process, false color images result. These allow the scientist to detect variations in the subject very easily. For example, gases of different temperatures will show up clearly in contrasting colors, and, in wind-tunnel work, variations in air density around moving objects are easy to see. For utmost sensitivity, it is important to use high-quality lenses that are free from chromatic aberration. For this reason, scientists often use mirror systems (see *Catadioptric lenses,* p. 191).

Applications of Schlieren photography
Schlieren pictures (left and below) have many uses. The vivid illustration of the air flow round the model of an airplane (left) was produced by combining Schlieren and wind tunnel techniques. The photograph records the differences in refraction and pressure in air that is traveling at different speeds and in various directions. Schlieren photography is therefore used widely in aerodynamic research. It is also useful in showing the heat patterns created by apparatus such as gas jets (below). These results can be helpful in designing the most efficient components in a wide range of products, from domestic heating to auto engines.

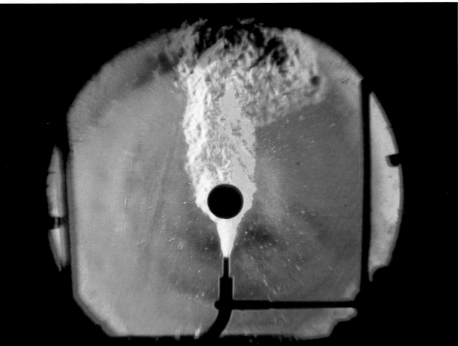

Kirlian photography

This branch of photography, named after its inventor Semyon Kirlian, is a form of image-making that is controversial, because it also seems to involve parapsychology. Kirlian photography is a method of recording the "auras", or invisible energy forms, which are thought to emanate from many objects, particularly living organisms.

The special Kirlian camera sandwiches the subject against a sheet of photographic film or paper between two electrodes. An electrical system passes high-voltage (but low-current) electricity to the electrodes for about one or two seconds. When the material is processed, it shows an image that displays either a flared outline of the subject, as if glowing, or a pattern

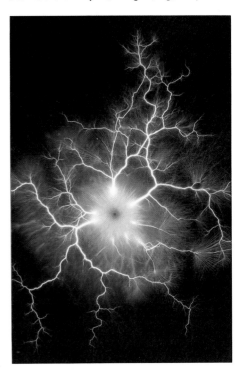

The Kirlian image
The dramatic image (above) was created with a Kirlian camera, by dropping a steel ball on to a sheet of color film in a high-energy electronic field. Scientists are researching the use of Kirlian photography for locating cracks in metal.

that resembles static electricity originating from the subject's center.

Subjects can be plants, seeds, or parts of the human body, particularly finger tips. Advocates claim that Kirlian images can help distinguish non-germinating from good seed, detect metal fatigue, and even offer a means of diagnosing cancer. Others argue that perspiration, aerial humidity, and temperature adequately account for the results. The colors formed on photographic paper differ with every emulsion. Kirlian pictures vary widely, especially with living subjects, and it is difficult to assess their practical usefulness. But extensive research will enable scientists to make a more accurate appraisal of Kirlian photography's value.

Holography

Holography is a method of producing three-dimensional photographic images without using a camera. It is useful in all fields that require a three-dimensional record of a subject, and for the detailed scanning of inaccessible subjects, such as the interiors of nuclear reactors. It is also invaluable in the production of optical components, and in stress analysis.

The essential equipment for holography is a laser. This produces "coherent" light, with all rays running parallel, limited to one wavelength, and with all the crests and dips of their waveform in unison. In the most common layout, a semi-silvered mirror splits the laser beam in two. One beam illuminates the subject, while the other illuminates a large glass plate coated with light-sensitive emulsion. Exposure takes place in a darkened room, with both equipment and subject secured in place.

During exposure, which usually lasts for about 10 sec, light reflected from the subject toward the plate acts like ripples spreading across water. Where it meets the beam of direct light waves at the emulsion surface, interference occurs. Minute fringes record on the plate, and, when developed, it shows a fine, abstract pattern of lines. After fixing, the

Producing holograms

The parallel (or "coherent") light waves from a laser are split in two. One beam lights the subject, the other acts as a reference beam and passes through a lens to the film. The light in the reference beam remains coherent, while the illumination reflected from the subject has random waveforms. This creates an interference pattern on a photographic plate, producing the image.

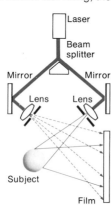

photographer bleaches the silver, leaving an image in etched gelatin.

To view the completed hologram, oblique rear illumination from a laser is necessary. Looking through the glass you see a complete three-dimensional monochrome reconstruction of the original scene. Unlike other stereo images, the hologram plate gives an image that changes appreciably depending on the viewer's position. For example, looking through the glass from a high angle, you can see areas behind near objects in the scene that become obscured when you view the hologram from lower down. It is possible to view most holograms accurately by any point light source, such as direct sunlight, or a distant spotlight. It helps to filter the spotlight, to reduce its range of wavelengths.

The main value of holograms in science and technology is their realism and detail. Images resemble models more than photographs. It is also possible to make schlieren holograms (see *Revealing the invisible,* pp. 280-3) in which shock waves, or mixtures of gases, record as solid forms. A powerful pulsed laser allows shorter exposures for photomicrographic holograms of living organisms.

Periphery photography

One of the most difficult aspects of record photography is to show the entire outer or inner surface of a cylindrical object. The first attempts to do this accurately were made in the late nineteenth century, when officials at the British Museum, London, wanted to photograph the decorated surfaces of Greek vases. More recently, applications of periphery photography have spread to industry, where scientists use the technique for analysis of wear of pistons, gear wheels, and fuel rods,

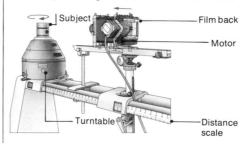

The photography of cylindrical objects

The periphery camera (above) has a turntable conected to a moving film back. As the turntable revolves, the film travels at the same rate, giving an accurate record of the entire surface. This makes it possible to record objects such as antique vases (below) and mechanical components such as cylinders. The photograph of a flame tube (bottom) shows the areas (outlined in black) where the heat has been most intense.

and for assessing heat patterns in gas tubes. A camera designed to do this work produces one continuous photograph detailing the full cylindrical surface.

The subject is placed centrally on a horizontal revolving turntable. To record the surface, the photographer uses a sheet film camera with a specially designed film back that slowly moves a piece of film sideways behind a fixed slit. The motors that rotate the turntable and move the film are linked, so that the film takes the same time to travel from side to side as the subject does to turn through 360°.

The photographer lights the face of the subject nearest the lens (the only one viewed at any one time) to emphasize important detail. Provided that subject and film movement are geared correctly, a time exposure, during which the subject rotates completely, should give an undistorted record.

If the subject has deep cavities or sharp protrusions, some distortions will occur, since these areas will move at a slightly different speed from the film. Complete objectivity only occurs with a truly cylindrical subject. To record the inner surface of a hollow cylinder, the photographer points the camera into the subject and uses the swing back camera movement (see *Improving depth of field,* pp. 122-3) to keep the film vertical. If the interior of the subject is very narrow, the photographer can reduce the turntable speed by half, in order to produce a larger negative of the object's inner surface.

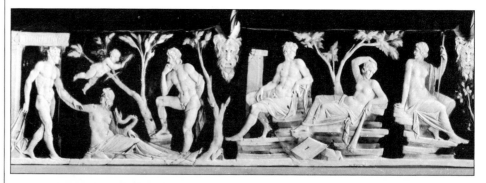

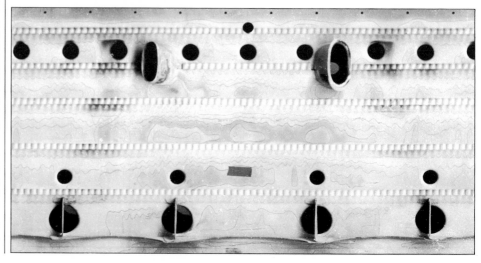

Medical and forensic photography

Photographers who work for hospitals and police forces have similar aims and often use the same techniques. Both fields use photography to reveal a subject's salient features, without distortion or misleading embellishments. It often takes great skill to show the information with the utmost clarity, and provide accurate documentation.

The final results are important documents. For doctors, they may confirm or disprove a diagnosis, while in a court of law they can provide the crucial evidence that proves a suspect's innocence or guilt. The photographer therefore has great responsibility, though much of the work is routine.

Medical and forensic photography have a history almost as long as photography itself, because pioneers soon recognized the new medium's accuracy as a means of recording detail. In 1840 the Parisian daguerreotype photographer Alfred Donne started to use a microscope to record teeth and bones. With the coming of the wet collodion process in 1851, several European hospitals began to keep comparative medical records in photographic form. In Switzerland, police also started to use photography at this time for identity purposes, and a few years later the governors of several British jails began to keep photographic records of all their prisoners.

Medical photography
Doctors use photography to aid diagnosis, monitor the effects of treatment, and to record the techniques of surgery and specimens of all kinds. These applications call for ultraviolet or infrared lighting to pick out cells or areas of infection, or the use of an endoscope to take pictures deep inside the human body. Images are sometimes made by means of heat or high-frequency sound.

Radiography has a wide range of applications, often in combination with X ray scanning devices that provide cross-section images of the living body. The medical photographer requires experience of most of these techniques, together with knowledge of human anatomy and clinical procedure.

Forensic photography
The forensic photographer provides evidence for most serious police cases. This covers detailed pictures of accident and crime scenes, records of injuries and stolen goods, and identity pictures. Forged or burnt documents may require photographing with infrared or ultraviolet techniques to reveal hidden details. Footwear impressions, fingerprints, and stains on clothes can call for painstaking macro and photomicrographic techniques.

See also
Manipulating film response *Special black and white films*, p. 157. Special color films, p. 159. Special effects lighting *Ultraviolet lighting*, p. 183. Scientific and technical photography *Equipment and techniques*, p. 274; *Revealing the invisible*, pp. 280-3.

Equipment and techniques

Both medical and forensic work involve some use of the latest image-recording devices, but a great number of functions still require only conventional camera equipment. Macro facilities are especially important. For work within the laboratory, most photographers use a 5 × 4 ins (12.5 × 10 cm) sheet film camera set on a bench column stand. When conditions permit, forensic photographers cover a great deal of "scene-of-crime" work with sheet film cameras. They use 35 mm cameras largely for color slides. Usually the subjects allow sets of identical transparencies, exposed at one time, giving better quality than duplicates.

Flash is an important light source. In police work on location it is often useful to help "fill in" daylight for maximum detail. Flash can also act as a hard, oblique light to emphasize abrasions, tire marks, and similar details. In medical photography too, flash gives consistent color, and is more comfortable for patients than tungsten lamps, with their high temperature. The ability of flash to freeze movement is invaluable.

To ensure accuracy of color rendition, it is often useful to include a scale of color patches alongside the subject. In black and white work, color filters or orthochromatic film are often required. Both can help emphasize differences in color – for example, when the main subject is pale in color against a flat, background.

Tasks such as the copying of fingerprints, which usually require images the same size as their subjects, may be undertaken so frequently that it is best to use an automatic camera system. This can be a specially-built unit, similar to a passport camera (see *Special cameras*, p. 208), or any regular camera adapted to fixed-focus close ups, with a spacing bracket to ensure correct subject distance (see *Technical aids*, p. 197).

A forensic photographer must always be mobile. Usually this means having transport pre-packed with basic camera kits, lighting, tripods, and a ladder for high shots.

Record photography

Straightforward records of accessible parts of the body and items of evidence work best against plain, contrasting tone backgrounds. Lighting must emphasize the most relevant details. To increase the amount of useful information in the picture, the photographer usually includes distance, tone, or color scales beside the subject.

The forensic photographer often has to demonstrate how two pieces of evidence fit together. For example, a chip of paint found on an assault victim may make an edge and color match with a scratched area on the bodywork of a suspect's car. Similarly, the plaster cast of a shoe impression at the scene of a crime can be shown alongside the corresponding part of the suspect's footwear.

To make fingerprints show up clearly, the investigator must dust them with powder. Black, white, gray, and fluorescent substances are used, the choice depending on which shows up best against the surface where the prints are found. When it is impossible to remove objects for photography in the studio, fingerprints often cause lighting problems. Prints on window glass may be best side-lit against a dark background. Prints left on strongly patterned or printed surfaces are especially difficult to photograph. Filters in conjunction with black and white film provide the best way of subduing an obtrusive design. The photographer views the subject through a range of filters to find the one that shows up the fingerprint most clearly.

One of the most valuable forensic routines is crime-scene photography. At the initial stages of investigation, significant details may not be evident, although later they may be vitally important. When a serious crime has occurred, a record of the entire area is required, showing it exactly as it was found after the event. It is essential to do this before investigations start to disturb the scene. With indoor crimes, police photographers record rooms from two or three corners, to show their entire contents. This may call for several flash heads (see *Using multihead flash*, p. 178) used to give both direct and bounced lighting. Close-ups of important details are then taken, but these are photographed so that the viewer can relate them to the whole scene. Forensic photographers use standard and wide-angle lenses. Long lenses are required far less often.

Medical photographers often use straight recording techniques to show specimens in jars. Knowledge of antisepsis, and the effects preserving fluids have on color appearance are necessary, and the photographer must use filters to make color appear natural.

Footprint and shoe comparisons
It is often possible to match pictures of footprints at the scene of a crime (above left) with a suspect's shoe (above right). Arrows on the photograph of the shoe mark the main points of comparison – the signs of wear on the heel and sole. In this case the image of the footprint was so clear that it was also possible to match the pattern of the socks worn by the suspect with the visible impression

Radiography

Images formed from X ray wavelengths use the technique known as radiography. "Soft", or short-wave, X rays have been used in medicine since soon after the discovery of X rays in 1895. Their main use is diagnostic — revealing conditions inside the patient's body.

Unlike industrial work (see *Revealing the invisible,* pp. 280-3), X ray intensity and exposure duration must be kept to a minimum in diagnostic work. An additional problem is that X rays can only cast shadows. Radiographers have devised a number of methods to reveal maximum body information within these limitations. For example, soft organs, such as the stomach, appear much more clearly visible if the patient drinks a "meal" containing substances opaque to X rays, like barium. Injections of iodine trace solutions make organs such as the kidney and the urinary tract visually separable from surrounding tissues.

Tomography

The human body consists of an overlapping mixture of bones, organs, and tissue. Tomography provides a radiographic method of revealing organs that are normally shielded by other parts, blurring irrelevant detail. First the

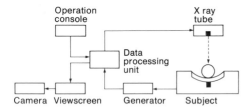

Scanning the body

The patient is positioned between the X ray tube and the detectors (above). Readings from the detector pass to a computer. This correlates them and converts them to an image, which the operator examines on a viewing console, recording the image with a camera. In tomography, the X

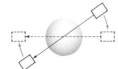

ray tube and detectors turn in the same direction around the subject (above) to make a cross-sectional scan.

radiographer estimates how deep inside the body the important area lies. Both the X ray tube, and the X ray film behind the patient, are programed to move in opposite directions, pivoting about this point.

Judged correctly, the shadows of the important detail remain on the same part of the film throughout the exposure, whereas everything at other distances is blurred because of movement. Results are similar to an image using differential focus.

The principle of tomography is also used in body scanning, to provide even more information about the subject. Tomography, a computer, and a photographic output combine to produce an image of a complete "slice" of a patient's body. The patient lies inside a frame while a fan-shaped beam of X rays is projected through the body to a line of about 30 detectors. Each detector feeds a density reading to a computer memory. Every reading corresponds to the energy absorbed by the body at that point. The whole frame rotates in stages through 180°, making exposures through the body at every 10°, over a period of about 20 seconds. Altogether, the scanner takes approximately three hundred thousand density readings in this time, and the computer relates these to the angles of exposure to build up a total image of a single "slice" through the body. This large number of density readings ensures an image of much higher definition than a conventional X ray picture. It is this excellent image quality that makes the process particularly suitable for brain scanning, where soft tissue is enclosed in a hard, more opaque bone structure.

A high-resolution cathode ray tube displays the final result, and the radiographer uses instant picture or regular film to photograph the scan. As with heat scanning (see *Thermography,* p. 287) it is possible to code areas of different density, so that the various organs of the body, and the diseased areas, are clearly distinguished. The use of a cathode ray tube has other advantages. The system allows the image to be recorded and instantly played back, increasing examination time without using extra radiation. Contrast control is also easy with the cathode ray tube.

Computerized tomography

The color body scan (left) was taken with computerized tomographic equipment. The initial X ray scan produced a black and white image, which doctors then color coded. Fats and fluids appear red and muscle tissue blue or green. Bones are coded pink and mauve. It is possible to produce this type of result quickly with a computer, and subsequent photography can provide a permanent record. The computer can also display data such as the time and details of the scan, and a key.

Using ultraviolet

In both medical and forensic work, it is often necessary to reveal subject details that are not apparent to the eye. Often invisible ultraviolet (UV) radiation provides the answer. All photographic materials are sensitive to these wavelengths, which are present in sunlight, as well as in the radiation from "black light" type fluorescent tubes and lamps.

It is possible to use UV in two ways — directly, to show how different parts of a subject reflect these wavelengths, or to make the subject glow visibly and record this fluorescent appearance on film.

UV reflectance

With direct reflected UV photography, a visually black, UV-transmitting filter is used over the lens during exposure, so that the only parts of the subject to record are the UV-reflective areas. It is possible to use any black and white film: color film has no advantage, since results are monochromatic.

In medical work, UV reflectance is useful to dermatologists, because it reveals certain differences in skin conditions. The pigment in normal skin absorbs UV, but some skin diseases cause de-pigmentation. This effect is too subtle to record in regular photographs, but shows up clearly in a UV picture. The affected areas appear starkly white.

UV reflectance can also be a worthwhile technique for the forensic photographer to use on documents. Sometimes faded or altered lettering shows up boldly against the different UV-reflective properties of the paper base. Printing on charred documents also shows up more clearly in UV radiation. In photomicrography, it is possible to benefit from UV's shorter wavelengths, because they are less prone to diffraction than light. Replacing light with UV radiation therefore improves image resolution appreciably.

UV fluorescence

Some materials emit visible light when subjected to UV radiation, and glow either white or in their own or another color. To achieve this effect, the photographer works in a darkened room, using lamps or flash units filtered to give out only UV. To record the fluorescence only (exactly as it appears to the eye) a clear, UV-absorbing filter over the camera lens is essential. Daylight film is usually used to record the various fluorescent tints.

The most common use of UV fluorescence in forensic photography is in detecting forgeries. In normal light there may be no visible signs of ink erasure and overwriting. But under a UV lamp, traces of the original ink (or patches where fluorescent characteristics have changed) show up clearly. Similarly, fingerprint traces on confusing multicolored or patterned surfaces are revealed when dusted with fluorescent powder and photographed with a UV set-up. On location, the most convenient source for this work is a pair of powerful electronic flash units filtered to emit only UV radiation.

UV fluorescence is also valuable in medical photomicrography. Structural details of tissues and cells appear with increased clarity if stained with substances that exhibit strong fluorescence. These bind to certain molecules more readily than others, but do not alter their structure in any way.

Differences in fluorescent color occur according to variations in the content of tissue, often in samples that appear uniform to the naked eye. The technique can therefore provide a way of distinguishing between malignant and non-malignant cells. The darkfield method of illumination (see *Photomicrography*, pp. 278-9) generally gives the clearest image of the specimen, using a high-pressure mercury lamp with a filter that passes only UV.

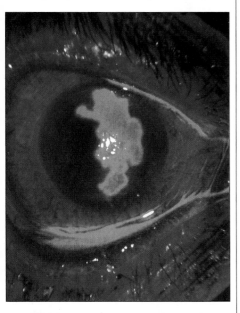

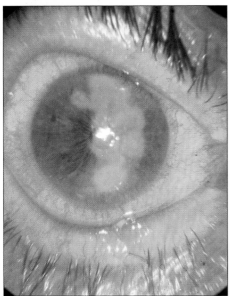

UV fluorescence photograph
The two pictures (above and top) show a dendritic ulcer of the cornea. The picture taken with UV fluorescence (top) shows the details of the ulcer with even greater clarity than the normal result on color film (above).

Thermography

Scanning a subject photographically to produce a representation of the heat it emits is a technique known as thermography. Infrared emulsions can record the temperatures of materials only between about 250° and 500°C. Objects at lower temperatures, such as the human body, emit medium or far-infrared radiation and are therefore outside the recording range of most IR photographic materials. Instead, the medical or forensic photographer can turn to thermal imaging devices that are electronic, but give a final photograph.

One form of thermal camera scans the subject point by point with a revolving mirror. This

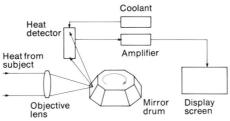

Heat scanning
An objective lens (above) gathers heat from the subject. A mirror on a rotating drum reflects the rays to a group of detectors, and these send a signal to an amplifier. The camera converts this signal to produce a visible image on a display screen, by means of a cathode ray tube. The mirrors on the drum are set at different angles, so that, as the drum turns (right), the camera scans a different zone of the subject. The camera's video circuitry gives a screen image.

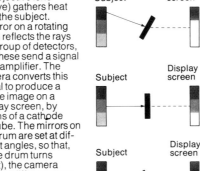

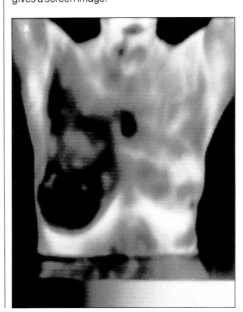

reflects each piece of IR information to a super-cooled detector cell, which converts the incoming radiation into a stream of electrical signals. These are fed to a color television tube. A temperature profile image appears displayed on the tube face, and the photographer can record this on color film.

The resulting picture represents variations in subject temperature by differences in image

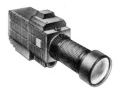

Thermographic camera
The heat camera (right) is small enough for surveillance photography. It produces a TV-type image, and it is possible to use the unit with a telescope.

brightness. Usually the electronics convert each tone on this "heat scale" so that it appears as a contrasting color on the screen. All parts showing the same color are equal in temperature so heat differences are clear.

Thermography allows the researcher to identify or analyze any warm object without direct contact. Medical photographers use this technique for the early detection of tumors and circulation disorders. It is possible to compare images with normal human heat patterns. Thermography can also measure the severity of burns, or show when a transplanted organ is functioning in the recipient's body.

The forensic photographer can also use thermal cameras. For detecting the previous presence of people, patches of slightly higher temperature left on carpets and other heat-absorbent materials can often be revealing.

Medical heat scanning
The heat pictures (below) show a tumor in a woman's breast. Because the growth is colder than the surrounding tissue, it stands out clearly in the black and white version (below left). The color-coded image (below right) gives an accurate display of temperatures on a scale from blue (cold) to white (hot).

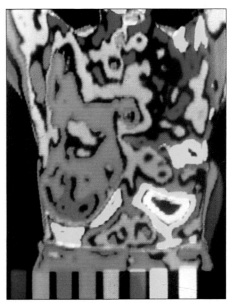

Using infrared

The main advantage of forming images with infrared (IR) is the radiation's penetrative power. The wavelengths most commonly used in forensic and medical photography are between 1 and 10 microns. These are known as the "near-infrared" wavelengths, because they are nearest to those in the visible spectrum. Only specially sensitized photographic materials respond to these wavelengths. Both black and white and color IR materials are available. Most respond only to the near-infrared wavelengths. Sensitivity to the middle and far bands (up to 1000 microns) would have few practical applications, since the photographer's body heat, or warmth from the camera itself, could fog the film. But there are a few materials that will respond to wavelengths up to 1000 microns.

Sources of IR include sunlight and all types of photographic lamps and flash units. Photographic lamps are a more effective source than IR sunlamps that mainly emit heat and far-infrared wavelengths.

Black and white techniques

An opaque filter that passes only IR radiation is essential when using black and white IR film. The photographer places this over either the camera lens or the light source. When using the filter on the lens, it is vital to focus first, or to use a distance scale to focus the camera. Whichever method of focusing is used, the focus distance setting must then be transferred to the IR setting on the lens barrel (see *Special black and white films,* p. 157).

In forensic work, IR is used extensively for copying documents, paintings, and all articles suspected of being forged or damaged. IR film often renders quite differently inks and pigments that look equally dark to the eye. Some inks become almost transparent. Others, non-reflective to IR, appear very dark. The police frequently deal with modified documents and paintings. If these have been altered or over-painted with a substance less opaque to IR than the original, the photograph will reveal the original appearance underneath.

IR photography can also clarify writing on documents that are too old, worn, or charred by burning to read. If the traces of the original ink are opaque to IR, and the base is IR reflective, the resulting picture may be easily readable. But this technique will only work if the document is still largely in one piece. Results vary with paper and ink types. Sometimes,

identifiable fingerprints have become clear on IR pictures of burnt documents.

The photography of IR luminance provides a variation on these detection tests. A lamp with a blue-green IR-absorbing filter is directed at the subject, and the camera photographs through a dark, IR-transmitting filter. With this technique only the lit subject areas that actually emit IR will record on film. The method is invaluable for distinguishing writing in one ball point pen from writing in another — something impossible by any other method.

Near-infrared wavelengths will also penetrate human skin to a depth of about 3 mm. This makes it possible to reveal the pattern of outer blood vessels. These show up as dark lines beneath the paler, translucent-looking flesh surface. Information from vein patterns is invaluable to doctors, indicating the development of cancer, vascular tumors, cirrhosis of the liver, and heart and varicose conditions hidden from normal vision and undetectable by X ray techniques.

Another important field for medical IR recording is the outer tissues of the eye. It allows the eye surgeon to "see through" opaque cataracts revealing the size and shape of the pupil. This information is essential for planning a corneal transplant.

Color techniques

Infrared color slide film (see *Special color films,* p. 159), generally used together with unfiltered electronic flash, offers even more information than black and white types. IR slide film combines emulsion that will record visible light, with IR sensitivity, so that a complex mixture of false colors records. Penetration is less marked than with black and white, but the extra visual contrast and separation given by colors often makes up for this.

IR color film can serve most medical applications, and often provides more useful results than black and white. In photomicrography, specimens such as red blood cells record in colors that vary with their oxygen content. For ophthalmology, IR color film enables the scientist to look into the eye and record the retina, even when the subject's eyeball is clouded with blood. This type of film is also useful to the forensic photographer. Pictures of tampered documents, and comparative shots to match fabrics or paint found on a suspect with similar items found at the scene of a crime, become still more definitive in color image form.

Surveillance and inspection

Low-light photography is frequently necessary in law enforcement, enabling the gathering of evidence without the suspect's knowledge. Techniques of medical inspection photography involve the introduction of both light source and optics into parts of the body that are not accessible to regular photographic equipment.

Endoscopy

An endoscope — a device that will convey an image along a tube — is ideal for pictures taken within inaccessible locations. With an endoscope it is possible to photograph inside the stomach of a living patient, or to record the interior of a closed room through its keyhole. For these types of shots, the photographer attaches the endoscope to an SLR, in place of the standard lens.

A common type of endoscope consists of a rigid tube a few millimeters wide and about 12 ins (30 cm) long. It has a small wide-angle lens at its tip, and contains relay lenses along its length that focus the image on the film. The rod will slip into small holes and straight tubes. For photography where there is no internal light, an endoscope with an outer covering of fiber optic strands is used. These convey the

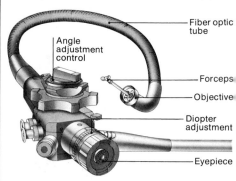

Fiber optic tube

Angle adjustment control

Forceps

Objective

Diopter adjustment

Eyepiece

The flexible endoscope
Doctors use the fiber optic endoscope (above) to examine internal organs, particularly the colon. The control at the eyepiece end allows the user to adjust the tip. The endoscopic image (below) shows the human esophagus. The light object in the lower right-hand corner is the anesthetist's tube, and the pale swelling is a vallecular cyst.

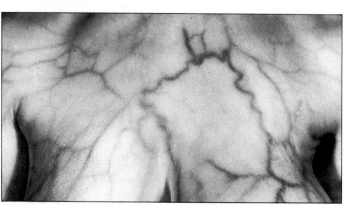

Medical infrared
The patient (left) suffered a benign growth in the left breast. Because the human skin is relatively transparent to the near infrared wavelengths, photography on IR film through an IR-passing filter shows the enlarged blood vessels several milimeters below the skin. This allows doctors to diagnose blood conditions, and to discover skin diseases before their effects show.

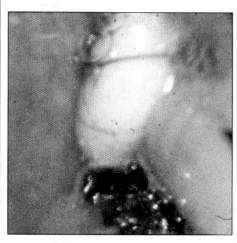

illumination from a bright tungsten lamp down to the tip of the endoscope.

For photography inside the digestive system, lungs, and bile duct, a thinner, flexible endoscope is required to pass along the curved passages. This device uses fiber optics to transmit the image itself. The lens at the tip forms an image on the ends of thousands of microscopic, tightly packed glass fibers. These have exactly the same pattern at each end of the tube, but are loose, and therefore flexible, along the middle. This means that each point of light trapped within its fiber makes up part of a recognizable image at the camera end of the endoscope, and here a second lens system copies it on film. The subject is lit by illumination from fiber optics around the edge of the tube. Because of their dot-type image formation, such endoscopes give poorer definition than straight designs, but they are much more versatile. It is possible to move them in any direction, and some types also enable the user to take tissue samples.

Surveillance

To photograph human subjects without them being aware of the photographer's presence, an electronic flash unit, covered with a filter that passes only infrared radiation, is ideal. It is then possible to take pictures on black and white IR film. Police photographers usually set up cameras at hidden vantage points, prefocusing them for a particular subject distance. The cameras are triggered by IR detectors, which sense the presence of a suspect.

Outdoors, and particularly with distant subjects, an image intensifier is sometimes used

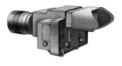 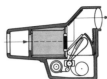

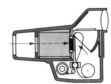

Surveillance camera
The camera (above) can produce images in very low light. At its heart is an image intensifier tube. The photographer examines the subject through a binocular viewer (above right). At the moment of exposure (right), the lower mirror moves out of the light path. The film springs forward, and presses against the fiber optic rear plate of the image intensifier tube. The resulting pictures are

Viewing

Exposing

valuable in surveillance work in the dark. The picture (below) was taken in starlight.

instead. This is a battery-powered, electronic device, placed between the camera body and telephoto lens, capable of amplifying image brightness several thousand times. It allows the photographer to take pictures by existing light, even on a moonless night, at exposures of 1/125 sec on regular black and white film. Starlight, or the streetlighting of a distant town reflected off cloud, is ample for identifiable portraits at 60 ft (18 m). The unit is similar in design to an image converter (see *Special-purpose, high-speed shutters,* p. 131). Other forms of surveillance units work by converting IR radiation into a bright, visible image. These are intended for use with a battery-powered IR searchlight with a narrow beam.

Forensic scientists also use computer image enhancement to improve poor quality images taken in difficult conditions. With a computer, it is possible to analyze the information, filter out irrelevant content, and produce a sharper, more detailed result. The most common system divides the image into points, treating each separately. The technology is similar to that used in astronomy (see *Photography and space exploration,* pp. 292-5).

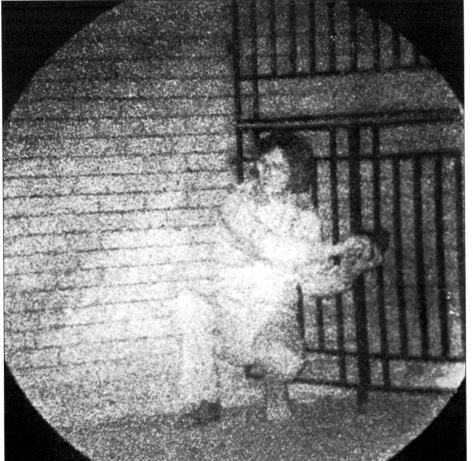

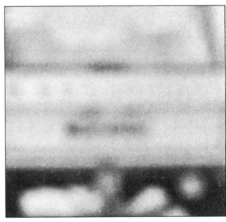

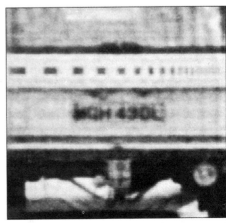

Reconstructing blurred images
Forensic scientists were able to reconstruct the blurred picture (top) using a computer to produce the result (above). Because of the computer's point-by-point enhancement, vital details of the vehicle license plate are now visible.

Isotope scanning and sonography

These techniques use small quantities of gamma radiation (wavelengths of 0.1-0.01 Ångstroms) for medical diagnosis. Photography is used only as the final medium for displaying the results, but it forms an essential link in making scientific findings visible. Isotope scanning uses a combination of electronics, radiography, and photography to reveal the inside of the human body.

When the patient is injected with an isotope emitting a small amount of gamma radiation, the rays become localized in certain organs such as the spine and pelvis. A gamma-ray-sensitive detector then scans the body, in a similar way to the heat-sensitive cell of a thermographic camera (see *Thermography*, p.287). The glow of the radiation appears color coded on a television screen, and this can be photographed for a permanent record. As a diagnostic system, isotope scanning can provide evidence of spinal tumors before these would be apparent using X radiography.

Sonography

Images formed with ultra-high-frequency sound (with the technique known as sonography) are used increasingly in medicine. A probe, or "transducer", is pressed against the patient's body and transmits sound waves that are reflected back. The reflections differ according to the distance of the organs they strike from the outside of the body. It is possible to build up images similar to those pro-

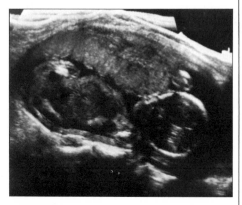

Ultrasound scanning
Doctors used a sound scan to produce the image of a four-month-old fetus. Safer than X rays, this method is suitable for photographing babies before birth, to confirm pregnancy, establish delivery date, and determine how the baby is lying in the womb.

duced by X ray body scanning (see *Radiography,* p. 286), allowing computer processing, color coding, display on a television screen, and photography.

The uses of sonography are growing rapidly. They are especially useful for examining liquid-filled organs such as the eye. In addition, the lack of danger from radiation makes sonography an important method for monitoring the development of unborn babies. In the field of obstetrics, sonography is likely to replace radiography completely for this reason.

Astronomical photography

Astronomical photographers record subjects that are outside the earth's atmosphere. Such pictures form a vital part of space exploration and fundamental research into the nature of the universe. Photography has had an important influence on astronomy — it is the most important tool to be developed since Galileo improved the telescope in the early seventeenth century and started to use it to observe the sky. But even with much more advanced telescopes, the eye has limitations. If objects are too dim, it is impossible to see them, but a photographic emulsion can accumulate light from weak, distant sources over an extended period.

The introduction of relatively fast "dry" plates in the 1870s for cameras attached to telescopes revolutionized human knowledge. Time exposures could gather the light from distant stars, and showed substantially more of the sky's contents than scientists knew to exist. Later the extended spectral sensitivity of infrared emulsions revealed yet more celestial bodies.

The traditional "refracting" telescope uses glass lenses of the widest possible diameter. Lenses up to 40 ins (100 cm) across are possible before weight and cost make such optics impracticable. Most modern telescopes work by reflection. They use a concave parabolic mirror, which can be as wide as 200 ins (500 cm), to focus the light. This design usually allows much larger apertures than the refracting telescope. Both types give an angle of view of about 1°.

Exposure times in astronomical photography are usually very long, and this imposes problems with loss of film speed and with the earth's rotation during exposure. The latter is easily overcome with a turning camera mount. But the most serious limitation to ground-based telescopes is the distortion caused by the atmosphere itself. This is what gives stars their characteristic "twinkling" appearance. Siting observatories on mountains where the air is clear provides a solution.

Photography from satellites and space probes has further helped overcome problems of atmospheric distortion. Spacecraft carrying electronic scanners pick up X ray and gamma radiation from stars at great distances.

See also
Choice of film *Reciprocity failure,* p. 152. Film and paper image formation *Effects of reciprocity failure,* p. 220. Scientific and technical photography *Equipment and techniques,* p. 274.

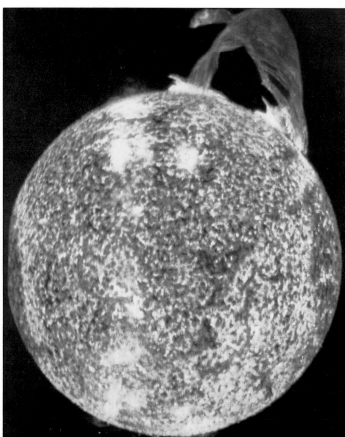

The sun
This direct photograph of the sun shows a flare, extending some 360,000 miles (576,000 km) into space above the solar surface. Such a flare lifts as much as one-thousandth of all the sun's surface gases at one time. The picture was taken from Skylab. Designed especially as an observatory, Skylab was the first spacecraft to make extensive surveys of the sky from outside the earth's atmosphere. The picture also shows sunspots — the dark patches that occur at points where intense magnetic forces break up the surface gas to reveal darker substances beneath.

Equipment and techniques

An ordinary tripod-mounted camera and a lens of moderately long focal length will produce satisfactory pictures showing the entire surface of the moon. On ASA 200 film, a typical exposure for the moon high in the sky is 1/60 sec at f 8 on a clear night. Pictures of other parts of the sky call for exposures of several minutes, and this often causes stars to record as curved tracks, centring on the pole star, which alone remains stationary.

Equatorial camera mounts
To prevent stars appearing as light trails, astronomical photographers use an equatorial telescope mount. This pans the camera and telescope very slowly against the earth's rotation, so that stars seem to remain still throughout exposures of minutes or even hours. The whole telescope pivots on a slow-motion rotating device with its axis pointing at the pole of the sky. The angle of this axis varies according to the latitude of the observatory. It is possible to turn the telescope in any direc-

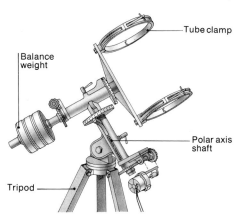

Tube clamp

Balance weight

Polar axis shaft

Tripod

Telescope mount
It is possible to connect the equatorial mount (above) to a slow-motion drive, to compensate for the earth's rotation. In order to track a star, it is neces- | sary to rotate the telescope about the polar axis. A ball-bearing mechanism cuts down friction when the telescope is turning.

tion to include the required area of the sky, but once there, it will keep the same area in view throughout the night, as though the earth were still. A vibration-free motor drives the mount, at a rate equivalent to a movement of 360° in 23 hours 56 min.

Refracting and reflecting telescopes
Astronomical photographers use both refracting telescopes (with lenses) and reflecting types (using mirrors). All types must be of the highest possible optical quality. Distortion is totally unacceptable for accurate recording of the sky's contents.

In a refracting telescope the front, compound lens elements collect the light, and an eyepiece at the viewing end magnifies the image. Most instruments work at an aperture between f 11 and f 16. The world's largest telescope of this type (Yerkes Observatory, USA) has a refracting element 40 ins (100 cm) in diameter. A larger lens would sag under its own

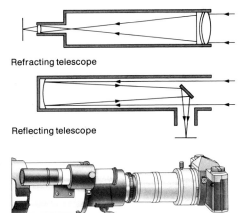

Refracting telescope

Reflecting telescope

Adaptor

Types of telescope
The refracting telescope (top) works like an extreme telephoto lens, with a large light-collecting element, and a small eyepiece. The reflecting type (center) | uses one mirror to collect the light, and another to reflect the image to the eyepiece. For photography, a camera adaptor is necessary (above).

weight, creating aberrations that would be unacceptable to scientists producing accurate records of the sky.

Reflecting telescopes collect light via a concave mirror. Some also have a second mirror to reflect light rays back through a hole in the main mirror, to increase the focal length. This is the same principle as that of the photographic mirror lens (see *Catadioptric lenses*, p. 191). An alternative design reflects light at right angles out of the side of the tube to a point of focus. The mirror system's advantages are its wider aperture (usually f 5), its lighter weight, and its freedom from chromatic aberrations. In order to photograph an astronomical subject directly, the telescope must be attached to the camera with a purpose-built

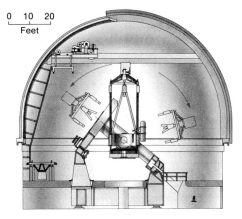

0 10 20
Feet

Giant reflecting telescope
The reflecting telescope (above) requires a large dome to accommodate the 10 ft (3.5 m) mirror, its massive support, and the mechanism that | turns and directs it. The purpose-built instrument allows scientists to observe stars billions of light years away.

adaptor. This allows you to photograph the image formed by the telescope mirror or lens, and it is also possible to obtain high magnifications by leaving the telescope eyepiece in position.

There are two major problems in using a camera attached to a telescope in this way. First, a heavy duty tripod and cable release are necessary to eliminate camera shake. Second, focusing can be difficult, particularly with the dark background of most astronomical subjects. With many focusing screens, the microprism area is shadowed and the image unclear. It is therefore best to use a matte screen on the camera, preferably together with a magnifying camera eyepiece.

In the world's largest reflectors, such as the 16 ft (5 m) diameter telescope at Palomar, the observer sits in a cage inside the telescope tube, over 80 ft (25 m) from the reflective surface at the point of prime focus. The reflector consists of a support coated with a thin, reflective aluminum film. The shape of this film is crucial. Is must be uniform in thickness, and

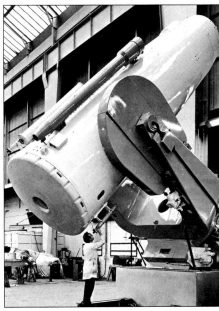

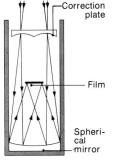

Correction plate

Film

Spherical mirror

The Schmidt camera
This large 48 ins (1.2 m) Schmidt camera (above) is sited at Siding Spring, N.S.W., Australia. It uses a spherical mirror and a shaped correction plate (left) to overcome the distortion of point light sources produced by the lens aberration coma. The camera produces a flat image field and permits very large apertures.

must not vary with temperature changes if the unit is to produce images of consistent optical quality. With such a powerful telescope, it is possible to observe stars situated billions of light years away from earth.

For a wider angle of view, the Schmidt camera employs a single mirror, plus a glass correcting plate to counter spherical aberrations. The photographic material, usually on a curved surface, is positioned inside the lens barrel, facing the mirror. As well as its greater angle of view, the Schmidt camera offers an aperture of approximately f 1.

Sensitivity and exposure
In spite of the low light levels involved, a high-speed emulsion is not necessarily the best choice for astronomical work. It is most important to ensure that the material has sufficient speed under actual working conditions. Some films that are fast for conventional photography suffer badly from reciprocity failure (see *Reciprocity failure,* p. 152) when used for long exposures to weak light. When exposed for hours, their effective speed can prove slower than another, medium-speed, film used in the same conditions. Special emulsions are available for astronomical photography that give their fastest speed under these conditions. Some black and white emulsions of this type are coated on glass, for maximum flatness and dimensional stability in critical survey work. For color photography, modern high-speed daylight color transparency film on a plastic base is satisfactory.

In practice, the major limiting factor when recording stars from a ground-based position is scattered light within the earth's atmosphere. The moon, or light from a nearby town, can illuminate the sky to such an extent that the weakest stars are lost in luminous fog. It is best to judge exposure by trial and error with particular telescope equipment. When the sky is bright enough to outshine faint stars, 5 minutes is usually the longest useful exposure time with a small reflecting telescope. On a dark, clear night, it is possible to extend this to 1 or 2 hours, recording increasing numbers of weak stars. With all these exposure times, an equatorial mount is necessary to prevent stars recording as light trails.

Radical developments in electronic light-detecting devices have limited the growth in size of really large telescopes. The charge coupled device (CCD), which may replace film in still photography (see *Future design trends,* p. 211), is already used in the world's major observatories. Over small image areas they can equal the recording power of photographic emulsions, but they have much greater sensitivity. Gains in effective light response of one hundred or more times are possible with this type of electronic image receptor.

Photographing the solar system
It is possible to produce acceptable pictures showing the whole of the larger planets (Jupiter and Saturn) or nearest planets (Venus and Mars) as well as parts of the moon, using a 4 or 5 ins (10-13 cm) reflecting telescope. As with all three-dimensional subjects, hard side-lighting gives the strongest impression of form. Craters on the moon therefore appear clearest when at or near the "terminator" – the boundary between the light and dark sections of the moon during its half and crescent phases. It is here that sunrise or sunset forms the longest shadows. Exposure times for the moon and planets should not exceed 10 sec, unless the telescope has a suitably geared equatorial mount to compensate for the earth's rotation.

The sun
Looking at the sun through a telescope is extremely dangerous and can permanently damage the observer's eyesight. One method of examining the sun's bright surface – revealing the details such as sunspots – is to use a very deep filter (see *Neutral density filters,* p. 201). Another safe method is to project its image on a surface such as a piece of white cardboard. Even then it is essential to use a neutral density filter. Photographic exposures must be as short as possible. To minimize the effects of the sun's heat turbulence on the earth's

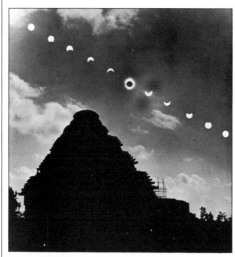

Solar eclipse
This time-lapse sequence of the solar eclipse in 1980 was taken at fifteen-minute intervals. The central image shows the

moment of total eclipse. An eclipse is the safest time to photograph the sun, since its brilliant disk is covered by the moon's dark silhouette.

atmosphere (which gives shimmering and destroys detail) exposures of 1/1000 sec or less are required.

The best time to take pictures of the sun's corona – the luminous haze surrounding the disk and spreading out irregularly into space – is during a solar eclipse. A coronagraph provides an alternative method. This consists of a special telescope with a circular mask to block out the sun's central disk, producing an effect like an artificial eclipse. Its optics are designed to minimize scattered light.

Photography and space exploration
Photography plays a central role in the exploration of outer space, and in increasing scientists' knowledge of the solar system. To make full use of photography's power of recording information, it is necessary to use a range of specialized techniques to create images in difficult circumstances, to transmit them to earth, and to interpret them in the laboratory.

Retrieving the image
In the most advanced areas of astronomical photography – especially of the planets of the solar system – scientists have turned to observations made from space itself. This has raised technical problems in transmitting the images back to earth. The earliest manned exploration of the moon allowed the return of exposed photographic film to earth for processing. Recent work involving space shuttles also has this advantage. Silver halide images obtained directly in this way give maximum detail and information. But most spacecraft are unmanned and do not return to earth, so that sophisticated image-retrieval techniques are necessary before results can be seen.

The first Lunar Orbiter craft developed silver halide film on board, scanned the negatives electronically by television, and transmitted the signals. On earth, the picture was reconstituted on a television tube, copied, and printed. More recent craft carry high-resolution television cameras on board. An electronic processor on the spacecraft converts the image signals to digital form and sends them to earth as a stream of numbers. For example, the first pictures of Mars from Mariner 9 each comprised 700 lines, every line consisting of 832 minute points of light, known as picture elements (or "pixels"). By using the digital signal, it is possible to code each pixel to any one of 512 brightness levels, and read out the lines slightly overlapped, so that the full picture appears free of the usual television linear grid.

This system allows the transmission of good quality pictures across millions of miles of space. It can also work in the low lighting conditions prevalent in the outer solar system. (For example, sunlight on Saturn is only one-hundredth its intensity on earth.)

Using invisible wavelengths
Astronomical image recording makes use of invisible radiation, as well as light that is visible to the human eye. Astrophysicists have used these wavelengths to discover unknown and invisible stars in distant space that are sources of ultraviolet or X rays. Even familiar objects, such as the sun, give new information when recorded in this way.

Scanning cameras that use electronics rather than emulsion-coated film are necessary since there are no adequate optics or film to form or record a full image in the normal way. In addition, the earth's atmosphere filters out most of this radiation, so observations must be made from space itself, using satellites and spacecraft. Here the stream of signals from a scanning electronic camera can easily be stored on magnetic tape and relayed to a receiving station on earth. Scientists use electronics to translate the received signals into visible photographic images or video results that it is possible to photograph later.

Cameras of this type have a sensing cell that scans the subject as a thermographic camera does (see *Thermography,* p. 287). Oscillating mirrors, or the cell itself, move in a continuous path that covers the entire subject area. But the cell only takes a reading from one minute area at a time. At the receiving station the camera activates a moving spot of visible light, which "writes" an image on a sheet of film or displays it on a cathode ray tube. The spot follows the same scan pattern made by the cell in the camera. Its scan lines overlap sufficiently for the final picture to be free of the linear pattern typical of television images.

The more sophisticated the scanning device and receiving equipment, the more numerous the pixels, and the better the total image resolution on the screen.

In practice, satellites and space probes usually have an array of several scanners, each designed to sense information in a dif-

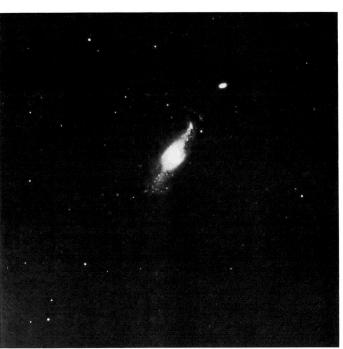

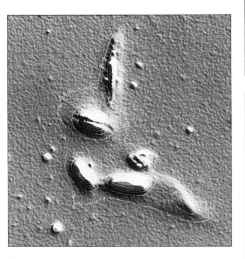

Stephan's Quintet

The group of distant galaxies known as Stephan's Quintet (above) is one of the most mysterious phenomena in space.

Computer image enhancement can clarify the galaxies' energy emission as contour lines, with a graphic "relief" effect.

The observation of galaxies
Evidence from computer-enhanced images has played an important part in scientific research into the galaxy NGC 1097 (left and below). The original black and white photograph (left) shows a distant spiral formation, similar to our own galaxy. The enhanced image (below) was produced by increasing contrast and programing the computer to outline areas of equal intensity. This reveals a distinct ring of light around the galaxy's edge. The close contours, like those on a terrestrial map representing a steep gradient, show areas of sudden change of intensity. Further stages of image enhancement, including color coding (see following page) provide additional information.

ferent region of the electromagnetic spectrum, but all viewing the same part of the sky. This allows the scientist to compare each set of images recorded at the same time, superimposing them in contrasting colors to emphasize their differences visually. In a similar way, the more remote space probes transmit blue, green, and red separation images, and scientists on earth reconstitute these as yellow, magenta, and cyan electronic pictures. Superimposing these produces a full-color picture, in the same way that the three dye images in color film form an image (see *Chromogenic film and paper theory,* pp. 217-19).

Cameras positioned above the earth's atmosphere allow scientists to tune into X rays — the most powerful radiation that illuminates the universe. X ray scanners show a view of space quite unlike its appearance by visible light. Deep chasms appear in the sun, and quasars,

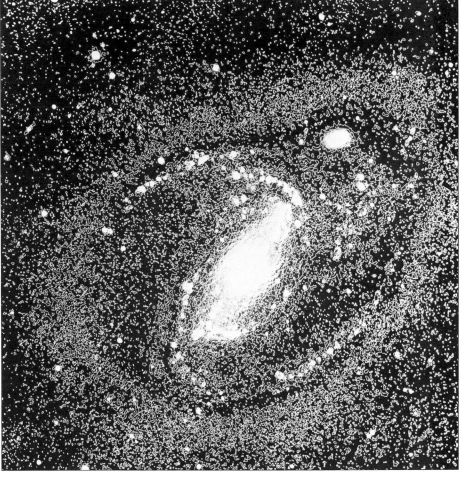

Types of image enhancement

The pictures of galaxy NGC 1097 (right and below) show further degrees of image enhancement of the original black and white image (see previous page). The contour image (right) shows the lines of equal intensity, including the galaxy's surrounding halo, very clearly. The color result (below) is based on an electronic scan of the black and white pictures. The dramatic false colors illustrate vividly a range of image brightnesses much greater than the range that the eye can distinguish in a regular black and white photograph. In this image, it is the differences between the colors that are important, not the colors themselves, which are chosen arbitrarily to encode particular brightnesses.

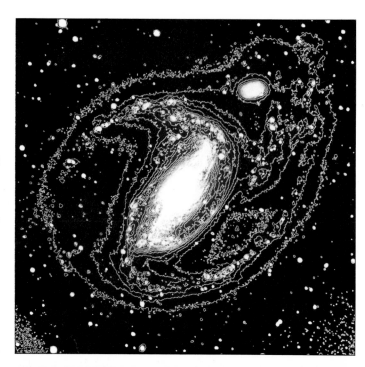

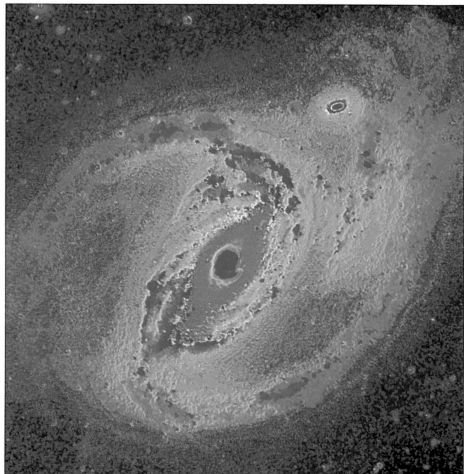

dense neutron stars, and "black holes" show up as intense energy sources in what previously seemed to be empty space.

The penetration of radar waves has also been used in astronomical photography. The planet Venus, for example, is shrouded in dense, chemical clouds that prevent direct observation. This cloud is also so corrosive that it has destroyed several spacecraft because they approached too close. Radar wavelengths (see *Remote sensing*, pp. 298-9) as well as infrared radiation, have proved invaluable in photographing this planet.

It is possible to make large mosaics from pictures formed by invisible wavelengths. They create picture maps that cover large areas of the sky, or the face of an entire planet. Copying the mosaic and reducing it in size gives a convenient, pictorial map.

Image enhancement

Scanned image signals — either direct from a spacecraft sensor or fed from a light scanner camera viewing a processed astronomical plate — are recorded on tape as a digital code. At any time, replaying the tape will reproduce the image on a television monitor for photographic copying or writing directly on film. But before this happens, the scientist can use a computer to modify the signals in a number of ways, so that interesting aspects of the image appear more strongly, while unwanted features are suppressed.

Effects are similar to photographic masking during printing (see *Masks and overlays,* p. 263), but the process is much faster and more sophisticated. For example, certain computer programs will "clean up" images by detecting and removing transmission errors. Other programs enhance local contrast, improving image sharpness and detail. It is also possible to delete objects larger or smaller than a particular size and add the results of one scan to another, like sandwiching negative and positive masks.

Computer enhancement can also turn tonal images into line results, allowing the researcher to plot the distribution of radiation around each astronomical source. It is also easy to code scans in color, making subject differences much more obvious to the eye than with tone variations. Details common to two areas of an image stand out in a color coded result.

With informed use of a computer, the astronomer can program whatever combination of features it is necessary to assess in a subject, allowing the computer to search and present these as a map or diagram, with contours or blocks of color. Enhancement techniques can be applied to any image in electronic form, and are available for medical, forensic, and general scientific work.

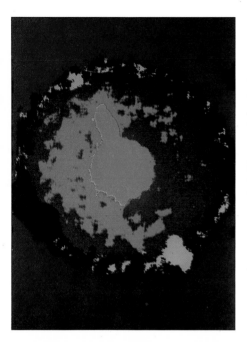

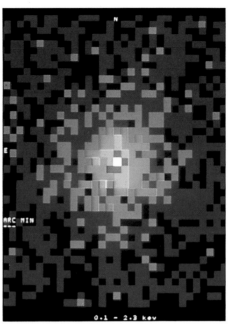

Analyzing starlight

Astrophysicists collect a great deal of important information by analyzing the actual radiation emitted or reflected by stars and planets. This is done with a spectrograph. This device admits light through a slit, forms it into a parallel beam by means of a lens, and passes it through a prism. Since refraction varies with wavelength, the incoming light splits into separate bands of colored rays that are focused by a second lens as a long, strip-shaped spectrum of colors. The prism also refracts infrared radiation beyond the red end of the visible spectrum, and, if the lens and prism are made of quartz, it will place UV before the blue end.

The "spread" band of radiation records on photographic plates, sometimes through a gradated gray filter in front of the emulsion. The filter's density gradient is at right angles to the spectrum, so that the processed plate carries a "wedge" spectrogram. This shows the relative strength of each wavelength band

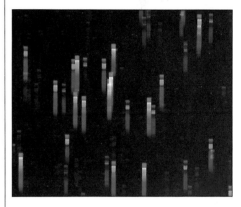

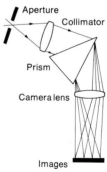

Galaxy M87
The three color-enhanced pictures show galaxy M87, the largest galaxy known to man. They demonstrate how astrophysicists can use different types of color enhancement to reveal varied aspects of subjects in outer space. The image (above left) shows the galaxy's central jet in blue, but this area has been burned out to show the structure of the surrounding gas in red and green. The more abstract picture (above) shows the enlarged picture elements of an X ray image, computer-processed to reveal the strength of the galaxy's radiation emissions. The white square at the center represents the zone of the most intense X ray emission in the black hole at the center of the galaxy. Scientists believe that this black hole causes the massive central jet. The more realistic image (left) shows the jet's shape in more detail, with the black central core, and the galaxy itself in red and orange.

The spectrograph
The image (above) shows the effect of spectral analysis of light. The spectrograph (left) contains an aperture and a collimating lens, which makes light rays run parallel. As these rays pass through the prism and the camera lens they are dispersed into component colors to produce a spectrum. Different substances show varying colors.

by their density and position against a scale.

The sun (including sunlight reflected from planets) gives a different distribution of energy from light that comes from stars and distant nebulae. This often consists of a bright continuous rainbow background crossed by a few dark lines (known as "absorption lines") caused by the presence of particular gases. It is these lines that give the radiation source its own "signature", varying according to its atmosphere (if any) and surface temperature. A body moving toward the earth records with a slight shift in its spectrogram toward blue light, while one moving away shows a slight red shift. This is due to the Doppler effect — an apparent change in the wavelengths emitted by objects when they are in motion.

Aerial photography

Photography of the earth's surface from air or space is known as aerial photography. Cameras may be as low as the length of a kite string, or as high as a satellite far above the earth's atmosphere. Satellite cameras can produce images of an entire continent, while cameras carried by low-flying aircraft and kites can take pictures of quite small areas of the earth's surface. The results of aerial photography play an invaluable role in city planning, archaeological research, cartography, oceanography, forestry, military intelligence, and the surveying of the earth's resources.

Low-altitude work involves oblique views that reveal ground features with familiar depth, width, and height. Vertical views from higher altitudes are used for surveys and mapping. Another facet of aerial photography is air-to-air work – producing pictures of aircraft in flight. Earth satellites several hundred miles high serve some of the functions of aerial photography. Their main advantage is that they permit continuous monitoring of the earth's surface – ideal in meterological work, for detecting pollution and other environmental changes, and for charting the growth of crops. The use of invisible radiation makes it possible to pick out specialist information, such as water temperature or vegetation diseases. In most cases satellites carry electronic cameras that operate under remote control. They send back pictures regularly to earth. Some of this equipment is designed for photography from space shuttles, so that retrievable film can be used.

In all aerial photography, the aircraft or satellite's movement means that a sequence of photographs automatically gives an overlapping series of ground-cover images. Vertically shot pictures produced in this way can be viewed as stereo pairs, or combined as a mosaic picture map. This is particularly useful for inaccessible regions, where field surveys would be difficult and costly to carry out.

Aircraft and earth-resource satellites carry banks of cameras and scanners sensitive to different wavebands. These give different information and images that can be color coded and superimposed to pick out chosen detail. It is also possible to enhance results electronically, with the same equipment used for astronomical pictures.

See also
Special cameras and lenses *Special cameras*, pp. 208-9. Scientific and technical photography *Equipment and techniques*, p. 274. Astronomical photography *Photography and space exploration*, pp. 292-5.

Photographic materials and techniques

Conventional film emulsions are suitable for most low-level aerial photography. Hand-held aerial cameras accept bulk film, either 70 mm or 5 ins (127 mm) wide. To help in haze penetration, black and white films for aerial work have their sensitivity extended into the near-infrared wavelengths. For the same reason, development to a slightly higher contrast than normal is recommended with these films. Color aerial films are similiar in performance to their 35 mm counterparts.

Survey camera films come in sizes up to $9\frac{1}{2}$ ins (24 cm) wide on a non-stretch base. Rolls as long as 1200 ft (365 m) are available. Like most aerial films they are designed for machine processing. Because subject conditions in aerial work differ from those in regular photography, special aerial film speed (AFS) ratings are given. These range from AFS 8, for high-altitude, high-resolution film, to AFS 400 for high-speed infrared. All films normally require a pale-yellow haze filter, to absorb excessive ultraviolet radiation. False color infrared color film requires a deep-yellow filter, and black and white IR film, a visually opaque, deep-red filter on the lens.

Lighting

The direction and quality of natural lighting is very important in aerial photography. For oblique shots at altitudes below 1000 ft (300 m) and vertical pictures that emphasize buildings and ground shapes, it is advisable to work before mid-morning or after mid-afternoon. Harsh, slanting evening light is excellent for archaeological surveys, to reveal the almost invisible undulations and patterns that denote the sites of early settlements. Sometimes maximum overall detail and absence of shadow is required instead – to allow multi-spectral sensors to read every visible surface. Flat, midday lighting is ideal for this type of work. Cloud is often a major problem. Developments such as radar and thermal photography make it possible to penetrate haze or cloud, and to photograph at night.

Basic aerial photography

The simplest and least expensive method of taking aerial pictures is to attach a small, lightweight camera to a kite or model airplane. Kits for both types of carrier are available commercially. A kite with a wingspan of 6 ft (2 m) can carry a $6\frac{1}{2}$ lb (3 k) camera and motordrive up to heights over 650 ft (200 m). A high-wing model aircraft with a 10 cc engine and 6 ft (2 m) wingspan will carry the same load, to an altitude of approximately 1150 ft (350 m). In both cases a radio control unit is required to trigger the shutter. Fast shutter speeds (1/500 sec or 1/1000 sec) are essential to overcome the effects of vibration.

The disadvantage of these systems is the difficulty of aiming the camera accurately, although with practice it is possible to use a radio-controlled plane with precision. The method is useful for archaeologists and others who require an economical alternative to helicopter or airplane rental.

Small airplanes provide the best transportation for simple commercial air-to-ground photography. The market for this work includes local government authorities, news media, agricultural interests, and the construction industry. A two- or three-seater, high-wing cabin airplane is usually preferable to a helicopter, as it gives less vibration and is much cheaper to rent. Airplanes operate at minimum altitudes of 1000 ft (300 m) in congested areas, and 500 ft (150 m) elsewhere. It is vital to read local regulations.

For this work a top-quality rollfilm SLR camera with a large hand grip is satisfactory. Pictures can be taken through an open window or removable door, using standard, wide-angle, and sometimes telephoto lenses. Those longer than 400 mm are difficult to use hand-held unless the camera has a gyro stabilizer to eliminate vibration. This device can be bulky in a small cabin. Exposures of 1/250 sec and faster are advisable, and it is best to avoid high-speed films and push processing, since aerial pictures generally require fine detail if they are to be useful for survey work.

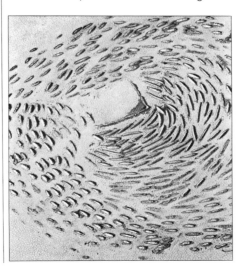

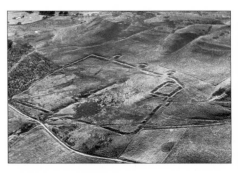

Applications of aerial photography
Georg Gerster's picture of an emergent volcano (left) provides an excellent example of the airplane's ability to reach inaccessible subjects. The archaeological image of a British hill fort (above) illustrates slight undulations and changes in vegetation that would have been invisible to an observer on the ground.

Medium-altitude photography

Most work at altitudes of 1000-10,000 ft (300-3000 m) is concerned with reconnaissance and air-to-air photography. Airforce and naval personnel and coastguards normally carry out reconnaissance work, ranging from photography of shipping or airplanes, to taking pictures as part of military maneuvers. Air-to-air work also includes publicity photography, undertaken by the staff of aircraft manufacturers, showing airplanes in flight.

Air-to-air photography

This type of photography requires a hand-held aerial camera taking 70 mm perforated film. Military and intelligence photographers regard this as the minimum size that resolves sufficient detail to be useful. Typically, each clip-on magazine carries up to 43 ft (13 m) of film. The camera is designed for ease of use with gloved hands in a confined space. Controls are large and there is a frame or rifle-type viewfinder. The more sophisticated models connect to the airplane's flight computer. This causes LEDs to print data, such as time, date, flight direction, and latitude and longtitude at the edge of each frame. Such information is

Photographing airplanes
The photographer used a motorized, hand-held aerial camera (right) to produce the dramatic image of a combat aircraft (below). To fill the frame tightly, the two airplanes had to fly close together.

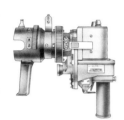

essential when the photographer is monitoring subjects, such as military equipment, that are likely to move over a period of time.

In air-to-air publicity photography, lighting and choice of background are very important, as well as the selection of the best possible angle on the subject. The work is difficult and potentially dangerous. Pre-planning of movements and maneuvers between camera and target aircraft is vital. Both airplanes must have compatible speeds, and the photographer must be in continuous radio contact with the pilot of the aircraft to be photographed.

Reconnaissance photography

To show the ground details of troop movements and the effects of raids, military photographers often use an array of six or more cameras. These are typically 5 × 5 ins (12.5 × 12.5 cm) types, housed in a unit carried beneath a fast airplane. The cameras can provide a complete, fan-shaped panorama of ground detail between left and right horizons. Wide-aperture lenses and fast shutter speeds are essential. Picture-taking rates must be geared to the speed and altitude of the airplane. A 60 per cent overlap between pictures is advisable both for compiling mosaics of contact prints and using consecutive images as stereo pairs. To do this a viewer that allows the photographer to examine prints is ideal. This device uses a pair of mirrors to reflect the images up to a stereo eyepiece. An alternative viewer, for high image magnification, is a stereoscopic zoom microscope. Some models provide a range of magnifications between × 4 and × 100.

Photogrammetry

This technique involves determining a subject's size and position by taking measurements from photographs. These may be single images or stereo pairs. Photogrammetry is used principally in map making. Land surveyors use airplanes at altitudes of over 15,000 ft (4600 m) with cameras set in shock-proof mountings in the fuselage floor. Although they are high-precision machines, these cameras are relatively simple to operate. They generally take $9\frac{1}{2}$ ins (24 cm) wide roll-film. One problem with film of this size is keeping it flat during exposure, so that the image is not distorted. Since film flatness is vital for map making, the camera incorporates a glass pressure plate that holds the material flat to within 0.013 mm. The glass also carries engraved crosses that appear on every image. These are invaluable for ground measurement, and they also help detect any film stretch or distortion during processing.

The cartographer examines contact prints, or the film images themselves, either visually or electronically as stereo pairs. Using a special "floating marker" it is possible to trace points of common height around hills and protrusions. The device feeds out the information to a plotting table and automatically draws contour lines and other details.

Infrared color film is often an important aid in this type of work. The false colors produced

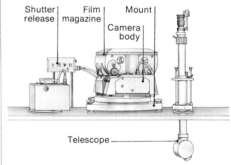

Shutter release | Film magazine | Mount | Camera body | Telescope

Aerial survey camera
The wide-angle mapping and survey camera (above) uses 9 × 9 ins (23 × 23 cm) film. It has a 153 mm lens that gives a 93° angle of view and has apertures from f 4 to f 11. Aerial photographers use the camera in conjunction with a special viewing telescope and a computer distortion rectifier to compensate for slight altitude changes. It is designed to give a 30 per cent image overlap.

help to separate tones and hues that would appear similar on regular film. (IR film was originally made for camouflage detection, showing up growing from cut foliage, or green-painted buildings.) Because healthy vegetation reflects more IR than diseased growth, infrared film is of great value in forestry surveys. It is also possible to detect different crop types by their different degrees of IR reflectance.

For purposes of comparison it is possible to make a simultaneous survey using IR, panchromatic, and filtered panchromatic films. This technique is known as multiband photography. It gives scientists the essential infor-

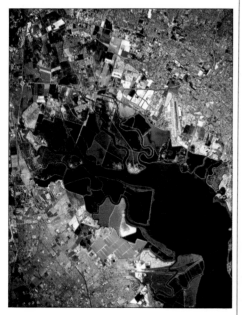

San Francisco Bay area
The aerial image of San Francisco Bay area was taken on IR film. It shows the type of detailed picture required for surveying and mapping. IR film separates streets (blue) from buildings (red) and water (dark blue) to give a clear indication of land uses.

mation that tells them which films are best suited to particular types of vegetation.

Land surveyors also use stereo pairs (see *Medium-altitude photography,* p. 297) to examine areas of the earth's surface in detail. These give the viewer striking, realistic images of features on the ground, but for making direct measurements from the image, single, vertical pictures are necessary.

Vegetation survey
Infrared scanners surveying timber in Oregon (below) detected disease before it was apparent on the ground. Trees infested by insects are blue, while healthy vegetation is red or pink on the image. The graph (right) shows the different quantities of radiation reflected by healthy and diseased vegetation.

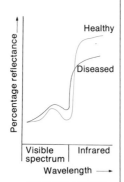

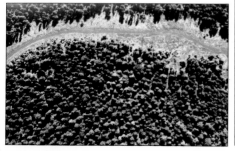

Remote sensing

Certain areas of earth survey work require the use of special techniques, such as forming images from the heat emitted by objects, or from radar. In addition, for the most sophisticated form of aerial survey, orbiting satellites provide the most consistent results. These branches of aerial photography, which rely on producing visible results from phenomena that are invisible to the naked eye, are known as remote sensing.

Thermal surveys
Thermography (the production of heat images) is used in aerial reconnaissance and survey work to distinguish warm objects from their surroundings. The equipment consists of a super-cooled scanning detector sensitive to

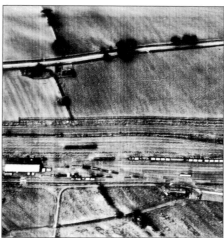

Thermal imagery
The heat emitted at night by a railway marshalling yard (above) produced a graphic illustration of items invisible to the eye. The hottest areas appear in white. These range from the large building on the left, to the trucks to the right which are warm and in use. Stationary items on the tracks appear black.

medium-infrared radiation, similar to a medical heat camera (see *Thermography,* p. 287). For military purposes it is possible to detect vehicles and grounded airplanes by the heat of their engines. Temperature differences also appear on the surfaces of lakes and rivers where waste discharge is taking place. In estuaries, river water mixing with the warmer sea discloses the pattern of currents. Scientists can code pictures so that temperature differences contrast starkly. Thermal pictures have the further advantage that they are unaffected by haze or poor light.

Side-looking radar
A recently developed survey device known as "side-looking airborne radar" (SLAR) gives high-quality aerial pictures with strong textural detail. It is known as an "active" system, because the operator transmits a pulse of radar wavelengths from the airplane itself, and then records and measures the reflected radiation.

The narrow radar beam fans out at an acute angle to one side of the aircraft. A large fixed antenna on the same or another plane receives

the reflected signals and translates them electronically to spots of light recorded on a strip of photographic film that moves at a speed proportional to the airplane's rate of travel. A computer on board the airplane compensates for the inevitable changes in altitude that occur. When returned to earth, a special optical system reconstitutes the spots into recognizable photographic images, at the same time correcting the oblique angle of view. The result is an apparently vertical photograph of land illuminated by strong light from one side. Radar can penetrate dense cloud, rain, and

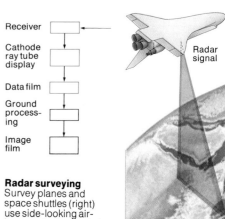

Radar surveying
Survey planes and space shuttles (right) use side-looking airborne radar to penetrate cloud cover and produce striking relief shots of the earth's surface. The diagram shows the 50° angle of the fan-shaped radar scan. The picture of the San Cristobal volcano (below) was taken using this method.

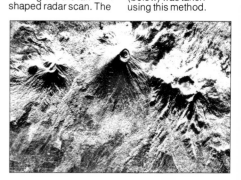

even the vegetation canopy of jungle areas, during both day and night. It reveals surface detail with excellent clarity. In addition to its use in mapping, SLAR can monitor boats, ice conditions at sea, and oil slicks. It can also help to locate valuable mineral resources in remote regions by means of the strong radar reflectance of certain metallic ores. SLAR images are always black and white, but it is possible to combine them with other aerial pictures, such as infrared images (see *Photogrammetry,* pp. 297-8) to produce dramatic color relief maps of an area.

Earth resources satellites
Orbiting satellites such as the Landsat series provide the most sophisticated aerial surveys of the earth. The Landsat series alone produces over two million images every year. A

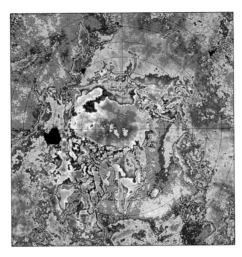 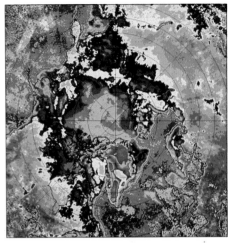

typical Landsat satellite travels in a continuous orbit, several hundred miles above the earth, passing north/south over both poles fourteen times a day. Meanwhile the earth spins relatively slowly from west to east, so that each time the satellite crosses the sunlit equator it passes over land 99 miles (160 km) west of its last circuit. The satellite covers the entire earth in overlapping parallel tracks, taking 252 orbits (18 days) to make one complete survey. An advantage of this system is that the sun always lights any one area at a constant angle.

Solar panels provide the satellite with power for all on-board functions. The survey equipment consists of four image detectors, each sensitive to a different group of visible or near-infrared wavelengths. These sensors share the same view of the earth. The satellite transmits their recorded signals when in range of ground receiving stations.

Sensitivities to different wavelengths provide information on a variety of features on the ground. A camera that scans only green-filtered light is used for sediment studies of rivers and lakes; red wavelengths highlight roads and other man-made features; infrared sensors separate vegetation types. These surveys provide visual information over the whole year, and enable scientists to relate the well-known to the sparsely surveyed parts of the planet. Computers give further information. They allow the researcher to read out satellite data in the form of air pictures or color maps illustrating the distribution of particular crops, fresh water resources, and relative areas of residential and agricultural develop-

Color satellite images
The two pictures of the North Pole show the area in summer (above left) and winter (above right). They chart changes in ice formation that are impossible to survey in any other way. The images are coded according to "brightness temperature" (microwave radiation multiplied by surface temperature). Coldest (green) areas remain the same, while the central polar zone becomes warmer (changing from brown to red) in the summer. The Landsat picture (below) is coded according to height above sea-level. It shows part of north-west England. Low-lying and coastal areas appear light blue, while higher areas are red, and still higher zones are green.

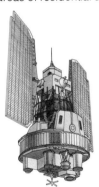

Landsat
NASA launched the first Landsat satellite in 1972. The current Landsat produces several different types of image. It carries a range of scanners, including types sensitive to near-infrared wavelengths, red light, and green light. The red-light wavelengths give the best black and white pictures, but composite color-enhanced pictures give the most valuable information.

ment. Scientists can then assess the significance of these millions of satellite readings by field checks at selected sites on the ground. This system is known as "ground truth" checking. In this way researchers are gradually building up a much fuller understanding of the spectral signatures of objects on the ground, and forming a visual index for the reading of these multiscan surveys.

Other earth satellites maintain a watch on the world's weather. They operate from a greater height than land survey devices, and orbit in the same direction and at the same speed as the earth, to effectively "hover" above key regions. Visual, infrared, and micro-wavelength scanners chart the complex movements of vast weather systems.

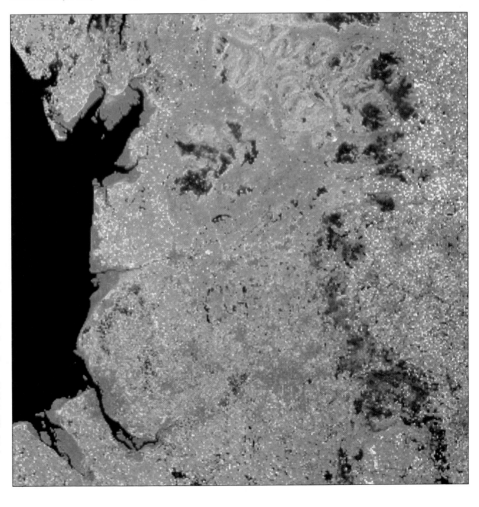

Natural history photography

Photography is an important way of illustrating living things clearly and accurately. For the scientist, it provides a means of identifying and cataloging species, and recording rare or nocturnal animals with accuracy and detail. The demand for such pictures is broad, covering the requirements of natural scientists, as well as books and specialized magazines.

The development of natural history photography dates from the early 1890s, with the arrival of hand-held cameras, and shutters offering relatively fast speeds. Later developments that have influenced nature photography range from flash, with its action-freezing properties, to color film, giving accurate records of specimens.

Photographing natural history subjects calls for a variety of skills. It involves the precise, scientific recording of specific facts, together with the creative selection and presentation of visually rewarding subject matter, and finding the best specimen in the most appropriate setting. Knowledge of the subject is vital. The most successful professional nature photographers are frequently trained biologists or zoologists.

Working conditions
Most photographers prefer to work in natural habitats rather than the artificial environment of a studio, and this can demand great versatility of approach. Hides and remote controlled cameras are usually required, as well as high-speed flash equipment, sometimes specially manufactured to the photographer's own specifications.

Having the knowledge to locate the habitat, and understanding the activities of the potential subject are essential. Natural history photographs must also be carefully documented. Apart from specialized scientific work, their main uses are in educational and general interest publications, and as illustrations for lectures. In all cases, users require accurate captions for each picture, containing details such as species, habitat, and the subject's precise activity. In the picture itself, it is essential to show the subject clearly, but some indication of environment should also be included. Differential focus, and contrast by tone or color, are both ways of emphasizing the main subject without excluding the background. The photographic equipment need not be especially elaborate or specialized, but must be rugged and easily portable.

See also
Light and subject properties *Lighting contrast and color,* p. 26. **The shutter** *Shutter and aperture relationships,* p. 125; *Shutter firing systems,* p. 126. **Close-up equipment,** pp. 195-7.

Equipment and techniques

Natural history subjects range from distant animals that call for telephoto lenses, to small insects and flowers, requiring macro equipment. The most popular camera type is the 35 mm SLR because of its portability and range of lenses. Natural history photographers also use rollfilm cameras if larger format transparencies are essential. Most naturalists carry at least two camera bodies, for different film types and to ensure against breakdown when photographer and equipment are isolated in a hide. For low-level work a waist-level finder or right-angle attachment is helpful, though for most pictures the standard pentaprism finder is most widely used.

A focusing macro lens, and extension tubes or bellows are essential for small subjects. Telephoto lenses of between 100 and 200 mm are adequate for most animals, and an 80-200 mm zoom is also excellent, especially for birds. Timid creatures and wild animals may call for a lens of about 400 mm — preferably a light, compact mirror design (see *Catadioptric lenses,* p. 191).

Camera supports are vital and require careful selection. A tripod should be sufficiently sturdy for the equipment, but not unnecessarily heavy in the field. Sometimes it is possible to weight down a tripod on location by filling a bag with earth or water and attaching it to the tripod to increase stability. If a tripod is too cumbersome, or takes too long to unfold, a monopod is often helpful (see *Tripods and camera supports,* p. 203). Working at ground level, or from an automobile window, a "bean bag" can support a telephoto lens. This consists of a canvas bag filled with dried peas or beans that adapts itself to the base of the lens. A ground spike, consisting of a ball and socket head attached to a tent peg, is another good camera support for small, close objects.

Flash is the best artificial light source for most small-scale subjects because it is portable and freezes movement. Two heads, with a generous length of cord, give greater versatility. For pictures of birds' nests and animal lairs, a camera with motor drive and remote trigger are useful. It is also worth carrying a sensitive hand-held exposure meter for inaccessible subjects. In particular, a spot meter gives accurate readings from small areas of distant subjects. It can also be valuable for local readings of flowers, and other subjects that are close to the camera.

Film choice depends on circumstances, but most naturalists avoid the fastest types, because their graininess may conceal fine detail. It is advisable to use the slowest material that subject and lighting conditions will permit. Color is preferable for most natural history subjects. Even when pictures are required for reproduction in black and white, it may be best to shoot in color and make black and white prints. In this way the naturalist has a color record of the subject on file, for possible future use. When using color work, books and magazines usually prefer to reproduce from slides rather than prints, and these are also ideal for talks and lectures.

Animals

Animal photography requires great patience, and knowledge of the subject's behavior. Animals are creatures of habit. By observation, the photographer can take advantage of their pattern of activities, or even set up new ones — for example, by leaving food in a particular place every day.

Captive animals
The existence of bars, wire, or protective glass poses the major problem when photographing zoo animals. For most natural history work it is best to wait until the animal moves toward the back of the enclosure. A wide-aperture or telephoto lens will ensure that foreground detail becomes too blurred to record. With glass, the photographer must find a clean area and use a standard lens pressed close against the surface. A rubber lens hood provides protection and a shield against reflections when this technique is used.

Ugly and unnatural backgrounds pose another problem. If differential focus techniques will not destroy this detail, it may be necessary to wait until the back of the cage falls into shadow, or to select a high viewpoint so that only floor details appear in the picture. Electronic flash is useful for "filling in" awkward daylight, and creates little disturbance. When used through glass, the light must be angled to avoid reflections.

Animals in the wild
It takes patience to locate and identify animals in the wild. A knowledgeable guide is useful, together with experience of animal behavior. A viewpoint downwind of any place where animals are known to eat or drink regularly is a good choice. It is best to work early or late in the day, especially in bush or desert regions near the Equator, where most activity occurs between dawn and 10 pm, and between 4 pm and dusk. At these times there is also much less presence of haze and heat, and the light-

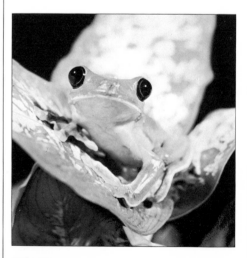

Flying frog
Heather Angel's picture of a Costa Rican flying frog makes good use of limited depth of field to isolate the subject against the background. Strong artificial lighting has emphasized the highlights on the subject's skin and eyes.

ing and sky effects are more interesting than in the middle of the day. In addition, most species will be resting in the shade around midday, and will be difficult to photograph.

Some photographers work from a fixed or portable hide, but this is not always necessary – an improvised camera support such as a bean bag can often give more flexibility. A telephoto zoom, or 500 mm mirror lens is invaluable.

It is vital to be prepared, setting the exposure controls and lens focus in advance, in anticipation of a subject appearing. When the opportunity for a picture does occur, you will often have to release the shutter immediately, with minimal adjustment of the camera settings.

Lighting should emphasize the animal's characteristic features, particularly the textural qualities of fur and hide (see *Texture as a design element*, p. 44). Panning at slow shutter speeds is a technique that can communicate a flowing sense of movement when a group is on the move or an animal is chasing its prey. At all times a combination of patience and quick reactions is necessary to take good pictures of animals in their own habitat.

Nocturnal species
Photographing animals that are mainly active at night calls for special care. The photographer must watch a known habitat for several nights, from a position downwind late at dusk. It may also be necessary to bait the intended picture area regularly, days before shooting. When the habitat is prepared, photographic

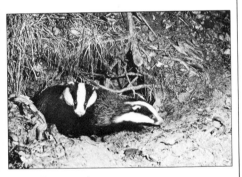

Night photography
The study of badgers outside their sett was taken at night using flash. In order to observe these creatures, the naturalist must be quiet and unobtrusive, but photographic flash lighting does not usually disturb them once they have become accustomed to it.

equipment is gradually introduced. It is best to select a particular object on which to focus. The naturalist can then fire the camera and flash from a distant vantage point using a long air or electric cable release. This allows complete choice of moment, but with subjects in total darkness an infrared trigger is best (see *Insects*, p. 302). Most photographers use flash when photographing nocturnal species. It does not disturb most animals any more than the sound of the camera, so there is little point in using infrared materials. It is much more important that the photographer is completely concealed. The most effective night pictures benefit greatly from the freezing power and extra depth of field made possible by flash.

Birds

Although it is possible to photograph individual specimens or flocks on the wing, birds are best photographed near the nest, or at some regular eating or drinking place. The simplest location is a bird table with an overhanging branch arranged near an open house window. Birds will regularly perch on the bough as a look-out before feeding, and you can organize this so that it has a simple background, not too varied in tone to cause exposure difficulties. A telephoto lens will give good results when aimed through a narrow gap in the curtains.

Most nature photography at feeding sites involves building a hide or using a remote-controlled or automatic camera. It is advisable to build the hide gradually so that the birds accept the changes that are taking place in their environment. The photographer can then narrow down the area that the birds will occupy by netting off parts of the food source or water until only a small, controllable area is in use. With an automatic set-up, high-speed flash can then be added, together with a trigger. (Flash is ideal to freeze action and allow small apertures for depth of field, provided that its position gives natural-looking lighting.)

Nests are important as locations because they pinpoint the frequent arrival and departure of a particular species. Still life details of eggs and nest materials are also interesting to the ornithologist. Pictures of birds at the nest

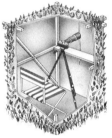

The hide
A hide (above) is often essential for photographing birds. Ample room is vital for both tripod and photographer. The observation slit should allow you to move the lens around, so that you can focus on subjects at different angles.

Nightjar
Eric Hosking took the picture of a male nightjar hovering immediately above the ground (right). High-speed flash froze the bird's rapid wingbeats. Nocturnal birds like the nightjar are very sensitive to light, so you should never mount the flash unit where it will be close to the subject.

can often record the types of food they bring to their young. The camera must view the perch the birds use to feed the young, or the entrance to the nest if it is enclosed. For automatic work, you must gradually assemble the camera, flash, motor drive (preferably with a sound-proof housing), and a radio or direct remote trigger. You can then observe the nest site through binoculars from a convenient distance, taking pictures at chosen moments.

Nocturnal birds have extremely keen eyesight, and this makes a hide essential. (With birds, scent is relatively unimportant.) At dusk, two people should enter the hide, one leaving soon afterwards. Birds will then assume that the hide is empty.

An alternative method is to use an infrared beam to trigger the camera. Setting up the beam across the flight path to the nest gives the best results, as it will capture the birds leaving the nest, and arriving with food.

In all bird photography it is essential not to disturb the subjects. Damage to nests, and any other intrusion may cause birds to abandon their eggs.

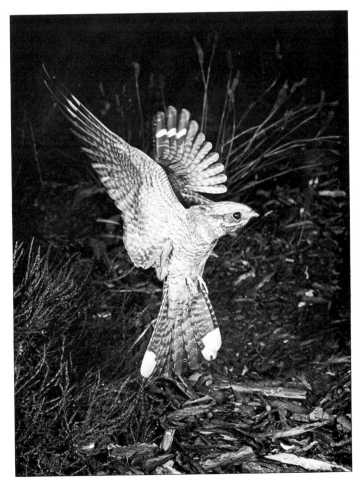

Insects

Butterflies, moths, and insects of all types pose special problems for the photographer because of their small size and fast, unpredictable movements. A macro lens of about 100 mm is essential. Flash is almost obligatory to allow small apertures for the depth of field required.

You can photograph some slow-moving insects in their natural habitat. A multihead flash unit attached to the camera is invaluable for this. It gives lighting of controlled duration and consistent intensity for a narrow range of subject distances. It is helpful to prefocus the lens. You can use a part of your hand or a small object about the same size as the insect as a guide. Then it is easy to move the camera until the image is perfectly sharp.

Another method is to capture the insect, treat it so that it only moves sluggishly, and photograph it in the studio. Photographers do this harmlessly by chilling the insect in the food compartment of a refrigerator until natural hibernation instincts make it sleepy and slow. It is then easy to place the specimen on material gathered from its natural surroundings, and light it with multihead flash.

Showing insects in flight is a particular challenge. It is necessary to restrict their flight path or "action field", to keep them within the camera's field of view and focus. One good way of achieving this is to use a dark tube of cardboard, leading from a specimen box toward a distant lamp. When you open the box, the in-

sects will be attracted to the light. The camera must be prefocused for a narrow zone across the tube mouth, where an infrared beam, connected to the camera shutter, is set up. Any insect flying toward the light will then break the beam, triggering camera flash. Foliage and other small items placed near the tube mouth provide a realistic setting. Using a strobe flash, it is possible to shoot short action sequences.

Slow, high-resolution color film, and specially made, high-intensity flash units are required. Very short duration flash is essential to freeze every detail of fast-moving insects — flashes of 1/25,000 sec are ideal.

Photographing insects in flight

The British naturalist Stephen Dalton devised the set-up (right) for recording insects in flight. Specimens released from the box fly toward the light and break an infrared trigger beam. Extreme high-speed flash can freeze wing movements, and a special fast shutter also helps to keep the image sharp. The use of more than one flash head gives good modeling.

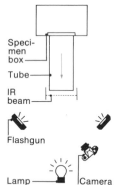

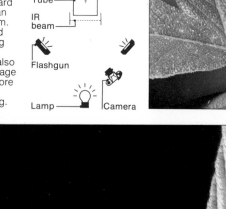

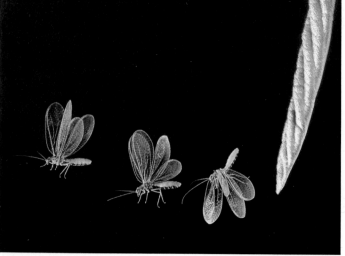

The movement of insects

The photographs of a moth (above) and a green lacewing (left) were both taken by Stephen Dalton. In both instances he used limited depth of field, so that the subjects are picked out against a plain background, and both feature an object on which the photographer could prefocus. To illustrate the flight of the lacewing, Dalton used a controlled sequence of flashes exposed on one frame of film.

Underwater life

Studies of fish are possible both in tanks and in their natural underwater habitat. Tank photography of small fish is relatively simple. Placing a glass partition across the width of the tank narrows the swimming area until it matches the depth of field of a camera lens positioned at the front of the tank. Plants can then be added in the part of the tank behind the partition, and carboard used as a background behind the tank. The best illumination is flash directed from the top front. It is essential to angle both camera and flash, to avoid reflections. To prevent optical distortions, it is also vital to use a tank that has flat sides.

A tank is also useful for underwater work in clear, shallow rock pools. You use it to house a camera with a waist-level viewfinder, lowering it partly into the water.

For true underwater pictures, a special camera is necessary. Excellent pictures of fish are possible at shallow depths if the photographer uses a snorkel. But aqualung equipment gives

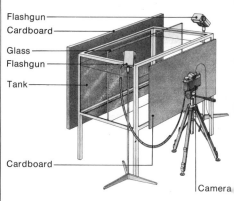

Flashgun
Cardboard
Glass
Flashgun
Tank
Cardboard
Camera

Aquaria
When photographing fish in an aquarium, the set-up (above), with dividing glass and background cardboard, is best. The sides of the tank should be flat and free from faults that will cause distortion. Cardboard round the lens help's reduce reflections.

Pike
Jane Burton's picture of a pike catching a small stickleback (below) was taken using an enlarged version of the set-up (above). It demonstrates how even an artificial arrangement can show interesting details of marine life, giving a realistic effect.

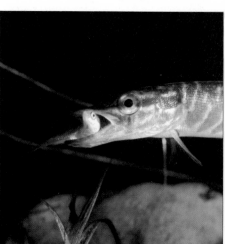

much greater freedom at depths down to about 16 ft (5 m).

Most fish are naturally inquisitive, and come quite close if the photographer stays still. The main problems are poor visibility due to sediment, and the color filtering effects of water. Working as close as possible to the subject therefore produces the best results, using a wide-angle lens to give the required angle of view. Telephoto lenses are of little use because of the haze effect of sediment. It is futile to at-

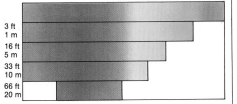

Colors underwater
The diagram (above) illustrates how daylight changes with depth. The deeper the water, the greater the loss of red, yellow, and green.

Schooling fish
Bill Wood's photograph of fish schooling off a reef gives a good sense of the whole group, as well as showing individual specimens.

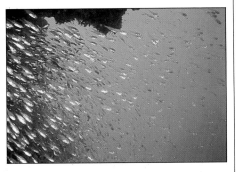

tempt camera-to-subject distances of more than one-third of maximum visibility.

Available light is only satisfactory at shallow depths and in the middle of the day when the sun is at right angles to the water surface, giving it greater penetration. Lower down the brilliant colors of marine life disappear because water filters out the red wavelengths of the spectrum leaving a blue twilight. Down to about 14 ft (4.5 m) some compensation is possible using red or magenta color balancing filters. Beyond this depth, underwater flash is essential, and it must be mounted on a support that places the head close to the subject, but well off the lens axis. This helps avoid the fog-like light scatter caused by debris in the water. Exposure is often a problem with underwater photography. A semi-automatic camera (see *TTL systems,* p. 135) is best, as you can use it with a dedicated flash, to give the correct flash output for the exposure set.

Specialized deep-water units are available for remote control work. These use a sonar mechanism to detect marine life and trigger the camera. Some types use closed-circuit television through the camera viewfinder to allow the photographer to select the moment of exposure.

Plants and flowers

The aim in recording plants and flowers is to reveal their structure, color, texture, and form. Specimens in perfect condition are essential. Deformations, insect bites, and other defects are obvious in close-up and it is vital to avoid them unless the purpose of the photograph is to reveal disease or infestation. Showing scale is often essential. A small ruler set at one end of the subject at the frame edge gives an accurate gauge of size.

It is advisable to photograph most plants and flowers in their natural habitat, since they cannot be moved without damage. This also gives a genuine sense of environment. But a studio allows total control of lighting and background and there is no problem with movement due to wind. A studio is also more convenient for plant pathology studies. A further use for a studio is to provide the controlled conditions necessary for pictures taken by ultraviolet or infrared radiation. These are valuable for diagnosing plant diseases.

The main technical challenges when working in this field are producing a suitably large image, obtaining sufficient depth of field, avoiding wind movement, and removing confusing detail in backgrounds. It is usually best to make a large image by working close up rather than using a telephoto lens. Close-ups avoid the form-flattening effect given by a distant viewpoint. With an SLR, the photographer can use a reversed lens, close-up attachment, extension tubes, or bellows, but a focusing macro lens is most convenient for close-ups. With non-reflex cameras, a spacing bracket used with a close-up lens is effective and quick (see *Technical aids,* p. 197).

Shallow depth of field at close distances limits the range of detail and makes it easy to lose sharp focus at the moment of shooting. Unless strongly differential focus is helpful to pick out one chosen element, it is best to support the camera on a tripod to allow a longer exposure at a smaller aperture. But subject movement caused by wind can still create difficulties. Staking the plant, or using a board as a wind shield may be necessary. Another solution is to freeze the subject's movement with flash. Cardboard is ideal for backgrounds, to act as a reflector, and to cut out any green tint from adjacent foliage. Tracing paper or a muslin "light tent" can diffuse harsh sunlight.

Weymouth pine
Alfred Lammer's picture (right) shows a close-up of the flower of the North American Weymouth Pine. To achieve a large image of this small subject, the photographer used a 50 mm standard lens, with two supplementary close-up lenses. This also gives limited depth of field, which emphasizes the sharp central flower spike. The surrounding pine needles also enhance the composition, acting as lead-in lines to the middle of the frame. It was photographed in situ, using diffused daylight.

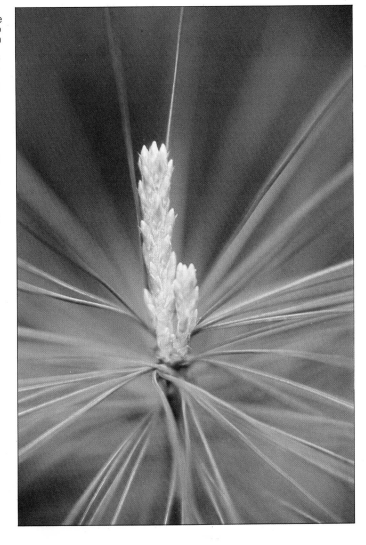

Sports photography

Sports provide a wide range of subject matter, in which action, excitement, and human drama play major roles. Capturing these elements effectively on film is often difficult and relies on extensive knowledge of the subject. Successful sports photographers are often ex-competitors themselves, or at least knowledgeable enthusiasts. The market for good sports pictures is wide. It ranges from newspapers, general and specialized magazines and books, to calendars, posters, and advertisements. Certain pictures have an immediate, short-lived news value, but many have a timeless quality that sums up human effort in sport.

Approaches to the subject

A good sports photographer must have patience, fast reactions, and the flexibility to solve problems and exploit unexpected situations. It is essential to have the right photographic equipment, and to use it in original ways. Astute choice of viewpoint and moment of exposure, together with techniques that help to convey the sense of action, are all vital. The photographer must also watch the scene carefully. The competitors' expressions and body language, as well as the reaction of spectators, can express the atmosphere of a sport more effectively than a record of the winners.

Conveying these qualities pictorially demands experience and understanding of each particular sport. The photographer can then anticipate peaks of action, and be ready one step ahead of the moments of greatest effort, triumph, or agony.

Some sports are easier to cover than others. Athletics events such as high jump, weight lifting, and pole vaulting have a fixed location and involve repetitive action. Other sports have inherent photographic difficulties. In football and golf, for example, the action covers a wide area, while in swimming, part of the competitor's body is always hidden under the water. Activities such as caving, mountaineering, and air sports also present problems of conditions.

Sports photography itself is very competitive. To produce good results, the photographer must research any unfamiliar event, to understand its techniques and help decide the best approach. It is vital to realize, for example, that a tennis player's or golfer's expression will show the greatest effort during and immediately after the stroke, rather than before.

The best sports pictures are not always of famous competitors, but often show unknown (and sometimes unrecognizable) figures at obscure events. But whoever they portray, the pictures should communicate dramatically the essential excitement, atmosphere, and skill of sport.

See also
Timing and movement, pp. 86-92. Dynamism, pp. 357-60.

Equipment and techniques

The vast majority of sports photographers use 35 mm SLR equipment, although for quiet indoor events, where noisy shutters are obtrusive, some still favor a good direct vision type. The body should accept a motor drive, and have controls that are easy to adjust in adverse outdoor conditions. A shutter offering speeds up to 1/1000 sec is preferable.

Lens choice varies with individual sports, but a 200 mm telephoto or 80-200 mm zoom is generally most useful. These lenses must have reasonably wide maximum apertures, to suit bad weather conditions or indoor sports. "One-touch" zooms, with one control for focusing and zooming, are the easiest to use when the action is fast.

For crowd pictures, general scenes, and dramatic close shots, a 28 mm or 35 mm wide-angle is useful. A wide-angle is also the prime lens for specialized sports such as caving. The most serious sports photographers also use a long telephoto of about 600 mm, with the widest maximum aperture available. Such a lens is excellent for filling the frame with an individual athlete's face, or to emphasize one person and subdue distracting surroundings with differential focus.

A motor drive is a particularly important item. Its main use is to wind on individual exposures, so that the photographer can look continuously through the viewfinder. To support a camera body and long lens, a monopod is invaluable, especially in sports that demand mobility. But a tripod is essential when you can leave the camera preset at a particular point. It is also useful for zooming at slow shutter speeds (see *Zooming effects,* p. 194) and to support long lenses.

Extra camera bodies are necessary in a field where speed of operation is vital. They allow rapid film changes, and save time when changing lenses. Sometimes a remote shutter release allows you to use two cameras – one preset on a tripod, the other hand held – to give a double chance of covering an event. Flash is of limited value. It interferes with the action of many sports, and has little effect with telephoto lenses. But it can sometimes help outdoors to fill in harsh sunlight, and is essential for underground caving.

With all equipment, the photographer must learn to load film, change lenses, and alter camera settings quickly, without looking, and in poor weather. It is also essential to practice altering the focus and zoom controls at the correct rate to keep a moving subject sharp and filling the frame. The precise time at which you press the shutter is crucial. If the peak of action is visible in the SLR viewfinder it is already too late. You must release the shutter a few milliseconds before the key moment arrives. For this reason, a direct vision viewfinder camera may be preferable because you can still see the action during exposure.

Most sports photographers use film in the ASA 64-400 range, occasionally uprating it to ASA 800 when light is poor. (The resulting graininess can add atmosphere.) For black and white work, especially when lighting conditions are fluctuating, dye-image negative film (see *Chromogenic film and paper theory,* pp. 217-19), with its wide exposure latitude, is an excellent choice.

Individual sports

It is vital to anticipate the particular climax of any action in individual sports such as athletics, skating, golf, and archery. This moment may be the point at which a competitor rolls over a high jump bar, or releases a javelin, or finally crosses a finishing line. The photographer must also observe individuals' characteristics of style. In throwing events, for example, it is important to know whether the athlete is left- or right-handed. In jumping, knowledge of the competitor's technique helps you choose viewpoints and camera angles. Capturing the best moments in sports like skiing usually means finding the place (often on a bend) where the most interesting shots will occur. Conditions are also difficult, resembling those experienced by mountaineers (see *Climbing and mountaineering,* p. 308).

Golf

Before photographing a golf tournament, it is essential to walk the course noting suitable backgrounds, and the likely position of the sun at different points. Wide-aperture telephoto lenses are essential to mask inappropriate background details by shallow depth of field. They also allow you to keep well back. A 500 mm mirror lens and an 85-200 mm zoom are ideal, and a monopod provides convenient, portable camera support. Even with this range of focal lengths, a golf tournament involves a great deal of walking and it is advisable to carry only a minimum of equipment.

Some of the best pictures occur at the green during the critical stages of putting. Here there is usually ample time to focus and compose as the players prepare their putts. The photographer must avoid distracting the players with a noisy camera, especially during the period of silence between addressing the ball and the moment of impact. Pictures showing reactions after this moment of concentration are also particularly effective.

Athletics

For track and field events, a 300 mm lens, and a zoom covering the shorter telephoto lengths are useful. A camera position inside the track gives greatest flexibility of viewpoint and subject matter, but the permission of the organizers is usually required.

Sports such as hammer throwing and discus are hard to photograph well because of the protective fence. You may have to use a wide-angle lens looking through the mesh. Shot-putting and javelin-throwing can be seen more easily. For the pole vault and high jump, a low, close viewpoint, and a wide-angle lens give good results. When a high-jumper uses the backward "flop" technique, it is essential to stand behind the bar in order to show the athlete's face.

Track sports pose different problems. Sprint events give the photographer little time, and it is best to concentrate on the finishing line. You can pre-focus the camera on the tape, using a low viewpoint to dramatize the effort of the last few yards. Middle-distance races require more flexibility. If your camera position is fixed, it is best to wait by the finishing line. But to photograph the early stages of the race, it is vital to look beyond this point, using a telephoto lens to pick out distant competitors. The most dramatic moment is often at the bell before the last lap, as the athletes strain to make their final effort to win the race.

Indoor events pose additional problems of confusing backgrounds, and light of uncertain color temperature. Bracketing with different color filters can be time consuming and some photographers prefer to use color negative film and make corrections during printing. Often maximum aperture is the deciding factor in lens choice. A wide maximum aperture is helpful in low light, and allows selective focus for eliminating confusing backgrounds.

Certain indoor sports, such as wrestling, are

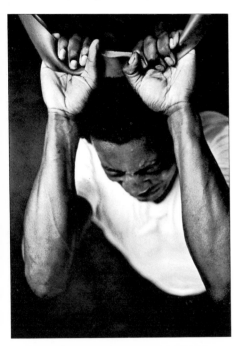

Training
The photograph of an athlete training (left) is by Milton Colindres. The impression of strain given by the downward-pulling arms dominates the image. Close framing strengthens the composition.

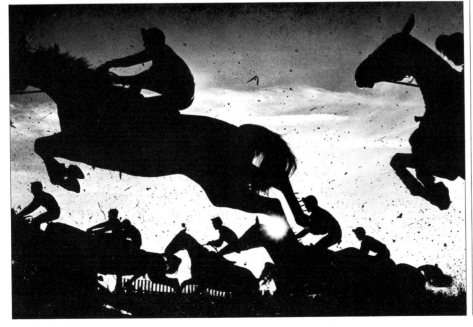

relatively slow-moving. Pictures rely mostly on the contestants' expressions. Others, like boxing, involve extremely fast movements that require a shutter speed of 1/500 sec or less to make them sharp on film. But sometimes an element of blur is acceptable, communicating, for example, the rapid movement of a fighter's glove (see *Blur as a movement device,* p. 91).

Horse racing
The most popular lenses for horse racing are an 85-200 mm zoom, a standard lens, and a wide-angle for close crowd shots. A position against the barrier flanking a straight stretch of the track is excellent for fast panning shots (see *Panning moving subjects,* p. 128) taken at shutter speeds of 1/125 sec or 1/60 sec. This abstracts ugly backgrounds and gives an impression of speed. You pre-focus the lens on the ground at the point on the track where the horses will pass.

Another good position is a low-angle viewpoint looking into an outside curve of the track. From here a 200 mm lens can capture the horses, their hooves throwing up turf as they round the bend. Some photographers set up two or three cameras with different lenses concentrated on one key point. These are fired by long cable releases. It is also possible to take spectacular steeplechase pictures with a camera pre-positioned inside one of the fences, and triggered remotely.

Horse racing
Chris Smith took the dramatic horse racing picture (below). By using a remote-controlled camera with a wide-angle lens from a low viewpoint, and exposing for the sky, Smith could show horses and flying mud in silhouette.

Team sports
The variety of action and the large area of ground involved makes team sports difficult to photograph. Intimate knowledge of the pattern of play is essential. Professional photographers have the advantage of positions close to the field at important games, but anyone can photograph from a similar position at regular amateur events, which can yield equally good pictures and where there will usually be fewer people blocking the line of view.

Many team sports present similar challenges to the photographer. Ice hockey, for example, combines the difficulties of football's large playing area with the problems of lighting and color temperature posed by baseball. An additional common problem is that a telephoto lens is often necessary because the photographer cannot get close enough to the action to fill the frame with a standard type. But following a fast moving subject is often difficult with a lens giving narrow depth of field. In some sports, such as baseball, it is easy to predict where the action will occur. But in others, like ice hockey, the action moves very quickly.

American football
To reduce excessive movement as much as possible, it is important to choose the most flexible basic camera position. This may be half way down the field, concentrating on the central area, but allowing you to photograph situations at either end with a 300 mm or 400 mm lens.

When taking overall views of the action, it is important to include the ball in the majority of pictures. This is less essential for smaller groups or individual players. Here a viewpoint close to ground level gives more dramatic results, allowing you to show players against a clear background of sky. With experience of the game it is often possible to anticipate the next move, but predicting who is going to receive a pass, or where the player will be, is difficult. At all points in the game, you should aim to capture both the peaks of action, and reactions of players and spectators.

Soccer
It is easiest to cover midfield play with a telephoto lens at the touchline, but a camera position at one side of the goal may result in close action pictures with an 85 mm or 50 mm lens. A 400 mm lens from here will also fill the frame with midfield play. But the limitation of this position is that it commits the photographer to covering one half of the field. This may be the half in which the least action occurs.

A more sophisticated arrangement is possible with two cameras. Using a hand-held camera with a telephoto lens to cover midfield play, you can set up a camera with a wide-angle lens on a tripod near the goal mouth. A tripod position at which the goal net fills the frame can produce dramatic pictures at key points in the match. A motor drive and radio-controlled shutter release allow you to operate the camera whenever there is any activity around the goal.

Baseball
To photograph a baseball game successfully, a long telephoto lens is necessary to cover the large playing area. A 300 mm or 400 mm lens

of the widest possible aperture is best. A tripod is also vital with lenses of this length. Because many baseball games take place at night flood-lighting can pose problems with film color balance (see *Color temperature,* p. 151). Using a special meter (see *Color temperature meters,* p. 164) or shooting on color negative film and correcting during printing are two possible solutions to this problem.

To outline the pattern of play against the ground, a high viewpoint is best. But most ac-

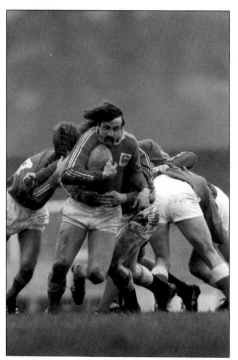

tion occurs at the bases and the batter's plate. Here it is possible to use a motor drive to shoot players as they run to a base, pulling focus if the subject is moving in relation to the camera. Immediately after a catch is taken, or a player reaches a base, there is a rich source of pictures showing individuals' reactions.

Cricket
Sports that take place over a long period of time, such as cricket, require utmost concentration and patience on the part of the photographer. Long periods when there is little to photograph may be broken at any time by sudden drama. In addition, the playing area has dimensions of over 330 ft (100 m), so it is essential to use a camera with a long lens mounted on a tripod. The most useful lens is a 600 mm, with the widest possible aperture.

Some sports photographers use a remote-controlled camera with a telephoto lens to cover the wicket continuously. Another valuable technique is to use a motor drive to take a short series of pictures of a bowler's run-up, pulling focus if necessary as the player moves toward the camera.

To an experienced eye, the field placing will suggest where catches may take place. When fielders are placed close in for a fast bowler, for example, the best camera position may be behind the batsman. There is also a rich source of pictures in the reactions of individual players immediately after a wicket has fallen.

Photographing footballers
In the pictures of rugby (left) and American football (below) Leo Mason approached two similar situations in different ways. For the rugby shot, the photographer used a low viewpoint to isolate the players against the sky, including the ball to give the picture a sense of direction. The tension in the football shot, more closely cropped, comes from the way the players converge in a clash of bright colors.

Water sports
All scenes that combine light and water have great visual potential. Water sports add action and excitement, but they also impose their own technical problems. Locating the best viewpoint is particularly difficult — especially as many water sports involve subjects that move very rapidly. Metering can also be a problem. Bright specular highlights on the water surface can easily mislead camera meters, and a spot meter gives the most accurate readings. Another method is to take a reading from a substitute object, or increase the exposure indicated by the camera's meter.

Water skiing
All three types of water skiing — slalom, ski jumping, and trick skiing — can yield dramatic photographs. In slalom work the towing boat travels in a straight line while the skier weaves through a line of buoys, plowing up a rear wall of spray. The best viewpoint is from the towing boat, looking back with a 100 mm or 200 mm lens and using shutter speeds of 1/500 sec or less. The rope remains the same length for the entire run, so that the lens requires no adjustment once you have focused on the skier. In addition, the competitor looks continuously toward the camera. You can take other shots, showing the boat and the skier, from the bank of the river.

Ski jumping is more dangerous, competitors being towed at speeds of around 40 mph (65 kph) up an inclined ramp into the air about 6 ft (2 m) above the water. If you use a telephoto lens from the bank you will be able to produce fast panning shots.

The third branch of water skiing, trick skiing, is the easiest to photograph, because the skier travels relatively slowly. The boat tows the competitor at speeds of 10-20 mph (16-32 kph), allowing the skier to perform complex maneuvers. The photographer requires a telephoto lens to capture these movements from the bank. A wide maximum aperture is ideal, since it allows the fast shutter speeds necessary to freeze movement.

Powerboat racing
As one of the fastest of sports, powerboat racing is difficult to photograph. A low-flying helicopter provides the most effective vantage point for offshore events. Working from a boat gives a more dramatic viewpoint, but usually calls for a 500 mm or 600 mm lens. Since a tripod is useless on a boat, the photographer is forced to use the lens hand-held, supported with a monopod or harness. Fast, ASA 400 color film is often essential, since you will have to stop down the lens to give some latitude of focus. To protect the lens, an ultraviolet filter is ideal, since it also reduces blue casts caused by the water. Turning points and rough-water sections of the course give most action, while the acceleration over a straight run puts the boats into dramatic angles.

Sailing
Compared to powerboats, sailboats offer larger area subjects that move more slowly. The photographer can also get closer to the boats, and a standard lens is often adequate. Some photographers work from a powerboat, which is highly maneuverable and allows rapid

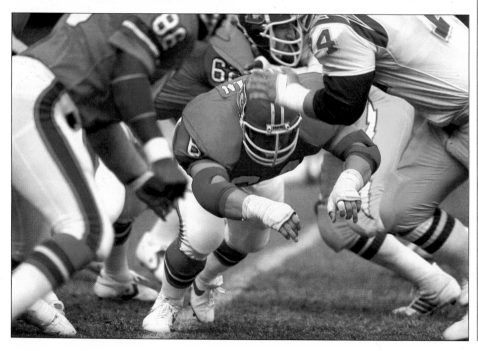

Sailboats
Leo Mason's picture of yachts in the Admiral's Cup 1979, shows the best time to photograph sailing events – when the boats are running before the wind. By framing close, the photographer has filled the frame with color, so that the bright sails contrast with the gray sea. The characteristic rounded shapes of the sails are still clear in spite of the close cropping.

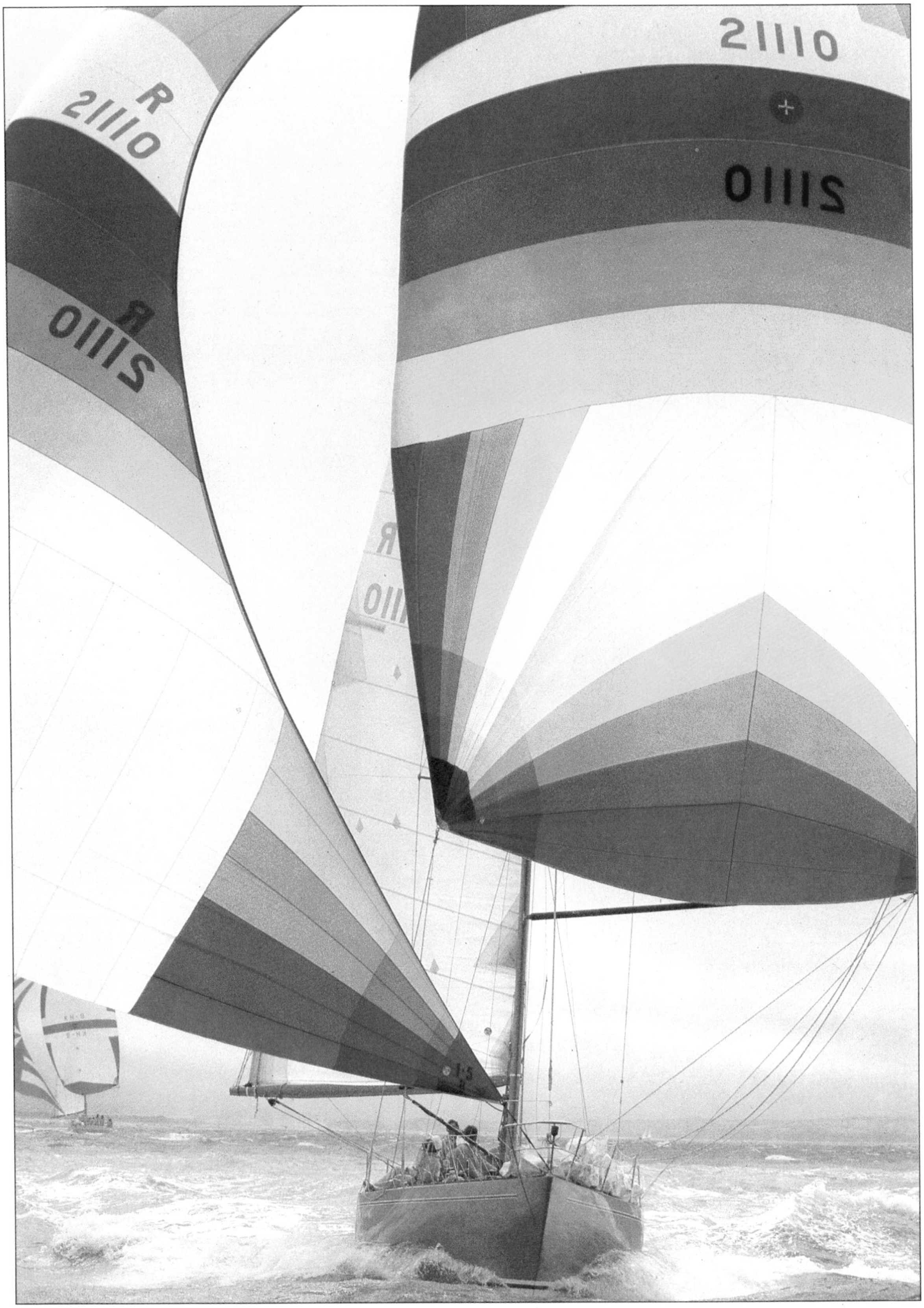

changes of location. A camera with a water-proof housing is ideal — it can be used immediately above the water to show the hulls sweeping upward.

The boats' graceful lines, shapes, and colors make attractive subjects, particularly when backlit or silhouetted, and the sails are filled with the wind. The most colorful shots show boats running before the wind, with their spinnakers filled. When time permits, it is helpful to use gradated color filters or polarizers to strengthen skies.

Canoeing

Canoe activities on rivers and streams allow a wide range of approaches. The effect produced largely depends on viewpoint. A bridge or nearby building can provide a good vantage point for mass starts to canoeing competitions. This is also an ideal viewpoint for pictures of rowing events. You can "stack up" the canoes' colorful shapes with a 200 mm or 300 mm lens from a lower, more distant viewpoint. From a point downstream, the photographer can show the skill and strength required to maneuver a canoe through a rock-strewn river. In this situation, a telephoto zoom lens is ideal. As well as making it easier to fill the frame with distant subjects, zooming the lens during an exposure of 1/8 sec gives radiating blur lines from the canoe and figure, shown head-on.

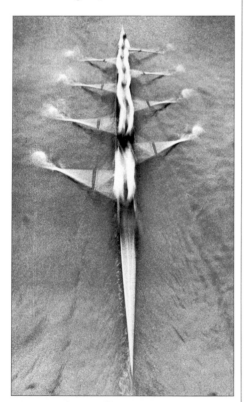

Rowing eight
To produce this rowing picture, Chris Smith used a slow shutter setting to give a blurred effect, conveying an impression of speed.

A high viewpoint from a bridge shows the shape of boat and oars much more clearly than a camera position on the bank.

Climbing and mountaineering

There are two broad types of photographs taken by climbers and mountaineers. These are views (see *Landscape photography*, p. 312), and pictures illustrating the human aspects of climbing itself. To obtain successful images, the photographer must be a climber. One of the world's foremost mountaineers, Chris Bonnington, is also among the best photographers of climbers and mountain scenery. The range of pictures possible from the lower slopes is very limited, even with a telephoto lens. It is therefore essential to keep the weight and bulk of equipment to a minimum. It is best to limit lenses to a 75-150 mm zoom for distant views, and a 28 mm wide-angle.

Climbing is a non-competitive pastime. It is therefore possible for the photographer to "direct" the subject, asking climbers to hold positions, or even to reposition themselves within the camera's field of view. But the restrictions of working on the rock face often mean that the adjustments must be only minimal. The photographer must know enough about climbing to realize when and how much

Photography on the rock face
The picture of a climber illustrates the effort and isolation of the mountaineer on the rock face. The tight rope, leading out of the frame toward the climber's goal, shows the figure's dependence, helping to communicate tension, while the rugged, vertical crag illustrates the hostile environment. The photograph is by John Cleare.

the subjects will be able to move.

A wide-angle lens will include close-proximity subjects, stressing depth, distance, and the steepness of the ascent. Ropes can lead in from a few inches away to a distant climber on the skyline, preferably with space visible between the climber's body and the rock (see *Lead-in lines*, p. 72).

Mountain conditions

The higher the altitude, the more important it is to use an ultraviolet or haze filter at all times, since more UV radiation penetrates the thinner atmosphere. Without a filter this would result in a blue cast on the film. Conditions at high altitudes can also affect the functioning of equipment. In particular, low temperatures can make the camera's internal electronic systems unreliable, and may affect the focusing movement and shutter. Where possible, climbers keep equipment under their outer clothing, to benefit from body heat. Conditions that are both cold and damp are worst. They can freeze a camera, and cause permanent damage.

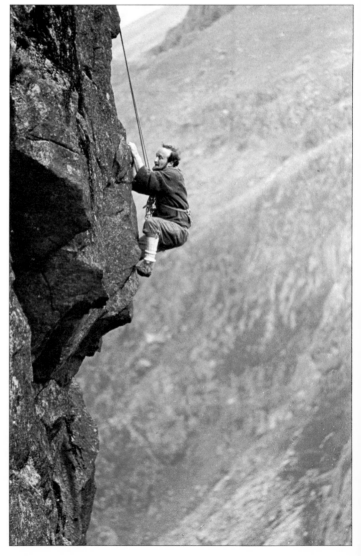

Caving

Underground caving presents the most hostile environment of all sports. Water, mud, atmospheric humidity of 95-100 per cent, and lack of light are coupled with enormous physical difficulties in transporting equipment. As with mountaineering, the photographer must be as involved in the activity as the other participants.

The equipment is less exceptional than the way the photographer must protect and use it. A regular 35 mm camera with wide-angle and standard lenses is adequate, provided that it offers time exposures. It is essential to shield the camera from damp, preferably using a transparent plastic bag incorporating a glass window that you attach to the front of the lens. This bag should have glove-type insets that accommodate the photographer's hands, making adjustment of the camera controls easy. A tripod is essential, together with flash. Underwater flash units are best, although they are bulky. Conventional electronic flash units often fail in the humid atmosphere of caves, even if kept in sealed waterproof containers for transportation. Flash bulbs or bars are often preferable because they are more robust and powerful. But it is vital to halve flash factors because of the dark cave surroundings.

It is possible to take close-up pictures of the cavers themselves with a flashgun mounted on the camera. But owing to the misty atmos-

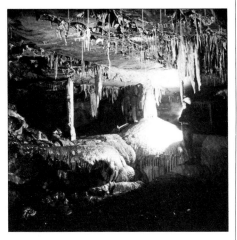

Photography underground
Chris Howes took this photograph of subterranean rock formations in a cave in South Wales. With the shutter locked open on the "B" setting, he used two flash units — one weak flash from the left-hand side, and a stronger one held by the caver on the right of the picture.

phere you cannot light general views of cave interiors in this way. Instead, it is best to place the camera on a tripod and leave the shutter open. You can then illuminate the scene with flash units set off at different points. Even with this technique, fast film is essential.

To provide back-lighting in the moist atmosphere, a useful technique is to direct one flash toward the camera, shielding it with a figure. This can give dramatic misty effects, and a strong sense of depth. Similarly, you can illuminate narrow passages from the far end, or from concealed corners, to show the conditions under which cavers explore.

Architectural and landscape photography

The subjects of architectural photography range from new developments to archaeological sites, taking in both interiors and exteriors. Landscapes include industrial subjects and townscapes as well as more traditional views of countryside. This wide variety of subject matter poses a number of similar photographic problems. The most important is the challenge of emphasizing the subject's essential features. Aspects that stand out in the camera viewfinder frequently become insignificant or dull in the final photograph. It is easy to lose the sense of panoramic space and distance in a landscape, or to distort perspective in architectural pictures. But photographs that cope with these problems can convey a scene's essential elements and form strong creative images.

Both landscape and architectural images have a wide-ranging market. They can provide objective records of the environment, and show clearly the relationship between natural and man-made structures. They can advertise real estate and tourism, and form interesting and expressive images in their own right. All these types of image are used in books and magazines, in specialist publications as well as on postcards, calendars and other illustrated material.

Architectural and landscape subjects were among the most popular for early photographers — primarily because they are static, so that it was possible to record them with long time exposures. The early landscape photographers used large format cameras (often known as view cameras). These were capable of giving large contact-printed photographs and used small-aper-

ture lenses for maximum detail. Explorers and geological survey teams employed their own photographers. For example, photographic images were vital in revealing the far western regions of the United States to the public.

Modern approaches
Photographers still use sheet film cameras for this type of work. This is due partly to the usefulness of the extensive camera movements to control perspective and depth of field, and partly to the grain-free quality of the large negatives. A sheet film camera, slow to focus and compose, also encourages care and contemplation of the subject.

The landscape photographer must be selective, deciding on the salient features of a scene, waiting for the right conditions, and emphasizing the elements that can help to express these. Viewpoint, lighting, and framing are all important. Successful architectural photography must also bring the subject to life, conveying its form, texture, setting, and relationship to people.

See also
Viewpoint, pp. 62-6. Camera types *Sheet film cameras,* pp. 108-9. Focal length and camera size, pp. 120-3. Straight photography, pp. 342-6.

Figure in a landscape
In Martin Dohrn's atmospheric picture, architectural and landscape elements combine to give a strong impression of locality. The long lines of the houses echo the edges of the vegetation in the foreground, and the figure helps to add atmosphere.

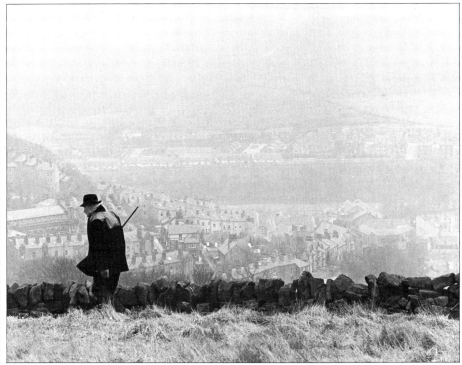

Equipment and approach

It is possible to take good architectural and landscape photographs with all types of camera equipment. The portability and convenience of small-format equipment make 35 mm and rollfilm cameras popular for landscapes. The wide lens range available for these camera types is a further advantage. Some specialist photographers prefer a sheet film camera. They are often influenced by the impressive control over depth of field obtained by great "straight" photographers such as Edward Weston and Ansel Adams (see *Individuals and movements of Straight photography,* pp. 343-6). The camera movements of a sheet film type make it especially useful.

A good 35 mm kit for architectural and landscape work would include a 21-35 mm zoom lens, and a 28 mm perspective control (or "shift") lens, in addition to a standard lens. A 135 mm telephoto, or an 85-200 mm zoom, are useful for selecting small areas of a subject, compressing buildings in the frame to compare or contrast their styles, or emphasizing aerial perspective in landscapes.

The largest sheet film cameras are generally too cumbersome for location work, so most photographers prefer the 5 × 4 ins (12.5 × 10 cm) format. The basic equipment for photography with this camera type is the camera, a 180 mm convertible lens (see *Special lenses,* p. 210), a 90 mm wide-angle with bag bellows, and film holders. A 65 mm extreme wide-angle lens is also helpful for cramped interiors. All these lenses should have covering power (see *Angle of view,* p. 120) sufficiently in excess of 5 × 4 ins (12.5 × 10 cm) to allow free use of camera movements. In addition, a highly sensitive hand meter is essential, and an instant picture back is useful to preview results.

All photographers also require a tripod, cable release, and spirit level. A compass is a useful extra item. It can help you predict the lighting direction at other times of the day. Filters are also important. The most valuable types are color filters to enhance contrast in black and white work, gradated filters for color film, polarizers, and UV or skylight types. A powerful flash gun, or a blue-filtered photographic lamp, are useful for improving the lighting of interiors. Slow or medium-speed films are ideal — the graininess of faster films masks detail.

The point of emphasis

Architectural and landscape subjects can look lifeless and uninteresting in the absence of a point of emphasis. A single dominant feature, with other elements in the picture subordinated, helps to establish a picture structure. Figures can also play an important role. They can provide a focal point, show scale, and suggest human environment. An open landscape seems more vast and empty when it includes a small distant figure. Figures are specially relevant in architectural pictures, since buildings are designed for human use. The figures included must relate to the subject — it is often possible to make them act as symbols. For example, children playing in frothing surf, or the solitary outline of a person at a window in a vast office block, can each represent the photographer's feelings about the scene.

Architectural exteriors

Photographing architecture involves similar techniques to those used for landscapes. But a building is more than a landscape of man-made materials and structures. It is also the product of a particular age, reflecting the patterns of life, forms of construction, and decorative style of the time at which it was made. The most imaginative architectural photographs are therefore more than a mere record of the architect's work. To photograph a building, it is best to have a point of view about its essential qualities and the way in which it is used. Professional photographers often have to adapt this approach to suit clients' requirements. Architects, owners, and historical groups will each have their own priorities.

The main visual influences on architecture are lighting and viewpoint. The way one part of a building casts a shape on another may either confuse or reveal its design. False attachments that join certain lines and separate others (see *Overlap and false attachment,* pp. 83-4) can transform the apparent geometry of structures. A local area of light may emphasize a good or bad feature, just as a pale colored background structure or light patch of cloud may act in a similar way. It is sometimes necessary to obscure unwanted or confusing features such as parked cars or street signs in shadow, or behind foreground objects giving an uncluttered effect.

It is frequently best to photograph a complete building "straight", examining all its features closely. You can then move in closer and move around the subject for more effective views. It will also be useful to return at different times of the day and under different weather conditions observing lighting changes.

Showing a building's setting is an excellent way to express mood. It can appear remote or hemmed in, and can blend or contrast with its surroundings. Often a change of viewpoint entirely alters a subject's appearance, simply because of the foreground and background elements included. A building may seem to be situated in the country from one angle, and clearly part of a city from another viewpoint.

The architectural photographer is frequently forced to shoot from a close viewpoint to avoid obstructions, using a wide-angle lens to include the whole subject. With tall buildings the camera is usually closer to the ground than the top of the building, so that you have to tilt the camera to include the roof, producing an image with converging verticals. A shift lens (see *Movements on 35 mm cameras,* p. 121) or a rising front movement on a view camera (see *Movements on view cameras,* p. 121) will help to correct the perspective. Choosing a higher camera position will have a similar effect. A viewpoint from the upper window of another

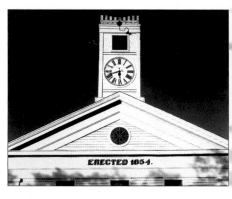

Approaches to architecture
Ansel Adams' straight photograph of a pediment and clock tower (above) is a precise, objective record of the subject, with correct perspective. The image of an office block (below) by Clive Frost, illustrates a more interpretative approach. A low viewpoint makes the verticals converge, emphasizing the building's height. Lighting enhances the reflective surface. The branches provide contrast.

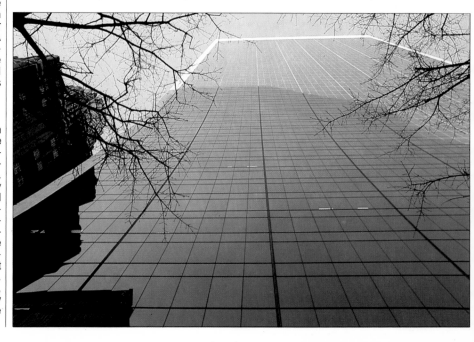

building is often ideal, while an aerial viewpoint may be the only way of showing environmental features that are horizontal.

Lines that lead in to important areas of the subject are often useful to emphasize particular parts of buildings (see *Lead-in lines,* p. 72). It is also possible to use framing devices (see *Finding frames,* p. 60) in a similar way. Quite minor framing objects, such as foliage, can also suggest a building's setting.

Architectural details
Well-chosen details can epitomize a building's character as well as a whole view. It is even possible to show a whole town in this way. Roof lines, decorations, ceiling bosses, or small areas of pattern can all be informative. The severe lines of a concrete structure, or a cluttered pattern of balcony shadows on an older building, can sum up an entire locality.

Two-dimensional decoration requires even frontal lighting, and three-dimensional detail is most effective in soft, directional illumination. Weather conditions, such as glistening rain, will also alter these features.

Careful use of viewpoint and focal length can often allow you to combine architectural details, juxtaposing colors, textures, and patterns in the same frame. They can divide the picture into contrasting areas, forming a semi-abstract design. It is also worth finding a camera position that will combine an architectural detail together with a more distant view. Showing one wing of a building reflected in the window of another is a good method of doing this.

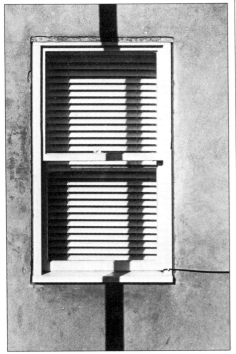

Isolating details
Carol Sharp took the picture of a window (above). Her choice of a small detail produced a strong simple composition. The hard lighting, giving a graphic pattern of offset shadows, gives a striking effect.

Cities and industrial landscapes

Buildings and man-made structures such as bridges and industrial plant play the same role in a townscape as trees and rocks in a landscape. As with landscape photography it is essential to select from these elements and emphasize the most important ones. Aspects that the photographer may wish to express range from the quiet atmosphere of a small town to the impressive skyscrapers of New York.

Subject blur can convey the speed and bustle of city life, while it is possible to show the claustrophobic quality of many modern cities with the cramped perspective of an extreme telephoto lens. A wide-angle lens, used from a low, close viewpoint, will emphasize the

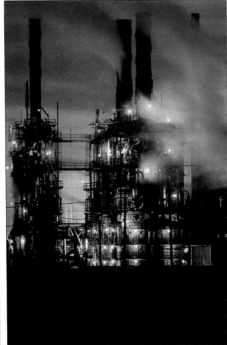

Industrial plant
The image of a chemical plant (above) is by Gabe Palmer. The turquoise smoke and
strong light tints the sky, to offset the stark, intricate outlines of the factory's pipework.

city's dynamism, and the height of office blocks. Heavy overcast weather makes these buildings look foreboding, while sun and slight haze can make them shimmer with light.

Lighting can completely alter the appearance of a scene. A cityscape that appears cluttered and untidy in the revealing light of day can become transformed at dusk, its roads illuminated by neon signs and the lights of vehicles. Bridges turn into delicate silhouettes, their angles and curves standing out clearly against the evening sky.

Industrial plants, waste heaps, factory chimneys, and power lines all form dramatic silhouettes at dusk. Some industries, such as oil refining, offer a wide range of shapes. Mining or engineering sites require a high viewpoint, such as the top of a crane or a helicopter. At night factories look striking, with walkways illuminated and buildings floodlit.

Interiors

A tripod is essential for both general architectural interiors and details. The most useful lens is a wide-angle, but care is necessary in handling this lens. The photographer must keep the camera back upright. If the image includes features well above the camera, a shift lens, or a view camera offering the rising front movement (see *Controlling converging lines,* p. 121) are necessary.

The main technical problems with interiors concern lighting, especially between window and wall detail. If possible, it is best to shoot with the light, keeping the windows behind you so that the room is illuminated evenly. Otherwise it will be vital to average exposure readings taken from both windows and walls, or slightly overexpose the window detail and light the interior with multihead flash. For the best effect, bounce flash illumination off a wall behind the camera. The "painting with light" technique (see *Lighting large areas,* p. 175) is also useful, especially with dark interiors such as churches.

Details can be particularly revealing. Fan vaulting, staircases, or glimpses of rooms through doorways are all elements that show an interior's character. When showing a whole room, you can often stress its best, or most important, features by rearranging the furnishings so that they fit better within the picture area. Domestic interiors frequently look better in photographs if some of the furniture is removed. In all cases an apparently slight adjustment to room contents can make the picture seem much less cluttered.

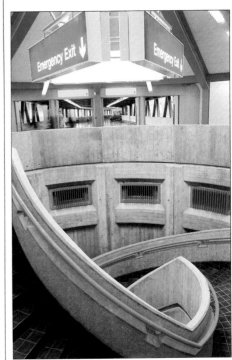

Architecture indoors
Ian McKinnell took the picture of an airport interior (above). The curving stairways and bright colors contribute
to a strong composition that is suitable for an illustration in an architectural book or magazine article.

Landscape photography

To take a successful landscape photograph, it is essential to decide on the subject's vital elements, and exclude, obscure or play down, the unwanted and irrelevant parts. Sometimes the picture has to serve a particular function – for example, showing a geological feature, or making some point about a region's agriculture or geography. It may also have to fill a specific format in a book or magazine. At other times the photographer is free to respond more subjectively to a scene – to its pattern, color, or scale, or to its sense of grandeur or its atmosphere of calm.

In all cases lighting and atmospheric conditions have an important influence on the picture's appearance. It is advisable to examine scenes in varying weather, and at different times of the day (see *Time of day,* p. 23). But it is also necessary to work fast when conditions are changing.

Viewpoint is another essential element in composing landscape pictures. Looking at a subject from different viewpoints can make it change completely in shape, color, or lighting direction. To gain a high viewpoint, some professionals use an automobile with a reinforced roof as a camera platform. It is possible to use a very low camera position to conceal unwanted mid-distance items with foreground detail. A telephoto lens can also help exclude unwanted detail, and produce a flattened composition from subject pattern and texture.

In many parts of the world, landscape appearance changes radically according to the season of the year. Sometimes a particular lighting effect can only occur a few times in the year, such as around the longest or shortest day. Tone and color scheme greatly influence mood in landscapes and depend largely on lighting. But it is possible to modify natural colors to produce the effect required by the careful use of filters. With pale color filters you can strengthen particular hues in a scene without making the effect obvious or artificial. A filter that matches the subject's natural colors will give the best results.

Black and white photography permits the use of strong color filters for fine adjustment of the tone values of blue sky or colored vegetation in relation to neutral rock or clouds. Filters that are too strong produce a dramatic sky that dominates land detail. But a strong, filtered sky can itself form a worthwhile subject.

Occasionally, when a sense of fantasy is required, infrared materials are useful. They transform familiar landscape elements into tone and color values quite different from those seen by the naked eye. Color IR slide film (see *Special color films,* p. 159) gives striking color distortions. But it is not easy to use, because of the difficulty of forecasting the resulting colors. It is best to make tests, especially with a range of color filters.

Black and white IR film can give unreal tonal appearances. With the appropriate filter, sunlit distant landscapes take on a new intensity, with deep haze penetration, darkened skies, and a snow-like glow to vegetation. The less green foliage present, the more subtle the effects of IR film become.

Hills and mountains

It is usually advisable to photograph hills and mountains early or late in the day when oblique light emphasizes their form. Trees or figures help to give scale and suggest distance. Bad weather (such as storms, rain clouds or light mist over peaks, frost, or snow) gives more character to a scene than a conventional fine day. Snow cover is most effective side or backlit to show its pattern and reflective quality. And because snow-covered land requires less exposure, sky detail in the picture appears darker and richer.

Wide-angle lenses help to relate the pattern of foreground rocks to distant peaks. Telephotos allow you to exclude irrelevant foreground details, and seem to place the farthest elements close behind mid-distance features.

The presence of water in the foreground of a landscape allows the pattern and color of distant mountains and sky to be repeated. Change of viewpoint and irregularities in the water surface offer variety, possible effects ranging from a symmetrical mirror image to a generalized mass of tone or color. Haze is also more frequent where there is water. Late dusk shots, in which hill ranges appear as black cutouts against light reflected from the sky above and its reflection in water below, form especially effective images.

Panoramas

A recurring problem in translating landscape scenes into pictures is that the eye can scan a much broader view of the subject than the camera. The photographer usually has to select from this wealth of information. But it is possible to present a wider panorama as one long image. If reproduced large, and viewed from fairly close, a panoramic picture encompassing a 180° angle of view can represent the original scene very realistically.

With a 35 mm panoramic camera (see *Special cameras,* pp. 208-9) it is possible to make such a picture with a single image. If only a regular camera is available, you can build up the panorama as a mosaic with a series of images. When exposing component images in this way, it is essential to keep the camera horizontal, to preserve a straight horizon. A tripod is ideal for this. A standard or short telephoto lens is more likely to give images that join up in foreground and background than a wide-angle. After each exposure you turn the camera on a vertical axis sufficiently to give a 30-40 per cent overlap with the subject area previously recorded. It is vital to match the prints in size, tone, and color balance. When joined as one long print, you can view the panorama bowed into a concave shape.

Another effective way of presenting panoramic landscapes is to shoot color slides with a minimal overlap, and show them with a bank of projectors. Each slide is mounted with a soft edge mask to fade off the image at the sides, so that one joins with the next.

Mountain landscape
This view of Half Dome, Yosemite Valley, is one of Ansel Adams' early "straight" landscape photographs, taken in 1927. Lighting, viewpoint, and a time of year when exposure for the snow-covered ground detail renders the blue sky dark, all add to the mountain's predominant shape. Adams' landscape pictures of the American West have a characteristic sense of grandeur.

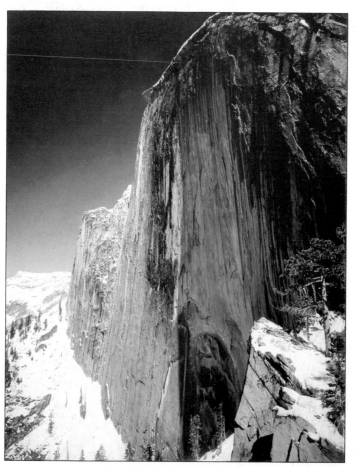

Infrared landscape
The landscape (right) by Trevor Crone was taken on black and white infrared film. The unusual tone qualities of this film type are particularly effective when used with vegetation. Leaves and grass, rich in chlorophyll, are highly reflective to the IR wavelengths in sunlight, appearing light on the film. This effect results in the striking contrast between foliage and sky, with the tones of tree and background opposite to the usual results with panchromatic film. There is also extreme haze penetration.

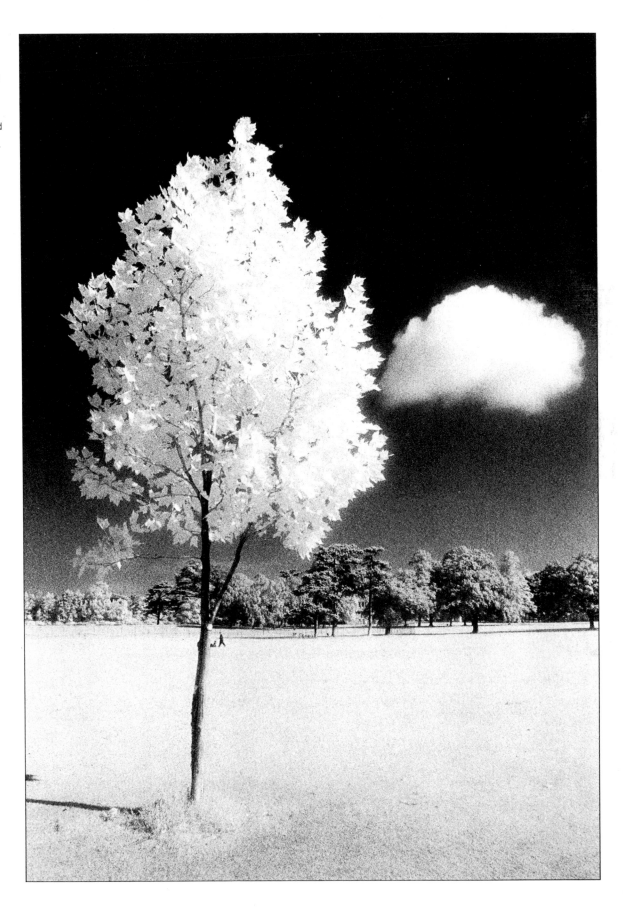

Editorial and advertising photography

One of the most common applications of photography is to help sell products and services through the advertising media. Advertising photography is extremely diversified in subject matter – from simple catalog illustration, to high fashion photographs using distant locations and complex skills and techniques, intended to fill the most costly advertising space.

Advertising work is an area of exacting demands on the photographer's expertise and organizational skills, and of high rewards. It is, by definition, a professional area of photography. Organized team work is essential, and the demands are often highly restrictive to the photographer, who is paid as much for painstaking technical reliability as for imaginative approach. Often, for example, photographers work to an agreed layout or "rough" produced by an art director, and must produce pictures that fill a prescribed space.

Most advertising shots are commissioned through an agency. The photographer has to work with visualizers, art directors, and copywriters, as well as specialists such as stylists, hairdressers, and make-up artists. The investment, including the purchase of advertising space, can be vast, and the photographer's responsibility to produce exactly the right image is very high. The work is also competitive and highly specialized. Agencies choose photographers for a particular ability, such as skill with meticulously constructed still lifes, flair with clothes, ingenuity in devising special effects, or the ability to organize large numbers of people in elaborate, studio sets.

Advertisers tend to be very cautious, and are anxious to appeal to a wide range of potential customers. They can seldom risk images that may shock or offend. But an imaginative team can produce striking results, the best images being impressive even when removed from the context for which they were conceived.

Pictures for magazine editorial features offer less money to the photographer, but greater scope for innovation, though images must complement the text. The size of the final picture, and its structural relationship to other images on the same page are also important considerations.

In successful advertising and editorial photographs props, models, settings, and products must all appear perfect because the resulting image must appear more attractive than life. This means meticulous selection, the construction and adaptation of settings, and the cosmetic treatment of everything, from machinery to foods, product packs to human bodies.

See also
Light sources, pp. 162-6. Lighting in the studio, pp. 167-70. Controlling mixed lighting, pp. 174-6. Advanced flash techniques, pp. 176-8. Surrealism, pp. 378-83.

Equipment and techniques

Photographers use all camera formats, from 10 × 8 ins (25 × 20 cm) to 35 mm. Some still-life specialists prefer the large sheet film formats because of the impressive appearance of final full-page-size color transparencies. These large images are also simple for the designer to relate to layouts, and they allow text to be added easily. For products, room sets, and studio food pictures, the large camera is as convenient to work with as other formats, provided that there is sufficient light for the small lens apertures essential for reasonable depth of field.

For location still-life product work, 5 × 4 ins (12.5 × 10 cm) and rollfilm are the most common formats, while fashion photographers favor the freedom of rollfilm and 35 mm cameras. Camera systems offering a wide range of top-quality lenses are essential. All lens types are required for advertising photography, including fisheyes for special effects.

Studio flash with modeling lamps (see *Flash lighting units,* pp. 165-6) is the most universal source of lighting. It is also possible to use studio flash equipment on location, powered by mobile generators. For room sets and most work on 10 × 8 ins (25 × 20 cm) film, powerful flash equipment giving an output of 10,000 joules or more may also be required.

Color transparency film is most frequently used. To test exposure, lighting effects, and composition before taking the final shot, an instant picture back is invaluable. Often assignments involve working to precise image formats. On sheet film cameras, the photographer can scale down the image to the required height-to-width proportions, and mark them on the focusing screen.

To produce the most appropriate background, it is often necessary to build room sets in the studio, constructing them like theater scenery. For low-budget work, or to supply location-type backgrounds, some photographers use projection techniques (see *Back projection,* p. 181, and *Front projection,* p. 182). A large studio is necessary for products such as automobiles, but as far as possible, real locations are preferable when dealing with big subjects. Location photography provides cheaper and often more authentic results than studio work, though there can be problems with lighting away from the controlled environment of the studio.

Leading advertising photographers work on a freelance basis, though publishers' in-house photographic staff handle some editorial work. All photographers in this field rely heavily on a range of back-up services. Costumiers supply garments, from period dress to futuristic uniforms. Stylists and prop gatherers furnish sets, while location finders offer the addresses and make arrangements for photographic sessions to take place all around the world. Model agencies, hairdressers, and make-up artists are also essential. It is possible to rent every form of technical aid, from fisheye lenses and smoke machines to fully equipped studios complete with staff. High-quality processing laboratories provide a rapid service, together with collection from and delivery to the studio. The photographer must also have an assistant to help in the production of complex images in the studio, as well as an agent to negotiate commissions and fees.

Still life

The best method of building up a set for still-life photography is to work gradually, in stages. It is usual to start by choosing the background or setting, and positioning the subject. Then set up the camera, on a tripod or studio stand, and make adjustments to viewpoint, camera angle, and focus. The appropriate props are then added. These should complement the shape, color, and texture of the subject without dominating it or confusing the composition. At this stage, the photographer establishes the quality, strength, direction, and distribution of the lighting. Again, it is best to do this gradually, observing the effects of each change to the illumination on the camera's focusing screen (see *Controlling lighting,* p. 169). When the lighting is satisfactory, and the exposure set, it is advisable to use an instant picture back to test the result. The photographer can then make further fine adjustments before exposing the final picture.

Food

With certain subjects, such as foods, color and condition are critical. Only the very finest specimens are acceptable – the slightest defects

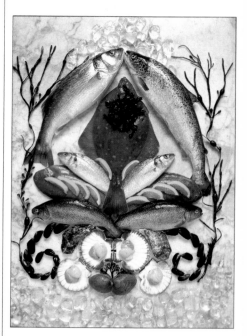

Arranging food
The highly symmetrical picture of fish (above) is by photographer Tessa Traeger, who specializes in elaborate studies of food. The ice and marble slab give the fish an appropriate background, setting off the ingenious arrangement. Perfect examples of the produce were required.

will ruin the final image. To photograph cooked foods, it is best to use meats and vegetables that are slightly undercooked, so that they retain their form and structure.

Photographers often have to compensate for the fact that the naked eye sees things differently from the camera. The imagination often enhances objects that the camera renders lifeless and flat. Most codes of advertising practice permit photographers to compensate for this by treating subjects in certain ways. Steaks and sausages may be frequently coated with glycerine to increase surface shine, while photographers add detergent to beer to enhance the head. Some substances, such as red wine, are difficult to photograph effectively. It is common practice to dilute red wine, to avoid underexposure. Certain items, such as cut and peeled fruit, deteriorate rapidly. Citric acid may be used for treating fruit, to prevent the cut surfaces from turning brown.

A further problem in food photography is that publishing dates make it necessary to

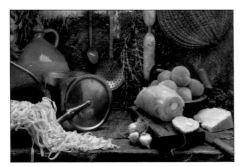

Food in a setting
Robert Golden's study (above) places pasta, garlic, meat, and cheese in a context of glowing surfaces, rich textures, and warm colors, making the food

inviting and appetizing. The surrounding kitchen equipment, wooden table surface, basket, and hanging herbs all enhance the total effect.

shoot months ahead, so that ingredients are not necessarily in season. Photographers often have to locate specimens and have them flown in. Choice of settings, and props such as plates, bowls, and cutlery is critical. These items must create the right atmosphere, without distracting the eye from the picture's main subject. But even the most elaborate treatment and the best props cannot disguise inferior subject matter.

Exploded views
Products that are designed for assembly or dismantling by the purchaser can be illustrated in an "exploded view". For example, a model airplane kit can appear with its components shown separately, as if floating in the air, but in the same configuration as when they are assembled. A sheet film camera is ideal, because the photographer can align the separate items by marking the focusing screen with wax pencil lines. Clamps are used to support each component from behind, at the height and angle that appear correct from the camera position. A retoucher removes the images of the supporting clamps with an airbrush, and the photographer copies the print.

Scale models
Photography of model figures, cars, and projected architectural developments requires particular care. A small lens aperture is necessary to maximize depth of field when working close up. Lighting must look natural – a single main source is best – and the correct camera-to-subject distance is vital to give realistic

perspective. The model's scale dictates camera distance, and height above the model's base. For example, you must photograph a 1:100 scale model with the camera at one-hundredth normal eye height. With small models, achieving a close camera position is

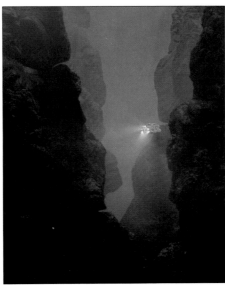

Using scale models
Nic Tompkin's picture of a model submarine (above) was made for an oil company. The image suggests themes of power and exploration.

The problem subject
Ray Massey's shot of a glass (below) shows mastery of a difficult subject. He inverted the image for a mysterious effect.

often difficult. Sometimes the only method of achieving the correct viewpoint from within the model is to use a right-angled endoscope (see *Surveillance and inspection,* pp. 288-9), in place of a normal camera lens.

Problem subjects
Some of the most difficult subjects for lighting have highly reflective surfaces. These range from metals such as polished chrome or silver, to glass. Coins, and similar flat objects can be lit through a 45° semi-silvered mirror (see *Using mirrors,* p. 183). A light tent is ideal for items such as chrome furniture and cutlery. It is also possible to backlight these items. This is especially suitable for glass (see *Lighting glass,* p. 174).

The main aim is to express the material's essential visual qualities, and the object's design, in as interesting and eye-catching a way as possible. Sometimes, for an editorial feature, a general theme is more important than particular subject qualities. For example, a still life may be required to epitomize nostalgia, or life in the future.

There are a number of devices that advertising photographers use to alter the appearance of subjects. For example, a cobweb machine and gray powder can produce a sinister, haunted atmosphere. Dry ice makes products appear to float on clouds. Sometimes, the subject itself may require extensive modification to achieve a startling effect. For example, a client may want a bare light bulb to glow, even though it is clearly disconnected and lying on a table. This requires running wires to the bulb filament from the back of the glass, and linking them to the electricity supply through a concealed hole in the table.

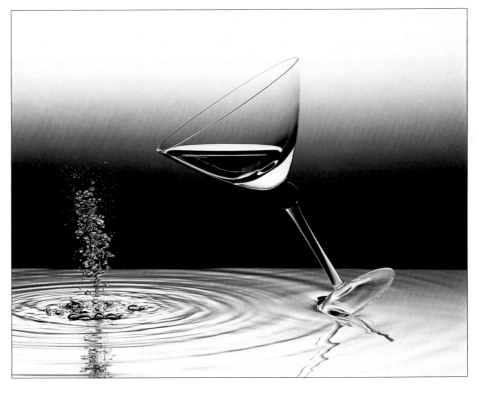

Fashion photography

The work of the fashion photographer ranges from recording garments accurately and objectively for mail order catalogs, to creating the settings that surround the latest designs for the world's foremost fashion magazines. The photographers who produce pictures for these publications usually aim to create ideas and illusions as much as reproducing the factual details of the garments. This is the most competitive and exclusively professional field of all photography.

Fashion is changing continuously, so exploratory, adventurous photography plays an important part in encouraging new ideas and "looks". This has led to dramatic changes in the styles of fashion photography, reflecting similar alterations in fashion itself. For example, the elegance of Baron de Meyer's 1920s fashion plates reflects a period when designers were concerned only with creating highly priced, exclusive garments. In the 1950s and 1960s, fashion designers turned their attention increasingly to ready-to-wear designs, less expensive and of more interest to young wage-earners. This development was mirrored in the image fashion designers wished to convey through photography. A lively, youthful approach replaced the elegance of the mid-century, typified by the work of Helmut Newton and David Bailey in the 1960s. This dynamic style of photography was not limited to pictures of ready-to-wear garments, but had a widespread influence on high-fashion photography. This development is revealed in the fashion magazines, which since the 60s have featured more pictures and fewer words, as well as using color more liberally.

The change of approach affected models as well as clothes. The frozen, statuesque figures in De Meyer's pictures gave way to the dynamic models of the 50s and 60s. Models and photographers no longer worked only in the studio, but also used real environments—from palaces to scrapyards, lonely beaches to crowded markets. Dramatic illumination from spotlights gave way to daylight, matched in the studio by soft, directional flash.

Today's photographers create their own individual approach to garments through choice of models, make-up, lighting, setting, and poses. The most successful photographers have an excellent rapport with their models, and are also capable of producing high-quality portraits. They work better within the less restricted, more exploratory, approach of editorial photography than within the rigorous confines of advertising assignments.

Make-up
Most models have neutral faces that can produce widely differing impressions according to the make-up used. Make-up is therefore a vital element in fashion photography, streng-

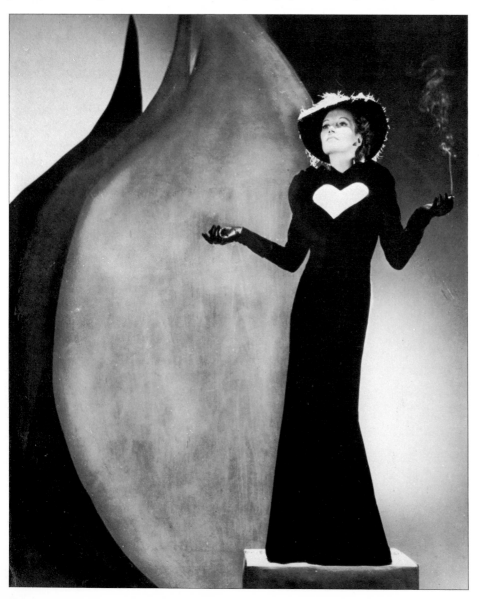

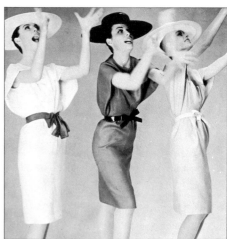

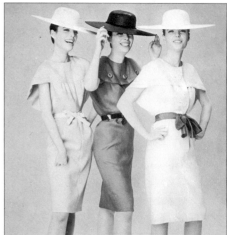

The statuesque pose
Constantin Joffé's fashion picture (left), taken in the 1930s, shows the elegance of the period. (Photograph courtesy of Sotheby's, Belgravia.)

Fashion in the 1960s
The two pictures from 1964 (above) are by Norman Parkinson. They show the informal approach, with expressive use of movement typical of the 60s.

thening the particular "look" the client wants to convey. The most important role of make-up is in enhancing mood and atmosphere. This type of make-up may be soft and romantic, bright and artificial, or theatrical and bizarre.

In most cases, make-up for photography must be more exaggerated than for normal wear. As well as helping to convey mood, the make-up should enhance the shape and tonal contrasts of the model's face. To do this, it is essential to pay special attention to the bone structure, and give the face a zone of emphasis, such as the eyes or lips. The photographer can strengthen shape and contrast further by making adjustments to lighting and altering viewpoint, while the model can emphasize these aspects by changing pose.

Model release
Everyone who models for a commercially used picture is normally asked to sign a "model release" form. Either the photographer or the art editor can organize this, and both agencies and publishers insist on releases that cover every recognizable person in a picture. Signing a release form means that the model foregoes any legal claim to influence the use of the picture later, usually in return for a modeling fee. This gives the photographer, agency, and client the freedom to use results from a photographic session in any way they wish, provided it is not offensive to the model as a private individual.

Modern approaches to fashion
Wayne Gunther's picture (below) illustrates a straightforward approach to fashion photography showing off the clothes to their best advantage. The studio shot (below center) by Diana Miller displays the garments clearly, but complements the mood with the stark silhouetted pattern of the wire.

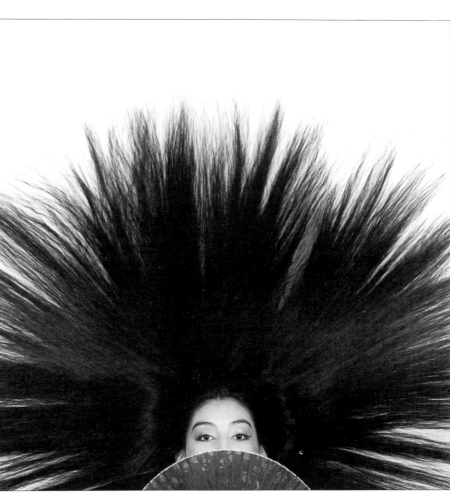

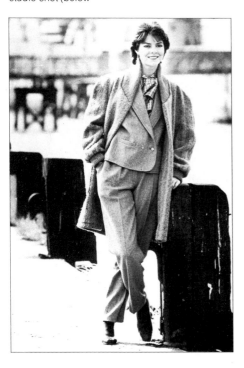

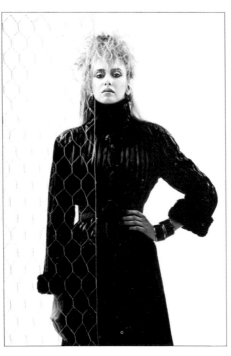

Hairstyles
The graphic study of a model's hair (above) is by Diana Miller. The bold shapes of fan, face, and hair mirror each other.

Make-up
Bob Carlos Clarke concentrated on one model's face to show her make-up (below). Soft lighting gives a delicate effect.

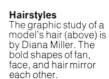
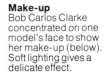
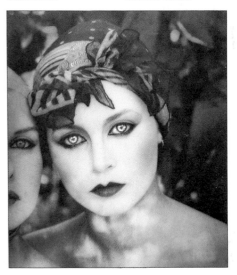

Advertising approaches

A successful advertising photographer must be able to identify closely with the purpose and ideas behind a particular campaign. Usually advertisements are of two types. "Hard sell" approaches feature the actual product, or its packaging, very prominently. The product is often shown in surroundings that set a scene, making the viewer wish to identify with it, but this background remains strictly subsidiary to the subject. Manufacturers often commission specially made "perfect" packs and contents intended only for photography.

If it is not easy or desirable to show the product itself, advertisers adopt a "soft sell" approach. For example, it is easier to advertise gasoline, insurance, and air conditioning by expressing their benefits to the purchaser. This approach gives greater scope for staged situations, and these may be humorous, bizarre, or romantic. Surrealism also exerts a strong influence on contemporary advertising style.

Photographers often build commercially successful themes around goals of universal appeal such as security, status, and affluence. Sometimes the photograph is designed purely for its arresting effect, the simple presence of a well-known product name being enough to promote the client's interests.

Another factor conditioning approach is the form in which the final advertisement will appear. Billboard posters must be direct and simple — they are scanned rapidly and must convey their message with immediacy. Book, magazine, and record covers should also have a strong, direct appeal. Like the pictures on packaging and can labels, they can often encourage impulse buying. Advertisements in particular magazines and newspapers, and point-of-sale material, all have slightly different aims, and are directed at a thoroughly researched audience. It is therefore often necessary to illustrate the same product or service in subtly different ways. It is also vital to take pictures of different formats. These requirements force the photographer to be flexible in composition, taking into account how a client may wish to use an image.

All these requirements impose restrictions, few of which apply to independent, self-expressive photographers. But an imaginative photographer and a sympathetic art director can still initiate original ideas, at the same time as matching a client's visual demands with the photographer's individual creative approach.

An advertiser may turn to one photographer for a moody, atmospheric approach, to another for a strictly objective, or dynamic shot. Some photographers work with immense patience and care, gradually producing meticulous still lifes of products, for example, or special effects montages. Others have a more spontaneous, intuitive approach, particularly when working with people, and so produce lively, expressive pictures. There is always a danger of photographers becoming increasingly specialized, and art directors making obvious choices of photographer when they want images of a particular type. In such an environment, pictures can easily become repetitive and stale. For this reason art directors are always looking for photographers with new ideas and fresh approaches, who are also sufficiently experienced and reliable.

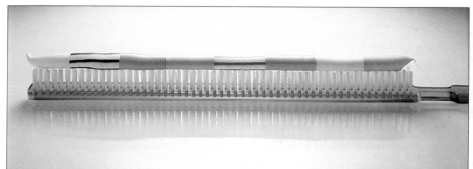

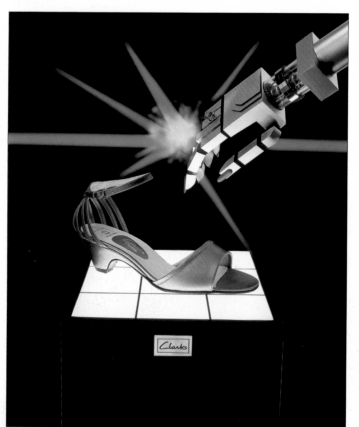

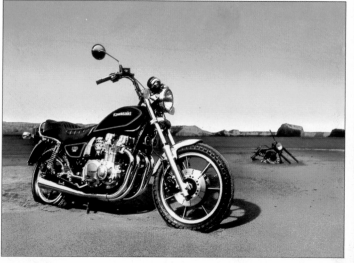

Hard-sell image
Nic Tompkin's picture for a shoe manufacturer (left) combines accurate recording of the product with a surrealist element — the mechanical hand. The striking green light rays complete the composition. Tompkin made a separate exposure for the light rays, and shooting the rest of the picture on the same frame of film.

Soft-sell image
The picture of an elongated toothbrush (above) was designed to advertise a range of products relating to dental care. The result is a clear, unified symbol, more effective than a cluttered illustration of a large number of items. The different colors suggest a variety of products. The picture is by Ray Massey.

Varying treatments
To create the bright, aggressive picture (facing page), Nic Tompkin used a multiple exposure for the light trails. These emphasize the bike's smooth lines, suggesting speed. Bob Carlos Clarke produced the softer effect (below), using montage, and coloring the shot with an airbrush.

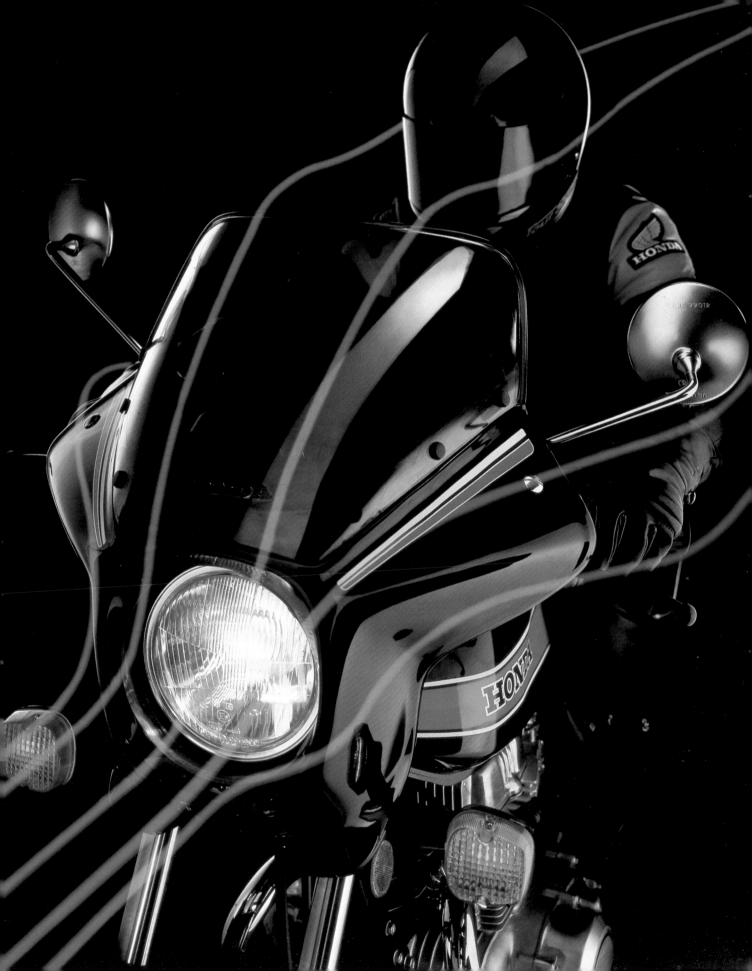

The human figure

Photographers, like painters before them, have always been keenly interested in portraying other people. Portraiture is highly commercial. As early as 1841, daguerreotype studios were established in France and England, and proved popular at once. Because exposures took several minutes, sitters often held stiff, self-conscious poses, but these early portraits were still impressive.

As photographic emulsions with greater sensitivity to light became common, portrait photography developed into an important part of everyday life. The 1930s and 40s brought further advances. Flexible spotlights and floods allowed flattering "glamor" lighting, while heavy negative retouching gave sitters apparently flawless features. Modern portrait methods allow the photographer complete control over results. Sometimes the intention is to flatter the subject, by stressing attractive and pleasing aspects. On other occasions the subject's public image is most important – the picture must suggest power, intellect, or charisma. The sitters themselves often commission these pictures, encouraging photography to fulfil a role similar to portrait painting. Third parties also frequently commission photographs of particular people. These range from relatives of the sitter, to companies, magazine editors, or calendar designers. Each will have opinions about the final result of the photographic session.

Specialized areas of portraiture pose their own problems. Stage photography, for example, involves difficulties with the use of existing light and the depiction of moving subjects. Nude photography is probably the most difficult aspect of all photography of the human figure. Although painters have depicted the nude for centuries, the clinical and revealing camera creates problems of its own. As a result nude photography has been confused by conflicts between art and morals, changes in attitudes to nakedness, and a market in pornography. The best nude photographers overcome these limitations by using a personal style to make original statements about their subjects' qualities.

Leading portraitists aim for pictures that give a perceptive interpretation of their subjects. A fine balance is required between the photographer's own style and the sitter's individual personality and physical characteristics. To achieve this balance, it is vital to be adept at putting people at their ease. At the same time, the photographer must make resourceful use of equipment, to stress wanted characteristics and conceal others.

See also
Lighting, pp. 160-1. Print finishing *Retouching and spotting,* p. 252. The documentary approach, pp. 347-57.

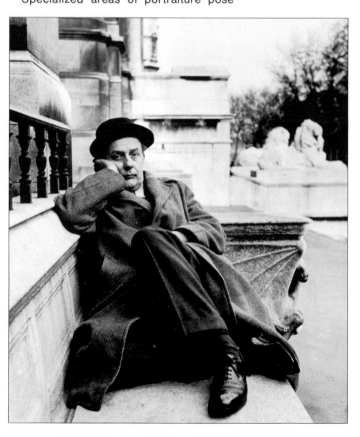

Sir John Betjeman
Cecil Beaton's portrait of the English poet Sir John Betjeman makes a special point of emphasizing his face. The architectural details, and the subject's leg and arm act as lead-in lines to the head (which is placed at the intersection of thirds). The poet's pensive expression, and the unusual, casual pose, give a strong impression of his character. The old building alerts the viewer to the poet's interest in architecture and his concern for his country's heritage.

Equipment and techniques

Early portrait photographers used sheet film cameras, in order to produce negatives large enough to retouch. Today most photographers use rollfilm or 35 mm equipment for portraiture, because of its convenience and speed of use. But the sheet film formats are still valuable for color images of superb quality, particularly when clients require oversize prints with minimal graininess.

The disadvantage with all sheet film cameras for portraiture is the inevitable delay between focusing and shooting – while you insert the film holder and close the shutter. A few sheet film cameras have cable links to speed up these actions. Some photographers solve the problem by using a 5 × 4 ins (12.5 × 10 cm) twin lens reflex camera.

Short telephoto lenses are generally more useful for portraits than standard or wide-angle types. With 35 mm equipment, for example, a 100 mm or 135 mm lens allows you to take full-frame head-and-shoulders portraits from a sufficient distance to avoid steep perspective. An 80-200 mm zoom is also useful, together with a 100 mm macro for big close-ups. For available light photography, the fastest possible lens is essential. With telephotos, a maximum aperture greater than f 4 is ideal. All lenses also require hoods – especially when shooting against the light.

Most photographers find that a motor drive and long cable release help in capturing fleeting expressions and poses. A tripod is always useful when composing, making it easier to adjust lighting and setting. A few special effects attachments, such as a diffuser, can sometimes help add atmosphere.

The most comfortable lighting is vital in the studio. Multihead electronic flash, with modeling lamps and large umbrella reflectors, is often best. These are portable enough for use at any location with a power supply. Most studios have a selection of props – chairs, stools, paneling, drapes, and other background materials such as paper rolls. None of these should be assertive or colorful enough to distract from the main subject.

Reflector boards and light diffusers (see *Lighting accessories,* p. 166) are very important both in the studio and on location. Folding reflectors are ideal for setting up on the shadow side of a bay window or porch to create an area of controlled illumination enclosing the subject and photographer. This arrangement helps to give fill-in light with the same quality as bounced studio lighting, yet has the advantage of allowing the photographer to show a real environment.

Each subject presents its own problems and priorities, but the main factors to consider are choice of setting, camera angle and distance (and accordingly the best lens focal length), lighting, pose, and expression. The last two of these variables are by far the most important, but also the least controllable.

Choice of film varies with lighting conditions. It is best to avoid graininess by using the slowest film that will allow a practical exposure. But occasionally a grainy pattern, eliminating fine detail, helps to give a coarse, rugged appearance to a portrait, especially when enlarged. Grain can also give an interesting texture to nudes.

Groups

Before photographing a group of people, it is necessary to decide whether to arrange them formally, or to choose an informal grouping. This will depend partly on the subject, and partly on the size of the group – it is very difficult to photograph a large informal group effectively. For a formal group, you first have to decide how to arrange the collection of people into an overall shape, preferably with a main feature or focal point. With subjects such as wedding parties and athletic teams this treatment can work well. It is easy to arrange everyone symmetrically on either side of the married couple or team captain. You may have to arrange large, seated groups in tiers, or shoot them from a high viewpoint, although this results in distortion, foreshortening the front row. The larger the group, the closer the members will have to be in order to fill the final picture with faces of a recognizable size. With formal groups, it is essential to show each member's face clearly. It is often best to shoot a large number of frames to do this, especially with a large group, since some results are likely to be ruined if one person moves slightly at the moment of exposure. Often the photographer must draw everyone's attention in some way at the moment of exposure – by giving a prearranged signal, blowing a whistle, or by asking the subjects themselves to sing or shout. If the group is too large to photograph with conventional equipment, a panoramic camera (see *Special cameras,* pp. 208-9) may provide the best solution to the problem.

Smaller group portraits usually work best if the subjects pose naturally, using relevant local backgrounds and settings as much as possible. A family in their home, athletes in a gymnasium, or even a group of firemen around their fire engine, are all excellent combinations of setting and subject. But the photographer must make adjustments, for example giving one person a more dominant position than another, introducing props where necessary, filling ugly gaps in the composition, and creating an overall structure for the image.

The less obvious and regimented this grouping appears the better. To create the impression of spontaneity, it is often preferable to encourage individuals to relate to each other rather than to the camera. Sympathy, and an inquiring interest in the subjects is essential to produce a spontaneous result.

Lighting is important in all group portraits. The best illumination is soft and even, avoiding any confusing shadows cast by one figure on the next. It is also essential to avoid strong light that shines in the subjects' eyes, making them squint.

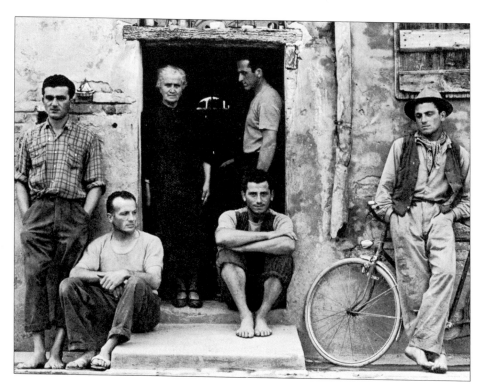

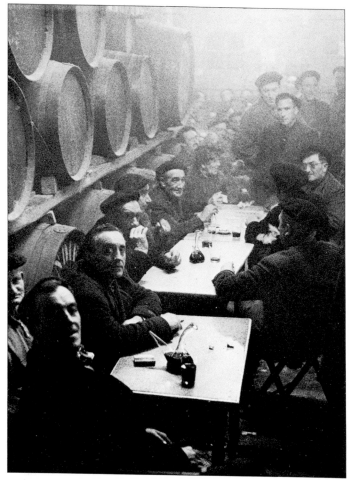

"The Family Luzzara, Italy"
Paul Strand took the serene portrait of an Italian family (above) in 1953. The figures are grouped around their front door, which acts as a framing device, emphasizing the importance of the mother. The poses are casual, but Strand has obviously arranged them to produce a finely balanced picture – the different directions of the subject's gazes help cement the structure. By breaking away from the traditional arrangement of people in rows, the photographer has produced an integrated image of patterns and shapes. ("The Family. Luzzara, Italy, 1953", Copyright © 1 1953, 1955, 1971, 1976, The Paul Strand Foundation, as published in Paul Strand: *Sixty Years of Photographs* Aperture, 1976.)

Informal group
This informal, atmospheric picture of men in a French wine cellar is by Edouard Boubat. The grainy effect helps to convey the mood of the location and brings out the character of the subjects' faces. The strong perspective leads the viewer's eye along the line of heads.

Individual portraits

In all portraiture, the photographer must decide what the sitter's strongest characteristics are. Some of these features will be physical, but psychological attributes are most important. The photographer must concentrate on these characteristics — which can range from vivacity and self-confidence to reserve and contemplation — and find the best ways of expressing them photographically.

To reveal the subject's physical features, close attention to composition and lighting is necessary. To capture personality, you must have a good relationship with the sitter, as well as the ability to shoot at the right moment. A relaxed atmosphere during shooting, together with the ability to put subjects at their ease by conversation, is essential. It is therefore best to avoid lighting set-ups that involve critical, time-consuming adjustments, as these force subjects into rigid poses. At all stages, the photographer must not be so involved in the technicalities of the camera and lighting that the sitter feels like an inanimate object. It is best to use conversation to create a relaxed atmosphere in the studio.

The setting

Whether the picture is taken outdoors, inside a room, or in the studio, the subject's surroundings are critical. An environment that is directly relevant to the sitter will be most revealing. This can involve showing the subject at home, at work, or in a studio set containing relevant props.

Using an existing setting is always worthwhile if the familiar surroundings make the sitter less self-conscious than if you had been working in an artificial studio environment. But it will require some adaptation — objects in the background such as wall hangings, desk lamps, or chairs, will probably need repositioning. It is also possible to alter viewpoint to exclude irrelevant and confusing items (see *Moving in close,* p. 62) or to transform the surroundings completely (see *Change of background,* p. 63).

Another approach is to create a simple austere portrait against a plain background, with soft overall lighting. To produce this effect, diffused studio lighting may be best.

Techniques for individual portraits

A tripod, although not always technically necessary, means that the photographer does not have to look through the viewfinder continuously. This allows more natural communication with the subject. The photographer can watch the sitter's face, noting the slightest changes in expression, and exposing enough film to capture each alteration. A small-format camera is ideal for shooting a large number of exposures in a short time.

Camera angle is also critical. You can use it to emphasize important features and suppress others. Seen from the front, for example, a long nose appears shorter and a broad nose wider than from a profile or three-quarter view. A low viewpoint emphasizes chin and mouth. Often an eye-level viewpoint is best because the eyes are the most dominant and influential facial features. But a full face view of the subject may be too symmetrical — often a three-quarter portrait is more interesting, with the nose dividing the face into unequal segments.

The other major influence on the appearance of a portrait is lighting. Most photographers prefer to keep the arrangement simple, using existing light as much as possible. This can be modified slightly to control contrast and composition. Fill-in flash and reflector boards are especially useful to reduce shadows.

Character portrait

In Clive Frost's portrait directional lighting gives the picture structure by lighting half the background and half the subject's face. The picture conveys the man's concentration, as he tilts the desk forward to benefit from the light coming in from the window.

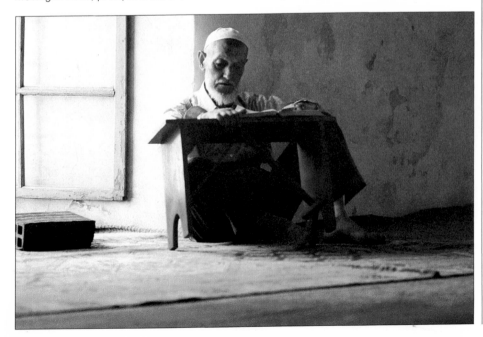

Photographing stage performers

Photographers of theater, ballet, and film productions once always used sheet film cameras. They produced static images of entire sets, and portraits of the stars that it was possible to retouch. Today, the more portable 35 mm and rollfilm equipment is preferred by stage photographers taking pictures for press publicity, programs, and front-of-house illustrations. These photographs are also used in magazines and books about the theater.

Theater work is a specialist area of photography, relying on a close working relationship with directors and actors, as well as a wide knowledge of the theater. Access to rehearsals, photo-calls, and performances when photography can take place comes through commissioning from producers.

The photographer must be able to use available stage lighting. In the theater this is often adequate in strength, but too harsh and contrasty for photography. Where possible (at photo-calls, for example) the house lights can remain up, to reduce this problem. For single

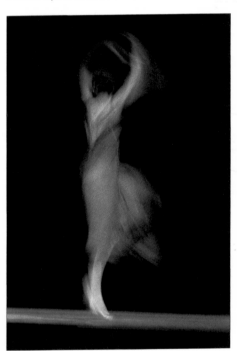

Movement in the theater

John Starr used blur to capture this dancer's graceful movements. By keeping some elements (such as foot and earring) sharp and bright, Starr emphasized the moving parts of the figure.

portraits in the theater, some photographers use mobile lighting kits to create a miniature "studio". But it is more usual to take pictures without interrupting the performance. Here even the noise of the shutter can be a distraction, and some photographers use a soundproof camera housing.

The contrast between figures and dark settings on stage often creates exposure difficulties. TTL meters are frequently misled. A spot meter (see *Using a hand-held meter,* p. 136) provides the best solution.

The nude

Most people find that nudes are the most difficult of all subjects to photograph well. In drawing and painting, the nude human body has always been recognized for its grace, beauty of line, and purity of form. But photography, with its detail-recording ability, can more easily arouse a sense of voyeurism and eroticism, even when the photographer's intention is to convey youth, freedom, or a sense of sculptural form. Another reason why many nude studies do not succeed is a barrier of mutual embarrassment between photographer and model. Photographic sessions become furtive, with neither party having a clear idea of what sort of images to produce.

The serious photographer goes to great lengths to find a relaxed model and create a good working relationship (detached, but not excessively formal) so that they are both aiming at a good set of pictures. All models feel vulnerable, even for simple facial studies. A nude model is especially vulnerable and needs to have confidence in the photographer's ability to create worthwhile results.

A wide range of interpretative approaches is possible, from harshly objective to abstract, from the explicit to the sentimental or romantic. The landscape of the human body can appear innocent or erotic, romantic or stark. It may be distorted into new forms, or translated into visual fantasy.

The photographer must visualize and plan the image well in advance. The result may be influenced by market requirements, but if free interpretation is possible it is sensible to avoid eroticism as the sole aim, preventing it from becoming a substitute for other qualities.

The model

A good nude model is never embarrassed about being naked. Experience need not be important. Professional models can all too easily lapse into predictable routine poses, just as lazy photographers sometimes adopt a set working formula. Painters' models are often unsuitable, because they are used to static posing over long periods. A photographic model, on the other hand, must be prepared to change poses rapidly, and should understand how the lighting and other equipment will affect the final pictures. This will result in an ability to understand the photographer's requirements that is much more important than any acquired posing habits. Personality and expression are also crucial. The model's character should be responsive and outgoing, and the expression natural.

Approaches to nude photography

Locations should connect with the ideas and associations the photographer wants to convey. They must also afford privacy. Ferns and long grasses suit a romantic image better than a background filled with harsh, rocky texture. Soft, directional daylight often suits the body's rounded forms, unless it is important to emphasize silhouette shape or skin texture. Lighting should also contribute to mood. Low-key lighting helps to convey a sense of intimacy and mystery, while stronger light and cast shadow patterns may suit a more dynamic or provocative pose.

Some of the most rewarding nude photo-graphs are made by isolating small areas of the body and treating these like still-life, land-scape, or abstract compositions. Backs and shoulders, hands and sides work well this way — and this is also a good method of beginning when working with a new model, as it can help break down any barriers of embarrassment that exist between photographer and model.

For pictures with a romantic emphasis, a typical choice of setting may be an interior with pale, muted colors, or, outdoors, a backlit water scene. It is best to avoid intricate textures and patterns.

The choice of model, lighting, and props, as well as camera accessories such as diffusers and starburst attachments, should convey a sense of softness. Hard illumination given by direct flash on the camera would destroy the illusion totally. Any garments should be loose and flowing, and light in texture. It is advisable to avoid extreme focal length lenses, contrived camera angles, or forced, unnatural poses when creating a romantic image.

Whatever approach is adopted, the photographer must capture the expression, pose, or movement that shows most clearly the picture's central theme.

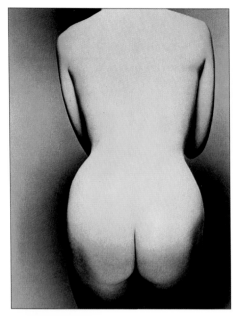

Flattened form
Bob Carlos Clarke's delicate nude study (above) uses slight shading on the edges of the figure to give a suggestion of subject form. But the central area of the back is unshaded, to give a flattened effect unusual in nude photographs. This, together with the overall light-brown coloring, and the tightly cropped head and legs, gives the image a haunting, statuesque quality.

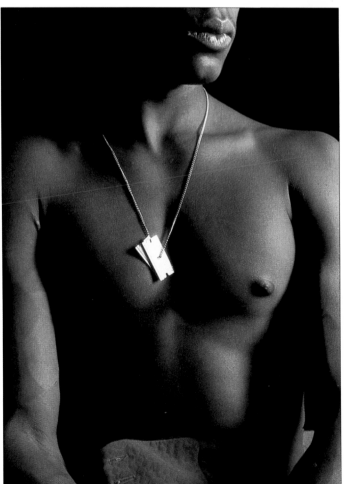

Texture and detail
The strong shadows and sense of form in the male nude by Will McBride (left) show a realistic approach. Use of directional lighting and a very dark background have also allowed the photographer to convey clearly the texture and quality of the subject's skin, with clear highlight areas. The rich, dark skin coloring is complemented by the red garment.

Reportage photography

Photographs for newspapers and illustrated magazines have a special importance. They provide permanent visual records of news events, putting faces to names, and showing the actual detail of what happened. Above all, they have the weight of authenticity and truth.

Reportage photography divides into two main areas: press photography and photojournalism. Press photography is concerned with summing up an event in a single picture, against all odds (including rival photographers), and in time to make the paper's next edition. A good press picture has strong news content – it should be memorable, and should make the reader want to read the article. It should therefore ideally contain the distilled essence of a situation, a revealed moment of truth.

Photojournalism is the communication of a situation, a place, or an event through picture essays. Here, the photographer's own point of view is all-important. More time is usually available for photography, and greater space in the publication, allowing the photographer to make personal comments on the subject.

The evolution of reportage photography

Although photography is an ideal medium for reportage, it was not until the late nineteenth century that photographs occasionally began to appear in print. The reason for this was the technical difficulty of making metal printing plates directly from photographs, preserving a full range of gray tones. There was also the reluctance of newspaper propietors and craftsmen who had vested interests in an industry where illustrations were drawn and engraved.

But by 1904, the world's first newspaper illustrated exclusively with photographs, the British *Daily Mirror*, had appeared. It quickly acquired a vast new readership among people who found the usual solid pages of text intimidating or dull. Within a few years photographs ousted drawn engravings in print. Newspapers employed their own photographers and also bought in pictures from newly created press photo agencies, who sent out cameramen to cover the main news events.

The evolution of wider aperture lenses and the flash bulb increased the press photographer's versatility, but hand-held plate cameras were still in use until the 1950s. Meanwhile, in Germany in the 1920s and 1930s, the editors of magazines such as the *Berliner Illustrierte Zeitung* began publishing sets of interrelated pictures. This coincided with new smaller format cameras such as the Ermanox and the Leica, which for the first time allowed the taking of candid pictures. Journalists turned photojournalists, presenting human interest stories in pictorial forms.

The idea of the picture magazine proved popular and spread around the world. Soon dozens of titles, such as *Vu, Life,* and *Picture Post,* were established, providing work for a new generation of mainly European photographers and picture editors. Many of these, including Alfred Eisenstaedt, Felix Mann, Brassaï, André Kertész, and Henri Cartier-Bresson, established international reputations largely as a result of this work.

The 1940s and 1950s proved the boom years for the picture magazines. During the 60s, with the wide availability of television, their popularity and advertising revenues declined, and many magazines closed. Since then the situation has stabilized. Many newspapers now run magazine supplements, and in Europe magazines such as *Paris Match* and *Stern* still survive independently. More modern layout, and the increasing use of color, have meant that contemporary photojournalists have had to evolve a more flexible technique.

See also
Timing and movement *Framing the action,* pp. 86-7; *The critical moment,* p. 88; *Controlling the setting,* p. 90; *Juxta-position and transient relationships,* p. 92. **The documentary approach,** pp. 347-57.

Equipment and techniques

Early press photographers used hand-held 5 × 4 ins (12.5 × 10 cm) plate cameras. These were simple to operate and reliable. They allowed photographers to rush-process individual exposures, and enlarge them while still wet. Their rangefinder focusing and wire frame viewfinders were designed to facilitate fast focusing and viewing. But plate cameras were also large and obtrusive, and eventually most press photographers turned to rollfilm twin lens reflex cameras. The TLR was smaller, quieter, and convenient for holding high or low (see *TLR cameras,* p. 107). Its design also allowed quick and easy picture composition.

Although some press photographers still favor the TLR, most now use 35 mm equipment. This has the convenience of interchangeable lenses, and is even less bulky than rollfilm equipment. Its ability to take 36 pictures at a single loading is an advantage in both photojournalism and press work. The photographer can cover fast-changing situations with a motor drive attached to the camera, often holding the cameras above the heads of a crowd. In spite of these advantages, the 35 mm format took a long time to become accepted for press work, due to the inconvenience and care required when fast-processing small negatives, and the mechanical unreliability of early SLRs. Today the majority of press photographers and photojournalists prefer 35 mm equipment, though some avoid the SLR in preference to the extra shutter quietness and bright viewfinder of a rangefinder direct vision type.

Press photographers usually carry at least two camera bodies, reducing the risk of running out of film at a critical moment. It is also possible to equip the bodies with different lenses. Wide-aperture standard and wide-angle lenses are the most useful for confined situations, especially indoors. While each photographer has a comprehensive lens kit covering the most useful focal lengths, newspapers and agencies often hold specialist items such as extreme telephotos and high-speed cameras capable of shooting about 100 frames per second.

Electronic flash is the universal, hand-held light source, but wherever possible, photographers prefer to work in existing light. This produces pictures that have a more naturalistic appearance, and allows the photographer to be discreet. Automatic internal camera meters are now so reliable that it is possible to use them confidently for exposure measurement in press work.

For black and white photography, medium or fast (ASA 400) film is most widely used. Chromogenic types are particularly popular for their exposure latitude, although they require more elaborate processing. Virtually all color photography is handled on slide materials. If necessary, push-processed ASA 400 color film helps the photographer cope with dim lighting conditions. But many photojournalists prefer slow ASA 24 color transparency film for its high resolution, where subject conditions permit.

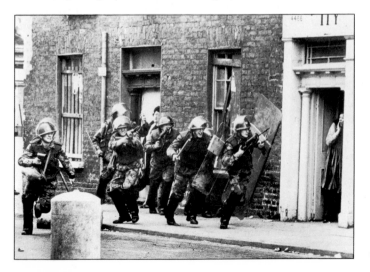

British soldiers, Northern Ireland
This dramatic picture taken in Londonderry, Northern Ireland is by Donald McCullin. It shows the horror on the faces of women watching in their doorways as soldiers of the Royal Anglian Regiment charge after an outbreak of stoning. The picture illustrates movingly the contrast between the violence of street warfare and ordinary, everyday urban life. McCullin is well known for his compassionate and provocative pictures of the victims of war that have been published widely.

Press photography

Photographs of a day's events must be produced fast, to meet printing deadlines. Speed is more important than top technical quality — no matter how well composed and printed a picture may be, its news value will be severely limited if it misses an edition. Reliable transport, and resourcefulness in finding the best viewpoints in diverse situations, are also vital.

Today the task of finding newsworthy stories is mainly the job of the picture editor. But competition is fierce, and it is essential for the photographer to find the most forceful pictures of a particular event. Not all press photography is of the "hot news" type. Much of the work is routine coverage of public events and appearances by people who are potentially newsworthy. If there is a shortage of good news stories, it is often up to the photographer to supply topical pictures to fill space.

Most press photographers are on the staff of newspapers or agencies. The news agencies specialize in fast distribution of images to leading papers and television networks. They also supply other markets, from local newspapers to specialist magazines.

Everyone involved in press photography, from the photographer to the printer, must make use of all the available technical aids. For the photographer, this means rapid processing and sometimes the use of high-quality instant picture cameras to short-cut the processing stages. As electronic still cameras are introduced (see *Future design trends,* p. 211) it will be possible for the photographer to telephone the camera's picture signal direct to the news desk soon after the picture is taken. Meanwhile, advanced electronics already play an important role in the production of many international magazines. Satellites facilitate the rapid scanning and transmitting of pictures from one part of the world to another, so that it is possible to print the magazine in a different country from that in which it is produced.

But such devices, although they save valuable production time, do not help the photographer on location. The difference between a good news shot and a failure may be a matter of fractions of a second. Often there is no second chance, so it essential to carry loaded cameras, with focus and exposure set to the most useful values — this is commonly 10 ft (3 m) for focusing, 1/250 sec for shutter speed, and f 4 for aperture.

When approaching a press assignment, the photographer must remember that editors are continuously looking for new angles on subjects. It is pointless to join a dozen other photographers, all covering an event from roughly the same viewpoint, unless this is literally the only position. A different camera position, revealing original aspects of the subject, will prove much more worthwhile. Exclusivity of approach is not always possible, but a good press picture should be animated and clear, and contain meaning, avoiding anything that is irrelevant to the story. Picture caption information is also vital. It should not describe what is obvious from the picture, but supply editorial staff with concrete information such as names, locations, dates, and occasions.

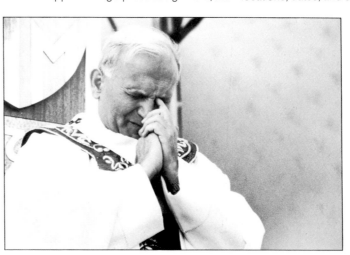

Pope John Paul II
Gianfranco Gorgoni took the photograph of Pope John Paul II during a visit to the pope's native country, Poland. The photographer captured a moment of intense concentration, a point during a public occasion when the subject's personal thoughts became apparent. The picture sums up the subject's thoughtfulness and concern.

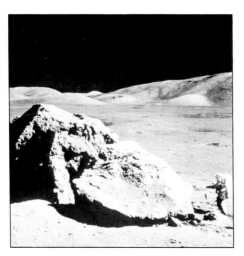

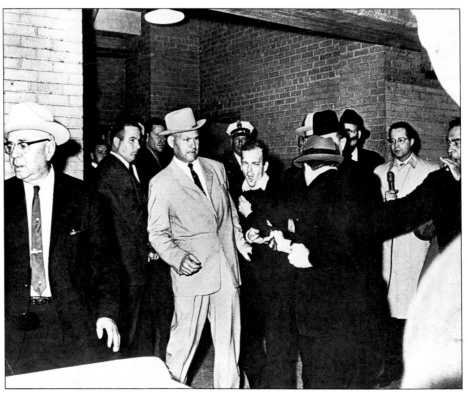

Picture from the moon
Astronaut Eugene A. Cernan took the picture of the lunar surface and his colleague Harrison H. Schmidt during the Apollo 17 mission. Pictures from manned space flights in the 60s and 70s repeatedly captured public interest for relating man to this previously unknown environment.

The murder of Lee Harvey Oswald
The news picture (right) was taken at the moment when Jack Ruby shot John F. Kennedy's assassin, Lee Harvey Oswald. The photographer, Bob Jackson, pressed the shutter before he knew what was happening, realizing a newsworthy event was occurring.

Photojournalism

The photojournalist has more time and space in which to present a story than the press photographer. Working alongside a writer, the photojournalist must research picture content with great care, as far as possible bearing in mind the emphasis of the narrative. Both writer and photographer must aim for a structured article, with a beginning, a middle, and an end.

In a good picture sequence, the individual images must be strong, but each should add something different to the whole sequence, presenting varied facets of an event or situation (see *Picture sequences,* pp. 88-9). It is possible to give variety by alterations in distance, angle, and picture shape, but it is advisable to make these changes relevant to the subject, avoiding visual gimmicks.

An assignment may take weeks, or a single day, but it will invariably involve the taking of hundreds of pictures. The photographer generally narrows down this vast choice before submitting slides or contact prints to the picture editor. But a wide selection is still required, including pictures of the same scene in both vertical and horizontal formats, giving freedom for page layout.

In making a final choice of pictures it is essential to take into account the shapes and colors, as well as the picture content, that appears on each double-page spread. Variety is important, but the pictures must interrelate.

Page layout is the art editor's responsibility. The photographer must be prepared for the editor to crop and arrange pictures to fit the page, and so that they conform with the emphasis of the story.

Working methods

Most photojournalists work on a freelance basis, commissioned by magazines or through agencies for particular assignments that suit their skills and specialities. Some photographers may have an affinity for social documentary picture stories, others for wars, or travel and landscape. Photojournalists receive a credit line for their work, which appears alongside the printed pictures, whereas press pictures usually appear anonymously. Many photojournalists have therefore become well known to the public. Photographers such as Don McCullin and Eve Arnold have built up considerable international reputations.

The best photojournalists express a point of view, caring passionately for their theme. One of the best examples of this is W. Eugene Smith's picture essay on the death and brain damage inflicted on the inhabitants of Minamata due to poisoning by industrial effluent (see *Magnum Photos,* pp. 353-4).

Truth and manipulation

Reportage photographs appear truthful, but in practice can easily be deceptive. However responsible a press photographer or photojournalist may be, it is impossible not to influence pictures' subject matter to a certain extent. No two people will take exactly the same picture of an event, and although a good photograph will seem to have the last word, it is rarely definitive. Sometimes the mere fact that an observer with a camera is present alters the events themselves. For example, if demonstrators, or anyone seeking publicity, notice a photographer or television crew, events can take a different turn.

Another factor is the photographer's choice of viewpoint and framing. For example, two politicians isolated in the viewfinder may seem to smile at each other, when in fact they are communicating with others outside the frame.

Similarly, someone brandishing a stick may look more menacing when photographed close-up with a wide-angle lens than in a telephoto shot taken from farther away.

Timing is a further important influence. In covering a confrontation, the photographer may choose to take pictures only when one group is looking aggressive, even though for most of the time the reverse was true. Well-known people may be photographed in public momentarily bored, puzzled, or happy, and these images may imply that this is typical of their behavior at all times.

Occasionally photographers miss shots, and ask the participants to repeat an event. This can work with such occasions as presentations and opening ceremonies, but taken to extremes it can lead to posed and totally manufactured news situations.

It is often possible to confuse deception with legitimate emphasis. The FSA photographer Arthur Rothstein (see *The Farm Security Administration project,* pp. 352), was severely criticized by the Administration's political opponents for moving a cattle skull from under scrub, and repositioning it in a patch of bare earth a few feet away. He argued that what he had done in no way altered the point his picture was making, but only helped communicate the area's drought and the cattle's starvation much more strongly.

Child laborer
The picture of a child (below) is by Lewis Hine. Hine is well known for his depiction of the social ills that resulted from industrialization. In 1908 the National Child Labor Committee employed him to collect evidence of exploited children in factories and mines. Most of the pictures he took are simple and direct, but use strong composition, showing children as they were found in their working environments.

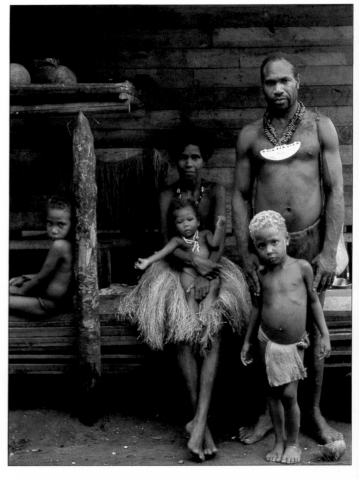

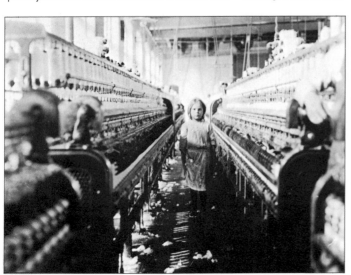

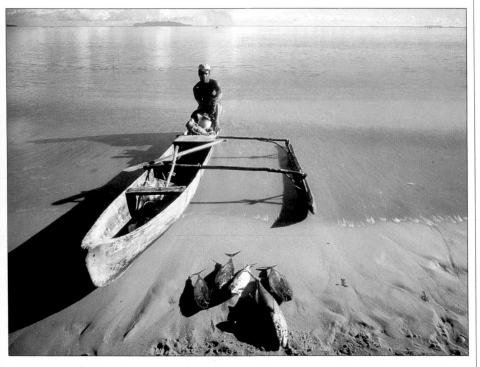

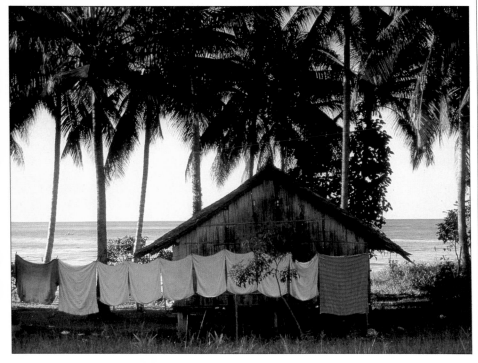

Manipulation after shooting

The presentation of documentary photographs on the printed page can also result in various forms and degrees of deception. Distortion can take place through cropping, retouching or montage, the way pages are designed, and the captions and headlines that run alongside the pictures.

It is common for newspaper pictures to be cropped strongly in reproduction. Space is at a premium, and editors have to think in terms of pictures that fit one, two, or three columns, as well as responding to the pressure of other stories that may change from one edition to the next. Sometimes editors use extreme picture proportions for effect (see *Horizontal image,* p. 56, and *Vertical format,* p. 57). It is sometimes necessary to mask confusing detail by using a spray, and retouchers sometimes paint in a "divider", or thin edge line to stop a white face fading into a light background.

Tight cropping can make gaps between objects in a picture become objectionable. This may necessitate the discreet removal of a central slice of the print, so that the two items move closer to each other. Equally, when several exposures exist of a group of people, it is possible to combine parts of different images to juxtapose the best expressions or actions. This is only a step away from erasing individuals from pictures or combining parts of totally different events, procedures that only the least scrupulous editors allow. Montage or composite printing techniques can be very convincing and have been used both surruptitiously and openly for propaganda purposes.

Page layout

A picture may also be influenced by adjacent material on the page. An editor can add extra meaning by coupling one picture with another — perhaps contrasting themes of rich and poor, or young and old. Photojournalistic stories that make use of several double-page spreads offer the greatest scope for inventive layout. The art editor can make points of emphasis by means of relative size and position of images, producing a total visual statement that may be at variance with the photographer's views. The tone of caption writing, too, can easily slant the effect of a picture, or suggest false implications, even if the factual information in the text is accurate. Photojournalism therefore calls for responsibility from those who supply and present the images, and a degree of skepticism from the public who view the results. If photographer and art editor work closely and in harmony, however, the resulting combination of pictures and text can form a powerful way of presenting ideas and information.

The Solomon Islands
The three color pictures (facing page, above, and top) are from a series taken by Kenneth Griffiths in the Solomon Islands. The whole sequence shows the people, their homes, and the surrounding landscape. It also illustrates the life of non-native people on the islands, such as Japanese (top), Australians, and Chinese. To document such a rich source of material, discriminating selection was essential, with the editor choosing pictures showing a variety of subject shapes, and types of composition. These examples show a family (facing page), a typical fishing boat (top), and a hut in its setting of palm trees (above).

Photographic styles

The skill involved in composing images in a camera viewfinder and turning them into permanent pictures is only a part of the creative process in photography. Decisions about what to photograph and why are far more personal, and they can take a lifetime to explore. *The specialized subject* shows that external requirements can preempt these decisions — the photographer has a particular job to do, whether it is to identify, measure, report, or to sell. But in this section, a large and important area of photography is identified that has no actual function other than to act as a means of communication or self-expression. These pictures are made to please the photographer and to express thoughts and ideas to others. There is freedom to develop a highly individual approach.

The evolution of style

A picture which displays a definite photographic style shows the photographer's attitude as strongly as it does the subject content. Often it is possible to identify the photographer by looking at the work alone — the subject approach, treatment, and form of presentation have similar distinguishing features that are characteristic of that person's work. This kind of strident individuality does not arise from safe, inoffensive, and technically conventional work. It is frequently the product of an approach that alienates some people at the same time as it attracts others.

A distinctive style evolves from the photographer's discovery of original ideas, opinions, and interests, which are developed irrespective of people's reactions and criticisms. The photographer does not develop a style by consciously trying to be different, or by merely mastering the complexities of techniques and equipment — it has to arise naturally from a combination of a unique way of looking at things and the right measure of self-confidence. Both of these take time to mature. Having once achieved a style, it is all too easy for the photographer to become typecast. A recognizable style may lead people to expect the photographer to go on producing the same kinds of imagery. Work exhibited successfully, published, or sold as a commission, may result in requests for more work of the same kind.

It is also easy for young photographers to become too specialized too early — turning away from unknown areas that are worth exploring in favor of something that the photographer knows that he or she can do well, without great effort or risk of failure. The long-term result may be work that is stale or dull. Photography, like any other art form, should be controversial, and even revolutionary, in order to progress and develop.

Talented photographers make the effort to keep their work fresh and new, reflecting in an individual way the spirit of their time. In photographer Ralph Gibson's view, it takes 15 years to develop a style, and then another 15 to throw it off again and persuade people that your work has changed. A lack of sympathy and understanding with a photographer's work may not always be the fault of collective narrow-mindedness but be produced by the photographer. Edward

Steichen once wrote about the harm that can be done by the photographer to his or her own work, saying that the most damaging restrictions on a photographer's liberty are, ironically, self-imposed. What begins as an original idea becomes routine, reduced to habit, which eventually has a deadening effect on the work. Steichen also wrote about the equally destructive effects of egoism and conceit, saying that a certain humility toward the subject and the medium will open up new possibilities for the photographer.

Groups and individuals

Since photography was first invented, photographers have worked together in groups. But as time elapses, members react against the ideals of the rest of the group, and create breakaway movements of their own. Today, the tendency is to work alone and concentrate on personal concerns, aims, and means of self-expression. Present-day photographic clubs and societies have a social role and offer a critique, but tend to service the average and encourage the conformist. Like the salons and academies of the fine artists at the turn of the century, these societies grow more conservative with age, tending to impede change and experiment rather than encourage it.

Artists of all kinds are expected to be experimental, although their work is judged in terms of the established norm. All eight exhibitions held in Paris by the Impressionist painters were received with hostility and contempt. Innovative work by photographers such as Julia Margaret Cameron and Alvin Langdon Coburn was sneered at in its day, while other photographs which were acclaimed at the time are now considered hollow and meaningless.

In this section photographers' work is divided into nine broad areas: *High Art photography, Pictorialism, Straight photography, The documentary approach, Dynamism, Structuralism and Abstraction, Metaphor and Symbolism, Romanticism and the dramatic,* and *Surrealism.* In the nineteenth century, photography was such an unexplored medium and so few practiced it that the trends and movements were far more clear cut than they are today. Photographers worked together with a common aim under recognized "labels". In the early decades of this century, after photography had been largely accepted as an expressive medium, a young generation adopted the direct, "straight" approach. They discarded the subject matter and technical manipulations which had previously made photographs resemble paintings, and followed the example set by the severe styles of modern art in fashion at the time.

The documentary role of photography is a style which spans all periods of photography, but owes much to the popularity of illustrated magazines, which began to publish photographs in the 1930s. Photographic styles such as Dynamism, Structuralism and Abstraction have strong connections with modern movements in the art world, but each group contains work from a cross-section of periods. Under the heading of Structuralism, for example, it is possible to compare the approaches of modern photographers with others who were popular forty years earlier. Other categories, such as Metaphor and Symbolism, and Surrealism, merge with other approaches and are glimpsed in the work of highly individual contemporary photographers.

Some photographers fit neatly into one particular category. For example, Jerry Uelsmann is a Surrealist, and Cecil Beaton is a Romantic, but others (notably André Kertész) maintain an individual style over a long career of continuous experimentation. Kertész has been influenced by, and in turn, has influenced many changes of style. For this reason, he and several other photographers appear in more than one category.

The intention of this section is to present a broad cross-section of photographic styles from photography's invention up to the present day, showing how different blends of vision, ideas, and techniques make photography such a diverse and expressive medium.

The study of photographs
Photographs deserve to be studied with the same care as any other expressive medium. Some pictures communicate their content and meaning immediately, making a complete statement that leaves little to the imagination. Others are perhaps more difficult to grasp at first, but challenge the viewer. Such pictures are likely to attract more sustained attention — the viewer will return to discover new things.

Photographs can be read at different levels. For example, a picture by Henri Cartier-Bresson may appeal because of its humorous glimpse of humanity, but it can give equal pleasure for the geometry of its design, or for the surreal interrelationships of its various elements. The more photographs you look at and become familiar with, the more you will discover in each one. As when you study any art form, you can soon notice the influence of other photographers, or current social and political conditions, in the work of each particular individual.

It will be possible also to identify stylistic developments in a photographer's work that relate to movements in the art world. In the early days of photography, timidity and a sense of inferiority caused photographers to imitate the art styles that were fashionable at the time, so that connections between art and photography were very obvious. Today, the work of painters remains influential, but there is such extensive cross-fertilization between the two media that it is dangerous to pin down the influences of art too firmly.

A sense of the technical history of photography will enrich an analysis of photographs, too. The most notable events to become familiar with are: the invention of hand-held cameras in the 1890s, which meant that the photographer was freed from the constraints of using static viewpoints; the invention of the mobile studio lamp in the 1930s, which encouraged the glamorous Hollywood style of "overlighting"; and the arrival of acceptable color print materials in the 1940s, which added a completely new dimension to the photographic image.

As new technical developments come on the scene, they inevitably expand the number of ways in which visual ideas can be expressed. From silver and dye images to electronic images, each new picture-forming material has its own qualities and limitations. It is interesting to imagine how the early Pictorialists would have made use of today's color materials, or how the Vorticists and other abstract photographers could have exploited modern lens attachments. One day, perhaps, the same feelings will be expressed about holograms, thermographs, and other kinds of enhanced electronic pictures.

The addition of color to photography, like the addition of sound to silent movies, created a new dimension that many photographers found difficult to adapt to. It has taken several generations to produce photographers who have been brought up to "think" in color. Yet the character and perception of individual photographers emerges, whatever medium happened to be available at the time. The essential qualities of romantic Impressionism, or uncompromising Straight photography are still the same after a period of 60 or 70 years, even though materials have altered substantially from gum bichromate to Ektachrome.

High Art photography

"High Art" photography was established as a style by a group of British photographers who wanted their work to have the same high status as the popular art of the day. They wanted recognition and the right to hang their photographs in galleries alongside paintings. The style reached the height of its popularity between 1850 and 1870, when photography was still in its infancy and drawing considerable public interest, but, because photography was still thought to be a "mere" recording device, heated discussions took place as to whether it was in fact an art or a science. In an attempt to gain acceptance, High Art photographs therefore resembled paintings as strongly as possible, both in theme and character. They portrayed genre themes, often highly sentimental, and were made by a variety of special manipulative effects.

High Art photography eventually lost popular appeal and became unfashionable when a series of new developments in equipment (such as the hand-held camera and roll film) meant that amateur photographers could make an impact on photographic styles. Most of these people had little desire to be "artists" – although many were serious enough to arrange their own exhibitions. Their work was far more interpretative and naturalistic. As a result, the High Art approach gradually developed into the pictorialist movement.

Detail and allegory

The Victorians were impressed by a picture if it was large, highly detailed and had clearly taken hours of painstaking labor to produce. As detail and accuracy were so important, many artists commissioned professional photographers to make studies of figures and landscapes which they copied in their paintings. This way of working in turn strongly influenced photographers when they made their own pictures. Art critics advised photographers that the best way to raise their new "mechanical aid" to a high art was to avoid using the actuality of everyday situations, instead borrowing the subject matter of contemporary artists. This meant allegory – pictures which contained a story or message, often sentimental, and featuring subjects popular in poems, operas, and novels of the time. Since it was impossible to find such scenes in real life, they had to be constructed deliberately. Photographers consequently became expert stage managers, constructing elaborate studio tableaux, and arranging costumed models and props.

One technique that was particularly popular with the High Art photographers was multiple printing. Each component in the scene was photographed separately (figures, landscape, and sky), and then combined by being printed together as one on a single sheet of paper. These composite pictures demanded infinite technical skill and many hours of work.

See also
Alternative printing techniques *Multiple printing*, p. 126.

The themes of High Art

Mid-Victorian society in Britain had definite ideas on what constituted a suitable subject theme for a work of art. Genre scenes, representing a "slice" of everyday life, were usually avoided unless they were highly sentimentalized. Photographers were earnestly advised by art critics to "draw a veil over the ordinary and ugly", and to follow the example set by painters who constructed anecdotal and allegorical scenes that were intended to pass on a moral message and be used for the purposes of instruction.

Photographers and painters often borrowed themes from popular poetry, historical legends and the Bible. Oscar Rejlander's composite photograph *Two Ways of Life* (1855) (see *Pictures and exhibitions of the High Art movement,* p. 333) is the largest and most well-known photograph to follow an allegorical theme. William Lake Price in the 1850s, and Julia Margaret Cameron in the 1870s were both well-known photographers who favored poetic themes (Cameron gained inspiration from Shakespeare and Tennyson). In America, Fred Holland Day later produced a large series on the life of Christ (1898).

The Victorian preoccupation with death can

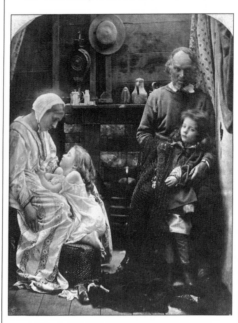

"Pray God Bring Father Safely Home" (c. 1870)
Taken by Julia Margaret Cameron, this narrative picture typifies sentimental High Art photography. It shows how innocent of the absurd Cameron was, and how careless she could be in her structuring of groups.

be found in many High Art pictures. Robinson's *Fading Away* (1858), and *The Lady of Shalott* (1861), Rejlander's *A Night Out, Homeless* (c. 1857), and pictures by Cameron such as *Pray God Bring Father Safely Home* are all typical examples. Such themes fitted in perfectly with what was considered to be artistic, and at exhibitions arranged by the newly formed photographic societies, the works received great acclaim.

The Pre-Raphaelite influence

Allegory was taken to its wildest extremes in High Art photography, but it had already become well known and popular because of its coverage by artists of the Romantic movement who favored historical themes.

In France, Delacroix was master of this style, with paintings such as *Liberty on the Barricade* (1831), and in America, Thomas Cole's *The Voyage of Life* and *The Architect's Dream* (1840) contained a similar blend of realism and fantasy. But since High Art was essentially an English movement, the style of painting which most influenced it during the 1850s was the work of the Pre-Raphaelite Brotherhood.

The Pre-Raphaelites were young ex-Royal Academy School art students such as John Millais, William Holman Hunt, and Dante Gabriel Rossetti, who banded together under the then fashionable term "brotherhood". Its members insisted on the importance of serious subjects, and often chose to illustrate episodes from novels and poems. They opposed what they considered to be the slipshod drawing and painting styles in most post-Renaissance European art, and wanted to return to what they thought of as the "purity" of Italian religious painting before the time of Raphael and the High Renaissance.

In particular, they were in rebellion against aesthetic precepts laid down by Sir Joshua Reynolds, the Royal Academy's first president, who encouraged English painters to use overdramatic lighting, stereotyped composition, and open styles of brushwork. The Brotherhood condemned Reynolds, along with Rubens and Rembrandt, for their lax treatment of three-dimensional form.

Each individual in the Brotherhood differed in his approach, but shared a belief that the gloominess of subject and color in Old Masters had been overdone, the Dutch choice of subjects too dull and earthy. Since art could have great moral power, it was time to offer something spiritually useful to mankind. Deep feeling about what they were doing and concern for "truth to nature" was consciously expressed by a mixture of romantic medievalism and an almost obsessive concentration on extreme detail. They considered that being humble before nature and faithful in its description was all part of recapturing a religious reverence that academic painting had lost.

Probably the greatest innovation of the Brotherhood was their realistic portrayal of family and friends, but applied to their romanticized, and often spiritual, themes.

The Pre-Raphaelites' painting technique was characterized by strong, vibrant colors. Other characteristics such as incisive, hard-edged outlines, and meticulous accuracy, have been attributed to the influence of photography. Both Millais and Rossetti used photographs as convenient and accurate reference sources for painting accurate portraits and landscapes.

One of the major criticisms made about the Pre-Raphaelite style of painting was that its insistence on truth to nature could lead to a general acceptance of photography. This idea was scandalous, since few believed that pictures made with a "machine" could possibly be capable of spiritual interpretation. The relationship between painters and photographers was therefore awkward – neither was quite sure what the role of photography was really supposed to be.

From the 1850s onward, Pre-Raphaelite painters received widespread support from the new, prosperous middle classes. The style appealed because the meticulously detailed method of painting, the bright colors, the clearly defined moral message through the use of symbols (lilies for innocence and books for virtue), all signified value to the Victorian.

Subjects and symbols
Where the Pre-Raphaelite artists were influenced by the detail available in photographs, so the photographers were influenced by the Pre-Raphaelites' picture content. Compare Robinson's composite photograph *The Lady of Shalott* with Millais' *Ophelia* (see below), painted nine years earlier. Cameron favored scenes from Shakespeare (for example, *King*

Lear and His Daughters – see *High Art's leading exponents,* pp. 332-3), which reflects the Pre-Raphaelite interest in poetic drama.

Symbols were borrowed, too. Late afternoon light, which was intended to imply a sense of death, is evident in several of Robinson's photographs, while children, designed to add pathos to a scene, are used in Pre-Raphaelite paintings and High Art photography.

The demise of the movement
Paintings by the Pre-Raphaelites dominated the prestigious Royal Academy exhibitions in Britain during the 1850s. Although the Brotherhood had actually disbanded by 1856, it had become very popular and had influenced other artists immeasurably. (The Surrealists, for example, have paid the same attention to detail.) Eventually, the movement was condemned as being affected, nostalgic, and creatively second-hand.

Techniques

Overall image sharpness was considered to be essential by the High Art photographers, but the technical capabilities of cameras at the time made this very difficult. The advent of High Art photography also coincided with the change to collodion glass plates in the early 1850s. These were extremely slow (the equivalent to ASA 1) and the maximum lens aperture in exhibition-sized cameras was seldom wider than f 11. The very long exposures therefore required meant that subject move-

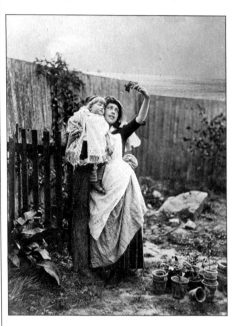

"The Gilly Flower" (1880)
A simple two-negative composite print by Henry Peach Robinson. The negative of the foreground and figures was printed first, and the background (which is only actually sharp on the horizon) was printed second.

ment was a constant problem. In addition, the combination of long-focus lenses and large cameras meant that it was often impossible to render foreground figures and background detail sharp unless the lens was stopped down even further. Consequently, different parts of a picture were often taken separately, and then combined to form a single image. This was achieved either by montaging or by making multiple prints.

Multiple printing
Landscape photographers were the first to attempt to print from more than one negative. This was because the blue-only sensitive plates could not reproduce cloud detail in the sky as well as dark, usually green-colored ground detail, at the same level of exposure. The solution was to make two separate negatives from the same viewpoint, and expose one correctly for the sky, and the other correctly for the land. By carefully masking the unwanted areas of each negative, they could be printed in turn on the same sheet of self-darkening paper, so that detail showed up clearly in both areas.

"The Lady of Shalott" (1861)
Henry Peach Robinson used Tennyson's poem for inspiration and created a modest set-up in his own back garden (right).

"Ophelia" (1852)
John Millais' conception of a scene from *Hamlet* (below) displays attention to detail, brilliant coloring, and hard outlines. These were all typical features of the Pre-Raphaelites' style, which greatly influenced the High Art photographers.

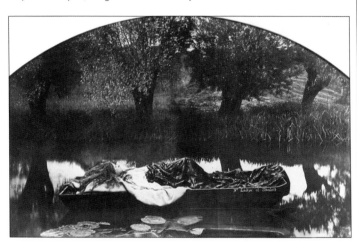

Photographers of High Art made use of this technique by first sketching the scene on paper, and then making negatives and prints of each figure or group of figures. Each component had to be carefully lit, posed, and viewed on the focusing screen at exactly the same position and size as it had appeared on the original sketch.

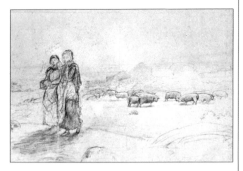

"Carolling" (1887)
To make his composition (below), Henry Peach Robinson firstly made a sketch (above) of the picture he wanted to create. This technique was also used by painters. Figure and landscape negatives were then made separately, and printed on the same sheet of albumen paper.

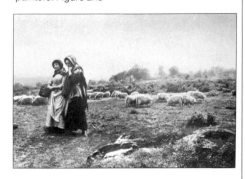

To prepare the final composite print, unwanted areas on the negatives had to be covered with lamp black or opaque paper, and contact printed one at a time, in exact register, on a large sheet of self-darkening albumen paper. Then, previously made prints of the figures were carefully cut out, and placed over all the figure images on the paper to act as masks while the whole sheet of albumen was exposed again behind a negative containing the background detail. Finally, any noticeable joins were retouched out of the print.

This technique was workable because of the large size of cameras and plates at the time, the practice of contact printing instead of enlarging the negative, and the self-darkening characteristic of the paper which allowed density and positioning to be checked after each individual exposure. Even so, the scale of the operation was daunting. To make *Two Ways of Life,* Rejlander photographed 25 models in separate groups (some of them appear twice), and then printed his 30 negatives over different parts of the 16 × 31 ins (40 × 79 cm) sheet of printing paper.

High Art's leading exponents

While there were a few exponents of the High Art style in America (such as John E. Mayall of Philadelphia) it reached its extreme levels in Britain. Most of the major practitioners came to photography possessing a traditional art background and training.

William Lake Price
An artist in water colors, William Lake Price changed to photography in 1854. He soon built up a reputation for specially constructed, stage-managed studies, such as *The Baron's Feast* and *Don Quixote in His Study,* and he was the first British photographer to make photographs by combining several negatives. His most successful work was portraiture, his sitters including the British royal family.

Oscar Rejlander
Rejlander rose very rapidly to fame with his work *Two Ways of Life,* but he had previously worked as a portrait painter. He took up photography in 1853 so that he could use it to make references for his work. Two years later, he changed his career and opened a photographic studio in the Midlands area of England. A part of his business was concerned with supplying figure studies for artists, and *Two Ways of Life* was, in a sense, a catalog of this aspect of his work. But its main purpose was to prove to others that this new "process", photography, was more than merely a mechanical aid for artists. However, the publicity and controversy over the picture appears to have discouraged Rejlander, for he made few other allegorical works, and he never made one

again on such a grand scale. Later commissions of any importance included work for Charles Darwin to illustrate *The Expression of Emotion in Man and Animals* (1872).

Henry Peach Robinson
Trained in drawing and painting, Henry Peach Robinson began collodion landscape photography after seeing a show of daguerrotypes at the Great Exhibition in London (1851). He

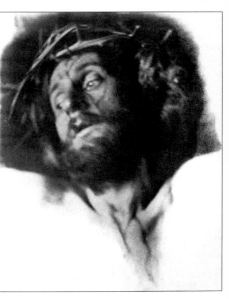

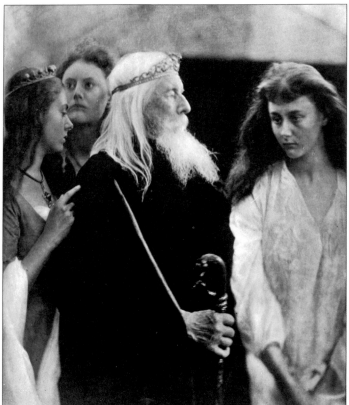

"The Last Seven Words" (1898)
One of a close-up sequence (above) of self portraits made by Fred Holland Day illustrating the Crucifixion. To create the right effects, Day starved himself for a year and grew his hair to shoulder length.

"King Lear and His Daughters"
One of Julia Margaret Cameron's many tableaux (left) inspired by Pre-Raphaelite themes. In this one her husband played Lear.

"Portrait of a Lady Seated" (1914)
Richard Polak, an American amateur photographer, imitated portraits (right) and domestic scenes as he thought Vermeer and De Hooch would have painted them. He used theatrical costumes and authentic Dutch settings. Although many of the small details were anachronistic, he did manage to capture the quality of light seen in paintings of the Dutch school.

was very impressed by Rejlander's creative work, and from 1858 onward, he produced pictures for exhibition purposes which were designed to show that photography was as capable of influencing the emotions as paintings. Most, but not all, of his pictures were produced by the multiple printing technique. His first, and most famous, work *Fading Away* was made from five negatives, while *Dawn and Sunset* was made from six. All his work is remarkable for its meticulous detail and craftsmanship – the joins between the negatives are virtually invisible.

Robinson wrote numerous books, such as *Picture Making by Photography* (1884), expounding his techniques and theories. But from this time onward, he increasingly turned to a single-negative approach to pictorial subjects, following the style of academy painting.

Julia Margaret Cameron
As well as producing striking portraits of her family and friends (see *Early documentary photographers,* pp. 348-9), Cameron produced numerous stage-managed photographs in the High Art style. Many of them now seem clumsy and crude, containing improvised props and makeshift costumes, but they catered precisely for the public demand for allegory and sentimentality at the time. Her constructed work received acclaim from photographers of the Photographic Society of London whereas her portraits were condemned.

Fred Holland Day
In America, the eccentric secessionist photographer, Fred Holland Day, continued to produce his own pictorial brand of High Art work late into the 1890s, long after the movement had lost impetus in Britain. He produced hundreds of pictures on biblical themes, the most famous of which is *The Crucifixion* (1898). In this he featured himself as Christ on the cross.

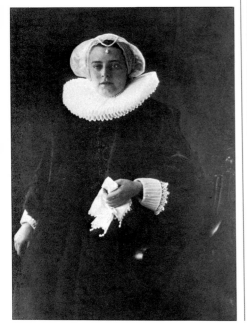

Pictures and exhibitions of the High Art movement

In the early 1850s, photographic societies were opening in many cities world wide. Their annual exhibitions were open to everyone, and they received wide press coverage. Consequently, exhibitions were vital for building up a photographer's reputation. For the professional, they were an important means of advertising – photographs were sold and orders placed. In England the Manchester Art Treasures exhibition of 1857 was an opportunity for Rejlander, and his contemporaries, to show just what was possible in the field of photographic allegory. For the first time photographs were exhibited alongside well-known paintings and sculptures and so took on an importance of their own. Rejlander showed several works, but the most popular by far was *Two Ways of Life*. The public flocked to see it to unravel the allegory, and Rejlander explained its meaning in *The Journal of the Photographic Society of London* of April 1858. The picture shows "...two youths have been fondly reared, the time has arrived when duty calls them to perform their part in the busy haunts of men." One youth is willing to be led into a virtuous life of religion and knowledge, while the other chooses a life of idleness, gambling, and vice.

Such was Victorian prudery that many people thought certain figures indelicate, and

the left side of the picture had to be covered when it was later exhibited in Scotland. However, Rejlander finally received a seal of approval when Queen Victoria bought a print for Prince Albert. Copies of the picture, and of another with slight variations, were sold to the public either at the full size of 16 × 31 ins (40 × 79 cm), or reduced.

Fading Away, Robinson's first composition to be exhibited, was shown at the Photographic Society of London annual exhibition in 1858. It shows a scene beloved of the Victorians – a dying girl surrounded by her grieving relatives. The photograph met with remarkable acclaim when it was subsequently shown at other exhibitions elsewhere in Britain, and then in Europe and America. Its success encouraged Robinson to produce a new multiple print for each annual exhibition of the society – a ritual which he continued for a period of over 20 years.

Cameron's High Art photographs were exhibited by the Photographic Society during the 1860s and were highly praised by critics and artist friends. Success seems to have had a bad effect on her work. Some of her later compositions, such as *Faith, Hope and Charity* and *Rosebud Garden of Girls,* lacked the sense of balance and grouping which is evident in her other work.

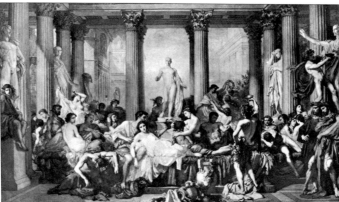

"Les Romains de la Décadence" (1847)
This orgy scene (left) by Thomas Couture became well known as a foremost example of nineteenth century High Art.

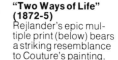

"Two Ways of Life" (1872-5)
Rejlander's epic multiple print (below) bears a striking resemblance to Couture's painting.

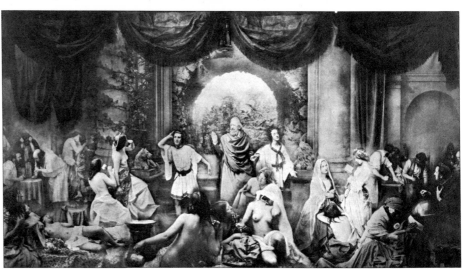

Pictorialism

A "pictorial" image is one in which the subject matter is less important than its appeal to our sense of beauty. Harmony of tone, line, and balance as a means of unifying the picture elements, are all more important than factual statements. Mundane or ugly subjects are avoided, and detail is often replaced by a softness of definition and tone manipulation, for aesthetic effect.

The Pictorialist movement developed during the 1880s and lasted into the 1920s and early 1930s. In the last decades of the nineteenth century, it was a reaction against the cosy, exclusive world of the High Art photographers, and was the result of a feeling that artists of all kinds should express their own individuality and talent, rather than comply with a strict set of traditions. This dissatisfaction resulted in the formation of numerous secessionist movements.

The world of photography was changing rapidly and dramatically at this time, and by the 1880s, photography was becoming a popular pursuit for anyone who could afford it. Talented amateurs began to make an impact on the photographic scene. From 1890 to 1900, pictorialist photographers set up their own international exhibitions, both in Europe and America. In London, the Linked Ring Brotherhood was formed in 1892, and from 1893 until 1909 ran an annual photographic salon. Meanwhile, in New York, Alfred Stieglitz formed the Photo-Secessionists in 1902, a group of photographers with their own gallery and publication.

The Pictorialists were determined to show that photography could be a fine art in its own right. Eventually Pictorialism proved itself to be a broad movement, embracing a number of very different disciplines and concepts, including Naturalism and Impressionism. New inventions such as soft-focus lenses and the hybrid gum bichromate and carbon printing processes allowed extensive control over results.

The secessionist threat
Collectively, the secessionist groups presented a serious threat to the conservative photographic societies, and were seen as dangerous, *avant-garde* dissidents. But they fought for and won acceptance in photographic exhibitions. From 1908 onward, however, rifts developed between the Pictorialists themselves, but the style itself had already caught the imagination of the general public. Pictorial photography had become the predominant style of serious amateur photographers, and it continued to be practiced in clubs and societies around the world, even though it had become increasingly inward-looking and conventional. The movement had contributed immeasurably to the acceptance of photography as an art form, but Pictorialism had finally become the new establishment.

See also
Special cameras and lenses *Special lenses,* p. 210.
Alternative printing techniques *Liquid emulsions,* p. 259.

The major influences on Pictorialism

The pictorialist movement was a product of the growing unrest in art circles between the established tradition and new, unconventional ideas. Many serious photographers believed that the High Art style was totally misguided, and that the aesthetics of photography should evolve as a more independent art form. The move was toward greater naturalism of subject matter, but portrayed without clinical realism.

The detailed work of the Pre-Raphaelite Brotherhood was still popular with the public, but Turner's use of light was, for some Pictorialists, an influence which directed them toward less "photographic", more interpretative images. The contemporary artist, Whistler, had a strong following among photographers. He believed that beauty should be sought in the picture itself, rather than in its subject matter. In his paintings and etchings he suppressed details in favor of using broad tonal treatment, which emphasized atmosphere. He transformed mundane objects into works of art as a conscious reaction to the subjects in typical Victorian paintings. This attitude is echoed in Whistler's choice of poetic titles, such as *Nocturne* and *Symphony,* which were imitated by photographers, too.

In France, the soft tones and blurred details in landscape paintings by Corot became popular from the late 1850s onward. But the impressionist painters made most impact from 1870 onward. The influence of Degas appears in the themes and composition of the French Pictorialists, and particularly in Demachy's work. It is interesting to note that the way artists worked was affected by photography, too. Degas and Monet both admitted that photography influenced their painting. Examples of this are the ways in which it could record movement, and crop scenes strangely.

Japanese art began to reach the West in the late nineteenth century. The unfamiliar compositions and structural use of strong, graphic shapes influenced artists greatly. Some of these effects could be adapted for the photographer's purpose through careful use of lighting and exposure, and it appears in Edward Steichen's early work, and in some pictures by Fred Holland Day and Alvin Langdon Coburn.

The publication of photographs
New processes in the printing world, which allowed photographs to be published in magazines and books for the first time, meant that photography received a much wider audience. Pictures could now be seen by the public all around the world. By the late 1860s, the Woodburytype process was used to illustrate expensive art books, and by the 1880s half-tone plates gave realistic reproductions in journals and newspapers.

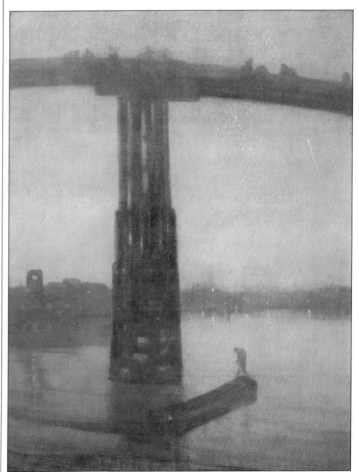

"Nocturne in Blue: Old Battersea Bridge" (1872-5)
Whistler's moonlight scene was inspired by a boat trip along the river Thames, London. Using subdued tones and details, he created a nocturnal mood — open areas spattered with firework sparks from a nearby pleasure garden are set off by the simple shapes of the bridge. For its time, the painting was a daring asymmetrical balance of forms and shapes, strongly influenced by Japanese composition. Whistler became the hero of interpretative painting in England toward the end of the nineteenth century.

Techniques

Manufacturers strove to improve the resolution of lenses and the detail-recording abilities of plates and printing processes, while ironically, the Pictorialists were trying to achieve the opposite effects. But fortunately the invention of gelatin plates had produced a greatly expanded market for photographic equipment, which meant that lens manufacturers, such as Dallmayer, could produce special "soft-focus" lenses for pictorial work. Photographers who could not afford them used pinholes in place of lenses, or even shook the tripod during exposure to get the desired effect.

It was important for Pictorialists to be able to retouch their negatives, so that selected details could be either omitted or emphasized. Glass plates of the time could be easily worked with graphite, dyed on the back, or sandwiched with tissue to create a textured effect. Some photographers pre-exposed their plates to textured surfaces before shooting, to help destroy the image's photographic look.

Many special monochrome printing processes were marketed or devised by photographers themselves, to give images with particular qualities. Each had his own favorite method — sometimes adaptations of processes which he tried to keep secret.

Platinum papers
Even the Pictorialists who adopted the naturalistic approach and never retouched their negatives used the "platinotype" (platinum printing) process, which was introduced in 1883. The paper was gelatin-free and impregnated with light-sensitive and platinum salts. It was very slow and had to be contact printed, after which a full image of silver and metallic platinum was developed in oxalate solution. Local control of tones during actual processing was possible by spreading glycerin over the print.

The main advantages of platinum prints over regular albumen papers were their richness of tone, and lack of surface shine due to the fact that the image was embedded in the paper fibers themselves. Platinum printing required skill, and the paper was costly. Purists such as P. H. Emerson and Frederick Evans regarded platinum paper as a fundamental ingredient of their art. It was considered to be so important that, when it ceased to be produced in 1916, several Pictorialists gave up photography altogether.

Carbon printing
Carbon printing dates from about 1866. The paper support was purchased ready-coated with gelatin containing either carbon or a pigmented dye of any chosen color. This "carbon tissue" was made light-sensitive in a potassium bichromate solution, and then contact printed behind the negative. Light hardened the gelatin so that "processing" consisted of washing away unexposed areas with warm water. Usually this was done with the tissue in face contact with the receiving paper, so that tissue and soluble gelatin peeled away together, leaving a full tone range image on the paper. Results contained rich shadows, clear highlights, and a choice of image color.

Although Platinotype and, to a large extent, carbon printing, were acceptable to naturalistic photographers, the more highly manipulated processes such as gum bichromate and bromoil were not. Today, the differences may not seem particularly distinct, but at the turn of the century, they were fiercely argued over.

Gum bichromate
To make "gum prints", drawing paper is brushed with a mixture of gum and a watercolor pigment of any chosen hue, plus potassium bichromate solution. When this is dry, it is contact printed with the negative. Washing in warm water removes unhardened areas corresponding to the dark parts of the negative, and so leaves a positive image in a colored pigment. The results are controlled through choice of paper texture, and coating tech-

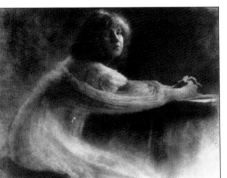

nique. Image "body" can be built up by re-coating and re-exposing to the negative, using the same color, or a totally different-colored pigment.

Robert Demachy helped to perfect the gum-bichromate process, and he was a master in producing delicate impressionistic images with it. He preferred to call the process "Photo-aquatint". Experts, such as Fred Holland Day, and J. Dudley Johnston devised their own variations of the method, for example gum platinum. They would first make a platinum print, then coat it with gum bichromate and re-expose it to the negative in exact image register. Results showed a subtle variety of tones, with rich blacks, and were excellent for making low-key pictures (see *The impressionistic approach,* pp. 338-40.)

"Lecture interompue" (c. 1905)
This is a typical example (left) of Robert Demachy's technique and style. He believed in working up his pictures from a basic, simple idea. Using the gum bichromate process, of which he was an acknowledged master, he added rough brushstrokes to achieve the strongly impressionistic effects he desired.

Girl in red (1908)
When Alvin Langdon Coburn took this auto-chrome (below), the process had only been in existence for a year. It shows how it could produce pleasing warm coloring, particularly in the red and pink area of the color spectrum.

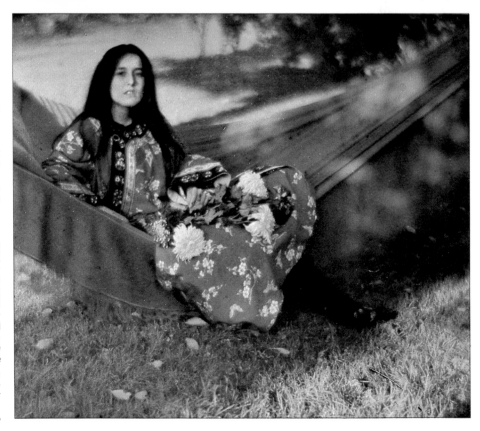

Oil pigment and bromoil

The oil processes, which date from 1904, allow the greatest amount of manipulation of all the processes. The paper can be of any texture, provided that it is coated with gelatin and sensitized with potassium bichromate. It is then exposed in contact with the negative and immersed in water so that the unexposed (unhardened) areas swell and become waterlogged. Oil pigment or lithographic ink is next applied by "dabbing" with a special short-haired brush. The oily color is rejected by swollen areas, but accepted by hardened gelatin. An image is gradually built up, under great control.

The bromoil version of this process was introduced when enlarging became common. After exposing and processing an enlargement on special bromide paper, the silver image is bleached in a solution which leaves the gelatin in a condition similar to that of an oil print. Then inking-up proceeds in the same way as for gum bichromate.

Pictorialists who used the gum or oil processes were often derided by the exponents of naturalism. Frederick Evans described their hand-worked results as "low-toned, treacly things". Certainly the resulting pictures often looked very unlike photographs — and photographers who worked in this way were often accused of seeking a "fine art" effect that had nothing to do with photography.

Photogravure

Photogravure is a method of mechanically printing photographs from an etched copper plate — quite unlike other manipulative processes. It allows the use of a range of printers' inks and papers, and produces images containing rich blacks. First, carbon tissue is transferred to a prepared copper plate. Then the soluble parts of the image are washed away, and the plate is etched, producing minute "wells" of different depths. When the plate is rolled with ink and the surplus removed, the deeper wells retain larger amounts of ink than the shallow ones. The plate is then faced with paper, and the sandwich is run through a press, to produce a print with a rich tonal range. Today, hardly any photographers use photogravure as a personal method, but at the time of its invention, in 1895, dedicated pictorialists would prepare plates, and pull prints just like any other artist.

Autochrome

The later years of the pictorialist movement coincided with the first materials to be made for commercial color photography, Lumière Autochrome plates (1907). These used the mosaic system to produce plate-sized color transparencies. The eye mixes different dots of primary color to see subject colors and shading — the same principle as the paint dot system used by Pointillist painters. Stieglitz, Steichen, and Coburn all used autochrome for pictorial landscapes and portraiture and in more recent years Lartigue has used it too. The results were soft in detail and contained muted tones and colors which could be particularly atmospheric (see previous page). It was not possible to manipulate autochromes or to produce color prints on paper.

Exhibitions and seccessionist movements

Despite the developments in the printing world in the late nineteenth century exhibitions remained the most important platform for photographers to communicate with each other and with the public.

The Photographic Society of London became The Photographic Society of Great Britain in 1894, and twenty years later added "Royal" to its name under the patronage of Queen Victoria. It was recognized as being the most important society for the promotion and display of photography. By the 1880s its annual exhibition had grown so much that it had developed into an exposition covering every aspect of photography, from scientific to artistic.

The Linked Ring Brotherhood

In 1891 a row developed over the selection of photographs for the Photographic Society of Great Britain exhibition. There was pressure from scientists on one side, who were complaining at the lack of scientific photography in previous exhibitions, and pressure from Pictorialists on the other, who complained that the society was uninterested in promoting photography as an art form.

Events came to a head when diffused, impressionistic work by Davison, such as *The Onion Field,* was rejected from the exhibition. A group of the most eminent Pictorialists, including Robinson and Davison, resigned from the society. The following year they set up a secessionist group, calling it the Linked Ring Brotherhood.

The Linked Ring, due to the energy and enthusiasm of its members, rapidly became the center of photography as a fine art in Britain. From the outset, the founders decided to make the membership international, and an invitation to join was considered a great honor. It was a democratic organization — each "link" became a "center link", or presiding officer, for one month at a time in rotation. During the following 18 years of its existence, most of the leading photographers in Britain, Europe, and America were to become members at some point. They created a network of communication which helped to account for the international growth and development of pictorial photography. Every year, from 1893 to 1909, the Links held an exhibition in London, which was devoted solely to the recognition of photography as art — the Photographic Salon.

The American pictorial photography exhibition

In 1900 the wealthy Fred Holland Day and his nephew Alvin Langdon Coburn took to London a major exhibition of nearly 400 photographs by American Pictorialists. The show was hung at the Royal Photographic Society, and called "The New School of American Pictorial Photography". The following year it traveled to Paris. This meant that British and European photographers could compare their work with this comprehensive cross section of American work. The Americans tended to choose more simplified subject matter, sacrificing detail for effect (particularly in portraits), and placing more emphasis on personal interpretation and the emotions.

The Photo-Secession

In America, the secessionist movement pivoted about one man, Alfred Stieglitz. As a leading member of the Camera Club of New York he was invited to devise and select an exhibition at the prestigious National Arts Club in 1902. He called the show the Photo-Secession, and enrolled most of the exhibitors to be the first members of the Photo-Secessionist Group. These included Frank Eugene, Gertrude Käsebier, Clarence White, and Edward Steichen. Several of these people were already members of the Linked Ring Brotherhood. The following year the group produced the first issue of the superbly produced quarterly magazine *Camera Work,* which was edited by Stieglitz. In 1905 he opened a gallery specially for the exhibition and sale of Photo-Secessionist work at 291 Fifth Avenue, New York, which soon became known as 291 Gallery.

Although the Photo-Secessionists were similar to the Linked Ring Brotherhood in that membership was by invitation only, and that the emphasis of the group's function was on exhibition work, the Photo-Secession differed in two respects. First, it was dedicated to the

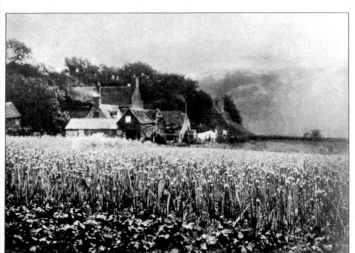

"The Onion Field, Mersea Island, Essex" (1890)
This picture was taken by George Davison using a pinhole instead of a lens. It was his first impressionistic photograph to be exhibited, and its slight overall diffusion created a sensation.

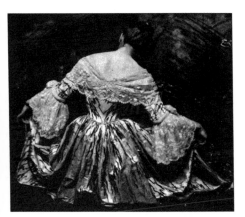

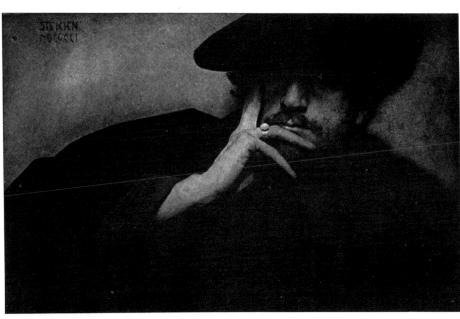

"Minuet" (1910)
Frank Eugene's pictures (above) were among the most painterly of all the Photo-Secessionists. Eugene worked his negatives over to create a *cliché-verre* appearance.

"Solitude: Fred Holland Day, Paris" (1901)
This portrait (right), with its dramatic posing and lighting, enhanced by gum bichromate printing, is typical of Edward Steichen's early work.

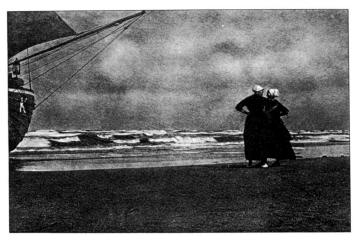

"Spring Showers, New York" (1902)
This cityscape (right) by Alfred Stieglitz shows his strong feelings for the natural elements as well as his skill in creating unaffected pictorial photographs.

"Gossip, Katwyk"
Taken in the year that Alfred Stieglitz was elected to the Linked Ring Brotherhood, this picture (left) shows how he was changing from his manipulative and contrived work to actuality subjects, with an emphasis on mood.

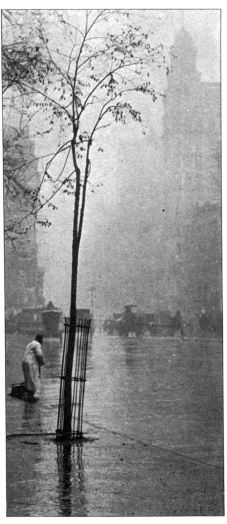

promotion of American photography, largely in competition with European and British work. Second, it was dominated and run by one person, rather than by the group. Stieglitz was solely responsible for selecting all the work, either for hanging at 291 Gallery, or for sending abroad in group shows. Within a few years, the influence of the Photo-Secessionists made them leaders world-wide in pictorial photography. Almost single-handed, Stieglitz had transferred the center of creative photography from Britain to America.

The demise of secessionist movements
By 1908, relations between the British Pictorialists and the Photo-Secessionists had deteriorated. The Photographic Salon of that year had excluded many Link members in favor of American photographers, and there was also argument between the Links themselves. In 1910, the Photographic Salon of the Linked Ring was replaced by the London Salon, and leading members such as George Davison and Craig Annan were excluded

from it. For a brief period these excluded Link members attempted to form another group to compete with the London Salon. Significantly they named it the London Secession.

The London Salon was also showing the work of individual American photographers who had lost Stieglitz's favor. Stieglitz blamed these people for their arrogance, while they, in turn, accused him of becoming increasingly intolerant of the painterly themes and impressionistic treatments used by pictorial photographers. Between 1910 and 1917 Stieglitz mounted only three photographic shows at 291 Gallery. The space, both in the gallery and in *Camera Work,* was devoted increasingly to new styles of non-photographic art from Europe, modern painting which eventually helped to replace Pictorialism with "straight" photography.

The Photo-Secessionists drifted apart, turning professional or forming their own pictorial groups. By 1917, both 291 Gallery and *Camera Work* had closed. Pictorialism was never an *avant-garde* movement again.

The impressionistic approach

All pictorial photographers believed in the importance of the image rather than the significance of the subject, but some favored styles which were "impressionistic" in character, while others were "naturalistic". The work of the French Impressionist painters, in which "truth to nature" was translated as individual impressions of natural scenes, was a strong influence during the 1890s. They encouraged a softness of outline which some photographers adopted by destroying fine detail throughout the image and replacing it by broad tonal treatments.

Impressionist painting

The name "Impressionism" was coined from the title of the picture by Monet, *Impression: Sunrise,* which was shown at a secessionist painting exhibition in Paris in 1874. Renoir, Sisley, Pissarro, and Degas all hung work which was structured by the play of light, rather than by firm subject outlines. They used brief, discontinuous brushstrokes, which looked "natural" to the eye when seen from a normal viewing distance. This style of working was quite different to traditional painting techniques, and it was totally free from historical influences. A further seven Impressionist exhibitions were held in France between 1876 and 1886. The work was received with hostility and contempt at the first exhibition in London (1889). But the movement had a marked influence on younger painters and photographers. The photographers could not try to imitate the Impressionists' use of color, but they seized upon their delicate use of lighting, the precise control of tone, and the soft quality of outlines.

Impressionists in the Linked Ring Brotherhood

Members of the Linked Ring who favored the impressionistic approach included George Davison, Alexander Keighley, Robert Demachy, and J. Dudley Johnston. Their work differed however, because each used his own personal techniques (both for printing and picture-taking), which were sometimes highly manipulative.

Davison was managing director for Kodak Limited in London, and he practiced straightforward photography to advertise his firm's products, but he exhibited his own impressionistic work. Several of his pictures (including *The Onion Field*) were taken with a camera which had a pinhole in place of a lens, to achieve a soft-focus effect over the whole image. He also used the gum bichromate process for additional manipulations.

In his early work, Keighley used sharp focus for a realistic look, but, influenced by Davison, he gradually evolved his own characteristically romantic style of impressionistic photography. He achieved unusual effects by doing extensive work by hand on his negatives, to strengthen or subdue details. He then printed them using the carbon process.

Demachy, the prolific leader of the aesthetic photography movement in France, was especially skilled in print manipulation. His uses of the gum bichromate process were both admired and condemned. His critics said that he went too far in destroying the photographic

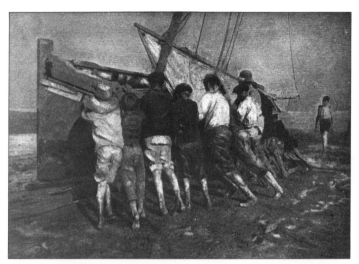

"L'Effort" (1904)
This gum bichromate print by Robert Demachy (left) is one of many similar impressionistic studies by him depicting figures in a landscape. Demachy was leader of the pictorial movement in France.

"A Sunlit Street, Berne" (1907)
J. Dudley Johnston's gum print in sepia and blue (below) shows how well suited the process was to creating impressionistic effects. His choice of subject matter and his composition are equally sympathetic to the style.

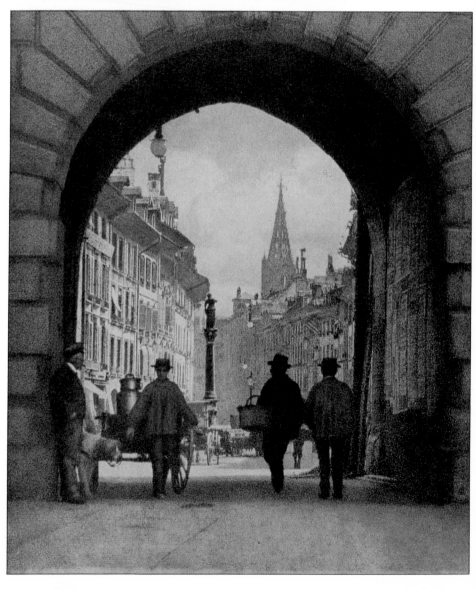

qualities of his images — his results often displayed pronounced brushstrokes, or even resembled drawings in charcoal or red crayon. Sometimes he would crosshatch negatives to make them resemble etchings — a technique that was also used by a founder-member of the Photo-Secessionists, Frank Eugene. Demachy wrote extensively on his approach, explaining that he had no time for objectivity, and pointing out that all the best paintings show an intervention between "commonplace reality" and the final result.

Impressionists of the Photo-Secession

The early work of Alfred Stieglitz, prior to 1894, consists of genre scenes with a strong romantic, manipulative element. But Rudolf Eickemeyer was perhaps the most notable photo-impressionist working in America. His work was strongly influenced by Whistler's

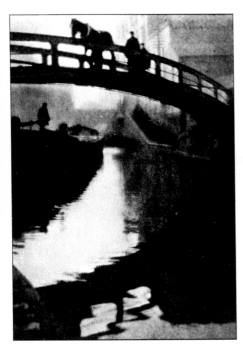

"Regent's Canal, London" (c. 1905)
Alvin Langdon Coburn, like J. Dudley Johnston, favored broad tonal treatments and a simplification of form. Compare the style and composition of this photograph with Whistler's *Nocturne* (p. 334).

An adventurous, experimental photographer, Coburn was elected to the Linked Ring Brotherhood at the age of 21.

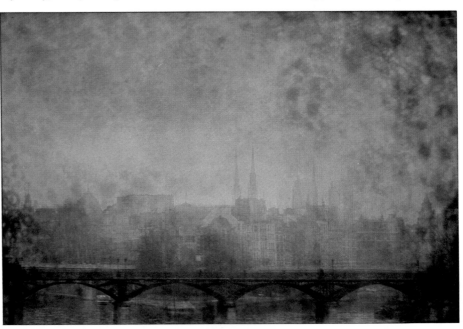

"Ile de la Cité, Paris"
Francisco Hidalgo is well known for his use of special effects in portraying landscapes. Results such as this (above) are produced by sandwiching two color slides — one a soft-focus shot of foliage, the other a blue, filtered, sharply focused picture of the landscape. It is tempting to relate the result to paintings, particularly to Claude Monet's studies of the Thames, London (1901-3). The possibilities for achieving impressionistic effects are considerably greater today than around the turn of the century. Modern color films, plus color filters, effects attachments, and the ability to print from sandwiched slides all allow a wide range of impressionistic results.

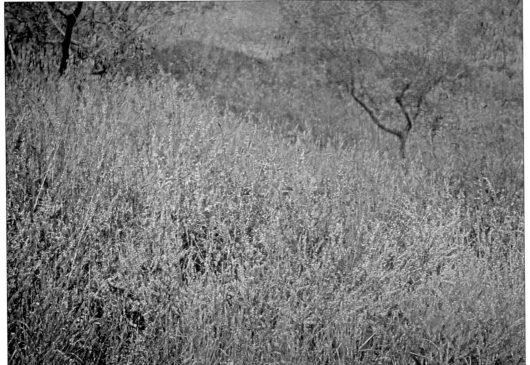

"The Creation: Summer" (1964)
This impressionistic interpretation of rich vegetation (left) by Ernst Haas was achieved by making a double exposure. Firstly, part of the landscape was photographed out of focus and underexposed. Then the same frame of film was used to expose the full scene, this time sharply focused.

"impressions" of Japanese painting, although earlier he had produced pictures which were much closer to Henry Peach Robinson's anecdotal pictures.

Clarence White was consistently impressionistic in his approach to photography, even though his style is distinctly personal. Typically, his pictures show simple scenes and figures, often backlit. His favorite subjects are women, usually wearing flowing white robes, solitary figures in hazy landscapes, and interiors containing family scenes. All his pictures have a romantic atmosphere (see *The pictorial origins of Romanticism,* p. 374).

Alvin Langdon Coburn, the transatlantic photographer who experimented with a variety of styles, adopted an impressionistic approach between 1904 and 1912. His cityscapes and portraits taken in London during this period are made with soft-focus lenses and gum bichromate printing, achieving tonal effects which contribute mood and atmosphere to the scenes.

Edward Steichen, like Stieglitz, was a fine impressionistic photographer during his period with the Linked Ring Brotherhood (1901-1910). His landscapes, consisting of misty, atmospheric effects were achieved by simple lens diffusion. He also used papers and printing processes which allowed soft contours, and the merest suggestion of form in his often low-key pictures.

Modern Impressionism
The impressionistic style of pictorial photography is often used today, whenever the mood of the subject demands it. Color now adds an important new ingredient. Ernst Haas (see *The major exponents of Dynamism,* pp. 358-60) often derives softness of outline in action and landscape shots by using intentional blur or differential focus. Sarah Moon (see *The leading exponents of Romanticism and the dramatic,* pp. 375-7) exploits the grain potential of the film itself to break up detail, to reduce contrast, and to desaturate colors. David Hamilton's use of lens diffusion spreads out highlights and adds a romantic mood to his pictures of adolescent girls.

The 1970s brought a considerable return of interest in manipulative pictorial photography, which had been dismissed for over a generation as "art for art's sake". This was partly due to a vogue for nostalgic things of all kinds, and the resurgence of interest in impressionistic painting. In addition, technical advances in photography, such as the availability of various light-diffusion attachments for lenses, and silver dye bleach printing papers for color printing, which were able to give purer colors, have made it technically easier to create impressionistic effects. At the same time, some of the old processes, such as gum bichromate, have been revived by photographers looking for more expressive ways of printing.

The naturalistic approach

Among the Pictorialists there was much argument and debate over the rival merits of the impressionistic and naturalistic approaches (especially within the Linked Ring, which was always less tolerant of variety than the Photo-Secession). Both trends were in fact a reaction against the influence of Henry Peach Robinson. For 28 years Robinson had dominated photography. First, in terms of the High Art movement (see *High Art's leading exponents,* pp. 332-3), and second, in pictorial photography, with his belief in the importance of following the traditions of academic paintings. He believed vehemently in the difference between "truth" and "fact". Mere facts, he said, were everywhere, but truth is an absence of falsehood — to be arrived at by avoiding "unprincipled" reality and correcting what was unpicturesque. For years, photographers had been following this advice, and by the mid-1880s British photography had built up a reputation for being polite, safe, unadventurous, and quite unoriginal.

P.H. Emerson
In 1889, this safe, predictable state of affairs was shattered by a treatise named *Naturalistic Photography for Students of the Art* by P.H. Emerson. An English physician and naturalist, he had his own opinions on Pictorialism. He was interested in "truth to nature", which meant in his view, truth to sentiment, but using real scenes that were completely free from artificiality. He found it quite unnecessary and unacceptable to imitate the methods of painters — photographers, he said, should study the picture on the camera's ground glass screen, and compose from what they saw there. He considered selection and care over viewpoint important, but said that composition should be determined by the contents of each scene, and not have "rules of art" imposed upon it. Having once visualized a picture, he said, the photographer should

work rapidly, and retain a spontaneous approach. Retouching and multiple printing were to be avoided so that photography was as pure and close to seeing as possible.

Emerson was a brilliant observer and photographer and a forceful lecturer and writer. He published several albums of platinum prints depicting the lives, work, and surroundings of people in rural East Anglia, England, the most well known of which was *Life and Landscapes on the Norfolk Broads.*

Some of Emerson's personal theories on art were based on scientific principles. For example, he maintained that the human eye did not see scenes with the same uncompromising detail as the stopped-down camera lens. The camera was therefore showing a distortion of real life. Instead of being concerned about achieving the utmost sharpness, he maintained that far more natural effects could be obtained by recording only a part of the scene sharply and showing full detail. And that the remaining areas should be kept soft in definition.

Surprisingly, several years later, in 1891, Emerson recanted these views in a dramatic pamphlet, which maintained that photography was a science, and not an art. But his ideas had already taken root in the imaginations of both photographers and the general public. Naturalism was considered to be a welcome new approach to pictorial photography — fresh and new, and capable of expressing ideas beyond the reach of High Art and established pictorial techniques. It was adopted by many different photgraphers, both those who belonged to the Linked Ring Brotherhood, and those within the Photo-Secession. Emerson's influence on photographic style was both lasting and far-reaching. It can be seen in the work of Frederick Evans and Alfred Stieglitz, Paul Strand and the photographers of the later "straight" movements, André Kertész, and Henri Cartier-Bresson.

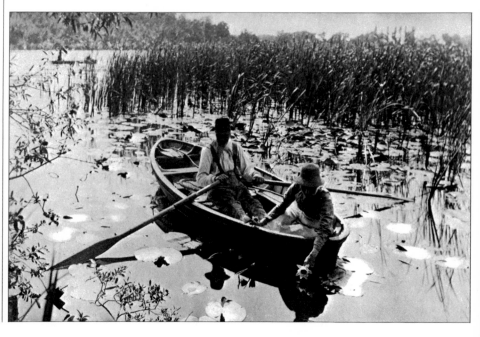

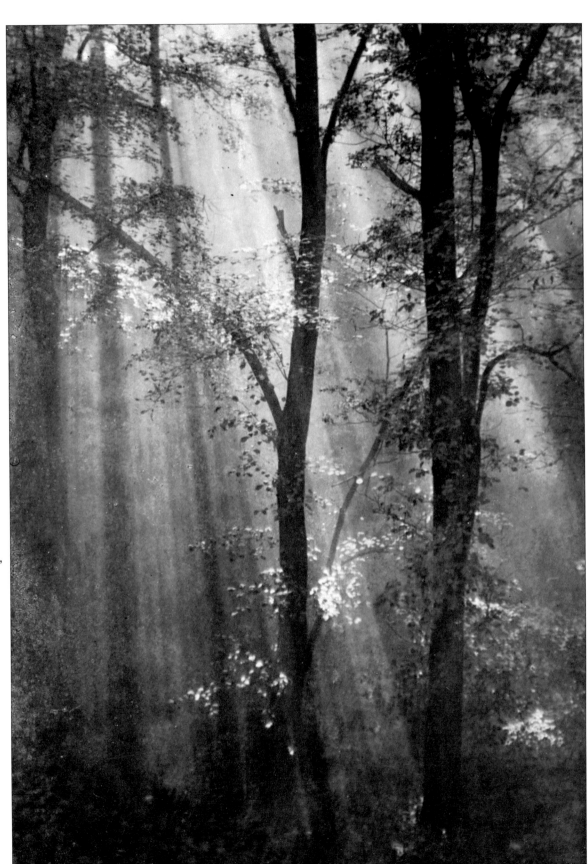

"The Dayspring From on High" (1917)
Alexander Keighley was primarily an impressionistic photographer, but this carbon print image is essentially true to nature. It differs little from the way it would have appeared to the photographer on the ground-glass screen.

"Gathering Waterlilies" (1885)
This picture by P.H. Emerson is perhaps the most well-known of the platinum print illustrations from his book *Life and Landscapes on the Norfolk Broads.* Emerson used these photographs to demonstrate his naturalistic approach to photography — avoiding all retouching, and gum or oil processes which could be manipulated.

Straight photography

"Straight" photography and the "New Realism" are terms that were given to one of the major movements to break away from Pictorialism around 1920. Disenchanted with the picturesque and also the allegorical themes and contrived subjects of High Art, a number of photographers were influenced by the revolutionary movements in modern art, and turned instead to making realistic, highly detailed images. Subjects were now naturalistic, ranging from dramatic landscapes and uncompromisingly direct portraits, to close-ups of intricate plant forms, from naturally weathered structures such as wood and stone, to man-made mechanical objects.

Tone richness and sharp detail
The images were free from any kind of image diffusion or manipulation in printing. Instead, qualities that were inherent in the photographic medium were exploited to the full. This meant its natural richness of tone, its ability to show extreme detail and to capture the play of light. Today, we take and use these characteristics without questioning, but in the early 1920s, the idea of making serious photographs from "ordinary", often mundane, subjects was considered revolutionary.

It is possible to see the origins of Straight photography in the pictorial photography of Frederick Evans, and the post-1910 work of Alfred Stieglitz. But the main photographers in the field were Paul Strand and Edward Weston in America, and Albert Renger-Patzsch in Europe.

Reactions to the Straight approach
The photographic societies of the pictorialist movement, with their ritual judging of what was suitable for exhibition purposes and what was not, were understandably hostile to the developments of Straight photography. In Britain, professional photographers rapidly adopted the ideas and theories behind the movement, but in amateur clubs, where tradition was valued more highly than experiment, Straight photography was dismissed as a modern aberration.

Right from the last issue of *Camera Work* (1917), which Stieglitz devoted to Strand's early work, Straight photography developed into a major style, and it was strengthened by the simultaneous growth of human documentary photography.

See also
Texture, pp. 43-5. **Aperture** *Standards of sharpness; Maximum depth of field*, p. 119. **Close-up equipment** *Standars of sharpness*, p. 197. **Architectural and landscape photography** *Equipment and approach*, p. 310

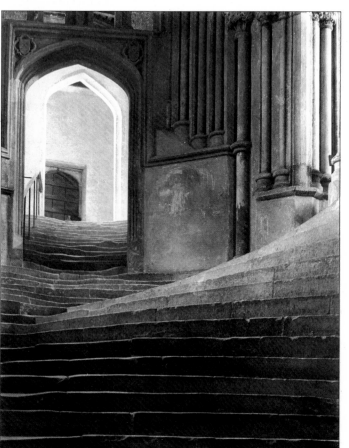

"Sea of Steps" (1903)
Frederick Evans became a member of the Linked Ring Brotherhood a few years after its inception, but he always remained a fervent believer in "plain", "straightforward" pictorial photography. For architectural studies such as this, he would spend long hours deciding on which viewpoint to use, and then return at different times of the day to study natural lighting effects. The negative was made with a 10 × 8 ins (25 × 20 cm) stand camera, and contact printed without any retouching on platinum paper. Stieglitz frequently published Evans' work in *Camera Work* (1904-7).

The influences of art on Straight photography

Art and photography had a noticeable influence on each other during the early years of this century. In the world of painting, Impressionism had undermined the Pre-Raphaelite urge to represent subjects in accurate detail. The spread of photographic images, both as prints and reproductions on the printed page, strongly competed with paintings as sources of information. Some painters reacted to this by using increasingly larger canvases, or by placing a much greater emphasis on the use of color, the technique of using noticeable brushstrokes, and the very character of the paint itself.

In its move away from precise representation, painting became less a "window on the world" and more a two-dimensional piece obviously worked by hand. The formal ingredients and elements of a painting's structure, the texture of the paint, and even the frame itself, became as important as, or even more important than, the subject depicted in the painting itself.

During the first decade of this century, Paris was the center of revolutionary movements in modern art. Painters such as Picasso, Matisse, and Braque followed and developed the interpretative style of Cézanne. And Cubism set out to present strange new concepts in the way form was shown. "Ideas" about subject were presented, rather than factual, descriptive views.

In America, Stieglitz, who was always anxious to explore new ideas, arranged for drawings and paintings by these unknown, revolutionary artists to be sent to New York. From 1908 onward, the work of modern artists was shown in 291 Gallery, and then at the major 1913 Armory Show of modern painting. The movement was known as "Modernism". Most of the members of the Photo-Secession were puzzled, and even shocked, by the strange imagery, which even defied the principles of perspective that had been practiced since Renaissance times. Such radical moves toward distortion and abstraction could hardly be matched by photography, they thought. But Modernism did encourage Coburn, Stieglitz, Steichen, and others to move away from expressing moods and impressions, and become concerned with the design content and structure of their photographs.

In both America and Europe, subject matter began to be explored in new ways. Photographers adopted unusual viewpoints, made extreme close-ups, and chose intentionally "unpicturesque" objects. Sharp focus gradually became accepted as a virtue — something to be taken advantage of rather than avoided. The years between 1910 and 1930 were when photography finally separated itself from the influences of painting. It was recognized that each medium was offering something quite different as a means of personal expression, and that each particular one had its own special qualities to offer.

Techniques

Although some Straight photographers prefer to use the large stand cameras of the nineteenth century in order to contact print their negatives, many have taken advantage of technical developments and quality improvements in cameras, lenses, and materials.

Stieglitz and Strand both favored hand-held cameras. The most popular of these at the time was the American-made Graflex single lens reflex plate camera. Both Edward and Brett Weston began their careers with Graflex cameras, but both in turn graduated to 10 × 8 ins (25 × 20 cm) view cameras for landscape and still life work, keeping the smaller cameras for portraits and work which required spontaneity. Edward Weston contact printed his work on platinum matte paper before changing over to using improved glossy bromide paper in the mid-1920s.

Brett Weston and Ansel Adams are both users of top-precision 6 × 6 cm rollfilm cameras, but Adams still uses plate cameras for the majority of his work. One major advantage, apart from image size, is the ability to process each negative individually, for optimum control of contrast and density.

The Zone System

Adams practices a technical philosophy which he has devised himself, based on the idea of pre-visualizing the final black and white image exactly, at the time of shooting. His approach to Straight photography includes the skilled manipulation of exposure and development in order to yield the most appropriate tone values from each particular subject. He has published his technique, the Zone System, and it has become an established method of tone control in photographic exposure and is taught in many American schools and colleges.

In essence, a photographer using the Zone System tests the materials, processing and printing techniques, in order to forecast how different subject brightnesses result in particular tones of gray on the final print. Each gray tone is called a "zone", and numbered from I through IX, with zone V as the middle gray. The nine zones are marked as a scale of tones on the calculator dial of a hand exposure meter. Careful measurement of each of the significant areas of brightness in a scene is essential to the success of the system. As you change shutter or aperture by one stop, the reproduction of all brightness moves up or down the scale. Development is adjusted to expand or contract the negative characteristics, compensating for subjects with high or low brightness ranges — and so consistently giving these zone values.

Individuals and movements of Straight photography

Straight photography had a marked influence on photographic style in many different countries, but its strongest disciples were American and German. In New York, "New Realism" was the label given to the kind of work produced from 1917 onward by such photographers as Paul Strand and Charles Sheeler. Meanwhile, from 1924 onward in Europe, an independent movement began called Neue Sachlicheit, or "New Objectivity". During the 1920s examples of these new approaches to photography and publications began to appear in international exhibitions and publications and its influence gradually began to spread. On the west coast of America this influence eventually resulted in the formation, in 1932, of a "school" which was to have a dramatic influence over the development of photographic styles world-wide — group f64.

Paul Strand

A recent high school graduate in 1909, Paul Strand was a frequent visitor to the 291 Gallery, and he was strongly influenced by the works of art from Europe which had been imported there by Stieglitz. Strand was impressed by the style, and in the years that followed, he set out to experiment by photographing everyday objects and creating abstract still lifes. His subjects included ordinary things such as a white picket fence, the close-up of a pile of bowls, the shadows cast from an overhead railroad, and the porch of a rural homestead. He also made straight photographs of city scenes in New York and the characters who inhabited them. These were intended to be pictures in their own right, rather than acting as factual, documentary records.

Stieglitz had an uncanny ability for recogniz-

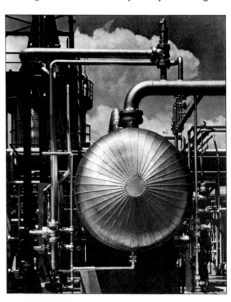

"Oil refinery, Tema, Ghana" (1963)
Paul Strand, more influenced by European modernist art than by the styles of Pictorialism, produced straight, semi-abstract studies of man-made subjects. Such things had been regarded as being too mundane by the Pictorialists to merit attention.
(Copyright © 1971, 1976, The Paul Strand Foundation, as published in Paul Strand: *Sixty Years of Photographs,* Aperture, 1976).

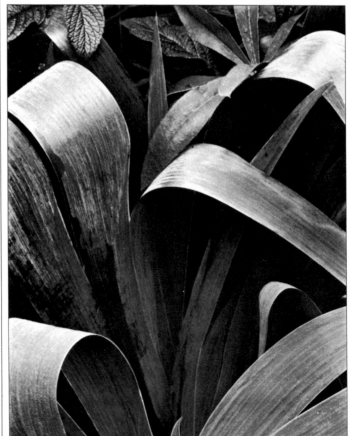

"Iris, Georgetown, Maine" (1928)
Strand's fascination with linear structures and pattern is particularly evident in this abstract of leaf forms. He invites the viewer to study and compare apparently similar natural shapes.
(Copyright © 1950, 1971, 1976, 1977 The Paul Strand Foundation, as published in Paul Strand: *Time in New England,* Aperture, 1980).

ing talent, and he was struck by Strand's work, both for his approach and his subject content. His pictures seemed to echo Stieglitz's own work, and Steichen's, too. In 1916, Strand was given his own exhibition at 291 Gallery, and in the following year, the final issue of *Camera Work* was devoted solely to his pictures. Today, Strand's particular choice of subject, his technical approach and straight treatment are all familiar photographic styles. But in comparison with the Pictorialists' soft, manipulative approach, and idealized, romantic subject

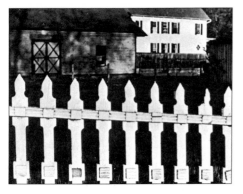

"The White Fence, Port Kent, New York" (1916)
Strand's most well-known photograph is strangely lacking in perspective, and strident in its design. (Copyright © 1971,
1976, The Paul Strand Foundation, as published in Paul Strand: *Sixty Years of Photographs,* Aperture, 1976).

matter, Strand's pictures were startling innovations. Even Stieglitz referred to them as being "brutally direct".

Strand went on to make less abstract, more objective images, but still choosing as subjects the mundane things around him, and always using straight photographic techniques. Photo-Secessionists such as Fred Holland Day and Rudolf Eickemeyer, and many of the British Pictorialists, were quite unable to come to terms with this style of photography and rejected it out of hand. In London it was bitterly despised by all, and cuttingly referred to as the "dustbin" school of American photography.

Strand's originality and energy was matched by his ability to express his ideas clearly in words. Writing in *Camera Work* he pointed out that "objectivity is the very essence of photography and at the same time its limitation". He goes on to point out that the photographer's main difficulty is to see both the potential quality and the limitations of a photograph, and that an honest approach as well as an "intensity of vision" is vital for personal expression, to be achieved with a straight photographic approach. "It is precisely here that honesty no less than intensity of vision is the prerequisite of a living expression... accomplished without tricks of process or manipulation".

Later on, in another magazine article which was an attempt to convert the unwilling British photographers to take up Straight photography, Strand summed up his philosophy in the following way, "Look at the things around you, the immediate world around you. If you are alive it will mean something to you, and if you

care enough about photography, and if you know how to use it, you will want to photograph that meaningness. If you let other people's vision get between the world and your own, you will achieve that extremely common and worthless thing, a pictoral photograph".

The New Objectivity
German photographers Albert Renger-Patzsch and Karl Blossfeldt were independently exploring the possibilities for using natural and man-made subjects for Straight photography during the very early 1920s. Renger-Patzsch believed that within the limitations of photography there was endless scope for exploring its creative potential by isolating and revealing forms and motifs which

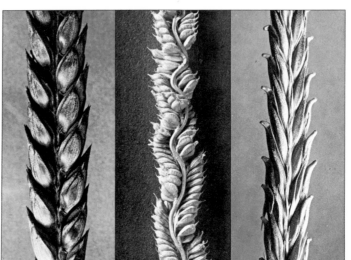

could quite easily be overlooked, or simply taken for granted. He thought that the photographer should remain the patient observer, without allowing personality to intrude, and without trying to achieve painterly effects. Renger-Patzsch's work was published in *The World is Beautiful,* published in 1928, featuring details of architecture, machinery, landscape, plants, and animal forms. Blossfeldt's book *Art Forms in Nature,* published a year later in 1929, contained enlarged close-ups of plant structures in soft, diffused light set against plain backgrounds. The similarity between natural things and man-made objects added further strength to the revelations of New Objectivity. Like the work of Strand and Straight photographers in America, the Germans made

Three plant forms (1929)
These three close-ups by Karl Blossfeldt reveal the "architectural" qualities of natural objects. The similarity between these simple stalks and various kinds of man-made decoration is remarkable.

"Aluminium Töpfe" (1925)
This powerful composition, using repeating shapes and tight framing, is typical of Albert Renger-Patzsch's choice of subject. He referred to them as "ordinary things".

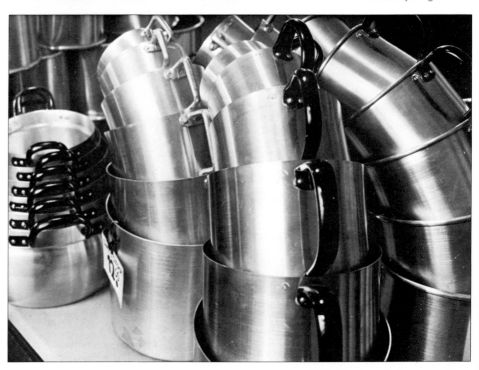

the fullest possible use of photography's ability to display details with maximum richness and dramatic tonal gradations. However, the Pictorialists criticized such pictures finding them "dull", and German photographers involved in the growing field of social documentary photography regarded the work as being merely superficial and "seeing for the sake of seeing".

Edward Weston and Group f 64

Straight photography was being pioneered by one man, who was working virtually in isolation in California – Edward Weston. In 1911, Weston had opened his own studio as a professional portrait photographer. He had also exhibited his pictorial images internationally – photographs that were heavily retouched, and

printed using the oil process. But a few years later, he changed his approach completely. Influenced by an exhibition of modern paintings and a visit in 1922 to New York, where he met Stieglitz and Strand, Weston changed his style to pin-sharp, unretouched photography. Initially, he concentrated on abstract compositions, but after a four-year stay in Mexico, he began to concentrate on straight, realistic images of people, landscapes, and everyday objects. Weston's time in Mexico was crucial to the development of his Straight style. He became acquainted with mural painters Orozco and Rivera, and he discovered the sun-bleached façades of rural architecture, and the strong faces of the Mexican people themselves. Weston captured the quality of the light and the detail he sought with his 10 × 8 ins

(12.5 × 10 cm) camera and his practice of contact printing. He became a master of his materials. The hallmarks of his work, which are widely imitated even today, are meticulous detail resulting from maximum depth of field, all-over sharpness, and a magnificent richness of tonal values.

When he returned to California in 1927, Weston devoted his time to photographing sand dunes, nudes, and close-ups of shells, fruit, and vegetables. His pictures were not intended to be a personal expression or an interpretation, although his choice of subject and his sensitivity to form were, in a sense, just that. He was striving to portray the "quintessence" of the object – a revelation of the thing itself. His work in fact celebrates the richness of sight – it shows the beauty which is an intrin-

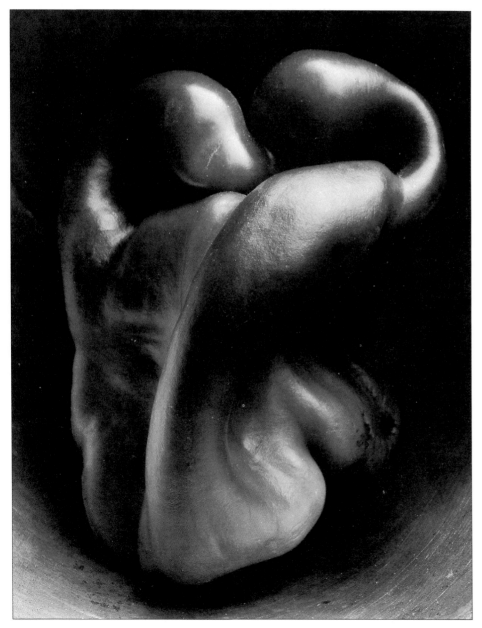

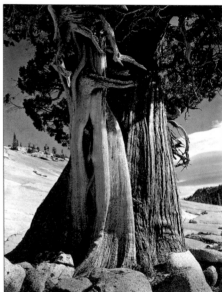

"Juniper, Lake Tenaya" (1938)
This picture (above) demonstrates Edward Weston's talent for using superb print quality to show his heightened awareness of form and texture. He used the smallest possible aperture to achieve maximum depth of field. Unlike Strand, Weston was relatively restrictive in his choice of subjects. Weston, in turn, was impressed by Strand's approach, but regarded some of the subjects he chose as tasteless. (Copyright © 1981 Center of Creative Photography, University of Arizona, Arizona Board of Regents. Used by permission.)

"Pepper No. 30" (1930)
The most renowned of Edward Weston's many studies of peppers (left). Weston always used natural light, often diffusing the sun's direct rays with muslin. In this photograph an old funnel is used to form the background. He took a week to make the flow of lines and sense of three-dimensional form work together to create this strongly suggestive image. (Copyright © 1981 Center of Creative Photography, University of Arizona, Arizona Board of Regents. Used by permission.)

sic part of the material and form of ordinary, commonplace objects.

In 1932 a group of photographers (including Ansel Adams, Imogen Cunningham, and Willard Van Dyke) joined Weston and called themselves Group f 64. The name was taken from the smallest aperture available on lenses of the time, which offered maximum depth of field. This was a vital requirement of the Straight approach to photography. Soft focus and fuzzy detail were totally rejected. The Group made their beliefs public, and produced exhibitions which were in direct competition with the photographic societies who were unwilling to show Straight work. Their reputation and ideas spread internationally because of these exhibitions, and although Group f 64 was only actually in existence for a period of a few years, it had immense impact and made a lasting contribution to styles of realism in photography – many of which are strongly evident in photographers' work today.

Ansel Adams
Of the original members of Group f 64, Ansel Adams was to become the most sustained exponent of Straight photography. He is a committed conservationist, as well as a writer and teacher, and he has spent most of his life photographing the landscape of California. His pictures all possess an attention to detail similar to Weston's, plus a definition and extreme

depth of field required to achieve a clarity of form, and meticulous attention to print quality. Strand's Straight photography was one of Adams' main influences, and another was the work of Stieglitz, who first exhibited his work in 1932 at An American Place, which he set up to continue the tradition of the 291 Gallery. Adams, like Weston, believes in "pre-visualizing" the final print, even before shooting, by studying the subject on the camera's viewing screen in a very considered way. He devised his "Zone System" to predict the tone values of each part of the subject as it appears on the camera's viewing screen.

What seems to be a strong technical emphasis is all part of Adams' insistence on good visual "description" of the subject. His pictures describe the grandeur of nature, the monumental or delicate structure of a landscape, the intricate flow of growth, and the drama of weathering and decay. His world is unpopulated, nature-dominated, and often dependent on transient light effects. His pictures are among the most popular Straight photographic works of art of our time.

The influences of Straight photography

Of all the photographic styles, the Straight approach has been the one most widely absorbed into the commercial world. For advertising a product, the qualities of photography can describe an object sensitively and powerfully – particularly when precision and craftsmanship must be implied. Straight photography in this form became familiar long before it was acceptable on the exhibition walls of photographic societies.

Edward Steichen turned professional in 1923, and until 1937 he worked as chief photographer for Condé Nast. His fashion photography and celebrity portraiture for *Vanity Fair* and *Vogue* magazines led him eventually to lucrative work in advertising photography.

Brett Weston, son of Edward Weston, has inherited his father's eye for creating pictures through the exploration of natural detail using Straight photography. He employs lines and shapes to make striking abstracts, completely free from manipulation. Ralph Gibson (see *Leading exponents of Structuralism and Abstraction,* pp. 364-8) also uses the extreme

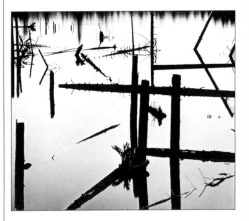

"Logging pond, Alaska"(1973)
This composition by Brett Weston shows a natural subject treated in a highly graphic and linear fashion. Unlike his father Edward's style, which was to show dramatic three-dimensional form, the result is virtually two-dimensional.

detail and realism of Straight photography in a highly personal way. Surfaces become patterns, clothing, parts of buildings or the human figure, clothed, are depersonalized by cropping, and are transformed into minutely described still lifes.

As a creative style, Straight photography can be both a strength and a limitation. Since superb detail of line and tone will portray unwanted parts of a scene with the same clarity as important elements, selection of viewpoint and lighting are critical. Also, it is all too easy for a justified fascination for the technical performance of the camera and film to tempt the photographer into making pictures which are no more than a display of craftsmanship. For example, there are photographers who, inspired by the work of Ansel Adams, have matched his technique, only to discover that their work fails to express his insight.

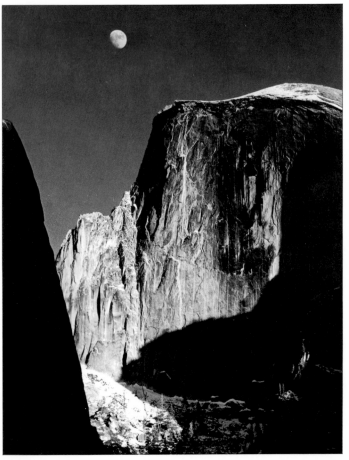

"Moon and Half Dome, Yosemite National Park" (1960)
This photograph, with its sense of natural grandeur, balance, and its powerful use of lighting and tonal contrast is characteristic of Ansel Adams' work. His studies of mountain country and unpopulated west coast landscapes demonstrate how powerful a means of expression Straight photography can be. Here Adams has selected exactly the right time to show dramatic interplay between flat shadow areas and sidelit, textured rock face.

The documentary approach

The documentary approach to photography is concerned essentially with the subject – the camera is used to communicate significant facts about people and their surroundings. As a style, it should be objective, but in practice the way the photographer reacts to a situation, particularly where people are involved, inevitably colors the approach and affects results.

The photographer's interest in, and choice of, the subject, the personal selection of a particular gesture or expression, and the use of surroundings, all add up to the creation of a recognizable personal style.

The first documentary photographers

Many early documentary photographers worked in virtual isolation. They were not members of brotherhoods or societies – their pictures would have been considered too ordinary, as well as a misuse of an artistic medium. The acceptance of Paul Strand's pictures of New York street people in 1915 did not prevent photographers who documented everyday life from being regarded as a race apart, operating outside the boundaries of aesthetic photography.

These few photographers consequently lacked the publicity and status of salon exhibitions, and even when the arrival of illustrated magazines in the 1930s meant that their work was published and found a wide audience, it was at first uncredited. But magazines did mean that photographers had the opportunity to travel the world in search of picture stories, and through "photojournalism" they could build up a reputation for their own distinctive styles. Some chose human documentary photography as a vehicle for expressing themselves (for example, their view of society), and they were given the label "social realist". Gradually, since the 1960s, there has been such interest in documentary styles that publishers and galleries have increasingly devoted monographs and one-person shows to work of this kind. In its early days documentary photographs were naïve both compositionally and technically, and the results were often misunderstood. Today, photographers and their audiences are more visually experienced and sophisticated, and composition, the use of lighting and viewpoint are used intuitively to reinforce the subject content.

See also
Reportage photography, pp. 324-7

Equipment and techniques

The technical developments which had the most impact on documentary photography were improvements in hand-held camera design. Early disguised or self-adapted cameras used by Paul Strand and Paul Martin were superseded by the German-made Ermanox f 1.8 camera for 4.5 × 6 cm plates in 1925. This same year, the first Leica appeared, but until 1932, the larger camera scored on the grounds of having a faster lens and giving better-quality enlargements. However, the unobtrusive and quiet Leica quickly became the camera of the photojournalist, ideally suiting the approach and techniques of such documentary photographers as Henri Cartier-Bresson and Alfred Eisenstaedt.

Some photographers, for whom spontaneity and the candid approach were not necessary, continued to use plate (now sheet film) cameras, or compromised with twin and then single lens reflex cameras, as they appeared on the market. In recent years, photographers have adopted the 35 mm SLR camera in preference to direct vision designs. A wide range of in-

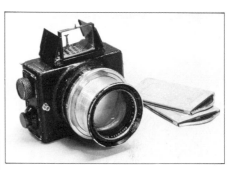

The Ermanox camera
This little f 1.8 camera was vital to the development of the candid style of documentary photography. It was introduced in Germany in 1925, the same year as the first Leica. It was widely used by press photographers and professionals because of its fast lens. (At the time it was the fastest in the world.)

terchangeable lenses has contributed great visual scope.

Improvements in the reproduction of photographs have been equally important. Black and white half tones replaced engraved interpretations of photographs in newspapers and magazines. During the 1960s electron scanners and webb offset printing machinery improved the quality and lowered the cost of color reproduction. The change to color photography is not yet complete. But only a minority of young documentary photographers still work exclusively in black and white – a factor largely determined by the immense demand made by color magazines for photographs in full color.

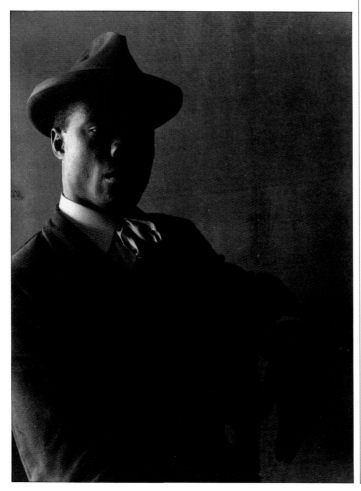

Untitled portrait (c. 1900)
Although so much of Fred Holland Day's work is highly staged (his *Crucifixion,* for example), some of his portraits are remarkably natural and were stylistically decades ahead of their time. Judging from his choice of lighting, his use of shape, and his straight portraiture technique, this picture could be mistaken for a modern documentary study. Unfortunately, the majority of Day's negatives were destroyed by fire in 1914, and only the negatives he had given to friends still remain – so his full output of work cannot be adequately assessed.

Early documentary photographers

Documentary photography goes right back to David Octavius Hill and Robert Adamson, and their project (begun in 1843) to make reference photographs for a giant historical work of 470 Scottish ministers. This was to commemorate the founding of the Free Church of Scotland. The photographs, which were all set pieces posed by Hill, have a directness and a sense of character which is unusual for their time. In the course of this project, Hill and Adamson developed an enthusiasm for their task and the calotype process, and they went on to build up a fine collection of pictures documenting Scottish celebrities and the inhabitants of Scottish fishing villages.

In Boston, Albert S. Southworth and Josiah J. Hawes went into partnership in 1841 and began photographing such well known personalities as Longfellow and Jenny Lind. They are now thought to be among the most skilled of American daguerrotypists, and among the first photographers to curtail exposure enough to take "snapshots" in ordinary settings.

Lewis Carroll, in England, also "collected" celebrities, but his main interest was photographing children, attracting widespread public disapproval. Today, the pictures are noted for their beauty and graceful composition.

Battlefield photographers

The first wars to be recorded by photography were the Crimean War by Roger Fenton in 1855, and the American Civil War by Matthew Brady and his photographers between 1861 and 1865. For the British and American public, the realism of photography replaced the imaginative and heroic painting which had glorified warfare in the past.

The problems imposed by operating the wet collodion process from a mobile, horse-drawn darkroom were immense, and photographers consequently produced views of battlefields long after the battle was over. However, some of Brady's pictures showing gutted towns and corpses at Gettysburgh, capture the horrific atmosphere of war.

Nadar and Julia Margaret Cameron

From 1851 until about 1880, most photographers used the wet plate process, which involved using collodion to attach silver halides to glass. Because of the slowness of the plates (equivalent to about ASA 2), long exposures were necessary, so portraits tended to be stiff and unlifelike. Very few portraits from that period actually communicate the subject's personality as well as giving a reasonable "likeness". There are two notable exceptions to this — Nadar (real name Gaspard Felix Tournachon) and Julia Margaret Cameron.

Nadar, a well-known Parisian photographer, caricaturist, and writer is perhaps best known for his portraits of leading French intellectuals and artists during the 1860s and 1870s. His pictures have static qualities, but he did encourage his sitters to pose themselves in his very simple settings. Because of this they look natural. Each portrait is a revealing study, full of expression and personality.

Cameron was an amateur photographer who adopted an equally uncompromising, direct attitude to portraiture. More daring than Nadar, she restricted the daylight in her studio

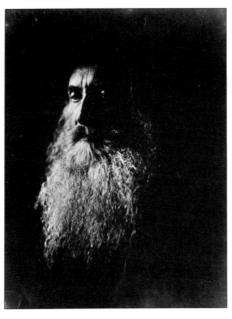

"Sir Henry Taylor"(c. 1867)
Despite the technical problems of the collodion process, Julia Margaret Cameron succeeds in showing character in this stern, moody portrait. Long exposures revealing subject movement and shallow focus were commonplace features of portrait photographs of the time.

so much that her portraits were Rembrandt-like in their somber tones. Her sitters were leading English poets, scientists, and artists of the late 1860s, and she had great admiration for them. She was determined to document "their inner greatness" as well as their external appearance. Some of her portraits are over-dramatized, but each one shows remarkably strong character. These pictures are quite unlike the contrived, allegorical compositions which she was also producing at this time (see *High Art's leading exponents*, pp. 332-3). They were heavily criticized for underexposure, subject movement, and for being "original at the expense of all photographic qualities".

John Thomson

Photographing the underprivileged was, in the 1870s, considered to be an unsuitable, tasteless subject, unless it was treated in a sentimental way. John Thomson is remembered for his frank coverage of London's poor. He set out to document their different occupations in as detached and unsentimental a way as possible. His pictures were to be used as references for engravings in his book *Street Life of London,* which he intended to bring about social reform.

Lewis Hine

At the beginning of this century, in about 1910, Lewis Hine was using photography in a similar way, on behalf of the National Child Labor Committee. He was a self-taught amateur, and one of his first projects was to make a complete coverage of the lives of impoverished immigrants. As a NCLC investigator Hine traveled around America exposing the plight of working children. He often had to smuggle his Graflex camera into cotton mills to take pictures of them minding dangerous machinery.

Hine believed that art should have a social purpose, and he was probably the first photographer consciously to use composition and technical skills to reinforce the points he wanted to make. His pictures were reproduced in NCLC pamphlets and used in traveling exhibitions, and they directly influenced the passing of Federal laws on labour abuse.

Paul Martin

In London during the 1890s, Paul Martin was recording everyday street life with a hand-held plate camera disguised as a parcel. He was a professional photographer, but he delighted in the realism and spontaneity afforded by candid photography. Intensely interested in people, he was an observer of life rather than a

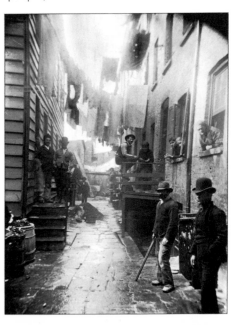

"Bandits' Roost, Mulberry Street" (c. 1888)
Jacob Riis took his camera into every dark, dingy street. He recorded this scene, and others like it, to show the world just what conditions were like in crowded, poverty-stricken areas of Manhattan, New York.

reformer — and he was quite content to portray the passing crowds without influencing and posing his subjects. His pictures recall the past precisely, and with sensitivity.

Jacob Riis

Making an impassioned plea for social justice, newspaper reporter Jacob Riis took photographs of New York's poor during the 1880s to 90s. Using the newly invented light source, flash powder, his pictures were indisputable evidence of facts which the better-off citizen chose to ignore. He made the photographs into lantern slides, which were used to illus-

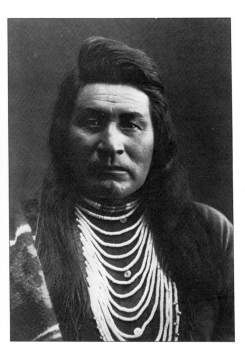

"Typical Nez Percé" (1899)
One of the 1500 pictures which were eventually published in 20 volumes to document the American Indians by Edward Curtis. (Courtesy of Philadelphia Museum of Photography. Photographed by Philadelphia Museum of Art.)

trate his public lectures, and were crudely reproduced in several of his books including *How The Other Half Lives* (1890). Riis was a reformer who was astute enough to realize how much people believed in the accuracy and truthfulness of photography, and thus how much it could influence their social awareness.

Edward Curtis
In the late 1880s, Edward Curtis began to make a record of the remaining North American Indians, tribe by tribe, on their reservations. He made numerous expeditions, sometimes with teams of anthropologists, to photograph for posterity fast-disappearing Indian customs, dress, and ways of life. He won acceptance within the tribes through his honest approach and his dedication to their interests.

Eugène Atget
In Paris, the work of Thomson and Martin was being echoed by Eugène Atget. Pitifully poor all his life, he made his living by selling reference pictures to artists. Between 1900 and 1925, he photographed the views and details of Paris that he considered to be important. The people who bought the photographs were mainly artists from the academic schools, and official bodies concerned with architectural records and historic monuments. The eight thousand large-format plates he made cover street scenes, gardens and trees, the interiors and exteriors of buildings, as well as street characters such as peddlers.

Atget's style grew directly out of his subjects – he took pictures in an objective way, oblivious of current artistic styles. His work went unrecognized until after his death in 1927, when

American photographer Berenice Abbott rescued his negatives and publicized his work.

Erich Salomon
The photographer for whom the term "candid camera" was originally coined was Erich Salomon, who specialized in attending court hearings, diplomatic conferences, important social gatherings, and musical performances, and taking highly revealing photographs. He used a small, wide-aperture Ermanox camera, which allowed him to shoot using existing indoor lighting. He went to great trouble, dressing scrupulously for the occasion, and putting to good use his quiet, polite manner, and his ability to speak several languages. His pictures of leading politicians have been unequalled – he shows them bored, animated, worried and relaxed.

August Sander
The German people were the obsession of professional portraitist, August Sander. During the 1920s he set himself the monumental task of finding and photographing exemplary "specimens" of the ranks and occupations of German society. He sought out a vast range of people – a gamekeeper, a clerk, a young aristocrat – taking straight, often full-length portraits, usually outdoors, and always in soft, overcast lighting. His pictures capture unerringly the exact stance and setting, summing up the person's role and personality.

Sander's work came to an end with the Second World War, and afterwards he felt unable to complete the project. Fortunately, hundreds of the pictures remain, and collectively, they are a unique and fascinating social record.

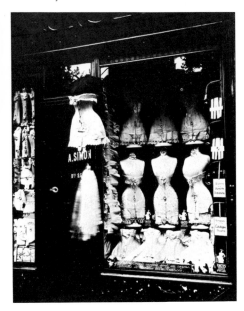

"Boulevard de Strasbourg" (c. 1910)
Many of Eugène Atget's pictures of Paris depict shop window displays. (Courtesy of Philadelphia Museum Art. Given anonymously. Photographed by Will Brown.)

"Man and Wife" (1928)
August Sander's project encompassed all walks of life and all classes. This photograph captures the seriousness and self-awareness of a middle-class architect and his wife.

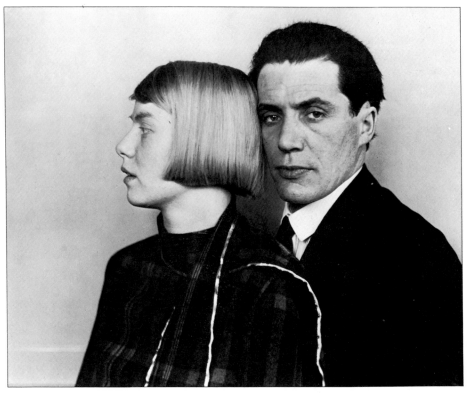

The external influences

Documentary photography, and particularly human documentary, has been more strongly influenced by printed mass communication than by other areas of photography. People are always interested in pictures of other people, and long before the advent of half-tone printing processes (see *Screens*, pp. 264-5) it was common to purchase photographs printed on albumen paper. Stores sold *cartes-de-visite* (small mounted prints the size of a visiting card) — the subject matter ranged from popular politicians and actors to circus performers and freaks. Stereoscopic prints were also widely collected. These often showed staged "actuality" scenes, such as "kissing the maid in the parlor", and were really the forerunners of today's television and video. Lantern slide shows were popular, too, attracting large audiences.

By the 1890s photographs were being reproduced on the pages of newspapers, which also coincided with growing moves for social reform. Nineteenth century concepts of helping the unfortunate through charity were gradually changing into what eventually became the social programs of the 1920s and 1930s, and photography, with its truthfulness and fact-recording ability, was a very persuasive and influential media in this cause.

Germany in the mid-1920s was the world center of the printing industry, as well as the country in the fore of camera and lens design. It was therefore natural that Germany should be the birthplace of the first magazines illustrated by photography. These publications used photographs arranged in sequences, forming photo-essays, through which photographers could report on an event and express an opinion. A new generation began to see photography as a serious, significant form of communication, quite different from the functions it had served previously.

The drastic upheaval of two world wars and subsequent events created a need for photoreporting. Photographs were taken to show the violence and cruelty of war, and they were seen by millions. Since that time protest movements and groups campaigning on behalf of neglected and maltreated minority groups have continued to use photography in this way.

During the 1950s and 1960s, the growth of television reduced the demand for picture magazines, but human documentary photography found new outlets in newspaper color magazines, books of photographs, and traveling photographic exhibitions. Centers which regularly exhibit photography increased ten-fold during the 1970s, and for the first time since the 1850s, the public began to visit exhibitions in large numbers. Henri Cartier-Bresson, Bill Brandt, Diane Arbus, and August Sander have all attracted larger audiences than many international painting exhibitions.

The illustrated magazines

Picture magazines, which began in Germany in the late 1920s, spread to America with *Life* in 1936, to Britain with *Picture Post* in 1936, and to France with *Paris Match* in 1949. They increased in popularity until the 1960s, when *Life* issued eight million copies, reaching a readership exceeding 30 million per issue. During this short period, the magazines discovered many young photographers who were committed to social realism. Newspapers of course ran individual news photographs, but the picture magazines covered stories in depth through sequences of photographs which took precedence over the text, often running to 15 or 20 pages.

Alfred Eisenstaedt

The work of Salomon, and other candid photographers, encouraged Alfred Eisenstaedt to change his style from impressionistic pictorialism, as an amateur, to straight human documentary photography. In 1929, he turned professional, achieving fame for his work on the *Berliner Illustrierte Zeitung,* and then fleeing Nazi Germany for America. There he joined Margaret Bourke-White and others as the first staff photographers on the newly launched *Life* magazine. His work is characterized by its simplicity of design and his frequent use of lines and shapes to frame subjects. He has photographed over 1300 assignments and 50 covers, and is the longest-serving member of the *Life* photographic team.

Margaret Bourke-White

Like Eisenstaedt, Margaret Bourke-White spent a large part of her professional career as a *Life* photographer. One of the toughest and most adventurous of the photojournalists of the time, her strongest work was in revealing bad social conditions. For her, pictures of people were lacking if they did not contain some reference to their work, living environment, and their relationships with others. Every object should contribute to the main subject of the picture. Her work is remarkable for its fastidious selection of subject material, without manipulation. Essays on Gandhi's India (1946) and the Nazi Buchenwald extermination camp are high points in her coverage of important historical events.

Bill Brandt

British photographer Bill Brandt learned photography in Paris under Man Ray, and after returning to England in 1931 he devoted most of his time to the newly developing documentary photography. He freelanced for *Picture Post* from its inception, along with Kurt Hutton and Felix Mann. Brandt's work from this time focuses on contrasting ways of English life — from the tough existence of miners in the northern towns, to the genteel life-style of middle-class Londoners, with their parlormaids, table silver, and lace curtains. His pictures starkly compare the class differences of the 1930s, and his sympathies lay firmly with the working-class families, whom his pictures portray with great respect and sensitivity.

Arnold Newman

Since 1946 Arnold Newman has spent the majority of his time working for magazines

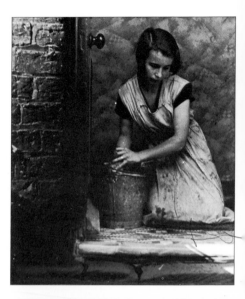

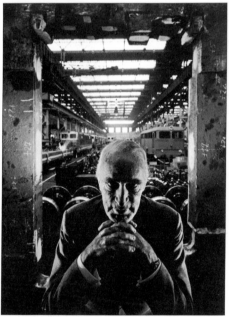

such as *Harper's Bazaar*. His pictures have a distinctive style — he makes a point of using his subject's home or workplace as a setting, and making it a vital compositional ingredient in the picture. These settings are natural and genuine, though very considered, and he makes subtle use of lighting. Shapes and patterns made out of these settings add structure to the pictures as well as information about the sitter. Sometimes the lighting and setting Newman chooses are strongly opinionated, but this exaggeration is used to emphasize what he has already researched and found to be present, although often in a lesser form. He also chooses unconventional positioning of the subject — using unorthodox frame divisions and shapes. His pictures are very instructive for their examples of people-handling and picture-building.

"Young Housewife, Bethnal Green" (1937)
This picture (left) is one of Bill Brandt's series on British classes and conditions, and it was used in *Picture Post.* It shows a young woman's pride and dignity as she goes about her menial work. Brandt's documentary work is sympathetic and expressive, but detached and reflective rather than militant. He is usually careful not to influence his subjects in any way.

"Alfried Krupp" (1963)
In this portrait of the armaments manufacturer (left) Arnold Newman makes an expressive statement without his subject's knowledge. He uses double side-lighting to produce a satanic, almost macabre, image. Not surprisingly, the portrait received public acclaim, but it incurred the subject's extreme wrath. (Photograph © Arnold Newman.)

"David Hockney" (1979)
In this portrait (right) Arnold Newman used props from the artist's studio, and added the painting to achieve a Mondrianesque composition. He used a distant viewpoint and telephoto lens to produce a flat-perspective effect, which echoes Hockney's own frequent use of flattened depth in his paintings. (Photograph © Arnold Newman.)

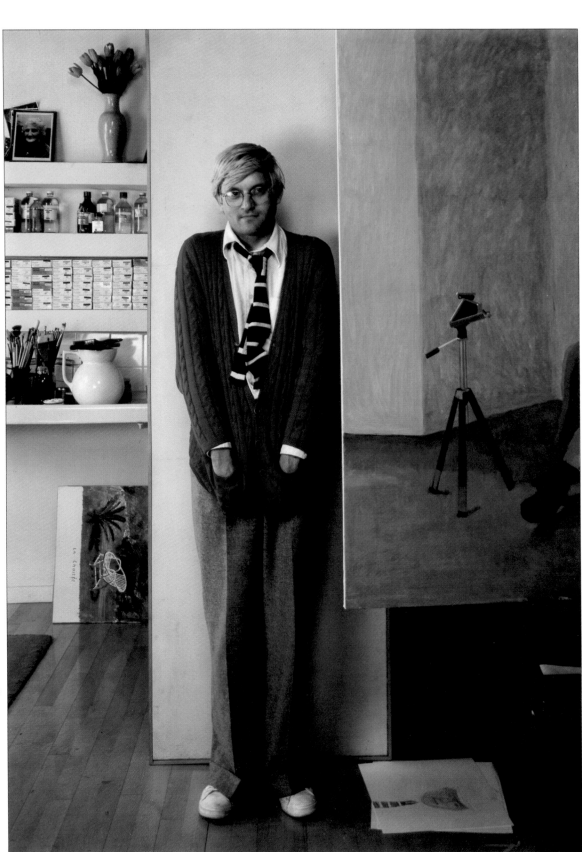

The Farm Security Administration project

During the 1930s in America, the Depression drastically affected the tenant farmers and migrant farm laborers of the Midwest. The banks refused to give credit and a prolonged drought meant that many farmers went bankrupt, while the demand for seasonal laborers disappeared. The people were dispossessed of their small holdings, and trekked westward toward California in the hope of finding work, living in makeshift roadside camps on the way. The Farm Security Administration was formed and a team of photographers was sent out to make a record of the situation which would eventually draw attention to the plight of all poor farming people at this time. The most well known FSA photographers, mostly employed at different times, were Dorothea Lange, Walker Evans, Jack Delano, Arthur Rothstein, Russell Lee, and Ben Shahn. The project was a landmark in the history of documentary photography — directly instrumental in obtaining aid from private individuals and government sources.

Dorothea Lange

The photographer whose work most captured the public's imagination was perhaps Dorothea Lange, an ex-member of Group f 64 (see *Individuals and movements of Straight photography*, pp. 343-6), and proprietor of a small portrait studio in San Francisco. Her direct approach to photography, combined with infinite compassion and respect for her subjects produced powerful, memorable images which successfully sidestepped sentimentality. Her subjects are dignified in their exhaustion and hopelessness. Between 1935 and 1942 she sought out and photographed this desperate situation in a revealing but sensitive way. Her pictures make a shocking contrast with the popular image of America in the 1930s — the glamorous world of Hollywood. Originally, the FSA photographs were intended to support text material, but the pictures had such strength and impact that the text came second. Picture essays were shown in city exhibitions and distributed to the press — the public was shocked. John Steinbeck credited Dorothea Lange's pictures as the inspiration for his novel *The Grapes of Wrath*.

Walker Evans

Lange's strength, as a member of the FSA team, lay in her pictures of people, which complemented perfectly the work of Walker Evans, who is known for his photographs of man-made subjects as well as portraits. Sharecroppers' dwellings, made out of wood and corrugated iron, are shown in pinsharp detail, lit by hard, directional sun. They are made to look beautiful. A deeper examination of Evans' subjects reveals an expressive content, too. His pictures of humble interiors depict not so much the spartan way of life, but a sense of the pride, care, and love which went into looking after them.

Evans' most well-known work was a book about the sharecroppers, *Let Us Now Praise Famous Men* (1941), which he produced in collaboration with the writer James Agee.

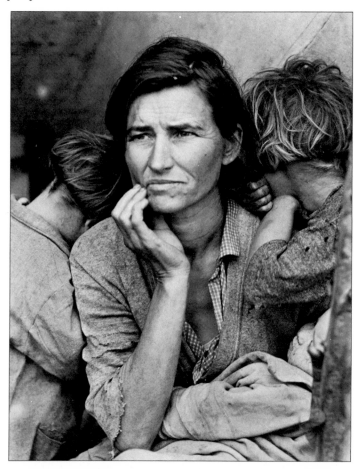

"Migrant Mother, California" (1936)
This is Dorothea Lange's most well-known FSA photograph. According to her notes, she found the family camped on the edge of a field where the pea crop had failed. The tires from their automobile had just been sold to buy food. The woman was 32 years old, with seven children.

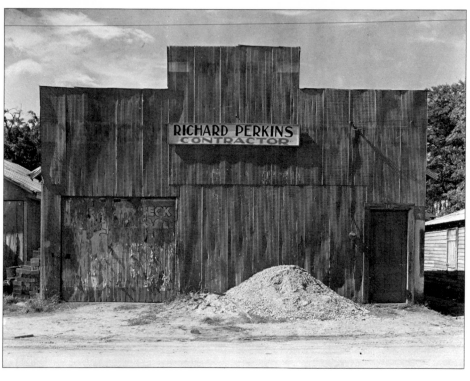

"Moundville, Alabama" (1936)
Harsh Midwestern sunlight produces a meticulously detailed rendering of this shanty building by Walker Evans. When working for the FSA project he tended to concentrate on portraying the textural qualities of architecture and the minute details of homestead interiors.

Magnum Photos

Magnum Photos is an agency which was formed in Paris in 1947, shortly after the Second World War. Six documentary photographers from six different countries decided to form a cooperative and take control of their own work by selecting their own picture stories, and shooting, editing and selling them to magazines. It was conceived as a profit-sharing organization with no set style of photography other than a determination to bear a "credible witness to life".

Hungarian Robert Capa, a war photographer, was first president and business manager. The five other founder members were Henri Cartier-Bresson (France), Werner Bischof (Switzerland), David Seymour (America), Ernst Haas (Austria), and George Rodger (Britain).

The agency rapidly earned an international reputation for human-interest picture stories that were apolitical. Although within nine years, Capa, Bischof, and Seymour had been killed on assignment, many other photographers have since joined Magnum as full or associate members, including W. Eugene Smith, Bruce Davidson, Eve Arnold, and Marc Riboud. An invitation to join Magnum is not given lightly — newcomers must first prove their ability to the other members. Today, Magnum is a flourishing agency, with offices in Paris, New York, and London. It supplies pictures of all kinds to every type of publication — from color magazines to industrial journals.

Henri Cartier-Bresson

Famous for his "invisibility", Henri Cartier-Bresson never attempts to influence what happens in front of his camera. This attitude is coupled with an ability to react rapidly to "key" moments. His subjects are situations which occur in real life, involving people — available to anyone with a camera. Cartier-Bresson notices the gesture, the relationship, the juxtaposition of elements and the brief moment, when all the picture components create a whole and have a meaning. Like Paul Martin was (see *Early documentary photographers,* pp. 348-9) he is an observer, happy to "take notes" on the human condition, rather than attempt to change it, or to draw conclusions from it. A typical Cartier-Bresson photograph shows a real situation but possessing an eccentric flavor, often existing only for a split second. His shots are tightly composed and have a warm sense of life, often with a touch of ambiguity.

Cartier-Bresson first became interested in photography through studying the work of Man Ray and Eugène Atget. Since 1930 he has traveled the world, covering both major events and small everyday happenings. In keeping with his approach to photography, he carries a 35 mm camera with him at all times, and limits his equipment to a single lens. He always uses black and white film, and has no interest in printing, which is done for him. Each picture is printed full frame, without being cropped. Cartier-Bresson has an instinctive sense of geometry and timing.

Eve Arnold

A long-standing member of Magnum Photos, Eve Arnold is a truly international photogra-

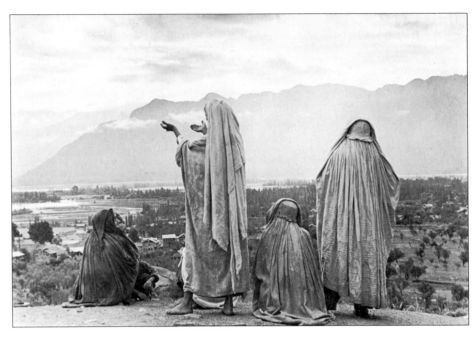

Srinagar, Kashmir (1948)
Muslim women, in this picture by Henri Cartier-Bresson, pray toward the sun rising over the distant Himalayas. The image conjures up an atmosphere of peace, contemplation, and thanksgiving. Cartier-Bresson avoids scenes that are staged or manufactured, preferring to use the camera as a sketchbook to capture spontaneous shapes and gestures.

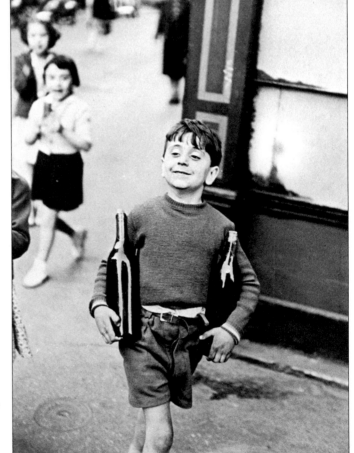

"The Provisions for Sunday lunch: Rue Mouffetard, Paris" (1954)
Henri Cartier-Bresson captures the cheeky pride of this small boy taking the family wine home. Even from this close viewpoint, Cartier-Bresson succeeds in taking the picture unobserved. He excels in showing the little, ordinary events of life with warmth and affection.

pher. She was born in America, is of Russian extraction, operates from Britain, and has traveled the world extensively. The wide-ranging, human-interest picture essays she has trackled typically cover themes such as poverty, compassion, integrity and human foibles of all kinds. She frequently manages to show a general situation through her studies of particular incidents. Her pictures always show a strong awareness of form, structure, and color.

Arnold is particularly well known for her pictures of women. She avoids the typically glamorous and idealized images of women, and manages to show her subjects naturally, in unguarded moments, instead. Her work is the result of strong personal commitment, as shown, for example, in her book *The Unretouched Woman,* which presents the lives and work of women.

W. Eugene Smith
A member of Magnum Photos from 1955 to 1959, W. Eugene Smith had already made his reputation on *Life* magazine, where he had worked for the previous 20 years. He special-ized in large-scale pictures stories, such as *Spanish Village* (1941), *Nurse Midwife* (1951), and *A Man of Mercy* (1954), and would spend several months getting to know his subjects, so that they did not feel that he was an intruder. Like Cartier-Bresson, Smith had a strong sense of composition, and this was combined with a preference for dramatic chiaroscuro lighting and low-key printing, which he some-times used to disguise unwanted information and contribute to the serious mood of many of his picture stories.

He was greatly respected by the staff of *Life* magazine, but he was highly sensitive about the way they arranged and presented his work on the printed page. Eventually, because of a row over the way they had treated one of his stories, he left.

Smith cared almost too passionately for the themes he photographed. Many, particularly his coverage of war, were based on the theme of man's inhumanity to man. His last and most influential project (produced as a book *Minamata: A Warning to the World*) disclosed the long-term effects of mercury poisoning from industrial waste on the inhabitants of a Jap-anese fishing village. As a result, he was badly assaulted by men from the chemical company, and after his return to America he turned from active photojournalism to lecturing and holding exhibitions.

Bruce Davidson
Unlike other members of Magnum Photos, Bruce Davidson works with a 5 × 4 ins (12.5 × 10 cm) view camera and uses artificial lighting on location. His best-known photographs come from self-chosen themes, such as one which concerns the affluence of Los Angeles, and another which describes the lives of the residents of one block on East 100th Street, New York. Through his careful choice of people and settings, he succeeded in showing ugliness in affluence, and found beauty in poverty. Describing his own style of human documentary photography, Davidson has called his pictures tense, silent, and like "landscapes" of people. Although his work often expresses an opinion that is extremely personal, David-son makes a conscious effort not to preach, preferring instead that we should look at his pictures and make our own decisions.

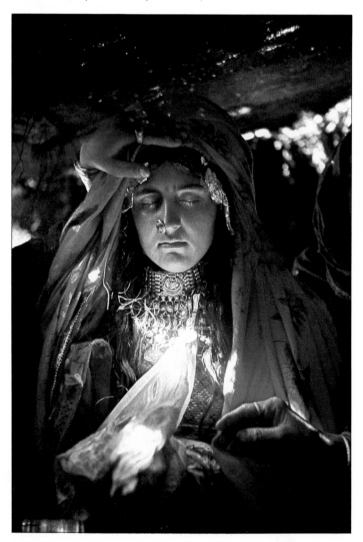

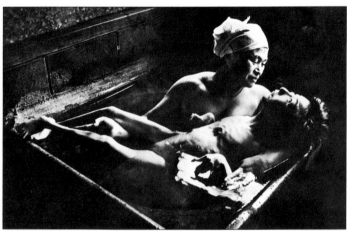

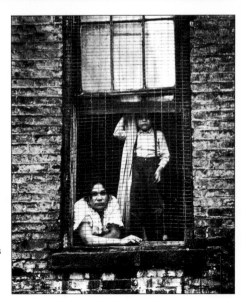

"Minamata Disease" (1971-4)
A Japanese mother (above) bathes her disfigured daughter, poisoned before birth. The picture, by W. Eugene Smith, is one of his series revealing the effects of industrial pollution.

"A Nomad Wedding in the Hindu Kush" (c. 1970)
From a series by Eve Arnold on veiled women (left) – at the wedding ceremony, the veil is lifted only when the groom arrives.

"East 100th Street" (1969)
Part of Bruce Davidson's in-depth coverage of a New York tenement building and its occupants.

The war photographers

Each war is a separate tragedy, and each war photographer has tried to express its horror and futility in a personal way. Today's photographers are reluctant to act as impartial observers – they play an active role, provoking reaction from a complacent public.

Robert Capa

Between 1936 and 1954 Robert Capa covered the Spanish Civil War, almost every major offensive in the Second World War, the struggles of Israeli independence, and the Indochina War. Capa adhered to his own slogan "If your pictures aren't good enough, you aren't close enough" by always being near the heart of the action, as it happened – the viewer has a sense of being there. His pictures of the D-Day landings in Europe were taken crawling through water alongside the troops, and they communicate dramatically the danger and apprehension. His best pictures are active both in content and construction.

Don McCullin

British photographer Don McCullin has continued Capa's tradition of exposing the horror of war. He has a compulsion to record what he calls "the destruction business", but his pictures are far more explicit than Capa's. He photographs decaying corpses and starving refugees with the intention of shocking. His bravery has resulted in some of the most telling shots taken of war situations in Vietnam, Biafra, Pakistan, and Northern Ireland (see *Reportage photography,* pp. 324-7). His work, which has been widely published in newspapers, books and the publications of relief organizations has done much to raise the consciousness of the general public.

Philip Jones Griffiths

War photographer Philip Jones Griffiths uses a more investigative approach than McCullin. His work, published in newspapers and magazines, and in his book *Vietnam Inc,* looks behind the scenes at the degrading existence of the people who bring war, and at the lives of their innocent victims. He juxtaposes pictures of horrific details with, for example, computer-run army headquarters, questioning the reasoning behind war, and the justification for it. Some of his strongest pictures show through actual situations how normal family life is overturned and destroyed by war.

The individualists

Some photographers of people have an expressionistic rather than a documentary approach to their work. The photography of Weegee, Brassaï, Robert Frank, Diane Arbus, and Robert Doisneau, for example, is personal, highly interpretative, unique and controversial. Each of them has had a far-reaching influence on other photographers, too.

Weegee

From 1931 to 1935 Weegee (real name Arthur Fellig) worked for the police department in New York full time, and from then on worked as a printer in a news agency darkroom by day and freelanced as a press photographer by night. He was a gritty news scavenger who occupied a room opposite the police headquarters in Manhattan, sleeping in his clothes alongside his 5 × 4 ins (12,5 × 10 cm) Graphic camera and a shortwave receiver, perma-

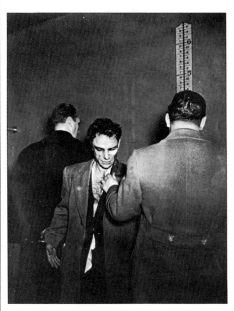

"Booked on Suspicion of Killing a Policeman" (1930)
One of Weegee's many frank pictures of crime in New York. Although his subjects are today unknown faces, they epitomize human violence. (Photograph courtesy of Sotheby's Belgravia.)

nently monitoring police frequencies. Consequently, he was always among the first on the scene of the crime – whether it was a gangland execution, a fire, or a suicide.

Because of his working hours Weegee's New York exists almost entirely at night, in pictures frontally lit with a flash on the camera. His foregrounds are brutally bright and his backgrounds murky. Weegee's technique was a set formula, but his subjects cover the entire range of human disasters. Collectively, his work presents a pitiless mixture of degradation, the extremes of life and death, the grotesque, the ridiculous, the desperate, and the violent. He often turned the camera on sightseers at the scene of the crime to record their expressions of ghoulish curiosity. Unlike Jacob Riis and Lewis Hine, who also worked

"The Normandy Invasion" (1944)
Robert Capa took this picture (right) from water level, under fire, as United States troops landed on the French beaches. Most of the pictures taken on this occasion were unfortunately lost or spoiled.

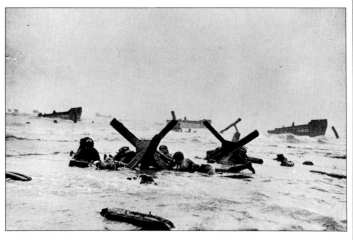

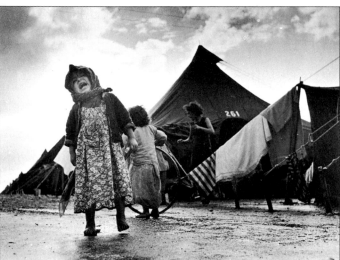

"Israel" (1948)
Robert Capa encapsulates the anguish of life in refugee camps in this strongly constructed picture (left). The child's stance gives the picture extraordinary tension – she is a Yemenite beggar in the Chaar Aliyah Receiving Center.

in similar tough areas, producing pictures which were intended to encourage social reform, Weegee was quite content to be in the right place at the right time and sell his work next day to the newspapers — even in direct competition with their own staff photographers. His large press camera and conspicuous flash equipment were somehow an integral part of the scene he was showing — there was no question of his being a discreet, invisible observer. The average newspaper shot of this period was stale the day after the event had taken place, but Weegee's hard-bitten work has lasting value as the documentation of human crises.

"Regard Oblique" (1953)
From a discreet camera position, Robert Doisneau's fast reaction (right) captures a fleeting glance. His pictures are witty, often satirical, but never caustic.

"Chattanooga, Tennesee"
Typical of many of Robert Frank's pictures which are intended to deglamorize modern life, this image (below) at first glance seems casual — almost a random snapshot. It is a poignant statement about the loneliness and isolation experienced by people in crowded cities. This young, aloof couple display despondency and tenderness — they are both sophisticated and vulnerable. (Photograph courtesy of Sotheby's Belgravia.)

Brassaï
Born Gyula Halász in Hungary, Brassaï renamed himself after his home town, Brassov, when he went to live in Paris in 1924. Initially he pursued a career as a journalist, but encouraged by fellow Hungarian André Kertész he began to take photographs in 1929 "to translate all the things that so enchanted me." For several years he worked at night, photographing the hidden night life of Paris. He shared Diane Arbus's taste for unusual personalities and he photographed them with their full complicity, using a camera mounted on a tripod and open flash to give dramatic lighting effects. Brassaï's Paris of the 1930s

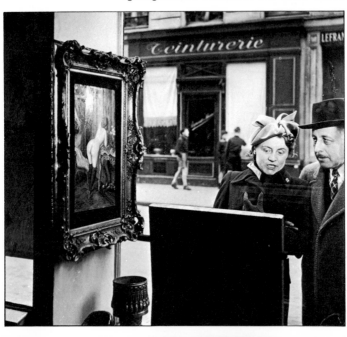

features prostitutes, pimps, transvestites, down-and-outs, and lovers by the Seine. Some of his strongest pictures are taken in bars, and backstage at the Folies Bergère.

His photographs seem more journalistic in character than Arbus's, but he never intended them to be wholly photojournalistic, and unlike Weegee's press photographs, each image stands as a picture in its own right. Brassaï's work has mainly been published in books on subjects such as Picasso, graffitti, and life in Paris of the 1930s, accompanied by his own extensive text.

Robert Doisneau
Famous for his witty, often humorous, documentary photographs, Robert Doisneau has been capturing aspects of Parisian life for thirty years. His pictures are purely informative on one level, making a record of a scene or an event. But at another level they are comments of greater importance. Doisneau is preoccupied by the major events and features of life such as love, marriage, ageing and youth, and he remarks on these using his precise sense of timing. He always succeeds in capturing the smallest incident — the stolen kiss, the briefest, chance expression, the juxtaposition of two incongruous objects, and the ambiguous relationships of people to their surroundings. He avoids obscure symbolism and is not interested in aesthetic photography, or in technical details. He shows scenes just as he sees them, using straight photographic techniques. Viewpoint selection is his main method of controlling the image.

Robert Frank
In the 1950s, Robert Frank's style of photography was perhaps the most original, and eventually, the most widely imitated new style of the 1950s. He is an American citizen, Swiss by birth, and an ex-fashion photographer turned freelance documentary photographer. Since 1958 he has devoted his time to filmmaking, but during 1955-6 he traveled across America, and as a comparative newcomer to the country, photographed all that struck him as significant about the American way of life. Frank's photographs are, at face value, casual. They dwell on the superficiality, loneliness, smugness, eccentricity, drabness, and ritual patriotism of certain aspects of modern American culture, as he observed it.

The result of this project was Frank's book *The Americans* (1959), which was considered shocking because it was hard, and unpatriotic at a time when patriotism was fashionable. But for young people of the 1950s and 1960s, Frank's pictures seemed to reveal all the inadequacies of "the system" and show it for what it was. His approach produced new schools of "urban realism" photography, influencing other photographers such as Lee Friedlander and Elliot Erwitt. Frank acknowledges his own debt to Bill Brandt and Walker Evans.

Diane Arbus
Diane Arbus began to take portrait photographs in the early 1940s, but it was only in 1957, while enrolled on a course taught by the photographer Lisette Model, that she began to devote her time exclusively to the work for

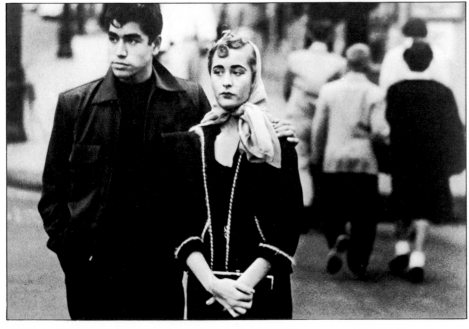

which she has come to be known. Throughout the 1960s, until her suicide in 1971, she made portraits of people – those she encountered randomly in her routine travels and those that were less accessible, whom she sought systematically. They ranged from the very public to the private.

Each person is shown from a frontal viewpoint with clinical detail, often lit with flash on her square-format camera. Each shot is taken with the knowledge and full participation of the subject. Her portraiture both documents external details and deals with private realities.

Exhibitions and published examples of Arbus's pictures since her death have created

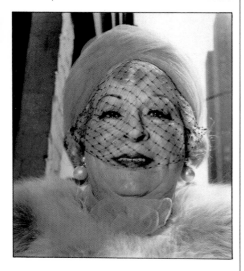

**"Woman With a Veil on
5th Avenue" (1968)**
(Photograph © 1968
The Estate of Diane
Arbus.)

public interest on an international scale, and have considerably influenced many younger photographers. Arbus's approach can be traced to the influences of August Sander, Bill Brandt, and Weegee. Her pictures are not intended (like the work of Lewis Hine or the photographers of the Farm Security Administration project) to generate sympathy and support for change. She admired Weegee particularly for the rough honesty of his work and his formalized manner of presentation. They both seem to share common ground – producing pictures which can be read at several levels.

Dynamism

A dynamic picture is one that suggests forceful movement and action. Often it shows forms which do not actually exist for the naked eye at any particular moment, but which can be created by a time exposure. This can be any moving subject, from a network of lines built up by moving traffic at night, to a hollow sphere created by a swirling dancer. Dynamism is also found in objects that move too rapidly for the eye to follow normally, but which can be recorded as frozen, detailed images. In addition, Dynamism is an element which is created by the way the picture is structured – through active lines and shapes that travel diagonally across the frame. Dynamic types of image form an important part of every photographer's "vocabulary", and some have made it the main characteristic of their style.

In the early years of the century, "dynamism", "force", and "motion" were important words in the revolutionary art world. The futurist and vorticist painters, in particular, were concerned with portraying the world in new ways, using forms of abstraction based on vitality and action. This was part of the modern art movement called "Cubism". The period from 1910 to 1930 was a time of extensive experimentation. Artists broke away from the illusion of reality in painting and assimilated some of the images that the camera offered, such as movement blur, multi-images, and frozen detail.

At the same time, photographers were experimenting and discovering just what forms of dynamic abstraction effects their medium could make. Features that had long been considered errors, such as subject blur, were explored, as well as devices which could "chop up" the exposures of moving objects for scientific analysis. Mirrors, too, were used to make geometric patterns. Doctrines such as Futurism, a movement in both painting and photography, were shortlived. But they revealed that still photography, seemingly ill-equipped to portray movement, can produce its own dynamic symbols.

Possibilities for Dynamism in photography have been increased more recently by developments such as electronic flash, stroboscopic lamps, color film, and zoom lenses. But it is often possible to create powerfully dynamic results with a minimum of special equipment and techniques.

See also
Line, pp. 36-7. Using slow shutter speeds, pp. 127-8. Using fast shutter speeds, pp. 129-31. Advanced flash techniques *The freezing power of flash*, p. 178. Special effects lighting *Creating light trails*, p. 180. Zoom lenses, pp. 192-4. Alternative printing techniques, *Image distortion*, p. 256. Scientific and technical photography *High-speed photography*, pp. 275-7. Sports photography, pp. 304-9.

The influences of modern art on Dynamism

All the modern art movements that were taking place in the first two decades of this century were aimed at overthrowing the styles of painting concerned with fine detail and realistic subject portrayal. Instead, artists sought status for paintings as two-dimensional objects in their own right.

In the 1910s, the prevailing atmosphere was one of optimism – a sense of having entered a new century in which a move toward modernity and mechanization would bring change and progress. Taller buildings, faster transportation, the advent of moving pictures, scientific photography, and the birth of the "snapshot" were all contributing to a changed visual conception of people's surroundings. Artists were interested in the characteristics of new processes (and particularly in photography) and how they could use and adapt them in order to sever links with the past traditions of fine art.

The most important new movement was Cubism. In this, the subject's most important aspects were broken down into simplified, cube-shaped forms and combined. Cubism originated in Paris and was a parent to many smaller movements, including two directly concerned with Dynamism – the Italian futurist group, and the British Vorticists.

Futurism
According to their 1910 manifesto, futurist painters held that previous art forms were outmoded and "static". Instead, Futurism was capable of expressing time as well as space by denoting the movements of objects through "lines of force". Futurism was concerned with mechanization and speed, and some of its followers were very strongly influenced by photo-sequences of locomotion by Eadweard Muybridge (see *The camera's portrayal,* p. 90), and the multi-image chronophotographs made in France by Étienne Marey. As Futurists pointed out, "A running horse does not have four hooves; it has twenty, and their movements are triangular".

Science seemed to prove that what the naked eye sees as "normal" is only a small part of what actually exists. The long time exposures of early photography presented moving broken water as "unnaturally" smooth. Moving clouds, people walking or running, the branches of wind-blown trees, the moon and stars at night, were shown as being either partially erased, or elongated.

Two leading Italian painters of the futurist movement were Umberto Boccioni and Giacomo Balla. During the years 1912 and 1913 Balla made a series of paintings based directly on the repetition of figures, influenced by Marey's chronophotography. They include *Dynamism of a Dog on a Leash,* a light-hearted work showing a "multi-legged" basset hound on a walk, and *The Rhythm of the Bow.* In Rome, photographer Antonio Bragaglia made experimental "fotodynamic portraits", in which the subject, set against a dark background, moved during a time exposure. In Paris, Marcel Duchamp painted his controversial cubo-futurist work *Nude Descending a Staircase,* inspired by images that both Eadweard

Muybridge and Etienne Marey had photographed some 25 years earlier. It was exhibited in 1913 at the Armory Show in New York.

Vorticism
The Vorticists were a small and exclusively British movement, primarily painters, sculptors, and writers, who gathered around founder Wyndham Lewis during the period from 1912. Their art was more abstract than that of the Futurists, but it clearly related to their work, as well as that of the Cubists. Much of their painting was based on stark, angular forms, often derived from the severe modern architecture which seemed to express the vitality of the new century.

Individuals actively (though in some cases briefly) associated with the movement included writer Ezra Pound, sculptor Jacob Epstein, and photographers Alvin Langdon Coburn and Malcolm Arbuthnot. Coburn, the irrepressible experimentalist, produced a large number of "Vortographs". They were made by pointing the camera lens down an angled mirror at small pieces of glass and wood, creating dynamic abstract-pattern images. He also made multi-image portraits.

Addressing photographers in 1917 in the staid photographic annual *Photograms of the Year,* Coburn discussed his approach, then wrote in exasperation, "If it is not possible to be 'modern' with the newest of all arts, then we had better simply bury our black boxes". His views had absolutely no effect on the Pictorialists. When one of his vortographs was reproduced in the next issue of *Photograms of the Year* a critic warned that experiment had lead Coburn into "a wild region. Something strange was bound to happen when the sane guidance of nature was rejected".

Francis Bacon
Many other individual painters have subsequently been influenced by photography's blurred representation of movement. The British figurative painter Francis Bacon, an important and influential force in contemporary painting, has based many of his works on different kinds of photographic imagery. His subject matter concentrates on evocations of men, dogs, and carcases, often partially blurred, and expressing a screaming world of revolution, dissolution, and terror. His style returns again and again to Muybridge's studies of male nudes, caught in strange frozen stances, isolated against plain, backgrounds.

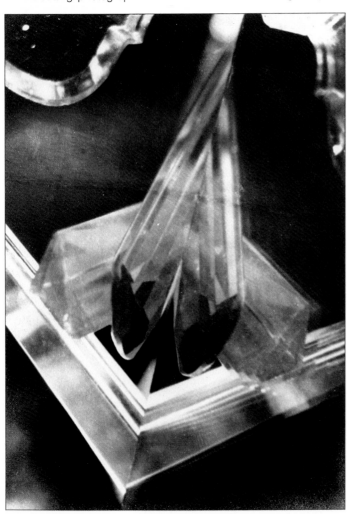

"Vortograph" (1917)
A tireless experimenter, Alvin Langdon Coburn devoted considerable energy to liberating photography from the recording of reality. He was encouraged by poet Ezra Pound (who suggested the name "vortograph") and artists of the English vorticist group to produce many abstract dynamic pictures, of which this is an example. Half the image is seen in a mirror, creating a symmetrical pattern from small angular pieces of reflective paper or glass. Vortographs were probably the first totally abstract photographs.

The major exponents of Dynamism

A dynamic style has been used by photographers for a wide variety of reasons. Some see it as a natural choice when they want to symbolize the action and drama in sport, the flow of dance, to communicate aggression in documentary photography, or to make pictures which attract and hold attention in advertising. For some, such as Harold Edgerton, dynamic photographs of a frozen moment in time — for example, a bat hitting a ball, or a droplet falling into a liquid — are graphic ways of enhancing a purely object analysis. Other photographers select a dynamic structure because it expresses what they want to say in their pictures.

Andy Earl
British photographer Andy Earl uses sharpness and blur together in the same photograph to express his interest in form, movement, and color. His technique is to shoot in weak daylight, using electronic flash and a short time exposure while moving his hand-held camera. The flash intensifies the color, heightens the effect of "unrealistic" lighting, and provides highly detailed foreground areas. Background, which is largely unaffected by the flash shows blur due to camera movement, although the effect is seldom apparent in the sky. This technique is difficult to control exactly and Earl admits to an element of uncertainty and surprise. Spontaneity and chance juxtapositions in the final image are inherent features of his style. His pictures are active and eventful — frequently showing people and animals erratically framed. Earl works mostly with a 5 × 4 ins (12.5 × 10 cm) camera, and may use between three and five flashes per exposure.

Eric Staller
Primarily involved in "drawing with light", to create dynamic images, Eric Staller selects real street scenes at night, which he transforms into settings for light trails. These form lines curving and weaving through space. They are all done by extremely long exposures, sometimes as long as 20 minutes, during which time Staller moves around the scene with lamps or sparklers attached to posts or frames. Since he is dressed in dark clothing, and keeps moving throughout the exposure, no trace of him or the light supports are recorded.

Staller is therefore concerned with creating images which the eye cannot experience at the time of shooting. Each expresses a form of movement or a pattern set in a stage-like environment, mixing real and unreal elements. The results are planned from beginning to end, with several trial run-throughs. Each picture is a precise ritual, which is almost mathematical, leaving little margin for error. He works with a wide-angle lens, and an ordinary 35 mm camera on a tripod. He gives enough additional exposure to show some detail in the settings, retaining a vital element of realism in the composition (see *Creating light trails,* p. 180). Apart from photography, Staller is interested in choreography, architecture, and drawing. Since 1977, he has organized dance "happenings", and light shows involving the projection of images on sculpture, and three-dimensional screens. It is interesting to note that his photographs are sold through a fine art gallery.

Ernst Haas

Since the early 1950s, America-based photographer Ernst Haas has devoted much of his time to making photo-essays, in color, for books and illustrated magazines. His early use of slow-speed Kodachrome film had caused him image-movement problems, because of the exposure times necessary. But gradually, he discovered the possibilities of using movement blur intentionally, often combined with camera-jog or panning, to convey a dynamic sense of action. He uses the technique to great creative effect in his pictures of galloping horses, birds in flight, boats, bull fights, and all kinds of sporting events.

Haas believes in "transformation, not reproduction" for this style of picture, where an active atmosphere is more evocative and exciting than precise accuracy of detail. Color is a vital ingredient in his action studies — the colored bands and whirls separate out different elements which would otherwise merge confusingly in the absence of sharpness. The majority of his work has been done on a direct vision, 35 mm camera. This allows him to follow the action continuously while the shutter remains open.

John Starr

John Starr is a British photographer who is concerned with dance as a subject, combined with a dynamic approach to photographic style. He is primarily interested in photographing classical ballet. For Starr, ballet photography is an extension of his main professional activity — sports photography. He works in the dancer's own environment, the theater, rather than in the studio (unlike Barbara Morgan — see over). He accepts and deals with the problems of lighting contrast and the frequent necessity for wide-aperture lenses, and has devised ways of creating undefined backgrounds, so that the setting does not compete with the moving figures.

Starr portrays the movement of the dance through the dynamism of his pictures. Often, the dancers are partially obscured by blur effects, which are used to give an impression of the constant movement of forms. It is interesting to note that he has applied several techniques in his treatment of dance that are usually used in sports photography. He makes full use of zooming, panning, and multi-faceted lens attachments whenever they will help in the emphasis of movement or to enhance dramatic pattern effects.

Francisco Hidalgo

It is just as possible to apply a dynamic effect to a static subject as to a moving one, and an excellent subject for this is modern architecture, with its dramatic lines and spatial effects. Francisco Hidalgo has made a speciality of portraying cityscapes in a highly stylized manner, so that they seem to "breathe" life and character. Born in Spain, and working in Paris, Hidalgo turned to photography from television graphic design, and his pictures of buildings show strong graphic qualities, which are very

Lighted windows
Eric Staller made frames carrying light bulbs to fit around each window, then pivoted them smoothly to a downward position — producing a series of curved light trails.

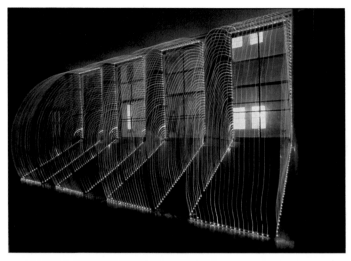

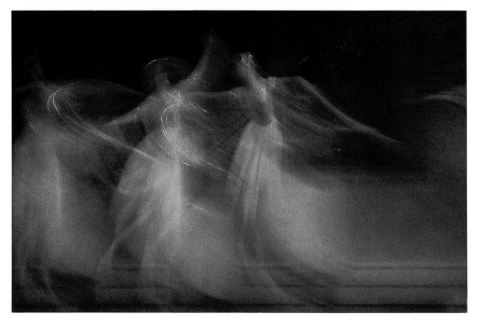

"Football motions"
Part of an assignment (left) by Ernst Haas commissioned by *Sports Illustrated* in the 1950s to see how a European would react to an unfamiliar game. Fascinated by the vibrant atmosphere and brilliant colors, Haas panned the camera, and used a shutter speed of 1/10 sec, producing a mixture of detail and swirling, dynamic action.

Dancers
John Starr used a slow shutter speed (below) to suggest the dynamic activity of classical ballet. Bright details form trails of light.

reminiscent of the work of German Cubist painter, Lyonel Feininger.

Hidalgo's pictures of New York, in particular, show dizzy panoramas, and streets fragmented into angular streaks of color. He uses several special effect techniques in his work — fish-eye lenses, zoom lenses, and various diffuser and filter attachments, as well as sandwiched transparencies and double exposure. His critics call him "the king of special effects", and accuse him of gimmickry. He defends his methods by arguing that to use accessories it is important to have an idea first — then reinforce that idea. He uses them when he wants to capture an atmosphere which is not there, or add something he can already see. (See also picture p. 339.)

Jacques-Henri Lartigue
The French photographer Jacques-Henri Lartigue has always been fascinated by the way fast emulsions and the briefest shutter speeds can capture transient events. His instinctive feel for the fleeting moment, plus a love for life, gives his photographs a light-hearted feel, and a spirit of energy and fun. Many of his best-known photographs were taken before the First World War, when he was still in his boyhood and adolescence. These pictures are high-speed snapshots of family and friends and were never intended to be any more than a personal record. Naturally attracted by speed and excitement, Lartigue photographed his adult relatives indulging in such activities as car-racing, flying, horseback riding, and tennis. He was never lacking in subject matter. Many of his pictures show a dynamism created by split-second timing. His subjects are shown suspended in mid-air, or crashing into water,

or distorted into speed-induced shapes by his camera shutter (see picture p. 131).

Barbara Morgan
The movement and interrelationship of forms are vital elements in dance, and many photographers at different times have used it as a subject, to create dynamic images. Barbara Morgan, formerly a painter, has devoted most of her time since 1953 to photographing dance. During the early part of this period, she spent several years working with choreographer Martha Graham.

Morgan works mostly in the studio, and uses highly controlled lighting brilliantly in her pictures. Her sources include multiple flash sources and stroboscopic speedlamps. This combination of "constructed" lighting and subject movement offers her just the scope she requires for the simplification of form, symbol, and gesture which she desires. She previsualizes the final appearance of the movement in the same way that Ansel Adams previsualizes tones (see *Individuals and movements of Straight photography*, pp. 343-6), and creates images with differing degrees of blurred or frozen detail specially to suit the spirit of the particular dance. Morgan also combines images of dancers with close-ups of plant forms and landscapes in photo-montages.

"Lamentation" (1935)
Barbara Morgan uses interrelated forms both in her dance and plant studies. This picture shows the same dancer in a carefully planned double exposure. The change of position in the frame adds to the sense of dynamic movement.

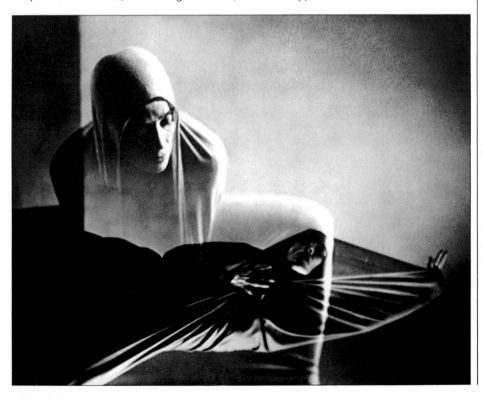

Techniques
The forerunners of many images of Dynamism were Eadweard Muybridge and Etienne Marey. Muybridge used a row of cameras with fast mechanical shutters to give detailed, frozen images of fast-moving subjects. His picture sequences had been published in both America and Europe, and by 1887, he had given several lecture tours to painters, sculptors, and scientists in both continents. In 1881, he worked for a short time with Marey in Paris. Marey invented a disk shutter camera, which allowed about twelve separate phases of a movement to record overlapped on a single plate. The resulting images describe a "flow" of action which relates directly to the futurist painters' "lines of force".

During the early 1930s, Harold Edgerton, of the Massachusetts Institute of Technology pioneered the design of two main forms of electronic flash. One gave a single flash of extremely short duration, freezing all moving elements, and eliminating camera shake. The other type was the repeating, or stroboscopic, flash which pulses at controlled speeds. This made Marey's type of complicated, special cameras quite redundant — overlapping images could now be made by anyone who had an ordinary camera.

Multi-flash techniques were applied to many new forms of subject matter, producing kinetic pictures which allowed accurate measurement of each stage of the action — they were often aesthetically interesting, too. Futurist painters would have delighted in such equipment if only it had been invented a generation earlier.

Exposure time effects
During the 1910s and '20s, in Jacques-Henri Lartigue's boyhood, large-format cameras, which were designed to be hand-held, often had focal plane shutters. When these were set at a high speed, fast-moving or panned subjects were sometimes distorted in shape (see *Focal plane distortion*, p. 131). Shape change occurs only rarely in Lartigue's work, but the

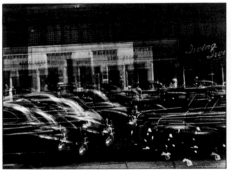

"Detroit" (1943)
To create a bustling impression of America's "automobile city", Harry Callahan made three exposures on one frame, shifting the camera sideways each time. The picture was taken at about the time that he was working for General Motors. Later, influenced by Minor White, he used multiple exposure techniques to make more metaphoric images. (Photograph courtesy of Light Gallery.)

Structuralism and Abstraction

effects were common in press photographs at the time — particularly in pictures of motor racing. The effect was soon adopted by illustrators of the time to suggest acceleration or braking, an effect which has been much imitated since as a symbol of dynamism particularly in advertising photography.

Photographically recorded light trails have long been used to analyze continuous movement, and to measure it against time. This has important functions in time-and-motion analysis and medical photography (recording the limitations or distortions of the patient's movements — see *Contracting time* p. 275). The slit shutter camera, which can be used to make race finish records, is another device that causes time and space to create their own characteristic and often dramatic, images.

Using ordinary equipment
Most kinds of dynamic photography require not so much special equipment as special care over the use of ordinary cameras and lenses. Working at 1/1000 sec or using flash for frozen action demands sufficiently fast reactions to choose one exact moment in time to shoot. But Ernst Haas's flowing images depend on his choice of a slow shutter speed plus any movement he makes with the camera. The same applies to Francisco Hidalgo's cityscapes — except that he sometimes makes a zooming or focusing shift during exposure. Eric Staller's "drawings with light" rely on the consistency of speed and smoothness of movement as the lights travel through the picture during exposure.

Whenever a photographer's lighting (lamps or flash) is to be combined with an exposure to existing light, the relative balance of intensity and color requires careful control. Often a test run-through with instant picture material is the best way of judging this — few of these images which rely on a time exposure for their success can be exactly predicted in advance.

Another technique for dynamic pictures is to divide up a normal exposure into several short segments of time, and allow the subject or camera to move between each. For example, using a neutral density filter, an outdoor scene requiring 1/15 sec can be given four exposures of 1/60 sec, or eight of 1/125 sec. Panning the camera slightly between such a series of part exposures gives a multi-image, often with a confused sense of action (see picture facing page).

The work of some photographers is characterized by the way design, form, and structure take precedence over the subject itself. This emphasis on deliberate structure and design can apply to a wide range of different images — from natural Straight photography, to manipulated abstractions.

Historically, Cubism and movements like it in the art world opened up new possibilities for photography in terms of portraying pattern and form. Individual photographers and painters during the 1920s were fired by ideas of visual experiment. Photograms, optical distortions, and solarization, plus other manipulative techniques were all discovered to be effective ways of changing conventional photographic images.

Manipulation was not done to make photographs look painterly, but to create new sources of abstract and semi-abstract design. They included experiments in Dynamism, such as Alvin Langdon Coburn's vortographs, which were probably the first abstract photographs ever to be made. Other photographers, particularly in Europe, used light and light-sensitive paper "raw" to create photograms. In Germany, during the late 1920s, all these methods were accepted as a creative tools in art schools, long before other countries.

Cameras began to be used to reveal patterns and design that had previously gone unnoticed. These included views from unusual viewpoints, oblique angles, close-ups, reflections, and shadow patterns. Subjects would often be distorted to bring out their design aspects.

Today, there is a wide general acceptance of the photography of expressive form and pattern, and its ability to show a highly structured design within the frame. Images may be simplified, austere linear patterns, abstract bands of color, or structure integrated within recognizable subjects.

See also
Shape, pp. 38-9. Pattern, pp. 40-2. Structure, pp. 72-9. Focal length and camera size, pp. 120-3. Alternative printing techniques *Photograms*, p. 257. Image manipulation *Solarization*, pp. 267-8.

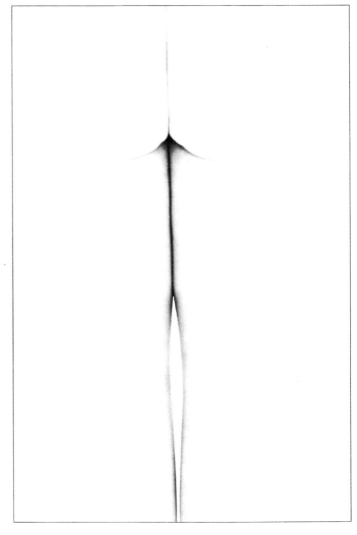

"Embrace 3" (1970)
Eikoh Hosoe abstracts his subject to create a highly simplified, almost austere, structure. His technique is to take a straight photograph, making use of soft frontal lighting and then printing to give a very light, contrasty result.

Mixed media images

Just as photographers have taken ideas, images, and techniques from the world of art so have painters used photographic images as an integral part of their work, particularly in the areas of Structuralism and Abstraction.

Richard Hamilton often uses a photograph together with diagrams, line drawings, and highly textured paint – an extension of earlier work when he incorporated three-dimensional objects in his paintings. Robert Rauschenberg often uses torn photographic illustrations and postcards to express the way the camera brings different worlds into our imagination simultaneously. And Andy Warhol's mosaic-like structures of repeated portraits seem to mimic the multiple nature of photographs themselves.

Mari Mahr
Born in Chile, Mari Mahr took up photography in Budapest, and now works in London. Her work, a mixture of photography, drawing and painting, increasingly appears in international exhibitions devoted to photography as a fine art. Her pictures are often concerned with picture-making itself. She takes simple, inanimate objects and makes them seem strangely significant. A photograph may be rephotographed so that its borders and rough edges are visible. The resulting image makes the original photograph seem very two-dimensional. She also places real still life objects on the surface of prints, and photographs this mixture of two and three dimensions.

Much of Mahr's work is basically black and white, selectively hand-colored and often printed using the gum bichromate process. She uses instant picture material too, sometimes painting the top or back surface. All these techniques help to destroy familiar photographic realism, and in extreme cases give strongly abstract results. Her talent lies in the way "abuse" of photographic materials and processes is used to produce compelling conceptual images.

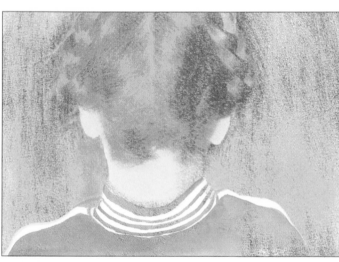

"Another Colored Photograph" and **"Green" (1978)** Both gum bichromate prints by Mari Mahr, these images show her delicate use of color and her mainly two-dimensional use of space. Mahr uses the process to create "unphotographic" image quality, with tonal values similar to an electrostatic (xerox) print. Her use of water color paints allows complete freedom in her choice and control of coloring.

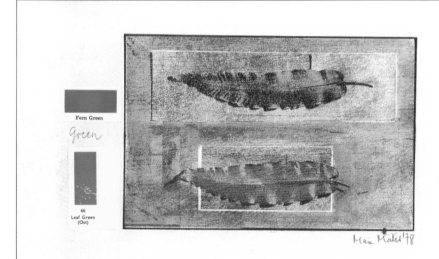

The influences of art on Structuralism and Abstraction

The earliest serious experiment in abstract and semi-abstract images came not from photographers, but from artists. The two most influential movements in the art world (both stemming from Cubism) were Dadaism and Constructivism.

Dadaism began in Zurich during the First World War, and was a revolutionary "anti-art" movement. Dadaists rebelled against the use of conventional artistic styles and materials and set out intentionally to outrage and scandalize the art establishment and break with tradition. They exhibited "art" made out of manufactured objects, and collages fashioned from fragments of newspapers and old photographs. They placed objects on light-sensitive paper and created abstract "photograms". The black and white reversed tones, free from traditional painterly techniques and concepts of perspective and composition suited their philosophy perfectly. Christian Schad, Marcel Duchamp, Man Ray, and John Heartfield were all Dadaists who explored the possibilities of photography as a major part of their work.

Constructivism was a non-objective art movement which was begun in Russia in 1913. Common materials such as glass, iron, and plaster were used, with the intention of bridging the gap between everyday life and art, and also revolutionizing industrial design. Alexander Rodchenko and Naum Gabo produced abstract hanging and relief constructions and collages.

Both dadaist and constructivist movements were an attitude to life involving the spontaneous use of materials to produce unfamiliar new effects. Different forms of photographic image therefore resulted through the experimental work of individual artists.

Christian Schad
An artist working in Zurich, Christian Schad used discarded objects as materials for his work. From 1918 onward he began making photograms of these objects. Fellow Dadaists called these cameraless images "Schadographs" after him.

Schad experimented with superimposed opaque and semi-transparent objects, both plain and structured. The reversal of tones and the stark outlines seemed to demonstrate that realism in photography is only relative. Some of these results were similar to Alvin Langdon Coburn's vortographs.

Man Ray
Man Ray studied architecture and engraving as a young man, and in New York frequented Stieglitz's 291 Gallery. Here he met painters and photographers of the modern school, and taught himself photography at first to record his own art works. By 1917 he was experimenting with combined drawing and photographic techniques in his own form of *cliché-verre*. He would draw on to the gelatin emulsion of existing glass negatives with a needle or etching tool. When this was contact printed, clear black outlines appeared around the photographic image. Ray traveled to Paris in 1921 and, influenced

by the European Dadaists, produced a wide range of photograms, which he named "Rayographs". He also used the principle of fogging the film during development, so that partial reversal occurred and black lines formed around harsh tone boundaries. This is known as the "Sabattier effect", but is usually called "solarization". Results have some similarities to *cliché-verre,* but are less crude. Ray applied solarization techniques to many of his figure studies and portraits. He experimented with shape distortions too — for example, creating elongated images

of hands by photograming them with an obliquely placed light source for exposure.

Ray's chief interest was in the way a subject's appearance could be deformed through light and chemistry. In the spirit of Dadaism, ordinary objects lost their identity and were translated into strange new structures and forms. His work was of more interest to painters than to other photographers, who were often unaware of current trends in the art world, and dismissed such images completely, calling them "puzzle" pictures and "trick photography".

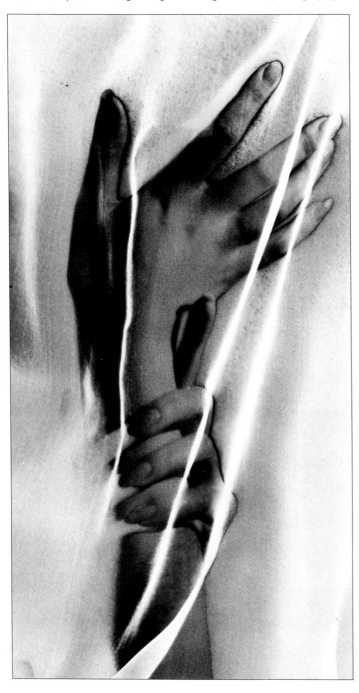

"Mano" (1931)
This study by Man Ray, taken in the 1920s, is an intriguing combination of photograph and photogram. The black outline is a characteristic of solarization; the muslin is printed in contact with the paper. Ray produced many images of hands, skillfully using their flowing shapes.
(Photograph courtesy of Sotheby's Belgravia.)

The Bauhaus

The Bauhaus school of art and design at Dessau in Germany was Europe's leading center for experiment in every aspect of art during the 1920s. Dadaist and constructivist-influenced artists who taught there included Lyonel Feininger (father of photographer Andreas Feininger), Paul Klee, Wassily Kandinsky and László Moholy-Nagy. They explored new materials and processes enthusiastically, and photography was used widely to provide sources of design for graphic and industrial purposes, fine art, and architecture.

László Moholy-Nagy
The most influential of experimental photographers teaching at the Bauhaus between 1923 and 1928 was Hungarian painter László Moholy-Nagy. As a Constructivist he encouraged the students to take, and make use of, all kinds of photographs, ranging from pictures clipped from magazines made into collages, through aerial photographs and high speed analytical images, to straight or manipulated shots.

Several years before, in 1912, Alvin Langdon Coburn had made a series of photographs called *New York From Its Pinnacles,* and now Bauhaus students were encouraged to explore the possibilities of high and low viewpoints, to make use of cast shadow patterns, forms, and textures, and use them as elements of design. Moholy-Nagy advocated "photographic vision" as a way of developing individual sensitivity, and he used mixed photographic and drawn images, montage, and every kind of technical manipulation to change or enhance photographic structure.

Photograms were considered to be important, as well as reticulation, solarization, light trails created by movement, double exposure, and constructivist devices for "light modulating" (spilled and reflected light-forming structures and patterns made directly on other surfaces).

Moholy-Nagy's own work was concerned with the exploration and expression of space-time, which he achieved by making semi-abstract movies, and using repetitive images in still photography. Like other Dadaists, he regarded the impressionistic-pictorialist ap-

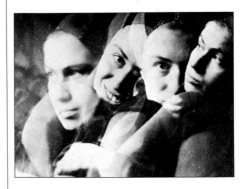

Multiple portrait (1927)
Renowned as a Bauhaus teacher, László Moholy-Nagy's own photographs were often ambiguous, exploring the themes of time and space, as well as the fundamentals of design.

Leading exponents of Structuralism and Abstraction

The two main influences on Structuralism in photography have been the straight approach of America-based photographers Paul Strand and Edward Weston, and the abstract design-conscious European approach of László Moholy-Nagy, Man Ray, and the Bauhaus.

Individual photographers have been affected by more transient influences. The challenge of experimenting with a particular subject or creating a certain look was irresistible. Hence, for example, photographs from high viewpoints were taken in the 1920s by Alexander Rodchenko and André Kertész — and Kertész, in particular, has returned again and again to using vertical shots of ground detail as a rich source of picture structure. Similar parallels can be found in the use of reflections, or tightly cropped man-made structures echoing the spirit of the New Objectivity movement.

It is interesting to compare the way Weston, Kertész, and Brandt have each structured their pictures of nudes. Weston used the qualities

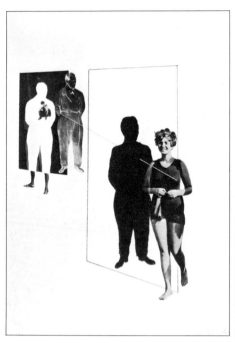

"Jealousy" (1930)
One of László Moholy-Nagy's many combined drawn and photographic images, exploiting both realistic and reversed tones and the representation of depth and scale.

proach to photography as work of aspiring painters who misunderstood the "photographic" nature of the camera.

Effects of Bauhaus
The teaching of the Bauhaus was important. It linked earlier revolutionary art movements with outlets in practical design and craftsmanship. These were to influence greatly the look of buildings, consumer products, posters and books, and photographs themselves. It gradually taught photographers to look at and think about the basic structures in pictures — the relationships of tones, lines, spaces, and forms could be discovered and considered objectively.

The Bauhaus was closed in 1933, and its teachers resettled in many different countries. Moholy-Nagy went to America, where in 1937 he set up the New Bauhaus, an art school, later to become part of Chicago's Institute of Design.

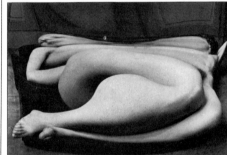

"Distortion, Paris" (1933)
An example (above) of André Kertész's nude studies made by using a fairground distorting mirror. It allowed manipulation of form yet retained the basic photographic image qualities.

Untitled nude
One of Bill Brandt's series (below) taken in the early 1950s. The distorted, semi-abstracted body form relates closely to rocks and pebbles on the seashore. Surrounding textures contrast strongly with the form.

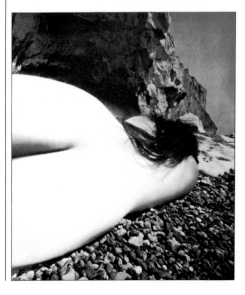

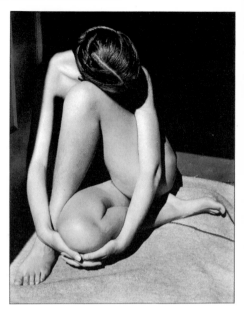

"Nude" (1936)
Like those of Kertész and Brandt, Edward Weston's nude (above) is completely depersonalized. But his unfailing use of the straight photographic approach and technique means that structure and shape are derived directly from the subject herself.

and form of the subject itself, plus the power of the photographic medium to resolve full tone and detail. He achieved flow of line through lighting, and the arrangement of limbs and body. Kertész, influenced by cubist friends, was taking pictures of nudes at this time, but achieving total structural distortion by abstracting them into deformed, rounded shapes (by photographing reflections in a fairground distorting mirror).

Brandt, who studied under Man Ray in Paris, has taken many pictures of nudes distorted by steep perspective and tight cropping. He depersonalizes them, so that they form part of the structure of the seashore, the landscape, or the room interior. He often uses very low viewpoints and prints flesh starkly white, so that it looks like bleached, smooth stone. Many of his best-known nude studies were taken with an extremely wide-angle lens, with a pinhole-sized aperture to maximize depth of field.

Ralph Gibson
Extreme cropping is an effective way of producing an abstract image, and American Ralph Gibson has produced a striking series of photographs of people, which puts this into practice. Backs of heads, half faces, and details of the clothed body are shown as stark areas of shape and pattern. Gibson's gritty detail and severe use of the frame edges as part of his picture structure depersonalize his subjects and transform them into still lifes. He is greatly concerned with the way in which hard light affects a surface and its relationship with visual texture and pattern.

Gibson looks for resonance and impact. He frequently succeeds in making the ordinary subject seem fresh and extraordinary — his

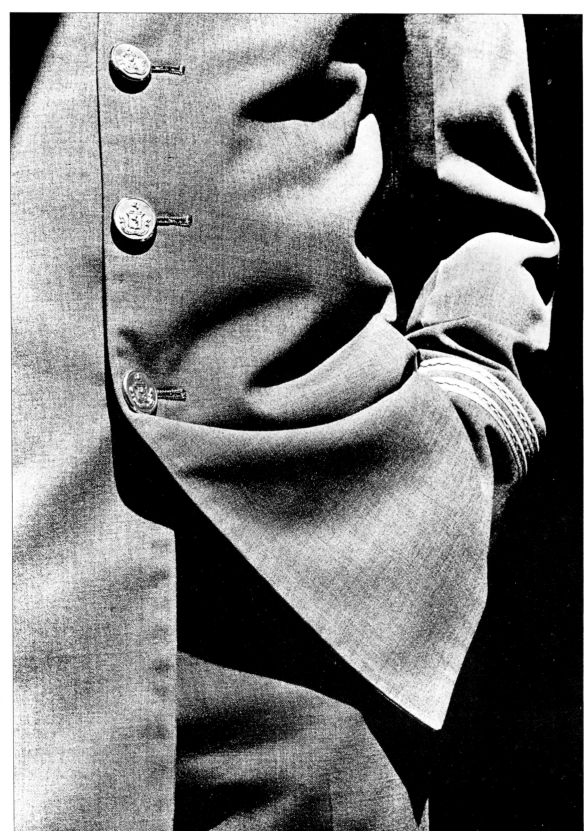

**From "Quadrants"
(1975)**
This picture by Ralph
Gibson is typical of his
tightly cropped close-
ups of people and
architecture. It was
taken with a 50 mm lens,
from a distance of 3 ft
(1 m) and makes use of
hard sunlight to give an
intense impression of
crisp textures and
pattern. By making a
16 × 20 ins (40 × 50 cm)
print, there is no re-
duction in scale be-
tween subject and
image, which should be
viewed from a distance
of 3 ft (1 m) or from
15 ins (38 cm) as repro-
duced here. Scale to
Gibson is as important
as framing as a means
of structuring images.
He is not concerned
with making abstract
photographs as such,
but is absorbed by the
abstract element in
ordinary things, pre-
sented by essentially
straight forms of
photography.

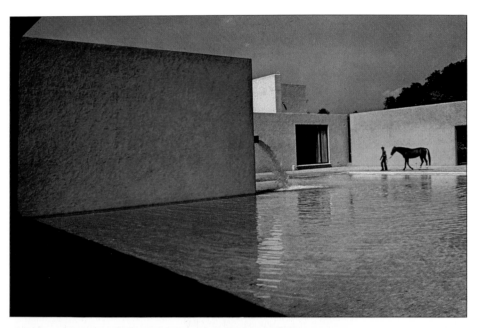

pictures are deceptively simple, but considered, striking designs. Compare his black and white work with Christian Vogt's bold use of color in similarly simple subjects.

René Burri
Swiss photographer René Burri works in color as well as in black and white, and he uses his strong structural sense of design to communicate the obscurity of things, as well as their ordered appearance. Hence, he often uses ambiguous cast shadows and bold blocks of color to produce geometric effects which approach semi-abstraction. Burri's picture essays have covered modern architecture, particularly the work of Le Corbusier, but in his professional work he is a photojournalist who is greatly concerned with human documentary work.

Franco Fontana
Italian photographer Franco Fontana uses structures and colors to create abstractions, yet his photography is primarily straight. He shows what the camera sees, but not through close-up. He most frequently uses distant viewpoint and telephoto lenses to turn the folds in a landscape into bands of color. Sometimes he makes time exposures from a moving vehicle to destroy detail by creating blur (see *Abstraction by blur,* p. 91). His pictures often conceal reality by their unfamiliar flattening of perspective, their overall sharpness, and their lack of scale references. Each picture appears to be all on one surface plane, as interrelated color shapes, tones, and textures, which he determines by choice of light direction. The proportions of one zone to another are gauged precisely within the frame. Cast shadows and false attachments are also used, to bring all parts of the image on to a common flat surface.

Christian Vogt
Much of the work of another Swiss photographer, Christian Vogt, is marked by its dramatic simplicity, depersonalization, and sense of form. Vogt studied commercial photography in Basel, then worked with photographers in Munich and London before setting up his own professional studio in Switzerland. This formal

"Mexico City" (1972)
An example (above) of René Burri's work, showing his eye for "clean-cut", stylish composition, using strong lines and powerful, vibrant colors.

Structure and shadows
Blocks of color (left) and critically gauged viewpoint make the structure of Franco Fontana's picture dominate subject.

From "Red Series" (1976-7)
One of Christian Vogt's series (below) using the color red. A still life of great simplicity, showing his concern for light on form.

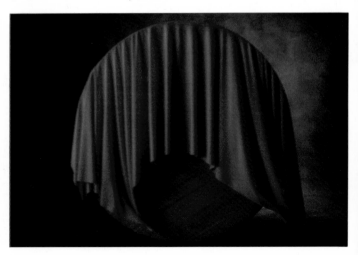

training gave him outstanding technical control of his medium. The commercial success of his studio allowed him time for other, more personal, projects, which began as experiments alongside his professional work.

Vogt often works out visual themes as sequences or "portfolios" of pictures – each individual image is complete in itself, but is reinforced by others with a common element or structure. Some have been concerned with time and space, others with color, or light on form, a few with the effects of false attachment (see *Using false attachment,* p. 84). He often adopts a still-life approach to his pictures and when he photographs people, they are frequently anonymous. Vogt suggests that this is indicative of the photographer's own anonymity. Certainly there is a degree of detachment and contemplation in much of his work, which gives it a dreamlike quality. In Vogt's own words "My pictures are not intended to be merely good or beautiful, but to stimulate the viewer to thought".

Aaron Siskind

A documentary photographer until the late 1940s, Siskind changed his approach from portraying the subject for its own worth to using semi-abstract effects. His interest centers on the textural qualities of surfaces, often taken in close-up, so that the identity of the subject becomes subordinated to design. Using straight photographic methods, Siskind photographs peeling paint, worn timber, stained walls, and other inanimate objects that often pass unnoticed. He is concerned with organizing lines and shapes by selection, suggesting order, character, and mood. The care he takes over composition and picture structure is matched by the extreme richness and superb detail in his prints. His cryptic images have been described as "art wrestled from junk". Although today subjects of this kind are frequently used as sources of abstract design, the originator was Siskind. His images relate to the work of the abstract expressionist painters of the 1950s, such as Jackson Pollock and Willem de Kooning.

André Kertész

In a long professional career in photography, which began in Paris during the 1920s and continued in America from the 1930s, André Kertész's work has ranged from photo-reportage to specialized interior shots for *Vogue* magazine. His style reflects both the European developments in small-format documentary photography and the New Vision concerns for design and space. But his aim in photography is less to produce a picture of epic subjects, than present the unexpected aspects of ordinary situations.

Kertész's pictures are characterized by their intriguing, satisfying geometrical structures as much as by their content. Like László Moholy-Nagy, he is intrigued by the way pattern and space in a scene are translated into shapes on the flat picture plane of the final print. He is also a master of false attachment, and the use of frame edges, tones, and lines, to give a structure to his images. He has an unfailing

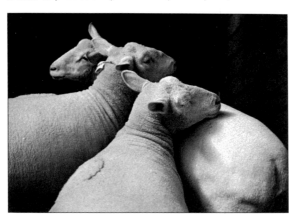

"Sheep, Paris" (1931)
André Kertész places great importance on structure in his pictures. Here (left), the lines formed by the animals flow together, seeming to relate to the companionship of the sheep themselves.

"Chez Mondrian" (1926)
Kertész treats this interior, home of Piet Mondrian (below), as a carefully composed still life. Its curves, circles, horizontal and vertical lines interrelate harmoniously and simply. There are subtle suggestions of Mondrian's own geometric abstractions.

"Kentucky" (1951)
Aaron Siskind uses objects such as this urban fence (below) as raw material for abstract images. Working close up and using straight techniques, he recasts the subject to make an abstract expressionist design, yet its origins are not completely obscured.
(Photograph courtesy of Light Gallery.)

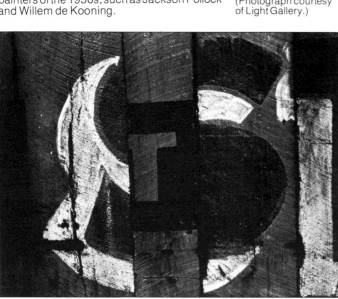

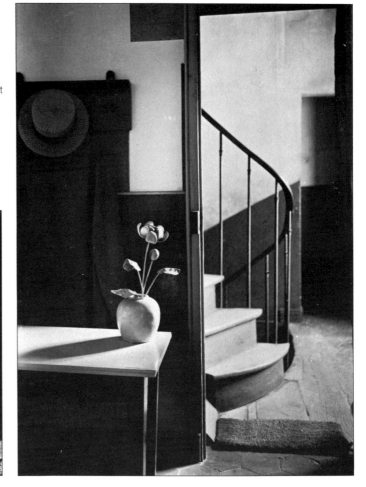

eye for the unexpected, telling detail.

It is possible to read Kertész's pictures on two levels — either as deceptively simple and original designs, or as results of his warm but detached enjoyment of people, situations, and the little oddities of everyday life. It is interesting to compare his work with that of Henri Cartier-Bresson — at times their work has much in common, although Kertész's has less to do with capturing the critical moment, and more to do with his leanings on a more personal and experimental level.

Joel Meyerowitz

It is sometimes possible to add structure to a picture by using light itself. Joel Meyerowitz, in his picture essay on Cape Cod, America, makes use of transient lighting effects to provide compositional design as well as atmosphere. His use of a large-format 10 × 8 ins (25 × 20 cm) view camera for the series has allowed him to "slow down" and make a detached assessment of his subjects by viewing the image upside down, and benefit from the compositional disciplines that this very simple device imposes.

Meyerowitz's images are spare. They often make combined use of the shapes of real objects and patches of light, carefully related to the frame edges. He considers color to be a vital, though often subtle, factor in describing the atmosphere and mood of "ordinary" scenes. His pictures often form series in which

the passage of time is represented by changing shadow shapes and hues.

Andreas Feininger

A documentary journalist turned teacher, Andreas Feininger has a special concern for the structures of the natural world. He shows rocks and shells as sculptural forms in close-up, so that they lose their scale and remind us of complex architectural shapes. Some of Feininger's work parallels Karl Blossfeldt's New Objectivity style (see *Individuals and movements of Straight photography*, pp. 343-6), but he makes greater use of lighting as a means of dramatically revealing structures. Unlike Harry Callahan's simplified linear studies, Feininger's work often stresses volume and the complexity of form. He uses straight photographic techniques, believing this to be a way of extending and sharpening the human vision.

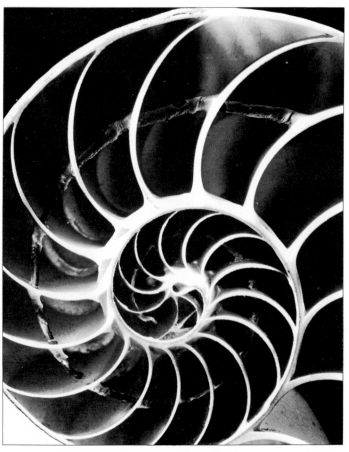

"Nautilus Shell" (1970)
The complex, almost architectural interpretation of this half shell is typical of Andreas Feininger's close-ups of natural subjects. Although the method of photography is straight, the subject matter itself is almost irrelevant — design and composition are all-important. (Feininger urges his students to study abstract and semi-abstract paintings to develop a sense of composition.) The styles of the Bauhaus and the New Objectivity are evident in his work — both influenced him when he was a student. (Compare this picture with the X ray photograph of a shell, p. 280).

Metaphor and Symbolism

Pictures that are concerned with metaphor describe things which are not directly connected with the subject matter itself. We are familiar with the concept of seeing things "in" other things. A sunlit, frosted window pane can evoke a wave or a tune. Rippled water, rocks, clouds, and plant forms can all be interpreted as different kinds of emotional experience.

Photographs can be vehicles for metaphor — either unintentionally or in a planned way. Because interpretation is often very personal, the viewer has an important role to play — contributing his or her own emotions to it. A photograph can have a personal significance, it can act as a catalyst to recalling our former experiences, other photographs, and other kinds of image. Such pictures can be ambiguous at first sight, but they are always a challenge — the viewer is forced to think. As photographer Wynn Bullock said "Only those things that happen in one's mind can one really know".

Uses for symbols

Photographs can also be, or can contain, symbols, which thought associations allow us to recall. The color white can suggest purity, and televisions and automobiles can suggest the consumer society. This area is greatly exploited in advertising. Symbols are used by human documentary photographers as well as by expressionist photographers. Robert Frank's subject matter — solitary figures, flags, and automobiles, and Bill Brandt's details of English middle-class life are both symbols and subjects. Whereas Dorothea Lange's pictures have become symbols in themselves — of deprivation in general, and of the Depression in the 1930s in particular.

Of the two, metaphor is the more subtle and personal. Photographically, its roots lie in the pictures Alfred Stieglitz took in the last fifteen years of his working life (1922-37). At a time when photographs were just beginning to be used on the printed page, and lucrative advertising and illustration work had attracted away leading pictorialist talent, Stieglitz began to take intensely personal photographs which he named "equivalents". These were mostly cloud studies, which were to represent emotional states and inner meanings.

This same metaphoric approach was kept alive in their own individual way by Minor White, Aaron Siskind, and Harry Callahan. It has had a strong following in photographic schools and colleges as a self analytical, contemplative form of expression. Ralph Eugene Meatyard, Wynn Bullock, and Duane Michals are photographers who, working in black and white, use tone values as a major element in their symbolic, often mystical, images.

See also
Light as the main picture ingredient, pp. 32-3. Editorial and advertising photography, pp. 314-19.

Equivalents

The concepts of symbolism, metaphor, and mysticism were noticeable features of the photographic brotherhoods of the turn of the century. The Photo-Secessionists even adopted a symbol, a transparent balloon-like sphere, as their trademark, and it appears in many of their photographs, particularly those of Clarence White and Fred Holland Day.

Alvin Langdon Coburn had produced semi-abstract studies of clouds as poetic symbols in 1912. Like these, Alfred Stieglitz's equivalents were born out of his fascination for, and study of, clouds. He was interested in them, not necessarily for their aesthetic qualities, but because of the ways they appeal to day dreamers and children. Clouds seemed to recall his most profound experiences — and he felt that, through them, he could express his personal philosophy of life.

Stieglitz also wanted to prove that his success as a photographer was not merely due to the choice of sitters available to him — some of whom were exceptionally photogenic — but that it extended to subjects that were free for anyone to portray. When he was working on this natural subject matter, he shunned anything but a completely straight technique, "My aim is increasingly to make photographs look so much like photographs, that unless one has *eyes* and *sees,* they won't be seen and still everybody will never forget them having once looked at them".

Stieglitz's earliest equivalents, made in 1922, were his metaphors for music. Later, as he became increasingly introspective and self-contained, the equivalent developed a metaphysical stature, and the concept of equivalence acquired disciples.

Minor White

The ideas and theories behind equivalents were adopted, developed, and popularized in America, by Minor White. His approach to photography was shaped and influenced by his early associations with Alfred Stieglitz, Edward Weston, and Ansel Adams. He became prominent during the mid-1950s as a teacher of photography at the Rochester Institute of Technology. Here he conducted photographic workshops, where he expected a high degree of intellectual analysis and involvement from his students.

In his own photography, Minor White seems to combine the introspective qualities of Stieglitz with Adams's technical mastery of tone values through previsualization and the Zone System. His pictures are mostly small, intimate studies of rock formations, moving water, and natural landscape. His aim was to endow these natural phenomena with his own emotion and empathy. It is significant that before turning to photography, White studied natural science, English, and was a devotee of Zen Buddhism and the art of meditation. He appreciated the difficulty of finding the inner meaning expressed by the photographer, and he wrote extensively on the concept of equivalence.

White's theory was that a photographer's mind must be "sensitized", made blank and open (perhaps through meditation), before taking a picture. When a mood of openness is reached, he said, vision is highly charged and there is a feeling that is close to mysticism.

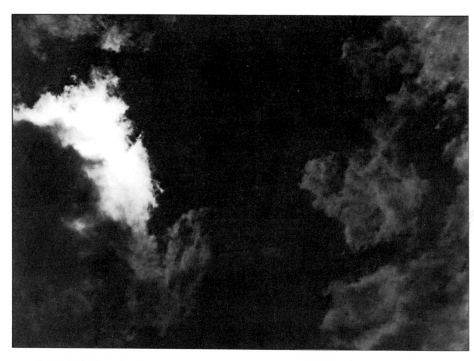

"Equivalent" (c. 1925)
In his advancing years Alfred Stieglitz became increasingly absorbed in making a series of equivalents, of which this cloud study is an example. Like reading meanings into flames in a hearth, their changing shapes and moods seem to be expressions of his most profound emotions.

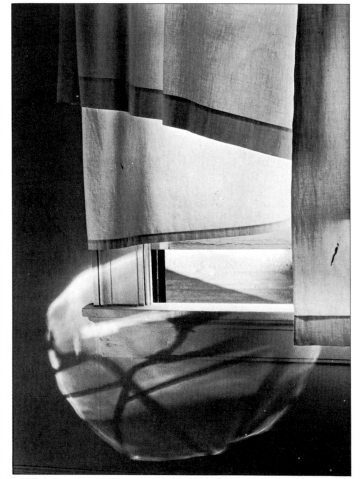

"Windowsill Daydreaming, Rochester, New York" (1958)
Light spilling beneath curtains produces an ephemeral effect — it resembles a liquid, or a cloud flowing into a room, rather than a still reflection. An unusual subject for Minor White, but invested with his characteristically ambiguous "inner meaning". (Photograph courtesy of Philadelphia Museum of Art. Purchased from the artist. Photographed by Eric Mitchell.)

The photographer must be prepared for anything to happen before shooting and afterwards, when looking at the print, must adopt an attitude of analytical criticism. His equivalents do not have a definite appearance since equivalence is a function or an experience rather than an object for a given person at a given instant, or a symbol or metaphor for something beyond the subject. The idea is that the photographer should find a subject which will evoke feelings that cannot be photographed. Subjects that change all the time,

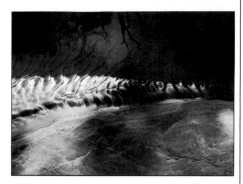

"Light Spine, Burr Trail, Utah" (1966)
This picture demonstrates Minor White's sophisticated sense of design and form in natural objects, plus his ability to use an ordinary subject for equivalence.

(Photograph courtesy of Philadelphia Museum of Art. Purchased from the artist. Photographed by Eric Mitchell.)

such as water, flames, clouds, ice, and light are all perfect for this because they suggest emotions, tactile encounters, and intellectual speculations.

The concept of equivalence took on the status of a cult during the 1960s and 1970s among a minority of American and British photographers. As well as writing widely, White co-founded and edited the magazine *Aperture* from 1952 until his death in 1976. It was conceived as a showcase for modern aesthetic photography, particularly metaphoric and symbolic work, using the highest possible quality reproduction. The publication introduced Paul Caponigro, Frederick Sommer, Walter Chappell, and many others. In the spirit of *Camera Work*, 50 years earlier, *Aperture* magazine and books became an international communications channel. *Aperture* monographs, published many years before such books became fashionable, did much to lay the foundations for recording photography for posterity.

The leading exponents of Metaphor and Symbolism

Not all the major photographers of Metaphor and Symbolism are devotees of equivalence, but all rely on the ability of the viewer to read significance into their images. Understanding the photograph, and adding an individual interpretation makes a substantial contribution to the photographer's personal statement.

Wynn Bullock

American photographer Wynn Bullock's work is, at its simplest level, concerned with portraying nature — often in combination with the human body. Influenced both by the Bauhaus and the photography of Edward Weston, Bullock discovers mirages and visions in the elements of landscape. His rocks and gnarled trees have faces, and eroded soil takes the shape of a procession of hooded figures. The nudes which adorn his landscapes are naturalistic, and seem to be an intrinsic part of their surroundings. His picture of a naked child lying face down in a forest glade (see below) is possibly the best known of all his photographs. It was used in Edward Steichen's *The Family of Man* exhibition (1955), which traveled the world representing the work of hundreds of photographers from all countries, showing their interpretations of the cycle of human life, in its myriad variations.

Another of Bullock's preoccupations is space-time — the symbolic addition of a fourth

"Child in the Forest" (1951)
A technically straight photograph by Wynn Bullock which is imbued with symbolism. It was used to signify the creation of man in *The*

Family of Man exhibition. (Photograph © Wynn Bullock, Wynn and Edna Bullock Trust. Courtesy of the Center for Creative Photography.)

dimension to his images. He has said that he is less concerned with showing objects than with making pictures of light. To him, light is similar to sound for its scope for personal expression. Both are found everywhere, and have psychological and physiological impact.

Clarence John Laughlin
Based in New Orleans, Clarence John Laughlin is involved in exploring the psyche through photography. His other interests include writing prose poems and macabre fiction. His pictures, which are often semi-abstract or surreal, have a mystical quality. Typical subjects include patterns of sunlight coming through curtains, reflections in everyday objects, superimpositions of faces on stone, and semi-transparent figures related to old monuments.

These elements are less things and people than symbols of his own thoughts. Many of

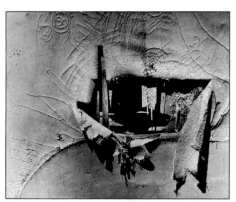

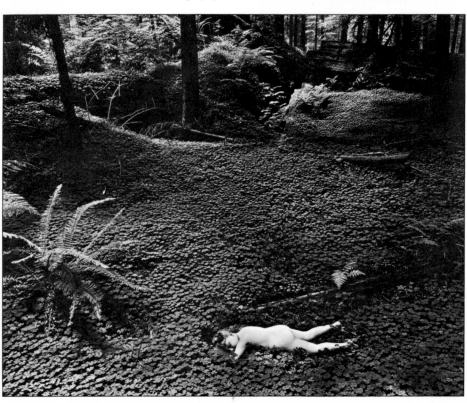

"Entrance to a Sub-World" (1954)
Many of Clarence John Laughlin's pictures show one subject framed in another, and make maximum use of natural texture and pattern. Of this photograph (left), Laughlin writes "Close-up of a small torn opening in the canvas wall of a homemade trailer.... To the eye, its meaning was almost imperceptible. But through the camera plus the human imagination — its meaning has been completely altered by a) scale has been increased so greatly that graphic values, previously lost, are now completely visible, and b) generating a magic which makes this small opening like the setting of a sinister stage — an ominous aperture into another world."

"The Portent in the Shadow" (1954)
One of a series (right) devoted to commonplace subjects, aiming to reveal meaning which has nothing to do with actual appearance. Clarence John Laughlin writes the following: "A traffic sign throws a shadow on an old Vieux Carré wall in New Orleans. But looking closely, we discover in the shadow a one-eyed face, with a helpless mouth — while the arrow points to nothingness. This image speaks to us in a secret language, a language which exists everywhere, even in the most 'inanimate' objects — it speaks to us, disquietingly, of our confusion, of our loss of direction. It is the language with which man impregnates all the objects around himself, when defending himself against the inhumanity of things...." (Photographs and captions © Clarence John Laughlin.)

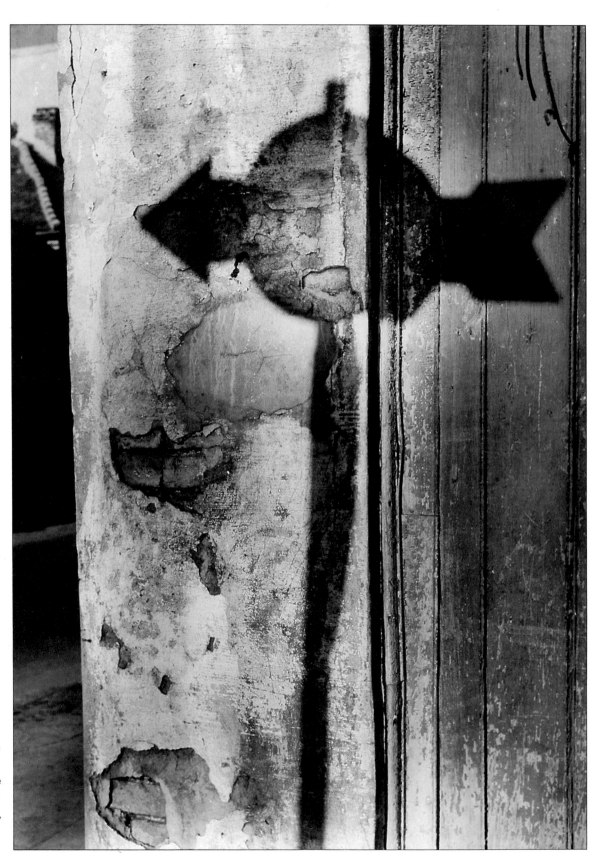

Laughlin's pictures suggest and conjure up the atmosphere of spirits and ghosts. In old age, he has preserved a fresh, almost child-like sensory perception, an almost disinterested view of simple things, and a talent for communicating them as significant. One of his most 'successful collections of pictures is *Ghosts Along the Mississippi,* which was published in 1948.

Ralph Eugene Meatyard

Something of an eccentric, with a strong sense of the macabre, Ralph Eugene Meatyard was an optician and businessman as well as a serious amateur photographer. As a young man he studied briefly under Minor White, and art historian Van Deren Coke. The main influences on him were literary — writers such as Gertrude Stein, Ezra Pound, and the literature of Zen. Many of his contacts were contemporary writers and poets.

His pictures were taken in and around his home town, and most of the people he used as subjects are depersonalized by shadow, by movement blur, or because they are wearing masks (usually of old men's faces). Sometimes the whole scene dissolves into a double image, or seems to shake like an earthquake. He is concerned with the strange but simple effects of light, as well as shadows. His figures relate to marks on walls, and patches of spilled light which create restless, uneasy patterns. His pictures possess a foreboding sense of disquiet. His people are always a part of the environment — either full-length or half-length, but never close-up. Sometimes, because of movement blur, real faces become masks, and masks (held still) become real faces. In some of his work there are noticeable simi-larities with the strange, expressive paintings of Edward Munch.

A friend, Wendell Berry, has explained that the imagery which Meatyard uses is clearly the product of a highly complex plot, which is not actually in evidence. This is not because Meatyard wants to keep it from us deliberately, but because the mystery of it is real. The plot is not made evident because he does not know what it is any more than we do.

Harry Callahan

The work of Harry Callahan is highly personal and self-exploratory. His recurring themes are details of pastoral structures and architectural façades, people and patterns of light in city streets, and highly personal pictures which include his wife and child. Sometimes, like Bullock's, his nudes are additions to a landscape, others are formal silhouette shapes, at times dominated by the structure of a room interior. He has also superimposed landscapes and figures, and has created images that are almost surreal.

Callahan discusses his work mostly in terms of the importance of self-expression, "if a man wishes to express himself photographically he must understand, surely to a certain extent, his relationship to life". Photographs that are different, he says, are usually so because the individual is making a point of expressing his own personality. Callahan thinks that more

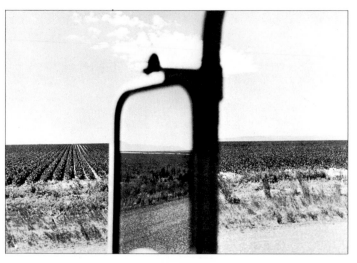

"Idaho" (1972)
This mysterious image by Lee Friedlander typifies his fascination with reflections in relation to the picture plane, and the critical division of the picture area. Open expanses of country are bisected by an automobile mirror, which plays tricks on perspective and implies both physical and spiritual emptiness.

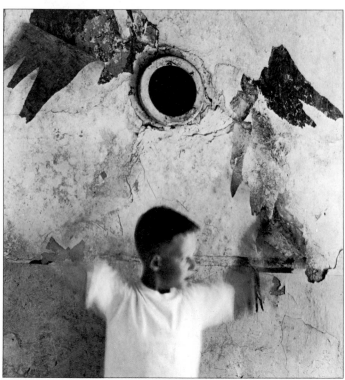

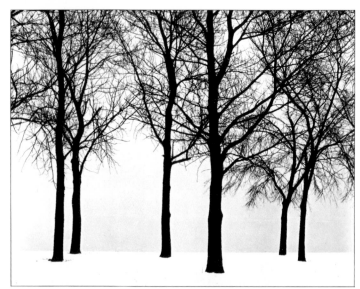

"Untitled" (1960)
This picture by Ralph Eugene Meat-yard revolves around shape simi-larities which seem to have strong symbolic overtones. The boy's head and blurred, "flapping" arms are linked with the circular and wing — like shapes above.

"Chicago" (1950)
One of Harry Callahan's austere, graphic images of natural pattern. Interlacing branches and stark, black trunks seem to symbolize growth and relationship. (Photograph courtesy of Light Gallery.)

people than do could find photography an exciting adventure and could discover that their individual feelings are worth expressing.

Duane Michals

A generation younger, Duane Michals is concerned with the spirit, just as Laughlin is. He is a freelance photographer, working in New York, and he is best known for his personal work. Since 1969, his work has taken the form of sequences of pictures — each one containing a slight variation, like consecutive frames from a movie. But unlike a movie, each frame is a frozen instant of time, offering gaps for the viewer to imagine and fill in. He or she is influenced by expectations and associations. Michals uses this device to tell stories or fables, which frequently contain a supernatural element. Mysterious blurred or semi-transparent figures move through the frames. Death is a recurring theme, with suggestions of the journey of the spirit leaving the body, or the figure of death returning to collect another soul. Sometimes, the main subject remains identical, but each picture is taken from a different position — the camera moving in a complete circle.

All these events are planned precisely, and acted out like playlets, in ordinary surroundings. The camera functions as a detached observer, but the viewer is drawn in and feels involved — as if he is standing outside himself, watching his own actions (see *Picture sequences*, pp. 88-9).

Lee Friedlander

An illustrative documentary photographer of great originality, Lee Friedlander's reputation rests on his apparently casual glimpses of city life. His pictures, though seemingly spontaneous, use doorways, windows, or lampposts to divide up the frame in a very deliberate way (see *Forming related compartments*, p. 61). In another side to his work, Friedlander uses a more atmospheric, less structural, approach, to symbolize modern life. Sometimes both these and his street scenes have strong surreal qualities.

Friedlander has produced a book of largely figurative self-portraits — many of the pictures include his own shadow cast apparently randomly on buildings, foliage, and on other people. The head and shoulders shape, sometimes in the form of dense shadow, sometimes a mysterious reflection in a mirror or window, seems to be symbolic of humanity trapped in a modern urban environment. His pictures of bleak motel rooms inhabited only by a face on a television screen seem to be concerned with the loneliness of the individual.

His choice of subject matter is influenced by the early work of Robert Frank, and he has a close working relationship with Jim Dine, the pop art-surrealist artist, whose work frequently parodies self-expression and the methods of painting itself.

Romanticism and the dramatic

Romantic and dramatic styles of imagery are concerned with mood, the emotions, and illusion. The manner in which the picture is made, and its treatment of the subject is as important as the subject itself. When applied to photography, it is the complete antithesis of the direct candid approach of Henri Cartier-Bresson, Robert Frank, or the photojournalism of Bill Brandt.

The roots of Romanticism in photography are seen in the constructed sets used in most nineteenth-century professional portrait studios. The painted backdrops, the props and decorations reflect the decorative tastes of the times. In addition, the pictorial-impressionistic techniques of soft focus and the hand manipulation of prints were perfect for romantic effects.

Many of the stylistic developments of Romanticism came to their peak in work from the top photographic portraitists of the 1920s and 1930s — the period when fashionable portrait studios were enjoying a heyday. Another significant impetus at this time came from the fashion magazines. Photographers found themselves with an immense new audience, and fierce competition built up between them in the portrayal of elegance and glamor. Pioneer fashion photographers such as Baron de Meyer successfully combined a theatrical approach with Pictorialism. De Meyer influenced, and

was influenced by, a glamorous style of lighting used for the new sound movies.

In the years following the 1930s the influence of the New Objectivity movement in Europe, and the Straight movement in America produced a reaction against Romanticism.

The influence of Romanticism on Realism still persisted into the 1950s, and early 1960s, in the dramatic low-key portraits by photographers such as Yousuf Karsh. At the same time, there was a surge of commercial photography which was used to publicize industry, and its style echoed this dramatic approach.

In the 1970s, the vogue for all things nostalgic brought a return to the romantic styles of the 1930s and, for the same reason, there has been a resurgence in interest in some of the manipulative techniques of Pictorialism. But apart from a few present-day photographers who use variations of the techniques of Romanticism, there is, as yet, no widespread revival of the decorative, constructed sets and elaborate lighting schemes of the romantic photographic movement. The best work of the style exists in *Vogue, Harpers Bazaar,* and *Vanity Fair,* of the 1930s.

See also
High Art photography, pp. 330-3. Pictorialism pp. 334-40.

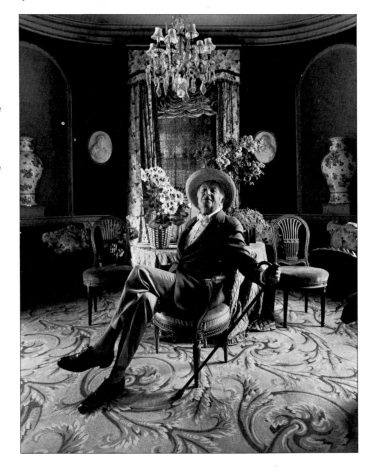

"Sir Cecil Beaton, Photographer and Designer, Broadchalke, Salisbury, Wilts" (1978) Although he is not a photographer of the romantic, Arnold Newman has succeeded in capturing the flamboyant personality and love of romantic settings in a pastiche of one of its greatest exponents. It was taken in collaboration with the subject in his own home, and it well illustrates how the use of environment can contribute to a portrait. During the 1930s, Beaton was producing photographs in this style, but constructed in the studios of the leading fashion magazines. (Photograph © Arnold Newman.)

The pictorial origins of Romanticism

By 1910, Alfred Stieglitz was directing the Photo-Secessionists toward the new Straight photographic approach epitomized by Paul Strand. Several members disagreed with his attitude and left the group, including most of the photographers who favored the impressionistic approach. In 1916, Clarence White, Gertrude Käsebier, and Alvin Langdon Coburn set up a rival concern — Pictorial Photographers of America, and White was its first president. Both he and Käsebier employed simple, romantic imagery, and made a deliberate and distinctive use of light.

Gertrude Käsebier

After studying painting at the Pratt Institute, Brooklyn, Gertrude Käsebier opened a photographic portrait studio in Paris, and then in New York (1897).

The pictures she exhibited widely in England and America were romantic in both subject matter and approach. Typically, her studies were taken in or around the home, and showed naturalistic scenes, usually of women and children. Their content is described by straightforward titles such as *The Dance, The Letter,* and *The Sketch.* But occasionally titles were sentimentalized, as in, for example, *The War Widow,* and *Blessed Art Thou Among Women.* But these titles appear to be afterthoughts — the pictures themselves are, in their own right, finely composed human studies. She preferred to use soft top- or back-lighting, sometimes combined with a slightly soft-focus lens to give an additional glow to white areas in the pictures. These were often set off by deep shadows, and given body and depth by her platinum paper prints.

Clarence White

Like Käsebier, Clarence White was internationally known for delicate studies of women and girls. Inevitably, they are posed in simple, family settings, often rimlit from the rear, giving a romantic touch especially to outdoor scenes. Many of his pictures, for example *The Ring Toss,* are powerful reminders of Degas' paintings of ballet scenes.

White's compositions have an assured graphic touch, but his people never seem quite real. They are more a romantic impression of grace and elegance — each personality dissolved by soft focus, movement, or the angle of light. White exhibited in almost every important show in America during a twenty-year period before and after the turn of the century. From 1906 he held the then unusual appointment of lecturer in photography at Columbia University, where he later founded the Clarence White School of Photography.

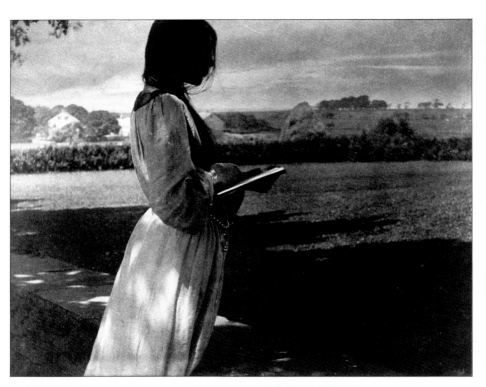

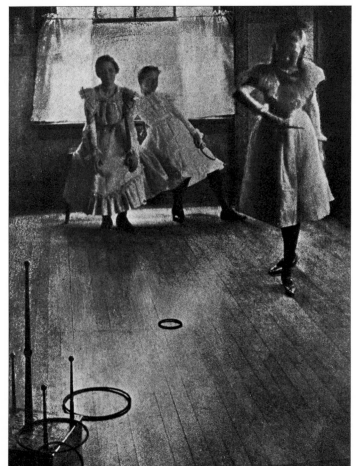

"The Sketch" (c. 1900)
This example (above) of Gertrude Käsebier's work shows the delicacy and feeling with which she treated her subjects, plus a certain originality of composition and style. Her experience as a painter is evident in the subtleties of line and the use of selective focus. A confirmed romantic, Käsebier left the Photo-Secessionists when Stieglitz began to advocate a revolutionary, straight approach.

"The Ring Toss" (1903)
Clarence White often used subjects similar to Käsebier (left), but his studies are usually more high key. This particular example is a daring composition, bearing in mind the technical problems of creating depth of field with a large-format camera, using existing light.

The leading exponents of Romanticism and the dramatic

The romantic and dramatic approaches to photography encompass a wide variety of different photographers and their individual subject preferences.

Baron de Meyer

The photographer whose style most closely links the largely amateur work of the Photo-Secessionists with the professional world of fashion and advertising between the two World Wars was Baron Adolf de Meyer. As an amateur, De Meyer was influenced by Alfred Stieglitz, and he joined the Photo-Secessionists. He began to develop his own original style of lighting to achieve romantic effects. Using largely high-key settings, he directed several lamps at the subject from the top or rear, and using a soft-focus lens, he was able to create flattering pictures which had a "magical" atmosphere. But his results were not merely due to technique. De Meyer had a gift for choosing the right locations for his sitters – in his pictures of women every surface is rich and glossy, from the satin dresses and upholstery and the marble floors, to the glinting highlights in glass and jewelry. He was also a master of styling. The drapes of curtains, the way a dress flows, and the flowers in his pictures were all styled by him. Even the flowers were sprayed lightly with water, to resemble dew.

From 1913 to the early 1940s, De Meyer worked for *Vogue,* and then *Harpers Bazaar* as a fashion and celebrity photographer. He had invented glamor photography before Hollywood talkies had made it the most universally copied and desirable of looks. His sitters were invariably picked out in an aura of light – their hair transformed into a glowing halo. But often his decorative treatment eclipsed their character and individuality. De Meyer's style became so fashionable that a reaction against it was bound to arrive eventually, but it says much for his talent that he was able to survive for so long in a field which was so highly competitive.

Cecil Beaton

Photographer Cecil Beaton, although clearly influenced by De Meyer, used his talent for a wide variety of different purposes. He was a stage and costume designer, as well as a photographer, author, and painter – a sense of romantic elegance pervades all his work. As a photographer, he worked chiefly in fashion and portraiture for *Harpers Bazaar* and other Condé Nast publications from the late 1920s until the 1950s, creating a distinctive, flamboyant style.

Beaton's pictures are characterized by elaborate decorative studio sets, which seem alive with light and flowers. He often went to immense trouble to build settings that looked like stage scenery for a romantic epic theater production, or a dreamland environment for a portrait by Gainsborough or Fragonard. These suited the particular personalities of the actors, actresses, writers, and members of high society he photographed. Usually, the effect was high key and delicate, but never static – the constructions and sets often made witty visual reference to other styles of the art world, such as Rococo, Surrealism, or Art Deco. Beaton's experience in other spheres helped to give his pictures originality and eye-catch-

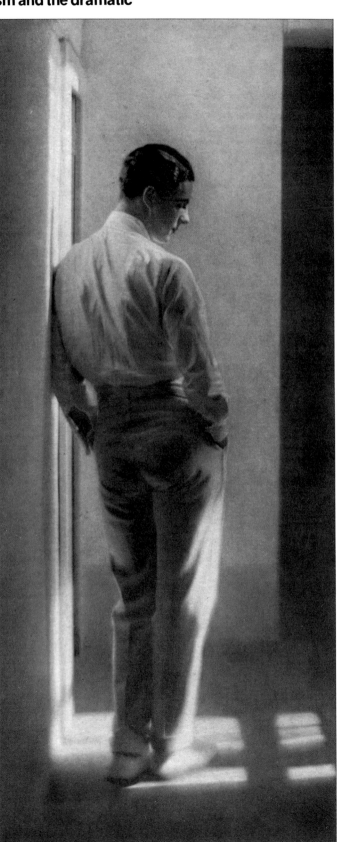

"Teddie" (1912)
This stylish portrait shows Baron de Meyer's typical preference for back-lighting and his elegant use of the lines of doorways, windows, or picture frames for framing his subjects. In later years he developed this style in elaborate fashion studies, using artificial light, for *Vogue* magazine.

ing appeal. Sometimes, they seem to reveal a hollowness which echoes the subject matter. When elegance and romance began to give way to the forthright styles of the 1960s, his approach seemed overcontrived and dated.

Yousuf Karsh

Canada-based professional photographer Yousuf Karsh specializes in dramatic portraits of male celebrities. His philosophy is evident in the titles of some of his published collections of pictures – *Faces of Destiny, Portraits of Greatness,* and *In Search of Greatness.*

Karsh has inherited some of Julia Margaret Cameron's obsession for revealing the inner power of the great men of the day – scientists, musicians, artists, and writers. He expresses it with dramatic, Hollywood-style, low-key lighting. The typical Karsh portrait shows the sitter's head and shoulders, lit in a highly controlled manner, with several harsh light sources. This illumination produces rich textures, and his lens is able to pick out every pore and wrinkle. He also makes frequent use of hands consciously to suggest character and to draw attention to the face. His prints have an immaculate, rich tonal range.

The technical qualities of Karsh portraits create pictures with great dramatic appeal – but the overperfect effects of light and pose frequently make the results seem static and overly contrived. Instead of real people, his sitters sometimes resemble statues.

Karsh's style was immensely successful and had great impact. During the 1940s and 1950s, in particular, he photographed many of the world's political leaders. His style was so influential that it was widely imitated by every main street photographer, and is still popular, to a certain extent, today. Early in his career, Karsh worked exclusively with 10 × 8 ins (25 × 20 cm) equipment, but he has since moved progressively to 5 × 4 ins (12.5 × 10 cm) and even to 35 mm formats.

Walter Nurnberg

European photographers who learned their skills during the 1930s were much influenced by the New Objectivity style, and the work of Albert Renger-Patzsch. After the Second World War, many specialized in advertising and publicity photography, and for some time during the late 1940s an 1950s industry, which was striving to re-establish itself after the war, became an important market for photography. Leading photographers such as Walter Nurnberg and Adolf Morath in Britain, and Art d'Aison in America turned from advertising to new dramatic forms of photographing industry and its procedures.

Nurnberg specialized in highly stylized black and white images, designed to advertise the facilities and craftsmanship of an industry. In a similar way to Karsh, he applies Hollywood-style lighting effects and pin-sharp detail to give a dramatic and romanticized view of industry and its processes. Nurnberg's affinity for the basic forms and structures found in machinery and industrial plant gave his work a dynamic force and a powerful structure. He made a masterly use of unusual angles, and he brought quantities of spotlights to the factories to turn them into film sets. By careful

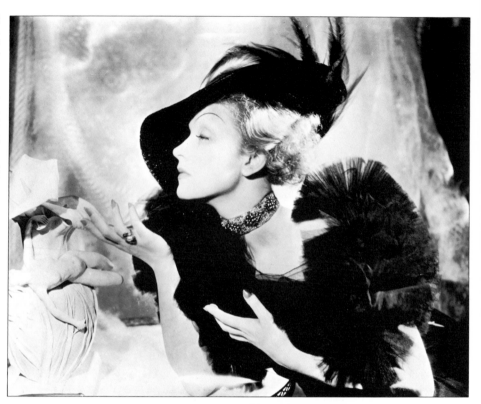

"Marlene Dietrich" (1935)
A portrait (above) by Cecil Beaton of this "very personification of screen glamour 'thirties' style". It shows Beaton's typically extravagant use of props and posing. (Photograph courtesy of Sotheby's Belgravia.)

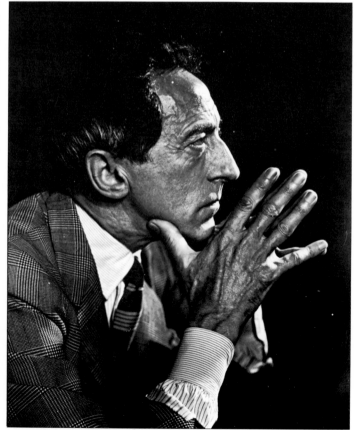

"Jean Cocteau"
Yousuf Karsh (Karsh of Ottawa) uses bold, low-key lighting (left) and extremely sharp detail in this dramatic portrait of the poet and playwright. It is a precisely planned pose, in which the hands make a significant contribution, suggesting an artistic, thoughtful personality. (Photograph courtesy of Camera Press London.)

organizaton and a total control of lighting, he banished the dirt and untidiness of the surrounding work environment by sinking it into the vague, dark backgrounds.

The activities he shows are real and accurate industrially, but presented in a highly theatrical manner. He portrays industry in the most flattering way possible, as part of a calculated expression of precision, quality, and care.

Marcus Adams

The realism of the New Objectivity had little immediate effect on the portraiture of women and children by the majority of serious amateurs and professional photographers during the 1930s. Instead, the most popular approach involved diffused details and top-lighting, plus the use of painted backdrops which suggested outdoor scenes. Marcus Adams, a leading exponent of this style, was unusual and particularly successful in his treatment and posing of young children, and he was regularly commissioned to take portraits of the British royal family. He often created soft-image detail in the darkroom by diffusing during enlarging — an effect which expanded the shadow areas. These results helped to give his work a flavor which was highly individual.

David Hamilton

A furniture designer and magazine art director, David Hamilton turned his attention to photography during the late 1960s. He works in the south of France, specializing in highly romanticized pictures of young girls. Typically, they are soft-focus studies, often mildly erotic. The settings are all real, the sun has a rose-colored effect, and the softness of detail makes the most ordinary subjects in the scene seem luminous, with a life of their own. Hamilton works almost entirely in color. His work appears in picture books which are compilations of his photographs, and editorial commissions for magazines.

Sarah Moon

Similar in style to Hamilton, Sarah Moon favors a soft-focus technique, and uses young girls as models. But her approach to her subjects is noticeably more innocent and naïve. Her pictures have an unusual grainy appearance, and their colors are more muted. Her work has qualities which many of the impressionist photographers would have used, had color materials been available to them. Moon is an ex-model, who turned to photography in the 1960s. She works in Paris, producing strongly romantic fashion studies, which often possess a haunting Victorian atmosphere. Her grainy effects, which have become one of her trademarks, are achieved by shooting the picture on small-format, fast color film, and enlarging considerably from this image, using a condenser enlarger.

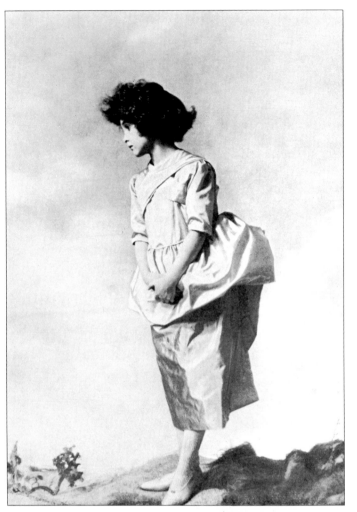

"Lady Pamela Smith"
Outstanding in his natural posing of children, Marcus Adams achieves a charming Raeburnesque result using a studio backdrop. The overall effect resembles the technique and style of mid-nineteenth century *carte-de-visite* photographers.

Reflections
This modern fashion shot (below) by Sarah Moon has a strongly romantic "thirties" flavor, and her use of bold grain enhances the mood. The repeated images create a frieze effect — each section is sufficiently different to make the eye glance from one section to the next, making comparisons.

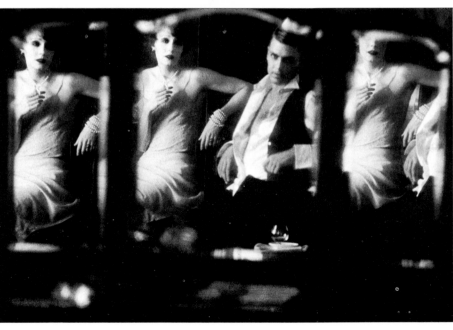

Surrealism

Images of Surrealism are founded in the subconscious – usually based on fantasy and daydreams – but expressed with maximum realism and detail. And it is this which makes photography an ideal medium for making surrealistic images. Its detail-recording ability, plus its reputation for truth and accuracy can make fantasy and reality become one. In the same way that dreams seem so believable at the time, so surreal images are often pervaded by strange occurrences and juxtapositions which appear perfectly realistic.

Anything is possible in Surrealism, and surreal photographs, like surreal poetry or drama, can make the impossible real. The sky has cracks in it, and a window, once removed from a room, carries the view away along with the glass. Surreal images therefore express irrational, haunting, and occasionally repellent themes, and they are today much used for advertising, as well as a means of self-expression. They may be light-hearted or deeply symbolic, or used to make social or political statements.

Origins
Surrealism was born out of the dadaist constructions of the early 1920s, when artists such as Raoul Hausmann discovered the creative possibilities of montage to form new composite images. Some of these montages were rough and angular, but other images, such as paintings by Magritte or Dali, took realism to extremes.

Modern Surrealism
Recent developments in photographic techniques, such as color slide sandwiching, double printing, and front- and back-projection are ideally suited for combining two images so that they look natural. Many photographers use ordinary montage techniques combined with air-brushing and hand coloring. Other photographers discover and isolate surreal situations and images from everyday life, which they can communicate through Straight photography. The brief juxtaposition between people and the shapes and patterns of their surroundings, the momentary glance or expression, and the many quite natural but strange-looking things that people do, are all subjects for the Surrealist.

Surreal pictures can be cheap and jokey, profound and disquieting, or concerned with visual puns. Since Surrealism is of the mind, ideas are all-important. Strangeness on its own is not enough – the photographer must develop a sense of free association and observation. After this, photographic techniques are available to carry the idea through in the most appropriate way.

See also
Special effects lighting *Back projection*, p. 181; *Front projection*, p. 182. Print finishing *Airbrushing*, pp. 252-3. Alternative printing techniques *Sandwich printing*, p. 260; *Multiple printing*, pp. 260-1. Workroom techniques *Toning*, p. 268; *Montage*, p. 269; *Hand coloring*, pp. 269-70. Editorial and advertising photography, pp. 314-18.

Art origins and influences

For dadaist and constructivist artists, it was a short step from making collages on canvas out of scraps of paper to doing the same thing with fragments of photographs. The combination of realism and antilogic, plus the use of a machine process (photographs were cut from printed material) was in accord with the dadaist rejection of the traditional techniques and methods of art.

Raoul Hausmann, together with George Groz, Hannah Hoch, and John Heartfield, were the first to construct images by photomontage. Hausmann and Hoch made grotesque images out of cut-out photographs and type. Some artists, such as László Moholy-Nagy and Paul Citroën made semi-abstract use of repetitive images. They carefully organized perspective and scale to give a realistic sense of depth, and intentionally mixed and disarranged it to suit the incoherence of the theme.

Heartfield, like many of the Berlin Dadaists, was strongly motivated politically. He made montages out of photographs and newspaper cuttings to produce posters and magazine illustrations for anti-Nazi propaganda. In Cologne, Max Ernst's photomontages created highly self-expressive, dream-like images which were a definite transition to Surrealism. The surrealist manifesto of 1924 described the new movement as the expression of thought, free from the exercise of reason, and outside all "aesthetic" or moral preoccupations. It returned to the concept of a painting acting as a "window". But it now opened on to a mental landscape, an interior world.

The movement had a liberating influence, and its tantalizing images had more popular public appeal and understanding than Cubism and Dadaism, which it replaced. Surrealism inherited several artists from Dadaism, such as Ernst and Man Ray. Others, such as Magritte, were attracted by the freedom it afforded the imagination in contrast with the formal structural concerns of Cubism.

Some surrealist artists adopted a style which was "photographic". Dali, a Surrealist since 1929, simulates photography in minutely detailed, illusionary paintings. He uses a method which he calls "hand-done color photography" to convey hallucinatory thought and fantasy. Magritte's paintings, by contrast, are less strident, less theatrical, and less remote from the possibilities of real life.

Painter and photographer Man Ray was influenced by the surrealist movement in Paris during the late 1920s. He joined the sometimes feverish search for the unexpected, always attracted to the unusual and experimental. His photographs include double exposures and strange juxtapositions of still life objects, occasionally solarized.

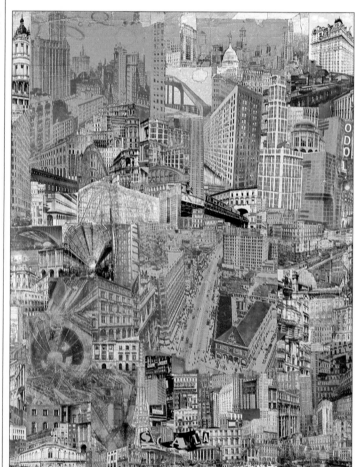

"Metropolis" (1923)
A collage made up of photographs, magazine illustrations, and postcards by Paul Citroën. Different perspectives and scales intermingle to produce a sense of profusion and disorder. In a similar way, dadaist and surrealist films used lap-dissolves to create collage effects. Collage and montage deliberately broke with the logic of earlier art forms and were the first steps toward Surrealism.

Techniques

Surrealist photographers who assemble their own images use a high level of darkroom and workroom techniques. Their results must look as lifelike and convincing as possible. Printing from several negatives on one piece of paper is a valuable method of blending components, and it allows a mixture of scale and perspective. Sometimes, experts such as Jerry Uelsmann contact print a film positive or make laterally reversed duplicate negatives. These are then sandwiched with the original and enlarged to give negative images or symmetrical patterns. The same techniques can apply to color transparencies. Component images can be photographed to the correct scale and accurately positioned within the viewfinder, then the resulting transparencies sandwiched and enlarged on pos/pos paper.

A relatively simple method of combining two or more images is to project them as slides on the surfaces of objects, and then to photograph the result. Using this method, portraits can be projected over the sides of buildings at dusk, or "sized down" to fill half an eggshell. By directing two projectors on a common screen, a pair of slide images can be montaged, and then the screen copied. Shading one or both light beams allows part of one image to be inserted inside the other, or scenes to merge imperceptibly (see *Projecting slides on objects,* p. 181).

Montage plus image toning and dye or hand coloring with crayon provides great flexibility. The photographer can see the effects instantly and modify at every stage. Air-brushing, in particular, allows very subtle control of tones and colors, especially for combining one component within another. But the work is laborious and time-consuming, and the final print is unique. When several copies are required, the photographer works on an oversized print, then rephotographs it and makes copies that are reduced in size.

Quite small technical preferences can often help to create an individual and highly characteristic image quality. For example, Paul de Nooijer shoots most of his pictures with a wide-angle lens, to give a looming, depth-enhancing effect. His black and white prints are made using a condenser equipped with a small projector-type lamp. This point source exaggerates negative grain in enlargements and gives a "gritty", high-resolution image, like a print from a metal etching plate.

The leading exponents of Surrealism

Many major photographers have, in the course of their careers, experimented with Surrealism. Some have chosen it as the most powerful way of reflecting a quizzical attitude to life, and they find their subjects in the natural environment around them. Others take a different approach, and construct elaborate surrealistic effects in the studio and darkroom, using a multitude of props and special photographic effects such as montage, double exposure, sandwiching transparences, and multiple printing.

The candid approach

Jacques-Henri Lartigue's early pictures, which he took during his childhood, actually precede the surrealist movement in art, but the extraordinary images he caught with his fast shutter speed have a definite surrealistic atmosphere — the people and situations he portrays are both eccentric and humorous. For example, in one of his photographs, a formally dressed man elegantly hurls his terrier across a brook. Many of Lartigue's pictures are spontaneous reactions to events going on around him, but others are the result of his own imagination — he led the subjects on, daring them to perform ever more ambitious feats, and photographed their efforts.

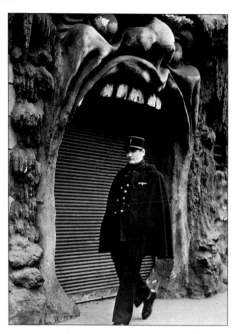

"Cabaret de l'Enfer" (1952)
Robert Doisneau illustrates (above) the surreal possibilities of timing in this picture of a gendarme passing a doorway. People are often unaware of their relationship with the scene around them — posters, signs, and shapes in the background can create bizarre effects.

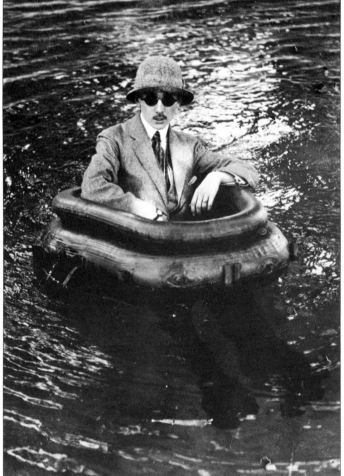

"Zissou in his Tire-Boat" (1906)
Jacques-Henri Lartigue's most surrealistic and humorous pictures were taken when he was very young. Here, Lartigue's brother stands immaculate in his "boat", which is made out of rubber waders attached to a tire.

Many of André Kertész's candid photographs show the strange juxtapositions that people, shadows, and objects make, producing surrealistic effects. He likes to show situations that have an ironic flavor, such as a tree reflected in a puddle along with a model ship being carried on dry land. Or a picture in which an overhead viewpoint shows a stone horse "galloping" in a garden, while outside a dog and its owner take exercise. High viewpoints are a favorite compositional device of Kertész's. They allow him to show two areas that are totally unrelated, or show two separate situations simultaneously.

This enables him to form surrealistic relationships between unconnected elements.

Henri Cartier-Bresson is best known as a photojournalist, but all his training was in Surrealism, and at heart he says he still feels primarily a Surrealist. His surrealistic pictures frequently capture elements together, but his split-second timing of the moment of pressing the shutter creates situations which have far deeper meanings. For example, a crowd watches a procession, while below, out of their sight, a man lies fast asleep on a pile of newspapers. Unlike may of the Surrealists, Cartier-Bresson makes a point of avoiding self-conscious strangeness and contrived oddness. Many of his pictures contain elements which happen to conflict, and which "spark" each other off naturally.

Elliott Erwitt has a gift for capturing humor, and his witty compositions have qualities which are strongly surrealistic. Animals, and particularly dogs, seem to perform especially for his camera, and many of his pictures present the world from an animal's point of view. He shows their relationships with anonymous human beings. For example, a large dog slumps miserably on a sidewalk while human feet hurry, unheedingly, by. Erwitt also delights in showing animals as revealing shapes. He makes witty comparisons with inanimate objects that are similarly shaped and happen to be near by. He is a long-standing member of Magnum Photos, and he makes his living chief-

ly from editorial and advertising photography. Most of his surrealistic, humorous work is done for fun, for his own satisfaction rather than for professional purposes.

The constructed approach

Surrealism is widely used in advertising, fashion photography, and portraiture – and it is usually the result of meticulously planned studio shots, or special effects in the darkroom. Angus McBean, a leading theatrical photographer for over 30 years, made a speciality of creating surrealistic portraits for the *Sketch* during the 1930s, as well as making a series of personal Christmas cards in a similar vein. His pictures were conceived and planned in minute detail, often using specially painted and constructed sets. He used montage techniques and multiple printing to show theater personalities of the day in often outrageous settings. The props used to create these settings often had associations with the show in which the actor or actress was appearing. Usually, McBean would get an idea, then think of a person who would best suit the setting he had in mind. Pictures made the other way around were never quite as successful. His Christmas cards were a *tour de force* – always showing a picture of himself incorporated with a well-known classical figure. He gives rein to his imagination, occasionally allowing a flamboyant, theatrical style to swamp the surrealistic elements.

Cecil Beaton's highly romanticized portraits of English society during the same period (see *The leading exponents of Romanticism and the dramatic,* pp. 375-7) also frequently exploited Surrealism. Evidence of his love for the flamboyant and the incongruous appears in many of his fashion plates made for *Vogue.*

"Florida" (1968)
Elliott Erwitt observes a small occurrence (left) and creates a picture possessing gentle humor. Its simplicity of content helps to emphasize the similar shapes.

"Mexico" (1934)
This picture by Henri Cartier-Bresson (below) shows his strong feel for geometric constructions, plus his ability to observe odd similarities between dissimilar objects (such as the hands and the shoes).

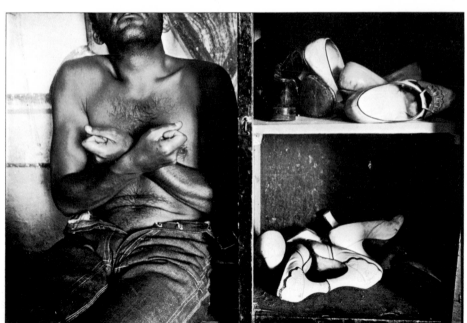

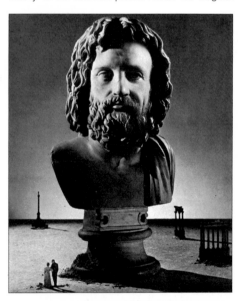

"My Dear I Think it Must be Battersea Park"
Angus McBean describes this Christmas card (above) as "One of the most difficult shots I ever made... we had to do it 51 times before it was right". It is a mixture of double printing, montage, and studio construction.

More decorative in taste and meticulous in style than McBean, Beaton did not make the same elaborate use of technical special effects, but relied on props and staging to achieve his ends. Having spent part of his working life as a theatrical set designer, Beaton was an expert at creating settings, and he placed great emphasis on them in his pictures.

Jerry Uelsmann

The American creative photographer Jerry Uelsmann constructs his surrealistic images in the darkroom. He uses multiple printing techniques to create images, drawing from a vast file of both black and white negatives and positive prints. His pictures frequently involve rocks, trees, human figures, and fragments of landscapes.

Uelsmann uses what he describes as "in-process discovery". He works with a bank of six enlargers and uses them sequentially to combine, merge, or overlap individual components on one image. In this way, the characteristics of photographic materials are allowed to make their own strong contribution to the final image.

He is not forthcoming about the statements his pictures make, preferring that the viewer should decide on their significance. But he has certain favorite themes, which can be found in many of his images — for example, common forms in dissimilar objects, and symbols of renewal and growth. He makes a point of showing weird landscapes, symmetrical

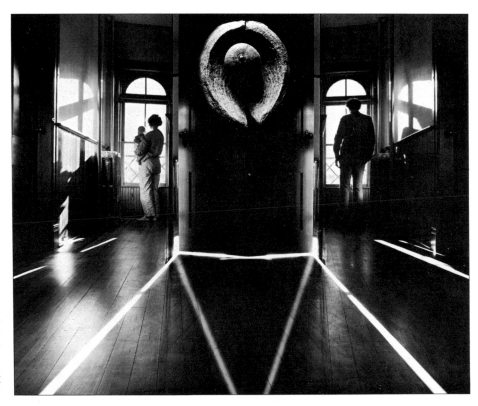

Untitled (1979)
The picture (above) by Jerry Uelsmann seems to concern the family and relationships. At first glance it seems to be a completely symmetrical picture, but a closer look reveals subtle differences — a feature which Uelsmann uses frequently in his work.

Untitled (1980)
Also by Uelsmann, this image (left) is a highly surrealistic use of natural subjects. The block of sky casts its shadow with great realism on the silver sea. Uelsmann goes to great lengths to match up lighting and perspective.

structures, and double reflections in a mixture of negative and positive forms. His much-quoted personal motto is "Robinson and Rejlander live!"

Paul de Nooijer

Like Angus McBean in his early black and white constructions, Paul de Nooijer uses elaborate studio set-ups, but adds extra elements by double-printing. These are usually surrealistic views through doors, windows, and in picture frames. Unlike McBean, De Nooijer hand-colors his prints to add a further sense of fantasy, and so that he can control color emphasis very precisely. His images are bright and often colored unrealistically. He dresses his models outlandishly, and they often look as though they are made out of wax, or are characters from a circus. He is intrigued by pattern — whether it appears in his subjects' costumes, on the walls, or floor coverings. His figures seem even more static and unlifelike because of this.

Sam Haskins

A South African working in Britain, Sam Haskins is an advertising and editorial photographer, shooting mostly in color. He specializes in surreal images, many of them mildly erotic, and with a strong graphic structure. It is easy to see the influence of Magritte in his work — he favors simple, streamlined structures, often spiked with humor. For example, in one of his pictures a giant fish lurks under a tiny boat.

The meaning of Haskins' pictures is easier to understand than are Uelsmann's. His technical skills — particularly his use of sandwiched transparencies and composite color printing — have allowed him to apply successfully the self-expression of Surrealism to the exacting commercial requirements of glossy magazines, calendars, and large-format books.

Bob Carlos Clarke

British photographer Bob Carlos Clarke has a stylized approach to Surrealism. His pictures seem unreal because of his methods of construction. He uses high-contrast black and white prints, montaging, hand-coloring and airbrushing. The resulting scenes sometimes appear lit by moonlight rather than daylight, with deep, black shadows and unexpected color combinations. His pictures are often produced for magazine features and record sleeves. They sometimes incorporate artwork as well, to the extent that they become a hybrid of photography and drawn illustration.

Carlos Clarke's total control over color and his specially photographed components, which are crisp and hard-edged, give figures a metallic, dream-like quality. Often, his themes are erotic, but he satirizes this through witty exaggeration of clothes, pose, and setting. His work is immediately recognizable through his dynamic use of line and his startling, sometimes nightmarish situations, combined with a super-sharp, glossy presentation.

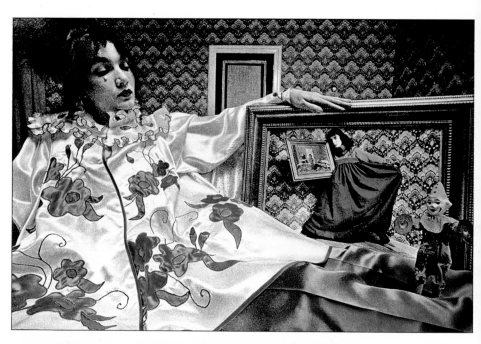

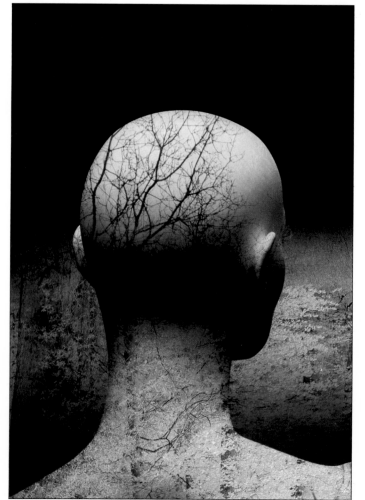

"Pierrot" (1977)
This hand-colored black and white print (above) demonstrates Paul de Nooijer's pre-occupation with pattern and the use of frames.

Figure in landscape (1980)
This picture (left) by Sam Haskins is made from two sandwiched color slides. The spreading branches and tree trunk seem to relate to the body's inner structure of blood vessels and nervous system.

"Pompeii" (1976)
Bob Carlos Clarke's figure in an urban landscape (facing page) is a combination of montage, hand-coloring, and sandwiching on lith paper. Cracked plaster and concrete forms or figures resembling statues recur in his work. This image seems to suggest disintegration — both architectural and human.

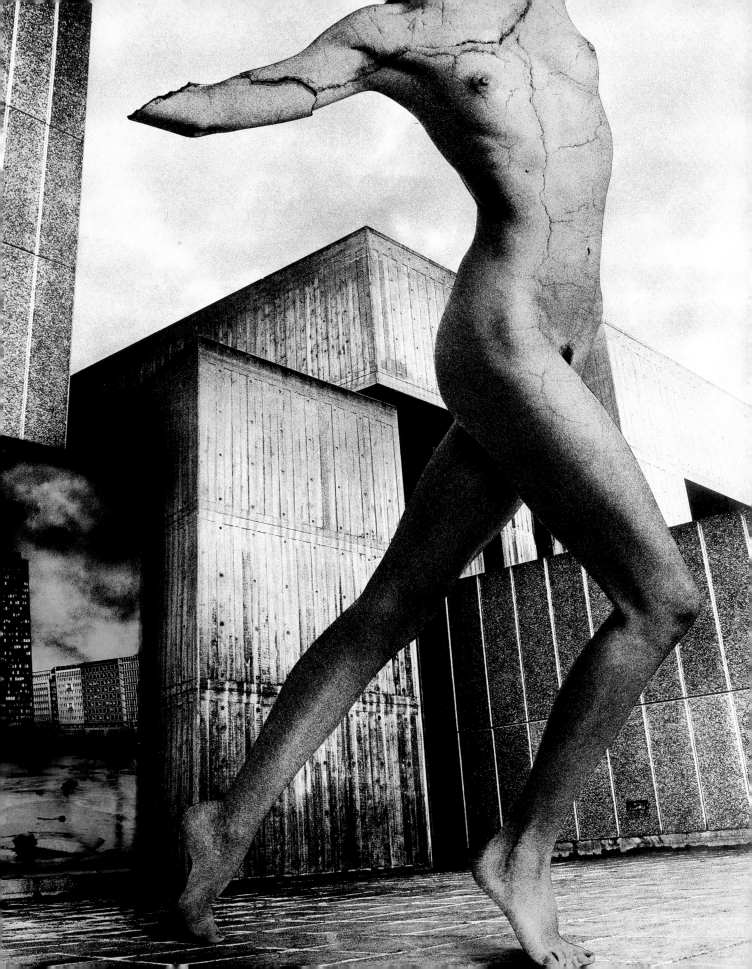

Subject glossary

The information which follows is a concise, practical guide to a range of 47 popular subjects, in alphabetical order. It is designed to be used as a quick reminder of the main points to watch for, the types of equipment required, and some possible approaches and techniques to try. The emphasis is on the basic methods of working, using a minimum of specialized equipment. It highlights the usefulness of certain items such as telephoto and close-up lenses, flash and additional lighting of all kinds, motor drives, and camera supports — so helping the planning of a complete photographic outfit.

Unless otherwise stated, all camera and focal length information applies to 35 mm format equipment. (To calculate the approximate equivalent focal lengths required for the 6 × 6 cm format camera, multiply by a factor of 1.6.)

Aerial views
Choose a window seat on the shaded side of the aircraft. Hold the camera parallel to a clean, unscratched part of the window — thick glass or plexiglass will distort the image if you shoot at an angle. Have the lens close to the window, but not braced against it — vibrations will produce blur on film. Set focus on infinity or the hyperfocal distance and use a fast shutter speed — at least 1/250 sec. A skylight filter will reduce blue cast and haze in air-to-ground shots. Just after take-off or before landing, photograph landscapes and city-scapes — especially as the aircraft banks and you get a more downward-looking view. Long shadows early or late in the day will help to add a sense of depth to the picture and will emphasize textural effects, too. At high altitudes

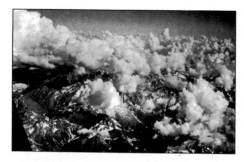

take pictures of dramatic cloud formations. Including part of the aircraft wing in the picture will suggest scale.

Animals see *Pets, Wild Animals,* and *Zoo animals*

Aquaria
Confine photography to flat-sided aquaria — curved bowls can distort the image. Use a tripod and ensure that both glass and water are clean. To avoid reflections mask the camera with a large piece of black cardboard or fabric, leaving a hole for the lens. A second piece of

midtone cardboard, well behind the back of the tank will provide a plain background. Restrict the fish's movements and aid focusing by inserting a sheet of glass to narrow the front-to-back dimensions of the tank, then use the water-filled rear compartment for natural vegetation. Flash gives the most satisfactory lighting — a single unit can be held above and from one side, but far enough back to illuminate the whole picture area evenly.

Architecture
Skillful use of lighting and viewpoint will enhance a building's most impressive features. Study it at different times, and from various angles. Strong angular light will bring out texture and modeling; front-lighting will flatten form but reveal color; back-lighting will emphasize a striking shape, while a white building will take on a pink glow at dawn or sunset. A front-on view will emphasize symmetry or patterning, while shooting from an oblique angle can exaggerate depth by creating a double-perspective effect. A high viewpoint may show a building's relationship with its surroundings, while a low angle will exaggerate height. But tilting the camera upward will cause vertical lines to converge — an effect that is accentuated by a wide-angle lens. Either use this strongly to give a dynamic impression of part of the structure, or avoid it by selecting a higher viewpoint or by using a telephoto lens from a distance. A 28 mm or 35 mm perspective control (or shift) lens will correct converging verticals. But a sheet film camera provides unequalled perspective control and image quality. A wide-angle lens is useful when shooting in cramped conditions, especially interiors, but focal lengths shorter than about 24 mm may exaggerate shapes near at hand. A telephoto lens of about 135 mm or 200 mm will enable you to photograph inaccessible architectural details. A slow to medium film (ASA 25 to 125) will help to resolve maximum detail. A tripod is invaluable indoors. With black and white film, use a deep-yellow or orange filter to darken skies and dramatize clouds. With color film, a polarizing filter will darken skies, increase color saturation, and reduce glare from windows. Try multifacet attachments to help give interpretative results.
See also **Interiors**

Babies and children
When photographing babies, try to fill the frame with the subject — either by using an 85 mm or 135 mm lens or by getting in close with a standard lens. At close range, depth of field is minimal, so focus accurately. It will be necessary to prop up a very young baby with cushions, or hold him or her looking over someone's shoulder (or the back of an armchair), unless you want to photograph the baby lying down. Show the baby occupied — playing, feeding, or being bathed. Avoid cluttered, distracting backgrounds, and try to shoot in soft lighting. Indoors, natural light from a window or bounced flash is best; outside, hazy or overcast conditions provide the

most comfortable lighting. Use medium speed (ASA 125) film and preset exposure at 1/125 sec or flash speed setting. Babies are unpredictable subjects and tire easily, so you must be ready to shoot when an opportunity arises.

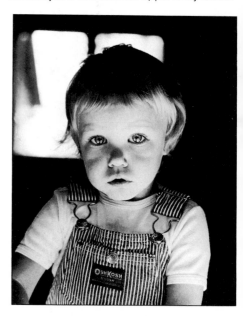

Children become bored and restless, very easily although they are excellent photographic subjects. A low viewpoint is essential, since a picture taken from adult height looking down will distort the subject. Unless you are taking formal portraits, use a hand-held camera and follow movements and expressions through the viewfinder at all times.

Birds
Before selecting a camera position, study the bird's movements and behavior. In a garden, a table or bird bath near the house will help to keep the subject in one spot, and allows a concealed vantage point. Preset focus and exposure, and shoot through a slightly open window, masked with a curtain. Have the camera on a tripod, and use a lens of about 100-200 mm. In open country, leave a food bait to lure birds and facilitate planning your shots. A good way of creating cover for yourself and the camera is to use a hide. Even here a zoom lens of 200-300 mm or a 500 mm lens may be essential to get a reasonable image from a distance, without disturbing the subject.

Another way of working is to set a camera and normal lens on a tripod, wait until birds have accepted its presence, then trigger the shutter by remote control. A motor drive or power winder may also be useful. Choose film fast enough to allow shutter speeds of 1/250 sec or less, especially if you wish to capture movement or use the camera hand-held. If light is insufficient or from the wrong direction when photographing a nest, use flash. The shutter speed required to freeze wing movement of birds in flight using natural light will vary according to subject size, distance, and direction of movement. Preset your exposure reading from ground detail similar in tone to the bird. Try panning the camera.

Candid portraits
The secret of expressive candid portraiture is to remain as unobtrusive as possible, either by concealing the camera or yourself, or by shooting when the subject is occupied in some activity. A wide-aperture, or a 100 mm or 135 mm telephoto lens allows you to take pictures from a distance without too much flattening of perspective. And by taking advantage of its limited depth of field you can isolate the subject from distracting surroundings. If it is impossible to remain unobserved, shoot frequently so that your presence begins to be taken for granted.

Smooth camera handling and a good sense of timing will help to capture the climax in a verbal exchange, or the momentary gesture or expression that sums up the subject's character. Set exposure in advance, reading

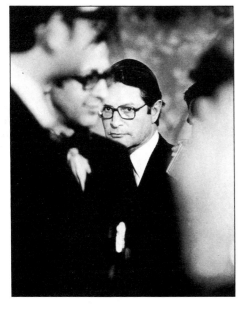

off your hand. You may also be able to pre-focus, using the distance scale or focusing on something about the same distance away in another direction. Try to use a shutter speed of 1/250 sec or faster. ASA 400 film and an f 2 or f 2.8 lens will allow hand-held shutter speeds in most indoor conditions. Sometimes the camera can be rested on a table or against a door frame. Always shoot by existing light — flash will tend to destroy mood and realism.

Candlelight
Candlelight creates an evocative atmosphere and, with the proper equipment, it can be used successfully for photography. As it has a low color temperature it records with a deep-orange cast on daylight-type slide film, and a warm cast on tungsten-light slide film, or negative film. This often adds atmosphere. Using ASA 400 film and an f 1.8 lens, you can take portraits close to candles at 1/15 or 1/30 sec. If the subject is a still life (a celebratory cake, or a church statue, for example) stop down

and use a tripod to allow long exposures. For candlelit portraits, be aware of dramatic contrast that such a localized light source creates a bank of several candles gives softer, more even, illumination. If you want a larger area to be illuminated, make careful use of diffused flash or low-level room lighting for fill-in. Direct, on-camera flash will destroy the realism of candlelight.

Carnivals and processions
Carnivals and processions are ideal for photographing colorful displays and lively candid portraits. At a formal procession, research the route beforehand and choose a strategic viewpoint. Consider lighting direction, and the possibilities of a high viewpoint for a clear view. If this is not feasible, shoot above other spectators' heads by holding the camera up high, with outstretched arms. A waist-level viewfinder camera can be held upside-down. In a restricted area, such as a narrow street, concentrate on close-ups of costumes and faces, using a medium-length telephoto lens. Also take wide-angle shots within the jostling crowd. Most processions move slowly, so shutter speed is not a problem, and you are free to stop down for maximum depth of field. Try a few shots at 1/15 or 1/8 sec with the camera firmly supported. This will give impressionistic images with a sense of flowing movement and color.

Celebrations see *Parties and celebrations*

Ceramics see *Silver and ceramics*

Circuses
Obtain permission to take photographs and then see the show through once before you begin shooting. This enables you to plan viewpoint and note the most photogenic peaks in the performance. If possible, choose an aisle seat several rows back from the ring, and try to include spectators in some of your shots. An f 2 or f 1.8 standard lens will be useful for high-wire and trapeze acts. Circuses tend to have dim overhead lighting, plus spotlights, centered on the ring. Use tungsten-light film and attach a lens hood to prevent flare. First take exposure readings from the ring when it is lit generally, and in a pool of spotlight. These are the main settings for the show, which you can vary as conditions change. Many circus acts are slow-moving, but sometimes it will be difficult to get a fast enough shutter speed to stop the action. Either uprate the film or shoot the peak of action — for example, when a trapeze artist reaches the top of a swing. With equestrian acts, try panning. Never use flash.

Clouds see *Skies and clouds*

Coins and medals
Close-up equipment is essential to fill the frame adequately with an object as small as a coin. Shoot from above, with the camera mounted on a tripod, and expose on slow film for maximum resolution. Use a diffused flood well back and at an oblique angle to the subject, with a reflector on the other side to reveal form and detail. A spotlight directed across the surface will emphasize relief, but will also cast a shadow on the subject's far side. To avoid this, either photograph it on a

plain, dark, non-reflective material, or increase the distance between the subject and background. Place it on a pedestal of modeling clay, so that the background and shadow is out of focus, or photograph it raised on a sheet of glass, or on a light box. Axial light through thin glass placed at 45° below the lens gives the best wholly frontal illumination. Use a lens hood to prevent flare.

Concerts see *Stage performances*

Copying objects
When you are making an exact copy of a painting, print, stamp, or any other flat object, make sure that the lens is precisely centered and that the camera back is parallel to the subject. A simple method is to put the camera on a tripod and attach the subject to the wall or floor. A standard lens is best for large subjects, but if it is as small as a stamp, use a macro lens, extension tubes or bellows. A more sophisticated method for small subjects is to use a copypod or copying stand.

Lighting must be even, whether it is daylight, tungsten lamps, or flash. With artificial lighting, place a lighting unit on either side of the camera at 45° to the subject, and far enough away to evenly illuminate the whole surface. If you must use glass to keep the subject flat, or you have to photograph a painting behind glass, mask off the tripod with black cardboard to prevent reflections. Ideally, eliminate glare from a glossy surface by using polarizing filters over both the lens and light sources. Use slow film to record maximum detail. When copying engravings or ink drawings in black and white use high-contrast line or lith film.

Crowds see *Groups and crowds*

Dance see *Stage performances*

Fireworks
Multiple firework explosions in the sky make far more spectacular pictures than single bursts. You can either make a double or triple

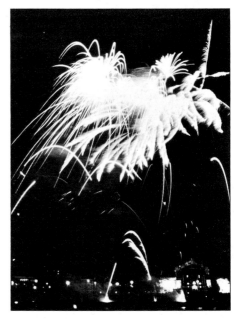

exposure, or mount the camera on a tripod and record the light trails of several bursts during a time exposure, covering the lens between explosions to avoid over-recording local illumination. Try using an aperture of f 8 or f 11 with ASA 200 film. Keep the lens open long enough to record the full burst of a firework, and if shooting several, try to expose them in different parts of the frame. A TLR or direct vision camera will allow you to observe the subject continuously while you are shooting.

Try to include reflective water or interesting silhouettes in the foregrounds of general views of displays. If shooting on transparency film, daylight-type film will give the most accurate color record of fireworks. If you are using ASA 400 film, you will be able to make short (1/30 sec) exposures of spectators' faces, provided that they are brightly lit either by fireworks or by a nearby bonfire.

Fish see *Aquaria, Underwater life*

Flowers and plants
When photographing flowers your results will be far more informative and appealing if you restrict your shots to a single flower head or a few blooms, rather than incorporating a large mass. To get right up close and fill the frame, you require a macro lens, extension tubes or bellows. Depth of field is limited close up, and focusing is critical, so camera and subject must be kept quite still. Use a tripod and windshield (which can double as a reflector if necessary).

Choose unobtrusive surroundings, remove distracting objects, but keep the setting natural. Use plain cardboard as a backdrop, and shoot tall plants against the sky. At close range, selective focusing will blur the background. Back-lighting reveals translucent petals, while side-lighting emphasizes delicate texture. Strong but diffused daylight is best for bringing out a flower's color. You can spray flowers lightly with water to add a dewy effect. Another approach, if the photograph is to show the flower as a botanical specimen, is to place it on a lightbox, and position a reflector or light over it. Mask off the glass outside the picture area in order to minimize flare.

Fog see *Weather*

Frost see *Snow, ice, and frost*

Glass
Photographing glassware can be problematic because it is transparent and it both transmits and reflects light. Choose lighting and background with care, and pay careful attention to controlling where highlights fall if you intend to show the form and outline of glass objects with maximum clarity and bring out their sparkling quality.

The choice of lighting set-up will depend on which feature of the glass you want to accentuate. Back-lighting by illuminating white or pale-toned background placed well behind the glass objects emphasizes their shape and translucency. (Tracing paper hung in front of a window has a similar effect.) It is particularly effective for etched or cut glass, or glass containing colored liquid. Using a dark background instead and lighting the glass from

above highlights rims and creates strong tonal contrast. And directing light up at a glass object from underneath highlights the base and lower surfaces. Work with one main light source, adding a subsidiary one if you want to highlight or gradate the background area or reduce shadows.

Always diffuse the light sources which are used directly on the glass, whether you use tungsten or flash, or you will cause glaring specular highlights. With a light background you can position black cardboard on both sides of the subject to create dark edgelines. With a dark background use white cardboard instead. Slow film will help to reveal fine detail. When using a light background arrangement read exposure off the background alone. With directly lit glass and a dark background, take the exposure reading of mid-gray cardboard placed near the subject.
See also **Stained glass**

Groups and crowds
Formal groups demand skillful organization. Tallest people should be at the back, smallest in front. All faces should be clearly visible and evenly lit. For strict uniformity, ask people to sit in the same way. When the group is to appear informal, take care over timing and atmosphere. Try to avoid excessive gaps. Heads should be at different levels and the atmosphere should be as relaxed as possible. Place props in the foreground to help contribute mood and unity (if the people are musicians, include their instruments, or if they are sports team, add some of their items of equipment).

For crowd shots, use a high viewpoint if possible, framing so that colors and shapes create a pleasing pattern. Outdoors, make sure that faces are not obscured by ugly shadows, or eyes squinting into the light. Diffused, even lighting is usually the most flattering. Indoors, existing light may necessitate the use of ASA 400 film. If using flash instead, make sure that all your subjects are within flash range by keeping the flash source as high as possible.

Ice see *Snow, ice, and frost*

Insects
Good close-up equipment is vital for photographing all but the largest insects. A lens (preferably macro) of about 100 mm plus extension tubes is useful for subjects that you are unable to approach very closely. Accurate focusing is critical when working close up as depth of field is extremely limited. You will find that it is easier to preset the focus, and then move very slightly back and forth, stopping to release the shutter only when focus is perfectly sharp.

If you are photographing *in situ* use fast (ASA 400) film – you will often have to compromise between a small enough aperture for adequate depth of field and a fast enough shutter to prevent camera shake. Generally it is best to rely on flash as your light source – especially ring flash, which can be attached to the end of the lens as one unit. Photographing insects in the field demands a high degree of patience and a sound knowledge of your subject's habits. You will often have to wait until an insect stops to feed

before there is enough time to obtain a finely detailed shot.

It is simpler to achieve good pictures of insects in the studio – background and lighting can be carefully chosen and controlled to simulate natural conditions. Back-lighting, for example, will bring out the detailed pattern and translucency of an insect's wing. Insect's life cycles are very good subjects for time-lapse photography. Photographing insects on the wing is extremely difficult, if not impossible, unless you construct a special set-up that includes high-speed flash and an automatic triggering device.

Interiors
Photographing a domestic interior allows maximum control over the subject – you can move furniture and alter lighting. Shoot from a high viewpoint for a broad view, or concentrate on a particular corner. Ensure that the floor is level and that verticals align with the frame sides. A wide-angle lens of 35 mm or 28 mm will be essential when working in cramped conditions. A shift lens will help to correct converging verticals, but a sheet-film camera offers the greatest range of camera movements. Available lighting will usually show the subject most atmospherically, but you may have to deal with excessive contrast and decide between exposing for highlights and so recording black shadows, or allowing very bright areas such as windows to burn out. (Although with careful control, artificial or mixed lighting can reduce contrast and give good natural results, too.) Another way to balance daylighting is by filling in shadow areas with diffused flash. At night, light the room with domestic tungsten lights and lamps, and use tungsten-light film for natural effects. Reduce contrast in dark areas or in large, dim corners by painting with light.

Landscapes
Weather, time of day, and the seasons are all factors which affect dramatically the appearance of landscapes, so select lighting conditions which enhance the subject's most striking features. In summer, light before mid-morning or after mid-afternoon will create long shadows that emphasize form. Or use glowing skies at dawn or sunset to backlight a landscape silhouette. High, midday sun will flatten form and cast short, dense shadows.

Strong composition is essential in landscape photography. Try to compose your pictures around a center of interest and avoid general views. Position the horizon low if the sky is dramatic, or high to emphasize foreground. Use foreground objects to produce a sense of scale, or to frame a scene. Lead the viewer's eye into the picture, perhaps with a river or road receding into the distance, or suggest scale by including a small figure. Use a low viewpoint to make foreground elements dominate the picture and set landscape features against the sky.

A wide-angle lens, to show breadth and space, offers sharp focus throughout the scene. It exaggerates linear perspective, especially when combined with a low viewpoint. A telephoto lens will add impact to distant elements by making them appear stacked up close behind each other. A UV filter will reduce excessive blueness in atmospheric haze, and a polarizing filter can intensify blue skies. Experiment with gradated filters, too. When using black and white film, use a medium-yellow filter to brighten greens and define clouds. It is advisable to tilt the camera downward slightly when measuring exposure, so that ground detail is calculated for precisely, rather than the sky exclusively. See also **Mountains, Seascapes**

Lightning
It is impossible to predict exactly when lightning will occur, so it is best to work during a storm at night, when the shutter can be left open without overexposing. Mount the camera on a tripod and set the shutter on B. Hold it open to incorporate several flashes, as when shooting fireworks. The more flashes you incorporate in the shot, the lighter the rest of the sky and the landscape will be. Look for interesting shapes on the skyline that will appear in silhouette and add a sense of scale. A wide-angle lens will enable you to maintain surveillance over a large area of sky. Focus the lens on infinity and set an aperture of f 11 (ASA 200 film). Then bracket the aperture widely so that you have a variety of results.

Medals see Coins and Medals

Mist see Weather

Moon
Taking a picture of the moon with a regular camera is perfectly possible, although the relative movement of earth and moon during exposures longer than a few minutes will record the moon as an elongated white shape. The best time to shoot is when the moon is full, or a few days before, when it rises early. If the moon is to form part of a landscape use a lens between 85 mm and 135 mm, to include the horizon and trees or other foreground objects. At twilight the exposure that is required for the landscape will be the same as that necessary to photograph the moon. Continue to take pictures at regular intervals as the last daylight fades from the sky.

Typical exposure for the moon is 1/60 sec at f 8 (ASA 200 film). Color film should be daylight-balanced. For pictures featuring the moon alone use your longest-possible focal length lens, perhaps with a tele-converter. A 500 mm lens with a × 2 converter gives a moon image about 1 cm diameter on the film. Also try shooting through one eyepiece of a pair of binoculars. Have both binoculars and

camera on tripods, the camera and its standard lens about 30 cm from the eyepiece. Close the gap with a black cardboard tube, and set the camera to its widest lens aperture, and infinity. Adjust focus with the binocular controls alone. The best time to shoot these pictures is when the moon is only half or three-quarters illuminated. The terminator, or boundary, between the lit and unlit parts will emphasize the moon's uneven surface.

Mountains
Conveying the sheer scale of mountain landscape can be a problem. A too distant or too wide-angle view may make a mountain range seem disappointingly small, while a near view may distort perspective and leave out foreground. The best solution is often to choose a viewpoint from which a telephoto lens of about 100 mm to 200 mm will enlarge distant mountains, so that their height is magnified and any aerial perspective effects present are accentuated, and yet still include some elements in the mid-distance in order to add a frame to the view.

When shooting on black and white film, use a yellow or orange filter, and for color a haze filter to combat the bluish UV haze common at high altitudes. If the scene is snowy, take care that the exposure meter is not misled by the brilliant glare into underexposing the scene and losing shadow detail. Bracket by half a stop over and under the recommended exposure. Early morning or late afternoon, when long shadows help to model contours, are excellent times of day to shoot, or at sunrise or sunset, when warm light reduces the blue appearance of shadows.

Nudes
When photographing the nude, you are dealing with the tones, shapes, and textures of the human body. You can portray the entire body in a flattering way, or concentrate on parts of it, to create an abstract composition of lines and forms. Take advantage of the exaggerated perspective of a wide-angle lens when used close up, to attenuate limbs. Use a lens of a focal length of 85 mm or 135 mm to fill the frame with small areas of the body, or use longer lenses to compress depth and scale. By experimenting with different viewpoints and lighting, you can do much to compensate for a model's shortcomings or emphasize the best qualities. For example, it is possible to enhance a long, graceful neck if the head is stretched back.

It is usually more comfortable to photograph nudes indoors, where you have privacy, warmth, and lighting control. Shooting near a window, with the subject lit softly from behind creates a silhouette. If you expose for the window, the contours of the body will be stressed even more. Strong side-lighting models form and reveals texture. You can reduce excessive contrast by using reflectors or diffused flash to fill shadows. When shooting with artificial illumination, diffuse or bounce your lights to bring out the smooth texture of skin and soften contours. Or use a diffusion or effects filter to achieve a romantic, soft-focus effect. Out of doors, directional lighting will give dramatic effects, but an overcast sky will flatter skin tones. Nude photography is equally successful in black and

white and color. Black and white tends to be more mysterious and graphic and is useful for suppressing distracting colors in the background. Most pictures are taken on slow film to preserve tonal and tactile qualities of the subject, but the graininess of high-speed (or pushed) film gives interesting impressionistic results, too.

Occupations
Always obtain permission before photographing people in their place of work. Before starting, watch work in progress, and plan shots carefully. Choose angles that give a clear view of the activity against an appropriate background which is not too assertive. A lens of about 85 mm or 100 mm will offer a narrow angle of view and shallow depth of field, which will make the subject stand out from a busy environment. It will also allow you to close in on details such as hands or faces without disturbing the subject. If conditions are cramped and space limited, use a wide-angle lens to include more information in the picture or to create a sense of dramatic perspective.

Choose a viewpoint which accentuates the relationship of the person with the work they are doing, and which unifies the two. Close-ups of hands or still lifes of tools can make telling pictures. Available light will often capture the atmosphere of a place, and in very dim conditions you may require fast film of ASA 400, possibly uprated. Find out existing lighting conditions in advance and take the necessary balancing filters if you are shooting in color, especially on slide film. In mixed lighting be prepared for color casts. Either make a feature of them, or switch off one source and match film or filtration for the other. If you require any additional lighting, bounce flash off a nearby, light-colored surface, or light up the entire setting with a multihead flash unit.

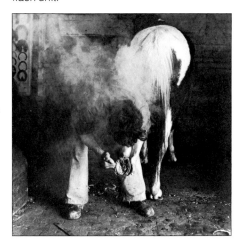

Parties and celebrations
Quick candid shooting is best for photographing parties and celebrations, to capture unrepeatable moments and fleeting expressions. Plan a sequence of shots to show the whole occasion. At Christmas, for example, your pictures might include unwrapping presents, the dinner spread, the tree, as well as family groups. Wherever possible preserve the spirit of the occasion by shooting in existing light

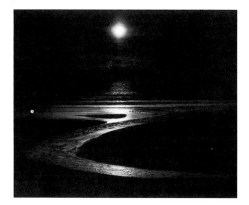

(daylight, domestic tungsten lamps, or candlelight). Even if you use daylight film in tungsten light, the orange cast often adds an acceptable warm appearance to the shots. Alternatively, use compatible tungsten slide film or a color-balancing filter. Flash may kill the mood of a party shot unless it is skillfully controlled. Try to use it bounced, or off camera, or combine it with daylight from a window to fill in shadow areas. When shooting by available light you will need your widest aperture lens and you must focus carefully or use an autofocus camera. (Remember, too, the advantages of an instant picture camera for these occasions.) The wider angle of view and depth of field of a 28 mm or 24 mm lens are useful to incorporate a group seated around a table. Make sure that faces close to the camera, at sides or corners of the picture are not distorted. Use a low viewpoint, at table height, to pick out individual faces. Or use a high viewpoint to give a more general view showing everyone, and making a feature of table contents. Remember, too, that it is always effective to use features such as a mirror, an archway, a window, or a doorway to act as a frame for a scene.

Pets

Plan pet photography to take into account the best lighting arrangements and viewpoints to bring out the animal's most striking qualities. Find a way of holding its interest before you start shooting — for example, by photographing it while eating or playing. Use someone else to attract attention at the moment of pressing the shutter, so that the animal looks alert. Choose a viewpoint at its own level — shot from above, a cat or dog's head will look out of proportion, while the legs and body will appear flattened by foreshortening. Kneel down or squat, focusing on the eyes, and choose a viewpoint that shows them with

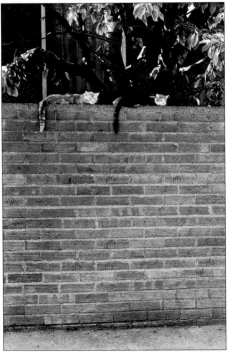

highlights. A telephoto lens of up to 135 mm is the best for close-up shots — it records proportions faithfully and allows you to use the camera without crowding the animal. And its shallow depth of field can be useful for putting a distracting background out of focus. Avoid using a close viewpoint and wide-angle lens for portraits of pets — otherwise the head will appear distorted.

Go for backgrounds of a plain, contrasting tone that isolate and emphasize the subject — perhaps by lead-in lines. Outdoors, a grass lawn or the sky is suitable, but a brightly colored mass of flowers is best avoided. Indoors, use a blanket or carpet. Small, active pets, such as hamsters or mice, may have to be held firmly. It can be a mistake to over-enlarge small puppies or kittens. Keep them fairly small in the frame and stress their size by including an object of known size for the sake of comparison.

Wherever possible, use natural lighting — or off-camera flash. Side-lighting will model the animal's body and bring out the texture of the fur, while back-lighting will surround the animal with a halo of lit fur, but you may require a reflector to preserve some shadow detail. When taking action shots of pets, you can freeze movement with flash or a shutter speed of 1/500 sec if lighting conditions permit. Excellent results are also possible by panning at 1/30 or 1/60 sec as the animal runs past. In general, work at about 1/125 sec using film of ASA 200 or faster.
See also **Aquaria**

Plants see *Flowers and plants*

Portraits

Many people become self-conscious and stiff in front of the camera, so look for ways of relaxing your subject and shoot rapidly and unobtrusively. Choose an environment where your subject feels at home and move around, studying the face from all sides. Choose a camera angle that makes the most of features — a low viewpoint makes a long face seem shorter, a head-on one broadens a wide face.

A medium telephoto lens of about 100 mm is generally preferred for close-up portraits as it permits shooting from some distance and so records the face without exaggerated perspective effects. Only use the steep perspective given by close viewpoint and a wide-angle lens if you want to make a virtue of the distortions — as in caricatures or special effects. A standard lens is quite suitable for taking either a head-and-shoulders or full-length portrait.

Shoot when your subject's pose and expression are characteristic, paying particular attention to the eyes and mouth. Always focus on the eyes and measure exposure from the face, averaging shadow and highlight readings. Always take lighting direction and quality into consideration. Oblique, diffused lighting is often the most flattering for outdoor portraits, giving good modeling and skin texture. Back-lighting accentuates the shape of the head and rimlights the hair or profile. Avoid direct light from overhead sun — it causes heavy shadow in the eyes and under the nose and chin and is usually unflattering. Facing directly into the sun will also force your subject to screw up the eyes in order to avoid the

harsh effects of glare.

Indoors, use natural light if it is bright enough — you may require ASA 400 film if hand-holding the camera, or use a tripod. Place your subject near a window for a dramatic contrast of highlights and shadows, or create a softer, more romantic mood by diffusing the light with gauze or net and using a paper reflector nearby to fill in shadow areas. Moving your subject away from the window, toward a facing reflective wall also reduces contrast.

Studio portraiture offers maximum control of lighting. Tungsten illumination allows you to see how light models features; with flash you must predict the effect, unless your flash head has a modeling light. It is generally best not to use on-camera flash for portraits. When shooting with more than one light source, use one light as the main one and another to bounce light into the shadows or to illuminate one specific area of the subject or the background details.
See also **Candids, Groups and crowds, Self portraits.**

Processions see *Carnivals and processions*

Rain see *Weather*

Sculpture

When photographing sculpture or bas-reliefs, choose camera angle and lighting with care to avoid such results as dominant foreground features or deeply shadowed eye sockets. The best viewpoint may be the one from which the sculptor intended the piece to be seen. But sometimes an unusual angle can create a more dynamic effect or relate the work dramatically to its setting. A low, close viewpoint will exaggerate height and solidity and relate it to trees and sky; a high one will foreshorten the subject and draw attention to upper surfaces and ground detail. For an abstract work several different angles may be required to give a comprehensive record. Often a close-up detail of the work will show the sculptor's craftsmanship better than a view of the whole piece. A telephoto lens of about 100 mm, if necessary with an extension tube, records subject detail without exaggerated perspective. A longer, 150-300 mm zoom is an asset for photographing inaccessible sculptural details on buildings such as distant gargoyles and decorative moldings. A sturdy tripod with a pan-and-tilt head offers support for long telephoto lenses and during a time exposure. When photographing sculpture you are unlikely to have total control over lighting levels. Outdoors, soft, even lighting often reveals form well, but harder side-lighting may be useful if you want to enhance rough texture or bas-relief. Harsh front-lighting tends to flatten form, while back-lighting emphasizes outline. A reflector or flash unit can be used to fill in shadow areas of small or large pieces respectively. If blue sky is to form the background, use a dark-yellow filter with black and white film, or a polarizing filter with color film. In churches, sculpture is often unevenly lit — ask permission if you want to supplement existing lighting with flash. Art galleries usually offer more sensitive lighting, but you may have to add a reflector or use flash to reduce or increase contrast, perhaps to accentuate a particular quality.

Seascapes

A head-on view, looking straight out to sea, may lack interest unless lighting conditions are dramatic. Broad expanses of water and sand, undifferentiated in tone, tend to look flat and uninteresting. Move back and include a strong shape in the foreground to add a sense of distance, or shoot along the shoreline, from a low viewpoint, to capture turbulent waves. Including foreground reflections in wet sand also adds interest. To photograph waves at their best, time your shots so that you press the shutter just before a wave breaks. Try a range of shutter speeds – from 1/500 sec, which should freeze movement, to 1/8 sec to show its flow.

Watch the sea carefully to observe how it changes in appearance with weather and lighting direction. At midday, colors are flat, and overhead sun suppresses texture. Lit by an overcast sky, the sea may look leaden. Low, angular lighting will enhance the sea's broken surface, while back-lighting will bring out its shimmering quality. Take care over exposure. By exposing for highlights, you will capture the water's sparkling quality, but you may lose shadow areas – so increase this exposure by at least one stop. A reading averaged from shadow and highlit areas is often the best solution, then make bracketed exposures (on slide film they can be underexposed at half-stop intervals). A lens hood is essential for sunlit seascapes. Use a UV or skylight filter to reduce bluish haze as well as to protect the lens from salt spray. An polarizing filter helps to intensify colors and minimize glare, and a gradated sky filter is sometimes useful to influence mood.

Self portraits

The main ways of photographing yourself are by using the delayed action release, remote control, a long cable release, or a mirror. A delayed action release or attachment gives you time to take up position in a pre-arranged spot after setting focus and lighting for a stand-in object or person. (A mirror behind the camera helps you to pose quickly.) You can use this method for including yourself in a group, too. Using a remote control or a long cable or electrical release makes the process much easier – you can conceal the release behind you or operate it with your foot.

Taking a self portrait in a mirror makes it harder to predict exactly what will be included in the viewfinder. You mount the camera on a tripod, then take a picture of your own reflection with the camera either against your face or at arm's length, slightly angled from one side of the mirror. Focus on a stand-in subject and stop down to maximize depth of field. Bear in mind that the reflection is effectively the same distance behind the mirror as the subject is in front. A window on the same wall as the mirror gives the best lighting. If you add lighting, make sure tht it does not shine directly on either the mirror or the lens.

Silver and ceramics

To shoot both polished silver and glazed ceramic subjects, you must know how to control reflections, and avoid distortion. Eye-catching views of the camera or surroundings will distract attention away from the subject and confuse its shape. You can minimize them by diffusing or bouncing the light source or by using a matting spray on the object. Or, with less reflective ceramics, you can position a simple outline in front of the main light to reflect as a window or some other shape. If the subject is highly reflective it can be set up on a large sheet of white cardboard, which is bent to pass under and behind it. Use a large, diffused light source close to one side to model the subject, or behind it to show its shape. If desired, you can use a second light to illuminate the background, on the side of the subject, that falls in shadow, so that it stands away from it.

Another approach is to use a tent of muslin or a drum-shaped arrangement of tracing paper to envelop the set. Direct lights on to its outer surface, and make a hole for the camera lens to look through. Ornamental or engraved pieces require side-lighting to show relief. Select a camera distance and angle that record the true proportions of an object. Use a lens focal length slightly longer than standard. A viewpoint above center is preferable to a low one which makes short, round objects look oval-shaped. A large-format camera with drop front is very useful in order to avoid creating vertical lines that converge toward the bottom of the frame.

Skies and clouds

The sky is at its most dramatic when it is changing (during storms, at dawn or sunset, and in spring or fall). It is so variable in color, shape, and mood that it can make a picture in itself. Flat, open expanses of land are good foundations for skyscapes, providing an uninterrupted vista of sky and clouds. A wide-angle lens takes in the broadest view and conveys a sense of limitless space, while a telephoto lens reduces perspective and allows you to concentrate on one striking area. In most cases you should read exposure from clear areas of the sky, not the land or sea. When conditions are stormy, exposing for the bright shafts of light will intensify colors and make the clouds stand out. With black and white film, use a yellow, orange, or red filter to dramatize the contrast between white clouds and sky. With color, intensify the blue of the sky with a polarizing filter, or tint it with a gradated filter. To take a picture of a rainbow, use a suitable focal length lens to include the whole setting (a wide-angle lens will probably be the best choice) and a UV filter to darken the sky and intensify color generally. Underexpose by at least one stop in order to increase color saturation, and select a slow film.

Snow, ice, and frost

Snow provides a perfect background for bright, vibrant colors and it outlines shapes. Use slow film (ASA 25 to 100) as snow is bright and highly reflective. Daylit snow looks best when shot in the glancing light of morning or evening sun, when long shadows add depth and modeling while enhancing the snow's crisp texture. In general, avoid overcast conditions, when snow will appear flat and predominantly gray. Shooting at dawn adds a cold, blue cast to snow; at sunset it takes on glowing sky colors. The greatest problem when photographing sunlit snow is accurate exposure due to the extreme contrast – bracketing is essential. Large areas of bright snow will fool the camera meter into under-exposing small but important darker areas if you take a general reading. Add at least half a stop to help pick out detail in the shadow areas, or average the highlight and shadow readings. Or take one reading from a hand or face to get an average.

To emphasize falling snow, choose a viewpoint which gives a dark background. A shutter speed of 1/250 sec shows falling snow as clear-cut specks. Photographed with a shutter speed of 1/4 or 1/8 sec, they will be recorded as blurred white streaks, to give a blizzard-like effect. In sunlit snow, use a lens hood to cut down flare, and a UV or haze filter to reduce the excessive blue cast from the sky in shadow areas.

Ice and frost details must be photographed in early morning, lit from the side or from behind. Frame tightly and take a reading from the very bright, glittering detail itself, so that the background is made much darker and more subdued.

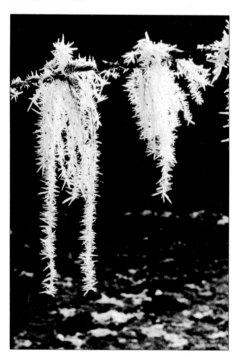

Sport

For any kind of sports photography, you need a wide-aperture lens, since you are frequently dealing with rapid action and will require sufficient light to give a fast shutter speed. In addition, fast film is preferable – especially for indoor activities (black and white film is available in higher speeds than color). Knowledge of the sport you are shooting will enable you to anticipate key moments. With some sports, such as high jump or gymnastics, you can take advantage of repetitive movements in order to select actions or postures that are typically expressive of that particular sport. To freeze movement, you must have quick reflexes to react instantly to the action, as well as a very fast shutter speed. The exact speed you use will depend on how far away your subject is, and the direction of the movement. Attach a power winder to your camera, so that it can be kept up to your eye.

When shooting indoors, you are seldom able to use flash for sports photography. If you have to rely on poor available light, however, convey speed and energy by letting the action blur with a slower shutter speed. Zooming also creates a dynamic effect. At track events pan the camera to freeze the subject and create a blurred background and give an impression of speed. This technique will also help to separate the subject from its surroundings.

A telephoto lens of at least 200 mm is essential to give a sufficient-sized image of subjects such as baseball players and cricketers, but it does tend to flatten perspective and dwarf the subject with the background. For subjects that you can shoot from a close viewpoint, a standard lens is a better choice, while a wide-angle lens will dramatize action by exaggerating perspective, when used from a close, low viewpoint. Select a viewpoint close to the main area of action – near the goal at a soccer match, or by a jump at a horse show, for example. Do not try to follow the action by constantly moving around – wait until it comes near and be ready to shoot, with focus and exposure preset. A motor drive allows you to record fast action sequences. *See also* **Winter sports**

Stage performances
You must obtain permission beforehand if you want to photograph a public performance. An amateur company is more likely to grant permission, while a professional one may allow you to attend a dress rehearsal or photocall. See the whole show through once before shooting, so that you can plan what equipment and viewpoints to use, and note climaxes in the action. Try to sit off-center and above stage level. A central view may give your pictures a two-dimensional and over formal impression. Use fast black and white film, or tungsten-balanced color film with a fast lens. Take a tripod.

Stage lighting can be very colorful, but it is also unpredictable and variable in intensity. Exposure is easier to gauge accurately when the whole stage is lit for a large group. When one or two figures are spotlit on a large, darkened stage, you will overexpose them if you take a general light reading. As a rough guide, keep to the exposure you used when the whole stage was illuminated. With a spot meter (or a spare body with TTL metering, and equipped with a telephoto lens) you can take exact readings of small areas from a distance. Also shoot from the wings, to get intimate shots of small spotlit groups, or the tense last moments before a member of the cast goes on stage. Ask if you can go backstage and, using ASA 400 film, photograph the cast either before or after the performance. Do not use flash – it will annoy your subjects and tend to produce an unnatural atmosphere.

When photographing dance, you may be able to use flash to obtain a sharp image in rehearsal or at a photocall. With a slow shutter speed you will be able to achieve highly effective results with blur – and this may express the rhythmic flow of movement in a far more effective way than pinsharp definition is capable of.

Stained glass
Successful photography of stained glass relies on getting sufficiently close and square-on to your subject, and using compatible lighting conditions and background. Framing a small area of the glass often makes a more striking picture than one which includes the whole window. To show a small detail of stained glass, use a telephoto lens from a balcony on the opposite wall, or clamp the camera to a ladder or steps. Make sure that the film plane is exactly parallel to the window. If you want to photograph the whole of a large, high window from ground level, a shift lens or camera with rising front will be necessary. In most cases you will also require a tripod, as the lighting is likely to be dim. For best color rendition, choose a day with bright but diffused sunlight, white cloud forming a background outside the window. Avoid times of day when the sun is shining directly through the glass, as it may affect both exposure and color reproduction and accentuate the shapes of subjects, such as trees, outside. If this is unavoidable, open the aperture right up in order to minimize depth of field. Always read exposure from the glass, not from the building interior – close-up exposure readings averaged from a variety of colors will give the truest exposure. When taking photographs of stained glass lit by daylight from outside, always use daylight film. For transparencies of stained glass lit from inside at night, but taken from outside, use a tungsten-balanced film.

Stamps see *Copying objects*

Sun
Photograph the sun at dawn or sunset, when atmospheric scatter reduces the contrast between sun and sky, and produces richest sky colors. Monitor exposure closely and bracket. Expose for the sun itself, or measure exposure off the surrounding sky. This will render foreground objects in silhouette. As the sun grows closer to the horizon it seems bigger, and this is most effectively represented by using a lens of 300 mm or longer, so that it dominates the frame. The sun is least photogenic around midday, when it is high in the sky. Never point your camera directly at bright overhead sun unless using dense filtering – you may damage your eyes as well as the exposure meter.

Try shooting the sun when it is diffused by mist, light cloud, or smog, or shining from behind a storm cloud. In a clear sky use a wide-angle lens to render the sun as a small point source. Use slow film and a neutral density or deep-colored filter. You may find iris flare a problem, especially if you use a wide-angle lens and shoot with the sun near the edge of the frame. If you want to eliminate flare spots altogether, make sure that the sun is near to the center of the viewfinder. To add a "radiant" effect to a small image of the sun, use a starburst filter.

Television screen
It is not difficult to get good results when photographing a television screen. But the images must be for personal use – as with photographing from a magazine or book, copyright prevents you from selling them. Do not use flash. Mount the camera on a tripod so that you can easily frame the center of the screen, and darken the room. Television images tend to be excessively contrasty when photographed, so reduce this by altering the television contrast control until some detail is just visible in the picture's shadows and highlights. Set the color controls as accurately as possible. Daylight-type color film will give you correct color reproduction. It is vital to use the correct shutter speed. Each television picture takes 1/30 sec to form (1/25 sec in the UK). Faster shutter speeds leave a dark band across the screen (see picture). The best speed to use is 1/8 sec, but if subject movement is occurring on the screen this setting could be reduced to 1/15 sec. The longer the exposure the more scans are included, giving better tone range. It is easiest to first make a video recording. This can then be replayed as many times as you wish while you take your photographs at different points, also giving bracketed exposures if necessary. Read exposure from the entire screen, or make an averaged reading from shadow and highlight areas, in the same way as if copying a picture. (Some modern silicon cells will fail to give an accurate measurement of the flickering television image. If your meter gives a reading that fluctuates rapidly, you will find it necessary to use a CdS or selenium cell hand meter instead.

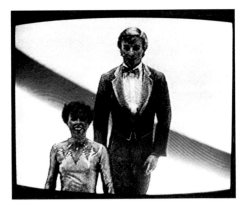

Theater see *Stage performances*

Townscapes
When photographing a town or city, take a wide range of shots to cover all its aspects and try to capture its atmosphere as well as its more obvious architectural features. Each town is unique, and it is possible to convey its qualities not just by showing its streets and buildings but also by photographing its street characters, transportation systems, crafts, graffiti, and the occupations of its inhabitants. Plan camera angles carefully, and watch for favorable lighting conditions. Use selective focus to simplify shots, or use a dark foreground element to lead the eye into the picture, or to frame the view. Foliage can act as a foil to the hard lines and cold textures of modern architecture. It can also mask ugly or incongruous features, such as lines of parked automobiles.

Use a wide-angle lens for a high, panoramic view, framed to give an interesting skyline, or for street scenes, shooting from a corner to benefit from the effects of double perspective.

A telephoto lens is useful for photographing close-up details — street signs, letter boxes, flights of steps, archways, windows, and doorways. It will also "concertina" closely packed buildings and pick out abstract patterns from modern architecture.

People add vitality and scale to townscapes, but should not appear conscious of your presence or dominate the picture. Catch candid groups as part of the general scene in markets, shops, and pedestrian precincts. Do not overlook the possibility of photographing scenes at dusk, with its mixture of sky light and illuminated buildings. When using slide film, shoot these on tungsten light film, or use a blue conversion filter.

Travel
Before embarking on a journey, consider the equipment you will need carefully. As well as a camera and flash, it is well worth taking a choice of lenses, lens hoods and filters, a tripod and cable release (for interior and night shots), spare batteries, and a plentiful supply of films of different speeds (slow for bright daylight, fast for nights shots and interiors). If you possess two camera bodies, use one for color and the other for black and white. A useful basic lens kit might consist of a 135 mm telephoto (for candid shots and details) and a 28 mm wide-angle lens (for interiors, landscapes, and groups) as well as a standard. A 40 mm plus an 85-200 mm zoom is a wider-ranging alternative.

If you have any specialist interests, such as flowers or underwater subjects, be sure to include the appropriate accessories. All your equipment should be carried in a moisture-resistant, foam-lined gadget bag to protect it from sand, water, and sudden knocks.

There is a wealth of colorful picture-making material in foreign places, ranging from costumes and handicrafts to food and townscapes. Try to cover all aspects of a journey, from departure to return. Take shots from the aircraft, boat, or through the windows of trains, automobiles, or coaches, using a fast shutter speed and precise timing.

In any location, take time to choose the most favorable views and lighting conditions (although the first impressions of a place can often be very telling). Be sure to observe local regulations and customs — do not photograph in churches, museums, or on military property without permission.

Never leave your equipment in a hot place, such as the back shelf of a vehicle parked in the sun. When passing through X-ray baggage checks, always have your film (both exposed and unexposed) examined by hand.

Trees
Season, lighting, and viewpoint are major considerations when photographing trees. In spring, you can take delicate close-ups of pastel-colored blossom and buds; in fall, when light is redder, make the most of the vast variety of leaf tones, setting them against rich evergreens; in winter shoot bare skeletal branches against a stormy or sunset sky. Mist and fog diffuse shape and create romantic effects. The stronger oblique light of late afternoon casts long shadows, modeling form as well as bringing out colors. Avoid front-lighting, which will give a two-dimensional

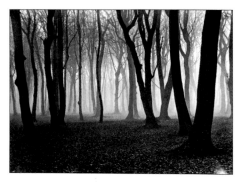

impression, and overhead lighting, unless it is filtered by branches.

Isolate a single tree from its setting by careful viewpoint and background choice. The sky often provides the simplest background, especially if you shoot with the camera resting on the ground. Do not shoot when skies are predominantly overcast, as light, colorless patches seen through branches can be dull. Choose a high viewpoint to incorporate the whole of a large tree, or use a shift lens to avoid the tree looking as though it is falling backward, because of converging verticals. Beware of branches that point toward the camera and may record in distorted perspective, unless you want this effect. Often you must compromise between stopping down to obtain sharp focus on twigs or the trunk, and opening up to put a distracting background out of focus. Pick out a pattern of foliage or branches from ground level with a 200 mm telephoto lens or zoom. Do not forget the possibilities of taking macro lens photographs of bark and leaf structures.

Underwater life
The simplest methods of photographing underwater life are to take pictures through an observation window in a boat, or to wade into the water with the camera in a watertight vessel with a glass or plastic bottom. To work below the surface, use an underwater camera or equip your camera with a watertight plastic or metal housing. You can also buy an underwater flash and exposure meter.

If necessary you can calculate underwater exposure roughly by reading off the back of your hand above the water, and then increasing it by two stops for 6 ft (2 m) down, three stops for 30 ft (9 m) down. Always bracket underwater shots widely so that you have a really large selection of results. Use 36-exposure ASA 400 film, so that you do not have to return to the surface to reload the camera too frequently.

Most underwater photographs are taken with a fast, short focal-length lens, which allows you to include the subject from a close distance, minimizing the light-scattering effect of the water. (Angle of view is reduced under water and focal length increased, so a 35 mm lens will have an effective focal length similar to a standard lens.) It may be quicker to preset focus before you dive — to 2 or 3 ft (1 m approx.) for smaller fish, 6 ft (2 m) for people or large fish. Working close also enables you to record colors more accurately, although the color of daylight becomes increasingly blue the deeper you go. Lighting intensity is

greatest under water when the sun's rays are almost perpendicular to the surface. Try to shoot between 10 am and 2 pm, and when the water is calm and clear. At depths below about 12 ft (4 m), you will require flash to capture the true colors of underwater life. Use flash off camera and directed at an angle to your subject to reduce the effects of backscatter. If flash is close to the lens, particles of water are illuminated and light is scattered, reducing contrast dramatically.

Water
Water reflects the color and light of the sun, while its form is dictated by wind and tide. In color it can range from translucent green at midday to golden pink at sunset. Its sparkle is best revealed by oblique lighting; its smooth reflective quality shows best in early morning or during late afternoon, when it is less likely to be windy.

Moving water presents more problems than still water — the way it looks in a photograph depends on the length of exposure. A fast shutter speed (at least 1/500 sec with a waterfall) will freeze movement but may make moving water look unnaturally static. Experiment with a range of slower speeds, down to 1 sec, observing the way the water softens to a blur. Use a neutral density filter and have the camera mounted on a tripod. When photographing streams or waterfalls with a hand-held camera, you are often prevented from using a fast shutter speed by poor light and the need to stop down for sufficient depth of field. If you want to shoot both the surface of the water and what lies beneath, beware of including surface reflections that may distort and break up the image. Often a polarizing filter can help to get rid of these reflections.

Weather
Some of the most atmospheric pictures are taken under bad weather conditions. Storms, fog, mist, and rain can produce shimmering color effects and transform the mood of an outdoor photograph. Storms provide striking high-contrast lighting effects and convey a sense of drama. Rain, fog, and mist diffuse light, muting colors and softening shapes. Rain makes flat surfaces wet and reflective and showers leaves and flowers with droplets. In fog or mist, the background fades into obscurity. Go for strong backlit shapes to act as a foil to the light surroundings. Measure exposure mostly for highlights, to throw darker shapes into silhouette. A haze filter (or orange filter on black and white film) will minimize the effects of haze, while a diffusion filter or other soft-focus filter will increase them. Take advantage of the predominantly muted tones to include small patches of isolated color to act as accent points in the picture.

To take sharp pictures of rain, use a shutter speed of at least 1/250 sec and try to frame the rain against a dark background. Show its effect on the surface of puddles and tops of automobiles. You can usually shoot from the shelter of a porch or through a window. If you are shooting outdoors, an underwater camera is ideal, but keep spots of water off the glass in front of the lens.

Keep your regular equipment as protected as possible in all adverse conditions. Put a UV filter over the front of the lens and use a lens

hood. A fast lens and fast film are vital for poor lighting conditions and a monopod or tripod may be useful when a slow shutter speed is called for. Always bracket exposure when lighting is unpredictable.
See also **Lightning, Snow, ice, and frost**

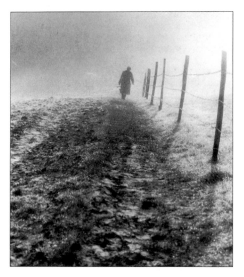

Weddings

If you are the only photographer present at the wedding, try to cover as many different aspects of the occasion as possible. If you are working alongside another photographer, divide up the work and concentrate on certain aspects of the day only.

Take plenty of film – mostly medium speed, but some ASA 400, or faster, for indoor, existing-light pictures. Expect to take several pictures of each subject, so that you have a choice of results. Concentrate, above all, on recording the spirit of the day. Standard, 85 mm, 135 mm, and 28 mm (or equivalent zooms) will cover your lens requirements. A diffusion filter, or some other soft-focus technique (such as breathing on a clear filter placed over the lens or covering it with a nylon stocking) may be useful if you want to enhance the romantic mood of a picture in a very traditional way.

Begin shooting before the ceremony – cover, for example, the preparations at the bride's house. Be early at the church to record the arrival of guests, then the groom, and finally the bride and her father. Shoot from within the church doorway, using it as a frame. You should have previously obtained permission to photograph inside the building, found the best viewpoints, and decided on focal lengths. Shoot by available light during the ceremony, using a tripod, making as little noise as possible. Include wide-angle general views from a balcony and closer shots with an 85 mm lens from one side of the altar.

When the ceremony is over, photograph the couple signing the register, then move outside to photograph people coming out. Take both head-and-shoulder as well as full-length shots of the bride and groom. If they are facing direct, hard sunlight, try to move them to a more shaded area. Take exposure readings for face tones. Watch out for distracting details in the background or foreground. Wedding

groups require good organization and a sense of timing. Flank the bride and groom with relatives from their respective sides of the family. Shoot with a normal lens, then change to 135 mm to pick out pairs and individuals.

At the reception, a wide-aperture, telephoto lens is also an asset for candids and for close-ups of decorative details, such as the wedding cake and bridal bouquet. A wide-angle lens is useful for general views of the wedding feast. Flash will probably be necessary for groups at table, or the formal cutting of the cake, if existing lighting is too dim to allow hand-held shutter speeds.
See also **Groups and crowds, Parties and celebrations**

Wild animals

You may have to track or stalk your subject, so equipment should be light, easy to carry, and versatile. If possible have a powerful telephoto such as a 500 mm mirror lens, so that you can work without disturbing the animal. Most photography will probably be done on a 80-200 mm or 200-300 mm zoom. If your subject is nervous, lay bait and conceal the camera, mounted on a tripod, in a hide, if necessary using remote control plus a motor drive attachment to operate it from a distance. Use fast film to allow small enough apertures for sufficient depth of field, and fast enough shutter speeds to freeze movement. Or, use slower film to photograph an animal moving rapidly across your field of vision, panning the camera to keep the animal sharp, blurring the background in order to convey an impression of speed.

If possible, choose a simple background that contrasts in color and texture with the animal's own. If you have to include surroundings which are confusing or detract from the main subject, open up the aperture to soften obtrusive shapes and colors. Including an object of known size can add a sense of scale to pictures of large animals, such as elephants and giraffes.

Lighting is of primary importance in bringing out the various features, textures, and colors. If you can choose when to shoot, low angular light is usually best. Back-lighting will rimlight an animal's coat and it can create strong dramatic shapes. Open shade will offer freedom from the problems caused by bright sunshine (such as very high contrast) but it may have the effect of making animal fur appear dull and lifeless.

Winter sports

A telephoto lens of at least 200 mm (preferably 300 mm or 400 mm) is necessary to photograph winter sports events such as skiing and bobsleighing, since you will not be able to shoot from close by. Take a monopod to help steady your longest lenses. Use medium or fast film, as although conditions are likely to be bright, you will want to use both your fastest shutter speed to arrest action and a small aperture to maximize depth of field with such long-focus lenses. The exact shutter speed required will depend on the distance of the subject and the direction of movement. Most winter sports are extremely fast-moving, so you must pre-determine the most promising location and be there ready to shoot. Prefocus on a spot you know the action will pass and

read exposure from your hand.

Snow appears dull without sunshine – so shoot when the sun is shining obliquely across the slopes, casting long shadows and bringing out the sparkling quality of snow. Photographing a skier emerging over the crest of a hill, raising clouds of snow behind, looks particularly striking if the subject is backlit. Pan the camera at 1/125 sec to suggest movement as a skier races past. For ski-jumping, shoot from below and to one side of the jump, and freeze the competitor in mid-air, at 1/1000 sec.

When shooting bobsled or toboggan racing, position yourself on a corner, where speed and excitement are likely to be at a peak. Always use a lens hood when shooting sunlit snow and a UV filter to reduce excessive blue in the shadows, and protect the lens from thrown-up ice or snow. For ice hockey, choose a location near one of the goals, and avoid the temptation to move around and follow the action. You will require flash here to freeze movement.

Work see *Occupations*

Zoo animals

Photographing animals in zoos can be difficult because of unattractive surroundings, unwanted shade, and the fact that animals are often lying down. But with a little knowledge of the animal's habits, plus patience and timing, you may be able to obtain some good results. Try to shoot when the animal is in the sun and the background is either in the shade, or acceptably plain. Once you have selected your location, prefocus on the spot you expect the animal to stand or lie down, and wait for it to assume position. If the animal is a different tone from the preselected spot, read exposure from a similarly toned object closer at hand. Focus on the eyes when there is time for accuracy. A 135 mm telephoto lens or a 80-200 mm zoom is an asset for zoo photographs – not only because it allows you to fill the frame from a distance but because its shallow depth of field helps you to isolate your subject by putting the surroundings out of focus. If the cage bars are in the way and you cannot avoid them, wait until the animal is well back from the bars, then shoot at a wide aperture so that they are not recorded.

Glossary

Abbe number Number denoting the degree of refraction of light of different wavelengths to different extents, given by a transparent material such as glass. The lower the Abbe number, the greater the dispersion of colors.

Aberration Inability of a lens to produce a perfect, sharp image, especially toward the edge of the lens field. Such faults can be reduced by compound lens constructions, and the use of small apertures.

Abrasion marks Marks on the emulsion surface of a film caused by scratching. Can be due to traces of dirt trapped between layers of film as it is wound on the spool, or to grit on the pressure plate.

Absorption Process by which light falling on a surface is partially absorbed by that surface (and generally converted to heat).

Abstract A subjective, non-realistic image. An abstract photograph generally contains a design of patterns or shapes where the identity of the subject is not evident.

Accelerator Chemical added to a developing solution to speed up the slow-working action of the reducing agents in the solution. Such chemicals are usually alkaline.

Acceptance angle See *Angle of view.*

Accessory shoe Fitting on top of a camera that supports accessories such as flashgun, viewfinder, or rangefinder. It does not normally have electrical contacts with the camera mechanism. See *Hot shoe.*

Acetate base A flame-proof base support for the emulsion layers of 35 mm and rollfilms. Consists of cellulose triacetate or cellulose acetate butyrate. This replaced the highly inflammable cellulose nitrate base used for the earliest films.

Acetic acid Chemical used in stop baths (a 2 per cent solution is generally recommended) and to acidify fixing solution. In the latter case a buffer is required to prevent the acid decomposing the compounds used in fixation.

Acetone Solvent chemical used in certain processing solutions that contain materials not normally easily soluble in water.

Achromatic Lens system corrected for chromatic aberration.

Acid Chemical substance with a pH value below 7. It is often used in photographic processing to stop the action of an alkaline solution.

Acid hardener Substance used in acid fixer to help harden the gelatin of the emulsion.

Acid rinse Weak acid solution used after development and before fixation. By neutralizing

alkaline developer left on the photographic material it arrests development.

Actinic The ability of light to cause a chemical or physical change in a substance. The actinic power of light during exposure causes the sensitive crystals in a photographic emulsion to change their structure, forming black metallic silver that creates an image.

Actinometer Early type of exposure calculator. A sample of self-darkening light-sensitive paper was exposed to subject lighting. As the material darkened, it was compared to a standard tint. The time taken for it to reach this standard formed the basis of exposure calculations.

Acuity Subjective term for the visual sharpness of an image.

Acutance Objective measurement of image sharpness. The steepness of the angle of the edge gradient between density boundaries in an image is used to express its sharpness. The steeper the angle between these boundaries, the greater the sharpness. As the angle becomes less acute, the difference between the two densities becomes more diffuse, and the image less sharp. Such measurements do not always correlate with subjective judgments as other factors play a part in the final effect.

Adapter ring Circular mount, available in several sizes, enabling accessories such as filters to be used with lenses of different diameters.

Additive printing Printing process employing the principle of additive synthesis. Some early color photography processes used this system. The method is still used for certain image manipulations.

Additive synthesis A method of producing full-color images by mixing light of the three primary color wavelengths, blue, green, and red. Mixed in equal proportions they produce white. Mixed in varying proportions, they can produce all the colors of the spectrum. Early color transparency processes using mosaic screens were based on additive synthesis.

Aerial perspective Depth and distance effect caused by atmospheric haze, and most noticeable with landscapes. Haze creates a large amount of scatter of short wavelength (blue and ultraviolet) light to which photographic emulsions are sensitive. This produces a reduction of warm colors and lowering of contrast and detail with distance. Contributes greatly to the illusion of depth in distant views.

Afocal lens Lens attachment that alters the focal length of a camera lens without disturbing the distance between the lens and the film plane. A range of attachments is available: some of these increase and others decrease the focal length of the prime lens.

Aftertreatment The treatment of negatives and prints to correct certain faults in exposure and development, or to create special effects.

Agitation Method used to keep fresh processing solution in contact with the emulsion surface during photographic processing. The manufacturer's recommendations for the degree of agitation required for particular materials must be followed, because agitation can markedly affect the total processing effect.

Air bells Bubbles of air clinging to the emulsion surface during processing. If the manufacturer's recommended agitation times are followed, air bells can generally be avoided.

Air brushing Method of retouching in which dye or pigment is sprayed, by means of compressed air, over selected areas of the negative or print.

Air-to-air photography The photography of aircraft in flight from another aircraft.

Albert effect Effect that creates a reversed image. An exposed frame of film, treated with dilute chromic acid is exposed to light. Development then gives a positive image by darkening the film grains that were not initially affected by exposure.

Albumen paper Photographic paper coated with a solution of albumen (prepared from egg white) and an ammonia salt, and sensitized with silver nitrate. Now obsolete.

Alcohol thermometer Instrument used for measuring temperature. Inexpensive, but less accurate version, of the mercury thermometer. Photographic alcohol thermometers should have blue-dyed contents, for easy reading in red or yellow safelighting.

Alkalinity Denotes the degree of alkali in a solution, measured in pH values. All values above pH 7 are alkaline. Most developers contain alkali in some form. The higher the alkalinity, the more active the solution.

Allegory Work of art that treats one subject in the guise of another. An allegorical photograph usually illustrates a subject that embodies a moral "inner meaning".

Alum Chemical used in acid hardening fixing baths. Two types are available, chrome alum and potassium alum. Potassium alum is preferred for fixing prints, since chrome alum is inclined to stain metallic silver green. The useful life of any hardening agent is generally shorter than that of an acid fixing bath.

Aluminum compounds Groups of chemicals often used as hardeners in fixing baths. They include aluminum ammonium sulfate, aluminum chloride, and aluminum sulfate.

Ambrotype Photographic process which

was a direct offshoot of the collodion process introduced in 1851 by Frederick Scott Archer. The process uses weak collodion glass negatives (which may be bleached to make the black silver image gray-white) and backed by a black background, producing the effect of a positive image. Ambrotypes replaced the earlier daguerreotypes, and became immensely popular because they were both cheaper and easier to view.

Amidol Soluble reducing agent that works at low pH values.

Ammonium chloride Chemical used in toners, bleaches, and concentrated liquid hardener solutions. Also known as sal-ammoniac.

Ammonium persulfate Chemical used in super-proportional reducers. It is inclined to precipitate in solution and give erratic results.

Ammonium sulfide Pungent chemical used in sulfide and sepia toning. It is also an ingredient in some intensifiers. The sulfurous fumes have a strong fogging effect on unprocessed photographic materials.

Ammonium thiosulfate Highly active, easily soluble fixing agent used in rapid fixing solutions. It works by converting unused silver halides to soluble complexes.

Amphitype Mid-19th century process based on an underexposed albumen-on-glass negative. This was viewed by reflected light against a black background to give a positive image similar to an ambrotype.

Anaglyph A positive stereoscopic pair of images, each dyed a different color, usually green and red. The two images are either printed on a single sheet of paper slightly out of register, or mounted as two separate images in a specially designed viewer or projector. In both cases they are viewed through colored filters complementary to the colored image. Each eye sees its appropriate left- or right-hand image only, and these fuse together to produce a three-dimensional effect.

Analyzer Chart, grid or (more expensive but more accurate) an electronic instrument used to determine correct color filtration when making color prints.

Anamorphic lens Lens with special cylindrical elements that allow it to compress one dimension of a two-dimensional image without affecting the other. Allows a picture of long, narrow proportions to be accommodated within a standard frame. A similar projection or printing system can be used to reform the image on a wide screen or produce a panoramic print. Originally developed for wide-screen cinematography, but also usable with still cameras.

Anastigmat Compound lens that has been corrected for the aberration astigmatism.

Angle of coverage See *Covering power*.

Angle of incidence Angle formed between an incident light ray striking a surface and a "normal", or line at right-angles to the surface.

Angle of reflection Angle formed between the reflection of an incident ray of light and a "normal" drawn at right-angles to the surface. The angle's measurement is equal to the angle of incidence.

Angle of view Angle subtended at the lens between the most widely separated parts of a distant subject which it will just image within the diagonal of the picture format. Varies with focal length and format size.

Angstrom Unit of measurement (equal to one ten-millionth of a millimeter) once used to indicate wavelengths within the electromagnetic spectrum. Visible light rays occur between 4000 Å (blue light) and approximately 7000 Å (red light). The indices between represent a variety of colors and saturations.

Angular field Angle subtended at the lens by the diameter of the largest circle within which the lens gives an image of acceptable sharpness and even illumination. Varies with focal length and lens design.

Anhydrous Dehydrated form of chemical. More concentrated, so that less weight is needed in a formula than the crystalline kind. Where a chemical is available in both forms its state must be quoted — either Anhyd. or Cryst.

ANSI speed Speed rating system for photographic materials. Devised by the American National Standards Institute. Doubling the ANSI number denotes material twice as sensitive to light.

Anti-fogging agent Constituent of a developer that inhibits or reduces fogging during development.

Anti-halation backing Light-absorbing dye coating within, or on the back of, most film bases, or between the base and the emulsion. It absorbs any light that passes straight through the emulsion layer, and prevents this extraneous light being reflected back to form a "halo" around bright highlights.

Antinous release Alternative term for camera cable release.

Anti-reflection coating See *Coated lens*.

Antiscreen plates Photographic plates containing dyes that reduce the blue sensitivity. Used unfiltered, they can give results similar to those obtained with yellow-filtered orthochromatic plates.

Aperture Circular hole in front of or within a lens that restricts the amount of light passing through the lens to the photographic material. On the majority of lenses the size of the aperture can be varied, and controlled by an iris diaphragm. This can be set to a series of "stops" calibrated in f numbers.

Aperture priority camera Semi-automatic camera exposure system in which the photographer selects the aperture, and the camera meter then automatically sets the shutter speed.

Aplanat Lens corrected for spherical and chromatic aberrations.

Apochromat Lens corrected to bring the three primary colors of the spectrum to common focus.

Apodization Lens treatment designed to cut down diffraction fringes that appear around the images of bright points of light.

Aquatint In fine art, an etching technique allowing control of tonal areas to produce almost unlimited gradations from pale gray to rich black. For this reason it has also been used in photography as an alternative term for gum bichromate process.

Archival permanence treatments Various treatments (such as special washes, selenium or gold toning) given to prints to make them fade-resistant. These techniques are often expensive and are mostly used by museums and galleries.

Arc lamp Powerful electric artificial light source in which the illumination is provided by glowing particles that cross the gap between a pair of electrodes. Early arc lamps burned carbon electrodes in air. Modern xenon arcs (used for movie projection) work in an enclosed quartz envelope.

Argentotype Mid-19th century silver print process, on which the kallitype and sepia paper processes are based.

Aristotype Early commercial print types made on collodion-chloride or gelatin-chloride paper.

Artificial daylight Artificial light having a similar color temperature to daylight. Often produced by filtering away some of the long wavelengths in tungsten lamp illumination.

Artificial light All light not originating from a natural source — normally the sun. The commonest artificial sources in photography are flash, and tungsten filament bulbs.

Artificial light film Color film balanced for use in tungsten artificial light, usually of 3200 K. Packs are usually marked "Tungsten" or "Type B". These films will only render the color of daylight illuminated scenes correctly if used with an orange correcting filter over the camera lens, to alter the light's color temperature.

ASA Speed rating for photographic materials devised by the American Standards Association. The rating is based on an arithmetical progression using an average gradient system. Films are classified by ASA number: doubling the number indicates a film of twice the light sensitivity.

Aspherical Of a lens, having a surface curvature that does not form part of a sphere. Aspherical elements are used to reduce optical aberrations in many modern lenses.

Assembly printing Method of printing using image separations. For example, yellow, magenta, and cyan (or blue, green, and red) films are stacked to make a final, full-color print.

Astigmatism Lens aberration making a single-point light source impossible to focus as a true point. It is imaged instead as either of two short lines, at right-angles at different distances from the lens.

Atmospheric perspective Alternative term for aerial perspective.

Autochrome process The first practical method of producing photographic images. Introduced by the Lumière brothers in France in 1907. Starch grains dyed in the primary colors created a color "screen" on the photographic plate. The plate was coated with panchromatic emulsion, and exposure made through the back of the plate. The image was given reversal black and white processing, and when held up to the light appeared as a colored transparency.

Autofocus Device used on certain cameras, projectors, and enlargers that focuses the image automatically. No manual adjustment is necessary to achieve sharp focus.

Automatic aperture Lens aperture mechanism that stops down to a preset size just as the shutter is fired, returning to maximum aperture again for focusing and composing the next image.

Automatic exposure control System of exposure setting in a camera, in which the electric current produced or inhibited by the action of light on a photoelectric cell operates a mechanism that adjusts the aperture and/or shutter speed automatically.

Automatic lens See *Automatic aperture.*

Auxiliary lens See *Supplementary lens.*

Available light General term applying to light normally occurring in a scene, not supplemented by illumination intended specifically for photography.

Average gradient See $\bar{G}$ *curve.*

Azo dyes Compounds forming colors of great strength and purity. Used in camera filters, and for integral tripack dye-bleach materials. Here processing reduces dye in contact with the silver image to a colorless substance.

Back focus The distance between the back surface of the lens and the image plane, when the lens is focused at infinity. This distance is not always equal to the focal length of the lens, particularly with telephoto lenses and with wide-angle lenses given inverted telephoto (retrofocus) construction to gain more space behind the lens.

Background Area shown behind the main subject in a picture. This can be anything from distant landscape or sky, to colored paper, a projected transparency or a specially built set.

Background density The density of any section of a negative or print on which there is no image. See also *Fog level.*

Backing Dark coating, normally on the back of a film, but sometimes between emulsion and base, to reduce halation. The backing dye disappears during processing.

Back-lighting Light coming from behind the main subject. Special care in exposure estimation is required with scenes lit in this way. Some automatic cameras have a back-lighting compensation button, which ensures that extra exposure is given.

Back projection Projection system often used to create the illusion of location backgrounds in the studio. Location scenes are photographed and then projected from behind a suitable translucent screen in the studio to create a background for objects placed in front of the screen. It is important that the direction of the lighting on the foreground objects matches that of the projected transparency and that background color and intensity are balanced with the subject situated in the foreground.

Bag bellows Short, baggy, flexible sleeve used on large-format cameras in place of the normal bellows unit, when short focal length (wide-angle) lenses are employed. It allows all the normal camera movements.

Ball and socket Swiveling mount used for attaching a camera to a tripod, consisting of a large ball joint designed to move in a cup. It enables the camera to be moved at any angle, and clamped in position.

Barium sulfate Whitening compound used in the manufacture of photographic printing paper (fiber-based). Gives brighter highlights in the final print than is possible from the white paper alone.

Barn doors Accessory used on spotlights and floodlamps to reduce light spill, and control the direction and width of the beam. Consists of four hinged metal flaps on a square rotatable frame.

Barrel distortion One of the most common lens aberrations in simple lenses, causing straight lines at the edge of the field to appear curved and bulge outward. These barrel-shaped lines are caused by an asymmetrical lens construction, in which the diaphragm is placed toward the front of the optical system.

Baryta Coating of barium sulfate applied as the foundation to fiber-based printing papers.

Base Support for a photographic emulsion. It is usually made from plastic, paper or glass, but may include metal or fabric.

Baseboard camera Portable folding large format sheet film camera in which the lens and bellows are supported on a baseboard. It allows limited use of camera movements.

Bas-relief Picture made to imitate the form of low-relief sculpture in which the subject projects slightly from its background, as in medals and coins. Produced by combining negative and positive images of the same subject, slightly out of register, to give the effect of shadows and highlights produced by a side-lit relief.

Batch numbers Set of numbers printed on packets of sensitive materials to indicate a common production coating. The batch number is given because slight variations of contrast and speed sometimes occur between batches of the same type of photographic material. This information is particularly important to the photographer using color materials and where automated systems are being used for monochrome printing.

Bauhaus School of architecture and design founded at Dessau, Germany by Walter Gropius in 1919. It aimed to reconcile aesthetics of design with new materials and industrial processes. Closed by Hitler in 1933. A prominent photographer teaching at the Bauhaus in the 1920s was László Moholy-Nagy, who set up the New Bauhaus in the USA in 1937.

B ("Bulb") Shutter speed setting at which the shutter will stay open as long as the shutter release is depressed. Used for exposures longer than the numbered settings. The term is derived from early mechanical blind shutters, fired by squeezing an air bulb at the end of a rubber tube.

Beam splitter Mirror or prism system capable of partly reflecting and partly transmitting light. Used in some reflex viewing systems, and optical devices such as front projection units, holographic rigs, and microscopes.

Belitski's reducer Solution used as a chemical reducer for negatives. Consists of ferric potassium citrate or oxalate in an acid fixing bath.

Bellows Light-tight, extendable sleeve fitted between the lens and the film plane. Used on sheet film (and some rollfilm) cameras to allow focusing. Smaller format cameras also often accept bellows units to increase the lens-to-film distance for close-up work.

Bellows shutter Obsolete shutter consisting of a pair of bellows that, when closed together, form a hemisphere enclosing the lens. The two bellows units part silently to expose the film.

Between-the-lens shutter Shutter placed within a compound lens, usually close to the iris diaphragm. Also known as a leaf or bladed shutter.

Bichromate Refers to potassium bichromate or (more commonly) potassium dichromate, used for bleaching and as a sensitizer for gelatin in gum bichromate and similar processes. Toxic chemical.

Bi-concave lens Simple lens, or lens element within a compound lens, whose surfaces curve toward the optical center. Such a lens causes light rays to diverge.

Bi-convex lens Simple lens, or lens element within a compound lens, whose surfaces curve outward, away from the optical center. Such a lens causes light rays to converge.

Binocular vision Observation made from two separate viewpoints at the same time, as with a pair of human eyes. Gives the visual ability to determine three dimensions. Stereoscopic photography depends on the use of binocular vision.

Bi-pack Combination of two films, differently sensitized, but exposed as one.

Bi-refringence Splitting of light passing through certain kinds of crystals into two rays at polarized right-angles to each other. Viewed in polarized light, colors are formed. Used in adapted form for polarizing filters.

Bispheric lens Lens having different curvatures at the center and the edge, each of which forms part of a sphere. The different edge curvature brings the peripheral rays more closely to the same point of focus as the center rays.

Bitumen Viscous substance formed by the mixture of certain mineral hydrocarbons. Used by Niépce in his heliography process.

Black silver Finely divided metallic silver formed from silver halides by exposure and development.

Bleach Chemical bath used to remove all or part of an image. For example, it can convert a silver image into a halide, which may then be fixed away or toned.

Bleach/fix Chemical bath in which the bleach and fixer have been combined. Used in many color processes. Also known as "Blix" solution.

Bleach-out Method of producing line drawings from photographic images. The photograph is processed in the normal way, its outlines sketched in waterproof ink, and the black metallic silver image then bleached away to leave the drawn outline.

Bleed Of a picture, having no borders, printed to the edge of the paper.

Blister Blemish on prints or negatives appearing as the result of incorrect processing. Caused by bubbles of gas or processing liquid under the emulsion surface, often occurring due to chemical reactions between different processing solutions, when rinsing is inadequate.

Blocking out The use of opaque paint on a (large format) negative surface to obscure unwanted details in the image. Used often to remove ugly background around large industrial subjects. Results in clean white surround when printed.

Blue print Alternative term for cyanotype.

Blue-sensitive Sensitive to blue light only (also known as "ordinary" sensitivity). All silver halides used in black and white emulsions are sensitive to blue light, but early photographic materials had only this sensitivity.

Blur Unsharp image areas, created or caused by subject or camera movement, or by selective or inaccurate focusing.

Boom Adjustable metal arm, attached to a firm stand, on which a lighting unit can be mounted. Extendable boom arms are also made to support cameras — either for remote positioning at great height, or as a cross-piece to a studio stand to allow a viewpoint directly over the subject.

Borax Sodium tetraborate. Weak alkaline compound used, for example, in fine grain developers.

Border The edge of a photographic print — either left white, or printed black.

Boric acid Compound used in certain fixers to prolong their hardening life. Also contained in some fine-grain developers.

Bounced light Illumination reflected from a ceiling, wall, or similar surface. Used to give softer illumination over a wider area than that provided by direct lighting, cutting down harsh or obtrusive shadows.

Box camera Simplest box-shaped type of camera, first introduced by George Eastman in 1888. Consists of a simple, often single-element lens, a light-tight body, and a place for the film. Shutter speed is usually fixed at 1/25 sec, and lens aperture at f 11. No focusing is necessary as the lens is set to its hyperfocal distance, giving acceptable images provided that the subject is not too close.

Bracketing The technique of shooting a number of pictures of the same subject and viewpoint at different exposure levels in order to obtain the most accurate result. Changes may be made with shutter or aperture settings. Exposure variations of half or one full setting, over or under, are usually selected, depending on subject and film type.

Brightfield Method of illumination used in photomicrography, created by transmitting light to the subject from below, reflecting sunlight from a mirror or using a microscope having a built-in lamp. Suitable for translucent and transparent specimens, but not for opaque subjects.

Brightline viewfinder Viewfinder in which the subject is outlined by a bright frame, apparently suspended in space. This may show parallax correction marks, or lines indicating the fields of view of different focal length lenses.

Brightness range Term describing the difference in luminance between the darkest and lightest areas of the subject, in both negative and print.

Brilliance The intensity of light reflected from a surface. Alternative term for luminosity.

Brometching Obsolete, special method of producing a bromide print. The result acquired the texture of its support and appeared similar to an etching. The method involved overexposing and overdeveloping the print, to which an etching solution was then applied.

Bromide paper Most common type of photographic printing paper. Coated with a light-sensitive emulsion of silver bromide to reproduce black and white contonous tone images.

Bromoil process Old printing process invented in 1907, consisting of three main stages. **1** An enlargement is made on suitable bromide paper, and processed. **2** The silver image is removed in a bleacher which also modifies the gelatin so it will accept lithographic ink or oil pigment only where the image originally existed. **3** While still damp the gelatin is "inked up" by hand, using special brushes and a light, stippling action. Use of different brushes, pigments and brushstrokes give a hand-finished appearance if required. The ink image can also be transferred by contact on another sheet of paper, using a press (bromoil transfer).

Brush development Method of development in which developer is applied to the material with a brush, sponge or squeegee. Most useful with prints too large for tray processing.

BSI British Standards Institute. Issues film speed ratings identical to ASA numbers.

Bubble chamber photography Method of analyzing the paths of minute, high-speed sub-atomic particles. When the particles pass through or collide in the chamber, they produce streams of gas bubbles in their wake, which can be photographed using high-speed electronic flash with several cameras working simultaneously from different positions. This enables the particles' path to be plotted in three dimensions.

Buffer Chemical substance used to maintain the alkalinity (and therefore the activity) of a developing solution, particularly in the presence of bromine, a developer restrainer that is produced as a by-product during development. Any compound or chemical that assists in maintaining the characteristics of a solution is also known as a buffer.

Bulk film Film purchased in long lengths. Used in bulk camera backs (on occasions that demand fast, extensive use of film), or with bulk film loaders (to reload cassettes cheaply).

Burning-in Method of increasing printing exposure in specific local areas of an image. Also known as printing-in.

Cable release Flexible cable used for firing a camera shutter. Particularly useful for slow shutter speeds and time exposures, when touching the camera may cause camera shake and subsequent blur in the image.

Cadmium sulfide (CdS) cell Photo-sensitive cell used in exposure meters. Fed by an electric current from a battery, its electrical resistance varies according to the amount of light it receives.

Calotype process The first negative/positive process, invented by W.H. Fox Talbot in 1839. Paper was coated with silver iodide and further sensitized with a solution of silver nitrate and gallic acid. After several minutes' exposure in the camera, the paper was developed to a negative in the same silver nitrate solution, and fixed. Negatives were contact printed in sunlight on paper coated with silver chloride solution. Also known at the time as the Talbotype process.

Camera lucida An artist's aid – a simple lens and prism system through which a virtual image is seen, apparently on the surface of the sheet of drawing paper. Invented in 1674 and still sold by art suppliers.

Camera movements Adjustments allowed by mechanical systems most common on large format cameras which provide the facility for lens and film plane movement from the normal positions. Can create increased depth of field in specific planes, and correct or distort image shape as required.

Camera obscura In its simplest form, a darkened room with a small hole in one wall. Light rays pass through the hole to form an inverted image of the scene outside on a screen. First mentioned by Aristotle in the fourth century BC, and developed through the centuries as an aid to drawing, forerunner of the camera lucida. During the 16th century, bi-convex lenses were added to the basic apparatus, and it became the ancestor of the present-day camera. Thomas Wedgwood, son of the English potter Josiah, attempted to combine the camera obscura with light-sensitive materials in about 1800. In 1826, the Frenchman Niépce succeeded in this, creating the first permanent record.

Capacitor Device that builds up and stores electrical charges. Comprises a pair of electrical conductors with insulating material between them. When a current is applied to one conductor, the charge builds up, and can be discharged when the conductors are joined. Used in electronic flash and some forms of electronic shutter.

Capping shutter An extra shutter used in some medium format SLR cameras or in conjunction with any one of a group of extreme high-speed shutter types offering exposures of only a few microseconds. The capping shutter opens, then the high-speed shutter fires, followed by re-closure of the capping shutter.

Carbon arc lamp Type of arc lamp using an electric current passing between two carbon rods. The earliest form of artificial lighting used by professional photographers.

Carbon process Contact printing process, introduced in 1866, and using tissue coated with pigmented gelatin. Colors available ranged from red chalk to bottle green, plus rich carbon black. The paper was sensitized in potassium bichromate, and contact printed behind a negative in sunlight. Gelatin hardened according to light received. Then the tissue was placed in face contact with paper or glass and unhardened gelatin washed away, leaving a transferred pigment image. Little manipulation was possible.

Carbon tetrachloride Liquid used for removing grease and finger marks from negatives.

Carbro process Early color print process, 1905-50, a development of the carbon process, but working from bromide print enlargements. The tri-chrome carbro version used yellow, magenta, and cyan tissues to assemble a print from blue, green, and red separation negatives.

Carte-de-visite Portrait photograph on a mount about the size of a visiting card. Introduced by Disderi in 1854, carte-de-visite portraits became a social craze in many countries during the 1860s, but died away in the 70s.

Cartridge Film in a light-tight container designed for quick, drop-in loading without threading. Used in 110 and 126 cameras.

Cassette Cylindrical metal or plastic film spool container. A light-trap allows handling and film threading in the camera in daylight. Used in 35 mm cameras and some bulk-loaded rollfilm magazines.

Cast Overall bias toward one color in a color photograph.

Catadioptric lens Compound lens that uses a combination of mirrors and glass elements within its construction. This allows the light path to be "folded", so that a very long focal length will fit within a short barrel. The aperture of a catadioptric lens is usually fixed. Also known as a mirror or reflex lens.

Cathode ray tube Evacuated bulb of glass containing pairs of plates between which electrodes pass. A voltage applied to the plates makes the electrons change their path. They provide a trace, which can be displayed on a screen. The cathode ray tube forms the heart of a television receiver, as well as oscilloscopes and similar devices.

Caustic potash (Potassium hydroxide) Highly active alkaline substance used in high-contrast developing solutions, such as lith developer, to promote vigorous development.

CC filters Pale color conversion filters, used in various hues and degrees of saturation for correcting or inducing color casts when shooting, and for balancing color in subtractive color printing processes. The color shift values are calibrated, and the filters are available in sets of yellow, magenta, and cyan, blue, green, and red.

Centigrade scale Scale of temperature on which the freezing point of water is equal to 0°C, and its boiling point to 100°C.

Changing bag Opaque fabric bag, with long, tight sleeves to fit over the photographer's arms. Allows the loading of sheet filmholders or a processing tank with light-sensitive materials in normal lighting conditions. Useful on location.

Characteristic curve Performance graph showing the relationship between exposure and density under known developing conditions. It can provide immediate comparative information on factors such as emulsion speed, fog level, and contrast effect. The study of photographic materials in this way is known as sensitometry.

Chemical focus Point at which a lens brings the actinic rays to focus. In a modern fully corrected lens, chemical focus and visual focus coincide. This may not, however, apply to infrared photography (see *Infrared focus*).

Chemical fog Veil of metallic silver formed over unexposed parts of a developed image. May be caused through overdevelopment, or prolonged use of exhausted solution. Even correct development causes an unobtrusive layer of chemical fog.

Chemical reducer Solution capable of diminishing the density, and so lightening and/or altering contrast on a photographic emulsion, usually by turning some of the black silver into soluble salts, e.g. Farmer's reducer.

Chiaroscuro Light and shade effect. The way in which objects can be emphasized by patches of light, or obscured in shadow. Rembrandt excelled in this technique.

Chlorhydroquinone Developing agent contained in warm-tone developers.

Chloride paper Printing paper with a silver chloride emulsion. Much less sensitive than bromide paper and containing additives giving a bluish-black image. Mainly used for contact printing, and also known as contact paper.

Chlorobromide paper Photographic paper coated with an emulsion made up of both silver chloride and silver bromide. Used for producing enlargements with a warm, slightly brownish-black image, especially if processed in warm tone developer. The proportions of chloride and bromide dictate the emulsion's sensitivity to light.

Chlorquinol Alternative term for chlorhydroquinone.

Chromatic aberration The inability of a lens to bring different colors of light reflected from the same plane in the subject to a common point of focus in the image. The aberration results in a color fringe around white objects imaged near the edges of the picture.

Chromaticity Objective measurement of the color of an object or light source. Determined mathematically by two numbers known as chromaticity coordinates. A chromaticity diagram plots these values for all mixtures of spectrum colors.

Chromatype Early type of extremely slow paper used for contact printing, coated with potassium dichromate and copper sulfate. Produced a yellow positive image that could be toned with silver nitrate or gold chloride.

Chrome alum Alternative term for potassium chromium sulfate. Hardening ingredient in certain stop baths and fixers.

Chromogenic development Process in which the oxidation products of development combine with color couplers to form dyes of a precise and known character. Used to develop many color photographic materials.

Chromogenic materials Color photographic films and papers that form dyes during processing (from the oxidation products of development and color couplers).

Chronocyclograph Photograph used for the analysis of complex cyclic movements. Lamps or reflectors are attached to the moving parts of the object to be photographed, and a time exposure is made against a black background. This lasts for the duration of a single cycle of the movement. Low ambient lighting or infrared film are often used to avoid the problems of overexposure.

Chronophotography Technique, pioneered by Eadweard Muybridge, for recording objects in motion by taking photographs at regular intervals. High-speed rotating mirror cameras and similar devices are used for chronophotography today.

Cibachrome See *Silver dye-bleach material.*

CIE standards System of standards adopted by the Commission Internationale de l'Eclairage. allowing accurate descriptions of colors.

Circles of confusion Disks of light on an image, formed by the lens from points of light in the subject. The smaller these disks, the sharper the image. Once they reach a size that can be perceived as disks rather than points, that part of the image is considered to be unsharp.

Clayden effect The desensitizing of an emulsion by means of exposure to a strong, brief flash of light. If a second, low-intensity exposure is made, a direct positive of the first exposure may result, causing the light to appear black on the final print. Also known as 'black lighting effect'.

Clearing agent Processing solution used to remove stains or to cancel out the effect of chemicals left on the sensitive material from previous stages in the process.

Clearing time The length of time needed for a negative to clear, depending on the emulsion and on the strength, temperature and agitation of the fixer.

Clear-spot focusing Method of lens focusing achieved by examining the image through a transparent area in a specific plane – e.g. the clear central section of a camera focusing screen.

Cliché-verre Designs painted on glass in varnish or oil paint, or scratched into the emulsion of a fogged and processed plate using an etching needle. Results are then printed or enlarged on photographic paper. Many cliché-verres were made by Camille Corot, and the Photo-secessionist Frank Eugene devised his own version, needle-etching the backgrounds to photographic negatives.

Click stops Lens aperture control using a series of bearings that click audibly into place at each numbered setting. Common to most enlarging lenses because they can readily be adjusted in the dark.

Clip test A short sample of film, cut from the main exposed roll, used to determine the most appropriate development time.

Close-up General term for an image of a close subject, filling the frame.

Close-up attachment Accessory that enables a camera to focus on subjects nearer than the lens normally allows. This is usually achieved by extending the lens-to-film distance.

Coated lens Lens with air-to-glass surfaces that have been coated (or "bloomed") with one or more antireflection layers.

Coherent light Light waves that vibrate with constant phase relationships. Can be produced by a laser (essential for making holograms) or a combination of two prisms.

Coincidence rangefinder See *Rangefinder.*

Cold cathode illumination Type of blue-rich fluorescent lighting with a low operating temperature. Used mainly in 10 × 8 ins enlargers where its even light and low heat increase operating convenience. Also allows a low, flat-topped enlarger lamphouse, because a condenser is not required. It is inclined to reduce contrast and edge definition in the image, and is unsuitable for color.

Cold colors. Colors at the blue end of the spectrum (green and cyan, as well as blue itself) that suggest a cool atmosphere, and often seem to recede when combined with warm colors in an image.

Cold-light enlarger Enlarger using cold cathode illumination.

Collage Composition (usually abstract) employing various different materials (such as photographs, newspaper clippings, fabrics, and wood) combined with original artwork and attached to canvas or card.

Collodion Soluble gun-cotton, dissolved in a mixture of ether and alcohol.

Collodion (or "wet plate") process Photographic process in which the plate was user-coated, and exposed and processed while still wet. Collodion was used as the clear agent for binding the silver halides to the glass. The process, invented in 1851 by Frederick Scott Archer, was a great improvement on the earlier daguerreotype process, because wet plates allowed unlimited numbers of prints. It gave excellent image quality and was cheap and slightly faster than most current processes. But it had the disadvantage of requiring bulky darkroom equipment that the photographer had to carry around on location. It was the most widely used photographic process until the introduction of the dry plate in the late 1870s.

Color balance Adjustment in color photographic processes ensuring that a neutral scale of gray tones is reproduced accurately, so that a gray subject will have no color bias.

Color balancing filters Filters used to balance color film with the color temperature of the light source and prevent the formation of color casts. An 85B filter is used with tungsten film in daylight, an 80A filter with daylight film in tungsten light.

Color circle Chart of spectrum hues presented as a circle. Often divided into sectors with the three primary colors (red, blue, and green) opposite their complementaries.

Color compensatory filters Pale-colored filters used to "warm" or "cool" subject colors.

Color contrast Subjective judgment on the apparent luminous difference or intensity of two colors when placed close to one another.

Color conversion filters See *CC filters.*

Color developer Developer designed to reduce exposed silver halides to black silver and at the same time create oxidation by-products that will react with color couplers to form specific dyes, allowing color development.

Color development Chemical treatment in the color processing cycle that produces the colored dye image. Oxidation products from the developing silver image link with color couplers to form dye at a rate related to the amount of silver image reduced. Hence a heavy deposit of silver, produced by exposure in negatives, or by reversal fogging in slides, gives a heavy deposit of dye.

Color head Enlarger illumination system that has built-in adjustable filters or light sources, for color printing.

Color masking Pink or orange mask built into color negative film to improve final reproduction on the print.

Color mixing The practical application of either additive or subtractive color synthesis.

Color saturation The purity or strength of color, due to the absence of black, white, or gray.

Color sensitivity The response of a light sensitive material to colors of different wavelengths.

Color sensitometry Method of determining the sensitivity of color materials by making a number of controlled exposures at different illumination levels, and assessing the results with a densitometer.

Color synthesis Combinations of colored light or dye layers that will collectively produce a colored image. Such systems are either additive or subtractive.

Color separation Process of photographing an image through filters to produce three black and white negatives that represent red, green, and blue content. Used today in photomechanical printing, and some manipulative processes.

Color temperature Convenient way of expressing the color quality (content) of a light source. The color temperature scale is usually measured in Kelvins (K).

Color temperature meter Device for measuring the color temperature of a light source. Usually compares the relative proportions of blue and red wavelengths present in the light.

Color toning System of changing the color of a black and white photographic image by converting black metallic silver into a colored compound or dye. Sepia toning is the most common color toning process.

Color weight Visual characteristic of fully saturated colors. Some of these colors appear darker (or heavier) than others. A color's visual weight may have a different appearance to the eye to its appearance on film – especially if a black and white image is being produced. For example, on panchromatic film, greens appear slightly darker and blues lighter than these colors appear to the eye.

Coma Lens aberration producing asymmetrical distortion of points in the image.

Combination printing Producing a composite image by printing more than one negative on a single sheet of paper.

Compact camera Camera of a design allowing easy portability. Usually a 35 mm or 110 direct vision type.

Compensating developer Developer designed to compress the general contrast range in a negative without influencing gradation in shadows and highlights to any appreciable degree.

Compensating positive Image on translucent film or glass that can be printed together with the negative of the same image. When they are combined in register, the resulting tonal range makes the satisfactory printing of very contrasty negatives much easier. See also *Masking.*

Complementary color The color of light which, when combined with another already specified color in the correct proportion, will form gray or white. Equally, when one color is subtracted from the full spectrum remaining wavelengths combine to form a color complementary to the missing hue. The term is mostly used in photography to describe the colors yellow, magenta, and cyan, because each is the complementary to one of the primaries – blue, green, and red.

Completion State of development when all the exposed silver halides have been reduced to metallic silver, and the image density will not increase with further development.

Composite printing Alternative term for combination printing.

Compound lens Lens system consisting of two or more elements. Compound lens designs can allow the lens designer to reduce lens aberrations, make maximum apertures larger and improve resolution.

Compound shutter Shutter consisting of a number of metal leaves arranged symmetrically around the edge of the lens barrel. Produces a central opening when released. See also *Between the lens shutter.*

Compur shutter Well known German brand of compound shutter.

Concave lens See *Bi-concave lens.*

Condenser In an enlarger or projector, the optical system that concentrates diverging rays from a light source into a beam focused on the main lens. Gives concentrated, even illumination to the negative or slide. In a spotlight, the fresnel lens which directs the light into a controlled beam.

Cones Sensory organs on the retina of the eye, allowing color vision. The human retina contains approximately six million cones. It is thought that there are three types, in pigments absorbing red, green, and blue light.

Constructivism Art movement begun in Russia c. 1913. Characterized by the use of everyday materials (such as glass, iron, and plaster) in abstract compositions. A development of Cubist relief-constructions, an attempt to bridge everyday life and art. Among its major exponents were the artist and photographer Alexander Rodchenko and the sculptor Naum Gabo.

Contact paper Printing paper used for contact printing with a bright light source. It is usually coated with silver chloride emulsion of a very slow speed.

Contact print Negative-sized photograph made by exposing printing paper in direct contact with the negative.

Contact printing frame Simple apparatus with a flat foam plastic bed and a hinged glass cover. Allows negatives to be held in firm, even contact with printing paper, so that contact prints can be made.

Contact screen Type of half-tone screen in which the dots consist of slightly unsharp halos. Used to make half-tone images, by contact printing through the screen on to line film.

Continuous tone Black and white negative or print with an image containing black, and a continuous range of gray tones through to white, representing a variety of subject luminosities.

Contour film Special print film producing an equidensity line image from a continuous tone negative or positive.

Contrast Subjective judgment of the difference between densities or luminosities and their degree of tonal separation in a subject, negative, or positive image. Contrast control is an important element in photography and is affected by a number of factors. Inherent subject contrast, subject lighting, lens flare, type of negative material, degree of development, enlarger type, and grade and surface quality of the printing paper are all important influences on final image contrast.

Contrast filters Filters used in black and white photography to darken or lighten the film's rendition of particular colors. They enable the photographer to record in contrasting tones colors that would normally appear similar in a black and white image.

Contre-jour Back-lighting. Photograph taken with the camera pointing directly at the light source.

Converging lens See *Convex lens.*

Converter lens Lens attachment that converts an existing camera lens to a longer or shorter focal length.

Convex lens Simple lens that causes rays of light from a subject to converge and form an image.

Copper chloride Chemical contained in certain bleaches, toners, and intensifiers.

Copper sulfate Chemical used in certain bleaches, toners, intensifiers, and reducers.

Copper toning Chemical process used for toning black and white prints. The image color produced ranges from brown to light red. See *Toners.*

Copyright Law governing the legality of ownership of particular photographs, works of art, etc.

Cronographic camera Camera used to photograph the sun. A special telescope attachment has a circular mask, which blocks out the sun's central disk, creating a simulated solar eclipse. By this means, the sun's corona can be photographed directly at any time. Normally the sun can only be photographed indirectly or during an eclipse.

Correction filter Lens attachment that alters the color rendition of a scene to suit the color response of the eye. Most black and white panchromatic films, although sensitive to all colors of the spectrum, do not have the same response to these colors as the human eye. Correction filters help compensate for this difference, and are usually yellow or yellow-green.

Coupled exposure meter Exposure meter that is linked to the lens aperture and/or shutter speed controls, so that an indication of correct or incorrect exposure settings can be given directly.

Coupled rangefinder Focusing system in which a rangefinder and the lens focusing mechanism are linked. As the lens is adjusted, a central area of the viewfinder indicates when lens focus is correct for the subject distance.

Coupler **1** Chemical present in different forms in all three layers of substantive color material. Each coupler is combined with oxidation by-products of the color development process to form yellow, magenta, or cyan dye. **2** Chemical incorporated in developer solution, which develops all halides into one color, as with some forms of toning, and non-substantive color film processes.

Covering power The maximum area of image of usable quality that a lens will produce. This must exceed the negative format – generously so if camera movements are to be used. The angle subtended at the lens by the usable portion of the image circle is known as the angle of coverage.

Coving Concave molding used to bridge the angle between floor and wall in a studio set, producing a continuous background curve.

CP filters Color printing filters. These are types of color compensating filters made of low-cost acetate instead of glass or gelatin. They are used in the filter drawer of the enlarger, not under the lens.

Critical aperture Setting at which a lens gives its best performance (usually about the middle of the number range). This setting offers the best compromise between diffracting due to small aperture and lens aberrations increasingly apparent at wide apertures.

Cropping Removing unwanted areas of an image during printing, by trimming a print, or masking a transparency.

Crossed polarization Technique of using two crossed polarizing filters, one over the light source, and one between the subject and the lens. With certain subjects, particularly plastic materials, bi-refringence then causes colored bands to appear. Crossed polarization can also be used to eliminate all reflections when copying artwork behind glass.

Cross front Camera movement allowing the lens to be moved laterally from its usual position.

Crown glass Low dispersion optical glass.

Cubism Early twentieth-century European art movement characterized by the rendering of forms as simplified planes, lines, and geometrical shapes. These are often arranged to depict the form as if seen simultaneously from several points of view.

Curvature of field Lens aberration causing the sharp image of a flat subject at 90° to the lens to be formed on a saucer-shaped plane. Stopping down reduces the effect.

Cut film (sheet film) Film available in flat sheets. The most common sizes are 5 × 4 ins (12.5 × 10 cm) and 10 × 8 ins (25 × 20 cm).

Cyan Blue-green subtractive color, complementary to red. Absorbs red but reflects (or transmits) the remaining two-thirds of the spectrum of white light.

Cyanotype Contact printing process producing a blue image on a white background. Once used for making prints from plans and similar translucent documents.

Dadaism Artistic movement that flourished in Europe between c. 1916-20. Based chiefly on willful irrationality, anarchy, and the overturning of traditional artistic and social values.

Daguerreotype The first practical and commercial photographic process, introduced by Louis Daguerre in 1839. The sensitive material comprised silver iodide, deposited on a polished silver-plated copper base. A positive image was produced by camera exposure and mercury "development", which turned light-struck halides gray-white. The image was made permanent by immersing the plate in a solution of sodium chloride or weak sodium thiosulfate. The image was often gold chloride-toned, to strengthen the result. Extremely popular for portraits, but superceded in the 1850s by the collodion process.

Darkcloth Cloth made of dark material placed over the photographer's head and the camera back to facilitate the viewing of images on the ground glass screen of sheet film cameras.

Darkfield Method of illumination used in photomicrography that will show a specimen against a dark or black background.

Darkroom Light-tight room used for processing and printing. Usually incorporates safelighting suitable for the materials in use.

Darkslide **1** On sheet film cameras, a slide-in plastic sheet used over the front of the film holder to protect the emulsion from light. **2** On rollfilm SLR film magazines, a slide-in metal sheet that prevents film fogging when changing magazines.

Daylight color film Color film intended for use with daylight or a light source of similar color temperature. These sources include both blue flashbulbs and electronic flash. The film is color balanced to 5400 K.

Daylight enlarger **1** Early type of enlarger using light from a hole in a window blackout to provide illumination of the negative. Outside the room a white-painted board was used to reflect even light from the sky. **2** Modern enclosed enlarger that allows the exposing process to be carried out in regular room lighting. The exposed paper (normally in roll form) must then be removed from the enlarger in the dark and processed as usual.

Daylight loading tank Light-tight film processing tank specially designed to allow loading in normal light.

Daylight tank (or drum) Light-tight container for film or paper processing. The exposed material is loaded in the dark, after which all the processing steps are carried out in normal light.

Dedicated flash Flash gun designed for use with a specific camera or group of cameras. It links directly into the internal camera circuitry, for example re-programing the shutter, using the TTL meter, receiving ASA data.

Definition Subjective term used to describe the clarity of a negative or print. It can also apply to a lens or photographic material, or the product of both, and commonly refers to the resolving power achieved.

Delayed action Operation of the shutter some time after the release is depressed. Most shutters have a delayed action timer built in.

Densitometer Instrument for measuring the density of silver deposits on a developed image by transmitted light (films) or reflected light (prints).

Density Amount of silver deposit produced by exposure and development. Measured in terms of the logarithm of opacity, where opacity is the amount of incident light divided by the amount transmitted or reflected, as measured by the densitometer.

Depth of field Distance between the nearest and farthest points in a subject that are brought to acceptably sharp focus on the film plane at one setting of the lens. For most subjects, it extends one-third of the distance in front of, and two-thirds behind the precise part of the subject focused on. The nearer the subject is to the camera, the shallower the depth of field therefore becomes.

Depth of field scale Scale on a lens barrel showing the near and far limits of depth of field possible when the lens is set at any particular focus and aperture.

Depth of focus The distance that the film plane can be moved while maintaining an acceptably sharp image without re-focusing the lens. It extends between two points equidistant in front of and behind the plane of optimum focus. The nearer the subject the greater the depth of focus permissable.

Desensitizing Reducing an exposed emulsion's sensitivity to light. This can be done by the application of certain dyes, or by using powerful oxidation agents. Also used to remove completely the latent image.

Detective camera Popular nineteenth-century novelty camera type. Cameras were disguised as hats, pocket watches, or binoculars. Used, allegedly, by private investigators.

Developer Chemical bath containing reducing agents, which converts exposed silver halides to black metallic silver, so making the latent image visible. Other chemicals, such as accelerator, preservative, and restrainer, are added to the bath to maintain the action of the reducing agents. There are three basic types of black and white developer. The formulae given below are typical examples of each type.

General purpose MQ developer
This developer can be used for both film and paper, depending on the dilution. The formula is as follows:

Metol	2 g
Hydroquinone	12 g
Sodium carbonate	7 g
Sodium sulfite	50 g
Potassium bromide	1 g
Water to 1 liter (Use 1 + 5 for films; or 1 + 3 for paper)	

Fine grain developer
This general-purpose developer for negative materials gives a fine grain image, and can be used with most film types.

Metol	2 g
Hydroquinone	5 g
Borax	2 g
Sodium sulfite	100 g
Water to 1 liter	

High-contrast developer
This developer produces a very high-contrast result, for line film.
Solution A

Hydroquinone	25 g
Potassium metabisulfite	25 g
Potassium bromide	25 g
Water to 1 liter	

Solution B

Potassium hydroxide	50 g
Water to 1 liter	

A working solution is prepared by mixing equal parts of A and B immediately before use. At a temperature of 68°F (20°C) full development should occur in 2-3 minutes.

Development The process of converting exposed silver halides to a visible image. Accurate development is achieved with an appropriate developer, suitably diluted at the right temperature. Length of development and amount of agitation also affect the degree of development.

Diaphragm The adjustable aperture of a lens, controlling the amount of light passing into the camera. It may be in front of, within, or behind the lens.

Diaphragm shutter Between-the-lens camera shutter that also performs the function of the iris diaphragm. Pressing the release causes a set of interposing blades to open to the preset aperture.

Diapositive Positive image produced on a transparent base for viewing by transmitted light, i.e. a transparency.

Diazo Abbreviation of diazonium compounds, which decompose under the action of intense blue or ultraviolet radiation, forming an image in an azo dye.

Dichroic Displaying two colors – one by transmitted, the other by reflected light.

Dichroic filters Filters produced by metallic surface coatings on glass to form colors by interference of light. Part of the separation is transmitted, the remainder reflected (for example, a magenta filter appears green by reflected light). Since they contain no dye, these filters are fade-free, but they are more expensive than dyed filters. Used in best-quality color enlarger heads.

Dichroic fog Colored veil of finely divided metallic silver over the surface of a negative, having different colors when viewed by reflected and transmitted light. Caused by faulty processing, particularly in developer solutions incorporating silver halide solvent. May also occur if strong developer is followed by exhausted fixer, without use of a stop-bath. Removable with ferricyanide reducer.

Differential focusing Setting the camera controls to produce minimum depth of field, so that image sharpness is limited to a particular subject element, isolating it against an unsharp background or foreground.

Diffraction Light scatter caused when rays pass through a small hole or close to the edge of an opaque surface. When a lens is stopped down to a very small aperture (e.g. f 45), diffraction affects image quality. Optimum image quality is usually achieved at settings about half-way through the aperture range, where aberrations are reduced but diffraction does not yet occur.

Diffraction grating Optical attachment that separates light into its constituent colors. Generally comprises a transparent surface on which a fine grid of opaque lines is etched. Diffraction at each edge disperses the light by different amounts according to wavelength. It has an effect similar to a prism.

Diffuser Any material that can scatter light. The effect is to soften the illumination. The closer a diffuser is placed to the light source, the less light is scattered.

Diffusion transfer Process in which development produces a negative and at the same time releases unexposed halides (a form of controlled dichroic fog). The released compounds migrate as a positive image to a receiving surface pressed in face contact with the negative. The process forms the basis of the original instant picture materials.

Dilution Reduction in the strength of a liquid by mixing it with an appropriate quantity of water. Dilution is often specified in "parts", either as an addition, or a ratio. For a dilution of 1 + 4, one part of stock solution must be dissolved in four parts of water. If "1:5" is specified, the same degree of dilution is required, one part of the solution being diluted until the final volume is five parts.

Dimensional stability A substance's ability to remain unchanging in size when subjected to processing and drying, to alterations in temperature and humidity, or the effects of ageing.

DIN Abbreviation of Deutsche Industrie Normen (German Industrial Standards). The DIN scale of film speed ratings indicates a doubling of film sensitivity by an increase of 3 in the rating.

Diopter Unit used in optics to express the light-bending power of a lens. The diopter value of a lens is the number of times its focal length will divide into one meter. The power of a convex lens is prefixed by a positive sign, that of a concave lens by a negative sign.

Direct vision viewfinder Sighting device with which the subject is viewed directly, without the aid of a prism or mirror.

Discharge lamp Light source that provides illumination when an electrical charge is applied to gas particles in a glass tube. As used in electronic flash.

Dispersion The splitting of white light into its component colors, normally due to different degrees of refraction (or diffraction) according to wavelength. A glass prism, for example, will disperse sunlight into a spectrum. The amount of dispersion depends on the type of glass, the angle of incident light, and the refractive index of the glass. Dispersive properties of a glass are expressed by its Abbe number – the lower the number the greater the dispersion.

Dissolve projector Projector with a dual lens system so aligned that successive slides fade in or out of each other during projection, without a black interval. A dissolve unit is used to gain the same effect using two (or more) single lens projectors in series.

Distance gauge See *Spacing bracket.*

Distance symbols Symbols used on the focusing control of simple cameras, as an aid to focus. The most common symbols (and distance ranges) are: portrait outline (3 to 6 ft/0.9 to 1.8 m), half-figure outline (6 to 9 ft/1.8 to 2.7 m), full figure (10 to 20 ft/3 to 6 m), and mountain (20 ft/6 m to infinity).

Distortion Alteration in shape and/or proportions of an image. May occur at any stage in the photographic process. Can be produced deliberately with lens attachments or via darkroom manipulation for unusual effects. Also occurs with certain lenses, particularly fisheye and anamorphic types.

Diverging lens Lens that causes light rays from a subject to bend away from the optical axis, i.e. a concave or negative lens.

Documentary photography The taking of photographs to provide a record of social and political situations, with the aim of conveying information, and sometimes adding social comment.

Dodging Control of exposure in photographic printing achieved by shading and so reducing exposure of specific areas of the paper.

Dolly Frame with lockable wheels, designed to support a tripod, and allow easy movement around a studio.

Double exposure See *Multiple exposure.*

Double extension Characteristic of sheet film monorail cameras, having sufficient bellows to extend to twice the focal length of the standard lens. Employed in close-up photography, allowing up to same-size images.

Drying cabinet Vented cabinet equipped with suspending rods for drying films after processing. Air is drawn into the cabinet by an electric fan, passed over the films, and emitted from the top of the cabinet.

Drying marks Marks on film emulsion caused by uneven drying and resulting in areas of uneven density, which show up on the final print. Marks on the back of the negative, caused by scum, can be removed, but there is no satisfactory way of removing drying marks on the emulsion side.

Dry mounting Method of attaching prints to flat surfaces by heating a shellac layer, under pressure, between the print and the mount.

Dry plate Term used in the late nineteenth century to distinguish gelatin-coated plates from the older collodion (wet) plates they replaced.

Dyad **1** A pair of complementary colors. **2** Any two colors considered visually harmonious.

Dye Chemical that imparts its color to another substance when mixed with it or applied to its surface. The color is transferred when the dye is absorbed into the material, unlike pigment, which transfers its color as a surface coating only.

Dye coupling Process creating a colored image from the reaction between by-products of color development and couplers. The couplers form part of the emulsion or the developing solution.

Dye destruction process Method of producing a colored image by partially bleaching fully formed dye layers incorporated in the sensitive material.

Dye-image monochrome films Black and white negative films designed for color processing. The final image is formed in a warm-colored dye, free of silver. These films offer better resolution and much greater exposure latitude than traditional silver image film.

Dye sensitizing Method of extending the color sensitivity of silver halides, by adding traces of suitable dyes during emulsion manufacture.

Dye transfer print Print made by transferring dyes from three separately prepared images,

in register, on a single sheet of paper. The images are enlargements, made on matrix film from three color separation negatives.

Dynamism Picture structuring which relates to a sense of movement, thrust and action generally. Often communicated by diagonal lines, acute angles, steep linear perspective, and similar devices.

Eberhard effect Border effect occurring in a developed image. Appears as a dense line along an edge of high density and as a light line along an edge of low density. It occurs most often in plates developed flat in solution not sufficiently agitated. The effect was described by Gustav Eberhard in 1926.

Edge numbers Reference numbers printed by light at regular intervals along the edge of 35 mm and rollfilms during manufacture. Permits the easy location of particular negatives. With an otherwise blank film the existence of visible numbers proves that the emulsion has been processed.

Electroluminescence The conversion of electrical energy directly into visible light. Used in image intensifiers, image converters, and similar devices.

Electronic flash Artificial lighting produced by an electronic discharge in a gas-filled tube. A single tube will produce a large number of flashes.

Electronic shutter Shutter system timed by electronic rather than mechanical means. Often such shutters are fired by closing electrical contacts through a button switch, rather than exerting purely mechanical pressure.

Electrophotography The creation of images by alteration to the electrical properties of the sensitive material as a result of the action of light. In the most common process (xerography), exposure renders the light-struck areas of the material conductive. A charge applied to the material is retained in the unexposed areas, giving a latent image with shadows represented by charged, resistant areas, and highlights by the uncharged, conductive sections. Pigmented powder, attracted to the charged areas, makes the image visible. The most widely used application of this process is in document-copying equipment.

Element A single lens-shaped piece of glass that forms part of a compound lens system.

Elon Methylaminophenol sulfate, commonly known as metol.

Emulsion Basically a mixture of light-sensitive compounds, such as silver halides, and gelatin. In this form, the chemicals can be coated on various bases to make films and printing papers.

Emulsion speed See *Speed.*

Endoscope Optical device allowing the

viewing and photography of small, inaccessible subjects. Usually consists of a long, narrow tube or bundle of fiber optics with a minute lens at the tip. Used mainly in medical work for taking photographs inside the human body.

Enlargement Print that is larger than the negative used to produce it. Sometimes known as a projection print.

Enlargement ratio Ratio denoting the amount of linear (not area) enlargement between a print and the negative image from which it is made. Thus a 360 mm-wide print from a 36 mm-wide negative represents an enlargement ratio of 10:1 or "times ten" ($\times$ 10). The same size print from a 6 cm-wide negative is a 6:1 enlargement.

Enlarger Apparatus for producing prints by projecting a negative or transparency on sensitive paper. Often allows the production of prints both smaller and larger than the original.

Enprint Small enlarged print, with dimensions of a fixed ratio, produced commercially in an automatic printer. Usually made on paper $3\frac{1}{2}$ ins (9 cm) wide.

Entrance pupil Size of the beam of light which, entering the elements of a compound lens that are in front of the aperture, completely fills the iris diaphragm. The diameter of the entrance pupil forms the effective diameter of the aperture of a camera lens.

Equivalent focal length Distance in a lens between the front nodal point and the focal plane when the lens is set to focus a subject at infinity sharply. In a telephoto lens the equivalent focal length is shorter than the back focus. The reverse is true in a retrofocus wide-angle lens.

Etching Dissolving away selected areas of a surface while shielding the other parts with a resist. The process is used as a creative drawing medium as well as for making half-tone plates on copper and zinc.

Ever-ready case Camera case that can be opened, allowing the camera to be used without removing it completely. A front flap hinges down to uncover lens, viewfinder, and the controls on the camera top plate.

Everset shutter Simple camera shutter mechanism on which a single depression of the release both tensions and fires the shutter.

Exit pupil Image of the iris diaphragm formed on the back surface of a compound lens by the elements behind the aperture.

Expendable flash See *Flash bulb.*

Expiry date Numbers printed on most film boxes indicating the date before which the material should be processed if it is to maintain its stated speed and contrast. In practice this also depends greatly upon storage conditions.

Exposure In photographic terms, the product of the intensity of light that reaches the film or paper (controlled by lens aperture), and the length of time this intensity is allowed to act (controlled by the camera shutter or enlarger timer).

Exposure calculator Device for assessing correct exposure times and lens apertures. Often found on hand meters, and used to convert a light reading into the required combinations of aperture and shutter settings, relative to film speed.

Exposure index See *Speed*.

Exposure latitude The amount by which it is possible to over- or underexpose a light-sensitive material and, with standard processing, still produce an acceptable result. Least latitude occurs with slow films, high-contrast materials, and when the subject has a wide brightness range.

Exposure meter Instrument for measuring the amount of light falling on or being reflected by a subject. Usually equipped to convert this measurement into usable information, such as the shutter speed and aperture size required. Often the meter will directly program these camera settings.

Exposure meter booster Device designed to increase the sensitivity of a (hand-held) exposure meter.

Exposure value (EV) A series of values marked on cameras having meshed aperture and shutter controls, so that as one control is altered the other changes to maintain the same exposure. For example, EV8 sets 1/15 sec at f 4 or 1/8 sec at f5.6 and so on. EV9 sets 1/30 sec at f4 or 1/15 sec at f5.6 and so on. Exposure values can also be used to indicate the sensitivity of range of a TTL or off-camera meter. A typical EV range on 35 mm SLR through-the-lens meters is EV3 to EV18. This range provides sufficient sensitivity for most requirements.

Extension tubes Metal or plastic tubes added to small or medium format cameras, to extend lens-to-film distance, often permitting magnification greater than × 1.

Extinction meter Early device for exposure calculation, consisting of a tube with an eyepiece at one end and a series of increasingly dark translucent numbers at the other. The photographer noted the number that was just barely visible, and a chart related this to plate speed, to show the exposure settings required.

Fahrenheit scale Scale of temperature named after its German originator, G. D. Fahrenheit. In this scale, the freezing point of water is 32°F, and its boiling point is 212°F.

False attachment Part of one object seen behind another so that lines, shapes or tones seem to join up. A compositional device used in various ways to produce images in which foreground and background objects appear to occupy the same plane.

Farmer's reducer Solution of potassium ferricyanide and sodium thiosulphate used for bleaching silver image negatives and prints. Invented by Howard Farmer, 1883. See *Reducers*.

Farraday shutter High-speed shutter using a pair of crossed polarizers, between which is a glass block within a coil. When a voltage passes through the coil, the plane of polarization changes, allowing light to pass through to the second polarizer.

Fast film Film which has an emulsion that is very sensitive to light. Such films have high ASA ratings.

Fast lens Lens with a wide maximum aperture (low f number).

Ferric chloride Bleaching solution sometimes used on negative materials.

Ferrotype plate Sheet of highly polished chromed steel, used for glazing fiber-based glossy prints.

Ferrotype process Method of creating direct positive images with dark enameled metal plates as a base. Also known as the tintype process.

Fiber optics Optical system using bunched strands of glass to transmit light. Fiber optics provide a flexible "light pipe" able to duct light from a lamp placed against one end of the strands and a remote optical system (such as the working tip of an endoscope) at the other. Provided the strands are bunched together in exactly the same order at each end, fiber optics allow images to be transmitted. A lens forms an image on the flat face of the fiber ends. At the far end of the fibers they are pressed into contact with an emulsion, or the picture on this end face is re-imaged. Resolution is limited by the number and diameter of the fibers.

Field camera Sheet film camera suitable for use in location work outdoors. Term also used for view camera.

Fill-in Light used to illuminate the shadow areas of a scene.

Film Photographic material consisting of a thin, transparent plastic base coated with light-sensitive emulsion. Two kinds of film base are in general use. Cellulose triacetate has greatest flexibility, as required for 35 mm or rollfilm. Polyethylene terephthalate or polyester is used in a thicker form for sheet film. Polyester has greatest dimensional stability.

Film clips Metal or plastic clips used to prevent the curling of a length of drying film. One grips the top of the film; another, hung at the bottom, is weighted to pull the film straight.

Film pack Container holding several sheets of film, so devised that when fitted to the camera the photographer can pull a tab to re-move an exposed sheet from the focal plane and replace it with another.

Film plane In a camera, the plane at the back of the camera across which the film lies. In an enlarger, the flat plane of the negative carrier aperture, across which the film is positioned. It is normally parallel to the enlarger baseboard.

Film speed See *Speed*.

Filter Transparent lens attachment, made of glass, plastic, or gelatin, which subtracts some wavelengths from the light passing through it.

Filter factor Number by which an unfiltered exposure reading must be multiplied to give the same effective exposure through a filter. This compensates for the absorption of light by the filter.

Filtration Use of a filter. In color printing, the use of color filters to control the color balance of an enlarged image, and so of the resulting print.

Finality development Prolonged development, reducing silver halides affected by light to silver until no further image density improvement occurs. If negative materials are treated in this way, contrast, grain, and fog levels tend to be unacceptably high. Printing papers respond more favorably to finality development.

Finder Abbreviation for viewfinder.

Fine-grain developer Film developer used to keep grain size in a photographic image to a minimum by reducing the tendency of the image-forming silver halides to join together in clumps. Most modern fine-grain developers are capable of achieving excellent results without loss of film speed.

Fisheye lens Extreme wide-angle lens in which correction of curvilinear (barrel) distortion is sacrificed in favor of extreme angle of view. Over 180° is therefore possible. Depth of field is practically infinite and focusing is often not required. Fisheye lenses produce highly distorted images.

Fixation Removal of unexposed and undeveloped halides by converting them to soluble salts that may be washed from the emulsion. Makes images permanent in white light.

Fixed focal length lens Lens with unvariable focal length, as opposed to a zoom lens.

Fixed focus lens Lens set at one fixed distance from the film and offering no method of focusing adjustment. It remains focused for a fixed point, usually at the hyperfocal distance. With the use of a small aperture (f 11), all subjects at distances from 6 ft (2 m) to infinity can be rendered reasonably sharp. Most cheap cameras use this system.

Fixer Chemical solution used for fixation.

Flare Non-image-forming light scattered by the lens, or reflected from the camera interior.

It is much reduced when glass-air surfaces within the lens are coated (or "bloomed") with metallic fluorides, and the camera interior is matte black. Flare has greatest effect on image shadows, which it degrades, lowering image contrast.

Flash Artificial light source giving brief but very bright illumination when triggered by the camera. There are two types: electronic, which may be used repeatedly, and expendable, in which the bulb must be replaced after a single firing.

Flash bulb Replaceable bulb for use in expendable flash units. A glass bulb contains pyrotechnic wire or paste which burns out in a brilliant flash when a low-voltage firing current is applied.

Flash factor Number providing a guide to correct exposure when using flash. Each flash unit or bulb is assigned a flash factor according to film speed and working conditions. The photographer must divide this figure by the flash-to-subject distance to give the correct f number.

"Flashing" Briefly and evenly exposing photographic material to white light. Most often used to lower the contrast of printing paper, when the flashing exposure is made in addition to the regular printing exposure. Also used to prevent loss of highlight detail when producing half-tone negatives.

Flashlight Alternative term for a battery-powered hand torch. Term also used for early photographic flash unit.

Flash powder Chemical powder consisting of a mixture of metallic magnesium and oxidation agent. Ignited by heat (from touch paper or a spark) to produce bright light.

Flash synchronization Method of ensuring that flash light duration and maximum shutter opening coincide. There are often two settings on a camera, X and M. X is the setting used for electronic flash, in which peak output is almost instantaneous on firing. M is for expendable flash, which normally requires a delay in shutter opening of about 17 milliseconds, to allow the bulb output to build up.

Flat-bed camera Camera designed for copying. Mounted on a vertical column, like an enlarger, allowing the photographer to accommodate different-sized documents in the same negative format.

Flat gradation Subjective term used to describe low-contrast values. May refer to the original lighting, or to a negative or positive photographic image.

Floating elements One or more elements in a lens which adjust position relative to other components during focusing or zooming. Used to maintain optimum correction of lens aberrations at all settings.

Floodlight Artificial light source with a broad dish-shaped reflector, producing evenly spread, soft illumination.

Fluorescent whites Brilliant highlights produced by applying fluorescent agent to printing paper base. The print can also be treated after washing with a fluorescent whitener or dye in solution, to create a similar result.

f number Sequence of figures printed on a lens barrel, indicating the aperture settings. The scale applies to all lenses, and is derived from the focal length of the lens divided by its effective apertures. Each higher f number halves the exposure given at the preceding one. The numbers progress by the square root of 2 (1.4). Aperture settings are also referred to as f stops.

Focal length The distance between the rear nodal point of a lens and the focal plane, when the lens is focused at infinity. The primary classification of a lens is by its focal length, usually measured in millimeters.

Focal plane Imaginary line in an optical system perpendicular to the optical axis, passing through the focal point. Forms the plane of sharp focus, which must coincide with the emulsion plane to record a sharp image. The position of focal point and focal plane varies according to subject distance.

Focal plane shutter Shutter consisting of a pair of blinds placed immediately in front of the focal plane. Film positioned at the focal plane is progressively exposed as the blinds move in sequence across it. Exposure duration is determined by the gap between the blinds.

Focal point Point of light on the optical axis, where all rays of light from a given subject meet at a common point of sharp focus.

Focusing Moving the lens in relation to the image plane, so as to obtain the required degree of sharpness.

Focusing hood Light-proof cowl used on TLR and most rollfilm SLR cameras to prevent extraneous light falling on the focusing screen.

Focusing magnifier Device to magnify the optical image and aid visual focusing. On a camera this may consist of a magnifier placed at a suitable distance from the focusing screen. For enlarging, the magnifier has a mirror which reflects part of the projected image upward, where it is examined through a magnifying lens on a ground-glass screen.

Focusing scale Scale of distances marked on a lens focusing ring. To focus the lens for a particular subject distance, the photographer lines this up with a reference mark on the barrel.

Focusing screen Glass or plastic surface mounted in a camera at an image-forming plane, enabling the image to be viewed and focused accurately.

Fogging Producing an overall veil of density on a negative or print, which does not form part of the image. This can be done either with chemicals, or by exposing the sensitive material to light.

Fog level Density formed in unexposed areas of film or paper during processing. Tends to be highest with ultra-fast emulsions, or films which have been push processed.

Foreground Area in an image closer than the main subject.

Format Size or shape of negative, slide, printing paper, or camera viewing area.

Frame **1** Single exposure on a roll of film. **2** Viewfinder image boundary. **3** Decorative border applied to finished, mounted print, for display purposes.

Frame numbers See *Edge numbers.*

Fresnel lens Condenser lens consisting of a set of concentric rings, each with a convex surface. Used in spotlights to concentrate the light beam. Also used (in a molded plastic sheet form) behind camera focusing screens to improve the even illumination of the image seen by the eye.

Frilling Wrinkling and separation of the emulsion along the edges of its support material.

Front-element focusing System of lens focusing in which only the front component of a compound lens moves backward and forward to adjust focus. Found in many early hand cameras.

Front projection Technique in which a studio subject can be combined with a previously photographed background. The background scene is projected from in front of the set, through a semi-silvered mirror over the camera lens, on a special reflective screen behind the main subject.

Futurism Art movement started in Italy c. 1910, characterized by an aggressive rejection of tradition, and the representation of the dynamic movement of machinery.

Galvanography Technique of electroplating a gelatin relief image created photographically to produce a photomechanical printing plate.

Gamma Measurement used in sensitometry to describe the angle made between the straight line portion of the characteristic curve of a photographic emulsion and the base of the graph. The gamma (γ) is the tangent of the angle so formed.

Ḡ curve Average gradient of a characteristic curve, describing similar characteristics to gamma, but measuring the slope from a line joining the lower and upper limits of the curve actually used in practice. More indicative of emulsion contrast than gamma values. Recommended development times for films are often related to specific Ḡ levels.

Gelatin Natural protein used as the transparent medium to hold light-sensitive silver halide crystals in suspension, binding them to the printing paper or film, yet swelling to allow entry of processing solutions and washing away of by-products.

Gelatin filters Filters cut from dyed gelatin sheet and held in front of the lens or studio light. They are cheaper than glass or plastic filters but less durable.

Gelatin-sugar process Daylight printing process using paper with a sugar and dichromate coating, which hardens on exposure to light.

Ghost Flare spot on the film caused by reflection of intense light from shiny surfaces. It may be corrected by using a polarizing filter or adjusting the light source, or intensified with a lens diffuser.

Glaze The smooth glossy surface produced on the surface of some printing papers. On fiber-based glossy paper this is produced by squeegeeing the wet print face down on a heated, highly polished surface to dry. Glossy resin-coated paper dries naturally with a glaze. Glazed prints exhibit a wider, richer range of tones than matte finishes.

Glazer Machine on which wet fiber base prints are placed face downward in contact with a polished surface, such as chromed steel, and held by a tensioned cloth. The surface is heated to dry the print.

Glossy paper Printing paper with a smooth shiny surface finish, to give maximum detail and tonal range.

Gold chloride Soluble crystals used in gold toners.

Golden Mean Compositional technique used to determine the "ideal" position for the main subject in the frame. It is based on creating a rectangle from a square. A line drawn from the center of one side of the square to the opposite corner becomes the radius of an arc. The side of the square is then protracted until it meets the arc, and from this point a rectangle is constructed. The side of the square which remains in the rectangle indicates the point at which the subject should be placed. Also known as the Golden Section.

GOST Arithmetical system of rating film speed, used in Soviet bloc countries.

Gradated filter Filter with colored section, which gradually reduces in density toward the center of the filter. The rest of the filter is clear. Gradated filters are used to reduce the contrast between a bright sky and the rest of the scene, or for special color effects.

Gradation Range of contrast found in the tones of an image, from white through gray to black. Gradation is termed "soft" where the tonal contrast is low, "normal" with normal contrast and "hard" or "contrasty" where contrast is great.

Grade System of terms and numbers used to denote the contrast characteristics of black

and white printing papers. 0-1 are soft; 2 is normal; 3 hard; 4 and 5 very hard. Similar grade numbers from different manufacturers may not represent identical characteristics.

Graduate Vessel used for measuring liquids, having a scale of figures to indicate volume.

Graininess Irregular clumps of black metallic silver making up the developed image. Graininess limits the image detail recording ability of the film. It shows up mostly in plain mid-tone areas such as sky. Dye images developed chromogenically from silver halides form a spread of much smaller dye molecules from each silver grain. However, in all cases graininess increases with the speed of the emulsion and degree of development.

Grains Exposed, developed silver halides which have formed black metallic silver grains to produce the visible photographic image.

Granularity The degree to which the silver halide grains have clumped together within the emulsion, measured objectively by a microdensitometer.

Gray card Card with an 18 per cent gray tint, used to determine exposure by taking a meter reading from light reflected by the card. The card simulates mid-tones in the subject, since an average scene represents around 18 per cent gray when reduced to monotones.

Gray scale Transparency or print with regular steps of tone from white (or clear) to black (or opaque), used to judge exposure or color balance. Also known as a neutral scale or a step wedge.

Ground glass screen Translucent glass sheet etched on one side only and used for viewing and focusing on sheet film and reflex cameras. The image is viewed from the clear side of the sheet.

Group f64 Influential school of American photographers which existed briefly in the 1930s. Its alumni included Edward Weston, Ansel Adams, Willard Van Dyke, and Imogen Cunningham. They used large format cameras at small apertures (hence the group's name) to give outstanding image detail and depth of field. Allied to impeccable printing techniques, their straightforward visual approach gave a fidelity which invested their often commonplace subjects with a profound significance and sense of identity.

Guide number The figure given to a light source such as an electronic flash unit to indicate its power. Also known as the flash factor, it is usually given for use with both feet and meters, since dividing the guide number by the subject distance gives the correct aperture to use for a given film speed. Unless otherwise stated, a single guide number quoted for a unit refers to use of 100 ASA film, with distances in feet.

Gum arabic Water soluble gum obtained from the Acacia tree, used in coatings in a number of photographic processes.

Gum bichromate Contact printing process once very popular for the manipulative, impressionistic effects it makes possible. Images are formed in water color pigment. Drawing paper is first coated with a mixture of gum, potassium bichromate and pigment of any chosen color. This is then exposed to sunlight or UV-rich light behind a negative. Light hardens the bichromate, and "processing" in hot water removes unexposed image areas. Images can be built up by successive coatings and exposures. Also known as the photo aquatint process.

Gum platinum process Combination of gum and platinum printing. Having made a conventional platinum print this is then sensitized with pigmented gum bichromate (see above) as if drawing paper. It is then re-exposed to the negative. Gum platinum prints therefore show a combination of colored and black images.

Gyroscopic camera mount Device employing a gyroscope to help stabilize hand-held cameras subject to movement or vibration from outside sources.

Halation Diffused ring of light typically formed around small brilliant highlight areas in the subject. It is caused by light passing straight through the emulsion and being reflected back by the film base on the light-sensitive layer. This records slightly out of register with the original image. Largely eliminated in modern films and plates by anti-halation dye.

Half-frame Negative format of 18 × 24 mm. Images are recorded on a vertical axis on standard 35 mm (24 × 36 mm) film, thus giving 72 half-frame images on film designed for 36 exposures.

Half-frame camera Camera designed to use 35 mm film in half-frame format.

Half-plate Picture format measuring $4\frac{3}{4} \times 6\frac{1}{2}$ ins; some early cameras produced negatives or plates of this size.

Half-silvered mirror Glass sheet evenly coated with a substance which transmits part of the light incident upon it and reflects the remainder. Used for beam-splitting devices in holography, and for front projection.

Half tone Mechanical process for printing apparently continuous tone images in ink. The image is formed of a pattern of dots. Large dots correspond to dark areas of the original; highlights are represented by much smaller dots. This method is used in the printing of books, newspapers and magazines. Continuous-tone photographs are converted into half-tone images by re-imaging through an even but slightly unsharp screen pattern, on high-contrast film. This dot image is then converted into printing plates.

Halogens Collective term for the elements chlorine, bromine, and iodine, which are combined with silver to produce the light-sensitive crystals used as the basis of most photographic emulsions.

Hand coloring Process of applying color tints — usually in the form of dyes or paint — to a photographic image to create or enhance color effects.

Hardener Chemical — often potassium or chrome alum — used in film manufacture and as a bath in some processing sequences. It strengthens the physical characteristics of the gelatin and therefore the emulsion, particularly in high-temperature processing.

Hard gradation Term denoting the quality of harsh contrast in a photograph, or the light source which produces this quality in the subject.

Heat filter Optical attachment, usually of thick infrared-absorbing glass, used to absorb heat radiation from a light source without diminishing its light output. The filter itself becomes hot, and so must be ventilated.

Herschel effect Destruction of an exposed image by infrared radiation. It can occur with silver halide emulsions, which are otherwise insensitive to this region of the spectrum.

Hide Camouflaged barrier, hut or tent used by natural history photographers to conceal themselves from birds or animals which might otherwise be disturbed by their visual presence.

High Art photography General term for early form of artistic photography (1851-70) in which workers set out to match the style and subject matter of paintings of the period. Often scenes were literary and allegorical, staged in front of the camera, or constructed from individual negatives into one composite print.

High-contrast developer/film Solution and materials designed to be used together to produce high-contrast images.

High key Photograph in which light or pale tones predominate, rather than dark, deeper tones.

Highlights The brightest areas of the subject, represented by the lightest areas in the transparency or by darkest deposits of black metallic silver on the negative (which reproduce as light tones on the positive print).

Hill cloud lens Lens with a 180° angle of view, used for photographing cloud formations and for meteorological work — the progenitor of the fisheye lens.

Holding back **1** Shortening the development time given to a film, to help compensate for over-exposure, or reduce image contrast. **2** Method of decreasing the exposure given to selective areas of the print by shading or masking the corresponding area of the negative for all or part of the exposure.

Holography System of photography, using neither camera nor lens, in which laser beams create an interference pattern recorded directly on appropriate light-sensitive sheet film or plates. After processing, viewing the image by the light of a laser or point source gives a three-dimensional monochrome image similar to viewing the object itself through a window.

Horizon The line at which earth and sky appear to meet. Its position, which can be altered by tilting the camera or by cropping the image, determines whether the sky or the landscape forms the principle interest in the picture. A low horizon concentrates interest in the sky, while the landscape is emphasized by a high horizon.

Hot shoe Fitting on top of many cameras designed to hold accessories, such as a flashgun. It contains electrical contacts which are part of the synchronizing circuits between flash and shutter.

Hot-spot Undesirable concentration of the central beam of a flood or spotlight on the subject.

Hue The name of a color (e.g. red, blue, yellow) or the property of color wavelength that distinguishes a pure color from any other color.

Hydrobromic acid Acid liberated during the developing process by reduction of the bromide. It slows down the process, but can be offset by using an accelerator.

Hydrochloric acid Highly corrosive chemical used in dilute form in some bleaching solutions.

Hydrogen peroxide Chemical used in hypo clearing agents.

Hydroquinone Reducing agent with strong developing action, giving high contrast when used in conjunction with a vigorous alkali. Also used with metol or phenidone to provide general-purpose and fine grain solutions (MQ/PQ). It becomes virtually inactive at temperatures below 55°F (13°C).

Hyperfocal distance The distance between the camera and the hyperfocal point.

Hyperfocal point The nearest point to the camera which is considered acceptably sharp when the lens, set at a particular aperture, is focused on infinity. If the lens is focused on this point, depth of field will extend from infinity to a point half-way between the camera and the hyperfocal point.

Hypersensitizing Early method of increasing the light sensitivity of a photographic emulsion prior to exposure. A 50 per cent speed increase can be gained by soaking the film (in total darkness) in a mixture of one part of 0.880 ammonia to 8 parts of pure alcohol and 24 parts of water. Dry the film carefully and use as quickly as possible.

Hypo Term used today to mean fixing solutions in general. It is an abbreviation of hyposulfite of soda, a name used incorrectly for the sodium thiosulphate used as a fixer in the nineteenth century.

Hypo eliminator Chemical bath used to remove the fixing agent from an emulsion, thus reducing the washing time.

"Ideal" format A film format in the proportion of 4 to 3, e.g. 6 × 4.5 cm. This ratio is considered an ideal shape by some manufacturers and photographers for both vertical and horizontal composition.

Illuminance Term quantifying the illumination of, or incident light falling on, a surface. Can be measured by meters.

Image Two-dimensional representation of a real object, produced by focusing rays of light.

Image amplifier Miniature television-like electronic device placed between the lens and the camera body to intensify the brightness of the image.

Image plane A plane commonly at right angles to the optical axis at which a sharp image of the subject is formed. The nearer the subject is to the camera, the greater the lens-image plane distance.

Image tube Device in which light, striking a front target plate in the form of an image, is transformed into a stream of electronic signals. An image tube may amplify the information, then return it to a light image by bombarding a phosphor screen at the back of the tube with electrons. Some image tubes are used to act as ultra fast shutters, others to intensify an image greatly under dim lighting conditions.

Impressionism Art movement in which painters broke away from the techniques of continuous brushstrokes and clearly expressed detail. They were largely concerned with the effects of light and color. Many works are in bright colors and high key. The first Impressionist exhibition was held in France in 1874, the last in 1886.

Incident light Light falling on a surface, as opposed to reflected by it.

Incident light attachment Accessory for a hand exposure meter, which allows it to give incident light readings.

Incident light reading The measurement by exposure meter of the amount of incident light reaching a subject. The meter is fitted with an incident light attachment and held close to the subject, pointing toward the main light source.

Indicator chemical Neutral chemicals which can be added to the sample of a solution to indicate pH level or the presence of hypo or other chemicals, by means of a color change.

Infectious development Development in which the image begins to build up slowly at first, then gains density more rapidly because the developer oxidation products formed are themselves highly active developing agents. Infectious development is utilized in most lith developers, and gives extreme contrast provided it is used on appropriate thin emulsion lith films.

Infinity The focusing position (marked ∞) at which objects so distant that light from them reaches the lens as parallel rays are brought to focus on the film. In practice it can be taken to mean objects on the distant horizon.

Infrared Band of wavelengths beyond the red end of the electro-magnetic spectrum. They are invisible to the human eye, but can be recorded on suitably sensitized film.

Infrared focus See *IR setting.*

Instamatic camera Compact camera popular in the 1960s and 70s with very simple controls, taking 126 film yielding 28 × 28 mm negatives. Some models have built-in flash.

Instant picture camera Camera, usually with simple controls, producing a finished photographic print within minutes of the film being exposed.

Integral tripack Light-sensitive material used for color photography consisting essentially of three emulsion layers, responding to blue, green, and red, coated on a base.

Integrating Term used to describe a method of arriving at an exposure by mixing all the light from bright and dim parts of the image or subject, to give a single reading. Results are therefore influenced by relative areas as well as brightness range.

Integration to gray Integrated method of exposure reading often applied to enlarging. A diffuser or other light-scrambling device is fitted over the lens and measurement made of the resulting "gray" value.

Intensification Chemical method of increasing the density of the photographic image. It is only suitable for treating negative materials and works better on negatives which have been underdeveloped rather than underexposed. The process involves bleaching and subsequent re-development. There are a number of formulae. For chromium intensifier it is as follows:
Solution A
    Potassium bichromate   25 g
    Water to 500 ml
Solution B
    Hydrochloric acid, concentrated   25 g
    Water to 500 ml
As a standard procedure, use 10 parts of A to 5 parts of B. Increase the amount of A to achieve a greater degree of intensification. If, when the negative is completely bleached, a yellow stain remains, rinse in a weak 2 per cent solution of potassium metabisulfite. Rinse in water and re-develop in a general purpose MQ developer, low in sulfite. Fine grain developers are not suitable. Wash and dry the intensified negatives in the usual way.

Intensity scale Exposure scale in which the

time of exposure remains constant but the intensity of light increases in regular stops.

Interchangeable lens system System of lenses of different focal lengths made to fit the same camera body. The lens mounts of one manufacturer, however, may not be compatible with those of another.

Interference The interaction of light waves when they meet and either reinforce or cancel each other. It can also produce colors or a complete image, as in a hologram.

Interleaving Method of agitating more than one sheet of photographic paper in the same tray. The bottom sheet is lifted to the top continuously.

Intermittency effect Phenomenon whereby a series of short, separate exposures will not produce the same photographic result as a single exposure of equivalent total duration.

Internegative Negative made on special color film designed for making copy prints from color slides. Internegative color film is manufactured with a built-in mask to control color and contrast.

Intersection of thirds Compositional technique whereby the image area is divided horizontally and vertically into equal thirds by means of four imaginary lines. The main subject is considered strongly placed if it is positioned at the intersection of any two of these lines.

Inverse square law The intensity of light reaching a surface is quartered each time the distance from the light source is doubled. This law applies to all forms of lighting emitted from a point (or compact) source, and is used to calculate flash guide numbers.

Inverted telephoto Type of lens constructed to provide a short focal length with a long back focus or lens-to-film distance. Most wide-angle lenses built for small format cameras are constructed in this way to allow space for the operation of the mirror and shutter.

Iodine Chemical used in reducers and bleachers.

Iris diaphragm The device within, behind or in front of the lens using a set of interleaving blades to control the size of the aperture, which is continuously variable.

Iris mount Mount which stands proud of the lens panel and accommodates the whole lens in the grip of an oversize iris diaphragm. Used on some old view cameras to accept lenses of any diameter — the mount is simply closed down to a size which will hold the lens.

Irradiation The scattering of light within the emulsion layer. It causes loss of definition, noticeable on overexposed negatives.

IR setting Mark, usually a red dot or line, found on many lenses to indicate the focus change required for infrared photography. Infrared light comes to focus at a point in front of

visible light from the same source, and so compensation has to be made.

I setting Speed setting denoting "instantaneous" found on some older cameras without stepped shutter speeds. It usually indicates a fixed shutter speed of around 1/30-1/60 sec, but this is often inconsistent.

ISO Initials of the International Standards Organization. The ISO film speed system is gradually replacing the ASA index. Both use identical numbers.

Ivorytype Obsolete printing process designed to give the impression of a painting on ivory. A hand-colored print was impregnated with wax and squeegeed face down on hot glass. The paper base was then backed by ivory-tinted paper.

Joule Unit used to quantify the light output of electronic flash. A joule is equal to one watt-second or 40 lumen-seconds. The measure is used to compare flash units in terms of power output.

Kallitype Obsolete printing process, resembling the platinum process. The image is formed in metallic silver rather than expensive platinum.

Kelvin (K) Unit of measurement on the absolute temperature scale, used to describe the color content of continuous spectrum light sources.

Kerr cell High-speed shutter without moving parts, using two crossed polarizing filters at either end of a cylinder filled with nitrobenzine. When a momentary high voltage pulse is applied to electrodes in the liquid, light being admitted by the first filter is rotated by 90°, and thus for the duration of the pulse allowed to pass through the second filter.

Keyed emulsion sensitivity Term used to describe the color response of color printing papers which have peak sensitivities to the three dye colors present in the same manufacturer's color negatives, and not to the full visible spectrum. The precise keying of sensitivity allows weak safelights to be used which emit wavelengths between the peaks, and helps control color balance in the print.

Key light The principle or dominant light source illuminating the subject.

Kilowatt Unit of 1000 watts, used to measure the power of an electrical light source.

Kinetic Concerned with movement and motion. Contributed to the word kinematograph, the first device for recording moving pictures.

Knifing Method of removing marks and other blemishes from the surface of a print by gentle scraping with the tip of a sharp knife.

Kostinsky effect Development effect in which dense image points are inclined to move apart, relative to each other, and light image points to move together. This occurs because developer is not being equally distributed over the image points, and is rapidly exhausted where two heavily exposed image points are close together. Because development continues on their outer surfaces, they appear to move apart. Agitation distributes developer and prevents the effect occurring.

Kromskop Early viewing instrument invented by F.E. Ives, embodying a system of mirrors and color filters to synthesize a full color image. This enabled monochrome transparencies made from separation negatives to be rear-illuminated through blue, green, and red filters, and then be seen combined in register as a single image.

Lamp General term used to describe the various kinds of artificial light sources used in photography.

Lamp black A pure carbon pigment, made from soot deposited from burning oils.

Lamphouse The light-tight housing of a projector or enlarger, which contains a light source.

Lantern slide Transparency sandwiched between glass plates and viewed by projection.

Large format camera General term for any camera having a picture format of 5 × 4 ins or larger.

Laser Abbreviation for Light Amplification by Stimulated Emission of Radiation. It is an intense collimated coherent light source of a very narrow band width. The strength of this source varies considerably between 1 milliwatt and 1 megawatt. Some lasers produce an effectively continuous emission of light, others give an intense pulse. At the moment its main photographic use is in producing holograms.

Latensification Method of increasing relative film speed by fogging after exposure and before development. It can be achieved by chemical or light means. There are three methods of intensification:
Chemical bath
   0.5 % solution potassium metabisulfite
   0.5 % solution sodium sulfite
Immerse exposed negatives in a mixture containing equal parts of the solutions. Rinse and continue normal processing cycle.
Chemical vapor
The exposed negatives are placed in a closed container with a small amount of mercury of sulfur dioxide. After about 24 hours the film is processed as usual. The amount of exposure needed varies with different types of sensitive material and should be assessed by trial and error. Results tend to be inconsistent.
Light
The film is briefly exposed to a low intensity light before development. The best light source is an evenly illuminated out-of-focus surface. The correct amount of exposure is best established by trial and error.

Latent image The invisible image formed in the emulsion by exposure to light and made visible by development.

Lateral reversal Mirror-image reversal of the subject from left to right, as found in the viewfinders of some reflex cameras.

Latitude The degree of over- and underexposure which a photographic emulsion will tolerate and still give an acceptable image. Faster films and softer grade papers generally have the greatest latitude.

LCD (Liquid crystal diode) Electronic, solid state display system commonly used for the face of wrist watches, and also used to display exposure information in the viewfinder of some camera types. A surface can be temporarily changed from transparent to dense black by application of a charge. The LCD can be programed to display any required black shape.

Lead acetate Crystalline, highly poisonous powder used in some toning and intensifying solutions.

Leader The beginning of a roll of film, which is attached to the camera's take up spool.

Leaf shutter See *Between-the-lens shutter*.

LED Visual display (by light emitting diodes) of such information as shutter speed, aperture and over/underexposure in the camera's viewfinder.

Lens Optical device made of glass or plastic and capable of bending light. A photographic lens may be constructed of single or multiple elements. There are two basic types of simple lens: convex (positive), which cause rays to converge to a point; and concave (negative), which cause rays to diverge. Both are used in compound lens constructions in which several elements are combined to give an overall converging effect.

Lens barrel Metal or plastic tube with blackened inner surface, in which the lens elements and mechanical components of the lens are mounted.

Lens cap Plastic, rubber or metal cover which fits over the front or back of the lens to protect it when not in use.

Lens hood Opaque tube, either cylindrical, square or funnel-shaped, used to shield the lens from stray light from outside the field of view. They may be of plastic, rubber or metal. The length and diameter of the lens hood should be carefully matched to the angle of view of the lens to avoid image cut-off. Some bellows lens hoods for large format cameras are adjustable in length.

Light Visible radiated energy which forms that part of the electro-magnetic spectrum in the wavelength range 400 - 720 nm (4000 - 7000 A). This range of wavelengths indicates the change in color along the visible spectrum, from violet to dark red.

Light box Surface used for viewing transparencies or negatives, consisting of a number of fluorescent tubes balanced for white light and covered by a sheet of translucent material.

Light meter Alternative term for exposure meter.

Light source General term for any source of light used in photography, whether natural or artificial.

Light tent Tent-like structure made of translucent material hung around a frame. The fabric diffuses the light coming from outside the tent so that highly reflective subjects placed inside it can be photographed without reflections of the camera, lamps or surroundings appearing in the picture. A hole is cut in the tent for the lens to look through.

Light-tight Term denoting a material or piece of equipment that is impervious to light.

Light trail Image track recorded on photographic material when a point of light is shifted during exposure.

Light trap Method of preventing entry of light. For example, a labyrinth used with film developing tanks, darkroom doors and ventilators, to prevent light entering while still allowing ready access for liquid or air circulation where necessary.

Light value Alternative term for exposure value, a scale which yields a range of shutter/aperture combinations possible in specific lighting situations. Also used, less precisely, to denote subject and lighting conditions with some exposure meters and tables.

Linear perspective The apparent convergence of parallel lines with increasing distance in a two-dimensional image. Changing the angle or distance of viewpoint makes lines converge more or less sharply, thus increasing or reducing the illusion of depth.

Line image Photographic image consisting of black areas and clear film (i.e. white), without any intermediate gray tones. Such images can be produced from other line images or from continuous tone subjects, by using high-contrast film, developer and papers.

Linked Ring Brotherhood Group of pictorialist photographers who broke away from the Photographic Society of Great Britain. Existed between 1892-1910. Membership, by invitation, was international.

Lippman process Early color process invented by Prof. Gabriel Lippmann (1845-1921). Light first passed through an almost transparent emulsion layer and was then reflected back by a layer of mercury. The interference between reflected and incident light produced a latent image in the emulsion which could be given black and white processing, but when set up backed with a mirror appeared in color.

Lith film An extreme form of line film with a thin coating of slow, high-contrast emulsion. Produces very high-contrast images, but only when used with a special lith developer. It is used as an intermediate process in creating a number of photographic color effects in the darkroom.

Local control Method of controlling the final quality of a print by increasing ("printing in") or decreasing ("dodging", or "holding back") the exposure given locally to selected areas of the image.

Log e The logarithmic values (to the base 10) of the relative brightnesses exposed on the film when undergoing sensitometric testing.

Long focus lens Any lens whose focal length is appreciably greater than the diagonal of the negative in the format in which it is used.

Low key Photograph in which heavy, dark tones predominate, with few highlights. Also applied to the lighting which produces such results.

Lumen Unit expressing the power of a light source. It is the amount of light which provides illumination of one foot candle intensity over a surface area of one square foot.

Luminance Measurable amount of light emitted by or reflected from a source or surface.

Luminescence Visible light produced from a surface submitted to invisible radiation such as UV, X rays and so on. Unlike fluorescent light, it continues to be emitted after the existing source is removed, gradually fading away.

Luminosity Brightness of either a light source or reflective surface.

Mackie line Effect sometimes found on a negative or print, in which a light line forms along the boundaries of the darkest image areas. It may be caused during processing by the diffusion of exhausted developer, lack of agitation, or by solarization.

Macro attachment Supplementary elements attached to the front of a normal lens to give an extreme close-up facility.

Macro lens A lens specially designed to give accurate resolution of very near subjects without the need for supplementary close-up attachments. Sometimes called a micro lens.

Macrophotography Extreme close-up photography in which images larger than the original subject are recorded without the use of a microscope.

Magazine Light-tight container holding film in bulk lengths.

Magenta Purple-red color composed of blue and red light.

Magnification Ratio of the height of the image to the height of the subject. Also applied to the ratio between print size and negative size (i.e. the degree of enlargement), or the ratio of lens-to-image distance to subject-to-lens distance. When subject and image are the same size, magnification is said to be × 1.

Main light See *Key light*

Mask 1 Opaque material used to cover the edges of the printing paper, and thus produce borders when the paper is exposed to light. **2** Weak positive image on film which, when registered with a negative, adds density to the shadow areas, and so reduces contrast. **3** Dyes incorporated into the non-image areas of color negatives, to improve color accuracy when printed.

Masking System of controlling a negative's density range or color saturation through the use of light-blocking masks (usually unsharp).

Masking frame Adjustable frame used to hold printing paper in position under the enlarger.

Mastic varnish Varnish used for negatives, extracted from the resin of *Pistachia lentiscus*.

Mat Alternative term for matte. Also describes the cardboard surround in a picture frame.

Matrix Relief image usually made from gelatin, used for processes such as dye transfer printing.

Matte Term used to describe a non-reflective, non-textured surface.

Matte box Mask used to make images suitable for wide-screen projection, by cutting off the top and bottom of the picture while retaining the existing width.

Meniscus lens Simple lens consisting of a single piece of glass, thicker at the center than at the edges. It has one concave and one convex face. If the curvature of the convex surface is the greater, the lens will cause light rays to converge. If the concave surface has the greater curvature, it will make light rays diverge.

Mercuric chloride/iodide/perchloride Toxic chemicals used in intensifiers.

Mercury vapor lamp Arc lamp in which the glowing arc is contained in an evacuated glass tube containing vaporized mercury, through which a current is passed.

Metal print Photographic print made on a sensitized metal surface.

Methyl alcohol Volatile, poisonous spirit commonly known as wood spirit. Used as a substitute for pure alcohol in some photographic processes.

Metol Reducing agent with mild developing action (to give medium/low contrast) when used in conjunction with a soft working alkali. It can form a balanced normal contrast solution when used with hydroquinone. These two reducing agents form the basis of most first developers in slide processing.

Metoquinone Combination of metol and hydroquinone, used as a developing agent (MQ developer).

Microfilm Slow 16 or 35 mm panchromatic film, having extremely fine grain and used in special cameras to copy documents, etc.

Microflash Extremely short-duration flash, measured in millionths of a second, used to photograph subjects such as projectiles or high-speed machinery.

Micron (μ) Unit of one millionth of a meter, sometimes used to express the wavelength of light in preference to the Angstrom unit.

Microphotography The production of extremely small photographs, using ultra fine-grain film in special cameras. The images are enlarged for viewing through a microfilm reader. Used to copy and reduce documents, printed circuits, etc.

Microprism collar Grid-type cluster of microprisms in the center of a camera's focusing screen, used as an aid to focusing.

Mid-tone Area of brightness midway between deepest shadow and brightest highlights.

Millimicron (mμ) The thousandth part of a micron.

Miniature camera General term applied to any 35 mm (or smaller) camera.

Mired Abbreviation of MIcro-REciprocal Degrees, a scale of measurement of color temperature. To calculate the mired value of a light source, divide one million by its color temperature in Kelvins. Color conversion filters are often given mired shift values.

Mirror Device for reflecting images, normally without distortion or diffusion. Mirrors used in photographic equipment are mostly surface coated, unlike hand mirrors which are coated behind glass. This prevents a double image — one from the glass surface, the other from the mirror silvering.

Mirror box Box containing one or more mirrors, usually angled to the light beam, as in the main body of an SLR camera.

Mirror camera High speed camera able to expose 30 or so frames at over a million frames per second. The film remains stationary behind a series of lenses (one per frame) while the light is reflected from the subject using a mirror forming part of a light speed turbine.

Mirror lens Telephoto lens using mirrors in its construction to allow an extremely long focal length to be accommodated within a short, squat barrel. The aperture is usually fixed. Such lenses are also known as reflex or catadioptric types.

Mode The programed operating function of automatic SLR cameras, e.g. aperture priority mode, shutter priority mode.

Modeling light Light used to create a three-dimensional effect achieved through the perception of form and depth.

Modelscope Device employing a short, rigid endoscope fitted with a right angle mirror at its tip, used to photograph scale models from a seemingly eye-level viewpoint.

Modular enlarger Enlarger with interchangeable filtration heads and/or illumination systems.

Monobath Single solution combining developer and slower working fixer, for processing black and white negatives. It is a quick, simple system but does not allow for development control.

Monochromatic illumination Lighting using rays of only one wavelength, used to eliminate chromatic aberration where sharpness is critical, e.g. in photomicrography.

Monochrome Single colored. Most frequently applied to black and white photographs, but can also describe sepia or other toned images in one color scheme. Similarly light rays of one color wavelength, i.e. a single, pure color.

Monopack Largely obsolete term for describing a film carrying several emulsions stacked as one.

Monorail camera Sheet film camera, of modular construction, mounted on a single rail to give maximum camera movements.

Montage Composite picture made from a number of photographs or other two-dimensional image sources mounted together, either overlaid or side by side.

Mordant Colorless, but dye-absorbing substance used in some forms of toning. The silver image is converted into a mordant, then soaked in dye.

Mosaic Composite made up from a patchwork of partly overlapping photographs. Extensively used in the past for the preparation of maps from sets of air-to-ground vertical survey photographs. Each component print must be accurately matched in tone and image size.

Motor drive Automatic power-driven wind-on mechanism that can be attached to some cameras. With the shutter release depressed the film will continue to wind on after each exposure until the pressure is released or a preset number of pictures have been taken. The wind-on rate is variable.

Mottle Processing fault characterized by random print density differences.

Mount Frame and/or backing used to support and protect prints or transparencies.

Mountant Adhesive used for mounting prints. It must not contain any chemical which may damage the image.

MQ/PQ developing solutions Developing solutions containing the reducing agents metol and hydroquinone (MQ), or phenidone and hydroquinone (PQ).

M-synch Flash setting or socket which synchronizes the firing of the shutter with the peak light output of a flash bulb.

Multi-band photography Method of aerial photography using cameras and scanners which are sensitive to different wavelength bands in the spectrum to record different characteristics of the subject.

Multimode camera 35 mm camera which will operate in several modes, e.g. automatic shutter priority, automatic aperture priority, manual, or totally automatic program.

Multiple exposure Technique of making more than one exposure on the same film frame, normally so that the images are superimposed.

Multiple flash The use of more than one flash unit, usually operating simultaneously, to light the subject.

Munsell system Method of precise color description, based on comparison with comprehensive hue and saturation charts. Has closest application to pigments, whereas the CIE system relates directly to light.

Nanometer Unit of measurement of light wavelength. A nanometer (nm) is one millionth of a millimeter.

Naphtha Volatile petroleum-based solvent such as benzine or gasoline (but not kerosene).

ND Abbreviation of neutral density.

Near ultraviolet Wavelengths from about 400 nm down to 250 nm. Practically all photographic emulsions are sensitive to these bands. Below 250 nm there is strong opacity to UV by the emulsion gelatin itself.

Negative Developed photographic image with reversed tones. Subject highlights appear dark and shadows appear light. With color materials, each subject color is represented by its complementary hue. A negative is usually made on a transparent base, so that light can be passed through it to expose another, similarly designed sensitive material, and so form a positive image.

Negative carrier Metal or plastic-hinged frame that supports and holds the negative flat between the light source and the lens in the enlarger.

Negative lens A lens which causes a parallel beam of light passing through it to diverge away from its original direction. Such lenses are thinner in the center than at the edges.

Negative/positive paper Paper used to print a positive image from a negative. Normally refers to color paper.

Neo-coccine Red dye used in retouching to stain the gelatin.

Neutral density Gray, colorless density. In color printing, it is caused by using some filters of all three subtractive colors at once. The color pack should be simplified by removing the filter of the lowest value, which indicates the level of neutral density within the pack. The other two color values are adjusted by subtracting an equal value from each.

Neutral density filter A gray filter used to reduce the amount of light entering the camera when aperture and speed settings cannot be altered. It has equal effect on all colors of the spectrum and so does not affect the color balance of the final image.

Neutral filtration In color printing, the filtration at which color balance is achieved, rendering a neutral gray on the film image as neutral gray on the color paper.

Neutralizer Normally a chemical designed to counteract and make inactive another chemical solution.

"New Objectivity" *(Neue Sachlichkeit)* A new objective approach to the subject matter of photography and cinema originating in Germany in the early 1920s. The photographer remains an impartial observer, intensifying the appreciation of forms and structures in ordinary things, but de-personalizing his approach.

"New Realism" Alternative name for *New Objectivity.*

Newton's rings Concentric colored rings produced when two flat, transparent surfaces are laid together in partial contact. The colors are formed by interference patterns. The effect is often seen in glass negative carriers and glass slide mounts.

Nitraphot Over-run tungsten filament lamp, similar to a photoflood but with a longer working life.

Nitrate base Cellulose nitrate base first used as an emulsion support for 35 mm film. Not used nowadays because of its highly inflammable nature.

Nitric acid Highly corrosive fluid used in the manufacture of silver halides.

Nodal plane An imaginary line passing through the front or rear nodal point perpendicular to the optical axis.

Nodal points Points in a compound lens where rays of light entering the lens appear to aim (front nodal point) or where the rays of light appear to have come from when they have passed through the lens (rear nodal point). Nodal points are used in many optical measurements instead of plotting refraction at every air/glass surface, for example in calculating the focal length of the lens.

Non-silver processes Image-making processes that do not require the use of metallic silver. Gum bichromate and cyanotype are non-silver processes.

Non-substantive film Color film which does not contain dye-forming couplers in each emulsion layer. These must be processed by the manufacturer, who can fog and couple each layer in separate chemical stages.

Normal lens Lens whose focal length is approximately equal to the diagonal of the film format with which it is used. It yields an image which most closely approximates to normal eye vision. Also referred to as the prime or standard lens for the format.

Notch A V or U shape cut into one edge of the film. With sheet film denotes the location of the sensitive side in the dark. Some automatic color printing machines use notches punched into the side of 35 mm film to position each image automatically in the negative carrier.

Objective The lens used closest to the specimen in microscopes or telescopes.

Oil reinforcement Method of altering the tonal range of prints on matte or textured fiber papers. Shadows can be deepened and highlights emphasized. The dried print is rubbed with a medium consisting of two parts of turpentine to one of mastic varnish and one of linseed oil. Some artists' oil color is then mixed with a little of the medium and applied locally to the print using a cotton ball.

One-shot color camera Obsolete plate camera making three-color separation negatives from a single exposure. It contained semisilvered mirrors and a primary colored filter in front of each emulsion, and used a long focus lens with a leaf shutter.

One-shot developer Developer that is used once only and then discarded.

Opacity Light-stopping power of a material. The greater the opacity of a substance, the more light it stops. In photography, opacity is expressed as a ratio of the amount of light falling on the surface of the material to the amount of light transmitted by it.

Opalescent Like opal, a material with a cloudy-white, translucent appearance.

Opal glass Glass with a translucent opal tint, used as a diffuser for enlargers, light boxes, and exposure meters.

Opal lamp Filament lamp with an opal glass bulb, giving good diffusion, but with considerable loss of light.

Opalotype Obsolete printing process in which a carbon-process image is transferred on to translucent opal glass. Alternatively, the image can be printed directly on to emulsion-coated opal glass.

Opaque, liquid Dense red or black pigment, dissolved in water to form a liquid paint used to fill in film areas that are required to print pure white. Used to create clean white backgrounds. Can be removed and re-applied if necessary.

Open flash Technique of firing the flash while the shutter remains held open on its B setting. The flash can be repeated as often as required before the shutter is closed, as in the "painting with light" technique.

Opening up Increasing the size of the lens aperture to admit more light to the film.

Optical axis Imaginary line passing horizontally through the center of a compound lens system.

Optical bench Device for measuring the optical performance of lenses. It consists of a track on which is mounted a light source, a screen and the lens to be tested. The image of the light source formed by the lens is examined on the screen.

Optical sensitizing Method of increasing the spectral sensitivity of an emulsion by using dyes.

Optical wedge Strip of material, clear at one end and gradually increasing in opacity toward the other, which is used to judge the effect of a range of light intensities on sensitized material.

Optics The science dealing with the behavior of light.

Orthochromatic Photographic materials sensitive to all colors of the visible spectrum except deep orange and red.

Ortho-phenylene diamene Fine-grain developing agent.

Overdevelopment The result of exceeding the degree of development recommended by the manufacturer. It can be caused by prolonged development time, increased temperature or over-agitation. It results in an increase of density and contrast, leading to fog and stains.

Overexposure The result of giving a light-sensitive material excessive exposure, either by exposing it to too bright a light source or by allowing light to act upon it for too long. On negative/positive materials this gives an increase in density and a reduction in contrast, especially in highlights. On slides the color is weakened to a point where it can be totally absent in highlight areas.

Over-run lamp Tungsten light source specifically used at a higher voltage than normal to increase light output and achieve constant color temperature. It has a very short life

and is best worked at normal voltage except when exposure readings are being made.

Oxalic acid Soluble white crystals used in some toners.

Oxidation product Chemical produced by a color developer during the conversion of exposed silver halides to black metallic silver. It is capable of creating a dye to allow primary color development. With modern color materials it is common for the oxidation product to be coupled with another chemical compound known as a color coupler so that a dye of precise and known character is formed. This procedure is known as chromogenic development.

"Painting with light" Technique of lighting large, dark interiors. The camera, mounted on a tripod, is given a long time exposure. The photographer, wearing dark clothing, moves continuously around the interior, giving flash or battery-powered photoflood illumination to the shadow areas.

Pan and tilt head Tripod head allowing the camera to be tilted up and down or turned through 360° while still remaining stable on the tripod. Can be locked in any position.

Panchromatic Photographic materials sensitive to all colors of the spectrum, including red.

Panchromatic vision filter Filter through which the subject can be viewed approximately as it would appear in monochrome as recorded on a panchromatic emulsion.

Panning Swinging the camera horizontally in a smooth arc to follow a moving subject. The subject's position in the viewfinder remains roughly constant. The shutter is released during panning so the subject records sharply against a blurred image of static surroundings.

Panorama Picture presenting a continuous view of the landscape, produced either by using a panoramic camera or from a composite of several photographs taken in an arc from the same viewpoint.

Panoramic camera Camera with a special horizontally scanning lens which rotates about its rear nodal point. It produces an image on a curved plate or film and can cover a very wide angle of view.

Paper base Support for the emulsion used in printing papers. May be plain fiber or resin-coated. Resin paper is water-repellent, allowing quicker processing, less washing, and faster drying.

Paper safe Light-tight container for unwrapped photographic papers, with an easy opening, positive closing lid for use in the dark.

Parabolic mirror Silvered glass or metal reflector with a parabolic axial cross-section, used to produce near-parallel rays from a light source positioned at its geometrical focus. Used for some color head enlarger lamps as well as some studio lighting units.

Parallax The difference between the image as seen through the viewfinder and the image as recorded on the film. It occurs in non-reflex and twin lens reflex cameras because of the slightly different viewpoints of lens and viewing system. The problem of parallax error, which does not occur with single lens reflex and sheet film cameras, is particularly evident at close subject distances.

Paraphenylenediamine Reducing agent used in some color developers whose oxidation products combine with phenol and amines (color couplers) to form dye.

Paraphotography General term for non-silver-halide image forming processes — for example thermography and gum bichromate.

Paraxial The rays nearest the optical axis of a lens.

Patch chart The squared-pattern test strip often made when color printing by the additive method.

Pellicle (pellicule) Thin film used in one-shot color cameras as a semi-reflecting surface.

Pentaprism Five-sided silvered prism used in single lens reflex cameras to give a laterally corrected left-to-right viewing of the image on the focusing screen.

Percentage solution Solution containing a given quantity of a dissolved substance in a stated volume of the solvent.

Periphery photography Technique used to photograph the entire inner or outer surface of a cylinder or tube. The camera is fitted with a special film back in which the film moves sideways behind a fixed slit, at a speed proportional to the rotation of the subject on a turntable. The resultant image made by photographing the subject from a fixed position is continuous, showing the entire surface of the cylinder.

Permanence test Chemical tests for permanence in finished negatives or prints. For example, sodium sulfide 2 % solution diluted 1 + 9 is left as a droplet on the clear rebate of the material for 2-3 minutes. Any color beyond pale cream left after blotting off denotes that silver compounds are present and the material requires rewashing, or first refixing and then washing.

Perspective System of representing three-dimensional objects on the two-dimensional surface of a photograph or drawing to give a realistic impression of depth.

Petzval lens Type of lens designed in 1840 by Josef Petzval, characterized by its wide aperture, but having a curved field. This f 3.6 lens first made daguerreotype portraiture possible, reducing exposures to a minute or so in bright sunlight. Used nowadays principally for projectors, where only a narrow

angle in comparison to the total field is used to form the image.

Phenidone Reducing agent used in general-purpose and fine-grain developers as a less toxic substitute for metol.

Phenol varnish Resin that sets when warmed. Used to produce a hard, durable top surface.

Phosphorescence Property held by some materials of absorbing light of one wavelength and emitting it (often for some time afterwards) as light of a different wavelength.

Phosphorophotography Technique of projecting an infrared image on a phosphorescent surface. Since infrared rays have the property of being able to reduce some kinds of phosphorescence, the glow of the surface will diminish in proportion to the intensity of the light, thus giving a negative image which can be photographed or contact-printed to give a positive image.

PEC see *Photo-electric cell*

Photo-Club de Paris Leading French amateur club for artistic photography, a pictorial group which broke away from the Société Française de Photographie in 1894. Largely dominated by Robert Demachy. Disbanded in 1900.

Photo color transfer (PCT) Method of making color enlargements by exposing on a full-size sheet of film, which is then soaked in a single activator solution and rolled in face contact with receiving paper. The sandwich can be left in normal light for 6-8 minutes, then peeled apart to give a finished paper print. Prints can be made from color negatives or slides, by using the appropriate transfer film.

Photo-elasticity Method of determining stress patterns in structures with the aid of polarized light.

Photo-electric cell Light-sensitive cell, used in exposure meters and for remote triggering of the shutter. A selenium cell generates electricity in proportion to its surface area and the amount of light falling on it. A cadmium sulfide (CdS) cell offers a resistance to a small electric charge when light falls upon it, and is therefore very responsive in dim light conditions. Cadmium sulfide cells are more sensitive than selenium, especially at low light levels. However, their sensitivity to red is poor by comparison. The most advanced cells use silicon.

Photo-engraving The production of a relief printing surface by chemical or mechanical means, with the aid of photography.

Photo-etching Technique of contact-printing an image on lith film on a presensitized zinc plate which is then processed and chemically etched to give a relief image.

Photoflood See *Over-run lamp.*

"Photogenic drawing" Original name given by William Fox Talbot to his earliest method

of recording camera images on chemically treated writing paper.

Photogram Pattern or design produced by placing opaque or transparent objects between a light-sensitive emulsion and a light source. By this method, images can be produced directly on printing paper without the use of a camera. After exposure to light, the photographic material is developed normally. At one time "photogram" was used as an alternative term to photograph, particularly for images of an artistic rather than functional nature.

Photogrammetry Method of making precise measurements from photographs. Used extensively in map-making (from aerial photograps), architectural planning and engineering drawing.

Photography Literally writing or drawing with light (from the Greek words *photos* meaning light and *graphos*, writing). First suggested by Sir John Herschel to William Fox Talbot in 1839.

Photogravure A method of printing photographs from an etched copper plate. Used in the mechanical printing of books and magazines to give high-quality results, and also for making short runs of prints by the artist. This latter use was popular among some pictorialists early this century. A piece of carbon tissue, exposed under the negative, was transferred to a grained copper plate, and unexposed areas washed away. Next the plate was etched in perchloride of iron, forming depths which varied according to the tones of the picture. It was then covered with a thin printers' ink, which was retained mostly in shadows, and printed on paper of the photographer's choice.

Photolamp Tungsten filament photographic lamp with a large diffused bulb, giving light of 3.200 K.

Photolithography Lithographic printing process using an image formed by photographic means.

Photolinen A laminate of linen and paper coated with black and white photographic emulsion, usually purchased in sheets or rolls. Used for photographic wall coverings, and techniques such as hand embroidery of prints.

Photometer Optical instrument, now obsolete, for measuring light being reflected from a surface. It works by comparing the reflected light with a standard source produced within the photometer. The small angle of acceptance means that often light from small areas of a subject can be measured from the camera position.

Photomicrography System of producing larger-than-life images of minute subjects by attaching the camera to a microscope.

Photon Particle of light energy. The smallest quantity of radiant energy that can be transferred between two systems.

Photo-reportage The use of photographs in newspapers and magazines, to supplement or replace written journalistic accounts.

Photo-resistor Photo-electric cell which varies in its electrical resistance according to light received.

Photo-secession Name of a breakaway group of US pictorialists led by Alfred Stieglitz, formed in New York in 1902. Disbanded 1917.

Photo-silkscreening Method of silk-screening images, using a stencil produced photographically.

Phototelegraphy The transmission of pictures between two points by means of radio or telegraph. A print (or negative) is wrapped around a cylinder and scanned by a small spot of light. Reflected light values are transmitted as a stream of signals. They control an exposing light source at the receiving station, which exposes light-sensitive material on a similar moving drum.

Photo-transistor Light-sensitive electronic component which functions as a switch. Used extensively for the slave firing of electronic flash heads.

pH scale Numerical scale running from 0 to 14, used to indicate the alkalinity or acidity of a chemical solution. 7 is neutral, while solutions with a lower pH value are increasingly acidic.

Physical development A form of development in which silver is contained in suspension within the developer and is attracted to the silver halides which have received exposure, i.e. a form of "plating" or intensification. Pure physical developers have not been successful, partly because proportional development is difficult to control.

Physiogram Photographic pattern produced by moving a regulated point of light over a sensitive emulsion.

Pictorialism Photographs which are a picturesque, decorative art in their own right, and appeal to the viewer's sense of beauty.

Piezo-electric flash Tiny flash bulbs (normally housed in flash cubes) which can be fired by the very low current produced by striking a piezo-electric crystal. Such bulbs can therefore be used without a battery – the shutter mechanism includes a tiny crystal which is struck as the shutter blades begin opening, firing the flash.

Pigment A coloring material that is insoluble in the liquid carrier with which it is mixed. Colors objects by spreading over their surfaces. Examples include paint or poster color.

Pigment processes Any method of making a positive print by using the property of bichromated colloids of changing their physical characteristics when exposed to light. Gum bichromate and bromoil are examples of pigment processes.

Pinacryptol Soluble dye powders used in desensitizers.

Pincushion distortion Lens aberration causing parallel, straight lines at the edge of the image to curve toward the lens axis.

Pinhole camera Camera without a lens, which has a very small hole pierced in one end. This allows light to pass through and form an image on the back of the camera, which is covered by photographic film or paper. Diffraction and light fall-off determine the optimum pinhole size and image distance needed to achieve maximum image quality.

Pixels Abbreviation for picture elements. The tiny squares of light making up the pictures are transmitted in digital form (as from cameras in space) and reconstituted as a visual image, either by scanning light direct on film or via a TV display.

Plane A surface. In lens optics an imaginary straight line on which image points may lie or which passes through a set of points perpendicular to the optical axis.

Plate Glass plates coated with emulsion. Originally the term referred to the daguerreotype metal plate, but continued when these were replaced by emulsion on glass.

Plate camera Camera designed to take glass plates, often adapted to take sheet film.

Plate rack Rack used to hold photographic plates when drying, allowing free drainage and air circulation.

Platinotype Obsolete contact printing process popular among pictorialists. The paper was impregnated with silver halide and platinum salts. Light caused reduction to a faint image of metallic platinum, and the full image was produced by development in an oxalate acid bath. The image, unlike any other papers, was embedded in the paper fibers. It gave exceptional depth and richness of tones. Platinotype papers became very expensive and were discontinued after 1918.

Point source lamp Strictly, an arc type lamp producing light from a small gap between two carbon rods. In practice, most compact filament, clear-glass slide projector or spotlight lamps act as point sources. Such a lamp provides hard shadows. In an enlarger, it gives maximum contrast and grain.

Polarization Light is said to travel in a wave motion along a straight path, vibrating in all directions at right angles to this plane. Polarization can be brought about with a polarizing filter, which causes light to vibrate in a single plane only, reducing its strength.

Polarized light Rays of light that have been restricted to vibrate in one plane only.

Polarizing filter Colorless gray filter made from stressed plastic. Polarizing filters are used over light sources or camera lenses to reduce or remove specular reflection from certain types of surfaces.

Polaroid camera Instant picture camera designed for polaroid materials.

Pola-screen Polarizing filter.

Portrait lens Lens used specifically for portraiture, usually having a focal length of between 85-105 mm in the 35 mm format. Some portrait lenses are also designed to produce a slightly diffused image.

Positive Photographic image (on paper or film) in which light and dark areas correspond to the highlights and shadows of the original subject. In a color image, colors are represented truly. The tones and colors of a positive are opposite to those of a negative.

Positive lens Simple lens that causes parallel light rays to converge to a point.

Positive/positive printing Process for printing a color transparency directly on paper to produce a positive print. Positive/positive materials include silver dye-bleach, reversal chromogenic paper, or photo color transfer types.

Posterization Photographic printing technique using a number of tone-separated negatives which are printed on high contrast material. A master negative is made by printing these in register on continuous tone film. The final print from this contains selected areas of flat tone in place of continuous tone.

Potassium bichromate Chemical used in chrome intensifier, and as a light sensitizer for gum or gelatin in various manipulative print processes.

Potassium bromide Chemical used as a restrainer in most developers, and as a re-halogenizing agent in some bleaches preceding toning.

Potassium carbonate Highly soluble, alkaline accelerator used in most general purpose and print developing solutions.

Potassium chloride Chemical used in some bleaches and sensitizers.

Potassium citrate Chemical used in blue and green toners.

Potassium dichromate Sensitizer used in gum bichromate and other processes. Similar in application to potassium bichromate.

Potassium ferricyanide Chemical used in Farmer's reducer as a bleach, and as a bleaching agent in many toning processes.

Potassium hydroxide Caustic potash. Highly active alkali (high pH). Used as the accelerator in many developers.

Potassium iodide Chemical used in bleachers, toners and intensifiers.

Potassium metabisulfite Acidifier used in fixers and stop baths. Also used as a preservative in some developers.

Potassium permanganate Chemical used extensively in reducers and bleachers, also as a dish cleaner. Acts as a test for the presence of fixer.Potassium persulfate Chemical sometimes used in super-proportional reducers.

Potassium sulfide Chemical used in sulfide (sepia) toning, and as a test for effective fixing.

Potassium thiocyanate Chemical used in some fine-grain developers as a silver solvent. It is also used in gold toners.

Pre-hardener Chemical solution used to harden gelatin of an emulsion prior to processing. Helps to protect emulsion against damage when high processing temperatures are being used.

Preservative Chemical, commonly sodium sulfite, used in developing solutions to prevent rapid oxidation of the reducing agents in use. It oxidizes rapidly in air and "immunizes" the developing solution until it becomes exhausted.

Pre-soak Preparatory water bath for film or paper prior to processing, preventing uneven development. Pre-soak is essential in certain color processes.

Press focus lever Lever found on the between-lens shutter of many large format cameras. Allows the shutter blades to be held open for lens focusing no matter what shutter speed has been set.

Primary colors In light, the three primary colors of the spectrum are blue, green, and red. Each comprises about one-third of the visible spectrum and they can be blended to produce white light or any other hue. In painter's pigments, the primaries are considered to be yellow, blue, and red.

Principal axis In a compound lens, an imaginary line which passes through the centers of curvature of all the lens elements.

Principal planes Imaginary lines which pass through the nodal planes of a lens system at right-angles to the principal axis.

Print In photography, an image (normally positive) which has been produced by the action of light (usually passed through a negative or slide) on paper or similar material coated with a light-sensitive emulsion.

Printing Process employed to make one or a number of images on paper or similar material. The sensitized material is exposed to light passed through a negative or positive.

Printing-in Technique for giving additional exposure to selected areas when making a print, other areas being shaded from the light.

Printing out processes Light-sensitive printing materials which visibly darken during exposure. The result may then require fixing only. All printing papers once worked by this method. The paper was very slow, being suitable only for printing by direct daylight.

Prism Transparent glass or clear plastic block with non-parallel flat surfaces. Used to reflect, refract or disperse light.

Processing General term used to describe the sequence of steps whereby a latent image is converted into a visible, permanent image. Normally involves chemicals, but may take place purely electronically, as with a video camera.

Process lens Lens designed specifically for the highest quality reproduction of flat, two-dimensional originals. Used mostly in the printing industry.

Projection cutting Any method of printing in which the image is optically projected on the sensitized material.

Projector Apparatus for showing enlarged images on a screen.

Proportional reducer Chemical method of reducing excess density and contrasts from a photographic negative.

Protective toning Toning process used to protect black and white prints from fading, and give archival permanence. Usually carried out with selenium or gold toners.

Pulling Method of under-rating the normal ASA speed of a film to produce an overexposed latent image and compensating for this by subsequent underdeveloping.

Pushing Extending development, used in conjunction with uprating the ASA speed of the film when exposing. Used to increase speed and contrast.

Pyro Reducing agent once used in developing solutions.

Quarter plate Negative or print format measuring $3\frac{1}{4} \times 4\frac{1}{4}$ ins, i.e. one-quarter the size of a whole plate ($8\frac{1}{2} \times 6\frac{1}{2}$ ins).

Quartz-iodine lamp Compact tungsten filament lamp designed to maintain its color temperature and light intensity throughout its working life.

Rack and pinion focusing Mechanical focusing system used on copying or monorail cameras. A pinion engages a rack on a slide. Focusing is achieved by turning a knob or wheel, which moves the lens or image panel.

Radiography Technique of using X rays, gamma rays and charged particles to form shadow images on photographic materials. Widely used in medicine and industrial research because of its ability to penetrate opaque materials.

Rangefinder A built-in aid in some direct vision cameras. It assesses subject distance (usually by comparing the subject from two separated viewpoints), and displays this information in the viewfinder. The split-image type shows a discontinuous image across a fine central line. One of these shifts sideways as the lens is focused – a continuous image appears when the correct setting has been made. The coincident type shows a double image until focus is achieved. Either type is linked directly to the lens focus control, to give a coupled rangefinder.

Rapid fixer Fixing solution that uses ammonium thiocyanate or thiosulfate instead of hypo (sodium thiosulfate). Allows greatly reduced fixing time.

Rapid rectilinear Early lens design composed of two matching doublet lenses, symmetrically placed around the focal aperture. It was introduced by Dallmeyer and Sternheil, and removed many of the aberrations present in more simple constructions.

"Rayographs" Term coined by Man Ray and his friends for pictures made by placing objects directly on photographic paper (photograms). Similarly the German painter Christian Schad called the results he produced this way "Schadographs".

Rebate Margin on photographic film surrounding the image area. Also sometimes used to describe the white border around prints.

Reciprocity failure The increasing loss of sensitivity of photographic emulsion when exposures are extremely brief or long. In color materials this failure may vary according to color layer, giving a shift of color balance. Often occurs in color papers given 60 sec or more exposure.

Reciprocity law This states that exposure equals intensity multiplied by time, where intensity is equal to the amount of light and time is equal to the period for which that amount is allowed to act upon the emulsion.

Reconstituted image Photograph produced by translating light from the subject into electronic signals, which are then reconstituted into a visible image by electronic means.

Recycling time Period taken for a flash gun to recharge itself between firings.

Red eye Effect encountered when light from a flash unit travels parallel to the lens axis during exposure. Blood vessels at the back of the subject's eyes reflect red light back toward the camera so that pupils appear red instead of black. Red eye is avoided by moving the flash unit to one side, or by bouncing the flash.

Reducers Solutions which remove silver from negatives or prints. They are used to diminish density and alter contrast on a photographic emulsion.
Farmer's reducer
A cutting reducer which removes equal amounts of silver from the whole surface. The effect is a reduction in density and a slight increase in contrast. The formula is as follows:

Solution A
Sodium thiosulfate 100 g
Water to 1 liter
Solution B
Potassium ferricyanide 20 g
Water to 1 liter
To prepare a working solution, use 100 ml of A, 20 ml of B and 200 ml of water.
The reduction continues until it is stopped by immersion in running water, followed by a bath of sodium thiosulfate and then a final wash.

Proportional reducer
This removes image density in proportion to the amount of silver present. The result is density and contrast reduction. The formula is:
Solution A
Potassium permanganate 0.25 g
10 % solution sulfuric acid 15 ml
Water to 1 liter
Solution B
Ammonium persulfate 25 g
Water to 1 liter
Prepare a working solution by mixing 1 part of A to 3 parts of B. With constant agitation, reduction should take place in 1-4 minutes. After reduction, soak negatives in a 1 percent solution of potassium metabisulfite for a few minutes, then wash normally.

Ammonium persulfate reducer
This solution has the effect of reducing density, contrast and highlights. The formula for this reducer is:
Ammonium persulfate 3.3 g
Sulfuric acid, 10 % solution 10 ml
Distilled water to 1 liter
The mixture does not keep and must be used immediately. It should be discarded when it begins to go milky. Immerse negatives until the required amount of reduction has occurred, then dip them in an acid fixer or a 5 percent sodium sulfite solution.

Reducing agent Chemical in a developer which converts exposed silver halides to black metallic silver. In some color developers the oxidation products of the reducing agent combine with color couplers to produce color dye.

Reflected light reading Measurement, by light meter, of the amount of light reflected by a subject, as opposed to light falling on the subject.

Reflecting telescope Telescope using a concave parabolic mirror to increase focal length and focus light at a point. Such designs allow far wider apertures than are possible with refracting telescopes.

Reflection Rays of light which strike a surface and bounce back again. Specular reflection occurs on even, polished surfaces; diffuse reflection occurs on uneven surfaces when light scatters.

Reflector Any surface from which light can be reflected. In particular, a white or gray card, or similar material, used to reflect light from a main source into shadow areas.

Reflex camera Camera with a viewing and focusing system that uses a mirror between the lens and focusing screen to give an upright image.

Reflex lens Alternative term for mirror lens.

Refraction The change in direction of light rays as they pass obliquely from one transparent medium to another of different density, e.g. from air to glass.

Refracting telescope Telescope using very wide glass lenses. Compound front elements collect the light, and an eyepiece at the viewing end magnifies the image.

Refractive index Numerical value indicating the light-bending power of a medium such as glass. The greater the bending power, the greater the refractive index.

Register Exact alignment when overlaying several separate images. For example, stacking color separation film images, or sequence-printing several images, to make an accurately combined image.

Register punch Punch used to make alignment holes in film or paper for registering images.

Rehalogenization Process by which the black metallic silver of a processed image is converted back to silver halides. It is used in bleaching prior to toning, and for some forms of intensification.

Relative aperture Diameter of the effective aperture divided into the focal length of the lens. The result is expressed as an f number, marked on the lens barrel.

Replenishment The addition of extra chemicals to a processing solution to compensate for its repeated use and consequent partial exhaustion.

Resin-coated (RC) paper Printing paper with a water-repellent base. Such papers can be processed faster, require less washing and dry more quickly than fiber-based papers. All color papers and most black and white papers are now made with this base.

Resist Protective but removeable layer applied to a surface in the form of a pattern or image. Used to prevent chemical solutions reaching covered areas. After the rest of the surface has been treated with chemical (toner for example) the resist is removed, leaving the underlying image unchanged.

Resolving power The ability of a lens or photographic emulsion to resolve fine detail. Resolution can be expressed in terms of the lines per millimeter which are distinctly recorded or visually separable in the final image.

Restrainer Chemical constituent of developing solutions that helps prevent reducing agents from affecting unexposed halides and converting them to black metallic silver. It reduces chemical fog.

Reticulation Minute wrinkling of an emulsion surface giving a cracked appearance to film. It is caused by sudden gelatin shrinkage at extreme changes of temperature, or an acidity/alkalinity excess during processing.

Retouching After-treatment of negatives, slides or prints by hand to remove blemishes and/or change tonal values.

Reversal material Photographic materials specifically designed to give a direct positive after only one exposure (i.e. without producing a separate negative), by suitable processing.

Ring-around A series of color prints from one negative or positive at various color filtrations, mounted to display the effects of filtration changes. The ring-around can then be compared with other prints when assessing filtration.

Ring flash Ring-shaped electronic flash unit attached to the front of a lens. It is used to give even, frontal lighting for close subjects.

Rinse Brief intermediate wash in clean water between processing stages. It helps to remove residual chemicals and so prevents one solution from being carried over into another.

Rising front Camera movement on most sheet film and monorail cameras, allowing the front lens panel to be raised or lowered from its central position. This allows parts of the subject well above the lens axis to appear on the film (with equivalent loss of the bottom of the picture).

Rods Receptors forming part of the retina at the back of the eye sensitive only to variations in brightness, not color.

Rollfilm Today refers to 120/620 or 127 format film which has an opaque paper backing and is supplied on an open spool (rather than in a light-tight cassette). The term is however often applied to all camera films in roll form, including 35 mm cassettes. At one time there were many other widths of rollfilm.

Rollfilm adaptor Special attachment for cameras designed for sheet film or cassettes, enabling rollfilm to be used.

Sabattier effect The part-positive, part-negative effect formed when an emulsion is briefly re-exposed to white light during development, and then allowed to continue development. Also known as pseudo-solarization. See also *Solarization*.

Safelight Darkroom light of a color and intensity that will not noticeably affect light-sensitized photographic materials. Film and paper manufacturers' safelight recommendations are readily available and should be followed.

Safety film Term used to describe a film with a base that is not readily inflammable. Early films used a nitrate base, which was highly inflammable. All film used today is on safety base.

Sal-ammoniac Ammonium chloride, used in some high-speed fixers.

Sandwiching The combination of two or more negatives or film positives in the negative carrier or masking frame when printing. Transparencies may also be sandwiched in a single mount.

Saturated color A pure color hue, undiluted by other colors, white, or gray.

Scale The linear relation between the size of the subject and the size of its image, or between the size of the negative and the size of the enlargement.

Scanning electron microscope (SEM) Device used in photomicrography which bombards and scans electrons in the specimen individually. This is built up into a complete image which is formed on a screen and photographed using a parallel display screen.

Schadographs See *Rayographs*.

Scheiner speed Logarithmic system of speed-rating negative materials. Used mostly in Europe between 1894-1939. Devised by the German astronomer Prof. Julius Scheiner.

Schumann plate Plate coated with an emulsion with so little gelatin content that the silver halide grains protrude above its surface. Used for photography in the far ultraviolet region where normal gelatin materials would absorb the ultraviolet radiation.

Screening Conversion of a continuous tone image to a half-tone (dot or line pattern) image, normally by copying or printing through a fine screen of black and white lines.

Screen plate Plate used in early additive forms of color photography with an emulsion covered by a screen of minute color filter elements. The image is processed by the black and white reversal method and viewed as a color transparency. The autochrome process used the screen plate systems.

Scrim Lighting attachment which, when placed in front of a lamp, reduces its strength, usually by one stop, without affecting lighting quality or color.

Secondary color Alternative name for complementary color.

Selective focusing Method of adjusting the lens aperture and shutter speed to give a depth of field that will limit image sharpness to a particular area of the subject, isolating it against an unsharp background and/or foreground.

Selenium cell Photoelectric cell used in some metering systems. It generates electricity in direct proportion to the amount of light falling on its surface.

Self-darkening paper See *Printing out*.

Self-toning paper Obsolete silver chloride papers used for contact printing in daylight. (Also known as POP materials.)

Sensitive materials In photography, the term applied to the film or paper emulsions that react to light, by changing chemically when they are exposed. In a broad sense, also applies to charge coupled devices used in video still cameras.

Sensitivity The degree of response of a photographic emulsion to exposure to light.

Sensitometry Scientific study of the response of photographic materials to exposure and development. This establishes emulsion speeds and recommended development and processing times.

Separation images Technique of producing an image by combining photographs produced on a material or using equipment which is sensitive to one region of the spectrum only with photographs recording other regions of the spectrum. This cumulatively yields a full color image.

Separation negatives Black and white negatives (usually prepared in threes on panchromatic film), made by photographing a full-color original scene through primary color filters. Each records the original in terms of its blue, green, or red content. The three negatives can be synthesized in primary or subtractive color dyes (using a process such as dye transfer) to produce a full color image of the original.

Shading Method of controlling the final quality of a print by varying the exposure given to different areas of the print through selective interruption of the light during enlarging. Also known as dodging.

Shadow detail Details visible in areas that are darkest in the subject. These appear as the lightest parts of a negative.

Shadows Darkest areas in a photograph, corresponding to parts of the original subject that were less strongly illuminated by the light source.

Sheet film Large-format film in sheets cut to a specific size rather than in roll form. Also called cut film. In practice, sheets are cut slightly smaller than the nominal dimensions, so they will slip easily into film holders.

Shelf life The length of time an unused material or chemical will remain fresh, i.e. before decomposition sets in.

Shutter Mechanical system used to control the time that light is allowed to act on a sensitive emulsion. The two types most common on modern cameras are the focal plane shutter and the between-the-lens or diaphragm shutter.

Shutter priority camera 35 mm camera on which the photographer selects the shutter speed, and the camera automatically sets the correct aperture to suit subject conditions and film speed.

Shutter speed The action of the shutter that controls the duration of an exposure. The faster the speed, the shorter the exposure.

Shutter speed settings are given in fractions of a second. Each is half the duration of the preceding one in a constant scale, marked on the shutter speed dial or ring.

Silhouette Photographic image in which the subject is seen as a solid black shape against a light background.

Silicon release paper Thin, heat-resistant interleaving paper, used between a photographic print and textured material in a heated press. It allows remolding of the print surface, yet prevents the two materials sticking together.

Silk print Image made on silk by means of the diazo or dye printing methods.

Silk screen Method of applying inks to paper or similar materials using a nylon stencil produced by photographic means.

Silver dye-bleach (SDB) material Integral tripack printing material in which fully formed yellow, magenta and cyan dyes are incorporated in the blue-, green-, and red-sensitive emulsion layers during manufacture. During processing, dye areas unwanted for the image are bleached away. Used to produce single-stage positive prints from slides.

Silver halides Compounds formed between silver and alkali salts of halogen chemicals such as bromine; chlorine and iodine. Silver bromide, silver chloride and silver iodides are the light-sensitive silver halides used in photographic emulsions to record the image. Halides are reduced to black silver when exposed to light and developed.

Silver nitrate Chemical combination of silver and nitric acid. It is used in photographic emulsion manufacture, and also in intensifiers and physical developers.

Silver reclamation System of recovering silver from exhausted solutions (especially fixers and bleachers) practised by processing laboratories. Three methods are used: sludging, metal exchange, and electrolytic. Electrolytic silver recovery allows the solution to be replenished and re-used.

Silver salts Compounds of silver.

Simultaneous contrast The effect that adjacent color hues have upon each other. Complementary colors, for example, appear to increase their mutual intensity and contrast when juxtaposed.

Single lens reflex (SLR) Camera which allows the user to see the exact image formed by the picture-taking lens, by means of a hinged mirror between the lens and film (and usually a pentaprism to correct the image from left to right). The lens-to-focusing screen distance, via the mirror, must be identical to the lens-to-film distance when the mirror is raised.

Sizing Very dilute, gluey solution used to prepare surfaces for coating by filling in pores and giving even absorbency.

Skylight filter Filter, usually very pale pink, used in color photography to reduce blue casts, particularly those associated with UV and haze. It may be left permanently on the lens to protect it from dust and abrasions.

Sky shade Alternative term for lens hood.

Slave unit Mechanism which fires additional flash sources simultaneously when a photo-electric cell is activated by the light from a flash source connected to the camera.

Slide A positive transparency intended for viewing by projection.

Slit shutter A narrow vertical slit either just in front of the emulsion or at a similar distance in front of the lens. Film is wound through the camera at a constant speed (to match the image of a moving subject), giving one long image along the length of the film.

Slow film Film having an emulsion with low sensitivity to light. Typically such films have ASA speeds of 32 or less.

Slow lens A lens with a small maximum aperture, such as f8.

Snapshot Term once used to describe a photograph taken with the I (instantaneous) setting on cameras. It came originally from rifle-shooting, when little or no time is allowed for aiming. Used nowadays to describe a casual picture taken by amateurs, usually with simple equipment.

Snoot Cone-shaped shield used on spotlights to direct a circular patch of light over a small area.

Sodium bichromate Chemical used in intensifiers, bleachers, toners, and in carbro and gum bichromate as an alternative process to potassium bichromate.

Sodium bisulfite Chemical used as an acidifying agent in acid fixing baths.

Sodium carbonate Alkaline accelerator used in general purpose and print developing solutions.

Sodium chloride Common salt, used in some bleachers and reducers, and in some forms of blue toning.

Sodium hexametaphosphate Chemical used as a water softener.

Sodium hydrosulfite Chemical used as a fogging agent in reversal processing.

Sodium hydroxide Strong alkali used as an accelerator in conjunction with hydroquinone in high-contrast developers.

Sodium metabisulfite Chemical used as a preservative in developers and in fixing and stop baths.

Sodium sulfide Chemical used in sulfide (sepia) toners.

Sodium sulfite Multi-purpose chemical used as a preservative in some developers.

Sodium thiocyanate Chemical used as a fixer and as a silver solvent.

Sodium thiosulfate The chemical most commonly used in fixation to convert unused silver halides into a soluble form. Known also as "hypo".

Soft focus Purposely diffused image, often a mixture of sharp and unsharp definition. This can be achieved either at the camera or the enlarger stage.

Soft focus lens Lens, often uncorrected for spherical aberrations, used to produce a soft focus image.

Soft gradation Term used to describe a quality of low tonal contrast in a photograph. Also used to describe the quality of lighting that produces this effect.

Solarization Strictly, the reversal or partial reversal of tones in a photographic image caused by vast over-exposure. Today used (inaccurately) to describe the partial reversal effects caused by fogging photographic material to light, more correctly called pseudo-solarization or the Sabattier effect.

Solubility Generally, the ease with which a solid will mix homogenously with water to provide a chemical solution. Specifically, solubility of a substance is defined by the amount that will dissolve in a given amount of liquid at a specified temperature.

Spacing bracket Simple device used to position the camera at the right distance from the subject for the lens focus setting in close-up work. Can also indicate the subject area which will fill the frame.

Spectral sensitivity Relative response of a photographic emulsion to each of the colors of the spectrum. The natural response of the emulsion can be altered by the introduction of dye sensitizers during manufacture. In color films, these dye sensitizers are used to achieve the required spectral sensitivity in each of the three emulsion layers.

Spectrum Commonly, that part of the electromagnetic spectrum – between wavelengths 400 to 700 nm – which is visible to the human eye. It appears as colored bands from violet and blue through green and yellow to orange and red, according to wavelength. When all these wavelengths are seen together the light appears white.

Speed The sensitivity of a photographic emulsion to light. Films are given ISO, ASA, DIN or GOST numbers to indicate their relative speed characteristics. The higher the number, the faster the film reacts to light.

Spherical aberration Lens fault which causes loss of definition, particularly at the edges of the frame.

Spill rings Concentric rings mounted in front of narrow-angle lamps to prevent the spreading of light rays.

Split image rangefinder See *Rangefinder*.

Spool Bobbin-like object consisting of a narrow core with flat disks at either end, around which the film is wound.

Spotlight Artificial light source using a fresnel lens, reflector and usually a simple focusing system to produce a strong beam of light of controllable width.

Spot meter Narrow-angle exposure meter used to take accurate light readings from any small area of the subject, from some distance away.

Spotting The retouching of small (usually white) specks on prints, and sometimes negatives, using water-color, dye or pencil.

Sprocket holes The perforations on both edges of 35 mm film, which engage with the teeth of the film transport mechanism.

Squeegee Implement with rubber blade or roller, used to squeeze water out of wet prints, or to press prints into contact with a glazing sheet.

Stabilization Alternative method of fixing, where unused silver halides are converted to near-stable compounds. These are not sensitive to light and washing is not required.

Stabilizer Final solution often used in color processing which leaves the dyes produced by chemical development more stable and fade-resistant.

Staining developer Developer, such as pyro, in which the oxidation products give extra image density by staining the gelatin.

Stand Heavy-duty studio support for equipment such as sheet film cameras.

Standard lens Lens whose focal length is approximately equal to the film format with which it is used. Also called a normal or prime lens.

Stand camera A camera that is not normally used hand-held, e.g. a large format or sheet film camera.

Static marks Jagged fog marks on negatives as a result of a very dry film being rewound or unwound too rapidly, thus creating sparks from static electricity, which fog the emulsion.

Step wedge Printed series of density increases, in regular steps from transparent to opaque. A method of making exposure tests when enlarging.

Stereo pairs Aerial photograph made up of two overlapping images, viewed through a device using a pair of prisms or mirrors to reflect light into a stereo eyepiece.

Stereo projection Method of forming an

image with a three-dimensional appearance by projecting right- and left-hand stereo images with a pair of projectors. The system requires that the viewer watches the screen through glasses which limit each eye to its appropriate image only.

Stereoscope Viewer which accepts pairs of stereoscopic images so they can be viewed combined into a single image with apparent three-dimensional depth.

Stereoscopic camera A camera designed to take simultaneous images of the same subject from viewpoints separated by the same distance as that between the eyes. Most stereo cameras take two pictures, one uses four.

Stereoscopy Method of creating a three-dimensional effect on a two-dimensional surface, using two (or more) images taken from slightly different viewpoints. A special stereo viewer is usually required.

Still life An inanimate subject, either in the studio, or outdoors, normally arranged to make full use of form, shape and lighting.

Stock solution Chemical stored in concentrated liquid form, ready for dilution prior to use.

Stop Alternative term for aperture.

Stop bath Chemical bath (usually a weak acid solution) which stops development by neutralizing the developer. This prevents active developer from contaminating further processing solutions.

Stopping down Reducing the size of the aperture, i.e. by selecting a higher f number. This has the effect of reducing image brightness and increasing depth of field.

"Straight" photography Term used to describe picture-making with minimum manipulation of the photographic process. Often used to describe the approach of Edward Weston and Group f64.

Stress marks Short black streaks on films caused by pressure or friction being applied to the emulsion surface before processing.

Strobe light Low-power electronic flash that can fire repeatedly at regular, controlled intervals. Can be programed to flash at rates from about one per second to hundreds or even thousands of flashes per second.

Studio camera At one time, term given to a large, 15 × 12 in camera on a wheeled stand. Today describes any camera using large format film and allowing camera movements, which, by virtue of its size and bulk, is not readily portable.

Subbing Layer applied to a photographic support as a foundation for the emulsion.

Subject The person or thing photographed. Often refers to specific, animate things (as opposed to generalized inanimate things referred to as objects). However, the terms sub-

ject and object tend to be used interchangeably in photography.

Subjective photography An interpretative image of the subject, with results influenced by the attitude of the photographer or client. The opposite of an objective, "clinical" record.

Sub-miniature camera A camera using a film format smaller than 35 mm.

Substantive film Color film in which the color couplers are contained within the emulsion.

Subtractive color synthesis Process of producing a color image by subtracting appropriate amounts of unwanted primary colors from white light, using yellow, magenta, and cyan filters. Dye layers of these three colors (sometimes called primaries) are used in color films and papers to reproduce an image subtractively. For example, in a color slide, the yellow image is effectively a record of where blue was not present in the original scene. Magenta records absence of green, and cyan, red. The three images, superimposed, reform all the subject colors and tones.

Subtractive primaries Yellow, magenta, and cyan: the complementary colors to the light primaries blue, green, and red.

Successive color contrast Trick of eyesight by which the impression of a color is influenced by an immediately preceding color stimulus. For example, moving from a tungsten lit room to another lit by "daylight" fluorescent tubes the illumination appears exceptionally blue until the eye response adjusts. See also *Simultaneous contrast.*

Sulfide toning Chemical method of changing the image color of a bromide print to give brown or sepia tones instead of black.

Sulfuric acid Chemical solution used in reducers and clearing baths.

Supercoat Top coating of non-sensitized gelatin added to sensitized emulsions to form a protective layer.

Supplementary lens Additional lens element(s) used in conjunction with the prime lens to provide a different focal length. Generally used for close-up photography.

Surface development Development process in which the image forms primarily on the surface of the emulsion and then penetrates deeper.

Surge marks Streaks on the image from each of the sprocket holes of 35 mm film (or at the edge of sheet film) caused by excessive agitation.

Surrealism Originally an early 1920s artistic movement, now taken to indicate the production of unreal images which defy reason and are generally derived from the subconscious.

Swing back/front Movement of lens and

back panels of most view and monorail cameras, so that lens or film pivot about the lens axis. It allows manipulation of perspective and depth of field.

Symmetry The effect of an evenly balanced arrangement of visual information, such as pattern, on either side of a central division.

Synchronized flash Method of synchronizing flash light duration with maximum shutter opening. There may be two settings on a camera, X and M. X is the setting used for electronic flash, in which peak output is almost instantaneous on firing. M is for expendable flash, which normally requires a delay in shutter opening of about 17 milliseconds, to allow the bulb output to build up. If a synchronizing connection is unmarked it can be taken to be X. Flash bulbs can be safely fired with X synchronization provided the shutter is set to 1/30 sec or slower.

Synchro-sunlight System of combining daylight and flash to achieve a controlled lighting ratio.

Tacking iron. Heated tool used to stick part of the dry-mounting tissue to a print and its mounting board.

Tank Plastic or stainless steel container for holding paper or films while they are processed in one or a sequence of chemical solutions. Some tanks are for darkroom use only. Most must be loaded in the dark, but can be used in daylight. A few can be both loaded and used in daylight.

Tanning development Type of developer used for processes (such as dye transfer) that require a relief image. Tans or hardens the gelatin only in areas where the silver image is formed.

Technical camera Large-format stand camera, with a ground-glass screen at the image plane for viewing and focusing. Offers camera movements.

Telephoto lens Long focal length lens, which enlarges distant subjects within its narrow angle of view. Depth of field increases as focal length increases. Telephoto construction allows long focal length with short back focus, making for relative compactness.

Tempering bath Large tank or deep tray filled with water maintained at the correct temperature for processing, often by means of thermostatic control. Used to house tanks, drums or trays as well as containers of processing solutions. Also known as a water jacket.

Tessar lens Famous German non-symmetrical lens design by Zeiss. Based on the triplet. It used collective and dispersive lens elements to correct curvature of field and give wide maximum apertures. Introduced in 1902 and in various forms used extensively (in cameras such as the Rolleiflex) until 1950.

Test strip Strip of printing paper or film which is given a range of trial exposures and/or filtrations by shading, to test for correct image density and color.

Texture The character of a surface. This usually means its roughness or smoothness. In photography, careful control of lighting can be used to describe a surface by adding a tactile quality in terms of depth, shape and tone, suggesting three dimensions.

Texture screen Transparent film or glass printed with a fine background pattern. Screens are interposed beween the image and the paper (either sandwiched with the negative or placed in contact with the paper) to break up large areas of tone. These screens can give an effect superficially similar to halftone screens.

Thermography Recording images by means of the heat radiated or reflected from a subject.

"Thick" negative colloquial term to describe a dense negative image.

"Thin" negative Negative lacking in density, having been underexposed or underdeveloped.

Thyristor flash gun Automatic flash gun that cuts off the flash when sufficient exposure has been given. A light sensor views the subject, and the unit must be programed to suit the film speed and aperture in use. This system also conserves power, makes recycling quicker, and prolongs battery life.

Time and temperature Controlling factors of a chemical photographic process. They depend on timing for an exact period, and accurately maintaining the correct solution temperature.

Time exposure General term for an exposure longer than can be set using the camera's fixed shutter speeds.

Time gamma curve Graph showing how the gamma of a film's response changes with development.

Time-lapse photography Method of recording chemical and physical changes in a subject over a period of time by photographing it at regular intervals from the same viewpoint, usually under unchanged lighting conditions.

Timer Clock used to control processing or exposure. It may be linked directly to the enlarger, switching off the light source automatically.

Tinting Application of color tints – usually in the form of dyes or paints – to a photographic image to create or enhance color effects. Has greatest effect on the lightest parts of the image, unlike toning, which on a black and white print colors the originally black silver parts of the pinture.

Tin-type See *Ferrotype.*

Tomography Radiographic technique used in medical photography. Moving the X ray tube and film in opposite directions produces a limited depth of field. This blurs unwanted detail and enables particular areas of bone, tissue or organs to be isolated. The technique is used in conjunction with a computer to build up a body-scan of sections of the patient's anatomy.

Tone On a print or negative, an area which has a uniform density and which can be distinguished from darker or lighter parts.

Tone-line process Technique used to reproduce a photographic image so that it resembles a pen and ink drawing.

Toners Used to change the color of the photographic print by chemical baths. Through a system of bleaching and dyeing, the black metallic silver image is converted to a dye image.
Sepia (sulfide) toning
This produces warm brown tones. The formula is:
Bleach
   Potassium bromide   50 g
   Potassium ferricyanide 100 g
   Water to 1 liter
Dilute 1 part to 9 parts water just before use.
Sulfide toner
   Sodium sulfide   200 g
   Water to 1 liter
Dilute 1 part to 6 parts water just before use. Bleach the print in the first solution, until it turns a very light brown, then rinse briefly in running water. Immerse it in the sulfide bath for about 1 minute and wash thoroughly for about 30 minutes. Once used, the solutions should be discarded, but the stock solutions will keep indefinitely in dark bottles. Sodium sulfide has a characteristic pungent smell, and should only be used in a well-ventilated room.
Blue toning
This changes the black parts of a print to blue. The bleach and toner are combined in one solution.
Bleach
   Potassium ferricyanide   2 g
   Sulfuric acid concentrated 3 ml
   Water to 1 liter
Blue toner
   Ferric ammonium citrate   2 g
   Sulfuric acid concentrated 3 ml
   Water to 1 liter
Prepare a working solution by mixing equal parts of bleach and toner just before use. Immerse the washed prints until the required amount of toning has been reached, and wash to remove any slight yellowing of the white areas.
Copper toning
The tones produced range from warm brown to light red, depending on the time the chemicals are allowed to act. Once again, bleach and toner are combined in one solution.
Bleach
   Potassium ferricyanide   1 g
   Potassium citrate   28 g
   Water to 1 liter
Copper sulfate toner
   Potassium citrate   28 g
   Copper sulfate   7 g
   Water to 1 liter

Prepare a working solution by mixing equal parts of bleach and toner just before use. Keep prints immersed in the solution until the required tone has been reached.

Tone separation Process of reducing the tonal range of a photograph to a very restricted range. The final result has strong highlights and deep shadows, with a set number of intermediate tones. See also *Posterization.*

Tone values Various shades of gray between the extremes of black and white in a photographic image.

Transfer processes Methods of transferring a photographic image from one surface to another. These may be by chemical transfer, from one emulsion to another; by physical transfer of a pigment or dye; or by the transfer of the whole emulsion layer.

Transmission The passage of light through a transparent or translucent material

Transmitted light Light which is passed through a transparent or translucent material. The amount of light transmitted depends on the density of the medium through which it passes and the brightness of the original light source.

Transparency Positive image in color or black and white produced on transparent film

Transposing frame Frame used for printing pairs of stereoscopic negatives from a two-lens camera.

Tray development Processing carried out in open trays. Black and white print processing is still carried out in this way as results can be checked visually under safelighting.

Trichrome carbro process Method of making assembly color prints from separation negatives, using an adaption of the carbon process. Images were printed in yellow, magenta, and cyan-dyed tissue, then transferred, in exact register, to a final paper support. This skilled and very time-consuming process was widely used by professional color photographers in the 1930s.

Tri-color filters Filters in deep primary colors (generally a set of three: one blue, one green, and one red) used to expose color prints by the additive method, or to make three separation negatives.

Trigger Term used to describe a shutter release.

Tripack See *Integral tripack.*

Triple extension Camera system in which lens-image distance can be extended by as much as three times the focal length of the (normal) lens. It is particularly useful for close-up photography.

Triplet lens Lens consisting basically of three elements: a diverging lens sandwiched between two converging lenses.

Tripod Three-legged camera support. The legs are usually in sections to permit height adjustments.

T setting Camera speed setting indicating "time" exposure, i.e. longer than the numbered settings. The shutter opens when the release is pressed and closes when it is pressed again. Most cameras now use a B rather than T setting.

T stops More accurate measurement of light entering a lens than f numbers. Whereas f numbers represent the ratio between measured diameter and focal length, T stops also take into account light transmission losses due to the glass and other factors. Found today only on some movie cameras.

TTL Through the lens metering, in which light-sensitive cells within the camera body measure exposure from image-forming light that has passed through the lens.

Tungsten filament lamp Artificial light source using a tungsten filament heated by the passage of electricity, and contained within a glass envelope.

Tungsten halogen lamp Compact tungsten lamp which gives consistent color temperature as the glass envelope used is non-blackening.

Tungsten light film Color film balanced to suit tungsten light sources with a color temperature of 3200K.

Twin lens reflex (TLR) Camera having two lenses of the same focal length. One is used for viewing and focusing, the other for exposing the film. The lenses are mounted above each other.

Two-bath development Development of negatives in two stages. Developer without alkali is followed by an alkali bath, which activates development. The material can be alternated between the two, allowing fine control over the degree of development given.

Two-color photography Simple method of color photography which analyzes the spectrum into two parts instead of three, forming images which are combined with complementary printing colors. This method will not reproduce the whole spectrum.

Type A color film Obsolete type of artificial light color film balanced for hight sources with a color temperature of 3400K.

Type B color film Color film balanced for artificial light sources with a color temperature of 3200K.

Type D color film Obsolete title for film balanced for daylight.

Ultrasonic image recording Image formation by measurement of ultrasound echoes translated electronically into a scanned visual image on a TV display. Also known as sonography.

Ultraviolet (UV) That part of the electromagnetic spectrum from about 400 nm down to 1 nm. It is invisible to the human eye, but most photographic materials are sensitive to near UV bands, down to 250 nm. It records as increased haze, particularly in distant views and at high altitudes, and may give a blue cast to color images.

Ultraviolet light source Illumination such as sunlight, a UV sun lamp, or a "black light" fluorescent tube, all of which radiate some wavelengths from within the UV range.

Underdevelopment The result of too little development time or a decrease in the development temperature. Underdevelopment reduces density and contrast in the image.

Underexposure The result of too little exposure. On negative/positive materials, underexposure reduces density and may reduce contrast especially in shadow areas.

Universal developer Developing solution suitable (at different dilutions) for both negative and print processing.

Uprating An exposure technique in which the manufacturer's recommended film speed is deliberately exceeded, by setting a higher speed rating on the camera. This causes underexposure which is compensated for by overdevelopment. Also known as "pushing".

Uranium nitrate Chemical used in toners and developers.

UV filter Filter used to absorb UV radiation, to reduce its effect. Appears visually colorless.

Vacuum back Camera back with a perforated plate through which air is drawn by a pump. A sheet of film is therefore sucked flat against the plate and held firmly during exposure. Used for special large-format cameras such as copying devices where dimensional accuracy is critical.

Vacuum easel Contact printing frame which ensures firm contact between the film and paper by excluding all air between the surfaces. Some types are also used to hold the paper flat on the enlarger baseboard when enlarging.

Vanishing point The point at which parallel lines, viewed obliquely, appear to converge in the distance.

Vapor discharge lamp Lamp in which electrical current passes through a vapor or gas rather than through a wire filament, thus producing illumination.

Variable contrast paper Printing paper in which grade (contrast) can be varied during enlarging by changing the color of the printing light using different color filters.

Variable focus lens A lens whose focal length can be continually varied within a given range. Also known as a zoom lens.

Veil Uniformly distributed silver deposit in a photographic image, not forming part of the image itself. Also known as fog.

Video still camera Camera using an electronic charge coupled device instead of film. Each still picture is recorded on a magnetic disk or tape within the camera, and may be replayed immediately through suitable equipment to appear on any TV set, or to give color prints.

View camera Large-format camera, which has a ground-glass screen at the image plane for viewing and focusing.

Viewfinder Optical sighting aid on a camera, used for composing and usually for focusing on the subject. The viewfinder may also display exposure information in meter-fitted cameras.

Viewing filter See *Panchromatic vision filter*.

Viewpoint Position of the camera in relation to the subject. When viewpoint is altered, perspective is changed.

Vignetting Printing technique where the edges of the picture are gradually faded out to black or white. It also refers to a fall-off in illumination at the edge of an image, such as may be caused by a lens hood or similar attachment partially blocking the field of view of the lens.

Vinyl film Emulsion coating on a polyvinyl chloride acetate base, with less shrinkage than conventional film bases.

Viscose sponge Synthetic sponge used to wipe surplus water off films before they are hung up to dry.

Viscous processing Processes using chemicals carried in sticky semifluid substances instead of normal liquids. Avoids spill and so allows chemical processing inside the camera or between sandwiched dry materials. Used for instant picture processing.

Volt Unit of electrical potential difference and electromotive force.

Voltage stabilizer Transformer used to produce a steady output voltage despite fluctuations of input voltage. May be required between household supply and a color enlarger.

Vorticism Movement begun by small group of English painters (1912-15) concerned with abstract images, largely based on the dynamic forms of modern architecture.

Vortograph Abstract photograph made with a simple kaleidoscopic apparatus, first used by Alvin Langdon Coburn in 1917.

Warm color Any color which, by association, suggests warmth, such as red, orange, and yellow.

Warm-tone developer Developer producing image colors in chlorobromide papers ranging from warm black to reddish-brown, according to type.

Water bath Large water-filled container used to maintain processing trays, tanks or chemicals at the correct temperature.

Waterproof paper Printing materials coated on a base which does not itself absorb liquids. Resin-coated paper is of this type.

Water softening Method of eliminating most of the minerals and salts found in hard water. These can form scum marks on films or a layer of scale on equipment using large quantities of water, and might contaminate chemical solutions. Water softeners may use either physical filtration systems or chemicals.

Watkins factor Old system of development control, based on observation of the processing image under safelighting. The figure by which the time an image takes to appear for the first time must be multiplied in order to give the total time required for a fully developed image to form.

Watt Unit of power in electricity. A guide to the light output of tungsten lamps.

Watt-second Unit of energy, equal to the joule.

Wavelength Method of identifying particular electromagnetic radiation, considered as rays progressing in wave-like form. Wavelength is the distance between one wavecrest and the next. Different types of electromagnetic radiation have different wavelengths, and differ greatly in their characteristics. In the case of light, wavelength is measured in nanometers (nm) or angstrom units (Å). Different wavelengths of radiation in the visible spectrum are seen as colors.

Waxed paper process Very early form of photography. A variation of the calotype process, by which sensitized paper, exposed in the camera and processed, was waxed to make the negative more transparent before printing.

Weak A negative or print which is low in contrast or density.

Wedge spectogram Indication of the spectral sensitivity of a sensitized material by exposing it to a spectrum of light through a graduated gray wedge set at right angles to the colors.

Wet collodion process Early method of producing negatives on glass coated with iodized collodion which is immersed in silver nitrate prior to exposure to form a light-sensitive emulsion. Must be exposed and processed while still wet. Used from 1851 to about 1876.

Wet plate See *Wet collodion process.*

Wet processing Processing by the application of chemicals in liquids. The traditional method of photographic processing.

Wetting agent Chemical which, when used in minute quantities, reduces the surface tension of water. Usually added to the final wash of films and plates to improve draining and thus prevent drying marks forming.

White light An approximately even mixture of wavelengths of visible light, from 400-700 nm.

White light control Lever on a color head enlarger which instantly removes the color filtration set (for focusing) and returns it when required.

White light spectrum Electromagnetic wavelengths between 400-700 mm.

Whole plate Negative and print format, measuring $6\frac{1}{2} \times 8\frac{1}{2}$ ins.

Wide-angle lens Lens with a focal length considerably shorter than the diagonal of the format it fills. The lens gives a wide angle of view, and considerable depth of field.

Wide-angle rack Additional focusing rack used on large-format baseboard cameras. Allows the lens panel to be racked back and forward for focusing even when placed close to the focusing screen to accommodate a wide-angle lens.

Wind tunnel Device used to test the aerodynamic properties of a structure by placing it inside a sealed tube, through which currents of air or gas are passed. These currents can be photographed by coloring or heating them, and using color or heat-sensitive materials to record their behavior. Alternatively, the movement of indicators attached to the structure can be observed.

Wood print Print made on a wood surface which has been suitably prepared. It can then either be coated with emulsion or the image can be transferred to it by transfer coating.

Working aperture The widest aperture at which an acceptable image can be achieved, as distinct from the widest aperture to which the lens iris will open up.

Working solution Liquid chemical that has been mixed and diluted ready for use.

Xenon A rare gas used within some electronic flash tubes and enclosed arc light sources.

Xerography Photographic process which uses an electrically charged metal plate. On exposure to light the electrical charge is destroyed, leaving a latent image in which shadows are represented by charged areas. A powdered pigment dusted over the plate is attracted to the charged areas, producing a visible image. This is transferred to a sheet of or-dinary paper and heat — fused into its fibers. Also used for forming color images, making three exposures through primary colored filters, and using yellow, magenta, and cyan powders which are transferred on top of each other on the paper. Used universally for document copying.

Xography System of photography which produces prints and transparencies with a three-dimensional effect. A cylindrically embossed lenticular screen is placed in contact with the film and a shutter behind the lens is arranged to scan the subject during exposure.

X ray Electro-magnetic radiations beyond ultraviolet which, when passed through a solid object and allowed to act upon a sensitive emulsion, form a shadow image of the internal structure of the object.

X-ray film Spectral sheet film for radiography, having a thick emulsion coated on both sides of the support to increase the absorption of X rays.

Yellow The color formed by mixing red and green light. Yellow is complementary to blue, and is one of the three colors used in subtractive color synthesis.

Zirconium lamp Arc lamp used in powerful enlargers and projectors.

Zone focusing Method of focusing the lens so that the depth of field extends over a preselected range of distances. By this means, any fast-moving subject which passes through this zone of sharp focus will itself appear sharp in the image. Zone focusing is used when there is no time to focus on the subject in the normal way, or when its exact movements are unpredictable.

Zone system The method of determining exposure and development required for individual scenes, invented by Ansel Adams. It is based on analysis of subject luminosities in terms of nine gray tones, labeled Zones I through IX and previsualizing them as print densities. By measuring each subject luminance with a hand meter it is possible to determine how much the range of values must be contracted or expanded by negative development control to give the required values in the final print. The Zone System is primarily intended for individually processed monochrome sheet film negatives, and the use of a hand (preferably spot) meter.

Zoom lens Lens which is constructed to allow continuously variable focal length within a specific range. The effective aperture and focus settings remain unchanged throughout such adjustments.

Index

References to photographs
are shown in **bold**

A

Aberrations 113, 184
Absorption lines 295
Abstraction 361-8
  by blur 91
  with slow shutter speeds 128
Acetic acid 222, 240
Actinometer 132
Action finder 204
Action photography
  See *Movement; Sports pho-
tography*
Adams, Ansel 37, 46, 80, 82, 310,
310, **312**, 343, 345, 346, **346**, 369
Adams, Marcus 377, **377**
Adamson, Robert 348
Additive color 242, 248, 250-1, 258
Advertising photography 314-18
Aerial camera 208, 296-7
Aerial film speed (AFS) 296
Aerial perspective 82-3, 192
Aerial photography 296-9
Aerodynamics photography 281
Agar, David **73**, **89**, **151**, **171**
Agitation 221, 225, 226, 241
Airbrushing 252-3, 379
Air-to-air photography 297
Ames room 85
Anamorphic lens 210
Angel, Heather **300**
Angle of view
  and focal length 185
  of fisheye lens 188
  in portraiture 322
  of telephoto lens 189-90
  underwater 208
  of wide-angle lens 186
Animal photography 300-1
Annan, Craig 337
Antihalation layer 216
Antinous release
  See *Cable release*
Aperture
  automatic 118
  controls 101, 112
  and depth of field 118-23, 125
  diaphragm 100-1, 116-17
  f number system 117
  and image brightness 101, 117
  lens speed 117
  pinhole 112
  principle of 100
  -priority camera 135
  settings 116-17
  and shutter speed 125

and simple cameras 113
and standard lens 113
and telephoto lens 190
and wide-angle lens 186
  See also *Depth of field*
Arbus, Diane 356-7, **357**
Arbuthnot, Malcolm 358
Architectural photography 309-11
Arc lamps 164
Arnold, Eve 60, 353-4, **354**
ASA number 132
  See also *Film speed*
Aspherical lens 185
Astronomical photography 292-5
Atget, Eugène 31, 349, **349**, 353
Atmospheric perspective
  See *Aerial perspective*
Attachments
  close-up 195
  filters 198-201
  fisheye 188
  holders 201
  teleconverter 190
  telephoto 110
  wide-angle 187
Autochrome process 143, 336
Autofocus lenses
  contrast-comparing 115
  infrared 115
  for instant picture cameras 109,
110, 115
  for SLR cameras 211
  ultrasonic 109, 110, 115
Automatic cameras
  aperture-priority 135
  compact 105
  metering 134
  multimode 135
  shutter-priority 135
Automatic diaphragm 117
Autowinder 202
Available lighting 160, 162-3

B

Background paper 167, 168
Backgrounds
  black 174
  for glass 174
  lighting 172-4
  in natural history photography
300, 303
  sets 314
  for silhouettes 172
  in studio 167-9
  and viewpoint 63
  white 172-3
Back-lighting 14, 17, 20, 26, 27, 49,
137, 170

Back projection 181, 378
Bacon, Francis 358
Bag bellows 109
Bags, camera 203
Bailey, David 316
Balance
  composition 76-8
  lighting 150, 167, 175
Baltz, Lewis 67, 80
Barclay, Victoria **59**, **78**
Barlow, Nic **72**, **183**
Barnack, Oscar 99
Barn doors 166, 167
Barrel distortion 184, 186-7
Baryta 216
Baseboard camera 108
Bas-relief 265
Batch number 153
Bath, Robin **18**, **22**, **26**, **29**, **30**, **51**,
74, **90**, **119**, **137**
Bauhaus 363-4
Bayonet mount 104, 205
Bean bag 300
Beaton, Cecil **320**, 375-6, **376**, 380
Bell, Chris **66**
Bellows
  bag 109
  close-up 185, 195, 196, 207
  sheet film camera 108-9
Berliner Illustrierte Zeitung 324, 350
Birds 301
Birefringence 281
Bischof, Werner 353
Black and white film
  antihalation layer 216
  availability 148
  base 144, 216
  blue-only sensitive 155
  characteristic curve 155
  chromogenic 144-5, 152-5, 214,
217, 224-7
  developer 144-5, 222
  development time 226
  downrating 156
  drying 227
  emulsion 144-5, 216
  filters 156-7, 201
  fixing 216, 222
  grain 152, 154, 223
  high-speed 157
  infrared 157, 312
  lith 155, 157, 261-2, 263, 266
  orthochromatic 155
  panchromatic 143, 155
  prescreened 264
  processing 144, 214-16, 224-6
  response 155-7
  slides 144, 152, 214, 216, 226
  speed 152
  structure 144-7, 216
  tonal equivalents 79
  tone separation 266
  uprating 156

washing 227
Black and white paper
  bromide 215, 226, 232-3
  chlorobromide 232-3
  developer 222, 240-1, 244
  direct positive 232-3
  document-copying 232-3
  fiber-based 214, 216, 232
  fixing 216
  grade 243
  image formation 216
  orthochromatic 215, 232-3
  panchromatic 215, 232-3
  print from color negative 245
  processing 215, 216, 222, 232-3,
240-1
  resin-coated 214, 216, 232
  reversal 215
  solarization 267
  structure 216
  variable contrast 237, 243, 249
  washing 216
Bleaching
  black and white slide film 144, 226
  chromogenic materials 145, 217
  in retouching 252
  in toning 268
Blemishes
  See *Retouching*
Blossfeldt, Karl 34, 43, 344, **344**,
368
Blue-only sensitive film 135
Blur
  abstraction 91
  camera shake 130
  and movement 127-9
  and shutter speed 127
Boom 166
Boubat, Edouard **321**
Bounced light
  See *Flash; Lighting*
Bourke-White, Margaret 67, 350
Bown, Jane **44**
Box cameras 99
Bracketing 133
Brady, Mathew 348
Bragaglia, Antonio 357
Brain, Tony **9**, **279**
Brandt, Bill 16, 25, 49, 81, 187, 350,
350, 356, 357, 364, **364**, 373
Braque, Georges 342
Brightfield 278
Brightness range 154
Broadlights 164, 166
Brokaw, Dennis **15**, **35**, **42**, **43**, **46**,
119
Bromide paper 215, 226, 232-3
Bromoil process 336
B-setting 124, 125
  See also *Time exposures*
Bubble chamber photography 282
Buckland, David **87**, **127**, **128**, **158**,
209

Bulb flash
　　See *Flash*
Bulk film
　　brands available 148
　　magazines 206
Bullock, Wynn 368, 370, **370**, 387
Burning-in 248-9
Burri, René **366**
Burton, Jane **275, 302**

C

Cable release 126
Cadmium sulfide (CdS) cell 134, 136
Callahan, Harry 39, **360**, 368, **372**, 372-3
Calotype process 142
Camera
　　aerial 208, 296-7
　　automatic 105, 134-5
　　basic principles 100-1
　　compact 104-5
　　development of 98-9
　　direct vision 104-5
　　electronic scanning 292-3
　　high-speed 209, 275-6
　　instant picture 109
　　miniature 99
　　multiple image 208
　　panoramic 209
　　rollfilm 106-7, 206
　　rotating mirror 276
　　rotating prism 276
　　sheet film 108, 207
　　single lens reflex 102, 106, 111 205-6
　　Slit-shutter 361
　　stereoscopic 209
　　subminiature 209
　　35 mm 102-5, 205
　　twin lens reflex 107
　　underwater 208
　　video still 211
Camera cases 203
Camera movements
　　in architectural photography 309
　　and covering power 120
　　and depth of field 122, 277
　　and shape of subject 123
　　shift 120, 121, 122
　　swing 120, 121, 123
　　tilt 120, 121, 123
　　See also *Shift lens*
Camera obscura 98, 112
Camera shake 125, 130, 189
Camera Work 336, 337, 342
Cameron, Julia Margaret 160, 330, **330, 332**, 333, 348, **348**, 376
Capa, Robert 62, 353, 355, **355**
Caponigro, Paul 370
Carbon printing 143, 335
Carlos Clarke, Bob **269, 318, 323**, **382, 383**

Carroll, Lewis 348
Cartier-Bresson, Henri 60, 66, 88, **88**, 340, 347, 353, **353**, 368, 373, 378, 380, **380**
Cartridge film 149
Cases 203
Cassette film 149
Catadioptric lens 191, 283, 300, 304
Cathode ray tube 286, 287, 293
Cézanne, Paul 342
C41 processing 148, 214, 222, 226, 230
Chappell, Walter 370
Characteristic curves 154-5, 220, 223
Charge-coupled device (CCD) 211, 292
Chemicals
　　exhaustion 227
　　keeping properties 222
　　kits 220, 222, 240
　　measuring 221
　　one-shot 221
　　storage 221-2
Chitty, John **28, 33, 41, 61, 92**
Chopping shutter 131
Chromatic aberration 184
Chromogenic materials
　　black and white film 144, 145, 152, 154, 155, 214, 217, 224, 226, 227
　　color negative film 145-6, 217, 218
　　color paper 217, 232-3
　　color slide film 145-6, 217-18
　　compensation processing 224
　　negative/positive 217, 218
　　positive/positive 217, 218
　　processing 214, 217, 226
　　substantive 218
　　toning 217, 266-7, 268
Chronocyclograph 275
Cibachrome
　　See *Silver dye-bleach (SDB) paper*
Citroën, Paul **378**
Claudet, Antoine 160
Cleare, John **308**
Clearing agent 222, 226
Close-up photography
　　bellows 185, 195, 196, 303
　　close-up lens 195-6
　　depth of field 196, 197, 277, 302, 303
　　extension tubes 185, 186, 195, 196, 303
　　macro lens 195, 197, 277, 300, 302
　　macrophotography 277
　　medical lens 210
　　photomicrography 278-9, 280-
　　reversing rings 196
　　spacing bracket 197
Coating, lens 113, 184
Cobweb machine 315
Cohen, S. **279, 289**
Colindres, Milton **53, 73, 95, 305**
Collie, Keith **32, 48**

Collodion 142
Color
　　additive 143
　　associations 23, 50
　　balance 78-9
　　brightness 51
　　casts 148, 158, 242, 248, 251
　　circle 70
　　complementary 70
　　composition 70-1
　　contrast 26-7, 167
　　cool 50, 74
　　divisions 59, 61
　　emphasis 70
　　and exposure 132
　　false 257, 258, 294, 297
　　formation 144-7, 217
　　frames 60
　　and glossy surfaces 22, 170
　　hue 51
　　isolated 71
　　and light 17, 20, 22, 161
　　and matte surfaces 21, 22
　　monochromatic 75
　　muted 75, 82
　　opposed 74-5
　　pattern 42
　　and polarized light 171, 281
　　primary 142-3
　　related 74
　　saturation 27, 51
　　scales 285
　　silhouettes 172
　　strong 74-5
　　subtractive 242
　　suppression 26
　　and surface finish 22
　　temperature 151, 162-3, 164
　　themes 75
　　and time of day 23
　　visual response to 14, 23, 24, 50
　　warm 50
　　wavelengths 14, 32, 151, 161-2
　　and weather 23, 28, 30
　　weight 79
　　wheel 50
Color analyzer 238, 246
Color couplers 146-7, 150, 218, 268
Color film
　　assessing results 228
　　availability 148, 150
　　balance 150
　　bleach/fix 217
　　casts 148, 158, 242, 248, 251
　　characteristic curves 155
　　contrast 158, 161, 167
　　daylight 151
　　downrating 158
　　drying 227
　　image formation 144-7, 217
　　infrared 159
　　instant picture 146
　　negative 146, 150, 155, 158, 159
　　processing 214, 217, 222
　　processing faults 230-1
　　reciprocity failure 122, 152, 292

　　separations 266
　　slide 146, 150, 155, 158, 214, 217-19, 227
　　slide duplicating 159
　　stabilizer 227
　　structure 144-7, 217
　　tungsten 151
　　uprating 158
　　washing 227
Color filters
　　balancing 158-9, 163, 201
　　compensating 158-9, 163, 201
　　conversion (enlarger type) 237, 242-7, 250-1
　　correction (for black and white) 156-7, 201
　　gradated 198-9
　　multicolor 198
　　polarizing 198
　　skylight 201
　　Ultraviolet 190
Color meter 164
Color paper
　　negative/positive 215, 216-17, 232-3, 240-1
　　positive/positive 215, 217, 232-3, 240-1
　　processing 222, 240
　　solarization 267
Color printing
　　additive 250-1
　　black and white original 258
　　density control 248
　　faults 248
　　filtration 242-7
　　local color control 251
　　masking 263, 266-7
　　multiple prints 260-1
　　negative/positive 246
　　positive/positive 247
　　posterization 266
　　retouching 252-3
　　sandwiching 260
　　separations 262
　　solarization 267
　　subtractive 242
Color separations 262
Color temperature 151, 162-3
Color temperature meter 164
Color toning 217-18, 268
Compact cameras 104
Compensation processing 224
Composing frame 54, 65
Composition
　　balance 76-8
　　color 70-1, 74-5
　　contrast 68-9
　　depth 81-5
　　dividing picture area 59, 61
　　emphasis 67-70
　　false attachment 83-4
　　format 56-7
　　frames within frames 60-1, 73
　　framing 58-61
　　Golden Mean 68
　　image grammar 54
　　imbalance 79

juxtaposition 92
lead-in lines 72
line 36-7, 56, 82
moving subjects 86-8, 90-1
overlap 83
perspective 81-3
picture sequences 88-90
position of horizon 58
position of subject 67, 86
rule of thirds 67
shape 73
style 94
symmetry 76
tone 68-9
viewpoint 62-6
visual selection 54
Computer image enhancement 271, 289, 290, 293, 294
Condenser enlarger 223, 236
Constructivism 362
Contact prints
frame 238
making prints 242, 244
Continuous tone film 233, 264-5
Contrast
and color 26-7, 71
and composition 68-9
and development time 223, 228
and downrated film 156, 158
and enlarger type 223
and exposure 133
and lighting 24-7, 162-3, 167
masking 251
and paper grade 233
reducing with flash 176
simultaneous 25
and telephoto lenses 192
and texture 44
and uprated film 156, 158
visual response to 23, 24
and zoom lenses. 193
Contrast-comparing autofocus 115
Converging lens 113
Converging lines
and composition 36, 82
controlling 121, 122
correcting at printing stage 256
Converters
telephoto 190
wide-angle 187
Convertible lens 210, 310
Copying
lighting 171, 286
slides 159, 197
stand 197
Coronograph 292
Couture, Thomas 333
Covering power 113, 120, 121, 310
Crone, Trevor 157, 313
Cropping 364
Cross-screen attachment 199
Cubism 342, 357
Cunningham, Imogen 39, 62, 345
Currey, Amanda 45, 50, 74, 80, 260, 270, 387, 392
Curtis, Edward S. 348-9, 349

D

Dadaism 362
Daguerre, Louis 98, 142
Daguerreotype process 142
Dakin, H. S. 283
Dalton, Stephen 302
Darkfield 278
Darkroom
equipment 220-1
layout 234-5
Darkslide 106
Data back 202
Davidson, Bruce 353, 354, 354
Davison, George 336, 336, 337, 338
Degas, Edgar 338
Daylight 16-32, 160
-balanced film 150-1, 158, 162-3
enlarger 237
simulated 176
Defocusing 117
Delano, Jack 352
Delayed action timer 126
De Lory, Andrew 16, 17, 21, 23, 30, 37, 40, 44, 47, 48, 56, 57, 58, 60, 64, 65, 69, 77, 82, 86, 114, 115, 117, 118, 128, 129, 130, 133, 136, 150, 156, 188, 189, 192, 199, 200, 210, 243, 245, 247, 385
Demachy, Robert 335, 335, 338, 338, 339
De Meyer, Baron 316, 373, 375, 375
De Nooijer, Paul 270, 381-2, 382
Density
control 248
negative 133, 228-31
print 240-2
values 154-5
Depth
compression 189, 190, 191
and distance 80-1, 191
illusions 85
and perspective 81-3
and scale 84-5
and viewpoint 81
Depth of field
and aperture 112, 116, 118-19, 125
in close-up work 196, 197, 277, 302
and fisheye lens 188
and focal length 118
improving 122-3
and photomicrography 278
preview 116, 118
scale 118-19
Scheimpflug correction 122
and subject distance 118-19
and telephoto lens 189, 192
and wide-angle lens 186
Developer
black and white film 144-5, 214, 222
black and white print 215, 216, 222, 232-3, 240-1, 244
color 146-7, 222

exhaustion 227
fine-grain 222, 223
high-contrast 214, 222
keeping properties 222
lith 261-2
maximum acutance 222
speed-enhancing 222
strength 224
Developing tanks 220-1, 225
Development
agitation 221, 225, 226, 241
chemical effect 144-6
chromogenic 217-19
and contrast 223, 228, 152
dye destruction 219
and grain 223, 152
holding back 224
infectious 262
integral 145, 146-7
overdevelopment 228
pushing 224
temperature 224
time 224, 226, 240-1
underdevelopment 228
uneven 229
See also *Downrating; Uprating*
Diaphragm 100-1, 116-17
Diapositive
See *Slide film*
Dichlor acetoacetanilide 217
Dichlor naphthol 217
Diepraam, Willem 85
Differential focusing
See *Selective focusing*
Diffraction filter 199
Diffuser enlarger 223, 236
Diffusion filter 170, 200, 210
DIN number 132
Direct vision camera 104-5
Distortion
Ames room 85
anamorphic lens 210
barrel 184, 186-7
camera movements 120-3
color 159, 257, 258
enlarger 256
fisheye lens 188
focal plane shutter 131
form 49
pincushion 184
wide-angle lens 186
Diverging lens 113
Documentary photography 347-56
Dodging 248-9
Dohrn, Martin 309
Doisneau, Robert 39, 53, 53, 92, 92, 356, 356, 378, 379
Donne, Alfred 285
Doppler effect 295
Double exposure 92
Douglas, Andrew 179
Downrating
black and white film 155, 156
color film 158, 230-1
and effect on grain 223
processing compensation 224
Driffield, V.C. 132

Drum processing 221, 241
Dry ice 315
Drying
cabinet 221
film 227
marks 229
paper 239
squeegee 221
Dry mounting 239, 253
Duchamp, Marcel 362
Ducos du Hauron, Louis 143
Dudley Johnston, J. 335, 338, 338
Dulling spray 170
Duplex meter reading 136
Duplicating slides 159, 197
Dustin, Fred 75, 267
Dye
chromogenic 144-7, 217-18
couplers 144-7
hand coloring 268, 269-70
toning 268
Dynamic balance 77, 86
Dynamism 357-61

E

Earl, Andy 358
Eastman, George 99, 100, 142
Edgerton, Harold 277, 358, 360
Edison, Thomas 99
Eickemeyer, Rudolf 339, 344
Eide, Per 42, 70, 130, 249
Eisenstaedt, Alfred 67, 350
Ektaflex
See *Photo color transfer paper*
Electromagnetic spectrum 274
Electronic flash
camera-mounted 139-41
lighting techniques 175-8
studio 169
See also *Flash*
Electronic images 271
Electronic scanning camera 292-3
Emerson, P.H. 335, 340, 340
Emulsion
black and white film 144-5, 216
black and white paper 216
chromogenic 217
color film 145-7, 217
color paper 217
effect of reciprocity failure 152, 220
instant picture film 145, 146-7
liquid 259
negative/positive 218
photo color transfer 219
positive/positive 218
silver dye-bleach 219
Endoscopy 288-9
Enlargement 242-51
Enlargers 223, 236-7
See also *Printing*
Equatorial mount 291, 292
Ernst, Max 378

Erwitt, Elliott **84**, 86, 378, 380, **380**
E6 processing 148, 214, 222, 226
Estall, Robert **31**, **82**, **83**, **91**
ESTAR film base 261-2
Eugene, Frank 336, **337**, 339
Evans, Frederick 335, 336, 340, 342, **342**
Evans, Walker 43, **60**, 62, 352, **352**, 356
Ever-ready case 203
Exploded views 315
Exposure
  bracketing 133
  in close-up work 197
  and color 132
  compensation 137
  and contrast 133
  controls 101, 106, 110
  for flash 139-41, 175, 176, 178,
  latitude 152, 154-5, 158
  printing 228-31, 242-3, 246-7,
  251
  problems 137, 306
  symbols 105
  time exposure effects 180, 360-1
  timers 237-8
  and tone 132, 133
  values 137
  zone system 343
  See also *Aperture; Exposure
  meter; Shutter*
Exposure meter
  cell types 134, 136
  center-weighted 134, 188
  with deep-colored filters 157
  in dim light 137
  duplex reading 136
  early models 132
  flash meter 141
  hand-held 136-7
  incident light reading 136
  limitations 138, 188
  overall-averaging 134, 138
  reflected light reading 136
  spot 134, 136, 300
  through-the-lens (TTL) 103, 133-5,
  157, 188
Exposure sequences
  instant picture camera 110
  rollfilm SLR 106
  35 mm SLR 103
  TLR 107
  sheet film camera 108
Extension tubes 185, 186, 195, 196
Extinction meter 132
Eyepiece correction lens 204

F

False attachment 84
False color 257, 258, 294, 297
  See also *Infrared*
Farmer's reducer 252, 263

Farm Security Administration (FSA)
  project 352, 357
Farraday cell 275
Fashion photography 314-17
Faults
  film processing 228-31
  prints 248
Feininger, Andreas 83, 368, **368**
Feininger, Lyonel 363
Fenton, Roger 348
Ferric ammonium citrate 268
Fiber-based paper 214, 216, 232
Fiber optics 289
Fiennes, Mark **25**, **69**
Figures
  in architectural photography 310
  nude 323
  stage performers 322
  See also *Portraiture*
Film
  additive color 143
  aerial photography 296
  antihalation layer 216
  availability 148
  black and white *See separate
  entry*
  blue-only sensitive 155
  cartridge 149
  cassette 149
  characteristic curves 154-5
  chromogenic 145, 217
  color *See separate entry*
  continuous tone 264-5
  contrast 144-51
  downrating *See separate entry*
  early types 142-3
  emulsion 144-7, 217
  formats 148-9
  grain 152, 154, 223
  infrared black and white 157
  infrared color 159
  instant picture 143-7
  latent image 144-7
  light sensitivity 132
  line 155, 233
  lith *See separate entry*
  orthochromatic 155
  panchromatic 143, 155
  prescreened 264
  reciprocity failure 152
  response 148, 154, 155-7
  rollfilm 149-50
  sheet film 150
  speed 103, 132, 137, 148, 150
  storage 153, 225
  structure 144-7
  tungsten (Type B) 150, 151, 158,
  167
  uprating *See separate entry*
Filters
  black and white 156-7, 201
  built-in 187, 188
  center spot 199
  color balancing 156-7, 163, 166,
  201
  color compensating 158-9, 201,
  163

color conversion 237, 242-7, 250-1
color correction 156-7, 201
cross-screen 199
diffraction 199
diffusion 200, 210
enlarger 237, 242-3, 250-1
gradated 198-9
haze 190
holders 201
infrared 157, 159, 288
multicolor 198
multifaceted 200
neutral density 129, 201
polarizing 131, 171, 174, 198, 281
prism attachment 199
safelight 238
skylight 83, 201
soft focus 200, 210
split field 200
starburst 30, 170, 174, 199
Filtration 237, 242-3, 244, 246-7, 250-1
Finder
  See *Viewfinder*
Fisheye lens 188-9
Fixed focus lens 114
Fixer
  black and white 144, 222, 240
  exhaustion 227
  fixing time 226
  insufficient 229
Flare 30, 201
Flash
  accessories 165
  bar 139, 165
  bounced 139, 177, 178
  bulb 139, 161, 177
  in close-up work 165-6, 197
  for compact cameras 105
  cube 139, 165
  dedicated 141
  diffused 141, 166, 176
  duration 141
  electronic 139-41, 175-8
  exposure for 139-41, 175-8
  fall-off 140
  fill-in 176
  flipflash 139, 178
  gradated filters with 199
  guide numbers 140, 178, 309
  high-speed photography 275, 276-7
  hot shoe 139
  magnesium 138, 161
  in medical/forensic photography 285
  meter 141
  multihead 167, 169, 177, 179, 360
  off-camera use 141, 177
  red eye 178
  reducing contrast with 176
  reflectors 165, 166
  ring flash 165-6
  self-regulating 141
  sensor 141
  simulating sunlight 176
  slave units 169

  stroboscopic 166, 276-7, 360
  studio 166, 169
  synchronization 139-41
  system 165
  twin-tube 177
  umbrella 166
  underground 309
  underwater 208, 303
  UV-emitting 286
  See also *Lighting*
Floodlights 164, 166
  See also *Lighting*
Flowers 303
Fluorescent light 164, 286
  filters for 158-9
  f numbers 117
Focal length
  and angle of view 185
  and camera size 112, 120
  and focal plane 101
Focal plane shutter 124
Focus magnifier 237, 244
Focusing
  aids 103, 114-15, 204
  automatic 115, 211
  controls 101, 102, 105, 112
  depth of field *See separate entry*
  fixed-focus lenses 114
  fresnel screen 103
  infrared 159, 288
  instant picture cameras 108, 115
  microprism 103
  rangefinder 105
  reflections 116
  screens 103, 204
  selective 114, 116, 125, 186, 190
  sheet film cameras 108, 114
  SLR cameras 103, 106
  split-image 103
  and subject distance 114
  telephoto lens 189
  TLR cameras 189
  viewfinder attachments 204
Focus magnifier 237, 244
Fogging
  accidental 229, 230, 248
  black and white slide film 144
  color slide film 218
  solarization 267
Fontana, Franco **14**, **39**, **46**, **59**, **67**, **78**, **80**, **83**, **91**, 191, 366, **366**
Fonyat, Bina **25**, **40**, **77**
Food photography 314-15
Foo, Tony **51**, **91**
Foreground 58, 186
Forensic photography 285-8
Form
  distortion 49
  lighting 16, 19, 48
  shadow 28
  structure 48
  as subject 46-7
  suppression 49
Format
  camera 102-8
  film 148-9
  picture 56-7

Fox Talbot, William Henry 98, 138, 142, **142**, 274
Frame finder 105
Framing
divisions 59
frames within frames 60-1
horizon 58
light 27
moving subjects 86-8
shape 39
Frank, Robert 31, 66, 86, 356, **356**, 368, 373
Freed, Leonard **36**
Freezing movement 128-9, 130, 275-7
Fresnel screen 103, 204
Friedlander, Lee 31, **61**, 88, 356, **372**, 373
Front projection 181, 182, 378
Frost, Clive **175**, **310**, **322**
Futurism 362

G

Gamma rays 274, 280
Gelatin 144-5
Gerster, Georg **296**
Gibson, Ralph 54, 346, 364-6, **365**
Glare 17, 170, 171, 174
Glass 174
Glazers 239
Godfrey, Stephen **21**, **60**
Golden Mean 68
Golden, Robert **315**
Gorgoni, Gianfranco **325**
GOST number 132
Goto, John **93**, **257**
Gradated filters 198-9
Grade number 233, 243
Grain
and development 152, 154, 156, 223
and film type 152, 223
Griffiths, Kenneth **326**, **327**
Grosz, George 378
Group f 64 344-6
Group photographs 321
Guide number 140, 178, 309
Gum bichromate 259, 335
Gunter, Wayne **317**

H

Haas, Ernst 31, 50, 82, 93, **191**, **339**, 340, 353, 359, **359**, 361
Hag 8, 260-1
Half tone 405
Half-tone screen 264
Halogenization 217, 268

Hamilton, David 340, 377
Hamilton, Richard 362
Hand coloring 268, 269-70, 379
H and D speed 132
Hardener 406
Harper's Bazaar 350
Haskins, Sam 382, **382**
Hausmann, Raoul 378
Hawes, Joseph J. 348
Haze 82-3, 192, 308
Heartfield, John **269**, 362, 378
Heat-absorbing filter 276
Herschel effect 406
Hidalgo, Francisco 198, **255**, **339**, 359-60, 361
High Art photography 330-3
High key 25, 27, 173
Highlights
affecting meter reading 136
burning out 26
masking 266-7
High-speed cameras 209, 324
High-speed photography 275-7
High-speed shutters 131, 275
Hill, David Octavius 348
Hine, Lewis **326**, 348, 357
Hoch, Hannah 378
Holding back 155, 224
Holland Day, Fred 330, **332**, 333, 334, 335, 344, **347**, 369
Holman Hunt, William 330
Holography 284
Horizon 58
Hosking, Eric **301**
Hosoe, Eikoh **361**
Hot shoe 139
Howes, Chris **309**
Hue 406
Hurter, F.W. 132
Hyperfocal distance 119
Hypo eliminator 222

I

Image intensifier 289
Image quality
and agitation 226
black and white negatives 228-9
color negatives 230
color slides 231
and development time 224
prints 240-2
Image retrieval systems 292
Image tube unit 131
Impressionism 338-40
Incident light metering 136
Infectious development 262
Infrared autofocus 115
Infrared film
in aerial photography 296, 297
black and white 157
color slide 159
filters for 201, 288

focusing 159, 288
in landscape photography 312
in scientific photography 288
in thermography 288
Infrared shutter trigger 126, 301, 302
Insects 302
Instant picture backs 110, 169, 178
Instant picture cameras 109-10
Instant picture film
availability 148
black and white 145
color 146-7
formats 148-9
packs 150
reclaimable negative 145, 148
Integral film processes 146-7
Integral reflector lamp 164
Integral tripack 217
Interchangeable film backs
bulk film 202
instant picture film 110
rollfilm SLR 106, 206
studio uses 169, 178
Interchangeable lenses 184-94
Interiors, lighting 175, 311
Intervalometer 126, 202
Inverse square law 140
Iodine 252
Iris 100-1, 116-17
ISO number 132
Isotope scanning 290

J

Jackson, Robert **325**
James, Ronald C. **40**
Joffé, Constantin **316**
Jones Griffiths, Philip 355
Jones, Roger **47**
Juxtaposition 92

K

Kandinsky, Wassily 363
Karsh, Yousuf 25, 88, 373, 376, **376**
Käsebier, Gertrude 336, 374, **374**
Keighley, Alexander 94, 338, **341**
Kelvin scale 151
Kerr cell 131, 275
Kertész, André 49, **49**, 54, **68**, 94, 191, 340, **364**, **367**, 367-8, 378, 379-80
Kirlian photography 283
Kinns, G. **301**
Klee, Paul 363

L

Lammer, Alfred **34**, **303**
Lamps
See *Lighting*
Land, Edwin 143, **143**
Landscape photography 309-12
Langdon Coburn, Alvin **10**, 62, **143**, 334, **335**, 336, **339**, 340, 342, 358, **358**, 361, 369
Lange, Dorothea 352, **352**, 368
Large-format camera
See *Sheet film camera*
Lartigue, Jacques-Henri 57, 88, **131**, 360, 379, **379**
Lasers
in holography 284
in image scanning 271
Latent image 144-7
Latitude, exposure 152, 154-6, 158
Laughlin, Clarence John 28, **370**, **371**, 370-2
Laurance, Robin **66**
Lead-in lines 72, 187
Lee, Russell 352
Lens
aberrations 113, 184
anamorphic 210
angle of view 185
aperture See separate entry
aspherical 185
autofocus 115, 211
bayonet mount 104
built-in shutter 191
catadioptric 191
close-up 195-6
coatings 113, 184
converging 113
convertible 210
covering power 120, 121, 310
depth of field scale 118-19
design development 184-5
diverging 113
enlarger 237
fisheye 188-9
fixed focus 114
focal length 120, 185
focusing See separate entry
interchangeable 104, 185-95, 205-7
macro 195
medical 210
meniscus 184
mirror 191
movements 120-3
for natural history photography 300
perspective correction (PC) 121
retrofocus 187, 188
shift 121, 187
soft focus 210
speed 117
for sports photography 304
standard 112-23
supplementary 105, 110
telephoto 189-92
for underwater photography 208-9

wide-angle 186-7
zoom 192-3
Lens attachments
close-up 195
filters 198-201
fisheye 188
holders 201
teleconverter 190
telephoto 110
wide-angle 187
Lens hoods 187, 193, 201
Le Querrec, Guy **388**
Lester, Peter **72, 79**
Life 324, 350
Light
atmospheric conditions 24, 28, 82-3, 308
available light 158, 160, 162-3
characteristics 14
and color 17, 18, 20, 22, 26-7
and contrast 16, 18, 24-7
and detail 19
diffused 18, 19, 45
dim 137
direction 16
flare 30
fluorescent 162, 163, 164
and form 16, 19, 48, 173
frontal 14, 17, 20, 27, 49
hard 14, 18
high key 25, 27
low key 25, 27
mixed sources 28, 150, 162, 174-5
moonlight 31
moving sources 32
natural 14-32, 160
and opaque materials 20
polarized 171
response to 14, 16, 18
rim 17, 29
shadowless 18
side 16, 20, 26
size of source 19, 162
soft 14, 18, 19
as subject 28-9, 32
and surface finish 21, 22, 29
symbols 28
and texture 16-21, 45
and time of day 16-18, 23
and tone 20, 24
trails 180, 275
and translucent materials 20
and transparent materials 20
ultraviolet 183, 292
and viewpoint 17, 22, 29
wavelength 14, 113, 151, 162-3
and weather 23, 28, 30
See also *Lighting*
Light-emitting diode (LED) 134
Lighting
accessories 166
and avertising photography 314-15
and aerial photography 296
and architectural photography 310-11
arc lamps 164
available 158, 160, 162-3

axial 171
back-lighting 17, 20, 26, 27, 49, 137, 170
back projection 181
balance 150, 167, 175
booms 166
bounced 139, 162, 164, 165, 174, 177, 178
broadlight 164, 166
and color 23-7
colored sources 179
and color temperature 151, 162-3, 164
and contrast 16, 18, 24, 26-7, 162, 167
for copying work 171
diffused 19, 45, 169, 170, 172-3, 174-5, 176
diffusers 166
equipment 160-6
flash *See separate entry*
foodlights 164, 166
fluorescent 162, 163, 164
frontal 14, 17, 20, 27, 49, 171, 178
front projection 181, 182
glare 170, 171
hard 18, 164
high key 25, 27, 173
integral reflector lamp 164
limelight 160
local 170
low key 25, 27, 172
mixed sources 28, 150, 162, 174-5, 180
natural 16-32
and opaque materials 20
painting with light 164, 175
physiograms 180
polarized 171
and portraiture 160, 174-5, 320
reflected 164, 165, 167, 172, 174, 179, 181, 197
reflective surfaces 171, 173
rim-lighting 17, 29, 170
shadowless 19, 162, 171, 173
side-lighting 16, 20, 26
silhouettes 172
simulated sunlight 176
size of source 18, 162
spotlights 164, 166
stands 166
in studio 167-8
and surface finish 21, 29, 170, 171, 173
and texture 16-21, 45, 171
and time-lapse photography 275
and tone 20, 24
tungsten 151, 158, 160, 164, 167
ultraviolet 183, 292
Lighting tent 173
Light trail 180, 275, 361
Line 36-7
Linear perspective 81-2
Line film 155, 233
Linked Ring Brotherhood 336-7
Liquid crystal diode (LCD) 134, 211
Liquid light 259

Lith film
characteristic curve 155
contrast 157, 233, 261
exposure 157, 262
masking 261, 263, 266
posterization 266
processing 233, 262
separations 262-3
Lorre, Jean **293, 294, 295**
Low key 25, 27, 172
Low-light metering 137
Luminance 224

M

McBean, Angus 380, **380**
McBride, Will 323
McCullin, Don 324, 355
Machine prints 248
Mackie line effect 267
McKinnell, Ian **186, 190, 196, 197, 277, 311**
Macro lens 195, 197
in natural history photography 300, 302
Macrophotography 277
Macro zoom lens 193
Magnification
image 195, 277-8
ratios 196, 244
Magnifying finder 204
Magnum Photos 353, 380
Mahr, Mari 259, 362, **362**
Manual override 103
Marey, Etienne 90, 357, 360
Martin, Paul 349, 353
Masking
contrast 251, 263
correction 263
drop-out 263
highlight 255, 266-7
lith film 261-2
retouching 253
shadow 266-7
Masking frame 237
Mason, Leo **306, 307**
Massey, Ray **182, 315, 318**
Matisse, Henri 342
Matte surfaces
and color 21, 22
dulling spray 170
and light 21, 29
Meatyard, Ralph Eugene 368, 372, **372**
Medical lens 210
Medical photography 285-90
Medium-format camera
See *Rollfilm camera*
Meire, Hylton **290**
Melton, Trevor **6, 20, 24, 29, 36, 69, 120, 121, 122, 123, 140, 141, 169, 170, 172, 173, 174, 176, 177, 178, 180, 182**

Menneer, Neil **20, 39, 62**
Metaphor and symbolism 368-73
Methyl ethyl ketone 217
Meyerowitz, Joel 368
Michals, Duane 89, 368 , 373
Michaud, Roland and Sabrina 3, 27, 39, 55
Microphotography 277, 280
Microprism 103
Microscopes 278-9, 297
Millais, John Everett 330, **331**
Miller, Diana **317**
Miller, Freeman D. **295**
Miniature camera 99
See also *35 mm camera*
Mirror lens 191, 283, 300, 304
Mirrors
focusing on 116
for local lighting 170
reflections 31
Mixed media images 362
Model, Lisette 356
Model release 317
Moholy-Nagy, László 62, **363**, 363-4, **364**, 367
Monet, Claude 338
Monopod 203, 300
Monorail camera 108
Montage 268, 269, 318, 378, 379
Moon, Sarah 340, 377, **377**
Morath, Adolf 376
Morgan, Barbara 360, **360**
Mosaics 294, 297, 312
Motor drive 202
Mounting 252-3
Mounts 227
Movement
blurring 91, 128-9
composition 57, 86-8, 90-1
critical moment 87-8
framing the subject 86, 128
freezing 128-9, 130
representing 275
and shutter speed 128-30
and viewpoint 91, 129
See also *Dynamism*
Multicoating 113, 184
Multicolor filter 198
Multifaceted filter 200
Multiple-image camera 208
Multiple printing 260-1, 331-2, 378-9
Muybridge, Eadweard 90, **90**, 274, 357, 358, 360

N

Nadar 348
Natural history photography 300-3
Naturalism 340
Natural light 16-32
Negative
assessing results 228
faults 228

filing 227
instant picture film 145, 148
processing 220-7
structure 144-8
See also *Black and white film; Color film*
Negative carrier 237
Negative/positive paper 216-19, 232-3
false color 258
photograms 257
processing 240-1
printing 246
ring-around 246
Neue Sachlichkeit 343-4
Newman, Arnold 18, 54, 67, 72, 73, 350, **350, 351, 373**
New Objectivity 343-4, 373, 376
New Realism
See *Straight photography*
Newton, Helmut 316
Niépce, Nicéphore 98, 142, **142**, 184
Night photography 31, 305
Non-substantive film processes 214, 219
Normal lens
See *Standard lens*
Nude 323, 364
Nurnberg, Walter 376

O

Oil pigment process 335-6
Oliver, Stephen **85**
110 cameras 104-5, 208
Orthochromatic film 155
Overdevelopment 228
Overexposure 154-5, 228, 230-1
Overlays 263-4
Oxidation products 147, 217, 218

P

Painting with light 164, 175
Palmer, Gabe **311**
Panchromatic film 143, 155
Panning 128, 301, 305
Panoramas 310
Panoramic camera 209, 321
Paper
black and white *See separate entry*
distortions 257
fiber-based 216, 232-3
grade 233, 243
negative/positive 215, 216-18, 232-3
photo color transfer 217, 219, 232-3

positive/positive 215, 216-19, 232-3
resin-coated 214, 215, 216, 232-3
silver dye-bleach 217, 219
surface 233
textured 43
variable-contrast 237, 243, 249
weight 233
Parallax error 104-5, 107
Paris Match 324, 350
Parkinson, Norman **316**
Parsons, Grubb **291**
Patch chart 250
Pattern 32, 40-2
Peach Robinson, Henry 330, 331, **331, 332**, 332-3, 336, 340
Pearson, David **246, 253**
Peel-apart film 145, 146
Pelham, Erik **384**
Penn, Irving 18
Pentaprism 102, 107
Periphery photography 284
Perspective
aerial (atmospheric) 82-3
and camera movements 122, 123
correcting distortion 256
and depth 81-3
linear 81-2
and telephoto lens 189, 192
and viewpoint 63-4, 82
and wide-angle lens 186, 187
Perspective control (PC) lens 121
Petzval, Josef 160
Photo color transfer paper 217, 219, 232-3
processing 241
Photogrammetry 297
Photograms 256, 363
Photogravure 336
Photojournalism 326, 350-6
Photomicrography 278-9, 281
Photo-secession 336-7, 374
Physiograms 180
Picasso, Pablo 342
Pictorialism 334-40
Picture Post 324, 350
Pincushion distortion 184
Pinhole image 112
Pissarro, Camille 338
Plants 303
Plate camera
See *Sheet film camera*
Platinotype process 335
Polak, Richard **333**
Polarized light 171, 278, 281
Polarizing filter 131, 171, 174, 198, 281
Portraiture 320-2
Positive/positive paper 216-19, 232-3
contrast 247
photograms 257
printing 247
processing 240-1
ring-around 247
Posterization 266
Potassium bichromate 259
Potassium bromide 217, 268

Potassium ferricyanide 217, 268
Potassium iodide 252
Pre-Raphaelite Brotherhood 330-1
Prescreened film 264
Press photography 325-6, 350-6
Price, William Lake 330, 332
Print
contact 242
faults 248
machine-processed 248
storage 253
Print tongs 238-9
Printing
additive 248, 250-1
black and white 245
burning-in 248-9
color 246-51
contact 242
contrast masking 251
density control 249
distortions 256
dodging 248-9
equipment 236-9
exposure 242-3, 244, 246, 247, 250
faults 248
filtration 237, 242-3, 244, 246-7, 250-1
multiple 260-1, 331-2, 379
processing solutions 240
retouching 252-3
sandwiching 260, 378, 379
screens 264
special effects 256-69
subtractive 242
vignetting 248
Prism attachment 199
Processing
agitation 221, 225, 226, 241
assessing 228
black and white film 224-6
C41 148, 214, 222, 226, 230
chemicals 222
chromogenic materials 217
color negative film 214, 217
compensation 224, 229
contact sheets 244
contrast 223
equipment 220-1
E6 148, 214, 222, 226
faults 228-31
grain 223
lith film 262
loading film 225
negative/positive materials 215, 218, 233
non-substantive slide film 214, 218-19, 222
photo color transfer material 219
positive/positive materials 215, 218-19, 233
silver dye-bleach material 219
substantive slide film 214, 218-19, 222
temperature 224
time 224, 226
Program mode 135

Proportion 63
Props 314-15, 321
Pulling
See *Downrating*
Pushing
See *Uprating*

Q

Quarter-plate camera 99

R

Radiography 280, 286
Rangefinder 105, 115
Rauschenberg, Robert 362
Ray-Jones, Tony **66**
Ray, Man **268**, 350, 353, 362-3, **363**, 378
Reciprocity failure 122, 152, 220, 292
Reclaimable negative 145, 148
Reconnaissance photography 297
Rectilinear projection 186
Red eye 178
Reflected light reading 136
Reflections
avoiding with light tent 173
avoiding with shift lens 120
controlled 173
using dulling spray 170
focusing on 116
glare 17, 170, 171, 174
and polarized light 171
shape and 38
specular 21
as subject 31
Reflectors 165, 172, 174, 179, 181, 197
Refraction 20, 112
Reflex cameras
single lens 102, 106, 109
twin lens 107
Registration systems 261
Rejlander, Oscar 330, 332, **333**
Remote releases
infrared 126, 301, 302
with motor drive 202, 304
triggered by subject 126, 276, 301, 302
ultrasonic 126
Renger-Patzsch, Albert 34, 82, 342, 344, **344**, 376, **391**
Reportage photography 324-6, 350-6
Resin-coated paper 214, 216, 232
Retouching
exploded views 315
in pictorialism 335
techniques 252-3, 271

Retrofocus lens design 187, 188
Reversing rings 196
Riboud, Marc 353
Right-angle finder 204
Riis, Jacob **348**, 349
Rim-lighting 17, 29, 170
Ring-around
    negative/positive 246
    positive/positive 247
Ring flash 165-6
Rodchenko, Alexander 364
Rodger, George 353
Rollfilm camera 106-7
    in aerial photography 296
    in architectural photography 310
    early designs 98-9
    exposure measurement 106
    in fashion photography 314
    film 149-50
    in portraiture 320
    single lens reflex 106
    system 206
    telephoto lens 191
    tripods 203
    twin lens reflex 107
    wide-angle lens 186
Romanticism 373-7
Rosetti, Dante Gabriel 330
Rotating mirror camera 276
Rotating prism camera 276
Rothstein, Arthur 352
Rozelaar, Paul **181**
Rule of thirds 67
Rybolt, Brian **31**

S

Sabattier effect 363
Safelights 233, 238
Salomon, Erich 349
Sander, August 349, **349**, 357
Sandwiching 378, 379
Sandwich printing 260
Satellite photography 298-9
Saturation 27, 51
Scale
    and depth 84-5
    and pattern 42
Scale models 315
Scatter
    See Flare
Schad, Christian 362
Schadeberg, Jurgen **116**
Scheimpflug correction 122
Schlieren photography 282-3
Schulze, Johann 142
Scientific photography
    aerial 296-9
    aerodynamics 281
    astronomical 290-5
    bubble chamber 282
    chronocyclographs 275
    endoscopy 288-9

forensic 285-8
high-speed 275-7
holography 284
hydrology 281
Kirlian 283
medical 285-90
microphotography 277, 280
periphery 284
photomicrography 278-9, 281
radiography 280, 286
Schlieren 282-3
sonography 290
surveillance 289
thermography 287, 298
Scott Archer, Frederick 142
Screens
    focusing 103, 204
    printing 264
Scrim 166, 167
Selective focusing 114, 116, 125
Selenium cell 134, 136
Separation printing 262, 266
Sepia toning 268
Sequence photography 88-90
Seymour, David 353
Shading 248-9
Shadows
    coloring 182
    controlling 169-77
    and direction of light 16, 17, 19
    printing manipulations 267
    shadowless lighting 162, 171, 173
    shape and form 28, 38
    See also Lighting
Shahn, Ben 352
Shape
    and balance 77
    and camera movements 123
    counterpoint 39
    and direction of light 16-17
    distortions 120-3, 188, 256
    and reflections 38
    and shadow 28, 38
    and structure 73
    and viewpoint 38, 39, 65
Sharp, Carol **28, 32, 44, 80, 94, 311**
Sharpness 119, 129, 130, 154
    See also Focusing
Sheet film cameras 108-9
    in close-up work 197, 277
    in fashion photography 314
    in medical and forensic pho-
      tography 285
    movements 120-3, 187, 207
    shutter 124, 125
    system 207
    tripod 203
Shift
    See Camera movements
Shift lens 121, 122, 187, 310
Shutter
    and aperture 125
    chopping 131
    development of 124
    firing systems 126
    flash synchronization 140
    focal plane 103, 106, 124-5

high-speed 131
leaf 106, 124
principle of 100
-priority cameras 102, 111, 135
sector 124
slit 361
speeds 101, 125, 127-30
timing 125
universal 108
Shutter releases 126
    See also Remote releases
Side-looking airborne radar 298
Silhouettes
    in natural light 17, 29
    in studio lighting 172, 174
Silicon blue cell (SBC) 134, 136
Silver dye-bleach (SDB) paper 217, 219, 233-4
    effect of reciprocity failure 220
    in masking 266
    processing 240
Silver halides 144-8, 216-19, 223, 259
Silver transfer system 145
Silvester, Hans **38, 71, 86-7**
Sims, John **50, 71, 75, 79, 116, 159, 198**
Single lens reflex (SLR) cameras 102-4, 106, 109-10
    automatic 103, 111, 135
    in close-up work 195
    development of 99
    in medical and forensic pho-
      tography 285
    multimode 135-6
    in natural history photography 300, 303
    in sports photography 304
    systems 205, 206
Siskind, Aaron 361, **367**, 368
Sisley, Alfred 338
Skylight filter 83, 201
Slide copying 159, 197
Slides
    black and white 144, 152, 214, 216, 226
    color 155, 214, 217-19
    mounts 227
    sandwiching 260
    See also Color film
Slit-shutter camera 361
Smith, Chris **9, 305, 308**
Smith, W. Eugene 67, 353, 354, **354**
Smyth, Forrest **22, 28**
Snoot 166, 181
Sodium carbonate 217
Sodium sulfide 268
Sodium sulfite 217
Sodium thiosulfate 240
Soft focus
    to diffuse glare 170
    filter 200
    in impressionism 340
    lens 210
    in pictorialism 335
Solarization 267, 363
Sommer, Frederick 370

Sonography 290
Southworth, Albert S. 348
Spacing bracket 197
Special effects
    anamorphic lens 210
    back projection 181
    bas-relief 265
    cobweb machine 315
    color separations 262
    dry ice 315
    false color 257, 258, 294, 297
    filters See separate entry
    fisheye lens 188-9
    gum bichromate 259
    hand coloring 269-70
    image distortions 256
    lighting 179
    light trails 180
    liquid emulsions 259
    masks 263-4
    montage 268, 269
    multiple printing 260-1
    panoramic camera 209
    paper effects 256
    photograms 256
    physiograms 180
    posterization 266
    sandwiching 260, 378, 379
    solarization 267, 363
    stereoscopic camera 209
    tone separations 262
    toning 268
Spectral signature 295, 299
Spectrograms 295
Specular reflection 21
Split field attachment 102
Split image 102
Sports photography 304-9
Spotlights 164, 166, 179, 276
    See also Lighting
Spot meter 134
Spotting 252
Squeegee 221, 227
Staller, Eric 358, **359**
Standard lens 112-23
Stands, lighting 166
Starburst filter 30, 170, 174, 199
Starr, John **187, 194, 200, 267, 322, 359, 359**
Steichen, Edward 334, 336, **337**, 340, 342, 346
Stephens, Tim **246, 247, 250, 251, 258, 262, 263, 264, 265, 266, 384**
Stereoscopic photography 209, 297
Stern 324
Stieglitz, Alfred 52, 336-7, **337**, 339, 340, 342, 343, 346, 368, 369, **369**, 374
Still life 314
Stop bath 222, 226, 240
Storage
    film 153
    negatives 225
    prints 253
Straight photography 310, 342-6
Strand, Paul **321**, 340, 342, 343, **343**, **344**, 347, 364, 374

Stroboscopic flash
  See *Flash*
Structuralism 361-8
Studio
  equipment 164-6
  layout 167-8
  lighting techniques 169-83
Subminiature cameras 209
  film for 148
Substantive film processes 214, 218
Subtractive color 242
Sulfuric acid 268
Summers, Roger **285**
Supports, camera 203, 300
Surface finish 21, 29, 170, 171, 173
Surge marks 229
Surrealism 378-82
Surveillance photography 289
Swing
  See *Camera movements*
Symbolism 28, 48, 52-3
  See also *Metaphor and symbolism*
Symmetry 58, 76
Synchronization 139-41
Systems
  flash 165
  rollfilm SLR 206
  sheet film camera 207
  35 mm SLR 205

T

Tanks 220-1, 225
Technical camera
  See *Sheet film camera*
Technical photography
  See *Scientific photography*
Teleconverter 190
Telephoto lens 189-92
  in landscape photography 312
  in natural history photography 300
  in portraiture 320
  in sports photography 304
  supports for 203
Telescopes 290-1
Temperature
  and development 224, 241
  effect on camera functions 308
  processing control 220-1, 224
Tempering box 220-1, 224, 239, 241
Test trips 242, 244, 246, 247, 250
Texture
  as design element 44
  detail 43
  lighting 16-21, 45
  paper 43
Thermography 287, 298
Thermometer 221, 239
35 mm camera 102-5
  in advertising photography 314
  in architectural photography 310
  automatic 103, 111, 135
  in fashion photography 314

historical development 99
in natural history photography 300
in photojournalism 347
in portraiture 320
in reportage photography 324
systems 205
Thomson, John 348
Three-dimensional images 81, 209
Through-the-lens (TTL) meter 103, 133-5, 157, 188
Tilt
  See *Camera movements*
Time exposure 127-8
  and blurring 91
  chronocyclographs 275
  light trails 180, 275
  physiograms 180
Time-lapse photography 275
Tomography 286
Tompkin, Nic **183, 315, 318, 319**
Tone
  balance 77
  and composition 68-9
  emphasis 69
  equivalents 79
  and exposure 132, 133
  high key 25, 27, 173
  and lighting 20, 24
  lith film 261-2
  low key 25, 27, 172
  scales 285
  separations 262, 266
  visual response to 23, 24
Toning
  chromogenic 217, 266-7, 268
  iron 268
  sepia 268
Traeger, Tessa **314**
Traverso, Giuliana **47**
Tray development 220, 221, 238, 240
Triggers
  infrared 126, 301, 302
  light-sensitive 126, 276, 302
  remote 202
  ultrasonic 126
Tripods 203
Truckel, Peter **259**
Tungsten
  film 150, 151, 158, 167
  lighting 150, 151, 158-9, 160, 163, 164, 167
Turner, Pete 50
Twin lens reflex (TLR) camera 107
  See also *Rollfilm camera*

U

Uelsmann, Jerry 72, 379, 380, **381**
Ultrasonic autofocus 115
Ultrasonic trigger 126
Ultraviolet (UV) filter 83, 183, 190
Ultraviolet light 183, 259, 286, 292
Ultra-wide-angle lenses 186-9

Umbrella reflector 165
  See also *Reflectors*
Underdevelopment 228
Underexposure 154-5, 228, 230-1
Underwater photography 208, 302-3
Ung, Jan **5, 52, 53, 73, 77, 93**
Uprating
  black and white film 155, 156
  color film 158, 230-1
  and grain 223
  processing compensation 224

V

Van Dyke, Willard 345
Vanity Fair 346
Variable-contrast paper 237, 243, 249
Video still camera 211, 271
View camera
  See *Sheet film camera*
Viewfinder
  action finder 204
  direct vision 100, 104-5
  displays 134
  eye-level finder 204
  with fisheye lens 188
  instant picture camera 109
  interchangeable 204
  magnifying finder 204
  microprism 103
  rangefinder 105, 115
  right-angle finder 204, 300
  rotary finder 204
  sheet film camera 100
  SLR 100, 103, 106
  split-image 103
  TLR 100, 101
  waist-level finder 106, 107, 204, 300
Viewpoint
  in architectural photography 310-11
  and background 63
  changing 65
  and composition 62-6
  and depth 84-5
  high 63, 64
  and landscapes 312
  and lighting 17, 22, 29
  and line 36
  and linear perspective 82
  low 63, 64
  and movement 91
  moving in close 63
  and pattern 40, 42
  and perspective 63-4
  and reflections 31
  and shape 38, 39, 65
  and silhouettes 29
  and subject meaning 66
  and wide-angle lens 186
Vignetting 193, 249

Vogt, Christian **46, 84, 366**, 366-7
Vogue 346
Vorticism 357

W

Waist-level finder 204
Walster, Nick **16, 45, 76**
Warhol, Andy 362
War photography 348, 355
Washers 221, 239
Washing
  fiber-based papers 216, 239
  film 144, 227
  resin-coated papers 239
  times 226
Waterproof housings 208, 308
Watson, Andrew 30, **263**
Weather 23, 28, 30
  See also *Light*
Wedge spectrogram 295
Weegee (Arthur Fellig) **355**, 355-6, 357
Weight, paper 233
Weston, Brett 346, **346**
Weston, Edward 28, 34, 43, 94, 310, 342, 344-6, **345**, 364, **364**, 369
Wetting agent 222, 227
Whistler, James McNeill 334, **334**, 339
White, Clarence 28, 336, 369, 374, **374**
White, Minor 368, 369, **369**, 370
Wide-angle lens 186-8
  underwater use 208

Wilson, Henry **6, 19, 63, 67, 94, 127, 128, 138, 175**
Wind-on mechanisms 101
Wind tunnel 280-1
Wolcott, Alexander 160
Wood, Bill **303**
Woodburytype process 334

X

Xenon arc spotlight 276
X rays
  in astronomical photography 292, 293,
  effect on film 153
  in radiography 274, 280-1, 288

Z

Zone system 343
Zoom lens 192-3

Acknowledgments

Author's acknowledgments

Producing a book of this size was a major task which relied absolutely on being one of a team. I was fortunate to be able to work with an intelligent and highly professional group of designers and editors who really cared for their subject, imposed high standards, and enjoyed working together. I would especially like to thank Joanna Godfrey Wood, who was involved with the project from its earliest conception and also Joss Pearson for setting things in motion. Jonathan Hilton and Michelle Stamp are respected colleagues from previous books. Caroline Lucas was tireless in her vital role of obtaining pictures from archives and photographers around the world. The cooperation of so many distinguished photographers is greatly appreciated. I also thank fellow teachers Tim Stephens and Sidney Ray for their expert help and information. Finally I would like to thank my wife Pamela, for her encouragement, perseverence – and for typing well over a quarter of a million words.

Michael Langford

Dorling Kindersley would like to extend special thanks to: Tim Stephens and Lucy Lidell for editorial contribution; Tim Shackleton, Richard Dawes, and Judith More for additional editorial work; Christopher Davis and Alan Buckingham for editorial advice; Alun Jones, Peter Moore, Rosamund Gendle, and Gary Marsh for design assistance; David McGrail for design research and development; Elly Beintema for preliminary picture research; Andrew de Lory, Trevor Melton, and Ian McKinnell for special photography; Reg Icke, Ramón Peypoch, and José Tacias of Reprocolor Llovet; Roy Thomas and John Marshall from Smeets; Sidney Ray for technical advice; and Lesley Gilbert for typing.

Illustrations by:
Alun Jones
Kuo Kang Chen
Diamond Arts
Alan Suttie
Venner Artists
Norman Lacey MISTC
Les Smith MSIAD
Jackson and Day
Tony Lodge
Andrew Popkiewicz
Gary Marsh
David Ashby

Photographic services by:
Arka Cartographics Ltd
Chris Barker
Negs
Paulo Color
Pelling and Cross
W. Photo
Photo Summit
Process Supplies
Studio 287
Frank Thomas

Prop hire and locations by:
H. R. Owen Ltd
Paxman Musical Instruments Ltd
J. J. Spiller (Hire) Ltd
Steam Age Mechanical Antiquities

Information and technical assistance was kindly provided by:
J. A. Allen (School of Oriental and African Studies, London University)
Aerofilms Ltd
Agfa-Gevaert Ltd
Barr and Stroud Ltd
Bowens Sales and Service Ltd
British Aerospace Dynamics Group
De Vere (Kensington) Ltd
Ford Motor Company Ltd
Fox Talbot
A. Gallenkamp and Co Ltd
GEC Medical Equipment Ltd
John Hadland (Photographic Instrumentation) Ltd
Hasselblad (GB) Ltd
Hunting Geology and Geophysics Ltd
Ilford Ltd
International General Electric Company of New York Ltd
Introphoto Ltd
KeyMed (Medical and Industrial Equipment) Ltd
Kodak Ltd
Light Optics Ltd
Linhof Professional Sales
Hylton Meire (Division of Radiology, Clinical Research Centre, Northwick Park Hospital, Harrow, Middx.)
Nikon UK Ltd
Olympus Optical (UK) Ltd
Osawa (UK) Ltd
NEI Parsons Ltd
Minolta UK Ltd
Salim Patel, Science Photo Library
Paterson Products Ltd
Pentax (UK) Ltd
Philips Electronic and Associated Industries Ltd
Polaroid (UK) Ltd
Pye Unicam Ltd
Research Engineers Ltd
Royal Greenwich Observatory
Royal Observatory Edinburgh
J. J. Silber Ltd
Sony (UK) Ltd
Thorn EMI Ltd
Vivitar (UK) Ltd
Carl Zeiss (Oberkochen) Ltd, London

Picture credits

Ansel Adams 37b, 310t, 312, 346l
Marcus Adams (Weidenfeld & Nicolson Archives) 377t
Aerofilms Ltd 296br
David Agar 73t, 89r, 151, 171
Heather Angel 300
Diane Arbus (© c. 1968 The Estate of Diane Arbus) 357
Eve Arnold (Magnum from John Hillelson Agency) 354l
Eugène Atget (Philadelphia Museum of Art: Given anonymously: Photographed by Will Brown, 1979) 349bl
Victoria Barclay 59t, 78t
Nic Barlow 72t, 183b
Robin Bath 18b, 22tl, 26r, 29b, 30bl, 51tl & r, 74l, 90b, 119br, 137
Cecil Beaton Photography (Courtesy of Sotheby's Belgravia) 320, 376t
Chris Bell 66b
Karl Blossfeldt (Galerie Wilde, Köln) 344tr
Edouard Boubat (Agence Top) 321b
Jane Bown 44t
Dr Tony Brain (Science Photo Library) 9t, 279b
Bill Brandt 350t, 364b
British Aerospace Dynamics Group 297
Dennis Brokaw 15, 35, 42b, 43, 46t, 119bl
David Buckland 87bc & r, 127b, 128tl, 158, 209
Wynn Bullock (Wynn & Edna Bullock Trust: Center for Creative Photography) 370b, 387l
René Burri (Magnum from John Hillelson Agency) 366t
Jane Burton (Bruce Coleman Ltd) 275b, 302br
Harry Callahan (Light Gallery) 360r, 372br
Julia Margaret Cameron (Royal Photographic Society) 330, 332br, 348t
Robert Capa (Magnum from John Hillelson Agency) 355tl & bl
Bob Carlos Clarke 269b, 318br, 323t, 383
Henri Cartier-Bresson (Magnum from John Hillelson Agency) 88, 353t & b, 380bl
CERN (Science Photo Library) 282t & b
John Chitty 28bl, 33, 41, 61, 92t & c
Paul Citroën (University of Leiden) 378
John Cleare (Mountain Camera) 308r
Dr S. Cohen (Science Photo Library) 279t, 289tr
Milton Colindres 53tl, 73br, 95, 305t
Keith Collie 32t, 48br
Thomas Couture (Mansell/Alinari) 333t
Trevor Crone 157, 313
Amanda Currey 45t, 50b, 74r, 80b, 260l, 270tr & l, 387r, 392

Edward S. Curtis (Philadelphia Museum of Art: Purchased with funds from the American Museum of Photography: Photographed by Philadelphia Museum of Art) 349t
H. S. Dakin (Science Photo Library) 283r
Stephen Dalton (Natural History Photographic Agency) 302t & bl
Bruce Davidson (Magnum from John Hillelson Agency) 354tl
George Davison (Royal Photographic Society) 336
Andrew de Lory 16t, 17, 21r, 23, 30cr, 37t, 40t, 44br, 47tl, 48tr, 56, 57l & c, 58, 60tr, 64, 65c & b, 69bl, 77tr, 82t, 86tl, lc & bl, 114, 115, 117, 118, 128bl, 129, 130tl & r, 133, 136, 150, 156bl & r, 188, 189, 192, 199, 200tl, 210, 243, 245, 247b, 385
Robert Demachy (Royal Photographic Society) 335t, 338t
Baron de Meyer (International Museum of Photography, George Eastman House) 375
Paul de Nooijer 270b, 382t
Willem Diepraam 85t
D. O. E. Hydraulics Research Station 281t
Martin Dohrn 309r
Robert Doisneau (Rapho) 53br, 92b, 356t, 379t
Andrew Douglas 179
Louis Ducos du Hauron (International Museum of Photography, George Eastman House) 143c
J. Dudley Johnston (Royal Photographic Society) 338b
Fred Dustin 75b, 267t
Dr Harold Edgerton (Science Photo Library) 277l
Per Eide 42t, 70, 130bl & r, 249l
P. H. Emerson (Royal Photographic Society) 340
Elliott Erwitt (Magnum from John Hillelson Agency) 84t, 380t
Robert Estall 31r, 82b, 83t, 91c
Frank Eugene (International Museum of Photography, George Eastman House) 337tl
Frederick Evans (Royal Photographic Society) 342
Mary Evans Picture Library 160
Walker Evans 60b, 352b
Andreas Feininger (Weidenfeld & Nicolson Archives) 368
Mark Fiennes 25t, 69br
Franco Fontana 14, 39t, 59b, 78b, 83br, 91b, 366c
Bina Fonyat 25b, 40b, 77b
Tony Foo 51b, 91t
Ford Motor Company 281b
William Henry Fox Talbot (Science Museum) 142r
Robert Frank (Courtesy of Sotheby's Belgravia) 356b
Leonard Freed (Magnum from John Hillelson Agency) 36bl
Lee Friedlander 61b, 372t

Clive Frost (Ace Photo Agency) 175tr & br, 310b, 322l
Georg Gerster (John Hillelson Agency) 296bl
Ralph Gibson 365
Stephen Godfrey 21l, 60tl
Joanna Godfrey Wood 83c
Robert Golden (Octopus Books Ltd) 315tl
Gianfranco Gorgoni (Colorific!) 325t
John Goto 93r, 257b
Kenneth Griffiths (© Sunday Times) 326r, 327t & b
Wayne Gunter 317bl
Ernst Haas (Magnum from John Hillelson Agency) 191, 339b, 359c
Hag 8, 260-1b
Sam Haskins 382b
Hawker Siddeley Dynamics Ltd (Science Photo Library) 298c
John Heartfield 269t
Francisco Hidalgo (Image Bank) 255, 339tr
Frank Hilton 193
Lewis Hine (International Museum of Photography, George Eastman House) 326l
Fred Holland Day (Royal Photographic Society) 332tr, 347l
Eric Hosking 301r
Eikoh Hosoe 361
Chris Howes 309l
India Office of Information (Courtesy of New Scientist magazine) 292
Robert Jackson (Camera Press Ltd) 325br
Ronald C. James 40c
Constantin Joffé (Courtesy of Sotheby's Belgravia) 316l
Roger Jones 47tr
Karsh of Ottawa (Camera Press Ltd) 376b
Gertrude Käsebier (Royal Photographic Society) 374t
Alexander Keighley (Royal Photographic Society) 341
André Kertész 49, 68, 364c, 367t & br
G. Kinns (Natural Science Photos) 301l
Kodak Museum 98bl, 99t & c, 132, 138t & br, 161br, 280r
Alfred Lammer 34, 303r
Alvin Langdon Coburn (Royal Photographic Society) 10, 143t, 335b, 339tl, 358
Dorothea Lange (Library of Congress) 352t
Michael Langford 18t, 19t & c, 48tl & bl, 65t, 152, 154, 156tl & r, 201, 223, 249tl & r, 256, 257t, 389, 390
Jacques-Henri Lartigue (John Hillelson Agency) 57r, 131t, 379b
Clarence John Laughlin 370tr, 371
Robin Laurance 66t
Guy le Querrec (Magnum from John Hillelson Agency) 388
Peter Lester 72b, 79l
Dr Jean Lorre (Science Photo Library) 293, 294, 295tl & bl
Mari Mahr 259l, 362t & b
Dr R. J. Marshall (Welsh National School of Medicine) 287tl & bl, 288bl
Leo Mason 306, 307
Ray Massey 182b, 315b, 318t
Angus McBean 380br

Will McBride (Image Bank) 323b
Don McCullin (© Sunday Times) 324
Ian McKinnell 186, 190, 196, 197, 277r, 311br
Ralph Eugene Meatyard (Courtesy of Christopher Meatyard) 372bl
Hylton Meire (Clinical Research Centre) 290l
Trevor Melton 6t, 20c, 24, 29t, 36t & br, 69t, 120, 121, 122, 123, 140, 141, 169, 170, 172, 173, 174, 176, 177, 178, 180, 182t
Neil Menneer 20b, 39br, 62
Duane Michals 89l
Roland and Sabrina Michaud (Rapho) 3, 27t & b, 39bl, 55
John Everett Millais (Tate Gallery) 331bl
Diana Miller 317t & bc
Dr Freeman D. Miller (Science Photo Library) 295r
László Moholy-Nagy (László Moholy-Nagy Fotografische Sammlung Im Museum Folkwang) 363r, (International Museum of Photography, George Eastman House) 364tl
Sarah Moon (Photograph printed by Bill Rowlinson) 377b
Barbara Morgan 360l
Eadweard Muybridge (Kingston-upon-Thames Library & Museum) 90t
NASA (Science Photo Library) 298tl & bl
Arnold Newman 350 b, 351, 373
Nicéphore Niépce (University of Texas, Gernsheim Collection) 142l
Patrick Nugent 26
Stephen Oliver 85cl
Gabe Palmer (Image Bank) 311t
Norman Parkinson (Camera Press Ltd) 316tr & br
Grubb Parsons 291
David Pearson 246b, 253t, (Alun Jones airbrushed) 253c & b
Erik Pelham 384r
Phonogram Ltd 85cr
Richard Polak (Royal Photographic Society) 333bl
Polaroid 143b
Man Ray (Courtesy of Sotheby's Belgravia) 268, 363l
Tony Ray-Jones (John Hillelson Agency) 66c
Oscar Rejlander (Royal Photographic Society) 333br
Albert Renger-Patzsch (Galerie Wilde, Köln) 344b, 391
Research Engineers Ltd 284cr & b
Jacob A. Riis (Jacob A. Riis Collection, Museum of the City of New York) 348b
Henry Peach Robinson (Kodak Museum) 331r & tl, 332tl & bl
Royal Aircraft Establishment, Farnborough 299b
Paul Rozelaar 181
Bryan Rybolt 31l
August Sander (Galerie Wilde, Köln) 349br
Jurgen Schadeberg 116b
Science Museum 161t & bl, 347r
Science Photo Library 131b, 278, 280l, 283 lt & lb, 286, 287bc & br,

288br, 289tr & br, 290r, 295tc, 299tl & r, 325bl
Tim Shackleton 112
Carol Sharp 28t, 32b, 44bl, 80t, 94r, 311bl
Hans Silvester (Rapho) 38, 71b, 86-7
John Sims 50t, 71t, 75 l & c, 79r, 116t, 159, 198
Aaron Siskind (Light Gallery) 367bl
Chris Smith 9b, 305 b, 308l
W. Eugene Smith (Magnum from John Hillelson Agency) 354tr
Forrest Smyth 22bl, 28br
Eric Staller 359t
John Starr 187, 194, 200c, 267bl, 322r, 359b
Edward Steichen (International Museum of Photography, George Eastman House) 377tr
Tim Stephens 246t, 247t, 250, 251, 258, 262, 263r, 264, 265, 266, 384l
Alfred Stieglitz (International Museum of Photography, George Eastman House) 337cl & cr (Zabriskie Gallery) 369t
Paul Strand (The Paul Strand Foundation) 321t, 343t & b, 344tl
Roger Summers (Derbyshire Constabulary) 285
Nic Tompkin 183t, 315tr, 318bl, 319
Tessa Traeger 314
Giuliana Traverso 47b
Peter Truckel 259r
Jerry Uelsmann 381
Jan Ung 5, 52, 53tr & bl, 73bl, 77tl, 93l
U. S. Dept. of Environment (Science Photo Library) 276
Christian Vogt 46b, 84b, 366b
Nick Walster 16b, 45b, 76
Andrew Watson (Vision International) 30t, 263l
Weegee (Arthur Fellig) (Courtesy of Sotheby's Belgravia) 355r
Brett Weston 346r
Edward Weston (© 1981 Center for Creative Photography, University of Arizona, used by permission) 345, 364tr
James McNeill Whistler (Tate Gallery) 334
Clarence White (International Museum of Photography, George Eastman House) 374b
Minor White (Philadelphia Museum of Art: Purchased from the Artist: Photographed by Eric Mitchell) 369b, 370tl
Henry Wilson 6b, 19b, 63, 67, 94t & bl, 127t, 128r, 138bl, 175tl
Bill Wood (Bruce Coleman Ltd) 303l

Key: t: top, c: center, b: bottom, l: left, r: right